# CONFLICT OF LAWS: CASES, MATERIALS AND PROBLEMS

## Revised Second Edition

By

**David H. Vernon**
*Allan D. Vestal Professor of Law*
*University of Iowa*

**Louise Weinberg**
*Holder of the Bates Chair*
*and Professor of Law*
*The University of Texas*

**William L. Reynolds**
*Jacob A. France Professor of Judicial Process*
*University of Maryland*

**William M. Richman**
*Distinguished University Professor of Law*
*University of Toledo*

LexisNexis™
Matthew Bender®

**Library of Congress Cataloging-in-Publication Data**

Weinberg, Louise.
   Conflict of laws: cases, materials and problems/Louise Weinberg, William L. Reynolds,
William M. Richman—2nd ed.
     p.  cm.
   Rev. ed. of: Conflict of laws/David H. Vernon. . .[et al].
   Includes index.
   ISBN 0-8205-4158-3
   1. Conflict of laws—United States—Cases. I. Reynolds, William L., 1945-II. Richman,
William M. III. Conflict of laws. IV. Title.
KF410.W45 2002
340.9'0973—dc21
               2002072420
               CIP

LexisNexis, the knowledge burst logo, and Michie are trademarks of Reed Elsevier Properties Inc.,
used under license. Matthew Bender is a registered trademark of Matthew Bender Properties Inc.

2003 Reprint

ISBN:0820557463

Editorial Offices
744 Broad Street, Newark, NJ 07102 (973) 820-2000
201 Mission St., San Francisco, CA 94105-1831 (415) 908-3200
701 East Water Street, Charlottesville, VA 22902-7587 (804) 972-7600
www.lexis.com

To Steve and Elizabeth

L.W.


To Bill, Catherine and Sarah

W.L.R.


To Carol

W.M.R.


To David, Our Colleague and Friend:
We Will Miss You.

L.W., W.L.R., W.M.R.

# PREFACE TO THE SECOND EDITION

In the decade since the publication of the first edition of this book, there have been steady changes in most of the areas covered. None has been revolutionary on its own, but together the developments have had a substantial impact; those changes are reflected throughout this edition. We have also revised Chapter IV considerably in that we reorganized the material on modern choice-of-law theory and added a new discussion of the choice-of-law provisions of the Restatement (Second) of Conflict of Laws. Although the Second Restatement has become the dominant choice-of-law methodology in over half the states, it sometimes gets short shrift in conflicts courses. We hope that this edition's expanded treatment of the Second Restatement will help teachers cover the topic in a way that more accurately reflects its importance in contemporary choice-of-law practice. Finally, we have added a new section on cyberspace jurisdiction.

We have received ample and enthusiastic support from our schools in preparing these materials. Thus we are grateful to: Dean Michael Sharlot and Dean William Powers of the University of Texas Law School for generous research support; Dean Karen Rothenberg, Yvette McMorris, and Amanda Lesher of the University of Maryland School of Law; and, Dean Phillip Closius and Associate Dean Beth Eisler of the University of Toledo College of Law.

During the preparation of this second edition David Vernon, our co-author, died. David was a fine scholar and an even better person. He published two editions (1973 and 1982) of the predecessor of this book, and then graciously welcomed us as co-authors of the first edition of the current book in 1990. We are grateful to have been able to collaborate with him. Also between the first and second editions, we suffered the losses of Roy Reynolds, Bernice C. Richman, and Jacob L. Richman — all of blessed memory. We will miss them. Once again, thanks to our families for their support: Steve and Elizabeth Weinberg; Carol, Emily and Nathan Richman, and Teddy, Bill, Catherine and Sarah Reynolds.

# SUMMARY TABLE OF CONTENTS

# TABLE OF CONTENTS

# Chapter 1

# INTRODUCTION

*The conflicts course.* This course deals with problems and disputes having contacts with more than one sovereign. One of the parties may be a nonresident of the forum;[1] out-of-state property may be in dispute; or the underlying events may have occurred outside the forum. The theory of recovery may be more suited to national than to state governance, or to governance by another country. The Constitution may constrain the forum's power to take jurisdiction over a nonresident, choose its own law, or relitigate a claim or issue decided in another sovereign's courts.

The conflicts course has become increasingly important to preparation for a sophisticated practice of law, whether in counseling or litigation. Because modern choice-of-law methodologies are undergoing significant and complex changes in many states, some formal training in choice-of-law methodology is particularly desirable.

*Plan of the book.* This book is divided classically into the three broad subject areas of the course: jurisdiction (Chapter 3), choice of law (Chapters 4-6), and judgments (Chapter 7). Chapter 2 leads into the substantive concepts of the course through readings on domicile, a problem pervasive throughout the course. The concluding chapter (Chapter 8) is devoted to domestic relations litigation, since that subject furnishes a convenient and interesting wrap-up of most of the concepts in the course. The book develops the conflicts concepts wherever possible with substantive material of great current interest: tort reform legislation, complex and mass litigation, international cases, and cases on the impact of the Constitution and federal supremacy.

Just to get your feet wet, consider the following case:

---

[1] The "forum" is the place of trial. Note, also, that often the word "foreign" is employed in conflicts cases to refer both to sister states and foreign countries as nonforum sovereigns.

## ROSENTHAL v. WARREN

*United States Court of Appeals for the Second Circuit*
*475 F.2d 438 (1973)*

Before LUMBARD, FEINBERG and OAKES, CIRCUIT JUDGES.

OAKES, CIRCUIT JUDGE:

This appeal in a diversity case raises the question whether New York would apply a Massachusetts damage limitation to the death of a New York domiciliary occurring in Massachusetts. The appeal . . . is from an order of the district court granting partial summary judgment in favor of the plaintiff in an action for wrongful death. The partial summary judgment struck the affirmative defense based upon the Massachusetts wrongful death statute limiting recoverable damages to " . . . not less than five thousand nor more than fifty thousand dollars, to be assessed with reference to the degree of [the tortfeasor's] culpability . . . ." The district court held that New York law was applicable. That law places no fixed value on wrongful death or limitation upon the damages in a wrongful death action . . . . We affirm.

The relevant facts are simple, the legal issue difficult. The decedent, Dr. Martin C. Rosenthal, was a citizen of New York. Decedent and his wife, who as executrix is plaintiff here, went to Boston where he was examined and diagnosed by Dr. Warren, whom the plaintiff describes as a world-renowned physician and surgeon treating patients from all over the world. On March 27, 1969, eight days after an operation performed by Dr. Warren at the New England Baptist Hospital, decedent died in the hospital while under the care of the defendant Warren.

Suit, alleging malpractice and asking for $1,250,000 in damages, was brought in New York state court. Jurisdiction of Dr. Warren to the extent of his insurance coverage was obtained by attachment levied on the St. Paul Fire & Marine Insurance Company, a Minnesota corporation doing business in New York, the malpractice insurer of a clinic where Dr. Warren is employed.[2] Jurisdiction of New England Baptist Hospital, of which Dr. Warren is surgeon in chief, a trustee, a member of the planning committee and an officer of the corporation, was obtained by service upon another officer of the hospital while soliciting funds in New York City. Defendants removed the suit to the federal district court on the basis of diversity of citizenship.

It is undisputed that although the hospital is a Massachusetts corporation, approximately one-third of its patients in 1969 came from outside Massachusetts and approximately 8 per cent of its patients in the same year were from New York. Indeed, the hospital claimed in its 1969 annual report that it was "not a local or community hospital in the usual sense because its patients come from literally everywhere." An affidavit of the head of the casualty underwriting department of the Boston office of St. Paul Fire & Marine, which issued the liability policy under which defendant Warren was covered, indicates that a general surgeon's liability policy in Massachusetts has a basic limit premium of $192, while a New York City surgeon pays a basic limit premium of $1,139,

---

[2] Jurisdiction was obtained under *Seider v. Roth*, 17 N.Y.2d 111, 269 N.Y.S.2d 99, 216 N.E.2d 312 (1966).

and that one factor contributing to the difference is the "dollar exposure" in New York, which has no wrongful death limitation. Dr. Warren's policy, however, makes no reference to coverage limitation in wrongful death cases.

This being a diversity case, it is, of course, elemental that we must look to the choice of law rules of the forum state, that is, to New York law. *Klaxon Co. v. Stentor Electric Manufacturing Co.,* 313 U.S. 487 (1941). Formerly New York probably would have applied the law of Massachusetts under the simplistic rule of *lex loci delicti* . . . .

In *Kilberg v. Northeast Airlines, Inc.,* 9 N.Y.2d 34, 172 N.E.2d 526, 211 N.Y. S. 2d 133 (1961), however, the New York Court of Appeals characterized the Massachusetts wrongful death limitation as "procedural" and refused to apply it in a suit brought in New York by a New York decedent's estate arising from the crash of an airplane flight originating in New York but fatally ending at Nantucket, Massachusetts. The court said that "[m]odern conditions make it unjust and anomalous to subject the traveling citizen of this State to the varying laws of other States through and over which they move," and pointed out that there were only 14 states limiting death case damages as of that time. The court also characterized wrongful death recovery limitations as "absurd and unjust" and emphasized the strong New York policy against such limitations, at least as to its domiciliaries, enshrined in a constitutional prohibition against them. Said the court, "The absurdity and injustice have become increasingly apparent in the six decades that have followed [the adoption of the New York constitutional prohibition]. For our courts to be limited by [the Massachusetts] damage ceiling (at least as to our own domiciliaries) is so completely contrary to our public policy that we should refuse to apply that part of the Massachusetts law. . . . "

*Kilberg* foreshadowed New York's total break with the wooden rule that the law of the place of the tort inevitably governed. The break became complete in the landmark *Babcock v. Jackson,* 12 N.Y.2d 473, 240 N.Y.S.2d 743,191 N.E.2d 279 (1963), where the Court of Appeals chose to apply New York law even though a statute of the place of the tort foreclosed rather than merely limited liability. . . . The opinion [in *Babcock*] laid the foundation for an "interest analysis" approach to choice of law problems, looking to "the law of the Jurisdiction which, because of its relationship or contact with the occurrence or the parties has the greatest concern with the specific issue raised in the litigation." [T]he *Babcock* court concluded that application of the inflexible rule of *lex loci delicti* could lead to "unjust and anomalous results . . . ."

Appellants contend that Massachusetts is the situs of the events leading to this law suit and, in effect, that the intent, either actual or constructive, of the parties was for the Massachusetts limitation on damages to govern in the event of a malpractice claim. This argument fails for many reasons. Quite probably it never occurred to Dr. Rosenthal, Dr. Warren or to the New England Baptist Hospital that a choice of law problem would arise; at least one does not ordinarily think of wrongful death limitations even when undertaking surgery. This is not a case where the conduct of the Massachusetts doctor or hospital vis a vis the decedent was patterned upon the Massachusetts death limitation. It is therefore not unfair to apply New York's compensatory policy to them. Additionally, it cannot be said that the defendants purchased insurance with the expectation Massachusetts law would govern damage recovery in this case . . . . [T]he specific insurance policy here does not distinguish between liability coverage for wrongful death and personal injuries, nor does it distinguish between medical practice on Massachusetts and out of state citizens. Finally, neither the hospital nor the doctor named here as defendants operate provincially; the doctor has a world-wide following and the hospital actively solicits funds from outside the Commonwealth of Massachusetts (including New York) and treats patients from "literally everywhere." It is thus impossible to say with any certainty what the parties' actual "expectations" as to choice of law were.

Even if expectations, real or constructive, could be hypothesized, they would be legally irrelevant. Despite the argument that looking to the expectations of the parties to solve choice of law problems promotes " 'an unconscious acceptance of legality and [the] legal order.' " *Miller v. Miller,* 22 N.Y.2d 12, 28, 290 N.Y.S.2d 734, 747, 237 N.E.2d 877, 886 (1968) (dissenting opinion), this contractual type of approach to multistate tort problems has been "summarily rejected" by the New York Court of Appeals . . . .

Rather, as we view it, the New York courts would balance against the New York interest in protecting its domiciliaries against wrongful death limitations the interests of Massachusetts in limiting damages for wrongful deaths allegedly caused by Massachusetts citizens or occurring in Massachusetts. Consideration of Massachusetts' interests in this case should, however, be from the perspective that the damage limitation is not confined to wrongful deaths resulting from medical malpractice but applies to all wrongful deaths however caused. Thus, any interest Massachusetts has in keeping medical liability insurance premiums down so as to avoid passing the increased costs on to Massachusetts citizens in the form of higher medical fees is simply one facet of whatever larger interest it may have in limiting in death as distinguished from personal injury cases the size of damage recovery against its citizens generally.[8]

That interest we think the New York courts would say is one not based upon logic, reason or social policy, but is really the vestigial remains of the mistaken view that there was no common law action for wrongful death . . . . In any event, it is our considered view that the New York Court of Appeals would view the Massachusetts limitation . . . as so "absurd and unjust" that the New York policy of fully compensating the harm from wrongful death would outweigh any interest Massachusetts has in keeping down in this limited type of situation the size of verdicts (and in some cases insurance premiums). If as *Kilberg* pointed out, "The absurdity and injustice [of wrongful death recovery limitations] have become increasingly apparent [since 1894] . . . , "since *Kilberg* they have become even more so. Since *Kilberg,* a number of

---

[8] If this case presented the converse fact situation where the decedent was a Massachusetts domiciliary and defendant doctor and hospital New York based, it is by no means clear a New York court would apply the Massachusetts wrongful death limitation. For, in addition to its interest in providing adequate compensation to those New York domiciliaries who suffer a wrongful demise, . . . unlimited . . . possible recovery in New York can be said to deter resident doctors and medical facilities from acts of malpractice. Thus New York would have an interest in regulating the tortfeasors. . . .

states have repealed their wrongful death limitations or increased the amounts so that at the present time there are only seven which have an outright limit, although some jurisdictions place a limit on a component of the damages and various states impose a limit in suits against certain governmental bodies. Indeed, Massachusetts itself recently increased its limits. Our examination indicates that Massachusetts is unique, moreover, in both imposing minimum and maximum damage limitations and assessing damages in proportion to the degree of the wrongdoer's culpability. Thus, the "absurdity and injustice" of death recovery limitations in general is heightened insofar as Massachusetts is concerned, because it relates damages recoverable not to the damages sustained, but to the degree of culpability, however that can be measured, on the part of the defendant. A respected, famous surgeon like Dr. Warren might well be held liable, were the Massachusetts statute applicable, for only $5,000 in damages, regardless of the damages sustained by the decedent's survivors. Thus the anachronistic concept embodied in the Massachusetts act is hardly one that the New York courts can be expected to embrace in the case of the death of a New York domiciliary with whose wife and children New York is "vitally concerned . . ." The New York policy favors "a just recovery" and "principles of fair play," that is to say, the "just, fair and practical result" which would not be furthered by applying the idiosyncratic Massachusetts law here. Our educated guess as to what the New York courts would do is to follow *Kilberg* and . . . apply the New York law of damages.

The constitutional argument, skillfully set forth in the dissent, was not raised by the parties below or on this appeal. We believe that in this case . . . New York has a significant interest—its domiciliary is the one who died and his next of kin are New York's charges—and the "incident" in Massachusetts is not purely "a local one," since the decedent was from out of state, and the defendant hospital is a national one in terms of its patients, its staff, its reputation and its efforts to obtain out-of-state contributions. In these circumstances, the refusal by New York to apply the Massachusetts death act's qualitative and quantitative limitations, even as it applies the remainder of the death act, is not so unreasonable as to violate the full faith and credit clause. The fact that Massachusetts was the situs of the tort and the residence of the defendant would not be sufficient to require as a matter of full faith and credit that the limitations in the Massachusetts law control, in light of the very strong New York policy against wrongful death limitations in connection with its citizens and next of kin and in light of the interstate aspects of the transaction. . . .

We agree with the court below and affirm the judgment.

LUMBARD, CIRCUIT JUDGE (dissenting):

The majority has concluded that the New York courts, on the facts of this case, would refuse to apply the Massachusetts wrongful death damage limitation. Accordingly, it has held that the federal district court, sitting in diversity, correctly refused to apply the Massachusetts damage limitation. From this holding I must dissent both because I do not agree that this [is] a proper appraisal of applicable New York law and because I believe that the Full Faith and Credit Clause of the United States Constitution bars the New York courts, and federal district courts sitting in diversity, from refusing to apply the Massachusetts limitation on the facts of this case. . . .

The majority purports to decide this case on interest-analysis grounds. However, the sole interest that it has found in New York emanates from the facts of plaintiff's and decedent's New York residence. Such an analysis simply proves too much; for it is tantamount to a *per se* rule that the courts will not apply such foreign damage limitations when the plaintiff is a resident of the forum state. Thus, I believe the majority's approach amounts to an insupportable abandonment of interest-analysis principles with regard to foreign damage limitations.

Appellee has correctly noted that the New York courts have never honored a foreign damage limitation such as that in issue. However, it is also true that the New York courts have never considered a case in which the interests of New York, in relation to those of the foreign state, were as minimal as they are here. The incident at the root of this litigation, the alleged malpractice of Dr. Warren, does not have the inter-state flavor of the *Kilberg* facts-death caused while in transit from one state to another. Here the decedent made a deliberate choice to undergo the operation in Massachusetts at defendant hospital. Hence, he journeyed into Massachusetts and registered in defendant hospital where he was under the care of defendant, Dr. Warren. The alleged negligence that resulted in decedent's death, the operation by Dr. Warren, occurred wholly within Massachusetts under the care of Massachusetts residents and in a Massachusetts institution. New York's only connection with this occurrence was the patient's permanent residence in New York. I do not see that New York's interest in this occurrence is enhanced by the fact that this Massachusetts physician and Massachusetts institution have such an eminent reputation that a substantial number of their patients, many from New York, are not Massachusetts residents and choose to come into Massachusetts and undergo treatment there; for there is no evidence that either defendant solicited patients from outside Massachusetts—their popularity is due solely to their reputation and the choice of the individual patients.

In my opinion the Massachusetts interests and contacts with the occurrence underlying this litigation should predominate. In addition to its interest in protecting its citizens and institutions from excessive recoveries, an important consideration behind the Massachusetts limitation is its policy of keeping liability premiums as low as possible for its residents. The significant differential that the majority has noted between malpractice insurance premiums in New York and those in Massachusetts is some testimony to the success of this policy. This interest of Massachusetts is fortified by the fact that the insurance policy from which any recovery will be paid was issued in Massachusetts. The fact that the policy has no coverage limitation in wrongful death cases, as noted by the majority, is irrelevant; for the difference in premiums makes it clear that the Massachusetts damage limitation is considered by insurance companies in calculating premiums for liability insurance issued in Massachusetts. Therefore, if we are to take the New York courts at their word that they follow an interest-analysis approach to torts conflict of laws problems, I can see no escape from the conclusion that Massachusetts interests predominate here and that the New York Court would on these facts be impelled to apply the Massachusetts damage limitation. . . .

In any event, even if the majority were correct that the New York courts would refuse to apply the Massachusetts damage limitation against a New

York plaintiff, I would hold that such an approach, when applied to a case in which the contacts with Massachusetts are as great as they are here, violates the Full Faith and Credit Clause of the United States Constitution. In *Pearson v. Northeast Airlines,* 309 F.2d 553 (en banc) (1962), *cert. den.* 372 U.S. 912 (1962), this circuit held that "the ruling of the New York Court of Appeals in *Kilberg* was a proper exercise of the state's power to develop conflict of laws doctrine." Thus, there was no breach of the Full Faith and Credit Clause when the New York Court ignored the Massachusetts damage limitation on the *Kilberg* facts. However, the majority in *Pearson* explicitly recognized that, in a case in which the Massachusetts interests were greater relative to the New York interests, it would be a constitutional violation for the New York courts to refuse to honor the foreign damage limitation. In this regard, Judge Kaufman wrote for the majority:

> We may concede that the Wrongful Death Statute of Massachusetts, almost certainly designed with an eye toward the regulation of occurrences transpiring wholly within Massachusetts, should be honored fully and completely when the incident under litigation is a local one. . . . But we cannot concede that Massachusetts has a constitutionally protected claim to the unqualified application of its statute in cases where there is an overwhelmingly interstate flavor.

I cannot see how the alleged malpractice and subsequent death of plaintiff's decedent can be classified as anything other than a local incident. Therefore, it appears to me that the clear import of this court's language in *Pearson* is that, in a case such as that presently before us, the Full Faith and Credit Clause would mandate the New York courts to apply the Massachusetts Wrongful Death Statute in its entirety, including the damage limitation. Hence, even if the majority and the district court are correct in their appraisal of New York law, the district court was nevertheless in error in refusing to apply the Massachusetts damage limitation to this case.

Accordingly, I would reverse the order of the district court.

## NOTES ON *ROSENTHAL:* A CONFLICTS MENU

(1) *Jurisdiction.* How did the New York court obtain jurisdiction over Dr. Warren? He lived and worked in Massachusetts and, as far as the opinion reveals, lacked "minimum contacts" with New York. Further, he did not seek out Dr. Rosenthal as a patient; rather, Rosenthal came to Dr. Warren's home state. Should we insist on pre-litigation connections between the defendant and the forum as a constitutional prerequisite to an exercise of jurisdiction? Why?

Putting contacts to one side for a moment, was the exercise of jurisdiction fair or reasonable? Which party would suffer greater inconvenience from litigation away from home? Where were the witnesses and the evidence? Should the court have dismissed the action on forum non conveniens grounds or transferred it to a federal court in Massachusetts?

In fact, the court did not assert personal jurisdiction over Dr. Warren, but rather attached a piece of his property. What property might he have had in

New York? This rather strained use of attachment jurisdiction was eventually held unconstitutional in *Rush v. Savchuk, see* § 3.16, *infra.*

The court's jurisdiction over the co-defendant hospital was based in part on personal service on an officer soliciting funds in New York. Should that be a constitutional basis for jurisdiction? If so, should the jurisdiction be limited to claims related to the officer's New York presence (i.e. claims related to fund raising), or should the jurisdiction extend to unrelated claims, like the ones in the instant case?

Why was the plaintiff so insistent on the New York forum anyway? Was it really because litigation in Boston would be a hardship?

(2)  *The Role of the Federal Courts.* Why does the federal court feel obliged to apply New York's choice-of-law rules? If New York and Massachusetts have different views on limiting wrongful death recovery, should the choice-of-law rules of either state be relied on to settle the matter? Why not use a set of neutral federal choice-of-law principles, at least when the forum is a federal court?

(3)  *Choice of Law.*

(a) *Tradition.* The court tells us that New York formerly employed the traditional "rule of *lex loci delicti*" (apply the law of the place of the wrong). This is known as a "territorialist" choice-of-law rule because it looks to the *place* where events occurred, things were located, or parties resided. "Territorialism" is the underlying assumption that the legislative jurisdiction of each sovereign is exclusive within its boundaries and ends at its boundaries. What result would the place-of-the-wrong rule produce in *Rosenthal?* Would it produce the same result regardless of whether the suit was brought in the New York or Massachusetts courts? That consequence—same result regardless of forum—is a good one, isn't it? At least it would avoid the jurisdictional jockeying that obviously occurred in *Rosenthal.*

If New York still followed the traditional territorialist rule, would it also apply Massachusetts' rules on hearsay and motion practice during the trial? If not, is it because those rules are "procedural?" Is the wrongful death damage limitation statute "procedural" in the same way? If New York still followed the traditional rule, would it apply a Massachusetts wrongful death damage rule that had different provisions for different races?

(b) *The Expectations of the Parties.* The court rejects the defendants' argument that the parties intended and expected Massachusetts law to apply. Realistically, did the parties have any expectations at all on this score? Do you think Dr. Warren was surprised when his attorneys told him New York's unlimited damages rule might be applied? Supposing that the defendants or their insurers really did expect Massachusetts law to apply, should that matter? Does your answer change in a case involving a contract rather than a tort issue?

(c) *Evaluating Rules; Weighing Interests.* The *Rosenthal* court seems to think that wrongful death damage limitation statutes are absurd, unjust and increasingly unpopular in other states. Should that be relevant in a choice-of-law discussion? Or should the court choose without considering the merits of the two competing substantive rules? Would the answer change if the issue were slavery rather than wrongful death damages? See Louise Weinberg, *Methodological Interventions and the Slavery Cases: or, Night-Thoughts of a Legal Realist*, 56 MD. L. REV. 1316 (1997).

After rejecting the *lex loci delicti* rule, the court seems to decide the case by comparing or weighing the "interests" of Massachusetts and New York in the case. Do states really have "interests" in litigation between private persons? If they do, how are we to divine what those interests are? Once we do, how can we weigh or compare interests to determine the stronger? Suppose the case had been brought in Massachusetts and it also used an "interest analysis." Would the result be the same? If not, how serious a problem is that?

*See* PROBLEMS 1-1. THE CAR RENTAL; 1-2. UNIFORMITY WHATEVER THE FORUM.

(4) *The Constitution and Choice of Law.* Should it be unconstitutional for New York to apply its law in a case like *Rosenthal*? If so, is it because such a ruling shows too little respect for Massachusetts, or because it would be too unfair to Dr. Warren?

(5) *Judgments.* Suppose plaintiff ultimately prevails and wins a judgment that exceeds both the Massachusetts damage limitations and the limits of his liability coverage. Should a Massachusetts court have to enforce such a judgment against the personal assets of Dr. Warren? Should the answer change if the New York court had obtained personal jurisdiction over Dr. Warren? Could the Massachusetts court refuse to enforce such a judgment on the ground that unlimited recoveries violate the important public policy of Massachusetts?

(6) *Bibliography.* Conflicts jurisprudence has long been fortunate in receiving the attention of distinguished authorities and commentators. This casebook will refer to many excellent articles and books. In this section, we call attention to several comprehensive works which students may find useful and enlightening.

General works on Conflicts include the AMERICAN LAW INSTITUTE'S RESTATEMENT (SECOND) OF THE CONFLICT OF LAWS (1971); RUSSELL WEINTRAUB, COMMENTARY ON THE CONFLICT OF LAWS (4th ed. 2001); ROBERT LEFLAR, LUTHER McDOUGAL & ROBERT FELIX, AMERICAN CONFLICTS LAW (4th ed. 1986); WILLIAM RICHMAN & WILLIAM REYNOLDS, UNDERSTANDING CONFLICT OF LAWS (3d ed. 2002); EUGENE SCOLES, PETER HAY, PATRICK BORCHERS & SYMEON SYMEONIDES, CONFLICT OF LAWS (3d ed. 2000); and DAVID CAVERS, THE CHOICE-OF-LAW PROCESS (1965).

Additional reading on jurisdiction can be found in ROBERT CASAD & WILLIAM RICHMAN, JURISDICTION IN CIVIL ACTIONS (3d ed. 1998); RESTATEMENT (THIRD) OF THE FOREIGN RELATIONS LAW OF THE UNITED STATES (1987); and, on judgments in the RESTATEMENT (SECOND) OF JUDGMENTS (1982). Further discussion of federal jurisdiction can be found in ERWIN CHEMERINSKY, FEDERAL JURISDICTION (3d ed. 1999), CHARLES WRIGHT, THE LAW OF FEDERAL COURTS (5th ed. 1994). More complete consideration of complex litigation appears in the American Law Institute's complex litigation project—COMPLEX LITIGATION: STATUTORY RECOMMENDATIONS AND ANALYSIS (1994)—and in LINDA MULLENIX, MASS TORT LITIGATION (1996). Finally, H. CLARK, THE LAW

OF DOMESTIC RELATIONS IN THE UNITED STATES (2d ed., 1987), provides a good secondary treatment of that field.

# Chapter 2

# DOMICILE

## § 2.01 The Concept

At common law it was thought that every person must have a domicile at all times from birth to death, and, for any single purpose, a person could have but one domicile at one time. Domicile is an important concept in conflicts law. Choice-of-law decisions often are influenced by the domicile of the parties. Jurisdiction of courts often depends on the domicile of one or both of the parties. And an individual's relationship to a governmental unit—including the individual's rights and duties—often depends on his or her domicile. As you consider the materials in this Chapter, ask yourself why domicile should be a controlling factor in determining the rights and duties of the parties.

When domicile is volitional and does not arise by operation of law, it exists as the result of a relationship—physical and mental—of a person to a place. It normally calls for physical presence coupled with a mental attitude towards the place that indicates some degree of permanence. The following three sections of the Restatement (Second) of Conflict of Laws (1971) detail the various forms domicile may take at common law.

## RESTATEMENT (SECOND) CONFLICT OF LAWS (1971)[*]

§ 11. Domicil[1]

(1) Domicil is a place, usually a person's home, to which the rules of Conflict of Laws sometimes accord determinative significance because of the person's identification with that place.

(2) Every person has a domicil at all times and, at least for the same purpose, no person has more than one domicil at a time.

§ 12. Home Defined.

Home is the place where a person dwells and which is the center of his domestic, social and civic life.

Comment

c. Factors important in determining home. In determining whether a dwelling place is a person's home, consideration should be given to:

    1.   Its physical characteristics;

    2.   The time he spends therein;

    3.   The things he does therein;

    4.   The persons and things therein;

---

[*] Copyright American Law Institute. Reprinted with permission.

[1] The term is sometimes spelled without the "e"-*viz.*, domicile.

5.   His mental attitude toward the place;

6.   His intention when absent to return to the place;

7.   Other dwelling places of the person concerned, and similar factors concerning them.

Justice Holmes provided a more succinct definition. Domicile, he wrote, is a person's "pre-eminent headquarters". *Bergner & Engel Brewing Co. v. Dreyfuss,* 172 Mass. 154, 157, 51 N.E. 531, 532 (1898).

## *Related Concepts*

1. *Citizenship.* Nationality and citizenship can be very important concepts in conflicts law. An American citizen living abroad, for example, can be required to return to this country to testify, even though he is domiciled abroad. *Blackmer v. United States,* 284 U.S. 421 (1932) (upholding contempt citation of an American citizen living in France for his failure to testify as required by federal law). The concept of citizenship or nationality is also important for choice-of-law purposes in many continental legal systems. Within our own federal system, however, a person's domicile or residence tends to be of much more importance than the state of citizenship. (On the concept of state citizenship, see generally Jonathan D. Varat, *State "Citizenship"and Interstate Equality,* 48 U. Chi. L. Rev. 487 (1981).) *See* PROBLEM 2-1. ENEMY NATIONALS.

2. *Residence.* Residence and domicile may be, but are not necessarily, the same. You can be a temporary resident, but not a temporary domiciliary. You can have two or more residences, but only a single domicile for any one purpose. Further, you cannot rely on the usage in legislation designed to grant rights or impose duties based on contacts with a physical location. Words such as "resident," "inhabitant," "citizen," and the like seem to be used interchangeably. At times, any of the words may mean: domicile itself (as in legislation dealing with jurisdiction of courts); less than domicile (school eligibility laws); or more than domicile (the homestead exemption laws, for example). In light of the inconsistent usage, you must be careful about the sense in which the word is used. *See* PROBLEMS 2-2. ONE VOTE SHORT; 2-3. ON THE MOVE AGAIN.

3. *Habitual residence.* The Hague Convention on Private International Law uses the term "habitual residence" in place of the common law concept of domicile. The main difference between habitual residence and domicile is that the former does not focus on intent. The term, however, suffers from the defect that some individuals wander so much that it is not easy to determine whether they have a habitual residence. Consider the example of the student attending law school in a state different from the place where her parents live, and who works for the summer in still a third state. Although habitual residence has won widespread use in international circles, it seems unlikely that it will see much use in this country. *See generally* David Cavers, *"Habitual Residence": A Useful Concept?,* 21 Am.U. L. Rev. 475 (1972).

## § 2.02  Domicile of Origin

A child acquires a domicile at birth, known as the domicile of origin. That domicile is that of the child's parents. Restatement (Second) of Conflict of Laws § 14(1).[2] A lot of metaphysics attaches to questions involving the abandonment of one's domicile of origin and the acquisition of a new domicile, a problem further complicated if the person in question later returns to a former home.

There are some wonderful illustrations. The following is one of those cases that, if it did not exist, a casebook editor would have had to invent.

### IN RE ESTATE OF JONES

*Iowa Supreme Court*
*192 Iowa 78, 182 N. W. 227 (1921)*

[Evan Jones, an "industrious and hard-working" native of Wales, emigrated to America when he was thirty-three in order to avoid an impending bastardy proceeding. He ended up in Iowa, where he was naturalized, but he apparently always longed for the lush green hills of his native Wales. In 1915, he sold his property, left most of the proceeds on deposit in a bank in Iowa, and boarded the ill-fated Lusitania to return to Wales. He died when a German submarine sank the Lusitania. Before leaving Iowa, he told his banker that he intended to live with his sister in Wales. The question for the court was whether Jones had achieved a new domicile in the British empire. If he had, then his property would not pass to his illegitimate child; if he was still domiciled in Iowa at the time of his death, then his property would pass to her as his sole heir under Iowa law.]

Faville, J.: A person may have his residence in one place while his domicile is in another. A person may have more than one residence at the same time, but can only have one domicile, at least for purposes of succession. It is well settled that every person, under all circumstances and conditions, must have a domicile somewhere.

The "domicile of origin" of every person is the domicile of his parents at the time of his birth. The "domicile of choice" is the place which a person has elected and chosen for himself to displace his previous domicile.

[I]t is obvious that the domicile of the decedent at the time of his death must in any event be determined by the assumption of a fiction. All will agree that the decedent did not have a domicile on the Lusitania. In order to determine his domicile, then, one of two fictions must be assumed, either that he retained the Iowa domicile until one was acquired in Wales or that he acquired a domicile in Wales the instant he abandoned the Iowa domicile and started for Wales, with the intent and purpose of residing there. [The court then

---

[2] *But see Elliott v. Krear,* 466 F. Supp. 444 (E.D. Va. 1979) (mother, domiciled in California, let child be raised by grandparents who were domiciled in Virginia; child held to be domiciled in Virginia). In *Martinez v. Bynum,* 461 U.S. 321 (1983), however, the Supreme Court permitted Texas to prohibit an alien child, who lived with a sister in Texas, from attending Texas public schools.

examined the English rule that presumed that, "A party abandoning the domicile of choice with the intent to return to his domicile of origin regains the latter the instant that the former domicile is abandoned."]

While there may have been a good reason for the establishment of the English rule we do not believe that any good reason exists for the recognition of such a rule under the circumstances disclosed in this case.

It therefore follows that the domicile of the decedent was in the state of Iowa until a new domicile had been actually acquired in Wales. No such domicile having been acquired, at the time of his death, his personal estate must be administered according to the laws of Iowa.

*See* PROBLEM 2-4. GAINING A NEW DOMICILE.

## NOTES ON *JONES*

(1) Do you think the court was influenced by the fact that its decision enabled the illegitimate daughter to inherit, obviously the just result? Or should the fact that the daughter, now an adult, had been shunned by her father his entire life lead to a different conclusion? (Remember that Jones originally left Wales in order to avoid a paternity proceeding.)

(2) The *Lusitania,* as a ship of the Cunard Line, flew the British flag. Should Jones have reacquired his British domicile when he stepped aboard the British ship with the intention of returning to British soil? The British version of domicile of origin is discussed in Cheshire & North's Private International Law 159-62 (1987).

## § 2.03  Domicile of Choice

### WHITE v. TENNANT

*West Virginia Supreme Court*
*31 W. Va. 790, 8 S.E. 596 (1888)*

[The White family owned a single tract of land which straddled the Pennsylvania-West Virginia border. The "mansion-house" was located in West Virginia, and there Michael White grew up. After marriage he lived with his wife Lucinda for several years on a farm on Day's Run, fifteen miles away. He still retained an interest in the family farm, and eventually the White family reached an arrangement in which Michael agreed to move to the Pennsylvania part of the farm and live there. He then sold the Day's Run farm to prepare to move to Pennsylvania.

Having sent some goods on ahead, on the morning of April 2, 1885, he left his old house with his wife and remaining furnishings with the declared intent of making the Pennsylvania house his home that evening. "He with his team, wife and goods and live-stock" arrived in Pennsylvania about sundown and unloaded their goods. The house being damp and uncomfortable, and Lucinda "complaining of feeling unwell," the couple returned to the mansion-house in West Virginia for the evening. Lucinda, it transpired, was sick with typhoid fever, and unable to leave the mansion-house. Although Michael returned to the Pennsylvania house several times to take care of the stock and generally "to look after it," he was destined never to live there—for he, too, was attacked with typhoid fever and died shortly thereafter, at the mansion-house in West Virginia. His wife survived.

The question before the court was the domicile of Michael at his death. If he was domiciled in West Virginia, Lucinda would receive his whole personal estate; if in Pennsylvania, she would be entitled to only half of the estate.]

SNYDER, J.: [I]f it is shown, that a person has entirely abandoned his former domicile in one state with the intention of making his home at a fixed place in another state with no intention of returning to his former domicile and then establishes a residence in the new place for any period of time, however brief, that will be in law a change of domicile, and the latter will remain his domicile until changed in like manner. The facts in this case conclusively prove, that Michael White, the decedent, abandoned his residence in West Virginia with the intention and purpose not only of not returning to it, but for the expressed purpose of making a fixed place in the State of Pennsylvania his home for an indefinite time. When he left his former home without any intention of returning, and in pursuance of that intention did in fact move with his family and effects to his new home with the intention of making it his residence for an indefinite time it became [when he arrived] eo instanti his domicile, and that his leaving there with the intention of returning the next day, did not change the fact. By the concurrence of his intention to make the Pennsylvania house his permanent residence with the fact that he had actually abandoned his former residence and moved to and put his goods in the new one, he made the latter his domicile. His leaving the Pennsylvania house, after he had moved to it with his family and goods, to spend the night, did not revive his domicile at his former residence on Day's Run because he had sold that, and left it without any purpose of returning there. By going from his new home to the house of his relatives to spend the night he certainly did not make the house thus visited his domicile; therefore, unless the Pennsylvania house was on the evening of April 2, 1885, his domicile, he was in the anomalous position of being without a domicile anywhere, which is a legal impossibility; and, that house having become his domicile, there is nothing in this case to show that he ever did in fact change or intend to change it or to establish a domicile elsewhere.

## NOTES AND QUESTIONS ON *WHITE v. TENNANT*

(1) *The Real Issue.* Is the opinion in *White* overly technical? Should Michael's subjective intention have been determinative? Does the requirement of physical presence add anything of significance to the intent requirement? And does the court's inquiry have anything to do with the real question in the case? Isn't that question whether Lucinda should take all of Michael's intestate estate or share it with his relatives? Should Michael's technical domicile control the answer to that question? If not, what should the answer turn on?

(2) *A Comparison of Two Chestnuts.* Both the *Jones and White* courts must decide if a decedent had achieved a new domicile in order to determine

intestate succession at death. Both cases are preoccupied with the technicalities of domicile; neither grapples at all with the relation between domicile and succession; nor does either address issues like the expectations of the decedent or the needs of the survivors ("succession"-type issues). Why do you think that is? And why do the two cases end up differently? Is reaching new soil really that important? Does the talisman of reaching new domicile remind you of the peppercorn you studied in first-year property which was paid as rent?

*In White,* the concept of domicile is used to solve a choice-of-law problem. It is also used by courts to determine both personal and divorce jurisdiction and is the contact that triggers the benefits and burdens of state citizenship, e.g., voting rights and estate taxes. The case of *In re Dorrance's Estate* deals with the latter problem.

See PROBLEMS 2-5. ESTABLISHING DIVERSITY FOR PURPOSES OF SUIT; 2-6. A FAMILY THAT STAYS TOGETHER; 2-7. BONDED ALIENS

## IN RE DORRANCE'S ESTATE

*Pennsylvania Supreme Court*
*309 Pa. 151, 163 A. 303,*
*cert. denied, 288 U.S. 617 (1932)*

FRAZER, C.J.

Dr. John T. DORRANCE was born November 11, 1873, in Bristol, Bucks county, Pa., where he spent the early years of his life with his parents. In 1897 he entered the employ of the Joseph Campbell Preserve Company in Camden, N.J. He remained with that firm and its corporate successor, the Campbell Soup Company, until his death.

At the start of his business career he established his residence at a boarding house in Camden, living there until 1905, when he moved to the Robeson Apartments in the same city. In 1906 he married Miss Ethel Mallinckrodt of Baltimore, Maryland, who survives him as his widow. Dorrance and his wife made their home at the Robeson Apartments until 1908, at which time they moved to Philadelphia and retained in that city until 1911. In 1909 Dorrance purchased a country place known as Pomona Fanns in Cinnaminson township, Burlington County, N.J. The Commonwealth concedes that from this date until November 14, 1925, decedent's domicile was in New Jersey.

During the years which passed from the time of his first association with the Campbell Company, Dorrance rose rapidly in the management and control of the business. Dorrance became the head of the company, and from 1915 until his death was the owner of all its capital stock. In 1922 the company was reorganized as the Campbell Soup Company, a New Jersey corporation with offices in Camden. At the time of his death, Dorrance had amassed an immense fortune, which both parties agreed is to be estimated at a figure exceeding $115,000,000.

In 1925 he purchased a large and attractive estate known as "Woodcrest" located in Radnor, Delaware county, Pa., in the suburbs of Philadelphia. The property was taken in the joint names of Doctor and Mrs. Dorrance, and including subsequent additions of surrounding acreage and furnishing of the mansion, the cost was approximately a million dollars. Speaking of the purchase of the Radnor estate, Mrs. Dorrance, the widow, testified as follows:

> "It was purchased so that our children would be more in contact with children and where they could go to school more easily with children with their prospects in life, and where we could do some entertaining from my oldest daughter who was then coming of age and who mingled with the world; and where I would be nearer my associates."

The house at Radnor was first occupied by the Dorrance family on November 14, 1925, at which time their entire personal effects were removed from Cinnaminson to Radnor. The commonwealth contends that from this date until his death, almost five years later, Dorrance was domiciled in Pennsylvania. Despite an attempt on the part of the executors to demonstrate that the former home in New Jersey was maintained as the principal home and establishment of decedent, and that there was a mere occasional occupancy of the Radnor place, it is our opinion the evidence clearly indicates that from 1925 until the autumn of 1930, the Radnor estate was the real and only home of the Dorrances, and, except for occasional visits to Cinnaminson and sojourns in Bar Harbor, Palm Beach, and other resorts, as well as trips to Europe, "Woodcrest" was occupied continuously by decedent and his family until his death, and at present is the family home.

There are a number of facts which, in our opinion, establish beyond question that continuously since 1925 the true home of Dorrance and his family was in Pennsylvania, and that the New Jersey residence was retained by him merely to lend weight to the fiction that he was domiciled there. Before 1925 Dorrance employed ten servants at Cinnaminson. After 1925 there was never more than four, and after the death of Dorrance's mother in 1929 only two. At "Woodcrest" sixteen servants were employed in the house and ten to twelve others worked on the grounds. There was a corresponding difference in the running expenses of the two properties. In 1924 the living expenses at Cinnaminson were slightly over $29,000. After 1925 the expenditures were considerably diminished, and in 1929 amounted to approximately $6,500. On the other hand, the maintenance of the Radnor estate exceeded $90,000 in 1929, and the year before amounted to approximately $95,000.

Although the comparative size of two residences is not conclusive of the fact of domicile, it is evidence of the intention to make one place the principal home. The expenditure of a very large sum of money for a residence which is not adapted to nor designed for mere seasonal occupancy is strong indication of an intention to make it the principal residence and main establishment of the family, particularly where the new residence is more elaborate and pretentious than any former abode. A few figures will readily show the marked difference between the Dorrance estates. The Cinnaminson property consisted of approximately seven acres located in a country district and surrounded by truck farms. The homestead was more than fifty years old, and had been remodeled in 1911. Although situated among fine old trees and surrounded by an extensive lawn, the house "was an ordinary brick mansard roof house of the time that it was built; very ugly," as Mrs. Dorrance testified.

On the other hand, "Woodcrest" was considered one of the most beautiful estates in the suburbs of Philadelphia. It originally comprised 119 acres, but subsequent additions to protect the boundaries brought the total acreage over 137.

Testimony as to the time Dorrance spent with his family at Cinnaminson after 1925 is extremely vague and uncertain. A fair conclusion from the evidence is that Dr. Dorrance and his wife made occasional trips to Pomona Farms, remaining one or two nights at a time, and that, upon their return from Bar Harbor or Jamestown at the end of the summers, a longer period was spent there, but only for the purpose of waiting until the servants had opened the Radnor house and made it fit for occupancy. When leaving for Europe or starting on summer vacations, their trunks and other baggage were sent from Radnor and shipped directly back to that place upon returning. Considering the nature of the occupancy of the Radnor estate, as well as the length of time spent there out of each year, all the facts clearly indicate that it was the principal establishment of Dorrance and his true family home after 1925.

The sumptuous residence in Pennsylvania was consistently chosen by Dorrance himself, as well as his wife and children, for all the outstanding events of their social life. Dorrance gave a number of large dinner parties there for men, principally business associates and friends, at which more than sixty guests were usually present. He and his wife entertained smaller groups for dinner quite frequently. His children invited their friends to "Woodcrest" for parties. One of the daughters was married in 1926 at the Radnor Church, and the wedding reception was held at "Woodcrest"; another, who was at the debutante age, was presented to society at an elaborate affair there in 1929.

[Dorrance] traveled back and forth daily from Radnor to his office in Camden. His weekends were spent at the Radnor place, several witnesses testifying that Dorrance took great interest in his estate, and on Sundays walked around the extensive grounds inspecting the property and conversing with caretakers. The children were entered in schools from the Radnor residence, and with their mother regularly attended St. Martins's Church in Radnor township. Dorrance himself did not transfer his membership to the Radnor church, but maintained his affiliation with a church in Riverton, N.J. This latter was only one of the many things which he did to avoid the appearance of identifying himself with the community in which he resided with his family; and that these acts, together with his declarations of residence in New Jersey, were intended to bolster his assertions that he remained domiciled in New Jersey, there can be little doubt. His real motive and the reasons which prompted this course of conduct are apparent.

With a remarkable demonstration of the same business acumen and sagacity which enabled him to accumulate his enormous personal fortune, he carefully drew his wills with the intent of retaining for his children after his death his 100 per cent interest in the Campbell Soup Company. This he would be able to do under the laws of New Jersey by the accumulation of income for the payment of inheritance and estate taxes, and with the assurance that his wife could not elect to take personally against his will, which would not be possible under the laws of Pennsylvania. In addition, it was a matter of considerable importance for him to declare himself a resident of New Jersey in respect to the payment of annual taxes on personal property, as his stock in the soup company, as well as United States and New Jersey government securities, were exempt from the tax in that state. By claiming a residence in New Jersey, Dorrance was able to effect a large annual saving in taxation. For that reason Dorrance informed others he hesitated to take up residence at Radnor, and when contemplating the purchase of "Woodcrest," he consulted his attorney, who advised him that retention of his New Jersey domicile "was largely a matter of intention." Consequently, following his removal to the estate at Radnor, he scrupulously endeavored to declare in formal documents and on many occasions that he was a resident of New Jersey. Upon the advice of his attorney, he executed an agreement with his wife that their residence should remain at Cinnaminson despite the occupancy of "Woodcrest" during "a portion of each year". The agreement stated that both would refrain from voting elsewhere than in Burlington county, N.J., and contained other clauses of a similar nature. Dorrance refused to accept a directorship in the Pennsylvania Railroad until assured by the president of the company that it was not necessary for more than a majority of the directors of that corporation to be residents of Pennsylvania. On many occasions and in various formal documents executed after 1925 he stated his residence to be at Cinnaminson, but counsel for the commonwealth has indicated several instances in which Dr. Dorrance did give his address at Radnor.

A circumstance of considerable importance was the fact that, after 1925, many of Dorrance's friends and acquaintances assumed he had become a resident of Pennsylvania. Dorrance discussed this with his lawyer, stating he had denied to them any intention of giving up his domicile in New Jersey. But in letters and conversations several of his friends expressed to him their belief that he had become a legal resident of Pennsylvania.

We come now to an examination of the law applicable in determining the domicile of decedent. The precise question is as follows: May expressions of a man to the effect that he desires to retain a domicile of choice in one state prevail over the intention to make a new home manifested by an actual removal to the new residence in another state, and accompanied by a manner of living which can leave no doubt that the new abode is the principal residence and establishment, particularly where the wish to retain the old domicile is colored by the motive of regulating his affairs after death in a manner not permitted by the laws of the state removed to, and is also bound up with the purpose of avoiding payment of substantial taxes on personal property? We are of the opinion that such is not the law, and that John T. Dorrance was domiciled in Pennsylvania at the time of his death.

With a few scattered expressions to the contrary, the law is generally settled that, as regards the determination of domicile, a person's expression of desire may not supersede the effect of his conduct.

[R]ecitals in deeds and wills are not given particular weight in determining domicile in comparison with the evidence supplied by the daily life of the individual and his acts and conduct. "More weight will be given to a person's acts than to his declarations, and when they are inconsistent, the acts will control." 19 C.J. 438.

In holding that a domicile of choice may not be retained by intention alone, we do not mean to disturb the well-settled rule that absence from a place of legal residence, for purposes of health or other unavoidable necessity, will not result in a loss of that domicile. Nor do we mean that, where a man has two actual residences, either one of which might be his domicile, he is not free to choose between them.

An attempt was made by counsel for appellees during the argument and in the briefs to show that Dorrance at no time intended to make his Radnor estate a permanent home and that he contemplated returning to Cinnaminson at an indefinite future time. Assuming such to be the case, there is no doubt that such vague intention of resuming a former domicile will not prevent the acquisition of a new one. "If a person has actually removed to another place, with an intention of remaining there for an indefinite time, and as a place of fixed present domicile it is to be deemed his place of domicile notwithstanding he may entertain a floating intention to return at some future period." *Gilbert v. David*, 235 U.S. 561, 569, quoting Story's "Conflict of Laws".

It is argued by appellees that, before a new domicile of choice can be acquired, there must be proof of the abandonment of the old. In our opinion, this contention is unsound, for the intention to make one's home in a new place necessarily includes the abandonment of the former home.

[B]y the act of removing his home and family from New Jersey to Pennsylvania, Dorrance acquired a domicile in the latter state. That he was unaware that such action would result in a change of domicile is irrelevant to the issue. His intention to maintain a home, indeed, a very lavish home, at Radnor, is undoubted. We fail to find in the record, after careful search, any convincing testimony of a bona fide intention upon his part or that of any member of his family, to occupy "Woodcrest" for any other than an indefinite period, and in fact to make it the "technically pre-eminent headquarters" of himself and family after November, 1925. "The intention requirement for the acquisition of a domicile of choice is an intention to make a home in fact, and not an intention to acquire a domicile." Restatement of the Law of Conflict of Laws, § 2 1. The evidence indicates that beyond all question Dorrance's family home and principal establishment was at Radnor. When either he or the members of his family went away of vacations, they started from "Woodcrest" and returned there afterwards. Practically his entire time, except when absent on vacations, was spent there. His friends and acquaintances considered it his home. Indeed, we may readily believe that in his heart Dr. Dorrance knew "Woodcrest" to be his true and only home, but for personal reasons, he preferred to state in public that it was not his home when every fact and circumstance pointed to the contrary. As already indicated, his mere declarations, undoubtedly made solely for personal reasons, did not prevent the acquisition of a domicile in Pennsylvania. In our opinion, the evidence clearly establishes the legal domicile of Dr. Dorrance to be in Pennsylvania, and accordingly there is due the commonwealth an inheritance transfer tax, based upon the agreed value of his estate at the time of his death.

## NOTES AND QUESTIONS ON *DORRANCE*

(1) *Death Taxes.* The dispute in *Dorrance* was over which state could tax his enormous fortune when he died. Domicile is the generally accepted basis

for taxing intangibles at death. *See* EUGENE SCOLES, ET AL., CONFLICT OF LAWS § 4.4 (3d ed. 2000). Why is that the required nexus?

(2) *Planning for Death.* Dorrance said that he "intended" to be a New Jersey domiciliary and he certainly took enough concrete steps to make that intention manifest. Should the decedent's intention control, at least when there are substantial contacts with the designated state? If you had represented Dorrance before his death, what advice would you have given him? Can he satisfy both his lifestyle and tax-minimizing goals?

(3) *Same Facts, Different Result.* What do you think New Jersey did? Not surprisingly, the court had no trouble in finding him a domiciliary of the Garden State. In *In Re Dorrance's Estate,* 115 N.J. Eq. 268, 170 A. 601 (1934), *cert. denied,* 298 U.S. 678 (1936), the New Jersey court found that the mere fact of residence was not dispositive in that it is "thoroughly well settled" law that a man's domicile, once acquired, does not change until a new domicile is acquired; and acquisition of a new domicile requires an intention to make his home permanently in the new residence. The evidence showed that Dorrance never intended permanently to reside in the Radnor residence, but moved there temporarily to accommodate the needs of his wife and children. The very factors which the Pennsylvania court found to be a ruse for taxation purposes the New Jersey court found to be persuasive in establishing that Dorrance never intended permanently to abandon his New Jersey residence (voting in Cinnaminson, motor vehicle registration and driver's license issued in New Jersey, declarations in his will, and so forth).

How could the Pennsylvania and New Jersey courts reach different conclusions on the same facts? What about the rule that a person can have *one-and only one-domicile* at a time for any one purpose?

*Compare* the laundry list of factors for determining domicile set out in *Simmons v. Skyway of Ocala,* 592 F. Supp. 356 (S.D. Ga. 1984):

> Several objective factors indicate whether domicile has been established for statements of intent can be given little weight if they conflict with objective facts. Those factors include: location of employment; home ownership and ownership of other real property; location of one's household furnishings; registration and title of one's automobiles; driver's license; voter registration; payment for utilities; banking; acquiring a telephone number and listing it; receiving mail; and establishing membership in local professional, civic, religious, or social organizations.

Do you find that list helpful?

(4) *The Utility of the Concept. The Dorrance* case involved a state's authority to tax; the White and Jones cases, discussed earlier, involved succession at death. What is it about domicile that makes it so useful a legal tool? Should a rational legal system make important decisions concerning the rights and responsibilities of individuals on the basis of technical domicile? What are the advantages of using domicile as a controlling factor? On balance, do the advantages overcome the difficulties of using domicile? And if you conclude that technical domicile is too uncertain and tenuous a concept to constitute

the foundation for rational judicial decision-making, what alternative do you suggest?

## MULTIPLE DOMICILE AND STATE TAXATION

(1) *The Difficulty of Being Ambulatory and Wealthy. Dorrance's Estate* illustrates the pitfalls that lie in wait for the wealthy who try to fudge their domicile in order to save on estate taxes. The double taxation of Dr. Dorrance's estate led to the adoption of the Federal Interpleader Act, 28 U.S.C. § 1335, in an attempt to solve the problem.

The idea was that interpleader could provide a forum to resolve conflicting claims such as those Pennsylvania and New Jersey made on Dorrance's estate. *See* Zachariah Chafee, *Federal Interpleader Since the Act of 1936,* 49 YALE L.J. 377 (1940). The Supreme Court quickly scotched those hopes by holding that the Eleventh Amendment barred a federal interpleader action against a state, *Worcester County Trust Co. v. Riley,* 302 U.S. 292 (1937). Two years later, however, the Court did provide the super-rich with a ray of hope. In *Texas v. Florida,* 306 U.S. 398 (1939), the Court accepted jurisdiction of a case where four states claimed the right to tax the decedent's estate; what made the case unusual was that the tax claims exceeded the value of the estate.

(2) *Howard Hughes Lives.* The death a number of years ago of Howard Hughes, the notorious billionaire recluse, provided the Supreme Court with an opportunity to review the area.

(a) *Hughes I.* California and Texas both claimed Hughes as a domiciliary, and, therefore, each also claimed the right to tax his estate. California sought to avoid the double taxation problem by suing Texas, invoking the Court's original jurisdiction. Although the Court refused jurisdiction, four Justices suggested that the estate file an interpleader action to test the continuing validity of *Worcester County; see California v. Texas,* 437 U.S. 601 (1978).

(b) *Hughes II.* When the administrator of Hughes' estate followed that suggestion, however, the Court reaffirmed Worcester County and held the action barred by the Eleventh Amendment. (Imagine how the administrator felt when he read this decision.) *Cory v. White,* 457 U.S. 85 (1982).

(c) *Hughes III.* But there still was an out. On the day it rejected *Hughes II,* the Court permitted California to file an original action against Texas on the ground that the tax claims against the Hughes estate exceeded its value. *California v. Texas,* 457 U.S. 164 (1982). Hence, a justiciable due process claim was raised.

(d) *Who Cares?* Are cases like *Dorrance* a necessary price to pay for a federal system? If the Supreme Court's original jurisdiction is available only when the tax claims exceed the value of the estate, double taxation can be avoided only by the ultra-wealthy. Does that make sense?

(3) Another form of relief is available in some states under the Uniform Arbitration of Death Taxes Act, 8A U.L.A. 521 (1943).

## § 2.04  Involuntary Domicile

What is the status of persons who have no choice where they live? In the old days, a woman who married acquired the domicile of her husband, see

Restatement (First) of Conflict of Laws § 21, but such a presumption is no longer constitutional today, is it? *See, e.g., Mas v. Perry,* 489 F.2d 1396 (5th Cir. 1974), *cert. denied,* 419 U.S. 842 (1974). Three other examples of involuntary domicile come quickly to mind:

— *Students.* In *Newburger v. Peterson,* 344 F. Supp. 559 (D.N.H. 1972), a Dartmouth student challenged a New Hampshire statute which prevented him from voting if he had a firm intention of leaving his college town at a fixed time in the future (thus lacking the requisite intent to establish domicile there). The Court held the statute unconstitutional: "[T]he challenged New Hampshire law forces persons who are in every meaningful sense members of New Hampshire political communities to vote in communities elsewhere which they have long departed and with whose affairs they are no longer concerned, if indeed the former community still recognizes the right." *See* PROBLEM 2-8. VOTING RIGHTS.

— *Minors and Person Under a Disability.* The federal rule that a person represented by a guardian has the same domicile, at least for diversity purposes, as the guardian. 28 U.S.C. §1332 (6).

— *Military Personnel.* A number of states provide by statute that members of the armed forces who live in the state for a period of time are residents for purposes of marriage dissolution. *See generally* Robert Leflar, *Conflict of Laws and Family Law,* 14 ARK. L. REV. 47 (1960). State courts often are willing, in the proper circumstances, to hold that members of the armed forces can acquire a domicile, at least if they live off base. *See, e.g., Sasse v. Sasse,* 41 Wash. 2nd 363, 249 P.2d 380 (1952). The Supreme Court, in *Carrington v. Rash,* 380 U.S. 89 (1965), invalidated a constitutional provision of Texas which forbade servicemen stationed in the state from acquiring a domicile there in order to vote.

— *Prisoners.* Although the Second Conflicts Restatement (§ 17) says that it is "impossible for a person to acquire a domicil in the jail in which he is incarcerated", recent case law does not support the generality of that provision. *See, e.g., Stifel v. Hopkins,* 477 F.2d 116 (6th Cir. 1973) (prisoner can establish domicile in state where he is incarcerated). That result is compelled, is it not, by the fact that domicile is used for determining jurisdiction to divorce and the right to vote—both of which are subject to strong constitutional protection? *See* PROBLEM 2-9. THE PRISONER.

For more good writing on domicile, see also Rhonda Wasserman, *Domicile and Divorce: Time to Sever the Knot,* 39 WM. & MARY L. REV. 1 (1997); Marc S. Klein, *A Critical Analysis of New Jersey's Domicile—Driven Choice of Law Methodology,* 17 SETON HALL L. REV. 204 (1987); Bernard Corr, *Interest Analysis and Choice of Law—The Dubious Dominance of Domicil,* 1983 UTAH L. REV. 651.

# Chapter 3

# JURISDICTION

## PART A  THE BASIC CONCEPTS

### § 3.01  Jurisdiction in Conflict of Laws

Jurisdiction is treated fully in courses in civil procedure, but there the focus is on the single-state context. In conflicts, by contrast, we consider more narrowly the problems of litigating the case when the defendant and his property are elsewhere. Here we focus not so much on dragging the defendant into court, but on dragging him into the state. Accordingly many jurisdiction problems (notice, service, etc.) that are just as acute in the single-state setting as in the conflicts setting, receive only summary treatment in this chapter.

Another difference is the treatment of choice-of-law implications. In civil procedure, the jurisdictional discussion largely ignores these issues; in this chapter, they are a major sub-theme.

Part A recapitulates briefly the basic jurisdictional concepts learned in civil procedure. Part B then treats the history of the due process restrictions on state court jurisdiction. This part begins with the Supreme Court's establishment of the territorial power theory of jurisdiction, proceeds through the theoretical and practical problems with that view, and ends with the Court's rejection of it in favor of the minimum contacts standard of *International Shoe*. Part C, the heart of the chapter, addresses the current constitutional limits on jurisdiction set out in the flurry of Supreme Court decisions since 1977.

The law of jurisdiction is not, however, purely constitutional law because a court cannot exercise jurisdiction unless it is empowered by local law; the state law bases for jurisdiction, both statutory and common law, are the subject of Part D. The focus changes in Part E from the defendant to her property and the Court's major reconceptualization of in rem jurisdiction in *Shaffer v. Heitner*. Finally, Part F treats the non-constitutional limits upon state court jurisdiction, and Part G considers jurisdiction in cyberspace.

### § 3.02  Lawyering Note

It would be difficult to overstate the importance of jurisdictional issues to the practicing lawyer involved in a choice-of-law case. Choice of forum often means the difference between winning and losing, or between a large or a small judgment. This may present a challenge to the attorney, because a forum with the most favorable choice-of-law rule from the plaintiff's perspective may be questionable in terms of jurisdiction. The plaintiff's counsel then must balance the potentially favorable substantive result with the danger of being thrown out of court on jurisdictional grounds. If the forum is the only one in which a favorable substantive result is likely, the jurisdictional issue must be faced and litigated. If another forum is available in which a favorable substantive result is somewhat less likely, but in which jurisdiction is clear, a hard decision must be made.

How should the lawyer proceed? Should the lawyer file in both states? Is it an abuse of process to file in both states and test the water in the courts of the state having the more favorable substantive rule while leaving the suit in the other state quiescent if possible? If double or triple filing is ethical, what problems will face the plaintiff's counsel, and how would you, as defense counsel, respond?

The substantive law as such is not the only consideration in selecting a forum. A plaintiff prefers a state with a history of large plaintiff's verdicts to one with a contrary history. A sophisticated understanding of jurisdictional requirements often permits the lawyer greater flexibility than would otherwise be possible.

The lawyer faces a potential conflict of interest in forum selection and must take great care to assure that the client's interest controls the decision. There normally is a financial incentive to try the case in the lawyer's home state. Whatever fee is generated in the home state need not be shared. If the case is referred to counsel in another state, the recovery, and thus any contingent fee, may be larger, but the referring lawyer normally must share the larger fee with cooperating attorneys and the "take home" may be smaller. The matter is sensitive, but the lawyer's obligation is clear: The client's interest must control the decision.

Knowledge of the constitutional limitations on state-court jurisdiction emphasized in this Chapter is essential. Keep in mind, however, that the Constitution is only a starting point. In many states, jurisdiction is governed by statutes or rules that may not extend jurisdiction to the full extent permitted by the Constitution. In such states a two-level analysis—one constitutional and the other statutory—is required.

Finally, after picking the forum likely to yield the most favorable result and carefully analyzing the constitutional and statutory law of amenability, the plaintiff's lawyer must consider the possibility that the defendant will assert one of the defenses or limits to jurisdiction discussed in Part F.

## § 3.03  Selecting the Proper Court—Jurisdiction and Related Concepts

Judicial jurisdiction in the most inclusive sense refers to the power or ability of a court to hear a dispute and render a valid judgment—valid in the sense that it will be recognized by other courts. Courts and scholars have used the word "jurisdiction" as a label for several different questions: Does the state have sufficient connections with the defendant to render a judgment against her? Has the state given this particular court the authority to hear actions of this type? Is the court properly located to hear the action?

Of these questions only the first is properly the subject of a chapter in a book on conflict of laws. But as the other questions indicate, the enterprise of allocating judicial business or selecting the proper court is a good deal more complicated than simply determining which state is the proper one in which to bring suit. Accordingly, before embarking on an extended discussion of the first question—jurisdiction over person and property—it is useful to consider that issue in a preliminary and general way and to distinguish it from the other two questions—jurisdiction over the subject matter and venue.

---

**BUCHANAN v. RUCKER,** 9 East 192, 103 Eng. Rep. 546 (Court of King's Bench, 1808.) Plaintiff sued defendant in an English court seeking to enforce a judgment of the Island Court in Tobago. Defendant had been served in the Tobago action by nailing a copy of the declaration and summons to the courthouse door, but there was no proof that defendant had ever been on the island of Tobago or had any connection with the island.

*Held:* For the defendant, the judgment of the Island Court in Tobago need not be recognized in England. There was some question whether the Toboggan statute provided for jurisdiction on these facts, but even if it did, England need not recognize the judgment.

> LORD ELLENBOROUGH, C.J . . . . Supposing however that the Act had said in terms, that though a person sued in the island had never been present within the jurisdiction, yet that it should bind him upon proof of nailing up the summons at the Court door; how could that be obligatory upon the subjects of other countries? Can the island of Tobago pass a law to bind the rights of the whole world? Would the world submit to such an assumed jurisdiction?

---

## NOTES ON JURISDICTION AND RELATED CONCEPTS

(1) *The Need for a Jurisdictional Basis.* The source of Lord Ellenborough's indignation in *Buchanan* is not hard to understand. The Island court had attempted to exercise territorial jurisdiction (or power) over a person who had no connection of any sort with Tobago. Thus, *Buchanan* teaches one of the fundamental principles of jurisdiction: the state must have some connection or relationship with defendant or his property to exercise power over him. *See* RESTATEMENT (SECOND) OF CONFLICT OF LAWS, ch. 3, introductory n. (1971). The kinds of connections that suffice for jurisdiction are referred to by courts and scholars as jurisdictional bases (or predicates).

(2) *Categories of Jurisdiction.* The type of connection or relationship that exists between the state and the defendant or her property determines the category of territorial jurisdiction that the court can exercise and the type of judgment it may render. If the defendant has personal contacts with the state (the sort that are discussed in Parts C and D of this chapter), the court may exercise in personam jurisdiction over the defendant. A court with that sort of jurisdiction may render a personal judgment against the defendant that can be satisfied out of any property of hers within the state. A personal

judgment creates a judgment debt against her that may be enforced in other states (against her property in those states), by operation of the Full Faith and Credit Clause. By contrast, if the state asserts its power because of a connection with the defendant's property (the sort of connection discussed in Part E) and not with her person, the court exercises some form of in rem jurisdiction. The only judgment the court can render then is one that affects only that particular piece of the defendant's property. *See generally* WILLIAM RICHMAN & WILLIAM REYNOLDS, UNDERSTANDING CONFLICT OF LAWS 18, 121-122 (3d ed. 2002).

(3) *Consequences of Lack of Jurisdiction.* Absent any sort of jurisdictional basis (or predicate), the court has no jurisdiction over the defendant and cannot proceed to hear the action. If it does, its judgment will not be valid. RESTATEMENT (SECOND) OF JUDGMENTS § 1 (1982). But a mistaken exercise of jurisdiction is not like any other legal mistake that a court makes. A typical mistake of law (for instance, application of the wrong substantive rule or misallocation of the burden of proof) must be corrected, if at all, on appeal, that is, by *direct* attack. If the mistake is incorporated into a judgment and all appeals are exhausted, however, the error may not be asserted in a separate proceeding—a *collateral* attack.

A jurisdictional error, however, may be the subject of a collateral attack. Suppose, for example, that a California court exercises jurisdiction over a New Yorker who has had no connection with California. If the New York defendant defaults, the victory may be an empty one for the California plaintiff since it is likely that the defendant has no property in California out of which to satisfy the judgment. The plaintiff may decide to sue the defendant in New York upon the California judgment. In that action, the defendant will certainly raise the lack of jurisdiction of the California court as a defense. The assertion of lack of jurisdiction of the rendering (California) court as a defense to a subsequent suit on the judgment in another state is the classic form of collateral attack. For more on the distinction between direct and collateral attack, see RESTATEMENT (SECOND) OF JUDGMENTS, ch. 5, introductory n. (1982).

(4) *Subject Matter Jurisdiction Distinguished.* Jurisdiction over the subject matter (often called "competence") differs from territorial jurisdiction (jurisdiction over person and property) in two principal respects. First, territorial jurisdiction is concerned with whether the state, through any of its courts, has power to hear the case and render a judgment. But once it is clear that a state has power to hear a case, another question remains. Which court within the state has been given the competence to hear this type or class of case? States customarily divide up the judicial business among their several courts according to legal subject matter and amount in controversy. Whether a case falls within the class of cases that the state has assigned to the particular court that the plaintiff has chosen is a question of subject matter jurisdiction or competence.

A second distinction concerns the notion of waiver. A defendant can always waive an objection to jurisdiction over the person. If the defendant is willing to submit to the jurisdiction of a state with which he lacks a connection sufficient to constitute a jurisdictional basis, he may do so. The only interest at stake is the defendant's right not to be compelled to litigate in a distant forum. If he is willing to forego the assertion of that interest, the court will not raise it on its own motion. *See* RESTATEMENT (SECOND) OF CONFLICT OF LAWS, § 32, cmt. b (1971).

The situation is different with subject matter jurisdiction or competence. The litigants, of course, have an interest in having their dispute heard by a competent court, but the state has an interest as well. It has determined how the judicial business is to be divided up among its courts, and the agreement of the parties cannot thwart that scheme. Thus, it is often said that jurisdiction over the subject matter cannot be conferred on a court by the agreement of the parties. Further, the court must notice lack of competence on its own motion, even if the parties do not raise the issue. *See, e.g.,* FED. R. CIV. P. 12(h)(3).

For more on the distinction between subject matter jurisdiction and jurisdiction over the person and property, see RESTATEMENT (SECOND) OF JUDGMENTS, ch. 2, introductory n. (1982).

(5) *Venue Distinguished.* Whether a state has sufficient contacts with a dispute so that any of its courts can hear it is a question of territorial jurisdiction. But even after the plaintiff has established that there is some court within a state which can hear a dispute, he must still answer the question: which court? This question is partially answered by considerations of subject matter jurisdiction—the way in which states divide the judicial business among their courts according to the type or class of litigation involved. States also divide up the judicial business geographically by rules that indicate which county or judicial district within the state is the appropriate place to bring the action. These are rules of venue. A typical set of venue provisions might require, for instance, that the action be brought in the county or district where plaintiff lives, or where defendant lives, or where the cause of action arose, or where the property is located. *See, e.g.,* 28 U.S.C. § 1391 (specifying the districts within the federal system in which the action may be brought).

Venue differs fundamentally from territorial jurisdiction and from subject matter jurisdiction. Rules of venue give the defendant a privilege not to be sued in an inconvenient forum; they do not affect the power or competence of the court. This rather abstract sounding distinction can be rendered more concrete by considering the question of waiver. A venue objection, unlike an objection based upon lack of subject matter jurisdiction, can always be waived by the defendant. Furthermore, unlike an objection to jurisdiction over the person, a venue objection can be raised only if the defendant appears and seasonably asserts it. A defaulting defendant may raise the defense of lack of jurisdiction over her person in a collateral attack, but she has lost her venue objection forever. For more on the distinction between venue and jurisdiction, see 1 ROBERT CASAD & WILLIAM RICHMAN, JURISDICTION IN CIVIL ACTIONS 6-8 (3d ed. 1998), FLEMING JAMES, GEOFFREY HAZARD & JOHN LEUBSDORF, CIVIL PROCEDURE § 2.1 (5th ed. 2001).

(6) *Jurisdiction and the Constitution.* In the United States, there are limits upon the jurisdiction of state and federal courts imposed by the Due Process Clauses of the Fifth and Fourteenth Amendments. A court that exercises

jurisdiction over a defendant in the absence of a proper jurisdictional basis has violated the defendant's right not to be deprived of property without due process, and, therefore, its judgment is invalid. The kind of connection or relationship between defendant and the state that suffices to support an exercise of jurisdiction is a question of federal law, and the Supreme Court is the final arbiter.

Just as the Due Process Clause limits the states' exercise of judicial jurisdiction, the Full Faith and Credit Clause controls the states' obligations to recognize and enforce the judgments of the courts of sister states. Subject only to a few controversial exceptions, the two constitutional clauses are co-extensive; thus, if a state has a jurisdictional contact sufficient to satisfy the Due Process Clause, the judgment of its courts must be given full faith and credit in other states.

To understand fully the impact of the Constitution on the jurisdiction and judgments of the states, it is helpful to compare the states with totally independent sovereigns. Suppose that the law of France regards residence of the plaintiff as a sufficient basis upon which to exercise judicial jurisdiction over the defendant but that Canadian law does not. If a French court exercises jurisdiction over a defendant on that basis, its judgment will not be recognized in Canada. The Canadian court will not feel itself bound by comity to enforce a foreign judgment based upon a jurisdictional contact that would not support the judgment of a Canadian court. *See Schibsby v. Westenholz*, L. R. [1870] 6 Q.B. 155. Nevertheless, although unenforceable abroad, the French judgment is perfectly valid at home. Since the Canadian and French courts recognize no common superior sovereign, they can only agree to disagree.

This problem cannot occur between states of the United States. There is one constitutional standard that limits state court jurisdiction and one final decision on the contents of that standard—the Supreme Court's. Thus, a judgment that perfectly satisfies the law of the rendering state, but fails to meet the due process standard, is invalid both at home and in sister states.

Commentators have begun to question whether there should be due process or, indeed any constitutional, restrictions on state-court territorial jurisdiction. *See* Patrick Borchers, *Jurisdictional Pragmatism: International Shoe's Half-Buried Legacy*, 28 U. C. DAVIS L. REV. 561 (1995), Roger Transgrud, *The Federal Common Law of Personal Jurisdiction: A Theoretical Evaluation*, 57 Geo. WASH. L. REV. 849 (1989). *But see* John Oakley, *The Pitfalls of "Hint and Run" History: A Critique of Professor Borchers's "Limited View" of Pennoyer v. Neff*, 28 U. C. DAVIS L. REV. 591 (1995). Assuming that there should be a due process limit on jurisdiction, how should it relate to the larger body of due process jurisprudence? Is the restriction on jurisdiction a function of procedural or substantive due process, or does it fit in its own separate category? *See* Jay Conison, *What Does Due Process Have to Do with Jurisdiction?*, 46 RUTGERS L. REV. 1071 (1993), William Richman, *Understanding Personal Jurisdiction*, 25 ARIZ. ST. L. J. 599, 609 (1993), Patrick Borchers, *The Death of the Constitutional Law of Personal Jurisdiction: From Pennoyer to Burnham and Back Again*, 24 U. C. DAVIS L. REV. 19, 90 (1990).

## § 3.04  Notice

**MULLANE v. CENTRAL HANOVER BANK AND TRUST CO.,** 339 U.S. 306 (1950). New York had a statute that provided for the existence and administration of common trust funds. Those funds were formed by pooling numerous small trust estates into one fund for purposes of investment administration. The accounts of the common fund were to be settled from time to time by a judicial proceeding called an accounting; beneficiaries of the constituent trusts (some of whose interests, names and addresses were known to the corporate trustee and others not) were to be notified of the accounting by publication. Central Hanover set up such a common fund; and at the first accounting, Mullane, special guardian and attorney for persons known or unknown who might have an interest in the common trust fund, objected that, notice by publication was constitutionally inadequate.

*Held:* Notification by publication was *adequate* for the *unknown* beneficiaries but *inadequate* for the *known* beneficiaries. The means [of notification] employed must be such as one desirous of actually informing the absentee might reasonably adopt to accomplish it. The reasonableness and hence the constitutional validity of any chosen method may be defended on the ground that it is in itself reasonably certain to inform those affected  .  .  .  or, where conditions do not reasonably permit such notice, that the form chosen is not substantially less likely to bring home notice than other of the feasible and customary substitutes.

## NOTES ON *MULLANE* AND THE REQUIREMENT OF ADEQUATE NOTICE

(1) *Relationship of Notice to Jurisdictional Basis.* The Due Process Clause, which requires the existence of an acceptable jurisdictional basis, also requires that defendant be given adequate notice of the pendency of the proceeding and an opportunity to be heard. The requirement of adequate notice is entirely separate from the requirement for a jurisdictional basis. No matter what sort of jurisdictional basis exists, and no matter whether jurisdiction is exercised *in personam* or *in rem,* the judgment will be invalid if the defendant has not been given adequate notice. Similarly, no matter how adequate the notice the defendant receives, the judgment will be invalid absent a satisfactory jurisdictional basis.

It is easy to understand why courts and lawyers confuse the two requirements. According to early jurisdictional theory, personal service of process was the only adequate basis for *in personam* jurisdiction over a non-domiciliary defendant. In hand service amply satisfied the notice requirement as well because even the most stouthearted defendant was likely to have at least his attention arrested by the marshall's hard knock at the door and his classic recitation: "I have something for you." Thus, at one stroke, the notice and basis requirements were satisfied, leading courts to confuse the two. Now that other bases for jurisdiction are constitutionally acceptable, it is crucial to distinguish between the two requirements. For more on the relationship between basis and notice, see 1 ROBERT CASAD & WILLIAM RICHMAN, JURISDICTION IN CIVIL ACTIONS 6-8 (3d ed. 1998).

(2) *The* Mullane *Test. Mullane* seems to require a two-part inquiry: (1) Is the method of notice chosen reasonably likely to reach those affected? (2) If conditions do not reasonably permit such notice, is the method chosen about as good as any other? On this standard the result in *Mullane* was clear. Notice by publication failed the first part of the test for both known and unknown beneficiaries. For known beneficiaries, publication failed the second test as well, because notice by mail (possible because their names and addresses were known), was clearly more likely to inform them than notice by publication. For the unknown beneficiaries, notice by publication was adequate, not because it was likely to inform them, but because it passed the second part of the test; no other technique was more likely to give them actual notice.

(3) *Methods of Giving Notice.* There are numerous ways of giving constitutionally adequate notice. Most are justified because they comply with the first part of the *Mullane* test; they are reasonably likely to inform the persons affected. The paradigm, of course, is personal service of process by an official of the court or a private process server. *See* FED. R. CIV. P. 4(c)(2)(B) and 4(d)(1). Also constitutionally adequate are service upon an authorized agent; service by mail, *see* FED. R. CIV. P. 4(c)(2)(C)(ii); and substituted personal service, in which the process server leaves the summons and complaint at defendant's house with "some person of suitable age and discretion then residing therein." *See* FED. R. CIV. P. 4(d)(1).

Notice by publication is much more troublesome. It clearly fails part (1) of the *Mullane* test. In the words of the *Mullane* court:

> It would be idle to pretend that publication alone . . . is a reliable means of acquainting interested parties of the fact that their rights are before the courts. . . . Chance alone brings to the attention of even a local resident an advertisement in small type inserted in the back pages of a newspaper, and if he makes his home outside the area of the newspaper's normal circulation the odds that the information will never reach him are large indeed.

If publication is to be considered constitutionally adequate notice, it must be because it satisfies the second part of the *Mullane* test. When the identity, interest, or address of persons affected by legal action are unknown, notice by publication, although not likely to reach them, is no less likely to give actual notice than any other method. It is only in those situations that publication alone is constitutionally adequate.

(4) *Non-constitutional Requirements.* A finding of constitutional adequacy does not end the inquiry into the sufficiency of notice. Each state has technical statutes and rules of court which specify the form of process and the way in which it must be served. A method of notification that satisfies due process standards may yet fail to satisfy these technical requirements and may result in an invalid judgment. Service by certified mail is a constitutionally acceptable means of giving notice, for example, but not every state permits it. A judgment based upon certified mail service will be invalid if state law deems the defect sufficiently serious; if the judgment is invalid according to the law of the rendering state, it is not entitled to full faith and credit in sister states.

(5) *Notice in In Rem Actions.* The measure of adequate notice does not change when the court exercises power over defendant's property instead of

his person. There is language in older cases which indicates that, because property is deemed to be in the possession of its owner, seizing or posting the property (especially if accompanied by publication) constitutes adequate notice to its owner. *See Pennoyer v. Neff,* 95 U.S. 714 (1878). After *Mullane,* however, the Supreme Court explicitly rejected this notion in two state condemnation cases. *See Walker v. City of Hutchinson,* 352 U.S. 112 (1956), and *Schroeder v. City of New York,* 371 U.S. 208 (1962).

Thus, the measure of adequate notice for in rem as well as in personam actions is the two-part *Mullane* test. Posting property and publication in local newspapers will rarely pass part (1) since they are unlikely to give actual notice to defendant. Nor will such forms of notice satisfy part (2) of the *Mullane* test because typically they are not the best means of notice available. The names and addresses of property owners are usually available from public records, and notice by mail (considerably more reliable than posting or publication) will often be possible. Based on this analysis, the Court has rejected notice by publication and posting of premises in a wide variety of contexts. See *Greene v. Lindsey,* 456 U.S. 444 (1982) (posting notice on tenant's apartment door insufficient notice in eviction action); *Mennonite Board of Missions v. Adams,* 462 U.S. 791 (1983) (posting and publication of property inadequate notice to mortgagee of tax sale); *Tulsa Professional Collection Services, Inc. v. Pope,* 485 U.S. 478 (1988) (published notice of probate proceeding insufficient notice to creditors of the estate).

# PART B    HISTORY: FROM POWER AND TERRITORIALITY TO CONTACTS AND FAIRNESS[1]

## § 3.05   Early Dogma

In *Pennoyer v. Neff*, 95 U.S. 714 (1877), the Supreme Court announced a theory of state court jurisdiction that was to hold sway for nearly seventy years,[2] and this analytical framework, rather than the holding of *Pennoyer* is important here.[3] The theory, which may be labeled conveniently "the territorial power theory" relied on a conception of the states as nearly independent sovereigns. In the words of Justice Field:

> The several States of the Union are not, it is true, in every respect independent, many of the rights and powers which originally belonged to them being now vested in the government created by the Constitution. But, except as restrained and limited by that instrument, they possess and exercise the authority of independent States, and the principles of public law to which we have referred are applicable to them. One of these principles is, that every State possesses exclusive jurisdiction and sovereignty over persons and property within its territory. . . . The other principle of public law referred to follows from the one mentioned; that is, that no State can exercise direct jurisdiction and authority over persons or property without its territory.

95 U.S. at 722

The result of these two "principles of public law" was that physical power over the defendant or his property was *necessary* for a constitutional exercise

---

[1] The historical notes in Part B draw heavily upon, 1 ROBERT CASAD & WILLIAM RICHMAN, JURISDICTION IN CIVIL ACTIONS 63-91 (3d ed. 1998), WILLIAM RICHMAN & WILLIAM REYNOLDS, UNDERSTANDING CONFLICT OF LAWS §§ 17-20 (3d ed. 2002), and David Vernon, *Single-Factor Bases of In Personam Jurisdiction–A Speculation on the Impact of Shaffer v. Heitner*, 1978 Wash. U.L.Q. 273, 274-278. For more historical discussion, specifically directed to the link between jurisdiction and due process, see Patrick Borchers, *The Death of the Constitutional Law of Personal Jurisdiction: From Pennoyer to Burnham and Back Again*, 24 U.C.DAVIS L. REV. 19 (1990)

[2] *International Shoe v. Washington*, 326 U.S. 310 (1945), was decided in 1945, sixty-eight years after Pennoyer.

[3] In *Pennoyer,* Neff, a Californian, filed suit in Oregon against Pennoyer seeking recovery of a tract of land in Oregon. Neff based his claim on a patent issued to him by the United States. Pennoyer claimed superior title by virtue of a later purchase of the property at a sheriff's sale in execution on a judgment that a third person, Mitchell, had obtained several years earlier in a quasi-in-rem proceeding against Neff.

In sustaining Neff's claim to the property, the Court held that the judgment Mitchell had obtained, the basis of the sheriff's sale, was rendered by the Oregon court without jurisdiction. Since the court lacked personal jurisdiction over Neff, the only basis of its power in the proceeding brought by Mitchell was the property Neff owned in Oregon. Mitchell, who followed the directions of the existing Oregon statutes, had failed to attach the property in question at the time he commenced his action against Neff. That failure was deemed fatal because, with neither Neff nor his property before it, the Oregon court had no basis for asserting jurisdiction over Mitchell's claim against Neff. Had Mitchell attached the property when he filed his suit, the earlier proceeding in Oregon would have been proper and Neff would have failed in his effort to reclaim the property.

of jurisdiction. In other words an exercise of jurisdiction could not be sustained, no matter how close defendant's ties with the state, *unless* the state had some sort of physical power. Further, physical power was *sufficient* for the constitutional exercise of jurisdiction; in other words, power would *always* justify the exercise of jurisdiction no matter how weak the defendant's ties with the state were.

In practice, only two jurisdictional bases perfectly satisfied the theory.[4] A state court could exercise some form of *in rem* jurisdiction if it seized a piece of defendant's property within the state's borders, and it could exercise *in personam* jurisdiction if defendant had been served with process while present within the state. This second basis for jurisdiction followed not literally, but only metaphorically from the territorial power theory. Personal service traced its ancestry to the English writ of *capias ad respondendum* according to which the sheriff arrested the defendant and held him to await the sovereign's pleasure. Service of process, where the sheriff is physically situated to seize the defendant, is simply the modern and civilized analogue of the arrest.

The opinion in *Pennoyer* recognized three additional bases for in personam jurisdiction that could be derived from the territorial power theory with only a bit more stretching.[5] (1) Jurisdiction based upon appearance or consent made some sense under the theory. If a defendant actually appeared in court, she could be said to be within the court's power; and if she consented to the exercise of jurisdiction, she could be held to have submitted to the court's power. (2) Domicile within the state did not guarantee that the defendant was at any given moment subject to the court's power, but it did mean that she had a permanent territorial affiliation with the state and was regularly subject to its laws.[6] (3) Jurisdiction over a corporation based upon its incorporation within the state also is consistent with the territorial power theory. A corporation is not only a "domiciliary" of its charter state, but also owes its legal life to that state's laws. Further, a state could require a corporation's consent to suits in its courts in return for allowing its existence as a limited liability association.

In summary, the Supreme Court's adoption in *Pennoyer* of the territorial power theory limited jurisdictional practice to a very few jurisdictional bases— known in the literature today as the traditional bases for jurisdiction. WILLIAM RICHMAN & WILLIAM REYNOLDS, UNDERSTANDING CONFLICT OF LAWS §§ 28-30 (3d ed. 2002). A court could exercise some form of in rem jurisdiction if there was some piece of defendant's property located within the state; it could exercise in personam jurisdiction if the defendant was personally served with

---

[4] Another jurisdictional basis was carefully preserved by the *Pennoyer* court even though it did not fit the territorial power theory very well. In a long dictum the Court indicated that its opinion should not be read to question the jurisdiction of the state of domicile over the marital status of its domiciliaries. *Pennoyer v. Neff,* 95 U.S. 714, 734-735 (1877). The fiction used to legitimate such jurisdiction over status was that the marriage was a thing or res that had a situs at the domicile of the parties. Thus the state of domicile could exercise some form of in rem jurisdiction. *See* 1 ROBERT CASAD & WILLIAM RICHMAN, JURISDICTION IN CIVIL ACTIONS 75-76 (3d ed.1998).

[5] Dicta in *Pennoyer* ratified these bases for jurisdiction even though they did not fit perfectly under the theory. 95 U.S. 714, 733-736 (1877). *See also* Casad & Richman, *supra* note 4, at 72-73.

[6] Once again dicta in *Pennoyer* legitimized this basis for jurisdiction. 95 U.S. 714, 735 (1877). *See also Developments in the Law-State Court Jurisdiction,* 73 HARV. L. REV. 909, 919 (1960).

process while present in the state, if he was a domiciliary of the state, or if he consented to the court's jurisdiction. Similarly a court could exercise in personam jurisdiction over a corporation if it was chartered in the state.

## § 3.06  Stretching the Dogma by Fictions

The territorial power theory and the exceedingly narrow jurisdictional practice that it required proved too confining for the courts as modern methods of transportation, communication and commerce made interstate litigation more common. For example, a simple interstate automobile accident could produce a very distressing result under the traditional theory. If a defendant from Pennsylvania drove his car to Massachusetts, injured the plaintiff there, and returned to Pennsylvania,[7] the plaintiff might well find herself remediless in Massachusetts because the defendant was not a domiciliary of Massachusetts, was not served with process in Massachusetts, and had not consented to the jurisdiction of Massachusetts. Similarly a foreign (out-of-state) corporation could send its products into the forum state and derive substantial revenue from the sales, yet not be amenable in a suit by a consumer in the state's courts.

Burdened with a jurisdictional theory that ill fit the realities of modern transportation and commerce, the courts and legislatures faced a choice: they could scrap the outmoded theory or stretch, it to reach more out-of-state defendants. Initially they chose the second, more conservative strategy, stretching the traditional theory with the doctrine of implied consent. The consent that was implied, of course, was fictional. A defendant did not actually consent to the court's jurisdiction; rather the defendant conducted certain activities in the forum, and consent was inferred from those activities. Thus, for example, some early long-arm statutes declared that by operating a motor vehicle upon the roads of the state, the non-resident motorist was deemed to have appointed the registrar of motor vehicles his agent for receipt of service of process. *See, e.g., Hess v. Pawloski*, 274 U.S. 352 (1927). By driving into the state, the non-resident "consented" to the jurisdiction of the state's courts.

The Supreme Court upheld such statutory fictions on the argument that the state had the right to exclude a motorist (resident or non-resident) from the use of its highways. It could therefore condition his permission to drive its roads upon his execution of an actual consent to jurisdiction. *See Kane v. New Jersey*, 242 U.S. 623 (1935). Finally, if it could extort an actual consent in return for the privilege of using its highways, it could infer a consent from the non-resident's exercise of the privilege.

The same fiction could be used to support jurisdiction over a defendant who engaged in any sort of closely regulated activity within the state. It would not serve, however, to reach an out-of-state defendant whose in-state conduct was more mundane. In *Flexner v. Farson*, 248 U.S. 289 (1919), the Supreme Court held that a state could not exclude non-residents from simply traveling through or conducting ordinary business in the state because natural persons (unlike corporations) are entitled to the privileges and immunities of national citizenship, one of which is the right to travel through and conduct ordinary

---

[7] This hypothetical is based on *Hess v. Pawloski*, 274 U.S. 352 (1927).

business in any of the states. Because the state could not exclude non-resident natural persons, it could not extract a consent from them or infer their consent to jurisdiction from their ordinary activities within the state.

The consent fiction also authorized jurisdiction over foreign corporations. The Privileges and Immunities Clause does not apply to corporations, *Paul v. Virginia,* 75 U.S. (8 Wall.) 168 (1868), so a state could prohibit a corporation from conducting any activities within its territory. *Lafayette Ins. Co. v. French,* 59 U.S. (18 How.) 404 (1855). If the state could completely exclude the foreign corporation, it could also condition the corporation's right to enter on its express consent to the jurisdiction of the state's courts. Once again, if the state could extort an actual consent, it could infer the corporation's consent from the entity's decision to engage in business in the forum.[8]

The courts also used the fiction of corporate "presence" as another doctrine-stretching device to justify the exercise of jurisdiction over foreign corporations. The idea was that if a corporation was conducting activities in the forum it could be deemed to be "present" there. In the words of Justice Brandeis: "A foreign corporation is amenable to process to enforce a personal liability, in the absence of consent, only if it is doing business within the State in such a manner and to such an extent as to warrant the inference that it is present there." *Philadelphia & Reading Ry. Co. v. McKibbin,* 234 U.S. 264 (1917).

The fictions of "consent" and "presence" proved to be adequate theoretical justifications for the exercise of jurisdiction over foreign corporations. The remaining question was how much contact between the defendant and the state was required in order to find that the corporation "consented" to jurisdiction or to find that it was "present" in the forum. Under both theories, the courts settled upon the practical test of "doing business." If the defendant was doing business in the forum, jurisdiction existed; otherwise, it did not.

Exactly what activities constituted "doing business" was not entirely clear; it is clear, however, that by modern standards the "doing business" test required a fairly substantial connection between the defendant and the forum. If the defendant's forum-related activities were continuous and systematic, the courts were likely to find it amenable; otherwise not.[9]

---

[8] The theoretical basis for the doctrine of implied consent suffered a serious blow when the Supreme Court began to expand the definition of "commerce among the several states." A state could not prevent a corporation from conducting "interstate commerce" within its borders, *International Text Book Co. v. Pigg,* 217 U.S. 91 (1910), and as the definition of interstate commerce" expanded, it became doubtful that a state could constitutionally exclude a corporation from its territory. Lacking the ability to exclude the corporation, the state could not require an express or implied consent as a condition of inclusion. By the 1940's, therefore, the basic premise of the theory of implied consent had eroded considerably.

[9] Minimal or isolated contacts within the forum did not constitute doing business. Even regular but intermittent activities—such as a retailer's periodic buying trips into the forum—were not enough. *Rosenberg Bros. & Co. v. Curtis Brown Co.,* 260 U.S. 516 (1923). The presence in the forum of a corporate agent and the maintenance of an office were factors to be considered but were not determinative. *Green v. Chicago, Burlington & Quincy Ry. Co.,* 205 U.S. 530 (1907). Mere solicitation of business in the forum was also deemed insufficient, although "solicitation plus" some additional activity might be enough. *Hutchinson v. Chase & Gilbert, Inc.,* 45 F.2d 139 (2d Cir. 1930).

## § 3.07 Contacts and Fairness

By the middle of this century the territorial power theory had proved its inadequacy. Its limited reach was out of step with modern advances in communication and transportation, which allowed persons (natural and legal) to conduct business in several states over a relatively short period of time. The changes in transportation, communication, and commercial practice resulted in more and more claims by state citizens against non-domiciliary persons and corporations, but often the territorial power theory could not justify jurisdiction over such defendants.

Another serious defect of the territorial power theory was that it depended upon fictions. Applied strictly, the theory would uphold jurisdiction in only a narrow band of cases. In other cases, the fiction of "implied consent" or "presence" was required. Thus, the theory lacked power in that it failed to reach many non-resident defendants, and it lacked elegance in that it needed a good deal of stretching to reach many others.

By the 1940's, the defects of the territorial power theory had rendered it obsolete, and the law of jurisdiction was ready for a major overhaul. The doctrinal overhaul, which began in *International Shoe v. Washington* and continues today, is best viewed as a shift in the conceptual basis of state-court jurisdiction from power to fairness. State-court jurisdiction is no longer based on physical power over the person or property of the defendant. Today the law is much more concerned with fairness, convenience, and the justified expectations of the parties. Nevertheless, remnants of power and territoriality analysis recur in the Supreme Court's opinions. The beginning of the shift from power to fairness is the subject of the cases and notes in this section. The current state of the law is explored in Part C, *infra*, of this Chapter.

## INTERNATIONAL SHOE CO. v. STATE OF WASHINGTON

*United States Supreme Court*
*326 U.S. 310 (1945)*

MR. CHIEF JUSTICE STONE delivered the opinion of the Court.

The questions for decision are (1) whether, within the limitations of the due process clause of the Fourteenth Amendment, appellant, a Delaware corporation, has by its activities in the State of Washington rendered itself amenable to proceedings in the courts of that state to recover unpaid contributions to the state unemployment compensation fund enacted by state statutes, and (2) whether the state can exact those contributions consistently with the due process clause of the Fourteenth Amendment.

The statutes in question set up a comprehensive scheme of unemployment compensation, the costs of which are defrayed by contributions required to be made by employers to a state unemployment compensation fund. The contributions are a specified percentage of the wages payable annually by each employer for his employees' services in the state. . . .

In this case notice of assessment for the years in question was personally served upon a sales solicitor employed by appellant in the State of Washington, and a copy of the notice was mailed by registered mail to appellant at its address in St. Louis, Missouri. Appellant appeared specially before the office of unemployment and moved to set aside the order and notice of assessment on the ground that the service upon appellant's salesman was not proper service upon appellant; that appellant was not a corporation of the State of Washington and was not doing business within the state; that it had no agent within the state upon whom service could be made; and that appellant is not an employer and does not furnish employment within the meaning of the statute.

[The administrative agency and the Washington courts ruled that the state had jurisdiction over appellant]. . . .

. . . Appellant is a Delaware corporation, having its principal place of business in St. Louis, Missouri, and is engaged in the manufacture and sale of shoes and other footwear. It maintains places of business in several states, other than Washington, at which its manufacturing is carried on and from which its merchandise is distributed interstate through several sales units or branches located outside the State of Washington.

Appellant has no office in Washington and makes no contracts either for sale or purchase of merchandise there. It maintains no stock of merchandise in that state and makes there no deliveries of goods in intrastate commerce. During the years from 1937 to 1940, now in question, appellant employed eleven to thirteen salesmen under direct supervision and control of sales managers located in St. Louis. These salesmen resided in Washington; their principal activities were confined to that state; and they were compensated by commissions based upon the amount of their sales. The commissions for each year totaled more than $31,000. Appellant supplies its salesmen with a line of samples, each consisting of one shoe of a pair, which they display to prospective purchasers. On occasion they rent permanent sample rooms, for exhibiting samples, in business buildings, or rent rooms in hotels or business buildings temporarily for that purpose. The cost of such rentals is reimbursed by appellant.

The authority of the salesmen is limited to exhibiting their samples and soliciting orders from prospective buyers, at prices and on terms fixed by appellant. The salesmen transmit the orders to appellant's office in St. Louis for acceptance or rejection, and when accepted the merchandise for filling the orders is shipped f.o.b. from points outside Washington to the purchasers within the state. All the merchandise shipped into Washington is invoiced at the place of shipment from which collections are made. No salesman has authority to enter into contracts or to make collections. . . .

Historically the jurisdiction of courts to render judgment *in personam* is grounded on their de facto power over the defendant's person. Hence his presence within the territorial jurisdiction of a court was prerequisite to its rendition of a judgment personally binding him. *Pennoyer v. Neff,* 95 U.S. 714, 733. But now that the *capias ad respondendum* has given way to way to personal service of summons or other form of notice, due process requires only that in order to subject a defendant to a judgment *in personam*, if he be not present within the territory of the forum, he have certain minimum contacts with it such that the maintenance of the suit does not offend "traditional notions of fair play and substantial justice."

Since the corporate personality is a fiction, although a fiction intended to be acted upon as though it were a fact, it is clear that unlike an individual its "presence" without, as well as within, the state of its origin can be manifested only by activities carried on in its behalf by those who are authorized to act for it. To say that the corporation is so far "present" there as to satisfy due process requirements, for purposes of taxation or the maintenance of suits against it in the courts of the state, is to beg the question to be decided. For the terms "present" or "presence" are used merely to symbolize those activities of the corporation's agent within the state which courts will deem to be sufficient to satisfy the demands of due process. L. Hand, J., in *Hutchinson v. Chase & Gilbert,* 45 F.2d 139, 141. Those demands may be met by such contacts of the corporation with the state of the forum as make it reasonable, in the context of our federal system of government, to require the corporation to defend the particular suit which is brought there. An "estimate of the inconveniences" which would result to the corporation from a trial away from its "home" or principal place of business is relevant in this connection.

"Presence" in the state in this sense has never been doubted when the activities of the corporation there have not only been continuous and systematic, but also give rise to the liabilities sued on, even though no consent to be sued or authorization to an agent to accept service of process has been given. Conversely it has been generally recognized that the casual presence of the corporate agent or even his conduct of single or isolated items of activities in a state in the corporation's behalf are not enough to subject it to suit on causes of action unconnected with the activities there. . . .

While it has been held, in cases on which appellant relies, that continuous activity of some sorts within a state is not enough to support the demand that the corporation be amenable to suits unrelated to that activity, there have been instances in which the continuous corporate operations within a state were thought so substantial and of such a nature as to justify suit against it on causes of action arising from dealings entirely distinct from those activities.

Finally, although the commission of some single or occasional acts of the corporate agent in a state sufficient to impose an obligation or liability on the corporation has not been thought to confer upon the state authority to enforce it, *Rosenberg Bros. & Co. v. Curtis Brown Co.,* 260 U.S. 516, other such acts, because of their nature and quality and the circumstances of their commission, may be deemed sufficient to render the corporation liable to suit. *Cf. Kane v. New Jersey,* 242 U.S. 160; *Hess v. Pawloski,* [274 U.S. 352 (1927)]. True, some of the decisions holding the corporation amenable to suit have been supported by resort to the legal fiction that it has given its consent to service and suit, consent being implied from its presence in the state through the acts of its authorized agents. But more realistically it may be said that those authorized acts were of such a nature as to justify the fiction.

It is evident that the criteria by which we mark the boundary line between those activities which justify the subjection of a corporation to suit, and those which do not, cannot be simply mechanical or quantitative. The test is not merely, as has sometimes been suggested, whether the activity, which the corporation has seen fit to procure through its agents in another state, is a little more or a little less. Whether due process is satisfied must depend rather upon the quality and nature of the activity in relation to the fair and orderly administration of the laws which it was the purpose of the due process clause to insure. . . .

[T]o the extent that a corporation exercises the privilege of conducting activities within a state, it enjoys the benefits and protection of the laws of that state. The exercise of that privilege may give rise to obligations, and, so far as those obligations arise out of or are connected with the activities within the state, a procedure which requires the corporation to respond to a suit brought to enforce them can, in most instances, hardly be said to be undue.

Applying these standards, the activities carried on in behalf of appellant in the State of Washington were neither irregular nor casual. They were systematic and continuous throughout the years in question. They resulted in a large volume of interstate business, in the course of which appellant received the benefits and protection of the laws of the state, including the right to resort to the courts for the enforcement of its rights. The obligation which is here sued upon arose out of those very activities. It is evident that these operations establish sufficient contacts or ties with the state of the forum to make it reasonable and just, according to our traditional conception of fair play and substantial justice, to permit the state to enforce the obligations which appellant has incurred there. . . .

Only a word need be said of appellant's liability for the demanded contributions to the state unemployment fund. The Supreme Court of Washington, construing and applying the statute, has held that it imposes a tax on the privilege of employing appellant's salesmen within the state measured by a percentage of the wages, here the commissions payable to the salesmen. This construction we accept for purposes of determining the constitutional validity of the statute. The right to employ labor has been deemed an appropriate subject of taxation in this country and England, both before and since the adoption of the Constitution. And such a tax imposed upon the employer for unemployment benefits is within the constitutional power of the states.

Appellant having rendered itself amenable to suit upon obligations arising out of the activities of its salesmen in Washington, the state may maintain the present suit *in personam* to collect the tax laid upon the exercise of the privilege of employing appellant's salesmen within the state. For Washington has made one of those activities, which taken together establish appellant's "presence" there for purposes of suit, the taxable event by which the state brings appellant within the reach of its taxing power. The state thus has constitutional power to lay the tax and to subject appellant to a suit to recover it. The activities which establish its "presence" subject it alike to taxation by the state and to suit to recover the tax.

*Affirmed.*

JUSTICE JACKSON took no part in the consideration or decision of this case.

[JUSTICE BLACK'S concurring opinion is omitted.]

## NOTES AND QUESTIONS ON *INTERNATIONAL SHOE* AND THE MINIMUM CONTACTS STANDARD

(1) *Commentary.* There is a wealth of commentary on *International Shoe*; nearly every modern jurisdiction opinion cites it and quotes its most important passages, and nearly every commentator recites its facts and holding. For a sample of the commentary, see WILLIAM RICHMAN & WILLIAM REYNOLDS, UNDERSTANDING CONFLICT OF LAWS § 20 (3d ed. 2002); Phillip Kurland, *The Supreme Court, The Due Process Clause and the In Personam Jurisdiction of State Courts—From Pennoyer to Denckla: A Review*, 25 U. CHI. L. REV. 569, 586-593 (1958). A useful collection of recent commentary appears in Symposium, *Fifty Years of International Shoe: The Past and Future of Personal Jurisdiction*, 28 U. C. DAVIS L. REV. 513-1038 (1995).

(2) *Adjudicatory and Legislative Jurisdiction.* Whether the defendant was amenable to the jurisdiction of the Washington courts is a question of adjudicatory jurisdiction. Another problem dealt with in the opinion is the issue of legislative jurisdiction—whether Washington could subject the defendant to its laws, in this case its law requiring employers to make contributions to an unemployment compensation fund. There are constitutional restrictions on the states' exercise of legislative jurisdiction, just as there are on their exercise of adjudicatory jurisdiction. The limitations on the states' legislative jurisdiction are the subject of Chapter 5, *infra*. Should the limits be the same in each case? Are the relevant factors the same?

(3) *Long-Arm Jurisdiction.* One important consequence of the decision was that it authorized the states to enact long-arm statutes, extending their courts' jurisdiction toward the newly expanded constitutional limits. Those statutes are considered in § 3.13, *infra*.

(4) *Discarding Old Doctrine.* The Supreme Court could have reached the same result in *International Shoe* under the traditional standard of "doing business." The defendant derived substantial revenue from its business in Washington; it solicited business in Washington; and it employed between eleven and thirteen salesmen in Washington. In the words of the opinion: "[The activities of the defendant] were neither irregular nor casual. They were systematic and continuous throughout the years in question."

If the Court could reach the right result under the old doctrine, why did it discard it and establish a new test? The standard answer is that the territorial power theory could explain jurisdiction in cases like *International Shoe* only by resort to the fictions of "presence" and "consent." But how does the Court, or any court, decide when to stretch existing doctrine just a bit more and when to discard the old theory and write on a clean slate?

(5) *"Minimum Contacts" or "Fair Play and Substantial Justice."* The new test established by *International Shoe* requires that the defendant "have certain minimum contacts with [the forum] such that the maintenance of the suit does not offend 'traditional notions of fair play and substantial justice.'"

This famous passage, however, is ambiguous, leading to inconsistent judicial interpretations. One reading focuses on the words "minimum contacts" and has led courts to require some sort of physical pre-litigation connection between the defendant and the forum. The other reading focuses on "fair play and substantial justice." Using that approach, courts have considered a wide range of factors (the inconvenience to the defendant of defending in the forum, the inconvenience to the plaintiff of bringing the action elsewhere, the interest of the forum state in the litigation, the relative wealth of the parties, the location of witnesses and evidence) to determine whether the exercise of jurisdiction is "fair."

The opinion in *International Shoe* contains numerous passages that support one interpretation or the other. For a more complete discussion of the two approaches and numerous citations to cases using each one, see 1 ROBERT CASAD & WILLIAM RICHMAN, JURISDICTION IN CIVIL ACTIONS 84-87 (3d ed. 1998). *See also* Kevin Clermont, *Restating Territorial Jurisdiction and Venue for State and Federal Courts*, 66 CORNELL L. REV. 411, 416-417 (1981).

In addition to the courts, commentators regularly do battle over the issue of contacts versus fairness. *Compare, e.g.,* Arthur Weisburd, *Territorial Authority and Personal Jurisdiction*, 63 WASH. U. L.Q. 377, 422 (1985), with Russell Weintraub, *Due Process Limitations on the Personal Jurisdiction of State Courts*, 63 OR. L. REV. 485, 486 (1984).

It is easy to see how the fairness approach derives from the Due Process Clause, which has been held to require "fair" treatment of persons in other contexts. But how is the "minimum contacts" view grounded in due process? Is the contacts requirement merely instrumental—a sort of bright-line test to measure fairness? Or is the insistence on pre-litigation connections between the defendant and the state simply a remnant of the territorial power theory?

(6) *McGee and Hanson.* Following *International Shoe,* the Supreme Court decided two cases, *McGee v. International Life Insurance Co.*, 355 U.S. 220 (1957), and *Hanson v. Denckla*, 357 U.S. 235 (1958), which highlighted the tension between the "fairness" and "contacts" approaches to jurisdiction.

**McGEE v. INTERNATIONAL LIFE INSURANCE CO.,** 355 U.S. 220 (1957). Franklin, a California resident, purchased a life insurance policy from the Empire Mutual Insurance Company. The defendant later contracted with Empire to assume its insurance obligations and mailed to Franklin in California a reinsurance certificate. The certificate contained an offer to insure Franklin upon the same terms as the policy he held with Empire. Franklin accepted the offer and mailed his policy premiums from California to defendant's offices in Texas. Apart from this one contact, the record revealed no other connection between defendant and California. The plaintiff, Franklin's mother (the beneficiary of the policy), claimed the death benefit after Franklin's death; but defendant refused to pay on the ground that Franklin had committed suicide. The plaintiff sued on the policy in California, serving the defendant by mail in Texas pursuant to the California Unauthorized Insurers Process Act. When the defendant failed to appear, the Plaintiff took a default judgment and sued the defendant in Texas to enforce that judgment. The Texas courts refused to give full faith and credit to the California judgment on the ground that the California court lacked jurisdiction.

*Held:* Reversed. The Texas courts' refusal to give full faith and credit to the California judgment was improper; California had jurisdiction over the defendant. The opinion endorsed the trend toward expanded state court jurisdiction, relying on changing patterns of business and commerce to justify it:

> [A] trend is clearly discernible toward expanding the permissible scope of state jurisdiction. . . . In part this is attributable to the fundamental transformation of our national economy over the years. Today many commercial transactions touch two or more States and may involve parties separated by the full continent. With this increasing nationalization of commerce has come a great increase in the amount of business conducted by mail across state lines. At the same time modern transportation and communication have made it much less burdensome for a party sued to defend himself in a State where he engages in economic activity.

The opinion seemed to emphasize the "fair play and substantial justice" component of the *International Shoe* test:

> Turning to this case we think it apparent that the Due Process Clause did not preclude the California court from entering a judgment binding on respondent. It is sufficient for purposes of due process that the suit was based on a contract which had substantial connection with that State. The contract was delivered in California, the premiums were mailed from there and the insured was a resident of that State when he died. It cannot be denied that California has a manifest interest in providing effective means of redress for its residents when their insurers refuse to pay claims. These residents would be at a severe disadvantage if they were forced to follow the insurance company to a distant State in order to hold it legally accountable. When claims were small or moderate individual claimants frequently could not afford the cost of bringing an action in a foreign forum—thus in effect making the company judgment proof. Often the crucial witnesses—as here on the company's defense of suicide—will be found in the insured's locality. Of course there may be inconvenience to the insurer if it is held amenable to suit in California where it had this contract but certainly nothing which amounts to a denial of due process.

The Court's concern with the relative inconvenience of the plaintiff and the defendant, the regulatory interest of the forum state, and the ease of access to sources of proof make it clear that *McGee* is a "fairness" case. After *McGee*, it appeared that the Supreme Court would adopt the "fairness" approach decisively and expand steadily the limits on state court jurisdiction. The court's next jurisdiction decision, however, moved in quite the opposite direction.

**HANSON v. DENCKLA,** 357 U.S. 235 (1958). In 1935 Mrs. Donner, a Pennsylvania domiciliary, created a trust in Delaware, naming a Delaware trustee. She directed that the income be paid to her during her life and reserved a power of appointment over the corpus. Mrs. Donner moved to Florida where, in 1949, she executed both her will and the power of appointment. The appointment directed that $400,000 from the trust go to the children of her daughter Elizabeth; the rest of her estate—about one million dollars—she left to her other two daughters, who were the legatees in her will.

After Mrs. Donner's death, the residuary legatees brought an action in Florida, naming as defendants (among others) Elizabeth (the executrix) and the Delaware trustee. They sought a determination that the trust corpus passed to them through the residuary clause. The Florida Supreme Court held that Florida had jurisdiction over the Delaware trustee and that under Florida law the trust was invalid because the settlor had retained too much power over the trustee and the trust corpus. The result was that nearly all of Mrs. Donner's estate (the $400,000 appointed to her grandchildren plus the one million bequeathed to the two daughters) passed through the residuary clause to the two daughters.

After the Florida suit began, but before the Florida judgment, Elizabeth, the executrix, began a declaratory judgment proceeding in Delaware to determine who was entitled to the trust assets. When the Florida decree was entered, the residuary legatees urged it as res judicata in Delaware, but the Delaware courts refused full faith and credit on the ground that the Florida court lacked jurisdiction over the Delaware trustee. The Supreme Court granted certiorari in both cases.

*Held:* Florida lacked jurisdiction over the Delaware trustee; the Delaware court was justified in refusing to give full faith and credit to the Florida judgment:

> [The residuary legatees] urge that the circumstances of this case amount to sufficient affiliation with the State of Florida to empower its courts to exercise personal jurisdiction over this nonresident defendant. Principal reliance is placed upon *McGee v. International Life Ins. Co.*, 355 U.S. 220. In *McGee* the Court noted the trend of expanding personal jurisdiction over nonresidents. . . . But it is a mistake to assume that this trend heralds the eventual demise of all restrictions on the personal jurisdiction of state courts. *Those restrictions are more than a guarantee of immunity from inconvenient or distant litigation. They are a consequence of territorial limitations on the power of the respective States.* However minimal the burden of defending in a foreign tribunal, a defendant may not be called upon to do so unless he has had the "minimal contacts" with that State that are a prerequisite to its exercise of power over him. *See Int'l Shoe Co. v. Washington*, 326 U.S. 310, 319. [Emphasis supplied.]

> We fail to find such contacts in the circumstances of this case. The defendant trust company has no office in Florida, and transacts no business there. None of the trust assets has ever been held or administered in Florida, and the record discloses no solicitation of business in that State either in person or by mail.

> The cause of action in this case is not one that arises out of an act done or transaction consummated in the forum State. In that respect, it differs from *McGee v. International Life Ins. Co.*, 355 U.S. 220, and the cases there cited. In *McGee*, the nonresident defendant solicited a reinsurance agreement with a resident of California. The offer was accepted in that State, and the insurance premiums were mailed from there until the insured's death. . . . In contrast, this action involves the validity of an agreement that was entered without any connection

with the forum State. The agreement was executed in Delaware by a trust company incorporated in that State and a settlor domiciled in Pennsylvania. The first relationship Florida had to the agreement was years later when the settlor became domiciled there, and the trustee remitted the trust income to her in that State. From Florida Mrs. Donner carried on several bits of trust administration that may be compared to the mailing of premiums in *McGee*. But the record discloses no instance in which the trustee performed any acts in Florida that bear the same relationship to the agreement as the solicitation in *McGee*. Consequently, this suit cannot be said to be one to enforce an obligation that arose from a privilege the defendant exercised in Florida. *Cf. Int'l Shoe Co. v. Washington*, 326 U.S. 310, 319. This case is also different from *McGee* in that there the State had enacted special legislation (Unauthorized Insurers Process Act) to exercise what *McGee* called its "manifest interest" in providing effective redress for citizens who had been injured by nonresidents engaged in an activity that the State treats as exceptional and subjects to special regulation.

The execution in Florida of the powers of appointment under which the beneficiaries and appointees claim does not give Florida a substantial connection with the contract on which this suit is based. . . . The unilateral activity of those who claim some relationship with a nonresident defendant cannot satisfy the requirement of contact with the forum State. The application of that rule will vary with the quality and nature of the defendant's activity, but it is essential in each case that there be some act by which the defendant purposefully avails itself of the privilege of conducting activities within the forum State, thus invoking the benefits and protections of its laws. *International Shoe Co. v. Washington*, 326 U.S. 310, 319. . . .

It is urged that because the settlor and most of the appointees and beneficiaries were domiciled in Florida the courts of that State should be able to exercise personal jurisdiction over the nonresident trustees. This is a non sequitur. . . . As we understand [Florida] law, the trustee is an indispensable party over whom the court must acquire jurisdiction before it is empowered to enter judgment in a proceeding affecting the validity of a trust. It does not acquire that jurisdiction by being the "center of gravity" of the controversy, or the most convenient location for litigation. The issue is personal jurisdiction, not choice of law.

## NOTES AND QUESTIONS ON *MCGEE* AND *HANSON*

(1) *Distinguishing the cases.* Are you satisfied with the Court's attempt to distinguish *Hanson* from *McGee*? Were not the Delaware trustee and the International Life Insurance Co. both commercial enterprises in one state with a single customer in another state? *See* WILLIAM RICHMAN & WILLIAM REYNOLDS, UNDERSTANDING CONFLICT OF LAWS § 20[c] (3d ed. 2002); Phillip Kurland, *The Supreme Court, The Due Process Clause and the In Personarn Jurisdiction of State Courts—From Pennoyer to Denckla: A Review*, 25 U. CHI. L. REV. 569, 622 (1958).

(2) *Hanson and Territoriality.* What passages in the quoted portion of the *Hanson* opinion make it clear that *Hanson* is a contacts case and not a fairness case? Is there language that is even more territorial than a simple insistence on pre-litigation contacts between the defendant and the forum—language that suggests a return to the territorial power theory of *Pennoyer*? *See* Harold Lewis, *The Three Deaths of "State Sovereignty" and the Curse of Abstraction in the Jurisprudence of Jurisdiction*, 58 Notre Dame L. Rev. 699, 709-711 (1983).

(3) *Jurisdiction and Choice of Law.* The opinion in *Hanson* is notable for its clear indication that more contact between the defendant and the state may be required to justify the state's exercise of adjudicatory jurisdiction than is required to justify the application of the state's law to the defendant's conduct: "[A state] does not acquire . . . jurisdiction by being the 'center of gravity' of the controversy, or the most convenient location for the litigation. The issue is personal jurisdiction, not choice of law."

Was choice of law the hidden motive behind the Court's decision? The Florida courts applied Florida law to determine that the trust and the power of appointment were invalid and that the corpus thus passed to the residuary legatees. The Delaware courts instead applied Delaware law and concluded that the trust and power of appointment were valid and that the corpus passed to Mrs. Donner's grandchildren. In order for the Supreme Court to permit a *per stirpes* distribution of Mrs. Donner's estate (and give the grandchildren their fair share), the Court had to reverse the Florida judgment and affirm the Delaware judgment. The direct route would have been to hold unconstitutional the Florida courts' choice-of-law decision, but that path was precluded by recent decisions of the Court that minimized the constitutional restrictions on state court choice-of-law decisions. See *Alaska Packers Ass'n v. Indus. Accident Comm'n*, 294 U.S. 532 (1935); *Pac. Employers Ins. Co. v. Indus. Accident Comm'n*, 306 U.S. 493 (1939). The Court was forced to use the constitutional restrictions on jurisdiction to do the dirty work instead.

(4) *The Influence of Hanson.* The obvious ulterior motive for the decision led many to believe that *Hanson* was bad law (made by a hard case), a jurisdictional oddity that went against the national trend. *See* Geoffrey Hazard, *A General Theory of State-Court Jurisdiction*, 1965 Sup. Ct. Rev. 241, 244 (1965). In fact, however, the later decisions of the Supreme Court have relied heavily on *Hanson* and its requirement that "there be some act by which the defendant purposely avails itself of the privilege of conducting activity in the forum State." The subsequent histories of *McGee* and *Hanson* are summarized in Christopher Cameron and Kevin Johnson, *Death of a Salesman? Forum Shopping and Outcome Determination Under International Shoe*, 28 U. C. Davis L. Rev. 769, 850-851 (1995).

## PART C   JURISDICTION AFTER 1977

### § 3.08   Introductory Note

For two decades, between *Hanson v. Denckla,*  357 U.S. 235 (1958), and *Shaffer v. Heitner,*  433 U.S. 186 (1977), the Supreme Court issued no major decisions on the constitutional limitations upon state court jurisdiction. After 1977, the Court ended its twenty-year silence with a vengeance—issuing twelve major decisions in the next thirteen years. Part C considers that period of extraordinary productivity.

As you read the notes and opinions in this part, be aware that the Court is not merely struggling to determine exactly how much connection between the defendant and the forum constitutes "minimum contacts." In addition, its opinions attempt to locate the constitutional basis for the minimum contacts test. Is the requirement based solely upon the unfairness of subjecting the defendant to litigation in a distant and inconvenient forum, or is there something about the states' relationship to each other that also limits their exercise of jurisdiction? Also try to see how the Court struggles with the ambiguity of the *International Shoe* formula: Must the defendant have purposefully established pre-litigation connections with the forum (contacts approach), or is it sufficient that the state's exercise of jurisdiction not be seriously unfair (fairness approach)? Or must the exercise of jurisdiction satisfy both the contacts and the fairness standards? Finally give some attention to the different types of arguments that the Court finds relevant to each of the two standards.

### § 3.09   Note on *Shaffer v. Heitner*

*Shaffer v. Heitner,* 433 U.S. 186 (1977), is most famous for its unification of in personam and in rem jurisdictional analysis under the *International Shoe* standard (*see* § 3.07, *infra,* for the text of the opinion), but the opinion also contains a significant discussion of the power, contacts and fairness themes we have been considering.

Plaintiff, a shareholder in Greyhound—a Delaware corporation with its principal place of business in Arizona—brought a derivative action in Delaware against several of Greyhound's officers and directors. He claimed that they had violated their duties to Greyhound by causing it to incur substantial civil and criminal antitrust liabilities based on activities that took place in Oregon. The Delaware court asserted quasi-in-rem jurisdiction over defendants, based not on their minimum contacts with Delaware, but on their ownership of Greyhound stock with a situs in Delaware according to a unique Delaware statute. The Supreme Court, invalidated the exercise of jurisdiction and held that all attempts to exercise jurisdiction must satisfy the minimum contacts test of *International Shoe.*

From the point of view of the development of jurisdictional theory, the opinion in *Shaffer*  is a mixed bag. Several passages bode well for a jurisdictional theory based largely on fairness; others do not. On the one hand, the opinion clearly rejects the territorial power theory of *Pennoyer:* "Thus, the relationship among the defendant, the forum, and the litigation, rather than the mutually exclusive sovereignty of the States on which the rules of *Pennoyer* rest, became the central concern of the inquiry into personal jurisdiction." *Id.* at 204. A footnote to this passage also dismisses the brief resurgence of the territorial power theory in the Court's opinion in *Hanson*.

> Nothing in *Hanson v. Denckla* is to the contrary. The *Hanson* Court's statement that restrictions on state jurisdiction "are a consequence of territorial limitations on the power of the respective States," simply makes the point that the States are defined by their geographic territory. After making this point, the Court in *Hanson* determined that the defendant over which personal jurisdiction was claimed had not committed any acts sufficiently connected to the State to justify jurisdiction under the *International Shoe* standard.[1]

Further, in a sweeping dictum, the Court asserted that "all assertions of state-court jurisdiction must be evaluated according to the standards set forth in *International Shoe* and its progeny." *Id.* at 212. This proposition, if rigorously applied, might have resulted in the abandonment of transient service or technical domicile as sufficient jurisdictional bases, since it is difficult to argue that they satisfy the *International Shoe* standard. After the Court's ruling in *Burnham v. Superior Court*, 110 S.Ct. 2105 (1990), § 3.12[A] *infra,* however, these traditional jurisdictional bases appear secure. *See* Part D of this chapter.

On the other hand, other parts of the opinion are not as supportive of a theory of jurisdiction based on fairness. Part IV contains a very restrictive view of the ability of Delaware to exercise jurisdiction over the absent officers and directors. Because defendants had no other contacts with Delaware and the cause of action was based on activities in Oregon, the issue resolved itself into one narrow question: Can the state in which a corporation is chartered exercise jurisdiction in a derivative action over directors of the corporation even if there is no other contact between the directors and the forum? Plaintiff first argued that in personam jurisdiction would have been proper because Delaware had a strong interest in regulating the supervision and management of Delaware corporations; Delaware law, after all, established the corporation and set up the duties owed by officers and directors. Plaintiff's second argument was that by accepting positions as directors, defendants received considerable benefit from Delaware's corporation law; in return for that benefit they could be required to respond to Delaware's summons in a cause of action related to their fiduciary duties. The Court rejected both arguments:

> [T]his line of reasoning establishes only that it is appropriate for Delaware law to govern the obligations of appellants to Greyhound and its stockholders. It does not demonstrate that appellants have "purposefully avail[ed themselves] of the privilege of conducting activities within the forum State" . . . in a way that would justify bringing

---

[1] *Id.* at 204, n. 20. Several commentators have noted this second death of the territorial power theory in the *Shaffer* footnote. *See* David Seidelson, *Recasting* World-Wide Volkswagen *as a Source of Longer Jurisdictional Reach,* 19 TULSA L.J. 1, 8 (1983); Harold Lewis, *The Three Deaths of "State Sovereignty" and the Curse of Abstraction in the Jurisprudence of Personal Jurisdiction,* 58 NOTRE DAME L. REV. 699, 711 (1983).

them before a Delaware tribunal. Appellants have simply had nothing
to do with the State of Delaware.

433 U.S. 186, 216 (1977).

Does the passage, just quoted, particularly the last sentence, suggest that
the Court is looking for some actual physical contact between defendants and
the forum? Is that asking for too much? After all, Delaware had created an
entity and allowed certain people (defendant directors) to have power and
control over it. Should Delaware be prohibited from monitoring their conduct
by asserting jurisdiction over them in a cause of action arising out of their
duties? Regardless of whether we approve of the Court's holding, it is clear
that this passage seems committed to the "contacts" rather than the "fairness"
interpretation of International Shoe. *See* Earl Maltz, *Reflections on a Landmark:* Shaffer v. Heitner *Viewed From a Distance,* 1986 B.Y.U. L. Rev. 1043,
1058-60. For more recent commentary on the opinion, see 1 Robert Casad
& William Richman, Jurisdiction in Civil Actions 91-95 (3d ed. 1998).

## § 3.10  The More Recent Cases

### WORLD-WIDE VOLKSWAGEN CORP. v. WOODSON

*United States Supreme Court*
*444 U.S. 286, 100 S. Ct. 559, 62 L. Ed. 2d 490 (1980)*

Mr. Justice White delivered the opinion of the Court.

The issue before us is whether, consistently with the Due Process Clause
of the Fourteenth Amendment, an Oklahoma court may exercise *in personam*
jurisdiction over a nonresident automobile retailer and its wholesale distributor in a products-liability action, when the defendants' only connection with
Oklahoma is the fact that an automobile sold in New York to New York
residents became involved in an accident in Oklahoma.

Respondents Harry and Kay Robinson purchased a new Audi automobile
from petitioner Seaway Volkswagen, Inc. (Seaway), in Massena, N. Y., in 1976.
The following year the Robinson family, who resided in New York, left that
State for a new home in Arizona. As they passed through the State of Oklahoma, another car struck their Audi in the rear, causing a fire which severely
burned Kay Robinson and her two children.

The Robinsons subsequently brought a products-liability action in the District Court for Creek County, Okla., claiming that their injuries resulted from
defective design and placement of the Audi's gas tank and fuel system. They
joined as defendants the automobile's manufacturer, Audi NSU Auto Union
Aktiengesellschaft (Audi); its importer, Volkswagen of America, Inc. (Volkswagen); its regional distributor, petitioner World-Wide Volkswagen Corporation
(World-Wide); and its retail dealer, petitioner Seaway. Seaway and World-
Wide entered special appearances,[3] claiming that Oklahoma's exercise of

---

[3] Volkswagen also entered a special appearance in the District Court, but unlike World-Wide
and Seaway did not seek review in the Supreme Court of Oklahoma and is not a petitioner here.
Both Volkswagen and Audi remain as defendants in the litigation pending before the District
Court in Oklahoma.

jurisdiction over them would offend the limitations on the State's jurisdiction imposed by the Due Process Clause of the Fourteenth Amendment.

The facts presented to the District Court showed that World-Wide is incorporated and has its business office in New York. It distributes vehicles, parts, and accessories, under contract with Volkswagen, to retail dealers in New York, New Jersey, and Connecticut. Seaway, one of these retail dealers, is incorporated and has its place of business in New York. Insofar as the record reveals, Seaway and World-Wide are fully independent corporations whose relations with each other and with Volkswagen and Audi are contractual only. Respondents adduced no evidence that either World-Wide or Seaway does any business in Oklahoma, ships or sells any products to or in that State, has an agent to receive process there, or purchases advertisements in any media calculated to reach Oklahoma. In fact, as respondents' counsel conceded at oral argument, there was no showing that any automobile sold by World-Wide or Seaway has ever entered Oklahoma with the single exception of the vehicle involved in the present case.

Despite the apparent paucity of contacts between petitioners and Oklahoma, the District Court rejected their constitutional claim and reaffirmed that ruling in denying petitioners' motion for reconsideration. Petitioners then sought a writ of prohibition in the Supreme Court of Oklahoma to restrain the District Judge, respondent Charles S. Woodson, from exercising *in personam* jurisdiction over them. . . . The Supreme Court of Oklahoma denied the writ, holding that personal jurisdiction over petitioners was authorized by Oklahoma's "long-arm" statute. . . .

## II

As has long been settled, and as we reaffirm today, a state court may exercise personal jurisdiction over a nonresident defendant only so long as there exist "minimum contacts" between the defendant and the forum State. *International Shoe Co. v. Washington,* [326 U.S. 310 (1945)]. The concept of minimum contacts, in turn, can be seen to perform two related, but distinguishable, functions. It protects the defendant against the burdens of litigating in a distant or inconvenient forum. And it acts to ensure that the States, through their courts, do not reach out beyond the limits imposed on them by their status as coequal sovereigns in a federal system.

The protection against inconvenient litigation is typically described in terms of "reasonableness" or "fairness." We have said that the defendant's contacts with the forum State must be such that maintenance of the suit "does not offend 'traditional notions of fair play and substantial justice.'" *International Shoe Co. v. Washington, supra,* at 316, quoting *Milliken v. Meyer,* 311 U.S. 457, 463 (1940).

The relationship between the defendant and the forum must be such that it is "reasonable . . . to require the corporation to defend the particular suit which is brought there." 326 U.S. at 317. Implicit in this emphasis on reasonableness is the understanding that the burden on the defendant, while always a primary concern, will in an appropriate case be considered in light of other relevant factors, including the forum State's interest in adjudicating the dispute, *see McGee v. International Life Ins. Co.*, 355 U.S. 220, 223 (1957); the plaintiff's interest in obtaining convenient and effective relief, *see Kulko v. California Superior Court*, [436 U.S. 84, 92 (1978)] at least when that interest is not adequately protected by the plaintiff's power to choose the forum, *cf. Shaffer v. Heitner*, 433 U.S. 186, 211, n. 37 (1977); the interstate judicial system's interest in obtaining the most efficient resolution of controversies; and the shared interest of the several States in furthering fundamental substantive social policies, *see Kulko v. California Superior Court, supra,* at 93, 98.

The limits imposed on state jurisdiction by the Due Process Clause, in its role as a guarantor against inconvenient litigation, have been substantially relaxed over the years . . . .

Nevertheless, we have never accepted the proposition that state lines are irrelevant for jurisdictional purposes, nor could we, and remain faithful to the principles of interstate federalism embodied in the Constitution. The economic interdependence of the States was foreseen and desired by the Framers . . . . But the Framers also intended that the States retain many essential attributes of sovereignty, including, in particular, the sovereign power to try causes in their courts. The sovereignty of each State, in turn, implied a limitation on the sovereignty of all of its sister States—a limitation express or implicit in both the original scheme of the Constitution and the Fourteenth Amendment.

Hence, even while abandoning the shibboleth that "[t]he authority of every tribunal is necessarily restricted by the territorial limits of the State in which it is established," *Pennoyer v. Neff*, [95 U.S. 714, 720 (1877)], we emphasized that the reasonableness of asserting jurisdiction over the defendant must be assessed "in the context of our federal system of government," *International Shoe Co. v. Washington*, 326 U.S. at 317, and stressed that the Due Process Clause ensures not only fairness, but also the "orderly administration of the laws," id., at 319. . . .

Thus, the Due Process Clause "does not contemplate that a state may make binding a judgment *in personam* against an individual or corporate defendant with which the state has no contacts, ties, or relations." *International Shoe Co. v. Washington, supra,* at 319. Even if the defendant would suffer minimal or no inconvenience from being forced to litigate before the tribunals of another State; even if the forum State has a strong interest in applying its law to the controversy; even if the forum State is the most convenient location for litigation, the Due Process Clause, acting as an instrument of interstate federalism, may sometimes act to divest the State of its power to render a valid judgment. *Hanson v. Denckla*, [357 U.S. 235, 251, 254 (1958)].

### III

Applying these principles to the case at hand, we find in the record before us a total absence of those affiliating circumstances that are a necessary predicate to any exercise of state-court jurisdiction. Petitioners carry on no activity whatsoever in Oklahoma. They close no sales and perform no services there. They avail themselves of none of the privileges and benefits of Oklahoma law. They solicit no business there either through salespersons or through advertising reasonably calculated to reach the State. Nor does the record show that they regularly sell cars at wholesale or retail to Oklahoma customers or residents or that they indirectly, through others, serve or seek to serve the Oklahoma market. In short, respondents seek to base jurisdiction on one, isolated occurrence and whatever inferences can be drawn therefrom: the fortuitous circumstance that a single Audi automobile, sold in New York to New York residents, happened to suffer an accident while passing through Oklahoma.

It is argued, however, that because an automobile is mobile by its very design and purpose it was "foreseeable" that the Robinsons' Audi would cause injury in Oklahoma. Yet "foreseeability" alone has never been a sufficient benchmark for personal jurisdiction under the Due Process Clause. In *Hanson v. Denckla, supra,* it was no doubt foreseeable that the settlor of a Delaware trust would subsequently move to Florida and seek to exercise a power of appointment there; yet we held that Florida courts could not constitutionally exercise jurisdiction over a Delaware trustee that had no other contacts with the forum State. In *Kulko v. California Superior Court,* 436 U.S. 84 (1978), it was surely "foreseeable" that a divorced wife would move to California from New York, the domicile of the marriage, and that a minor daughter would live with the mother. Yet we held that California could not exercise jurisdiction in a child-support action over the former husband who had remained in New York.

If foreseeability were the criterion, a local California tire retailer could be forced to defend in Pennsylvania when a blowout occurs there, *see Erlanger Mills, Inc. v. Cohoes Fibre Mills, Inc.,* 239 F.2d 502, 507 (CA4 1956); a Wisconsin seller of a defective automobile jack could be haled before a distant court for damage caused in New Jersey, *Reilly v. Phil Tolkan Pontiac, Inc.,* 372 F. Supp. 1205 (NJ 1974); or a Florida soft-drink concessionaire could be summoned to Alaska to account for injuries happening there, *see Uppgren v. Executive Aviation Services, Inc.,* 304 F. Supp. 165, 170-171 (Minn. 1969). Every seller of chattels would in effect appoint the chattel his agent for service of process. His amenability to suit would travel with the chattel. We recently abandoned the outworn rule of *Harris v. Balk,* 198 U.S. 215 (1905), that the interest of a creditor in a debt could be extinguished or otherwise affected by any State having transitory jurisdiction over the debtor. *Shaffer v. Heitner,* 433 U.S. 186 (1977). Having interred the mechanical rule that a creditor's amenability to a *quasi in rem* action travels with his debtor, we are unwilling to endorse an analogous principle in the present case.

This is not to say, of course, that foreseeability is wholly irrelevant. But the foreseeability that is critical to due process analysis is not the mere likelihood that a product will find its way into the forum State. Rather, it is that the defendant's conduct and connection with the forum State are such that he should reasonably anticipate being haled into court there. The Due Process Clause, by ensuring the "orderly administration of the laws," *International Shoe Co. v. Washington,* 326 U.S. at 319, gives a degree of predictability to the legal system that allows potential defendants to structure their primary conduct with some minimum assurance as to where that conduct will and will not render them liable to suit.

When a corporation "purposefully avails itself of the privilege of conducting activities within the forum State," *Hanson v. Denckla,* 357 U.S. at 253, it has clear notice that it is subject to suit there, and can act to alleviate the risk of burdensome litigation by procuring insurance, passing the expected costs on to customers, or, if the risks are too great, severing its connection with the State. Hence if the sale of a product of a manufacturer or distributor such as Audi or Volkswagen is not simply an isolated occurrence, but arises from the efforts of the manufacturer or distributor to serve, directly or indirectly, the market for its product in other States, it is not unreasonable to subject it to suit in one of those States if its allegedly defective merchandise has there been the source of injury to its owner or to others. The forum State does not exceed its powers under the Due Process Clause if it asserts personal jurisdiction over a corporation that delivers its products into the stream of commerce with the expectation that they will be purchased by consumers in the forum State.

But there is no such or similar basis for Oklahoma jurisdiction over World-Wide or Seaway in this case. Seaway's sales are made in Massena, N. Y. World-Wide's market, although substantially larger, is limited to dealers in New York, New Jersey, and Connecticut. There is no evidence of record that any automobiles distributed by World-Wide are sold to retail customers outside this tristate area. It is foreseeable that the purchasers of automobiles sold by World-Wide and Seaway may take them to Oklahoma. But the mere "unilateral activity of those who claim some relationship with a nonresident defendant cannot satisfy the requirement of contact with the forum State." *Hanson v. Denckla, supra,* at 253.

In a variant on the previous argument, it is contended that jurisdiction can be supported by the fact that petitioners earn substantial revenue from goods used in Oklahoma. The Oklahoma Supreme Court so found, drawing the inference that because one automobile sold by petitioners had been used in Oklahoma, others might have been used there also. While this inference seems less than compelling on the facts of the instant case, we need not question the court's factual findings in order to reject its reasoning.

This argument seems to make the point that the purchase of automobiles in New York, from which the petitioners earn substantial revenue, would not occur *but for* the fact that the automobiles are capable of use in distant States like Oklahoma. Respondents observe that the very purpose of an automobile is to travel, and that travel of automobiles sold by petitioners is facilitated by an extensive chain of Volkswagen service centers throughout the country, including some in Oklahoma. However, financial benefits accruing to the defendant from a collateral relation to the forum State will not support jurisdiction if they do not stem from a constitutionally cognizable contact with that State. *See Kulko v. California Superior Court,* 436 U.S. at 94-95. In our view, whatever marginal revenues petitioners may receive by virtue of the fact that their products are capable of use in Oklahoma is far too attenuated a contact to justify that State's exercise of *in personam* jurisdiction over them. . . .

*Reversed.*

Mr. Justice Brennan, dissenting.*

Because I believe that the court reads *International Shoe* and its progeny too narrowly, and because I believe that the standards enunciated by those cases may already be obsolete as constitutional boundaries, I dissent.

I

The Court's opinions focus tightly on the existence of contacts between the forum and the defendant. In so doing, they accord too little weight to the strength of the forum State's interest in the case and fail to explore whether there would be any actual inconvenience to the defendant. The clear focus in *International Shoe* was on fairness and reasonableness. The Court specifically declined to establish a mechanical test based on the quantum of contacts between a State and the defendant. . . . The existence of contacts, so long as there were some, was merely one way of giving content to the determination of fairness and reasonableness.

Surely *International Shoe* contemplated that the significance of the contacts necessary to support jurisdiction would diminish if some other consideration helped establish that jurisdiction would be fair and reasonable. The interest of the State and other parties in proceeding with the case in a particular forum are such considerations. *McGee v. International Life Ins. Co.,* 355 U.S. 220, 223 (1957), for instance, accorded great importance to a State's "manifest interest in providing effective means of redress" for its citizens.

Another consideration is the actual burden a defendant must bear in defending the suit in the forum. Because lesser burdens reduce the unfairness to the defendant, jurisdiction may be justified despite less significant contacts. . . . [T]he constitutionally significant "burden" to be analyzed relates to the mobility of the defendant's defense. For instance, if having to travel to a foreign forum would hamper the defense because witnesses or evidence or the defendant himself were immobile, or if there were a disproportionately large number of witnesses or amount of evidence that would have to be transported at the defendant's expense, or if being away from home for the duration of the trial would work some special hardship on the defendant, then the Constitution would require special consideration for the defendant's interests.

That considerations other than contacts between the forum and the defendant are relevant necessarily means that the Constitution does not require that trial be held in the State which has the "best contacts" with the defendant. The defendant has no constitutional entitlement to the best forum or, for that matter, to any particular forum. Under even the most restrictive view of *International Shoe,* several States could have jurisdiction over a particular cause of action. We need only determine whether the forum States in these cases satisfy the constitutional minimum.

---

* [Justice Brennan combined his dissent to the *World-Wide* opinion with his dissent to *Rush v. Savchuk. Rush* is discussed in § 3.16, *infra.*]

## II

In [this case] . . . , I would find that the forum State has an interest in permitting the litigation to go forward, the litigation is connected to the forum, the defendant is linked to the forum, and the burden of defending is not unreasonable. Accordingly, I would hold that it is neither unfair nor unreasonable to require these defendants to defend in the forum State. . . . [T]he interest of the forum State and its connection to the litigation is strong. The automobile accident underlying the litigation occurred in Oklahoma. The plaintiffs were hospitalized in Oklahoma when they brought suit. Essential witnesses and evidence were in Oklahoma. *See Shaffer v. Heitner,* 433 U.S. at 208. The State has a legitimate interest in enforcing its laws designed to keep its highway system safe, and the trial can proceed at least as efficiently in Oklahoma as anywhere else.

The petitioners are not unconnected with the forum. Although both sell automobiles within limited sales territories, each sold the automobile which in fact was driven to Oklahoma where it was involved in an accident. It may be true, as the Court suggests, that each sincerely intended to limit its commercial impact to the limited territory, and that each intended to accept the benefits and protection of the laws only of those States within the territory. But obviously these were unrealistic hopes that cannot be treated as an automatic constitutional shield.

An automobile simply is not a stationary item or one designed to be used in one place. An automobile is *intended* to be moved around. Someone in the business of selling large numbers of automobiles can hardly plead ignorance of their mobility or pretend that the automobiles stay put after they are sold. It is not merely that a dealer in automobiles foresees that they will move. The dealer actually intends that the purchasers will use the automobiles to travel to distant States where the dealer does not directly "do business." The sale of an automobile *does purposefully* inject the vehicle into the stream of interstate commerce so that it can travel to distant States. . . .

The Court accepts that a State may exercise jurisdiction over a distributor which "serves" that State "indirectly" by "delivering its products into the stream of commerce with the expectation that they will be purchased by consumers in the forum State." It is difficult to see why the Constitution should distinguish between a case involving goods which reach a distant State through a chain of distribution and a case involving goods which reach the same State because a consumer, using them as the dealer knew the customer would, took them there. In each case the seller purposefully injects the goods into the stream of commerce and those goods predictably are used in the forum State.

Furthermore, an automobile seller derives substantial benefits from States other than its own. A large part of the value of automobiles is the extensive, nationwide network of highways. Significant portions of that network have been constructed by and are maintained by the individual States, including Oklahoma. The States, through their highway programs, contribute in a very direct and important way to the value of petitioners' businesses. Additionally, a network of other related dealerships with their service departments operates throughout the country under the protection of the laws of the various States, including Oklahoma, and enhances the value of petitioners' businesses by facilitating their customers' traveling.

Thus, the Court errs in its conclusion . . . that "petitioners have no 'contacts, ties, or relationship'" with Oklahoma. There obviously are contacts, and, given Oklahoma's connection to the litigation, the contacts are sufficiently significant to make it fair and reasonable for the petitioners to submit to Oklahoma's jurisdiction.

## III

It may be that affirmance of the judgments . . . would approach the outer limits of *International Shoe's* jurisdictional principle. But that principle, with its almost exclusive focus on the rights of defendants, may be outdated. . . . *International Shoe* inherited its defendant focus from *Pennoyer v. Neff,* 95 U.S. 714 (1878), and represented the last major step this Court has taken in the long process of liberalizing the doctrine of personal jurisdiction. Though its flexible approach represented a major advance, the structure of our society has changed in many significant ways since *International Shoe* was decided in 1945. Mr. Justice Black, writing for the Court in *McGee v. International Life Ins. Co., 355* U.S. 220, 222 (1957), recognized that "a trend is clearly discernible toward expanding the permissible scope of state jurisdiction over foreign corporations and other nonresidents."

As the Court acknowledges, both the nationalization of commerce and the ease of transportation and communication have accelerated in the generation since 1957. The model of society on which the *International Shoe* Court based its opinion is no longer accurate. Business people, no matter how local their businesses, cannot assume that goods remain in the business' locality. Customers and goods can be anywhere else in the country usually in a matter of hours and always in a matter of a very few days. . . .

The conclusion I draw is that constitutional concepts of fairness no longer require the extreme concern for defendants that was once necessary. Rather, as I wrote in dissent from *Shaffer v. Heitner* (emphasis added), minimum contacts must exist "among the *parties,* the contested transaction, and the forum State."[15] The contacts between any two of these should not be determinative. "[W]hen a suitor seeks to lodge a suit in a State with a substantial interest in seeing its own law applied to the transaction in question, we could wisely act to minimize conflicts, confusion, and uncertainty by adopting a liberal view of jurisdiction, unless considerations of fairness or efficiency strongly point in the opposite direction. . . . " Assuming that a State gives a nonresident defendant adequate notice and opportunity to defend, I do not think the Due Process Clause is offended merely because the defendant has to board a plane to get to the site of the trial.

The Court's opinion suggests that the defendant ought to be subject to a State's jurisdiction only if he has contacts with the State "such that he should

---

[15] In some cases, the inquiry will resemble the inquiry commonly undertaken in determining which State's law to apply. That it is fair to apply a State's law to a nonresident defendant is clearly relevant in determining whether it is fair to subject the defendant to jurisdiction in that State. *Shaffer v. Heitner* (Brennan, J., dissenting); *Hanson v. Denckla,* 357 U.S. 235, 258 (1958) (Black, J., dissenting).

reasonably anticipate being haled into court there." There is nothing unreasonable or unfair, however, about recognizing commercial reality . . . . When an action in fact causes injury in another State, the actor should be prepared to answer for it there unless defending in that State would be unfair for some reason other than that a state boundary must be crossed.

In effect the Court is allowing defendants to assert the sovereign rights of their home States. The expressed fear is that otherwise all limits on personal jurisdiction would disappear. But the argument's premise is wrong. I would not abolish limits on jurisdiction or strip state boundaries of all significance; I would still require the plaintiff to demonstrate sufficient contacts among the parties, the forum, and the litigation to make the forum a reasonable State in which to hold the trial.

I would also, however, strip the defendant of an unjustified veto power over certain very appropriate fora—a power the defendant justifiably enjoyed long ago when communication and travel over long, distances were slow and unpredictable and when notions of state sovereignty were impractical and exaggerated. But I repeat that that is not today's world. If a plaintiff can show that his chosen forum State has a sufficient interest in the litigation (or sufficient contacts with the defendant), then the defendant who cannot show some real injury to a constitutionally protected interest should have no constitutional excuse not to appear.

Mr. Justice Marshall, with whom Mr. Justice Blackmun joins, dissenting. . . .

This is a difficult case, and reasonable minds may differ as to whether respondents have alleged a sufficient "relationship among the defendant[s], the forum, and the litigation," *Shaffer v. Heitner,* 433 U.S. 186, 204 (1977), to satisfy the requirements of *International Shoe.* I am concerned, however, that the majority has reached its result by taking an unnecessarily narrow view of petitioners' forum-related conduct. The majority asserts that "respondents seek to base jurisdiction on one, isolated occurrence and whatever inferences can be drawn therefrom: the fortuitous circumstance that a single Audi automobile, sold in New York to New York residents, happened to suffer an accident while passing through Oklahoma." If that were the case, I would readily agree that the minimum contacts necessary to sustain jurisdiction are not present. But the basis for the assertion of jurisdiction is not the happenstance that an individual over whom petitioners had no control made a unilateral decision to take a chattel with him to a distant State. Rather, jurisdiction is premised on the deliberate and purposeful actions of the defendants themselves in choosing to become part of a nationwide, indeed a global, network for marketing and servicing automobiles.

Petitioners are sellers of a product whose utility derives from its mobility . . . . Petitioners know that their customers buy cars not only to make short trips, but also to travel long distances. In fact, the nationwide service network with which they are affiliated was designed to facilitate and encourage such travel. Seaway would be unlikely to sell many cars if authorized service were available only in Massena, N. Y. Moreover, local dealers normally derive a substantial portion of their revenues from their service operations and thereby obtain a further economic benefit from the opportunity to service cars which were sold in other States. It is apparent that petitioners have not attempted to minimize the chance that their activities will have effects in other States; on the contrary, they have chosen to do business in a way that increases that chance, because it is to their economic advantage to do so . . . .

The majority apparently acknowledges that if a product is purchased in the forum State by a consumer, that State may assert jurisdiction over everyone in the chain of distribution. With this I agree. But I cannot agree that jurisdiction is necessarily lacking if the product enters the State not through the channels of distribution but in the course of its intended use by the consumer. We have recognized the role played by the automobile in the expansion of our notions of personal jurisdiction. Unlike most other chattels, which may find their way into States far from where they were purchased because their owner takes them there, the intended use of the automobile is precisely as a means of traveling from one place to another. In such a case, it is highly artificial to restrict the concept of the "stream of commerce" to the chain of distribution from the manufacturer to the ultimate consumer.

I sympathize with the majority's concern that persons ought to be able to structure their conduct so as not to be subject to suit in distant forums. But that may not always be possible. Some activities by their very nature may foreclose the option of conducting them in such a way as to avoid subjecting oneself to jurisdiction in multiple forums. . . .

MR. JUSTICE BLACKMUN, dissenting.

I confess that I am somewhat puzzled why the plaintiffs in this litigation are so insistent that the regional distributor and the retail dealer, the petitioners here, who handled the ill-fated Audi automobile involved in this litigation, be named defendants. It would appear that the manufacturer and the importer, whose subjectability to Oklahoma jurisdiction is not challenged before this Court, ought not to be judgment-proof. It may, of course, ultimately amount to a contest between insurance companies that, once begun, is not easily brought to a termination. Having made this much of an observation, I pursue it no further.

For me, a critical factor in the disposition of the litigation is the nature of the instrumentality under consideration. It has been said that we are a nation on wheels. What we are concerned with here is the automobile and its peripatetic character. One need only examine our national network of interstate highways, or make an appearance on one of them, or observe the variety of license plates present not only on those highways but in any metropolitan area, to realize that any automobile is likely to wander far from its place of licensure or from its place of distribution and retail sale. Miles per gallon on the highway (as well as in the city) and mileage per tankful are familiar allegations in manufacturers' advertisements today. To expect that any new automobile will remain in the vicinity of its retail sale—like the 1914 electric car driven by the proverbial "little old lady"—is to blink at reality. The automobile is intended for distance as well as for transportation within a limited area.

It therefore seems to me not unreasonable—and certainly not unconstitutional and beyond the reach of the principles laid down in *International Shoe*

*Co. v. Washington,* 326 U.S. 310 (1945), and its progeny—to uphold Oklahoma jurisdiction over this New York distributor and this New York dealer when the accident happened in Oklahoma. I see nothing more unfair for them than for the manufacturer and the importer. All are in the business of providing vehicles that spread out over the highways of our several States. It is not too much to anticipate at the time of distribution and at the time of retail sale that this Audi would be in Oklahoma. Moreover, in assessing "minimum contacts," foreseeable use in another State seems to me to be little different from foreseeable resale in another State. Yet the Court declares this distinction determinative. . . .

My position need not now take me beyond the automobile and the professional who does business by way of distributing and retailing automobiles. Cases concerning other instrumentalities will be dealt with as they arise and in their own contexts. . . .

## NOTES AND QUESTIONS

(1) *Interstate Federalism.* The territorial Power theory has the persistence of original sin. After the Court abandoned the theory in *International Shoe v. Washington,* 326 U.S. 310 (1945) (*see* § 3.07, *supra*), it resurfaced as dictum in *Hanson v. Denckla,* 357 U.S. 235 (1958) (*see* § 3.07, *supra*). The Court again rejected the theory in footnote 20 of its opinion in *Shaffer v. Heitner,* 433 U.S. 186 (1977). Is that outmoded but hardy doctrine revived in *World-Wide,* this time in the guise of "interstate federalism"?

According to the majority, fairness to the defendant is not the only reason for the "minimum contacts" test. The requirement is also justified by "principles of interstate federalism embodied in the Constitution." The opinion makes it quite clear that the relationship of the states *to each other* (as constituent sovereigns in a federation) places a limit on their adjudicatory jurisdiction that is separate and distinct from any restriction based on fairness to the defendant. In other words, even if the forum's exercise of jurisdiction causes no unfairness to the defendant, it may yet be unconstitutional because of its infringement upon the sovereignty of the other states.

The Court's reliance on this argument is troubling. If the restrictions on jurisdiction are based not only on fairness to the defendant but also on the rights of other states, how can the defendant waive a jurisdictional objection? Individuals cannot waive the rights of states, can they? Certainly they cannot when the issue is subject matter jurisdiction; the court must raise that defect on its own motion, even if no party objects. *See* Fed. R. Civ. P. 12 (h)(3). It did not take long for the issue to present itself.

(2) **INSURANCE CORP. OF IRELAND LTD. v. COMPAGNIE DES BAUXITES DE GUINEE,** 456 U.S. 694 (1982). The defendants (foreign insurance companies) objected to an assertion of personal jurisdiction by a United States District Court. Plaintiffs attempted to use the discovery devices to show defendants' minimum contacts with Pennsylvania, but the defendants were recalcitrant. After repeated refusals to produce the requested documents, the district judge (pursuant to Fed. R. Civ. P. 37(b)) entered an order holding defendants amenable to the court's in personam jurisdiction as a discovery sanction.

*Held*: The defendants' refusal to comply with the district court's discovery orders constituted a waiver of their jurisdictional objections. The Court abandoned its reliance on interstate federalism as a foundation for the minimum contracts requirement—focusing exclusively instead on defendant's liberty interest. "The personal jurisdiction requirement recognizes and protects an individual liberty interest. It represents a restriction on judicial power not as a matter of sovereignty, but as a matter of individual liberty." *Id.* at 702. In footnote 10, the Court explained away the reliance on federalism in *World-Wide.*

> It is true that we have stated that the requirement of personal jurisdiction, as applied to state courts, reflects an element of federalism and the character of state sovereignty vis-a-vis other States. For example, in *World-Wide Volkswagen Corp. v. Woodson,* 444 U.S. 286, 291-292 (1980), we stated:
>
>> [A] state court may exercise personal jurisdiction over a nonresident defendant only so long as there exist "minimum contacts" between the defendant and the forum State. The concept of minimum contacts, in turn, can be seen to perform two related, but distinguishable, functions. It protects the defendant against the burdens of litigating in a distant or inconvenient forum. And it acts to ensure that the States, through their courts, do not reach out beyond the limits imposed on them by their status as coequal sovereigns in a federal system.
>
> The restriction on state sovereign power described *in World-Wide Volkswagen Corp.,* however, must be seen as ultimately a function of the individual liberty interest preserved by the Due Process Clause. That Clause is the only source of the personal jurisdiction requirement and the Clause itself makes no mention of federalism concerns. Furthermore, if the federalism concept operated as an independent restriction on the sovereign power of the court, it would not be possible to waive the personal jurisdiction requirement: individual actions cannot change the powers of sovereignty, although the individual can subject himself to powers from which he may otherwise be protected. . . .

The cyclic waxing and waning of the territorial power theory is discussed in Allan Stein, *Styles of Argument and Interstate Federalism in the Law of Personal Jurisdiction,* 65 TEX. L. REV. 689 (1987); Harold Lewis, *The Three Deaths of "State Sovereignty" and the Curse of Abstraction in the Jurisprudence of Personal Jurisdiction,* 58 NOTRE DAME L. REV. 699 (1983); David Seidelson, *Recasting World-Wide Volkswagen as a Source of Longer Jurisdictional Reach,* 19 TULSA L.J. 1, 5-10 (1983); John Drobak, *The Federalism Theme in Personal Jurisdiction,* 68 IOWA L. REV. 1015 (1983). For additional commentary on the constitutional source of the restrictions on state-court jurisdiction, see William Richman, *Understanding Personal Jurisdiction,* 25 ARIZ. ST. L. J. 599, 606-610 (1993), Robert Abrams & Paul Dimond, *Toward a Constitutional Framework for the Control of State Court Jurisdiction,* 69 MINN. L. REV. 75, 75-76 (1984).

(3) *A Two-Stage Test.*   Despite the doctrinal blind alley of interstate federalism, other elements in the *World-Wide* opinion have retained vitality. Chief among them is the Court's developing resolution of the contacts/fairness ambiguity in *International Shoe.*   Although the majority does not say so explicitly (as do more recent cases), it seems to adopt a weighted two-step methodology. The first (and, by far, the more important) step is the requirement that defendant establish purposeful contacts with the forum. If that threshold test is satisfied, the next step requires a weighing of the overall fairness of the exercise of jurisdiction—considering such factors as the inconvenience to the defendant, the plaintiff's interest in a ready forum, the state's regulatory interest in the cause of action and the ease of access to sources of proof.

Some of the commentators approve of *World-Wide's* emphasis on contacts over fairness. *See, e.g.,* Martin Louis, *The Grasp of Long Arm Jurisdiction Finally Exceeds its Reach: A Comment on World-Wide Volkswagen Corp. v. Woodson,* 58 N.C. L. REV. 407 (1980). The majority, however, favor greater emphasis on the fairness approach. *See, e.g.,* Martin Redish, *Due Process, Federalism and Personal Jurisdiction: A Theoretical Evaluation,* 75 Nw. U. L. REV. 112 (1981).

(4) *The Need for Contacts.*   What is the continuing justification for the first step in the Supreme Court's two-step test? In other words, why should the Court still require that a defendant purposefully establish contacts with the forum state? *Bauxites* conclusively disposes of the federalism rationale. If all that remains is the defendant's liberty interest, that interest seems to be adequately protected by the second step—the fairness step. Is the requirement of pre-litigation connections simply a device to make the fairness requirement more concrete, a bright-line test to keep judges from running amok in broad and expansive discussions of fairness? Or is the requirement justified because primary actors in our system really do have expectations about the jurisdictional significance of state boundaries? *See* Robert Mills, *Personal Jurisdiction Over Border State Defendants: What Does Due Process Require?*, 13 S. ILL. U. L. REV. 919 (1989). Another possibility, of course, is that there is no remaining reason for the contacts requirement. *See* Louise Weinberg, *The Place of Trial and the Law Applied: Overhauling Constitutional Theory,* 59 U. COLO. L. REV. 67, 102 (1988). *See also* David Welkowitz, *Beyond Burger King: The Federal Interest in Personal Jurisdiction,* 56 FORD. L. REV. 1, 26 (1987) (suggesting a threshold requirement of a state governmental interest instead of the current contacts requirement).

(5) *The Stream of Commerce.*   The stream of commerce doctrine developed in state courts during the Supreme Court's twenty-year silence on jurisdiction. *See, e.g., Gray v. American Radiator & Standard Sanitary Corp.,* 22 Ill. 2d 432, 176 N.E.2d 761 (1961); *Buckeye Boiler Co. v. Superior Court of Los Angeles City,* 71 Cal. 2d 893, 458 P.2d 57, 80 Cal. Rptr. 113 (1969). The doctrine held that a manufacturer of defective goods should be amenable to jurisdiction wherever those goods are distributed, either directly or indirectly, through the stream of commerce.

The *World-Wide* majority approves of the stream of commerce concept but adds the important limitation that jurisdiction may not exist where the product enters the forum not through the chain of distribution but rather as a result of the foreseeable action of a consumer who purchased it elsewhere. Does the limitation make sense?

For discussion of the stream of commerce doctrine, see WILLIAM RICHMAN & WILLIAM REYNOLDS, UNDERSTANDING CONFLICT OF LAWS, § 36 (3d ed. 2002). The doctrine was restricted even more by the Court's recent decision of *Asahi Metal Industry Co. v. Superior Court of California, see* § 3.10, *infra*.

(6) *Foreseeability.* The Court rejects foreseeability as an adequate substitute for purposeful connections between the defendant and the forum. In other words, foreseeability that defendant's product would cause injury in the forum is not a sufficient condition for jurisdiction.

A hypothetical case posed by Judge Sobeloff in *Erlanger Mills v. Cohoes Fibre Mills,* 239 F.2d 502 (4th Cir. 1956), shows the difficulty with foreseeability. Suppose a California filling station owner who has never ventured outside his native state. One day, a Pennsylvania tourist drives into the station and purchases a tire. Back home in Pennsylvania, the tire ruptures and causes the tourist severe injury. Was it foreseeable to the defendant that his sale of the tire would cause injury there? Certainly the license plates on the car made Pennsylvania a likely destination. But is the exercise of jurisdiction fair, or even sensible? If you think that there ought not be jurisdiction in Pennsylvania, try to isolate your reasons. Is it because the California defendant is a little guy? Is it because plaintiff came to him in California rather than vice versa? How could the defendant structure his primary conduct to avoid amenability in Pennsylvania?

Although the *World-Wide* majority holds foreseeability in the forum not sufficient for jurisdiction, it does indicate that foreseeability is a relevant concept. The foreseeability that is crucial is defendant's anticipation (given its forum-related activity) that it could be "haled into court" in the forum. In other words, a defendant is amenable to jurisdiction in the forum if it could foresee being amenable to jurisdiction in the forum. Enlightening, no?

Another problem with the majority's foreseeability-of-amenability standard is that it depends on the assumption that ordinary citizens have any expectations at all about jurisdiction. Do you agree? This is an empirical question, and, presumably, it could be investigated empirically; yet the jurisdictional literature contains not a shred of evidence in either direction. At least one commentator has begun to use empirical methods in the study of some jurisdictional issues. *See* Michael Solimine, *The Quiet Revolution in Personal Jurisdiction*, 73 TUL. L. REV. 1 (1998). For more discussion of foreseeability, see WILLIAM RICHMAN & WILLIAM REYNOLDS, UNDERSTANDING CONFLICT OF LAWS, § 36 (3d ed. 2002); Katherine Sheehan, *Predicting the Future: Personal Jurisdiction for the Twenty-First Century*, 66 U. CIN. L. REV. 385, 435-436 (1998). Leonard Ratner, *Procedural Due Process and Jurisdiction to Adjudicate,* 75 NW. U. L. REV. 363, 379 (1980).

(7) *The Motive for Joining Seaway and World-Wide.* A puzzle in *World-Wide* (noted in Justice Blackmuns's dissent) is why the plaintiffs were so insistent that the retailer (Seaway) and the distributor (World-Wide) be joined as defendants. The manufacturer (Audi) and the importer (Volkswagen of

America) were clearly amenable and had deep pockets. Do you think that the plaintiffs were afraid that the manufacturer and the importer would assert in their defense that the defect in the car resulted from wrongdoing by the dealer or the distributor?

In fact, however, plaintiffs' motive was concerned more with choice of forum than litigation strategy. The state court in Creek County, Oklahoma has a reputation for sympathy to plaintiffs and high damage awards; the federal court in Tulsa is a much less favorable forum for personal injury plaintiffs. Plaintiffs' counsel believed that plaintiffs retained a technical domicile in New York. Because they were not yet present in Arizona and had no intention of remaining in Oklahoma, they had not abandoned their New York domicile. By joining the dealer and the distributor, both New York corporations, he hoped to prevent removal of the case to federal court by destroying the "complete" diversity required for removal. *See* RUSSELL WEINTRAUB, COMMENTARY ON THE CONFLICT OF LAWS, 153 (4th ed. 2001).

For a lively and highly detailed account of the facts of the case and its progress through the courts, see Charles Adams, *World-Wide Volkswagen v. Woodson—The Rest of the Story*, 72 NEB. L. REV. 1122 (1993).

(8) *Justice Brennan's View.* Although Justice Brennan disagrees with the majority's application of the "minimum contacts" test, the more interesting part of his opinion is his rejection of the minimum contacts standard in favor of an approach based more on fairness. His two-step test considers the forum's interest and the potential inconvenience for the defendant: first, plaintiff must show that the forum has a sufficient interest in the litigation (or sufficient contacts with the defendant); second, if plaintiff makes such a showing, defendant can defeat jurisdiction by showing that the exercise of jurisdiction is "unfair for some reason other than that a state boundary must be crossed."

Is the difference between Brennan and the majority based upon two fundamentally different views of the position of the states within the federation? What is the jurisdictional significance of state boundaries for the majority? For Brennan? *See* WILLIAM RICHMAN & WILLIAM REYNOLDS, UNDERSTANDING CONFLICT OF LAWS, § 22 (3d ed. 2002), Sheehan, *supra* note 6, at 433-435. For favorable commentary on Brennan's dissent, see Luther McDougal, *Judicial Jurisdiction: From a Contacts to an Interest Analysis,* 35 VAND. L. REV. 1 (1982).

*See* PROBLEMS 3C-1. THE HITCH AND TRAILER; 3C-2. THE TRADE SHOW; 3C-3. THE AUDIT; 3C-4. SHE CAN'T GO HOME AGAIN; 3C-5. THE MICHELINS; 3C-6. A NIGHT TO FORGET.

## KEETON v. HUSTLER MAGAZINE, INC.

*United States Supreme Court*
*465 U.S. 770, 104 S. Ct. 1473, 79 L. Ed. 2d 790 (1984)*

JUSTICE REHNQUIST delivered the opinion of the Court.

Petitioner Kathy Keeton sued respondent Hustler Magazine, Inc., and other defendants in the United States District Court for the District of New Hampshire, alleging jurisdiction over her libel complaint by reason of diversity of citizenship. The District Court dismissed her suit because it believed that the Due Process Clause of the Fourteenth Amendment to the United States Constitution forbade the application of New Hampshire's long-arm statute in order to acquire personal jurisdiction over respondent. The Court of Appeals for the First Circuit affirmed, summarizing its concerns with the statement that "the New Hampshire tail is too small to wag so large an out-of-state dog." We granted certiorari, and we now reverse.

Petitioner Keeton is a resident of New York. Her only connection with New Hampshire is the circulation there of copies of a magazine that she assists in producing. The magazine bears petitioner's name in several places crediting her with editorial and other work. Respondent Hustler Magazine, Inc., is an Ohio corporation, with its principal place of business in California. Respondent's contacts with New Hampshire consist of the sale of some 10,000 to 15,000 copies of Hustler Magazine in that State each month. Petitioner claims to have been libeled in five separate issues of respondent's magazine published between September 1975 and May 1976.[1]

The Court of Appeals . . . held that petitioners's lack of contacts with New Hampshire rendered the State's interest in redressing the tort of libel to petitioner too attenuated for an assertion of personal jurisdiction over respondent. The Court of Appeals observed that the "single publication rule" ordinarily applicable in multistate libel cases would require it to award petitioner "damages caused in all states" should she prevail in her suit, even though the bulk of petitioner's alleged injuries had been sustained outside New Hampshire.[2]

. . . The court also stressed New Hampshire's unusually long (6-year) limitations period for libel actions. New Hampshire was the only State where petitioner's suit would not have been time-barred when it was filed. Under these circumstances, the Court of Appeals concluded that it would be "unfair" to assert jurisdiction over respondent. New Hampshire has a minimal interest in applying its unusual statute of limitations to, and awarding damages for, injuries to a nonresident occurring outside the State, particularly since petitioner suffered such a small proportion of her total claimed injury within the State.

We conclude that the Court of Appeals erred. . . . Respondent's regular circulation of magazines in the forum State is sufficient to support an assertion of jurisdiction in a libel action based on the contents of the magazine. This is so even if New Hampshire courts, and thus the District Court under *Klaxon Co. v. Stentor Co.,* 313 U.S. 487 (1941), would apply the so-called "single publication rule" to enable petitioner to recover in the New Hampshire

---

[1] Initially, petitioner brought suit for libel and invasion of privacy in Ohio, where the magazine was published. Her libel claim, however, was dismissed as barred by the Ohio statute of limitations, and her invasion-of-privacy claim was dismissed as barred by the New York statute of limitations, which the Ohio court considered to be "migratory." Petitioner then filed the present action in October 1980.

[2] The "single publication rule" has been summarized as follows: "As to any single publication, (a) only one action for damages can be maintained; (b) all damages suffered in all jurisdictions can be recovered in the one action; and (c) a judgment for or against the plaintiff upon the merits of any action for damages bars any other action for damages between the same parties in all jurisdictions." RESTATEMENT (SECOND) OF TORTS § 577A(4)(1977).

action her damages from "publications" of the alleged libel throughout the United States.

. . . Such regular monthly sales of thousands of magazines cannot by any stretch of the imagination be characterized as random, isolated, or fortuitous. It is, therefore, unquestionable that New Hampshire jurisdiction over a complaint based on those contacts would ordinarily satisfy the requirement of the Due Process Clause that a State's assertion of personal jurisdiction over a nonresident defendant be predicated on "minimum contacts" between the defendant and the State. *See World-Wide Volkswagen Corp. v. Woodson,* 444 U.S. 286, 297-298 (1980); *International Shoe Co. v. Washington,* 326 U.S. 310, 317 (1945). . . .

We think that the three concerns advanced by the Court of Appeals, whether considered singly or together, are not sufficiently weighty to merit a different result. The "single publication rule," New Hampshire's unusually long statute of limitations, and plaintiffs lack of contacts with the forum State do not defeat jurisdiction otherwise proper under . . . the Due Process Clause.

In judging minimum contacts, a court properly focuses on "the relationship among the defendant, the forum, and the litigation." *Shaffer v. Heitner,* 433 U.S. 186, 204 (1977). *See also Rush v. Savchuk,* 444 U.S. 320, 332 (1980). Thus, it is certainly relevant to the jurisdictional inquiry that petitioner is *seeking* to recover damages suffered in all States in this one suit. The contacts between respondent and the forum must be judged in the light of that claim, rather than a claim only for damages sustained in New Hampshire. That is, the contacts between respondent and New Hampshire must be such that it is "fair" to compel respondent to defend a multistate lawsuit in new Hampshire seeking nationwide damages for all copies of the five issues in question, even though only a small portion of those copies were distributed in New Hampshire.

The Court of Appeals expressed the view that New Hampshire's "interest" in asserting jurisdiction over plaintiffs multistate claim was minimal. We agree that the "fairness" of haling respondent into a New Hampshire court depends to some extent on whether respondent's activities relating to New Hampshire are such as to give that State a legitimate interest in holding respondent answerable on a claim related to those activities. But insofar as the State's "interest" in adjudicating the dispute is a part of the Fourteenth Amendment due process equation, as a surrogate for some of the factors already mentioned, see *Insurance Corporation of Ireland v. Compagnie des Bauxites de Guinee,* 456 U.S. 694, 702-703, n. 10 (1982), we think the interest is sufficient.

The Court of Appeals acknowledged that petitioner was suing, at least in part, for damages suffered in New Hampshire. And it is beyond dispute that New Hampshire has a significant interest in redressing injuries that actually occur within the State. . . . This interest extends to libel actions brought by nonresidents. False statements of fact harm both the subject of the falsehood and the readers of the statement. New Hampshire may rightly employ its libel laws to discourage the deception of its citizens. There is "no constitutional value in false statements of fact." *Gertz v. Robert Welch, Inc.,* 418 U.S. 323, 340 (1974). . . .

New Hampshire also has a substantial interest in cooperating with other States, through the "single publication rule," to provide a forum for efficiently litigating all issues and damages claims arising out of a libel in a unitary proceeding. This rule reduces the potential serious drain of libel cases on judicial resources. It also serves to protect defendants from harassment resulting from multiple suits. In sum, the combination of New Hampshire's interest in redressing injuries that occur within the State and its interest in cooperating with other States in the application of the "single publication rule" demonstrates the propriety of requiring respondent to answer to a multistate libel action in New Hampshire.

The Court of Appeals also thought that there was an element of due process "unfairness" arising from the fact that the statutes of limitations in every jurisdiction except New Hampshire had run on the plaintiff's claim in this case.[10]

Strictly speaking, however, any potential unfairness in applying New Hampshire's statute of limitations to all aspects of this nationwide suit has nothing to do with the jurisdiction of the court to adjudicate the claims. "The issue is personal jurisdiction, not choice of law." *Hanson v. Denckla,* 357 U.S. 235, 254 (1958). The question of the applicability of New Hampshire's statute of limitations to claims for out-of-state damages presents itself in the course of litigation only after jurisdiction over respondent is established, and we do not think that such choice-of-law concerns should complicate or distort the jurisdictional inquiry.

The chance duration of statutes of limitations in non-forum jurisdictions has nothing to do with the contacts among respondent, New Hampshire, and this multistate libel action. Whether Ohio's limitations period is six months or six years does not alter the jurisdictional calculus in New Hampshire. Petitioner's successful search for a State with a lengthy statute of limitations is no different from the litigation strategy of countless plaintiffs who seek a forum with favorable substantive or procedural rules or sympathetic local populations. Certainly Hustler Magazine, Inc., which chose to enter the New Hampshire market, can be charged with knowledge of its laws and no doubt would have claimed the benefit of them if it had a complaint against a subscriber, distributor, or other commercial partner.

Finally, implicit in the Court of Appeals' analysis of New Hampshire's interest is an emphasis on the extremely limited contacts of the *plaintiff* with New Hampshire. But we have not to date required a plaintiff to have "minimum contacts" with the forum State before permitting that State to assert personal jurisdiction over a nonresident defendant. On the contrary, we have upheld the assertion of jurisdiction where such contacts were entirely lacking. . . . In the instant case, respondent's activities in the forum may not

---

[10] Under traditional choice-of-law principles, the law of the forum State governs on matters of procedure. *See* RESTATEMENT (SECOND) OF CONFLICT OF LAWS, § 122 (1971). In New Hampshire, statutes of limitations are considered procedural. There has been considerable academic criticism of the rule that permits a forum State to apply its own statute of limitations regardless of the significance of contacts between the forum State and the litigation. But we find it unnecessary to express an opinion at this time as to whether any arguable unfairness rises to the level of a due process violation.

be so substantial as to support jurisdiction over a cause of action unrelated to those activities.[11] But respondent is carrying on a "part of its general business" in New Hampshire, and that is sufficient to support jurisdiction when the cause of action arises out of the very activity being conducted, in part, in New Hampshire.

The plaintiff's residence is not, of course, completely irrelevant to the jurisdictional inquiry. As noted, that inquiry focuses on the relations among the defendant, the forum, and the litigation. Plaintiff's residence may well play an important role in determining the propriety of entertaining a suit against the defendant in the forum. That is, plaintiff's residence in the forum may, because of defendant's relationship with the plaintiff, enhance defendant's contacts with the forum. Plaintiff's residence may be the focus of the activities of the defendant out of which the suit arises. But plaintiff's residence in the forum State is not a separate requirement, and lack of residence will not defeat jurisdiction established on the basis of defendant's contacts.

It is undoubtedly true that the bulk of the harm done to petitioner occurred outside New Hampshire. But that will be true in almost every libel action brought somewhere other than the plaintiff's domicile. There is no justification for restricting libel actions to the plaintiffs home forum.[12] The victim of a libel, like the victim of any other tort, may choose to bring suit in any forum with which the defendant has "certain minimum contacts . . . such that the maintenance of the suit does not offend 'traditional notions of fair play and substantial justice.' "

Where, as in this case, respondent Hustler Magazine, Inc., has continuously and deliberately exploited the New Hampshire market, it must reasonably anticipate being haled into court there in a libel action based on the contents of its magazine. *World-Wide Volkswagen Corp. v. Woodson,* 444 U.S., at 297-298. And, since respondent can be charged with knowledge of the "single publication rule," it must anticipate that such a suit will seek nationwide damages. Respondent produces a national publication aimed at a nationwide audience. There is no unfairness in calling it to answer for the contents of that publication wherever a substantial number of copies are regularly sold and distributed.

The judgment of the Court of Appeals is reversed, and the cause is remanded for proceedings consistent with this opinion.

---

[11] The defendant corporation's contacts with the forum State in [*Perkins v. Benguet Consolidated Mining Co.,* 342 U.S. 437 (1952)] were more substantial than those of respondent with New Hampshire in this case. In *Perkins,* the corporation's mining operations, located in the Philippine Islands, were completely halted during the Japanese occupation. The president, who was also general manager and principal stockholder of the company, returned to his home in Ohio where he carried on "a continuous and systematic supervision of the necessarily limited wartime activities of the company." The company's files were kept in Ohio, several directors' meetings were held there, substantial accounts were maintained in Ohio banks, and all key business decisions were made in the State. In those circumstances, Ohio was the corporation's principal, if temporary, place of business so that Ohio jurisdiction was proper even over a cause of action unrelated to the activities in the State.

[12] As noted in *Calder v. Jones,* we reject categorically the suggestion that invisible radiations from the First Amendment may defeat jurisdiction otherwise proper under the Due Process Clause.

[Justice Brennan's concurring opinion is omitted.]

*See* PROBLEM 3C-7. SENDING A LETTER.

---

## NOTES AND QUESTIONS

(1) *Three Fairness Issues.* The Court uses the two-step procedure it developed in *World-Wide,* first assessing contacts between the defendant and the forum and then evaluating the fairness of the exercise of jurisdiction. The Court's contacts holding is unremarkable, but its treatment of the three fairness concerns is instructive:

(a) *State Interests.* What two interests of New Hampshire does the Court find at stake in *Keeton?* Are they the sort of compelling interests found in *McGee, or* are they simply make-weights?

After *Bauxites'* rejection of "interstate federalism," is it appropriate for the Court to consider the forum's regulatory interest in the dispute as a factor in the jurisdictional calculus? Some commentators argue that the two concepts are very closely related, and that the rejection of "interstate federalism" requires that the Court eliminate all consideration of the forum's interest. William Knudsen, *Keeton, Calder, Helicopteros and Burger King— International Shoe's Most Recent Progeny,* 39 MIAMI L. REV., 809, 813 (1985); Harold Lewis, *The Three Deaths of "State Sovereignty" and the Curse of Abstraction in the Jurisprudence of Personal Jurisdiction,* 58 NOTRE DAME L. REV. 699, 701 (1983). Do you agree? Is consideration of the forum state's interest in exercising jurisdiction consistent with conventional due process analysis in areas other than jurisdiction? When determining what process is due before a state can deprive a person of liberty or property, is it appropriate to consider the strength of the state's interest as well as the importance of the deprivation to the individual?

(b) *Jurisdiction and Choice of Law.* Recall that in both *Hanson and Shaffer* the Court carefully distinguished the jurisdictional question from the choice-of-law issue. In each case, the Court held that the fact that a forum's law might apply to a dispute was not a good reason to hold that the forum had adjudicatory jurisdiction. In *Keeton* the Court holds the converse: that the fact that the forum's law should not be applied to a dispute is not a good ground to defeat the forum's adjudicatory jurisdiction. In other words, the applicability of the forum's law to a dispute is neither a necessary nor a sufficient condition for the exercise of adjudicatory jurisdiction. Allan Stein, *Styles of Argument and Interstate Federalism in the Law of Personal Jurisdiction,* 65 TEX. L. REV. 689, 729 (1987). Adjudicatory jurisdiction seems to depend mostly on assessing contacts under the "minimum contacts"/ "purposefully availing" standard. Constitutional restrictions on choice of law are governed by an assessment of contacts and state interests under the *Allstate/Phillips* standard. *See* § 5.04, Notes and Questions on *Shutts,* note (5), *infra.* Should the questions be kept so completely separate and distinct? This is a good question to reconsider after reading *Allstate.*

(c) *Plaintiff's Residence.* The Court held that plaintiff's contacts with the forum are not relevant except in so far as they tend to enhance the contacts between the defendant and the forum. That proposition is not controversial under orthodox minimum contacts analysis. However, the Court's treatment of this issue combined with its insistence on the irrelevance of choice of law to adjudicatory jurisdiction seems to provide plaintiffs with complete license to engage in forum shopping. *Intrastate* forum shopping (between federal and state courts) is enough of an evil to have spawned one of the landmarks of our jurisprudence. *Erie R.R. v. Tompkins* (*see* § 6.02, *infra*). Do we want to be as cavalier about *interstate* forum shopping as *Keeton* seems to be?

(2) *Keeton and World-Wide. Keeton* can be thought of as the mirror image of *World-Wide. In World-Wide,* the contacts analysis leads to a holding of no jurisdiction in spite of the fact that many of the fairness considerations point toward amenability. Quite the opposite is true in *Keeton*; the contacts analysis leads to a holding that jurisdiction exists even though many of the fairness factors point in the opposite direction. What does a comparison of the two cases say about the Court's position on the relative importance of contacts and fairness?

Recall the important "Even if . . . " passage in *World-Wide.* Using the same sentence structure we can fashion a rule to be taken from *Keeton*: even if the state has relatively little interest in the dispute, and even if the exercise of jurisdiction could result in an unfair choice-of-law decision, and even if the plaintiff has no significant connections with the forum, the forum may exercise jurisdiction over a defendant who has purposefully established significant contacts with the state.

**CALDER v. JONES,** 465 U.S. 783, 104 S. Ct. 1482, 79 L. Ed. 2d 804 (1984). Offended by an article in the National Enquirer, plaintiff, Shirley Jones, brought a defamation action in California against the Enquirer, its local distributing company, the author of the article, and the Enquirer's editor. The Enquirer had very substantial contacts with California, as did the distributor; about 600,000 copies of the weekly magazine were sold in the state, and it was the Enquirer's largest single market. The author and the editor had much less contact with California, consisting mostly of telephone calls and business and pleasure trips. The Enquirer and its distributor raised no objection to California's jurisdiction; the individual defendants, however, objected basing their challenge on their status as employees and on the protection supplied them by the First Amendment.

*Held:* The California court had jurisdiction over both individual defendants. Their status as employees did not give them immunity:

> [Defendants] argue that they are not responsible for the circulation of the article in California. A reporter and an editor, they claim, have no direct economic stake in their employer's sales in a distant State. Nor are ordinary employees able to control their employer's marketing activity. . . . [They] liken themselves to a welder employed in Florida who works on a boiler which subsequently explodes in California. Cases which hold that jurisdiction will be proper over the manufacturer, should not be applied to the welder who has no control over and

derives no direct benefit from his employer's sales in that distant State.

[The] analogy does not wash. Whatever the status of their hypothetical welder, [defendants] are not charged with mere untargeted negligence. Rather, their intentional, and allegedly tortious, actions were expressly aimed at California. . . . And they knew that the brunt of that injury would be felt by respondent in the State in which she lives and works and in which the National Enquirer has its largest circulation. . . .

[Defendants] are correct that their contacts with California are not to be judged according to their employer's activities there. On the other hand, their status as employees does not some how insulate them from jurisdiction. Each defendant's contacts with the forum State must be assessed individually. . . .

Also discounted was defendants' argument that the First Amendment places special limitations on jurisdiction in defamation cases:

We . . . reject the suggestion that First Amendment concerns enter into the jurisdictional analysis. The infusion of such considerations would needlessly complicate an already imprecise inquiry. Moreover, the potential chill on protected First Amendment activity stemming from libel and defamation actions is already taken into account in the constitutional limitations on the substantive law governing such suits. To reintroduce those concerns at the jurisdictional stage would be a form of double counting. We have already declined in other contexts to grant special procedural protections to defendants in libel and defamation actions in addition to the constitutional protections embodied in the substantive laws.

## NOTES AND QUESTIONS

(1) *The Fiduciary Shield.* The position of Calder and South that their status as employees should insulate them from amenability is known as the "fiduciary shield" doctrine. Professors Casad and Richman suggest that the doctrine is a reflection of the substantive law of agency in contract cases; an agent typically is not bound personally by contracts that he signed on behalf of the principal. *See* 1 ROBERT CASAD & WILLIAM RICHMAN, JURISDICTION IN CIVIL ACTIONS 487-494 (3d ed. 1998). The use of the doctrine in torts cases seems clearly inappropriate. Employees are not insulated from tort liability merely because they acted for their principal; similarly they should not be insulated from amenability for that reason. For criticism of the doctrine, see Thomas Sponsler, *Jurisdiction over the Corporate Agent: The Fiduciary Shield,* 35 WASH. & LEE L. REV. 349 (1978).

The Court says that the "welder" analogy "does not wash" because the defendants in *Calder* were not charged with "untargeted negligence." Is the Court's distinction based upon the difference between negligent and intentional tortious conduct, or is it based on the geographical "targeting"? Suppose the hypothetical welder knew the boiler would end up in California because California was the only market for his employer's boilers. For discussion of the issue, see William Knudson, *Keeton, Calder, Helicopteros and Burger King—International Shoe's Most Recent Progeny,* 39 U. MIAMI L. REV. 809, 821 (1985).

(2) *Jurisdiction and the First Amendment.* The Court emphatically rejects the suggestion that the First Amendment calls for a more rigorous standard of amenability for out-of-state publishers than for other defendants. For commentary on this issue, see David Levine, *Preliminary Procedural Protection for the Press from Jurisdiction in Distant Forums After Calder and Keeton,* 1984 ARIZ. ST. L.J. 459; Paul Carrington and James Martin, *Substantive Interests and the Jurisdiction of State Courts,* 66 MICH. L. REV. 227 (1967). Professor Levine suggests that the publishers most likely to be chilled by the possibility of libel actions in a distant forum are major daily newspapers such as the Atlanta Constitution or the Detroit Free Press which distribute only a few newspapers in distant states. A sensible reaction for such publishers might well be to stop such marginally beneficial distributions—an outcome that does raise serious First Amendment concerns.

Was the Court right to reject special jurisdictional limitations for First Amendment cases? What of the strong possibility that a publisher will be haled into a forum with which it has relatively little contact to face a local jury infuriated by the out-of-state newspaper's coverage of local events? *See New York Times v. Connor,* 365 F.2d 567, 572 (5th Cir. 1966). Is it pertinent that the Court first applied First Amendment limitations to state defamation law in *New York Times v. Sullivan,* 376 U.S. 254 (1967)? That decision overturned a $500,000 Alabama jury verdict (a huge sum at the time) based on an advertisement placed in an issue of the New York Times by civil rights groups attacking racial segregation in Alabama; only 394 copies of the advertisement were distributed in Alabama. Does your position on the jurisdictional issue depend on whether the offending article is a political statement or a less "worthy" form of expression as in *Keeton* and *Calder?* Does the First Amendment draw that distinction?

The central issue, of course, is whether the substantive law controlling the claim should affect the jurisdictional issue. The Court suggests that the use of the First Amendment in the jurisdictional calculus would be a form of "double counting" since the protection of free speech is already adequately ensured by the substantive law. This is a weak argument. Of course, it would be a form of "double counting," but sometimes our law requires such procedural substantive redundancy (*e.g.,* the special pleading requirements for fraud in FED. R. CIV. P. 9), and sometimes it does not. Why is double counting required in other contexts but not here? *See also Bose Corp. v. Consumers Union of the United States,* 466 U.S. 485 (1984) (requiring appellate courts to review the record independently with respect to the facts constituting "actual malice" in libel claims).

(3) *A Query.* One final thought on the subjects of both Notes (1) and (2) above: Why did plaintiffs join the author and the editor? Surely the Enquirer had deep enough pockets to satisfy the judgment.

## HELICOPTEROS NACIONALES de COLOMBIA v. HALL

*United States Supreme Court*
*466 U.S. 408 (1984)*

JUSTICE BLACKMUN delivered the opinion of the Court.

We granted certiorari in this case to decide whether the Supreme Court of Texas correctly ruled that the contacts of a foreign corporation with the State of Texas were sufficient to allow a Texas state court to assert jurisdiction over the corporation in a cause of action not arising out of or related to the corporation's activities within the State.

### I

Petitioner Helicopters Nacionales de Colombia, S.A. (Helicol), is a Colombian corporation with its principal place of business in the city of Bogota in that country. It is engaged in the business of providing helicopter transportation for oil and construction companies in South America. On January 26, 1976, a helicopter owned by Helicol crashed in Peru. Four United States citizens were among those who lost their lives in the accident. Respondents are the survivors and representatives of the four decedents.

At the time of the crash, respondents' decedents were employed by Consorcio, a Peruvian consortium, and were working on a pipeline in Peru. Consorcio is the alter ego of a joint venture named Williams-Sedco-Hom (WSH).[1] The venture had its headquarters in Houston, Tex. Consorcio had been formed to enable the venturers to enter into a contract with Petro Peru, the Peruvian state-owned oil company. Consorcio was to construct a pipeline for Petro Peru running from the interior of Peru westward to the Pacific Ocean. Peruvian law forbade construction of the pipeline by any non-Peruvian entity.

Consorcio/WSH needed helicopters to move personnel, materials, and equipment into and out of the construction area. In 1974, upon request of Consorcio/WSH, the chief executive officer of Helicol, Francisco Restrepo, flew to the United States and conferred in Houston with representatives of the three joint venturers. At that meeting, there was a discussion of prices, availability, working conditions, fuel, supplies, and housing. Restrepo represented that Helicol could have the first helicopter on the job in 15 days. The Consorcio/WSH representatives decided to accept the contract proposed by Restrepo. Helicol began performing before the agreement was formally signed in Peru on November 11, 1974. The contract was written in Spanish on official government stationery and provided that the residence of all the parties would be Lima, Peru. It further stated that controversies arising out of the contract would be submitted to the jurisdiction of Peruvian courts. In addition, it provided that Consorcio/WSH would make payments to Helicol's account with the Bank of America in New York City.

Aside from the negotiation session in Houston between Restrepo and the representatives of Consorcio/WSH, Helicol had other contacts with Texas.

---

[1] The participants in the joint venture were Williams International Sudamericana, Ltd., a Delaware corporation; Sedco Construction Corporation, a Texas corporation; and Horn International, Inc., a Texas corporation.

During the years 1970-1977, it purchased helicopters (approximately 80% of its fleet), spare parts, and accessories for more than $4,000,000 from Bell Helicopter Company in Fort Worth. In that period, Helicol sent prospective pilots to Fort Worth for training and to ferry the aircraft to South America. It also sent management and maintenance personnel to visit Bell Helicopter in Fort Worth during the same period in order to receive "plant familiarization" and for technical consultation. Helicol received into its New York City and Panama City, Fla., bank accounts over $5,000,000 in payments from Consorcio/WSH drawn upon First City National Bank of Houston.

Beyond the foregoing, there have been no other business contacts between Helicol and the State of Texas. Helicol never has been authorized to do business in Texas and never has had an agent for the service of process within the State. It never has performed helicopter operations in Texas or sold any product that reached Texas, never solicited business in Texas, never signed any contract in Texas, never had any employee based there, and never recruited an employee in Texas. In addition, Helicol never has owned real or personal property in Texas and never has maintained an office or establishment there. Helicol has maintained no records in Texas and has no shareholders in that state. None of the respondents or their decedents were domiciled in Texas,[5] but all of the decedents were hired in Houston by Consorcio/WSH to work on the Petro Peru pipeline project.

Respondents instituted wrongful death actions in the District Court of Harris County, Tex., against Consorcio/WSH, Bell Helicopter Company, and Helicol. Helicol filed special appearances and moved to dismiss the actions for lack of *in personam* jurisdiction over it. The motion was denied. After a consolidated jury trial, judgment was entered against Helicol on a jury verdict of $1,141,200 in favor of respondents.

. . . In ruling that the Texas courts had *in personam* jurisdiction, the Texas Supreme Court first held that the State's long-arm statute reaches as far as the Due Process Clause of the Fourteenth Amendment permits. Thus, the only question remaining for the court to decide was whether it was consistent with the Due Process Clause for Texas courts to assert *in personam* jurisdiction over Helicol.

## II

The Due Process Clause of the Fourteenth Amendment operates to limit the power of a State to assert *in personam* jurisdiction over a nonresident defendant. *Pennoyer v. Neff,* 95 U.S. 714 (1877). Due process requirements are satisfied when *in personam* jurisdiction is asserted over a nonresident corporate defendant that has "certain minimum contacts with [the forum] such that the maintenance of the suit does not offend 'traditional notions of fair play and substantial justice.'" *Int'l Shoe Co. v. Washington,* 326 U.S. 310

---

[5] Respondents' lack of residential or other contacts with Texas of itself does not defeat otherwise proper jurisdiction. *Keeton v. Hustler Magazine, Inc., ante,* 465 U.S. 770, 780; *Calder v. Jones,* 465 U.S. 783, 788. We mention respondents' lack of contacts merely to show that nothing in the nature of the relationship between respondents and Helicol could possibly enhance Helicol's contacts with Texas. The harm suffered by respondents did not occur in Texas. Nor is it alleged that any negligence on the part of Helicol took place in Texas.

(1945). When a controversy is related to or "arises out of" a defendant's contacts with the forum, the Court has said that a "relationship among the defendant, the forum, and the litigation" is the essential foundation of *in personam* jurisdiction. *Shaffer v. Heitner,* 433 U.S. 186 (1977). [8]

Even when the cause of action does not arise out of or relate to the foreign corporation's activities in the forum State, [9] due process is not offended by a State's subjecting the corporation to its *in personam* jurisdiction when there are sufficient contacts between the State and the foreign corporation. *Perkins v. Benguet Consol. Mining Co.,* 342 U.S. 437 (1952); *see Keeton v. Hustler Magazine, Inc.* 465 U.S. 770 (1984). In *Perkins,* the Court addressed a situation in which state courts had asserted general jurisdiction over a defendant foreign corporation. During the Japanese occupation of the Philippine Islands, the president and general manager of a Philippine mining corporation maintained an office in Ohio from which he conducted activities on behalf of the company. He kept company files and held directors' meetings in the office, carried on correspondence relating to the business, distributed salary checks drawn on two active Ohio bank accounts, engaged an Ohio bank to act as transfer agent, and supervised policies dealing with the rehabilitation of the corporation's properties in the Philippines. In short, the foreign corporation, through its president, "ha[d] been carrying on in Ohio a continuous and systematic, but limited, part of its general business," and the exercise of general jurisdiction over the Philippine corporation by an Ohio court was "reasonable and just."

All parties to the present case concede that respondents' claims against Helicol did not "arise out of," and are not related to, Helicol's activities within Texas." [10] We thus must explore the nature of Helicol's contacts with the State

---

[8] It has been said that when a State exercises personal jurisdiction over a defendant in a suit arising out of or related to the defendant's contacts with the forum, the State is exercising "specific jurisdiction" over the defendant. *See* Arthur von Mehren & Donald Trautman, *Jurisdiction to Adjudicate: A Suggested Analysis,* 79 HARV. L. REV. 1136, 1144-1164 (1966).

[9] When a State exercises personal jurisdiction over a defendant in a suit not arising out of or related to the defendant's contacts with the forum, the State has been said to be exercising "general jurisdiction" over the defendant. *See* Lea Brilmayer, *How Contacts Count: Due Process Limitations on State Court Jurisdiction,* 1980 S. CT. REV. 77, 80-8 1; von Mehren & Trautman, 79 HARV. L. REV., at II *36-1144; Calder v. Jones, ante,* 465 U.S. at 786-787.

[10] Because the parties have not argued any relationship between the cause of action and Helicol's contacts with the State of Texas, we, contrary to the dissent's implication, assert no "view" with respect to that issue.

The dissent suggests that we have erred in drawing no distinction between controversies that "relate to" a defendant's contacts with a forum and those that "arise out of" such contacts. This criticism is somewhat puzzling, for the dissent goes on to urge that, for purposes of determining the constitutional validity of an assertion of specific jurisdiction, there really should be no distinction between the two.

We do not address the validity or consequences of such a distinction because the issue has not been presented in this case. Respondents have made no argument that their cause of action either arose out of or is related to Helicol's contacts with the State of Texas. Absent any briefing on the issue, we decline to reach the questions (1) whether the terms "arising out of" and "related to" describe different connections between a cause of action and a defendant's contacts with a forum, and (2) what sort of tie between a cause of action and a defendant's contacts with a forum is necessary to a determination that either connection exists. Nor do we reach the question whether, if the two types of relationship differ, a forum's exercise of personal jurisdiction in a situation where the cause of action "relates to," but does not "arise out of," the defendant's contacts with the forum should be analyzed as an assertion of specific jurisdiction.

of Texas to determine whether they constitute the kind of continuous and systematic general business contacts the Court found to exist in *Perkins*. We hold that they do not.

It is undisputed that Helicol does not have a place of business in Texas and never has been licensed to do business in the State. Basically, Helicol's contacts with Texas consisted of sending its chief executive officer to Houston for a contract-negotiation session; accepting into its New York bank account checks drawn on a Houston bank; purchasing helicopters, equipment, and training services from Bell Helicopter for substantial sums; and sending personnel to Bell's facilities in Fort Worth for training.

The one trip to Houston by Helicol's chief executive officer for the purpose of negotiating the transportation-services contract with Consorcio/WSH cannot be described or regarded as a contact of a "continuous and systematic" nature, as *Perkins* described it, see also *International Shoe Co. v. Washington,* 326 U.S. at 320, and thus cannot support an assertion of in personam jurisdiction over Helicol by a Texas court. Similarly, Helicol's acceptance from Consorcio/WSH of checks drawn on a Texas bank is of negligible significance for purposes of determining whether Helicol had sufficient contacts in Texas. There is no indication that Helicol ever requested that the checks be drawn on a Texas bank or that there was any negotiation between Helicol and Consorcio/WSH with respect to the location or identity of the bank on which checks would be drawn. Common sense and everyday experience suggest that, absent unusual circumstances, the bank on which a check is drawn is generally of little consequence to the payee and is a matter left to the discretion of the drawer. Such unilateral activity of another party or a third person is not an appropriate consideration when determining whether a defendant has sufficient contacts with a forum State to justify an assertion of jurisdiction. . . .

The Texas Supreme Court focused on the purchases and the related training trips in finding contacts sufficient to support an assertion of jurisdiction. We do not agree with that assessment, for the Court's opinion in *Rosenberg Brothers & Co. v. Curtis Brown Co.,* 260 U.S. 516 (1923) (Brandeis, J., for a unanimous tribunal), makes clear that purchases and related trips, standing alone, are not a sufficient basis for a State's assertion of jurisdiction.

The defendant in *Rosenberg* was a small retailer in Tulsa, Okla., who dealt in men's clothing and furnishings. It never had applied for a license to do business in New York, nor had it at any time authorized suit to be brought against it there. It never had an established place of business in New York and never regularly carried on business in that State. Its only connection with New York was that it purchased from New York wholesalers a large portion of the merchandise sold in its Tulsa store. The purchases sometimes were made by correspondence and sometimes through visits to New York by an officer of the defendant. The Court concluded: "Visits on such business, even if occurring at regular intervals, would not warrant the inference that the corporation was present within the jurisdiction of [New York]."

This Court in *International Shoe* acknowledged and did not repudiate its holding in *Rosenberg.* In accordance with *Rosenberg,* we hold that mere purchases, even if occurring at regular intervals, are not enough to warrant a State's assertion of *in personam* jurisdiction over a nonresident corporation in a cause of action not related to those purchase transactions. [12] Nor can we conclude that the fact that Helicol sent personnel into Texas for training in connection with the purchase of helicopters and equipment in that State in any way enhanced the nature of Helicol's contacts with Texas. The training was a part of the package of goods and services purchased by Helicol from Bell Helicopter. The brief presence of Helicol employees in Texas for the purpose of attending the training sessions is no more a significant contact than were the trips to New York made by the buyer for the retail store in *Rosenberg* . . .

## III

We hold that Helicol's contacts with the State of Texas were insufficient to satisfy the requirements of the Due Process Clause of the Fourteenth Amendment. [13] Accordingly, we reverse the judgment of the Supreme Court of Texas.

JUSTICE BRENNAN, dissenting.

Decisions applying the Due Process Clause of the Fourteenth Amendment to determine whether a State may constitutionally assert *in personam* jurisdiction over a particular defendant for a particular cause of action most often turn on a weighing of facts. To a large extent, today's decision follows the usual pattern. Based on essentially undisputed facts, the Court concludes that petitioner Helicol's contacts with the State of Texas were insufficient to allow the Texas state courts constitutionally to assert "general jurisdiction" over all claims filed against this foreign corporation. Although my independent weighing of the facts leads me to a different conclusion, the Court's holding on this issue is neither implausible nor unexpected.

What is troubling about the Court's opinion, however, are the implications that might be drawn from the way in which the Court approaches the constitutional issue it addresses. First, the Court limits its discussion to an assertion of general jurisdiction of the Texas courts because, in its view, the underlying cause of action does "not aris[e] out of or relat[e] to the corporation's activities within the State." Then, the Court relies on a 1923 decision in *Rosenberg Brothers & Co. v. Curtis Brown Co.,* [260 U.S. 516], without

---

[12] This Court in *International Shoe* cited *Rosenberg* for the proposition that "the commission of some single or occasional acts of the corporate agent in a state sufficient to impose an obligation or liability on the corporation has not been thought to confer upon the state authority to enforce it." Arguably, therefore, *Rosenberg* also stands for the proposition that mere purchases are not a sufficient basis for either general or specific jurisdiction. Because the case before us is one in which there has been an assertion of general jurisdiction over a foreign defendant, we need not decide the continuing validity of *Rosenberg* with respect to an assertion of specific jurisdiction, i.e., where the cause of action arises out of or relates to the purchases by the defendant in the forum State.

[13] As an alternative to traditional minimum-contacts analysis, respondents suggest that the Court hold that the State of Texas had personal jurisdiction over Helicol under a doctrine of jurisdiction by necessity." *See Shaffer v. Heitner,* 433 U.S. 186, 211, n. 37, 97 S. Ct. 2569, 2583, n. 37, 53 L. Ed. 2d 683 (1977). We conclude, however, that respondents failed to carry their burden of showing that all three defendants could not be sued together in a single forum. It is not clear from the record, for example, whether suit could have been brought against all three defendants in either Columbia or Peru. We decline to consider adoption of a doctrine of jurisdiction by necessity—a potentially far-reaching modification of existing law—in the absence of a more complete record.

considering whether that case retains any validity after our more recent pronouncements concerning the permissible reach of a State's jurisdiction. By posing and deciding the question presented in this manner, I fear that the Court is saying more than it realizes about constitutional limitations on the potential reach of *in personam* jurisdiction. In particular, by relying on a precedent whose premises have long been discarded, and by refusing to consider any distinction between controversies that "relate to" a defendant's contacts with the forum and causes of action that "arise out of" such contacts, the Court may be placing severe limitations on the type and amount of contacts that will satisfy the constitutional minimum.

In contrast, I believe that the undisputed contacts in this case between petitioner Helicol and the State of Texas are sufficiently important, and sufficiently related to the underlying cause of action, to make it fair and reasonable for the State to assert personal jurisdiction over Helicol for the wrongful death actions filed by the respondents. . . . I therefore dissent.

I

. . . .

The Court . . . looks for guidance to our 1923 decision in *Rosenberg,* which until today was of dubious validity given the subsequent expansion of personal jurisdiction that began with *International Shoe,* in 1945. In *Rosenberg,* the Court held that a company's purchases within a State, even when combined with related trips to the State by company officials, would not allow the courts of that State to assert general jurisdiction over all claims against the nonresident corporate defendant making those purchases.[1] Reasoning by analogy, the Court in this case concludes that Helicol's contacts with the State of Texas are no more significant than the purchases made by the defendant in *Rosenberg.* The Court makes no attempt, however, to ascertain whether the narrow view of *in personam* jurisdiction adopted by the Court in *Rosenberg* comports with "the fundamental transformation of our national economy" that has occurred since 1923. This failure, in my view, is fatal to the Court's analysis.

[Justice Brennan describes the transformation and the jurisdictional expansion that accompanied it.]. . . .

As a foreign corporation that has actively and purposefully engaged in numerous and frequent commercial transactions in the State of Texas, Helicol clearly falls within the category of nonresident defendants that may be subject to that forum's general jurisdiction. Helicol not only purchased helicopters and other equipment in the State for many years, but also sent pilots and management personnel into Texas to be trained in the use of this equipment and to consult with the seller on technical matters. Moreover, negotiations

---

[1] The Court leaves open the question whether the decision in *Rosenberg* was intended to address any constitutional limits on an assertion of "specific jurisdiction." *Ante,* n. 12 *(citing Int'l Shoe,* 326 U.S., at 318). If anything is clear from Justice Brandeis' opinion for the court in *Rosenberg,* however, it is that the Court was concerned only with general jurisdiction over the corporate defendant. The Court's resuscitation of *Rosenberg,* therefore, should have no bearing upon any forum's assertion of jurisdiction over claims that arise out of or relate to a defendant's contacts with the State.

for the contract under which Helicol provided transportation services to the joint venture that employed the respondents' decedents also took place in the State of Texas. Taken together, these contacts demonstrate that Helicol obtained numerous benefits from its transaction of business in Texas. In turn, it is eminently fair and reasonable to expect Helicol to face the obligations that attach to its participation in such commercial transactions. Accordingly, on the basis of continuous commercial contacts with the forum, I would conclude that the Due Process Clause allows the State of Texas to assert general jurisdiction over petitioner Helicol.

## II

The Court also fails to distinguish the legal principles that controlled our prior decisions in *Perkins* and *Rosenberg.* In particular, the contacts between petitioner Helicol and the State of Texas, unlike the contacts between the defendant and the forum in each of those cases, are significantly related to the cause of action alleged in the original suit filed by the respondents. Accordingly, in my view, it is both fair and reasonable for the Texas courts to assert specific jurisdiction over Helicol in this case.

By asserting that the present case does not implicate the specific jurisdiction of the Texas courts, the Court necessarily removes its decision from the reality of the actual facts presented for our consideration.[3] Moreover, the Court refuses to consider any distinction between contacts that are "related to" the underlying cause of action and contacts that "give rise" to the underlying cause of action. In my view, however, there is a substantial difference between these two standards for asserting specific jurisdiction. Thus, although I agree that the respondents' cause of action did not formally "arise out of" specific activities initiated by Helicol in the State of Texas, I believe that the wrongful death claim filed by the respondents is significantly related to the undisputed contacts between Helicol and the forum. On that basis, I would conclude that the Due Process Clause allows the Texas courts to assert specific jurisdiction over this particular action.

The wrongful death action filed by the respondents was premised on a fatal helicopter crash that occurred in Peru. Helicol was joined as a defendant in the lawsuit because it provided transportation services, including the particular helicopter and pilot involved in the crash, to the joint venture that employed the decedents. Specifically, the respondents claimed in their original complaint that "Helicol is . . . legally responsible for its own negligence through its pilot employee." Viewed in light of these allegations, the contacts between Helicol and the State of Texas are directly and significantly related to the underlying claim filed by the respondents. The negotiations that took place in Texas led to the contract in which Helicol agreed to provide the precise

---

[3] Nor do I agree with the Court that the respondents have conceded that their claims are not related to Helicol's activities within the State of Texas. Although parts of their written and oral arguments before the Court proceed on the assumption that no such relationship exists, other portions suggest just the opposite. . . .

Thus, while the respondents' position before this Court is admittedly less than clear, I believe it is preferable to address the specific jurisdiction of the Texas courts because Helicol's contacts with Texas are in fact related to the underlying cause of action.

transportation services that were being used at the time of the crash. Moreover, the helicopter involved in the crash was purchased by Helicol in Texas, and the pilot whose negligence was alleged to have caused the crash was actually trained in Texas.

This is simply not a case, therefore, in which a state court has asserted jurisdiction over a nonresident defendant on the basis of wholly unrelated contacts with the forum. Rather, the contacts between Helicol and the forum are directly related to the negligence that was alleged in the respondents' original complaint. Because Helicol should have expected to be amenable to suit in the Texas courts for claims directly related to these contacts, it is fair and reasonable to allow the assertion of jurisdiction in this case.

Despite this substantial relationship between the contacts and the cause of action, the Court declines to consider whether the courts of Texas may assert specific jurisdiction over this suit. Apparently, this simply reflects a narrow interpretation of the question presented for review. *See ante, n.* 10. It is nonetheless possible that the Court's opinion may be read to imply that the specific jurisdiction of the Texas courts is inapplicable because the cause of action did not formally "arise out of" the contacts between Helicol and the forum. In my view, however, such a rule would place unjustifiable limits on the bases under which Texas may assert its jurisdictional power.

Limiting the specific jurisdiction of a forum to cases in which the cause of action formally arose out of the defendant's contacts with the State would subject constitutional standards under the Due Process Clause to the vagaries of the substantive law or pleading requirements of each State. For example, the complaint filed against Helicol in this case alleged negligence based on pilot error. Even though the pilot was trained in Texas, the Court assumes that the Texas courts may not assert jurisdiction over the suit because the cause of action "did not 'arise out of,' and [is] not related to," that training. If, however, the applicable substantive law required that negligent training of the pilot was a necessary element of a cause of action for pilot error, or if the respondents had simply added an allegation of negligence in the training provided for the Helicol pilot, then presumably the Court would concede that the specific jurisdiction of the Texas courts was applicable.

Our interpretation of the Due Process Clause has never been so dependent upon the applicable substantive law or the State's formal pleading requirements. At least since *International Shoe,* the principal focus when determining whether a forum may constitutionally assert jurisdiction over a nonresident defendant has been on fairness and reasonableness to the defendant. To this extent, a court's specific jurisdiction should be applicable whenever the cause of action arises out of *or* relates to the contacts between the defendant and the forum. It is eminently fair and reasonable, in my view, to subject a defendant to suit in a forum with which it has significant contacts directly related to the underlying cause of action. Because Helicol's contacts with the State of Texas meet this standard, I would affirm the judgment of the Supreme Court of Texas.

---

## NOTES AND QUESTIONS

(1) *Fairness and Convenience.* Can the result in *Helicopteros* be justified on grounds of fairness and convenience? Who was more able to litigate away from home, Helicol or plaintiffs? Was Helicol (or its insurer) able to mount a credible pre-trial, trial, and appellate defense in Texas? With their Texas judgment reversed for lack of jurisdiction, what forums were open to the plaintiffs? Could they successfully pursue their claims in Colombia or Peru? What effect would economic differences between North and South America have on the measure of plaintiffs' damages? Is the contingent fee arrangement upon which American tort plaintiffs depend available in Colombia or Peru? Based on factors such as these, one commentator concluded that "a dismissal on jurisdictional grounds in a case like *Helicopters* is tantamount to a dismissal for all purposes." Louise Weinberg, *The Helicopteros Case and the Jurisprudence of Jurisdiction,* 58 S. CAL. L. REV. 913, 934 (1985). For additional commentary emphasizing the progress of the case through the lower courts, *see* Dennis Terez, *The Misguided Helicopters Case: Confusion in the Courts Over Contacts,* 37 BAYLOR L. REV. 913(1985).

(2) *General and Specific Jurisdiction.* The Court adopts explicitly the general/ specific jurisdiction dichotomy proposed in Arthur von Mehren & Donald Trautman, *Jurisdiction to Adjudicate: A Suggested Analysis,* 79 HARV. L. REV. 1121 (1966). "General jurisdiction" exists when defendant's contacts with the state are sufficient to support jurisdiction even in an action completely unrelated to those contacts. "Specific jurisdiction" applies in a case where defendant's forum connections are fewer and less significant, but the cause of action arises out of those contacts.

(3) *General Jurisdiction in Helicol.* Is the Court's narrow holding—no general jurisdiction over Helicol in Texas—correct? Were Helicol's connections with Texas sufficient to support a claim that is completely unrelated to those contacts? Suppose a Louisianan flew to Colombia and negotiated with Helicol there to lend Helicol a substantial sum of money to buy fuel from a Colombian supplier. If Helicol defaulted, could the Louisianan obtain jurisdiction over Helicol in Texas in an action for payment of the debt? If not, does that mean that the Court's general jurisdiction holding is correct? For commentary on this portion of the Court's opinion, see RUSSELL WEINTRAUB, COMMENTARY ON THE CONFLICT OF LAWS 162 (4th ed. 2001); William Knudsen, *Keeton, Calder, Helicopters and Burger King—International Shoe's Most Recent Progeny,* 39 U. MIAMI L. REV. 809, 826-832 (1985).

*See* PROBLEM 3C-8. WHO OWES WHAT TO WHOM?

(4) *Out-dated Authority.* To bolster its plausible general jurisdiction holding, the Court resurrects the *Rosenberg* case in spite of the fact that *Rosenberg* was decided twenty years before *International Shoe* debunked *Pennoyer* and the territorial power theory of jurisdiction. Was this reliance on *pre-International Shoe* authority predictable to the bench, the bar, the

scholars? What effect does it have on the legal process? How does it affect the very practical problem of conducting research on jurisdictional issues?

(5) *Foreign Trade.* The United States and the Motor Vehicle Manufacturers Association filed amicus briefs in *Helicopteros,* arguing that holding a foreign purchaser amenable to general jurisdiction would discourage foreign firms from purchasing American goods—a result that is especially troubling given the current balance of trade deficit. Is that a real worry? What empirical assumptions does this argument presuppose? How could they be tested?

If the Supreme Court considered the argument, it did not say so. If the foreign trade problem affected the Court, *Helicopteros* would be a classic example of a case where the abstract manipulations in the opinion have nothing to do with the real reason for the decision. For a discussion of that possibility, see Louise Weinberg, *The Helicopteros Case and the Jurisprudence of Jurisdiction,* 58 S. CAL. L. REV. 913 (1985).

(6) *Necessity.* Plaintiffs argued that jurisdiction over Helicol was justified by the doctrine of "jurisdiction by necessity." The Court has flirted with this concept in the past in *Mullane v. Central Hanover Bank and Trust,* 339 U.S. 306 (1950) and *Shaffer v. Heitner,* 433 U.S. 186 at n. 37 (1977) (*see* § 3.16, *infra),* but declined the opportunity to develop it further here. *See* n. 13. Under what circumstances, if any, should the plaintiff's need for a forum justify jurisdiction over a defendant who does not meet the "purposefully availing" test? *See* Ian Fraser, *Jurisdiction by Necessity—An Analysis of the Mullane Case,* 100 U. PA. L. REV. 305 (1951).

---

## NOTES ON GENERAL AND SPECIFIC JURISDICTION

(1) *Dispute-Blind and Dispute-Specific.* The distinction between general and specific jurisdiction has generated significant commentary. In an impressive article, Professor Mary Twitchell offered a useful clarification. She recast the general/specific dichotomy as a distinction between exercises of jurisdiction which are "dispute-blind" (the decision is made without regard to the nature of the claim) and "dispute-specific" (the decision considers the nature of the claim). The point of the reformulation is to help the courts restrict the use of general jurisdiction to cases in which the defendant's forum connections are so pervasive as to justify jurisdiction over any claim against him. *See* Mary Twitchell, *The Myth of General Jurisdiction,* 101 HARV. L. REV. 610 (1988). Does the reformulation add clarity? For commentary, see Lea Brilmayer, *Related Contacts and Personal Jurisdiction,* 101 HARV. L. REV. 1444 (198 8); Mary Twitchell, *A Rejoinder to Professor Brilmayer,* 101 HARV. L. REV. 1465 (1988).

(2) *Hard Questions.* The general/specific distinction raises some difficult questions. Is general jurisdiction still justified now that long-arm statutes facilitate specific jurisdiction?

*Compare* Linda Silberman, *"Two Cheers" for International Shoe (and None for Asahi): An Essay on the Fiftieth Anniversary of International Shoe,* 28 U.C.

DAVIS L. REV. 755 (1995), *with* Harold Maier & Thomas McCoy, *A Unifying Theory for Personal Jurisdiction and Choice of Law*, 39 AM. J. COMP. L. 249, 271 (1991). Is the justification for jurisdiction in each of the two paradigms the same? An influential article argues that it is not. General jurisdiction is justified by the state's relationship to those who, through the political process, can influence the state's decision-making; by contrast specific jurisdiction is justified by the state's authority to control activities within its territory. *See*
  Lea Brilmayer, Jennifer Haverkamp, Buck Logan, Loretta Lynch, Steve Neuwirth, and Jim O'Brien, A *General Look at General Jurisdiction,* 66 TEX. L. REV. 721, 726 (1988).

What relationships between the state and the defendant suffice to support an exercise of general jurisdiction? Pretty clearly, domicile for a natural person is adequate, as are incorporation and principal place of business for a corporation. In other cases, what level of forum-related activity is required? *See id.* at 727-741; Russell Weintraub, *A Map Out of the Personal Jurisdiction Labyrinth*, 28 U. C. DAVIS L. REV. 531, 555-557 (1995); Mary Twitchell, *The Myth of General Jurisdiction, supra,* at 667-679; B. Glenn George, *In Search of General Jurisdiction,* 64 TUL. L. REV. 1097, 1129 (1990).

Perhaps the most controversial question raised by the general/specific jurisdiction distinction is the definition of "claim related" contacts. When is a defendant's contact with the forum "related" to plaintiffs claim so that it can furnish a basis for specific jurisdiction? The question is significant because contacts that are not "claim related" must be so numerous and significant that they justify general jurisdiction.

Professor Brilmayer proposes a narrow standard of substantive relevance to plaintiff's claim: "A contact is related to the controversy if it is the geographical qualification of a fact relevant to the merits." In other words, a contact between the forum and the defendant is claim-related only if it is an event that is relevant under the substantive law. *See* Lea Brilmayer, *How Contacts Count: Due Process Limitations on State Court Jurisdiction,* 1980 SUP. CT. REV. 77, 82; Brilmayer, Haverkamp, Logan, Lynch, Neuwirth, and O'Brien, *supra* at 738. Professor Twitchell finds the test too narrow and would consider for purposes of specific jurisdiction defendant's forum activities that are similar to the acts that gave rise to the claim. *See* Twitchell, *The Myth of General Jurisdiction, supra,* at 650-665.

To focus the Brilmayer-Twitchell debate, consider this case: defendant, a trucker who regularly drives his truck on business into and out of the forum, injures plaintiff on such a trip, but the collision occurs one mile outside the forum. For Twitchell, the defendant's forum contacts are "claim-related" because they are similar to the event that caused the claim; for Brilmayer, they are not because driving a truck in the forum on other occasions is not relevant to plaintiffs claim under the substantive law of negligence.

## NOTES ON GENERAL JURISDICTION, SPECIFIC JURISDICTION, AND THE SLIDING SCALE

(1) *The Sliding Scale.* * The general/specific jurisdiction distinction is certainly a useful way to talk about the defendant's forum contacts and the relationship between those contacts and plaintiff's claim. The distinction raises an interesting question: Is jurisdiction proper in a case that falls between the two paradigms—one where the defendant has substantial contacts with the forum, but not so many as to justify general jurisdiction, and where plaintiff's cause of action does not arise out of defendant's forum activities, although it is not totally unrelated to the them? In other words, is jurisdiction proper where the case fails to satisfy the requirements for either general or specific jurisdiction but partially satisfies the requirements for both? *Helicopteros* seems to be such a case, but in footnote 10 of its opinion, the Court carefully ducks the issue of specific jurisdiction, and, *a fortiori,* the question of whether jurisdiction exists in cases that fall between the two paradigms.

Some commentators have argued that there should not be jurisdiction in cases that fall between the two paradigms. *See* Lea Brilmayer, *How Contacts Count: Due Process Limitations on State Court Jurisdiction,* 1980 SUP. CT. REV. 71. *But see* Harold Lewis, *A Brave New World for Personal Jurisdiction: Flexible Tests Under Uniform Standards,* 37 VAND. L. REV. 1 (1984). On that view, claim-relatedness seems to be on an all-or-nothing issue; like an electrical switch, it is either "on" or "off." Contacts that do not meet the specific jurisdiction test are important only if there are enough of them to justify general jurisdiction. In his dissenting opinion, Justice Brennan disagreed with this view. Between the two extremes, he argued for a third discrete category where plaintiff's claim does not "arise out of" the defendant's forum contacts but is nevertheless "related" to them. Thus, Brennan seems to view claim-relatedness as a three-position switch with two of those positions adequate for specific jurisdiction.

In fact, the relationship between the plaintiff's claim and the defendant's forum connections does not fit well into two or even three discrete categories; it resembles a continuum more than a two-or three-position switch. At one extreme are cases where an element of the plaintiff's claim consists of some act by the defendant purposefully done in the forum. At the other extreme are cases where the plaintiff's claim simply has nothing to do with the defendant's forum contacts. In between, the variations and gradations are too numerous to catalogue. For instance, some portion of the plaintiff's claim might be closely connected with the defendant's forum contacts while another portion might be unconnected. *See, e.g., Keeton v. Hustler Magazine Inc.* § 3.10, *supra.* Or the plaintiff's claim might arise from activities outside the forum that breached a duty created by a relationship centered in the forum. *See,*

---

* This Note is adapted from William Richman, *Review Essay,* 72 CALIF L. REV. 1328, 1336-1346 (1984). Copyright © California Law Review, 1984; reprinted with permission.

*e.g., Shaffer v. Heitner,* § 3.16, *infra.* Or the plaintiff's claim might arise from an extra-forum act of the defendant that nevertheless is part of an ongoing activity that is significantly connected to the forum. *See, e.g., Cornelison v. Chaney,* 16 Cal. 3d 143, 545 P.2d 264, 127 Cal. Rptr. 352 (1976). It bears repetition; the variations seem endless.

A continuum model of the relationship between the plaintiff's claim and the defendant's forum contacts permits plotting that relationship against another phenomenon that is clearly a continuum—the extent of the defendant's connections with the forum. The result is a typical Cartesian graph.

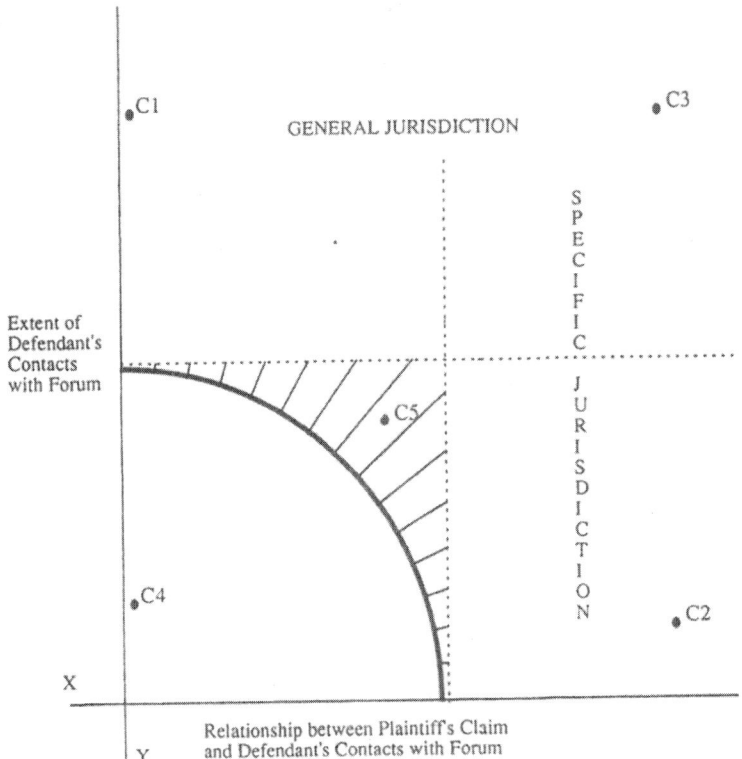

The extent of the defendant's contacts with the forum is plotted on the Y (vertical) axis, and the relationship between the plaintiff's claim and the defendant's forum contacts is plotted on the X (horizontal) axis. The horizontal dotted line indicates the point at which the defendant's contacts with the forum are sufficiently extensive to justify exercising general jurisdiction. The vertical dotted line indicates the point at which the defendant's contacts, however few, are so closely related with the plaintiff's claim that specific jurisdiction is justified.

*C1* is a case where the defendant has very extensive contacts with the forum, but the plaintiff's cause of action has nothing to do with the defendant's forum connections. An example is an action in California against a California domiciliary based on an automobile accident in New York. The classic

Supreme Court case is *Perkins v. Benguet Consolidated Mining Co.,* 342 U.S. 437 (1952), in which the defendant, a Philippine corporation conducting extensive operations during World War II "in exile" in Ohio, was sued there on a cause of action arising out of activities in the Philippines.

In paradigm *C2,* the defendant has very few connections with the forum, but the plaintiff's claim arises directly out of those contacts. A well-known example *is McGee v. International Life Insurance Co.,* 355 U.S. 220 (1957), in which the defendant's only contact with California was an offer mailed into the state to insure a California domiciliary. The action, however, a claim for the death benefit under the policy, arose directly out of the one contact.

*C3* represents a situation that receives little comment because jurisdiction based on either theory is so clear. The defendant has numerous connections with the forum, and the plaintiff's claim is closely related to those contacts. An example is an action in Ohio against an Ohio domiciliary based upon a contract made and performed in Ohio.

The result in *C4* is also uncontroversial, but in the other direction. The defendant has few contacts with the forum and the cause of action does not arise out of those contacts. Suppose, for example, a Canadian citizen is sued in New York based upon an automobile accident in Vermont. The case meets neither paradigm and jurisdiction does not exist.

*C5* in the shaded area of the graph is *Helicopteros.* It is controversial because it satisfies neither paradigm. The defendant's contacts with the forum are not so extensive as to justify general jurisdiction, nor does the plaintiff's claim directly arise out of the defendant's forum contacts, thus justifying specific jurisdiction. Nevertheless, because the case is a *near-miss on both* paradigms, the exercise of jurisdiction should be upheld.

To encompass all the proper cases, the general/specific jurisdiction dichotomy must be supplemented by a *sliding scale* model of the relationship between the two key variables: the extent of the defendant's forum contacts on the one hand and the proximity of the connection between those contacts and the plaintiff's claim on the other. As the quantity and quality of the defendant's forum contacts increase, a weaker connection between the plaintiff's claim and those contacts is permissible; as the quantity and quality of the defendant's forum contacts decrease, a stronger connection between the plaintiff's claim and those contacts is required. The concepts of general jurisdiction and specific jurisdiction are simply the two opposite ends of this sliding scale.

Besides accounting for the cases that fall between general and specific jurisdiction, the sliding scale model has an additional advantage. The view that requires a case to satisfy one of the two paradigms invites an excessively conceptualistic analysis of the notion of claim-relatedness. Reading Justice Brennan's dissent in *Helicopteros,* it is easy to foresee careful scholarly and judicial treatments of this notion. Must an element of the plaintiff's claim consist of one of the defendant's forum-connected acts, or are mere similarity, and geographical proximity sufficient? Must all or only part of the plaintiff's claim spring from the defendant's contacts with the forum? This sort of mechanical jurisprudence elevates characterization and conceptual manipulation to the level they once achieved under the choice-of-law regime of the original RESTATEMENT OF CONFLICT OF LAWS. *See* § 4.11, *infra*. In fact, however, claim-relatedness, like general and specific jurisdiction, is simply an analytical tool—a convenient summary of some of the factors that make an exercise of jurisdiction fair or unfair. Because the sliding scale does not treat claim-relatedness as an all-or-nothing phenomenon, it reduces the temptation to manipulate that concept and thus helps the court focus on the issue: the underlying factors that ensure the fairness of a particular exercise of jurisdiction.

"General jurisdiction" and "specific jurisdiction" are just useful analytical tools that identify two sorts of cases in which the basic underlying factors—the defendant's benefit from the forum, the foreseeability of forum litigation, lack of serious inconvenience, defendant's initiation of the transaction—in one mix or another make jurisdiction fair. It seems rigid and wrongheaded to suggest that no intermediate mixtures are permissible.

(2) *Critique*. For commentary critical of the sliding scale, see Linda Simard, *Hybrid Personal Jurisdiction: It's Not General Jurisdiction, Or Specific Jurisdiction, But Is It Constitutional?*, 48 CASE WESTERN L. REV. 559 (1998), Flavio Rose, *Related Contacts and Personal Jurisdiction*, 82 CAL. L. REV. 1545 (1994).

(3) *Judicial Solutions.*[*] Without guidance from the Supreme Court, the lower courts have had to develop their own criteria for 'relatedness.' Some refuse to find specific jurisdiction unless the plaintiff's claim arises directly from defendant's forum-related activity. *See, e.g., Pizarro v. Hoteles Concorde Int'l C.A.*, 907 F.2d 1256, 1259 (1st Cir. 1990); *Sybaritic Inc. v. Interport Int'l, Inc.*, 957 F.2d 522, 525 (8th Cir. 1992). Others follow Justice Brennan's disjunctive formulation of specific jurisdiction and require only that plaintiff's claim "arise out of" *or* be "related to" defendant's forum contacts. *Ruston Gas Turbines, Inc. v. Donaldson Co.*, 9 F.3d 415, 418 (5th Cir.1993). Still others permit specific jurisdiction over a claim that has a "substantial relation to" defendant's contacts, *see Third Nat'l Bank v. WEDGE Group, Inc.*, 882 F.2d 1087, 1091 n. 2 (6th Cir.1989), *cert. denied*, 493 U.S. 1058 (1990), is "made possible by" those contacts, *see Lanier v. American Board of Endodontics*, 843 F.2d 901, 908-909 (6th Cir.*), cert. denied*, 488 U.S. 926 (1988) or "lies in the wake of" defendant's forum-connected activities. *Deluxe Ice Cream Co v. R.C.H. Tool Corp.*, 726 F.2d 1209, 1215-1216 (7th Cir.1984).

The federal appellate courts disagree on whether a 'but for' relationship is adequate for specific jurisdiction: If plaintiff's claim does not arise out of defendant's forum-connected activities, can the court base specific jurisdiction on the fact that the claim would not have arisen *but for* those activities? The Sixth, Seventh, Ninth and Tenth Circuits have approved the 'but for' test for specific jurisdiction; the First and Eighth Circuits have reached results inconsistent with it; and the Fifth Circuit has waffled on the issue. For citations, see 1 ROBERT CASAD & WILLIAM RICHMAN, JURISDICTION IN CIVIL ACTIONS 159-162 (3d ed. 1998). For commentary on the cases and arguments in favor of the "but for" test, see Mark Maloney, *Note, Specific Jurisdiction*

---

[*] This note draws heavily on the discussion in 1 ROBERT CASAD & WILLIAM RICHMAN, JURISDICTION IN CIVIL ACTIONS 159-162 (3d ed. 1998).

*and the "Arise From or Relate To" Requirement. . .What Does It Mean?*, 50 WASH. & LEE L. REV. 1265 (1993).

---

## BURGER KING CORP. v. RUDZEWICZ

*United States Supreme Court*
*471 U.S. 462, 105 S. Ct. 2174, 85 L. Ed. 2d 528 (1985)*

JUSTICE BRENNAN delivered the opinion of the Court.

The State of Florida's long-arm statute extends jurisdiction to "[a]ny person, whether or not a citizen or resident of this state," who, *inter alia,* "[b]reach[es] a contract in this state by failing to perform acts required by the contract to be performed in this state," so long as the cause of action arises from the alleged contractual breach. The United States District Court for the Southern District of Florida, sitting in diversity, relied on this provision in exercising personal jurisdiction over a Michigan resident who allegedly had breached a franchise agreement with a Florida corporation by failing to make required payments in Florida. . . .

### I

### A

Burger King Corporation is a Florida corporation whose principal offices are in Miami. It is one of the world's largest restaurant organizations, with over 3,000 outlets in the 50 States, the Commonwealth of Puerto Rico, and 8 foreign nations. Burger King conducts approximately 80% of its business through a franchise operation that the company styles the "Burger King System"—"a comprehensive restaurant format and operating system for the sale of uniform and quality food products." Burger King licenses its franchisees to use its trademarks and service marks for a period of 20 years and leases standardized restaurant facilities to them for the same term. In addition, franchisees acquire a variety of proprietary information concerning the "standards, specifications, procedures and methods for operating a Burger King Restaurant." They also receive market research and advertising assistance; ongoing training in restaurant management; and accounting, cost-control, and inventory-control guidance. By permitting franchisees to tap into Burger King's established national reputation and to benefit from proven procedures for dispensing standardized fare, this system enables them to go into the restaurant business with significantly lowered barriers to entry.

In exchange for these benefits, franchisees pay Burger King an initial $40,000 franchise fee and commit themselves to payment of monthly royalties, advertising and sales promotion fees, and rent computed in part from monthly gross sales. Franchisees also agree to submit to the national organization's exacting regulation of virtually every conceivable aspect of their operations. . . .

Burger King oversees its franchise system through a two-tiered administrative structure. The governing contracts provide that the franchise relationship established in Miami and governed by Florida law, and call for payment of all required fees and forwarding of all relevant notices to the Miami headquarters. The Miami headquarters sets policy and works directly with its franchisees in attempting to resolve major problems. Day-to-day monitoring of franchisees, however, is conducted through a network of 10 district offices which in turn report to the Miami headquarters.

. . . The appellee John Rudzewicz, a Michigan citizen and resident, is the senior partner in a Detroit accounting firm. In 1978, he was approached by Brian MacShara . . . , who suggested that they jointly apply to Burger King for a franchise in the Detroit area. MacShara proposed to serve as the manager of the restaurant if Rudzewicz would put up the investment capital; in exchange, the two would evenly share the profits. . . .

Rudzewicz and MacShara jointly applied for a franchise to Burger King's Birmingham, Michigan, district office in the autumn of 1978. Their application was forwarded to Burger King's Miami headquarters, which entered into a preliminary agreement with them in February 1979. During the ensuing four months it was agreed that Rudzewicz and MacShara would assume operation of an existing facility in Drayton Plains, Michigan. MacShara attended the prescribed management courses in Miami during this period, and the franchisees purchased $165,000 worth of restaurant equipment from Burger King's Davmor Industries division in Miami. Even before the final agreements were signed, however, the parties began to disagree over site-development fees, building design, computation of monthly rent, and whether the franchisees would be able to assign their liabilities to a corporation they had formed. During these disputes Rudzewicz and MacShara negotiated both with the Birmingham district office and with the Miami headquarters.[7] With some misgivings, Rudzewicz and MacShara finally obtained limited concessions from the Miami headquarters, signed the final agreements, and commenced operations in June 1979. By signing the final agreements, Rudzewicz obligated himself personally to payments exceeding $1 million over the 20-year franchise relationship.

The Drayton Plains facility apparently enjoyed steady business during the summer of 1979, but patronage declined after a recession began later that year. Rudzewicz and MacShara soon fell far behind in their monthly payments to Miami. Headquarters sent notices of default, and an extended period of negotiations began among the franchisees, the Birmingham district office, and the Miami headquarters. After several Burger King officials in Miami had engaged in prolonged but ultimately unsuccessful negotiations with the franchisees by mail and by telephone,[9] headquarters terminated the franchise

---

[7] Although Rudzewicz and MacShara dealt with the Birmingham district office on a regular basis, they communicated directly with the Miami headquarters in forming the contracts; moreover, they learned that the district office had "very little" decision-making authority and accordingly turned directly to headquarters in seeking to resolve their disputes.

[9] Miami's policy was to "deal directly" with franchisees when they began to encounter financial difficulties, and to involve district office personnel only when necessary. In the instant case, for example, the Miami office handled all credit problems, ordered cost-cutting measures, negotiated for a partial refinancing of the franchisees' debts, communicated directly with the franchisees in attempting to resolve the dispute, and was responsible for all termination matters.

and ordered Rudzewicz and MacShara to vacate the premises. They refused and continued to occupy and operate the facility as a Burger King restaurant.

## B

Burger King commenced the instant action in the United States District Court for the Southern District of Florida in May 1981. . . . Burger King alleged that Rudzewicz and MacShara had breached their franchise obligations . . . by failing to make the required payments "at plaintiff's place of business in Miami, Dade County, Florida," and also charged that they were tortiously infringing its trademarks and service marks through their continued, unauthorized operation as a Burger King restaurant. . . . Rudzewicz and MacShara entered special appearances and argued, *inter alia,* that because they were Michigan residents and because Burger King's claim did not "arise" within the Southern District of Florida, the District Court lacked personal jurisdiction over them. The District Court denied their motions. . . .

After a 3-day bench trial, the court . . . concluded that it had "jurisdiction over the subject matter and the parties to this cause." Finding that Rudzewicz and MacShara had breached their franchise agreements with Burger King and had infringed Burger King's trademarks and service marks, the court entered judgment against them, jointly and severally, for $228,875 in contract damages. The court also . . . awarded costs and attorney's fees to Burger King.

Rudzewicz appealed to the Court of Appeals for the Eleventh Circuit. A divided panel of that Circuit reversed the judgment, concluding that the District Court could not properly exercise personal jurisdiction over Rudzewicz. . . .

## II

### A

The Due Process Clause protects an individual's liberty interest in not being subject to the binding judgments of a forum with which he has established no meaningful "contacts, ties, or relations." *International Shoe Co. v. Washington,* [326 U.S. 310, 319 (1945)].[13] By requiring that individuals have "fair warning that a particular activity may subject [them] to the jurisdiction of a foreign sovereign," *Shaffer v. Heitner,* 433 U.S. 186, 218 (1977) (STEVENS, J., concurring in judgment), the Due Process Clause "gives a degree of predictability to the legal system that allows potential defendants to structure their primary conduct with some minimum assurance as to where that conduct will and will not render them liable to suit." *World-Wide Volkswagen Corp. v. Woodson,* 444 U.S. 286, 297 (1980).

Where a forum seeks to assert specific jurisdiction over an out-of-state defendant who has not consented to suit there, this "fair warning" requirement

---

[13] Although this protection operates to restrict state power, it "must be seen as ultimately a function of the individual liberty interest preserved by the Due Process Clause" rather than as a function "of federalism concerns." *Insurance Corp. of Ireland, v. Compagnie des Bauxites de Guines,* 456 U.S. 694, 702-703, n. 10 (1982).

is satisfied if the defendant has "purposefully directed" his activities at residents of the forum, *Keeton v. Hustler Magazine, Inc.,* 465 U.S. 770, 774 (1984), and the litigation results from alleged injuries that "arise out of or relate to" those activities, *Helicopteros Nacionales de Colombia, S.A. v. Hall,* 466 U.S. 408, 414 (1984). . . . And with respect to interstate contractual obligations, we have emphasized that parties who "reach out beyond one state and create continuing relationships and obligations with citizens of another state" are subject to regulation and sanctions in the other State for the consequences of their activities. *See* . . . *McGee v. Int'l Life Ins. Co.,* 355 U.S. 220, 222-223 (1957).

We have noted several reasons why a forum legitimately may exercise personal jurisdiction over a nonresident who "purposefully directs" his activities toward forum residents. A State generally has a "manifest interest" in providing its residents with a convenient forum for redressing injuries inflicted by out-of-state actors. Moreover, where individuals "purposefully derive benefit" from their interstate activities, it may well be unfair to allow them to escape having to account in other States for consequences that arise proximately from such activities. . . . And because "modern transportation and communications have made it much less burdensome for a party sued to defend himself in a State where he engages in economic activity," it usually will not be unfair to subject him to the burdens of litigating in another forum for disputes relating to such activity. *McGee v. Int'l Life Ins. Co., supra,* at 223.

Notwithstanding these considerations, the constitutional touchstone remains whether the defendant purposefully established "minimum contacts" in the forum State. Although it has been argued that foreseeability of causing *injury* in another State should be sufficient to establish such contacts there . . . , the Court has consistently held that this kind of foreseeability is not a "sufficient benchmark" for exercising personal jurisdiction. *World-Wide Volkswagen Corp. v. Woodson,* 444 U.S., at 295. Instead, "the foreseeability that is critical to due process analysis . . . is that the defendant's conduct and connection with the forum State are such that he should reasonably anticipate being haled into court there." *Id.,* at 297. In defining when it is that a potential defendant should "reasonably anticipate" out-of-state litigation, the Court frequently has drawn from the reasoning of *Hanson v. Denckla,* 357 U.S. 235, 253 (1958):

> "The unilateral activity of those who claim some relationship with a nonresident defendant cannot satisfy the requirement of contact with the forum State. The application of that rule will vary with the quality and nature of the defendant's activity, but it is essential in each case that there be some act by which the defendant purposefully avails itself of the privilege of conducting activities within the forum State, thus invoking the benefits and protections of its laws."

This "purposeful availment" requirement ensures that a defendant will not be haled into a jurisdiction solely as a result of "random," "fortuitous," or "attenuated" contacts or of the "unilateral activity of another party or a third person."[17] Jurisdiction is proper, however, where the contacts proximately result from actions by the defendant *himself* that create a "substantial connection" with the forum State . . . .[18]

Jurisdiction in these circumstances may not be avoided merely because the defendant did not *physically* enter the forum State. Although territorial presence frequently will enhance a potential defendant's affiliation with a State and reinforce the reasonable foreseeability of suit there, it is an inescapable fact of modem commercial life that a substantial amount of business is transacted solely by mail and wire communications across state lines, thus obviating the need for physical presence within a State in which business is conducted. So long as a commercial actor's efforts are "purposefully directed" toward residents of another State, we have consistently rejected the notion that an absence of physical contacts can defeat personal jurisdiction there.

Once it has been decided that a defendant purposefully established minimum contacts within the forum State, these contacts may be considered in light of other factors to determine whether the assertion of personal jurisdiction would comport with "fair play and substantial justice." *Int'l Shoe Co. v. Washington,* 326 U.S., at 320. Thus courts in "appropriate case[s]" may evaluate "the burden on the defendant," "the forum State's interest in adjudicating the dispute," "the plaintiff's interest in obtaining convenient and effective relief," "the interstate judicial system's interest in obtaining the most efficient resolution of controversies," and the "shared interest of the several States in furthering fundamental substantive social policies." These considerations sometimes serve to establish the reasonableness of jurisdiction upon a lesser showing of minimum contacts than would otherwise be required. On the other hand, where a defendant who purposefully has directed his activities at forum residents seeks to defeat jurisdiction, he must present a compelling case that the presence of some other considerations would render jurisdiction unreasonable. Most such considerations usually may be accommodated through means short of finding jurisdiction unconstitutional. For example, the potential clash of the forum's law with the "fundamental substantive social policies" of another State may be accommodated through application of the

---

[17] Applying this principle, the Court has held that the Due Process Clause forbids the exercise of personal jurisdiction over an out-of-state automobile distributor whose only tie to the forum resulted from a customer's decision to drive there, *World-Wide Volkswagen Corp. v. Woodson, supra;* over a divorced husband sued for child-support payments whose only affiliation with the forum was created by his former spouse's decision to settle there, *Kulko v. California Superior Court, supra* ; and over a trustee whose only connection with the forum resulted from the settlor's decision to exercise her power of appointment there, *Hanson v. Denckla,* 357 U.S. 235 (1958). In such instances, the defendant has had no "clear notice that it is subject to suit" in the forum and thus no opportunity to "alleviate the risk of burdensome litigation" there. *World-Wide Volkswagen Corp. v. Woodson, supra,* at 297.

[18] So long as it creates a "substantial connection" with the forum, even a single act can support jurisdiction. *McGee v. Int'l Life Ins. Co.,* 355 U.S., at 223. The Court has noted, however, that "some single or occasional acts" related to the forum may not be sufficient to establish jurisdiction if "their nature and quality and the circumstances of their commission" create only an "attenuated" affiliation with the forum. *Int'l Shoe Co. v. Washington,* 326 U.S. 310, 318 (1945); *World-Wide Volkswagen Corp. v. Woodson,* 444 U.S., at 299. This distinction derives from the belief that, with respect to this category of "isolated" acts, *id.,* at 297, the reasonable foreseeability of litigation in the forum is substantially diminished.

forum's choice-of-law rules.[19] Similarly, a defendant claiming substantial inconvenience may seek a change of venue.[20] Nevertheless, minimum requirements inherent in the concept of "fair play and substantial justice" may defeat the reasonableness of jurisdiction even if the defendant has purposefully engaged in forum activities. *World-Wide Volkswagen Corp. v. Woodson, supra,* at 292; *see* also RESTATEMENT (SECOND) OF CONFLICT OF LAWS §§ 36-37 (1971). As we previously have noted, jurisdictional rules may not be employed in such a way as to make litigation "so gravely difficult and inconvenient" that a party unfairly is at a "severe disadvantage" in comparison to his opponent.

B

(1)

Applying these principles to the case at hand, we believe there is substantial record evidence supporting the District Court's conclusion that the assertion of personal jurisdiction over Rudzewicz in Florida for the alleged breach of his franchise agreement did not offend due process. At the outset, we note a continued division among lower courts respecting whether and to what extent a contract can constitute a "contact" for purposes of due process analysis. If the question is whether an individual's contract with an out-of-state party *alone* can automatically establish sufficient minimum contacts in the other party's home forum, we believe the answer clearly is that it cannot. The Court long ago rejected the notion that personal jurisdiction might turn on "mechanical" tests, *International Shoe Co. v. Washington, supra,* at 319, or on "conceptualistic . . . theories of the place of contracting or of performance." Instead, we have emphasized the need for a "highly realistic" approach that recognizes that a "contract" is "ordinarily but an intermediate step serving to tie up prior business negotiations with future consequences which themselves are the real object of the business transaction." It is these factors—prior negotiations and contemplated future consequences, along with the terms of the contract and the parties' actual course of dealing—that must be evaluated in determining whether the defendant purposefully established minimum contacts within the forum.

In this case, no physical ties to Florida can be attributed to Rudzewicz other than MacShara's brief training course in Miami. Rudzewicz did not maintain offices in Florida and, for all that appears from the record, has never even visited there. Yet this franchise dispute grew directly out of "a contract which had a *substantial* connection with that State." *McGee v. Int'l Life Ins. Co.,* 355 U.S., at 223 (emphasis added). Eschewing the option of operating an independent local enterprise, Rudzewicz deliberately "reach[ed] out beyond" Michigan and negotiated with a Florida corporation for the purchase of a long-term franchise and the manifold benefits that would derive from affiliation with a nationwide organization. Upon approval, he entered into a carefully structured 20-year relationship that envisioned continuing and wide-reaching

[19] *See Allstate Ins. Co. v. Hague,* 449 U.S. 302, 307-313 (1981) (opinion of Brennan, J.). *See generally* RESTATEMENT (SECOND) OF CONFLICT OF LAWS §§ 6, 9 (1971).

[20] *See, e.g.,* 28 U.S.C. S 1404(a). . . . [This statute and the doctrine of forum non conveniens are discussed in Part F, *infra*].

contacts with Burger King in Florida. In light of Rudzewicz' voluntary acceptance of the long-term and exacting regulation of his business from Burger King's Miami headquarters, the "quality and nature" of his relationship to the company in Florida can in no sense be viewed as "random," "fortuitous," or "attenuated." Rudzewicz' refusal to make the contractually required payments in Miami, and his continued use of Burger King's trademarks and confidential business information after his termination, caused foreseeable injuries to the corporation in Florida. . . .

The Court of Appeals concluded, however, that in light of the supervision emanating from Burger King's district office in Birmingham, Rudzewicz reasonably believed that "the Michigan office was for all intents and purposes the embodiment of Burger King" and that he therefore had no "reason to anticipate a Burger King suit outside of Michigan." This reasoning overlooks substantial record evidence indicating that Rudzewicz most certainly knew that he was affiliating himself with an enterprise based primarily in Florida. The contract documents themselves emphasize that Burger King's operations are conducted and supervised from the Miami headquarters, that all relevant notices and payments must be sent there, and that the agreements were made in and enforced from Miami. Moreover, the parties' actual course of dealing repeatedly confirmed that decision-making authority was vested in the Miami headquarters and that the district office served largely as an intermediate link between the headquarters and the franchisees. When problems arose over building design, site-development fees, rent computation, and the defaulted payments, Rudzewicz and MacShara learned that the Michigan office was powerless to resolve their disputes and could only channel their communications to Miami. Throughout these disputes, the Miami headquarters and the Michigan franchisees carried on a continuous course of direct communications by mail and by telephone, and it was the Miami headquarters that made the key negotiating decisions out of which the instant litigation arose.

Moreover, we believe the Court of Appeals gave insufficient weight to provisions in the various franchise documents providing that all disputes would be governed by Florida law. The franchise agreement, for example, stated:

> "This Agreement shall become valid when executed and accepted by BKC at Miami, Florida; it shall be deemed made and entered into in the State of Florida and shall be governed and construed under and in accordance with the laws of the State of Florida. The choice-of-law designation does not require that all suits concerning this Agreement be filed in Florida."

The Court of Appeals reasoned that choice-of-law provisions are irrelevant to the question of personal jurisdiction, relying on *Hanson v. Denckla* for the proposition that "the center of gravity for choice-of-law purposes does not necessarily confer the sovereign prerogative to assert jurisdiction." This reasoning misperceives the import of the quoted proposition. The Court in *Hanson* and subsequent cases has emphasized that choice-of-law *analysis*— which focuses on all elements of a transaction, and not simply on the defendant's conduct—is distinct from minimum-contacts jurisdictional analysis—which focuses at the threshold solely on the defendant's purposeful connection to the forum.[23] Nothing in our cases, however, suggests that a choice-of-law *provision* should be ignored in considering whether a defendant has "purposefully invoked the benefits and protections of a State's laws" for jurisdictional purposes. Although such a provision standing alone would be insufficient to confer jurisdiction, we believe that, when combined with the 20-year interdependent relationship Rudzewicz established with Burger King's Miami headquarters, it reinforced his deliberate affiliation with the forum State and the reasonable foreseeability of possible litigation there. . . .

(2)

Nor has Rudzewicz pointed to other factors that can be said persuasively to outweigh the considerations discussed above and to establish the *unconstitutionality* of Florida's assertion of jurisdiction. We cannot conclude that Florida had no "legitimate interest in holding [Rudzewicz] answerable on a claim related to" the contacts he had established in that State . . . .[25] Finally, the Court of Appeals' assertion that the Florida litigation "severely impaired [Rudzewicz'] ability to call Michigan witnesses who might be essential to his defense . . . " is wholly without support in the record. And even to the extent that it is inconvenient for a party who has minimum contacts with a forum to litigate there, such considerations most frequently can be accommodated through a change of venue. . . .

The Court of Appeals also concluded, however, that the parties' dealings involved "a characteristic disparity of bargaining power". . . . Rudzewicz [contended in the District Court] that Burger King was guilty of misrepresentation, fraud, and duress; that it gave insufficient notice in its dealings with him; and that the contract was one of adhesion. After a 3-day bench trial, the District Court found that Burger King had made no misrepresentations, that Rudzewicz and MacShara "were and are experienced and sophisticated businessmen," and that "at no time" did they "ac[t] under economic duress or disadvantage imposed by" Burger King. . . . Rudzewicz was represented by counsel throughout these complex transactions and, as Judge Johnson observed in dissent below, was himself an experienced accountant. . . . Rudzewicz was able to secure a modest reduction in rent and other concessions from Miami headquarters; moreover, to the extent that Burger King's terms were inflexible, Rudzewicz presumably decided that the advantages of affiliating with a national organization provided sufficient commercial benefits to offset the detriments.[28]

---

[23] *Hanson v. Denckla,* 357 U.S., at 253-254. *See also Keeton v. Hustler Magazine, Inc.,* 465 U.S., at 778; *Kulko v. California Superior Court,* 436 U.S., at 98; *Shaffer v. Heitner,* 433 U.S., at 215.

[25] Complaining that "when Burger King is the plaintiff, you won't 'have it your way' because it sues all franchisees in Miami," Brief for Appellee 19, Rudzewicz contends that Florida's interest in providing a convenient forum is negligible given the company's size and ability to conduct litigation anywhere in the country. We disagree. Absent compelling considerations, *cf. McGee v. International Life Insurance Co.,* 355 U.S., at 223, a defendant who has purposefully derived commercial benefit from his affiliations in a forum may not defeat jurisdiction there simply because of his adversary's greater net wealth.

[28] We do not mean to suggest that the jurisdictional outcome will always be the same in franchise cases. Some franchises may be primarily intrastate in character or involve different decision-

## III

Notwithstanding these considerations, the Court of Appeals apparently believed that it was necessary to reject jurisdiction in this case as a prophylactic measure, reasoning that an affirmance of the District Court's judgment would result in the exercise of jurisdiction over "out-of-state consumers to collect payments due on modest personal purchases" and would "sow the seeds of default judgments against franchisees owing smaller debts." We share the Court of Appeals' broader concerns and therefore reject any talismanic jurisdictional formulas. . . . We . . . have emphasized that jurisdiction may not be grounded on a contract whose terms have been obtained through "fraud, undue influence, or overweening bargaining power" and whose application would render litigation "so gravely difficult and inconvenient that [a party] will for all practical purposes be deprived of his day in court." Just as the Due Process Clause allows flexibility in ensuring that commercial actors are not effectively "judgment proof" for the consequences of obligations they voluntarily assume in other States, *McGee v. International Life Insurance Co.,* 355 U.S., at 223, so too does it prevent rules that would unfairly enable them to obtain default judgments against unwitting customers.

For the reasons set forth above, however, these dangers are not present in the instant case. . . . The judgment of the Court of Appeals is accordingly reversed, and the case is remanded for further proceedings consistent with this opinion.

JUSTICE POWELL took no part in the consideration or decision of this case.

JUSTICE STEVENS, with whom JUSTICE WHITE joins, dissenting.

In my opinion there is a significant element of unfairness in requiring a franchisee to defend a case of this kind in the forum chosen by the franchisor. . . .

. . . [The opinion of the Court of Appeals is] more persuasive than what this Court has written today:

> "Nothing in the course of negotiations gave Rudzewicz reason to anticipate a Burger King suit outside of Michigan. The only face-to-face or even oral contact Rudzewicz had with Burger King throughout months of protracted negotiations was with representatives of the Michigan office. Burger King had the Michigan office interview Rudzewicz and MacShara, appraise their application, discuss price terms, recommend the site which the defendants finally agreed to, and attend the final closing ceremony. There is no evidence that Rudzewicz ever negotiated with anyone in Miami or even sent mail there during negotiations. . . .
>
> "Given that the office in Rudzewicz' home state conducted all of the negotiations and wholly supervised the contract, we believe that he

---

making structures, such that a franchisee should not reasonably anticipate out-of-state litigation. Moreover, commentators have argued that franchise relationships may sometimes involve unfair business practices in their inception and operation. *See* H. BROWN, FRANCHISING REALITIES AND REMEDIES 4-5 (2d ed. 1978). For these reasons, we reject Burger King's suggestion for "a general rule, or at least a presumption, that participation in an interstate franchise relationship" represents consent to the jurisdiction of the franchisor's principal place of business.

had reason to assume that the state of the supervisory office would be the same state in which Burger King would file suit. Rudzewicz lacked fair notice that the distant corporate headquarters . . . would later seek to assert jurisdiction over him in the courts of its own home state. . . .

"Just as Rudzewicz lacked notice of the possibility of suit in Florida, he was financially unprepared to meet its added costs. . . . [T]he typical franchise store is a local concern serving at best a neighborhood or community. Neither the revenues of a local business nor the geographical range of its market prepares the average franchise owner for the cost of distant litigation. . . .

"The particular distribution of bargaining power in the franchise relationship further impairs the franchisee's financial preparedness. In a franchise contract, 'the franchisor normally occupies [the] dominant role'. . . .

"We discern a characteristic disparity of bargaining power in the facts of this case. There is no indication that Rudzewicz had any latitude to negotiate a reduced rent or franchise fee in exchange for the added risk of suit in Florida. He signed a standard form contract whose terms were non-negotiable. . . . Burger King resisted price concessions, only to sue Rudzewicz far from home. In doing so, it severely impaired his ability to call Michigan witnesses who might be essential to his defense. . . .

*See* PROBLEMS 3C-9. TURBINES FOR SALE; 3C-10. ALCOHOL ABUSE TRAINING; 3C-11. THE LIQUIDATION.

## NOTES AND QUESTIONS

(1) *Contracts and Planning. Burger King* is the first contract case the Supreme Court dealt with since *McGee v. International Life Insurance Co.* (discussed in § 3.07, *supra),* and both decisions contain expansive interpretations of the minimum contacts standard. Should the fact that contractual transactions entail considerable planning lead to more relaxed jurisdictional holdings than is appropriate in tort cases? Should there be any difference between the jurisdictional analysis of contract and tort cases? *See* Martin Louis, *Jurisdiction Over Those Who Breach Their Contracts: The Lessons of Burger King,* 72 N. C. L. Rev. 55 (1993).

(2) *Brennan's Reformulation.* Justice Brennan obviously was constrained by the two-stage analysis adopted by the Court in *World-Wide.* Just as clearly, however, he had his own view of the matter, which he articulated so forcefully in his *World-Wide* dissent. In part II A of the *Burger King* opinion, he found the opportunity to reformulate the two-stage test subtly to bring it closer to his own expansive fairness-oriented theory.

Consider his treatment of the first stage, the "contacts" stage. Physical entry by the defendant into the forum is not required. This observation is more of a useful clarification than a reformulation because the cases prior to *Burger King* do not require physical entry. What reasons does Justice Brennan give for this proposition? Is he right? Instead of physical entry, the requirement seems to be that defendant "purposefully direct" his activities toward the forum state. Is this standard more liberal than *Hanson's* requirement that defendant "purposefully avail itself of the privilege of conducting activities within the forum state, thus invoking the benefits and protections of its laws"? For a favorable appraisal of this portion of the opinion, see Margaret Stewart, *A New Litany of Personal Jurisdiction,* 60 U. COLO. L. REV. 5, 38-40 (1989).

Justice Brennan's contribution to the second stage—the fairness stage—of the analysis is more significant. For one thing, he identifies the five factors that should be considered in the fairness calculation. He also seems to suggest that once plaintiff has shown that defendant has purposefully established minimum contacts with the forum, the burden of persuasion on the fairness issue is on the *defendant,* who "must present a compelling case that the presence of some other considerations would render jurisdiction unreasonable." This burden shift is a significant reformulation of the *World-Wide* two-step analysis, which seemed to place the persuasion burden on both the contacts and the fairness issues on plaintiff. Finally, and most surprisingly, Justice Brennan got five of his colleagues to agree that the fairness considerations could "sometimes serve to establish the reasonableness of jurisdiction upon a lesser showing of minimum contacts than would otherwise be required." This passage is the strongest support in recent memory for the fairness interpretation of the *International Shoe* formula.

Justice Brennan's re-tooling of *World-Wide's* two-stage test has led some commentators to conclude that at least this once he was able to have it "his way" and that his opinion is indeed a "whopper." Rex Perschbacher, *Minimum Contacts Reapplied: Mr. Justice Brennan Has It His Way in Burger King Corp. v. Rudzewicz,* 1986 ARIZ. ST. L.J. 585; Pamela Stephens, *The Single Contract as Minimum Contacts: Justice Brennan "Has It His Way,"* 28 WM. & MARY L. REV. 89 (1986).

(3) *Conceptualism and Realism.* The Court rejected any sort of conceptualist or formalist analysis based on where the contract was executed or was to be performed. Does this "highly realistic" jurisdictional analysis have a parallel in the development of contract choice-of-law theory? Compare the First Restatement treatment of contract cases in § 4.07, *infra,* to the more modern approaches considered in Chapter 4, Parts D, E, and F. *See also* § 4.30, *infra.*

(4) *The Choice-of-Law Clause.* Justice Brennan's use of the contract's choice-of-law clause is intriguing (See Part II B(l) of the opinion). The Court in *Hanson, Shaffer, and Keeton* carefully distinguished the issues of choice of law and jurisdiction, and held that the fact that a state's law might govern a dispute was neither a necessary nor a sufficient condition for that state's courts to exercise adjudicatory jurisdiction. How does Justice Brennan answer this challenge? Does it make any sense to conclude, as he does, that Rudzewicz purposefully invoked the benefits and protections of Florida law by signing *Burger King's* form contract? Did *Burger King* insert the clause in its contracts because Florida law "protects" and "benefits" franchisees?

On the subject of the choice-of-law clause, why did *Burger King* fail to insert a consent-to-jurisdiction clause? Professor Weintraub points out that consent-to-jurisdiction clauses were forbidden by the Michigan Franchisee Investment

Act while choice-of-law clauses were not. *See* R. WEINTRAUB, COMMENTARY ON THE CONFLICT OF LAWS 167 (4th ed. 2001). Did Justice Brennan's ingenious but perhaps disingenuous use of the choice-of-law clause allow *Burger King* to accomplish indirectly what it could not have done directly?

If, in spite of the Michigan statute, the contract had contained a consent-to-jurisdiction clause, would a Florida court have been required to refuse to exercise jurisdiction? *See* the materials on the constitutional restrictions on choice of law in Chapter 5, *infra*.

(5) *Relative Wealth and Power.* The disagreement between the majority and the dissent raises a question that has troubled courts and commentators: should the relative wealth and power of the parties affect the constitutional propriety of the forum's exercise of jurisdiction? These factors seem to be relevant at both stages of the Court's two-stage jurisdictional calculus. At the "contacts" stage, the defendant's economic strength is indirectly relevant; an economically powerful defendant is more able to "reach out beyond" his home state and so is more likely to have purposeful contacts with the forum than is a smaller enterprise. At the "fairness" stage, the relative wealth and power of the parties is more directly relevant since conducting litigation away from home can be prohibitively expensive for consumers or small business enterprises. See Russell Weintraub, *A Map Out of the Personal Jurisdiction Labyrinth*, 28 U. C. DAVIS L. REV. 531, 547 (1995) (suggesting that the fairness attack on jurisdiction should be reserved for such defendants). Based on its ability to rouse judicial disagreement at several stages of the litigation, the factual setting in *Burger King* must be close to the line. What arguments convinced the majority? The dissent?

Another closely related issue raised in *Burger King* is the effect to be given to jurisdiction-consent clauses and choice-of-law clauses. According to the Court, such clauses are valid unless they are procured by fraud, duress, or overweening bargaining power. The Court's concern about "overweening bargaining power" may be limited to forum-selection clauses in adhesion contracts between mail order sellers and consumer buyers. Mere inequality of bargaining power—as certainly existed in *Burger King*—is probably not enough. In *National Equipment Rental v. Szukhent,* 375 U.S. 311 (1964), for instance, the defendants were Michigan farmers, not consumers, who signed an adhesion contract appointing the wife of an officer of National Equipment Rental their agent for receipt of service in New York. The Supreme Court upheld New York's exercise of jurisdiction in a 5-4 decision. *Szukhent* and consent-to-jurisdiction clauses are treated in more detail in § 3.12[C][2], *infra,* of this chapter. *See also* WILLIAM RICHMAN & WILLIAM REYNOLDS, UNDERSTANDING CONFLICT OF LAWS § 30[c] (3d ed. 2002). The concern about such clauses being used against mail order consumers has been termed "the mail order specter;" it is discussed in detail in 2 ROBERT CASAD & WILLIAM RICHMAN, JURISDICTION IN CIVIL ACTIONS 170 (3d ed. 1998).

# ASAHI METAL INDUSTRY COMPANY, LTD. v. SUPERIOR COURT

*United States Supreme Court*
*480 U.S. 102, 107 S. Ct. 1026, 94 L. Ed. 2d 92 (1987)*

JUSTICE O'CONNOR announced the judgment of the Court and delivered the unanimous opinion of the Court with respect to Part I, the opinion of the Court with respect to Part II-B, in which THE CHIEF JUSTICE, JUSTICE BRENNAN, JUSTICE WHITE, JUSTICE MARSHALL, JUSTICE BLACKMUN, JUSTICE POWELL, and JUSTICE STEVENS join, and an opinion with respect to Parts II-A and III, in which THE CHIEF JUSTICE, JUSTICE POWELL, and JUSTICE SCALIA join.

This case presents the question whether the mere awareness on the part of a foreign defendant that the components it manufactured, sold, and delivered outside the United States would reach the forum state in the stream of commerce constitutes "minimum contacts" between the defendant and the forum state such that the exercise of jurisdiction "does not offend 'traditional notions of fair play and substantial justice.' "

## I

On September 23, 1978, on Interstate Highway 80 in Solano County, California, Gary Zurcher lost control of his Honda motorcycle and collided with a tractor. Zurcher was severely injured, and his passenger and wife, Ruth Ann Moreno, was killed. In September 1979, Zurcher filed a product liability action in the Superior Court of the State of California in and for the County of Solano. Zurcher alleged that the 1978 accident was caused by a sudden loss of air and an explosion in the rear tire of the motorcycle, and alleged that the motorcycle tire, tube, and sealant were defective. Zurcher's complaint named, inter alia, Cheng Shin Rubber Industrial Co., Ltd. (Cheng Shin), the Taiwanese manufacturer of the tube. Cheng Shin in turn filed a cross-complaint seeking indemnification from its codefendant and from petitioner, Asahi Metal Industry Co., Ltd. (Asahi), the manufacturer of the tube's valve assembly. Zurcher's claims against Cheng Shin and the other defendants were eventually settled and dismissed, leaving only Cheng Shin's indemnity action against Asahi.

California's long-arm statute authorizes the exercise of jurisdiction "on any basis not inconsistent with the Constitution of this state or of the United States." Asahi moved to quash Cheng Shin's service of summons arguing the State could not exert jurisdiction over it consistent with the Due Process Clause of the Fourteenth Amendment.

In relation to the motion, the following information was submitted by Asahi and Cheng Shin. Asahi is a Japanese corporation. It manufactures tire value assemblies in Japan and sells the assemblies to Cheng Shin, and to several other tire manufacturers, for use as components in finished tire tubes. Asahi's sales to Cheng Shin took place in Taiwan. The shipments from Asahi to Cheng Shin were sent from Japan to Taiwan. Cheng Shin bought and incorporated into its tire tubes 150,000 Asahi valve assemblies in 1978; 500,000 in 1979; 500,000 in 1980; 100,000 in 1981; and 100,000 in 1982. Sales to Cheng Shin accounted for 1.24 percent of Asahi's income in 1981 and 0.44 percent in 1982. Cheng Shin alleged that approximately 20 percent of its sales in the United States are in California. Cheng Shin purchases valve assemblies from other suppliers as well, and sells finished tubes throughout the world.

In 1983 an attorney for Cheng Shin conducted an informal examination of the valve stems of the tire tubes sold in one cyclery in Solano County. The attorney declared that of the approximately 115 tire tubes in the store, 97 were purportedly manufactured in Japan or Taiwan, and of those 97, 21 valve stems were marked with the circled letter "A", apparently Asahi's trademark. Of the 21 Asahi valve stems, 12 were incorporated into Cheng Shin tire tubes. . . . An affidavit of a manager of Cheng Shin whose duties included the purchasing of component parts stated: " 'In discussions with Asahi regarding the purchase of valve stem assemblies the fact that my Company sells tubes throughout the world and specifically the United States has been discussed. I am informed and believe that Asahi was fully aware that valve stem assemblies sold to my Company and to others would end up throughout the United States and in California.' " An affidavit of the president of Asahi, on the other hand, declared that Asahi " 'has never contemplated that its limited sales of tire valves to Cheng Shin in Taiwan would subject it to lawsuits in California.' " . . .

Primarily on the basis of the above information, the Superior Court denied the Motion to quash summons. . . .

The Court of Appeal of the State of California issued a peremptory writ of mandate commanding the Superior Court to quash service of summons. . . .

The Supreme Court of the State of California reversed and discharged the writ issued by the Court of Appeal. The court observed that "Asahi has no offices, property or agents in California. It solicits no business in California and has made no direct sales [in California]." Moreover, "Asahi did not design or control the system of distribution that carried its valve assemblies into California." Nevertheless, the court found the exercise of jurisdiction over Asahi to be consistent with the Due Process Clause. It concluded that Asahi knew that some of the valve assemblies sold to Cheng Shin would be incorporated into tire tubes sold in California, and that Asahi benefited indirectly from the sale in California of products incorporating its components. The court considered Asahi's intentional act of placing its components into the stream of commerce—that is, by delivering the components to Cheng Shin in Taiwan—coupled with Asahi's awareness that some of the components would eventually find their way into California, sufficient to form the basis for state court jurisdiction under the Due Process Clause.

We granted certiorari and now reverse.

## II

### A

The Due Process Clause of the Fourteenth Amendment limits the power of a state court to exert personal jurisdiction over a nonresident defendant. "[T]he constitutional touchstone" of the determination whether an exercise of personal jurisdiction comports with due process "remains whether the defendant purposefully established 'minimum contacts' in the forum State." *Burger King Corp. v. Rudzewicz,* 471 U.S. 462, 474 (1985). Most recently we have reaffirmed the oft quoted reasoning of *Hanson v. Denckla,* 357 U.S. 235, 253 (1958), that minimum contacts must have a basis in "some act by which the defendant purposefully avails itself of the privilege of conducting activities within the forum State, thus invoking the benefits and protections of its laws." *Burger King,* 471 U.S., at 475. . . .

Applying the principle that minimum contacts must be based on an act of the defendant, the Court in *World-Wide Volkswagen Corp. v. Woodson,* 444 U.S. 286 (1980), rejected the assertion that a consumer's unilateral act of bringing the defendant's product into the forum State was a sufficient constitutional basis for personal jurisdiction over the defendant. It had been argued in *World-Wide Volkswagen* that because an automobile retailer and its wholesale distributor sold a product mobile by design and purpose, they could foresee being haled into court in the distant States into which their customers might drive. The Court rejected this concept of foreseeability as an insufficient basis for jurisdiction under the Due Process Clause. . . .

In *World-Wide Volkswagen* itself, the state court sought to base jurisdiction not on any act of the defendant, but on the foreseeable unilateral actions of the consumer. Since *World-Wide Volkswagen,* lower courts have been confronted with cases in which the defendant acted by placing a product in the stream of commerce, and the stream eventually swept defendant's product into the forum State, but the defendant did nothing else to purposefully avail itself of the market in the forum state. Some courts have understood the Due Process Clause, as interpreted in *World-Wide Volkswagen,* to allow an exercise of personal jurisdiction to be based on no more than the defendant's act of placing the product in the stream of commerce. Other courts have understood the Due Process Clause and the above-quoted language in *World-Wide Volkswagen* to require the action of the defendant to be more purposefully directed at the forum State than the mere act of placing a product in the stream of commerce. . . .

We now find this latter position to be consonant with the requirements of due process. The "substantial connection" between the defendant and the forum State necessary for a finding of minimum contacts must come about by an action of the defendant purposefully directed toward the forum State. The placement of a product into the stream of commerce, without more, is not an act of the defendant purposefully directed toward the forum State. Additional conduct of the defendant may indicate an intent or purpose to serve the market in the forum State, for example, designing the product for the market in the forum State, advertising in the forum State, establishing channels for providing regular advice to customers in the forum State, or marketing the product through a distributor who has agreed to serve as the sales agent in the forum State. But a defendant's awareness that the stream of commerce may or will sweep the product into the forum State does not convert the mere act of placing the product into the stream into an act purposefully directed toward the forum State.

Assuming, arguendo, that respondents have established Asahi's awareness that some of the valves sold to Cheng Shin would be incorporated into tire tubes sold in California, respondents have not demonstrated any action by Asahi to purposefully avail itself of the California market. Asahi does not do business in California. It has no office, agents, employees, or property in California. It does not advertise or otherwise solicit business in California. It did not create, control, or employ the distribution system that brought its valves to California. There is no evidence that Asahi designed its product in anticipation of sales in California. On the basis of these facts, the exertion of personal jurisdiction over Asahi by the Superior Court of California[*] exceeds the limits of Due Process.

## B

The strictures of the Due Process Clause forbid a state court from exercising personal jurisdiction over Asahi under circumstances that would offend "traditional notions of fair play and substantial justice." *International Shoe Co. v. Washington,* [326 U.S., 310, 316 (1945)], quoting *Milliken v. Meyer,* [311 U.S. 457, 463 (1940)].

We have previously explained that the determination of the reasonableness of the exercise of the jurisdiction in each case will depend on an evaluation of several factors. A court must consider the burden on the defendant, the interests of the forum state, and the plaintiff's interest in obtaining relief. It must also weigh in its determination "the interstate judicial system's interest in obtaining the most efficient resolution of controversies; and the shared interest of the several States in furthering fundamental substantive social policies." *World-Wide Volkswagen,* 444 U.S., at 292 (citations omitted).

A consideration of these factors in the present case clearly reveals the unreasonableness of the assertion of jurisdiction over Asahi, even apart from the question of the placement of goods in the stream of commerce.

Certainly the burden on the defendant in this case is severe. Asahi has been commanded by the Supreme Court of California not only to traverse the distance between Asahi's headquarters in Japan and the Superior Court of California in and for the County of Solano, but also to submit its dispute with Cheng Shin to a foreign nation's judicial system. The unique burdens placed upon one who must defend oneself in a foreign legal system should have significant weight in assessing the reasonableness of stretching the long arm of personal jurisdiction over national borders.

When minimum contacts have been established, often the interests of the plaintiff and the forum in the exercise of jurisdiction will justify even the serious burdens placed on the alien defendant. In the present case, however, the interests of the plaintiff and the forum in California's assertion of

---

[*] We have no occasion here to determine whether Congress could, consistent with the Due Process Clause of the Fifth Amendment, authorize federal court personal jurisdiction over alien defendants based on the aggregate of national contacts, rather than on the contacts between the defendant and the State in which the federal court sits. *See Max Daelwyler Corp. v. R. Meyer,* 762 F.2d 290, 293-295 (CA3 1985); *DeJames v. Magnificence Carriers, Inc.,* 654 F.2d 280, 283 (CA3 1981); *see also* Born, *Reflections on Judicial Jurisdiction in International Cases,* to be published in 17 GA. J. INT'L & COMP. L. I (1987); Lilly, *Jurisdiction Over Domestic and Alien Defendants,* 69 VA. L. REV. 85, 127-145 (1983).

jurisdiction over Asahi are slight. All that remains is a claim for indemnification asserted by Cheng Shin, a Taiwanese corporation, against Asahi. The transaction on which the indemnification claim is based took place in Taiwan; Asahi's components were shipped from Japan to Taiwan. Cheng Shin has not demonstrated that it is more convenient for it to litigate its indemnification claim against Asahi in California rather than in Taiwan or Japan.

Because the plaintiff is not a California resident, California's legitimate interests in the dispute have considerably diminished. The Supreme Court of California argued that the State had an interest in "protecting its consumers by ensuring that foreign manufacturers comply with the state's safety standards." The State Supreme Court's definition of California's interest, however, was overly broad. The dispute between Cheng Shin and Asahi is primarily about indemnification rather than safety standards. Moreover, it is not at all clear at this point that California law should govern the question whether a Japanese corporation should indemnify a Taiwanese corporation on the basis of a sale made in Taiwan and a shipment of goods from Japan to Taiwan. *Phillips Petroleum v. Shutts,* 472 U.S. 797, (1985); *Allstate Ins. Co. v. Hague,* 449 U.S. 302, 312-313 (1981). The possibility of being haled into a California court as a result of an accident involving Asahi's components undoubtedly creates an additional deterrent to the manufacture of unsafe components; however, similar pressures will be placed on Asahi by the purchasers of its components as long as those who use Asahi components in their final products, and sell those products in California, are subject to the application of California tort law.

*World-Wide Volkswagen* also admonished courts to take into consideration the interests of the "several States," in addition to the forum state, in the efficient judicial resolution of the dispute and the advancement of substantive policies. In the present case, this advice calls for a court to consider the procedural and substantive policies of other nations whose interests are affected by the assertion of jurisdiction by the California court. The procedural and substantive interests of other nations in a state court's assertion of jurisdiction over an alien defendant will differ from case to case. In every case, however, those interests, as well as the Federal interest in its foreign relations policies, will be best served by a careful inquiry into the reasonableness of the assertion of jurisdiction in the particular case, and an unwillingness to find the serious burdens on an alien defendant outweighed by minimal interests on the part of the plaintiff or the forum State. "Great care and reserve should be exercised when extending our notions of personal jurisdiction into the international field." *United States v. First Nat'l City Bank,* 379 U.S. 378, 404 (1965) (Harlan, J., dissenting). *See Born, Reflections on Judicial Jurisdiction in International Cases,* 17 GA. J. INT'L & COMP. L. 1 (1987).

Considering the international context, the heavy burden on the alien defendant, and the slight interests of the plaintiff and the forum State, the exercise of personal jurisdiction by a California court over Asahi in this instance would be unreasonable and unfair.

### III

Because the facts of this case do not establish minimum contacts such that the exercise of personal jurisdiction is consistent with fair play and substantial justice, the judgment of Supreme Court of California is reversed, and the case is remanded for further proceedings not inconsistent with this opinion.

*It is so ordered.*

JUSTICE BRENNAN, with whom JUSTICE WHITE, JUSTICE MARSHALL, and JUSTICE BLACKMUN join, concurring in part and in the judgment.

I do not agree with the plurality's interpretation of the stream-of-commerce theory, nor with its conclusion that Asahi did not "purposely avail itself of the California market." I do agree, however, with the Court's conclusion in Part II-B that the exercise of personal jurisdiction over Asahi in this case would not comport with "fair play and substantial justice," *International Shoe Co. v. Washington,* 326 U.S. 310, 320 (1945). This is one of those rare cases in which "minimum requirements inherent in the concept of 'fair play and substantial justice' . . . defeat the reasonableness of jurisdiction even [though] the defendant has purposefully engaged in forum activities." *Burger King Corp. v. Rudzewicz,* 471 U.S. 462, 477-478 (1985). I therefore join Parts I and II-B of the Court's opinion, and write separately to explain my disagreement with Part II-A.

The plurality states that "a defendant's awareness that the stream of commerce may or will sweep the product into the forum State does not convert the mere act of placing the product into the stream into an act purposefully directed toward the forum State." The plurality would therefore require a plaintiff to show "[a]dditional conduct" directed toward the forum before finding the exercise of jurisdiction over the defendant to be consistent with the Due Process Clause. I see no need for such a showing, however. The stream of commerce refers not to unpredictable currents or eddies, but to the regular and anticipated flow of products from manufacture to distribution to retail sale. As long as a participant in this process is aware that the final product is being marketed in the forum State, the possibility of a lawsuit there cannot come as a surprise. Nor will the litigation present a burden for which there is no corresponding benefit. A defendant who has placed goods in the stream of commerce benefits economically from the retail sale of the final product in the forum State, and indirectly benefits from the State's laws that regulate and facilitate commercial activity. These benefits accrue regardless of whether that participant directly conducts business in the forum State, or engages in additional conduct directed toward that State. Accordingly, most courts and commentators have found that jurisdiction premised on the placement of a product into the stream of commerce is consistent with the Due Process Clause, and have not required a showing of additional conduct.

The plurality's endorsement of what appears to be the minority view among Federal Courts of Appeals represents a marked retreat from its analysis in *World-Wide Volkswagen v. Woodson,* 444 U.S. 286 (1980). . . .

The Court in *World-Wide Volkswagen* . . . took great care to distinguish "between a case involving goods which reach a distant State through a chain of distribution and a case involving goods which reach the same State because a consumer . . . took them there." 444 U.S., at 306-307 (Brennan, J., dissenting). The California Supreme Court took note of this distinction, and correctly concluded that our holding in *World-Wide Volkswagen* preserved the stream-of-commerce theory.

In this case, the facts found by the California Supreme Court support its finding of minimum contacts. The Court found that "[a]lthough Asahi did not design or control the system of distribution that carried its valve assemblies into California, Asahi was aware of the distribution system's operation, and it knew that it would benefit economically from the sale in California of products incorporating its components." Accordingly, I cannot join the plurality's determination that Asahi's regular and extensive sales of component parts to a manufacturer it knew was making regular sales of the final product in California is insufficient to establish minimum contacts with California.

JUSTICE STEVENS, with whom JUSTICE WHITE and JUSTICE BLACKMUN join, concurring in part and concurring in the judgment.

The judgment of the Supreme Court of California should be reversed for the reasons stated in Part II-B of the Court's opinion. While I join Parts I and II-B, I do not join Part II-A for two reasons. First, it is not necessary to the Court's decision. An examination of minimum contacts is not always necessary to determine whether a state court's assertion of personal jurisdiction is constitutional. *See Burger King Corp. v. Rudzewicz.* Part II-B establishes, after considering the factors set forth in *World-Wide Volkswagen Corp. v. Woodson,* that California's exercise of jurisdiction over Asahi in this case would be "unreasonable and unfair." This finding alone requires reversal; this case fits within the rule that "minimum requirements inherent in the concept of 'fair play and substantial justice' may defeat the reasonableness of jurisdiction even if the defendant has purposefully engaged in forum activities." Accordingly, I see no reason in this case for the Court to articulate "purposeful direction" or any other test as the nexus between an act of a defendant and the forum State that is necessary to establish minimum contacts.

Second, even assuming that the test ought to be formulated here, Part II-A misapplies it to the facts of this case. The Court seems to assume that an unwavering line can be drawn between "mere awareness" that a component will find its way into the forum State and "purposeful availment" of the forum's market. Over the course of its dealings with Cheng Shin, Asahi has arguably engaged in a higher quantum of conduct than "[t]he placement of a product into the stream of commerce, without more. . . . " Whether or not this conduct rises to the level of purposeful availment requires a constitutional determination that is affected by the volume, the value, and the hazardous character of the components. In most circumstances I would be inclined to conclude that a regular course of dealing that results in deliveries of over 100,000 units annually over a period of several years would constitute "purposeful availment" even though the item delivered to the forum State was a standard product marketed throughout the world.

## NOTES AND QUESTIONS

(1) *The Reasonableness Holding.* The holding of *Asahi,* contained in Part II B of Justice O'Connor's plurality opinion, commanded an eight-to-one majority of the Justices. Although not controversial among them, the holding nevertheless breaks new ground. Since *World-Wide* the Court has been committed to the two step jurisdictional test: minimum contacts plus

reasonableness. The notion that a strong showing by the defendant on the reasonableness tests could overcome a finding of minimum contacts appears most forcefully in dictum in *Burger King.*

> On the other hand, where a defendant who purposefully has directed his activities at forum residents seeks to defeat jurisdiction, he must present a compelling case that the presence of some other consider-ations would render jurisdiction unreasonable. . . . Nevertheless minimum requirements inherent in the concept of "fair play and substantial justice" may defeat the reasonableness of jurisdiction even if the defendant has purposefully engaged in forum activities.

Until *Asahi,* however, the Supreme Court had never *held* that a case could fail the reasonableness test even though the defendant had minimum contacts with the forum.

Is it wise for the Court to insist on the reasonableness step when the con-tacts test is passed, or does the added hurdle simply encourage more threshold litigation in our already burdened courts? *Compare* Linda Silberman, *"Two Cheers" for International Shoe (and None for Asahi): An Essay on the Fiftieth Anniversary of International Shoe,* 28 U. C. Davis L. Rev. 755 (1995), Russell Weintraub, *Asahi Sends Personal Jurisdiction Down the Tubes,* 23 Tex. Int'l L.J. 55, 62 (1988), *with* Courtland Peterson, *Jurisdiction and Choice of Law Revisited,* 59 U. Colo. L. Rev. 37, 50 (1988). Does the reasonableness test merely duplicate at the constitutional level the inquiry mandated under state law by the doctrine of forum non conveniens? Is such redundancy desirable?

(2) *Plaintiffs' Settlement.* To what extent is the Court's reasonableness holding based on the fact that the claims of the dead and injured Californians had been settled? Is the Court's holding on this point consistent with its pronouncement in *Keeton* that plaintiff's "lack of residence [in the forum] will not defeat jurisdiction established on the basis of defendant's contacts?" *See* Earl Maltz, *Unravelling the Conundrum of the Law of Personal Jurisdiction: A Comment on Asahi Metal Industry Co. v. Superior Court of California,* 1987 Duke L.J. 669, 686; Weintraub, *supra* note (1) at 61.

How does the Court's treatment of this point affect litigation strategy? If you represented a manufacturer in the position of Cheng Shin, might you advise delaying the settlement of the plaintiff's primary claim pending the resolution of the issue of jurisdiction over the impleaded foreign component part maker? *See* David Seidelson, *A Supreme Court Conclusion and Two Ra-tionales That Defy Comprehension: Asahi Metal Industry Co., Ltd. v. Superior Court of California,* 53 Brooklyn L. Rev. 563, 584 (1987).

Justice O'Connor is surely correct in her balancing of the interests of Cheng Shin and Asahi. But has she underestimated California's interest in deterring the flow of unsafe component parts into the state? For critical commentary on Part II B of the *Asahi* opinion, *see* Weintraub, *supra* Note (1), at 59.

(3) *The Stream of Commerce Modification.* The stream of commerce theory began in the state courts with cases like *Gray v. American Radiator & Standard Sanitary Corp.,* 22 Ill. 2d 432, 176 N.E.2d 761 (1961). Titan Valve Manufacturing Company manufactured a safety valve in Ohio and sold it to

American Radiator who incorporated it into a hot water heater in Pennsylvania. The hot water heater "in the course of commerce" was sold to a consumer in Illinois, where the valve malfunctioned and injured the plaintiff. The Supreme Court of Illinois held Titan amenable to in personam jurisdiction and announced that "[a]s a general proposition, if a corporation elects to sell its products for ultimate use in another State, it is not unjust to hold it answerable there for any damage caused by defects in those products."

The idea behind the stream of commerce theory is that a manufacturer should not be insulated from amenability in the forum simply because the distribution and sale of its products in the forum are accomplished through middle men (distributors and retailers) instead of directly by the manufacturer.

In *World-Wide* (*see* note (5), § 3.10, *supra*) the majority added a significant limitation to the theory: although jurisdiction over the manufacturer exists when the product arrives in the forum state via the chain of distribution, there is no jurisdiction when the chain of distribution ends outside the forum and the foreseeable acts of a consumer bring the product into the forum, where it causes injury.

The O'Connor plurality in *Asahi* would place a much tighter restriction on the theory: the mere fact that the chain of distribution or stream of commerce brings the product into the forum is not sufficient to conclude that the manufacturer of the product has minimum contacts with the forum. What additional facts must be shown to conclude that a manufacturer has purposefully directed its activity toward the forum state? Are these additional contacts necessary to insure that the manufacturer be able to anticipate being haled into court in the forum? After *Asahi*, how would you advise a foreign component parts manufacturer? Is this part of Justice O'Connor's opinion simply "a primer for a non resident defendant seeking to enjoy economic benefits of a forum state's market while retaining immunity from jurisdiction in the state?" *See Seidelson, supra* note (2) at 578. A careful discussion of the history of the stream of commerce theory, both before and after *Asahi,* appears in Mollie Murphy, *Personal Jurisdiction and the Stream of Commerce Theory: A Reappraisal and a Revised Approach,* 77 KY. L. REV. 243 (1988).

(4) *Product Plaintiffs' Problems.* The plurality's conclusion that Asahi did not have minimum contacts with California applies not only to the indemnity claim of Cheng Shin against Asahi, but also to a direct claim by the California victims against Asahi. Professor Weintraub describes the plurality's holding as "ominous" because the reasons given apply to the typical component part manufacturer. *See* Weintraub*, supra* Note (1), at 66-71. Does the opinion establish a requirement of "jurisdictional privity" to replace the contractual privity requirement abolished by *Henningsen v. Bloomfield Motors, Inc.,* 161 A.2d 69 (N.J. 1960), and § 402A of the RESTATEMENT (SECOND) OF TORTS? *See* Christine Wiseman, *Reconstructing the Citadel: The Advent of Jurisdictional Privity*, 54 OHIO ST. L.J. 403 (1993).

What problems would Justice O'Connor's view create for the product liability plaintiff? The forum state would still have jurisdiction over the maker of the finished product. But what if the finished product manufacturer is a relatively small enterprise and the component part maker has the deep pocket? What if the component part maker is liable under the appropriate substantive law, but the manufacturer of the finished product is not? Note also that the plurality's no-minimum-contacts holding may apply not only to component part makers but also to a finished product manufacturer that insulates itself from the forum's jurisdiction with one or more layers of intermediate independent distributors.

Now that the stakes are clear, what is your prediction? Is the O'Connor plurality's view of the stream of commerce likely to become the law? Justice Stevens is the swing vote; for analysis of his brief opinion, see Lawrence Dessem, *Personal Jurisdiction After Asahi: The Other (International) Shoe Drops,* 55 TENN. L. REV. 41, 74-77 (1987). For discussion of the lower court cases following the two stream-of-commerce views, see 1 ROBERT CASAD & WILLIAM RICHMAN, JURISDICTION IN CIVIL ACTIONS 157-158, nn.300, 301 (3d ed. 1998), Russell Weintraub, *A Map Out of the Personal Jurisdiction Labyrinth,* 28 U. C. DAVIS L. REV. 531, 554 (1995).

*See* PROBLEMS 3C-12. A HIGH-SPEED BOAT; 3C-13. IMPORTED ASBESTOS.

(5) *Alien Defendants. Asahi* and *Helicopteros* (*see* § 3.10, *supra*) raise the issue of the constitutional limitations on state court jurisdiction over alien defendants. For the most part, the courts have used the same contacts/fairness analysis that controls jurisdiction over defendants who are citizens of different states.

There are, however, significant differences between litigating against alien defendants and sister state defendants, which might call for a different result. On the one hand, an American plaintiff injured by an alien defendant could make a strong argument that the *International Shoe* test should permit jurisdiction upon a weaker showing of contacts than would be required against an American defendant. A plaintiff whose action against an American defendant is dismissed for lack of jurisdiction usually can litigate the claim in the courts of a sister state, where the defendant has more contacts. The jurisdictional ruling seldom has the effect of entirely precluding plaintiff from relief. Where the defendant is an alien, however, a negative ruling on jurisdiction often means that the plaintiff must pursue her claim in another country. There the plaintiff must face not only increased litigation expenses but also a foreign legal system that might be much less sympathetic to personal injury plaintiffs than is ours. The combination of those factors will often leave the plaintiff remediless for all practical purposes. *See* Louise Weinberg, *The Helicopteros Case and the Jurisprudence of Jurisdiction,* 58 S. CAL REV. 913, 934 (1985); Mark Toran, *Federalism, Personal Jurisdiction, and Aliens,* 58 TUL. L. REV. 758, 788 (1984).

On the other hand, the alien defendant can turn the argument around and urge that a stronger showing of contacts should be required. An American defendant sued in a sister state has to contend only with moderate litigation inconveniences and sister state courts that do not differ fundamentally from the courts of his home state. The foreign defendant typically will face greater costs, a legal system that differs profoundly from his own country's, and, perhaps, xenophobic bias. There is, however, no empirical evidence that foreign litigants' *results* in American litigation are worse than those of domestic litigants. *See* Kevin Clermont & Theodore Eisenberg, *Xenophila in American Courts*, 109 HARV. L. REV. 1120 (1996).

Besides the relative burdens on the parties, other considerations may modify the jurisdictional calculus when the defendant is an alien. Historically courts have been reluctant to issue judgments that are unenforceable. A judgment of an American court against an alien defendant might be enforceable only by the courts of the defendant's domicile; should that nation's law of recognition of judgments affect an American court's willingness to exercise jurisdiction? *See* Ronan Degnan & Mary Kay Kane, *The Exercise of Jurisdiction Over and Enforcement of Judgments Against Alien Defendants*, 39 HASTINGS L.J. 799, 844-854 (1988); Arthur von Mehren & Donald Trautman, *Jurisdiction to Adjudicate: A Suggested Analysis*, 79 HARV. L. REV. 1121, 1126-27 (1966).

Another factor to consider is the impact of a state court's exercise of jurisdiction on the foreign relations and foreign trade of the United States. *See Maltz, supra* note (2), at 687-790. Expansive exercises of jurisdiction by American courts may trigger political, judicial or economic retaliation. *See* Raymond Paretsky, *A New Approach to Jurisdictional Questions in Transnational Litigation in U.S. Courts*, 6 U. PA. J. INT. BUS. L. 663, 678 (1988).

A final issue raised but not decided in *Asahi* concerns not the quantity or quality of the alien defendant's contacts, but their focus. Must the alien defendant have minimum contacts with the forum state, or is it sufficient that he have minimum contacts with the United States as a whole? In other words, can an American court "aggregate" the defendant's contacts with several states to produce the constitutionally required "minimum"? Should the answer to this question depend upon whether the forum court is a state court or a federal court? If the question comes up in a federal court, should the court's basis for subject matter jurisdiction (diversity or federal question) make a difference? *See* FED. R. CIV. P. 4(k)(2). The aggregation issues are especially significant when the alien defendant has a substantial number of contacts with the United States, which are distributed very thinly among several states. The Court cites Gary Born, *Reflections on Judicial Jurisdiction in International Cases*, 17 GA. J. INT'L & COMP. L. 1 (1987), and Graham Lilly, *Jurisdiction Over Domestic and Alien Defendants*, 69 VA. L. REV. 85 (1983). Both articles provide detailed and helpful discussions of the issues raised in this note. *See also* Degnan and Kane, *supra*.

(6) *Asahi* has provoked abundant commentary. *See, e.g., Symposium,* 39 S.C. L. REV. 729-896 (1988) (useful articles by Professors Stravitz, Weber, and Gelfand); Morton, *Contacts, Fairness and State Interests: Personal Jurisdiction After Asahi . . .* , 9 PACE L. REV. 451 (1989); WilliamVan Dercreek, *Jurisdiction Over the Person—The Progeny of Pennoyer and the Future of Asahi,* 13 NOVA L. REV. 1287 (1989).

# PART D  BASES FOR JURISDICTION

## § 3.11  Introduction

Part C of this Chapter dealt with the constitutional restrictions on the territorial jurisdiction of the state courts. The United States Constitution, however, is not the only source of law governing the jurisdiction of state courts. The mere fact that an exercise of jurisdiction does not violate the Due Process Clause does not mean that it is permissible. A state court can exercise jurisdiction only if state law (decisional or statutory) gives it the authority to do so.

Traditionally, state decisional law has authorized jurisdiction when (1) the defendant is served with process while present within the state's territory, (2) the defendant is a domiciliary of the state, or (3) the defendant consents to the state's exercise of jurisdiction. These three relationships between the defendant and the forum state are referred to as traditional bases for jurisdiction; they are treated in § 3.12, *infra*. In addition, all states now have statutes that extend their courts' jurisdiction beyond the traditional bases toward the constitutional limits. These provisions, known as long-arm statutes, are treated in § 3.13, *infra*.

## § 3.12  Traditional Bases for Jurisdiction

### [A]  Personal Service Within the State

---

### BURNHAM v. SUPERIOR COURT

*United States Supreme Court*
*495 U.S. 604 (1990)*

JUSTICE SCALIA announced the judgment of the Court and delivered an opinion in which THE CHIEF JUSTICE AND JUSTICE KENNEDY join, and in which JUSTICE WHITE joins with respect to parts I, II-A, II-B, and 11-C.

The question presented is whether the Due Process Clause of the Fourteenth Amendment denies California courts jurisdiction over a nonresident, who was personally served with process while temporarily in that State, in a suit unrelated to his activities in the State.

Petitioner Dennis Burnham married Francie Burnham in 1976, in West Virginia. In 1977 the couple moved to New Jersey, where their two children were born. In July 1987 the Burnhams decided to separate. They agreed that Mrs. Burnham, who intended to move to California, would take custody of the children. Shortly before Mrs. Burnham departed for California that same month, she and petitioner agreed that she would file for divorce on grounds of "irreconcilable differences."

In October 1987, petitioner filed for divorce in New Jersey state court on grounds of "desertion . . . " Mrs. Burnham, after unsuccessfully demanding that petitioner adhere to their prior agreement to submit to an "irreconcilable differences" divorce, brought suit for divorce in California state court in early January 1988.

In late January, petitioner visited southern California on business, after which he went north to visit his children. . . . [P]etitioner was served with a California court summons and a copy of Mrs. Burnham's divorce petition. He then returned to New Jersey.

Later that year, petitioner made a special appearance in the California Superior Court, moving to quash the service of process on the ground that the court lacked personal jurisdiction over him because his only contacts with California were a few short visits to the State for the purpose of conducting business and visiting his children. [The California courts upheld personal jurisdiction over petitioner based on the service of process in California.] We granted certiorari.

## II

### A

To determine whether the assertion of personal jurisdiction is consistent with due process, we have long relied on the principles traditionally followed by American courts in marking out the territorial limits of each State's authority. That criterion was first announced in *Pennoyer v. Neff,* 195 U.S. 704 (1878). . . . In what has become the classic expression of the criterion, we said in *International Shoe Co. v. Washington,* 326 U.S. 310 (1945), that a State court's assertion of personal jurisdiction satisfies the Due Process Clause if it does not violate "traditional notions of fair play and substantial justice." Since *International Shoe,* we have only been called upon to decide whether these "traditional notions" permit States to exercise jurisdiction over absent defendants in a manner that deviates from the rules of jurisdiction applied in the 19th century. We have held such deviations permissible, but only with respect to suits arising out of the absent defendant's contacts with the State.[1] *See, e.g., Helicopteros Nacionales de Colombia v. Hall,* 466 U.S. 408, 414 (1984). The question we must decide today is whether due process requires a similar connection between the litigation and the defendant's

---

[1] We have said that "[e]ven when the cause of action does not arise out of or relate to the foreign corporation's activities in the forum State, due process is not offended by a State's subjecting the corporation to its in personam jurisdiction when there are sufficient contacts between the State and the foreign corporation." *Helicopteros Nacionales de Colombia v. Hall,* 466 U.S., at 414. Our only holding supporting that statement, however, involved "regular service of summons upon [the corporation's] president while he was in [the forum State] acting in that capacity." *See Perkins v. Benguet Consolidated Mining Co.,* 342 U.S. 437, 440 (1952). It may be that whatever special rule exists permitting "continuous and systematic" contacts to support jurisdiction with respect to matters unrelated to activity in the forum, applies *only* to corporations, which have never fitted comfortably in a jurisdictional regime based primarily upon "de facto power over the defendant's person." *Int'l Shoe Co. v. Washington,* 326 U.S. 310, 316 (1945). We express no views on these matters—and, for simplicity's sake, omit reference to this aspect of "contacts"—based jurisdiction in our discussion.

contacts with the State in cases where the defendant is physically present in the State at the time process is served upon him.

## B

Among the most firmly established principles of personal jurisdiction in American tradition is that the courts of a State have jurisdiction over nonresidents who are physically present in the State. The view developed early that each State had the power to hale before its courts any individual who could be found within its borders, and that once having acquired jurisdiction over such a person by properly serving him with process, the State could retain jurisdiction to enter judgment against him, no matter how fleeting his visit. That view has antecedents in English common-law practice. . . . . Justice Story believed the principle, which he traced to Roman origins, to be firmly grounded in English tradition: "[B]y the common law[,] personal actions, being transitory, may be brought in any place, where the party defendant may be found," for "every nation may . . . rightfully exercise jurisdiction over all persons within its domains." J. Story, Commentaries on the Conflict of Laws §§ 554, 543 (1846). . . .

Recent scholarship has suggested that English tradition was not as clear as Story thought, see Hazard, *A General Theory of State-Court Jurisdiction,* 1965 Sup. Ct. Rev. 241, 253-260; Ehrenzweig, *The Transient Rule of personal Jurisdiction: The "Power"Myth and Forum Conveniens,* 65 Yale L.J. 289 (1956). Accurate or not, however, judging by the evidence of contemporaneous or near-contemporaneous decisions one must conclude that Story's understanding was shared by American courts at the crucial time for present purposes: 1868, when the Fourteenth Amendment was adopted. . . .

Decisions in the courts of many States in the 19th and early 20th centuries held that personal service upon a physically present defendant sufficed to confer jurisdiction, without regard to whether the defendant was only briefly in the State or whether the cause of action was related to his activities there. [citations omitted; decisions in 13 states] Although research has not revealed a case deciding the issue in every State's courts, that appears to be because the issue was so well settled that it went unlitigated. Opinions from the courts of other States announced the rule in dictum. [citations omitted; opinions from eight states] Most States, moreover, had statutes or common-law rules that exempted from service of process individuals who were brought into the forum by force or fraud, or who were there as a party or witness in unrelated judicial proceedings. These exceptions obviously rested upon the premise that service of process conferred jurisdiction. Particularly striking is the fact that, as far as we have been able to determine, not one American case from the period (or, for that matter, not one American case until 1978) held, or even suggested, that in-state personal service on an individual was insufficient to confer personal jurisdiction.[3]

---

[3] Given this striking fact, and the unanimity of both cases and commentators in supporting the in-state service rule, one can only marvel at Justice Brennan's assertion that the rule "was rather weakly implanted in American jurisprudence," and "did not receive wide currency until well after our decision in *Pennoyer v. Neff.*" . . . Justice Brennan cites neither cases nor commentators from the relevant period to support his thesis and instead relies upon modern secondary sources that do not mention and were perhaps unaware of, many of the materials I have discussed. . . .

This American jurisdictional practice is, moreover, not merely old; it is continuing. It remains the practice of, not only a substantial number of the States, but as far as we are aware all the States and the federal government—if one disregards (as one must for this purpose) the few opinions since 1978 that have erroneously said, on grounds similar to those that petitioner presses here, that this Court's due-process decisions render the practice unconstitutional. We do not know of a single State or federal statute, or a single judicial decision resting upon State law, that has abandoned in-State service as a basis of jurisdiction.

## C

Despite this formidable body of precedent, petitioner contends, in reliance on our decisions applying the *International Shoe* standard, that in the absence of "continuous and systematic" contacts with the forum, a non-resident defendant can be subjected to judgment only as to matters that arise out of or relate to his contacts with the forum. This argument rests on a thorough misunderstanding of our cases.

The view of most courts in the 19th century was that a court simply could not exercise in personam jurisdiction over a nonresident who had not been personally served with process in the forum. *Pennoyer v. Neff* . . . [held] that when proceedings "involv[e] merely a determination of the personal liability of the defendant, he must be brought within [the court's] jurisdiction by service of process within the State, or his voluntary appearance." We invoked that rule in a series of subsequent cases, as either a matter of due process or a "fundamental principle of jurisprudence."

Later years, however, saw the weakening of the *Pennoyer* rule. . . . We initially upheld [state long-arm statutes] under the Due Process Clause on grounds that they complied with *Pennoyer's* rigid requirement of either "consent" or "presence." As many observed, however, the consent and presence were purely fictional. Our opinion in *International Shoe* cast those fictions aside, and made explicit the underlying basis of these decisions: due process does not necessarily require the States to adhere to the unbending territorial limits on jurisdiction set forth in *Pennoyer* . . . . Subsequent cases have derived from the *International Shoe* standard the general rule that a State may dispense with in-forum personal service on nonresident defendants in suits arising out of their activities in the State. As *International Shoe* suggests, the defendant's litigation-related "minimum contacts" may take the place of physical presence as the basis for jurisdiction:

> "Historically the jurisdiction of courts to render judgment *in personam* is grounded on their de facto power over the defendant's person. Hence his presence within the territorial jurisdiction of a court was prerequisite to its rendition of a judgment personally binding on him. But now that the *capias ad respondendum* has given way to personal service of summons or other form of notice, due process requires only that in order to subject a defendant to a judgment *in personam,* if he be not present within the territory of the forum, he have certain minimum contacts with it such that the maintenance of the suit does not offend 'traditional notions of fair play and substantial justice.' "

Nothing in *International Shoe* or the cases that have followed it, however, offers support for the very different proposition petitioner seeks to establish today: that a defendant's presence in the forum is not only unnecessary to validate novel, nontraditional assertions of jurisdiction, but is itself no longer sufficient to establish jurisdiction. That proposition is unfaithful to both elementary logic and the foundations of our due process jurisprudence. The distinction between what is needed to support novel procedures and what is needed to sustain traditional ones is fundamental, as we observed over a century ago:

> "[A] process of law, which is not otherwise forbidden, must be taken to be due process of law, if it can show the sanction of settled usage both in England and in this country; but it by no means follows that nothing else can be due process of law. . . . [That which], in substance, has been immemorially the actual law of the land . . . therefore is due process of law. But to hold that such a characteristic is essential to due process of law, would be to deny every quality of the law but its age, and to render it incapable of progress or improvement. It would be to stamp upon our jurisprudence the unchangeableness attributed to the laws of the Medes and Persians." *Hurtado v. California,* 110 U.S. 516, 528-529 (1884).

The short of the matter is that jurisdiction based on physical presence alone constitutes due process because it is one of the continuing traditions of our legal system that define the due process standard of "traditional notions of fair play and substantial justice." That standard was developed by analogy to "physical presence," and it would be perverse to say it could now be turned against that touchstone of jurisdiction.

### D

Petitioner's strongest argument, though we ultimately reject it, relies upon our decision in *Shaffer v. Heitner,* 433 U.S. 186 (1977). . . .

It goes too far to say, as petitioner contends, that *Shaffer* compels the conclusion that a State lacks jurisdiction over an individual unless the litigation arises out of his activities in the State. *Shaffer,* like *International Shoe,* involved jurisdiction over an absent defendant, and it stands for nothing more than the proposition that when the "minimum contact" that is a substitute for physical presence consists of property ownership it must, like other minimum contacts, be related to the litigation. Petitioner wrenches out of its context our statement in *Shaffer* that "all assertions of state-court jurisdiction must be evaluated according to the standards set forth in *International Shoe* and its progeny," 433 U.S., at 212. When read together with the two sentences that preceded it, the meaning of this statement becomes clear:

> "The fiction that an assertion of jurisdiction over property is anything but an assertion of jurisdiction over the owner of the property supports an ancient form without substantial modern justification. Its continued acceptance would serve only to allow state-court jurisdiction that is fundamentally unfair to the defendant.

"We therefore conclude that all assertions of state-court jurisdiction must be evaluated according to the standards set forth in *International Shoe* and its progeny." *Ibid.* (emphasis added).

*Shaffer* was saying, in other words, not that all bases for the assertion of in *personam* jurisdiction (including, presumably, in-state service) must be treated alike and subjected to the "minimum contacts" analysis of *International Shoe,* but rather that *quasi in rem* jurisdiction, that fictional "ancient form," and in personam jurisdiction, are really one and the same and must be treated alike—leading to the conclusion that quasi in rem jurisdiction, . . . must satisfy the litigation-relatedness requirement of *International Shoe.* The logic of *Shaffer's* holding . . . does not compel the conclusion that physically present defendants must be treated identically to absent ones. As we have demonstrated at length, our tradition has treated the two classes of defendants quite differently, and it is unreasonable to read *Shaffer* as casually obliterating that distinction. *International Shoe* confined its "minimum contacts" requirements to situations in which the defendant "be not present within the territory of the forum," and nothing in *Shaffer* expands that requirement beyond that.

It is fair to say, however, that while our holding today does not contradict *Shaffer,* our basic approach to the due process question is different. We have conducted no independent inquiry into the desirability or fairness of the prevailing instate service rule, leaving that judgment to the legislatures that are free to amend it; for our purposes, its validation is its pedigree, as the phrase *"traditional notions* of fair play and substantial justice" makes clear. *Shaffer* did conduct such an independent inquiry, asserting that "traditional notions of fair play and substantial justice" can be as readily offended by the perpetuation of ancient forms that are no longer justified as by the adoption of new procedures that are inconsistent with the basic values of our constitutional heritage. Perhaps that assertion can be sustained when the "perpetuation of ancient forms" is engaged in by only a very small minority of the States. Where, however, as in the present case, a jurisdictional principle is both firmly approved by tradition and still favored, it is impossible to imagine what standard we could appeal to for the judgment that it is "no longer justified." While in no way receding from or casting doubt upon the holding of *Shaffer* or any other case, we reaffirm today our time-honored approach. For new procedures, hitherto unknown, the Due Process clause requires analysis to determine whether "traditional notions of fair play and substantial justice" have been offended. *Int'l Shoe,* 326 U.S., at 316. But a doctrine of personal jurisdiction that dates back to the adoption of the Fourteenth Amendment and is still generally observed unquestionably meets that standard.

## III

A few words in response to Justice Brennan's concurrence . . . .

[T]he concurrence's proposed standard of "contemporary notions of due process" . . . measures state-court jurisdiction not only against traditional doctrines in this country, including current state-court practice, but against each Justice's subjective assessment of what is fair and just. . . .

The subjectivity, and hence inadequacy, of this approach becomes apparent when the concurrence tries to explain why the assertion of jurisdiction in the present case meets its standard of continuing-American-tradition-plus-innate fairness. Justice Brennan lists the "benefits" Mr. Burnham derived from the State of California—the fact that, during the few days he was there, "his health and safety [were] guaranteed by the State's police, fire, and emergency medical services; he [was] free to travel on the State's roads and waterways; he likely enjoy[ed] the fruits of the State's economy." Three days' worth of these benefits strike us as powerfully inadequate to establish, as an abstract matter, that is "fair" for California to decree the ownership of all Mr. Burnham's worldly goods acquired during the ten years of his marriage, and the custody over his children. . . . Even less persuasive are the other "fairness" factors alluded to by Justice Brennan. It would create "an asymmetry," we are told, if Burnham were permitted (as he is) to appear in California courts as a plaintiff, but were not *compelled* to appear in California courts as defendant; and travel being as easy as it is nowadays, and modern procedural devices being so convenient, it is no great hardship to appear in California courts. The problem with these assertions is that they justify the exercise of jurisdiction over *everyone, whether or not* he ever comes to California. . . . In other words, even if one agreed with Justice Brennan's conception of an equitable bargain, the "benefits" we have been discussing would explain why it is "fair" to assert general jurisdiction over Burnham-returned-to-New-Jersey after-service only at the expense of proving that it is also "fair" to assert general jurisdiction over Burnham-returned-to-New-Jersey-*without* -service-which we *know* does not conform with "contemporary notions of due process."

There is, we must acknowledge, one factor mentioned by Justice Brennan that *both* relates distinctively to the assertion of jurisdiction on the basis of personal in-state service and is fully persuasive—namely, the fact that a defendant voluntarily present in a particular State has a "reasonable expectatio[n]" that he is subject to suit there. By formulating it as a "reasonable expectation" Justice Brennan makes that seem like a "fairness" factor; but in reality, of course, it is just tradition masquerading as "fairness." The only reason for charging Mr. Burnham with the reasonable expectation of being subject to suit is that the States of the Union assert . . . and have always asserted adjudicatory jurisdiction over the person, by serving him with process during his temporary physical presence in their territory. . . . Justice Brennan's long journey is a circular one, leaving him, at the end of the day, in complete reliance upon the very factor he sought to avoid. . . .

. . . Justice Brennan says that "[f]or these reasons (i.e., because of the reasonableness factors enumerated above), as a rule the exercise of personal jurisdiction over a defendant based on his voluntary presence in the forum will satisfy the requirements of due process." The use of the word "rule" conveys the reassuring feeling that he is establishing a principle of law one can rely upon—but of course he is not. Since Justice Brennan's only criterion of constitutionality is "fairness", the phrase "as a rule" represents nothing more than his estimation that, *usually,* all the elements of "fairness" he discusses in the present case will exist . . . . Thus, despite the fact that he manages to work the word "rule" into his formulation, *Justice Brennan's* approach does not establish a rule of law at all, but only a "totality of the circumstances" test, guaranteeing what traditional territorial rules of jurisdiction were designed precisely to avoid: uncertainty and litigation over the preliminary issue of the forum's competence. It may be that those evils, necessarily accompanying a freestanding "reasonableness" inquiry, must be accepted at the margins, when we evaluate non-traditional forms of jurisdiction newly adopted by the states. But that is no reason for injecting them into the core of our American practice, exposing to such a "reasonableness" inquiry the ground of jurisdiction that has hitherto been considered the very baseline of reasonableness, physical presence. . . .

JUSTICE WHITE, concurring in part and concurring in the judgment.

I join Part I and Parts II-A, II-B, and II-C of JUSTICE SCALIA'S opinion and concur in the judgment of affirmance.

The rule allowing jurisdiction to be obtained over a non-resident by personal service in the forum state, without more, has been and is so widely accepted throughout this country that I could not possibly strike it down, either on its face or as applied in this case, on the ground that it denies due process of law guaranteed by the Fourteenth Amendment. Although the Court has the authority under the Amendment to examine even traditionally accepted procedures and declare them invalid, *e.g., Shaffer v. Heitner,* 433 U.S. 186 (1977), there has been no showing here or elsewhere that as a general proposition the rule is so arbitrary and lacking in common sense in so many instances that it should be held violative of Due Process in every case. Furthermore, until such a showing is made, which would be difficult indeed, claims in individual cases that the rule would operate unfairly as applied to the particular non-resident involved need not be entertained. At least this would be the case where presence in the forum state is intentional, which would almost always be the fact. Otherwise, there would be endless, fact-specific litigation in the trial and appellate courts, including this one. Here, personal service in California, without more, is enough, and I agree that the judgment should be affirmed.

JUSTICE BRENNAN, with whom JUSTICE MARSHALL, JUSTICE BLACKMUN, and JUSTICE O'CONNOR join, concurring in the judgment.

I agree with Justice Scalia that the Due Process Clause of the Fourteenth Amendment generally permits a state court to exercise jurisdiction over a defendant if he is served with process while voluntarily present in the forum State. I do not perceive the need, however, to decide that a jurisdictional rule that "has been immemorially the actual law of the land," automatically comports with due process simply by virtue of its "pedigree . . . Unlike Justice Scalia, I would undertake an "independent inquiry into the . . . fairness of the prevailing in-state service rule." I therefore concur only in the judgment.

I

I believe that the approach adopted by Justice Scalia's opinion today—reliance solely on historical pedigree—is foreclosed by our decisions in *International Shoe Co. v. Washington,* and *Shaffer v. Heitner.* In *International Shoe,* we held that a state court's assertion of personal jurisdiction does not violate the Due Process Clause if it is consistent with "traditional notions of fair play and substantial justice." In *Shaffer,* we stated that "all assertions of state-court jurisdiction must be evaluated according to the standards set forth in *International Shoe* and its progeny." The critical insight of *Shaffer* is that all rules of jurisdiction, even ancient ones, must satisfy contemporary notions of due process. . . . We recognized that " '(t)raditional notions of fair play and substantial justice' can be as readily offended by the perpetuation of ancient forms that are no longer justified as by the adoption of new procedures that are inconsistent with the basic values of our constitutional heritage. . . . "

While our holding in *Shaffer* may have been limited to *quasi in rem* jurisdiction, our mode of analysis was not. Indeed, that we were willing in *Shaffer* to examine anew the appropriateness of the quasi in rem rule—until that time dutifully accepted by American courts for at least a century— demonstrates that we did not believe that the "pedigree" of a jurisdictional practice was dispositive in deciding whether it was consistent with due process. . . . If we could discard an "ancient form without substantial modern justification" in *Shaffer,* we can do so again. Lower courts,[4] commentators,[5] and the American Law Institute[6] all have interpreted *International Shoe and Shaffer* to mean that every assertion of state-court jurisdiction, even one pursuant to a "traditional" rule such as transient jurisdiction, must comport with contemporary notions of due process. . . .

## II

Tradition, though alone not dispositive, is of course *relevant* to the question whether the rule of transient jurisdiction is consistent with due process.[7]

---

[4] Some lower courts have concluded that transient jurisdiction did not survive *Shaffer.* Others have held that transient jurisdiction is alive and well. But even cases falling into the latter category have engaged in the type of due process analysis that Justice Scalia's opinion claims is unnecessary today.

[5] Although commentators have disagreed over whether the rule of transient jurisdiction is consistent with modern conceptions of due process, that they have engaged in such a debate at all shows that they have rejected the methodology employed by Justice Scalia's opinion today. *See* Bernstine, *Shaffer v. Heitner: A Death Warrant for the Transient Rule of In Personam Jurisdiction?,* 25 VILL. L. REV. 38, 47-68 (1979-1980); Brilmayer, et al. *A General Look at General Jurisdiction,* 66 TEX. L. REV. 721, 748-755 (1988); Fyr, *Shaffer v. Heitner: The Supreme Court's Latest Last Words on State Court Jurisdiction,* 26 EMORY L. J. 739, 770-773 (1977); Lacy, *Personal Jurisdiction and Service of Summons After Shaffer v. Heitner,* 57 ORE. L. REV. 505, 510 (1978); Posnak, A *Uniform Approach to Judicial Jurisdiction After Worldwide and the Abolition of the "Gotcha" Theory,* 30 EMORY L. J. 729, 735, n. 30 (1981); Redish, *Due Process, Federalism and Personal Jurisdiction: A Theoretical Evaluation,* 75 Nw. U.L. REV. 11 12, 1117, n. 35 (1981); Sedler, *Judicial Jurisdiction and Choice of Law: The Consequences of Shaffer v. Heitner,* 63 IOWA L. REV. 1031, 1035 (1978); Silberman, *Shaffer v. Heitner: The End of an Era,* 53 N.Y.U. L. REV. 33, 75 (1978); Vernon, *Single Factor Bases of In Personam Jurisdiction—A Speculation on the Impact of Shaffer v. Heitner,* 1978 WASH. U. L. Q. 273, 303; von Mehren, *Adjudicatory Jurisdiction: General Theories Compared and Evaluated,* 63 B.U. L. REV. 279, 300-307 (1983); Zammit, *Reflections on Shaffer v. Heitner,* 5 HASTINGS CONST. L. Q. 15, 24 (1978).

[6] *See* RESTATEMENT (SECOND) OF CONFLICT OF LAWS SECTION 2, cmt. b, p.29.

[7] I do not propose that the "contemporary notions of due process" to be applied are no more than "each Justice's subjective assessment of what is fair and just." Rather, the inquiry is guided by our decisions . . . and the specific factors that we have developed to ascertain whether a jurisdictional rule comports with "traditional notions of fair play and substantial justice," ( . . . including "the burden on the defendant, the interests of the forum State, and the plaintiff's interest in obtaining relief").

Tradition is salient not in the sense that practices of the past are automatically reasonable today; indeed, under such a standard, the legitimacy of transient jurisdiction would be called into question because the rule's historical "pedigree" is a matter of intense debate. The rule was a stranger to the common law[8] and was rather weakly implanted in American jurisprudence "at the crucial time for present purposes: 1868, when the Fourteenth Amendment was adopted." For much of the 19th century, American courts did not uniformly recognize the concept of transient jurisdiction, and it appears that the transient rule did not receive wide currency until well after our decision in *Pennoyer v. Neff,* 95 U.S. 714 (1878).[10]

Rather, I find the historical background relevant because, however murky the jurisprudential origins of transient jurisdiction, the fact that American courts have announced the rule for perhaps a century . . . provides a defendant voluntarily present in a particular State *today* "clear notice that [he] is subject to suit" in the forum. . . . The transient rule is consistent with reasonable expectations and is entitled to a strong presumption that it comports with due process. "If I visit another State, . . . I knowingly assume some risk that the State will exercise its power over my property or my person while there. My contact with the State, though minimal, gives rise to predictable risks." *Shaffer,* 433 U.S. at 218 (Stevens, J., concurring in judgment). . . .

By visiting the forum State, a transient defendant actually "avail(s)" himself of significant benefits provided by the State. His health and safety are guaranteed by the State's police, fire, and emergency medical services; he is free to travel on the State's roads and waterways; he likely enjoys the fruits of the State's economy as well. Moreover, the Privileges and Immunities Clause of Article IV prevents a state government from discriminating against a transient defendant by denying him the protections of its law or the right of access to its courts . . . . Without transient jurisdiction, an asymmetry would arise: a transient would have the full benefit of the power of the forum State's courts as a plaintiff while retaining immunity from their authority as a defendant. *See* Maltz, *Sovereign Authority, Fairness, and Personal Jurisdiction: The Case for the Doctrine of Transient Jurisdiction,* 66 WASH. U. L. Q. 671, 698-699 (1988).

The potential burdens on a transient defendant are slight. "[M]odern transportation and communications have made it much less burdensome for a party sued to defend himself" in a State outside his place of residence. *Burger King,* 471 U.S. at 474, quoting *McGee v. Int'l Life Ins. Co.,* 355 U.S. 220, 223 (1957). That the defendant has already journeyed at least once before to the forum—as evidenced by the fact that he was served with process there—is

---

[8] Justice Scalia's opinion acknowledges, American courts in the 19th century erected the theory of transient jurisdiction largely upon Justice Story's historical interpretation of Roman and continental sources. . . . [I]t now appears that as a historical matter Story was almost surely wrong. . . .

[10] One distinguished legal historian has observed that "notwithstanding dogmatic generalizations later sanctioned by the RESTATEMENT (OF CONFLICT OF LAWS), appellate courts hardly ever in fact held transient service sufficient as such" and that "although the transient rule has often been mouthed by the courts, it has but rarely been applied." Ehrenzweig, *The Transient Rule of Personal Jurisdiction: The "Power" Myth and Forum Conveniens,* 65 YALE L.J. 289, 292, 295 (1956).

an indication that suit in the forum likely would not be prohibitively inconvenient. Finally, any burdens that do arise can be ameliorated by a variety of procedural devices. For these reasons, as a rule the exercise of personal jurisdiction over a defendant based on his voluntary presence in the forum will satisfy the requirements of due process.

In this case, it is undisputed that petitioner was served with process while voluntarily and knowingly in the State of California. I therefore concur in the judgment.

JUSTICE STEVENS, concurring in the judgment.

As I explained in my separate writing, I did not join the Court's opinion in *Shaffer v. Heitner,* because I was concerned by its unnecessarily broad reach. The same concern prevents me from joining either Justice Scalia's or Justice Brennan's opinion in this case. For me, it is sufficient to note that the historical evidence and consensus identified by Justice Scalia, the considerations of fairness identified by Justice Brennan, and the common sense displayed by Justice White, all combine to demonstrate that this is, indeed, a very easy case.[*] Accordingly, I agree that the judgment should be affirmed.

## NOTES AND QUESTIONS ON *BURNHAM* AND TRANSIENT JURISDICTION

(1) *The Surprising Resurgence of Territoriality.* Did the result and the opinions *in Burnham* surprise you? Certainly, they shocked the post-*Shaffer* commentators, who almost unanimously predicted and urged the demise of transient jurisdiction. *See* the impressive array of authority cited in note 5 of Justice Brennan's opinion. *But see* Earl Maltz, *Sovereign Authority, Fairness and Personal Jurisdiction: The Case for the Doctrine of Transient Jurisdiction,* 66 WASH. U. L.Q. 671 (1988); Jeffrey Glen, *An Analysis of "Mere Presence" and Other Traditional Bases of Jurisdiction,* 45 BROOKLYN L. REV. 607 (1979).

The federal and state appellate courts were more evenly divided. *Compare Nehmiah v. Athletics Congress of the U.S.A.,* 765 F.2d 42 (3d Cir. 1985); *Duehring v. Vasquez,* 490 So. 2d 667 (La. App. 1986) *with Amusement Equipment, Inc. v. Mordelt,* 779 F.2d 264 (5th Cir. 1985); *Humphrey v. Langford,* 246 Ga. 732, 273 S.E.2d 22 (1980).

The American Law Institute weighed in with a limited approval of transient jurisdiction "unless the individual's relationship to the state is so attenuated as to make the exercise of such jurisdiction unreasonable." RESTATEMENT (SECOND) OF CONFLICT OF LAWS, § 28 (1986 Revisions); but few if any voices could be heard suggesting unqualified approval of jurisdiction based upon mere presence. As an indication of just how surprising the *Burnham* Court's holding is, the wife's brief in the Supreme Court did not even argue for the *per se* constitutionality of transient jurisdiction, but rather urged its sufficiency "as long as under all of the facts and circumstances of the case the exercise of such jurisdiction is reasonable." Brief on the Merits for Real Party in Interest at 23. *See also* Transcript of Oral Argument at 34-35.

---

[*] Perhaps the adage about hard cases making bad law should be revised to cover easy cases.

(2) *History.* As the opinions of Justice Scalia and Brennan indicate, the remote history of transient presence as a basis for jurisdiction is quite controversial. Although the predominant view (espoused by Justice Story) is that transient jurisdiction has respectable English antecedents, modern scholars have argued forcefully that alone it was never an adequate jurisdictional basis in England. *See, e.g.,* Albert Ehrenzweig, *The Transient Rule of Personal Jurisdiction: The Power Myth and Forum Conveniens,* 65 YALE L.J. 289, 299 (1956). Is that history relevant to a constitutional claim in 1990?

Note that the two opinions disagree over the status of transient jurisdiction in 1868, when the Fourteenth Amendment was adopted; why is that history particularly relevant? Justice Scalia thinks the proper inquiry "in any event" is what the rule was *thought to be*; why? *See generally* Edward Eberle, *Procedural Due Process: The Original Understanding,* 4 CONST. COMM. 339 (1987).

While there is debate about the remote history of transient jurisdiction, its more modern history is quite clear. In the one hundred years between *Pennoyer and Shaffer,* it was clearly sufficient to support an exercise of personal jurisdiction. Should this more recent history be relevant to the due process inquiry?

(3) *Tradition and Due Process.* Justices Scalia and Brennan differ sharply on the importance of tradition to due process; Scalia, believes a procedure's traditional acceptance is sufficient to show its compliance with due process, while Brennan insists on measuring even traditionally accepted practices against contemporary notions of fairness. This is not the first time the two have disagreed on this score. *See, e.g., Michael H. v. Gerald D.,* 491 U.S. 110 (1989) (traditional versus contemporary views of the conflicting parental rights of wife's adulterous lover (child's biological father) and wife's husband with respect to a child born to wife during the marriage). For commentary on the role of tradition in the jurisprudence of jurisdiction, see James Weinstein, *The Early American Origins of Territoriality in Judicial Jurisdiction,* 37 ST. LOUIS U. L.J. 1 (1992); L. Benjamin Young, *Justice Scalia's History and Tradition: the Chief Nightmare in Professor Tribes Anxiety Closet,* 78 VA. L. REV. 581 (1992).

Scalia's view is that resort to "contemporary notions of due process" is inherently subjective, reliance on tradition being the only hope of objectivity. How does Brennan respond? Who gets the better of this subjectively debate? *See* Russell Weintraub, *An Objective Basis for Rejecting Transient Jurisdiction,* 22 RUTGERS L.J. 611 (1991). Note that the issue of subjectivity in due process analysis is one that long pre-dates the tenure of either Justice. *See Calder v. Bull,* 3 Dall. 386 (1798) (dispute between justices Chase and Iredell); *Adamson v. California,* 332 U.S. 46 (1947) (dispute between Justices Frankfurter and Black).

(4) *Distinguishing Shaffer.*

a. *"Ancient Forms."* Given Justice Scalia's reliance on traditional acceptance as a gauge of due process, how does he distinguish *Shaffer v. Heitner,* 433 U.S. 186 (I 977) (*see* § 3.16, *supra,* for the text of the opinion)? After all, attachment, (quasi-in-rem) jurisdiction has as respectable a pedigree as does transient service. How does he respond to the admonition in *Shaffer* that

" 'traditional notions of fair play and substantial Justice' can be as readily offended by the perpetuation of ancient forms that are no longer justified as by the adoption of new procedures that are inconsistent with the basic values of our constitutional heritage"? Are you persuaded by his distinction based upon the number of states that currently approve of the "ancient form"?

The underlying problem, of course, is basic to Anglo-American jurisprudence: how to deal with an "ancient form" that now seems unfair. *Shaffer* and *Burnham* adopt diametrically opposed solutions. How should one choose between their two approaches?

b. *Dueling Dicta.* Leaving the tradition argument aside, *Shaffer* is still a problem for Justice Scalia. How does he explain away *Shaffer's* famous dictum that "all assertions of state-court jurisdiction must be evaluated according to the standards set forth in *International Shoe* and its progeny?" Are you persuaded by his minimalist interpretation of *Shaffer's* holding—as applicable only to quasi-in-rem cases? *See* Martin Redish, *Tradition, Fairness and Personal Jurisdiction: Due Process and Constitutional Theory After Burnham v. Superior Court*, 22 RUTGERS L. J. 675, 680 (1991). What about his textual argument that the minimum contacts/fair play and substantial justice standard of *International Shoe* applies only if defendant "be not present within the territory of the forum?" *See also Amusement Equip., Inc. v. Mordelt,* 779 F.2d 264 (5th Cir. 1985).

c. *Counter-distinctions.* In some respects, the practice that *Shaffer* struck down, attachment jurisdiction, seems more defensible under the due process clause than the one *Burnham* upheld. Defendant's ownership of some types of property in the forum often indicates a more substantial affiliation with that state than does temporary personal presence there. *See* Petitioner's Brief on the Merits at 24; Bruce Posnak, *A Uniform Approach to Judicial Jurisdiction After World-Wide and the Abolition of the "Gotcha" Theory,* 30 EMORY L.J. 730, 745-746 (1981). Further attachment jurisdiction jeopardizes only one piece of defendant's property, while transient jurisdiction—since it can result in a personal judgment—threatens all of defendant's property in every state.

(5) *Reasonable Expectations.* Justices Scalia and Brennan do agree on one justification for transient jurisdiction. A defendant has a reasonable expectation of amenability to suit in the forum if she is served with process there; thus, by entering the forum she assumes the risk. *See World-Wide Volkswagen Corp. v. Woodson,* § 3.10, *supra;* Glen, *supra,* at 611; *but see* Twitchell, *The Myth of* General *Jurisdiction,* 101 HARV. L. REV. 610, 670 (1988); Harold Lewis, *A Brave New World for Personal Jurisdiction: Flexible Tests Under Uniform Standards,* 37 VAND. L. REV. 1, 60 (1984). But are they right; do ordinary people really have any expectations at all about what will and will not render them amenable? The literature on jurisdiction reveals not a shred of empirical evidence in either direction. In the absence of evidence, the argument seems to depend on the legal fiction imputing knowledge of the law to the litigants. Is such fictional knowledge any sounder than the fictional consents required to justify long-arm jurisdiction before *International Shoe?*

Note also that the argument is quite circular. What the Court decides will control expectations, and those very expectations are then used to justify the decision. See Allan Stein, *Burnham and the Death of Theory in the Law of Personal Jurisdiction*, 22 RUTGERS L.J. 597, 604-605 (1991).

(6) *Benefits and Burdens.* Are you persuaded by Justice Brennan's attempt to justify transient jurisdiction based on the benefits that a transient receives while in the state; or is Justice Scalia right that those benefits are "powerfully inadequate" to support personal jurisdiction? *See also* Lewis, *supra.* Note (5).

Justice Brennan also argues that modern advances in transportation and communication remove much of the burden placed on a defendant subjected to transient jurisdiction. How does Justice Scalia respond? Note also that modern transportation supports a counterargument against transient jurisdiction. In the days of *Pennoyer,* transportation was sufficiently inconvenient that it was relatively unlikely that a defendant could be found in a state with which he lacked significant contacts. Today, of course, a defendant's casual presence in such a forum is much more likely.

(7) *Fact-Specificity.* Justices Scalia and White clearly are anxious to avoid in transient jurisdiction cases the kind of fact-specific due process inquiry required in a typical long-arm jurisdiction case. *See also Humphrey v. Langford,* 246 Ga. 732, 273 S.E.2d 22 (1980):

> We believe it is not practical to have classifications of sojourners in the state. Where does a court draw the line between sojourners here for an evening of bowling and sojourners who commute to the state on a daily basis?

It is easy to sympathize with the Justices' concern; certainty and ease of application are important for any rule of law, but especially so for one controlling jurisdiction, which must be settled at the beginning of the lawsuit. *But see* Erwin Chemerinsky, *Assessing Minimum Contacts: A Reply to Professors Cameron and Johnson*, 28 U. C. DAVIS L. REV. 863, 867 (1995) ("bright-line rules in the area of personal jurisdiction are generally worse than the more flexible minimum contacts test"). But if certainty is a principal goal, can "fundamental notions of fair play and substantial justice" be sacrificed on the alter of bright-line convenience? And if they can in a case involving transient service of process, why not in a typical long-arm case? For commentary on the issue, *compare* Linda Silberman, *Reflections on Burnham v. Superior Court: Toward Presumptive Rules of Jurisdiction and Implications for Choice of Law*, 22 RUTGERS L.J. 569, 578, 583 (1991); Winton Woods, *Burnham v. Superior Court: New Wine, Old Bottles*, 13 GEO. MASON L. REV. 199, 204 (1990) *with* Mary Twitchell, *Burnham and Constitutionally Permissible Levels of Harm*, 22 RUTGERS L.J. 659, 672 (1991).

Out of concern for administrative convenience, Justice White adopts a "presumptive constitutionality" test. Unless the defendant can show that the ruling is "arbitrary and lacking in common sense" in *most* cases, there is no need to consider the fairness of transient jurisdiction in each defendant's particular case. Professor Hay argues that an alien defendant might be able to make just such a showing, *i.e.*, that tag jurisdiction is "arbitrary and lacking in commonsense" in most cases involving *aliens. See* Peter Hay, *Transient Jurisdiction, Especially Over International Defendants: Critical Comments on Burnham the Superior Court of California*, 1990 U. ILL. L. REV. 593.

(8) *Justice Stevens.* For commentary on Justice Stevens brief opinion, see Stanley Cox, *Would That Burnham Had Not Come to be Done Insane! A Critique of Recent Supreme Court Personal Jurisdiction Reasoning, An Explanation Why Transient Presence Jurisdiction is Unconstitutional, and Some Thoughts About Divorce Jurisdiction in a Minimum Contacts World*, 58 TENN. L. REV. 497, 531-537 (1991) (title only slightly shorter than Stevens opinion).

(9) *General Jurisdiction and Forum Shopping.* According to *Burnham,* personal service within the state provides a basis for general jurisdiction, i.e., there need be no connection of any kind between defendant's transient presence in the state and plaintiff's claim. As you will see in Chapter 5, *infra,* the Supreme Court subjects a state's choice of its own law only to minimal scrutiny, *Allstate Insurance Co. v. Hague,* 449 U.S. 302 (1981); and a state can almost always apply its own statute of limitations, *Sun Oil Co. v. Wortman,* 486 U.S. 717 (1988). Does the *Allstate, Wortman, Burnham* trilogy encourage a plaintiff with a stale claim simply to lie in ambush for the defendant in the state with longest available statute of limitations?

(10) *Force, Fraud and Immunity.* Before the advent of modern long-arm statutes, service of process within the forum was the principal means of acquiring jurisdiction over non-resident defendants. In order to ameliorate the sometimes harsh results of that practice, the courts devised doctrines that the defendant could use to attack jurisdiction based on personal service. Thus, if the defendant was brought into the forum state by force or fraud and then served with process, most courts refused to exercise jurisdiction. *See, e.g., Wyman v. Newhouse,* 93 F.2d 313 (2d Cir. 1937). To the same effect was the doctrine of immunity from process, which protected defendants who were served while attending judicial proceedings in the forum as witnesses or civil defendants; some courts also extended the protection to criminal defendants, civil plaintiffs, and attorneys. *See* 1 ROBERT CASAD & WILLIAM RICHMAN, JURISDICTION IN CIVIL ACTIONS 40-47 (3d ed.1998). For a brief discussion of these defenses, see WILLIAM RICHMAN & WILLIAM REYNOLDS, UNDERSTANDING CONFLICT OF LAWS § 48 (3d ed.2002).

The limits on jurisdiction based upon force, fraud, and immunity are less important today than they once were because modern jurisdictional theory and modern long-arm statutes permit state courts to exercise jurisdiction over nonresidents without in-state service. Had the Supreme Court struck down transient service as a sufficient basis for jurisdiction, these once crucial doctrines would have had interest for historians only. After *Burnham,* however, they have a renewed lease on life.

*See* PROBLEM 3D-1. AN INVITATION TO ATTEND.

(11) *Non-Intentional Presence.* What is the result where defendant's presence in the forum is not intentional? For years, *Grace v. MacArthur,* 170 F. Supp. 442 (E.D. Ark. 1959), has been the favorite bete noir of jurisdiction scholars; the court upheld jurisdiction over a defendant who was served with process while on a commercial airline flight over Arkansas. Is *Grace* good law after *Burnham?* Clearly the Brennan group would say no, and Justice White's concurring opinion seems limited to cases where defendant's presence in the forum is "intentional." The future of cases like *Grace,* then, seems to hinge on what Justice White means by that legendary legal weasel-word.

(12) *The Subpoena Power.* Once largely dependent on personal service of process, state court jurisdiction has been expanded by advances in jurisdictional theory and the enactment of ambitious state long-arm statutes, *see* § 3.13, *infra.* The power to compel the attendance of witnesses, however, has not shown proportional growth; most state statutes still require in-state service. *See* Rhonda Wasserman, *The Subpoena Power, Pennoyer's Last Vestige,* 74 MINN. L. REV. 37, 67 (1989). Is this dichotomy justified? Who faces the greater burden of inconvenience, the out-of-state witness, or the out-of-state defendant?

## [B] Domicile, Residence, and Citizenship

## NOTES AND QUESTIONS

(1) *Justifications.* Domicile traditionally has been considered a constitutionally adequate basis for jurisdiction. At least three different reasons have been advanced for that conclusion:

(a) *Benefits and Burdens.* In *Milliken v. Meyer,* 311 U.S. 457 (1940), the Supreme Court said that:

> Domicile in the state is alone sufficient to bring an absent defendant within the reach of the state's jurisdiction for purposes of a personal judgment by means of appropriate substituted service . . . . As in case of the authority of the United States over its absent citizens *(Blackmer v. United States,* 284 U.S. 421), the authority of a state over one of its citizens is not terminated by the mere fact of his absence from the state. The state which accords him privileges and affords protection to him and his property by virtue of his domicile may also exact reciprocal duties. "Enjoyment of the privileges of residence within the state, and the attendant right to invoke the protection of its laws, are inseparable" from the various incidences of state citizenship. The responsibilities of that citizenship arise out of the relationship to the state which domicile creates. That relationship is not dissolved by mere absence from the state. The attendant duties, like the rights and privileges incident to domicile, are not dependent on continuous presence in the state. One such incident of domicile is amenability to suit within the state even during sojourns without the state, where the state has provided and employed a reasonable method of apprising such an absent party of the proceedings against him.

(b) *Fairness.* A second justification for domicile as an adequate jurisdictional basis was advanced by the court in *Hall v. Hall,* 585 S.W.2d 384, 386 (Ky. 1979):

> Certainly it does no violence to traditional notions of fair play and substantial justice to require a person to defend a claim conveniently at home, where he has every reason to anticipate that he may be sued and where the state has a strong general interest in his economic health.

(c) *Necessity.* A final justification is based on necessity; there should be some place where the defendant is continuously amenable to suit on any cause of action. *See* RESTATEMENT (SECOND) OF CONFLICT OF LAWS § 29 (cmt. a); Mary Twitchell, *The Myth of General Jurisdiction,* 101 HARV. L. REV. 610, 631 (1988). Absent such a jurisdictional basis, a defendant might be able to slip through the cracks of a state's long-arm statute and leave the plaintiff with no forum or only an inconvenient forum. *See* WILLIAM RICHMAN & WILLIAM REYNOLDS, UNDERSTANDING CONFLICT OF LAWS § 29 (3d ed. 2002). A thorough discussion of all of the justifications for using domicile as a jurisdictional basis appears in Lea Brilmayer, Jennifer Haverkamp, Buck Logan, Loretta Lynch, Steve Neuwirth, and Jim O'Brien, *A General Look at General Jurisdiction,* 66 TEX. L. REV. 721, 728-33 (1988).

(2) *Fairness and "Technical" Domicile.* According to *Shaffer v. Heitner, all* exercises of jurisdiction must satisfy the "minimum contacts . . . fair play and substantial justice" standard of *International Shoe.* Does jurisdiction based on domicile meet this standard? Are you satisfied with the rationales offered in Note (1)? If jurisdiction is justified in the typical domicile case, what about the cases in which defendant's domicile in the forum is based not on his actual home but rather on the technical rules for the domicile of prisoners or armed service personnel?

Another troublesome situation involves a defendant who has left her home permanently but has not yet established a new one. Suppose a domiciliary of New York leaves the state with all her belongings to seek her fortune in the West. On the trip her auto collides in Wyoming with one driven by another New Yorker. Some months later, while still wandering from one western state to another, and before settling on one as her new home, she is served with process from the New York court based on the Wyoming accident. Is the defendant a domiciliary of Wyoming or of any other western state? Why not? If she is not a domiciliary of one of the western states, where is her domicile? Is it consistent with "fair play and substantial justice" for New York to exercise jurisdiction over her based on the Wyoming accident even though she has terminated all her contacts with New York?

Does the Supreme Court's decision in *Burnham v. Superior Ct., supra* p. 111, insulate jurisdiction based upon technical domicile from any *Shaffer* -based attack? Do any of the opinions in *Burnham* provide a ground for distinguishing technical domicile from transient service?

For commentary on the propriety of domicile-based jurisdiction after *Shaffer,* see RUSSELL WEINTRAUB, COMMENTARY ON THE CONFLICT OF LAWS §§ 2.15, 2.15A, 2.15B (4th ed. 2001); David Vernon, *Single Factor Bases of In Personam Jurisdiction—A Speculation on the Impact of Shaffer v. Heitner,* 1978 WASH. U. L.Q. 273, 299-301 (1978).

(3) *General and Specific.* Domicile is a basis for general jurisdiction. If jurisdiction is based on domicile, plaintiff's cause of action need not arise out of defendant's connection with the state. In other words, a defendant can be sued in his domicile upon any cause of action no matter where it arises. If general jurisdiction is based on domicile, at what time must defendant be domiciled in the forum—the time of the commencement of the action or the time when the cause of action arose?

Domicile can also operate as a basis for specific jurisdiction. Suppose defendant has lived his entire life in Nebraska, married and started a family there, and moved a short time ago to Kansas. Defendant's wife brings an action against him in Nebraska for support. Certainly Nebraska will have jurisdiction over the defendant, but it will be specific jurisdiction based on a cause of action that arose out of defendant's connection with the forum, not general jurisdiction based on his long-time domicile there. Many long-arm statutes use domicile as a basis for specific jurisdiction in cases arising out of defendant's living in a marital relationship in the forum. *See, e.g.,* OHIO R. CIV. P. 4.3(A)(8).

When domicile is used as a basis for specific jurisdiction, when must the domicile exist—at the time of the commencement of the action or at the time the cause of action arose? For a discussion of these questions, see; 2 ROBERT CASAD & WILLIAM RICHMAN, JURISDICTION IN CIVIL ACTIONS 271-276 (3d ed. 1998), RUSSELL WEINTRAUB, COMMENTARY ON THE CONFLICT OF LAWS § 4.11 (4th ed. 2001).

(4) *Residence.* RESTATEMENT (SECOND) OF CONFLICT OF LAWS § 30 provides that a state may "exercise judicial jurisdiction over an individual who is a resident of the state unless the individual's relationship to the state is so attenuated as to make the exercise of such jurisdiction unreasonable." The Supreme Court has never ruled on the question. Residence is typically a weaker connection between a person and a state than is domicile. A "resident" need not have the intention to make the state his permanent home; moreover, a person may have several residences but only one domicile. Consider a person who is domiciled in New York but spends two months each winter in a condominium in Florida and two months each summer in a home in Maine. If jurisdiction can be based on residence, presumably Maine and Florida will have jurisdiction over this person, but will the jurisdiction be general or specific? In other words, could a court in Maine exercise jurisdiction over a defendant in this position based on a cause of action that arose in Florida?

(5) *Citizenship.* Can the federal courts exercise jurisdiction over a United States citizen who lives abroad? Relying on the reciprocal benefits and burdens rationale (*see* Note (1), *supra*), the Supreme Court in *Blackmer v. United States,* 284 U.S. 421 (1932), held that they could. Once again, is the jurisdiction acquired general, or should it be limited to claims which arise in the United States? Suppose a United States citizen who lives permanently in France, has an automobile accident in France and injures a vacationing Canadian. Should a federal court in Michigan be able to exercise *in personam* jurisdiction over the American expatriate to hear the Canadian's personal injury claim?

## [C]   Appearance and Consent

## [1]   Appearance

### INSURANCE CORPORATION OF IRELAND, LTD. v. COMPAGNIE DES BAUXITES DE GUINEE

*United States Supreme Court*
*456 U.S. 694, 102 S. Ct. 2099, 72 L. Ed. 2d 492 (1982)*

JUSTICE WHITE delivered the opinion of the court.

Rule 37(b), Federal Rules of Civil Procedure, provides that a district court may impose sanctions for failure to comply with discovery orders. Included among the available sanctions is:

> "An order that the matters regarding which the order was made or any other designated facts shall be taken to be established for the purposes of the action in accordance with the claim of the party obtaining the order." Rule 37(b)(2)(A).

The question presented by this case is whether this Rule is applicable to facts that form the basis for personal jurisdiction over a defendant. May a district court, as a sanction for failure to comply with a discovery order directed at establishing jurisdictional facts, proceed on the basis that personal jurisdiction over the recalcitrant party has been established? Petitioners urge that such an application of the Rule would violate due process: if a court does not have jurisdiction over a party, then it may not create that jurisdiction by judicial fiat. They contend also that until a court has jurisdiction over a party, that party need not comply with orders of the court; failure to comply, therefore, cannot provide the ground for a sanction. In our view, petitioners are attempting to create a logical conundrum out of a fairly straightforward matter.

### I

[Compagnie des Bauxites de Guinee (CBG) is a Delaware corporation whose principal place of business is in the Republic of Guinea, where it operates mining and processing facilities. Representatives of CBG instructed an insurance broker to obtain $20 million worth of business interruption insurance to cover CBG's operations in Guinea. The first half of the coverage was provided by Insurance Company of North America; the second half of the coverage, the excess insurance was obtained by the broker from foreign insurers through the London insurance market. No separate policy was issued for the excess insurance; the parties adopted the terms of the INA policy. CBG suffered mechanical problems in its operations in Guinea which resulted in a business interruption loss of $ 10 million. CBG claimed that the loss was covered by the business interruption insurance, but the insurers refused to indemnify CBG. CBG sued INA and the excess insurers in the Western District of Pennsylvania. INA did not contest the personal jurisdiction of the district court, but several of the excess insurers did. CBG attempted to use discovery in order to show that the excess insurers had sufficient contact with Pennsylvania for the district court to exercise jurisdiction over them. During a period of about two years the insurers resisted CBG's discovery requests on various grounds.

Despite several court orders, the excess insurers did not produce the requested information. Finally, the district judge warned the insurers that if they did not produce the requested information, he would rule (as a discovery sanction under F. R. CIV. P. 37(b)) that the court had personal jurisdiction over them. The excess insurers did not comply, and the district judge invoked the threatened sanction, ruling that the court had personal jurisdiction.]

## II

. . . Petitioners' basic submission is that to apply Rule 37(b)(2) to jurisdictional facts is to allow fiction to get the better of fact and that it is impermissible to use a fiction to establish judicial power, where, as a matter of fact, it does not exist. In our view, this represents a fundamental misunderstanding of the nature of personal jurisdiction.

The validity of an order of a federal court depends upon that court's having jurisdiction over both the subject matter and the parties. The concepts of subject-matter and personal jurisdiction, however, serve different purposes, and these different purposes affect the legal character of the two requirements. Petitioners fail to recognize the distinction between the two concepts— speaking instead in general terms of "jurisdiction"—although their argument's strength comes from conceiving of jurisdiction only as subject-matter jurisdiction. . . .

Subject-matter jurisdiction . . . is an Art. III as well as a statutory requirement; it functions as a restriction on federal power, and contributes to the characterization of the federal sovereign. Certain legal consequences directly follow from this. For example, no action of the parties can confer subject-matter jurisdiction upon a federal court. Thus, the consent of the parties is irrelevant, principles of estoppel do not apply, and a party does not waive the requirement by failing to challenge jurisdiction early in the proceedings. Similarly, a court, including an appellate court, will raise lack of subject-matter jurisdiction on its own motion. . . .

None of this is true with respect to personal jurisdiction. The requirement that a court have personal jurisdiction flows not from Art. III, but from the Due Process Clause. The personal jurisdiction requirement recognizes and protects an individual liberty interest. It represents a restriction on judicial power not as a matter of sovereignty, but as a matter of individual liberty.[10]

---

[10] It is true that we have stated that the requirement of personal jurisdiction, as applied to state courts, reflects an element of federalism and the character of state sovereignty vis-a-vis other States. For example, in *World-Wide Volkswagen Corp. v. Woodson,* we stated:

> "[A] state court may exercise personal jurisdiction over a nonresident defendant only so long as there exist 'minimum contacts' between the defendant and the forum State. The concept of minimum contacts, in turn, can be seen to perform two related, but distinguishable, functions. It protects the defendant against the burdens of litigating

Thus, the test for personal jurisdiction requires that "the maintenance of the suit . . . not offend 'traditional notions of fair play and substantial justice.' "

Because the requirement of personal jurisdiction represents first of all an individual right, it can, like other such rights, be waived. In *McDonald v. Mabee,* [243 U.S. 90 (1917)] the Court indicated that regardless of the power of the State to serve process, an individual may submit to the jurisdiction of the court by appearance. . . . [U]nlike subject-matter jurisdiction, which even an appellate court may review *sua sponte,* under Rule 12(h), Federal Rules of Civil Procedure, "[a] defense of lack of jurisdiction over the person . . . is waived" if not timely raised in the answer or a responsive pleading.

In sum, the requirement of personal jurisdiction may be intentionally waived, or for various reasons a defendant may be estopped from raising the issue. These characteristics portray it for what it is—a legal right protecting the individual. The plaintiff's demonstration of certain historical facts may make clear to the court that it has personal jurisdiction over the defendant as a matter of law—i.e., certain factual showings will have legal consequences—but this is not the only way in which the personal jurisdiction of the court may arise. The actions of the defendant may amount to a legal submission to the jurisdiction of the court, whether voluntary or not.

The expression of legal rights is often subject to certain procedural rules: the failure to follow those rules may well result in a curtailment of the rights. Thus, the failure to enter a timely objection to personal jurisdiction constitutes, under Rule 12(h)(1), a waiver of the objection. A sanction under Rule 37(b)(2)(A) consisting of a finding of personal jurisdiction has precisely the same effect. As a general proposition, the Rule 37 sanction applied to a finding of personal jurisdiction creates no more of a due process problem than the Rule 12 waiver. . . .

Petitioners argue that a sanction consisting of a finding of personal jurisdiction differs from all other instances in which a sanction is imposed, including the default judgment . . . because a party need not obey the orders of a court until it is established that the court has personal jurisdiction over that party. If there is no obligation to obey a judicial order, a sanction cannot be applied for the failure to comply. Until the court has established personal jurisdiction, moreover, any assertion of judicial power over the party violates due process.

---

in a distant or inconvenient forum. And it acts to ensure that the States, through their courts, do not reach out beyond the limits imposed on them by their status as coequal sovereigns in a federal system."

Contrary to the suggestion of Justice Powell, our holding today does not alter the requirement that there be "minimum contacts" between the nonresident defendant and the forum State. Rather, our holding deals with how the facts needed to show those "minimum contacts" can be established when a defendant fails to comply with court-ordered discovery. The restriction on state sovereign power described in *World-Wide Volkswagen Corp.,* however, must be seen as ultimately a function of the individual liberty interest preserved by the Due Process Clause. That Clause is the only source of the personal jurisdiction requirement and the Clause itself makes no mention of federalism concerns. Furthermore, if the federalism concept operated as an independent restriction on the sovereign power of the court, it would not be possible to waive the personal jurisdiction requirement: individual actions cannot change the powers of sovereignty, although the individual can subject himself to powers from which he may otherwise be protected.

This argument again assumes that there is something unique about the requirement of personal jurisdiction, which prevents it from being established or waived like other rights. A defendant is always free to ignore the judicial proceedings; risk a default judgment, and then challenge that judgment on jurisdictional grounds in a collateral proceeding. By submitting to the jurisdiction of the court for the limited purpose of challenging jurisdiction, the defendant agrees to abide by that court's determination on the issue of jurisdiction: that decision will be res judicata on that issue in any further proceedings. . . .

## III

Even if Rule 37(b)(2) may be applied to support a finding of personal jurisdiction, the question remains as to whether it was properly applied under the circumstances of this case. Because the District Court's decision to invoke the sanction was accompanied by a detailed explanation of the reasons for that order and because that decision was upheld as a proper exercise of the District Court's discretion by the Court of Appeals, this issue need not detain us for long . . .

[The Court held that the district judge's ruling was not an abuse of discretion]

JUSTICE POWELL, concurring in the judgment.

The Court rests today's decision on a constitutional distinction between "subject matter" and "in personam" jurisdiction. Under this distinction, subject matter jurisdiction defines an Art. III limitation on the power of federal courts. By contrast, the Court characterizes the limits on *in personam* jurisdiction solely in terms of waivable personal rights and notions of "fair play." Having done so, it determines that fundamental questions of judicial power do not arise in this case concerning the personal jurisdiction of a federal district court.

In my view the Court's broadly theoretical decision misapprehends the issues actually presented for decision. Federal courts are courts of limited jurisdiction. Their personal jurisdiction, no less than their subject-matter jurisdiction, is subject both to constitutional and to statutory definition. When the applicable limitations on federal jurisdiction are identified, it becomes apparent that the Court's theory could require a sweeping but largely unexplicated revision of jurisdictional doctrine. This revision could encompass not only the personal jurisdiction of federal courts but "sovereign" limitations on state jurisdiction as identified in *World-Wide Volkswagen Corp v. Woodson,* 444 U.S. 286, 291-293 (1980). Fair resolution of this case does not require the Court's broad holding. Accordingly, although I concur in the Court's judgment, I cannot join its opinion. . . .

Before today our decisions had established that "minimum contacts" represented a constitutional prerequisite to the exercise of in personam jurisdiction over an unconsenting defendant. In the absence of a showing of minimum contacts, a finding of personal jurisdiction over an unconsenting defendant, even as a sanction, therefore would appear to transgress previously established constitutional limitations. . . .

The Court's decision apparently must be understood as related to our state jurisdictional cases in one of two ways. Both involve legal theories that fail to justify the doctrine adopted by the Court in this case.

## A

Under traditional principles, the due process question in this case is whether "minimum contacts" exist between petitioners and the forum State that would justify the State in exercising personal jurisdiction. By finding that the establishment of minimum contacts is not a prerequisite to the exercise of jurisdiction to impose sanctions under Federal Rule of Civil Procedure 37, the Court may be understood as finding that "minimum contacts" no longer are a constitutional requirement for the exercise by a state court of personal jurisdiction over an unconsenting defendant. Whenever the Court's notions of fairness are not offended, jurisdiction apparently may be upheld.

Before today, of course, our cases had linked minimum contacts and fair play as *jointly* defining the "sovereign" limits on state assertions of personal jurisdiction over unconsenting defendants. *See World-Wide Volkswagen Corp v. Woodson, supra,* at 292-293; *see Hanson v. Denckla,* [375 U.S. 235, 251 (1958)]. The Court appears to abandon the rationale of these cases in a footnote. *See ante,* at 702-703, n. 10. . . . For the first time it defines personal jurisdiction solely by reference to abstract notions of fair play. And, astonishingly to me, it does so in a case in which this rationale for decision was neither argued nor briefed by the parties.

## B

Alternatively, it is possible to read the Court opinion, not as affecting state jurisdiction, but simply as asserting that Rule 37 of the Federal Rules of Civil Procedure represents a congressionally approved basis for the exercise of personal jurisdiction by a federal district court. On this view Rule 37 vests the federal district courts with authority to take jurisdiction over persons not in compliance with discovery orders. This of course would be a more limited holding. Yet the Court does not cast its decision in these terms. And it provides no support for such an interpretation, either in the language or in the history of the Federal Rules.

In the absence of such support, I could not join the Court in embracing such a construction of the Rules of Civil Procedure. There is nothing in Rule 37 to suggest that it is intended to confer a grant of personal jurisdiction. Indeed, the clear language of Rule 82 seems to establish that Rule 37 should *not* be construed as a jurisdictional grant: "These rules shall not be construed to extend . . . the jurisdiction of the United States district courts or the venue of actions therein." Moreover, assuming that minimum contacts remain a constitutional predicate for the exercise of a State's *in personam* jurisdiction over an unconsenting defendant, constitutional questions would arise if Rule 37 were read to permit a plaintiff in a diversity action to subject a defendant to a "fishing expedition" in a foreign jurisdiction. A plaintiff is not entitled to discovery to establish essentially speculative allegations necessary to personal jurisdiction. Nor would the use of Rule 37 sanctions to enforce discovery orders constitute a mere abuse of discretion in such a case. For me at least, such a use of discovery would raise serious questions as to the constitutional as well as the statutory authority of a federal court—in a diversity case—to exercise personal jurisdiction absent some showing of minimum contacts between the unconsenting defendant and the forum State. . . .

---

## NOTES AND QUESTIONS ON *BAUXITES* AND JURISDICTION BASED ON APPEARANCE

(1) *Scope of a General Appearance.* A defendant who makes a *general appearance* in the forum to litigate the merits of plaintiff's claim is subject to the forum's personal jurisdiction even if he has no other contact with the forum state. RESTATEMENT (SECOND) OF CONFLICT OF LAWS § 33. What is the scope of the jurisdiction generated by a general appearance? Clearly, there is jurisdiction over the defendant on the cause of action in which he appears, and it is equally clear that an appearance in one action is not a basis for jurisdiction in a totally unrelated suit. But what about a case where defendant appears generally in an action and plaintiff, pursuant to liberal amendment rules such as FED. R. CIV. P. 15, amends his complaint to add an additional claim? What arguments should a defendant make in such a case? For a general discussion of jurisdiction based upon defendant's appearance, see 1 ROBERT CASAD & WILLIAM RICHMAN, JURISDICTION IN CIVIL ACTIONS 254-288 (3d ed. 1998); WILLIAM RICHMAN & WILLIAM REYNOLDS, UNDERSTANDING CONFLICT OF LAWS § 30 (3d ed. 2002).

(2) *The Special Appearance.* A special appearance is a device which permits a defendant to appear for the sole purpose of litigating the court's jurisdiction without making a general appearance and thereby consenting to the court's exercise of jurisdiction. The right to make a special appearance is not guaranteed by the Due Process Clause, *York v. Texas,* 137 U.S. 15 (1890), but now all states permit some form of special appearance.

Suppose defendant appears specially and loses on the jurisdictional question in the trial court. If she proceeds to defend on the merits at trial, has she then submitted to the court's jurisdiction and thus lost her jurisdictional objection on appeal? The cases are divided. *Compare, e.g., Corbett v. Physicians' Casually Ass'n,* 135 Wis. 505, 115 N.W. 365 (1908), *with Harkness v. Hyde,* 98 U.S. 476 (1878).

The Federal Rules of Civil Procedure deal with the problems of appearance and jurisdictional objections in a more liberal and elegant manner. There is no longer a requirement for a special appearance. Defendant simply includes the jurisdictional objection in the answer or in a preliminary Rule 12 motion. Defendant does not waive the jurisdictional objection and submit to the court's jurisdiction by answering on the merits. In the words of Rule 12(b): "No defense or objection is waived by being joined with one or more other defenses or objections in a responsive pleading or motion." Defendant waives her jurisdictional objection only if (1) she makes a Rule 12 motion but does not include in it the objection to personal jurisdiction or, (2) she does not make a Rule 12 motion and she fails to include the jurisdictional objection in her answer. *See* F. R. Civ. P. 12 (b), (g), (h)(1). For a careful discussion of the special appearance and Rule 12, see 1 Casad & Richman, *supra* note 1.

(3) *Preclusion of the Jurisdictional Issue.* If defendant attacks the court's jurisdiction and the court erroneously finds against him, that erroneous finding has issue preclusion effect, unless reversed by the appropriate appellate court. *Baldwin v. Iowa State Traveling Men's Ass'n,* 283 U.S. 522 (1931). The issue cannot be relitigated in a subsequent collateral attack. Accordingly, a defendant who loses a jurisdictional challenge is well advised to stay in the forum and litigate the merits of the action. Otherwise, plaintiff will win a default judgment that can be enforced in any state where defendant has property. In an action on the judgment, defendant has no defense; the jurisdictional issue is precluded by the prior litigation, and the merits are merged into a judgment that is entitled to full faith and credit.

(4) *Bauxites Evaluated.* Notes (2) and (3), *supra,* make clear that the well-settled doctrines of waiver and preclusion can subject a defendant to jurisdiction in the forum even in the absence of minimum contacts. In other words, even if a defendant lacks minimum contacts with the forum, his conduct in the forum's courts can result in a relatively invulnerable, although erroneous, finding of jurisdiction.

Viewed from this perspective, the holding in *Bauxites* is clearly correct, isn't it? Does Justice White's concurrence, like the excess insurers' arguments, seem to be an attempt "to create a logical conundrum out of a fairly straightforward matter?" *But see* Lea Brilmayer, *Consent, Contract and Territory,* 74 Minn. L. Rev. 1, 27 (1989). Once it has been determined that jurisdiction can be "bootstrapped" by waiver or preclusion, the only remaining question is whether the court's ability to ensure compliance with its orders (discovery and otherwise) is as important as the policies that justify waiver and preclusion.

(5) *Plaintiff's Appearance.* The doctrines of appearance and submission have some application to plaintiffs as well. Suppose a plaintiff having no connection with the forum sues a defendant there, and defendant counterclaims against plaintiff. The forum has judicial jurisdiction over the plaintiff on the original claim as well as the counterclaim. *Adam v. Saenger,* 303 U.S. 59 (1938). By resorting to the state's courts, plaintiff has supplied a reasonable basis for the state's exercise of jurisdiction. If the rule were otherwise, an out-of-state plaintiff would have a considerable advantage over in-state litigants because he could use the courts to press his own claims without fear of a counterclaim.

## [2]  Consent

## NATIONAL EQUIPMENT RENTAL, LTD. v. SZUKHENT

*United States Supreme Court*
*375 U.S. 311, 84 S. Ct. 411, 11 L. Ed. 2d 354 (1964)*

Mr. Justice Stewart delivered the opinion of the Court . . . .

The respondents obtained certain farm equipment from the petitioner under a lease executed in 1961. The lease was on a printed form less than a page and a half in length, and consisted of 18 numbered paragraphs. The last numbered paragraph, appearing just above the respondents' signatures and printed in the same type used in the remainder of the instrument, provided that "The Lessee hereby designates Florence Weinberg, 47-21 Forty-first Street, Long Island City, N.Y., as agent for the purpose of accepting service of any process within the State of New York." The respondents were not acquainted with Florence Weinberg.

In 1962 the petitioner commenced the present action by filing in the federal court in New York a complaint which alleged that the respondents had failed to make any of the periodic payments specified by the lease. The Marshall delivered two copies of the summons and complaint to Florence Weinberg. That same day she mailed the summons and complaint to the respondents, together with a letter stating that the documents had been served upon her as the respondents' agent for the purpose of accepting service of process in New York, in accordance with the agreement contained in the lease. The petitioner itself also notified the respondents by certified mail of the service of process upon Florence Weinberg. . . .

We need not and do not in this case reach the situation where no personal notice has been given to the defendant. . . . The question presented here, on the other hand, is whether a party to a private contract may appoint an agent to receive service of process within the meaning of Federal Rule of Civil Procedure 4(d)(1), where the agent is not personally known to the party and where the agent has not expressly undertaken to transmit notice to the party.

The purpose underlying the contractual provision here at issue seems clear. The clause was inserted by the petitioner and agreed to by the respondents in order to assure that any litigation under the lease should be conducted in the State of New York. . . .

Under well-settled general principles of the law of agency, Florence Weinberg's prompt acceptance and transmittal to the respondents of the summons and complaint pursuant to the authorization was itself sufficient to validate the agency, even though there was no explicit previous promise on her part to do so. . . .

We deal here with a Federal Rule, applicable to federal courts in all 50 States. But even if we were to assume that this uniform federal standard should give way to contrary local policies, there is no relevant concept of state law which would invalidate the agency here at issue. . . .

It is argued, finally, that the agency sought to be created in this case was invalid because Florence Weinberg may have had a conflict of interest. This argument is based upon the fact that she was not personally known to the respondents at the time of her appointment and upon a suggestion in the record that she may be related to an officer of the petitioner corporation. But such a contention ignores the narrowly limited nature of the agency here involved. Florence Weinberg was appointed the respondents' agent for the single purpose of receiving service of process. An agent with authority so limited can in no meaningful sense be deemed to have had an interest antagonistic to the respondents, since both the petitioner and the respondents had an equal interest in assuring that, in the event of litigation, the latter be given adequate and timely notice which is a prerequisite to a valid judgment.

A different case would be presented if Florence Weinberg had not given prompt notice to the respondents, for then the claim might well be made that her failure to do so had operated to invalidate the agency. We hold only that, prompt notice to the respondents having been given, Florence Weinberg was their "agent authorized by appointment" to receive process within the meaning of Federal Rule of Civil Procedure 4(d)(1).

The judgment of the Court of Appeals is reversed and the case is remanded for further proceedings consistent with this opinion.

*It is so ordered.*

MR. JUSTICE BLACK, dissenting.

The petitioner, National Equipment Rental, Ltd., is a Delaware corporation with its principal place of business in greater New York City. From that location it does a nationwide equipment rental business. The respondents, Steve and Robert Szukhent, father and son farming in Michigan, leased from National two incubators for their farm, signing in Michigan a lease contract which was a standard printed form obviously prepared by the New York company's lawyers. Included in the 18 paragraphs of fine print was the following provision:

> " . . . the Lessee hereby designates Florence Weinberg, 47-21 Forty-first Street, Long Island City, N.Y., as agent for the purpose of accepting service of any process within the State of New York."

The record on the motion to quash shows that the Szukhents had never had any dealings with Mrs. Weinberg, their supposed agent. They had never met, seen, or heard of her. She did not sign the lease, was not a party to it, received no compensation from the Szukhents, and undertook no obligation to them. In fact, she was handpicked by the New York company to accept service of process in any suits that might thereafter be filed by the company. Only after this suit was brought was it reluctantly revealed that Mrs. Weinberg was in truth the wife of the one of the company's officers. . . .

Where one party, at its leisure and drawing upon expert legal advice, drafts a form contract, complete with waivers of rights and privileges by the other, it seems to me to defy common sense for this Court to formulate a federal rule designed to treat this as an agreement coolly negotiated and hammered out by equals. . . . It is hardly likely that these Michigan farmers, hiring farm equipment, were in any position to dicker over what terms went into the contract they signed. Yet holding this service effective inevitably will mean that the Szukhents must go nearly a thousand miles to a strange city, hire New York counsel, pay witnesses to travel there, pay their own and their witnesses' hotel bills, try to explain a dispute over a farm equipment lease to a New York judge or jury, and in other ways bear the burdens of litigation in a distant, and likely a strange city. The company, of course, must have had this in mind when it put the clause in the contract. It doubtless hoped, by easing into its contract this innocent-looking provision for service of process in New York, to succeed in making it as burdensome, disadvantageous, and expensive as possible for lessees to contest actions brought against them. . . . Rule 4(d)(1), designed in part to preserve the right to have a case tried in a convenient tribunal, should not be used to formulate federal standards of agency that defeat this purpose.

It should be understood that the effect of the Court's holding is not simply to give courts sitting in New York jurisdiction over these Michigan farmers. It is also, as a practical matter, to guarantee that whenever the company wishes to sue someone who has contracted with it, it can, by force of this clause, confine all such suits to courts sitting in New York. This Court and others have frequently refused to hold valid a contract which, before any controversy has arisen, attempts to restrict jurisdiction to a single court or courts. Here this contract as effectively ousts the Michigan courts of jurisdiction as if it had said so. Today's holding disregards Michigan's interest in supervising the protection of rights of its citizens who never leave the State but are sued by foreign companies with which they have done business. . . .

The Court's holding that these Michigan residents are compelled to go to New York to defend themselves in a New York court brings sharply into focus constitutional questions as to whether they will thereby be denied due process of law in violation of the Fifth and Fourteenth Amendments. While implicit in much of the oral arguments and in the briefs, these questions have not been adequately discussed. . . .

It has been established constitutional doctrine since *Pennoyer v. Neff,* 95 U.S. 714, was decided in 1878, that a state court is without power to serve its process outside the State's boundaries so as to compel a resident of another State against his will to appear as a defendant in a case where a personal judgment is sought against him. This rule means that an individual has a constitutional right not to be sued on such claims in the courts of any State except his own without his consent. . . .

The Court relies on the printed provision of the contract as a consent of the Szukhents to be sued in New York, making the *Pennoyer* rule inapplicable. . . . This Court should not permit valuable constitutional rights to be destroyed by any such sharp contractual practices. The idea that there was a knowing consent of the Szukhents to be sued in the courts of New York is no more than a fiction—not even an amiable one at that.

I would affirm the judgment.

MR. JUSTICE BRENNAN, with whom THE CHIEF JUSTICE and MR. JUSTICE GOLDBERG join, dissenting.

I would affirm. . . . It offends common sense to treat a printed form which closes an installment sale as embodying terms to all of which the individual knowingly assented. The sales pitch aims solely at getting the signature on the form and wastes no time explaining or even mentioning the print. Before I would find that an individual purchaser has knowingly and intelligently consented to be sued in another State, I would require more proof of that fact than is provided by his mere signature on the form. . . .

## NOTES AND QUESTIONS ON *SZUKHENT* AND JURISDICTION BASED ON CONSENT

(1) *Express Consent.* Defendant's general appearance is essentially a consent after the fact. After the court asserts jurisdiction, defendant consents by appearing to litigate the merits. But a defendant also may consent in advance. The consent may take the form of a document (often a power of attorney) nominating a particular state official or private person to be an agent to accept service of process. Often, a state regulatory scheme or corporation code compels such a consent in return for granting the privilege of conducting activities or engaging in business within the state. *See, e.g., Kane v. New Jersey,* 242 U.S. 160 (1916), in which the Supreme Court upheld a regulatory scheme which conditioned an out-of-state driver's permission to drive on New Jersey's highways on his executing an instrument, appointing the Secretary of State his agent for receipt of service of process. Such extorted consent provisions are now largely unnecessary. After *International Shoe,* modern long-arm statutes can provide for the exercise of jurisdiction over defendants who engage in activities within the state without resort to the conceptual expedient of consent.

(2) *Implied Consent.* Early long-arm statutes also relied on the doctrine of "implied consent." The consent implied, of course, was fictional. The statutory schemes did not require an extorted actual consent as in *Kane;* rather they provided that the defendant's conducting of certain activities in the forum (driving a car, for instance) constituted "implied consent" to the jurisdiction of the forum's courts for any cause of action arising out of those activities. *See, e.g., Hess v. Pawloski,* 274 U.S. 352 (1927).

Once again, the decision in *International Shoe* rendered the doctrine of implied consent obsolete. Legislatures were free to enact long-arm statutes providing for jurisdiction over defendants based directly on their activities in the forum without the need to infer from those activities a fictional consent. For a more complete account of the use of express and implied consent to expand state court jurisdiction in the *pre-International Shoe* era, see WILLIAM RICHMAN & WILLIAM REYNOLDS, UNDERSTANDING CONFLICT OF LAWS § 18 (3d ed. 2002).

(3) *Contractual Consent.* The defendant also may consent by contract to the court's jurisdiction. Consent-to-jurisdiction clauses, fairly common in commercial contracts, sometimes specify the jurisdiction of an arbitration panel in the forum instead of the forum's courts. Jurisdiction consent clauses, when combined with choice-of-law clauses, permit sophisticated contracting parties considerable freedom to plan for and bargain over the place and the manner in which their disputes will be resolved.

(4) *Adhesion Contracts.* Are you bothered by the Court's holding in *Szukhent* that Mrs. Weinberg was a proper agent, even though she was married to an officer of the plaintiff? Perhaps it might help to think about what it means to be an "agent" for service of process. Apparently, all that Mrs. Weinberg had

to do was forward promptly to the Szukhents the documents that had been served on her; this she did faithfully. Does it matter, therefore, that her interests were "antagonistic," as Justice Black put it, to those of her principals?

Does the holding violate at least the spirit of *International Shoe* by permitting New York courts to exercise jurisdiction in a way that offends "fundamental notions of fair play and substantial justice"? Or is it a sufficient answer that the Szukhents voluntarily waived their constitutional rights? After all, constitutional rights can be waived in other areas (think of plea bargaining, for example).

Is *Szukhent* good authority for the validity of consent-to-jurisdiction clauses in consumer adhesion contracts? Recall the Court's concern about this problem expressed in *Burger King,* § 3.10, *supra.* Can *Szukhent* be distinguished from such a case? *Szukhent* was decided before the Court decreed in *Shaffer v. Heitner,* 433 U.S. 186 (1977), that all assertions of jurisdiction must meet the "fair play and substantial justice" standard of *International Shoe.* Based on this oft-quoted passage, can you fashion an argument that *Szukhent* is no longer good law? *See* Richman & Reynolds, *supra* note 2 at § 30[c]; Rudolph Schlesinger, *Jurisdictional Clauses in Consumer Transactions: A Multifaceted Problem of Jurisdiction and Full Faith and Credit,* 29 HASTINGS L.J. 967, 974 (1978). How is your *Shaffer*-based argument affected by the Supreme Court's ruling in *Burnham v. Superior Court,* § 3.12[A], *supra?*

(5) *"Cognovit" Clauses.* It is common practice in a number of states to include confession of judgment or "cognovit" clauses in commercial contracts. The effect of a cognovit clause is to permit the creditor, upon default, to "confess" judgment on behalf of the debtor in an appropriate court. Creditors, of course, find this a very appealing procedure. The possibility of abuse is always present, however, because many of these clauses either are not the subject of express bargaining, or are part of a contract between parties of unequal bargaining power. Probably the Szukhents were surprised to find themselves sued in New York; imagine their surprise if they also found that they had confessed judgment there.

The Supreme Court, during a brief flirtation with consumer activism in the late 1960's, gave some reason to believe that confessed judgments might not pass constitutional muster. But in *D.H. Overmyer Co. v. Frick,* 405 U.S. 174 (1972), the Court re-affirmed its holding in *Szukhent* and held that "a cognitive clause is not, *per se,* violative of Fourteenth Amendment due process." The Court added, however, that "where the contract is one of adhesion, where there is great disparity in bargaining power, and where the debtor receives nothing by the cognovit provision, other legal consequences may ensue." (In other words be careful?)

Cognovit judgments can be affected by both state and federal legislation. *See* Schlesinger, *supra* Note (4).

(6) *Exclusive Jurisdiction Clauses.* A problem related to contractual consent-to-jurisdiction clauses is the exclusive jurisdiction clause. Suppose the parties to a contract agree to litigate any dispute arising from their contract in the courts of New York, but one party ignores the provision and sues in

Michigan, a jurisdiction that has ample contact with the dispute. Should a Michigan court refuse to exercise jurisdiction? *See* § 3.19, *infra.*

---

# PHILLIPS PETROLEUM CO. v. SHUTTS

*United States Supreme Court*
*472 U.S. 797, 105 S. Ct. 2965, 86 L. Ed. 2d 628 (1985)*

JUSTICE REHNQUIST delivered the opinion of the Court.

Petitioner is a Delaware corporation which has its principal place of business in Oklahoma. During the 1970's it produced or purchased natural gas from leased land located in 11 different States, and sold most of the gas in interstate commerce. Respondents are some 28,000 of the royalty owners possessing rights to the leases from which petitioner produced the gas; they reside in all 50 States, the District of Columbia, and several foreign countries. Respondents brought a class action against petitioner in the Kansas state court, seeking to recover interest on royalty payments which had been delayed by petitioner. They recovered judgment in the trial court, and the Supreme Court of Kansas affirmed the judgment over petitioner's contentions that the Due Process Clause of the Fourteenth Amendment prevented Kansas from adjudicating the claims of all the respondents, and that the Due Process Clause and the Full Faith and Credit Clause of Article IV of the Constitution prohibited the application of Kansas law to all of the transactions between petitioner and respondents. We granted certiorari to consider these claims. We reject petitioner's jurisdictional claim, but sustain its claim regarding the choice-of-law.

Because petitioner sold the gas to its customers in interstate commerce, it was required to secure approval for price increases from what was then the Federal Power Commission, and is now the Federal Energy Regulatory Commission. Under its regulations the Federal Power Commission permitted petitioner to propose and collect tentative higher gas prices, subject to final approval by the Commission. If the Commission eventually denied petitioner's proposed increase or reduced the proposed increase, petitioner would have to refund to its customers the difference between the approved price and the higher price charged, plus interest at a rate set by statute.

Although petitioner received higher gas prices pending review by the Commission, petitioner suspended any increase in royalties paid to the royalty owners because the higher price could be subject to recoupment by petitioner's customers. Petitioner agreed to pay the higher royalty only if the royalty owners would provide petitioner with a bond or indemnity for the increase, plus interest, in case the price increase was not ultimately approved and a refund was due to the customers. Petitioner set the interest rate on the indemnity agreements at the same interest rate the Commission would have required petitioner to refund to its customers. . . .

The . . . royalty owners [who did not provide the bond] received no royalty on the unapproved portion of the prices until the Federal Power Commission approval of those prices became final. . . . Petitioner paid no interest to the royalty owners although it had the use of the suspended royalty money for a number of years.

Respondents Irl Shutts, Robert Anderson, and Betty Anderson filed suit against petitioner in Kansas state court, seeking interest payments on their suspended royalties which petitioner had possessed pending the Commission's approval of the price increases. Shutts is a resident of Kansas and the Andersons live in Oklahoma. Shutts and the Andersons own gas leases in Oklahoma and Texas. Over petitioner's objection the Kansas trial court granted respondents' motion to certify the suit as a class action under Kansas law. The class as certified was comprised of 33,000 royalty owners who had royalties suspended by petitioner. The average claim of each royalty owner for interest on the suspended royalties was $100.

After the class was certified, respondents provided each class member with notice through first-class mail. The notice described the action and informed each class member that he could appear in person or by counsel; otherwise each member would be represented by Shutts and the Andersons, the named plaintiffs. The notices also stated that class members would be included in the class and bound by the judgment unless they "opted out" of the lawsuit by executing and returning a "request for exclusion" that was included with the notice. The final class as certified contained 28,100 members; 3,400 had "opted out" of the class by returning the request for exclusion, and notice could not be delivered to another 1,500 members, who were also excluded. Less than 1,000 of the class members resided in Kansas. Only a miniscule amount, approximately one quarter of one percent, of the gas leases involved in the lawsuit were on Kansas land. . . .

. . . The [trial] court found petitioner liable under Kansas law for interest on the suspended royalties to all class members. . . . The Kansas Supreme Court had held in [an unrelated class action] that a gas company owed interest to royalty owners for royalties suspended pending final Commission approval of a price increase. . . . [It] held as a matter of Kansas equity law that the applicable interest rates for computation of interest on suspended royalties were the interest rates at which the gas company would have had to reimburse its customers had its interim price increase been rejected by the Commission. . . .

The trial court in the present case applied the [same] rule . . . . and held petitioner liable for prejudgment and post-judgment interest on the suspended royalties, computed at the Commission rates governing petitioner's . . . price increases. . . . The trial court did not determine whether any difference existed between the laws of Kansas and other States, or whether another State's laws should be applied to non-Kansas plaintiffs or to royalties from leases in states other than Kansas.

Petitioner raised two principal claims in its appeal to the Supreme Court of Kansas. It first asserted that the Kansas trial court did not possess personal jurisdiction over absent plaintiff class members . . . [contending] that the "opt-out" notice to absent class members . . . was insufficient to bind class members who . . . did not possess "minimum contacts" with Kansas. Second, petitioner claimed that Kansas courts could not apply Kansas law to every claim in the dispute. The trial court should have looked to the laws of each State where the leases were located to determine, on the basis of conflict of laws principles, whether interest on the suspended royalties was recoverable, and at what rate.

The Supreme Court of Kansas . . . rejected both of petitioner's claims. . . .

I

As a threshold matter we must determine whether petitioner has standing to assert the claim that Kansas did not possess proper jurisdiction over the many plaintiffs in the class who were not Kansas residents and had no connection to Kansas. . . .

Respondents claim that petitioner is barred by the rule requiring that a party assert only his own rights; they point out that respondents and petitioner are adversaries and do not have allied interests such that petitioner would be a good proponent of class members' interests. They further urge that petitioner's interference is unneeded because the class members have had opportunity to complain about Kansas' assertion of jurisdiction over their claim, but none have done so.

. . . Petitioner seeks to vindicate its own interests. As a class-action defendant petitioner is in a unique predicament. If Kansas does not possess jurisdiction over this plaintiff class, petitioner will be bound to 28,100 judgment holders scattered across the globe, but none of these will be bound by the Kansas decree. Petitioner could be subject to numerous later individual suits by these class members because a judgment issued without proper personal jurisdiction over an absent party is not entitled to full faith and credit elsewhere and thus has no res judicata effect as to that party. Whether it wins or loses on the merits, petitioner has a distinct and personal interest in seeing the entire plaintiff class bound by res judicata just as petitioner is bound. The only way a class action defendant like petitioner can assure itself of this binding effect of the judgment is to ascertain that the forum court has jurisdiction over every plaintiff whose claim it seeks to adjudicate, sufficient to support a defense of res judicata in a later suit for damages by class members.

While it is true that a court adjudicating a dispute may not be able to predetermine the res judicata effect of its own judgment, petitioner has alleged that it would be obviously and immediately injured if this class-action judgment against it became final without binding the plaintiff class. We think that such an injury is sufficient to give petitioner standing on its own right to raise the jurisdiction claim in this Court. . . .

II

Reduced to its essentials, petitioner's argument is that unless out-of-state plaintiffs affirmatively consent, the Kansas courts may not exert jurisdiction over their claims. Petitioner claims that failure to execute and return the "request for exclusion" provided with the class notice cannot constitute consent of the out-of-state plaintiffs; thus Kansas courts may exercise jurisdiction over these plaintiffs only if the plaintiffs possess the sufficient "minimum contacts" with Kansas as that term is used in cases involving personal jurisdiction over out-of-state defendants. *E.g., Int'l Shoe Co. v. Washington,* 326 U.S. 310 (1945); *Shaffer v. Heitner,* 433 U.S. 186 (1977); *World-Wide Volkswagen Corp. v. Woodson,* 444 U.S. 286 (1980). . . .

Although the cases like *Shaffer* and *Woodson* which petitioner relies on for a minimum contacts requirement all dealt with out-of-state defendants or parties in the procedural posture of a defendant, petitioner claims that the same analysis must apply to absent class-action plaintiffs. In this regard petitioner correctly points out that a chose in action is a constitutionally recognized property interest possessed by each of the plaintiffs. An adverse judgment by Kansas courts in this case may extinguish the chose in action forever through res judicata. Such an adverse judgment, petitioner claims, would be every bit as onerous to an absent plaintiff as an adverse judgment on the merits would be to a defendant. Thus, the same due process protections should apply to absent plaintiffs; Kansas should not be able to exert jurisdiction over the plaintiffs' claims unless the plaintiffs have sufficient minimum contacts with Kansas.

We think petitioner's premise is in error. The burdens placed by a State upon an absent class-action plaintiff are not of the same order or magnitude as those it places upon an absent defendant. An out-of-state defendant summoned by a plaintiff is faced with the full powers of the forum State to render judgment against it. The defendant must generally hire counsel and travel to the forum to defend itself from the plaintiff's claim, or suffer a default judgment. The defendant may be forced to participate in extended and often costly discovery, and will be forced to respond in damages or to comply with some other form of remedy imposed by the court should it lose the suit. The defendant may also face liability for court costs and attorney's fees. These burdens are substantial, and the minimum contacts requirement of the Due Process clause prevents the forum State from unfairly imposing them upon the defendant.

A class-action plaintiff, however, is in quite a different posture. . . .

In sharp contrast to the predicament of a defendant haled into an out-of-state forum, the plaintiffs in this suit were not haled anywhere to defend themselves upon pain of a default judgment. As commentators have noted, from the plaintiffs' point of view a class action resembles a "quasi-administrative proceeding, conducted by the judge." 3B J. MOORE & J. KENNEDY, MOORE'S FEDERAL PRACTICE 123.45 [4.-5] (1984); Kaplan, *Continuing Work of the Civil Committee: 1966 Amendments to the Federal Rules of Civil Procedure (I),* 81 HARV. L. REV. 356, 398 (1967).

A plaintiff class in Kansas and numerous other jurisdictions cannot first be certified unless the judge, with the aid of the named plaintiffs and defendant, conducts an inquiry into the common nature of the named plaintiffs' and the absent plaintiffs' claims, the adequacy of representation, the jurisdiction possessed over the class, and any other matters that will bear upon proper representation of the absent plaintiffs' interest. Unlike a defendant in a civil suit, a class-action plaintiff is not required to fend for himself. The court and named plaintiffs protect his interests. Indeed, the class-action defendant itself has a great interest in ensuring that the absent plaintiffs' claims are properly before the forum. In this case, for example, the defendant sought to avoid class certification by alleging that the absent plaintiffs would not be adequately represented and were not amenable to jurisdiction.

The concern of the typical class-action rules for the absent plaintiffs is manifested in other ways. Most jurisdictions, including Kansas, require that a class action, once certified, may not be dismissed or compromised without the approval of the court. In many jurisdictions such as Kansas the court may amend the pleadings to ensure that all sections of the class are represented adequately.

Besides this continuing solicitude for their rights, absent plaintiff class members are not subject to other burdens imposed upon defendants. They need not hire counsel or appear. They are almost never subject to counter-claims or cross-claims, or liability for fees or costs. Absent plaintiff class members are not subject to coercive or punitive remedies. Nor will an adverse judgment typically bind an absent plaintiff for any damages, although a valid adverse judgment may extinguish any of the plaintiff's claims which were litigated.

Unlike a defendant in a normal civil suit, an absent class-action plaintiff is not required to do anything. He may sit back and allow the litigation to run its course, content in knowing that there are safeguards provided for his protection. In most class actions an absent plaintiff is provided at least with an opportunity to "opt out" of the class, and if he takes advantage of that opportunity he is removed from the litigation entirely. This was true of the Kansas proceedings in this case. The Kansas procedure provided for the mailing of a notice to each class member by first-class mail. The notice, as we have previously indicated, described the action and informed the class member that he could appear in person or by counsel, in default of which he would be represented by the named plaintiffs and their attorneys. The notice further stated that class members would be included in the class and bound by the judgment unless they "opted out" by executing and returning a "request for exclusion" that was included in the notice.

Petitioner contends, however, that the "opt out" procedure provided by Kansas is not good enough, and that an "opt in" procedure is required to satisfy the Due Process Clause of the Fourteenth Amendment. Insofar as plaintiffs who have no minimum contacts with the forum State are concerned, an "opt in" provision would require that each class member affirmatively consent to his inclusion within the class.

Because States place fewer burdens upon absent class plaintiffs than they do upon absent defendants in non-class suits, the Due Process Clause need not and does not afford the former as much protection from state-court jurisdiction as it does the latter. The Fourteenth Amendment does protect "persons," not "defendants," however, so absent plaintiffs as well as absent defendants are entitled to some protection from the jurisdiction of a forum State which seeks to adjudicate their claims. In this case we hold that a forum State may exercise jurisdiction over the claim of an absent class-action plaintiff, even though that plaintiff may not possess the minimum contacts with the forum which would support personal jurisdiction over a defendant.

If the forum State wishes to bind an absent plaintiff concerning a claim for money damages or similar relief at law, it must provide minimal procedural due process protection. The plaintiff must receive notice plus an opportunity to be heard and participate in the litigation, whether in person or through counsel. . . . [W]e hold that due process requires at a minimum that an absent plaintiff be provided with an opportunity to remove himself from the class by executing and returning an "opt out" or "request for exclusion" form to the court. Finally, the Due Process Clause of course requires that the named plaintiff at all times adequately represent the interests of the absent class members.

We reject petitioner's contention that the Due Process Clause of the Fourteenth Amendment requires that absent plaintiffs affirmatively "opt in" to the class, rather than be deemed members of the class if they do not "opt out." We think that such a contention is supported by little, if any precedent, and that it ignores the differences between class action plaintiffs, on the one hand, and defendants in non-class civil suits on the other. Any plaintiff may consent to jurisdiction. The essential question, then, is how stringent the requirement for a showing of consent will be.

We think that the procedure followed by Kansas, where a fully descriptive notice is sent first-class mail to each class member, with an explanation of the right to "opt out," satisfies due process. Requiring a plaintiff to affirmatively request inclusion would probably impede the prosecution of those class actions involving an aggregation of small individual claims, where a large number of claims are required to make it economical to bring suit. The plaintiff's claim may be so small, or the plaintiff so unfamiliar with the law, that he would not file suit individually, nor would he affirmatively request inclusion in the class if such a request were required by the Constitution. If, on the other hand, the plaintiff's claim is sufficiently large or important that he wishes to litigate it on his own, he will likely have retained an attorney or have thought about filing suit, and should be fully capable of exercising his right to "opt out."

In this case over 3,400 members of the potential class did "opt out," which belies the contention that "opt out" procedures result in guaranteed jurisdiction by inertia. Another 1,500 were excluded because the notice and "opt out" form was undeliverable. We think that such results show that the "opt out" procedure provided by Kansas is by no means *pro forma,* and that the Constitution does not require more to protect what must be the somewhat rare species of class member who is unwilling to execute an "opt out" form, but whose claim is nonetheless so important that he cannot be presumed to consent to being a member of that class by his failure to do so. Petitioner's "opt in" requirement would require the invalidation of scores of state statutes and of the class-action provision of the Federal Rules of Civil Procedure, and for the reasons stated we do not think that the Constitution requires the State to sacrifice the obvious advantages in judicial efficiency resulting from the "opt out" approach for the protection for the *rara avis* portrayed by petitioner.

We therefore hold that the protection afforded the plaintiff class members by the Kansas statute satisfied the Due Process Clause. . . .

[The portion of the Court's opinion dealing with the constitutionality of the Kansas court's choice of Kansas law to govern the case is reproduced in § 5.04, *infra.* ]

## NOTES AND QUESTIONS

(1) *Class Action Plaintiffs.* The Court relied heavily on the distinction between the position of class action plaintiffs and ordinary civil defendants. Are there enough distinctions to make a difference? One commentator argues forcefully that the application of the label "plaintiff" to non-opt-out class members is misleading. Such individuals bear little relationship to the traditional civil plaintiff. It is better to treat them as *sui generis,* as a type of litigant that did not exist in the relatively simple legal world that gave us the terms "plaintiff" and "defendant". John Kennedy, *The Supreme Court Meets the Bride of Frankenstein: Phillips Petroleum Co. v. Shutts and the State Multistate Class Action,* 34 U. KAN. L. REV. 255, 280 (1985). The author also argues that the opt-out class action reveals a fundamental change in the court's role from a passive non-initiating umpire to a quasi-administrative agency actively prosecuting the claims of persons who fail to object. *Id.* at 284.

Has the Court dismissed too cavalierly the possibility that members of a class might be subject to genuine burdens: discovery requests, counterclaims, cross claims, and court costs? *See* Arthur Miller & David Crump, *Jurisdiction and Choice of Law in Multistate Class Actions After Phillips Petroleum Co. v. Shutts,* 96 YALE L.J. 1, 26 (1986).

The Court's broad view of state class action jurisdiction (with no minimum contacts requirement) also poses another question: what if two or more state courts certify the same nationwide class? Would the result depend upon a race to judgment? Could the defendant manipulate the result by dilatory tactics in some states and cooperative acceleration in its favored state? *See id.* at 24.

*Shutts* dealt with a Rule 26(b)(3) class action, in which members of the plaintiff class have the opportunity to opt-out and thus avoid the preclusive effects of a decision. How should *Shutts* apply to plaintiffs in non-opt-out class actions under Rule 26(b)(1) and (2). Because such plaintiffs cannot opt out, must they have minimum contacts with the forum and otherwise be treated like defendants? Are there other possible solutions? *See* Linda Mullenix, *Class Actions, Personal Jurisdiction, and Plaintiffs' Due Process: Implications for Mass Tort Litigation,* 28 U. C. DAVIS L. REV. 871 (1995).

(2) *Consent or Necessity.* Is jurisdiction in an opt-out class action really based on consent? The inference of the consent of class members who do not opt-out is based entirely on their ability to understand the notice and its explanation of their rights and options. But much of what lawyers write and say is incomprehensible to non-lawyers, and there are well-known examples—some rather amusing—of the misreading of legal notices by laymen. *See* Miller & Crump, *supra* Note (1), at 22.

If the "consent" of the non-opt-out class members is as fictional as the implied consents of the early long-arm statutes, what is the real basis for jurisdiction in cases like *Shutts*? Arguably, it is a form of jurisdiction by necessity, similar to the doctrine which justifies jurisdiction over the interests of all the world in a true in rem action. A multi-state class action would be virtually impossible without some way to assert jurisdiction over absent class members. Why, then, did the Court fail to articulate that rationale? Possibly the Court is concerned about the scope and implications of such a doctrine. It has rejected arguments for jurisdiction based on necessity in some rather egregious cases, in which plaintiffs really had no other practical forum. *See Helicopteros Nacionale de Colombia v. Hall,* § 3.10, *supra.*

(3) In *Bauxites, Szukhent, and Shutts,* the Supreme Court permitted jurisdiction in cases in which the person had no minimum contacts with the forum. In *Bauxites* it relied on waiver, and in *Szukhent and Shutts,* on consent. But why are waiver and consent adequate substitutes for minimum contacts? Is it because waiver and consent are based on fairness? If so, do these cases show that pre-litigation contact, like waiver and consent, is just one way of guaranteeing fairness?

If "minimum contacts" is simply an instrument to ensure fairness, why not routinely permit jurisdiction in cases where defendant lacks minimum contacts with the forum, but could not be subject to any unfair burden in defending there? What if defendant, a citizen of Michigan, has no pre-litigation contacts with Ohio but lives so close to the border that the Ohio court is actually closer to his home than the appropriate Michigan court? How would it be unfair to him to defend in the Ohio court? *See* Robert Mills, *Personal Jurisdiction Over Border State Defendants: What Does Due Process Require?,* 13 S. ILL. U. L. REV. 919 (1989). Perhaps the unfairness would be in the Ohio court's propensity to apply its own law. If that is the real problem, then why not deal with it through meaningful constitutional restrictions on state court choice-of-law decisions rather than by clinging to the minimum contacts requirement?

On the question of whether a choice-of-law forecast should enter the jurisdictional calculation, see Louise Weinberg, *The Place of Trial and the Law Applied: Overhauling Constitutional Theory,* 59 U. COLO. L. REV. 67, 97-100 (1988).

## [D]   Traditional Bases for Jurisdiction over Corporations

*Domestic Corporations.* Traditionally, jurisdiction over the domestic corporation was not a problem; even under the restrictive territorial theory before *International Shoe,* there were ample jurisdictional bases for such defendants. A corporation is a domiciliary of its state of incorporation. Indeed, a particularly close relationship exists between a corporation and its home state because the laws of that state make the corporation's existence possible. Another traditional basis that applies without much stretching is consent. In return for giving it life, the state can require the corporation's consent to the jurisdiction of the state's courts. Whatever the rationale, and often there was no felt need to articulate any, courts have traditionally assumed jurisdiction over domestic corporations.

Under current jurisdictional theory, incorporation within the state remains a constitutionally adequate basis for jurisdiction over a corporation; and every state has statutes or rules that permit its courts to exercise jurisdiction on that basis. *See* RESTATEMENT (SECOND) OF CONFLICT OF LAWS § 41 (1971); 1 ROBERT CASAD & WILLIAM RICHMAN, JURISDICTION IN CIVIL ACTIONS 332-333 (3d ed. 1998). Further, incorporation within the state usually will support an exercise of general jurisdiction; thus the forum can adjudicate any claim against the corporate defendant, not merely those that arise in the forum.

Is the current state of the law consistent with *International Shoe's* command to safeguard "fair play" and "substantial justice"? What considerations support the fairness of incorporation within the forum as a basis for general jurisdiction? *See* William Richman & William Reynolds, Understanding Conflict of Laws § 31 (3d ed. 2002). What about a case where the corporation has no contact with the state beyond the purely formal connection of its charter of incorporation? What if, in such a case, the state of incorporation is the only state whose statute of limitations does not bar the plaintiff's claim? Is the defendant's claim of unfairness in such a case based on jurisdiction or choice of law? If it is based on choice of law, why might we be unsympathetic to it?

After *Burnham v. Superior Court, supra* § 3.12[A], how would you predict the Court would rule on any unfairness-based challenge to jurisdiction based on incorporation within the forum?

*"Qualifying" Corporations.* Every state provides conditions that an out-of-state corporation must satisfy in order to "qualify" to operate within the state. One such condition is that the foreign corporation consent to the jurisdiction of the state's courts. According to most such statutes, the consent is not limited to claims arising within the state. Is that result constitutional? One commentary argues that the forum court should look beyond the formal "consent" and exercise general jurisdiction only if the defendant's connections with the state are sufficiently substantial to warrant it without regard to the defendant's extorted submission. *See* 1 ROBERT CASAD & WILLIAM RICHMAN, JURISDICTION IN CIVIL ACTIONS 334-339 (1998).

*Doing Business.* Before the jurisdictional revolution of *International Shoe* and the advent of modern long-arm statutes, states exercised jurisdiction over foreign, non-qualifying corporations based upon "doing business" statutes. Many states retain such statutes, but their function has changed over the years. Once they provided a basis for specific jurisdiction, but in that capacity the statutes have been superseded largely by the "transacting business" provisions of modern enumerated act long-arm statutes. These new provisions require much less contact between the defendant and the forum than do the older "doing business" statutes. Often a single transaction is sufficient.

No longer needed for specific jurisdiction, the emerging modern role of the "doing business" statutes is as a basis for general jurisdiction. New York, for instance, has so construed a statute permitting "jurisdiction over persons, property or status as might have been exercised heretofore." *See* MCKINNEY'S CIVIL PRACTICE LAW & RULES § 301; *Frummer v. Hilton Hotels Int'l, Inc.,* 19 N.Y.2d 533, 281 N.E.2d 41, 227 N.Y.S.2d 851 (1967), *cert. denied,* 389 U.S. 923 (1967).

When used as a basis for general jurisdiction, the "doing business" statutes have been construed to require fairly significant contacts between the defendant and the forum. In the words of the RESTATEMENT (SECOND) OF CONFLICT

OF LAWS § 47(2), a state court can exercise jurisdiction "over a foreign corporation which does business in the state with respect to causes of action that do not arise from the business done in the state if this business is so continuous and substantial as to make it reasonable for the state to exercise such jurisdiction."

Thus, mere solicitation of orders does not meet the standard. Even if a corporation has agents in the state who solicit orders and even if products are then shipped into the state to fill those orders, the corporation is not "doing business" according to most courts. "Solicitation plus" some additional activity, such as maintaining a showroom or office in the state, however, may be sufficient. *See* B. Glenn George, *In Search of General Jurisdiction,* 64 TUL. L. REV. 1097, 1129 (1990). Cases involving regular but intermittent contact with the state, such as a retailer's periodic buying trips or a professional sports team's road trips, have produced inconsistent results.

Suppose a retail store in Kansas City, Kansas advertises in Kansas City, Missouri and sells a substantial portion of its merchandise to customers who come from Missouri. Is the store doing business in Missouri so that a plaintiff customer could maintain an action in Missouri based on a sale in Kansas? Would the exercise of jurisdiction violate due process? A very careful and complete study of "doing business" statutes and cases appears in 1 Casad & Richman, *supra,* 339-364. Professor Weintraub points out that the trend toward the expansive use of a "doing business" statute as a basis for general jurisdiction may have stalled as a result of the Supreme Court's very restrictive view of general jurisdiction in *Helicopleros Nacionale de Colombia v. Hall,* § 3.10, *infra.* Russell Weintraub, COMMENTARY ON THE CONFLICT OF LAWS 214 (4th ed. 2001).

*Parents and Subsidiaries.* Judicial jurisdiction over a subsidiary corporation does not guarantee judicial jurisdiction over the subsidiary's parent corporation. Similarly, jurisdiction over the parent does not guarantee jurisdiction over the subsidiary. If, however, the parent so controls the subsidiary that its separate legal existence is a mere fiction, courts will "pierce the corporate veil" for purposes of jurisdiction as well as substantive law and attribute the forum contacts of the subsidiary to the parent. Thus, if the subsidiary is found to be "doing business" in the forum, the parent will be also. *E.g. Cannon Mfg. Co. v. Cudahy Packing Co.,* 267 U.S. 333 (1925); RESTATEMENT (SECOND) OF CONFLICT OF LAWS § 52, cmt. b.

Even if the entities are not so close as to permit piercing the corporate veil, jurisdiction over the parent might still be available on an agency theory. Suppose, for instance, a national retailer conducts buying and other corporate business through a parent corporation but accomplishes its retail distribution through ten subsidiaries, each of which has a separate geographical territory. If the subsidiaries are each separately capitalized and separately controlled, piercing the veil will be extremely difficult; but if a subsidiary acts as the parent's agent in the forum, jurisdiction over the parent may be permissible upon that basis. *See* Russell Weintraub, COMMENTARY ON THE CONFLICT OF LAWS 192-193 (3d ed. 1986); Lea Brilmayer & Kathleen Paisley, *Personal Jurisdiction and Substantive Legal Relations: Corporations, Conspiracies, and Agency* 74 CALIF. L. REV. 1 (1986).

What other relationships between defendants should have jurisdictional significance? Consider *World-Wide Volkswagen v. Woodson,* § 3.10, *supra; Rush v. Savchuk,* § 3.16, *supra;* and *Calder v. Jones,* § 3.10, *supra:* In each, an argument was made that a relationship among the defendants should affect the jurisdictional calculus. How did the Court rule? Was it right?

*Partnerships and Unincorporated Associations.* Traditionally, partnerships and unincorporated associations did not have separate legal existence as did corporations. What that meant for jurisdictional purposes was that the forum had to obtain personal jurisdiction over each defendant partner or member in order to render a valid judgment. Now most states have statutes that permit a partnership or association to be sued in its own name based on its activities in the forum. A judgment in such an action can be satisfied only out of the property of the entity, unless, of course, the court obtains personal jurisdiction over the partners or members as well as the entity. A thorough discussion of this issue appears in 1 Casad & Richman, *supra,* at 364-370.

## § 3.13   Long-Arm Statutes

### [A]   In General

The preceding section examined traditional bases for personal jurisdiction. These bases, incorporated in state law, were adequate to extend the forum's jurisdiction as far as the Constitution would permit under the Supreme Court's restrictive territorial power theory of jurisdiction. When the Court jettisoned that theory in *International Shoe,* however, new state legislation was required to extend state court jurisdiction towards the new and expanded constitutional limits. State legislatures responded to the challenge by enacting long-arm statutes.

Long-arm statutes take two basic forms. The simpler type—the California statute is the paradigm—directs the court to exercise jurisdiction whenever permitted by the Constitution. The more complicated statutes, often called "enumerated act" statutes, direct the court to exercise jurisdiction over any defendant who commits one of several enumerated acts in the forum. With these statutes, Illinois and later Wisconsin and New York were the pioneers. The most influential formulation is probably the one adopted by the Commissioners on Uniform State Laws in the Uniform Interstate and International Procedure Act. The two types of long-arm statute are compared in WILLIAM RICHMAN & WILLIAM REYNOLDS, UNDERSTANDING CONFLICT OF LAWS § 33 (3d ed. 2002). A more detailed treatment of the comparison and of the early history of long-arm statutes appears in 1 ROBERT CASAD & WILLIAM RICHMAN, JURISDICTION IN CIVIL ACTIONS 380-392 (3d ed. 1998). *See also* Brainerd Currie, *The Growth of the Long Arm: Eight Years of Extended Jurisdiction in Illinois,* 1963 U. ILL. L. F. 533 (1963).

### [B]   The California Style Long-Arm Statute

California's long-arm statute reads as follows: "A court of this state may exercise jurisdiction on any basis not inconsistent with the Constitution of this state or of the United States." CAL. CIV. PROC. CODE § 410.10 (West 1973). The statute is simplicity itself; it tells the state courts to exercise jurisdiction to the fullest extent possible without violating the Due Process Clause. In other words, it puts no state-law-generated limits on the jurisdiction of state courts.

The argument for the California style statute is based on its simplicity and thoroughness. Because of the statute's simplicity, the court need not engage in any statutory construction at all. When faced with a jurisdictional challenge, it simply proceeds to the due process issue. If jurisdiction is constitutionally permissible, the statutory test is also satisfied. The thoroughness of the California type statute becomes apparent when compared to a typical enumerated act statute. The latter may fail to reach some defendants, who would be amenable under the Due Process Clause, because the defendant has not committed one of the statute's enumerated acts. Even careful legislative drafting cannot foresee all the possible constitutionally permissible jurisdictional bases. To rectify this, some states with enumerated act statutes have added catchall "any constitutional basis" provisions to the list of specific statutory bases.

The argument against the California style statute is based on vagueness and notice. The statute does not notify potential defendants specifically of the types of conduct that will render them amenable to the forum's jurisdiction. How serious is that concern? Do persons, natural or legal, often alter their primary conduct because of jurisdictional rules, or does this argument magnify the importance of lawyers' distinctions to the rest of the world? On the other hand, the Supreme Court in *World-Wide Volkswagen,* § 3.10, *supra,* indicated that the foreseeability of defendant's being haled into court is a crucial constitutional yardstick. Do statutes of the California type reduce the ability of defendants to foresee the jurisdictional consequences of their actions? For arguments for and against the California style statute, see RUSSELL WEINTRAUB, COMMENTARY ON THE CONFLICT OF LAWS § 4.9A (4th ed. 2001), Robert Leflar, *Barely Fair, Not Grossly Unjust,* 25 S.C.L. REV. 177 (1973).

## [C]  Enumerated Act Statutes

## UNIFORM INTERSTATE AND INTERNATIONAL PROCEDURE ACT

*13 U. L. A. 461 (1979)*

§ 1.03 [Personal Jurisdiction Based Upon Conduct]

  (a)  A court may exercise personal jurisdiction over a person, who acts directly or by an agent as to a [cause of action][claim for relief] arising from the person's

   (1)  transacting any business in this state;

   (2)  contracting to supply services or things in this state;

   (3)  causing tortious injury by an act or omission in this state;

(4)   causing tortious injury in this state by an act or omission outside this state if he regularly does or solicits business, or engages in any other persistent course of conduct, or derives substantial revenue from goods used or consumed or services rendered, in this state; or

(5)   having an interest in, using, or possessing real property in this state; or

(6)   contracting to insure any person, property, or risk located within this state at the time of contracting.

(b)   When jurisdiction over a person is based solely upon this section, only a [cause of action] [claim for relief] arising from acts enumerated in this section may be asserted against him.

## [D]   The Long Arm in Federal Court

## FEDERAL RULE OF CIVIL PROCEDURE 4(k)

(k)   Territorial Limits of Effective Service

(1)   Service of a summons or filing a waiver of service is effective to establish jurisdiction over the person of a defendant

(A)   who could be subjected to the jurisdiction of a court of general jurisdiction in the state in which the district court is located, or

(B)   who is a party joined under Rule 14 or Rule 19 and is served at a place within a judicial district of the United States and not more than 100 miles from the place from which the summons issues, or

(C)   who is subject to the federal interpleader jurisdiction under 28 U.S.C. § 1335, or

(D)   when authorized by a statute of the United States.

(2)   If the exercise of jurisdiction is consistent with the Constitution and laws of the United States, serving a summons or filing a waiver of service is also effective, with respect to claims arising under federal law, to establish personal jurisdiction over the person of any defendant who is not subject to the jurisdiction of the courts of general jurisdiction of any state.

---

## NOTES AND QUESTIONS ON STATE AND FEDERAL LONG-ARM PROVISIONS

(1) *Reference.* For section-by-section analysis of the Uniform Act, see WILLIAM RICHMAN & WILLIAM REYNOLDS, UNDERSTANDING CONFLICT OF LAWS § 33 (3d ed. 2002). Long-arm statutes are treated exhaustively in 1 ROBERT

CASAD & WILLIAM RICHMAN, JURISDICTION IN CIVIL ACTIONS 379-524 (3d ed. 1998).

(2) *General or Specific Jurisdiction.* Does the statute provide for the exercise of specific or general jurisdiction? What language in the statute makes this clear?

(3) *The Constitutional Limits.* Many courts have held that statutes patterned on § 1.03 of the Act were intended by the legislature to extend the state's jurisdiction to the outer limits of the Due Process Clause. For those courts, jurisdictional analysis is a one-step procedure; ignoring the language of the statute, they simply proceed to test the court's jurisdiction under the Supreme Court's constitutional standards. *See, e.g., Dwyer v. District Court,* 188 Colo. 41, 532 P.2d 725, 726 (1975).

As a matter of statutory construction, does this one-step analysis make sense? Why would a legislature use a complicated enumerated act statute to achieve the same result that the California statute reaches with only 24 words? One commentary suggests that opinions that interpret an enumerated act statute to reach to the limits of due process should not be read too literally. They may mean only that the specific provisions of the statute (the enumerated acts) should be very broadly construed. ROBERT LEFLAR, LUTHER McDOUGAL & ROBERT FELIX, AMERICAN CONFLICTS LAW 103 (4th ed. 1986).

(4) *Jurisdiction and the Merits.* Because of the language of the statute, the merits of plaintiff's claim can become entangled with the jurisdictional issue. For instance, when the statute enumerates causing "tortious injury in the state" as a jurisdictional basis, the same factual question—did defendant tortiously injure plaintiff—controls both the jurisdictional issue and the substantive merits of the claim. Does this mean that the merits of plaintiff's claim must be tried in order to determine whether the court has jurisdiction? Suppose that it does, and suppose further that defendant prevails on the merits: what kind of dismissal should the court order? If, on the one hand, it dismisses based upon a lack of jurisdiction, what will be the claim preclusive effect of defendant's victory? If, on the other hand, the court dismisses on the merits, will it have decided the merits of a claim over which, by its own findings, it had no jurisdiction?

A sensible approach to this conundrum is for the court to rule that the jurisdictional requirement that defendant cause "tortious injury in this state" is satisfied as soon as plaintiff can prove that defendant committed some act that affected the plaintiff in the forum; whether the act was "tortious" and "caused" an effect on plaintiff, and whether that effect constitutes "injury" are questions that should await a trial on the merits. *See Nelson v. Miller,* 11 Ill. 2d 378, 143 N.E.2d 673 (1957); 1 Casad & Richman, *supra* note 1, at 444-445.

(5) *Transacting business in the state (§ 1.03(a)(1)).*

(a) The statutory phrase "transacting any business" should not be confused with the earlier traditional formula "doing business." "Doing business" has been defined traditionally as activity of a systematic and continuous nature; because of the extensive contact required, it may be sufficient as a basis for general jurisdiction. "Transacting business," by contrast, serves only as a basis for specific jurisdiction; consequently it requires significantly less contact between the defendant and the forum.

(b) How much forum-directed activity is required for defendant to be transacting business? Some courts have taken an extremely expansive view. In *Parke-Bernet Galleries, Inc. v. Franklyn,* 26 N.Y.2d 13, 308 N.E.2d 337, 256 N.Y.S.2d 506 (1970), for example, the court held that a California defendant had "transacted business" in New York by making long-distance telephone bids in an auction held in New York. Not all courts have been so liberal. Some have found no transaction of business even when defendant had significant business dealings with a plaintiff based in the forum. *See, e.g., Scullin Steel v. Nat'l Ry. Utilization Corp.,* 676 F.2d 309 (8th Cir. 1982).

A fact pattern that occurs frequently involves a forum-based buyer who has commercial dealings with an out-of-state seller, primarily by telephone and mail. Are such contacts by the defendant with the forum sufficient to conclude that seller is "transacting business in the forum"? What should the crucial factual variables be? Based on a survey of the cases, the leading study on long-arm jurisdiction concludes that the key variables are whether the seller or his agents have physically entered the forum during negotiations and whether the seller initiated contact with the buyer or vice versa. 1 Casad & Richman, *supra* note 1, at 399-405. Should it matter if the positions of the buyer and seller are reversed, with a forum seller attempting to assert jurisdiction over an out-of-state buyer? For a discussion of the relevance of initiation and of the buyer-seller distinction, see Richman & Reynolds, *supra* note 1, at § 37[f].

Is advertising in the state enough to constitute transacting business? Suppose defendant, an automobile dealer in Missouri, advertises in Oklahoma. Plaintiff, a resident of Oklahoma, travels to Missouri and purchases a car which turns out to be defective. Can plaintiff maintain a warranty action against defendant in Oklahoma based on the theory that defendant's advertising there constitutes transacting business? *See Acme Equip. Co. v. Metro Auto Auction of Kansas City, Inc.,* 484 F. Supp. 219 (W.D. Okla. 1979).

(c) Should "transacting business" be interpreted in terms of formal commercial law? In a transcontinental mail or telephone deal, should it matter where the contract was made or where title passed? What answer would you expect from a court that adhered to the vested rights theory of choice of law? *See* § 4.05, *infra.* A more modern, less formalistic court offered this observation:

> Commendable advocacy on both sides has been expended in an attempt to define the place where and the time when title passed, who paid the freight, who had the risk of loss, and which end of the transcontinental telephone conversation marked the point where the contract was made . . . .

> Here, the state's jurisdiction to try a case has been challenged on grounds of fairness and justice. The meaningful inquiry, therefore, is whether a foreign purchaser has produced effects in the forum of such significance that it is not manifestly unfair to require him to resolve a resulting legal dispute in this state.

*State ex rel. White Lumber Sales, Inc. v. Sulmonetti,* 252 Or. 121, 448 P.2d 57 1, 572-573 (1968).

(d) Review the facts in *Burger King v. Rudzewicz*, § 3.10, *supra*. Did the defendant transact any business in Florida?

(6) *Contracting to supply services or things in this state (§ 1.03(a)(2)).*

There is substantial overlap between this section and the preceding provision. Often a defendant who contracts to supply services or things in the forum does so by transacting business there. The present section, however, also reaches the defendant who makes an agreement outside the state to supply goods or services within the state. Thus, the language of the statute makes it irrelevant that the contract was negotiated or executed elsewhere. *E.g., Droukas v. Divers Training Academy, Inc.*, 375 Mass. 149, 376 N.E.2d 548, 553 (1978).

Further, the statute does not require that performance be rendered in the forum. Indeed, there is no requirement that defendant or his agents have entered the state. *E.g., Snyder v. Hampton Indus., Inc.*, 521 F. Supp. 130, 145 (D. Md. 1981). Suppose buyer, a resident of the forum, travels several thousand miles to seller's place of business and contracts for seller to supply widgets in the forum. Seller, who has had no other contact with the forum, breaches and does not deliver the widgets. Buyer sues seller for breach of contract in the forum. Does this long-arm provision apply? If it does, would the exercise of jurisdiction over seller pass muster under the Due Process Clause?

(7) *Causing tortious injury by an act or omission in this state (§ 1.03(a)(3)).*

(a) This provision is the lineal descendant of the old non-resident motorist statutes upheld in cases like *Hess v. Pawloski,* 274 U.S. 352 (1927), and is designed to reach a defendant who drives a car into the forum and causes tortious injury there. The statute does not require, however, that the injury occur in the forum; thus, the statute reaches a defendant whose tortious act *in the forum* (say negligent manufacture of a product) causes injury *outside the forum.* Uniform Interstate and International Procedure Act, § 1.03, Commissioner's Comments, 13 U.L.A. 468 (1986). Would the exercise of jurisdiction in such a case violate the Due Process Clause? Did defendant purposefully avail itself of the opportunity of conducting activities in the forum?

(b) The statute uses the phrase "tortious injury." Does that language limit its application to common law torts, or does it also cover other wrongs such as copyright and patent infringement and antitrust violations? Note also that the statute applies to an "act or omission." Less precise statutes refer only to "tortious acts" leaving the courts with the question of whether tortious nonfeasance constitutes a tortious act. *See* 1 Casad & Richman, *supra* note 1, at 440-444, for cases that treat the issues raised in this note.

(8) *Causing tortious injury in this state by an act or omission outside this state (§ 1.03(a)(4)).*

(a) The statute covers a defendant who performs an act outside the state that causes injury inside the state. Thus it reaches the typical products liability case in which defendant manufactures a defective product outside the state, and sends it either directly or through middle-men to the forum where it injures plaintiff, a consumer.

The reason the statute is so precise in separating the tort into the foreign act and local injury is that less precise statutes produced problems of interpretation. Consider, for example, *Gray v. American Radiator & Standard Sanitary Corp.,* 22 Ill. 2d 432, 176 N.E.2d 761 (1961), in which the statute provided for jurisdiction over a defendant who "commits a tortious act within the State." *Gray* involved a foreign act (manufacture of a defective product) that produced a local injury, creating a difficult problem of statutory construction. Was the "tortious act" committed in Ohio where the product was made or Illinois where the defective product caused injury? The court dealt with the problem by using the venerable choice-of-law rule that "the place of a wrong is where the last event takes place which is necessary to render the actor liable." Thus, the defendant "committed a tortious act" in Illinois because plaintiffs injury there was the last event necessary to produce liability.

Not all courts followed the approach in *Gray,* however. For example, in *Feathers v. McLucas,* 15 N.Y.2d 443, 209 N.E.2d 68, 261 N.Y.S.2d 8, *cert. denied,* 382 U.S. 905 (1965), the Court of Appeals of New York held that New York's long-arm statute, which required a "tortious act within the state," could not reach the foreign act/local injury situation. The statutory construction issue that split the *Gray* and *Feathers* courts is eliminated by the more careful wording of § 1.03(a) (4). By separating the tort into the foreign act and local injury, the statute removes the need to ask the question: Where was the tort?

With the ambiguity thus removed, the first clause of the section is very expansive. It grants jurisdiction over a defendant whose acts *anywhere* cause injury in the forum. Suppose a manufacturer in Maine makes fishing lures for the local market only. One of its products is purchased by a citizen of Maine and given as a gift to a Marylander, who loses it while fishing in Canada. It is found by a visiting Californian who takes it back to California where, because of a defective design, it injures plaintiff. Would the first clause of § 4, standing alone, make the Maine defendant amenable in California, even though he had no contact with California or any other state but Maine, and even though the product arrived in California through pure happenstance? Would such a result be constitutional?

To avoid reaching such cases, the statute requires that there be one of three "additional affiliations" between the defendant and the forum. For jurisdiction to exist under the section, the defendant must either (1) regularly do or solicit business, (2) engage in any other persistent course of conduct, or (3) derive substantial revenue from goods used in the forum. How does the requirement for an "additional affiliation" eliminate cases like the Maine fishing lure maker? What effect does the "additional affiliation" requirement have on the typical product liability case, in which the product that injured plaintiff is part of a stream of defendant's products that flows into the state?

(b) A useful exercise is to apply this provision to the facts of the Supreme Court's well known due process cases: *World-Wide, Keeton, Calder,* and *Asahi,* all in § 3.10 *supra.* Does the statute provide for jurisdiction in those cases? In *World-Wide,* the Supreme Court of Oklahoma held that the statute created jurisdiction over the New York Audi dealer and the New York distributor:

> In the case before us, the product being sold and distributed by the petitioners is by its very design and purpose so mobile that petitioners

can foresee its possible use in Oklahoma. This is especially true of the distributor, who has the exclusive right to distribute such automobile in New York, New Jersey and Connecticut. The evidence presented below demonstrated that goods sold and distributed by the petitioners were used in the State of Oklahoma, and under the facts we believe it reasonable to infer, given the retail value of the automobile, that the petitioners derive substantial income from automobiles which from time to time are used in the State of Oklahoma.

*World-Wide Volkswagen Corp v. Woodson,* 585 P.2d 351, 354 (1978). Was the court right? Were the dealer and the distributor deriving substantial revenue from goods used or consumed in Oklahoma?

(c) An interesting variation on the foreign act-local injury theory is the case in which the death of the victim (a forum resident) is caused outside the forum by defendant's negligent acts or omissions. Can plaintiff, the victim's spouse, successfully assert jurisdiction over defendant in a wrongful death action in the forum on the theory that defendant committed a tortious act outside the forum that caused financial injury and loss of companionship in the forum? *See, e.g., Von Seggern v. Saikin,* 187 Neb. 315, 189 N.W.2d 512 (1971); 1 Casad & Richman, *supra* note 1, at 466-469.

(d) In addition to the tort theory, product liability plaintiffs often assert claims based on breach of warranty. Accordingly, some state statutes have a variation on § 103(a)(4) providing for jurisdiction over a defendant who causes "injury in this state to any person by breach of warranty expressly or impliedly made in the sale of goods outside this state." *See, e.g.,* Ohio R. Civ. P. 4.3(5).

(9) *Having an interest in, using, or possessing real property in this state (§ 1.03(a)(5)).*

(a) Section (a)(5) provides for jurisdiction over the defendant in any cause of action arising out of defendant's ownership, use, or possession of real property in the state. An exercise of jurisdiction under this section almost always will be constitutional. Is that because an absentee landowner can almost always anticipate being "haled into court" in the situs state to defend a claim relating to the land, because such a defendant avails herself of the benefits and protection of the law of the situs, or because the situs state has such a strong interest in regulation of title, use and possession of land within its borders?

(b) The statute provides for jurisdiction in a wide variety of cases having to do with land: cases having to do with conveyances including sale, purchase, lease and mortgage; cases sounding in contract such as real estate listing agreements, and contracts to perform work or services on the property; and tort cases such as those involving injury to persons on the property (slip and fall) or misrepresentations made surrounding the sale of the property. A useful collection of cases construing the reach of the statute appears in Leflar, McDougal & Felix, *supra* note 3 at § 4.

(c) What type of jurisdiction does the court acquire under this statute—in personam or in rem? What practical difference does it make? If jurisdiction is based upon this section, when must the defendant have an interest in the property, at the time of the commencement of the suit or at the time the cause of action arose? *See* Richman & Reynolds, *supra* note 1, at § 33[c].

(10) *Contracting to insure any person, property, or risk located within this state at the time of contracting (§ 1. 03(a)(6)).*

This provision, incorporated in many state long-arm statutes, is sometimes referred to as a foreign insurers process act. Note that the contract may be negotiated and executed elsewhere, and by interstate or international communication, so long as the risk insured is within the forum. Further jurisdiction can be sustained even if the defendant has insured only one risk in the forum. A collection of cases liberally applying this provision can be found in 2 Casad & Richman, *supra* note 1, at 202-211.

Why is it constitutionally permissible for jurisdiction to be so expansive here? Surely one who insures a risk in the forum can "anticipate being haled into court there;" that basically is what the insurance business is all about. Also, the forum state has a strong interest in regulating out-of-state insurers to make sure that its citizens are not bilked by them. This latter argument carried the day in *McGee v. International Life Insurance Co.,* 355 U.S. 220 (1957), § 3.07, *supra,* the most expansive exercise of jurisdiction ever permitted by the Supreme Court. For general commentary on *McGee* and this provision, see Richman & Reynolds, *supra* note 1, at §§ 20[b], 33[c].

(11) *Federal Rule 4(k).* The current version of Rule 4, unlike earlier versions, separates the problems of basis and notice. The notice provisions of the rule— Rules 4(d), 4(e), and 4(f)—permit service on or solicitation of a waiver of service from a defendant anywhere in the world. Rule 4(k) then provides that service or waiver is sufficient to establish jurisdiction over a defendant only in the circumstance specified in subsections 4(k)(1)(A)-(D) and 4(k)(2).

(a) Rule 4(k)(1)(A) permits a federal court to exercise jurisdiction over the person of a defendant "who could be subjected to the jurisdiction of a court of general jurisdiction in the state in which the district court is located." This provision permits the exercise of jurisdiction over a defendant who would be subject to general jurisdiction, or long-arm (specific) jurisdiction in the state courts. Should the constitutional test for an exercise of jurisdiction under this provision require minimum contacts between the defendant *and the forum state* or is it sufficient that the defendant have minimum contacts with the United States as a whole? Should the answer be the same for federal question and diversity cases? These issues are treated fully in 1 Casad & Richman, *supra* note 1, at 551-560.

(b) Rule 4(k)(1)(B) permits the court to exercise personal jurisdiction over a party impleaded under Rule 14 or joined pursuant to Rule 19 as a person needed for a just adjudication if the party is served (or waives service) in the United States and within 100 miles of the federal courthouse where the action is pending. The bulge provision applies whether the case rests on federal question, diversity, or admiralty jurisdiction. The constitutional test for jurisdiction under the bulge provision is minimum contacts with either the forum state or the bulge state.

(c) Rule 4(k)(1)(D) provides that service or waiver of service is effective to establish jurisdiction over the person of a defendant "when authorized by a statute of the United States." This provision refers to federal statutes that provide for nation-wide or world-wide territorial jurisdiction for particular types of cases. Subdivision (C), which provides for jurisdiction over a defendant "who is subject to the federal interpleader jurisdiction under 28 USC § 1335," is thus superfluous. Interpleader jurisdiction is permitted, after all, by the Federal Interpleader Act, which is a federal statute and so comes within the terms of subsection (D). Presumably either subsection is satisfied by minimum contacts with the United States as a whole.

(d) Rule 4(k)(2) provides that service or waiver of service is sufficient to generate jurisdiction over defendants who are not subject to personal jurisdiction in any state court, in cases "arising under federal law," provided only that the assertion of jurisdiction is consistent with the constitution and federal law. Why is there a need for such a provision? What classes of defendants does it target? What about an alien that has diffuse contacts with the United States as a whole but lacks sufficient minimum contacts with any one state? What about an alien that has sufficient contacts with a state but falls outside the terms of the state's long-arm statute? Could this provision reach a citizen living abroad, who lacks minimum contacts with any state? Why is this section limited to cases arising under federal law?

The constitutional limitation on an assertion of jurisdiction under Rule 4(k)(2) comes from the Fifth Amendment, not the Fourteenth, and requires minimum contacts with the United States as a whole, rather than with the forum state. Further, the Fifth Amendment, like the Fourteenth, also prohibits the assertion of jurisdiction if the forum is so inconvenient to the defendant as to constitute a denial of "fair play and substantial justice" in spite of the defendant's minimum contacts with the United States. Remember *Asahi,* see § 3.10, *supra.*

The issues raised in this note are treated in detail in 1 Casad & Richman, *supra* note 1, at 551-560. *See also* David D. Siegel, *Supplementary Practice Commentaries*, FED. RULES CIV. PROC. Rule 4, 28 USCA 83-84 (1998 Pocket Part).

# PART E   JURISDICTION BASED ON PROPERTY

## § 3.14   The Traditional Taxonomy

### [A]   Jurisdiction In Rem and Jurisdiction In Personam

The territorial power theory of *Pennoyer v. Neff,* 95 U.S. 714 (1877), distinguished strictly between in personam jurisdiction and in rem jurisdiction. A court with in personam jurisdiction could bind the persons who were before it, while a court with in rem jurisdiction could bind only the property before it. Real consequences turned on this formal distinction. Notice requirements for in rem actions were considerably more lenient, and a court could exercise in rem jurisdiction over a piece of defendant's property in the forum even though the defendant had no other contact with the state.

The formal distinction lost some of its significance as jurisdictional theory matured. It became clear that every exercise of jurisdiction, whether styled "in rem" or "in personam" affects the interests of persons. *See* RESTATEMENT (SECOND) OF JUDGMENTS § 5, cmt. b (1982). Accordingly, the Supreme Court held in *Mullane v. Central Hanover Bank & Trust Co.,* 339 U.S. 306 (1950), and its progeny that the constitutional adequacy of notice-giving provisions does not depend on whether the action is in rem or in personam. Further in *Shaffer v. Heitner,* 433 U.S. 186 (1977), the Court held that every exercise of jurisdiction—in personam or in rem—must satisfy the "minimum contacts . . . fair play and substantial justice" standard of *International Shoe.*

Despite these developments, the in rem/in personam distinction retains descriptive as well as historical significance. It describes two very different ways in which a court can affect the interests of persons. *See* RESTATEMENT (SECOND) OF CONFLICT OF LAWS, ch. 3, topic 2, introductory n. (1971). The best way to understand the concepts is to concentrate on the different effects of in rem and in personam judgments.

A court exercising personal jurisdiction over a defendant can issue a judgment against him for any kind of legal or equitable relief. If plaintiff's claim is for damages, the court can issue a general money judgment that plaintiff can satisfy out of any property of defendant's within the forum. Further, the Full Faith and Credit Clause permits plaintiff to sue on the judgment debt in any other state and satisfy it out of defendant's property there. If, on the other hand, plaintiff's claim is for equitable relief, a court with personal jurisdiction over the defendant can order him to do or refrain from doing any act on pain of contempt. Thus, a court exercising personal jurisdiction can affect defendant profoundly and can give plaintiff any type of relief available under the substantive law.

A court exercising in rem jurisdiction acts in a much more limited fashion. It affects a defendant only by terminating his interest in the particular piece of property over which it has asserted jurisdiction. It cannot issue a general money judgment against him, nor can it grant equitable relief. From a plaintiff's point of view, therefore, in rem jurisdiction *usually* will be a second choice because the only relief an in rem judgment can grant plaintiff is to establish her title to the particular piece of property or order the property sold and the proceeds paid to her. Thus, if plaintiff's claim exceeds the value of the property over which the court exercises jurisdiction, an in rem judgment can give plaintiff only partial relief. *See* WILLIAM RICHMAN & WILLIAM REYNOLDS, UNDERSTANDING CONFLICT OF LAWS § 41 (3d ed. 2002). When might a plaintiff nevertheless prefer in rem to in personam jurisdiction?

## [B]  Jurisdiction In Rem, Jurisdiction Quasi-In-Rem and Attachment Jurisdiction

The traditional learning divided jurisdiction over property into three sub-classes: "true in rem" (often called, simply "in rem"), "quasi-in-rem type I," and "quasi-in-rem type II" (now usually called "attachment jurisdiction").

In a true in rem action, the court determines the interests of everyone, whether named in the proceedings or not, in the particular *res* or thing. In essence, the action is one "against all the world." RESTATEMENT (SECOND) OF JUDGMENTS § 6, cmt. a (1982). The practical effect of such a proceeding is to establish relatively unassailable title in the thing because no one, whether named as a party or not, can later claim exemption from the effect of the judgment on the ground that the court lacked personal jurisdiction.[1] Traditional examples of in rem actions are admiralty, forfeiture, eminent domain, probate, and land title registration, actions in which it is crucial that the court be able to extinguish the interests of persons who may be outside the forum's territory or whose interests, or even existence, may be unknown.

In a quasi-in-rem type I action, plaintiff asserts a pre-existing interest in a particular thing against certain named individuals only, and the judgment affects only the interests of the named parties, not those of "all the world." An example of such an action is a suit to remove a cloud on title, an action where plaintiff seeks to establish the right to the land against a particular person's rival claim.

The analytical significance of the distinction between in rem and quasi-in-rem jurisdiction has all but vanished. The constitutional prerequisites are the same in both cases. In both instances there must be a relationship between the forum and the *res* or thing sufficient to make the exercise of jurisdiction reasonable. RESTATEMENT (SECOND) OF JUDGMENTS § 6, cmt. a (1982). (Usually the presence of the thing in the state will suffice.) And in both, all persons likely to be affected are entitled to adequate notice. In a quasi-in-rem action that requirement means notice to the named parties, while in a true in rem action it means notice to everyone whose interest in the thing is known and reasonable efforts to insure that other interested persons will learn of the action. Thus, apart from any consequences state law attaches to the labels, the distinction between in-rem and quasi-in-rem type I jurisdiction has only historical significance.[2]

---

[1] RESTATEMENT (SECOND) OF CONFLICT OF LAWS, ch. 3, topic 2, introductory n. (1971). A latecomer could, however, assert the lack of proper notice. *See* Mullane v. Cent. Hanover Bank and Trust Co., 339 U.S. 306 (1950); Schroeder v. City of New York, 371 U.S. 208 (1962).

[2] The American Law Institute has abandoned the distinction completely. *See* Restatement (Second) of Conflict of Laws (1986 Revisions) § 6, cmt. a.

Quasi-in-rem type II jurisdiction (now more commonly called "attachment jurisdiction") is quite different. In both a true in rem action and in a quasi-in-rem type I action, plaintiff has a pre-existing claim to the *res* or thing, and that claim is the subject of the action. RESTATEMENT (SECOND) OF CONFLICT OF LAWS § 66, cmt. a (1986 Revisions). In other words, plaintiff asserts an interest in the thing, and the court adjudicates that claim. By contrast, in an attachment action, plaintiff does not assert a pre-existing interest in the thing; indeed the claim often has nothing at all to do with the attached property. Rather, plaintiff asserts a personal claim against defendant (a tort or contract claim, for example) and seeks to apply the thing to the payment of the claim.

## § 3.15    The Development of Attachment Jurisdiction.[3]

In *Pennoyer v. Neff,* 95 U.S. 714 (1978), the Supreme Court articulated the territorial power theory of jurisdiction and, as a corollary, the conceptual basis for attachment jurisdiction.

> Every State owes protection to its own citizens; and, when non-residents deal with them, it is a legitimate and just exercise of authority to hold and appropriate any property owned by such non-residents to satisfy the claims of its citizens. It is in virtue of the State's jurisdiction over the property of the non-resident situated within its limits that its tribunals can inquire into that non-resident's obligations to its own citizens. . . .

With this justification, *Pennoyer* permitted a court, if it attached real property of the defendant at the commencement of the action, to adjudicate a personal claim against the defendant even though there was no personal jurisdiction over her and even though the claim had no relation to the attached property. The principal limitation was that a court with attachment jurisdiction could not issue a personal judgment against the defendant; its power was limited to the authority to award the property to plaintiff or order the property sold and the proceeds paid to satisfy the claim.

When the holding of *Pennoyer* was extended to intangible personal property, it generated a question not raised in cases involving realty or tangibles. What is the *situs* of the intangible? In plain language, *where* is it? The question did not arise with respect to land or tangible personal property because its answer there was so obvious. The question of situs was crucial because the situs of the intangible determined which state could exercise jurisdiction over it. Thus, the issue of situs provided an opportunity to expand or contract the scope of attachment jurisdiction.

––––––––––

**HARRIS v. BALK,** 198 U.S. 215 (1905). Action by Epstein in Maryland against Balk, a domiciliary of North Carolina, for $344. The court acquired

---

[3] A full treatment of the historical development appears in Joseph Kalo, *Jurisdiction as an Evolutionary Process: The Development of Quasi-in-Rem and In Personam Principles,* 1978 DUKE L.J. 1147.

jurisdiction by personal service upon Harris, Balk's debtor, thus garnishing the debt ($180) Harris owed Balk. Pursuant to the court's order, Harris paid the $180 to Epstein and returned to his residence in North Carolina. Balk then sued Harris in North Carolina for the $180 debt. Harris relied on the Maryland judgment, which Balk attacked for lack of jurisdiction. Balk argued that the situs of the debt (his intangible personal property) was in North Carolina, not Maryland, where it was supposedly garnished.

*Held.* The Maryland court had attachment jurisdiction over Balk's property (the debt). "The obligation of the debtor to pay his debt clings to and accompanies him wherever he goes." The obligation represents intangible personal property of the *creditor,* which (according to *Pennoyer)* provides a basis for attachment jurisdiction, even though the creditor has no connection with the forum state.

---

**SEIDER v. ROTH,** 17 N.Y.2d 111, 269 N.E.2d 312, 216 N.Y.S.2d 99 (1966). Plaintiff, a New Yorker, was injured in an automobile accident in Vermont by Lemiux, a resident of Quebec. Lemiux had no contact with New York sufficient to support an exercise of in personam jurisdiction, nor did he have any real or tangible personal property in New York upon which to base attachment jurisdiction. The court obtained jurisdiction by attaching Lemiux's liability insurance policy with the Hartford Accident and Indemnity Company, which was doing business in New York.

*Held.* Hartford's obligation to defend and indemnify Lemiux constituted a "debt" to Lemiux and was, therefore, "property" of his which could be garnished by service on Hartford to provide the basis for an attachment action.

---

## NOTES ON *HARRIS* AND *SEIDER*

(1) *The Practical Effect of Harris.* The holding in *Harris* turned attachment jurisdiction into a very potent instrument of unfairness. Its practical effect was to make all debtors their creditors' agents for receipt of service of process. The creditor had to be prepared to defend an attachment action in any forum where the debtor could be found, even though the creditor had no contact with the forum and even though the attached property (the debt) had no relationship to plaintiff's claim. For example, a person who had a savings account in a bank in a distant state could be forced to defend any cause of action in the distant state. In the commercial context, a supplier was amenable to attachment jurisdiction in the home state of any customer who purchased on credit terms. Nevertheless, some courts pushed the concept even further.

(2) *Attaching Defendant's Insurance Policy.* Note that in *Seider* Lemiux's insurance policy was an even more ephemeral sort of property than the debt in *Harris.* In *Harris,* at least the debt was an unconditional obligation, while in *Seider,* the "debt" was conditioned upon the existence of Lemiux's liability, a fact not yet determined.

(3) *The Unfairness of Attachment Jurisdiction.* Comparison of *Seider* to *Harris* and both to *Pennoyer* shows how the exercise of attachment jurisdiction expanded from tangible property to intangible property to property whose existence was merely contingent. This steadily attenuating notion of property created a substantial possibility of unfairness to defendants. In the years before *International Shoe,* the expansive reach of attachment jurisdiction may have been worth that price because the concept operated as a proto-long-arm statute, allowing plaintiffs to sue out-of-state defendants who could not be reached under the restrictive territorial power theory. *See* Linda Silberman, *Commentaries on* Shaffer v. Heitner: *The End of an Era,* 53 N.Y.U. L. REV. 33, 48 (1978). But after *International Shoe* and the rise of state long-arm statutes, the expansive view of attachment jurisdiction was no longer necessary to assure fairness to plaintiffs. The remaining possibility of unfairness to defendants eventually attracted the attention of the Supreme Court.

## § 3.16   The In Rem Revolution

### SHAFFER v. HEITNER

*United States Supreme Court*
*433 U.S. 186, 97 S. Ct. 2569, 53 L. Ed. 2d 683 (1977)*

MR. JUSTICE MARSHALL delivered the opinion of the Court.

The controversy in this case concerns the constitutionality of a Delaware statute that allows a court of that State to take jurisdiction of a lawsuit by sequestering any property of the defendant that happens to be located in Delaware. Appellants contend that the sequestration statute as applied in this case violates the Due Process Clause of the Fourteenth Amendment . . . because it permits the state courts to exercise jurisdiction despite the absence of sufficient contacts among the defendants, the litigation, and the State of Delaware. . . .

### I

Appellee Heitner, a nonresident of Delaware, is the owner of one share of stock in the Greyhound Corp., a business incorporated under the laws of Delaware with its principal place of business in Phoenix, Ariz. [H]e filed a shareholder's derivative suit in the Court of Chancery for New Castle County, Del., in which he named as defendants Greyhound . . . and 28 [of its] present or former officers or directors. . . .In essence, Heitner alleged that the individual defendants had violated their duties to Greyhound by causing it . . . to engage in actions that resulted in the corporation being held liable for substantial damages in a private antitrust suit and a large fine in a criminal contempt action. The activities which led to these penalties took place in Oregon.

Simultaneously with his complaint, Heitner filed a motion for an order of sequestration of the Delaware property of the individual defendants pursuant to Del. Code Ann., Tit. 10, § 366 (1975). . . .The requested sequestration order was signed the day the motion was filed. Pursuant to that order, the sequestrator "seized" approximately 82,000 shares of Greyhound common stock belonging to 19 of the defendants, and options belonging to another 2 defendants. These seizures were accomplished by placing "stop transfer" orders or their equivalents on the books of the Greyhound Corp. So far as the record, shows, none of the certificates representing the seized property was physically present in Delaware. The stock was considered to be in Delaware, and so subject to seizure, by virtue of Del. Code Ann., Tit. 8, § 169 (1975), which makes Delaware the situs of ownership of all stock in Delaware corporations.[9]

All 28 defendants were notified of the initiation of the suit by certified mail . . . and by publication. . . . The 21 defendants whose property was seized (hereafter referred to as appellants) responded by entering a special appearance for the purpose of moving to quash service of process and to vacate the sequestration order. They contended that . . . under the rule of *International Shoe Co. v. Washington,* 326 U.S. 310 (1945), they did not have sufficient contacts with Delaware to sustain the jurisdiction of that State's courts. . . .

## II

The Delaware courts rejected appellants jurisdictional challenge by noting that this suit was brought as a *quasi in rem* proceeding. Since *quasi in rem* jurisdiction is traditionally based on attachment or seizure of property present in the jurisdiction, not on contacts between the defendant and the State, the courts considered appellants' claimed lack of contacts with Delaware to be unimportant. This categorical analysis assumes the continued soundness of the conceptual structure founded on the century-old case of *Pennoyer v. Neff,* 95 U.S. 714 (1878). . . .

From our perspective, the importance of *Pennoyer* is not its result, but the fact that its principles . . . became the basic elements of the constitutional doctrine governing state-court jurisdiction. As we have noted, under *Pennoyer* state authority to adjudicate was based on the jurisdiction's power over either persons or property. This fundamental concept is embodied in the very vocabulary which we use to describe judgments. If a court's jurisdiction is based on its authority over the defendant's person, the action and judgment are denominated *"in personam"* and can impose a personal obligation on the defendant in favor of the plaintiff. If jurisdiction is based on the court's power over property within its territory, the action is called *"in rem" or "quasi in rem."* The effect of a judgment in such a case is limited to the property that supports jurisdiction and does not impose a personal liability on the property owner, since he is not before the court. . . .

By concluding that "[t]he authority of every tribunal is necessarily restricted by the territorial limits of the State in which it is established," 95 U.S., at 720, *Pennoyer* sharply limited the availability of *in personam* jurisdiction

---

[9] Section 169 provides:

"For all purposes of title, action, attachment, garnishment and jurisdiction of all courts held in this State, but not for the purpose of taxation, the situs of the ownership of the capital stock of all corporations existing under the laws of this State, whether organized under this chapter or otherwise, shall be regarded as in this State."

over defendants not resident in the forum State. If a nonresident defendant could not be found in a State, he could not be sued there. On the other hand, since the State in which property was located was considered to have exclusive sovereignty over that property, *in rem* actions could proceed regardless of the owner's location. . . .

[The Court then summarized the expansion of personal jurisdiction theory from the territorial power model of *Pennoyer* to the minimum contacts/fairness formulation of *International Shoe. See* p. 38, *supra.* ] Thus, the relationship among the defendant, the forum, and the litigation, rather than the mutually exclusive sovereignty of the States on which the rules of *Pennoyer* rest, became the central concern of the inquiry into personal jurisdiction.[20] The immediate effect of this departure from *Pennoyer's* conceptual apparatus was to increase the ability of the state courts to obtain personal jurisdiction over nonresident defendants.

No equally dramatic change has occurred in the law governing jurisdiction in rem. . . .

We think that the time is ripe to consider whether the standard of fairness and substantial justice set forth in *International Shoe* should be held to govern actions *in rem* as well as *in personam.*

III

The case for applying to jurisdiction *in rem* the same test of "fair play and substantial justice" as governs assertions of jurisdiction *in personam* is simple and straightforward. It is premised on recognition that "[t]he phrase," judicial jurisdiction over a thing,' is a customary elliptical way of referring to jurisdiction over the interests of persons in a thing." RESTATEMENT (SECOND) OF CONFLICT OF LAWS § 56, introductory n. (1971) (hereafter Restatement). This recognition leads to the conclusion that in order to justify an exercise of jurisdiction *in rem,* the basis for jurisdiction must be sufficient to justify exercising "jurisdiction over the interests of persons in a thing."[23] The standard for determining whether an exercise of jurisdiction over the interests of persons is consistent with the Due Process Clause is the minimum-contacts standard elucidated in *International Shoe.*

This argument, of course, does not ignore the fact that the presence of property in a State may bear on the existence of jurisdiction by providing contacts among the forum State, the defendant, and the litigation. For example, when claims to the property itself are the source of the underlying controversy between the plaintiff and the defendant,[24] it would be unusual

---

[20] Nothing in *Hanson v. Denckla,* 357 U.S. 235 (1958), is to the contrary. The *Hanson* Court's statement that restrictions on state jurisdiction "are a consequence of territorial limitations on the power of the respective States," simply makes the point that the States are defined by their geographical territory. After making this point, the Court in *Hanson* determined that the defendant over which personal jurisdiction was claimed had not committed any acts sufficiently connected to the State to justify jurisdiction under the *International Shoe* standard.

[23] It is true that the potential liability of a defendant in an *in rem* action is limited by the value of the property, but that limitation does not affect the argument. The fairness of subjecting a defendant to state-court jurisdiction does not depend on the size of the claim being litigated.

[24] This category includes true *in rem* actions and the first type of *quasi in rem* proceedings.

for the State where the property is located not to have jurisdiction. In such cases, the defendant's claim to property located in the State would normally indicate that he expected to benefit from the State's protection of his interest. The State's strong interests in assuring the marketability of property within its borders and in providing a procedure for peaceful resolution of disputes about the possession of that property would also support jurisdiction, as would the likelihood that important records and witnesses will be found in the State. The presence of property may also favor jurisdiction in cases, such as suits for injury suffered on the land of an absentee owner, where the defendant's ownership of the property is conceded but the cause of action is otherwise related to rights and duties growing out of that ownership.[29]

It appears, therefore, that jurisdiction over many types of actions which now are or might be brought *in rem* would not be affected by a holding that any assertion of state-court jurisdiction must satisfy the *International Shoe* standard.[30] For the type of *quasi in rem* action typified by *Harris v. Balk* and the present case, however, accepting the proposed analysis would result in significant change. These are cases where the property which now serves as the basis for state-court jurisdiction is completely unrelated to the plaintiff's cause of action. Thus, although the presence of the defendant's property in a State might suggest the existence of other ties among the defendant, the State, and the litigation, the presence of the property alone would not support the State's jurisdiction. If those other ties did not exist, cases over which the State is now thought to have jurisdiction could not be brought in that forum.

Since acceptance of the *International Shoe* test would most affect this class of cases, we examine the arguments against adopting that standard as they relate to this category of litigation. Before doing so, however, we, note that this type of case also presents the clearest illustration of the argument in favor of assessing assertions of jurisdiction by a single standard. For in cases such as *Harris* and this one, the only role played by the property is to provide the basis for bringing the defendant into court. Indeed, the express purpose of the Delaware sequestration procedure is to compel the defendant to enter a personal appearance.[33] In such cases, if a direct assertion of personal jurisdiction over the defendant would violate the Constitution, it would seem that an indirect assertion of that jurisdiction should be equally impermissible.

The primary rationale for treating the presence of property as a sufficient basis for jurisdiction to adjudicate claims over which the State would not have jurisdiction if *International Shoe* applied is that a wrongdoer

> should not be able to avoid payment of his obligations by the expedient of removing his assets to a place where he is not subject to an in personam suit.

---

[29] *Cf. Dubin v. Philadelphia*, 34 Pa. D. & C. 61 (1938). If such an action were brought under the *in rem* jurisdiction rather than under a long-statute, it would be a *quasi-in rem* action of the second type.

[30] *Cf.*, Smit, *The Enduring Utility of In Rem Rules: A Lasting Legacy of* Pennoyer v. Neff, 43 BROOK. L. REV. 600 (1977). We do not suggest that jurisdictional doctrines other than those discussed in text, such as the particularized rules governing adjudications of status, are inconsistent with the standard of fairness.

[33] This purpose is emphasized by Delaware's refusal to allow any defense on the merits unless the defendant enters a general appearance, thus submitting to full *in personam* liability.

RESTATEMENT § 66, cmt. a. This justification, however, does not explain why jurisdiction should be recognized without regard to whether the property is present in the State because of an effort to avoid the owner's obligations. Nor does it support jurisdiction to adjudicate the underlying claim. At most, it suggests that a State in which property is located should have jurisdiction to attach that property, by use of proper procedures, as security for a judgment being sought in a forum where the litigation can be maintained consistently with *International Shoe.* Moreover, we know of nothing to justify the assumption that a debtor can avoid paying his obligations by removing his property to a State in which his creditor cannot obtain personal jurisdiction over him. The Full Faith and Credit Clause, after all, makes the valid *in personam* judgment of one State enforceable in all other States.[36]

It might also be suggested that allowing *in rem* jurisdiction avoids the uncertainty inherent in the *International Shoe* standard and assures a plaintiff of a forum.[37] We believe, however, that the fairness standard of *International Shoe* can be easily applied in the vast majority of cases. Moreover, when the existence of jurisdiction in a particular forum under *International Shoe* is unclear, the cost of simplifying the litigation by avoiding the jurisdictional question may be the sacrifice of "fair play and substantial justice." That cost is too high.

We are left, then, to consider the significance of the long history of jurisdiction based solely on the presence of property in a State. . . . This history must be considered as supporting the proposition that jurisdiction based solely on the presence of property satisfies the demands of due process, but it is not decisive. "[T]raditional notions of fair play and substantial justice" can be as readily offended by the perpetuation of ancient forms that are no longer justified as by the adoption of new procedures that are inconsistent with the basic values of our constitutional heritage. The fiction that an assertion of jurisdiction over property is anything but an assertion of jurisdiction over the owner of the property supports an ancient form without substantial modern justification. Its continued acceptance would serve only to allow state-court jurisdiction that is fundamentally unfair to the defendant.

We therefore conclude that all assertions of state-court jurisdiction must be evaluated according to the standards set forth in *International Shoe* and its progeny.[39]

---

[36] Once it has been determined by a court of competent jurisdiction that the defendant is a debtor of the plaintiff, there would seem to be no unfairness in allowing an action to realize on that debt in a State where the defendant has property, whether or not that State would have jurisdiction to determine the existence of the debt as an original matter.

[37] This case does not raise, and we therefore do not consider, the question whether the presence of a defendant's property in a State is a sufficient basis for jurisdiction when no other forum is available to the plaintiff.

[39] It would not be fruitful for us to re-examine the facts of cases decided on the rationales of *Pennoyer* and *Harris* to determine whether jurisdiction might have been sustained under the standard we adopt today. To the extent that prior decisions are inconsistent with this standard, they are overruled.

## IV

The Delaware courts based their assertion of jurisdiction in this case solely on the statutory presence of appellants' property in Delaware. Yet that property is not the subject matter of this litigation, nor is the underlying cause of action related to the property. Appellants' holdings in Greyhound do not, therefore, provide contacts with Delaware sufficient to support the jurisdiction of that State's courts over appellants. If it exists, that jurisdiction must have some other foundation.

Appellee Heitner did not allege and does not now claim that appellants have ever set foot in Delaware. Nor does he identify any act related to his cause of action as having taken place in Delaware. Nevertheless, he contends that appellants' positions as directors and officers of a corporation chartered in Delaware provide sufficient "contacts, ties, or relations," *International Shoe Co. v. Washington,* 326 U.S., at 319, with that State to give its courts jurisdiction over appellants in this stockholder's derivative action. This argument is based primarily on what Heitner asserts to be the strong interest of Delaware in supervising the management of a Delaware corporation. . . .

This argument is undercut by the failure of the Delaware Legislature to assert the state interest appellee finds so compelling. Delaware law bases jurisdiction, not on appellants' status as corporate fiduciaries, but rather on the presence of their property in the State. . . . Sequestration can be used in any suit against a nonresident, and reaches corporate fiduciaries only if they happen to own interests in a Delaware corporation, or other property in the State . . . .[43] If Delaware perceived its interest in securing jurisdiction over corporate fiduciaries to be as great as Heitner suggests, we would expect it to have enacted a statute more clearly designed to protect that interest.

Moreover, even if Heitner's assessment of the importance of Delaware's interest is accepted, his argument fails to demonstrate that Delaware is a fair forum for this litigation. The interest appellee has identified may support the application of Delaware law to resolve any controversy over appellants' actions in their capacities as officers and directors. But we have rejected the argument that if a State's law can properly be applied to a dispute, its courts necessarily have jurisdiction over the parties to that dispute.

> [The State] does not acquire . . . jurisdiction by being the 'center of gravity' of the controversy, or the most convenient location for litigation. The issue is personal jurisdiction, not choice of law. It is resolved in this case by considering the acts of the [appellants].

*Hanson v. Denckla,* 357 U.S. 235, 254 (1958).

Appellee suggests that by accepting positions as officers or directors of a Delaware corporation, appellants performed the acts required by *Hanson v. Denckla.* He notes that Delaware law provides substantial benefits to corporate officers and directors, and that these benefits were at least in part the incentive for appellants to assume their positions. It is, he says, "only fair and just" to require appellants, in return for these benefits, to respond in the State of Delaware when they are accused of misusing their power.

---

[43] Delaware does not require directors to own stock. DEL. CODE ANN., Tit. 8, § 141(b) (Supp. 1976).

But like Heitner's first argument, this line of reasoning establishes only that it is appropriate for Delaware law to govern the obligations of appellants to Greyhound and its stockholders. It does not demonstrate that appellants have "purposefully avail[ed themselves] of the privilege of conducting activities within the forum State," *Hanson v. Denckla,* in a way that would justify bringing them before a Delaware tribunal. Appellants have simply had nothing to do with the State of Delaware. Moreover, appellants had no reason to expect to be haled before a Delaware court. Delaware, unlike some States, has not enacted a statute that treats acceptance of a directorship as consent to jurisdiction in the State. And "[i]t strains reason . . . to suggest that anyone buying securities in a corporation formed in Delaware 'impliedly consents' to subject himself to Delaware's . . . jurisdiction on any cause of action.". . . .

. . . Delaware's assertion of jurisdiction over appellants in this case is inconsistent with [the *International Shoe* standard]. The judgment of the Delaware Supreme Court must, therefore, be reversed.

Mr. Justice Rehnquist took no part in the consideration or decision of this case.

Mr. Justice Powell, concurring.

I agree that the principles of *International Shoe Co. v. Washington,* 326 U.S. 310 (1945), should be extended to govern assertions of *in rem* as well as *in personam* jurisdiction in a state court. I also agree that neither the statutory presence of appellants' stock in Delaware nor their positions as directors and officers of a Delaware corporation can provide sufficient contacts to support the Delaware courts' assertion of jurisdiction in this case.

I would explicitly reserve judgment, however, on whether the ownership of some forms of property whose situs is indisputably and permanently located within a State may, without more, provide the contacts necessary to subject a defendant to jurisdiction within the State to the extent of the value of the property. In the case of real property, in particular, preservation of the common-law concept of quasi in rem jurisdiction arguably would avoid the uncertainty of the general *International Shoe* standard without significant cost to " 'traditional notions of fair play and substantial justice.' "

Subject to the foregoing reservation, I join the opinion of the Court.

Mr. Justice Stevens, concurring in the judgment. . . .

. . . I . . . agree with the Court that on the record before us no adequate basis for jurisdiction exists and that the Delaware statute is unconstitutional on its face.

How the Court's opinion may be applied in other contexts is not entirely clear to me. I agree with Mr. Justice Powell that it should not be read to invalidate *quasi in rem* jurisdiction where real estate is involved. I would also not read it as invalidating other long-accepted methods of acquiring jurisdiction over persons with adequate notice of both the particular controversy and the fact that their local activities might subject them to suit. My uncertainty as to the reach of the opinion, and my fear that it purports to decide a great deal more than is necessary to dispose of this case, persuade me merely to concur in the judgment.

MR. JUSTICE BRENNAN, concurring in part and dissenting in part.

I join Parts I-III of the Court's opinion. I fully agree that the minimum-contacts analysis developed in *International Shoe Co. v. Washington,* represents a far more sensible construct for the exercise of state-court jurisdiction than the patchwork of legal and factual fictions that has been generated from the decision in *Pennoyer v. Neff.* It is precisely because the inquiry into minimum contacts is now of such overriding importance, however, that I must respectfully dissent from Part IV of the Court's opinion. . . .

. . . I am convinced that as a general rule a state forum has jurisdiction to adjudicate a shareholder derivative action centering on the conduct and policies of the directors and officers of a corporation chartered by that State. Unlike the Court, I therefore would not foreclose Delaware from asserting jurisdiction over appellants were it persuaded to do so on the basis of minimum contacts. . . .

[T]he chartering State has an unusually powerful interest in insuring the availability of a convenient forum for litigating claims involving a possible multiplicity of defendant fiduciaries and for vindicating the State's substantive policies regarding the management of its domestic corporations. I believe that our cases fairly establish that the State's valid substantive interests are important considerations in assessing whether it constitutionally may claim jurisdiction over a given cause of action.

In this instance, Delaware can point to at least three interrelated public policies that are furthered by its assertion of jurisdiction. First, the State has a substantial interest in providing restitution for its local corporations that allegedly have been victimized by fiduciary misconduct, even if the managerial decisions occurred outside the State. . . . Second, state courts have legitimately read their jurisdiction expansively when a cause of action centers in an area in which the forum State possesses a manifest regulatory interest. *E.g., McGee v. Int'l Life Ins. Co.,* 355 U. S. 220 (1957) (insurance regulation); *Travelers Health Ass'n v. Virginia,* 339 U.S. 643 (1950) (blue sky laws). . . . Finally, a State like Delaware has a recognized interest in affording a convenient forum for supervising and overseeing the affairs of an entity that is purely the creation of that State's law.

. . . [T]he Court argues [that these considerations] pertain to choice of law, not jurisdiction. I recognize that the jurisdictional and choice-of-law inquiries are not identical. But I would not compartmentalize thinking in this area quite so rigidly as it seems to me the Court does today, for both inquiries "are often closely related and to a substantial degree depend upon similar considerations." In either case an important linchpin is the extent of contacts between the controversy, the parties, and the forum State. While constitutional limitations on the choice of law are by no means settled, important considerations certainly include the expectancies of the parties and the fairness of governing the defendants' acts and behavior by rules of conduct created by a given jurisdiction. These same factors bear upon the propriety of a State's exercising jurisdiction over a legal dispute. At the minimum, the decision that it is fair to bind a defendant by a State's laws and rules should prove to be highly relevant to the fairness of permitting that same State to accept jurisdiction for adjudicating the controversy.

Furthermore, I believe that practical considerations argue in favor of seeking to bridge the distance between the choice-of-law and jurisdictional inquiries. Even when a court would apply the law of a different forum, as a general rule it will feel less knowledgeable and comfortable in interpretation, and less interested infostering the policies of that foreign jurisdiction, than would the courts established by the State that provides the applicable law. Obviously, such choice-of-law problems cannot entirely be avoided in a diverse legal system such as our own. Nonetheless, when a suitor seeks to lodge a suit in a State with a substantial interest in seeing its own law applied to the transaction in question, we could wisely act to minimize conflicts, confusion, and uncertainty by adopting a liberal view of jurisdiction, unless considerations of fairness or efficiency strongly point in the opposite direction.

This case is not one where, in my judgment, this preference for jurisdiction is adequately answered. Certainly nothing said by the Court persuades me that it would be unfair to subject appellants to suit in Delaware. The fact that the record does not reveal whether they "set foot" or committed "act[s] related to [the] cause of action" in Delaware, is not decisive, for jurisdiction can be based strictly on out-of-state acts having foreseeable effects in the forum State. *E.g., McGee v. Int'l Life Ins. Co.* . . . . Further, I cannot understand how the existence of minimum contacts in a constitutional sense is at all affected by Delaware's failure statutorily to express an interest in controlling corporate fiduciaries. To me this simply demonstrates that Delaware did not elect to assert jurisdiction to the extent the Constitution would allow. Nor would I view as controlling or even especially meaningful Delaware's failure to exact from appellants their consent to be sued. . . .[6]

I, therefore, would approach the minimum-contacts analysis differently than does the Court. Crucial to me is the fact that appellants voluntarily associated themselves with the State of Delaware, "invoking the benefits and protections of its laws," by entering into a long-term and fragile relationship with one of its domestic corporations. They thereby elected to assume powers and to undertake responsibilities wholly derived from that State's rules and regulations, and to become eligible for those benefits that Delaware law makes available to its corporations' officials. . . . I thus do not believe that it is unfair to insist that appellants make themselves available to suit in a competent forum that Delaware might create for vindication of its important public policies directly pertaining to appellants' fiduciary associations with the State.

---

[6] Admittedly, when one consents to suit in a forum, his expectation is enhanced that he may be haled into that State's courts. To this extent, I agree that consent may have bearing on the fairness of accepting jurisdiction. But whatever is the degree of personal expectation that is necessary to warrant jurisdiction should not depend on the formality of establishing a consent law. Indeed, if one's expectations are to carry such weight, then appellants here might be fairly charged with the understanding that Delaware would decide to protect its substantial interests through its own courts, for they certainly realized that in the past the sequestration law has been employed primarily as a means of securing the appearance of corporate officials in the State's courts. Even in the absence of such a statute, however, the close and special association between a state corporation and its managers should apprise the latter that the State may seek to offer a convenient forum for addressing claims of fiduciary breach of trust.

## NOTES AND QUESTIONS ON *SHAFFER* AND THE CONTINUING UTILITY OF PROPERTY-BASED JURISDICTION

(1) *A Conceptual Revolution. Shaffer* represents a conceptual revolution of the first order. It does not merely change a rule about jurisdiction over property, but alters that very concept with the realization that "jurisdiction over property" is merely a "customary elliptical way of referring to jurisdiction over the interests of persons" in the property. *Shaffer* thus establishes a "unified field theory" of jurisdiction with all exercises to be based on the standards of *International Shoe. See* Geoffrey Hazard, *A General Theory of State-Court Jurisdiction,* 1965 SUP. CT. REV. 241, 282, for an early argument that a unified theory is required.

As a contribution to jurisdictional theory, *Shaffer* bears an interesting reciprocal relationship to *Shoe. Shoe* began the jurisdictional revolution by abandoning one tenet of the territorial power theory. After *Shoe,* territorial power was no longer a *necessary* condition for a constitutional exercise of jurisdiction. Three decades later, the Court held the converse in *Shaffer*; territorial power is not a *sufficient* condition either. Donald Werner, *Dropping the Other Shoe:* Shaffer v. Heitner *and the Demise of Presence-Oriented Jurisdiction,* 45 BROOK. L. REV. 565 (1979).

How secure is *Shaffer's* power-is-not-sufficient holding after the Supreme Court's decision in *Burnham v. Superior Court,* § 3.12[A], *supra?*

(2) *Orthodox In Rem and Quasi In Rem Type I.* It is clear from the Court's opinion that orthodox in rem and quasi-in-rem type I jurisdiction over land and tangible personal property survive *Shaffer's* in rem revolution. What passage in the opinion would you quote as authority for this proposition? This feature of *Shaffer* has not proved controversial. *See* Donald Fyr, *Shaffer v. Heitner: The Supreme Court's Latest Last Words on State Court Jurisdiction,* 26 EMORY L.J. 739 (1977).

Nevertheless, probing the Court's reasons is worthwhile. The opinion cites three: (1) defendant's claim to the property normally indicates that "he expected to benefit from the State's protection of his interest," (2) the state has a strong interest "in assuring the marketability of property within its borders and in providing a peaceful resolution of disputes about possession of that property," (3) the location of "important records and witnesses" in the situs state will usually make it a convenient forum to try claims to the property.

The reasons are weighty, to be sure; but they seem to address primarily the fairness and reasonableness portion of the *International Shoe* formulation, not the contacts portion. *World-Wide* and its progeny clearly indicate that both tests must be passed. Is the presence of the property in the forum enough of a "contact" with the defendant or is this one of those cases where fairness "considerations . . . serve to establish the reasonableness of jurisdiction upon a lesser showing of minimum contacts than would otherwise be required?" *See* Justice Brennan's majority opinion in *Burger King,* p. **** *supra.* If litigation convenience, strong state interest, and defendant's expectation of benefit are weighty enough to overcome a dearth of pre-litigation connections between the defendant and the state in the in rem context, why were they not in *Kulko* and *World-Wide?*

What about the "against all the world" feature of in rem jurisdiction? Does the situs have minimum contacts with the whole world? Clearly the justification for that feature of in rem jurisdiction must be based upon state interest, reasonableness and necessity—not contacts. Once again, why are such considerations sufficient here but not in *Helicopteros?* Professor Vernon argues that in rem jurisdiction can be justified under the *International Shoe* standard by treating an in rem action as a two-level process, requiring contacts at only one level:

> The first level involves what is in essence a quasi in rem proceeding in which claims of particular persons—those who are known or knowable—are determined. At this level, it is possible to establish an adequate nexus between the forum and the defendant. The second level, applying to the potential claims of all other persons in the world, operates somewhat as a nonclaim period would operate to cut off all unfiled claims against an estate, as a statute of limitations would operate to cut off claims against an individual defendant, or as the passage of the time period necessary to establish adverse possession would operate to cut off competing claims to the property. . . .
>
> . . . [A]t the second level, it seems realistic to view the true in rem decree as judicially, rather than a legislatively, established point in time after which claims of those not involved in the first (quasi in rem) level are barred. . . . Viewed in this manner, and conceding that notice would be necessary, a forum-defendant nexus would not be required.

David Vernon, *State-Court Jurisdiction: A Preliminary Inquiry into the Impact of* Shaffer v. Heitner, 63 IOWA L. REV. 997, 1003 (1978). *

Is the analogy perfect? Suppose plaintiff, a citizen of Ohio is injured in Michigan and brings an action in Ohio after the Michigan statute of limitations has run but within Ohio's limitations period. Must the Ohio court dismiss? Contrast this case with one in which an *in rem* proceeding (say, a probate action) in Michigan results in Beneficiary being awarded title to a particular res, an automobile. He drives the car into Ohio. Plaintiff, a resident of Ohio, who falls into the "all the world" category (i.e., her identity and possible claims were unknown) now brings an action against Beneficiary, asserting her rival claim to the car. Must the Ohio court dismiss?

(3) *Surviving Uses of Attachment Jurisdiction.*

(a) *Plaintiff's Claim Related to the Attached Property.* The Court indicates that attachment jurisdiction survives in cases "such as suits for injury suffered on the land of an absentee owner, where the defendant's ownership of the property is conceded but the cause of action is otherwise related to rights and duties growing out of that ownership." What arguments support jurisdiction in such cases? The same ones that apply in true in rem and quasi-in-rem type I cases? *See* David Vernon, *Single-Factor Bases of In Personam Jurisdiction—A Speculation on the Impact of* Shaffer v. Heitner, 1978 WASH. U. L.Q. 273, 296. How closely related must plaintiff's claim be to the attached property and what is the test for measuring "relatedness"? Keep these questions in mind for they surface again in the next case and the notes which accompany it.

(b) *Attachment with Minimum Contacts. Shaffer* requires that an exercise of attachment jurisdiction satisfy the standards of *International Shoe* and its progeny. Accordingly attachment jurisdiction over a piece of defendant's property in the forum is available if defendant has minimum contacts with the state. But the existence of minimum contacts would also justify an exercise of personal jurisdiction. Why then would a plaintiff settle for attachment jurisdiction? Suppose the facts of the case satisfy the minimum contacts standard, but the case does not fit within the state's in personam long-arm statute. Could plaintiff use attachment jurisdiction to fill the gap in the unambitious long-arm statute? *See, e.g., Banco Ambrosiano v. Artoc Bank & Trust Ltd.,* 62 N.Y.2d 65, 464 N.E.2d 432, 476 N.Y.S.2d 64 (1984). *See also* Joseph Zammit, *Reflections on* Shaffer v. Heitner, 1978 HASTINGS CONST. L.Q. 15, 20. Is there an argument against this sort of "gap-filling" based on the principles of statutory construction? *See* RESTATEMENT (SECOND) OF CONFLICT OF LAWS § 66, cmt. c (1986 Revisions).

*Shaffer* indicates that attachment jurisdiction and personal jurisdiction are governed by the same minimum contacts *standard.* But does that necessarily mean that the exact same *quantum* of contacts is required in both instances? Defendant's risk in an attachment action typically is much lower than in an in personam case. Should the difference in risk mean that the quantum of contacts required for an attachment action might be lower yet still satisfy "fundamental notions of fair play and substantial justice"? *See* RUSSELL WEINTRAUB, COMMENTARY ON THE CONFLICT OF LAWS, 256 (4th ed. 2001); Stefan Riesenfeld, Shaffer v. Heitner: *Holding, Implications, Forebodings,* 30 HASTINGS L.J. 1183, 1204 (1979).

(c) *Attachment to Enforce a Sister-State Judgment.* Footnote 36 and its accompanying text make it clear that the use of attachment jurisdiction to enforce an in personam judgment survives *Shaffer.* The typical case occurs when plaintiff obtains an in personam judgment in a state where defendant has no property out of which to satisfy the judgment. Plaintiff then sues to enforce the judgment in a state where defendant has property but no other contacts. How can the attachment jurisdiction of the enforcing state be justified under the standards of *International Shoe?* Often the defendant will have minimum contacts with the state relating to the attached property, but the presence of property is no guarantee. Indeed, the lasting lesson of *Harris v. Balk,* § 3.15, *supra,* is that defendant can have intangible personal property in a state where he has no other contacts. *See also Berger v. Berger,* 138 Vt. 367, 417 A.2d 921 (1980) (defendant's only contact with Vermont being an undistributed one-quarter of his mother's estate).

One argument is that defendant is not entitled to due process in the enforcing state since she has already had it in the rendering state. The enforcing state need not have minimum contacts with the defendant because the rendering state did. *See Bank of Babylon v. Quirk,* 192 Conn. 447, 472 A.2d 21 (1984); ROBERT LEFLAR, LUTHER MCDOUGAL & ROBERT FELIX, AMERICAN CONFLICTS LAW 133 (1986). This is a non sequitur, isn't it? The defendant is entitled to notice of the pendency of the enforcement action. Why should the contact and notice requirements be treated so differently? The Court's stated justification in footnote 36 is fairness. Is it so clear that an action to enforce a judgment can generate no unfairness? *See* Earl Maltz, *Reflections on a Landmark:* Shaffer v. Heitner *Viewed from a Distance,* 1986 B.Y.U. L. REV. 1043, 1046-1048. Suppose defendant defaults in the rendering state on the theory that it lacked jurisdiction over her. Is it fair to force her to litigate the jurisdiction of the rendering state in the enforcing state simply because she has a debtor (intangible personal property) there?

Perhaps the real justification lies in necessity and in the national policy favoring interstate enforcement of judgments. *See* David Vernon, *State-Court Jurisdiction: A Preliminary Inquiry into the Impact of* Shaffer v. Heitner, 63 IOWA L. REV. 997, 1008 (1978). If that is so, it seems to suggest that some state and national policies are powerful enough to trump defendant's right not to be sued in a place with which he has no pre-litigation connections. Are there other potential trumping policies in cases like *World-Wide* and *Helicopteros?* Shouldn't the Court be able to enumerate them and explain why they are not as powerful as the prevailing policy in enforcement cases? That sort of analysis would take the jurisprudence of jurisdiction beyond the current contacts-for-contacts-sake doctrine.

(d) *Attachment to Secure.* The Court also approves the attachment of defendant's property in a forum where he lacks minimum contacts if the purpose of the attachment is to provide security for a judgment being sought in a forum whose jurisdiction meets *Shoe-Shaffer* standards. What is the justification for the attachment-to-secure procedure? Should an attachment for this purpose require a lesser "showing of contacts" than would an attachment for other purposes? Why? *See Carolina Power & Light Co. v. Uranex,* 451 F. Supp. 1044, 1047-8 (N.D. Cal. 1977); ROGER CRAMTON, DAVID CURRIE, HERMA KAY & LARRY KRAMER, CONFLICT OF LAWS: CASES, COMMENTS, QUESTIONS 388 (5th ed. 1993).

(e) *Land.* The concurring opinions of Justices Powell and Stevens suggest that attachment jurisdiction should survive when the attached property is real estate. What arguments do they cite? Can you think of others? Are you convinced? *See* WILLIAM RICHMAN & WILLIAM REYNOLDS, UNDERSTANDING CONFLICT OF LAWS § 45[b][5] (3d ed. 2002); Linda Silberman, Shaffer v. Heitner: *The End of an Era,* 53 N.Y.U. L. REV. 33, 68-69 (1978). You will learn in the next chapter that land is often treated as a "special case" for choice-of-law purposes also. *See* §§ 4.08, 4.29, *infra.*

(f) *The Effect of Burnham.* How does the Supreme Court's decision in *Burnham v. Superior Court,* § 3.12[A], *supra,* affect the *Shaffer*–based arguments supporting orthodox *in rem* jurisdiction and attachment jurisdiction when used to secure or enforce a sister state judgment? Is there still a need after *Burnham* even to consider such fairness-based arguments, or is it enough to note that these practices are securely grounded in tradition? Does *Burnham* have the same effect on the arguments supporting attachment jurisdiction over land?

(g) *Necessity.* In footnote 37, the Court refuses to consider whether "the presence of defendant's property in a State is a sufficient basis for [attachment] jurisdiction when no other forum is available to the plaintiff." The question raises the problem of "jurisdiction by necessity," a doctrine with respectable antecedents.

In *Mullane v. Central Hanover Bank & Trust Co.,* 339 U.S. 306 (1950), the Court upheld a New York statute that provided for the existence of common trust funds formed by pooling numerous small trust corpuses into one fund for purposes of investment administration. The accounts of the common fund were to be settled from time to time in a judicial procedure called an accounting, which the statute made binding on all interested persons regardless of their contacts with New York. The Court's approval was based not on the in rem/in personam distinction, but rather on the practical necessity for an all-binding accounting procedure in order to make trust pooling possible:

> Without disparaging the usefulness of distinctions between actions *in rem* and those *in personam* in many branches of law, or on other issues, or the reasoning which underlies them, we do not rest the power of the State to resort to constructive service in this proceeding upon how its courts or this Court may regard this historic antithesis. It is sufficient to observe that, whatever the technical definition of its chosen procedure, the interest of each state in providing means to close trusts that exist by the grace of its laws and are administered under the supervision of its courts is so insistent and rooted in custom as to establish beyond doubt the right of its courts to determine the interests of all claimants, resident or nonresident, provided its procedure accords full opportunity to appear and be heard.

For commentary on *Mullane* and its emphasis on necessity, see Ian Fraser, *Jurisdiction by Necessity—An Analysis of the Mullane Case,* 100 U. PA. L. REV. 305 (1951).

What exactly does the Court mean by the phrase "when no other forum is available"? No other forum anywhere in the world, or just no other forum in the United States? *Compare Louring v. Kuwait Boulder Shipping Co.,* 455 F. Supp. 630 (D. Conn. 1977) (attachment jurisdiction exercised over defendant who lacked minimum contacts with Connecticut but had fair warning that its activities might subject it to suit somewhere in the United States), *with* John Leathers, *Forum Juridicum: The First Two Years After* Shaffer v. Heitner, 40 LA. L. REV. 907, 916 (1980) (critical of *Louring* and suggesting that the "no other forum" language in footnote 37 should be read literally). Did the Supreme Court answer this question in *Helicopteros,* § 3.10, *supra,* in which plaintiffs' claims were dismissed even though they had no alternative forum in the United States? In *Helicopteros,* plaintiffs sought to proceed against defendant personally rather than by attaching its property. Should that distinction matter in the "jurisdiction by necessity" context? Should cautious litigators, therefore, hedge their bets and attempt to attach defendant's property as well as proceed against him personally when lack of jurisdiction in an American state might consign plaintiff's claim to the tender mercies of a foreign, plaintiff-hostile judicial system?

The argument for jurisdiction by necessity takes an interesting turn in the multi-defendant context. The trend in modern procedural systems, as shown by liberal joinder provisions and expansive use of claim preclusion and issue preclusion, is to encourage the disposition of multiple claims involving multiple parties in a single law suit. Strict adherence to the minimum contacts formula and restrictive state long-arm statues, however, will sometimes leave plaintiff with no forum where all defendants can be joined. *See* Donald Fyr, Shaffer v. Heitner, *The Supreme Court's Latest Last Words on State Court Jurisdiction,* 26 EMORY L.J. 739, 771-772 (1977). In such situations, the case for jurisdiction by necessity is very appealing, indeed.

(4) *Overruling "Chestnuts."* What of the unlamented "chestnuts," *Harris* and *Pennoyer* ? Their rationale is overruled, but what about their facts? Would they pass the new *Shaffer-Shoe* test? Did the defendants in those cases have minimum contacts with the forum? Were plaintiffs' claims closely related to the attached property? In footnote 39, the court explicitly refused to re-examine the facts of those cases. A commentator has remedied the Court's omission. *See* Andreas Lowenfeld, *In Search of the Intangible: A Comment on* Shaffer v. Heitner, 53 N.Y.U. L. REV. 102 (1978).

(5) *The "Situs" Problem.* The holding in *Shaffer* has not done away completely with the problem of the situs of intangibles. Billions of dollars of assets in the United States are held through corporations and trusts organized under the laws of the Bahamas, the Cayman Islands, Liberia, Panama, etc. Suppose the Bahamas has a law like Delaware's that makes the islands the situs of all stock of corporations incorporated according to its laws. Launder Incorporated is a Bahamian corporation, whose shareholders live in Miami and whose principal assets are bank accounts in Miami. In a lightning coup détat, the Popular Front for the Redemption of the Bahamian People has seized control of the Bahamas and expropriated all foreign property in the islands, placing control of these assets in the Minister of Finance, as trustee for the Bahamian people. She brings an action in Miami against Launder's former American shareholders claiming title to the bank accounts. How should the court rule? When the new government seized all "property" located in the islands, did it successfully seize the stock of Launder? Does the answer depend on the "situs" of the stock? *See Lowenfeld, supra,* Note (4), at 118.

(6) *The Limited Appearance.* Traditional attachment jurisdiction under *Pennoyer, Harris,* and *Seider,* produced substantial possibilities of unfairness to defendants, who could be sued in distant states with which they had no real contact. Before the theoretical revolution of *Shaffer* eliminated the excesses of attachment jurisdiction, some courts developed the limited appearance concept as a device for mitigating the doctrine's unfair impact on defendants. To appreciate the value of the concept, consider the predicament of a defendant sued in a traditional attachment action. At the commencement of the action, a court in the forum attached a piece of defendant's property within the state, creating a dilemma for the defendant. Failure to appear and

defend the action resulted in default; the property then would be sold and the proceeds paid to plaintiff. On the other hand, an appearance to defend on the merits could be considered a consent to the court's personal jurisdiction.

The limited appearance concept removed one of the horns of the dilemma by permitting defendants to appear and litigate the merits of plaintiff's claim without submitting to the personal jurisdiction of the court. In other words, defendants could defend their interest in the property that was "held hostage" without risking a personal judgment. Thus, the limited appearance was a valuable dispensation for defendants.

The argument for the limited appearance was that forcing the defendant either to appear generally or to forfeit the property is so unfair as to violate fundamental notions of fair play. Accordingly, it was argued that the limited appearance was constitutionally required. *See Developments in the Law— State-Court Jurisdiction,* 73 HARV. L. REV. 909, 954 (1960).

The case against the limited appearance is based on judicial economy. Suppose the defendant is permitted to make a limited appearance, the parties fully litigate the merits, and plaintiff prevails, but the attached property is not worth enough to satisfy plaintiff's claim completely. To obtain complete relief, plaintiff would have to sue again (where the defendant is subject to in personam or attachment jurisdiction), and the parties would relitigate the merits of the action. Such a wasteful duplication of effort contravenes the important policies underlying the doctrine of res judicata. For a collection of authorities on both sides of the issue, see CHARLES WRIGHT & ARTHUR MILLER, FEDERAL PRACTICE AND PROCEDURE § 1123.

Does *Shaffer* do away with the need for the limited appearance? See Richman & Reynolds, *supra* note (3)(e), at § 43. Re-examine the surviving uses of attachment jurisdiction. Are there any in which the limited appearance retains its usefulness?

*See* PROBLEM 3D-2. THE ACCIDENTAL SHOOTING.

(7) *Default and Collateral Attack.* The holding in *Shaffer* leaves an interesting procedural question: Can a defendant in an attachment action assert the jurisdictional objection by default and collateral attack? That option has always been available to defendants sued personally; if a defendant is sued in personam in a forum where she has no contacts or property, she has always been able to default and then assert the rendering court's lack of jurisdiction as a defense to a subsequent enforcement action brought by plaintiff in a forum in which defendant does have property. In an attachment action, however, defendant, by definition, has property in the forum. If she defaults, the sheriff will sell the attached property at a judicial auction, perhaps to a third party.

Before Shaffer, the defendant had no grounds for collateral attack because the presence of the property in the forum sufficed for a constitutional exercise of jurisdiction. Now that *Shaffer* has rejected that rule, can the defendant assert the jurisdictional objection in a collateral attack by suing the third party for the property?

If such an avenue is open to the defendant, it would be a bit harsh on the third party. Given such a possibility, who would be willing to buy in at a judicial sale following an attachment action? Suppose the third party had already disposed of the property, would the defendant have a civil rights claim against the sheriff under 42 U.S.C.§ 1983 for taking the property without due process "under color of state law"? One possible solution is to prohibit a defendant in an attachment action from asserting the jurisdictional objection by default and collateral attack, i.e., to require the defendant to appear for the purpose of asserting the lack of jurisdiction or waive that objection forever. Is that solution precluded by *Shaffer's* requirement that all assertions of jurisdiction meet the standards of *International Shoe,* or is the remaining difference between in personam and attachment actions sufficient to permit significant procedural variations? For commentary on this issue, see Irving Younger, *Quasi in Rem Defaults After* Shaffer v. Heitner. *Some Unanswered Questions,* 45 BROOK. L. REV. 675 (1979); Robert Casad, Shaffer v. Heitner, *An End to Ambivalence in Jurisdiction Theory,* 26 U. KAN. L. REV. 61, 79-80 (1977).

(8) *Jurisdiction and Choice of Law. Shaffer* raises a recurrent theme in conflict of laws, the relationship between judicial and legislative jurisdiction (choice of law). Justice Marshall's majority opinion makes a strong distinction between the contacts necessary for a state to exercise adjudicative jurisdiction and those required to support the application of a state's law to a controversy, the implication being that the former is the higher standard. Subsequent holdings in choice-of-law cases seem to bear out this implication. *See Allstate Ins. Co. v. Hague* and *Phillips Petroleum v. Shutts,* both in § 5.04, *infra.* Justice Brennan in dissent "would not compartmentalize thinking in this area quite so rigidly." He sees many of the same factors as relevant to both questions. Some commentators have gone farther and asserted that "the constitutional dimensions of the exercise of long-arm act jurisdiction and the application of the forum's substantive law should be fully co-extensive." *See* Robert Sedler, *Judicial Jurisdiction and Choice of Law: The Consequences of* Shaffer v. Heitner, 63 IOWA L. REV. 1031, 1033 (1978).

Which side gets the better of the argument? Are the factors identical? What about litigation convenience, location of witnesses, proof and the like? Should those factors matter at all to the choice-of-law issue? If there is a difference between the two standards which should be higher? The Court's leaning is fairly clear, but from defendant's point of view, the Court seems to have it backwards. Professor Silberman's critique of the Court's priorities is both flippant and devastating; she suggests that "[t]o believe that a defendant's contacts with the forum state should be stronger under the Due Process Clause for jurisdictional purposes than for choice of law is to believe that an accused is more concerned with where he will hang than whether." Linda Silberman, Shaffer v. Heitner: *The End of An Era,* 53 N.Y.U. L. REV. 33, 88 (1978).

(9) *Seider After Shaffer.* Does *Seider v. Roth,* § 3.15, *supra,* survive the in rem revolution of *Shaffer?* Even before *Shaffer, Seider*–type attachment jurisdiction was controversial. The problem was that *Seider* relied upon a "bootstrap" argument. Under traditional theory, a court could exercise attachment jurisdiction only if some piece of defendant's property was found within the state and attached at the beginning of the action. In a *Seider* action, the attached intangible property was the "debt" that the insurer owed the

defendant-insured; but the "debt," the insurer's obligation to defend and indemnify the defendant, did not exist until the defendant had been sued. In other words, the *res* that formed the basis for attachment jurisdiction could not come into existence until the action was commenced, and the action could not be commenced without the res to exercise jurisdiction over.

A less conceptualistic critique of the *Seider* doctrine focused on its pragmatic effects rather than its formal justification. The doctrine made the limits on personal jurisdiction somewhat beside the point in any action in which the defendant had liability insurance with a national carrier. As long as defendant's insurer did business in the forum, defendant was amenable to attachment jurisdiction there, no matter where plaintiff's injury occurred. Thus, to take only one example, a California defendant who injured a New Yorker on a California highway could be forced to defend plaintiff's claim in New York even though he had not the slightest connection with New York. *Seider,* in other words, made every vacationing New Yorker into a "rolling transcontinental summons to a New York courtroom. See Richman & Reynolds, *supra* note (3)(e), at § 42[c]; David Siegel, *Jurisdiction Ad Infinitum: New York's "Rem" Seizure of the Insurance Policy for Jurisdiction in Accident Cases,* 20 INT'L & COMP. L.Q. 99 (1971).

The decision in *Shaffer* sparked serious debate about the continued vitality of the *Seider* doctrine. *See* the Symposia at 63 IOWA L. REV. 991 (1978) and 45 BROOK. L. REV. 493 (1979). The Court ended the debate three years after *Shaffer.*

---

**RUSH v. SAVCHUK,** 444 U.S. 320 (1980). Plaintiff and defendant, both residents of Indiana, were involved in a single car automobile accident in Indiana; plaintiff was a guest in defendant's car. Plaintiff moved to Minnesota after the accident and sued defendant there. Since defendant had no contacts with Minnesota, plaintiff obtained attachment jurisdiction by garnishing defendant's insurance policy with the State Farm Insurance Company. After the Minnesota courts approved the exercise of jurisdiction based on the *Seider* doctrine, defendant appealed to the Supreme Court, and the case was remanded for further consideration in light of *Shaffer.* On remand, the Minnesota Supreme Court again upheld the exercise of jurisdiction, this time on the ground that the case passed the *Shaffer* test. On a second appeal, the Supreme Court reversed:

> [T]he fictitious presence of the insurer's obligation in Minnesota does not, without more, provide a basis for concluding that there is any contact in the *International Shoe* sense between Minnesota and the insured. To say that "a debt follows the debtor" is simply to say that intangible property has no actual situs, and a debt may be sued on wherever there is jurisdiction over the debtor. State Farm is "found," in the sense of doing business, in all 50 States and the District of Columbia. Under appellee's theory, the "debt" owed to Rush would be "present" in each of those jurisdictions simultaneously. It is apparent that such a "contact" can have no jurisdictional significance.

---

## NOTES ON *RUSH* AND THE DEATH OF THE *SEIDER* DOCTRINE

(1) *The Relationship Between Plaintiff's Claim and the Attached "Property."* Plaintiff argued that *Seider*-type jurisdiction passed muster under *Shaffer* because the claim, based on an auto accident, was closely related to the attached property, the liability insurance policy. The Court was unimpressed:

> The insurance policy is not the subject matter of the case, nor is it related to the operative facts of the negligence action. The contractual arrangements between the defendant and the insurer pertain only to the conduct, not the substance, of the litigation, and accordingly do not affect the court's jurisdiction . . . .

444 U.S. at 329. Plaintiffs argument and the Court's response raise once again the knotty problem of "claim-relatedness." *See* Notes on General and Specific Jurisdiction §3.10, Note (2), *supra.*

(2) *The Direct Action Argument.* Plaintiff also argued that a *Seider* action is simply a judicially-created direct action procedure like the one approved by the Supreme Court in *Watson v. Employer's Liability Assurance Corp. See* § 5.02, *infra.* The "nominal defendant," he argued, has no real stake in the action because liability is limited to the policy amount. Thus, it is not unfair to conduct the trial in a forum with which the insurer, but not the insured, has minimum contacts. In footnote 20 of its opinion the Court responded that a *Seider* defendant might well have a significant economic stake in the proceeding if she were sued by multiple plaintiffs in several states for an aggregate amount greater than the policy limit. Further, some defendants (e.g., professionals sued for malpractice) will have significant noneconomic stakes in the action.

# PART F  LIMITATIONS ON THE EXERCISE OF JURISDICTION

## § 3.17  Scope Note

Sometimes a court will have constitutional power to assert jurisdiction and yet may decline to do so. The due process clause, of course, does not *require* a court to exercise jurisdiction. This Part of Chapter Three examines several situations in which a court may refuse to hear a case. The two most prominent areas involve the doctrine of forum non conveniens and contracts which contain forum selection clauses. The discussion concludes with a brief explanation of several other jurisdiction-limiting doctrines.

## § 3.18  Forum Non Conveniens

### PIPER AIRCRAFT CO. v. REYNO

*United States Supreme Court*
*454 U.S. 235 (1981)*

JUSTICE MARSHALL delivered the opinion of the Court.

I

A

In July 1976, a small commercial aircraft crashed in the Scottish highlands. . . . The pilot and five passengers were killed instantly. The decedents were all Scottish subjects and residents, as are their heirs and next of kin. There were no eyewitnesses to the accident. At the time of the crash the plane was subject to Scottish air traffic control.

The aircraft, a twin-engine Piper Aztec, was manufactured in Pennsylvania by petitioner Piper Aircraft Co. (Piper). The propellers were manufactured in Ohio by petitioner Hartzell Propeller, Inc. (Hartzell). At the time of the crash the aircraft was registered in Great Britain and was owned and maintained by Air Navigation and Trading Co., Ltd. (Air Navigation). It was operated by McDonald Aviation, Ltd. (McDonald), a Scottish air taxi service. Both Air Navigation and McDonald were organized in the United Kingdom. The wreckage of the plane is now in a hangar in Farnsborough, England. . . .

In July 1977, a California probate court appointed respondent Gaynell Reyno administratrix of the estates of the five passengers. Reyno is not related to and does not know any of the decedents or their survivors; she was a legal secretary to the attorney who filed this lawsuit. Several days after her appointment, Reyno commenced separate wrongful-death actions against Piper and Hartzell in the Superior Court of California, claiming negligence and strict liability. Air Navigation, McDonald, and the estate of the pilot are not parties to this litigation. The survivors of the five passengers whose estates are represented by Reyno filed a separate action in the United Kingdom against

Air Navigation, McDonald, and the pilot's estate. Reyno candidly admits that the action against Piper and Hartzell was filed in the United States because its laws regarding liability, capacity to sue, and damages are more favorable to her position than are those of Scotland. Scottish law does not recognize strict liability in tort. Moreover, it permits wrongful-death actions only when brought by a decedent's relatives. The relatives may sue only for "loss of support and society."

On petitioners' motion, the suit was removed to the United States District Court for the Central District of California [and then transferred] to the United States District Court for the Middle District of Pennsylvania, pursuant to 28 U.S.C. § 1404(a).[4]

## B

In May 1978, after the suit had been transferred, both Hartzell and Piper moved to dismiss the action on the ground of forum non conveniens. The District Court granted these motions. . . . It relied on the balancing test set forth by this Court in *Gulf Oil Corp. v. Gilbert,* 330 U.S. 501 (1947) . . . [where] the Court stated that a plaintiff's choice of forum should rarely be disturbed. However, when an alternative forum has jurisdiction to hear the case, and when trial in the chosen forum would "establish . . . oppressiveness and vexation to a defendant . . . out of all proportion to plaintiff's convenience," or when the "chosen forum [is] inappropriate because of considerations affecting the court's own administrative and legal problems," the court may, in the exercise of its sound discretion, dismiss the case. To guide trial court's discretion, the Court provided a list of "private interest factors" affecting the convenience of the litigants, and a list of "public interest factors" affecting the convenience of the forum . . . .[6]

[The Court of Appeals reversed, and the Supreme Court granted certiorari.]

## II

The Court of Appeals erred in holding that plaintiffs may defeat a motion to dismiss on the ground of forum non conveniens merely by showing that the substantive law that would be applied in the alternative forum is less favorable to the plaintiffs than that of the present forum. The possibility of a change in substantive law should ordinarily not be given conclusive or even substantial weight in the forum non conveniens inquiry. . . .

---

**4** Section 1404(a) provides: "For the convenience of parties and witnesses, in the interest of justice, a district court may transfer any civil action to any other district or division where it might have been brought."

**6** The factors pertaining to the private interests of the litigants included the "relative ease of access to sources of proof; availability of compulsory process for attendance of unwilling, and the cost of obtaining attendance of willing, witnesses; possibility of view of premises if a view would be appropriate to the action; and all other practical problems that make trial of a case easy, expeditious and inexpensive." The public factors bearing on the question included the administrative difficulties flowing from court congestion; the "local interest in having localized controversies decided at home"; the interest in having the trial of a diversity case in a forum that is at home with the law that must govern the action; the avoidance of unnecessary problems in conflict of laws, or in the application of foreign law; and the unfairness of burdening citizens in an unrelated forum with jury duty.

. . . Under *Gilbert,* dismissal will ordinarily be appropriate where trial in the plaintiff's chosen forum imposes a heavy burden on the defendant or the court, and where the plaintiff is unable to offer any specific reasons of convenience supporting his choice. If substantial weight were given to the possibility of an unfavorable change in law, however, dismissal might be barred even where trial in the chosen forum was plainly inconvenient.

. . . [T]his Court's earlier forum non conveniens decisions . . . have repeatedly emphasized the need to retain flexibility. . . . If central emphasis were placed on any one factor, the forum non conveniens doctrine would lose much of the very flexibility that makes it so valuable.

In fact, if conclusive or substantial weight were given to the possibility of a change in law, the forum non conveniens doctrine would become virtually useless. Jurisdiction and venue requirements are often easily satisfied. As a result, many plaintiffs are able to choose from among several forums. Ordinarily, these plaintiffs will select that forum whose choice-of-law rules are most advantageous. Thus, if the possibility of an unfavorable change in substantive law is given substantial weight in the forum non conveniens inquiry, dismissal would rarely be proper. . . .

If the possibility of a change in law were given substantial weight, deciding motions to dismiss on the ground of forum non conveniens would become quite difficult. Choice-of-law analysis would become extremely important, and the courts would frequently be required to interpret the law of foreign jurisdictions. First, the trial court would have to determine what law would apply if the case were tried in the chosen forum, and what law would apply if the case were tried in the alternative forum . . . Dismissal would be appropriate only if the court concluded that the law applied by the alternative forum is as favorable to the plaintiff as that of the chosen forum. The doctrine of forum non conveniens, however, is designed in part to help courts avoid conducting complex exercises in comparative law. As we stated in *Gilbert,* the public interest factors point towards dismissal where the court would be required to "untangle problems in conflict of laws, and in law foreign to itself."

Upholding the decision of the Court of Appeals would result in other practical problems. At least where the foreign plaintiff named an American manufacturer as defendant, a court could not dismiss the case on grounds of forum non conveniens where dismissal might lead to an unfavorable change in law. The American courts, which are already extremely attractive to foreign plaintiffs, would become even more attractive. The flow of litigation into the United States would increase and further congest already crowded courts.[19]

The Court of Appeals based its decision, at least in part, on an analogy between dismissals on grounds of forum non conveniens and transfers between federal courts pursuant to § 1404(a). In *Van Dusen v. Barrack,* 376 U.S. 612 (1964), this Court ruled that a § 1404(a) transfer should not result in a change

---

[19] . . .We recognize, of course, that Piper and Hartzell may be engaged in reverse forum shopping. However, this possibility ordinarily should not enter into a trial court's analysis of the private interests. If the defendant is able to overcome the presumption in favor of plaintiff by showing that trial in the chosen forum would be unnecessarily burdensome, dismissal is appropriate—regardless of the fact that defendant may also be motivated by a desire to obtain a more favorable forum.

in the applicable law. [T]he court below held that that principle is also applicable to a dismissal on forum non conveniens grounds. However, § 1404(a) transfers are different than dismissals on the ground of forum non conveniens.

Congress enacted § 1404(a) to permit change of venue between federal courts. Although the statute was drafted in accordance with the doctrine of forum non conveniens, it was intended to be a revision rather than a codification of the common law. District courts were given more discretion to transfer under § 1404(a) than they had to dismiss on grounds of forum non conveniens.

The reasoning employed in *Van Dusen v. Barrack* is simply inapplicable to dismissals on grounds of forum non conveniens. That case did not discuss the common-law doctrine. Rather, it focused on "the construction and application" of § 1404(a). Emphasizing the remedial purpose of the statute, *Barrack* concluded that Congress could not have intended a transfer to be accompanied by a change in law. The statute was designed as a "federal housekeeping measure," allowing easy change of venue within a unified federal system. The Court feared that if a change in venue were accompanied by a change in law, forum-shopping parties would take unfair advantage of the relaxed standards for transfer. The rule was necessary to ensure the just and efficient operation of the statute.

We do not hold that the possibility of an unfavorable change in law should never be a relevant consideration in a forum non conveniens inquiry. Of course, if the remedy provided by the alternative forum is so clearly inadequate or unsatisfactory that it is no remedy at all, the unfavorable change in law may be given substantial weight; the district court may conclude that dismissal would not be in the interests of justice.[22] In these cases, however, the remedies that would be provided by the Scottish courts do not fall within this category. Although the relatives of the decedents may not be able to rely on a strict liability theory, and although their potential damages award may be smaller, there is no danger that they will be deprived of any remedy or treated unfairly.

## III

The Court of Appeals also erred in rejecting the District Court's *Gilbert* analysis. . . .

## A

The District Court acknowledged that there is ordinarily a strong presumption in favor of the plaintiff's choice of forum, which may be overcome only when the private and public interest factors clearly point towards trial in the

---

[22] At the outset of any forum non conveniens inquiry, the court must determine whether there exists an alternative forum. Ordinarily, this requirement will be satisfied when the defendant is "amenable to process" in the other jurisdiction. In rare circumstances, however, where the remedy offered by the other forum is clearly unsatisfactory, the other forum may not be an adequate alternative, and the initial requirement may not be satisfied. Thus, for example, dismissal would not be appropriate where the alternative forum does not permit litigation of the subject matter of the dispute. . . .

alternative forum. It held, however, that the presumption applies with less force when the plaintiff or real parties in interest are foreign.

The District Court's distinction between resident or citizen plaintiffs and foreign plaintiffs is fully justified. In *Koster,* the Court indicated that a plaintiff's choice of forum is entitled to greater deference when the plaintiff has chosen the home forum.[23] When the home forum has been chosen, it is reasonable to assume that this choice is convenient. When the plaintiff is foreign, however, this assumption is much less reasonable. Because the central purpose of any forum non conveniens inquiry is to ensure that the trial is convenient, a foreign plaintiff's choice deserves less deference.[24]

## B

The forum non conveniens determination is committed to the sound discretion of the trial court. It may be reversed only when there has been a clear abuse of discretion; where the court has considered all relevant public and private interest factors, and where its balancing of these factors is reasonable, its decision deserves substantial deference. . . .

## (1)

In analyzing the private interest factors, the District Court stated that the connections with Scotland are "overwhelming." This characterization may be somewhat exaggerated. Particularly with respect to the question of relative ease of access to sources of proof, the private interests point in both directions. As respondent emphasizes, records concerning the design, manufacture, and testing of the propeller and plane are located in the United States. She would have greater access to sources of proof relevant to her strict liability and negligence theories if trial were held here.[25] However, the District Court did not act unreasonably in concluding that fewer evidentiary problems would be posed if the trial were held in Scotland. A large proportion of the relevant evidence is located in Great Britain.

The Court of Appeals found that the problems of proof could not be given any weight because Piper and Hartzell failed to describe with specificity the evidence they would not be able to obtain if trial were held in the United States. It suggested that defendants seeking forum non conveniens dismissal must submit affidavits identifying the witnesses they would call and the testimony these witnesses would provide if the trial were held in the alternative

---

[23] . . . As the District Court correctly noted in its opinion, the lower federal courts have routinely given less weight to a foreign plaintiff's choice of forum.

A citizen's forum choice should not be given dispositive weight, however. Citizens or residents deserve somewhat more deference than foreign plaintiffs, but dismissal should not be automatically barred when a plaintiff has filed suit in his home forum. As always, if the balance of conveniences suggests that trial in the chosen forum would be unnecessarily burdensome for the defendant or the court, dismissal is proper.

[24] . . . [T]he deference accorded a plaintiff's choice of forum has never been intended to guarantee that the plaintiff will be able to select the law that will govern the case.

[25] In the future, where similar problems are presented, district courts might dismiss subject to the condition that defendant corporations agree to provide the records relevant to the plaintiff's claims.

forum. Such detail is not necessary. Piper and Hartzell have moved for dismissal precisely because many crucial witnesses are located beyond the reach of compulsory process, and thus are difficult to identify or interview. . . .

The District Court correctly concluded that the problems posed by the inability to implead potential third-party defendants clearly supported holding the trial in Scotland. Joinder of the pilot's estate, Air Navigation, and McDonald is crucial to the presentation of petitioners' defense. If Piper and Hartzell can show that the accident was caused not by a design defect, but rather by the negligence of the pilot, the plane's owners, or the charter company, they will be relieved of all liability. It is true, of course, that if Hartzell and Piper were found liable after a trial in the United States, they could institute an action for indemnity or contribution against these parties in Scotland. It would be far more convenient, however, to resolve all claims in one trial. . . .

(2)

The District Court's review of the factors relating to the public interest was also reasonable. On the basis of its choice-of-law analysis, it concluded that if the case were tried in the Middle District of Pennsylvania, Pennsylvania law would apply to Piper and Scottish law to Hartzell. It stated that a trial involving two sets of laws would be confusing to the jury. It also noted its own lack of familiarity with Scottish law. Consideration of these problems was clearly appropriate under *Gilbert*; in that case we explicitly held that the need to apply foreign law pointed towards dismissal.[29]

Scotland has a very strong interest in this litigation. The accident occurred in its airspace. All of the decedents were Scottish. Apart from Piper and Hartzell, all potential plaintiffs and defendants are either Scottish or English. As we stated in *Gilbert,* there is "a local interest in having localized controversies decided at home." Respondent argues that American citizens have an interest in ensuring that American manufacturers are deterred from producing defective products, and that additional deterrence might be obtained if Piper and Hartzell were tried in the United States, where they could be sued on the basis of both negligence and strict liability. However, the incremental deterrence that would be gained if this trial were held in an American court is likely to be insignificant. The American interest in this accident is simply not sufficient to justify the enormous commitment of judicial time and resources that would inevitably be required if the case were to be tried here.

IV

The Court of Appeals erred in holding that the possibility of an unfavorable change in law bars dismissal on the ground of forum non conveniens. It also erred in rejecting the District Court's *Gilbert* analysis. The District Court

---

[29] Many forum non conveniens decisions have held that the need to apply foreign law favors dismissal.

properly decided that the presumption in favor of the respondent's forum choice applied with less than maximum force because the real parties in interest are foreign. It did not act unreasonably in deciding that the private interests pointed towards trial in Scotland. Nor did it act unreasonably in deciding that the public interests favored trial in Scotland. Thus, the judgment of the Court of Appeals is

*Reversed.*

JUSTICE POWELL took no part in the decision of these cases.

JUSTICE O'CONNOR took no part in the consideration or decision of these cases.

JUSTICE WHITE, concurring in part and dissenting in part.

I join Parts I and II of the Court's opinion. However, like JUSTICE BRENNAN and JUSTICE STEVENS, I would not proceed to deal with the issues addressed in Part III. To that extent, I am in dissent.

JUSTICE SEVENS, with whom JUSTICE BRENNAN joins, dissenting.

. . . I would simply remand the case to the Court of Appeals for further consideration of the question whether the District Court correctly decided that Pennsylvania was not a convenient forum in which to litigate a claim against a Pennsylvania company that a plane was defectively designed and manufactured in Pennsylvania.

———

## NOTES AND QUESTIONS ON FORUM NON CONVENIENS

(1) *Forum Non Conveniens.* The Court gives a long list of factors to use in determining whether a case should be dismissed on forum non conveniens grounds. Is that laundry list of standards helpful to litigants or lower court judges? Will it aid predictability in decision-making? *See* Allan Stein, *Forum Non Conveniens and the Redundancy of Court Access Doctrine,* 133 U. PA. L. REV. 781, 785 (1985), remarking on the "crazy quilt of ad hoc, capricious, and inconsistent decisions." Professor Stein observed that the motion to dismiss is less likely to be granted if the court finds a "forum interest in the litigation," *id.* at 834, and that "the residency of the parties seems to make an important difference in aircraft accident litigation." *Id.* at 835. Why do you think that is? It's not surprising, is it, given that long list of factors, that forum non conveniens decisions are reviewable only for "abuse of discretion"?

The Court distinguishes carefully between the "public" and "private" interests that need to be analyzed in deciding whether to dismiss. Is that a helpful dichotomy? Were you satisfied with the way in which the Court analyzed those interests? In particular, were the potential third-party defendants, Air Navigation and McDonald, really all that important to the case? If they were, then is the Court saying that forum non conveniens is really about finding a forum where all interested parties can be joined properly?

Did the Court pay enough attention to Pennsylvania's public interest in deterring wrongful conduct (making sure airplanes are manufactured property)? Isn't deterrence a large part of the reason why we have strict liability actions?

In footnote 19, the Court refers to "reverse forum-shopping." That term refers to defendants who have been able sufficiently to manipulate the system so that they are able to get a forum (here, Scotland) with the law (and/or procedure) that *they,* and not the plaintiffs, want. (Remember: defendants have already 1) removed the case to federal court, 2) transferred it to Pennsylvania, and 3) obtained a dismissal; pretty good maneuvering by their attorneys.) Does this bother you? Or is the real problem with this case simply that it had no business in the California courts in the first place? Can the same be said of the Pennsylvania courts?

(2) *Historical Background.* As the *Piper* opinion indicates, the doctrine of forum non conveniens has been around for quite a while, with roots in the law of admiralty and in the law of Scotland. *See generally* Robert Braucher, *The Inconvenient Federal Forum,* 60 HARV. L. REV. 908 (1947). Its reception in this country was a little more hesitant, however: "*Forum non conveniens* is a recent invention, having been proposed in 1929 by a member of the New York City defense bar, and adopted by only a few states before 1947." Peter McAllen, *Deference to the Plaintiff in Forum Non Conveniens,* 13 So. ILL. L.J. 191, 193 (1989), referring to Paxton Blair, *The Doctrine of Forum Non Conveniens in Anglo-American Law,* 29 COLUM. L. REV. 1 (1929). When *Gulf Oil* was decided in 1947, however, forum non conveniens was here to stay in the federal courts. For the recent history of the doctrine, especially the cases following *Piper*, see William Reynolds, *The Proper Forum for a Suit: Transnational Forum Non Conveniens and Counter-Suit Injunctions in the Federal Courts,* 70 TEX. L. REV. 1663 (1992).

(3) *Voluntary Judicial Abstention.* Why would a court ever decline to hear a case over which it has jurisdiction? Consider the remarks of Chief Justice Marshall in *Cohens v. Virginia,* 19 U.S. (6 Wheat.) 264 (1821) (a subject matter jurisdiction case):

> It is most true that this Court will not take jurisdiction if it should not; but it is equally true that it must take jurisdiction if it should. . . . We have no more right to decline the exercise of jurisdiction which is given, than to usurp that which is not given. The one or the other would be treason to the constitution.

Does the *Piper* Court convince you that it is not committing "treason to the constitution"?

Compare the more hospitable attitude of some foreign courts. Lord Denning once wrote that, "No one who comes to these courts asking for justice should come in vain. . . . The right to come here is not confined to Englishmen. It extends to any friendly foreigner." *The Atlantic Star,* [1973] Q.B. 364, 381-82, rev'd, [1974] A. C. 436. Professor Juenger reports similar attitudes are found in many countries, and that the European Court of Justice has decided that a plaintiff should have her choice of filing a tort action in the country where either the conduct or injury occurred. Friedrich Juenger, *Forum Shopping, Domestic and International,* 63 TUL. L. REV. 553, 564-70 (1989).

This, of course, brings up the question of what's wrong with forum shopping. Forget all of the factors and interests and tests discussed in *Piper* and ask yourself why it should be possible to deny plaintiff her chosen forum if venue and jurisdiction are proper there. It is important to remember that venue and jurisdictional statutes represent political compromises concerning the proper exercise of fundamental powers of a sovereign. Should a court upset those compromises lightly—or at all? *See* Stein, *supra* Note (1), at 786-95.

(4) *Possible Remedies.* Section 1404(a) establishes the mechanics for transferring cases within the federal system. Similarly, a number of states provide for forum non conveniens transfers within their own system. What happens, however, if the forum non conveniens problem involves different judicial systems? *Piper Aircraft* represents one possibility—dismissal. But what if some of the defendants are not amenable to jurisdiction in the desired forum? What options does a court then have?

Can it stay its proceedings pending service of process in a more convenient forum? Can it dismiss on condition that defendants (all? some?) consent to jurisdiction in the more convenient forum? *See* EUGENE SCOLES ET AL. 381-382 (3d ed. 1992).

(5) *Forum Non Conveniens and Section 1404(a).* Justice Marshall carefully distinguishes in *Piper* between the forum non conveniens doctrine and a transfer made pursuant to 28 U.S.C. § 1404(a) (quoted in footnote 4 of the *Piper* opinion). Why? Is the formal distinction between a transfer within the same system (§ 1404) and a dismissal in favor of an alternative forum outside of the system (forum non conveniens) a real one? Intra-system transfers, to be sure, do provide the parties with the same general set of procedural and evidentiary rules. But are those issues as important as the convenience and power questions discussed in *Piper?* Are they as important as the choice-of-law question? (Choice-of-law issues under § 1404(a) are discussed in § 3.19 and Chapter 7, Part B, *infra.)*

Do you think Congress, when it adopted § 1404(a), was really trying to accomplish something different from the common law of forum non conveniens? Or, is it more realistic to assume that Congress basically was giving the federal courts a new procedure—transfer rather than dismissal—to use in cases when plaintiff's choice of forum is inconvenient? Justice Marshall seems to have adopted this latter view, for he wrote in *Piper* that § 1404(a) "was drafted in accordance with the doctrine of forum non conveniens." In any event, the lower federal courts seem to treat the two concepts as closely related, *e.g., Vaz Borraltio v. Keydril Co.,* 696 F.2d 379 (5th Cir. 1983), although generally "a *lesser* showing of inconvenience" is required for a §1404 (a) transfer, *Norwood v. Kirkpatrick,* 349 U.S. 29, 32 (1955). *See also* Scoles et al. *supra* note (4), at 492. The lesser standard is consistent with the difference between intra-and inter-system transfers, is it not?

The language of § 1404(a) has caused one major problem, however, for the transfer can be only "to any other district or division where it might have been brought." Does this preclude a transfer to another district where the defendant could object to venue or jurisdiction, but is willing to waive those objections? *See Hoffman v. Blaski,* 363 U.S. 335 (1960).

Section 1404(a) was adopted in 1948, the year after the decision in *Gulf Oil Corp. v. Gilbert,* as part of the general revision of the Federal Judicial

Code—and two years after the seminal decision on minimum contacts in *International Shoe Co. v. Washington,* 326 U.S. 310 (1946). *See* Stein, *supra* Note (2), at 801-08. Does that history give you any clues as to how to interpret § 1404(a)?

---

## THE BHOPAL LITIGATION
## IN RE UNION CARBIDE CORPORATION GAS PLANT
## DISASTER

*United States District Court, Southern District of New York*
*634 F. Supp. 842 (1986)*

[In December of 1984 a gas leak at a chemical plant operated by Union Carbide India Limited (UCIL) in Bhopal, India resulted in the worst industrial disaster in history with over 2,000 deaths and injuries to more than 200,000 persons. Within days of the accident, the first of more than 100 lawsuits was filed in the United States against Union Carbide Corporation (UCC), which owned just over fifty percent of the stock of UCIL. The suits were filed in seven different federal districts and were consolidated for pre-trial proceedings in the Southern District of New York. UCC moved to dismiss the suits on grounds of forum non conveniens. The District Court, following the analytical framework provided by *Gulf Oil Corp. v. Gilbert* and extended in *Piper Aircraft,* found that the Indian courts would provide a more appropriate forum. The court found that private interest concerns, such as the availability of witnesses and other evidentiary materials, along with the need to view the scene of the accident, argued in favor of India as the more appropriate forum. The court further found that public interest concerns such as administrative difficulties, the relative interests of India (which the court labeled "immense") and the United States, and applicable law also pointed to India as the more appropriate forum. Finally, the Indian legal system was found to provide "an adequate alternative forum" for the litigation.]

KEENAN, DISTRICT JUDGE. *Gilbert* and *Piper* explicitly acknowledge that the need of an American court to apply foreign law is an appropriate concern on a *forum non conveniens* motion, and can in fact point toward dismissal. . . . A federal court is bound to apply the choice of law rules of the state in which an action was originally brought; even upon transfer to a different district, the transferee district court must be obligated to apply the state law that would have been applied if there had been no change of venue. Thus, this court, sitting over a multi district litigation, must apply the various choice of law rules of the states in which the actions now consolidated before it were brought. . . . [I]t is likely that Indian law will emerge as the operative law. An Indian court, therefore, would be better able to apply the controlling law than would this United States Court. . . . This public interest factor . . . weighs in favor of dismissal on the grounds of *forum non conveniens* . . .

This Court is firmly convinced that the Indian legal system is in a far better position than the American courts to determine the cause of the tragic event and thereby fix liability. Further, the Indian Courts have greater access to all of the information needed to arrive at the amount of the compensation to be awarded the victims.

[One argument raised by the plaintiffs against dismissal on grounds of *forum non conveniens* was that a judgment rendered against UCC by an Indian court could not be enforced in the United States without additional extensive litigation. India, on the other hand, recognized the res judicata effect of foreign judgments so that a United States judgment against UCC could be readily enforced in India.]

The possibility of non-enforcement of a foreign judgment by courts of either country leads this Court to conclude that the issue must be addressed at this time. Since it is defendant Union Carbide which, perhaps ironically, argues for the sophistication of the Indian legal system in seeking a dismissal on grounds of *forum non conveniens,* and plaintiffs . . . state a strong preference for the American legal system, it would appear that both parties have indicated a willingness to abide by a judgment of the foreign nation whose forum each seeks to visit. Thus, this Court conditions the grant of a dismissal on *forum non conveniens* grounds on Union Carbide's agreement to be bound by the judgment of its preferred tribunal, located in India, and to satisfy any judgment rendered by the Indian court, and affirmed on appeal in India. Absent such consent to abide by and to "make good" on a foreign judgment, without challenge except for concerns relating to minimal due process, the motion to dismiss now under consideration will not be granted. The preference of both parties to play ball on a distant field will be taken to its limit, with each party being ordered to be bound by the decision of the respective foreign referees.

*The appeal.* On appeal, the Court of Appeals for the Second Circuit modified the order, 809 F.2d 195 (2nd Cir. 1987). Judge Mansfield wrote:

> [W]e are satisfied that there was no abuse of discretion in . . . granting dismissal . . . On the contrary, it might reasonably be concluded that it would have been an abuse of discretion to deny *a forum non conveniens* dismissal. . . .
>
> In requiring that UCC consent to enforceability of an Indian judgment against it, the district court proceeded at least in part on the erroneous assumption that, absent such a requirement, the plaintiffs, if they should succeed in obtaining an Indian judgment against UCC, might not be able to enforce it against UCC in the United States. The law, however, is to the contrary. Under New York law, which governs actions brought in New York to enforce foreign judgments, . . . a foreign-country judgment that is final, conclusive and enforceable where rendered must be recognized and will be enforced as "conclusive between the parties to the extent that it grants or denies recovery of a sum of money" [with exceptions for failure to provide due process or lack of personal jurisdiction]. Art. 53, Recognition of Foreign Country Money Judgments, 7B N.Y.Civ. Prac. L. & R. sections

5301-09 (McKinney 1978). . . . . [5] Since the court's condition with respect to enforceability of any final Indian judgment is predicated on an erroneous legal assumption . . . and since the district court's purpose is fully served by New York's statute providing for recognition of foreign-country money judgments, it was error to impose this condition upon the parties.

---

## NOTE ON THE BHOPAL LITIGATION

(1) *Who Was Right?* Why did the defendants move for a dismissal? Do you think they were worried about problems of proof and production of evidence? What of forum bias against them? *See* Louise Weinberg, *Insights and Ironies: The American Bhopal Cases,* 20 Tex. Int'l. L.J. 307, 315 (1985): "It lieth not in a defendant's mouth to argue that it is vexatious, harassing, and inconvenient to be sued at home."

Should the result change if India's tort system had been found not to be up to the challenges presented by the Bhopal disaster? Professor Marc Galanter, who was an expert witness for the plaintiffs in the *Bhopal* litigation discusses the relevant Indian law in Marc Galanter, *When Legal Worlds Collide: Reflections on Bhopal, the Good Lawyer and the American Law School,* 36 J. Legal Educ. 292 (1986).

If the accident had occurred in Kentucky rather than in India, would it have been appropriate to transfer the case under § 1404(a)? If so, and if India's legal system really is up to the challenge presented by the disaster, the decision is unobjectionable, isn't it?

An imaginative approach to the Bhopal problem is suggested in Daniel Magraw, *The Bhopal Disaster—Structuring a Solution,* 57 U. Colo. L. Rev. 835 (1986) (suggesting the creation of a joint American/Indian tribunal, along the lines of the American/Iranian claims tribunal now sitting in The Hague, to resolve all claims).

How should forum non conveniens apply when the foreign plaintiff sues an American defendant for human rights abuse, and the foreign government is part of the problem? *See* Kathryn Boyd, *The Inconvenience of Victims: Abolishing Forum Non Conveniens in U. S. Human Rights Litigation,* 39 Va. J. Int'l. L. 41 (1998).

---

[5] New York's article 53 is based upon the Uniform Foreign Money-Judgments Recognition Act, *see* 13 U.L.A. 263 (1962), which has been adopted by 15 states in addition to New York. In states that have not adopted the Uniform Money-Judgments Recognition Act, foreign judgments may be recognized according to principles of comity. *See Hilton v. Guyot,* 159 U.S. 113 (1895) [discussed in § 7.05, *infra*].

UCC, as a New York business corporation, would be subject to personal jurisdiction in a court sitting in New York. An Indian money judgment could be enforced against UCC in New York by means of either an action on the judgment or a motion for summary judgment in lieu of complaint. In either case, once converted into a New York judgment, the judgment would be enforceable as a New York judgment, and thus entitled to the full faith and credit of New York's sister states. [Footnote by the court.—*Eds.*]

(2) *The Conditional Dismissal.* The trial court conditioned its dismissal on Union Carbide's agreeing to be bound by a final judgment rendered by an Indian court. Was that a proper exercise of the court's authority? Enforceability of foreign judgments is generally discussed in § 7.05, *infra.*

*See* PROBLEM 3F-1. IN TRINIDAD; 3F-2. CAIRO OR CONNECTICUT.

## § 3.19   Forum Non Conveniens, Transfer and Choice of Law

### FERENS v. JOHN DEERE CO.

*Supreme Court Of The United States*
*494 U.S. 516; 110 S. Ct. 1274; 108 L. Ed. 2d 443 (1990)*

KENNEDY, J., delivered the opinion of the Court, in which REHNQUIST, C. J., and WHITE, STEVENS, and O'CONNOR, JJ., joined. SCALIA, J., filed a dissenting opinion, in which BRENNAN, MARSHALL, and BLACKMUN, JJ., joined.

[While working on his Pennsylvania farm, Albert Ferens lost his hand when it became caught in his combine harvester, manufactured by Deere & Company. He delayed filing a tort suit, and Pennsylvania's 2-year limitations period expired. In the third year, and within Pennsylvania's longer contract limitations period, he and his wife brought a contract and warranty action based on diversity of citizenship against Deere in the United States District Court for the Western District of Pennsylvania. The Ferenses also filed a second diversity suit against Deere in the United States District Court for the Southern District of Mississippi, alleging negligence and products liability. The Ferenses chose Mississippi because the statute of limitations for torts had not yet run; they knew that, under *Klaxon Co. v. Stentor Electric Mfg. Co.,* 313 U.S. 487, 496 (1941) [*see* § 6.15, *infra* ], a federal diversity court would apply Mississippi choice-of-law rules, which would require application of Mississippi's statute of limitations. On the ground that Pennsylvania was a more convenient forum, the Ferenses then moved, under § 1404(a), to transfer the action to the federal court in Pennsylvania. They assumed, based on *Van Dusen* v. *Barrack*, 376 U.S. 612 (1964), that, after the transfer, the Mississippi statute of limitations would continue to govern the suit. Deere did not oppose the motion, and the court granted the transfer. The District Court in Pennsylvania, however, ruled instead that, because the Ferenses had moved for transfer as plaintiffs, the rule in *Van Dusen* did not apply. Accordingly, it applied Pennsylvania's two-year statute of limitations and dismissed the Ferenses' tort action. The Court of Appeals for the Third Circuit affirmed.]

Section 1404(a) of Title 28 states: "For the convenience of parties and witnesses, in the interest of justice, a district court may transfer any civil action to any other district or division where it might have been brought." In *Van Dusen* v. *Barrack*, 376 U.S. 612 (1964), we held that, following a transfer under § 1404(a) initiated by a defendant, the transferee court must follow the choice-of-law rules that prevailed in the transferor court. We now decide that, when a plaintiff moves for the transfer, the same rule applies.

## II

Section 1404(a) states only that a district court may transfer venue for the convenience of the parties and witnesses when in the interest of justice. It says nothing about choice of law and nothing about affording plaintiffs different treatment from defendants. We touched upon these issues in *Van Dusen,* but left open the question presented in this case. In *Van Dusen,* an airplane flying from Boston to Philadelphia crashed into Boston Harbor soon after takeoff. The personal representatives of the accident victims brought more than 100 actions in the District Court for the District of Massachusetts and more than 40 actions in the District Court for the Eastern District of Pennsylvania. When the defendants moved to transfer the actions brought in Pennsylvania to the federal court in Massachusetts, a number of the Pennsylvania plaintiffs objected because they lacked capacity under Massachusetts law to sue as representatives of the decedents. The plaintiffs also averred that the transfer would deprive them of the benefits of Pennsylvania's choice-of-law rules because the transferee forum would apply to their wrongful-death claims a different substantive rule. The plaintiffs obtained from the Court of Appeals a writ of mandamus ordering the District Court to vacate the transfer. We reversed. . . . [and] held that the Court of Appeals erred in its assumption that Massachusetts law would govern the action following transfer. . . . [Based upon the legislative history of § 1404, we concluded] that the law applicable to a diversity case does not change upon a transfer initiated by a defendant.

## III

[The opinion in] *Van Dusen* reveals three independent reasons for our decision. First, § 1404(a) should not deprive parties of state-law advantages that exist absent diversity jurisdiction. Second, §1404(a) should not create or multiply opportunities for forum shopping. Third, the decision to transfer venue under § 1404(a) should turn on considerations of convenience and the interest of justice rather than on the possible prejudice resulting from a change of law. . . . [W]e find it prudent to consider [the same three factors] in deciding whether the rule in *Van Dusen* applies to transfers initiated by plaintiffs. We decide that, in addition to other considerations, these policies require a transferee forum to apply the law of the transferor court, regardless of who initiates the transfer. . . .

## A

The policy that § 1404(a) should not deprive parties of state-law advantages. . .has its real foundation in *Erie R. Co. v. Tompkins,* 304 U.S. 64 (1938). . .We explained *Erie* in *Guaranty Trust Co. v. York,* 326 U.S. 99, 109 (1945), as follows:

> In essence, the intent of [the Erie] decision was to insure that, in all cases where a federal court is exercising jurisdiction solely because of the diversity of citizenship of the parties, the outcome of the litigation in the federal court should be substantially the same, so far

as legal rules determine the outcome of a litigation, as it would be
if tried in a State court. The nub of the policy that underlies *Erie R.
Co. v. Tompkins* is that for the same transaction the accident of a suit
by a non-resident litigant in a federal court instead of in a State court
a block away should not lead to a substantially different result. . . .

The *Erie* policy had a clear implication for *Van Dusen*. The existence of
diversity jurisdiction gave the defendants the opportunity to make a motion
to transfer venue under § 1404(a), and if the applicable law were to change
after transfer, the plaintiff's venue privilege and resulting state-law advantages could be defeated at the defendant's option. To allow the transfer and
at the same time preserve the plaintiff's state-law advantages, we held that
the choice-of-law rules should not change following a transfer initiated by a
defendant.

Transfers initiated by a plaintiff involve some different considerations, but
lead to the same result. Applying the transferor law, of course, will not deprive
the plaintiff of any state-law advantages. A defendant, in one sense, also will
lose no legal advantage if the transferor law controls after a transfer initiated
by the plaintiff; the same law, after all, would have applied if the plaintiff
had not made the motion. In another sense, however, a defendant may lose
a nonlegal advantage. Deere, for example, would lose whatever advantage
inheres in not having to litigate in Pennsylvania, or, put another way, in
forcing the Ferenses to litigate in Mississippi or not at all. . . .

Applying the transferee law, by contrast, would undermine the *Erie* rule
in a serious way. It would mean that initiating a transfer under § 1404(a)
changes the state law applicable to a diversity case. . . . In general, however,
we have seen § 1404(a) as a housekeeping measure that should not alter the
state law governing a case under *Erie*. . . . The Mississippi statute of
limitations, which everyone agrees would have applied if the Ferenses had
not moved for a transfer, should continue to apply in this case.

### B

*Van Dusen* also sought to fashion a rule that would not create opportunities
for forum shopping. . . . An opportunity for forum shopping exists whenever
a party has a choice of forums that will apply different laws. The *Van Dusen*
policy against forum shopping simply requires us to interpret § 1404(a) in a
way that does not create an opportunity for obtaining a more favorable law
by selecting a forum through a transfer of venue. In the *Van Dusen* case itself,
this meant that we could not allow defendants to use a transfer to change
the law.

No interpretation of § 1404(a), however, will create comparable opportunities for forum shopping by a plaintiff because, even without § 1404(a), a
plaintiff already has the option of shopping for a forum with the most favorable
law. The Ferenses, for example, had an opportunity for forum shopping in the
state courts because both the Mississippi and Pennsylvania courts had
jurisdiction and because they each would have applied a different statute of
limitations. . . . Applying the transferor law would not give a plaintiff an
opportunity to use a transfer to obtain a law that he could not obtain through

his initial forum selection. If it does make selection of the most favorable law more convenient, it does no more than recognize a forum shopping choice that already exists. . . .

C

*Van Dusen* also made clear that the decision to transfer venue under § 1404(a) should turn on considerations of convenience rather than on the possibility of prejudice resulting from a change in the applicable law. We reasoned in *Van Dusen* that, if the law changed following a transfer initiated by the defendant, a district court "would at least be reluctant to grant transfers, despite considerations of convenience, if to do so might conceivably prejudice the claim of a plaintiff." The court, to determine the prejudice, might have to make an elaborate survey of the law, including statutes of limitations, burdens of proof, presumptions, and the like. This would turn what is supposed to be a statute for convenience of the courts into one expending extensive judicial time and resources. Because this difficult task is contrary to the purpose of the statute, in *Van Dusen* we made it unnecessary by ruling that a transfer of venue by the defendant does not result in a change of law. This same policy requires application of the transferor law when a plaintiff initiates a transfer. . . .

Some might think that a plaintiff should pay the price for choosing an inconvenient forum by being put to a choice of law versus forum. But this assumes that § 1404(a) is for the benefit only of the moving party. By the statute's own terms, it is not. Section 1404(a) also exists for the benefit of the witnesses and the interest of justice, which must include the convenience of the court. . . . The desire to take a punitive view of the plaintiff's actions should not obscure the systemic costs of litigating in an inconvenient place.

D

This case involves some considerations to which we perhaps did not give sufficient attention in *Van Dusen*. Foresight and judicial economy now seem to favor the simple rule that the law does not change following a transfer of venue under § 1404(a). Affording transfers initiated by plaintiffs different treatment from transfers initiated by defendants may seem quite workable in this case, but the simplicity is an illusion. . . . The rule would leave unclear which law should apply when both a defendant and a plaintiff move for a transfer of venue or when the court transfers venue on its own motion. The rule also might require variation in certain situations, such as when the plaintiff moves for a transfer following a removal from state court by the defendant, or when only one of several plaintiffs requests the transfer, or when circumstances change through no fault of the plaintiff making a once convenient forum inconvenient. True, we could reserve any consideration of these questions for a later day. But we have a duty, in deciding this case, to consider whether our decision will create litigation and uncertainty. On the basis of these considerations, we again conclude that the transferor law should apply regardless of who makes the § 1404(a) motion.

## IV

Our rule may seem too generous because it allows the Ferenses to have both their choice of law and their choice of forum, or even to reward the Ferenses for conduct that seems manipulative. We nonetheless see no alternative rule that would produce a more acceptable result. Deciding that the transferee law should apply, in effect, would tell the Ferenses that they should have continued to litigate their warranty action in Pennsylvania and their tort action in Mississippi. Some might find this preferable, but we do not. . . .

Second, one might contend that, because no per se rule requiring a court to apply either the transferor law or the transferee law will seem appropriate in all circumstances, we should develop more sophisticated federal choice-of-law rules for diversity actions involving transfers. To a large extent, however, state conflicts-of-law rules already ensure that appropriate laws will apply to diversity cases. Federal law, as a general matter, does not interfere with these rules. In addition, even if more elaborate federal choice-of-law rules would not run afoul of *Klaxon* and *Erie,* we believe that applying the law of the transferor forum effects the appropriate balance between fairness and simplicity.

For the foregoing reasons, we conclude that Mississippi's statute of limitations should govern the Ferenses' action. We reverse and remand for proceedings consistent with this opinion.

*It is so ordered.*

JUSTICE SCALIA, with whom JUSTICE BRENNAN, JUSTICE MARSHALL, and JUSTICE BLACKMUN join, dissenting.

In *Erie R. Co. v. Tompkins*, 304 U.S. 64 (1938), we held that the [Rules of Decision] Act requires a federal court to apply, in diversity cases, the law of the State in which it sits, both statutory law and common law established by the courts. Three years later, in *Klaxon Co. v. Stentor Electric Mfg. Co.*, 313 U.S. 487, 494 (1941), we considered "whether in diversity cases the federal courts must follow conflict of laws rules prevailing in the states in which they sit." We answered the question in the affirmative, reasoning that, were the rule otherwise, "the accident of diversity of citizenship would constantly disturb equal administration of justice in coordinate state and federal courts sitting side by side," a state of affairs that "would do violence to the principle of uniformity within a state, upon which the *Tompkins* decision is based." . . .

In *Van Dusen v. Barrack*, 376 U.S. 612 (1964), we held that a result different from *Klaxon* is produced when a suit has been transferred under § 1404(a) on defendant's motion. Our reasons were two. First, we thought it highly unlikely that Congress, in enacting § 1404(a), meant to provide defendants with a device by which to manipulate the substantive rules that would be applied. That conclusion rested upon the fact that the law grants the plaintiff the advantage of choosing the venue in which his action will be tried, with whatever state-law advantages accompany that choice. A defensive use of § 1404(a) in order to deprive the plaintiff of this "venue privilege," would allow the defendant to "get a change of law as a bonus for a change of venue," and would permit the defendant to engage in forum shopping among States, a privilege that the *Klaxon* regime reserved for plaintiffs. Second, we concluded that the policies of *Erie* and *Klaxon* would be undermined by application of the transferee court's choice-of-law principles in the case of a defendant-initiated transfer because then "the 'accident' of federal diversity jurisdiction" would enable the defendant "to utilize a transfer to achieve a result in federal court which could not have been achieved in the courts of the State where the action was filed. . . ."The goal of *Erie* and *Klaxon*, we reasoned, was to prevent "forum shopping" as between state and federal systems; the plaintiff makes a choice of forum law by filing the complaint, and that choice must be honored in federal court, just as it would have been honored in state court, where the defendant would not have been able to transfer the case to another State.

We left open in *Van Dusen* the question presented today, viz., whether "the same considerations would govern" if a plaintiff sought a § 1404(a) transfer. In my view, neither of those considerations is served—and indeed both are positively defeated—by a departure from *Klaxon* in that context. First, just as it is unlikely that Congress, in enacting § 1404(a), meant to provide the defendant with a vehicle by which to manipulate in his favor the substantive law to be applied in a diversity case, so too is it unlikely that Congress meant to provide the plaintiff with a vehicle by which to appropriate the law of a distant and inconvenient forum in which he does not intend to litigate, and to carry that prize back to the State in which he wishes to try the case. Second, application of the transferor court's law in this context would encourage forum shopping between federal and state courts in the same jurisdiction on the basis of differential substantive law . . . . [By their file-and-transfer maneuver], [t]he plaintiffs were seeking to achieve exactly what *Klaxon* was designed to prevent: the use of a Pennsylvania federal court instead of a Pennsylvania state court in order to obtain application of a different substantive law. . . . The significant federal judicial policy expressed in *Erie* and *Klaxon* is reduced to a laughingstock if it can so readily be evaded through filing-and-transfer.

The Court expresses concern that if normal *Erie-Klaxon* principles were applied a district judge might be reluctant to order a transfer, even when faced with the prospect of a trial that would be manifestly inconvenient to the parties, for fear that in doing so he would be ordering what is tantamount to a dismissal on the merits. But where the plaintiff himself has moved for a transfer, surely the principle of *volenti non fit injuria* suffices to allay that concern. . . .

The Court suggests that applying the choice-of-law rules of the forum court to a transferred case ignores the interest of the federal courts themselves in avoiding the "systemic costs of litigating in an inconvenient place,". . . . The point, apparently, is that these systemic costs will increase because the change in law attendant to transfer will not only deter the plaintiff from moving to transfer but will also deter the court from ordering sua sponte a transfer that will harm the plaintiff's case. . . . I do not think that the prospect of depriving the plaintiff of favorable law will any more deter a district judge from transferring than it would have deterred a district judge, under the prior regime, from ordering a dismissal sua sponte pursuant to the doctrine of forum non conveniens. In fact the deterrence to sua sponte transfer will be considerably less, since transfer involves no risk of statute-of-limitations bars to refiling. . . .

Thus, even as an exercise in giving the most extensive possible scope to the policies of § 1404(a), the Court's opinion seems to me unsuccessful. But as I indicated by beginning this opinion with the Rules of Decision Act, that should not be the object of the exercise at all. The Court and I reach different results largely because we approach the question from different directions. For the Court, this case involves an "interpretation of § 1404(a)," and the central issue is whether *Klaxon* stands in the way of the policies of that statute. For me, the case involves an interpretation of the Rules of Decision Act, and the central issue is whether § 1404(a) alters the "principle of uniformity within a state" which *Klaxon* says that Act embodies. I think my approach preferable, not only because the Rules of Decision Act does, and § 1404(a) does not, address the specific subject of which law to apply, but also because, as the Court acknowledges, our jurisprudence under that statute is "a vital expression of the federal system and the concomitant integrity of the separate States." To ask, as in effect the Court does, whether *Erie* gets in the way of § 1404(a), rather than whether § 1404(a) requires adjustment of *Erie*, seems to me the expression of a mistaken sense of priorities.

For the foregoing reasons, I respectfully dissent.

## NOTES AND QUESTIONS ON TRANSFER, FORUM NON CONVEVIENS AND CHOICE OF LAW

(1) *Van Dusen.* When the Supreme Court first confronted the issue of choice of law in the transfer context in *Van Dusen v. Barrack*, 376 U.S. 612 (1964), discussed at length in the *Ferens* opinion, the question arose after the defendants moved for transfer under § 1404(a); the Supreme Court, relying on the history and purpose of § 1404(a), held that the transferee district court must apply the law (including the choice-of-law rules) that the transferor district court would have applied:

> [Section] 1404 (a) was not designed to narrow the plaintiff's venue privilege or to defeat the state-law advantages that might accrue from the exercise of this venue privilege . . . The legislative history . . . certainly does not justify the rather startling conclusion that one might "get a change of law as a bonus for a change of venue." . . . If a change in the law were in the offing, the parties might regard the section primarily as a forum-shopping instrument. And, more importantly, courts would . . . be reluctant to grant transfers despite considerations of convenience if to do so might conceivably prejudice the claim of a plaintiff who initially selected a permissible forum. . . .

*Id.* at 635-637.

Why should the court be reluctant to "defeat the state-law advantages that might accrue from the exercise of [plaintiff's] . . . venue privilege?" Given this solicitude for the plaintiff's options, why should the Court be so alarmed at the possibility of forum shopping by the defendant? Is the Court's stance justified by the difference between the parties' litigation burdens?

Should the *Van Dusen* rule apply when transfer is from one federal circuit to another and the two differ on the interpretation of federal law? *See* Robert Ragazzo, *Transfer and Choice of Federal Law: The Appellate Model,* 93 MICH. L. REV. 703 (1995).

(2) *Transfer Under § 1406.* Section 1404(a) permits transfer when plaintiff's initial choice of forum is authorized by the venue statutes. When instead plaintiff's initial choice is incorrect, the court can simply dismiss the case for improper venue. Another transfer statute, 28 U.S.C. §1406(a), however, gives the court the additional option of transferring the case to a "district or division in which it could have been brought." The difference between the two options will be crucial, of course, when the statute of limitations has run. In *Goldlawr v. Heiman,* 369 U.S. 463 (1962), the Supreme Court interpreted the statute liberally to apply to jurisdiction as well as venue; thus it permits transfer "however wrong the plaintiff may have been in filing his case as to venue, whether the court in which it was filed had personal jurisdiction over the defendants or not." *Id.* at 466.

Should the *Van Dusen* rule (law of the transferor district) apply when the court transfers under § 1406(a)? Nearly all courts have held that it should not and that the transferee district should apply its own state's law. How would you justify that result? *See* ROBERT CASAD & WILLIAM RICHMAN, JURISDICTION IN CIVIL ACTIONS §5-6 (3d ed. 1998).

(3) *The History of Ferens.* *Ferens* had been to the Supreme Court before and was remanded to the Third Circuit. Initially the Third Circuit had affirmed the district court dismissal and held that the application of the Mississippi statute of limitations violated the due process clause. The Supreme Court remanded in light of its decision in *Sun Oil Co. v Wortman,* 486 U.S. 717 (1988) (*see* § 4.35[B], *infra*), which held that "a State may choose to apply its own statute of limitations to claims governed by the substantive laws of another state without violating the Full Faith and Credit Clause or the Due Process Clause." The decision in *Wortman* relied in part on the venerable history of the rule that the forum applies its own statute of limitations even when it applies the substantive law of another state (" 'If a thing has been practiced her for two hundred years by common consent, it will need a strong case for the Fourteenth Amendment to affect it.' ")

However, the Court also relied on the principle that "[a] state's interest in regulating the workload of its courts and determining when a claim is too stale to be adjudicated certainly suffices to give it legislative jurisdiction to control remedies available in its courts by imposing statutes of limitations." Because of the transfer, however, Mississippi's interest in regulating its courts had evaporated; after all, the case would be tried in Pennsylvania, not Mississippi. So was the Third Circuit's initial decision then correct after all? If so, was the Supreme Court then wrong to remand in light of its holding in *Wortman*? *See* David Seidelson, *1 (Wortman) + 1 (Ferens) = 6 (Years): That Can't be Right—Can it? Statutes of Limitations and Supreme Court Inconsistency,* 57 BROOKLYN L. REV. 787, 792 (1991).

(4) *Transfer on Motion of the Plaintiff.* Strangely, the opinion in *Ferens* simply assumes without discussion that a plaintiff can obtain a transfer under 28 U.S.C. § 1404 (a). But is that assumption really so self-evident? After all,

the plaintiff chose the court to begin with; after making the choice, why should the plaintiff be able to obtain a transfer? Clearly it would make sense to permit the plaintiff to move for transfer if conditions change after filing. For example, the addition of parties under Rule 19 or the filing of counterclaims, third-party claims, or cross claims might well alter the convenience balance and render some other forum preferable to plaintiff's initial choice. But in *Ferens*, there were no such changes; the case that was transferred was the same one filed by the plaintiff. Under those circumstances, why permit the plaintiff to obtain a transfer? For discussion of this issue, see Seidelson, *supra* note 3, at pp. 793-95.

(5) *Forum Shopping.* It is easy to see how the *Van Dusen* rule discourages forum shopping by the defendant; by retaining the law of the transferor state, the rule removes any choice-of-law incentive for the defendant to seek a transfer. The *Ferens* corollary, however, seems to have the opposite effect of encouraging both intrastate and interstate forum shopping by plaintiffs. Clearly *Ferens* gives the plaintiff a strong incentive to choose the federal court in the transferor state over the corresponding state court; the federal court presents—and the corresponding state court does not—the option of a transfer to a convenient forum while retaining the law of the transferor state. Further, the end result of *Ferens* file-and-transfer maneuver is to give the plaintiff a choice-of-law result in the transferee federal court that would not have been possible in the corresponding state court. Thus from the standpoint of either the transferee or the transferor state, *Ferens* seems to promote rather than discourage intrastate forum shopping.

The effect of *Ferens* on interstate forum shopping is even more obvious since it removes the only disincentive (litigation in an inconvenient forum) attached to shopping for more favorable state law.

For more discussion of *Ferens* and its effect on forum shopping, see Kimberly Norwood, *Shopping for a Venue: the Need for More Limits on Choice,* 50 U. MIAMI L. REV. 267 (1995).

(6) *Compare Piper Aircraft.* In *Van Dusen* and *Ferens*, the Supreme Court compelled the transferee court to apply the law of the transferor state in order to prevent the change of venue from depriving the plaintiffs of the choice-of-law advantages gained from their initial forum selections. In *Piper Aircraft Co. v. Reyno* (§ 3.18), the Court was unable to guarantee that result; there are no U. S. district courts in Scotland, and the Scottish courts stubbornly refuse to acknowledge the supervisory authority of the U. S. Supreme Court. The Supreme Court could have guaranteed the plaintiff the choice-of-law advantages of her initial forum selection only by denying the defendant's forum non conveniens dismissal motion. Yet it refused to do so, holding explicitly that the likelihood of a plaintiff-unfavorable change in governing law was not sufficient to prevent a forum non conveniens dismissal. Is that holding inconsistent with the rationale of *Van Dusen* and *Ferens*? *See* WILLIAM RICHMAN & WILLIAM REYNOLDS, UNDERSTANDING CONFLICT OF LAWS § 47[c] (3d ed. 2002).

## § 3.20   Forum Selection Clauses

### THE BREMEN v. ZAPATA OFF-SHORE CO.

*United States Supreme Court*
*407 U.S. 1, 92 S. Ct. 1907, 32 L. Ed. 2d 513 (1972)*

Mr. Chief Justice Burger delivered the opinion of the Court.

. . . In November 1967, respondent Zapata, a Houston based American corporation, contracted with petitioner Unterweser, a German corporation, to tow Zapata's ocean-going, self-elevating drilling rig Chaparral from Louisiana to a point off Ravenna, Italy. . . .

Zapata had solicited bids for the towage . . . Unterweser was the low bidder . . . The contract submitted by Unterweser contained the following provision, which is at issue in this case:

"Any dispute arising must be treated before the London Court of Justice." In addition the contract contained two clauses purporting to exculpate Unterweser from liability for damages to the towed barge. . . .

On January 5, 1968, Unterweser's deep sea tug Bremen departed Venice, Louisiana, with the Chaparral in tow bound for Italy. On January 9, while the flotilla was in international waters in the middle of the Gulf of Mexico, a severe storm arose. The sharp roll of the Chaparral in Gulf waters caused its elevator legs, which had been raised for the voyage, to break off and fall into the sea, seriously damaging the Chaparral. In this emergency situation Zapata instructed the Bremen to tow its damaged rig to Tampa, Florida, the nearest port of refuge.

On January 12, Zapata, ignoring its contract promise to litigate "any dispute arising" in the English courts, commenced a suit in admiralty in the United States District Court at Tampa, seeking $3,500,000 damages against Unterweser in personam and the Bremen in rem, alleging negligent towage and breach of contract. Unterweser responded by invoking the forum clause of the towage contract, and moved to dismiss for lack of jurisdiction or on forum non conveniens grounds, or in the alternative to stay the action pending submission of the dispute to the "London Court of Justice." Shortly thereafter,

. . . Unterweser commenced an action against Zapata seeking damages for breach of the towage contract in the High Court of Justice in London, as the contract provided. Zapata appeared in that court to contest jurisdiction, but its challenge was rejected, the English courts holding that the contractual forum provision conferred jurisdiction. . . .

We hold . . . that far too little weight and effect were given to the forum clause in resolving this controversy. For at least two decades we have witnessed an expansion of overseas commercial activities by business enterprises based in the United States. The barrier of distance that once tended to confine a business concern to a modest territory no longer does so. Here we see an American company with special expertise contracting with a foreign company to tow a complex machine thousands of miles across seas and oceans. The expansion of American business and industry will hardly be encouraged if, notwithstanding solemn contracts, we insist on a parochial concept that all disputes must be resolved under our laws and in our courts. . . . We cannot have trade and commerce in world markets and international waters exclusively on our terms, governed by our laws, and resolved in our courts.

Forum-selection clauses have historically not been favored by American courts. Many courts, federal and state, have declined to enforce such clauses on the ground that they were "contrary to public policy," or that their effect was to "oust the jurisdiction" of the court. Although this view apparently still has considerable acceptance, other courts are tending to adopt a more hospitable attitude toward forum-selection clauses. This view . . . is that such clauses are prima facie valid and should be enforced unless enforcement is shown by the resisting party to be "unreasonable" under the circumstances. We believe this is the correct doctrine to be followed by federal district courts sitting in admiralty. It is merely the other side of the proposition recognized by this Court in *National Equipment Rental, Ltd. v. Szukhent*, 375 U.S. 311 (1964), holding that in federal courts a party may validly consent to be sued in a jurisdiction where he cannot be found for service of process through contractual designation of an "agent" for receipt of process in that jurisdiction. . . . This approach is substantially that followed in other common law countries including England. It is the view advanced by noted scholars and that adopted by the Restatement of the Conflict of Laws. It accords with ancient concepts of freedom of contract and reflects an appreciation of the expanding horizons of American contractors who seek business in all parts of the world. Not surprisingly, foreign businessmen prefer, as do we, to have disputes resolved in their own courts, but if that choice is not available, then in a neutral forum with expertise in the subject matter. Plainly, the courts of England meet the standards of neutrality and long experience in admiralty litigation. The choice of that forum was made in an arm's-length negotiation by experienced and sophisticated businessmen, and absent some compelling and countervailing reason it should be honored by the parties and enforced by the courts.

The argument that such clauses are improper because they tend to "oust" a court of jurisdiction is hardly more than a vestigial legal fiction. It appears to rest at core on historical judicial resistance to any attempt to reduce the power and business of a particular court and has little place in an era when all courts are overloaded and when businesses once essentially local now operate in world markets. It reflects something of a provincial attitude regarding the fairness of other tribunals. . . .

There are compelling reasons why a freely negotiated private international agreement, unaffected by fraud, undue influence, or overweening bargaining power, such as that involved here, should be given full effect. In this case, for example, we are concerned with a far from routine transaction between companies of two different nations contemplating the tow of an extremely costly piece of equipment from Louisiana across the Gulf of Mexico and the Atlantic Ocean, through the Mediterranean Sea to its final destination in the Adriatic Sea. In the course of its voyage, it was to traverse the waters of many jurisdictions. The Chaparral could have been damaged at any point along the route, and there were countless possible ports of refuge. That the accident occurred in the Gulf of Mexico and the barge was towed to Tampa in an emergency were mere fortuities. It cannot be doubted for a moment that the parties sought to provide for a neutral forum for the resolution of any disputes arising during the tow. Manifestly much uncertainty and possibly great inconvenience to both parties could arise if a suit could be maintained in any jurisdiction in which an accident might occur or if jurisdiction were left to any place where the Bremen or Unterweser might happen to be found.[15] The elimination of all such uncertainties by agreeing in advance on a forum acceptable to both parties is an indispensable element in international trade, commerce, and contracting. There is strong evidence that the forum clause was a vital part of the agreement, and it would be unrealistic to think that the parties did not conduct their negotiations, including fixing the monetary terms, with the consequences of the forum clause figuring prominently in their calculations. . . .

Thus, in the light of present-day commercial realities and expanding international trade we conclude that the forum clause should control absent a strong showing that it should be set aside. Although their opinions are not altogether explicit, it seems reasonably clear that the District Court and the Court of Appeals placed the burden on Unterweser to show that London would be a more convenient forum than Tampa, although the contract expressly resolved that issue. The correct approach would have been to enforce the forum clause specifically unless Zapata could clearly show that enforcement would be unreasonable and unjust, or that the clause was invalid for such reasons as fraud or overreaching. Accordingly, the case must be remanded for reconsideration. . . .

Courts have also suggested that a forum clause, even though it is freely bargained for and contravenes no important public policy of the forum, may nevertheless be "unreasonable" and unenforceable if the chosen forum is seriously inconvenient for the trial of the action. Of course, where it can be said with reasonable assurance that at the time they entered the contract, the parties to a freely negotiated private international commercial agreement contemplated the claimed inconvenience, it is difficult to see why any such claim of inconvenience should be heard to render the forum clause unenforceable. We are not here dealing with an agreement between two Americans to resolve their essentially local disputes in a remote alien forum. In such a case, the serious inconvenience of the contractual forum to one or both of the parties might carry greater weight in determining the reasonableness of the forum clause. The remoteness of the forum might suggest that the agreement was an adhesive one, or that the parties did not have the particular controversy in mind when they made their agreement, yet even there the party claiming should bear a heavy burden of proof. Similarly, selection of a remote forum to apply differing foreign law to an essentially American controversy might contravene an important public policy of the forum. For example, so long as

---

[15] At the very least, the clause was an effort to eliminate all uncertainty as to the nature, location, and outlook of the forum in which these companies of differing nationalities might find themselves. Moreover, while the contract here did not specifically provide that the substantive law of England should be applied, it is the general rule in English courts that the parties are assumed, absent contrary indication, to have designated the forum with the view that it should apply its own law. It is therefore reasonable to conclude that the forum clause was also an effort to obtain certainty as to the applicable substantive law.

*Bisso* governs American courts with respect to the towage business in American waters,\* it would quite arguably be improper to permit an American tower to avoid that policy by providing a foreign forum for resolution of his disputes with an American towee.

This case, however, involves a freely negotiated international commercial transaction between a German and an American corporation for towage of a vessel from the Gulf of Mexico to the Adriatic Sea. . . .

*Vacated and remanded.*

MR. JUSTICE DOUGLAS, dissenting.

It is said that because these parties specifically agreed to litigate their disputes before the London Court of Justice, the District Court, absent "unreasonable" circumstances, should have honored that choice by declining to exercise its jurisdiction. The forum-selection clause, however, is part and parcel of the exculpatory provision in the towing agreement which . . . is not enforceable in American courts. For only by avoiding litigation in the United States could petitioners hope to evade the *Bisso* doctrine.

Judges in this country have traditionally been hostile to attempts to circumvent the public policy against exculpatory agreements. . . .

The instant stratagem of specifying a foreign forum is essentially the same as invoking a foreign law of construction except that the present circumvention also requires the American party to travel across an ocean to seek relief. . . .

[T]hese parties may have been of equal bargaining stature. Yet we have often adopted prophylactic rules rather than attempt to sort the core cases from the marginal ones. . . .

## FORUM SELECTION CLAUSES

(1) *Freedom of Contract and Other Issues.* Why not routinely enforce forum selection clauses; are they not merely one facet of a general freedom to contract? Would a federal-court-created right to enforce such clauses run afoul of the doctrine of *Erie R.R. v. Tompkins*, 304 U.S. 64 (1938)? Isn't personal jurisdiction a right which can be waived? If so, why not permit it to be waived in advance? *See* Linda Mullenix, *Another Choice of Forum, Another Choice of Law: Consensual Adjudicatory Procedure in Federal Courts*, 57 FORD. L. REV. 291, 323 (1989).

Was the Court's reliance on the *Szukhent* decision (*see* § 3.12, *supra*) well-placed? Professor Mullenix argues that *Szukhent* is an "inappropriate" foundation for *The Bremen*, *id.* at 307-09, both because of its lack of reasoning and because it really involved the validity of service of process under Federal Rule 4. Do you agree?

Chief Justice Burger's opinion emphasizes the needs of the international economy. Do you find that persuasive? Would the argument have been as strong if the case were purely domestic?

---

\* *Bisso v. Inland Waterways Corp.*, 349 U.S. 85 (1955), had held invalid an exculpatory clause in a towage contract —*Eds.*

What of his emphasis on the parties' need for certainty, a goal which, if met, surely will reduce costs; does that answer all objections? Does Burger give any other reason for embracing forum selection clauses?

(2) *The Unreasonableness Problem.* The Court states that an unreasonable agreement should not be enforced; the clause, in other words, will be unenforceable if there exist "grounds for the revocation of any contract," e.g., fraud or "overwhelming economic power." *The Bremen,* of course, provided a paradigm case for enforcing forum clauses; the parties were sophisticated, knowledgeable international organizations.

How likely is it that a court will find a clause unreasonable under other circumstances? *See* Mullenix, *supra* note (1) at 352: "In almost every instance, without regard to the comparative size, skills, sophistication or assets of the parties, the courts find fair bargaining." Are you surprised? *See Hodes v. S.N.C Achille Lauro,* 858 F.2d 905 (3d Cir. 1988), where a passenger's ticket on the hijacked Achille Lauro cruise ship provided that all disputes would be controlled by Italian law and suit could be only in the courts of Naples; the complaint alleged inadequate security by the defendant. Should the clause be honored? The court thought so: "We adamantly refuse to wield the trump of American public policy. . . . American passengers, simply do not carry American public policy on their backs wheresoever they may venture." Do you agree? *See* Symeon Symeonides, *Choice of Law in the American Courts in 1988,* 37 AM. J. COMP. L. 457, 488 (1989).

Finally, should a choice-of-law provision in a forum selection clause count in the reasonableness equation? Does the decision in *Burger King v. Rudzewicz,* 471 U.S. 462 (1985), § 3.10, *supra,* help you answer this question? *See D'Antuono v. CCH ComputaxSystems,* 570 F. Supp. 708 (D.R.I. 1983) (it counts). Why is that? Is party autonomy the key factor or is it because the forum will also be familiar with governing law? Or does the presence of both jurisdiction and choice of law clauses merely show the overwhelming bargaining power of one party?

What if the contract stipulated that disputes must be heard in Iran, and then the Iranian revolution broke out? *See McDonnell Douglas Corp. v. Islamic Republic of Iran,* 758 F.2d 341 (8th Cir. 1985), *cert. denied,* 474 U.S. 948 (1985).

(3) *Public Policy in the States.* Occasionally, a statute has been construed to invalidate forum selection clauses. *See* RUSSELL WEINTRAUB, COMMENTARY ON THE CONFLICT OF LAWS 283 (4th ed. 2001). Some states are quite hostile to forum selection clauses. *See, e.g., Stewart Org. v. Ricoh,* 487 U.S. 22 (1988) (Alabama does not generally enforce forum selection clauses). Federal courts, however, "routinely and uncritically" use *The Bremen* to enforce forum selection clauses even in domestic cases. Mullenix, *supra* Note (1), at 313.

*See* PROBLEM 3F-3. PARTNERS IN DISPUTE.

(4) *The Problem of the Exculpatory Clause.* Why would a court not want its jurisdiction "ousted"? In the old days of the common law, when judges were paid by fees from litigants, hostility to jurisdiction-ousting provisions like arbitration clauses was easy to understand. But federal judges aren't paid by litigants' fees. Why should they be concerned with such clauses? Especially

given all the complaints today about overcrowded dockets. Surely the English court specified in *The Bremen* will provide a high standard of justice—at least of the procedural variety.

And therein might lie the rub, for is not the real fight over the enforceability of the exculpatory clauses? While Justice Douglas thought those clauses unenforceable under American precedent, the majority suggested they would be enforced in England. So the fight really becomes one of public policy; should the litigants be free to contract in such a way so as to avoid the strong public policy against exculpatory clauses? (Recall the converse situation in *Burger King v. Rudzewicz*, 471 U.S. 462 (1985) § 3.10, *supra*, where a choice-of-law clause was used because Michigan law forbade a forum selection clause in the franchise agreement.)

Put somewhat differently, the selection of a forum heavily influences the judicial decision concerning which law to apply, and, therefore, in *The Bremen*, whether the exculpatory clauses will be recognized. Should the parties be able to do that. In other words, why are not nonadhesive exculpatory clauses routinely enforced? Consider whether the American policy against exculpation is designed to benefit anyone other than the parties to the agreement. If not, and the contract is not unconscionable, then do we really care? On the other hand, does the reason behind the policy against exculpatory clauses suggest that the contracting parties should not be allowed to make them enforceable by using the back door of a forum—selection clause? In other words (and not for the first time), is jurisdiction as important as choice of law?

(5) *The Special Problem of Arbitration Clauses.* An arbitration agreement, like a forum selection clause, ousts a court of jurisdiction. But it also does more, for arbitration panels usually are not bound by precedent, and their decisions are generally unreviewable except for fraud. No judicial officer, in other words, decides whether an arbitration award is consistent with established law. Does that bother you? Arbitration eliminates some personal rights, but it is something the parties have agreed to do; is there any thing else involved? Consider *Scherck v. Alberto-Culver*, 417 U.S. 506 (1974), a case with an arbitration clause and international connections, but which was substantively governed by American antitrust law. The Court treated the arbitration clause as just another forum selection problem and reiterated some of the language from *The Bremen*:

> [A] contractual provision specifying in advance the forum for litigating disputes and the law to be applied is an almost indispensable precondition to achieving the orderliness and predictability essential to any international business transaction.

417 U.S. at 506. Justice Stevens, dissenting in another antitrust/international arbitration case, observed that "it is improper to subordinate the public interest in enforcement of antitrust policy to the private interest of resolving commercial disputes. . . . " *Mitsubishi Motors Corp. v. Soler Chrysler-Plymouth Inc.*, 473 U.S. 614, 665 (1985). Stevens' concern that an arbitrator will be less interested in policy and more interested in party expectations (the heart of commercial law) is realistic, isn't it? But does that mean that it necessarily trumps the commercial demand for certainty?

In any event, the Supreme Court has embraced arbitration clauses with all the fervor of the newly converted. The culmination of this trend was *Rodriguez de Quija v. Shearson/Am. Express, Inc.*, 109 S. Ct. 1917 (1989), overruling the long-standing decision of *Wilko v. Swan*, 346 U.S. 427 (1953) (holding that claims brought by customers of brokers under the 1933 Securities Act cannot be forced to arbitration).

*See* PROBLEM 3F-4. THE ARBITRATION.

(6) *See generally* Mullenix, *supra* Note (1); Rudolph Schlesinger, *Jurisdictional Clauses in Consumer Transactions: A Multifaceted Problem of Jurisdiction and Full Faith and Credit*, 29 HASTINGS L.J. 967 (1978); James Gilbert, *Choice of Forum Clauses in International and Interstate Contracts*, 65 KY. L.J. 1 (1976).

---

# CARNIVAL CRUISE LINES, INC. v. SHUTE

*United States Supreme Court*
*499 U.S. 585; 111 S. Ct. 1522; 113 L. Ed. 2d 622 (1991)*

OPINION BY JUSTICE BLACKMUN

In this admiralty case we primarily consider whether the United States Court of Appeals for the Ninth Circuit correctly refused to enforce a forum-selection clause contained in tickets issued by petitioner Carnival Cruise Lines, Inc., to respondents Eulala and Russel Shute.

[The Shutes, through a Washington travel agent, purchased a 7-day cruise on petitioner's ship, the Tropicale. They paid the fare to the agent who forwarded the payment to Carnival's headquarters in Florida. Carnival then sent a "contract ticket" to the Shutes in Washington. Each ticket contained the following forum selection clause:

> 8. It is agreed by and between the passenger and the Carrier that all disputes and matters whatsoever arising under, in connection with or incident to this Contract shall be litigated, if at all, in and before a Court located in the State of Florida, U. S. A., to the exclusion of the Courts of any other state or country.

The Shutes boarded the Tropicale in Los Angeles, and the ship sailed to Puerto Vallarta, Mexico, and then returned to Los Angeles. In international waters off the Mexican coast, Eulala Shute was injured when she slipped and fell during a tour of the ship's galley. The Shutes filed suit against Carnival in the United States District Court for the Western District of Washington, claiming that Mrs. Shute's injuries had been caused by the negligence of Carnival and its employees. The district court upheld the forum selection clause, but the Court of Appeals reversed.]

[T]he Court of Appeals acknowledged that a court concerned with the enforceability of such a clause must begin its analysis with *The Bremen v. Zapata Off-Shore Co.*, where this Court held that forum-selection clauses, although not "historically . . . favored," are "prima facie valid." The appellate court concluded that the forum clause should not be enforced because it "was not freely bargained for." As an "independent justification" for refusing to enforce the clause, the Court of Appeals noted that there was evidence in the record to indicate that "the Shutes are physically and financially incapable of pursuing this litigation in Florida" and that the enforcement of the clause would operate to deprive them of their day in court and thereby contravene this Court's holding in *The Bremen*. We granted certiorari to address the question whether the Court of Appeals was correct in holding that the District Court should hear respondents' tort claim against petitioner. Because we find the forum-selection clause to be dispositive of this question, we need not consider [Carnival's] constitutional argument [that it was not amenable to personal jurisdiction in Washington].

We begin by noting [that] we do not address the question whether respondents had sufficient notice of the forum clause before entering the contract for passage. . . Respondents essentially have conceded that they had notice of the forum-selection provision. Additionally, the Court of Appeals evaluated the enforceability of the forum clause under the assumption, although "doubtful," that respondents could be deemed to have had knowledge of the clause.

Within this context, respondents urge that the forum clause should not be enforced because, contrary to this Court's teachings in *The Bremen*, the clause was not the product of negotiation, and enforcement effectively would deprive respondents of their day in court.

Both petitioner and respondents argue vigorously that the Court's opinion in *The Bremen* governs this case, and each side purports to find ample support for its position in that opinion's broad-ranging language. This seeming paradox derives in large part from key factual differences between this case and *The Bremen*, differences that preclude an automatic and simple application of *The Bremen's* general principles to the facts here.

In *The Bremen*, this Court [held] . . . that, in general, "a freely negotiated private international agreement, unaffected by fraud, undue influence, or overweening bargaining power, such as that involved here, should be given full effect." The Court further generalized that "in the light of present-day commercial realities and expanding international trade we conclude that the forum clause should control absent a strong showing that it should be set aside." The Court did not define precisely the circumstances that would make it unreasonable for a court to enforce a forum clause. Instead, the Court discussed a number of factors that made it reasonable to enforce the clause at issue in *The Bremen* and that, presumably, would be pertinent in any determination whether to enforce a similar clause.

In this respect, the Court noted that there was "strong evidence that the forum clause was a vital part of the agreement, and [that] it would be unrealistic to think that the parties did not conduct their negotiations, including fixing the monetary terms, with the consequences of the forum clause figuring prominently in their calculations." Further, the Court observed that it was not "dealing with an agreement between two Americans to resolve their essentially local disputes in a remote alien forum," and that in such a case, "the serious inconvenience of the contractual forum to one or both of the parties might carry greater weight in determining the reasonableness of the forum clause." The Court stated that even where the forum clause establishes a remote forum for resolution of conflicts, "the party claiming [unfairness] should bear a heavy burden of proof."

*The Bremen* concerned a "far from routine transaction between companies of two different nations contemplating the tow of an extremely costly piece of equipment from Louisiana across the Gulf of Mexico and the Atlantic Ocean, through the Mediterranean Sea to its final destination in the Adriatic Sea." These facts suggest that, even apart from the evidence of negotiation regarding the forum clause, it was entirely reasonable for the Court in *The Bremen* to have expected Unterweser and Zapata to have negotiated with care in selecting a forum for the resolution of disputes arising from their special towing contract. In contrast, respondents' passage contract was purely routine and doubtless nearly identical to every commercial passage contract issued by petitioner and most other cruise lines. In this context, it would be entirely unreasonable for us to assume that respondents—or any other cruise passenger—would negotiate with petitioner the terms of a forum-selection clause in an ordinary commercial cruise ticket. Common sense dictates that a ticket of this kind will be a form contract the terms of which are not subject to negotiation, and that an individual purchasing the ticket will not have bargaining parity with the cruise line. But by ignoring the crucial differences in the business contexts in which the respective contracts were executed, the Court of Appeals' analysis seems to us to have distorted somewhat this Court's holding in *The Bremen*.

In evaluating the reasonableness of the forum clause at issue in this case, we must refine the analysis of *The Bremen* to account for the realities of form passage contracts. As an initial matter, we do not adopt the Court of Appeals' determination that a nonnegotiated forum-selection clause in a form ticket contract is never enforceable simply because it is not the subject of bargaining. Including a reasonable forum clause in a form contract of this kind well may be permissible for several reasons: First, a cruise line has a special interest in limiting the fora in which it potentially could be subject to suit. Because a cruise ship typically carries passengers from many locales, it is not unlikely that a mishap on a cruise could subject the cruise line to litigation in several different fora. Additionally, a clause establishing ex ante the forum for dispute resolution has the salutary effect of dispelling any confusion about where suits arising from the contract must be brought and defended, sparing litigants the time and expense of pretrial motions to determine the correct forum and conserving judicial resources that otherwise would be devoted to deciding those motions. Finally, it stands to reason that passengers who purchase tickets containing a forum clause like that at issue in this case benefit in the form of reduced fares reflecting the savings that the cruise line enjoys by limiting the fora in which it may be sued. We also do not accept the Court of Appeals' "independent justification" for its conclusion that *The Bremen* dictates that the clause should not be enforced because "there is evidence in the record to indicate that the Shutes are physically and financially incapable of pursuing this litigation in Florida." We do not defer to the Court of Appeals' findings of fact. In dismissing the case for lack of personal jurisdiction over petitioner, the District Court made no finding regarding the physical and financial impediments to the Shutes' pursuing their case in Florida. The Court of Appeals' conclusory reference to the record provides no basis for this Court to validate the finding of inconvenience. Furthermore, the Court of Appeals did not place in proper context this Court's statement in *The Bremen* that "the serious inconvenience of the contractual forum to one or both of the parties might carry greater weight in determining the reasonableness of the forum clause." The Court made this statement in evaluating a hypothetical "agreement between two Americans to resolve their essentially local disputes in a remote alien forum." In the present case, Florida is not a "remote alien forum," nor—given the fact that Mrs. Shute's accident occurred off the coast of Mexico—is this dispute an essentially local one inherently more suited to resolution in the State of Washington than in Florida. In light of these distinctions, and because respondents do not claim lack of notice of the forum clause, we conclude that they have not satisfied the "heavy burden of proof," required to set aside the clause on grounds of inconvenience.

It bears emphasis that forum-selection clauses contained in form passage contracts are subject to judicial scrutiny for fundamental fairness. In this case, there is no indication that petitioner set Florida as the forum in which disputes were to be resolved as a means of discouraging cruise passengers from pursuing legitimate claims. Any suggestion of such a bad-faith motive is belied by two facts: petitioner has its principal place of business in Florida, and many of its cruises depart from and return to Florida ports. Similarly, there is no evidence that petitioner obtained respondents' accession to the forum clause by fraud or overreaching. Finally, respondents have conceded that they were given notice of the forum provision and, therefore, presumably retained the option of rejecting the contract with impunity. In the case before us, therefore, we conclude that the Court of Appeals erred in refusing to enforce the forum-selection clause.

The judgment of the Court of Appeals is reversed.

*It is so ordered.*

JUSTICE STEVENS, with whom JUSTICE MARSHALL joins, dissenting.

The Court prefaces its legal analysis with a factual statement that implies that a purchaser of a Carnival Cruise Lines passenger ticket is fully and fairly notified about the existence of the choice of forum clause in the fine print on the back of the ticket. Even if this implication were accurate, I would disagree with the Court's analysis. But, given the Court's preface, I begin my dissent by noting that only the most meticulous passenger is likely to become aware of the forum-selection provision. . . .

Of course, many passengers, like the respondents in this case, will not have an opportunity to read [the clause] until they have actually purchased their tickets. By this point, the passengers will already have accepted the condition set forth in [the contract ticket] which provides that "the Carrier shall not be liable to make any refund to passengers in respect of . . . tickets wholly or partly not used by a passenger." Not knowing whether or not that provision is legally enforceable, I assume that the average passenger would accept the risk of having to file suit in Florida in the event of an injury, rather than canceling—without a refund—a planned vacation at the last minute. The fact that the cruise line can reduce its litigation costs, and therefore its liability insurance premiums, by forcing this choice on its passengers does not, in my opinion, suffice to render the provision reasonable. . . .

Forum-selection clauses in passenger tickets involve the intersection of two strands of traditional contract law that qualify the general rule that courts will enforce the terms of a contract as written. Pursuant to the first strand, courts traditionally have reviewed with heightened scrutiny the terms of contracts of adhesion, form contracts offered on a take-or-leave basis by a party with stronger bargaining power to a party with weaker power. . .

The common law, recognizing that standardized form contracts account for a significant portion of all commercial agreements. . . subjects terms in contracts of adhesion to scrutiny for reasonableness. Judge J. Skelly Wright set out the state of the law succinctly in *Williams v. Walker-Thomas Furniture Co.*:

> "Ordinarily, one who signs an agreement without full knowledge of its terms might be held to assume the risk that he has entered a one-sided bargain. But when a party of little bargaining power, and hence little real choice, signs a commercially unreasonable contract with little or no knowledge of its terms, it is hardly likely that his consent, or even an objective manifestation of his consent, was ever given to all of the terms. In such a case the usual rule that the terms of the agreement are not to be questioned should be abandoned and the court should consider whether the terms of the contract are so unfair that enforcement should be withheld."

The second doctrinal principle implicated by forum-selection clauses is the traditional rule that "contractual provisions, which seek to limit the place or court in which an action may . . . be brought, are invalid as contrary to public policy." Although adherence to this general rule has declined in recent years, particularly following our decision in *The Bremen v. Zapata Off-Shore Co.*, the prevailing rule is still that forum-selection clauses are not enforceable if they were not freely bargained for, create additional expense for one party, or deny one party a remedy. A forum-selection clause in a standardized passenger ticket would clearly have been unenforceable under the common law before our decision in *The Bremen*, and, in my opinion, remains unenforceable under the prevailing rule today.

*The Bremen*, which the Court effectively treats as controlling this case, had nothing to say about stipulations printed on the back of passenger tickets. That case involved the enforceability of a forum-selection clause in a freely negotiated international agreement between two large corporations providing for the towage of a vessel from the Gulf of Mexico to the Adriatic Sea. The Court recognized that such towage agreements had generally been held unen- forceable . . . but held that the doctrine of those cases did not extend to commercial arrangements between parties with equal bargaining power. . .

I would continue to apply the general rule that prevailed prior to our decision in *The Bremen* to forum-selection clauses in passenger tickets.

I respectfully dissent.

## NOTES ON FORUM SELECTION CLAUSES IN CONSUMER CONTRACTS

(1) *Unanswered Questions.* An arm's-length, international contract between sophisticated parties, *The Bremen* was an ideal case for the enforcement of a forum selection clause. Because it was an easy case, *The Bremen* left many questions unanswered: Under what circumstances would a forum-selection clause be unreasonable or unjust? When would it violate the forum's public policy? What should count as serious inconvenience? Should the rule apply only between sophisticated contracting parties, or should it embrace routine transactions involving consumers? *See* William M. Richman, *Carnival Cruise Lines: Forum Selection Clauses in Adhesion Contracts*, 40 AM. J. COMP. L. 977, 979 (1992). To what extent have these questions been answered in *Carnival Cruise*?

(2) *The Scope of the Holding.* Is there anything left of the reasonableness and inconvenience limitations of *The Bremen*, or does *Carnival Cruise* validate every agreement? The majority pointed to three factors that made the agreement reasonable: the possibility of suits in many fora, simplification of the threshold question of jurisdiction, and the possibility of savings to consumers from reduced transaction costs. But won't these factors be present in every transaction between a national or international seller and a local consumer? *See* Patrick J. Borchers, *Forum Selection Agreements in the Federal Courts after Carnival Cruise: A Proposal for Congressional Reform*, 67 WASH. L. REV. 55, 74 (1992).

The Court does acknowledge two *Bremen*–based limitations on forum-selection agreements that survive *Carnival Cruise*. First, "serious inconvenience" is still a ground for invalidating a forum-selection clause; however, the Court limits the scope of this exception to cases involving an "agreement between Americans to resolve their essentially local disputes in a remote alien forum." Second, a clause may be invalidated if the drafter uses it as a device for discouraging consumers from pursuing legitimate claims. In the next sentence, however, the court shows its reluctant to find evidence of such a bad faith motive as long as the chosen forum is the drafter's headquarters or a place where it does a substantial amount of business. Given the Court's narrow interpretation of the two remaining tests for validity, how likely is it that a forum-selection clause will ever fail either?

(3) *Contracts I.* One of the main justifications for validating forum-selection clauses is freedom of contract; the parties should be able to agree before hand on a method for resolving their disputes. Purely as a matter of contract law, was there a meeting of the minds in *Carnival Cruise* ? Is your answer affected by Justice Stevens' suggestion in that the Shutes had no opportunity to see the clause until they received their tickets, at which point their purchase was "non-refundable?" Should the Court have invalidated the clause as "unconscionable?" The doctrine is recognized in the Uniform Commercial Code (*see* § 2-302) and defined in the well-known case of *Williams v. Walker-Thomas Furniture Co.*, 350 F.2d 445 (D.C. Cir. 1965). Its hallmarks are a lack of meaningful

choice on the part of one party, terms which are unreasonably favorable to the other party, fine-print boilerplate provisions, and inequality of bargaining power (especially where one party lacks the knowledge or sophistication to understand terms drafted by the other). *See* Linda Mullenix, *Another Easy Case, Some More Bad Law: Carnival Cruise Lines and Contractual Personal Jurisdiction*, 27 TEXAS INT'L L.J. 323, 353-35 (1992). Does *The Bremen* allow explicitly for invalidation of a forum-selection clause based on unconscionability? If not, does the language concerning unreasonableness embrace the concept implicitly?

(4) *Economics 101.* Are you impressed by the Court's use of economics to conclude that "it stands to reason" that consumers will benefit from Carnival's savings as a result of the forum-selection clause? Most commentators were not:

> In order to justify [its] . . . conclusory recitation, the Court would need to postulate a competitive market and consider such variables as the competition in the local and national markets for cruise passengers, the primacy of price (as opposed to other factors) in the choices of passengers, the pressure on Carnival to offer price concessions in lieu of other inducements, the extent to which governmental regulations limit savings transmissions to passengers, the percentage of Carnival's revenues that would be devoted to legal expenses with and without forum-selection clauses, the likelihood that any possible savings would be transmitted to consumers rather than to shareholders, management or employees, and the likelihood that savings actually passed on would amount to any sum sufficient to consider a "benefit" to any particular passenger. Without serious consideration of those factors, the court's conclusory recitation is bad law and bad economics.

*See* Richman, *supra* note 1, at 984. As usual, Professor Weintraub was more eloquent and more succinct: The Court, "applying economic theory apparently gleaned from the back of a bubble gum wrapper, enforced the clause. . . . " *See Conference on Jurisdiction, Justice and Choice of Law for the Twenty-First Century: Case One: Choice of Forum Clauses*, 29 N. ENG. L. REV. 517, 555 (1995). Not all commentators have been so harsh, however. *See* Michael Solimine, *Forum Selection Clauses and the Privatization of Procedure,* 25 CORNELL INT. L. J.51 (1992).

(5) *The Chicago School.* The central tenet of the law and economics school is that freedom of contract produces the most efficient results for society; regulation by market forces is superior to government intervention. In a free market a rational actor will not enter a contract unless it improves her position. Form contracts are not an evil, but rather an efficient substitute for individual negotiation and drafting of instruments in similar repetitive transactions. Nor does the imposition of harsh terms by the stronger contracting party (the seller in a consumer transaction) call for government regulation because competition among sellers will result in an economically ideal allocation of resources. If one seller offers unattractive terms, other sellers will enter the market offering better terms in hopes of securing more sales. Even an information deficiency among consumers is not a worry; as long as some proportion of consumers are informed, sellers will compete for their

business, thus offering better terms to all. Further, if some sellers insist on oppressive terms, their competitors will have an economic incentive to inform consumers via advertising of their own willingness to forego the advantage. Thus, according to this view, there is no need for the courts to invalidate forum selection clauses in consumer contracts; the market will insure that consumers will have either a choice of a contract without the offensive term or a concession on some other term worth at least as much. For a much more complete rendition of the Chicago School argument, see Lee Goldman, *My Way and the Highway: the Law and Economics of Choice of Forum Clauses in Consumer Form Contracts*, 86 Nw. U. L. Rev. 700, 714-716 (1992).

In your own experience, how many of the economic assumptions of the preceding paragraph are justified? Do consumers always (typically) act rationally? Do they usually have enough information to assess the value of a forum-selection clause to the seller or its potential cost to the consumer? Is it rational for a consumer to incur the costs required to read and become informed about all terms in a sales contract? Do you read and understand them all? Given the low probability of a claim against the cruise lines for each consumer, would a rational consumer choose one supplier over another based upon a forum selection term? What about competitor advertising? Will Kathy Lee Gifford sing, "We've got the ships; we've got the fun; we've got the food; we've got the great destinations; AND, should you become injured on one of our ships, you can maintain an action against us in a court convenient to you instead of having to sue in a distant forum across the country"? *See* Goldman, *supra*, for a more complete critique of the Chicago School position.

---

## STEWART ORGANIZATION, INC. v. RICOH CORP.

*United States Supreme Court*
*487 U.S. 22, 108 S. Ct. 2239; 101 L. Ed. 2d 22 (1988)*

Justice Marshall delivered the opinion of the Court.

This case presents the issue whether a federal court sitting in diversity should apply state or federal law in adjudicating a motion to transfer a case to a venue provided in a contractual forum-selection clause.

The dispute underlying this case grew out of a dealership agreement that obligated petitioner, an Alabama corporation, to market copier products of respondent, a nationwide manufacturer with its principal place of business in New Jersey. The agreement contained a forum-selection clause providing that any dispute arising out of the contract could be brought only in a court located in Manhattan. . . . In September 1984, petitioner brought a complaint in the United States District Court for the Northern District of Alabama. . . .

Relying on the contractual forum-selection clause, respondent moved the District Court either to transfer the case to the Southern District of New York under 28 U. S. C. § 1404(a) or to dismiss the case for improper venue under 28 U. S. C. § 1406. The District Court denied the motion. It reasoned that the transfer motion was controlled by Alabama law and that Alabama looks unfavorably upon contractual forum-selection clauses. . . .

Both the panel opinion and the opinion of the full Court of Appeals referred to the difficulties that often attend "the sticky question of which law, state or federal, will govern various aspects of the decisions of federal courts sitting in diversity." A District Court's decision whether to apply a federal statute such as § 1404(a) in a diversity action,[3] however, involves a considerably less intricate analysis than that which governs the "relatively unguided *Erie* choice." Our cases indicate that when the federal law sought to be applied is a congressional statute, the first and chief question for the District Court's determination is whether the statute is "sufficiently broad to control the issue before the Court." This question involves a straightforward exercise in statutory interpretation to determine if the statute covers the point in dispute.

. . . Although we agree with the Court of Appeals that *The Bremen* case may prove "instructive" in resolving the parties' dispute, we disagree with the court's articulation of the relevant inquiry as "whether the forum selection clause in this case is unenforceable under the standards set forth in *The Bremen*." Rather, the first question for consideration should have been whether § 1404(a) itself controls respondent's request to give effect to the parties' contractual choice of venue and transfer this case to a Manhattan court. . . . [W]e hold that it does. . . .

A motion to transfer under § 1404(a) thus calls on the District Court to weigh in the balance a number of case-specific factors. The presence of a forum-selection clause . . . will be a significant factor that figures centrally in the District Court's calculus. . . . The flexible and individualized analysis Congress prescribed in § 1404(a) thus encompasses consideration of the parties' private expression of their venue preferences. . . .

Because § 1404(a) controls the issue before the District Court, it must be applied if it represents a valid exercise of Congress's authority under the Constitution. The constitutional authority of Congress to enact § 1404(a) is not subject to serious question. . . .

JUSTICE KENNEDY, with whom JUSTICE O'CONNOR joins, concurring.

I concur in full. I write separately only to observe that enforcement of valid forum selection clauses, bargained for by the parties, protects their legitimate expectations and furthers vital interests of the justice system. Although our opinion in *The Bremen* involved a federal district court sitting in admiralty, its reasoning applies with much force to federal courts sitting in diversity. The justifications we noted in *The Bremen* to counter the historical disfavor forum selection clauses had received in American courts, should be understood to guide the District Court's analysis under § 1404(a).

---

[3] Respondent points out that jurisdiction in this case was alleged to rest both on the existence of an antitrust claim, and diversity of citizenship. Respondent does not suggest how the presence of a federal claim should affect the District Court's analysis of applicable law. . . . Our conclusion that federal law governs transfer of this case, makes this issue academic for purposes of this case, because the presence of a federal question could cut only in favor of the application of federal law. We therefore are not called on to decide, nor do we decide, whether the existence of federal question as well as diversity jurisdiction necessarily alters a District Court's analysis of applicable law.

The federal judicial system has a strong interest in the correct resolution of these questions, not only to spare litigants unnecessary costs but also to relieve courts of time consuming pretrial motions. Courts should announce and encourage rules that support private parties who negotiate such clauses. Though state policies should be weighed in the balance, the authority and prerogative of the federal courts to determine the issue, as Congress has directed by § 1404(a), should be exercised so that a valid forum selection clause is given controlling weight in all but the most exceptional cases.

JUSTICE SCALIA, dissenting. I agree with the opinion of the Court that the initial question before us is whether the validity between the parties of a contractual forum-selection clause falls within the scope of 28 U.S.C. § 1404(a). I cannot agree, however, that the answer to that question is yes. Nor do I believe that the federal courts can, consistent with the twin-aims test of *Erie R. Co. v. Tompkins*, fashion a judge-made rule to govern this issue of contract validity.

. . . In deciding what is substantive and what procedural for these purposes, we have adhered to a functional test based on the "twin aims of the *Erie* rule: discouragement of forum-shopping and avoidance of inequitable administration of the laws."

Under the twin-aims test, I believe state law controls the question of the validity of a forum-selection clause between the parties. . . .

---

## NOTES AND QUESTIONS ON *STEWART ORGANIZATION v. RICOH*

(1) *What Happened to Erie?* The Court of Appeals (sitting en banc) thought the case presented a difficult *Erie* problem. Only one member of the Supreme Court agreed, however; the Court's sleight-of-hand statutory-interpretation-venue-approach certainly makes the *Erie* problem disappear. (The *Erie* doctrine is discussed in more detail in Section 6.01, *infra*.)

(2) *Is the Issue Dead?* Section 1404(a) does not apply when a foreign country is the preferred forum. The *Erie* issue, therefore, will have to be faced again. Does the policy in favor of forum clauses identified in *The Bremen* suggest how the Court might resolve the issue? *See* R. WEINTRAUB, COMMENTARY ON THE CONFLICT OF LAWS 268-269 (4th ed. 2001).

(3) *Whose Law of Forum Non Conveniens*? In *Chick Kam Choo v. Exxon Corp.*, 486 U.S. 140 (1988), plaintiff's decedent was killed while working in Singapore, where both he and plaintiff lived. Suit was brought against the defendant/employer in Texas federal district court, but was dismissed on forum non conveniens grounds. Plaintiff then filed a new action in a Texas state court; the defendant removed that case to federal court, but the Fifth Circuit ordered it remanded for lack of diversity. Defendant then sued in federal district court to enjoin the litigation pending in the Texas state courts. The lower courts granted the injunction, believing that it was necessary to protect the earlier forum non conveniens dismissal, and the injunction thus

fell within an exception to the Anti-Injunction Act, 22 U.S.C. § 1983, which generally forbids federal courts from enjoining actions in state court. The Supreme Court reversed, holding that the question whether federal or state *forum non conveniens* law controlled was not yet ripe for decision.

What happens when the Court finally has to face the issue?

The underlying causes of action in *Chick Kam Choo* were founded both in admiralty and in the Texas wrongful death act. Should a federal court apply different standards for forum non conveniens if its jurisdiction is based on diversity (the Texas wrongful death action), or on a federal question (the admiralty action)? Justice White, concurring, thought a different standard might apply due to the strong "federal interest in uniformity" in admiralty law. Do you agree? *See also* McAllen, *Deference to the Plaintiff in Forum Non Conveniens*, 13 So. ILL. U. L. REV. 191, 266-68 (1989).

*See* PROBLEMS 3F-5. THE AFFILIATION AGREEMENT; 3F-6. THE SALES AGENT.

## § 3.21   Local Actions

Conflicts law has long distinguished between "local" and "transitory" actions. The difference between the two is historical, deriving from the fact that some causes of action—the local ones—required that jurors be drawn from the jurisdiction in which the injury occurred. *See* Note, *Local Actions in the Federal Courts*, 70 HARV. L. REV. 708, 709 (1957). Although most anything could be called a local cause of action, the term was usually applied to problems involving land; in those cases venue was proper only at the situs. While that may seem natural enough in the case of title to land (a topic explored further in § 3.14, *supra*), the common law's fetish with real property has led many courts to conclude that even actions involving trespass to land can be heard only in the state where the land is located. The leading case is a famous opinion by Chief Justice Marshall, *Livingston v. Jefferson*, Fed. Cas. 666 (No. 8411) (D. Va. 1811). Many recent cases and commentators have rejected that rule, concluding that Chief Justice Marshall was wrong. *See, e.g., Reasor-Hill Corp. v. Harrison*, 220 Ark. 521, 249 S.W.2d 994 (1952); RESTATE- MENT (SECOND) OF CONFLICT OF LAWS §§ 87 and 88.

A transitory cause of action is one where the jurors can be drawn from anywhere; it is one, therefore, which can travel or migrate to other locations, and, hence, one which can be sued on anywhere. Some states have tried to keep actions at home by defining them as local; others have refused to entertain foreign causes of action. The constitutionality of those attempts is discussed in § 5.06, *infra. See generally* Brainerd Currie, *The Constitution and the "Transitory" Cause of Action*, 73 HARV. L. REV. 36 (1959).

## § 3.22   Tax and Penal Statutes, Public Policy, and Jurisdiction

"The Courts of no country execute the penal laws of another." So wrote Chief Justice Marshall in *The Antelope*, 23 U.S. (10 Wheat.) 66, 123 (1825) (dictum). The effect of that policy today is pretty much limited to criminal prosecutions.

Does that make sense? Why should a court refuse to enforce another state's criminal law? *See* WILLIAM RICHMAN & WILLIAM REYNOLDS, UNDERSTANDING CONFLICT OF LAWS, § 50[a] (3d ed. 2002). *See also* John Corr, *Criminal Procedure and the Conflict of Laws,* 73 GEO. L.J. 1217 (198 5); Robert Leflar, *Extrastate Enforcement of Penal and Governmental Claims,* 46 HARV. L. REV. 193 (1932).

A closely related version of this problem involves a state's attempt to enforce its tax laws in another state. In *Milwaukee County v. M.E. White Co.,* 296 U.S. 268 (1935), the Court wrote that it was an "open question" whether a court had to hear a tax claim brought by another state. Surely, that should not be a question today; why would any court want to "offer a legally respectable asylum to the tax dodger"? *Oklahoma ex rel. Oklahoma Tax Comm'n v. Neely,* 225 Ark. 230, 282 S.W.2d 150 (1955). *See* Richman & Reynolds, *supra,* at § 50[b].

Finally, there is the public policy problem. May a court properly decline to exercise jurisdiction when it does not like the policy that underlies the cause of action that it is asked to enforce? That's an easy question when the policy is that of another country which offends deeply-held American values. But what if the policy is that of another state? Justice Cardozo once wrote:

> The courts are not free to refuse to enforce a foreign right at the pleasure of the judges, to suit the individual notion of expediency or fairness. They do not close their doors, unless help would violate some fundamental principle of justice, some prevalent conception of good morals, some deep-rooted tradition of the common weal.

*Loucks v. Standard Oil Co.,* 224 N.Y. 99, 120 N.E. 198 (1918) (discussed in § 4.14, *infra*). Can a constitutionally valid law of an American state today ever be said to violate "some fundamental principles of justice"? *See generally* Monrad Paulsen & Michael Sovern, *"Public Policy" in the Conflict of Laws,* 56 COLUM. L. REV. 969 (1956).

## § 3.23 The Large Case, Consolidation, and Jurisdiction

The Bhopal disaster illustrates an increasingly common phenomenon: multiparty, multiforum litigation. A mass disaster in the form of a plane crash, a toxic product like asbestos, or a large securities fraud can generate enormous quantities of litigation, with many parties filing major lawsuits in a number of different jurisdictions. Not only does this kind of litigation impose enormous costs on the parties, but the entire judicial system also comes under stress. These cases are especially disruptive, eating up far more than their fair share of scarce judicial resources. Because the stakes are very high and the issues difficult, discovery and motion practice are often extensive and costly. Further, because it is difficult to join all parties in a single forum, complex litigation often entails the waste and injustice of multiple contests and inconsistent resolutions of similar factual and legal issues. The result is delayed and inconsistent compensation for victims and high legal fees and other transaction costs to the tortfeasors. *See* Gene Shreve, *Reform Aspirations of the Complex Litigation Project,* 54 LA. L. REV 1139, 1141 (1994); Thomas D. Rowe,

Jr. and Kenneth D. Sibley, *Beyond Diversity—Federal Multiparty, Multiforum Jurisdiction*, 135 U. PA. L. REV. 7 (1986).

One solution is to consolidate related cases, a procedure long available in more normal situations. In 1968, Congress, in response to 1,800 actions filed in 33 federal courts seeking damages from manufacturers of electrical equipment who had been convicted of price-fixing, adopted a procedure for dealing with complex litigation. Today, 28 U.S.C. § 1407 authorizes the Judicial Panel on Multidistrict Litigation to transfer to a single federal judge related actions which have been filed in more than one federal district court. Transfer, which is discretionary with the Panel, may be ordered when the cases involve "one or more common questions of fact," and a transfer "will promote the just and efficient conduct of such actions."

The transferee judge has authority only over pretrial motions (including discovery). As a practical matter, however, the transferee judge usually retains the transferred cases for trial. *See generally* Richard Marcus, *Conflicts Among Circuits and Transfers Within the Federal Judicial System*, 93 YALE L.J. 677 (1984); Wilson Herndon and Earnest Higginbotham, *Complex Multidistrict Litigation—An Overview of 28 U.S.C.A. Sec. 1407*, 31 BAYLOR L. REV. 33 (1979); Note, *The Judicial Panel and the Conduct of Multidistrict Litigation*, 87 HARV. L. REV. 1001 (1974).

There are, of course, other methods of gathering related cases together in a single forum. Federal Rules 19 and 20 joinder), Rule 23 (class actions), and Rule 24 (intervention) all serve that purpose, as does interpleader practice under either Rule 22 or the Federal Interpleader Act, 28 U.S.C. § 1335. (Interpleader is discussed in Chapter 2, *supra*.) Further, in particular areas of the law, such as bankruptcy, probate, and admiralty, additional specialized consolidation techniques have long been available. (Thus the true in rem proceeding does have its uses.) *See also* Comment, *The Consolidation of Multistate Litigation in State Courts*, 96 YALE L.J. 1099 (1986).

The American Law Institute's Complex Litigation Project is an ambitious set of proposals for state and federal legislation designed to facilitate further the consolidation of related cases in the state and federal systems. *See* Complex Litigation: Statutory Recommendations and Analysis (1994). The touchstone of the Project might be a quote from Professor Zachariah Chafee: "In matters of justice . . . the benefactor is he who makes one lawsuit grow where two grew before." *Id.* at 23, quoting Zachariah Chafee, *Bills of Peace with Multiple Parties*, 45 HARV. L. REV. 1297 (1932).

The Project's first major proposal is a federal statute to expand the current multidistrict litigation regime by providing for transfer and consolidation in one district (for trial as well as pretrial proceedings) of actions pending in several federal districts if they involve common factual or legal questions and if transfer and consolidation would promote the just, fair and efficient conduct of the actions, *id,* § 3.01. The consolidation decision would be entrusted to a special Complex Litigation Panel of federal judges, which could act sua sponte, on motion of any party, or at the suggestion of the court in which one of the actions is pending. Liberalized venue provisions and nationwide personal jurisdiction would permit transfer to any district or districts "where the just and efficient resolution of the actions will be promoted and fairness to individual litigants will be facilitated." *See id.*, § 3.04.

Another proposal is designed to consolidate in a single state court multiple actions pending in different state and federal courts. It recommends: (1) a federal statute permitting transfer of cases from federal courts for consolidation in a state court if other pending state cases and the events giving rise to the controversy are centered in one state, fairness and the interests of justice would be advanced, and the state court is more appropriate than other possible transferee forums; and (2) an interstate compact or uniform act to facilitate the transfer and consolidation in one state court of related cases pending in the courts of different states. *Id.*, §§ 4.01, 4.02.

A third proposal is for federal legislation that would facilitate the consolidation of state court actions in a federal court in which related litigation is pending. The proposal would significantly liberalize removal and supplemental jurisdiction in the context of complex multiforum litigation. *Id.*, §§ 5.01, 5.03.

The most controversial provisions of the project deal with anti-suit injunctions, involuntary consolidation, and choice of law in consolidated cases. Section 5.04 permits a transferee court to enjoin related proceedings in any state or federal court. Even more radically, § 5.05 permits a transferee court to enter an order informing nonparties that they may intervene and, even if they do not, will be bound by its determinations to the same extent as a party. Finally Chapter 6 proposes a code of federal choice-of-law rules to govern in complex consolidated cases.

Do you agree with the goal of the project? What values does the project sacrifice or compromise to achieve that goal? Is there something to be said for the plaintiff being able to choose where she wants her case tried? (Remember that the forum she chose is a perfectly proper one; it only becomes "inconvenient" because of a rash of related litigation elsewhere.) What of the extra expense to her and her lawyer of having to try the case in an inconvenient and distant forum; why should she, rather than the government (or the defendant), have to bear that cost? What do you think of mandatory intervention or of binding nonparties who refuse to intervene? Would the ALI proposals also increase the tendency to concentrate major litigation in a few urban centers? Probably most transfers will be made to large metropolitan areas that have the courtroom facilities, extra staff, and travel conveniences to handle mass litigation. The law and its practice may lose much of its richness, it has been argued, if certain types of very important cases are handled only in, say, Los Angeles and New York.

The ALI Project has had little practical impact; none of its legislative proposals have been implemented, and most of the commentary has been critical (especially of its choice-of-law proposals). For commentary, see Symposium, 1995 B.Y.U. L. Rev. 731-1155 (1995), Symposium, 54 La. L. Rev. 843-1160 (1994).

# PART G   THE CHALLENGE OF THE FUTURE

## § 3.24   Jurisdiction in Cyberspace

### CYBERSELL, INC. v. CYBERSELL, INC.

*United States Court Of Appeals For The Ninth Circuit*
*130 F.3d 414 (9th Cir. 1997)*

RYMER, Circuit Judge:

We are asked to hold that the allegedly infringing use of a service mark in a home page on the World Wide Web suffices for personal jurisdiction in the state where the holder of the mark has its principal place of business. [The plaintiff] . . . claims that [the defendant] . . . infringed its federally registered mark and should be amenable to suit in Arizona because cyberspace is without borders and a web site which advertises a product or service is necessarily intended for use on a world wide basis. The district court disagreed, and so do we. . . .[W]e conclude that it would not comport with "traditional notions of fair play and substantial justice," for Arizona to exercise personal jurisdiction over an allegedly infringing . . . web site advertiser who has no contacts with Arizona other than maintaining a home page that is accessible to Arizonans, and everyone else, over the Internet.

I

[Cybersell, Inc., an Arizona corporation referred to by the Court as Cybersell AZ, was incorporated in May 1994 to provide Internet and web advertising and marketing services.[1] In 1994, it filed an application to register the name "Cybersell" as a service mark; the application was approved, and Cybersell AZ operated a web site using the mark. In 1995 two Florida residents, formed Cybersell, Inc., a Florida corporation (Cybersell FL), with its principal place of business in Orlando, in order to provide business consulting services for strategic management and marketing on the web. At the time, Cybersell AZ had no home page on the web nor had the PTO granted its application for the service mark. Cybersell FL created a web page that proclaimed in large letters "Welcome to CyberSell!" Representatives of Cybersell AZ found the Cybersell FL web page and sent an e-mail protesting that use of the name. Cybersell FL then changed its name to WebHorizons, Inc. and replaced the CyberSell logo at the top of its web page. Cybersell AZ filed this action in the District of Arizona, alleging trademark infringement, unfair competition, fraud, and RICO violations. The district court granted Cybersell FL's motion to dismiss for lack of personal jurisdiction, and Cybersell AZ appealed.]

---

[1] [The principals of Cybersell AZ are Laurence Canter and Martha Siegel, known among web users for first "spamming" the Internet.] Spamming refers to the posting indiscriminately of advertisements to news groups on the web. Unlike crossposting, spamming individually posts the advertisement to each news group, requiring the recipient to delete the message from each news group to which she has subscribed.

## II

The general principles that apply to the exercise of personal jurisdiction are well known. As there is no federal statute governing personal jurisdiction in this case, the law of Arizona applies. Under Rule 4.2(a) of the Arizona Rules of Civil Procedure, an Arizona court may exercise personal jurisdiction over parties, whether found within or outside the state, to the maximum extent permitted by the Constitution of this state and the Constitution of the United States. . . .Thus, Cybersell FL may be subject to personal jurisdiction in Arizona so long as doing so comports with due process.

A court may assert either specific or general jurisdiction over a defendant. *See Helicopteros Nacionales de Colombia, S.A. v. Hall,* 466 U.S. 408 (1984). Cybersell AZ concedes that general jurisdiction over Cybersell FL doesn't exist in Arizona, so the only issue in this case is whether specific jurisdiction is available.

We use a three-part test to determine whether a district court may exercise specific jurisdiction over a nonresident defendant:

> (1) The nonresident defendant must do some act or consummate some transaction with the forum or perform some act by which he purposefully avails himself of the privilege of conducting activities in the forum . . .(2) the claim must be one which arises out of or results from the defendant's forum-related activities [and] (3) exercise of jurisdiction must be reasonable.

Cybersell AZ argues that the test is met because trademark infringement occurs when the passing off of the mark occurs, which in this case, it submits, happened when the name "Cybersell" was used on the Internet in connection with advertising. Cybersell FL, on the other hand, contends that a party should not be subject to nationwide, or perhaps worldwide, jurisdiction simply for using the Internet.

## A

Since the jurisdictional facts are not in dispute, we trun to the first requirement. . . .

We have not yet considered when personal jurisdiction may be exercised in the context of cyberspace, but the Second and Sixth Circuits have had occasion to decide whether personal jurisdiction was properly exercised over defendants involved in transmissions over the Internet, *see CompuServe, Inc. v. Patterson,* 89 F.3d 1257 (6th Cir. 1996); *Bensusan Rest. Corp. v. King*, 937 F. Supp. 295 (S.D.N.Y. 1996), *aff'd,* 126 F.3d 25 (2d Cir. 1997), as have a number of district courts. Because this is a matter of first impression for us, we have looked to all of these cases for guidance. Not surprisingly, they reflect a broad spectrum of Internet use on the one hand, and contacts with the forum on the other. As *CompuServe* and *Bensusan* seem to represent opposite ends of the spectrum, we start with them.

CompuServe is a computer information service headquartered in Columbus, Ohio, that contracts with individual subscribers to provide access to computing and information services via the Internet. It also operates as an electronic conduit to provide computer software products to its subscribers. Computer software generated and distributed in this way is often referred to as "shareware." Patterson is a Texas resident who subscribed to CompuServe and placed items of "shareware" on the CompuServe system pursuant to a "Shareware Registration Agreement" with CompuServe which provided, among other things, that it was "to be governed by and construed in accordance with" Ohio law. During the course of this relationship, Patterson electronically transmitted . . . software files to CompuServe, which CompuServe stored and displayed to its subscribers. Sales were made in Ohio and elsewhere, and funds were transmitted through CompuServe in Ohio to Patterson in Texas. In effect, Patterson used CompuServe as a distribution center to market his software. When Patterson threatened litigation over allegedly infringing CompuServe software, CompuServe filed suit in Ohio seeking a declaratory judgment of noninfringement. The court found that . . . Patterson had knowingly reached out to CompuServe's Ohio home and benefitted from CompuServe's handling of his software and fees. Because Patterson had chosen to transmit his product from Texas to CompuServe's system in Ohio, and that system provided access to his software to others to whom he advertised and sold his product, the court concluded that Patterson purposefully availed himself of the privilege of doing business in Ohio.

By contrast, the defendant in *Bensusan* owned a small jazz club known as "The Blue Note" in Columbia, Missouri. He created a general access web page that contained information about the club in Missouri as well as a calendar of events and ticketing information. Tickets were not available through the web site, however. . .Bensusan was a New York corporation that owned "The Blue Note," a popular jazz club in the heart of Greenwich Village. Bensusan owned the rights to the "The Blue Note" mark. Bensusan sued King for trademark infringement in New York. The district court distinguished King's passive web page, which just posted information, from the defendant's use of the Internet in CompuServe by observing that whereas the Texas Internet user specifically targeted Ohio by subscribing to the service, entering into an agreement to sell his software over the Internet, advertising through the service, and sending his software to the service in Ohio, King has done nothing to purposefully avail himself of the benefits of New York. King, like numerous others, simply created a Web site and permitted anyone who could find it to access it. Creating a site, like placing a product into the stream of commerce, may be felt nationwide-or even worldwide-but, without more, it is not an act purposefully directed toward the forum state.

Given these facts, the court reasoned that the argument that the defendant "should have foreseen that users could access the site in New York and be confused as to the relationship of the two Blue Note clubs is insufficient to satisfy due process."

"Interactive" web sites present somewhat different issues. Unlike passive sites such as the defendant's in *Bensusan*, users can exchange information with the host computer when the site is interactive. Courts that have addressed interactive sites have looked to the "level of interactivity and commercial nature of the exchange of information that occurs on the Web site" to determine if sufficient contacts exist to warrant the exercise of jurisdiction.

*See, e.g., Zippo Mfg. Co. v. Zippo Dot Com, Inc.*, 952 F. Supp. 1119, 1124 (W.D. Pa. 1997) (finding purposeful availment based on Dot Com's interactive web site and contracts with 3000 individuals and seven Internet access providers in Pennsylvania allowing them to download the electronic messages that form the basis of the suit) . . . .

*Inset Systems, Inc. v. Instruction Set, Inc.*, 937 F. Supp. 161 (D. Conn. 1996), is the case most favorable to Cybersell AZ's position. Inset developed and marketed computer software throughout the world; Instruction Set, Inc. (ISI) provided computer technology and support. Inset owned the federal trademark "INSET"; but ISI obtained "INSET.COM" as its Internet domain address for advertising its goods and services. . . . Inset learned of ISI's domain address when it tried to get the same address, and filed suit for trademark infringement in Connecticut. The court reasoned that ISI had purposefully availed itself of doing business in Connecticut because it directed its advertising activities via the Internet and its toll-free number toward the state of Connecticut (and all states); Internet sites and toll-free numbers are designed to communicate with people and their businesses in every state; an Internet advertisement could reach as many as 10,000 Internet users within Connecticut alone; and once posted on the Internet, an advertisement is continuously available to any Internet user . . . .

Some courts have also given weight to the number of "hits" received by a web page from residents in the forum state, and to other evidence that Internet activity was directed at, or bore fruit in, the forum state. *See, e.g., Heroes, Inc. v. Heroes Found.*, 958 F. Supp. 1 (D.D.C. 1996) . . .; *Pres-Kap, Inc. v. System One, Direct Access, Inc.*, 636 So. 2d 1351 (Fla. Dist. Ct. App. 1994). . . .

In sum, the common thread, well stated by the district court in *Zippo*, is that "the likelihood that personal jurisdiction can be constitutionally exercised is directly proportionate to the nature and quality of commercial activity that an entity conducts over the Internet." *Zippo*, 952 F. Supp. at 1124.

## B

Here, Cybersell FL has conducted no commercial activity over the Internet in Arizona. All that it did was post an essentially passive home page on the web, using the name "CyberSell," which Cybersell AZ was in the process of registering as a federal service mark. While there is no question that anyone, anywhere could access that home page and thereby learn about the services offered, we cannot see how from that fact alone it can be inferred that Cybersell FL deliberately directed its merchandising efforts toward Arizona residents.

Cybersell FL did nothing to encourage people in Arizona to access its site, and there is no evidence that any part of its business (let alone a continuous part of its business) was sought or achieved in Arizona. To the contrary, it appears to be an operation where business was primarily generated by the personal contacts of one of its founders. While those contacts are not entirely local, they aren't in Arizona either. No Arizonan except for Cybersell AZ "hit" Cybersell FL's web site. There is no evidence that any Arizona resident signed up for Cybersell FL's web construction services. It entered into no contracts in Arizona, made no sales in Arizona, received no telephone calls from Arizona, earned no income from Arizona, and sent no messages over the Internet to Arizona. The only message it received over the Internet from Arizona was from Cybersell AZ. Cybersell FL did not have an "800" number, let alone a toll-free number that also used the "Cybersell" name. The interactivity of its web page is limited to receiving the browser's name and address and an indication of interest—signing up for the service is not an option, nor did anyone from Arizona do so. No money changed hands on the Internet from (or through) Arizona. In short, Cybersell FL has done no act and has consummated no transaction, nor has it performed any act by which it purposefully availed itself of the privilege of conducting activities, in Arizona, thereby invoking the benefits and protections of Arizona law.

We therefore hold that Cybersell FL's contacts are insufficient to establish "purposeful availment." Cybersell AZ has thus failed to satisfy the first prong of our three-part test for specific jurisdiction. We decline to go further solely on the footing that Cybersell AZ has alleged trademark infringement over the Internet by Cybersell FL's use of the registered name "Cybersell" on an essentially passive web page advertisement. Otherwise, every complaint arising out of alleged trademark infringement on the Internet would automatically result in personal jurisdiction wherever the plaintiff's principal place of business is located. That would not comport with traditional notions of what qualifies as purposeful activity invoking the benefits and protections of the forum state . . . .

### III

Cybersell AZ also invokes the "effects" test employed in *Calder v. Jones*, 465 U.S. 783, with respect to intentional torts directed to the plaintiff, causing injury where the plaintiff lives. However, we don't see this as a *Calder* case. Because Shirley Jones was who she was . . . and was libeled by a story in the National Enquirer, which . . . had a nationwide circulation with a large audience in California, the Court could easily hold that California was the "focal point both of the story and of the harm suffered". . . . There is nothing comparable about Cybersell FL's web page . . . Cybersell FL's web page simply was not aimed intentionally at Arizona knowing that harm was likely to be caused there to Cybersell AZ. . . .

*Affirmed.*

## NOTES AND QUESTIONS ON JURISDICTION IN CYBERSPACE

(1) *Introduction to Cybertalk*. Before considering the jurisdictional problems posed by the information revolution, it is helpful to learn the lay of the land. In *Reno v. ACLU*, 521 U.S. 844, 849-53, the Supreme Court provided this explanation for the cyber-challenged:

> The Internet is an international network of interconnected computers. It is the outgrowth of what began in 1969 as a military program called

"ARPANET" . . . While the ARPANET no longer exists, it provided an example for the development of a number of civilian networks that, eventually linking with each other, now enable tens of millions of people to communicate with one another and to access vast amounts of information from around the world. The Internet is "a unique and wholly new medium of worldwide human communication."

The Internet has experienced "extraordinary growth." The number of "host" computers—those that store information and relay communications—increased from about 300 in 1981 to approximately 9,400,000 by the time of the trial in 1996. Roughly 60% of these hosts are located in the United States. About 40 million people used the Internet at the time of trial, a number that is expected to mushroom to 200 million by 1999.

Individuals can obtain access to the Internet from many different sources, generally hosts themselves or entities with a host affiliation. Most colleges and universities provide access for their students and faculty; many corporations provide their employees with access through an office network; many communities and local libraries provide free access; and an increasing number of storefront "computer coffee shops" provide access for a small hourly fee. Several major national "online services" such as America Online, CompuServe, the Microsoft Network, and Prodigy offer access to their own extensive proprietary networks as well as a link to the much larger resources of the Internet. These commercial online services had almost 12 million individual subscribers at the time of trial.

Anyone with access to the Internet may take advantage of a wide variety of communication and information retrieval methods. These methods are constantly evolving and difficult to categorize precisely. But, as presently constituted, those most relevant to this case are electronic mail ("e-mail"), automatic mailing list services ("mail exploders," sometimes referred to as "listservs"), "newsgroups," "chat rooms," and the "World Wide Web." All of these methods can be used to transmit text; most can transmit sound, pictures, and moving video images. Taken together, these tools constitute a unique medium—known to its users as "cyberspace"—located in no particular geographical location but available to anyone, anywhere in the world, with access to the Internet.

E-mail enables an individual to send an electronic message—generally akin to a note or letter—to another individual or to a group of addressees. . . . A mail exploder is a sort of e-mail group. Subscribers can send messages to a common e-mail address, which then forwards the message to the group's other subscribers. Newsgroups also serve groups of regular participants, but these postings may be read by others as well. There are thousands of such groups, each serving to foster an exchange of information or opinion on a particular topic . . . [T]wo or more individuals wishing to communicate more immediately can enter a chat room to engage in real-time dialogue—in other words, by typing messages to one another that appear almost immediately on the others' computer screens. . . .

The best known category of communication over the Internet is the World Wide Web, which allows users to search for and retrieve information stored in remote computers, as well as, in some cases, to communicate back to designated sites. In concrete terms, the Web consists of a vast number of documents stored in different computers all over the world. Some of these documents are simply files containing information. However, more elaborate documents, commonly known as Web "pages," are also prevalent. Each has its own address—"rather like a telephone number." Web pages frequently contain information and sometimes allow the viewer to communicate with the page's (or "site's") author. They generally also contain "links" to other documents created by that site's author or to other (generally) related sites. Typically, the links are either blue or underlined text—sometimes images.

Navigating the Web is relatively straightforward. A user may either type the address of a known page or enter one or more keywords into a commercial "search engine" in an effort to locate sites on a subject of interest. A particular Web page may contain the information sought by the "surfer," or, through its links, it may be an avenue to other documents located anywhere on the Internet. . . .The Web is thus comparable, from the readers' viewpoint, to both a vast library including millions of readily available and indexed publications and a sprawling mall offering goods and services.

From the publishers' point of view, it constitutes a vast platform from which to address and hear from a world-wide audience of millions of readers, viewers, researchers, and buyers. . . .Publishers include government agencies, educational institutions, commercial entities, advocacy groups, and individuals. Publishers may either make their material available to the entire pool of Internet users, or confine access to a selected group, such as those willing to pay for the privilege. "No single organization controls any membership in the Web, nor is there any centralized point from which individual Web sites or services can be blocked from the Web."

A more complete treatment of the basics can be found in David Wille, *Personal Jurisdiction and the Internet—Proposed Limits on State Jurisdiction over Data Communications in Tort Cases*, 87 KY. L.J. 95, 183-201.

(2) *Jurisdiction and the Worldwide Web.* "Just as the automobile challenged and exposed the weaknesses in the power theory of jurisdiction, so the internet is challenging modern jurisdiction theory." 1 ROBERT CASAD & WILLIAM RICHMAN, JURISDICTION IN CIVIL ACTIONS §2-5[7] (3d ed. 1999). The analogy is a good one, but the authors may have understated their case. The automobile stressed the power theory because it minimized distances and thus contracted space. But when a technology creates a whole new type of space, it poses a more fundamental challenge to the vestiges of territorialism in modern theory. A theory adequate for a world defined by borders and miles and compass points is likely to founder in one where those familiar concepts are increasingly irrelevant.

(3) *Easy Cases*. That said, it is a mistake to assume that every internet case is beyond the power of current jurisdiction theory. E-mail, for example, stresses current doctrine no more than the telephone since the sender is aware of and can limit the geographical target of the message. *See* Katherine Sheehan, *Predicting the Future: Personal Jurisdiction for the Twenty-first Century*, 66 U. CINN. L. REV. 385, 412 (1998). Many cases involving the World Wide Web also are not difficult for current theory. In breach of contract and product liability cases, there usually will be contacts between the defendant and the forum beyond defendant's mere construction of a web page that can be accessed in the forum. Typically there will be individual negotiations between the plaintiff and the defendant and often the delivery of a product or a service into the forum. While such cases will not always support jurisdiction, the extra contacts make them relatively easy to analyze under current theory. For a case dealing with contacts beyond the defendant's mere creation of a forum-accessible web page, *see CompuServe, Inc. v. Patterson*, 89 F.3d 1257 (6th Cir.1996). For commentary on cases of this type, *see* Martin Redish, *Of New Wine and Old Bottles: Personal Jurisdiction, the Internet, and the Nature of Constitutional Evolution*, 38 JURIMETRICS 575, 595 (1998).

(4) *General Jurisdiction*. These cases also have proved to be unproblematic. Not surprisingly, maintenance of a web site is not enough to render the defendant amenable to general jurisdiction in a state in which the web site can be accessed. *See Weber v. Jolly Hotels*, 977 F. Supp. 327, 333 (D.N.J. 1997) (Italian hotel's maintenance of a web site that could be accessed from New Jersey was not sufficient to render hotel amenable in New Jersey based on New Jersey plaintiff's injury in Italy when plaintiff had neither learned of the hotel nor made arrangements to stay there through the web site.)

(5) *The Hard Case*. The difficult issue for current jurisdictional theory is whether the author of a web page should be amenable to specific jurisdiction based solely on the fact that the page can be accessed in the forum. *Cybersell* and many of the cases it discusses (including *Zippo* and *Bensusan*) represent the emerging answer to the question; the defendant's maintenance of a web site that can be accessed from the forum is not enough, by itself, to generate jurisdiction over the defendant in the forum. Thus *Inset Systems*, also discussed in *Cybersell*, seems to swim against the tide. By exposing every web page owner to nationwide (or worldwide) jurisdiction, does the holding in *Inset Systems* threaten to "chill" activity on the web? Or is this just another example of the logocentrist fallacy, the tendency of lawyers to overestimate the effects of their doctrines and distinctions on the decisions of real people?

Cases posing the hard question, i.e., cases involving no contact beyond creation of the web site, usually involve a tort theory, most often one involving intellectual property. So far the most typical fact pattern mirrors *Cybersell* and involves a defendant that has chosen an internet domain name that allegedly violates the plaintiff 's trade name or service mark. When the defendant's page has resulted in substantial in-state business, the cases usually find jurisdiction, and some seem willing to find jurisdiction based on the number of in-state hits, whether they result in contracts for the defendant or not. Still others are willing to find jurisdiction based on the fact that the page is active rather than merely passive; i.e., it permits the reader to communicate with the page author, perhaps to place an order. Should it matter in web-page-only cases that the web server (the computer on which the web page was placed) is in the forum? What about the plaintiff? *See* Sheehan, *supra* note 3 at 417-421.

(6) *The Calder v. Jones Argument*. On facts similar to those in *Cybersell*, the *Inset Systems* court defended its opposite result as follows:

> In the present case, [the defendant] . . . has directed its advertising activities via the Internet and its toll-free number toward not only the state of Connecticut, but to all states. The Internet as well as toll-free numbers are designed to communicate with people and their businesses in every state. Advertisement on the Internet can reach as many as 10,000 internet users within Connecticut alone. Further, once posted on the Internet, unlike television and radio advertising, the advertisement is available continuously to any Internet user. [The defendant] has therefore, purposefully availed itself of the privilege of doing business within Connecticut.

*Inset Systems, Inc. v. Instruction Set, Inc.*, 937 F. Supp. 161,165 (D.Conn. 1996). Would the court have reached the same result if the trademark violation had occurred in a national print advertisement, or is there something especially significant about the electronic nature of the communication? Does *Calder v. Jones*, *supra* § 3.10, support the court's position? If not, is it because of the difference between defamation and trademark violation or because the defamation in *Calder* was intentionally targeted toward the plaintiff in forum?

(7) *The Initiation Argument*. In non-electronic jurisdiction cases, the courts have found the concept of initiation to be a useful device. Courts tend to find jurisdiction more readily when defendant has initiated contact with the plaintiff in the forum than when plaintiff seeks out the defendant in its home state. *See* WILLIAM RICHMAN & WILLIAM REYNOLDS, UNDERSTANDING CONFLICT OF LAWS § 37[f] (3d ed. 2002). How does this test work in a World Wide Web case? Does the Web page author initiate the transaction by creating the page, or does the user initiate the transaction by accessing the Web page? Do the details of the actual electronic transfers affect your decision? If so, consider this explanation of the typical Web page access:

> When an accessor "visits" a web site . . . the accessor does not make a visit analogous to a physical visit. A web site access involves a two-way data communication in a request/response protocol. The accessor's computer sends a request to the web site operator's computer, and the web server, in response to the request sends a copy of the web page to the accessor's computer. . . . A web site access is analogous to the . . . accessor sending a post card . . . requesting a free copy of a newspaper published by the web site operator, followed by the sending of the newspaper. . . . Of course, . . . the web site operator does not know exactly where the newspaper is being sent; the web site operator has instead employed automatic equipment for the distribution.

Wille, *supra* note 1, at 109.

(8) *Radical Solutions*. Not surprisingly, some jurisdiction scholars see the cyberspace cases as a welcome occasion for the general reexamination of

current jurisdiction theory. *See* Redish, *supra* note 3, at 601-610; Wille, *supra* note 1 at 115-139. Do you agree? If so, what sort of change do these cases suggest? Should there be more emphasis on litigational convenience and less on contacts? Is purposeful availment becoming irrelevant? If the law of jurisdiction moves in that direction, how will it affect choice of law? Is a diminution in state sovereignty inevitable?

Another radical solution to the problem of jurisdiction in cyberspace draws on the historical analogy of the law merchant and would involve a separate set of cyber-courts enforcing a separate law of cyberspace. This option would eliminate much of the inconvenience associated with out-of-state litigation. Is it a good idea otherwise? What effect would it have on state sovereignty? For discussion of the possibility, see David Johnson and David Post, *Law and Borders—The Rise of Law in Cyberspace*, 48 STAN. L. REV. 1367 (1996); I. Trotter Hardy, *The Proper Legal Regime for "Cyberspace,"* 55 U. PITT. L. REV. 993, 1019 (1974); Henry Perritt, Jr., *Jurisdiction in Cyberspace,* 41 VILL. L. REV. 1 (1996).

# Chapter 4

# CHOICE OF LAW

## § 4.01 Scope Note

This Chapter examines the question of what law should be applied to a multi-state problem. Part A addresses the preliminary problem of proving foreign law; Parts B and C discuss the traditional systems used in solving choice-of-law problems and the devices that were sometimes used to avoid the unhappy results produced by those traditional methods; Part D considers modern methods of analyzing choice-of-law problems; lastly, Part E considers selected aspects of choice of law today.

## PART A   A PRELIMINARY LOOK

## § 4.02   An Introductory Problem

### KALMICH v. BRUNO

*United States Court of Appeals for the Seventh Circuit*
*553 F.2d 549 (1977)*

PELL, CIRCUIT JUDGE.

This is a diversity case between plaintiff-appellant, Hayim Kalmich, a citizen of Quebec, Canada, and defendant-appellee, Karl Bruno, a citizen of Illinois . . . .

. . . In 1941, Kalmich, a Jew, resided in Belgrade in his native Yugoslavia and operated and owned a textile importing business. In April of that year, the armies of Nazi Germany invaded and conquered Yugoslavia, forcing the incumbent government of Yugoslavia into exile. The occupation forces shortly installed a General Plenipotentiary for the Economy in Serbia, whose responsibility was to "Aryanize" the economy by seizing and confiscating all businesses and property owned by Jews, solely because they were Jews.

Bruno is alleged to have voluntarily subordinated himself to the General Plenipotentiary,[3] and when an order for the seizure of Kalmich's business was issued on June 24, 1941, Bruno was given the duties of managing and operating the business. He seized the business and proceeded to run it. In March of 1942, Bruno substantially understated the value of the business to his superiors to enable him to purchase it from them at a bargain price. That same month, he bought the business from the General Plenipotentiary for even less than the value he had previously stated. Thereafter, he resold the business to one Guc, presumably at a profit.

---

[3] The complaint basically alleges that the conquering government in which the defendant of his own free will participated seized the plaintiff's business solely because of his religious beliefs.

The complaint alleges that sometime prior to the defeat of the German occupation forces in Yugoslavia, Bruno "to avoid, prevent and frustrate any prosecution for his knowingly willful and malicious conduct, fled Yugoslavia for places unknown to the Plaintiff." After the end of the war, Kalmich spent substantial time, money, and effort unsuccessfully attempting to find Bruno for redress in a search that covered five countries. It was only in May of 1972 that Kalmich discovered, from sources not disclosed, that Bruno was living in Chicago, Illinois. This lawsuit followed.

Count I of the complaint seeks damage recovery under statutory provisions of Yugoslavian law which are summarized therein to provide the notice of foreign law issues required by Rule 44. 1, FED.R.CIV.P. One general provision referred to in the complaint is a broad repeal of all statutes, ordinances, decrees, and regulations enacted prior to the date of the Nazi invasion, and all those enacted by the Nazi occupation forces; presumably this repeal provision was an attempt to clean the slate for new laws enacted after the war. The remaining [allegations of Count I are]:

> 23. That at a time unknown to the Plaintiff but after the termination of World War II the nation of Yugoslavia enacted Article 125 of the Criminal Code [Article 1251 which provides that anyone who confiscated belongings of another during World War II, for nonmilitary purposes, would be subject to criminal prosecution.
>
> 24. That in 1965, the nation of Yugoslavia enacted Article 134(a) of its Criminal Code [Article 134(a)] which provides that there shall be no statute of limitations upon the prosecution of those accused of violations of Article 125.
>
> 25. That on or about August 16, 1946, Sec. I of the Law Concerning the Treatment of Property. Taken Away From the Owner by the Enemy or its Helpers [Section I] became effective in Yugoslavia, said Law providing a civil cause of action for those whose belongings were confiscated by the German occupation force.
>
> 26. That, in 1953, Section 20 of the Yugoslavian Statute of Limitations, as amended [Section 20], became effective, said Section providing that the statute of limitations upon criminal actions shall serve as the statute of limitations upon civil actions if the conduct complained of in the civil action could subject the Defendant to a criminal prosecution.

Actual damages, interest, and punitive damages totalling $1,826,208, plus costs and any post-judgment interest were sought.

Count II of the complaint, referring generally to the allegations of Count I, asserts that Bruno obtained Kalmich's property (the business) in an unlawful and tortious manner, and seeks recovery under a constructive trust theory in the same amounts as mentioned above, plus all profits and proceeds received by Bruno from his possession and sale of the business . . . .

[I]n our opinion the ultimate resolution of the appeal turns upon the determination not only of Illinois law but also that of Yugoslavia, a "foreign country" under Rule 44. 1, Fed.R.Civ.P. Irrespective of the deference to which a district court judge's determination of the local law is entitled, we regard the matter of foreign country law as purely a "question of law," as it is characterized in Rule 44. 1, the resolution of which we are free to arrive at on the basis of our own independent research and analysis.

In diversity cases, of course, a federal court applies the substantive law of the state in which it sits. *Erie R.R. Co. v. Tompkins,* 304 U.S. 64 (1938). Where the laws of more than one jurisdiction are at least arguably in issue, the Erie reference to the law of the forum-state includes that state's choice of law rules. *Klaxon Co. v. Stentor Elec. Mfg. Co., Inc.,* 313 U.S. 487 (1941); *Griffin v. McCoach,* 313 U.S. 498 (1941).

We think it clear, and neither party disagrees, that the Illinois courts would choose to apply the substantive law of Yugoslavia to this case. Yugoslavia was the site of the tort and the injury, and we can think of no argument that would demonstrate that Illinois has a more significant relationship with this case than has Yugoslavia. *See Ingersoll v. Klein,* 46 Ill.2d 42, 262 N.E.2d 593, 595 (1970). Moreover, the district court's cogent analysis demonstrates beyond any real question that this is the type of foreign cause of action that the courts of Illinois will enforce. Although only Count I is expressly rooted in Yugoslavian law, these conclusions apply with full force to Count II as well. Even if Illinois courts would apply the principles of Illinois equity jurisprudence to Kalmich's constructive trust theory, the underlying premise of the theory, the asserted unlawfulness and tortiousness of Bruno's seizure of Kalmich's business, would have to be measured by Yugoslavian law.

The choice of the applicable statute of limitations poses a different, and, in this case, a more difficult problem. State law barring an action because of a statute of limitations is sufficiently "substantive," in the *Erie* sense, that a federal court in that state exercising diversity jurisdiction must respect it. *Guaranty Trust Co. v., York,* 326 U.S. 99 (1945). Illinois has a five-year statute of limitations governing actions for damages for injury to real or personal property. ILL. REV. STAT. 1975, ch. 83, § 16. As pleaded in the complaint, Yugoslavia's statute of limitations applicable here appears to be perpetual. The question then, if not the answer, may be simply put: which statute of limitations should be applied under Illinois' choice of law rules?

The basic choice of law rule pertaining to statutes of limitations, in Illinois as elsewhere, is that such statutes are "procedural in their nature," that they "generally affect only the remedy and not substantive rights," and, thus, that the limitations statutes of the forum will usually apply, even though the causes of action to which they are applied may have arisen in and been governed by the substantive law of another jurisdiction.

An exception, however, is recognized in certain circumstances where the foreign cause of action is statutorily based . . . .

The controlling premise of such an argument would be that statutes of limitations are considered "procedural" because they reflect basically procedural concerns of the forum: discouraging plaintiffs from sleeping on their rights, and limiting the use of the forum's courts to cases in which it is thought that the matters in question are fresh enough to allow a fair rendering of justice. The fact that a foreign jurisdiction has enacted a statutory right with a long specific limitation would, according to this argument, provide no basis for overriding the forum's important interests in the integrity of its judicial system. Where the specific limitation is shorter than that which the forum provides for, it may be said that there remains no right for the forum to enforce, even though the forum would otherwise be willing to enforce one.

The major premises of the contrary argument would be these: where the forum's choice of law rules point to another jurisdiction, that jurisdiction's law governs the substantive rights of the parties; a general statute of limitations of the locus jurisdiction reflects only the locus' procedural concerns for its courts, and need not concern the forum; a specific limitation, on the other hand, goes to the substance of the foreign right and should be applied in the forum . . . .

. . . In our opinion Section 20 and Article 134(a), read together, demonstrate a connection between the Yugoslavian limitation provision that is adequately specific to warrant honoring the perpetual limitation in this case.

If adequate specificity exists, it cannot matter that various of the Yugoslavian statutes involved were enacted at different times. Likewise, the fact that Section 20 must be applied through another statute, Article 134(a), does not weaken Kalmich's claim of specificity. Hypothetically, if Section 20 allowed the use of criminal limitations periods only in civil actions based on war crimes under Article 125, it is inconceivable that the reference to Article 134(a) that would be required to see what the criminal limitation was would flaw the otherwise obviously specific nature of Section 20 . . . .[4]

Nor, as a final matter, do we find any disturbing aspect contrary to Illinois public policy in the fact that litigation is being allowed some thirty years after the events on which the claim for recovery is based. This is true notwithstanding our earlier reference to a policy argument of limitation of the use of the forum's courts to cases in which it is thought that the matters in question are fresh enough to allow a fair rendering of justice. Policy also is involved because of the desirability of discouraging litigants from sleeping on their rights. There would appear to be no aspect of sleeping on rights here and as far as the freshness aspect is concerned, Illinois, as is the case probably in most states, statutorily recognizes circumstances which would permit access to the courts of its state notwithstanding a lapse of time which could be very substantial and which could under some circumstances even exceed that involved in the case before us. Thus, the statute of limitations is tolled in certain circumstances by the absence of the defendant from the state. Similarly the statute is tolled if the person entitled to bring an action is at the time of the accrual of the cause of action an infant under 18 years of age, is insane or mentally ill, or is imprisoned on a criminal charge, the tolling continuing for two years beyond the removal of the disability . . . .

---

[4] This conclusion is supported by the opinion letter of Kalmich's Yugoslavian law expert. The parties are in controversy over the proper role of this letter in the case. Kalmich argues that the district court was bound by the conclusions of this unsworn, uncross-examined letter, simply because it was the only expert opinion tendered in the case. Bruno argues that it should not have been offered or considered because it was first offered in support of Kalmich's motion to alter judgment and it would not be admissible in evidence. Both arguments are plainly wrong under FED.R.CIV. 44.1. As material relevant to the question of law as to foreign law, it was properly offered even at the late date it was offered, and properly considered both in the district court and in this court . . . .

[The dissenting opinion of Judge Swygert is omitted.]

---

## NOTES AND QUESTIONS ON *KALMICH*

Why did the court believe that the law of Yugoslavia should be applied? The suit, after all, was filed in Chicago against a resident of Illinois, and the plaintiff was from Quebec. The litigation involved events which had taken place a third of a century earlier. Of what relevance, therefore, was the law of Yugoslavia?

Once the decision was made to apply the War Crimes law of Yugoslavia, why was it necessary to discuss which statute of limitations controlled? Why would the court not routinely apply Yugoslavan law to all aspects of the case (e.g., admissibility of documents)? And why would it matter whether the Yugoslavian limitations period was tied in with the requisite "specificity" to the war crimes law?

Finally, what does "policy" have to do with the case? Is the court suggesting that if the circumstances were different, Illinois "policy" would keep the court from enforcing the Yugoslavian law? If so, what could that policy be? *See* PROBLEM 4A-1. FORUM'S POLICY.

The *Kalmich* opinion foreshadows many of the issues which will be covered in this Chapter. No attempt even to suggest answers is made here; rather the case is included to help students consider possible approaches to choice-of-law problems.

## § 4.03  A Very Brief History of Choice of Law Before the Twentieth Century

Choice-of-law problems occur whenever relatively advanced economic and legal systems come into contact with each other on a frequent basis. Thus, the ancient Greek city-states, the medieval Italians, the Renaissance Dutch, and the modern Americans have all developed sophisticated theories concerning what laws should be applied to a particular problem. *See* Friedrich Juenger, *A Page of History,* 35 MERCER L. REV. 419 (1984); Hessel Yntema, *The Historic Bases of Private International Law,* 2 AM. J. COMP. L. 297 (1953). Expressed differently, the need to resolve economic disputes in a peaceful fashion has led a number of very different societies to think seriously about how to choose a law to control multi-state transactions.

Anglo-American thinking about conflicts problems is usually traced to Justice Joseph Story's magisterial treatise, Commentary on the Conflict of Laws, Foreign and Domestic (1834) (the treatise went through a number of later editions). This extraordinary work was of great influence not just here, but in Britain and on the Continent as well. Story emphasized the use of comity, a duty of "mutual interest and unity" owed by one state to another.

In this century, the two Restatements of Conflicts of Laws have significantly influenced conflicts law. The first, promulgated in 1934 (a century after the publication of Story's work) with Professor Joseph Beale as Reporter, concentrated on a vested rights, territorially-based approach. The First Restatement is analyzed in Part B, *infra,* of this Chapter. The Second Restatement (1971), with Professor Willis Reese as Reporter, adopted a combination of territorial and policy approaches. Meanwhile, Professor Brainerd Currie began developing "Interest Analysis" in the late 1950's, a method which emphasized consideration of the policies behind the various rules at issue. The Second Restatement and Interest Analysis are discussed in Part D, *infra,* of this Chapter.

## § 4.04   Proving Foreign Law

### WALTON v. ARABIAN AMERICAN OIL CO.

*United States Court of Appeals for the Second Circuit*
*233 F.2d 541 (2d Cir.)*
*cert. denied, 352 U.S. 872 (1956)*

FRANK, CIRCUIT JUDGE.

Plaintiff is a citizen and resident of Arkansas, who, while temporarily in Saudi Arabia, was seriously injured when an automobile he was driving collided with a truck owned by defendant, driven by one of defendant's employees. Defendant is a corporation incorporated in Delaware, licensed to do business in New York, and engaged in extensive business activities in Saudi Arabia. Plaintiff's complaint did not allege pertinent Saudi Arabian "law," nor at the trial did he prove or offer to prove it. Defendant did not, in its answer, allege such "law," and defendant did not prove or offer to prove it. There was evidence from which it might have been inferred, reasonably, that, under well-established New York decisions, defendant was negligent and therefore liable to plaintiff.,The trial judge, saying he would not take judicial notice of Saudi-Arabian "law," directed a verdict in favor of the defendant and gave judgment against the plaintiff.

1. As jurisdiction here rests on diversity of citizenship, we must apply the New York rules of conflict of laws. It is well settled by the New York decisions that the "substantive law" applicable to an alleged tort is the "law" of the place where the alleged tort occurred. This is the federal doctrine; *see, eg., Slater v. Mexican Nat'l R.R. Co.,* 194 U.S. 120. This doctrine is often said to be based on the notion that to hold otherwise would be to interfere with the authority of the foreign sovereign.[2]

2. The general federal rule is that the "law" of a foreign country is a fact which must be proved. However, under Federal Rules of Civil Procedure Rule 43(a), 28 U.S.C.A., a federal court must receive evidence if it is admissible according to the rules of evidence of the state in which the court sits. At first

---

[2] A variant but related notion is that the foreign sovereign alone has the power to create a legal obligation resulting from an act done within the territory over which it has "jurisdiction", and that, if that sovereign does create such an obligation, that obligation accompanies the person of the defendant everywhere. For criticisms of this view, *see, eg.,* Walter Wheeler Cook, The Logical and Legal Bases of the Conflict of Law (1942).

glance, then, it may seem that the judge erred in refusing to take judicial notice of Saudi Arabian "law" in the light of New York Civil Practice Act, § 344-a. In *Siegelman v. Cunard White Star,* 2 Cir., 221 F.2d 189, 196-197, applying that statute, we took judicial notice of English "law" which had been neither pleaded nor proved. Our decision, in that respect, has been criticized; but it may be justified on the ground that an American court can easily comprehend, and therefore, under the statute, take judicial notice of, English decisions, like those of any state in the United States.[9] However, where, as here, comprehension of foreign "law" is, to say the least, not easy, then, according to the somewhat narrow interpretation of the New York statute by the New York courts, a court "abuses" its discretion under that statute perhaps if it takes judicial notice of foreign "law" when it is not pleaded, and surely does so unless the party, who would otherwise have had the burden of proving that "law," has in some way adequately assisted the court in judicially learning it.

3. Plaintiff, however, argues thus: The instant case involves such rudimentary tort principles, that the judge, absent a contrary showing, should have presumed that those principles are recognized in Saudi Arabia; therefore the burden of showing the contrary was on the defendant, which did not discharge that burden. But we do not agree that the applicable tort principles, necessary to establish plaintiff's claim, are "rudimentary": In countries where the common law does not prevail, our doctrines relative to negligence, and to a master's liability for his servant's acts, may well not exist or be vastly different. Consequently, here plaintiff had the burden of showing, to the trial court's satisfaction, Saudi Arabian "law."

This conclusion seems unjust for this reason: Both the parties are Americans. The plaintiff was but a transient in Saudi Arabia when the accident occurred and has not been there since that time. The defendant company engages in extensive business operations there, and is therefore in a far better position to obtain information concerning the "law" of that country. But, under the New York decisions which we must follow, plaintiff had the burden. As he did not discharge it, a majority of the court holds that the judge correctly gave judgment for the defendant.

4. In argument, plaintiffs counsel asserted that Saudi Arabia has "no law or legal system", and no courts open to plaintiff, but only a dictatorial monarch who decides according to his whim whether a claim like plaintiffs shall be redressed, i.e., that Saudi Arabia is, in effect, "uncivilized." According to Holmes, J.—in *Slater v. Mexican National Railroad Co.* —the lex loci does not apply "where a tort is committed in an uncivilized country" or in one "having no law that civilized countries would recognize as adequate." If such were the case here, we think the New York courts would apply (and therefore we should) the substantive "law" of the country which is most closely connected with the parties and their conduct in this case, American "law."[14A] But

---

[9] An American court may go astray even in taking judicial notice of English "law." The similarity in language may be deceptive by concealing significant differences. Indeed, just because the English language appears the same as the American language (although it is not), an American may understand the former less adequately, than he understands German or French, which is more obviously "foreign" and different.

[14A] . . . .As the tort rules, pertinent here, of New York, Delaware and Arkansas are doubtless substantially similar, there would be no need to choose one or the other.

plaintiff has offered no data showing that Saudi Arabia is thus "uncivilized." We are loath to and will not believe it, absent such a showing . . . .

Since the plaintiff deliberately refrained from establishing an essential element of his case, the complaint was properly dismissed. The majority of the court thinks that, for the following reasons, it is inappropriate to remand the case so that the plaintiff may have another chance: he had abundant opportunity to supply the missing element and chose not to avail himself of it. It does not appear whether Judge Bicks or counsel for the parties considered the application of Section 344-a of the New York Civil Practice Act. Since Judge Bicks specifically determined that he would not take judicial notice of the Arabian "law", he must have considered that in some circumstances he might take judicial notice of foreign "law". But in any event, as we have pointed out, it would have been an abuse of discretion under the New York cases to take notice of the foreign "law" here. The judgment of dismissal must therefore be affirmed.

The writer of the opinion thinks we should remand for this reason: Apparently neither the trial judge nor the parties were aware of New York Civil Practice Act, § 344-a; consequently, in the interests of justice, we should remand with directions to permit the parties, if they so desire, to present material which may assist the trial judge to ascertain the applicable "law" of Saudi Arabia.[16]

*Affirmed.*

---

## NOTES AND QUESTIONS

(1) *Proving Foreign Law. Walton* raises two quite interesting, but different, points: How does a party prove foreign law, and what happens when that proof fails or is not even attempted?

At common law, the proof of foreign law was a question of fact, a rule that dates back to the time of Lord Mansfield and Chief Justice Marshall, and survived well into this century. *See* Eugene Scoles, et al. Conflict of Laws 529-32 (3d ed 2000). Thus, the content of foreign law was a jury question (at least sometimes), and the jury's decision was reviewed (at least in some courts) under the clearly erroneous rule usually applied to questions of fact.

---

[16] Or that it has no "civilized' legal system; *see* point 4 of the text, *supra.*

Nussbaum, 3 Am. J. of Comp. Law (1954) 60, 63-64 —points to an important fact: the prohibitive expense to a party of modest financial means in obtaining an expert to explain foreign "law." Subsequently (pp. 66-67), Nussbaum suggests that the trial judge call his own expert; the judge, says Nussbaum, would require the parties to advance the expert's fee, or, "if this is not feasible, the court (hence eventually the losing party), may be charged with the fee as part of the court's business." But, as matters now stand, this solution is not feasible: In a federal criminal case, a trial judge may call upon his own expert whom the government will pay; *see* Criminal Rule 28, 18 U.S.C.A. However, in a civil case (at any rate, one to which the government is not a party) the government has no authority to pay an expert; and the use of the device—of taxing the expert's fee as part of the costs to the losing party may be beyond the judge's power (absent a statute); in any event, the expert will go unpaid if the losing party has not the funds to pay such costs.

Various reforms in recent years have changed all of this. Federal Rule 44. 1, adopted in 1966, provides that proof of foreign law is a question of law and a court "may consider any relevant material or source." Rule 44.1 provides:

> A party who intends to raise an issue concerning the law of a foreign country shall give notice by pleadings or other reasonable written notice. The court, in determining foreign law, may consider any relevant material or source, including testimony, whether or not submitted by a party or admissible under the Federal Rules of Evidence. The court's determination shall be treated as a ruling on a question of law.

The judge is not limited to material submitted by the parties, but may conduct research on her own. *See generally* Sass, *Foreign Law in Federal Courts,* 1 AM. J. COMP. L. 97 (1983); Arthur Miller, *Federal Rule 44.1 and the "Fact"Approach to Determining Foreign Law: Death Knellfor a Die-hard Doctrine,* 65 MICH. L. REV. 617 (1967).

*See* PROBLEM 4A-2. THE ISRAELI LAWYER.

Two uniform acts, the Uniform Judicial Notice of Foreign Law Act, and the Uniform Interstate and International Procedure Act provide a procedure similar to Rule 44.1 for state courts. (The latter Uniform Act supercedes the former). *See also* Alexander, *The Application and Avoidance of Foreign Law in The Law of Conflicts,* 70 Nw. U.L. Rev. 602 (1975).

What do you think caused these reforms? Was it because proof of foreign law as "fact" rather than "law" was too expensive, time-consuming, and cumbersome? Or was there more at stake—such as a desire to limit the discretion of the jury?

(2) *It May Not be as Easy as it Looks. Walton* is a comparatively easy case, a simple automobile accident. How would you like to have been the lawyer (or client!) in *Pancolto v. Sociedade de Safaris de Mozambique, S.A.R.L.,* 422 F. Supp. 405 (N.D. 111. 1976) (Mozambique law of negligence applied to a safari accident), or *Basch v. Westinghouse Elec. Corp.,* 777 F.2d 165 (4th Cir. 1985) (Iranian tort law applied to the employment of an American citizen by an American corporation during work in Iran)? Or consider the following case:

**KUNSTSAMMLUNGEN ZU WEIMAR v. ELICOFON,** 678 F.2d 1150 (2d Cir. 1982). [Action brought by the East and West German governments independently—to recover "two priceless Albrecht Duerer portraits . . . . They were stolen in 1945 and fortuitously discovered in 1966 in the Brooklyn home of an American citizen . . . ."]

MANSFIELD, J: The search for an answer to the deceptively simple question, "Who owns the paintings?," involves a labyrinthian journey through 19th century German dynastic law, contemporary German property law, Allied Military Law during the post-war occupation of Germany, New York State law, and intricate conceptions of succession and sovereignty in international law . . . .

\* \* \*

True to his word, Judge Mansfield takes uson a tour (albeit a quick one, except for his discussion of New York law) of that exotic jurisprudence. Do you think it really is possible that the litigants or the court mastered all of the nuances of the various laws involved in the case? (Remember Judge Frank's warning about "tacit assumptions.")

Expert testimony is often used to establish foreign law. Should a judge be bound by the testimony of the experts? *See Usatorre v. The Victoria,* 172 F.2d 434 (2d Cir. 1949) (not bound by experts under old foreign law-is-fact method), *Chantier Naval Voisin v. MIY Daybreak,* 677 F. Supp. 1563 (S.D. Fla. 1988) (not bound by expert testimony under Rule 44.1). *Usatorre* is a particularly interesting opinion by Judge Frank who roamed at scholarly will from Aristotle to Justice Story on his way to concluding that testimony by an expert on Argentine admiralty laws could be disregarded by the court. Do you think it possible that Frank really had all of the "tacit assumptions" of Argentine admiralty law under his command? Consider also Chief Justice Vanderbilt's comment in *Leary v. Gledhill,* 8 N.J. 260, 84 A.2d 725 (1951):

> In the instant case the transaction occurred in France. Our courts may properly take judicial knowledge that France is not a common law, but rather a civil jurisdiction. It would, therefore, be inappropriate and indeed contrary to elementary knowledge to presume that the principles of the common law prevail there.

(3) *The Consequences of Failure to Prove Foreign Law.* In *Leary v. Gledhill,* 8; N.J. 260, 84 A.2d 725 (1951), Chief Justice Vanderbilt discussed the consequences of failure to prove foreign law:

> The courts, however, were reluctant to dismiss an action for a failure to plead and prove the applicable foreign law as they would have dismissed it for a failure to prove other material facts necessary to establish a cause of action or a defense. Accordingly, the courts frequently indulged in one or another of several presumptions: that the common law prevails in the foreign jurisdiction; that the law of the foreign jurisdiction is the same as the law of the forum, be it common law or statute; or that certain fundamental principles of the law exist in all civilized countries. As a fourth alternative, instead of indulging in any presumption as to the law of the foreign jurisdiction, the courts would merely apply the law of the forum as the only law before the court on the assumption that by failing to prove the foreign law the parties acquiesce in having their controversy determined by reference to the law of the forum, be it statutory or common law. By the application of these various presumptions the courts have in effect treated the common law rule that foreign law could not be noticed but must be pleaded and proved as if it were a matter of fact merely as a permissive rule whereby either party could, if it were to his advantage, plead and prove the foreign law. Thus the failure to plead and prove the foreign law has not generally been considered as fatal . . . .

Vanderbilt identified four options—presumptions—available to the court when foreign law is not proven. First, the court could presume that foreign and domestic law are the same. This is a heroic assumption. Think about the variation in the laws of the fifty states on products liability, limitations on recovery for medical malpractice, and so forth. Second, and closely related to the first option, the court could presume that the common law is the law of the foreign jurisdiction; this presumption, however, makes little sense when the other jurisdiction is France or Saudi Arabia.

Third, the court could presume that certain fundamental legal principles exist in all civilized countries. Is that sensible? Do you think there is a kind of "natural law" (at least of highly industrialized societies) governing the law of debt, or the law of automobile negligence? The fourth option identified by Justice Vanderbilt—that the court could view the parties as having acquiesced in the application of forum law—is more consistent with modern realistic jurisprudence. If the parties do not care what law controls their problem, why should the court? Or is there a possibility that something other than party desires (or bad lawyering or laziness) may be involved? *See generally* William L. Reynolds, *What Happens When Parties Fail to Prove Foreign Law?* 48 MERCER L. REV. 775 (1997).

Another alternative, of course, is raised by *Walton:* dismissal for failure to prove an essential element of the cause of action. Do you approve of the dismissal in *Walton,* or is that solution too extreme? *Walton,* remember, involved an automobile accident between an American citizen and an American company. How easy would it have been for the plaintiff to establish Saudi law? How would you go about doing so? How expensive do you think those experts would be? If the plaintiff did not live in a major metropolis like New York, do you think he would even be able to find them? If the cost of proving Saudi law was high compared to the value of the case, would the case be brought? If not, has justice been done? (The difficulty of determining the Saudi law that the court wanted to apply in *Walton* is shown by the discussion of the case in Robert von Mehren and Donald Trautman, The Law of Multistate Problems 100-02 (1965).)

*See* PROBLEM 4A-3. THE LAW WHEN?

(4) *Why is Foreign Law Relevant?* Of course, all of this raises the question of just why we might care about the content of foreign law. Why not just routinely apply forum law—a tactic which certainly would save wear and tear on the judges. Surprisingly, this turns out to be an extremely difficult question; indeed, most of the rest of this lengthy Chapter will consider this problem in one way or another. Here are some introductory hints, however: Do the parties have "rights" based on where the transaction occurred? Are party expectations relevant? Should we consider the policies behind the various rules? Does one state owe some sort of deference to the laws of another state?

(5) *The Uncivilized State.* Judge Frank states that New York would not apply the law of an "uncivilized" nation. Why not? Is it because the laws of an uncivilized nation might be too rudimentary, either generally or in a particular area like commercial obligations? If the problem is only with a specific area is the reluctance based on some notion of party expectations? (This point is discussed in connection with the "party autonomy" rule in Part E, *infra,* of this Chapter.) What if the parties had relied on the law of the uncivilized state, however?

There is also the difficulty of defining an uncivilized state. How do you know an uncivilized State when you find one? Was the Soviet Union under Stalin uncivilized? Uganda under Idi Amin? Iran under Ayatollah Khomeni? The common thread among al of these states, of course, is a despotism of various levels of depravity. Why should that be revelant? Is it due to some basic due process or natural law notions? *See* PROBLEM 4A-4." I SHOT HIM FIVE TIMES IN SELF DEFENSE." What if the foreign law is arbitrary or discriminates on the basis of race, religion, or gender? *Compare Holzer v. Deutsche Reichsbahn-Gesellschaft,* 277 N.Y. 474, 14 N.E. 2d 798 (1938), *infra* in § 4.14, where the court enforced a Nazi law which discriminated against German Jews. An American court (or any civilized court, for that matter) cannot participate in such conduct, can it?

A final problem with applying the law of an uncivilized state may be that it has no "law." What if legal outcomes, for example, turn on the unbridled discretion of the sovereign, who can intervene and change results at her whim? What if the particular legal issue of transaction is simply beyond the sophistication of the foreign legal system, *e.g.,* a sale and lease-back in a country with a tribal or feudal system? In such cases, of course, there is no foreign "law" for an American court to apply, is there?

(6) *Certified Questions.* The Uniform Certification of Questions of Law Act (adopted in 31 states), provides an excellent method of getting foreign law decided correctly. The Act permits a federal court, or state appellate court, to avoid having to guess the content of foreign law by authorizing it to ask the highest court of another state to declare the law on a question which the certifying court believes "may be determinative" of the case and for which "no controlling" precedent exists.

There are drawbacks to the certification process, of course. Certification can cost both time and money. It can also lead to quasi-advisory opinions which may suffer from being divorced from the discipline imposed by the need to resolve the actual facts of a real case. Used properly, however, certification can be marvelously useful. *See* Bernard Corr & Ira Robbins, *Interjurisdictional Certification and Choice of Law,* 41 VAND. L. REV. 411 (1988). *See* PROBLEM 4A-5. DID TWO UNINSURED MOTORISTS MEET?

Should certification by state courts of federal issues be possible? State courts, remember, often pass on federal issues. Judge Bernard Meyer of the Court of Appeals of New York has advocated such a procedure. *See* Bernard Meyer, *Justice, Bureaucracy, Structure, and Simplification,* 42 MD. L. REV. 659, 673 (1983).

# PART B THE TRADITIONAL SYSTEM

## § 4.05 Introduction

### [A] The Vested Rights Theory and the First Restatement

The traditional system for choice of law in the United States was embodied in the Restatement of Conflict of Laws, published in 1934. The vested rights theory, the theoretical basis for the First Restatement, was a highly metaphysical account of the choice-of-law process formulated in reaction to the doctrine of comity, the dominant choice-of-law theory of the nineteenth century. Both vested rights and comity were answers to a highly conceptualistic question that modern conflicts theory wisely tends to ignore. When an Ohio court decides a conflicts case using a principle found in the law of Michigan, exactly what is it doing? Is it "applying" the Michigan law, enforcing a Michigan right, or creating an Ohio right that is modeled on a Michigan right that would have existed had the case been a wholly Michigan case? *See* Elliot Cheatham, *American Theories of Conflict of Laws: Their Role and Utility,* 58 HARV. L. REV. 361, 365-367 (1945).

Joseph Story, the first great American conflicts theorist, assumed the first approach. He believed that the forum court "applied" the foreign law based on the theory of comity—the customary respect given by one sovereign to another:

> The true foundation, on which the administration of international law must rest, is, that the rules, which are to govern, are those, which arise from mutual interest and utility, from a sense of the inconveniences, which would result from a contrary doctrine, and from a sort of moral necessity to do justice, in order that justice may be done to us in return.

JOSEPH STORY, COMMENTARIES ON THE CONFLICT OF LAWS, FOREIGN AND DOMESTIC 34 (1834).

The notion of comity was subject to two principal criticisms. First, comity suggested that in a conflicts case the forum court might "apply" foreign law, thus implying that the foreign law operated outside the territory of the foreign sovereign. This notion conflicted with the then-current territorial dogma that no law could have any effect outside the territory of the sovereign that promulgated it. Second, comity permitted too much judicial discretion. It seemed to suggest that a judge was free to decide on his own whether justice and convenience required the application of foreign law. This expanded view of judicial discretion was at odds with the prevalent notion of formalism, the view that judges had little freedom and that their decisions were the inevitable result of applying certain, relatively unchanging legal rules. On formalism, *see generally* Grant Gilmore, The Ages of American Law ch. 3 (1977).

The vested rights theory provided a view of the choice of law process that was more acceptable to the territorialist and formalist jurisprudence of the early twentieth century. The theory, propounded by Joseph H. Beale in this country and A.V. Dicey in England, held that foreign law could never operate outside the territory of the foreign sovereign. Rather, the forum's use of foreign law could be explained in terms of the forum's enforcement of a right that had vested as a result of an occurrence in the foreign jurisdiction. *See* 3 JOSEPH BEALE, A TREATISE ON THE CONFLICT OF LAWS, 1964-1965 (1935); A. V. DICEY, A DIGEST OF THE LAW OF ENGLAND WITH REFERENCE TO THE CONFLICT OF LAWS 17-25 (5th ed. 1932). In the words of Justice Holmes,

> When . . . liability is enforced in a jurisdiction foreign to the place of the wrongful act, obviously that does not mean that the act in any degree is subject to the *lex fori,* with regard to either its quality or its consequences. On the other hand, it equally little means that the law of the place of the act is operative outside its own territory. The theory of the foreign suit is that although the act complained of was subject to no law having force in the forum, it gave rise to an obligation, an *obligatio* which, like other obligations, follows the person, and may be enforced wherever the person may be found.

*Slater v. Mexican Nat'l R.R.,* 194 U.S. 120, 126 (1904). *See* PROBLEM 4B-1. A MEXICAN TRAIN CRASH.

The vested rights theory made it important to determine when and where a particular right vested because the law of that place would control the content of the right. This resulted in a system of rules each of which governed a major area of law by identifying a particular event (the tortious injury or the making of a contract, for example) as the trigger for the vesting of a right. Thus, questions in tort were decided by the law of the place of injury, questions in contract by the law of the place of making, etc.

For more on comity, vested rights and the theoretical basis of the First Restatement, *see* William Richman & William Reynolds, Understanding Conflict of Laws § 63 (3d ed. 2002); EUGENE SCOLES ET AL., CONFLICT OF LAWS 18-22 (3d ed. 2000), Kermit Roosevelt III, *The Myth of Choice of Law: Rethinking Conflicts,* 97 MICH. L. REV. 2448, 2455-2461 (1999).

## [B]  First Restatement Practice—Broad Rules and Escape Devices

Under the influence of Joseph Beale, the Reporter for the project, the American Law Institute incorporated the vested rights theory into the First Restatement. This traditional system prevailed in most American courts until the work of a new generation of judges and scholars, trained in legal realism, began to supplant it in the 1950's and 1960's. Even today, the First Restatement system retains a good deal of vitality. In perhaps a quarter of the states, it is alive and well as the dominant general choice-of-law methodology. *See* Symeon Symeonides, *Choice of Law in the American Courts in 1999: One More Year,* 48 AM. J. COMP. L. 143 (2000); William M. Richman & David Riley, *The First Restatement on the Twenty-fifth Anniversary of Its Successor: Contemporary Practice on Traditional Courts,* 56 MD. L. REV. 101 (1997); Gregory E. Smith, *Choice of Law in the United States,* 38 HASTINGS L.J. 1041, 1043-4 (1987); Herma Kay, *Theory into Practice: Choice of Law in the Courts,* 34 MERCER L. REV. 521, 582 (1983). Furthermore, even the states that have abandoned the First Restatement for most choice-of-law problems retain it for issues involving interests in land.

The traditional system for choice of law consists of a few broad, single-contract, jurisdiction-selecting rules coupled with an array of escape devices. Each of these features of the traditional system requires a brief comment. At first glance, the rules do not appear to be few or broad; the Restatement contains over 300 sections on choice of law. RESTATEMENT (FIRST) OF CONFLICT OF LAWS, §§ 119-428. Most of the sections, however, can be condensed into a few general summary rules. Nearly all questions in tort, for example, are governed by the law of the place of injury, and nearly all questions about property are governed by the law of the situs.

Professor Cavers has fixed on the First Restatement rules the label "jurisdiction-selecting," because they pick between competing states (jurisdictions), rather than between competing rules. David Cavers, The Choice of Law Process 9 (1965). Thus, the court does not consider the scope, content, or policy of the substantive rule of law until *after* choosing the state whose rule will control. In making the initial choice, the First Restatement rules are not concerned with which substantive rule is "better," or the parties' intentions, or policy; rather, they are concerned *only* with identifying a particular event and the jurisdiction (state) in which that event occurred.

Another feature of the First Restatement rules is that, unlike other choice-of-law systems, they rely upon *only one* salient connection between the dispute and the state. On the issue of the validity of a contract, for example, the Center of Gravity Theory *(see § 4.16, infra)* might look to several important contacts: the domicile of the parties, the place where the contract was made, the place where it was to be performed, the place where financial injury from breach might be felt. The First Restatement considers only one contact—the place of making.

The three sections that follow examine the Restatement's treatment of several substantive areas of law: torts, contracts, land, and personal property.

## § 4.06   Torts

## ALABAMA GREAT SOUTHERN RAILROAD CO. v. CARROLL

*Alabama Supreme Court*
*97 Ala. 126, 11 So. 803 (1892)*

McCLELLAN, J. The plaintiff W. D. Carroll is, and was at the time of entering into the service of the defendant, the Alabama Great Southern Railroad Company, and at the time of being injured in that service, a citizen of Alabama. The defendant is an Alabama corporation operating a railroad extending from Chattanooga in the State of Tennessee through Alabama to Meridian in the State of Mississippi. At the time of the casualty complained of, plaintiff was in the service of the defendant in the capacity of brakeman on freight trains running from Birmingham, Alabama, to Meridian, Mississippi, under a contract which was made in the State of Alabama. The injury was caused by the breaking of a link between two cars in a freight train which was proceeding from Birmingham to Meridian. The point at which the link broke and the injury was suffered was in the State of Mississippi. . . . It was shown to be the duty of certain employees of defendant . . . to inspect the links attached to cars to be put in trains . . . at Chattanooga, Birmingham, and some points between Birmingham and the place where this link broke, and also that it was the duty of the conductor of freight trains and the other train-men to maintain such inspection as occasion afforded throughout the runs or trips of such trains; and the evidence affords ground for inference that there was a negligent omission on the part of such employees to perform this duty, or if performed, the failure to discover the defect in and to remove this link was the result of negligence.

. . . This was the negligence not of the master, the defendant, but of fellow-servants of the plaintiff, for which at common-law the defendant is not liable. . . .

. . . [P]laintiff has shown no cause of action under the common-law as it is understood and applied both here and in Mississippi.

It is, however, further contended that the plaintiff, if his evidence be believed, has made out a case for the recovery sought under the Employer's Liability Act of Alabama, it being clearly shown that there is no such, or similar law of force in the State of Mississippi. Considering this position in the abstract, that is dissociated from the facts of this particular case which are supposed to exert an important influence upon it, there can not be two opinions as to its being unsound and untenable. So looked at, we do not understand appellee's counsel even to deny either the proposition or its application to this case, that there can be no recovery in one State for injuries to the person sustained in another unless the infliction of the injuries is actionable under the law of the State in which they were received. Certainly this is the well established rule of law subject in some jurisdictions to the qualification that the infliction of the injuries would also support an action in the State where the suit is brought, had they been received within that State.

But it is claimed that the facts of this case take it out of the general rule . . . and authorize the courts of Alabama to subject the defendant to the payment of damages under section 2590 of the Code, although the injuries counted on were sustained in Mississippi under circumstances which involved no liability on the defendant by the laws of that State.

This insistence is in the first instance based on that aspect of the evidence which goes to show that the negligence which produced the casualty transpired in Alabama, and the theory that wherever the consequence of that negligence manifested itself, a recovery can be had in Alabama. . . .

. . . It is admitted, or at least cannot be denied, that negligence of duty unproductive of damnifying results will not authorize or support a recovery. Up to the time the train passed out of Alabama no injury had resulted. For all that occurred in Alabama, therefore, no cause of action whatever arose. The fact which created the right to sue, the injury without which confessedly no action would lie anywhere, transpired in the State of Mississippi. It was in that State, therefore, necessarily that the cause of action, if any, arose; and whether a cause of action arose and existed at all or not must in all reason be determined by the law which obtained at the time and place when and where the fact which is relied on to justify a recovery transpired. Section 2590 of the Code of Alabama had no efficiency beyond the lines of Alabama. It cannot be allowed to operate upon facts occurring in another State so as to evolve out of them rights and liabilities which do not exist under the law of that State which is, of course paramount in the premises. . . . The negligent infliction of an injury here under statutory circumstances creates a right of action here, which, being transitory, may be enforced in any other State or country the comity of which admits of it; but for an injury inflicted elsewhere than in Alabama our statute gives no right of recovery, and the aggrieved party must look to the local law to ascertain what his rights are. Under that law this plaintiff had no cause of action, as we have seen, and hence he has no rights which our courts can enforce, unless it be upon a consideration to be presently adverted to. We have not been inattentive to the suggestions of counsel in this connection, which are based upon that rule of the statutory and common criminal law under which a murderer is punishable where the fatal blow is delivered, regardless of the place where death ensues. This principle is patently without application here. There would be some analogy if the plaintiff had been stricken in Alabama and suffered in Mississippi, which is not the fact. There is, however, an analogy which is afforded by the criminal law, but which points away from the conclusion appellee's counsel desire us to reach. This is found in that well established doctrine of criminal law, that where the unlawful act is committed in one jurisdiction or State and takes effect—produces the result which it is the purpose of the law to prevent, or, it having ensued, punish for—in another jurisdiction or State, the crime is deemed to have been committed and is punished in that jurisdiction or State in which the result is manifested, and not where the act was committed.

Another consideration—that referred to above—it is insisted, entitles this plaintiff to recover here under the Employer's Liability Act for an injury inflicted beyond the territorial operation of that act. This is claimed upon the fact that at the time plaintiff was injured he was in the discharge of duties which rested on him by the terms of a contract between him and defendant which had been entered into in Alabama, and, hence, was an Alabama contract, in connection with the facts that plaintiff was and is a citizen of this State, and the defendant is an Alabama corporation. . . .

The contract was that plaintiff should serve the defendant in the capacity of a brakeman on its freight train between Birmingham, Alabama, and Meridian, Mississippi, and should receive as compensation a stipulated sum for each trip from Birmingham to Meridian and return. The theory is that the Employer's Liability Act became a part of this contract; that the duties and liabilities which it prescribes became contractual duties and liabilities, or duties and liabilities springing out of the contract, and that these duties attended upon the execution whenever its performance was required—in Mississippi as well as in Alabama—and that the liability prescribed for a failure to perform any of such duties attached upon such failure and consequent injury wherever it occurred, and was enforceable here because imposed by an Alabama contract notwithstanding the remission of duty and the resulting injury occurred in Mississippi. . . . If this argument is sound, and it is sound if the duties and liabilities prescribed by the act can be said to be contractual duties and obligations at all, it would lead to conclusions the possibility of which has not hitherto been suggested by any court or law writer, and which, to say the least, would be astounding to the profession. . . . [T]he duties and liabilities incident to the relation between the plaintiff and the defendant which are involved in this case, are not imposed by and do not rest in or spring from the contract between the parties. The only office of the contract, under section 2590 of the Code, is the establishment of a relation between them, that of master and servant; and it is upon that relation, that incident or consequence of the contract, and not upon the rights of the parties under the contract, that our statute operates. . . .

## NOTES AND QUESTIONS ON *CARROLL* AND THE PLACE OF THE WRONG

(1) *The Place of the Wrong.* The Restatement contains over fifty sections on torts, but nearly all choose the law of "the place of the wrong." Thus, the law of the place of the wrong controls the existence of a legal injury (§ 378), defendant's standard of responsibility (§ 381), causation (§ 383), contributory negligence (§ 385), the fellow-servant rule (§ 386), vicarious liability (§ 387), defenses to liability (§ 388), survival of actions (§ 390), and the measure of damages (§ 412). *See generally* WILLIAM RICHMAN & WILLIAM REYNOLDS, UNDERSTANDING CONFLICT OF LAWS § 65[a] (3d ed. 2002).

(2) *The Impact Rule.* But where is "the place of the wrong?" Section 377 answers: the place "where the last event necessary to make an actor liable for an event takes place." In all but a few cases, the "last event" is the injury to the plaintiff. In the words of the Restatement, the forum should apply the law of "the place where the harmful force first takes effect upon the body," or in other words, the law of the place of impact.

The Restatement, following courts like *Carroll,* derived the "last event" or "place-of-impact" rule from the vested rights theory. Recall that the theory holds that the forum enforces a right that has vested in a foreign state; the right can vest only when all the elements of the plaintiff's claim have been satisfied. But why the fetish about time order? If each element of a tort is a necessary condition for liability, why should the last be singled out as more crucial than the first? If time order really is so crucial, which state's statute should govern in a wrongful death case, the state where defendant injures decedent, the state where decedent seeks medical treatment and eventually dies, or the state where decedent's family feels the economic loss from his death? The vested rights theory suggests the second or third option, but the Restatement follows the impact rule and chooses the first. *See* §   377, note 1 and § 391.

(3) *Exceptions:* The First Restatement contains a few limited exceptions to the place-of-injury rule:

(a) *Vicarious Liability.* Suppose P authorizes A to drive P's car in state X, and A exceeds his authority and drives the car into state Y where he injures V. Under the law of X, P would not be vicariously liable to V, while Y law would produce liability. Which law controls? *See Scheer v. Rockne Motors,* 68

F.2d 942 (2d Cir. 1934). Section 387 chooses the law of X; it provides that the vicarious liability of defendant for the acts of another is determined by the place of the injury *only if* the defendant authorized the person to act for him in the state. Comment a explains:

In order that the law of the state of the wrong may apply to create liability against the absentee defendant, he must in some way have submitted himself to the law of that state. It is sufficient if he has authorized or permitted another to act for him in the state in which the other's conduct occurs. . . .[*]

*See* PROBLEMS 4B-2. VICARIOUS LIABILITY BY NEW YORK LAW; 4B-3. OWNER'S LIABILITY.

(b) *Duty or Privilege to Act.* Suppose a health officer in state X is required to burn infected rags at a particular place and the burning causes a nuisance in state Y. According to § 382, there is no liability; a person who acts in one state pursuant to a legal duty or privilege is not liable even if his action causes injury in another state where the injury is actionable.

(c) *Reliance on Particular Standard of Care.* Section 380(2) provides that one who acts in state X in reliance upon a very particular standard of care will not be liable if his act causes injury in state Y where the particular standard is higher. Comment b provides an illustration: By the law of both X and; Y, a railroad is liable for fire if it acts negligently. In Y, failure to equip a locomotive with a spark arrester is negligence *per se*; in *X,* it is not. If a railroad operates a locomotive carefully in X without a spark arrester and causes a fire that damages property in Y, the railroad is not liable.

(d) *Poison.* Suppose defendant in state X mails poisoned candy to the plaintiff in state Y. She eats the candy in Y, falls ill in state Z and dies in state W. The law of Z controls. *See* § 377, comment a, illustration 2.

Are these exceptions consistent with the vested rights theory? If not what explains them? Can you see a link?

(4) *Prevalence of the Rule.* Eleven states still follow the place-of-injury rule for tort conflicts: Alabama, Florida, Georgia, Kansas, Maryland, Montana, New Mexico, North Carolina, South Carolina, Virginia, West Virginia and Wyoming. *See* Symeon Symeonides, *Choice of Law in the American Courts in 1998: Twelfth Annual Survey,* 47 AM. J. COMP. L. 327, 330 (1999), William Richman & David Riley, *The First Restatement of Conflicts on the Twenty-fifth. Anniversary of Its Successor,* 56 Md. L. Rev. 1196, 1202 (1997). Among the most recent cases are *Milton v. IIT Research Institute,* 138 F3d 519 (4th Cir 1998) (applying Virginia conflicts law); *Fitzgerald v. Austin,* 715 So.2d 795 (Ala. App. 1997).

(5) *Evaluating the Rule.* The place-of-injury rule, aside from the exceptions, is hard and fast. But is it wise?

(a) *Simplicity and Forum Neutrality.* One great virtue of the place-of-injury rule is that it is simple and easy to apply. This may seem trivial now, but after an exploration of the complete and confusing array of modern choice-of-law systems (*see* Parts D, E, & F, *infra*), simplicity may acquire the nostalgic allure of the ten-cent coke.

---

[*] Copyright American Law Institute. Reprinted with permission.

The rule is also forum-neutral; in other words, it produces the same result regardless of where the lawsuit is brought. The traditionalists thought that desirable:

> [T]here will be no justice unless cases are decided in accordance with law, that is, in the conflict-of-laws area, on a basis which will be accepted by other states, and will lead, in so far as humanly possible, to the same decision of a controversy no matter where the suit is brought. . . . This should be apparent on its face. It is made apparent when the question of forum-shopping is considered. If each court simply decides what it regards as "just", or, on the other hand, if it applies only its own law, then diverse precedents will surely develop, and counsel for plaintiffs will be remiss in their duty if they do not study all the cases in all the states, and file their suit (as they often can) in a state which will give them a favorable result.

> Not only is this a denial of true justice, a denial of the purpose of the conflict of laws, but also it is a denial of law itself. It provides no opportunity for certainty in the law. It makes it difficult to plan transactions having interstate elements.

> . . . We will not have law in this area, we will not fulfill the objectives of the conflict of laws, unless we can provide rules for cases under which the same cases will be decided the same way no matter where the suit is brought, to the extent that this is possible within the limits of human frailty.

DAVID CAVERS, THE CHOICE OF LAW PROCESS 22-23 (1965).[1]

If simplicity and forum-neutrality are desired goals, how much should be sacrificed to attain them? What about a rule requiring the choice of the law of the state first (or last) in alphabetical order?

(b) *Arbitrary and Mechanical.* Suppose the injury in *Carroll* had occurred one hundred yards before the Mississippi border instead of one hundred yards after it; would the result change? Does that make sense?

(c) *Proper Scope.* The place-of-injury rule applies to all sorts of torts from battery to negligence to deceit to alienation of affections. Is such broad applicability a good or bad thing? Is such a broad rule common in our legal system? It certainly makes for an elegant and simple system, but does it produce problems as well?

In addition to lumping together cases that are very different, the Restatement separates cases that are quite similar. Suppose a consumer from Illinois purchases a lawn mower in Iowa and then returns to Illinois where he is injured by the lawn mower. In the typical product liability action, the consumer will plead one count in strict tort and one in warranty. The two theories—one descended from tort, the other from contract—are designed to regulate the same sort of conduct and compensate the same sort of injury, yet the First Restatement will apply the law of Iowa (the place of making of

---

[1] The passage comes from the opinion of "Judge" Erwin Griswold. Professor Cavers posed a hypothetical case and then wrote a decision for each of several noted conflicts scholars whom he elevated to judge for the occasion.

the contract) to one and the law of Illinois (the place of injury) to the other. Does that make sense?

*See* PROBLEM 4B-4. WHEN EAST MEETS WEST.

(d) *Non-Physical Injuries.* The place-of-injury rule is even more problematic in cases involving non-physical injuries. What law should apply in a case of defamation published by a national magazine? Note that the "single publication" rule does not solve this problem. It provides that an entire edition of the magazine constitutes a single publication that gives rise to but one cause of action. It permits the plaintiff to sue in one forum for all of his damages, but it does not indicate what law that forum should apply. *See* WILLIAM PROSSER & W. PAGE KEETON, PROSSER AND KEETON ON TORTS 800 (5th ed. 1984). Where then is the place of injury? Every state in which plaintiffs reputation suffers? Does the rule mean that the law of each place of injury should apply to the publication that occurred there? *See* § 377, comment a, illustration 7; James Pielemeier, *Constitutional Limitations on Choice of Law: The Special Case of Multistate Defamation,* 133 U. PA. L. REV. 381, 393-94 (1985). That would require the jury to hear fifty separate sets of instructions. To avoid this bizarre and impractical result, courts attempted to pick one contact as most significant so that the entire case could be governed by one state's law. *See* William Prosser, *Interstate Publication,* 51 MICH. L. REV. 959, 971-978 (1953) (ten possible contacts, no consensus in the courts). But which contact should control? Plaintiff's domicile, defendant's domicile, the state in which the magazine is composed and edited, the state of the greatest circulation? How should the court choose?

Defamation is just one example. How does the place-of-injury rule work for other non-physical injuries such as misrepresentation (deceit), unfair competition, and alienation of affections? *See* PROBLEM 4B-5. ALIENATION OF AFFECTIONS.

## § 4.07 Contracts

### [A] The Place of Contracting

### MILLIKEN v. PRATT

*Massachusetts Supreme Judicial Court*
*125 Mass. 374, 28 Am. Rep. 241 (1878)*

The plaintiffs are partners doing business in Portland, Maine, under the firm name of Deering, Milliken & Co. The defendant is and has been since 1850, the wife of Daniel Pratt, and both have always resided in Massachusetts. In 1870, Daniel, who was then doing business in Massachusetts, applied to the plaintiffs at Portland for credit, and they required of him, as a condition of granting the same, a guaranty from the defendant to the amount of five hundred dollars, and accordingly he procured from his wife the following instrument:

"Portland, January 29, 1870. In consideration of one dollar paid by Deering, Milliken & Co., receipt of which is hereby acknowledged, I guarantee the payment to them by Daniel Pratt of the sum of five hundred dollars, from time to time as he may want—this to be a continuing guaranty. Sarah A. Pratt."

This instrument was executed by the defendant two or three days after its date, at her home in Massachusetts, and there delivered by her to her husband, who sent it by mail from Massachusetts to the plaintiffs in Portland; and the plaintiffs received it from the post office in Portland early in February, 1870.

The plaintiffs subsequently sold and delivered goods to Daniel from time to time until October 7, 1871, and charged the same to him, and, if competent, it may be taken to be true, that in so doing they relied upon the guaranty. . . . This action is brought for goods sold . . . [with] a balance due of $560.12. The one dollar mentioned in the guaranty was not paid, and the only consideration moving to the defendant therefor was the giving of credit by the plaintiffs to her husband. Some of the goods were selected personally by Daniel at the plaintiffs' store in Portland, others were ordered by letters mailed by Daniel from Massachusetts to the plaintiffs at Portland, and all were sent by the plaintiffs by express from Portland to Daniel in Massachusetts, who paid all express charges. . . .

Payment was duly demanded of the defendant before the date of the writ, and was refused by her.

The Superior Court ordered judgment for the defendant; and the plaintiffs appealed to this court.

GRAY, C. J. The general rule is that the validity of a contract is to be determined by the law of the state in which it is made; if it is valid there, it is deemed valid everywhere, and will sustain an action in the courts of a state whose laws do not permit such a contract. *Scudder v. Union Nat'l Bank,* 91 U.S. 406. Even a contract expressly prohibited by the statutes of the state in which the suit is brought, if not in itself immoral, is not necessarily nor usually deemed so invalid that the comity of the state, as administered by its courts, will refuse to entertain an action on such a contract made by one of its own citizens abroad in a state the laws of which permit it.

If the contract is completed in another state, it makes no difference in principle whether the citizen of this state goes in person, or sends an agent, or writes a letter, across the boundary line between the two states. . . . So if a person residing in this state signs and transmits, either by a messenger or through the post-office, to a person in another state, a written contract, which requires no special forms or solemnities, in its execution, and no signature of the person to whom it is addressed, and is assented to and acted on by him there, the contract is made there, just as if the writer personally took the executed contract into the other state, or wrote and signed it there; and it is no objection to the maintenance of an action thereon here, that such a contract is prohibited by the law of this Commonwealth.

The guaranty, bearing date of Portland, in the State of Maine, was executed by the defendant, a married woman, having her home in this Commonwealth, as collateral security for the liability of her husband for goods sold by the plaintiffs to him, and was sent by her through him by mail to the plaintiffs at Portland. The sales of the goods ordered by him from the plaintiffs at Portland, and there delivered by them to him in person, or to a carrier for him, were made in the State of Maine. The contract between the defendant and the plaintiffs was complete when the guaranty had been received and acted on by them at Portland, and not before. It must therefore be treated as made and to be performed in the State of Maine.

The law of Maine authorized a married woman to bind herself by any contract as if she were unmarried. The law of Massachusetts, as then existing, did not allow her to enter into a contract as surety or for the accommodation of her husband or of any third person. Since the making of the contract sued on, and before the bringing of this action, the law of this Commonwealth has been changed, so as to enable married women to make such contracts.

The question therefore is, whether a contract made in another state by a married woman domiciled here, which a married woman was not at the time capable of making under the law of this Commonwealth, but was then allowed by the law of that state to make, and which she could now lawfully make in this Commonwealth, will sustain an action against her in our courts.

It has been often stated by commentators that the law of the domicil regulating the capacity of a person, accompanies and governs the person everywhere. But this statement, in modern times at least, is subject to many qualifications; and the opinions of foreign jurists upon the subject, the principal of which are collected in the treatises of Mr. Justice Story and of Dr. Francis Wharton on the Conflict of Laws, are too varying and contradictory to control the general current of the English and American authorities in favor of holding that a contract, which by the law of the place is recognized as lawfully made by a capable person, is valid everywhere, although the person would not, under the law of his domicil be deemed capable of making it. . . .

The principal reasons on which continental jurists have maintained that personal laws of the domicil, affecting the status and capacity of all inhabitants of a particular class, bind them wherever they may go, appear to have been that each state has the rightful power of regulating the status and condition of its subjects, and, being best acquainted with the circumstances of climate, race, character, manners and customs, can best judge at what age young persons may begin to act for themselves, and whether and how far married women may act independently of their husbands; that laws limiting the capacity of infants or of married women are intended for their protection, and cannot therefore be dispensed with by their agreement; that all civilized states recognize the incapacity of infants and married women; and that a person, dealing with either, ordinarily has notice, by the apparent age or sex, that the person is likely to be of a class whom the laws protect, and is thus put upon inquiry how far, by the law of the domicil of the person, the protection extends.

On the other hand, it is only by the comity of other states that laws can operate beyond the limit of the state that makes them. In the great majority of cases, especially in this country, where it is so common to travel, or to transact business through agents, or to correspond by letter, from one state to another, it is more just, as well as more convenient, to have regard to the law of the place of the contract, as a uniform rule operating on all contracts of the same kind, and which the contracting parties may be presumed to have in contemplation when making their contracts, than to require them at their peril to know the domicil of those with whom they deal, and to ascertain the law of that domicil however remote, which in many cases could not be done without such delay as would greatly cripple the power of contracting abroad at all. . . .

It is possible also that in a state where the common law prevailed in full force, by which a married woman was deemed incapable of binding herself by any contract whatever, it might be inferred that such an utter incapacity, lasting throughout the joint lives of husband and wife, must be considered as so fixed by the settled policy of the state, for the protection of its own citizens, that it could not be held by the courts of that state to yield to the law of another state in which she might undertake to contract.

But it is not true at the present day that all civilized states recognize the absolute incapacity of married women to make contracts. The tendency of modern legislation is to enlarge their capacity in this respect, and in many states they have nearly or quite the same powers as if unmarried. In Massachusetts, even at the time of the making of the contract in question, a married woman was vested by statute with a very extensive power to carry on business by herself, and to bind herself by contracts with regard to her own property, business and earnings, and, before the bringing of the present action, the power had been extended so as to include the making of all kinds of contracts, with any person but her husband, as if she were unmarried. There is therefore no reason of public policy which should prevent the maintenance of this action.

*Judgment for the plaintiffs.*

## NOTES AND QUESTIONS ON *MILLIKEN* AND THE PLACE OF MAKING

(1) *Before the First Restatement:* Prior to the adoption by the Restatement of the place-of-making rule, the case law was divided on the question of the proper choice-of-law rule for contract cases. *Milliken* represented one line of authority. Another, represented by *Hall v. Cordell,* 142 U.S. 116 (1891), chose the law of the place of performance; a third, typified by *Pritchard v. Norton,* 106 U.S. 124 (1882), opted for the law of the state that would validate the contract; and a fourth used some combination of the first three approaches. *See Poole v. Perkins,* 126 Va. 33, 101 S.E. 240 (1919)(combining the validation and place-of-performance rules).

Professor Beale found this lack of uniformity distressing, all the more so because support for the three different rules often appeared within one state and sometimes within one case. 2 JOSEPH BEALE, A TREATISE ON THE CONFLICT OF LAWS 1077 (1935); Joseph Beale, *What Law Governs the Validity of a Contract,* 23 HARV. L. REV. 1, 2 (1909). (Beale's views didn't change much in the intervening three decades.) Accordingly, he set out to pick among the three possibilities. The validation principle was unsatisfactory because it "involves permission to the parties to do a legislative act. It practically makes a legislative body of any two persons who choose to get together and contract." *Id.* at

260. He rejected the place-of-performance rule as inconsistent with the vested rights theory and its territorial assumptions: "Any attempt to make the law of the place of performance govern the act of contracting is an attempt to give to that law exterritorial effect." *Id.* at 267.

(2) *Beale's Choice.* With the alternatives rejected, Beale settled on the place-of-making rule:

> That this rule is theoretically sound there can be no doubt. . . . The rule is based on the necessity of some law to raise an obligation between parties, and of this there can be no question. If two parties agree to do a thing, their agreement does not and cannot create any binding obligation to do it. The obligation created by the promise is merely a moral and social one, with which the law has nothing to do. It is only when the law affixes to the promise a legal obligation of performance that the parties can be said to have entered into a contract in a true sense. . . .
>
> The question whether a contract is valid, that is, whether to the agreement of the parties the law has annexed an obligation to perform its terms, can on general principles be determined by no other law than that which applies to the acts, that is, by the law of the place of contracting. If the law at that place annexes an obligation to the acts of the parties, the promise has a legal right which no other law has power to take away except as a result of new acts which change it. If on the other hand the law of the place where the agreement is made annexes no legal obligation to it, there is no other law which has power to do so.

*Id.* at 270-271. Beale was obviously impressed with arguments premised upon abstractions about sovereignty and territoriality. Are you?

Fortunately for the more modern-minded, Beale also made some practical arguments for the place-of-making rule. For one thing, he claimed it was certain of application. Was he right?

Beale also argued for the law of place-of-making on the ground that it was easier for the parties to ascertain and follow. Parties meeting at the place of making to negotiate their contract can seek legal counsel there to determine that state's governing law. The parties are unlikely to return to their respective domiciles to get legal advice, and they might not be able to find legal counsel expert in the law of the place of performance. This argument obviously contemplates a face-to-face meeting of the parties in the place of making. How well does it work in a case like *Milliken* where the contract is a result of interstate or international correspondence?

(3) *Other Alternatives.* Another possibility, at least for contractual capacity cases like *Milliken,* is the law of the promisor's domicile. *See, eg., Marks v. Loewenberg,* 143 La. 196, 78 So. 444 (1918). Why does the *Milliken* court reject that rule? Would the promisee's domicile be a better choice? As a final suggestion, what about the place of breach? Is that alternative more consistent with the vested rights theory? *See* JAMES MARTIN, CONFLICT OF LAWS: CASES AND MATERIALS 31 (1984). By analogy to the tort rule, isn't breach the last

event needed to generate liability? Remember *Alabama Great Southern Railroad v. Carroll,* § 4.06, *supra.*

(4) *Extent of the Rule.* Section 332 provides that the law of the place of making governs capacity to make the contract, the necessary form, if any, in which the promise must be made; the mutual assent or consideration, if any, required to make a promise binding; any other requirements for making a promise binding; fraud, illegality, or any other circumstances which make a promise void or voidable; except as stated in § 358, the nature and extent of the duty for the performance of which a party becomes bound; the time when and the place where the promise is by its terms to be performed; the absolute or conditional character of the promise.

(5) *Prevalence.* Ten states continue to follow the place-of-making rule for choice-of-law problems in contracts: Alabama, Georgia, Kansas, Maryland, New Mexico, Rhode Island, South Carolina, Tennessee, and Virginia, *See* Symeon Symeonides, *Choice of Law in the American Courts in 1998: Twelfth Annual Survey,* 47 AM. J. COMP. L. 327, 330 (1999), William Richman & David Riley, *The First Restatement of Conflicts on the Twenty-fifth Anniversary of its Successor,* 56 MD. L. REV. 1196, 1202 (1997). Among the most recent cases are *Shope v. State* Farm Ins. Co., 122 N.M. 398, 925 P.2d 515 (1996); *Rahmani v. Resorts Int'l., Inc.,* 20 F. Supp. 2d 392 (E.D. Va. 1998).

(6) *Determining the Place of Contracting: In General.* Section 311 provides that, "[t]he law of the forum decides as a preliminary question by the law of which state questions arising concerning the formation of a contract are to be determined, and this state is  .  .  .  called the 'place of contracting.'"

> Comment d then elucidates: "Under its Conflict of Laws rules, in deter-
> mining the place of contracting, the forum ascertains the place in
> which, under the general law of Contracts, *the principal event neces-
> sary to make a contract* occurs. [emphasis added]."

The "principal event" is "the final act  .  .  .  which made the prom-
ise  .  .  .  binding." 2 Joseph Beale, A Treatise on the Conflict of Laws 1045 (1934); Herbert Goodrich, Goodrich on Conflict of Laws 309 (3d ed. 1949). The Restatement supplies specific sections that define the "principal event" in different contractual situations; for a formal contract, the principal event is delivery (§ 312); for an informal unilateral contract, the offeree's performance (§ 323); for an informal bilateral contract, the offeree's promise (§ 325, illustrations 1-5).

*See* PROBLEM 4B-6. COME FLY WITH ME CLARICE.

(7) *Determining the Place of Contracting: Offer and Acceptance in Different States.*

(a) *The Mailbox Rule.* Section 326(b) adopts the mailbox or dispatch rule of the famous case of *Adams v. Lindsell,* 1 Bam. & Ald. 681 (K.B. 1818): "When an offer for a bilateral contract is made in one state and an acceptance is sent from another state to the first state in an authorized manner the place of contracting is  .  .  .  the state from which the acceptance is sent."

*Adams* was not a conflicts case, but rather a domestic contract case that posed the question whether a contract formed by mail is complete when the offeree dispatches his acceptance or when the offeror receives it. *Adams* chose the time of dispatch, the time when the offeree places the acceptance in the mailbox. Note that § 326(b) uses the mailbox rule in an entirely different context to determine *the place where* the contract was made for choice-of-law purposes, rather than *the time when* the contract was made for domestic contracts purposes. Does this make sense? Professor MacNeil demonstrates the dangers of plucking the technicalities of the mailbox rules out of their legal context and using them for a purpose they were not designed to serve:

[In] *Shurter v. Ricker* . . . [a] married woman living in New York made an offer by mail to a friend in Texas. He accepted the offer by telegram. If Texas law were applicable, the contract was unenforceable; if New York law were applicable, it was enforceable. The court held that because the offeree used a different means of communication from that used by the offeror [means of acceptance is a crucial technicality under the mailbox rule], the acceptance was only effective on receipt, and therefore the contract was made in New York and subject to New York law. The court, however, suggested that if the offeree had mailed his acceptance it would have been effective on dispatch, the agreement would have been made in Texas, Texas law would have applied, and the contract would have been unenforceable. It is rather difficult to see how the gallant interest of Texas in protecting married women from making ill-considered contracts is in any way reduced if an acceptance is sent by telegram or increased if an acceptance is sent by mail. Ian R. MacNeil, *Time Of Acceptance: Too many Problems for a Single Rule,* 112 U. PA. L. REV. 947, 950-951 (1964). * *See also* Arthur; Nussbaum, *Conflict Theories of Contracts: Cases Versus Restatement,* 51 YALE L.J. 893, 899 (1942).

(b) *The Mailbox Rule and Vested Rights.* Is the mailbox rule of § 326 consistent with the vested rights theory? Suppose Seller and Buyer negotiate a contract through the mail, Seller sending and receiving letters in Michigan, and Buyer sending and receiving letters in Ohio. Seller mails an offer that Buyer, in due course, receives. Michigan law makes the offer revocable, while under Ohio law it is irrevocable for a reasonable time. Within the reasonable time period, Seller mails and Buyer receives a purported revocation; then Buyer mails his acceptance. Is there a contract? Under the vested rights theory, should Michigan law control the offer and Ohio law the acceptance? What result under § 326? *See* WALTER W. COOK, THE LOGICAL AND LEGAL BASES OF THE CONFLICT OF LAWS 361-362 (1942).

(8) *Arbitrary Results.* "The greatest objection to the place of making rule is . . . that the results may often be fortuitous. Whether there is a contract or not . . . may depend upon chance." GEORGE W. STUMBERG, CONFLICT OF LAWS 231 (2d ed. 1951). Suppose in *Milliken* that the law of Massachusetts, as well as the law of Maine, removed the contractual disability of married women. Further suppose that Sarah had executed the guarantee in Massachusetts and had given it to Daniel who promptly forgot to mail it. He then attended a trade convention in Connecticut, a state that retained the common law incapacity rule, where he met one of the partners in Deering, Milliken & Co. and handed him the guarantee. What result?

---

* Reprinted with permission of U. OF PA. L. REV.

The mailbox rule can exacerbate the problem of arbitrary results. Seller in New York offers to sell radar detectors to Buyer in Miami; Buyer wants time to think. He makes up his mind on a Delta flight from Miami to San Francisco and telephones his acceptance from St. Louis where he changes airplanes. Radar detectors are legal in New York and Florida but contraband in Missouri. What result? Suppose the exact same facts but that Buyer gets a lower fare from US Air and changes planes in Chicago, where radar detectors are legal. Should the legality of the contract between Buyer and Seller depend on the airline price wars?

(9) *Manipulation by the Parties.* Can the place-of-making rule be manipulated by the parties to validate their pact?

**POOLE v. PERKINS,** 126 Va. 33, 101 S.E. 240 (1919). Action by plaintiff payee of a note made by defendant, a married woman. The note was made and delivered in Tennessee where married women's contracts were voidable and was to be paid in Virginia where married women had no contractual disability. The court validated the note using a combination of the rules listed in Note (1), *supra.* Of the place of making rule, it said: "It follows, therefore, beyond question, that if Mrs. Poole had merely stepped across the state line between Bristol, Tenn., and Bristol, Va., and signed the note in the latter state, she would be held liable. . . . "

Is the place of contracting rule, then, vulnerable to the same critique Beale launched against the intention validation rule? It seems to permit the parties, at least indirectly, "to do a legislative act." Does it make sense to deny the parties the right to choose their own law yet permit them to accomplish the same result by walking across the street? *See* PROBLEM 4B-7. SUPPORTING OUR CHILDREN.

(10) *Manipulation by the Courts.* In his treatise, Professor Beale writes:

> Practically [the place of contracting rule] . . . is the best rule. . . .
> In the first place, there is no uncertainty in the application of the rule.
> There can only be one place in which a contract is made, and what
> that place can never be subject to great or serious doubt. . . . The act
> of contracting is a momentary act, and the contract must arise at some
> particular moment as a result of an act done in some one state.

2 JOSEPH BEALE, THE CONFLICT OF LAWS 1091 (1935). Was Beale right? The court in *Milliken* held that the transaction was a unilateral contract (an exchange of a promise for a performance), formed when Deering Milliken accepted Sarah's offer to guarantee the contract by selling the goods to Daniel. Is it equally plausible to treat the case as a bilateral contract (an exchange of promises), formed when Deering Milliken's offer to sell to Daniel was accepted by Sarah's promise to guarantee?

And *Milliken* is really an easy case. What about the typical modern interstate commercial transaction? There may be preliminary chafering, serious negotiating, perhaps a "battle of forms," and eventually an exchange of consideration for goods or services, which in turn may be followed by some "service after the sale." Will it be clear which pieces of interstate mail or telephonic communication constitute offer, acceptance, counter-offer, rejection and breach? Are offers and acceptances, counter-offers and rejections, unilateral and bilateral contracts things or events in the world? Or are they rather labels that lawyers attach to events in order to convince courts? Isn't Contracts the course where there are no answers, only arguments? The legal/commercial indeterminacy of modern transactions prompted the drafters of the Uniform Commercial Code to provide that a contract may exist "even though the moment of its making is undetermined." U.C.C. § 2-204(2).

(11) *The Result in* Milliken. Given that the court had a fair amount of room to maneuver, did it get the right result? Do you think its decision was affected by the parties' expectations or the fact that Massachusetts had abandoned its antiquated policy concerning the contractual capacity of married women? If these factors were important, should the court have based its decision squarely on them and skipped the formalisms about the place of making? Would that sort of opinion be a better predictor of the court's future decisions?

## [B]  The Performance Exception

### LOUIS-DREYFUS v. PATERSON STEAMSHIPS, LTD.

*United States Circuit Court of Appeals for the Second Circuit*
*43 F.2d 824 (1930)*

Before L. HAND, CHASE, and MACK, Circuit Judges.

L. HAND, CIRCUIT JUDGE.

The libellants at Duluth shipped a parcel of wheat upon two ships of the respondent and received in exchange bills of lading, Duluth to Montreal, "with transshipment at Port Colbourne, Ontario." These contained an exception for "dangers of navigation, fire and collision," but nothing further which is here relevant. The respondent exercised its right of reshipment, unladed the wheat at Port Colbourne, stored it in an elevator, and reladed thirty-five thousand bushels in another ship, the Advance, belonging to one Webb, chartered by the respondent's agent, the Hall Shipping Company, for that purpose. This ship safely carried her cargo until she reached the entrance to the Cornwall Canal in the St. Lawrence River, where she took the ground, stove in her bottom and sank. The suit is for the resulting damage to the wheat.

The respondent defended on the ground that the strand, not being due to any fault in management, was a danger of navigation. Failing this, it relied upon the Harter Act (46 USCA §§ 190-195) and the Canadian Water—Carriage of Goods Act (9-10 Edward VII, Chap. 81), which covers among other ships those "carrying goods from any port in Canada to any other port in Canada." It,  . . .  like section three of the Harter Act provides that "if the owner of any ship transporting merchandise or property from any port in Canada exercises due diligence to make the ship in all respects seaworthy and properly manned, equipped and supplied, neither the ship, nor the owner, agent or charterer" shall be liable "for faults or errors in navigation or in the management of the ship." The respondent tried to prove that the Advance was seaworthy, and was therefore within both statutes. . . .

We shall assume arguendo that section three of the Harter Act did not cover the case; verbally it only includes "vessels transporting merchandise or property to or from any port in the United States." . . . Verbally at least section six [of the Canadian Act] covered the situation; the Advance was "transporting goods" "from" a Canadian port . . .

The important question is whether we should look to Canadian law at all. Here is a contract of carriage, made in Minnesota without any relevant exceptions, to be performed partly in the United States and partly in Canada; the carrier fails in performing that part of it which is to take place in Canada; he does not safely transport the grain from the entrance of the canal to Montreal. The law of the place of that performance excuses him for those faults in navigation which have caused the loss. Does that law control? *Liverpool, etc., Co. v. Phenix Insurance Co.,* 129 U.S. 397, decided that the validity of a provision in a contract of carriage, limiting the carrier's common-law duty, was to be determined by the law of the place where the contract was made, and this is well-settled law (section 366, Tentative Restatement No. 4, Conflict of Laws; American Law Institute), even when the parties expressly stipulate that all questions shall be decided according to some foreign law, which would require a different result. It is of course only an instance of the usual rule that the law of the place where promises are made determines whether they create a contract; that law alone attaches any legal consequences to acts within its territory.

On the other hand, it is always said that as to matters of performance the law of the place of performance controls, though in application the boundaries of this doctrine are not easy to find. . . . An exchange of mutual promises, or whatever other acts may create a contract for future performance, do not put the obligor under any immediate constraint, except so far as the doctrine of anticipatory breach demands. A present obligation arises only in the sense that it is then determined that when the time for performance arrives, his conduct shall not be open to his choice. For the present nothing is required of him; he can commit no fault and incur no liability. When the time comes for him to perform, if he fails, the law requires him to give the equivalent of the neglected performance; that compulsion is the sanction imposed by the state and the measure of the obligation. The default must indeed be at the place of performance, but the promisor need not himself be there, nor may he there have any property to respond. In such cases it is impossible to say that any liability arises under the law of that place; yet it would be exceedingly inconvenient to hold that it depended upon the law of the place where the promisor chanced to be at the time of performance, especially if such a doctrine were extended to all places where he has any property. In the interest of certainty and uniformity there must be some definite place fixed whose law shall control, wherever the suit arises. Whether the place of performance is chosen because of the likelihood that the obligor will be there present at the time of performance, or—what is nearly the same thing—because the agreement presupposes that he shall be, is not important. All we need say here is that the same law which determines what liabilities shall arise upon nonperformance, must determine any excuses for nonperformance, which are no more than exceptions to those liabilities.

. . . In the case at bar, the Canadian law says that performance of the contract of carriage, as respects navigation, shall be excused if the owner uses due care to examine his ship and make her fit for her voyage, to man and victual her and the like. The conduct so specified is thus made an excuse for his failure to carry the goods safely to their destination as he has promised to do. . . .

. . . We conclude that if the Advance was in fact seaworthy, the respondent was excused by virtue of the Canadian statute, and in that event we need not consider the issue of due diligence. . . .

Decree reversed; cause remanded to be reheard upon the issue [of the seaworthiness of the Advance.]

## NOTES ON THE EXCEPTION FOR ISSUES OF PERFORMANCE

(1) *Issues of Validity and Issues of Performance.* For issues of performance, the Restatement provides: *

§ 358. Law Governing Performance.

The duty for the performance of which a party to a contract is bound will be discharged by compliance with the law of the place of performance of the promise with respect to:

 (a)   the manner of performance;

 (b)   the time and locality of performance;

 (c)   the person or persons by whom or to whom performance shall be made or rendered;

 (d)   the sufficiency of performance;

 (e)   excuse for non-performance.

Combining § 358 with § 332 produces the facile formula: "issues of validity are governed by the place of contracting and issues of performance, by the place of performance." But how can issues of validity be separated from those of performance? Is the distinction really so clear? The Restatement recognized the problem and responded with uncharacteristic uncertainty. Comment c to § 332 provides:

A difficult problem is presented in deciding whether a question in a dispute concerning a contract is one involving the creation of an obligation or performance thereof. There is no distinction based on logic alone between determining the creation of the contract and the rights and duties thereunder on the one hand, and its performance on the other. . . . The point at which initiation ceases and performance begins is not a point which can be fixed by any rule of law of universal application to all cases. Like all questions of degree, the solution must depend upon the circumstances of each case and must be governed by the exercise of judgment.

From the point of view of the First Restatement, this is a rather astounding admission, especially since the principal virtues claimed for the First

---

Restatement are its certainty and its deduction via pure logic from the axioms of the vested rights theory. *See* WALTER W. COOK, THE LOGICAL AND LEGAL BASES OF THE CONFLICT OF LAWS 360-361 (1942).

(2) *Does the exception swallow the rule?* Professor Nussbaum wonders what is left of the "place of contracting" rule once issues of performance have been carved out:

[T]he Restatement assigns to this law [that of the place of performance] . . . the determination of whether the performance is sufficient, whether there is an excuse for non-performance, whether a breach has occurred, and whether there is a right to damages for a breach. Now, contract litigation most frequently revolves around these points. . . . Practically, what remains in this respect to the [place of making rule] under the Restatement's theory is no more than a shell, a dignity.

Arthur Nussbaum, *Conflict Theories of contracts: Cases Versus Restatement,* 51 YALE L.J. 893, 915-916 (1942).

(3) *The application in Louis-Dreyfus.* What would have happened in *Louis-Dreyfus* if the ship had sunk in American waters? Is it wise to make the carrier's liability for negligent operation turn on such a technicality? Does that rule of law make it more difficult for the carrier to set freight rates? To ensure against loss? Suppose again that the ship had sunk in American waters, but that the contract had contained a clause excusing the carrier's liability for negligence of the master and crew. Presumably the carrier would have been liable because, as Judge Hand says, "the validity of a provision in a contract of carriage, limiting the carrier's common-law duty was to be determined by the law of the place where the contract was made." In other words, according to Hand and the Restatement, the carrier's liability for negligence in navigation is governed by the law of the place of performance, but the validity of a clause limiting that liability is governed by the place of contracting. Does that make sense? *See* J. H. C.; Morris, *The Eclipse of the Lex Loci Solutionis—A Fallacy Exploded,* 6 VAND. L. REV. 505, 506-507 (1953).

Setting aside for a moment the wisdom of the validity/performance dichotomy, does the result in *Louis-Dreyfus* make sense? Consider some of the legal background Judge Hand alluded to. According to the traditional rule of American admiralty law, the carrier was liable for errors of navigation. Both the Harter Act and a similar Canadian statute had changed the rule by excusing the carrier for such errors if the carrier exercised due diligence to make the ship seaworthy and to insure that she was properly manned. The Harter Act did not apply because the voyage of the Advance from Port Colbourne to Montreal was not a voyage "to or from any port in the United States." Would it have made sense for Hand to deny the carrier the seaworthiness defense even though the statutory policy of both Canada and the United States favored it? For favorable commentary on Judge Hand's manipulation of the validity/performance dichotomy, *see* WILLIAM RICHMAN & WILLIAM REYNOLDS, UNDERSTANDING CONFLICT OF LAWS §66[b] (3d ed. 2002).

## § 4.08   Land—The Situs Rule

### IN RE BARRIE'S ESTATE

*Iowa Supreme Court*
*240 Iowa 431, 35 N. W.2d 658 (1949).*

HAYS, JUSTICE. . . .

Mary E. Barrie, domiciled in Whiteside County, Illinois, died owning real and personal property in Illinois and real property in Tama County, Iowa. The instrument in question was offered for probate in Whiteside County, Illinois. Although first admitted to probate, it was later denied probate after the Illinois Supreme Court had ruled that said instrument had been revoked by cancellation and that decedent died intestate.

Thereafter the instrument was offered for probate in Tama County, Iowa, by one of the beneficiaries named therein. To the petition for probate, decedent's heirs at law filed objections based upon the judgment of the Illinois Supreme Court, to the effect that the said last will and testament had been revoked. Objectors assert that this judgment is conclusive upon the Iowa Courts. Proponent's motion to strike said objections, for the reason that they do not constitute a valid basis for denying probate, being overruled by the trial court, this appeal was taken.

The instrument offered for probate was duly signed by decedent and witnessed by two witnesses. . . . When found, after the death of decedent, the instrument had the word "void" written across its face in at least five places, including the attestation clause. Also, upon the cover and upon the envelope containing same, appears the word "void" written with the name "M. E. Barrie" and "Mary E. Barrie". The Illinois Court found that the writing of the word "void" on the instrument, as above related, constituted a revocation by cancellation within the purview of the Illinois Statute. This statute provides for the revocation of a will by "(a) by burning, canceling, tearing, or obliterating it by the testator."

No question is raised as to the due execution of the instrument, either under the Illinois or the Iowa Statutes. No question is raised as to the testamentary capacity of decedent, nor is it claimed by the objectors that there has been a revocation under the Iowa statute. The question before this court for determination may be stated thus, "Is the judgment of the Illinois Court, holding that said instrument had been revoked and that decedent died intestate, conclusive and binding upon the Iowa Courts?"

. . . Decedent was a non-resident of the state and died owning property in Tama County which was subject to administration. Clearly the District Court of Tama County has original jurisdiction to probate this instrument. . . . That this is in accordance with the recognized rule, *see* Section 469 American Law Institute, Restatement, Conflict of Laws, which states: "The will of a deceased person can be admitted to probate in a competent court of any state in which an administrator could have been appointed had the decedent died intestate". . . .

Upon the general question as to the validity, operation, effect, etc., of a will by which property is devised, there are certain well established and generally recognized rules, and which definitely differentiate between movable (personal) and immovable (real) property. We are only concerned with immovables, in the instant case. The general rule as stated in Story Conflict of Laws, 8th Ed., p. 652, is, "The doctrine is clearly established at the common law, that the law of the place where the property (speaking of real immovable property) is located is to govern as to capacity or incapacity of the testator, the forms and solemnities to give the will or testament its due attestation and effect" . . . Upon the specific question as to revocation of a will, Beale, Conflict of Laws, Vol. 3, p. 972 states, "The revocation of a will is governed by the law of the state of situs of the land.". . . .

Under the above stated rule, Iowa courts are free to place their construction, interpretation, and sanction upon the will of a non-resident of the state who dies owning real property within the state . . . although it has been admitted to probate in the state of the domicil of testator.

Does a different rule pertain where instead of being admitted to probate in the domicil state, probate is denied? We think not. It is generally held that the full faith and credit provision of the Federal Constitution, Section 1, Article 4, does not render foreign decrees of probate conclusive as to the validity of a will, as respects real property situated in a state other than the one in which the decree was rendered, nor does the doctrine of res adjudicata or estoppel by judgment apply. *Robertson v. Pickrell,* 109 U.S. 608, where the court said the probate established nothing beyond the validity of the will in that state, and while conclusive there, the full faith and credit clause and the act of Congress enacted pursuant thereto, did not require that they shall have any greater force and efficacy in other courts than in the courts of the state from which they were taken, but only such faith and credit as by law and usage they had there. . . .

. . . To hold that an act which constitutes a revocation in one state is a revocation in another state where under the law the act does not constitute a revocation, is contrary to the general rule, which is stated in 57 Am. Jur. Wills, Sec. 493, to be, "Where a statute prescribes the method and acts by which a will may be revoked, no acts other than those mentioned in the statute are to operate as a revocation, no matter how clearly appears the purpose of the testator to revoke his will and his belief that such purpose has been accomplished". . . . [T]he acts held to be a revocation in Illinois, do not constitute such in Iowa, *see* Sec. 633.10, Code of 1946. [Iowa law required either destruction of the will or cancellation in the presence of two witnesses.]

Sec. 63.3.49, Code of 1946, provides:

> "A last will and testament executed without this state, in the mode prescribed by the law, either of the place where executed or of the testator's domicile, shall be deemed to be legally executed, and shall be of the same force and effect as if executed in the mode prescribed by the laws of this state, provided said last will and testament is in writing and subscribed by the testator."

This statute . . . is clearly a modification of the common law and should not be extended to include matters not clearly included therein. It specifically deals with the formalities in the execution of the will, and nothing more. No question of execution is here involved. That the legislature might have waived the common law rule, as applicable to revocations as well as to the formal execution, as it has done, cannot be denied. However the legislature has not seen fit to do so. . . .

We hold that the Illinois judgment denying probate to the will in question is not conclusive and binding upon the courts of this state, in so far as the disposition of the Iowa real estate is concerned. . . .

*Reversed and remanded.*

SMITH, JUSTICE (dissenting).

I am unable to agree with the majority opinion. It perpetuates an anomalous and confusing legal situation which our own statutes seem clearly designed to remove and which judicial thinking should seek a way to avoid. The importance of the question involved justifies, even requires, a statement of the grounds of dissent. . . .

It is true of course that Code section 633.49 refers to *execution* and not directly to *revocation;* and we have here a document, held in Illinois to be non-testamentary, because of *revocation* and not because of any defect in original *execution.* In other words, we have an instrument not merely "executed" but also *revoked* "without this state, in the mode prescribed by the law . . . of the testator's domicile."

But revocation is merely the converse of execution. The power to execute implies the power to revoke. A will can no longer be said to be *executed* after it has been *revoked.* Whether an instrument is a will is determined not only by the manner of its execution but also by the manner of its attempted revocation. Both acts are a part of the testamentary process. It is unthinkable that our legislature intended to require recognition of the laws of another jurisdiction in the matter of one and not of the other. . . .

The purpose of both Code sections 633.33 and 633.49 must have been to abolish or minimize confusion and conflict between states in the matter of handling wills. Foreign ownership of property has become common. Owners of property in different jurisdictions should not be required, in making and revoking their wills, to do more than comply with the law of their own domiciles, or with the law of the jurisdiction where the instrument is drawn or revoked. . . .

There is nothing sacrosanct about the "lex loci" anymore than about any other common law rule. Our statute provides: "The rule of the common law, that statutes in derogation thereof are to be strictly construed, has no application to this code. Its provisions and all proceedings under it shall be liberally construed with a view to promote its objects and assist the parties in obtaining justice."

Undoubtedly our will statutes are in derogation of the common law in many respects. . . . Code, section 633.49 is clearly in derogation of lex loci rei sitae as to *execution* of foreign wills. Its purpose is obvious. The majority opinion would construe it narrowly and technically by limiting the word "executed" to its strict and more common meaning—the performance of the acts by which the instrument is brought into being, specifically the signing and witnessing of it according to statutory requirements.

But ambiguity, justifying interpretation of a statute is not simply that arising from the meaning of particular words. It includes such as may arise in respect of the general scope and meaning of the statute when all its provisions are examined. . . .

[W]hen our statute speaks of a will "executed without this state in the mode prescribed by the law" of testator's domicile and provides that the instrument shall be deemed to be legally *executed,* and shall be of the same force and effect as if *executed in* the mode prescribed by the laws of this state," we should construe it as requiring us to recognize the validity of a revocation by the testator, consummated in a mode recognized by the law of his domicile. Any other construction would render the statute impotent as to an important part of the very mischief it was plainly designed to remedy. . . .

*See* PROBLEM 4B-8. LAW OF THE SITUS.

---

## NOTES ON *BARRIE* AND THE SITUS RULE

(1) *Movable and Immovable Property.* The First Restatement adopted the traditional civil law distinction between immovable and moveable property. *See* Restatement (First) of Conflict of Laws § 208, Special Note. The distinction corresponds to the common law distinction between real and personal property, except that a leasehold interest in land is classified as immovable property for conflicts purposes, while in general property parlance it is considered personal rather than real property.

(2) *The Situs Rule.* The rule is one of the most rigid of the traditional formulae. To lawyers schooled in the territorial theory, it seemed as much a part of the natural order as the laws of science. Of its history, general acceptance, and scope of application, Judge Goodrich, a leading advocate of the traditional choice-of-law system wrote:

Upon one general proposition in the Conflict of Laws there has been little if any difference of opinion among the authorities. The reference to the law of the state where land lies with regard to legal questions involving rights in the land is one of practically universal acceptance. The principle has been stated by courts and text writers in very broad terms. Thus, our pioneer American authority in the field, Mr. Justice Story generalizes: "All the authorities recognize the principle in its fullest import, that real estate is exclusively subject to the laws of the government, within whose territory it is situate.". . . .

Applications of the broad principle are easy to find. The law of the situs governs the requisites of a deed to land, the quantum of the estate conveyed, the validity of a will devising land, the determination of the question whether the will has been revoked, whether a trust can be created in real estate, whether a grantor has legal capacity to convey. It would be affectation to multiply instances, for the general principle is well known and thoroughly established.

Herbert Goodrich, *Two States and Real Estate,* 89 U. PA. L. REV. 417, 418 (1941*). See* also Restatement (First) of Conflict of Laws §§ 214-310.*

(3) *Reasons for the Rule.* Typically three reasons have been given for the situs rule:

(a) *Power.*

It will be at once seen that immovables, being unable to be taken away from the state in which they are, must always in the last analysis be governed by the laws of that state. Those laws alone can apply to the land since any contrary provision would be given no effect by the courts and the executive officers of the state of situs. It therefore follows that every question arising with regard to land is to be governed by the law of the situs.

2 JOSEPH BEALE, A TREATISE ON THE CONFLICT OF LAWS 938-939 (1935). Beale's argument, based on the de facto power of the situs state over the land, is that a non-situs court should always apply the law of the situs in order to ensure that the courts of the situs will willingly enforce the judgment.

Beale is right that the non-situs court cannot directly affect title to land in the situs. *See Fall v. Eastin* § 7.08[F], *infra* and the notes following it. But, if the non-situs court has personal jurisdiction over the defendant, can it provide other sorts of relief such as a money judgment or an order to defendant to make a conveyance on pain of contempt?

How helpful is Beale's power argument in cases like *Barrie* where the forum is also the situs and there is no possible worry about enforcement. *See* RUSSELL WEINTRAUB, COMMENTARY ON THE CONFLICT OF LAWS 504-517 (4th ed. 2001); Note, *Choice of Law Governing Land Transactions: The Contract-Conveyance Dichotomy,* 111 U. PA. L. REV. 482, 485 (1963).

(b) *Recording Systems.* This argument holds that the situs rule is necessary in order to prevent title searching from becoming a completely unmanageable task and to protect those who rely on the recording systems. Under modern recording systems, documents affecting title are recorded at the situs. The searcher should be able to examine the instruments in the chain of title and readily determine their construction and effect. That he can do only if they are governed by the law of the situs. If the validity or interpretation of a conveyance were determined by the law of the grantor's domicile, for example, the searcher would need to ascertain that domicile, a fact that might not appear on the face of the record. Moreover, instead of being able to rely upon the familiar law of the situs, the searcher would need to research the law of the grantor's domicile. Inevitably, errors and omissions would occur, and bona fide purchasers would suffer. *See* Herbert Goodrich, *Two States and Real Estate,* 89 U. PA. L. REV. 417, 418-419 (1941); Crawford D. Hening, *Is the Construction of Wills Devising Real Estate Governed by the Rules of Construction of the Domicil of the Testator or by the Rules of the Situs of the Property?,* 50 AM. L. REG. 718, 733 (1902).

---

* Reprinted with permission of U. OF PA. L. REV.

The recording statute rationale is a very strong argument for applying the situs rule in cases where a bona fide purchaser has relied on the situs' land records, but how is it relevant in a case like *Barrie* where the dispute is between two sets of gratuitous transferees (heirs v. testamentary devisees), none of whom had any occasion to check the land records? But could the use of non-situs law in a case like *Barrie* lay a trap for future purchasers of the land? If the *Barrie* court had used Illinois law, declared the will revoked, and ordered the distribution of the Iowa land to Mrs. Barrie's heirs, wouldn't that order have resulted in an unimpeachable title? Presumably, the Iowa probate court would have ordered some type of transfer or conveyance of the land to the heirs, and that instrument would then appear in the Iowa land records. How would it be possible for a later title searcher to be misled? If the searcher examined the will itself and had some concern about the adequacy of its revocation, that concern should be laid to rest by the preclusive effect of the Iowa probate court's judgment, shouldn't it? *See* RUSSELL WEINTRAUB, COMMENTARY ON THE CONFLICT OF LAWS 502 (4th ed. 2001); Moffatt Hancock, *Conceptual Devices for Avoiding the Land Taboo in Conflict of Laws: The Disadvantages of Disingenuousness,* 20 STAN. L. REV. 1, 22-23 (1967), reprinted in MOFFATT HANCOCK, STUDIES IN MODERN CHOICE OF LAW: TORTS, INSURANCE, LAND TITLES 372 (1984).

(c) *Our land.* A final argument for the situs rule focuses on the very strong concern of the situs state for land within its territory. In most land cases, the situs state will have a strong interest because in most cases the situs state will also be the location of other important contacts. Thus, the situs will have an interest in the division of marital property when it is also the marital domicile, and it will have an interest in the distribution of an estate when it is also the domicile of the decedent or her heirs or devisees. But what about cases like *Barrie* in which, so far as the opinion showed, Iowa's only contact with the dispute was as situs of the land. Why should Iowa care about the outcome of the will dispute? Would it be different if the case presented zoning, environmental, or perpetuities questions? *See* RUSSELL WEINTRAUB, COMMENTARY ON THE CONFLICT OF LAWS 527-528 (4th ed. 2001); Moffatt Hancock, *Full Faith and Credit to Foreign Laws and Judgments in Real Property Litigation: The Supreme Court and the Land Taboo,* 18 STAN. L. REV. 1299 (1966). Compare the scope of the situs rule, note (2), *supra,* with its rationales in this note. Is it a mismatch?

*See* PROBLEMS 4B-9. INCORPORATION BY REFERENCE; 4B-10. A GIFT TO CHARITY.

(4) *The Decision in Barrie and Statutory Construction.* Does *Barrie* make sense in light of the purposes behind the competing revocation rules of Illinois and Iowa? What wills were the two revocation statutes designed to control? Professor Hancock reasons:

> [T]he Illinois statute, which effectuated popular ideas by permitting various types of revocatory acts, was designed primarily for the benefit of Illinois citizens. By the same token, when the Iowa legislature decided to require more stringent probative safeguards for a valid revocation, it must have been concerned primarily with the protection of Iowa testators and beneficiaries. Since the testatrix was domiciled

in Illinois, these considerations suggest that her case fell within the policy scope of the Illinois statute and not within that of the Iowa statute.

Moffatt Hancock, *Conceptual Devices for Avoiding the Land Taboo* in *Conflict of Laws: The Disadvantages of Disingenuousness,* 20 STAN. L. REV. 1, 3 (1967),[*] republished in MOFFATT HANCOCK, STUDIES IN MODERN CHOICE OF LAW: TORTS, INSURANCE, LAND TITLES 353 (1984). Is Professor Hancock right?

What about the Iowa court's narrow interpretation of the foreign execution statute as applying to execution but not revocation of wills outside the state? Does it make sense as a matter of statutory construction? Once again Professor Hancock's critique is powerful:

> [T]he revocation of wills is clearly within the spirit if not the letter of the statute; no rational distinction can be drawn, in this context, between rules prescribing the mode of making wills and those prescribing the mode of revoking them. Both types of rules serve the same purpose: the establishment of techniques by which a testator can communicate his wishes to the judge. It would have been absurd for the lawmaker to say (in effect) to the foreign testator, "For your convenience we shall recognize your will as valid if made in compliance with our law, the law of your domicile, or the law of the place of making. But if you decide to revoke that will you can only do so in the mode prescribed by our law."

*Id* at 357. *See also* WILLIAM RICHMAN & WILLIAM REYNOLDS, UNDERSTANDING CONFLICT OF LAWS §67[a] (3d ed. 2002). By way of explanation, the court tells us that statutes in derogation of the common law are to be narrowly construed!

(5) *Current Status.* The situs rule is alive and well in the modern choice-of-law practice. It figures prominently in the Second Restatement, *see* § 4. 26, *infra*, and with only a few exceptions, contemporary judicial opinions apply it to nearly all questions involving real property. William Richman & William Reynolds, *Prologomenon to an Empirical Restatement of Conflicts,* 75 IND. L.J. 417 (2000).

## § 4.09   Movable Property

### [A]   Inter Vivos Transactions

**CAMMELL v. SEWELL,** 5 Hurl. & N. 728,157 Eng. Rep. 1371 (1860) (Court of Exchequer Chamber). [Plaintiffs were the English insurers of a cargo of lumber shipped on a Prussian vessel from a Russian port to England. The ship ran aground in Norwegian waters, and the cargo was unloaded and sold at auction pursuant to the request of the ship's master. The purchaser, Clausen, resold the lumber to defendants, English merchants. The plaintiffs brought suit in Norway against the master and the purchaser, seeking to have the auction sale invalidated, but the Diocesan Court confirmed it. Plaintiffs

---

[*] Copyright © 1967 by the Board of Trustees of the Leland Stanford, Jr. University. Reprinted with permission.

brought this action in trover in England. After the lower court held for the defendants, plaintiffs appealed.]

*Held:* Judgment for defendant affirmed. The court first determined that it need not recognize as conclusive the judgment of the Norwegian Diocesan court. On the choice-of-law question, however, the court held that Norwegian law applied:

> We think that the law on this subject was correctly stated by the Lord Chief Baron in the course of the argument in the Court below, where he says "if personal property is disposed of in a manner binding according to the law of the country where it is, that disposition is binding everywhere." And we do not think that it makes any difference that the goods were wrecked, and not intended to be sent to the country where they were sold. We do not think that the goods which were wrecked here would on that account be the less liable to our laws as to market overt, or as to the landlord's right of distress, because the owner did not foresee that they would come to England. . . .

> . . . [A]s, on the evidence before us, we cannot treat Clausen otherwise than as an innocent purchaser, and as the law of Norway appears to us, on the evidence, to give a title to an innocent purchaser, we think that the property vested in him, and in the defendants as sub-purchasers from him, and that, having once so vested, it did not become divested by its being subsequently brought to this country, and, therefore, that the judgment of the Court of Exchequer should be affirmed.

In defense of Norwegian law, the majority wrote:

> It does not appear to us that there is anything so barbarous or monstrous in this state of the law as that we can say that it should not be recognized by us. Our own law as to market overt is analogous; and though it is said that much mischief would be done by upholding sales of this nature, not justified by the necessities of the case, it may well be that the mischief would be greater if the vendee were only to have a title in cases where the master was strictly justified in selling as between himself and the owners. If that were so, purchasers, who seldom can know the facts of the case, would not be inclined to give the value, and on proper and lawful sales by the master the property would be in great danger of being sacrificed.

The dissent disagreed with the majority's appraisal of the Norwegian law:

> Can such a foreign law as the law of Norway is alleged to be, avail in England to take the property in the cargo out of the English owners?

> What is that law?. . . . [It] amounts to this, that if the ship has satisfied the single but indefinite condition of "wreck," the cargo, however large, valuable, uninjured and capable of transshipment, may be sold by the master.

> It is obvious that if a law of this nature were recognized by other countries as giving validity to the title of a purchaser, property at sea would be exposed to a species of confiscation. Although fraud, when

proved, might avoid the sale, yet great temptations to fraud would be held out, both to masters of vessels and to purchasers of cargoes. Such a law would encourage wrecking and discourage succour to vessels in distress. Small islands and petty states might be tempted to establish it, and thereby become public nuisances to the traffic of maritime nations. The personal liability of the master to the owners of ship or cargo is commonly of little value, and would not amount to any substantial indemnity.

## NOTES AND QUESTIONS ON *CAMMELL* AND THE SITUS RULE

(1) *Scope.* For nearly all *inter vivos* transactions of movables, the First Restatement prescribes the law of the place where the movable was located at the time of the transaction. Thus, the situs rule applies to conveyances (§§ 255-258), adverse possession (§ 259), mortgages (§ 265), conditional sale (§ 272), liens and pledges (§ 279), powers of appointment (§ 283), and trusts (§ 294). The most notable exceptions are the rules dealing with the rights of married persons in each other's property; they refer to the law of the parties' domicile. *See* Restatement (First) of Conflict of Laws §§ 259 and 290.

(2) *Rationale.* The argument for the situs rule was based upon convenience and party expectations. It was argued that the situs rule made a good deal more sense than the older notion that conveyances of movables should be controlled by the law of the domicile of the parties.

Several obvious objections can be made to that rule. First, the parties to a commercial sale may have different domiciles; whose then should control? Further, much modern business is conducted by corporations, and corporate domicile is often a mere legal technicality. Finally, corporations as well as individuals often conduct business far from their domiciles; a party to a sale of property far from home would not naturally expect the validity of the sale to be governed by the law of his domicile. *See* Herbert Goodrich, *Goodrich on Conflict of Laws,* 404-406 (2d ed. 1938).

An alternative to the situs rule was the law of the place where the contract for sale was made. This option was dealt with via the same contract/conveyance distinction that controlled in land transactions. *Id.* at 406-407. For more on the defense of the situs rule, *see* Wendell Carnahan, *Tangible Property and the Conflict of Laws,* 2 U. CHI. L. REV. 345 (1935).

(3) *Odd results.* The situs rule for movable property occasionally could produce strange results by picking the law of a state that had very little to do with the case. *Shanahan v. George B. Landers Construction Co.,* 266 F.2d 400 (1959), illustrates the problem. Seller, a Massachusetts Corporation and buyer, a New Hampshire Corporation entered a conditional sales contract for the sale of a trench hoe. Each party executed the documents in its home state and delivery was made in Vermont where buyer was performing a construction job; buyer thereafter moved the hoe to New Hampshire and used it there in

its construction business. Buyer failed to make the payments, and seller repossessed the hoe in New Hampshire, moved it to Massachusetts, and sold it there. Under New Hampshire law, the repossession was improper; Massachusetts law, however, sanctioned it. The Restatement, in adherence to the situs rule, would have applied the law of Vermont—the place where the hoe was at the time of the original conveyance. *See* Restatement (First) of Conflict of Laws § 281. In choosing New Hampshire law, the court explicitly rejected the Restatement solution. It concluded that the delivery of the hoe in Vermont was "only for the convenience of the purchaser in performing a single contract in that state" and accordingly was "immaterial" for choice-of-law purposes. 266 F.2d. at 404. *See also* David Cavers, *The Conditional Seller's Remedies and the Choice-of-Law Process—Some Notes on Shanahan,* 35 N.Y.U. L. Rev. 1126, 1134 (1960).

(4) *Intangible Property.* How should the situs rule apply with regard to an intangible? Where is its situs? Recall the difficulties that this concept produced in the discussion of attachment jurisdiction; *see Harris v. Balk* and *Shaffer v. Heitner,* §§3.15 and 3.16, *supra.*

(5) *The Law of Norway.* Note that the dispute between the majority and the dissent in *Cammell* centers not on the merits of the situs rule as a choice-of-law directive but rather on the merits of the Norwegian law it selects. What should a court do when a tried and true choice-of-law rule points toward a law that is immoral or offensive to the forum state?

## [B]   Testamentary Disposition and Intestate Succession

### WHITE v. TENNANT

*West Virginia Supreme Court of Appeals*
*31 W. Va. 790, 8 S.E. 596 (1888)*

(This case is reproduced in § 2.03, *supra.*)

### NOTES AND QUESTIONS ON THE DOMICILE RULE

(1) *Scope and Rationale.* The First Restatement refers questions concerning testamentary disposition of movables (§§ 306, 307) and intestate succession of movables (§ 303) to the law of the state in which decedent died domiciled.

The rationale for this major exception to the situs rule is that it is desirable to have an entire estate pass according to a single plan. If each item of a decedent's estate were distributed according to the law of its situs, no single plan could control. If decedent died intestate, for example, each piece of his property would be distributed according to the intestacy laws of its situs. If decedent died leaving a will, the will might be valid according to the law of the situs of some property and invalid according to the law of the situs of other property. In order to avoid this lack of uniformity, the reference for the entire estate is to the law of decedent's domicile. *See* 2 JOSEPH BEALE, A TREATISE ON THE CONFLICT OF LAWS, §§ 303.1 & 306.1 (1935).

Given the appeal of the uniformity rationale, why shouldn't it work for intestate distribution and testamentary disposition of land? *See* WILLIAM

RICHMAN & WILLIAM REYNOLDS, UNDERSTANDING CONFLICT OF LAWS §67[b] (3d ed. 2002).

(2) *Evaluation.* In many cases, the domicile rule for succession on death of movables makes good sense. But in some cases *(White,* for example) the technical rules of domicile produce very odd results. It is, of course, unlikely that Michael or Lucinda ever had given any thought to the matter, but if they had, would it have surprised them that Michael's estate would be distributed according to Pennsylvania law? The laws of intestacy basically serve to make a will for a decedent who has not done so himself. The legislature, with due regard for local family customs and relations, selects a pattern of distribution that would coincide with the wishes of the "average testator." Which legislature was better able to do that for Michael?

# PART C   ESCAPE DEVICES

## § 4.10   Introductory Note

The results produced by the simple, hard-and-fast rules of the First Restatement did not always satisfy the judges. When faced with a rule that required choice of Maryland law when justice and common sense favored the law of Delaware, the judges, in the way of all judges, sought to do justice, a search that led them to seek ways to avoid the rules of the vested rights regime.

Typically, they did not articulate the considerations of policy, fairness, and party expectations that motivated their decisions; both the conflicts theory and the general jurisprudence of the time were too rigidly formalistic to permit so frank a strategy. Rather, they invented "escape devices"—highly conceptual maneuvers that permitted them to avoid an undesirable outcome without breaking faith with the traditional system. Thus, they could recharacterize a property issue as a tort problem and escape the law of the situs in favor of the law of the place of injury, or find that a tort problem was really a question of procedure, which permitted escape from the law of the place of injury to the law of the forum. Another possibility was *renvoi*; if the forum's choice-of-law rule directed the choice of French law and the result was offensive, the court could read "the law of France" to mean the *whole* law of France—including French choice-of-law rules, which might refer the issue back to forum law.

Finally, courts occasionally took the bull by the horns and refused for reasons of "public policy" to apply the law suggested by the First Restatement's rigid rules.

Judges who used these devices in their quest for justice ran headlong into conflict with the vested rights theory's drive for certainty. This Part of Chapter IV examines the methods courts used to tame the First Restatement rules, as well as their efforts to cabin the exceptions they created—all in pursuit of the elusive, and often contending, goals of justice and certainty.

## § 4.11   Characterization

Results reached under the regime of the First Restatement depended on how the court characterized the problem—as a tort, as a contract, and so on. The First Restatement, however, did not explain how a court was to know what label to attach. This is not an insignificant problem. After all, as even first-year students know, legal problems do not come in tidy and neatly labeled packages. It is exceedingly curious, therefore, that the Restatement failed to deal with this critical issue.

### [A]   Substance/Procedure

All first-year law students wrestle with the distinction between substance and procedure, generally in the context of learning the *Erie* doctrine. They learn not only that the distinction is vital but also that it is a hard one to draw at times.

In conflicts, the importance of the distinction extends well beyond *Erie* and its progeny (discussed in Chapter 6, *infra)*. The traditional rule is easy to state: The forum applies its own procedural rules, and it applies the substantive law of the state determined by the vested rights theory *(e.g.,* the law of the place of wrong in torts). The reasons for the traditional rule are also straightforward. Sometimes the forum will have some important judicial policy codified in its procedural law. In the case of limitations, for example, the forum will apply its own statute having the effect of extinguishing a tort claim even though it would be timely under the law of the place of injury. A second major reason for the forum's use of its own procedural rules is simple convenience. It would be extremely burdensome in a contract case, for instance, for the forum court to have to learn and apply the hearsay or motion practice rules of the place of making.

Even though the traditional rule and its reasons are relatively clear, practice could be a bit more complicated. A familiar trilogy of Massachusetts cases illustrates the devilish difficulty of distinguishing substance from procedure.

1) *Duggan v. Bay St. Ry.,* 230 Mass. 330, 119 N.E. 757 (1918). The question here was whether a statute that allocated the burden of proof on contributory negligence was constitutional. The substance/procedure issue arose because the legislature had ordered the statute to be applied retroactively. The court held the statute to be procedural and, therefore, approved its retroactive application.

2) *Levy v. Steiger,* 233 Mass. 600, 124 N.E. 477 (1919). In *Levy,* a Massachusetts plaintiff was injured in an automobile accident in Rhode Island, a state that placed the burden of proof on contributory negligence on the plaintiff. The court had no trouble with the analysis; because the statute had already been classified as procedural (in *Duggan),* Massachusetts law rather than that of the place of injury (Rhode Island) would apply. Is *Duggan* good precedent for *Levy?* Do the underlying issues have anything in common beside the fact that they involved the same statute?

3) *Sampson v. Channell,* 110 F.2d 754 (1st Cir. 1940). This case was somewhat more complicated. It was an action in federal court in Massachusetts based on an automobile accident in Maine. The question was whose law on burden of proof was to govern—that of Massachusetts, Maine, or the federal court. In an initial application of *Erie,* which had been decided only two years earlier, Judge Magruder felt bound to apply state rather than federal law, because burden of proof rules were "substantive"; after all, the burden of proof can determine the outcome of the case. The court then had to choose which state's law to apply. This answer was easy: Massachusetts, had already classified the issue as "procedural" for choice-of-law purposes (in *Levy,* remember); and the federal court followed suit. In a neat *ipse dixit* the court, in other words, classified the issue as "substantive" for *Erie* purposes and "procedural" for choice-of-law purposes.

Does this make sense? Can burden of proof be both substantive and procedural? Did Judge Magruder demonstrate a better understanding of the different uses of the substance/procedure distinction than did the *Levy* court?

*See* PROBLEMS 4C-1. THE PROMISED LAND; 4C-2. COMMITTEE OF INQUIRY.

---

## MARIE v. GARRISON

*New York Supreme Court*
*13 Abb. N. Cas. 210 (1883)*

Dwight, Referee: [Plaintiff alleged that it had a contract with defendant and that it had modified some of its rights under that contract in consideration of oral promises made by defendant.]. . . .

To this proposition the defendant objects that the later oral agreement is in its turn subject to the provisions of the Statute of Frauds. . . .

[The referee held that there was adequate consideration alleged to support the modified contract.]

I have now arrived at the second inquiry. This is whether the New York Statute of Frauds can be applied in this case to exclude evidence of the consideration. . . . It is maintained by [defendant] . . . that the New York Statute of Frauds is a rule affecting the *remedy* upon a contract within its terms—a rule prescribing evidence and accordingly a rule of procedure. If this be so, they further argue that a rule of evidence is a branch of the law of the *forum* . . . . It is, on the other hand, insisted by the plaintiff that this New York law is so framed as to be a rule of substance, entering into the very existence of the contract. If so, . . . validity . . . is to be determined by the law of the place where the contract was made. If valid there, it is valid everywhere; if void there, it is void everywhere. . . .

[T]he New York statute . . . declares that a contract . . . not "*expressing the* consideration" shall be "*void* . . . ."

Can it fairly be said that a contract declared "void" by statute still subsists *as a contract,* and that the only effect of the statute is to deprive a party of a remedy? Is such a word as "void" a mere word of *evidence?*

I think not. I regard the word "void" as a word of substance, and not as a mere word of procedure. In that view, the statute cannot, by accepted rules under the "Conflict of Laws," be applied to contracts made in other States, and accordingly not to the present case. . . .

I now propose to examine the point whether the Statute of Frauds of Missouri has been violated. . . .

The contract for the sale of land is not made *void* in Missouri, if the statute is not complied with. It is only enacted that no "action shall be brought," in that case. . . . [T]he remedy *in Missouri only* is affected by these words. . . .

[Because the plaintiff sought no remedy in a Missouri forum, the Referee held that the Missouri Statute of Frauds did not apply.]

The conclusion then is that this letter, whether tested by the law of New York or Missouri does not trench upon any provision of the Statute of Frauds.

*See* PROBLEM 4C-3. SLOT MACHINE JURISPRUDENCE.

---

## NOTES AND QUESTIONS ON *MARIE v. GARRISON*

The opinion in *Marie* was written by a referee named Timothy Dwight, the founder of the Columbia Law School. *See* LAWRENCE M. FRIEDMAN, A HISTORY OF AMERICAN LAW 419 (1976). It has been *very* heavily edited. You may take our word for it that, while longer, it is no clearer in the unedited version.

Perhaps the opinion is unclear because its author wished to obscure the absurdity of his result (or maybe it's the other way around). Does it make sense to label the New York Statute of Frauds "substantive" and the Missouri Statute "procedural"?

Having said all of this—was the result in *Marie* just?

When you study "False Conflicts" in § 4.19, *infra,* of this Chapter, ask yourself whether *Marie* is one.

For statute of frauds cases, many traditionalist courts adopted Dwight's simplistic literal solution. They looked to the particular wording of the state statute of frauds: if it read "no contract shall be good," they treated the issue as substantive; if it read, "no action shall be brought," they used a procedural characterization. *Compare Houghtaling v. Ball & Chapin,* 20 Mo. 563 (1855) *with Brown v. Valentine,* 240 F. Supp. 539 (W.D. Va. 1965). This solution seems especially silly since both formulae are borrowed from the prototype English statute, one from section four, the other from section seventeen; and it is likely that the variation in the language in the original was purely accidental. Nevertheless, the First Restatement seems to have ratified the courts' literality. Restatement of Conflict of Laws § 334, Comment a (1934). For a critique of that position, see Comment, *The Statute of Frauds in the Conflict of Laws,* 43 CALIF. L. REV. 295 (1955).

*See* PROBLEMS 4C-4. STATUTES OF FRAUDS ARE SUBSTANTIVE; 4C-5. A FINDER'S FEE.

---

## GRANT v. Mc-AULIFFE

*California Supreme Court*
*41 Cal. 2d 859, 264 P.2d 944 (1953)*

TRAYNOR, JUSTICE. [The three plaintiffs were injured when their car collided in Arizona with a car driven by one Pullen, who later died. Defendant McAuliffe was later appointed administrator of Pullen's estate. All four persons involved in the accident were California residents, and McAuliffe had been appointed administrator by a California court. He rejected the claims filed by plaintiffs against the estate.]

The basic question is whether plaintiffs' causes of action against Pullen survived his death and are maintainable against his estate. The statutes of this state provide that causes of action for negligent torts survive the death of the tort feasor and can be maintained against the administrator or executor of his estate. Defendant contends, however, that the survival of a cause of action is a matter of substantive law, and that the courts of this state must apply the law of Arizona governing survival of causes of action. There is no provision for survival of causes of action in the statutes of Arizona, although there is a provision that in the event of the death of a party to a pending proceeding his personal representative can be substituted as a party to the action, if the cause of action survives. The Supreme Court of Arizona has held that if a tort action has not been commenced before the death of the tortfeasor a plea in abatement must be sustained.

Thus, the answer to the question whether the causes of action against Pullen survived and are maintainable against his estate depends on whether Arizona or California law applies. In actions on torts occurring abroad, the courts of this state determine the substantive matters inherent in the cause of action by adopting as their own the law of the place where the tortious acts occurred, unless it is contrary to the public policy of this state. "[No court can enforce any law but that of its own sovereign, and, when a suitor comes to a jurisdiction foreign to the place of the tort, he can only invoke an obligation recognized by that sovereign. A foreign sovereign under civilized law imposes an obligation of its own as nearly homologous as possible to that arising in the place where the tort occurs." Learned Hand, J., in *Guinness v. Miller,* D.C., 291 F. 769, 770. But the forum does not adopt as its own the procedural law of the place where the tortious acts occur. It must therefore, be determined whether survival of causes of action is procedural or substantive for conflict of laws purposes.

    . . . In many cases it has been held that the survival of a cause of action is a matter of substance and that the law of the place where the tortious acts occurred must be applied to determine the question. The Restatement of the Conflict of Laws, section 390, is in accord. It should be noted, however, that the majority of the foregoing cases were decided after drafts of the Restatement were first circulated in 1929. Before that time, it appears that the weight of authority was that survival of causes of action is procedural and governed by the domestic law of the forum. Many of the cases, decided both before and after the Restatement, holding that survival is substantive and must be determined by the law of the place where the tortious acts occurred, confused the problems involved in survival of causes of action with those involved in causes of action for wrongful death. . . . A cause of action for wrongful death is statutory. It is a new cause of action vested in the widow or next of kin, and arises on the death of the injured person. Before his death, the injured person himself has a separate and distinct cause of action and, if it survives, the same cause of action can be enforced by the personal representative of the deceased against the tortfeasor. The survival statutes do not create a new cause of action, as do the wrongful death statutes. . . . They merely prevent the abatement of the cause of action of the injured person, and provide for its enforcement by or against the personal representative of the deceased. They are analogous to statutes of limitation, which are procedural for conflict of laws purposes and are governed by the domestic law of the forum. Thus, a cause of action arising in another state, by the laws of which an action cannot be maintained thereon because of lapse of time, can be enforced in California by a citizen of this state, if he has held the cause of action from the time it accrued.

Defendant contends, however, that the characterization of survival of causes of action as substantive or procedural is foreclosed by *Cort v. Steen,* 36 Cal.2d 437, 442, 224 P.2d 723, where it was held that the California survival statutes were substantive and therefore did not apply retroactively. The problem in the present proceeding, however, is not whether the survival statutes apply retroactively, but whether they are substantive or procedural for purposes of conflict of laws. " 'Substance and Procedure,' . . . are not legal concepts of invariant content." *Black Diamond Steamship Corp. v. Robert Stewart & Sons,* 336 U.S. 386, 397; W. W. COOK, THE LOGICAL AND LEGAL BASES OF THE CONFLICT OF LAWS (1942), c. 6: "Substance and Procedure," and a statute or other rule of law will be characterized as substantive or procedural according to the nature of the problem for which a characterization must be made.

Defendant also contends that a distinction must be drawn between survival of causes of action and revival of actions, and that the former are substantive but the latter procedural. On the basis of this distinction, defendant concludes that many of the cases cited above as holding that survival is procedural and is governed by the domestic law of the forum do not support this position, since they involved problems of "revival" rather than "survival." The distinction urged by defendant is not a valid one. Most of the statutes involved in the cases cited provided for the "revival" of a pending proceeding by or against the personal representative of a party thereto should he die while the action is still pending. But in most "revival" statutes, substitution of a personal representative in place of a deceased party is expressly conditioned on the survival of the cause of action itself. If the cause of action dies with the tortfeasor, a pending proceeding must be abated. A personal representative cannot be substituted in the place of a deceased party unless the cause of action is still subsisting. In cases where this substitution has occurred, the courts have looked to the domestic law of the forum to determine whether the cause of action survives as well as to determine whether the personal representative can be substituted as a party to the action. Defendant's contention would require the courts to look to their local statutes to determine "revival" and to the law of the place where the tort occurred to determine "survival," but we have found no case in which this procedure was followed.

Since we find no compelling weight of authority for either alternative, we are free to make a choice on the merits. We have concluded that survival of causes of action should be governed by the law of the forum. Survival is not an essential part of the cause of action itself but relates to the procedures available for the enforcement of the legal claim for damages. Basically the question is one of the administration of decedents' estates, which is a purely local proceeding. The problem here is whether the causes of action that these plaintiffs had against Pullen before his death survive as liabilities of his estate. Section 573 of the Probate Code provides that "all actions founded . . . upon any liability for physical injury, death or injury to property, may be maintained by and against executors and administrators in all cases in which the cause of action . . . is one which may not abate upon the death of their respective testators or intestates. . . . Civil Code section 956 provides that "A thing in action arising out of a wrong which results in physical injury to the person . . . shall not abate by reason of the death of the wrongdoer and causes of action for damage to property are maintainable against executors and administrators under section 574 of the Probate Code. Decedent's estate is located in this state, and letters of administration were issued to defendant by the courts of this state. The responsibilities of defendant, as administrator of Pullen's estate, for injuries inflicted by Pullen before his death are governed by the laws of this state. This approach has been followed in a number of well reasoned cases. It retains control of the administration of estates by the local legislature, and avoids the problems involved in determining the administrator's amenability to suit under the laws of other states. The common law doctrine *actio personalis moritur cum persona* had its origin in a penal concept of tort liability. Today, tort liabilities of the sort involved in these actions are regarded as compensatory. When, as in the present case, all of the parties were residents of this state, and the estate of the deceased tortfeasor is being administered in this state, plaintiffs' right to prosecute their causes of action is governed by the laws of this state relating to administration of estates. . . .

GIBSON, C. J., and SHENK and CARTER, JJ., concur.

SCHAUER, JUSTICE. I dissent. In *Cort v. Steen,* this court held that under the doctrine of nonsurvivability the abatement of an action by the death of the injured person through the tortfeasor's act or otherwise, or by the death of the tortfeasor, abates the wrong as well; that the effect of a survival statute is to create a right or cause of action rather than to either continue an existing right or revive or extend a remedy theretofore accrued for the redress of an existing wrong; and that consequently a survival statute enacted after death of the tortfeasor did not apply to the tort or cause of action involved. And more recently, in *Re Estate of Arbulich* (1953), 41 Cal.2d 257 P.2d 433, we recognized the rule that the burden of proof provisions of the Probate Code sections (259 et seq.) dealing with reciprocal inheritance rights are not merely procedural in nature, but, rather, are substantive statutes regulating succession, and that consequently such rights are to be determined by the law as it existed on the date of decedent's death.

Irreconcilably inconsistent with the cases cited in the preceding paragraph, the majority now holds that "Survival is not an essential part of the cause of action itself but relates to the procedures available for the enforcement of the legal claim for damages. Basically the question is one of the administration of decedents' estates, which is a purely local proceeding." If the above stated holding is to prevail, then for the sake of the law's integrity and clarity, and in fairness to lower courts and to counsel, the cited cases should be expressly overruled. But even more regrettable than the failure to either follow or unequivocally overrule the cited cases is the character of the "rule" which is now promulgated: the majority assert that henceforth "a statute or other rule of law will be characterized as substantive or procedural according to the nature of the problem for which a characterization must be made," thus suggesting that the court will no longer be bound to consistent enforcement or uniform application of "a statute or other rule of law" but will instead apply one "rule" or another as the untrammeled whimsy of the majority may from time to time dictate, "according to the nature of the problem" as they view it in a given case. This concept of the majority strikes deeply at what has been our proud boast that ours was a government of laws rather than of men.

. . . Since this court has clearly held that a right or cause of action created by a survival statute is likewise substantive, rather than procedural, we should hold, if we would follow the law, that the trial court properly granted defendant's motions to abate.

SPENCE, J., concurs [with the dissent].

EDMONDS, Justice (dissenting).

I concur in [Justice Schauer's] conclusion that the order granting the defendant's motion to abate should be affirmed.

---

## *GRANT* AND THE SUBSTANCE/PROCEDURE PROBLEM

(1) *Distinguishing the Unprecedent. Grant* shows that a court can escape the place-of-injury rule via the substance/procedure route without being clumsy and mechanical. Note, for example, how deftly Justice Traynor disposes of the inconvenient precedent of *Cort v. Steen* and its characterization of the California statute as substantive for constitutional/retroactivity purposes. Compare the wooden way the Massachusetts court handled the same problem in *Levy v. Steiger.*

(2) *Survival of Actions.* Restatement (First) § 390 indicates clearly that survival of actions is a substantive matter to be governed by the law of the place of injury. For the *Grant* court to ignore such an explicit Restatement directive, its desire for escape must have been very strong. Is the court's result a good one? If so, is it because of the reasons that underlie the substance/procedure distinction? Would it have been very burdensome for the California court to apply Arizona's nonsurvival rule? Can't every court's docket benefit from one more pre-trial dismissal? If administrative convenience does not provide real justification for the court's escape from the First Restatement choice, what does?

(3) *Rebelling Against the Machine.* In a path-breaking study, Brainerd Currie applauded the court's result and flippantly described the mechanical manipulation required to reach such results under the rigid framework of the First Restatement:

> The judges fed the data into the machine in the usual way, but, when the machine's answer came out, they couldn't swallow it. They rebelled against the machine. They *adjudicated* the case. Using discretion and intelligence, and having regard to the fact that it was a lawsuit they were trying, they looked for a result they could live with. They saw

no purpose, in reason or policy, to be served by applying Arizona law to cut off the rights of the plaintiffs when the tortfeasor died. . . . So they decided the case *their* way. This was a kind of insubordination on their part. . . . Doubtless they felt a bit uncomfortable, as anyone might who has departed from the ordained path. So they went back to the machine and fed the same data into it again, this time using a somewhat different procedure. After pressing the button marked "Procedure is governed by the law of the forum, substance by the law of the place of the wrong," they pressed the button marked "Procedural" instead of the one marked "Substantive." This time the machine came up with the answer that the court had arrived at independently.

Brainerd Currie, *Survival of Actions: Adjudication Versus Automation in the Conflict of Laws,* 10 STAN. L. REV. 205 (1958),* reprinted in Brainerd Currie, *Selected Essays on the Conflict of Laws,* 138-139 (1963). Remarkably, Justice Traynor, the author of the majority opinion in *Grant,* publicly confirmed Currie's analysis in a law review article written six years after *Grant* was decided. Traynor defended the result, arguing that application of Arizona law would have frustrated California policy without advancing any Arizona policy. In a footnote, he offers a more limited defense of the manipulation required to reach the correct result:

It may not be amiss to add that although the opinion in the case is my own, I do not regard it as ideally articulated, developed as it had to be against the brooding background of a petrified forest. Yet I would make no more apology for it than in reaching a rational result it was less deft than it might have been to quit itself of the familiar speech of choice of law.

Roger Traynor, *Is This Conflict Really Necessary?,* 37 TEX. L. REV. 658, 670 n. 35 (1959).*

(4) *A Modern Example.* Contemporary First Restatement courts continue to use the tort-to-procedure re-characterization escape device. *See Baxter v. Sturm, Ruger & Co,* 644 A.2nd 1297 (Conn. 1994) (Re-characterization used to escape the eight year statute of repose of the place of injury in favor of the law of the forum, which had no statute of repose.)

## [B]   Tort and Contract

## LEVY v. DANIELS' U-DRIVE AUTO RENTING CO.

*Connecticut Supreme Court of Errors*
*108 Conn. 333, 143 A. 163 (1928)*

WHEELER, C. J. The complaint alleged these facts: The defendant, Daniels' U-Drive Auto Renting Company, Incorporated, rented in Hartford to Sack an

---

* Copyright © 1958 by the Board of Trustees of The Leland Stanford, Jr. University. Reprinted with permission.

* Published originally in 37 Texas Law Review 657-75 (1959). Copyright © 1959 by the Texas Law Review. Reprinted with permission.

automobile, which he operated, and in which Levy, the plaintiff, was a passenger. During the time the automobile was rented and operated, the defendant renting company was subject to section 21 of chapter 195 of the Public Acts of Connecticut, 1925, which provides:

> "Any person renting or leasing to another any motor vehicle owned by him shall be liable for any damages to any person or property caused by the operation said motor vehicle while so rented or leased."

[Plaintiff was injured in Massachusetts when the car in which he was a passenger was struck from the rear by another car. Alleging negligence on the part of both drivers, Plaintiff sued the other driver; he also sued the car rental company under the Connecticut statute.]. . . .

The complaint alleges a tortious operation of the automobile rented to Sack by the defendant, causing the injuries to the plaintiff as alleged, and constituting an action ex delicto. The statute gives, in terms, the injured person a right of action against the defendant which rented the automobile to Sack, though the injury occurred in Massachusetts. It was a right which the statute gave directly, not derivatively, to the injured person as a consequence of the contract of hiring. The purpose of the statute was not primarily to give the injured person a right of recovery against the tortious operator of the car, but to protect the safety of the traffic upon highways by providing an incentive to him who rented motor vehicles to rent them to competent and careful operators, by making him liable for damage resulting from the tortious operation of the rented vehicles. The common law would not hold the defendant liable upon the facts recited in the complaint for the negligence of Sack in the operation of this automobile. The rental of motor vehicles to any but competent and careful operators, or to persons of unknown responsibility, would be liable to result in injury to the public upon or near highways, and this imminent danger justified, as a reasonable exercise of the police power, this statute, which requires all who engage in this business to become responsible for any injury inflicted upon the public by the tortious operation of the rented motor vehicle. . . .

The statute made the liability of the person renting motor vehicles a part of every contract of hiring a motor vehicle in Connecticut. A liability ex delicto is created by the law of the place of the delict. A liability arising out of a contract depends upon the law of the place of contract, "unless the contract is to be performed or to have its beneficial operation and effect elsewhere, or it is made with reference to the law of another place." We will enforce rights of action on contracts arising in other jurisdictions unless these contravene our own law, or our own fundamental and important public policy imperatively requires their nonenforcement. It is a general rule, subject to the exceptions we have noted, that rights ex contractu may be enforced anywhere.

If the liability of this defendant under this statute is contractual, no question can arise as to the plaintiff's right to enforce this contract, provided the obligation imposed upon this defendant was for the "direct, sole and exclusive benefit" of the plaintiff. The contract was made in Connecticut; at the instant of its making the statute made a part of the contract of hiring the liability of the defendant which the plaintiff seeks to enforce. The law inserted in the contract this provision. The statute did not create the liability;

it imposed it in case the defendant voluntarily rented the automobile. . . . The right of the plaintiff as a beneficiary of this contract to maintain this action is no longer an open question in this state. The contract was made for him and every other member of the public. That the beneficiary was undetermined because each of the public was a beneficiary is of no consequence. His injury determines his identity and right of action. . . .

---

## NOTES AND QUESTIONS ON *LEVY*

An automobile accident is a tort, and the accident occurred in Massachusetts; so why was Connecticut law applied? The trick for plaintiff, of course, is to convince the court that it should characterize the problem differently. Plaintiff, in other words, must find a choice-of-law rule that will refer to Connecticut law.

The obvious candidate is to label the problem as one sounding in contract, but how did the court get away with that? Do you find its theory convincing? What does the car rental contract have to do with the plaintiff? In any event, is this theory really different from the tort concept of negligent entrustment? *See* FOWLER HARPER, FLEMING JAMES & OSCAR GRAY, THE LAW OF TORTS § 18.7 (3d ed. 1996).

The First Restatement treats vicarious liability issues in tort cases as "determined by the law of the place of wrong." § 387. If that provision had been available to the defendant in *Levy,* do you think it would have changed the result?

## THE ARKANSAS TELEGRAPH CASES

**WESTERN UNION TELEGRAPH CO. v. GRIFFIN,** 92 Ark. 219, 122 S.W. 489 (1909). Plaintiffs were the husband and father of Gerrie Griffin. The husband from his home in Arkansas sent this message via the defendant telegraph company to the father in Mississippi: "Gerrie died very suddenly at one p.m. today. Come at once. . . . " Because of the defendant's negligence, the wire was not received for several days, and the father missed Gerrie's funeral. The husband and father sued the telegraph company for "mental anguish and suffering" a remedy available under a specific Arkansas statute. No such remedy was available in Mississippi where the late delivery occurred.

*Held:* for plaintiffs *on the contract* made in Arkansas. "The statute makes mental anguish an element of recoverable damage for failure to receive, transmit, or deliver a telegram; yet the relation out of which the duty arises is created by contract, and the cause of action primarily grows out of the contract."

---

**WESTERN UNION TELEGRAPH CO. v. CHILTON,** 100 Ark. 296, 140 S.W. 26 (1911). From Missouri a friend of plaintiff sent the following telegram to plaintiff in Arkansas: "Come home at once, your baby is dead." Once again, the defendant's negligence resulted in late delivery, and the plaintiff missed the funeral.

*Held*: for plaintiff in *tort*:

[Defendant] contends that there can be no recovery on the contract in this case because the contract was made in Missouri, and in that state damages for mental anguish are not allowed. [This] contention cannot be sustained. While it is true that the cause of action under the statue grew out of a contract that was made in Missouri, yet the negligent breach of that contract constituting the tort . . . occurred in this state, and that under our statute makes the cause of action complete for damages for mental anguish.

## NOTE

Can *Griffin* and *Chilton* be distinguished? In the space of five years, the Arkansas courts decided eight interstate telegram cases. In three (including *Griffin*) where the message was sent from Arkansas to a state lacking a mental anguish statute, the court used a contract characterization and upheld plaintiffs' claims for mental anguish. In the other five (including *Chilton*) where the message was sent *to* Arkansas from a state having no mental anguish statute, the court also held for plaintiffs but was required to use a tort characterization to accomplish the job. *See* ROBERT LEFLAR, LUTHER McDOUGAL & ROBERT FELIX, AMERICAN CONFLICTS LAW 258 (4th ed. 1986).

A more recent example of the Arkansas-telegraph phenomenon is a series of cases construing a West Virginia statute that prohibits an insured from collecting uninsured motorist benefits for injury and damage caused by a hit-and-run driver unless there is physical contact between the two vehicles. Unsympathetic to the goal of the statute, the West Virginia courts permit recovery by characterizing the issue as a contract problem when the contract is made outside West Virginia and the injury occurs within the state, and as a tort issue when the contract is made within West Virginia and the injury occurs outside the state. *See Perkins v. Doe*, 350 S.E.2d 711, (W.Va. 1986), *Lee v. Saliga,* 373 S.E.2d 345 (W.Va. 1988). The only Virginia case construing the statute involved a Virginia contract and a West Virginia injury. Not surprisingly, the court characterized the issue as sounding in contract in order to avoid the West Virginia statute, which otherwise would have applied according to Virginia's place-of-injury rule. *See Buchanan v. Doe,* 431 S.E.2d 289 (Va.1993). For commentary on this series of cases see William Richman & David Riley, *The First Restatement of Conflict of Laws on the Twenty-fifth Anniversary of its Successor: Contemporary Practice in Traditional Courts,* 56 MD. L. REV. 1196, 1223 (1997).

## [C]  Property and Contract

### POLSON v. STEWART

*Massachusetts Supreme Judicial Court*
*167 Mass. 211, 45 N.E. 737 (1897)*

HOLMES, J. This is a bill to enforce a covenant made by the defendant to his wife, the plaintiff's intestate, in North Carolina, to surrender all his marital rights in certain land of hers. The land is in Massachusetts. The parties to the covenant were domiciled in North Carolina. According to the bill, the wife took steps which, under the North Carolina statutes, gave her the right to contract as a feme sole with her husband as well as with others, and afterwards released her dower in the defendant's lands. In consideration of this release, and to induce his wife to forbear suing for divorce, for which she had just cause, and for other adequate considerations, the defendant executed the covenant. . . .

But it is said that the laws of the parties' domicile could not authorize a contract between them as to lands in Massachusetts. Obviously, this is not true. It is true that the laws of other states cannot render valid conveyances of property within our borders which our laws say are void, for the plain reason that we have exclusive power over the res. But the same reason inverted establishes that the lex rei sitae cannot control personal covenants not purporting to be conveyances, between persons outside the jurisdiction, although concerning a thing within it. Whatever the covenant, the laws of North Carolina could subject the defendant's property to seizure on execution, and his person to imprisonment, for a failure to perform it. Therefore, on principle, the law of North Carolina determines the validity of the contract. . . .

If valid by the law of North Carolina, there is no reason why the contract should not be enforced here. . . . The competency of the wife to receive the covenant is established by the law of her domicile, and of the place of the contract. The laws of Massachusetts do not make it impossible for him specifically to perform his undertaking. He can give a release which will be good by Massachusetts law. If it be said that the rights of the administrator are only derivative from the wife, we agree, and we do not for a moment regard any one as privy to the contract except as representing the wife. But, if then it be asked whether she could have enforced the contract during her life, an answer in the affirmative is made easy by considering exactly what the defendant undertook to do. So far as occurs to us, he undertook three things: First, not to disturb his wife's enjoyment while she kept her property; second, to execute whatever instrument was necessary in order to release his right if she conveyed; and third, to claim no rights on her death, but to do whatever was necessary to clear the title from such rights then. All these things were as capable of performance in Massachusetts as they would have been in North Carolina. Indeed, all purposes of the covenant could have been secured at once in the lifetime of the wife by a joint conveyance of the property to a trustee upon trusts properly limited.

It will be seen that the case does not raise the question as to what the common law and the presumed law of North Carolina would be as to a North Carolina contract calling for acts in Massachusetts, or concerning property in Massachusetts, which could not be done consistently with Massachusetts law. . . .

*Demurrer overruled.*

FIELD, C. J. (dissenting). . . . As a conveyance made directly between husband and wife of an interest in Massachusetts land would be void although the parties were domiciled in North Carolina when it was made, and by the laws of North Carolina were authorized to make such a conveyance, so I think that a contract for such a conveyance between the same persons also would be void. It seems to me illogical to say that we will not permit a conveyance of Massachusetts land directly between husband and wife, wherever they may have their domicile, and yet say that they may make a contract to convey such land from one to the other, which our courts will enforce. It is possible to abandon the rule of lex rei sitae, but to keep it for conveyances of land and to abandon it for contracts to convey land seems to me unwarrantable. . . .

*See* PROBLEM 4C-6. THE COMMUNITY.

---

## NOTES AND QUESTIONS ON *POLSON* AND SOME ADDITIONAL RECHARACTERIZATION PLOYS

(1) *The Contract/Conveyance Distinction. Polson* is one of the earliest cases to make this distinction; later courts have used it to distinguish a contract to convey from the actual conveyance, a note from the mortgage securing it, and covenants personal to the parties from those running with the land. In each instance, the contractual facet of the transaction has been referred to the place of making and the conveyance facet to the situs. *See generally* RUSSELL WEINTRAUB, COMMENTARY ON THE CONFLICT OF LAWS 539-540 (4th ed. 2001); Note, *Choice of law Governing Land Transactions: The Contract-Conveyance Dichotomy,* 111 U. PA. L. REV. 482 (1963).

Does the distinction make sense in light of the "exclusive power" rationale for the situs rule—that only the situs courts can act directly to affect title to the land, but any court with personal jurisdiction over the defendant can order him to pay damages for breach of contract. *See* WILLIAM RICHMAN & WILLIAM REYNOLDS, UNDERSTANDING CONFLICT OF LAWS § 67[c][3] (2d ed. 2002).

(2) *The Use of the Distinction in Polson.* Does the result in *Polson* make sense? What married women did Massachusetts hope to protect with its incapacity rule, and what contracts did North Carolina wish to validate with its opposite stance? Does the result make sense in light of the policies underlying contract law generally? If the result in *Polson* makes sense, what about the reasoning? Consider the following:

> Holmes announced the court's allegiance to [the situs] formula in these words: "The laws of other States cannot render valid conveyances of property within our borders which our laws say are void, for

the plain reason that we have exclusive power over the res." On the other hand, he observed, a North Carolina court could, consistently with established doctrine, have enforced North Carolina law and compelled the husband to perform his covenant by subjecting his property to execution and his person to imprisonment. Having created this false and needless conflict between the laws of the two states, Holmes proposed a Gilbertian solution: During the wife's lifetime the Massachusetts court (though insisting that a conveyance from husband to wife would have been void) could nevertheless have ordered husband to make just such a conveyance and then held that conveyance to be valid!

Moffatt Hancock, *Conceptual Devices for Avoiding the Land Taboo in Conflict of Laws: The Disadvantages of Disingenuousness,* 20 STAN. L. REV. 1, 35 (1967),[*] reprinted in MOFFATT HANCOCK, STUDIES IN MODERN CHOICE OF LAW: TORTS, INSURANCE, LAND TITLES 385 (1984).

(3) **BURR v. BECKLER,** 264 Ill. 230, 106 N.E. 206 (1914). Husband and wife were citizens of Illinois. While the wife was temporarily in Florida, her husband persuaded her to execute a note in favor of plaintiff and a deed of trust (mortgage) on her Illinois land to secure the note. Plaintiff sued wife for foreclosure in Illinois. Under Illinois law, wife had capacity to make the note and mortgage, while under Florida law she did not.

*Held:* For the wife; Florida law applied.

The validity construction, force, and effect of instruments affecting title to land depend upon the law of the state where the land lies. But if the note was void, the trust deed, which was incidental and intended to secure a performance of the obligation created by the note, could not be enforced. It is a universal rule that the validity of a contract is to be determined by the law of the place where it is made, and if it is not valid there, it will not be enforced in another state in which it would have been valid if made there.

As a matter of choice of law, can the result in *Burr* be defended? Why did Florida want to protect Illinois wives from the fraudulent conduct of their husbands? Perhaps the equities influenced the court; there was evidence that the husband really had misled his wife and that the plaintiff may have known of the fraud. If so, should the court have justified the result by manipulating the internal law of Illinois rather than creating a highly questionable choice-of-law precedent to mislead other courts? For commentary on *Burr,* see RUSSELL WEINTRAUB, COMMENTARY ON THE CONFLICT OF LAWS 540 (4th ed. 2001).

## [D] Property or Tort

The contract/conveyance dichotomy is just one sort of re-characterization that courts used to escape the situs rule. Property cases can also be re-characterized as tort cases. Suppose a debtor attempts to frustrate his creditors by executing a conveyance in the forum of land in the situs. Can

---

[*] Copyright © 1977 by the Board of Trustees of Leland Stanford, Jr. University. Reprinted with permission.

a creditor's claim of fraud be referred to the law of the forum—the place of the wrong—instead of the situs? Judge Learned Hand permitted the recharacterization in *Irving Trust Co. v. Maryland Casualty Co.*, 83 F.2d 168 (2d Cir.), *cert. denied*, 299 U.S. 571 (1936):

We have no doubt therefore that title passed by the deeds delivered in New York to property situated in those of the three situs states whose laws did not forbid such transfers; yet the law of New York might still make receipt of the deed a wrong and impose a liability upon the grantee though he got good title. *But see James v. Powell*, 19 N.Y.2d 249, 225 N.E.2d 741, 279 N.Y.S.2d 10 (1967) (applying the law of the situs to the issue of compensatory damages but the law of the forum to the issue of punitive damages). *See generally* Albert Ehrenzweig & Peter Westen, *Fraudulent Conveyances in the Conflict of Laws: Easy Cases May Make Bad Law*, 66 MICH. L. REV. 1679 (1968).

## [E]   Characterization: What Kind of Property?

### DUCKWALL v. LEASE

*Indiana Appellate Court, In Banc.*
*106 Ind. App. 664, 20 N.E.2d 204 (1939)*

LAYMON, JUDGE. The facts were stipulated.

Ella Stevenson died testate on April 12, 1927, a resident of the state of Ohio and the owner in fee simple of a tract of real estate . . . in Miami county, Indiana. . . . Her will was probated on April 20, 1927, in the Probate court of Preble County, Ohio, and was duly probated as a foreign will in the Miami Circuit Court of Indiana. . . . By the terms of her will she gave to her husband, G. Curtin Stevenson, her personal property . . . provided: "that my said husband G. Curtin Stevenson, during his life, shall assume the full management and shall have the full use and benefit of all proceeds accruing from and on my farm situated near Bunker Hill, . . . Indiana, and at his demise, I direct that the said farm shall be sold and the proceeds divided equally, share and share alike, between my sister [and brother]." [Both the brother and the sister] . . . preceded the testatrix in death. Ella Stevenson [died leaving] only her husband, G. Curtin Stevenson.

G. Curtin Stevenson, . . . died testate, a resident of Preble County, Ohio, and his will was duly probated [in Ohio] . . . [and] probated as a foreign will in . . . Indiana. By the terms of his will he bequeathed and devised to his wife, "Ollie Stevenson, one thousand dollars in addition to the five hundred dollars allowed her by law." The balance of his estate was to be divided among his nieces and nephew. . . .

The General Code of the state of Ohio (section 10581) provides in effect that a devise or legacy to any relative does not lapse by reason of the death of the devisee or legatee before the death of the testator.

Appellants, as the heirs of [Ella Stevenson's brother], instituted this action to partition the real estate situated in Miami County, Indiana. . . . Appellees [devisees and legatees of G. Curtin Stevenson] . . . filed a cross-complaint upon the theory that the devise to [the brother and sister] lapsed, because both preceded the testatrix in death and the real estate passed to G. Curtin Stevenson, surviving husband of the testatrix, as in case of intestacy, and that upon his death, the devisees and legatees of said G. Curtin Stevenson became the owners of the land in controversy as tenants in common. . . .

Appellants contend that under the terms of the will of said decedent an equitable conversion of the real estate therein referred took place at the death of the testatrix; that the interests which the brother and sister named in the will would have taken, had they survived the testatrix, assumed the character of personal property from that date; and that the legacies to them did not lapse by virtue of the law of the state of Ohio.

Appellees insist that under the law of Indiana the devise to [the sister and brother] lapsed because both preceded the testatrix in death and the real estate passed to the heir or heirs of the testatrix as in case of intestacy, to-wit, the surviving husband of the testatrix . . . ; that the species of property involved in this action is real estate; and that therefore the law of the state in which the land is situated controls its transmission by will or its passage in case of intestacy. They insist . . . that since the brother and sister preceded the testatrix in death, the legacy to each of them having failed, there was no reason for the conversion of the property at the date of the death of the testatrix.

It must be conceded that the rule as to personal property is that the law of the place where the testator is domiciled at the time of his death governs as to the capacity of the testator to make a will and as to the forms to be observed in its execution and revocation, and as to its validity in every respect. . . . It is equally well settled that title to and the disposition of real property, whether by deed, a last will, or otherwise, must be governed exclusively by the law of the country where it is situated. . . .

It must be conceded that the law of the place where the realty is situated determines whether the testator's will effects an equitable conversion of realty into personalty.

Furthermore, whether a legacy or bequest, of personalty, lapses because the beneficiary dies, or otherwise becomes incapable of taking, before the death of the testator, is determined by the law of the testator's domicile, and whether a devise of realty lapses depends upon the law of the place where the land is situated. . . .

In the instant case, had the brother and sister named in the will survived the testatrix, under the doctrine of equitable conversion there could be no question but that the property which they were to receive by virtue of the provisions of the will was personal property, the distribution of which would be governed by the laws of the state of the domicile of the testatrix, which, in the instant case, was the state of Ohio.

The weight of authority seems to be that an equitable conversion of testatrix's real estate took place at the time of her death, and such conversion will not be postponed by the fact that the land is not to be sold until after the death of the life tenant. . . .

The doctrine of equitable conversion is a legal fiction invented to protect the beneficiaries and to sustain and carry out the intention of a testator or settlor, never to defeat it.

Here the testatrix did not contemplate that in any contingency her heirs at law or any of them would succeed to the title of the land. From the terms of the will it obviously was not her intention for the beneficiaries to receive the land, but only the proceeds thereof. In order to effect the intention of the testatrix, as expressed by the terms of her will, the property, under the doctrine of equitable conversion, for the purpose of succession and to accomplish the purposes of the will, will be regarded as of that species into which the testatrix directed or intended it to be, and, in the instant case, the bequests of the proceeds of the sale to her brother and sister named are to be regarded as bequests of personal property, and not as devises of interests in the land.

Appellees contend that since the brother and sister named in the will preceded the testatrix in death, the legacy to each of them having failed, there was no reason for the conversion of the property at the date of the death of the testatrix.

There would be merit in this contention if the law of Indiana governed the provisions of the will. It will be noted that if appellees were correct in this contention, the will of Mrs. Stevenson, so far as it disposes of her real estate, has no effect and must be disregarded. But, as heretofore concluded, in order to give effect to her will, the property must be considered as personalty, and, under the law of Ohio, the legacies did not lapse. . . .

[T]he property in controversy must be, as between the parties hereto, treated as personal property, and its distribution and disposition must be governed by the laws of the state of Ohio.

*Judgment reversed.* . . .

## NOTES ON EQUITABLE CONVERSION

(1) *Origin of the Concept.* The concept of equitable conversion did not originate in the choice-of-law context. Its original use was in English common law where different rules governed the descent of personal and real property; personal property passing to the personal representatives and real property passing by the rule of primogeniture to the heir. Suppose that testator's will ordered land sold and the proceeds paid to beneficiary, but that the beneficiary died intestate before the sale. Is his interest in the land real property that goes to his heir or personal property that goes to his personal representatives? Equity courts held that the will caused an equitable conversion of the land into personal property, which then went to the beneficiaries' personal representative. *See* AUSTIN SCOTT, ABRIDGMENT OF THE LAW OF TRUSTS §§ 130 -131 (1960).

In choice of law, equitable conversion performs the same transformation of real to personal property, but with a very different consequence; it changes the choice from the law of situs (the rule for real property) to the law of decedent's domicile (the rule for personal property). It can be dangerous, of course, to pick a concept, category or distinction from one context and use it in another without being aware that it serves very different functions in the new setting; recall the transplanting in *Levy v. Steiger* (§ 4.11[A], *supra*) of the substance/procedure distribution from the constitutionality/retroactivity discussion to the choice-of-law context. *See* Moffatt Hancock, *Fallacy of the Transplanted Category*, 37 CAN. B. REV. 535 (1959).

(2) *The Reasoning and Result in Duckwall.* The reasoning in *Duckwall is* obviously and—quite consciously—fictional; no actual conversion of the realty occurred at the death of the testatrix. Is the reasoning also circular? The legal issue was whether the gifts to the testatrix's brother and sister lapsed because they predeceased her. The court reasoned that the testatrix's will equitably converted the real estate to personalty and thus that the Ohio (domicile) anti-lapse statute applied. But if the gifts lapsed at the death of the brother and sister, what remained of them to be converted at the death of the testatrix? In other words, the court had to assume non-lapse—the very question in issue—in order for the equitable conversion fiction to work. *See* Moffatt Hancock, *Equitable Conversion and the Land Taboo in Conflict of Laws,* 17 STAN. L. REV. 1095 (1965), reprinted in MOFFATT HANCOCK, STUDIES IN MODERN CHOICE OF LAW: TORTS, INSURANCE, LAND TITLES 313 (1984).

What about the result in *Duckwall*? The question of lapse is really a question about the testatrix's intentions. Would she have wanted her husband's nieces and nephews on the one hand or her brother's and sister's children on the other to take the remainder after her husband's life estate? This question is much like the question of intestate distribution; who should take in the absence of the decedent's instructions? In both cases, lapse and intestacy, the legislature provides an answer based on its perceptions of what distribution the typical person would want. Which legislature—Ohio's or Indiana's—was better situated to answer the lapse question for the testatrix in *Duckwall ? See id.* at 313. *See also* WILLIAM RICHMAN & WILLIAM REYNOLDS, UNDERSTANDING CONFLICT OF LAWS § 67[c][1] (3d ed. 2002).

(3) *The Dangers of Fiction.* Is there any harm in using a fictional device like equitable conversion to produce sensible results in cases like *Duckwall*? What danger is there in using a fiction instead of attempting to state the real reasons that make the decision desirable?

---

**TOLEDO SOCIETY FOR CRIPPLED CHILDREN v. HICKOK,** 152 Tex. 578, 261 S.W.2d 692 (1953), *cert. denied,* 347 U.S. 936 (1954), shows one danger of resorting to a fiction. Testator, a wealthy Ohioan, owned as partnership property some mineral estates in Texas. A few months before his death he agreed with his partner to form a corporation and convey to it the mineral rights in exchange for stock in the corporation. In his will, he incorporated the contract by reference and directed the completion of the exchange. The residuary clause in his will (which included the Texas mineral estates) set up a trust whose income was to go to his wife and children (all Ohioans) for twenty years and the remainder to go to several Ohio charitable and religious organizations. Testator's children challenged the validity of the will in a Texas court. Under the Ohio deathbed gift statute (called a mortmain statute), the gift to the charities would fail because the will was executed less than a year before testator died. Under Texas law the will was valid. The children argued that the will equitably converted the mineral rights (realty) into stock (personalty) and thus that the law of Ohio as testator's domicile should control.

*Held:* Texas law applied and the gifts to the charities were valid.

> We are disposed to agree with the majority of the text writers, whose view appears to be also the view of the Restatement, that the fiction of equitable conversion from realty to personalty or vice versa, "can have no place in the Conflict of Laws." . . . If this view should impress some as legalistic in the sense of excluding the intent of the testator that his mineral interest should become corporate stock, it is hardly more of a "technical" approach than that of regarding as done "that which had not been done. . . . "

## NOTE AND QUESTIONS

Why would Texas want to apply its law to a dispute between the Ohio children and the Ohio charities? Was the court so overwhelmed by its unmasking of the fiction that it was unable to see that fiction's real function as a device to compensate for the rigidity and policy-blindness of the situs rule?

For additional commentary on the situs rule and equitable conversion, see Moffatt Hancock, *In the Parish of St. Mary le Bow, in the Ward of Cheap,* 16 STAN. L. REV. 561 (1964), reprinted in MOFFATT HANCOCK, STUDIES IN MODERN CHOICE OF LAW: TORTS, INSURANCE, LAND TITLES 225-293 (1984).

## [F] The Empty Promise of Recharacterization

## HAUMSCHILD v. CONTINENTAL CASUALTY CO.

*Wisconsin Supreme Court*
*7 Wis. 2d 130, 95 N. W.2d 814 (1959)*

CURRIE, JUSTICE. This appeal presents a conflict of laws problem with respect to interspousal liability for tort growing out of an automobile accident. Which law controls, that of the state of the forum, the state of the place of wrong, or the state of domicile? Wisconsin is both the state of the forum and of the domicile while California is the state where the alleged wrong was committed. Under Wisconsin law a wife may sue her husband in tort. Under California law she cannot. [The trial court applied California law and dismissed the wife's claim. She appealed.]

This court was first faced with this question in *Buckeye v. Buckeye,* 203 Wis. 248, 234 N.W. 342. (1931). In that case Wisconsin was the state of the forum and domicile, while Illinois was the state of the place of wrong. It was there held that the law governing the creation and extent of tort liability is that of the place where the tort was committed. . . . From this premise it was further held that interspousal immunity from tort liability necessarily is governed by the law of the place of injury. . . .

The principle enunciated in the *Buckeye* case and followed in subsequent Wisconsin cases, that the law of the place of wrong controls as to whether one spouse is immune from suit in tort by the other, is the prevailing view in the majority of jurisdictions in this country. . . . However, criticism of the rule of the *Buckeye* case, by legal writers, some of them recognized authorities in the field of conflict of laws, and recent decisions by the courts of California, New Jersey, and Pennsylvania, have caused us to re-examine the question afresh. . . .

The first case to break the ice and flatly hold that the law of domicile should be applied in determining whether there existed an immunity from suit for tort based upon family relationship is *Emery v. Emery,* 45 Cal.2d 421, 289 P.2d 218 (1955). In that case two unemancipated minor sisters sued their unemancipated minor brother and their father to recover for injuries sustained in an automobile accident that occurred in the state of Idaho, the complaint alleging willful misconduct in order to come within the provisions of the Idaho "guest" statute. All parties were domiciled in California. The opinion by Mr. Justice Traynor recognized that the California court, in passing on the question of whether an unemancipated minor child may sue the parent or an unemancipated brother, had a choice to apply the law of the place of wrong, of the forum, or of the domicile. It was held that the immunity issue was not a question of tort but one of capacity to sue and be sued, and rejected the law of the place of injury as "both fortuitous and irrelevant." In deciding whether to apply the law of the forum, or the law of the domicile, the opinion stated this conclusion:

> . . . We think that disabilities to sue and immunities from suit because of a family relationship are more properly determined by reference to the law of the state of the family domicile. That state has the primary responsibility for establishing and regulating the incidents of the family relationship and it is the only state in which the parties can, by participation in the legislative processes, effect a change in those incidents. Moreover, it is undesirable that the rights, duties, disabilities, and immunities conferred or imposed by the family relationship should constantly change as members of the family cross state boundaries during temporary absences from their home. . . .

The two reasons most often advanced for the common law rule, that one spouse may not sue the other, are the ancient concept that husband and wife constitute in law but one person, and that to permit such suits will be to foment family discord and strife. The Married Women's Acts of the various states have effectively destroyed the "one person" concept thereby leaving as the other remaining reason for the immunity the objective of preventing family discord. This is also the justification usually advanced for denying an unemancipated child the capacity to sue a parent, brother or sister. Clearly this policy reason for denying the capacity to sue more properly lies within the sphere of family law, where domicile usually controls the law to be applied, than it does tort law, where the place of injury generally determines the substantive law which will govern. . . .

We are convinced that, from both the standpoint of public policy and logic, the proper solution of the conflict of laws problem, in cases similar to the instant action, is to hold that the law of the domicile is the one that ought to be applied in determining any issue of incapacity to sue based upon family relationship.

However, in order to adopt such a conflict of laws rule it will be necessary it overrule at least six prior decisions of this court, and to partially overrule two others. If it ever is proper for a court to depart from *stare decisis,* we scarcely can perceive of a more justifiable situation in which to do so. In the first place, the rule being discarded is one lying in the field of conflict of laws as applied to torts so that there can hardly have been any action taken by the parties in reliance upon it. Secondly, strong reasons exist for supplanting such rule by a better one which does not unnecessarily discriminate against the citizens of our own state.

The most compelling argument against taking such step is that it departs from the rule of the Restatement, and disturbs the sought after ideal of establishing some uniformity in the conflict of laws field. However, as well appears from the cases hereinbefore cited, there is a clearly discernable trend away from the rule of the Restatement insofar as it requires that the law of the place of wrong is to be applied in determining questions of incapacity to sue based on family status. Furthermore, it must be recognized that, in the field of the conflict of laws, absolutes should not be made the goal at the sacrifice of progress in furtherance of sound public policy. . . .

Perhaps a word of caution should be sounded to the effect that the instant decision should not be interpreted as a rejection by this court of the general rule that ordinarily the substantive rights of parties to an action in tort are to be determined in the light of the law of the place of wrong. This decision merely holds that incapacity to sue because of marital status presents a question of family law rather than tort law. . . .

. . . While the appellant's counsel did not request that we overrule *Buckeye v. Buckeye,* and the subsequent Wisconsin cases dealing with this particular conflict of laws problem, he did specifically seek to have this court apply California's conflict of laws principle, that the law of the domicile is determinative of interspousal capacity to sue, to this particular case. However, to do so would violate the well recognized principle of conflict of laws that, where the substantive law of another state is applied, there necessarily must be excluded such foreign state's law of conflict of laws.

The reason why the authorities on conflict of laws almost universally reject the renvoi doctrine (permitting a court of the forum state to apply the conflict of laws principle of a foreign state) is that it is likely to result in the court pursuing a course equivalent to a never ending circle. For example, in the instant case, if the *Buckeye v. Buckeye* line of Wisconsin cases is to be followed, the Wisconsin court first looks to the law in California to see whether wife can sue her husband in tort. California substantive law holds that she cannot.

However, California has adopted a conflict of laws principle that holds that the law of the domicile determines such question. Applying such principle the court is referred back to Wisconsin law because Wisconsin is the state of domicile. Again the court applies Wisconsin law and, under the prior holdings of the *Buckeye v. Buckeye* line of authorities, would have to again refer to California law because such line of cases does not recognize that the law of domicile has anything to do with interspousal immunity, but holds that the law of the state of injury controls.

Wisconsin certainly should not adopt the much criticized renvoi principle in order not to overrule the *Buckeye v. Buckeye* line of cases, and still permit the plaintiff to recover. Such a result we believe would contribute far more to produce chaos in the field of conflict of laws than to overrule the *Buckeye v. Buckeye* line of cases and adopt a principle the soundness of which has been commended by so many reputable authorities.

Judgment reversed and cause remanded for further proceedings not inconsistent with this opinion.

FAIRCHILD, JUSTICE (concurring).

I concur in the reversal of the judgment, but do not find it necessary to reexamine settled Wisconsin law in order to do so. . . . It has been the rule in Wisconsin that the existence or non-existence of immunity because of family relationship is substantive and not merely procedural, and is to be determined by the law of the locus state. The law of California is that the existence or nonexistence of immunity is a substantive matter, but that it is an element of the law of status, not of tort. The tort law of California is no more concerned with immunity than is Wisconsin's. Thus it makes no difference under the facts of this case whether we look directly to the law of Wisconsin to determine that immunity is not available as a defense, or look to the law of Wisconsin only because California, having no general tort principle as to immunity, classifies immunity as a matter of status.

. . . Under the principle announced by the majority that the existence or nonexistence of immunity is a matter of status our courts must henceforth recognize immunity as a defense where the alleged tort occurred in Wisconsin, but the parties are married and are domiciled in an immunity state. This would mean that such an act is or is not a remedial wrong depending upon the state where the parties happen to be domiciled.

The determination of domicil is not always easy, yet the courts will henceforth be required to determine it in many cases where it has heretofore been considered immaterial. A good many married couples who may have domicil in other states are in Wisconsin for extended periods. Some for example, are students at colleges and universities, some stationed here for military duty, some temporarily assigned here by employers, and some vacationing. Under the rule abandoned by the majority, a tortious act done in Wisconsin by a non-resident and injuring his spouse gave rise to the same civil liability as if done by a permanent resident . . .

In summary, I would dispose of the present case upon the theory that California law governs the existence of the alleged cause of action and that in California the immunity question can not be decided by resort to the law of torts but rather the law of status. I would leave to a later case the consideration of whether the Wisconsin rule of choice of law as to the defense of family immunity should remain as heretofore or, if it is to be changed, which rule will be best.

I am authorized to state that MR. JUSTICE BROWN concurs in this opinion.

---

## NOTES AND QUESTIONS ON *HAUMSCHILD* AND ESCAPE FROM THE LAW OF THE PLACE OF INJURY

(1) *The Desire for Escape*: *Why?* One reason that *Haumschild* is so remarkable is that it overruled *Buckeye v. Buckeye,* the leading First Restatement authority on interspousal tort immunity. Besides enjoying a twenty-eight year reign at home, *Buckeye* was followed in six other jurisdictions. *See* Moffatt; Hancock, *The Rise and Fall of Buckeye v. Buckeye,* 1931-1959: *Marital Immunity for Torts in Conflict of Laws,* 42 U. CHI. L. REV. 237 (1962).

Before considering *how* the *Haumschild* court escaped the law of the place of injury, it is worthwhile to consider *why* it might have found the result of the place-of-injury rule so undesirable as to justify overruling a homegrown conflicts landmark. First, consider the merits of the two competing tort rules: Is spousal immunity the wave of the future or an outmoded relic of a common law system that treated a man and his wife as a single person? Another important consideration is the real alignment of the parties and issues. Is the case really a suit by the wife against the husband to establish fault, or is it rather a claim for compensation by the couple against the husband's insurer? Finally, consider the parties' expectations: Did Mrs. Haumschild believe that her ability to obtain compensation from her husband's insurer would vary depending upon what state they happened to be driving through?

(2) *The Means to Escape: How?* The court made good its escape by recharacterizing the issue. Dissatisfied with the result produced by the place-of-injury rule, the court changed the classification of the immunity issue from tort law to family law, and thus exchanged the law of the place of injury for the more palatable law of the marital domicile.

> The reasoning of the court may be described as "characterization" or "classificatory." The choice was considered to be one between tort law and family law. The policies of interspousal immunity were used to classify the immunity rule rather than to justify the result. The specific law-fact pattern did not appear in the formulation of the rule. The court established . . . a [new] jurisdiction-selecting rule.

Jayne, *Interspousal Immunity: Revolution and Counterrevolution in American Tort Conflicts,* 40 S. CAL. L. REV. 307, 327 (1967).[*]

Of course, the structure of the First Restatement favors this maneuver; a system composed of a few single-contact jurisdiction selecting rules, each governing one whole legal subject area, makes labeling the all important exercise.

---

[*] Reprinted with permission of Southern California Law Review.

This sort of decision procedure also means that often the reasons for the court's decision will diverge from the reasons given in the opinion. The "why," in other words, often will differ from the "how." Why is that so bad? How does it affect the ability of the bar to predict the future course of decision by examining the opinions in decided cases?

(3) *Where to Escape to: Another Jurisdiction-Selecting Rule?* Another difficulty with re-characterization, inherent in the structure of the First Restatement, is that it can result only in the application of a different First Restatement rule. Because all of these are broad, jurisdiction-selecting rules, there is always the strong possibility that the new rule (the result of the re-characterization) will produce questionable results in future cases.

*Haumschild* is a perfect example: The court re-characterized interspousal immunity from tort to domestic relations and thus switched from the law of the place of injury to the law of the couple's domicile. Unfortunately, the next Wisconsin case showed the inherent difficulty of a simple switch from one overbroad rule to another. Husband and wife, domiciliaries of Illinois, an immunity state, collided in Wisconsin with a car driven by defendant, a Wisconsin domiciliary. Wife sued the defendant who then impleaded the husband for contribution. Relying on the domicile rule of *Haumschild,* the Supreme Court of Wisconsin applied the Illinois immunity law and affirmed the dismissal of the impleader action. If the husband was immune from tort liability to his wife, he was similarly immune from the defendant's derivative claim for contribution. *Haynie v. Hanson* 16 Wis. 2d 299, 114 N.W.2d 443 (1962). The result was that the defendant was left holding the bag. He had argued that Wisconsin public policy and substantial justice required a different result, but the court was not impressed:

> The questions of public policy and substantial justice which have been raised by the appellants were fully considered in the *Haumschild* case, and we find no compelling basis for retreat. If the appellants' position were adopted it would mean that Mrs. Haynie could not sue her husband in her own state of Illinois, but she could do so in Wisconsin. It is the law of the domicile which should be applied to resolve the issue of immunities from suit which are based upon family relationships.

After reading *Haumschild* and *Haynie,* are you beginning to suspect that re-characterization is too blunt a tool for the job of seeking conflicts justice? Do you have an alternative suggestion? Post script: Eventually, the Wisconsin Supreme Court saw the light and overruled *Haynie* in *Zelinger v. State Sand and Gravel Co.,* 38 Wis. 2d 98, 156 N.W.2d 466 (1968).

(4) *One View of Characterization.* Does the following quotation capture the essence of the characterization problem: "Characterization encourages *reflexive,* mechanical choices rather than *reflective* inquiry into the reasons why a particular result is proper." WILLIAM RICHMAN & WILLIAM REYNOLDS, UNDERSTANDING CONFLICT OF LAWS § 57 (3d ed. 2002). *See also* Douglass Rendleman, *McMillan v. McMillan: Choice of Law in a Sinkhole,* 67 VA. L. REV. 315, 318 (1981).

## § 4.12   Depeçage

## CORPORATION VENEZOLANA DE FOMENTO v. VINTERO SALES CORP.

*United States Court of Appeals for the Second Circuit*
*629 F.2d 786 (1980)*

LUMBARD, CIRCUIT JUDGE. This appeal presents a complex of legal issues arising out of the default by Venezolana de Cruceros del Caribe, C.A., ("Cariven") a Venezuelan corporation, on notes issued by it and guaranteed by Corporacion Venezolana de Fomento, ("CVF"), a Venezuelan governmental entity, and purchased by The Merban Corporation ("Merban"), a Swiss corporation, and later resold in part to various United States and Canadian banks, who became intervenors in this action. CVF alleged in its complaint filed in the Southern District of New York that the guarantees were void both because CVF had never approved them and because CVF had been fraudulently induced to guarantee the notes by Vintero Sales Corporation and Vintero Corporation, both New York Corporations, by Vincent A. DeLyra, a United States citizen and principal in the Vintero companies (all parties to this action, and hereinafter collectively described as "the DeLyra interests"), and by Merban and several of Merban's officers. CVF appeals from the decision of the district court, Sweet, J., rejecting CVFs claims of non-approval and fraud, rendering judgment for Merban on its counterclaims to recover on the guarantees, and from the district court's supplemental opinion finding that it had subject matter jurisdiction, 477 F. Supp. 615 (S.D.N.Y. 1979). We affirm this portion of the district court's decision, but reverse and remand insofar as the judgment and opinion below absolves the DeLyra interests of actionable fraud . . . .

[T]he District Court had jurisdiction under the Edge Act, 12 U.S.C. § 632 . . . .

The ground for our reversal is that Judge Sweet applied the wrong law. Certain aspects of this transaction, such as the sufficiency of the [Venezuela] Comptroller General's approval [of the guarantees], are governed by New York law. This does not mean, as the district court apparently assumed, that New York law governs related issues, such as CVF's allegation that it was defrauded by the DeLyra interests. Using the choice of law technique of *depeçage,* [8] a court may—and in this case we think should have—separated this part of this case into two different portions for choice of law purposes. The first portion is the question of what law to apply to the question of the sufficiency of the Comptroller General's telegram as an approval under the Loan Agreements. Since there are enough contacts with New York to validate

---

[8] Depeçage occurs where the rules of one legal system are applied to regulate certain issues arising from a given transaction or occurrence, while those of another system regulate the other issues. The technique permits a more nuanced handling of certain multistate Situations and thus forwards the policy of aptness. *See generally* Reese, *depeçage. A Common Phenomenon in Choice of Law,* 73 COLUM. L. REV. 58 (1973). von Mehren, *Special Substantive Rules for Multistate Problems: Their Role and Significance in contemporary Choice of Law Methodology,* 88 HARV. L. REV. 347 (1974). *See also Pearson v. Northeast Airlines, Inc.,* 309 F.2d 553 (2d Cir. 1962) (en banc).

the parties' choice of New York law as governing under any choice of law analysis, we need not reach the question of what jurisdiction's law would be applied if a serious challenge to the parties' ability to choose New York law could be mounted.[*] Analysis is more difficult with respect to choice of law for the CVF-DeLyra fraud issues. Were this a diversity case, *Klaxon Co. v. Stentor Elec. Mfg. Co., Inc.*, 313 U.S. 487 (1941), would require that we look to the choice of law doctrines of the forum state. This is a federal question case, however, and it is appropriate that we apply a federal common law choice of law rule in order to decide which of the concerned jurisdiction's substantive law of fraud (ie., that of New York or that of Venezuela) should govern. The use of federal common law in specialized areas where jurisdiction is not based on diversity has been sanctioned by the Supreme Court since the day Erie was decided, see *Hinderlider v. LaPlata River Co.*, 304 U.S. 92 (1938); and the availability of a federal choice of law rule in a case like this, where jurisdiction is based on a statute meant to give a federal forum to nationally chartered banks, is supported by *Clearfield Trust Co. v. United States*, 318 U.S. 363 (1943).

In this case we think that the question of whether or not CVF was defrauded by the DeLyra interests is one best resolved under Venezuelan law. Unlike the validity of the guarantees, the resolution of this question has no repercussions in the world of international commercial transactions. It involves no choice of law decision made by the parties. Instead, it calls for a determination whether or not a Venezuelan corporation, Cariven (or its two principals, one of whom, Gascue, is Venezuelan) defrauded a second Venezuelan corporation, CVF, in Venezuela. The alleged fraud, moreover, concerned acts that were to take place in Venezuela and be of Venezuelan legal significance (*e.g.*, the increased capital contributions, the Ministry of Communications approval, and the securing of a "prenda naval", a civil law ship mortgage). Such allegations, in our view, should be evaluated under Venezuelan rather than New York law.

Because the district court thought that the fraud claim against the DeLyra interests was governed by New York law insofar as CVF sought to impose liability on the DeLyra interests in addition to negating CVFs guarantees, the district court did not resolve certain questions of fact and law (such as DeLyra's possible personal liability under the CVF-Cariven indemnity contract, and the sufficiency of proof of fraud under Venezuelan law). Accordingly, we direct a remand for the consideration of these and other issues connected with the resolution of CVFs claim of fraud against the DeLyra interests.

*Affirmed in part, reversed in part,*

*and remanded.*

---

[*] There were two loan agreements. The first expressly provided for application of New York law, and the court found the second one did so implicitly. —*Eds.*

---

## NOTES AND QUESTIONS ON *VINTERO*

(1) *Depeçage.* When a court applies the law of more than one jurisdiction to a case it is engaged in depeçage (from the French "depeçer," meaning "to dissect" or "to take to pieces"). The use of depeçage, to quote from the title of Professor Reese's article referred to in footnote 8 of *Vintero,* is a "common phenomenon."

Although analysis under the First Conflicts Restatement led to the selection of a jurisdiction whose law would determine the outcome of a case, depeçage was probably used in virtually every case in which a foreign law was chosen. Can you think of why that is? Consider an automobile accident which occurred outside of the forum; the court would apply the law of the place of the wrong, of course, but only to "substantive" issues. The forum, however, would still apply its own law to "procedural" issues. Occasionally, the First Restatement permitted depeçage in other settings; there is a dual reference in contract cases, for example, to the law of the place of making for formation problems and to the law of the place of performance for performance issues. *See* RESTATEMENT (FIRST) OF CONFLICT OF LAWS § 322, comment a.

(2) *A "Hybrid Camel."* Depeçage clearly is sensible in the ordinary case where foreign substantive law is applied. Certainly, there is every reason to apply the forum's procedural law to "non-substantive" issues. But depeçage can also be used as an escape device; and, like the other escape devices, it can be abused. Consider *Maryland Casualty Co. v. Jacek,* 156 F. Supp. 43 (D.N.J. 1957). There, a New Jersey couple had an automobile accident in New York. A suit between spouses could be maintained in New York, but not in New Jersey. On the other hand, New York law required an insurance carrier to pay liability arising from a suit between spouses only if the insurance policy expressly provided for that result. Using a vested rights approach, the New Jersey court characterized the immunity issue as a "tort" and controlled, therefore, by New York law (the accident site); and characterized the meaning of the insurance contract as a contract and, therefore, controlled by New Jersey law (where the contract was made). The end result was that the insurance company was liable.

What result would have been reached if the case had been decided using only New York or only New Jersey law? Does that answer help you understand why one commentator called the result "grotesque"? Comment, *False Conflicts,* 55 CALIF. L. REV. 74, 114 (1967). Professor Reese, however, liked *Jacek.* Willis L. M. Reese, *Depeçage: A Common Phenomenon in Choice of Law,* 73 COLUM. L. REV. 58, 67-68 (1973). Compare Brainerd Currie's observation about depeçage: "It is one thing to fall between two stools; it is quite another to put together half a donkey and half a camel; and then ride to victory on the synthetic hybrid." *Quoted* in DAVID CAVERS, THE CHOICE-OF-LAW PROCESS 39 (1965).

*See* PROBLEM 4C-7. APPLYING THE LAW OF DIFFERENT STATES?

(3) *The Vintero Decision. Vintero* represents a modern use of depeçage. The application of both New York and federal common law is most unusual; do you understand why the court chose those two laws and why it applied them to two different problems? The problem of contract choice-of-law clauses is discussed in more detail in § 4.30, *infra;* federal common law is discussed in Chapter 6, *infra.*

## § 4.13 Renvoi

### IN RE SCHNEIDER'S ESTATE

*New York Surrogate's Court, New York County*
*96 N.Y.S.2d 652 (1950)*

FRANKENTHALER, SURROGATE. This case presents a novel question in this State in the realm of the conflict of laws. Deceased, a naturalized American citizen of Swiss origin, died domiciled in New York County, leaving as an asset of his estate certain real property located in Switzerland. In his will he attempted to dispose of his property, including the parcel of Swiss realty, in a manner which is said to be contrary to the provisions of Swiss internal law. That law confers upon one's legitimate heirs a so called legitime, *i.e.,* a right to specified fractions of a decedent's property, which right cannot be divested by testamentary act. The precise issue, therefore, is whether this deceased had the power to dispose of the realty in the manner here attempted.

Ordinarily, the courts of a country not the situs of an immovable are without jurisdiction to adjudicate questions pertaining to the ownership of that property. Actions concerning realty are properly litigable only before the courts of the situs. However, in this case the administratrix appointed prior to the probate of the will has liquidated the foreign realty and transmitted the proceeds to this State. She is now accounting for the assets of the estate including the fund representing that realty. As a consequence this court is called upon to direct the administration and distribution of the substituted fund and to determine the property rights therein. In doing so, however, reference must be made to the law of the situs, as the question of whether the fund shall be distributed to the devisee of the realty under the terms of the will is dependent upon the validity of the original devise thereof which must be determined under the law of the situs of the land itself.

The court is confronted at the outset with a preliminary question as to the meaning of the term "law of the situs"—whether it means only the internal or municipal law of the country in which the property is situated or whether it also includes the conflict of laws rules to which the courts of that jurisdiction would resort in making the same determination. If the latter is the proper construction to be placed upon that term, then this court must, in effect, place itself in the position of the foreign court and decide the matter as would that court in an identical case.

The meaning of the term "law of the situs" can be ascertained best from a consideration of the reasons underlying the existence of the rule which requires the application thereof. The primary reason for its existence lies in the fact that the law-making and law-enforcing agencies of the country in which land is situated have exclusive control over such land. As only the courts of that country are ultimately capable of rendering enforceable judgments affecting the land, the legislative authorities thereof have the exclusive power to promulgate the law which shall regulate its ownership and transfer. When the land itself formed the estate asset upon which the will was intended to operate, the power of the sovereign to enforce such laws created rights therein between the parties in interest. If an instrument which was intended to transfer that land did not meet the standards set by that law or violated some provision thereof regarding the land, the courts had the physical power to deny it effect and enforce instead the rights decreed by the law of that country or the law of any other country which the law-making agencies deemed appropriate in a particular case.

Hence, the rights which were created in that land are those which existed under the whole law of the situs and as would be enforced by those courts which normally would possess exclusive judicial jurisdiction. Erwin Griswold, *Renvoi Revisited,* 51 HARVARD L. R. 1165, 1186 [1939]; *cf* Schreiber, *The Doctrine of Renvoi in Anglo-American Law,* 31 HARVARD L. R. 5231 559 [1918]. If another court, in this case our own, is thrust into a position where it is obliged to adjudicate the same questions concerning title to that land, or a substitute therefor, it should be guided by the methods which would be employed in the country of situs. The purely fortuitous transfer of the problem to the courts of another state by virtue of a postmortuary conversion of the land, effected for the purpose of administering the entire estate in the country of domicile, ought not to alter the character of the legal relations which existed with respect to the land at the date of death and which continued to exist until its sale. Consequently, this court, in making a determination of ownership, must ascertain the body of local law to which the courts of the situs would refer if the matter were brought before them.

It has been urged, however, that a reference to the conflict of laws rules of the situs may involve an application of the principle of renvoi, and if so, it would place the court in a perpetually-enclosed circle from which it could never emerge and that it would never find a suitable body of substantive rules to apply to the particular case. This objection is based upon the assumption that if the forum: must look to the whole law of the situs, and that law refers the matter to the law of the domicile, this latter reference must be considered to be the whole law of the latter country also, which would refer the matter back to the law of the situs, which process would continue without end. That reasoning is based upon a false premise, for as has been said by Dean Griswold, *Renvoi Revisited,* "Recognition of the foreign conflict of laws rule will not lead us into an endless-chain of references if it is clear for any reason that the particular foreign conflicts rules (or any rule along the line of reference) is one which refers to the internal law alone . . . ."

The precise question here considered, namely whether there shall be a reference to the entire law of the situs to determine the ownership of the proceeds of foreign realty, is one of first impression in this State. Nevertheless, the above stated principles, together with the rule enunciated in the Restatement of the Conflict of Laws, in the English authorities on the subject and in analogous cases in courts of this State and others require us to accept it as a part of our law and to hold that a reference to the law of the situs necessarily entails a reference to the whole law of that country, including its conflict of laws rules.

The rule as formulated in the Restatement is as follows:

"Section 8. Rule in questions of title to land or divorce. (1) All questions of title to land are decided in accordance with the law of the state where the land is, including the Conflict of Laws rules of that State. (2) All questions concerning the validity of a decree of divorce are decided in accordance with the law of the domicile of the parties, including the Conflict of Laws rules of that State."

In all other cases the Restatement rejects the renvoi principle and provides that where a reference is made to foreign law that law should be held to mean only the internal law of the foreign country . . . .

Concerning the actual content of Swiss law, the expert witnesses summoned by the respective parties are in agreement that the Swiss internal law would apply to the real and personal estate of a Swiss citizen domiciled in Switzerland, and that the laws of the country of domicile would, under the Swiss theory of unity of succession, apply to all of the Swiss property belonging to a foreign national.

The experts disagreed, however, upon the ultimate question in this case, i.e., the Swiss rule applicable to the distribution of the Swiss realty of a person of hybrid nationality domiciled not in Switzerland but in the country of his second citizenship. Under Swiss law the decedent herein was vested with dual nationality. The law of that country provides that a citizen, in order to divest himself of the cloak of citizenship must formally renounce his allegiance in the manner prescribed by statute. Such formal Act of renunciation was not performed by the decedent. The assumption of a new allegiance by naturalization in the United States did not of itself suffice to free him of fealty to Switzerland. In such event, he became a person of twin or dual citizenship, a status which is recognized under Swiss law.

The court has carefully examined the authorities and materials submitted by the experts and has formed its conclusion upon the basis of those authorities. None of the cases submitted involved the precise facts here presented. They rather present guides, signs and close analogies. From these indicia, however, the court concludes that the Swiss law would refer a matter such as this to the New York internal law, under which law the will is a valid disposition of the testator's property. The testamentary power of this decedent would not be curtailed by the *legitime*.

The language in the Swiss cases, most of which pertain only to the question of the jurisdiction of courts, indicated that the place in which "property is situated," as referred to in the [Swiss-American] Treaty, means, in the case of foreign domiciliaries, the country of domicile, upon the Swiss legal fiction that a decedent's entire estate follows his person and is located at his domicile. Such a rule amounts to a statement that the place of actual location of property (Switzerland) refers all questions to the law of the place of presumed location, i.e., the country of domicile. The Swiss courts treat the reference to its own law as a reference to its own conflict of law rules and policies concerning the devolution of estates of foreigners.

In the case of one who is of both Swiss and American nationality, but who is not a Swiss domiciliary, it appears that the same rule applies; domicile is controlling and its laws provide the substantive rules of decision . . . .

Consequently, the court holds that the testamentary plan envisaged by the testator and set out in his will is valid, even in its application to the Swiss realty. The proceeds of that realty must therefore be distributed pursuant to the directions contained in the will . . . .

## NOTES AND QUESTIONS ON RENVOI

(1) *The Decision.* The situation in *Schneider* was unusual because normally the proper disposition of the Swiss land could have been determined only by a Swiss court. But the administrator had sold the property and the proceeds were in New York awaiting distribution; hence the dilemma. The court believed that happenstance (that the proceeds from the sale of the property were now in New York) should not affect its analysis. Do you agree?

Having determined that situs law must apply, the court then had to define "law of the situs"—does that phrase refer to the "whole law" or "internal law" only? The court answered that question by referring to the exclusive power of Swiss courts over Swiss land, a reference which led to the conclusion that "the rights which were created in that land are those which existed under the whole law of the situs . . . ." Do you find that logic compelling?

Next, the *Schneider* court had to figure out what a Swiss court would do, a task which required analysis of "guides, signs, and close analogies." Those rather vague "indicia" referred the court back to New York internal law, where, of course, the court could have started. Was the long trek worth it?

Finally, what of the court's confidence that it could escape from the endless circle which the use of renvoi could create? If the only "indicia" as to how to break out of the circle are guides, signs and close analysis," how likely is it that the court can locate the right place to break from the circle—or even that there *is* a right place? (What if Swiss law, for example, also includes the doctrine of renvoi?) Renvoi, in other words, may permit an escape in *Schneider* from the *lex sitae,* but is its use cabined by *any* standard?

*See* PROBLEMS 4C-8. FROM ENGLAND TO FRANCE TO ENGLAND AND BACK?; 4C-9. FROM TINYER TO EVERS TO CHANCE I, II, AND III.

(2) *Renvoi in Land Cases.* Although traditionalist courts made some use of renvoi as an escape device (albeit sparingly) in torts and contracts cases, they did so without the authorization of the Restatement. The First Restatement is generally hostile toward renvoi, approving of the concept only for questions of title to land and the validity of a decree of divorce. RESTATEMENT (FIRST) OF CONFLICT OF LAWS §§ 7 and 8 (1934). Traditionalist scholars were similarly skeptical. JOSEPH BEALE, CONFLICT OF LAWS 55-58 (1935); HERBERT GOODRICH, CONFLICT OF LAWS § 10 (1927). In contrast, renvoi is an explicit part

of the Restatement's property provisions. Section 8 provides that "all questions of title to land are decided in accordance with the law of the state where the land is, including the Conflict of Laws rules of that state." The reason for the Restatement's view on renvoi in property cases harks back to the power argument for the situs rule. In Beale's words, it is "essential to the protection of the interests of all parties that . . . a title should be determined everywhere as the state of situs would determine it since that state alone must have final authority." 1 JOSEPH BEALE, THE CONFLICT OF LAWS 57 (1935). Why is that?

(3) *Renvoi: Escape from the Place of Injury.* Despite theoretical disapproval, courts which purported to follow the First Restatement occasionally used renvoi as an escape device in non-land cases. If the court could not live with the results of applying the law of the place of injury, it could read the word "law" to refer to the whole law of that state, including its choice-of-law rules, which might in turn refer to the law of some other state, perhaps the forum. An example is provided by Justice Fairchild's concurring opinion in *Haumschild,* § 4.11[F]*supra.* He proposed to treat the problem of interspousal immunity as one sounding in tort, leading to the application of California law. But because California would treat the problem as one involving "status," the issue would be resolved under the law of Wisconsin, the marital domicile.

Usually renvoi was futile in tort cases, however, because most American states applied the place of injury rule, and renvoi does not provide an escape from the vested rights result if both states have identical choice-of-law rules. It could have worked in *Haumschild* because, although both states used the place of injury rule, they used different characterizations of the spousal immunity issue.

(4) *Renvoi: Escape from the Place of Making.* The Restatement did not approve of renvoi in contract cases either (*see* § 7); nevertheless, traditionalist courts occasionally resorted to the concept to escape the place of making rule. In *University of Chicago v. Dater,* 277 Mich. 658, 270 N.W. 175 (1936), defendant, a married woman, and her husband executed a note in Michigan and mailed it to the lender in Illinois. The lender made the loan by check delivered to defendant and her husband in Chicago. The husband later died, the defendant defaulted, and the lender sued her in Michigan. Under Michigan law, defendant had no contractual capacity; under Illinois law she did. Both jurisdictions used the place-of-contracting rule; and that circumstance would ordinarily preclude an escape via renvoi. Illinois and Michigan, however, interpreted the rule differently. Michigan law held the place of contracting to be the place where the loan was actually made (Illinois), while Illinois had held in *Burr v. Beckler,* 264 Ill. 230, 106 N.E. 206 (1915), that the place of making was the place where the note was executed (Michigan). The Supreme Court of Michigan was able to use the *Burr* holding to escape the result of its own "law of the place of contracting" rule by interpreting the law of Illinois to include Illinois' choice-of-law rules which, as interpreted in *Burr,* selected Michigan law.

Does the use of renvoi in *Dater* make sense according to the justifications for renvoi advanced in *Schneider?* If not, might it be justified on the ground that the *Burr* case shows that Illinois had no interest in having its contractual capacity rule applied to the defendant? *See* Erwin Griswold, *Renvoi Revisited,*

51 HARV. L. REV. 1165, 1207-1208 (1938). If, instead, the Michigan court was simply using renvoi cynically as an escape device, what was its real motivation?

*See* PROBLEM 4C-10. A WIFE'S CAPACITY.

(5) *Renvoi Today.* The Second Restatement of Conflicts has little more use for renvoi than did its predecessor. Section 8 provides that renvoi should be used "When the objective of the particular choice-of-law rule is that the forum reach the same result on the very facts involved as would the courts of another state . . . ." Comment *h* explains:

> In at least two situations, the purpose underlying the forum's choice-of-law rule will be that the forum should reach the same result on the very facts involved as would the courts of the other state. This will usually be so when the other state clearly has the dominant interest in the issue to be decided and its interest would be furthered by having the issue decided in the way that its courts would have done . . . . The second situation where the purpose underlying the choice-of-law rule of the forum will usually be attainment of the same result as would have been reached by the courts of the other state is where there is an urgent need that all states should apply a single law in resolving a certain question . . . . Primarily for these reasons, the forum will apply the choice-of-law rules of the state of the decedent's domicil at death to determine questions relating to succession to interests in movables . . . .

The Restatement gives as an instance of the first situation the not surprising example of transfer of an interest in land—where the situs has the "dominant interest" and that interest "would be furthered" by deciding the case as would the situs courts. Will the situs *always* have the greatest interest in land cases? And why succession to interests in movables is renvoi appropriate in the "second situation," succession to interests in movables at death?

The two Restatements reflect well the limited acceptance of renvoi today. Although some commentators had expected it to be used more widely, that has not happened. Typical of contemporary judicial opinions concerning renvoi is *Maroon v. State Dept. of Mental Health,* 411 N.E. 2d 404, 413 (Ind. App. 1980), where the court referred to renvoi as an "ancient, disfavored doctrine . . . [which] is not and should not become, a part of our law."[1]

On the other hand, modern forms of choice-of-law analysis, which emphasize a state's interest in a problem, see Part H *infra,* should be receptive to renvoi: If a state is willing to refer the problem to the law of another jurisdiction, that shows that the first state lacks an "interest" in the problem and its law should not be applied. That is exactly the approach that was taken by the Maryland court in the *ARTRA* decision.

See PROBLEM 4C-11. THE TRUCK STOP.

---

[1] Because some provisions of the Uniform Commercial Code refer choice-of-law problems to the whole law of a jurisdiction, renvoi remains a possibility in certain commercial matters. *See, e.g.,* Schipani, *The Lender's Dilemma: National and International Automated Data Complications in Perfecting a Security Interest in Accounts,* 22 N. ENG. L. REV. 273 291-92 n. 69.

(6) *The Federal Tort Claims Act.* There is one common use of renvoi today. The Federal Tort Claims Act, 28 U.S.C.§ 1346(b), provides that the United States shall be liable "under circumstances where . . . a private person would be liable in accordance with the law of the place where the act or omission occurred." In *Richards v. United States,* 369 U.S. 1 (1962), the Court held that the whole law of the place of injury must be applied to a claim brought under the Act. The Court reasoned that only in that way could the same result be reached in cases where the United States was a defendant and in cases where the defendant is a private person. Uniformity in other words, required renvoi. Do you agree?

## AMERICAN MOTORISTS INSURANCE CO. v. ARTRA GROUP, INC.

*Court of Appeals of Maryland*
*338 Md. 560, 659 A.2d 1295 (1995)*

CHASANOW, Judge.

[The case involved a suit brought by ARTRA against an insurance company, American Motorists. ARTRA had brought suit against another company which had an insurance policy with the defendant covering pollution. The question was whether the policy protected a buyer such as ARTRA.]

\*    \*    \*

American Motorists's first suggestion is that we recognize that the rule of lex loci contractus is antiquated and should be abandoned in favor of some form of the more modern approaches to choice of law such as the one advocated by RESTATEMENT (SECOND) CONFLICT OF LAWS . . . American Motorists's second suggestion is that we engraft the doctrine of renvoi to our body of conflict of law rules. We need not determine today how far we should go in incorporating the doctrine of renvoi, but we do adopt a limited form of renvoi which will direct the application of Maryland law to resolve the substantive issues in the instant case.

[The Court first discussed whether it would abandon the lex loci contractus rule]. Absent a choice-of-law provision in the contract, our courts have applied the rule of lex loci contractus to matters regarding the validity and interpretation of contract provisions. We have recognized an exception to the application of lex loci contractus when application of a foreign jurisdiction's law would be contrary to a strong public policy of this State, but we do not find this exception applicable to the facts of the instant case.; Although American Motorists asks us to abandon our adherence to lex loci contractus, we need not consider such a sweeping change, for we adopt a limited application of renvoi which permits us to apply Maryland law where the application of lex loci contractus indicates that the foreign jurisdiction would apply Maryland law to the substantive issues of the controversy.

## RENVOI

The doctrine of renvoi is basically that, when the forum court's choice-of-law rules would apply the substantive law of a foreign jurisdiction to the case before the forum court, the forum court may apply the whole body of the foreign jurisdiction's substantive law including the foreign jurisdiction's choice-of-law rules. If, in applying renvoi principles, the foreign jurisdiction's conflict of law rules would apply the forum's law, this reference back of the forum to its own laws is called a remission. That is what is involved in the instant case . . . . It has been suggested that renvoi could have the danger of creating an endless cycle. In the instant case, Maryland choice-of-law rules apply the doctrine of lex loci contractus and, pursuant thereto, apply Illinois law. In applying Illinois law, we also adopt Illinois choice of law, which would apply Maryland law, which applies Illinois law, and back and forth. What breaks the endless cycle? As shall be seen, we adopt a limited form of renvoi in the instant case that does not have the endless cycle.

Where the forum would apply the law of the foreign jurisdiction and the foreign jurisdiction would apply the law of the forum, it would seem that the balance should tip in favor of the jurisdiction with the most significant contacts or, if not to the jurisdiction with the most significant contacts, then for ease of application and to prevent forum shopping, the law of the forum should be applied. In the instant case, Maryland is apparently the jurisdiction with the most significant contacts as well as the forum. Maryland courts should, in applying Illinois law, apply Illinois' most significant relationship choice-of-law rule and follow the law an Illinois court would follow if the case was instituted in Illinois—Maryland law. Thus, whether suit was filed in Maryland or Illinois, Maryland law would govern the contract . . . .

It is axiomatic that Maryland law is Maryland law because our courts and legislature believe the rules of substantive law we apply are the best of the available alternatives. From this fundamental principle, it is safe to assume our courts would prefer to follow Maryland law unless there is some good reason why Maryland law should yield to the law of a foreign jurisdiction. Our own substantive law is not only more familiar to and easier for Maryland judges to apply, but there has been a legislative or judicial determination that it is preferable to the available alternatives. Sometimes, however, there are good reasons why our courts should, and do, apply the law of a foreign jurisdiction. First, if Maryland does not defer to other states when they have a significant interest, they might not defer to Maryland when we have a significant interest. Second, we should discourage forum shopping and strive for some uniformity and predictability in resolving conflict of law issues regardless of where suit is filed. For simplicity, predictability, and uniformity in contract law, Maryland courts have, as have a majority of other state courts, followed the rule of lex loci contractus and have applied the substantive law of the place of contracting. In declining to apply Maryland law to a contract made in another state, we do so not because we deem the law of the other state preferable to Maryland law, but because our preference for Maryland law is outweighed by considerations of simplicity, predictability and uniformity. Where, however, the place of contracting applies Maryland law, then simplicity, predictability, and uniformity would be better achieved if Maryland courts followed the conflict of law rule of the place of contracting and apply Maryland law. In that case, there would be uniformity in choice of law regardless of in which jurisdiction suit was filed, and where, as in the instant case, suit was filed in Maryland, then Maryland courts would be applying Maryland law.

The limited renvoi exception which we adopt today will allow Maryland courts to avoid the irony of applying the law of a foreign jurisdiction when that jurisdiction's conflict of law rules would apply Maryland law. Under this exception, Maryland courts should apply Maryland substantive law to contracts entered into in foreign states' jurisdictions in spite of the doctrine of lex loci contractus when:

> 1) Maryland has the most significant relationship, or, at least, a substantial relationship with respect to the contract issue presented; and

> 2) The state where the contract was entered into would not apply its own substantive law, but instead would apply Maryland substantive law to the issue before the court.

Our holding that Maryland's adherence to lex loci contractus must yield to a test such as RESTATEMENT (SECOND) CONFLICT OF LAWS § 188 when the place of contracting would apply Maryland law pursuant to that test is not a total jettisoning of lex loci contractus.

Our case law gives some indication that our courts can give flexibility to our traditional choice-of-law rules. Perhaps some movement away from rigidly following the rule of lex loci contractus is indicated by our adopting RESTATEMENT (SECOND) CONFLICT OF LAWS § 187 and giving deference to the contracting parties' choice of applicable law. We are not yet, however, ready to jettison lex loci contractus except in those instances already noted. Lex loci contractus is still the law in the majority of jurisdictions, although there is a significant modern erosion of the rule. If that erosion continues, however, this Court may, in the proper case, have to reevaluate what the best choice-of-law rules ought to be to achieve simplicity, predictability, and uniformity.

## II.

[In the second part of the decision, the Court of Appeals considered various aspects of the insurance policies and contract interpretation. Considering the case in light of the tort suit against Sherwin-Williams and other evidence extrinsic to the case at bar, the court determined that the insurer had not duty to defend or indemnify ARTRA under the exclusionary clauses in the policy that are given effect under Maryland law].

RAKER, J., dissenting:

[Judge Raker's pithy dissent captured her exasperation with the court's seeming abandonment of the *lex locus contractus* rule. She captured that feeling in her lengthy quotation from a poem by Professor McLaughlin, only a part of which is here reproduced.]

### CONFLICT OF LAWS

> CONFLICT OF LAWS with its peppery seasoning,
> Of pliable, scarcely reliable reasoning,
> Dealing with weird and impossible things,

Such as marriage and domicil, bastards and kings,
All about courts without jurisdiction,
Handing out misery, pain and affliction,
Making defendant, for reasons confusing,
Unfounded, ill-grounded, but always amusing
Liable one place but not in another
Son of his father, but not of his mother,
Married in Sweden, but only a lover in
Pious dominions of Great Britain's sovereign.
Blithely upsetting all we've been taught,
Rendering futile our methods of thought,
Till Reason, tottering down from her throne,
And Common Sense, sitting, neglected, alone,

Give us once more our legitimate status.
Ah, Students, bewildered, don't grasp at such straws,
But join in the chorus of Conflict of Laws.

### Chorus

Beale, Beale, wonderful Beale,
Not even in verse can we tell how we feel,
When our efforts so strenuous,
To over-throw,
Your reasoning tenuous,
Simply won't go.
For the law is a system of
Wheels within wheels
Invented by Sayres and Thayers and Beales
With each little wheel
So exactly adjusted,
That if it goes haywire
The whole thing is busted.
So Hail to Profanity,
Goodbye to Sanity, lost if you stop to consider or pause,
On with the frantic, romantic, pedantic,
Effusive, abusive, illusive, conclusive,
Evasive, persuasive Conflict of Laws.

* * *

James McLaughlin, Conflict of Laws: *The New Approach to Choice of Law: Justice in Search of Certainty, Part Two,* 94 W. VA.L. REV. 73, 108 n. 65 (1991).

Today, the majority fails to shed new "light" on the murky maze of Conflict of Laws. Instead, in an unwarranted departure from the bedrock of Maryland choice of law in contract cases—lex loci contractus—the majority adopts a "limited renvoi exception." In so doing, it unwisely qualifies a solid, predictable rule in favor of the often criticized and rejected doctrine of renvoi. In my view, it makes no "sense" in the instant case to curtail Maryland's well-established rule . . . .

I believe that today's decision will lead to uncertainty, confusion, and unpredictability. Accordingly, I respectfully dissent.

## NOTES AND COMMENTS ON *ARTRA*

1. *Renvoi and the Modernists.* Advocates of policy-based choice-of-law analysis had looked to renvoi as a possible solution to the deadlock Currie saw in the case of a true conflict. To illustrate with ARTRA, if Illinois would apply Maryland law to resolve the alleged conflict, then Illinois policy will not be compromised by a Maryland court's choice of Maryland law. An apparent true conflict has been changed—through the alchemy of renvoi—into a false conflict. Explicit use of renvoi, however, in policy analysis has been quite unusual, *ARTRA* itself being a rare counter-example.

2. *Renvoi and Reform.* Maryland is or at least was one of the few states that still (pretend?) to follow the traditional choice-of-law rules. Why do you think the majority did not go all of the way and adopt full-blown modern analysis? Is a partial victory better than none at all? What is the proper judicial role in such a case? By the way, if you were a lawyer in Maryland today, what advice would you give a client concerning a tort choice-of-law problem?

Is *ARTRA* a practicable halfway measure? The case itself is easy enough because Illinois law was clear enough. But what if it had not been? It is difficult enough to figure out another state's policies; how much more difficult is it to determine that state's choice-of-law rules? How long do you think the *ARTRA* halfway house will last in Maryland?

*See* PROBLEMS 4C-12. FEDERAL TORT CLAIMS ACT APPLIED; 4C-13. NO SOVEREIGNTY AND NO FAULT; 4C-14. JUDGE SCALIA'S HYPO.

## § 4.14  Public Policy

### LOUCKS v. STANDARD OIL CO. OF NEW YORK

*New York Court of Appeals*
*224 N. Y 99, 120 N.E. 198 (1918)*

CARDOZO,J. The action is brought to recover damages for injuries resulting in death. The plaintiffs are the administrators of the estate of Everett A. Loucks. Their intestate, while traveling on a highway in the state of Massachusetts, was run down and killed through the negligence of the defendant's servants then engaged in its business. He left a wife and two children, residents of New York. A statute of Massachusetts provides [for recovery for wrongful death; recovery was to be "not less than $500, nor more than $10,000, to be assessed with reference to the degree of . . . culpability. . . . "]

The question is whether a right of action under that statute may be enforced in our courts.

1. "The courts of no country execute the penal laws of another." *The Antelope,* 10 Wheat. 66. The defendant invokes that principle as applicable

here. Penal in one sense the statute indisputably is. The damages are not limited to compensation; they are proportioned to the offender's guilt. A minimum recovery of $500 is allowed in every case. But the question is not whether the statute is penal in some sense. The question is whether it is penal within the rules of private international law. A statute penal in that sense is one that awards a penalty to the state, or to a public officer in its behalf, or to a member of the public, suing in the interest of the whole community to redress a public wrong. The purpose must be, not reparation to one aggrieved, but vindication of the public justice. The Massachusetts statute has been classified in some jurisdictions as penal, and in others as remedial. . . . The courts of Massachusetts have said that the question is still an open one. No matter how they may have characterized the act as penal, they have not meant to hold that it is penal for every purpose. Even without that reservation by them, the essential purpose of the statute would be a question for our courts.

We think the better reason is with those cases which hold that the statute is not penal in the international sense. . . . It is true that the offender is punished, but the purpose of the punishment is reparation to those aggrieved by his offense. The common law did not give a cause of action to surviving relatives. In the light of modern legislation, its rule is an anachronism. Nearly everywhere, the principle is now embodied in statute that the next of kin are wronged by the killing of their kinsman. The family becomes a legal unit, invested with rights of its own, invested with an interest in the continued life of its members, much as it was in primitive law. The damages may be compensatory or punitive according to the statutory scheme. In either case the plaintiffs have a grievance above and beyond any that belongs to them as members of the body politic. They sue to redress an outrage peculiar to themselves.

We cannot fail to see in the history of the Massachusetts statutes a developing expression of this policy and purpose. The statutes have their distant beginnings in the criminal law. To some extent the vestiges of criminal forms survive. But the old forms have been filled with a new content. The purpose which informs and vitalizes them is the protection of the survivors. They are moods and phases, the particular and varying expression, of a tendency in legislation as general as the common law. They are not to be viewed in isolation, apart from the stream of events. At first, the remedy was given only when the wrongdoer was a common carrier. That statute goes back to 1840, antedating Lord Campbell's Act in England. The remedy was by indictment and fine, the fine being payable to the widow and next of kin. If there were no survivors of the prescribed class, there could be no indictment. The reason was that even then the dominant purpose was reparation to the family. But later an alternative remedy by civil action at the suit of the executor or administrator became available even against carriers. Then other statutes gave a civil remedy exclusively. Some statutes were confined to cases where the defendant was the employer of the decedent. Finally there comes one which gave a remedy against all persons who had not otherwise been made liable. The remedy is civil; it is an action of tort.

Through all this legislation there runs a common purpose. It is penal in one element and one only; the damages are punitive. The courts of

Massachusetts do not give punitive damages even for malicious torts except by force of statute. That may have led them to emphasize unduly the penal element in such recoveries. But the punishment of the wrongdoer is not designed as atonement for a crime; it is solace to the individual who has suffered a private wrong. . . . There are crosscurrents and eddies in the stream. We follow the main course. The executor or administrator who sues under this statue is not the champion of the peace and order and public justice of the commonwealth of Massachusetts. He is the representative of the outraged family. He vindicates a private right.

2. Another question remains. Even though the statute is not penal, it differs from our own. We must determine whether the difference is a sufficient reason for declining jurisdiction.

A tort committed in one state creates a right of action that may be sued upon in another unless public policy forbids. That is the generally accepted rule in the United States. The question is whether the existence of a right of action for tort under the statutes of another state is to be conditioned upon the existence of a kindred statute here. . . . No case has yet arisen in which the statutes were so dissimilar that acceptance or rejection of the rule was necessary to a decision. The time has come to re-examine its foundations.

A foreign statute is not law in this state, but it gives rise to an obligation, which, if transitory, "follows the person and may be enforced wherever the person may be found." "No law can exist as such except the law of the land; but . . . it is a principle of every civilized law that vested rights shall be protected." Beale, *supra*, § 51. The plaintiff owns something and we help him to get it. We do this unless some sound reason of public policy makes it unwise for us to lend our aid. If aid is to be withheld here, it must be because the cause of action in its nature offends our sense of justice or menaces the public welfare. Our own scheme of legislation may be different. We may even have no legislation on the subject. That is not enough to show that public policy forbids us to enforce the foreign right. A right of action is property. If a foreign statute gives the right, the mere fact that we do not give a like right is no reason for refusing to help the plaintiff in getting what belongs to him. We are not so provincial as to say that every solution of a problem is wrong because we deal with it otherwise at home. Similarity of legislation has indeed this importance; its presence shows beyond question that the foreign statute does not offend the local policy. But its absence does not prove the contrary. It is not to be exalted into an indispensable condition. The misleading word "comity" has been responsible for much of the trouble. It has been fertile in suggesting a discretion unregulated by general principles. Beale, CONFLICT OF LAWS, § 71. The sovereign in its discretion may refuse its aid to the foreign right. The courts are not free to refuse to enforce a foreign right at the pleasure of the judges, to suit the individual notion of expediency or fairness. They do not close their doors, unless help would violate some fundamental principle of justice, some prevalent conception of good morals, some deep-rooted tradition of the common weal.

This test applied, there is nothing in the Massachusetts statute that outrages the public policy of New York. We have a statute which gives a civil remedy where death is caused in our own state. We have thought it so important that we have now imbedded it in the Constitution. (Const. art. 1, § 18.) The fundamental policy is that there shall be some atonement for the wrong. Through the defendant's negligence, a resident of New York has been killed in Massachusetts He has left a widow and children, who are also residents. The law of Massachusetts gives them a recompense for his death. It cannot be that public policy forbids our courts to help in collecting what belongs to them. We cannot give them the same judgment that our law would give if the wrong had been done here. Very likely we cannot give them as much. But that is no reason for refusing to give them what we can. We shall not make things better by sending them to another state, where the defendant may not be found, and where suit may be impossible. Nor is there anything to shock our sense of justice in the possibility of a punitive recovery. The penalty is not extravagant. It conveys no hint of arbitrary confiscation. It varies between moderate limits according to the defendant's guilt. We shall not feel the pricks of conscience, if the offender pays the survivors in proportion to the measure of his offense. We have no public policy that prohibits exemplary damages or civil penalties. We give them for many wrongs. To exclude all penal actions would be to wipe out the distinction between the penalties of public justice and the remedies of private law. Finally, there are no difficulties of procedure that stand in the way. We have a statute authorizing the triers of the facts, when statutory penalties are sued for, to fit the award to the offense. The case is not one where special remedies established by the foreign law are incapable of adequate enforcement except in the home tribunals.

We hold, then, that public policy does not prohibit the assumption of jurisdiction by our courts and that this being so, mere differences of remedy do not count. For many years the courts have been feeling their way in the enforcement of these statutes. A civil remedy for another's death was something strange and new, and it did not find at once the fitting niche, the proper category, in the legal scheme. We need not be surprised, therefore, if some of the things said, as distinguished from those decided, must be rejected today. But the truth, of course, is that there is nothing sui generis about these death statutes in their relation to the general body of private international law. We must apply the same rules that are applicable to other torts; and the tendency of those rules today is toward a larger comity, if we must cling to the traditional term. The fundamental public policy is perceived to be that rights lawfully vested shall be everywhere maintained. At least, that is so among the states of the Union. There is a growing conviction that only exceptional circumstances should lead one of the states to refuse to enforce a right acquired in another. The evidences of this tendency are many. One typical instance will suffice. For many years Massachusetts closed her courts to actions of this order based on foreign statutes. She has opened them now, and overruled her earlier decisions. If it has ever been accepted here we think it should be abandoned now. . . .

HISCOCK, C.J., and CUDDEBACK, POUND, CRANE, and ANDREWS, JJ., concur. COLLIN, J., dissents from decision of second question in opinion of CARDOZO, J., but otherwise concurs.

*See* PROBLEMS 4C-15. THE GOLDEN RULE AND PROSTITUTION; 4C-16. BUYING BACK YOUR OWN GOODS; 4C-17. A COUPLE IN A HURRY; 4C-18. INTERSPOUSAL IMMUNITY; 4C-19. A "TALAK" DIVORCE.

# NOTES ON *LOUCKS*

(1) *Escape Because the Law Chosen by the Rule is Penal.* Why would any state refuse to execute the "penal laws" of another? Does Judge Cardozo tell you? Does it help to reflect on what it means to be "penal" in the international sense? Suppose a prosecution of defendant in Maryland for violating a penal statute in Virginia. What frame of reference would the Maryland prosecutor use to determine how to exercise her prosecutorial discretion? What frame of reference would the judge use to inform her discretion in sentencing? *See* WILLIAM RICHMAN & WILLIAM REYNOLDS, UNDERSTANDING CONFLICT OF LAWS § 50[a] (3d ed. 2002).

Why was the Massachusetts wrongful death statute not "penal in the international sense"? What is the purpose of the minimum recovery of $500? Cardozo claims that the action serves only to benefit the family and not to "champion" the "public justice" of Massachusetts; but isn't deterrence of wrongful activity one of the purposes of tort law? Won't the deterrent effect of a judgment against the defendant further "peace and order" in Massachusetts?

(2) *Public Policy: Empowering the Judges.* Public policy was the ultimate escape device employed by traditionalist courts. It permitted forum judges to refuse to apply the law chosen by a First Restatement rule simply on the basis that the law chosen was morally odious. What is the rationale for giving such extraordinary power to the judges? Is this grant of power consistent with the traditionalist desires for certainty, forum neutrality, and mechanical decision procedures? If not, what should be done? How could a First Restatement court deal with an action in New York to enforce a contract—made in another country and legal there—to sell a human being?

(3) *Public Policy: Controlling the Judges.* The preceding hypothetical pretty clearly shows the need for a public policy escape device. But how to control this lightning in a bottle? It threatens to give the judges carte blanche to ignore the rules when they produce embarrassing results. The First Restatement carefully attempted to cabin the judges' discretion. The offending law must be "contrary to the strong public policy of the forum." RESTATEMENT (FIRST) OF CONFLICT OF LAWS § 612. The comments indicate that "mere difference between the laws of the two states" is not enough and that "the application of [the public policy doctrine] is extremely limited" especially between one American state and another. The classical judicial formulations are also quite strict: The foreign law must, as Cardozo wrote in *Loucks,* "violate some fundamental principle of justice, some prevalent conception of good morals, some deep-rooted tradition of the common weal" it must be "inherently vicious, wicked or immoral, and shocking to the prevailing moral sense." *Intercontinental Hotels Corp. v. Golden,* 15 N.Y.2d 9, 254 N.Y.S.2d 527, 203 N.E.2d 210 (1964).

On this standard, was Cardozo right in *Loucks?*

**HOLZER v. DEUTSCHE REICHSBAHN-GESELLSCHAFT,** 277 N.Y. 474, 14 N.E.2d 798 (1938). Breach of contract action brought by a German national against his former employer, a German corporation. Count one alleged that defendant discharged plaintiff solely because he was Jewish.

Count two relied upon a disability clause in the contract of employment that provided that "in the event the plaintiff should die or become unable, without fault on his part, to serve during the period of the contract the defendants would pay to him . . . 120,000 marks. . . ." The defendant relied upon the affirmative defense that plaintiff's discharge was required by a German law providing for the forced retirement of persons of non-Aryan descent.

*Held:* The second count could proceed to trial, but the first count should be dismissed. Under the decisions of this court and of the Supreme Court of the United States, the law of the country or state where the contract was made and was to be performed by citizens of that country or state governs. Within its own territory every government is supreme, and our courts are not competent to review its actions. We have so held, "however objectionable" we may consider the conduct of a foreign government. "Every sovereign State is bound to respect the independence of every other sovereign State, and the courts of one country will not sit in judgment on the acts of the government of another done within its own territory." *Oetjen v. Centr. Leather Co.,* 246 U.S. 297 (1918). . . . "It cannot be against the public policy of this State to hold nationals to the contracts which they have made in their own country to be performed there according to the laws of that country." *Dougherty v. Equitable Life Assurance Soc'y,* 266 N.Y. 71, 193 N.E. 897 (1934).

\* \* \*

If ever a case was ripe for the public policy escape, *Holzer* is it. Weren't the Nazi laws wicked and shocking to the prevailing moral sense? On the other hand, the case was decided in 1938, long before there was general awareness of the Nazi genocide. Without the wisdom of hindsight the Nazi statute is simply an example of de jure racism. Was New York in a position in 1938 to refuse application of all overtly racist foreign law? Another reason for the court's deference to German law is the "act of state" doctrine, which forbids a court from inquiring into the legality of the acts of foreign governments. *See Banco Nacional de Cuba v. Sabbatino,* § 6.08, *infra.* Does the act of state doctrine always trump the public policy device in cases of collision? What about "war crimes" trials? For a discussion of the jurisprudential problem, *see* the debate between Lon Fuller & H.L.A. Hart in volume 71 of the Harvard Law Review.

*See* PROBLEM 4C-20. "I SIMPLY OBEYED THE LAW."

Holzer must be compared with another public policy case from New York. *Mertz v. Mertz,* 271 N.Y. 466, 3 N.E.2d, 597 (1936), was an automobile negligence action brought in New York by one New York spouse against another. New York at the time had an interspousal immunity rule, but Connecticut, the place of injury, did not. Declaring that "a state can have no public policy except what is to be found in its Constitution and laws," the Court of Appeals of New York refused to apply the Connecticut law.

Can you reconcile *Holzer* and *Mertz?* Surely the Nazi forced retirement law was more evil than Connecticut's choice to do away with interspousal immunity. Might the distinction lie in the amount of contact and concern that New York—as compared to the foreign state—has with each case? What do the two cases tell you about the First Restatement's attempt to empower yet control the judges in their use of public policy?

(4) *Sources of Public Policy.* Where is the court supposed to find the forum state's public policy? Certainly in the state's constitution and statutes, *see Mertz, supra,* but what about other sources? In *Intercontinental Hotels Corp. v. Golden,* 15 N.Y.2d 9, 254 N.Y.S.2d 527, 203 N.E.2d 210 (1964), the court went further. Plaintiff, a Puerto Rican gambling casino operator sued defendant, a New Yorker, for gambling debts incurred in Puerto Rico. In holding that the Puerto Rican law permitting casino gambling did not violate New York public policy, the court found that policy revealed in: "prevailing social and moral attitudes of the community," "the changing attitudes of the people of the State of New York," "the legalization of pari-mutuel betting and the operation of bingo games," "a strong movement for legalized off-track betting," "our newspapers [which] quote the odds on horse races, football games [and] basketball games," and "informed public sentiment." What do you think of the plaintiff's attorney's job of creative lawyering? How would you have responded for the defendant?

(5) *Jurisdiction or Choice of Law.* Note that a court could use the public policy device in one of two different ways. Faced with a claim based upon an odious foreign law, the court could either refuse to exercise jurisdiction or, as a matter of choice of law, apply forum law instead. Does the choice of method make any difference? What are the claim preclusive effects of the two different maneuvers? Which shows more respect to the other state? Note also that the jurisdictional method is not always available; suppose, for instance, plaintiff's claim (say, a contract) does not violate the forum's public policy, but that defendant's defense (say, a contractual incapacity based on race) does. Denying jurisdiction will not solve the problem.

(6) *Public Policy and Gambling Contracts. Kramer v. Bally's Park Place, Inc.,* 311 Md. 387, 535 A.2d 466 (1988). Suit to enforce a gambling debt entered into in New Jersey. The gambling involved was legal in New Jersey, but not in Maryland.

*Held:* The debt is enforceable under *lex locus contractus* unless it offends a "very strong" public policy of Maryland.

[S]everal forms of gambling are legal in Maryland . . . including bingo, raffles, chance books, "paddle wheels," "wheels of fortune" "card parties," and games of skill. [A law] also broadly authorizes gambling activities in numerous counties by volunteer fire companies or by fraternal, civic, war veterans, religious or charitable institutions. . . .

. . . [T]he State has been extensively involved in the management and operation of various types of lotteries. . . .

In light of the . . . extent of legal gambling in Maryland, we cannot conclude that there is a sufficiently strong Maryland public policy against gambling debts that would justify disregarding the *lex loci contractus* principle.

The Court noted as well "the prevalence and type of gambling on horse races in colonial Maryland." *See also Intercontinental Hotels Corp. v. Golden,* 15 N.Y.2d 9, 203 N.E.2d 210, 254 N.Y.S.2d 527 (1964) ("The trend in New York

State demonstrates an acceptance of *licensed* gambling transactions as a morally acceptable activity. . . . Informed public sentiment is only against unlicensed gambling. . . . ") (Emphasis in original.)

Compare *The Casanova Club v. Bisharat,* 189 Conn. 591, 458 A.2d 1 (1983), in which, on analogous facts, the court refused to enforce a gambling debt that had been contracted in England. Judge Peters wrote that:

> Our General Assembly has made substantial inroads into the public policy against gambling. The legislature has sanctioned activities such as lotteries, off-track and parimutuel betting, and jai ali frontons. None of these statutes, however, permits gambling on credit, and that is the vice at which the underlying statutes forbidding wagering contacts are particularly directed.

Which opinion is right? RESTATEMENT (SECOND) OF CONFLICT OF LAWS § 202(1) applies the most significant relationship test to questions of illegality; which jurisdiction is that in a gambling case?

## KILBERG v. NORTHEAST AIRLINES, INC.

*New York Court of Appeals*
*9 N. Y2d 34, 211 N. Y.S.2d 133, 172 N.E.2d 526 (1961)*

DESMOND, CHIEF JUDGE. Defendant is a common carrier of passengers by air. Plaintiff's intestate, a passenger on one of defendant's planes, was killed in August, 1958 when the airship crashed and burned at Nantucket, Massachusetts, in the course of a flight from a New York airport. The complaint pleads three causes of action but this appeal has to do, immediately, with the second count only. That part of the complaint has been dismissed. . . .

The disputed second cause of action alleges that plaintiff's intestate before boarding the plane at La Guardia Airport bought from defendant a ticket for transportation to Nantucket, that defendant by causing his death in the crash breached its contract to carry him safely and that as a result the passenger's estate and his dependent suffered substantial damages (stated as $150,000) for which his administrator sues and which include "loss of accumulations of prospective earnings of the deceased." There was in effect at the time of this disaster section 2 of chapter 229 of the General Statutes of Massachusetts which gave a cause of action against a common carrier for negligently causing a passenger's death but limited to not less than $2,000 or more than $15,000 the damages to be awarded therefore. Special Term held that plaintiff could sue in contract and that the law of New York, the place of contract, governed such a cause of action and not the law of Massachusetts, the place of the wrong. The Appellate Division took the position that the second cause of action, however labeled or phrased, is in tort for negligently causing death and as such is subject to the damage limitation of the Massachusetts wrongful death statute.

Plaintiff's submission as to this second count is that it sounds in contract and so is governed for all purposes by the law of New York, the place of contract. If the alleged contract breach had caused injuries not resulting in death, a New York governed contract suit would, we will assume, be available. But it is law long settled that wrongful death actions, being unknown to the common law, derive from statutes only and that the statute which governs such an action is that of the place of the wrong. . . . It follows . . . that plaintiff as administrator has no separate right to sue this carrier in contract for causing his intestate's death.

That does not mean, however, that for this alleged wrong plaintiff cannot possibly recover more than the $15,000 maximum specified in the Massachusetts act. Modern conditions make it unjust and anomalous to subject the traveling citizen of this State to the varying laws of other States through and over which they move. The number of States limiting death case damages has become smaller over the years but there are still 14 of them. An air traveler from New York may in a flight of a few hours' duration pass through several of those commonwealths. His plane may meet with disaster in a State he never intended to cross but into which the plane has flown because of bad weather or other unexpected developments, or an airplane's catastrophic descent may begin in one State and end in another. The place of injury becomes entirely fortuitous. Our courts should if possible provide protection for our own State's people against unfair and anachronistic treatment of the lawsuits which result from these disasters. There is available, we find, a way of accomplishing this conformably to our State's public policy and without doing violence to the accepted pattern of conflict of law rules.

Since both Massachusetts and New York authorize wrongful death suits against common carriers, the only controversy is as to amount of damages recoverable. New York's public policy prohibiting the imposition of limits on such damages is strong, clear and old. Since the Constitution of 1894, our basic law has been (N.Y. Const. art 1, § 16), that "The right of action now existing to recover damages for injuries resulting in death, shall never be abrogated; and the amount recoverable shall not be subject to any statutory limitation." Each later revision of the State Constitution has included this same prohibition against limitations of death action damages. . . . New York's original wrongful death law, passed very soon after Lord Campbell's Act became law in Great Britain, had like the latter no restriction as to damages. The Legislature later imposed such limits but the Convention which drew the 1894 Constitution rejected and forbade them. "The argument which evidently controlled the convention [was] . . . that the arbitrary limitation was absurd and unjust in measuring the pecuniary value of all lives to the next of kin by the same arbitrary standard." The absurdity and injustice have become increasingly apparent in the six decades that have followed. For our courts to be limited by this damage ceiling (at least as to our own domiciliaries) is so completely contrary to our public policy that we should refuse to apply that part of the Massachusetts law. The Massachusetts cases likewise say that Massachusetts will enforce the *lex loci delicti* in wrongful death suits unless Massachusetts public policy forbids. . . .

Actually, we have in *Wooden v. Western N. Y. & Pac. R.R. Co.*, 126 N.Y. 10, 16-17, 26 N.E. 1050, 1051, a flat holding by our court that in an action brought for causing a wrongful death in Pennsylvania, the New York courts would enforce our limitation of damages (as it then existed) although Pennsylvania had no such limitation. The reason, equally pertinent here, is that the "restriction pertains to the remedy, rather than the right" and "does not strictly affect the rule of damages, but rather the extent of damages; and that extent, as limited or unlimited, does not enter into any definition of the right enforced, or the cause of action permitted to be prosecuted." *Loucks v. Standard Oil Co.,* 224 N.Y. 99, 120 N.E. 198, does not overrule *Wooden, supra.* Looking at the true holding of the *Loucks* case, rather than picking out language from the opinion, we find that the court was merely deciding that the minimum set for recovery in the Massachusetts wrongful death statute did not make it a "penal statute" unenforceable here because contrary to our public policy.

As to conflict of law rules it is of course settled that the law of the forum is usually in control as to procedures including remedies. However, as Professor Leflar says (CONFLICT OF LAWS, § 60), remedial and substantive "shade into each other constantly" and "the law of the forum normally determines for itself" whether a given question is one of substance or procedure. As to whether the measure of damages should be treated as a procedural or a substantive matter in wrongful death cases, there is authority both ways and no controlling New York decision. . . . It is open to us, therefore, particularly in view of our own strong public policy as to death action damages to treat the measure of damages in this case as being a procedural or remedial question controlled by our own State policies. . . .

From all of this it follows that while plaintiff's second or contract cause of action is demurrable, his first count declaring under the Massachusetts wrongful death action is not only sustainable but can be enforced, if the proof so justifies, without regard to the $15,000 limit. Plaintiff, therefore, may apply if he be so advised for leave to amend his first cause of action accordingly.

The judgment appealed from should be affirmed, with costs.

FULD, JUDGE (concurring). I, too, believe that the judgment dismissing the contract cause of action alleged in the second count of the complaint should be affirmed. However, having made that determination, I would go no further.

To expatiate on this, I would say that, while I agree that the second count— the only one before us—fails to state a cause of action, I find no warrant or justification for going beyond that single issue and considering, *sua sponte,* questions which underlie the complaint's first count alleging a cause of action for wrongful death under the Massachusetts statute. . . .

If this were a matter of first impression, it might be effectively argued that, where "two or more communities are touched or affected by a factual sequence," the "guide to the governing law" should be the jurisdiction having "the most significant contact or contacts" (Fowler Harper, *Policy Bases of the Conflict of Laws: Reflections on Rereading Professor Lorenzen's Essays,* 56 YALE L.J. 1155, 1161). And, since the contract of safe carriage was undertaken in New York and since this fact provides a more "significant contact" than the adventitious occurrence of the crash in Massachusetts, it might well be further urged, this State's wrongful death statute and not that of Massachusetts should apply.

Impressed though I am by the theoretical soundness of such a position, I am forced to the conclusion that it is foreclosed by our decisions. . . . Since, as is apparent, plaintiff's intestate could not have maintained the cause of action alleged in the second count, there was no right of action to survive his death.

In sum, then, limiting consideration to the only matter before us, it is my conclusion that no action ex contractu is available to the plaintiff under either the common law of New York or its wrongful death statute and that, therefore, the Appellate Division properly granted the defendant's motion to dismiss the second cause of action.

FROESSEL, JUDGE (concurring). We concur for affirmance of the judgment appealed from, dismissing plaintiff's second cause of action. We should reach no other question. In this case, defendant moved to dismiss the second cause of action for legal insufficiency, and nothing more; the subsequent notices of appeal were limited accordingly. . . .

It has long been recognized as the law of this State that the right to maintain an action for wrongful death is dependent upon the existence of a statute creating such a right at the place where the injury resulting in death occurred.

Plaintiff's right to maintain this action must therefore stem from the provisions of the Massachusetts statute. That statute, however, expressly limits the extent of the right given, and declares that the damages assessed thereunder shall not be more than $15,000. In effect, this is tantamount to providing that there shall be no cause of action for wrongful death beyond this amount. The majority, by giving extraterritorial effect to our prohibition against the limitation of recovery in such actions, would permit plaintiff to recover on the basis of the foreign law, and yet not be bound by its express limitation. Such action was vigorously condemned by the Supreme Court of the United States in *Slater v. Mexican Nat'l R.R. Co.* (194 U.S. 120, 126) where Mr. Justice Holmes, writing for the court stated; "It seems to us unjust to allow a plaintiff to come here absolutely depending on the foreign law for the foundation of his case, and yet to deny the defendant the benefit of whatever limitations on his liability that law would impose."

No sound reason appears why our courts, in enforcing such a right at all, should not enforce it in its entirety. This court has no power to determine what the public policy of Massachusetts should be and we may not ignore foreign law affecting the substantive rights of the parties merely because such law differs from our own.

In *Loucks v. Standard Oil Co.,* although it was suggested that our courts might refuse to enforce a right based upon a foreign statute "that outrages the public policy of New York", this court held that a Massachusetts act, very similar to the one with which we are now confronted, must be enforced—despite the fact that we "cannot give them the same judgment that our law would give if the wrong had been done here." Thus Judge Cardozo in his opinion clearly indicated that the maximum damages would be controlled by the Massachusetts statute. . . .

[Judge Froessel then discussed several New York precedents.] In our opinion, these precedents are conclusive, and may not be disregarded without being overruled. The principle which they affirm is clearly the well established law of this State. . . .

[T]he overwhelming weight of judicial authority in the United States is in accord with the view that the law of the place of injury governs not only the existence of the cause of action for wrongful death, but also the measure of damages.

Professor Leflar does note (§ 60, p. 109) that the procedural and substantive law "shade into each other constantly," he clearly states, in the same chapter, that "The size of the right is a part of the right?" and that, therefore, the "measure of damages should be treated as a substantive rather than a procedural matter, and that the amount of the award should be determined by the rules of law of the place of the tort . . . rather than by the rules of the forum, as such. There is some authority the other way, treating measure of damages as procedure merely, on the idea that it does not constitute the right but only the remedy given in substitution for the right. This carries a nice theory to a point at which it conflicts with common understanding." (LEFLAR, CONFLICT OF LAWS, § 65, p. 118). . . .

Furthermore, questions relating to such defenses as contributory (comparative) negligence, charitable immunity, incapacity of wife to sue, and the Statute of Limitations have all been regarded by this court as regulated by the law of the place of the injury rather than our own law, since, they involve the substantial rights of the parties. In each of these cases we applied a foreign rule of law, although such rule was clearly contrary to the law of our own State, and we applied it whether it benefitted the plaintiff or the defendant. In our opinion, the defense raised in the case at bar must be treated in the same manner—viz., by applying the law of Massachusetts, the place of death.

The majority would apply our own law of damages because the place of injury is entirely fortuitous. The same argument may be made with respect to each of the cases just referred to. We should not overrule well-established principles, nor "refuse to enforce a foreign right" at our pleasure, to suit our "individual notion of expediency or fairness" (Loucks v. Standard Oil Co.).

The position adopted by the majority may result in the situation where, in a single airplane crash in which numerous passengers from various States are killed, a different law will be applied in each action resulting therefrom. The courts of each State, if they followed the majority view, would then apply their own law of damages to the case. As Judge Cardozo pointed out in the Loucks case, supra, "The theory of the statute personal, a body of national law which the citizen carries about with him . . . is a theory which has yielded generally in this country to the principles of the territorial system and the doctrine of vested rights." We should not attempt to revive it now.

DYE, BURKE, and FOSTER, JJ., concur with DESMOND, C.J.; FULD, J., concurs in result in a separate opinion; FROESSEL, J., concurs for affirmance in a separate opinion in which VAN VOORHIS, J., concurs.

*Judgment affirmed.*

## NOTES AND QUESTIONS ON *KILBERG*

(1) *The Contract Recharacterization.* What reason did the majority give for rejecting plaintiff's attempt to recharacterize the case as a contract action to

be decided, under the vested rights theory, according to New York law, where the ticket was bought? Are you convinced?

(2) *Distinguishing Loucks.* The Massachusetts statute involved in *Kilberg* is, of course, a direct descendant of the one applied in *Loucks.* How is Chief Judge Desmond able to avoid the precedential effect of *Loucks*—a conflicts landmark authored by the estimable Cardozo and apparently squarely on point? Are you convinced, or is the distinction somewhat lame?

(3) *Public Policy or Procedure.* With *Loucks* out of the way, the court lurches hastily towards a conclusion, but what is it? Expressed in first-year law school terms, what is the holding in *Kilberg*? Is it based on public policy or the procedural recharacterization of the wrongful death damages limitation issue? The latter option was rejected in the following year in *Davenport v. Webb,* 11 N.Y.2d 392, 183 N.E.2d 902 (1963).

(4) *The Concurrences.* Judge Froessel is not satisfied with either of the possible holdings. He marshals a parade of horribles, arguing that cases dealing with other issues, such as capacity to sue and charitable immunity, would be affected by both. Was he right to be concerned?

Judge Fuld is obviously unhappy with both the majority and Judge Froessel's concurrence. Can you think of any reason (other than wanting to do things in the proper order—a perfectly valid reason, of course) why he wanted to delay resolving the sufficiency of the first count of the complaint until the parties had had a chance to brief it?

(5) *Public Policy and Candor.* Professors Paulsen and Sovem suggest that the immorality of the foreign law was not the real problem:

> "[P]ublic policy" is one way to avoid the application of a choice of law rule which the forum wishes to avoid. The objection of the forum, thus, is not *to the content of the foreign law but to its own choice of law rule.* Rather than to change or modify the supposedly applicable rule the court may refuse on public policy grounds to apply the law to which the rule makes reference. The closer the tie between the forum and the facts of a given transaction the more readily we may expect the forum to use its own law to judge the matter before it. In such a view the "public policy" doctrine becomes a kind of choice of law principle, imprecise, uncertain of application, but nevertheless discharging a choice of law function.

Monrad Paulsen & Michael Sovern, *"Public Policy" in the Conflict of Laws,* 56 COLUM. L. REV. 969, 981 (1956). In other words, public policy may be the most honest of the First Restatement escape devices, but it is still not very honest. How does that affect the predictability of decisions in future conflicts cases? Paulsen and Sovern suggest a more honest, more predictable approach:

> If judges honestly put the question whether the foreign law is barbarous in its provisions or frightfully unjust in the particular case, few cases will provide an affirmative answer. If a judge sees that, in a given case, public policy doctrine substitutes for choice of law, he should address himself directly to questions concerning choice of law policy.

*Id.* at 1016.

*(6) Contemporary Practice.* Use of the public policy device by First Restatement courts continues today; in fact, it is one most frequently litigated choice-of-law issues. *See* William Richman and David Riley, *The First Restatement of Conflict of Laws on the Twenty-fifth Anniversary of Its Successor: Contemporary Practice in Traditional Courts,* 56 Md. L. Rev. 1196, 1227 (1997). *See, e.g., Alexander v. General Motors Corp.,* 466 S.E.2d 607, 609 (Ga. 1995). Consistent with the findings of Professors Paulsen and Sovern, note 5, *supra,* a more recent study, *see* Richman & Riley, *supra,* found that some First Restatement courts use public policy as a device to import modern choice-of-law strategies, such as the center of gravity and interest analysis, into otherwise traditional practice. *See, e.g., Braxton v. Anco Electric, Inc.,* 409 S.E.2d 914 (N.C. 1991). As a result, First Restatement courts have held some relatively innocuous legal principles to be sufficiently wicked to violate the public policy of the forum. *See e.g. Alexander v. General Motors Corp.,* 478 S.E.2d 123, (Ga. 1996) (failure of place of injury to adopt strict liability in tort, relying instead upon negligence and warranty, violated forum's public policy), *Trahan v. E.R. Squibb & Sons Inc.,* 567 F. Supp. 505, 507 (M.D.Tenn. 1983) (same).

## § 4.15   A Concluding Note

This Part begins and ends with consideration of the two primary methods of attacking First Restatement methodology. The first, characterization, merely leads the court to other sections of the First Restatement, but as *Haumschild* vividly illustrates, does not free it from the vested rights prison Professor Beale constructed so cunningly. The second escape, public policy, leads only to ad hoc decisions; its apogee is *Kilberg.* The challenge for judges and scholars was to find a new solution, an effort treated in the next Part of this Chapter.

## PART D   THE CHOICE-OF-LAW REVOLUTION

### § 4.16   The First Shots: The Center of Gravity or Grouping of Contacts Theory

#### AUTEN v. AUTEN

*Court of Appeals of New York*
*308 N.Y. 155; 124 N.E.2d 99 (1954)*

FULD, J. In this action to recover installments allegedly due for support and maintenance under a separation agreement executed in this state in 1933, the wife's complaint has been dismissed, on motion for summary judgment, upon the ground that her institution of an action for separation in England constituted a repudiation and a rescission of the agreement under New York law. Determination of the appeal, involving as it does a question of conflict of laws, requires examination of the facts disclosed by the papers before us.

Married in England in 1917, Mr. and Mrs. Auten continued to live there with their two children until 1931. In that year, according to plaintiff, defendant deserted her, came to this country and, in the following year, obtained a Mexican divorce and proceeded to "marry" another woman. Unable to come to terms with the ocean between them, plaintiff made a trip to New York City to see and talk to defendant about adjustment of their differences. The outcome was the separation agreement of June, 1933, upon which the present action is predicated. It obligated the husband to pay to a trustee, for the "account of" the wife, who was to return to England, the sum of 50 pounds a month for the support of herself and the children. In addition, the agreement provided that the parties were to continue to live separate and apart, that neither should sue "in any action relating to their separation" and that the wife should not "cause any complaint to be lodged against [the husband], in any jurisdiction, by reason of the said alleged divorce or remarriage."

Immediately after the agreement was signed, plaintiff returned to England, where she has since lived with her children . . . .[D]efendant failed to live up to his agreement, making but a few payments under it, with the result that plaintiff was left more or less destitute in England with the children. About a year after the agreement had been executed, in August of 1934, plaintiff filed a petition for separation in an English court, charging defendant with adultery. This English action . . . was instituted upon advice of English counsel that it "was the only method" by which she "could collect money" from defendant; it was done, plaintiff expressly declares, to "enable" her "to enforce" the separation agreement, and not with any thought or intention of repudiating it.

The years passed, and in 1947, having realized nothing as a result of the English action and little by reason of the New York separation agreement, plaintiff brought the present suit to recover the sum of $26,564, which represents the amount allegedly due her, under the agreement, from January 1, 1935 to September 1, 1947.

In his answer, defendant admitted making the agreement, but, by way of a separate defense . . . claimed that plaintiff's institution of the separation suit in England operated as a repudiation of the agreement and effected a forfeiture of her right to any payments under it. Following a motion by the wife for summary judgment and a cross motion by the husband for like relief, the court at Special Term granted the husband's cross motion and dismissed the complaint. The Appellate Division affirmed . . . .

Both of the courts below, concluding that New York law was to be applied, held that under such law plaintiff's commencement of the English action and the award of temporary alimony constituted a rescission and repudiation of the separation agreement, requiring dismissal of the complaint. Whether that is the law of this state . . . need not detain us, since in our view it is the law of England, not that of New York, which is here controlling.

Choosing the law to be applied to a contractual transaction with elements in different jurisdictions is a matter not free from difficulty. The New York decisions evidence a number of different approaches to the question.

Most of the cases rely upon the generally accepted rules that "All matters bearing upon the execution, the interpretation and the validity of contracts. . .are determined by the law of the place where the contract is made," while "All matters connected with its performance. . .are regulated by the law of the place where the contract, by its terms, is to be performed." What constitutes a breach of the contract and what circumstances excuse a breach are considered matters of performance, governable, within this rule, by the law of the place of performance.

Many cases appear to treat these rules as conclusive . . . .[O]ther decisions, including the most recent one in this court, have resorted to a method first employed to rationalize the results achieved by the courts in decided cases . . . which has come to be called the "center of gravity" or the "grouping of contacts" theory of the conflict of laws. Under this theory, the courts, instead of regarding as conclusive the parties' intention or the place of making or performance, lay emphasis rather upon the law of the place "which has the most significant contacts with the matter in dispute."

Although this "grouping of contacts" theory may, perhaps, afford less certainty and predictability than the rigid general rules, the merit of its approach is that it gives to the place "having the most interest in the problem" paramount control over the legal issues arising out of a particular factual context, thus allowing the forum to apply the policy of the jurisdiction "most intimately concerned with the outcome of [the] particular litigation." Moreover, by stressing the significant contacts, it enables the court, not only to reflect the relative interests of the several jurisdictions involved but also to give effect to the probable intention of the parties and consideration to "whether one rule or the other produces the best practical result . . . ."

Turning to the case before us, examination of the respective contacts with New York and England compels the conclusion that it is English law which must be applied to determine the impact and effect to be given the wife's institution of the separation suit. It hardly needs stating that it is England which has all the truly significant contacts, while this state's sole nexus with the matter in dispute—entirely fortuitous, at that—is that it is the place where the agreement was made and where the trustee, to whom the moneys were in the first instance to be paid, had his office. The agreement effected a separation between British subjects, who had been married in England, had children there and lived there as a family for fourteen years. It involved a husband who, according to the papers before us, had willfully deserted and abandoned his wife and children in England and was in the United States, when the agreement was signed, merely on a temporary visa. And it concerned an English wife who came to this country at that time because it was the only way she could see her husband to discuss their differences. The sole purpose of her trip to New York was to get defendant to agree to the support of his family, and she returned to England immediately after the agreement was executed. While the moneys were to be paid through the medium of a New York trustee, such payments were "for account of" the wife and children, who, it was thoroughly understood, were to live in England. The agreement is instinct with that understanding; not only does it speak in terms of English currency in providing for payments to the wife, not only does it recite that the first payment be made to her "immediately before sailing for England," but it specifies that the husband may visit the children "if he should go to England."

In short, then, the agreement determined and fixed the marital responsibilities of an English husband and father and provided for the support and maintenance of the allegedly abandoned wife and children who were to remain in England. It merely substituted the arrangements arrived at by voluntary agreement of the parties for the duties and responsibilities of support that would otherwise attach by English law. There is no question that England has the greatest concern in prescribing and governing those obligations, and in securing to the wife and children essential support and maintenance. And the paramount interest of that country is not affected by the fact that the parties separate and provide for such support by a voluntary agreement. It is still England, as the jurisdiction of marital domicile and the place where the wife and children were to be, that has the greatest concern in defining and regulating the rights and duties existing under that agreement, and, specifically, in determining the circumstances that effect a termination or repudiation of the agreement.

Nor could the parties have expected or believed that any law other than England's would govern the effect of the wife's institution of a separation action. It is most unlikely that the wife could have intended to subject her rights under English law to the law of a jurisdiction several thousand miles distant, with which she had not the slightest familiarity. On the contrary, since it was known that she was returning to England to live, both parties necessarily realized that any action which she took, whether in accordance with the agreement or in violation of it, would have to occur in England. If any thought was given to the matter at all, it was that the law of the place where she and the children would be should determine the effect of acts performed by her.

It is, perhaps, not inappropriate to note that, even if we were not to place our emphasis on the law of the place with the most significant contacts, but were instead simply to apply the rule that matters of performance and breach are governed by the law of the place of performance, the same result would follow. Whether or not there was a repudiation, essentially a form of breach, is also to be determined by the law of the place of performance and that place, so far as the wife's performance is concerned, is England. Whatever she had to do under the agreement—"live separate and apart from" her husband, "maintain, educate and support" the children and refrain from bringing "any action relating to [the] separation"—was to be done in England. True, the husband's payments were to be made to a New York trustee for forwarding to plaintiff in England, but that is of no consequence in this case. It might be, if the question before us involved the manner or effect of payment to the trustee, but that is not the problem; we are here concerned only with the effect of the wife's performance.

Since, then, the law of England must be applied, and since, at the very least, an issue exists as to whether the courts of that country treat the commencement of a separation action as a repudiation of an earlier-made separation agreement, summary judgment should not have been granted.

The judgment of the Appellate Division and that of Special Term insofar as they dismiss the complaint should be reversed, with costs in all courts, and the matter remitted for further proceedings in accordance with this opinion.

## NOTES ON *AUTEN*, THE CENTER OF GRAVITY, AND THE BEGINNING OF THE CHOICE-OF-LAW REVOLUTION

(1) *The Academic Attack on Vested Rights*: The academic attack on the traditional system began thirty years before *Auten* with the work of Walter Wheeler Cook, who used the predictive theory of American Legal Realism, to destroy the vested rights theory even before the adoption of the Restatement in 1934. According to the Realists, a legal right is simply a prediction that a court will grant relief to the plaintiff. In Cook's words:

> "Right," "duty," and other names for legal relations are therefore not names of objects or entities which have an existence apart from the behavior of the officials in question, but merely terms by means of which we describe to each other what prophecies we make as to the probable occurrence of a certain sequence of events—the behavior of the officials. We must, therefore, constantly resist the tendency to which we are all subject to reify, "signify" or hypostatize "rights" and other "legal relations."

WALTER W. COOK, THE LOGICAL AND LEGAL BASES OF THE CONFLICT OF LAWS 30 (1942). Thus, according to the predictive theory, it made no sense to speak of "enforcing vested rights" in choice-of-law cases. Until the court decided, there simply was no "right" for it to enforce.

Cook also argued that the vested rights theory failed to explain adequately how courts actually treat choice-of-law problems. Once again, he used the predictive theory to show that courts do not enforce "foreign rights." A "foreign right" is simply a prediction about what a foreign court would do if faced with the exact facts of plaintiff's case. To make such a prediction, the forum court would have to apply the foreign choice-of-law rules as well as the foreign internal rule; in other words, the court would need to apply the doctrine of renvoi. Because courts do not routinely apply renvoi to all choice-of-law problems, Cook concluded that the vested rights theory was not an accurate description of actual practice in the courts. *Id.* at 19.

Cook proposed an alternative description, which came to be called the local law theory. According to that view, the forum court does not "apply" foreign law, nor does it enforce a "foreign right." Rather, it applies forum law (the only law it can apply); in a case with foreign elements, that law, for reasons of fairness and party expectations, may incorporate a principal or rule of decision drawn from the legal system of another state. In the words of Learned Hand:

> However no court can enforce any law but that of its own sovereign, and when a suitor comes to a jurisdiction foreign to the place of the tort, he can only invoke an obligation recognized by that sovereign. A foreign sovereign under civilized law imposes an obligation of its own as nearly homologous as possible to that arising in the place where the tort occurs.

*Guinness v. Miller,* 291 Fed. 769 (S.D.N.Y. 1923).

Cook's view is more economical than the vested rights theory because it can explain the forum's use of a foreign rule of law without the need to postulate a "foreign right" that exists prior to any court's enforcement of it. More importantly, it shifts the focus of the discussion away from a formalistic account of the choice-of-law process toward the more practical question: What reasons justify the forum's use of a principle found in another state's law?

(2) *The Academic Attack on Traditional Practice*: Leading the early academic attack on traditional practice, Professor David Cavers focused not on the vested rights theory, but rather on the traditional system's methods and results. *See* David Cavers, *A Critique of the Choice of Law Problem,* 47 Harv. L. Rev. 173 (1933). He characterized the traditional rules as "jurisdiction-selecting"; they chose a place or a jurisdiction and then applied its law regardless of the content of that law.

> When a case arises in which a foreign law is offered in evidence or in which the applicability of the law of the forum is denied, a court faithful to the conventional approach will turn in search of a conflict of laws rule to determine the jurisdiction whose law should govern the question at issue. The conflicts rule indicates in which jurisdiction the appropriate law may be found. Assuming the law offered to be from that jurisdiction, the court will then proceed with the case, employing that law as a rule of decision. Not until its admission for that purpose does the content of that law become material.

*Id.* at 178.

Cavers argued that the vested rights and territorial theories compelled this approach. With those theories discredited, he urged a choice-of-law method that explicitly recognized the considerations of justice and social expediency that "should be, and in many cases have been, the dominant determinants of [choice-of-law cases]." In particular, he urged the forum court to take account of the content of the competing rules and the results that a choice would produce. It should then "appraise these results in light of those facts in the event or transaction which, from the standpoint of justice between the litigating individuals or of those broader considerations of social policy which conflicting laws may evoke, link that event or transaction to one law or the other . . . ."

Although Cavers' work presaged the direction of modern choice-of-law thinking, he did not propose, at least in his early work, a detailed and systematic choice-of-law approach. However, a new generation of scholars, including Brainerd Currie, Willis Reese, Albert Ehrenzweig and Robert Leflar did just that, and their work is the subject of Parts E–G on modern choice-of-law methods.

(3) *Auten and the "Center of Gravity:"* Influenced by Cook, Cavers, and the more recent scholars, courts began to experiment with new choice-of-law approaches, and *Auten* is one of the first notable cases. Its center-of-gravity test is a significant advance over the traditional system since it allows consideration of multiple contracts unlike the single-contact rules of the First Restatement. The new test is still, however, a jurisdiction-selecting system, to use Cavers' term; in other words, the court determines the center of gravity of the litigation by adding up contacts without considering the content of the competing states' laws. To see the resulting problem, consider a variation of *Auten* where the laws of England and New York are reversed. Presumably England would still be the center of gravity, but should English law apply? Is it possible for a court to make the rational choice of law without knowing the content and underlying purposes of the competing legal rules?

(4) *Measuring Significance.* How did Judge Fuld determine which contacts to count when measuring the center of gravity? Consider a subsequent decision from the same court, also written by Judge Fuld:

**HAAG v. BARNES,** 9 N.Y.2d 554, 216 N.Y.S.2d 65, 175 N.E.2d 441 (1961). Action for support of an illegitimate child, brought by plaintiff-mother, a New York legal secretary, who had worked for defendant Barnes, an Illinois lawyer, whenever his business brought him to New York. A sexual liaison developed, Haag became pregnant, and then the relationship cooled. She went to Illinois to see Barnes but was directed instead to his lawyer. It was agreed that Barnes would pay for Haag's delivery at a Chicago Hospital, and the parties later signed an agreement under which he would pay $275 per month until the child was 16. Under Illinois law an unmarried mother's release of paternity liability was valid without judicial approval, if given for more than $ 800; under New York law the release was invalid without prior judicial approval. The agreement contained a choice-of-law clause specifying Illinois law.

*Held*: Illinois law would apply. [E]ven if the parties' intention and the place of making of the contract are not given decisive effect, they are nevertheless to be given heavy weight in determining which jurisdiction "has the most significant contacts with the matter in dispute". And when these important factors are taken together with other of the "significant contacts" in the case, they likewise point to Illinois law. Among these other Illinois contacts are the following: (1) both parties are designated in the agreement as being "of Chicago, Illinois," and the defendant's place of business is and always has been in Illinois; (2) the child was born in Illinois; (3) the persons designated to act as agents for the principals . . . are Illinois residents, as are the attorneys for both parties who drew the agreement; and (4) all contributions for support always have been, and still are being, made from Chicago.

Contrasted with these Illinois contacts, the New York contacts are of far less weight and significance . . . . [It] may not be gainsaid said that the "center of gravity" of this agreement is Illinois and that, absent compelling public policy to the contrary, Illinois law should apply . . . .

As a matter of fact, the agreement . . . clearly goes beyond "indemnification of the community" and the provision of "bare necessities." Whether we read it as a whole, or look only to the financial provisions concerned . . . we must conclude that "the welfare of the child" is fully protected.

———

Why was the location of the parties' agents and lawyers important in *Haag* but not in *Auten*? Why was it important in *Haag* that the agreement indicated that the parties were "of Chicago"? Why was the source of the income to make the payments for child and spousal support important in *Haag* but not in *Auten* ? Why was there no consideration in *Haag* of where the plaintiff received secretarial training or where the defendant went to law school? Surely, because these details are irrelevant to choice of law, but if they are irrelevant what is the relevance of the other trivial contacts that Judge Fuld emphasizes?

(5) The *Flaws of the Theory.* These questions reveal two basic problems with the center of gravity theory. First, it provides no measure of significance; that is, there is no way to decide whether a contact is significant to the choice of law or not. Absent a measure of significance, the alternative seems to be simply to count up contacts and choose the law of the state with the greatest number, but such a calculus is inherently and obviously manipulable. Could you manufacture new contacts in either case to shift the choice to your client's liking? When your opponent responded in kind, how would you convince the court that those fabricated contacts were any less relevant or worthy then your own?

The second major problem with the theory is that it does not permit explicit consideration of some of the obvious motivations behind the decisions in *Auten* and *Haag*. In both, for instance, Judge Fuld felt some desire to validate the contractual transaction. Further, he felt a pull in both cases toward the just result. Mr. Auten should have paid for the support of his children, and his wife's instituting an English lawsuit upon advice of counsel should have had no effect on his obligation. The Haag-Barnes agreement was relatively fair, considering the economics of the times, and there was little need for judicial intervention to assure the welfare of the child.

The center of gravity theory, however, could not accommodate directly the judicial desire to validate contracts nor the need to insure just results. In lieu of explicit consideration of these two motivations, Fuld had no choice but to place his thumb upon the scale of contacts, creating new and seemingly irrelevant contacts where necessary and adjusting the weights of others, according not to their choice-of-law significance, but rather their effect on the result. Does this process seem depressingly familiar?

Clearly the challenge of the choice-of-law revolution, and one that the center of gravity could not meet, was to formulate new methods that could consider more honestly the motivations behind the choice-of-law decisions of conscientious judges. The remainder of this chapter treats the efforts of the new generation of scholars to create such systems. Before considering those efforts, however, note 6 treats the current influence of the center of gravity, and § 4.17 provides a freeze-frame photo of the current state of the on-going choice-of-law revolution.

(6) *The influence of the center of gravity*. Despite its flaws as a modern choice-of-law methodology, the center of gravity has had enormous influence on the choice-of-law revolution, particularly in its effect on the Restatement (Second) of Conflict of Laws. In its early drafts, the American Law Institute adopted a method very much like the center of gravity, which called for application of the law of the state of the "most significant relationship" to the case. In subsequent drafts in 1963 and 1967, however, the Institute modified the approach to take account of more modern developments in choice-of-law theory, particularly, interest analysis. Eventually the Restatement Second settled on the current language of § 6 (Chapter 4, Part F, *infra*), which incorporates many of the insights of modern choice-of-law scholars and which adds considerable structure to the otherwise amorphous "most significant relationship" formula.

Some courts that claim to have "adopted" the Second Restatement, continue to use the center of gravity approach and choose the applicable law in the free-form way contemplated in *Auten, Haag,* and the Restatement's early drafts. Thus, these courts simply tote up contacts and conclude without further explanation that one state's law, rather than the other's should govern. *See, e.g., Ehredt v. DeHavilland Aircraft Co.,* 705 P.2d 446, 453 (Alaska 1985); *In re Asbestos Litigation,* 517 A.2d 697, 698 (Del. Super. Ct. 1986). Other states use the original "center of gravity" idea specifically detaching it from the Second Restatement. *See, e.g., Perkins v. Clark Equipment Co.,* 823 F. 2d 207 (8th Cir. 1987), *State Automobile Mutual Insurance Company v. Spray,* 547 F.2d 397 (7th Cir. 1977) (applying Indiana law). In all, six states use some variant of the free-form center-of-gravity approach. *See* Symeon Symeonides, *Choice of Law in the American Courts in 1997,* 46 AM. J. COMP. L. 233, 265 (1998).

## § 4.17 The Continuing Revolution

### O'CONNOR V. O'CONNOR

*Supreme Court of Connecticut*
*519 A.2d 13 (1986)*

JUDGES: Peters, C. J., Shea, Dannehy, Callahan and M. Hennessey, Js.

OPINION BY: PETERS

The sole issue on this appeal is whether, under the circumstances of this case, an injured person may pursue a cause of action under Connecticut law to recover for allegedly tortious conduct that occurred in a jurisdiction where such a cause of action would not be permitted. The plaintiff, Roseann O'Connor, brought an action against the defendant, Brian O'Connor, seeking damages for injuries that she suffered as a result of an automobile accident in Quebec . . . .[1]

The relevant facts are undisputed. The plaintiff was injured as a result of a one car automobile accident that occurred on September 3, 1981, in the province of Quebec, Canada. At the time of the accident, the defendant was operating the automobile and the plaintiff was his sole passenger. The parties, both of whom were Connecticut domiciliaries, were on a one-day pleasure trip that began, and was intended to end, in Vermont. The plaintiff underwent hospital treatment for her injuries in Quebec and has suffered continuing physical disabilities while residing in Connecticut.

The plaintiff brought an action against the defendant [under Connecticut law which] permits the victim of serious physical or economic injury caused by an automobile accident to sue the tortfeasor for damages. The defendant, however, moved to strike the complaint, on the ground that the applicable law in the case was the law of Quebec. Quebec law would not permit the plaintiff's tort action because . . . [it] provides instead for government funded [no-fault] compensation for victims of bodily injury caused by automobile accidents

After a hearing, the trial court . . . granted the motion to strike in an oral decision. The court expressly based its decision on this court's opinion in *Gibson v. Fullin,* our most recent decision affirming the doctrine that the nature and extent of tort liability is governed by the place of injury, hereinafter referred to as "lex loci delicti" or "lex loci."

On appeal to this court, the plaintiff argues that the trial court erred in granting the defendant's motion to strike. Recognizing that the trial court and the Appellate Court accurately applied the rules governing conflict of laws that our Connecticut cases have previously articulated, the plaintiff urges this court to reexamine the propriety of our continued adherence to the doctrine of lex loci delicti in cases of personal injury. In the particular circumstances of this case, the plaintiff maintains, we should no longer adhere rigidly to the doctrine of lex loci but should instead seek to discern and to apply the law of the jurisdiction that has the most significant relationship to the controversy. . . . Quebec, although it was the place of injury, has no significant interest in applying its statutory compensation scheme to the controversy because the location of the automobile accident in Quebec was purely fortuitous. Connecticut, by contrast, has a substantial interest in applying its law to the case because: (1) both parties are domiciled and employed in Connecticut; (2) both parties are subject to the requirements and entitled to the benefits of Connecticut. . .law, and that law embodies a policy of providing access to the courts for persons with serious bodily injuries; and (3) aside from her initial treatment after the accident, the plaintiff has received all of her post-accident medical care in Connecticut. We agree with the plaintiff.

This court has traditionally adhered to the doctrine that the substantive rights and obligations arising out of a tort controversy are determined by the

---

[1] The parties were not related at the time of the accident. They subsequently married each other . . . .

law of the place of injury, or lex loci delicti. Recently, however, we have recognized that there are circumstances in which strict application of the lex loci delicti rule frustrates the legitimate expectations of the parties and undermines an important policy of this state. In such circumstances, we have refused to apply the doctrine. *Simaitis v. Flood,* 182 Conn. 24, 437 A.2d 828 (1980).

*Simaitis* was a plaintiff's appeal of an adverse summary judgment in a negligence action arising out of an automobile accident that occurred in Tennessee. The parties were Connecticut domiciliaries employed by a Connecticut corporation. The accident occurred while they were traveling in the course of their employment. The dispositive issue on appeal was whether the governing law was the workers' compensation act of Tennessee, which barred the plaintiff's action for damages, or the Connecticut act, which permitted such an action. We held that application of the lex loci rule in these circumstances afforded an "unsatisfactory resolution" to the choice of law problem, noting that to employ the rule "would bestow upon temporary visitors injured in Connecticut all the relief which the Connecticut compensation act affords, but deny that same relief to Connecticut residents injured while on temporary business outside the state, even when all other incidents of employment . . . are in Connecticut." Although we expressly declined to reconsider the rule of lex loci for tort law in general, we decided that it was appropriate to pursue an alternate approach for choice of law issues in workers' compensation cases. . . .

Our decision in *Simaitis* has rightly been interpreted as a signal that we are not wholeheartedly committed to application of lex loci as the sole approach to choice of law in all torts cases . . . .

We have consistently held that "a court should not overrule its earlier decisions unless the most cogent reasons and inescapable logic requires it." We have also recognized, however, that "[p]rinciples of law which serve one generation well may, by reason of changing conditions, disserve a later one," and that "[e]xperience can and often does demonstrate that a rule, once believed sound, needs modification to serve justice better. Accordingly, we now undertake to analyze the policies and principles underlying the doctrine of lex loci delicti, as a preliminary step to determining whether "cogent reasons and inescapable logic" demand that we abandon the doctrine under the circumstances of the present case.

The doctrine of lex loci delicti, as first adopted by American courts in the late nineteenth and early twentieth centuries, presumes that the rights and obligations of the parties to a tort action "vest" at the place of injury. *See* 3 J. BEALE, CONFLICT OF LAWS (1935) p. 1968. Justice Cardozo, describing the vested rights theory in *Loucks v. Standard Oil Co.,* stated: "A foreign statute is not law in this state, but it gives rise to an obligation, which, if transitory, 'follows the person and may be enforced wherever the person may be found. . . .' [I]t is a principle of every civilized law that vested rights shall be protected." The vested rights theory was a guiding principle of the first Restatement of Conflict of Laws.

The vested rights theory of choice of law is an anachronism in modern jurisprudence. Its underlying premise, that the legislative jurisdiction of the place where a right "vests" must be recognized in every other jurisdiction, presupposes that a nationally uniform system of choice of law rules is necessary and desirable. See R. LEFLAR, AMERICAN CONFLICTS LAW (1968) pp. 205-206. Choice of law rules are not immutable principles, however. Subject to the limitations of the due process clause of the fourteenth amendment and the full faith and credit clause of article IV of the United States constitution; see *Phillips Petroleum Co. v. Shutts,* 472 U.S. 797(1985); *Allstate Ins. Co. v. Hague,* 449 U.S. 302 (1981), individual state courts are free to formulate choice of law rules as they deem appropriate. "[F]or a State's substantive law to be selected in a constitutionally permissible manner, that State must have a significant contact or significant aggregation of contacts, creating state interests, such that choice of its law is neither arbitrary nor fundamentally unfair."

Stripped of the mantle of constitutional authority, the vested rights doctrine is simply another legal theory, and one which has been the subject of extensive criticism for the past half century. See W. Cook, *"The Logical and Legal Bases of the Conflict of Laws,"* 33 YALE L.J. 457 (1924); E. Lorenzen, *"Territoriality, Public Policy and the Conflict of Laws,"* 33 YALE L.J. 736 (1924); H. Yntema, *"The Hornbook Method and the Conflict of Laws,"* 37 YALE L.J. 468 (1928). Professor David F. Cavers criticized the vested rights doctrine as ignoring the substantive content of legal rules and focusing exclusively on territorial concerns, "the law's content being irrelevant to the choice" of law. D. CAVERS, RE-STATING THE CONFLICT OF LAWS: THE CHAPTER ON CONTRACTS, IN XXTH CENTURY COMPARATIVE AND CONFLICTS LAW (1961) pp. 349, 350. Another, more fundamental criticism of the vested rights theory of conflicts of law is that it fails to explain "why the law of the place of wrong should be applied to cases which have arisen there. [It gives] us a guiding principle but without any raison d'Êetre." M. HANCOCK, TORTS IN THE CONFLICT OF LAWS (1942) p. 36.

The theoretical barrenness of the vested rights doctrine, from which the rule of lex loci delicti derives, is but one of the many reasons that a majority of state courts have rejected the rule of lex loci, and that legal scholars have virtually unanimously urged its abandonment. "The basic theme running through the attacks on the place of injury rule is that wooden application of a few overly simple rules, based on the outmoded 'vested rights theory,' cannot solve the complex problems which arise in modern litigation and may often yield harsh, unnecessary and unjust results." The lex loci approach fails to acknowledge that jurisdictions other than the place of injury may have a legitimate interest in applying their laws to resolve particular issues arising out of a tort controversy.

Having noted the perceived weaknesses of a categorical lex loci delicti rule, we now consider the principal reasons advanced for its retention. These are: (1) the desirability of allowing the legislature to alter established choice of law doctrines; (2) stare decisis; (3) the certainty and predictability of result afforded by a categorical choice of law rule and the concomitant ease of applying such a rule; and (4) the prevention of parochial applications of forum law in controversies involving foreign jurisdictions. We will examine each of these rationales in turn as they relate to the circumstances of the present case.

Because choice of law is a matter of "broad public policy," the defendant argues that it is the province of the legislature, and not the courts, to make doctrinal changes in established law. Some of the courts that have chosen to adhere to the lex loci doctrine have expressed similar sentiments. We disagree. The lex loci doctrine is the creation of jurists and scholars, not legislators. Statutes deal expressly with choice of law issues only rarely and episodically. . . .The legislature of course retains plenary authority, subject to constitutional mandates, to formulate statutory choice of law rules. Until the legislature chooses to act, however, this court has an independent responsibility to modernize rules of law that have traditionally reposed with the judiciary.

Regarding stare decisis, the second argument in favor of retaining lex loci, we have already noted that, while courts should not overrule established precedent except in compelling circumstances, the force of precedent will not hinder our rejection of a rule whose application no longer serves the ends of justice. The arguments for adherence to precedent are least compelling, furthermore, "when the rule to be discarded may not be reasonably supposed to have determined the conduct of the litigants, and particularly when in its origin it was the product of institutions or conditions which have gained a new significance or development with the progress of the years." In the present case, as in most unintentional tort cases, there is no reason to suppose that the defendant planned his conduct with the intention of availing himself of the benefits of Quebec law . . . . Our refusal to adhere to lex loci delicti in this case, therefore, does not defeat any legitimate prelitigation expectations of the parties founded in reliance on our prior decisions.

The third argument in favor of retention of the doctrine of lex loci is that it imparts certainty, predictability, and ease of application to choice of law rules. We do not underestimate these characteristics. "Simplicity in law is a virtue. Judicial efficiency often depends upon it." R. Leflar, *"Choice-Influencing Considerations in Conflicts Law,"* 41 N.Y.U. L. REV. 267, 288 (1966). The virtue of simplicity must, however, be balanced against the vice of arbitrary and inflexible application of a rigid rule . . . . In the present case, application of the lex loci delicti doctrine makes determination of the governing law turn upon a purely fortuitous circumstance: the geographical location of the parties' automobile at the time the accident occurred. Choice of law must not be rendered a matter of happenstance, in which the respective interests of the parties and the concerned jurisdictions receive only coincidental consideration . . . .

We note, furthermore, that lex loci's arguable advantages of uniformity and predictability have been undermined by its widespread rejection by courts and scholars, and by judicial constructions that avoid its strict application . . . . Even when it was the dominant American choice of law rule, courts frequently took advantage of various "escape devices" that allowed them to pay lip service to lex loci while avoiding its strict application. B. Currie, *"Notes on Methods and Objectives in the Conflict of Laws,"* 1959 DUKE L.J. 171, 175-78. Such devices included characterizing the issue at stake as procedural, rather than substantive, so that the law of the forum could be applied or characterizing a complaint framed in tort as a contract matter, thus allowing the law governing the place of contracting, rather than the place of injury, to control.

Because the use of such evasive devices undermines the predictability and ease of application of the lex loci doctrine, their use has been widely disparaged by scholarly commentators. "[I]t is a poor defense of the system to say that the unacceptable results which [lex loci] will inevitably produce can be averted by disingenuousness if the courts are sufficiently alert." B. Currie, *supra,* 176.

We now consider the fourth principal argument in favor of retention of lex loci, that application of the doctrine prevents forum courts from exercising parochial favoritism. Without lex loci, there is a risk that the forum will not take seriously the foreign jurisdiction's legitimate interest in the controversy. How seriously this risk is viewed depends upon an assessment of the available alternatives. "The alternative to a hard and fast system of doctrinal formulae is not anarchy. The difference is not between a system and no system, but between two systems; between a system which purports to have, but lacks, complete logical symmetry and one which affords latitude for the interplay and clash of conflicting factors . . ." F. Harper, *"Policy Bases of the Conflict of Laws: Reflections on Rereading Professor Lorenzen's Essays,"* 56 YALE L.J. 1155, 1157-58 (1947). Existing caselaw in other jurisdictions demonstrates that conflicts principles need not depend solely upon lex loci to assure proper deference to the legitimate claims of foreign law. A principled search for the local law of the state with the most significant relationship to the occurrence and the parties will often cause foreign law to be recognized as the law that should govern the controversy. "There is no reason why [a judge] should be less dispassionate in a conflicts case than in any other." R. Traynor, *"Is This Conflict Really Necessary?"* 37 TEX. L. REV. 655, 675 (1959).

We are, therefore, persuaded that the time has come for the law in this state to abandon categorical allegiance to the doctrine of lex loci delicti in tort actions. Lex loci has lost its theoretical underpinnings. Its formerly broad base of support has suffered erosion. We need not decide today, however, whether to discard lex loci in all of its manifestations. It is sufficient for us to consider whether, in the circumstances of the present case, reason and justice require the relaxation of its stringent insistence on determining conflicts of laws solely by reference to the place where a tort occurred.

In deciding how to assess a replacement for lex loci, we recognize that the legal literature offers us various alternative approaches . . . . [The court adopted the approach of the Restatement (Second) and applied the law of Connecticut.]

## NOTES AND QUESTIONS ON *O'CONNOR* AND THE CONTINUING CHOICE-OF-LAW REVOLUTION

(1) *The Pace of the Revolution.* In the first few decades, the choice-of-law revolution proceeded slowly, with only a few states adopting the new methods. The promulgation of the Restatement (Second) of Conflict of Laws in 1971 accelerated the pace somewhat so that by 1985 about half of the states had abandoned the First Restatement. Since then adherence to the traditional system has continued to decline steadily so that by 1997 only sixteen states relied on the First Restatement to any significant extent. *See* William M.

Richman and David Riley, *The First Restatement of Conflict of Laws on the Twenty-fifth Anniversary of Its Successor: Contemporary Practice on Traditional Courts,* 56 Md. L. Rev. 101 (1997). For the current report of the courts' dwindling allegiance to the First Restatement, see Symeon Symeonides, *1999: One More Year,* 48 Am. J. Comp. L. 142, 145-149 (2000) (13 adherents).

The total number clearly overstates the current prevalence of traditional choice-of-law methodology because First Restatement courts routinely deviate from the traditional system in worker's compensation, U.C.C., insurance, usury, and choice-of-law clause cases. Further, some courts import modern methods into traditional practice via the escape devices. Even more important, deviation from tradition tends to be progressive; a typical pattern within one state is to begin deviation from the lex loci rules in unusual cases and then adopt modern methods more generally, eventually abandoning the traditional system entirely. *See* Richman and Riley, *supra,* at 1230-1231. Do you see evidence of these trends in *O'Connor?*

(2) *Piecemeal Progress*: Within a single state, progress toward modern choice-of-law practice has been piecemeal. Following the common law tradition, a court faced with a tort choice-of-law case decided no more than the case at hand and sometimes adopted a modern method for torts cases, leaving contracts cases to be decided by the traditional place-of-making rule. Often, but not always, the court would adopt the new method for contract cases at the next opportunity. The sequence, torts-first-then-contracts, has been the norm although a few states (Indiana, Delaware, and Nevada, for example) have differed. Can you think of a reason for the typical sequence or for the exceptions? A possibility, of course, is simply that tort choice-of-law cases occur more commonly, appearing in the reported decisions about twice as often as contract cases. Very occasionally, a court has offered a principled reason for dividing its loyalties between traditional and modern systems. The Supreme Court of Florida, for example, opting to retain the traditional system for contract cases, even though it had opted for modernity in tort cases eight years before, offered this explanation:

> We recognize that this Court has discarded the analogous doctrine of lex loci delicti with respect to tort actions and limitations of actions. However, we believe that the reasoning controlling those decisions does not apply in the instant case. With tort law, there is no agreement, no foreseen set of rules and statutes which the parties had recognized would control the litigation. In the case of an insurance contract, the parties enter into that contract with the acknowledgement that the laws of that jurisdiction control their actions. In essence, that jurisdiction's laws are incorporated by implication into the agreement.

*See Sturiano v. Brooks,* 523 So. 2d 1126, 1129 (Fla. 1988). Are you convinced by the distinction? Will contract cases always involve reliance interests? Will tort cases never involve them? Are there reasons to abandon the traditional choice-of-law system that might outweigh reliance in particular contract cases? For a more complete discussion of the piecemeal progress problem, see Richman and Riley, *supra,* 1206-1213.

(3) *Reasons to Join the Revolution*:

(a) What reasons does the *O'Connor* court give for the initial deviation from the First Restatement in *Simiatis v. Flood*? Are these reasons especially applicable to worker's compensation cases or do they apply to tort cases generally or, even more generally, to choice-of-law cases across the board?

What additional reasons does the court advance for abandoning the place-of-injury rule generally? The opinion's treatment of the vested rights theory is fairly typical of modern courts. Few take it seriously; even those opinions that retain the traditional system in the face of a modernist challenge tend not to rely on the metaphysics of vested rights. Apart from faulty theoretical underpinnings, what other defects does the court attribute to the First Restatement?

(b) Are you convinced by the court's response to the stare decisis and let-the-legislature-do-it arguments? It is true as a general matter that the courts are always free to abandon common law doctrine, but are some judge-made doctrines so entrenched that it makes sense to leave fundamental reform to the legislature? In a state without a modern evidence code, for instance, would it be wise policy for the supreme court to abolish the hearsay rule?

(c) How does the court discount the purported advantages of the traditional system, its certainty, predictability, and ease of application? One argument relies on the widespread rejection of the traditional method by courts. This attack is not just the everybody-is-doing-it argument, which is, of course, vulnerable to the what-if-everybody-jumped-off-a-cliff response. Rather, the point has additional force in this context because one of the supposed virtues of the traditional system is national uniformity, and once a substantial number of states defect, national uniformity ceases to be a selling point.

(d) Are you tempted by the traditional system's supposed anti-parochialism? If so, remember the Arkansas telegraph cases, discussed in § 4.11[B].

*(4) Reactionaries*

(a) Not every contemporary court has chosen to join the revolution. The most spirited defense of tradition comes from the West Virginia Supreme Court of Appeals in *Paul v. National Life,* 352 S.E.2d 550 (W.Va. 1986), and ease of application was a major theme in the opinion. Deriding a modern choice-of-law system, which had been described as a "method of analysis that permitted dissection of the jural bundle constituting a tort and its environment," the *Paul* court responded:

> That sounds pretty intellectual, but we still prefer a rule. The lesson of history is that methods of analysis that permit dissection of the jural bundle constituting a tort and its environment produce protracted litigation and voluminous, inscrutable appellate opinions, while rules get cases settled quickly and cheaply.

The court suggested that much of the dissatisfaction with the First Restatement arose in cases involving guest statutes, intra-family immunity, and contributory negligence. These doctrines are rapidly disappearing, however, leaving reformist courts saddled with cumbersome modern choice-of-law systems long after the substantive-law evils that provoked them have disappeared. Are you convinced? What of the new choice-of-law issues generated by tort reform

legislation: damage caps, no-fault compensation regimes, arbitration requirements, and the like? Will the traditional lex loci rules generate satisfactory
solutions?

Finally, the court responded to the argument that the system of escape
devices had robbed the First Restatement of its claimed virtues of certainty,
uniformity, and predictability:

> There is some truth in this, and we generally eschew the more
> strained escape devices employed to avoid the sometimes-harsh effects
> of the traditional rule. Nevertheless, we remain convinced that the
> traditional rule, for all of its faults, remains superior to any of its
> modern competitors. Moreover, if we are going to manipulate conflicts
> doctrine in order to achieve substantive results, we might as well
> manipulate something we understand. Having mastered marble, we
> decline an apprenticeship in bronze.

(b) By far, the most frequently cited reasons to retain the traditional system
are the vices of the more modern alternatives. They are thought to be
confusing, unpredictable, manipulable, result-oriented, and incapable of
providing guidance to the courts. After reading Parts B and C and *Auten* and
*Haag,* you have some basis to evaluate these critiques, but you may wish to
reconsider the question after studying the materials in Parts E and F of this
chapter.

# PART E  INTEREST ANALYSIS

## § 4.18  Doing Interest Analysis

*Introduction.* Interest analysis is probably the methodology of most pervasive influence on courts today. Its purposive approach has been incorporated into other choice-of-law systems, and informs the work of even those courts and commentators that have formally adopted rival views. Here, our intention is not only to display the approach, but to provide some basic training in it. Like many lawyers who master interest analysis, you may find yourself using it in a preliminary way to get a handle on a conflicts case, whatever approach to conflicts you may actually prefer or find expedient to argue.

Although there are certain unique features, fundamentally the approach does not differ from ordinary purposive reasoning, or as Brainerd Currie described it, "ordinary construction and interpretation." That the task of courts in conflicts cases was essentially one of construction of domestic law was also recognized early by the Supreme Court. *Cf. Lauritzen v. Larsen,* 345 U.S. 571 (1953), *supra* (Jackson, J.): "[We] are simply dealing with a problem of statutory construction rather commonplace in a federal system by which courts often have to decide whether [a law] is to be applied to foreign events or transactions."

---

## NOTES ON THE EMERGENCE OF INTEREST ANALYSIS

(1) *The constitutional ground rules: the power of a state.* In the 1930s, in notable opinions particularly by Justices Stone and Brandeis, the Supreme Court began to develop a modern view of the nature of the *power* of a state to govern. These developments will be traced more fully in Chapter 5, *infra.* The Court based, and still bases, the legislative power of a sovereign not so much on its territory as on its *sphere of legitimate governmental interest.*

Obviously, spheres of interest, unlike territories, can overlap: that is why conflicts arise. Yet a "balancing" of interests, so typical of constitutional jurisprudence in other contexts, is not a feature here. In a conflicts case, the Court declines to require a state to "balance" its interests against those of another state. The other state, after all, can apply its own law in its own courts when the occasion arises.

*A fortiori,* the Court has declined to impose upon American courts any overriding duty of full faith and credit to laws (as opposed to judgments). The reasoning has been that it would be "absurd" if a court must always apply the other state's law but never its own. *Alaska Packers Ass'n v. Indus. Accident Comm.,* 294 U.S. 532, 542-43 (1935). So with fair consistency the Court has held that a state with a legitimate interest in applying its own law on the particular facts of a conflicts case will be free to do so, even when another state is equally, or even more, interested in applying *its* law. For extensive coverage of constitutional limits upon choices of law, see Chapter 5, *infra.*

Paul Freund, *Chief Justice Stone and the Conflict of Laws,* 59 HARV. L. REV. 1210 (1946): "The constitutional latitude afforded the states by virtue of their respective interests is not, of course, necessarily the measure of what may be desirable as a choice of law. But [it does] at least furnish a helpful point of departure for conflicts cases."

(2) *Brainerd Currie.* Building on the insights of Cook, Cavers, and the constitutional conflicts opinions of Justices Stone and Brandeis, Brainerd Currie published a series of brilliant essays on conflicts in the late 1950s. He showed how ordinary purposive reasoning could be applied to conflicts cases. He called the method, *"governmental interest analysis."* In the course of developing his ideas he discovered that many "conflicts" cases did not involve true conflicts of state interests, and therefore presented no real problem. He called these, *"false conflicts."* To impose a traditional choice of law upon a "false conflict" was not only unnecessary, but very often would produce irrational results.

## BRAINERD CURRIE AND INTEREST ANALYSIS

In what is widely thought to be the most influential conflicts writing of this century, *Married Women's Contracts,* 25 U. CHI. L. REV. 227 (1958), Currie was able to demonstrate, using interest analysis, precisely what was wrong with the traditional approach. Even more important, he showed that interest analysis was a powerful new tool for solving some conflicts problems and analyzing all of them. In the space of just a few years, Currie published an enormous amount of scholarship developing interest analysis; those writings revolutionized the field of choice of law.

Currie had two great insights. The first was to recognize that no law should be applied in a choice-of-law case unless (a) doing so would advance the policy interests of at least one state that (b) had a legitimate "interest" (or "contact") with the problem, an interest that must be evaluated in light of the facts of each case. That insight—anathema, of course, to adherents of the Vested Rights doctrine—actually has two components.

1) *Interest Analysis.* The first part of Currie's argument, that all judicial decisions should advance policy interests, was not novel; that view had been widely recognized in academic and judicial circles since the Legal Realists had become prominent in the early 1930s. Currie's genius lay in applying that doctrine to choice-of-law questions. ( Why it took until the late 1950s for the teachings of the Realists to reach Conflicts is a difficult question. For some speculation on the subject, *see* William L. Reynolds, *Legal Process and Choice of Law,* 56 MD. L. REV. 1371 (1997).) Currie summarized interest analysis in the following way:

> [T]he court should first of all determine the governmental policy . . . which is expressed in the law of the forum. The court should then inquire whether the relationship of the forum state to the case at bar— that is, to the parties, to the transaction, to the subject matter, to the litigation—is such as to bring the case within the scope of the state's governmental concern, and to provide a legitimate basis for the assertion that the state has an interest in the application of its policy in this instance.

Brainerd Currie, *The Constitution and the Choice of Law: Governmental Interests and the judicial Function,* 26 U. CHI. L. REV. 9, 9-10 (1958).

Or, as one scholar explained, Currie "argued that it is inherently unsound to choose between competing laws without reference to those laws, as the First Restatement did . . . .[I]n choosing between competing laws, courts should take into account the policies behind those laws and the facts of the particular case." Bruce Posnak, *Choice of Law: Interest Analysis and Its "New Crits,"* 36 AM. J. COMP. L. 681, 682 (1988).

2) *False (and True) Conflicts.* Currie's second insight followed from the first and was equally brilliant: If the law of only one state would be furthered by application in the case at bar, then only that state's law should be applied. In other words, it made no sense, when the facts of a case implicated the policies of one state but not another, to apply the law of any state but the one whose policies were implicated. That insight follows naturally from the Realist belief, captured in Currie's first insight, that all law should advance policy interests. This second insight, which Currie labeled a "false conflict," has proven to be the most enduring contribution of interest analysis to choice-of-law theory. Indeed, the false conflict insight has won near universal acceptance in American courts.

Currie also recognized a corollary to the recognition of false conflicts: there will be times when the interests of two or more states *will* be implicated; that is, the policies represented by the different laws would be furthered by the application of either one in the case at hand. Currie labeled this situation a "True" Conflict. The resolution of true conflicts has proven to be the most difficult task for interest analysis and, indeed, for any policy-based method of resolving choice-of-law problems.

3) *A Warning on Terminology.* Judges, lawyers, and sometimes even academics often use technical terms such as "interest analysis" loosely. Although the term, properly speaking, refers only to the Currie methodology, it often is used to refer to any method for approaching choice of law decision-making through policy analysis—a method sometimes called "modern" analysis in contrast to the dated methods of the First Restatement.

Currie's work has spawned a vast literature, pro and con. For general criticism of Interest Analysis, *see, e.g.,* LEA BRILMAYER, CONFLICT OF LAWS: FOUNDATIONS AND FUTURE DIRECTIONS, ch. 2 (1991); Harold Korn, *The Choice-of-Law Revolution: A Critique,* 83 COLUM. L. REV. 772 (1983); Alfred Hill, *Governmental Interests and the Conflict of Laws—A Reply to Professor Currie,* 27 U. CHI. L. REV. 463 (1960). For a general defense, see, e.g., Bruce Posnak, *Choice of Law: Interest Analysis and Its New "Crits,"* 36 AM. J. COMP. L. 681 (1988); Robert Sedler, *Interest Analysis and the Forum Preference in the Conflict of Laws: A Response to the 'New Crits,'* 34 MERCER L. REV. 593 (1983).

The rest of Part E develops Interest Analysis as a prelude to the examination of other forms of modern analysis including the Second Conflicts Restatement in Parts F and G of this Chapter.

*See* PROBLEM 4E-1. CURRIED CONFLICTS.

## NOTE ON LAW, POLICY, "SIGNIFICANT" CONTACTS, AND INTEREST ANALYSIS

The relation among the various terms employed in interest analysis can be conveniently displayed by diagraming actual cases. *See* William Richman, *Diagraming Conflicts: A Graphic Understanding of Interest Analysis,* 43 OHIO St. L.J. 317 (1982). Take, for example, the *Carroll* case, § 4.06, *supra.* It might be diagramed as follows:

|  | Alabama | Mississippi |
|---|---|---|
| Contacts | Forum<br>Worker<br>Employer<br>Employment contract<br>Wrongful conduct | Injury |
| Law | D vicariously<br>liable | D not liable |
| Policy<br>(Purpose) | Compensate<br>workers for<br>work injuries | Protect employers<br>from vicarious<br>liabilities |

An arrow can now be drawn from each "policy" to the "contact" to which the policy might be relevant. Alabama's policy of compensating workers points to the Alabama worker. The contact with the worker, then, becomes "significant;" the state has an "interest" in having its law applied in order to compensate its worker. A second arrow drawn from Mississippi's policy of protecting employers will point to the defendant employer; but now the arrow must cross columns, and point back toward an *Alabama* employer. Thus, Mississippi's contact with the case as place of injury is not "significant." Its employer-protecting "policy" cannot be advanced by applying its law (the fellow-servant rule), because the employer is not a Mississippi employer, employing workers in Mississippi.[1] Thus, Mississippi has no "interest" in applying its fellow-servant rule; and the forum, Alabama, should apply the law of the only interested state: Alabama. The case is a false conflict. Thus, when Alabama applied Mississippi law in that case it made a perverse choice. It defeated its own domestic policies without advancing any Mississippi policy.

---

[1] This conclusion may begin to shift as the defendant railway engages increasingly in activities in Mississippi requiring the employment of workers there. The argument that Mississippi is an interested state, and the case a true conflict, may then become available to that extent.

## STUBBORN QUESTIONS ABOUT INTEREST ANALYSIS

*Introduction.* The following questions are raised for you to think about as you read through the cases in this Chapter. They raise issues of continuing current controversy over interest analysis.

(1) *Interest in wilful governance?* Does a state have an interest merely by saying it does? In a long line of decisions, the Supreme Judicial Court of Massachusetts had established that Massachusetts "has an interest in always applying its own law." Is there a difference between a legitimate governmental interest and a unilateral declaration of power? Writers who have assumed that a sovereign can become an interested one by declaring itself to have an interest include Lea Brilmayer, *Governmental Interest Analysis: A House Without Foundations,* 46 OHIO L.J. 459 (1985); and Phaedon Kozyris, *Interest Analysis Facing Its Critics,* 46 OHIO St. L.J. 569 (1985). But interest analysts do not generally share this assumption.

(2) *Does A State Have an "Interest" in Everything?* A state certainly has an interest in some laws, especially those which concern its interests as sovereign or its pocketbook (examples include sovereign immunity and the state as property owner). But does a state really have an interest in its version of the parol evidence rule or Statute of Frauds?

(3) *Empowerment, "officiousness," and the "selfish state."* In *Milliken v. Pratt,* § 4.07, *supra* was Massachusetts *empowered* to legislate for all married women worldwide? Wasn't the state's legitimate sphere of governmental interest (the old-fashioned phrase would have been, "its police power") limited to providing for the general welfare of its residents? Of course Massachusetts must have power to govern all events, visitors, and objects on its territory, but such power is needed to enable it to provide for the general welfare of Massachusetts people.

Although the idea of empowerment was missing from Currie's formulation, it seems useful to a modern understanding of his work. *See* Louise Weinberg, *Choice of Law and Minimal Scrutiny,* 44 U. CHI. L. REV. 440, 445 (1982). Rather than basing his reasoning explicitly on a limit on state *power,* Currie simply said it would be "officious" of Massachusetts to try to protect all married women everywhere. He posited a "selfish state," rationally seeking to advance its own interest.

## § 4.19 False Conflicts

*Introduction.* The identification of the "false conflict" remains Brainerd Currie's signal achievement. Once analysis shows that there is only one interested state, there is overwhelming consensus that state's law should apply.

Understandably, courts have been most open to arguments for abandonment of the First Restatement approach when confronted with a false conflict. In the case that follows, note that, quite apart from arguments about the choice of law to be made, counsel presented the court with arguments about whether or not to abandon the traditional approach. What would you have added to those arguments?

## BABCOCK v. JACKSON

*New York Court of Appeals*
*12 N. Y. 2d 473, 240 N. Y.S.2d 743, 191 N.E.2d 279 (1963)*

FULD, JUDGE. On Friday, September 16, 1960, Miss Georgia Babcock and her friends, Mr. and Mrs. William Jackson, all residents of Rochester, left that city in Mr. Jackson's automobile, Miss Babcock as guest, for a weekend trip to Canada. Some hours later, as Mr. Jackson was driving in the Province of Ontario, he apparently lost control of the car; it went off the highway into an adjacent stone wall, and Miss Babcock was seriously injured. Upon her return to this State, she brought the present action against William Jackson, alleging negligence on his part in operating his automobile [Jackson having died after suit was filed, his executrix was substituted as defendant].

At the time of the accident, there was in force in Ontario a statute providing that "the owner or driver of a motor vehicle, other than a vehicle operated in the business of carrying passengers for compensation, is not liable for any loss or damages resulting from bodily injury to, or the death of any person being carried . . . ." [No] such bar is recognized under this State's substantive law of torts . . . .

The question presented is simply drawn. Shall the law of the place of the tort *invariably* govern the availability of relief for the tort or shall the applicable choice of law rule also reflect a consideration of other factors which are relevant to the purposes served by the enforcement or denial of the remedy?

The traditional choice of law rule, embodied in the original Restatement of Conflict of Laws, and until recently unquestioningly followed in this court, has been that the substantive rights and liabilities arising out of a tortious occurrence are determinable by the law of the place of the tort. It had its conceptual foundation in the vested rights doctrine, namely, that a right to recover for a foreign tort owes its creation to the law of the jurisdiction where the injury occurred and depends for its existences and extent solely on such law. Although espoused by such great figures as Justice Holmes and Professor Beale, the vested rights doctrine has long since been discredited . . . . [As] applied to torts, the theory ignores the interest which jurisdictions other than that where the tort occurred may have in the resolution of particular issues. It is for this very reason that, despite the advantages of certainty, ease of application and predictability which it affords, there has in recent years been increasing criticism of the traditional rule by commentators and a judicial trend towards its abandonment or modification.

Realization of the unjust and anomalous results which may ensue from application of the traditional rule in tort cases also prompted judicial search for a more satisfactory alternative in that area. In the much discussed case of *Kilberg v. Northeast Airlines, Inc.,* this court declined to apply the law of the place of the tort as respects the issue of the quantum of the recovery in a death action arising out of an airplane crash, where the decedent had been a New York resident and his relationship with the defendant airline had originated in this State . . . .

The emphasis in *Kilberg* was plainly that the merely fortuitous circumstance that the wrong and injury occurred in Massachusetts did not give that State a controlling concern or interest in the amount of the tort recovery as against the competing interest of New York in providing its residents or users of transportation facilities there originating with full compensation for wrongful death. Although the *Kilberg* case did not expressly adopt the "center of gravity" theory, its weighing of the contacts or interests of the respective jurisdictions to determine their bearing on the issue of the extent of the recovery is consistent with that approach.

Significantly, it was dissatisfaction with "the mechanical formulae of the conflicts of law" which led to judicial departure from similarly inflexible choice of law rules in the field of contracts, grounded, like the torts rule, on the vested rights doctrine . . . .

In *Auten v. Auten,* . . . this court abandoned such rules and applied what has been termed the "center of gravity" or "grouping of contacts" theory of the conflict of laws . . . . The "center of gravity" rule of *Auten,* has not only been applied in other cases in this State, as well as in other jurisdictions, but has supplanted the prior rigid and set contract rules in the most current draft of the *Restatement of Conflict of Laws* . . . .

Comparison of the relative "contacts" and "interests" of New York and Ontario in this litigation, vis-a-vis the issue here presented, makes it clear that the concern of New York is unquestionably the greater and more direct and that the interest of Ontario is at best minimal. The present action involves injuries sustained by a New York guest as the result of the negligence of a New York host in the operation of an automobile, garaged, licensed and undoubtedly insured in New York, in the course of a week-end journey which began and was to end there. In sharp contrast, Ontario's sole relationship with the occurrence is the purely adventitious circumstance that the accident occurred there.

New York's policy of requiring a tort-feasor to compensate his guest for injuries caused by his negligence cannot be doubted as attested by the fact that the Legislature of this State has repeatedly refused to enact a statute denying or limiting recovery in such cases and our courts have neither reason nor warrant for departing from that policy simply because the accident, solely affecting New York residents and arising out of the operation of a New York based automobile, happened beyond its borders. Per contra, Ontario has no conceivable interest in denying a remedy to a New York guest against his New York host for injuries suffered in Ontario by reason of conduct which was tortious under Ontario law. The object of Ontario's guest statute, it has been said, is "to prevent the fraudulent assertion of claims by passengers, in collusion with the drivers, against insurance companies" (Survey of Canadian Legislation, 1 U.Toronto L.J. 358, 366) and, quite obviously, the fraudulent claims intended to be prevented by the statute are those asserted against Ontario defendants and their insurance carriers, not New York defendants and their insurance carriers. Whether New York defendants are imposed upon or their insurers defrauded by a New York plaintiff is scarcely a valid legislative concern of Ontario simply because the accident occurred there, any more so than if the accident had happened in some other jurisdiction.

It is hardly necessary to say that Ontario's interest is quite different from what it would have been had the issue related to the manner in which the defendant had been driving his car at the time of the accident . . . .

The issue here, however, is not whether the defendant offended against a rule of the road prescribed by Ontario for motorists generally or whether he violated some standard of conduct imposed by that jurisdiction, but rather whether the plaintiff, because she was a guest in the defendant's automobile, is barred from recovering damages for a wrong concededly committed. As to that issue, it is New York, the place where the parties resided, where their guest-host relationship arose and where the trip began and was to end, rather than Ontario, the place of the fortuitous occurrence of the accident, which has the dominant contacts and the superior claim for application of its law. Although the rightness or wrongness of defendant's conduct may depend upon the law of the particular jurisdiction through which the automobile passes, the rights and liabilities of the parties which stem from their guest-host relationship should remain constant and not vary and shift as the automobile proceeds from place to place. Indeed, such a result, we note, accords with "the interests of the host in procuring liability insurance adequate under the applicable law, and the interests of his insurer in reasonable calculability of the premium." (Ehrenzweig, *Guest Statutes in the Conflict of Laws,* 69 YALE L.J. 595, 603) . . . .

VAN VOORHIS, JUDGE (dissenting).

The decision . . . of this appeal changes the established law of this State . . . . Attempts to make the law or public policy of New York State prevail over the laws and policies of other States where citizens of New York State are concerned are simply a form of extraterritoriality which can be turned against us whenever actions are brought in the courts of New York which involve citizens of other States . . . . Undoubtedly ease of travel and communication, and the increase in interstate business have rendered more awkward discrepancies between the laws of the States in many respects. But this is not a condition to be cured by introducing or extending principles of extraterritoriality, as though we were living in the days of the Roman or British Empire, when the concepts were formed that the rights of a Roman or an Englishman were so significant that they must be enforced throughout the world even where they were otherwise unlikely to be honored by "lesser breeds without the law . . . ."

*See* PROBLEM 4E-2. REVERSING *BABCOCK*.

## NOTES AND QUESTIONS ON *BABCOCK*

(1) *After* Babcock *came the deluge.* The decision provided the impetus for wide-spread modernization of choice-of-law doctrine by adopting analysis which focuses on the policies implicated by the competing legal rules. As noted in Part D of this Chapter, only a handful of states still follow the traditional choice-of-law rules exemplified by the First Restatement. Of course, the

under-lying question will always remain: Was the revolution ushered in by Currie and *Babcock* a good thing?

*See* PROBLEM 4E-3. THE CASE FOR THE OPPOSITION.

(2) *What is the choice-of-law method adopted by New York in* Babcock? The case contains elements of interest analysis, but Judge Fuld certainly tries to do as little violence as he can to the "place of most significant contact" method he adopted in *Auten and Haag.*

(3) **TOOKER v. LOPEZ,** 24 N.Y.2d 569, 301 N.Y.S.2d 519, 249 N.E.2d 394 (1969). Action for wrongful death. Catherina Tooker, a 20-year-old student at Michigan State University, was killed in a car driven by Marcia Lopez, her fellow student, who was also killed. (The accident also seriously injured another passenger, Susan Silk.) Tooker and Lopez were both New York domiciliaries. The automobile which Lopez was driving belonged to her father who resided in New York, where the car was registered and insured. The Michigan guest statute required a showing of willful misconduct or gross negligence, and thus would defeat recovery.

*Held* (Keating, J.): For the plaintiff. This case is one of the simplest in the choice-of-law area. It is a false conflict. New York has the only real interest in whether recovery should be granted. The application of Michigan law would defeat a legitimate interest of the forum State without serving a legitimate interest of any other State.

> The policy of this State with respect to all those injured in automobile accidents is reflected in the legislative declaration which prefaces New York's compulsory insurance law: "The legislature is concerned over the rising toll of motor vehicle accidents and the suffering and loss thereby, inflicted. The legislature determines that it is a matter of grave concern that motorists shall be financially able to respond in damages for their negligent acts, so that innocent victims of motor vehicle accidents may be recompensed for the injury and financial loss inflicted upon them."

> Neither this declaration of policy nor the standard required provisions for an auto liability insurance policy make any distinction between guests, pedestrians or other insured parties.

> New York's grave concern in affording recovery for the injuries suffered by Catherina Tooker, a New York domiciliary, and the loss suffered by her family as a result of her wrongful death is evident merely in stating the policy which our law reflects. On the other hand, Michigan has no interest in whether a New York plaintiff is denied recovery against a New York defendant where the car is insured here.

*Concurring separately* (Fuld, J.): The New York experience with guest-statute cases is now sufficient to justify New York in the formulation of clear choice-of-law rules.

\* \* \*

For further development of Judge Fuld's proposal and the state of choice of law in New York today, see *Neumeier v. Kuehner* and the Notes which follow it, § 4.25[C], *infra.*

See PROBLEMS 4E-4. PRESUMPTION OF DEATH; 4E-5. UNLIMITED RECOVERY?; 4E-6. THE U-TURN; 4E-7. THE MEXICAN SAFARI; 4E-8. THE STATE LINE TAVERN; 4E-9. KLM AND PAN AM; 4E-10. THE DANGERS OF RAIL TRAVEL; 4E-11. LIFE CAN BE DANGEROUS.

(4) *The "Miss Silk" problem.* Judge Keating was right, wasn't he, that the problem presented by Ms. Tooker's case was one of the easiest in the conflict of laws? But remember that at the time of the crash, there was another passenger in the car: Susan Silk. Unlike Tooker, she was not a New Yorker. Judge Keating, Judge Burke, and Judge Breitel all recognized that New York's rule in favor of complete recovery in auto accident cases could not be made to apply without strain to Silk's case, a case with which New York's only contact would be as residence of the defendant driver. Would it be proper for New York to reach different outcomes in cases brought by similarly situated co-passengers in the same vehicle? Judge Keating felt not at all sure that Silk would, in fact, be denied the benefit of New York law. But if she were, he argued, that was the consequence not of interest analysis, but of federalism.

(5) *The New York course of decision and the difficulty of policy analysis.* The results in New York conflicts cases both before and after *Tooker* have been erratic.

New York's problems were attributed by Judge Keating in *Tooker* to the difficulty of determining the policies underlying legal rules. Thus, in *Babcock, the* purpose behind the guest statute was thought to be to protect insurers from collusive suits. But in a later case, involving the Colorado guest statute and a second car, the New York court was deflected by a "teleological argument" that the purpose of a state's guest statute was not only to protect its auto insurers, but also to grant priority in the defendant's assets to innocent victims over "ungrateful guests." In *Tooker,* the New York court retracted that bit of reasoning, pointing out that the Colorado statute, like the Michigan statute in *Tooker,* did not bar the action, but merely raised the burden of proof. Such a statute could not rationally preserve the asserted priority.

The court might have added another argument to this. In a wrongful death case, it is hard to say that the surviving dependents of an "ungrateful guest" are less innocent than other victims of the accident in a second car. Or is the action for wrongful death analogous to an insurance policy, which is thought to benefit the insured, as well as the beneficiaries, and which will be forfeit if the insured breaches a material term? *See* BRAINERD CURRIE, SELECTED ESSAYS ON THE CONFLICT OF LAWS 295 (1963).

(6) *Analyze a state's rule? Or the absence in that state of the other state's rule?*

Which rule should a court submit to a policy (reason-for-the-rule) analysis? In the guest statute cases, New York's rule is, properly, its underlying tort law, providing full recovery for injuries caused by negligence. But courts sometimes seek the reason for not having a particular rule. In a guest-statute case, such a court might try to divine the reason why the forum does not have a guest statute. *See, eg., Schultz v. Boy Scouts of Am., Inc.,* 65 N.Y.2d 189, 491 N.Y.S.2d 90, 480 N.E.2d 679 (1985). Might the two sorts of questions yield different answers?

(7) *Fortuity in the conflict of laws.* Recall that in *Kilberg,* § 4.14, *supra,* New York thought it unfair that choice of law should be determined by the place where a plane fortuitously fell out of the sky. In *Auten,* § 4.16, *supra,* Judge Fuld thought it fortuitous that the contract was made in New York. In *Babcock,* Judge Fuld thought it fortuitous that the New York parties were injured in Ontario. Do questions about fortuitousness advance a choice-of-law inquiry? In *Tooker,* Judge Keating made short work of "adventitiousness:"

The dissent is, of course, correct that it was "adventitious" that Miss Tooker was a guest in an automobile registered and insured in New York. For all we know, her decision to go to Michigan State University as opposed to New York University may have been "adventitious." Indeed, her decision to go to Detroit on the weekend in question instead of staying on campus and studying may equally have been "adventitious." The fact is, however, that Miss Tooker went to Michigan State University; that she decided to go to Detroit on October 16, 1964; that she was a passenger in a vehicle registered and insured in New York; and that, as a result of all these "adventitious" occurrences, she is dead, and we have a case to decide.

(8) *The expectations of the parties and the "seat of the relationship."* The interesting debate among the judges in *Tooker* raises the question whether the parties might reasonably expect that Michigan law would apply to their dispute. They might have expected this simply because Michigan was the place of injury. Here, however, Michigan also seemed to be the "seat of the relationship" between the parties-both the guest-host relationship at issue, and the parties' general relationship with each other. The Second Restatement takes the position that in certain cases the "seat of relationship" of the parties might well be the place of most significant contact with the case. *See* § 159, Comment *b.* Moreover, *Tooker* and *Lopez,* arguably, were not New Yorkers for purposes of the case; they were settled in Michigan for the duration of their college educations. To this, Judge Keating responded,

The fact that the deceased guest and driver were in Michigan for an extended period of time is plainly irrelevant. Indeed, the Legislature, in requiring that insurance policies cover liability for injuries regardless of where the accident takes place has evinced commendable concern not only for residents of this State, but residents of other States who may be injured as a result of the activities of New York residents. Under these circumstances we cannot be concerned with whether Miss Tooker or Miss Lopez were in Michigan for a summer session or for a full college education.

What role should the expectations of the parties play in conflicts cases? Does it matter whether those cases involve contractual or settled property rights, rather than inadvertent tortious conduct? Can insurers, who defend many of this country's tort claims, ever be "surprised?" *See* RUSSELL WEINTRAUB, COMMENTARY ON THE CONFLICT OF LAWS 286-87 (3d ed. 1986); Richard Morris, *Enterprise Liability and the Actuarial Process: The Insignificance of Foresight,* 70 YALE L.J. 554 (1961). Don't insurers have full opportunity to adjust premiums in advance to take account of choice-of-law risks? Is it likely that party expectations can furnish more than buttressing arguments?

# HURTADO v. SUPERIOR COURT

*California Supreme Court (In Bank)*
*11 Cal. 3d.574, 114 Cal. Rptr. 106, 522 P. 2d 666 (1974)*

SULLIVAN, JUSTICE. [This was an action for wrongful death arising out of a 1969 car accident in California. The defendant driver, Manuel Hurtado, was the decedent Antonio Hurtado's cousin. The accident occurred when Hurtado's car collided with a pick-up truck owned and operated by defendant Jack Rexius. Both defendants were Californians; the plaintiff and his decedent were both Mexicans.]

Defendant Hurtado moved respondent court for a separate trial of the issue whether the measure of damages was to be applied according, to the law of California or the law of Mexico . . . .

In the landmark opinion authored by former Chief Justice Traynor for a unanimous court in *Reich v. Purcell* (1967) 67 Cal..2d 551, 63 Cal.Rptr. 31, 432 P.2d 727 *(see* Symposium, *Comments on Reich v. Purcell* (1968) 15 U.C.L.A. L. Rev. 551-654), we renounced the prior rule, adhered to . . . for many years, that in tort actions the law of the place of the wrong was the applicable law in a California forum regardless of the issues before the court. We adopted in its place a rule requiring an analysis of the respective interests of the states involved (governmental interest approach) . . . .

The issue involved in the matter before us is the measure of damages in the underlying action for wrongful death. Two states or governments are implicated: (1) California—the place of the wrong, the place of defendants' . . . residence, and the forum; and (2) Mexico—the domicile and residence of both plaintiffs and their decedent.

The fact that two states are involved does not in itself indicate that there is a "conflict of laws" or "choice of law" problem. There is obviously no problem where the laws of the two states are identical. Here, however, the laws of California and Mexico are not identical. [A calculation of the damages in this case under Mexican law will limit] recovery by the survivors of the decedent . . . to 24,334 pesos, or $1,946.72 at the applicable exchange rate of 12.5 pesos to the dollar. California provides that the heirs of the decedent are entitled to recover such sum, as under all the circumstances of the case, will be just compensation for the pecuniary loss which each heir has suffered by reason of the death of the decedent.

Although the two potentially concerned states have different laws, there is still no problem in choosing the applicable rule of law where only one of the states has an interest in having its law applied. "When one of two states related to a case has a legitimate interest in the application of its law and policy and the other has none, there is no real problem; clearly the law of the interested state should be applied." (B. CURRIE, SELECTED ESSAYS ON THE CONFLICT OF LAWS 189 (1963).

The interest of a state in a tort rule limiting damages for wrongful death is to protect defendants from excessive financial burdens or exaggerated claims . . . . Since . . . in this case, . . . Mexico has no defendant residents to protect, [it] has no interest in denying full recovery to its residents injured by non-Mexican defendants . . . .

[The] forum will apply its own rule of decision unless a party litigant timely invokes the law of a foreign state . . . .

In the case at bench, California as the forum should apply its own measure of damages for wrongful death, unless Mexico has an interest in having its measure of damages applied. Since, as we have previously explained, Mexico has no interest whatsoever in the application of its limitation of damages rule to the instant case, we conclude that the trial court correctly chose California law . . . .

[Defendant] contends that California has no interest in applying its measure of damages in this case because [under] *Reich v. Purcell, supra,* . . . the interest of a state in the law governing damages in wrongful death actions is "in determining the distribution of proceeds to the beneficiaries and that interest extends only to local decedents and beneficiaries." Decedent and plaintiffs were residents of Mexico and not "local decedents and beneficiaries" in California. Therefore, so the argument runs, California has no interest whatever in how plaintiff survivors, residents of Mexico, should be compensated for the wrongful death of their decedent, also a resident of Mexico, and conversely Mexico *does* have an interest.

Defendant's reading of *Reich* is inaccurate. It confuses two completely independent state interests: (1) the state interest involved in *creating* a cause of action for wrongful death so as to provide *some* recovery; and (2) the state interest involved *in limiting the amount* of that recovery. In *Reich* this court carefully separated these two state interests, although it referred to them in the same paragraph. The state interest in creating a cause of action for wrongful death is in "determining the distribution of proceeds to the beneficiaries;" the state interest in limiting damage is "to avoid the imposition of excessive financial burdens on them (defendants)."

In the case at bench, the entire controversy revolves about the choice of an appropriate rule of decision on the issue of the proper *measure* of damages; there is no contention that plaintiffs are not entitled under the applicable rules of decision to *some* recovery inwrongful death. The Mexican rule is a rule limiting damages. Thus, the interest of Mexico at stake is one aimed at protecting resident defendants in wrongful death actions and, as previously explained, is inapplicable to this case, because defendants are not Mexican residents. Mexico's. interest in limiting damages is not concerned with providing compensation for decedent's beneficiaries. It is Mexico's interest in, creating wrongful death actions which is concerned with distributing proceeds to the beneficiaries and that issue has not been raised in the case at bench.

The creation of wrongful death actions "insofar as plaintiffs are concerned" is directed toward compensating decedent's beneficiaries. California does not have this interest in applying its wrongful death statute here because plaintiffs are residents of Mexico. However, the creation of wrongful death actions is not concerned solely with plaintiffs. As to defendants the state interest in creating wrongful death actions is to deter conduct . . . . "Limitations of damages for wrongful death, however, have little or nothing to do with conduct. They are concerned not with how people should behave but with how survivors should be compensated . . . ."

Defendant's final contention is that California has no interest in extending to out-of-state residents greater rights than are afforded by the state of residence . . . . Defendant urges seemingly as an absolute choice of law principle that plaintiffs in wrongful death actions are not entitled to recover more than they would have recovered under the law of the state of their residence. In effect defendant argues that the state of plaintiffs' residence has an overriding interest in denying their own residents unlimited recovery.

Limitations of damages express no such state interest. A policy of limiting recovery in wrongful death actions "does not reflect a preference that widows and orphans should be denied full recovery." (CAVERS, THE CHOICE-OF-LAW PROCESS (1965), at p. 151) . . . .

---

## THE PLACE OF INJURY AND PROBLEMS OF POLICY ANALYSIS

(1) *A teaser.* If the parties are from different states with different laws, why isn't *Hurtado* a true conflict?

(2) *Reversing the Babcock facts.* Is it true that all cases in which the parties share a joint domicile are false conflicts? Does reversing the *Babcock* facts yield a false conflict? Suppose that in a guest statute case the parties are joint domiciliaries of Michigan, but the place of injury is New York. The action is brought in New York. Is Michigan, as joint domicile, the only interested state? Or does New York have an interest too? *See* Donald Trautman, *Kell v. Henderson: A Comment,* 67 COLUM. L. REV. 465, 467 (1967) (pointing out that at the place of injury "deterrent policies legitimately come into play"). Recall the discussion of analogous validating interests that come into play at the place of contracting, *see* § 4.18, *supra.*

(3) *Compensatory interests of the place of injury.* In *Bryant v. Sun West Airlines,* 146 Ariz. 41, 45, 703 P.2d 1190, 1194 (1985), an air crash case, the court remarked, "[The] state where the injury occurs does not have a strong interest in compensation if the injured plaintiff is a non-resident." In a footnote to this, the court added, "The only [compensatory] interest of the state of injury would be in the compensation of those who rendered medical aid and other assistance to the injured parties)." *See also Reich v. Purcell,* 67 Cal. 2d 551, 556, 432 P.2d 727, 731, 63 Cal. Rptr. 31, 35 (1967).

But wouldn't the place of injury have interests in furnishing a remedy for anyone injured there?

(4) *Undercutting deterrent policies of the place of injury.* Can the state effectually secure the safety of the territory for its "own" without simultaneously securing it for visitors? Would a court's refusal to give an injured visitor the

benefit of forum law be discriminatory? *See* Donald Trautman, *Kell v. Henderson: A Comment,* 67 COLUM. L. REV. 465, 467 (1967) (noting place of injury's "concern not to discriminate against nonresidents"). Are these concerns weaker in air crash cases like *Bryant?*

(5) **SCHULTZ v. BOY SCOUTS OF AMERICA, INC.,** 65 N.Y.2d 189, 491 N.Y.S.2d 90,480 N.E.2d 679 (1985). Action by parents of two young boys alleging child molestation by a Scoutmaster. The molestation occurred during a camping trip in New York. The New York Court of Appeals treated the case as one between joint domiciliaries of New Jersey. The issue was whether New Jersey's charitable immunity statute should be applied to immunize the defendant Boy Scouts from liability. In this reverse-*Babcock* situation, the court applied New Jersey law. The court reasoned that the deterrence interests of the place of injury were weak in this case because charitable immunity was "loss-allocating" rather than "conduct regulating." Thus, in effect, the case was a false conflict, and New Jersey, the joint domicile of the parties, was the only interested state. But wasn't New York's underlying tort law "conduct-regulating?"

(6) *Deterrence interests at the place of injury—Rationality and efficiency of rules.* It is sometimes argued that the deterrent interests of states are very weak in automotive accident cases. The defendant driver cannot be deterred from bad driving by liability rules, the argument goes, when she is already maximally deterred by her concern for her own safety. *See* RUSSELL WEINTRAUB, COMMENTARY ON THE CONFLICT OF LAWS 303 (3d ed. 1986); *Veasey v. Doremus,* 510 A.2d I 1 87, 103 N.J. 244 (3d Cir. 1986); *McSwain v. McSwain,* 420 Pa. 86, 215 A.2d 677 (1966). But why, then, do we impose liability for negligence in driving to begin with?

(7) *The problem of standard-of-living differentials.* Would it make a difference in *Hurtado* if the defendants were residents of Mexico? The California court is right, isn't it, when it says that its deterrent policies are advanced when money liability for the consequences of a tort is undiminished? But in an international case, like *Hurtado,* should widely divergent standards of living make a difference? The court does not tell us to what extent the Mexican cap on damages would approximate compensatory damages for this plaintiff. If damages are awarded by the standards of California juries, will the widow and her children return to Mexico to live in "ducal" splendor? *Cf.* Brainerd Currie, *The Silver Oar and All That: A Study of the Romero Case,* 27 U. CHI. L. REV. 1, 74 (1959).

What if the accident in *Hurtado* had occurred in Mexico? Wouldn't that take California's deterrent policies out of the picture? In *Hernandez v. Burger,* 102 Cal. App.3d 795, 162 Cal. Rptr. 564 (1980), the California Court of Appeal reasoned that although the plaintiff was Mexican, Mexico had an interest in keeping its damage ceiling low to encourage tourism, and, therefore, applied Mexican law.

The identification of false conflicts theoretically should simplify the judicial task. Do the foregoing problems of policy analysis shake your confidence in that statement? Or is policy analysis equally complex in nonconflicts cases?

## § 4.20   True Conflicts: Currie's Solution-Forum Law

*Introduction.* In the false conflict case, the obvious "solution" is to apply the law of the only interested state. But in the true conflict case, there is no obvious solution. In *Married Women's Contracts,* Currie wrote:

> There is no conceivable choice-of-law rule that will solve the [true conflict,] even though both states adopt it and consistently apply it . . . . The sensible and clearly constitutional thing for any court to do, confronted with a true conflict of interests, is to apply its own law . . . . [A] court should never apply any other law except when there is a good reason for doing so. That so doing will promote the interests of a foreign state at the expense of the interests of the forum is not a good reason.

Currie insisted that the interests of the concerned states should not be "weighed" or "balanced" at the forum. (Indeed, Currie once suggested that in the event of a true conflict, the court should apply the law of the state that comes first in the alphabet.) In this, his conflicts thinking was in the tradition of the constitutional conflicts cases in the Supreme Court. These cases hold that an interested state has power to apply its own law in its own courts, unqualified by any duty to "weigh" or "balance" the interests of another state. *See* Chapter 5, *infra.*

### THE ELUSIVE CONCEPT OF "PURPOSE"

Currie's whole line of analysis depends, of course, on the identification of the policy-or purpose-behind a state's law. The alleged inability of a court successfully to make that identification, especially when dealing with the laws of another state, has proven to be a prominent and frequent criticism of Interest Analysis. Critics have argued that the task Currie requires cannot be properly done. Thus, it is argued that statutes are ambiguous, that they seek to achieve multiple purposes, that the laws are really written by lobbyists representing "special interests," that legislative history is unreliable, that the "plain meaning" of the statute's language may conflict with extrinsic sources of meaning, and so forth.

There is, of course, little that is new under the legal sun and the debate described above is really a sub-set of a much larger debate concerning the proper method of statutory interpretation. Currie's search for legislative purpose was typical of the scholarly jurisprudence at the time he was writing about Conflicts. Indeed, his seminal article, *Married Women's Contracts,* was published in 1958, the very year when the Hart and Sacks treatise on Legal Process, the Bible of the purposive approach to interpretation, appeared. *See* HENRY M. HART, JR. AND ALBERT M. SACKS, THE LEGAL PROCESS: BASIC; PROBLEMS IN THE MAKING AND APPLICATION OF LAW 1370-83 (1958). (1994 ed., Eskridge & Frickey eds). (The current debate on interpretation is best captured in WILLIAM N. ESKRIDGE, JR. AND PHILIP P. FRICKEY, CASES AND MATERIALS ON LEGISLATION: STATUTES AND THE CREATION OF PUBLIC POLICY (2d ed. 1995).)

That debate certainly cannot be resolved here. But a simple question is in order. Did Currie ask judges to do anything different from what they do in every case? Don't judges always worry about purpose? The real problem, of course, lies not in the question but in ascertaining what is the purpose. But that problem should not—and does not—lead to deliberate efforts by judges to seek a judicial *tabula rasa* before deciding a case.

*See* PROBLEM 4E-12. EVEN STEVEN.

The following cases both involve application of forum law to true conflicts. Were they rightly decided?

# LILIENTHAL v. KAUFMAN

*Oregon Supreme Court*
*239 Or. 1, 395 P.2d 543 (1964)*

DENECKE, JUSTICE. This is an action to collect two promissory notes. The defense is that the defendant maker has previously been declared a spendthrift by an Oregon court and placed under a guardianship and that the guardian has declared the obligations void. The plaintiffs counter is that the notes were executed and delivered in California, that the law of California does not recognize the disability of a spendthrift, and that the Oregon court is bound to applythe law of the place of the making of the contract. The trial court rejected plaintiffs argument and held for the defendant.

This same defendant spendthrift was the prevailing party in our recent decision in *Olshen v. Kaufman,* 235 Or. 423, 385 P.2d 161 (1963). In that case the spendthrift and the plaintiff, an Oregon resident, had gone into a joint venture to purchase binoculars for resale. For this purpose plaintiff had advanced moneys to the spendthrift. The spendthrift had repaid plaintiff by his personal check for the amount advanced and for and for plaintiff's share of the profits of such venture. The check had not been Paid because the spendthrift had insufficient funds in his account. The action was for the unpaid balance of the check.

The evidence in that case showed that the plaintiff had been—unaware that Kaufman was under a spendthrift guardianship. The guardian testified that he knew Kaufman was engaging insome business and had bank accounts and that he had admonished him to cease these practices, but he could not control the spendthrift.

The statute applicable in that case and in this one is ORS 126.335:

"After the appointment of a guardian for the spendthrift, all contracts, except for necessaries, and all gifts, sales and transfers of real or personal estate made by such spendthrift thereafter and before, the termination of the guardianship are voidable."

We held in that case that the voiding of the contract by the guardian precluded recovery by the plaintiff and that the spendthrift and the guardian were not estopped to deny the validity of plaintiffs' claim. Plaintiff does not seek to overturn the principle of that decision but contends it has no application because the law of California governs, and under California law the plaintiff's claim is valid.

The facts here are identical to those in *Olshen v. Kaufman, supra,* except for the California locale for portions of the transaction. The notes were for the repayment of advances to finance another joint venture to sell binoculars. The plaintiff was unaware that defendant had been declared a spendthrift and placed under guardianship. The guardian, upon demand for payment by the plaintiff, declared the notes void. The issue is solely one involving the principles of conflict of laws . . . .

Under these circumstances our duty is threefold—to decide this case correctly, to indicate generally our views on the course to be taken in this particular part of the conflict of laws, but at the same time to refrain from making any pronouncements which might in the future restrain this court from taking a course which by that time has proved to be the most desirable.

Before entering the choice-of-law area of the general field of conflict of laws, we must determine whether the laws of the states having a connection with the controversy are in conflict. Defendant did not expressly concede that under the law of California the defendant's obligation would be enforceable, but his counsel did state that if this proceeding were in the courts of California, the plaintiff probably would recover. We agree . . . .

Defendant contends that the law of California should not be applied in this case by the Oregon court because the invalidity of the contract is a matter of remedy, rather than one of substance . . . .

Plaintiff contends that the substantive issue of whether or not an obligation is valid and binding is governed by the law of the place of making, California . . . .

In this case California had more connection with the transaction than being merely the place where the contract was executed. The defendant went to San Francisco to ask the plaintiff, a California resident, for money for the defendant's venture. The money was loaned to defendant in San Francisco, and by the terms of the note, it was to be repaid to plaintiff in San Francisco.

On these facts, apart from lex loci contractus, other accepted principles of conflict of laws lead to the conclusion that the law of California should be applied. [The] validity of a note is determined by the law of the place of payment . . . .

There is another conflict principle calling for the application of California law. Stumberg terms it the application of the law which upholds the contract. Ehrenzweig calls it the "Rule of Validation." Mr. Justice Harlan, speaking for the majority in *Kossick v. United Fruit Co.,* 365 U.S. 731 (1961) [in admiralty], stated such a rule . . . . The "rule" is that, if the contract is valid under the law of any jurisdiction having significant connection with the contract, i.e., place of making, place of performance, etc., the law of that jurisdiction validating the contract will be applied. This would also agree with the intention of the parties, if they had any intentions in this regard. They must have intended their agreement to be valid . . . .

In the general law of contracts we constantly strive to hold the contract valid and enforceable. The "rule of validation" has the same purpose in conflict of laws.

Thus far all signs have pointed to applying the law of California and holding the contract enforceable. There is, however, an obstacle to cross before this end can be logically reached. In *Olshen v. Kaufman, supra,* we decided that the law of Oregon, at least as applied to persons domiciled in Oregon contracting in Oregon for performance in Oregon, is that spendthrifts' contracts are voidable. Are the choice-of-law principles of conflict of laws so superior that they overcome this principle of Oregon law?

To answer this question we must determine, upon some basis, whether the interests of Oregon are so basic and important that we should not apply California law despite its several intimate connections with the transaction. The traditional method used by this court and most others is framed in the terminology of "public policy." The court decides whether or not the public policy of the forum is so strong that the law of the forum must prevail although another jurisdiction, with different laws, has more and closer contacts with the transaction. Included in public policy" we must consider the economic and social interests of Oregon. When these factors are included in a consideration of whether the law of the forum should be applied this traditional approach is very similar to that advocated by many legal scholars. This latter theory is that choice-of-law rules should rationally advance the policies or interests of the several states (or of the nations in the world community.

How "deep rooted (the) tradition of the common weal,"** particularly regarding spendthrifts, is illustrated by our decisions . . . . This court has decided that Oregon's policy voiding spendthrifts' contracts is not so strong as to void an Oregon spendthrift's marriage contract made in Washington [citation omitted] . . . .

The difficulty in deciding what is the fundamental law forming a cornerstone of the forum's jurisprudence and what is not such fundamental law, thus allowing it to give way to foreign law, is caused by the lack of any even remotely objective standards. [The problem of incapacity] of married women to contract illustrates the difficulty. *Milliken v. Pratt* is used in many case books as an example. There, the Massachusetts court held, under Massachusetts law, a Massachusetts married woman was incapable of contracting as a surety was not such a cornerstone of Massachusetts jurisprudence and economy that Maine law to the contrary could not be applicable . . . .

However, as previously stated, if we include in our search for the public policy of the forum a consideration of the various interests that the forum has in this litigation, we are guided by more definite criteria. In addition to the interests of the forum, we should consider the interests of the other jurisdictions which have some connection with the transaction.

Some of the interests of Oregon in this litigation are set forth in *Olshen v. Kaufman, supra.* The spendthrift's family which is to be protected by the establishment of the guardianship is presumably an Oregon family. The public authority which may be charged with the expense of supporting the spendthrift or his family, if he is permitted to go unrestrained upon his wasteful way, will probably be an Oregon public authority. These, obviously, are interests of some substance.

---

** A reference to Judge Cardozo's famous opinion on public policy in *Loucks v. Standard Oil Co.,* § 4.14, *supra. —Ed.*

Oregon has other interests and policies regarding this matter which were not necessary to discuss in *Olshen*. As previously stated, Oregon, as well as all other states, has a strong policy favoring the validity and enforceability of contracts . . . .

The defendant's conduct—borrowing money with the belief that the repayment of such loan could be avoided—is a species of fraud. Oregon and all other states have a strong policy of protecting innocent persons from fraud . . . .

It is in Oregon's commercial interest to encourage citizens of other states to conduct business with Oregonians. If Oregonians acquire a reputation for not honoring their agreements, commercial intercourse with Oregonians will be discouraged. If there are Oregon laws, somewhat unique to Oregon, which permit an Oregonian to escape his otherwise binding obligations, persons may well avoid Commercial dealings with Oregonians.

The substance of these commercial considerations, however, is deflated by the recollection that the Oregon Legislature has determined, despite the weight of these considerations, that a spendthrift's contracts are voidable.

California's most direct interest in this transaction is having its citizen creditor paid. As previously noted, California's policy is that [a] creditor . . . should be paid even though the debtor is a spendthrift. California probably has another, although more intangible, interest involved. It is presumably to every state's benefit to have the reputation of being a jurisdiction—in which contracts can be made and performance be promised with the certain knowledge that such contracts will be enforced. Both of these interests, particularly the former, are also of substance.

We have, then, two jurisdictions, each with several close connections with the transaction, and each with a substantial interest, which will be served or thwarted, depending upon which law is applied. The interests of neither jurisdiction are clearly more important than those of the other. We are of the opinion that in such a case the public policy of Oregon should prevail and the law of Oregon should be applied; we should apply that choice-of-law rule which will advance the policies or interests of Oregon.

Courts are instruments of state policy. The Oregon Legislature has adopted a policy to avoid possible hardship to an Oregon family of a spendthrift and to avoid possible—expenditure of Oregon public funds which might occur if the spendthrift is required to pay his obligations. In litigation Oregon courts are the appropriate instrument to enforce this policy. The mechanical application of choice-of-law rules would be the only apparent reason for an Oregon court advancing, the interests of California over the equally valid interests of Oregon. The present principles of conflict of laws are not favorable to such mechanical application.

We hold that the spendthrift law of Oregon is applicable and the plaintiff cannot recover . . . .

O'CONNELL, JUSTICE (specially concurring) . . . . In the *Olshen* case we had to choose between two competing policies; on one hand the policy of protecting the interest of persons dealing with spendthrifts which, broadly, may be described as the interest in the security of transactions, and on the other hand the policy of protecting the interests of the spendthrift, his family and the county. It was decided that the Oregon Legislature adopted the latter policy in preference to the former . . . .

To distinguish the *Olshen* case it would be necessary to assume that although the legislature intended to protect the interest of the spendthrift, his family and the county when local creditors were harmed, the same protection was not intended where the transaction adversely affected foreign creditors. I see no basis for making that assumption. There is no reason to believe that our legislature intended to protect California creditors to a greater extent than our own.

GOODWIN, JUSTICE (dissenting). I am unable to agree with the conclusion of the majority . . . . The plaintiff was a merchant in California who was approached in the ordinary course of business by a seemingly competent person and asked to enter into a business arrangement. The notes were executed, delivered, and made payable in California. If the parties gave any thought to law at all, which is unlikely, they would have assumed that California law would apply to their business. Consequently, if California law were to be applied, it would neither surprise the parties nor shock the conscience of the court . . . .

In the case before us, I believe that the policy of both states, Oregon and California, in favor of enforcing contracts, has been lost sight of in favor of a questionable policy in Oregon which gives special privileges to the rare spendthrift for whom a guardian has been appointed.

*Olshen v. Kaufman* held that there was a policy in this state to help keep spendthrifts out of the almshouse. I can see nothing, however, in Oregon's policy toward spendthrifts that warrants its extension to permit the taking of captives from other states down the road to insolvency.

SLOAN, J., joins in this dissent.

*See* PROBLEMS 4E-13. COMPARATIVE NEGLIGENCE; 4E-14. BEAUTIFUL HAWAII; PROBLEM 4E-15. THE LAURITZEN-ROMERO-RHODITIS TRILOGY; 4E-16. THE CARD COUNTER.

---

## NOTES AND QUESTIONS ON *LILIENTHAL*

(1) *Background.* Although the fact does not appear of record, it is reported that Lilienthal had been careful to make appropriate inquiries about Kaufman through two Portland banks, and that each bank independently (but erroneously) gave Kaufman a clean bill of health. *See* Roger Cramton, David Currie, & Herma Hill Kay, Conflict of Laws 273 (3d ed. 1981).

(2) *Validation preference.* Can *Lilienthal* be reconciled with *Milliken v. Pratt?* Interestingly, the *Lilienthal* court seems to have struggled hard to avoid its ultimate conclusion. The court saw the harm to Oregon commerce in applying Oregon law; toyed longingly with the rule of validation *(see* note (3), *infra);* pointed out that the parties must have intended their contract to be valid; and even called Kaufman's conduct a "species of fraud." These are not

the kinds of noises made by a court tooling up to leave the contract creditor holding an empty bag.

Why are courts so reluctant to invalidate agreements? Consider the various factors, for example, that in a domestic case will "take a contract out of the statute" of frauds. Clearly, the policies underlying contract law are subordinated whenever the legislature deems it necessary to create a local defense. But general contract policy is likely to be widely shared (cf the U.C.C.), while defenses like those in *Milliken and Lilienthal* tend to be local and idiosyncratic. Moreover, contracts are integrations of the parties' intentions, and so party "expectations" are relevant. If Sarah Pratt knew of and relied on the married women's defense, would that strengthen her case? Or would the court be likely to think her conduct a "species of fraud?" If she was ignorant of the defense, would she be surprised by being held to her agreement?

Given all this, what on earth could have induced the Oregon court to rule for its charismatic binoculars salesman, the deadbeat Kaufman? If you think the court felt bound by the *Olshen* case, wasn't that precedent distinguishable, as being on wholly domestic facts?

(3) *Ehrenzweig's "true rules" and the "rule of validation."* The court in *Lilienthal* mentions, among the reasons for its reluctance to apply forum law—as it eventually nevertheless did -that Ehrenzweig's, "rule of validation" pointed the other way. The late Professor Albert Ehrenzweig argued empirically that American courts tended to reach predictable results for given classes of cases. These empirically—derived rules Ehrenzweig called "true rules." In his article, *A Proper Law in a Proper Forum: A "Restatement" of the "Lex Fori Approach,"* 18 OKLA. L. REV. 340 (1965), and elsewhere, Ehrenzweig identified a number of "true rules." Among these was "the rule of validation." As an empirical matter, courts would not apply law that would upset planned transactions. With an equal ring of truth, Ehrenzweig pointed out that, in the absence of a specific "true rule" for a case, the residual "true rule" was to apply the law of the forum. Although Ehrenzweig argued normatively that a "proper" forum *should* apply its own law, his more general point was that courts in fact do tend to wind up applying their own law unless there is some good reason for doing otherwise.

(4) *The plaintiff at the unfavorable forum.* Why do you suppose the plaintiff went to Oregon to sue when there was favorable law at home in California? Did California have modern long-arm legislation in 1964? Should the fact that plaintiff was forced to an unfavorable forum have made a difference in the forum's choice of law? *See Hans Baade, Counter-Revolution or Alliance for Progress? Reflections on Reading Cavers, the Choice-of-Law Process,* 46 TEXAS L. REV. 141, 160 (1967).

(5) *Costs of departing from forum law.* In *Lilienthal,* what would have been the costs, if any, of departing from forum law? What was the purpose of Oregon's peculiar spendthrift law? Who institutes legal proceedings under that law? Is it possible that the court in *Milliken y. Pratt* would *not* have departed from forum law but for the post-transaction repeal of the married women's defense?

For criticism of *Lilienthal, see, e.g.,* DAVID CAVERS, THE CHOICE-OF-LAW PROCESS 192 (1965); RUSSELL WEINTRAUB, COMMENTARY OFF THE CONFLICT

OF LAWS 372 n. 72 (3d ed.1987). *But see* Louise Weinberg, *On Departing from Forum Law,* 35 MERCER L. REV. 595, 623 (1984); Robert Sedler, *Interest Analysis and Forum Preference in the Conflict of Laws. A Response to the "New Critics,"* 34 MERCER L. REV. 593, 604 (1983).

The tension in cases like *Lilienthal* seems to have to do with our concern that the creditor or tort plaintiff might be denied a chance to prove her case although "better" law, law that is more validating or remedial or in some sense fairer, is available at the place of transaction or occurrence. Laws that would frustrate these policies tend to be disfavored. For further exploration of the forum's perception of "better law" elsewhere, *see* §  4.24, *infra.*

(6) It might be thought that forum law would be least controversial when the interested forum would allow the plaintiff to try to prove her case, notwithstanding that some other interested state in its own courts would have barred the way. In such cases, forum law would tend to validate agreements and to remedy wrongs; thus, in such cases it is forum law that would tend to vindicate general policies. Nevertheless, true conflict cases applying plaintiff-favoring forum law evoke much criticism. The following materials explore the problem.

---

## HALL v. UNIVERSITY OF NEVADA [I]

*California Supreme Court, In Bank*
*8 Cal. 3d 522, 105 Cal. Rptr. 355, 503 P.2d 1363 (1972)*

PETERS, JUSTICE. Plaintiffs appeal from an order quashing service of summons and complaint on the defendants, University of Nevada, a corporation, and the State of Nevada.

Plaintiffs filed suit in the San Francisco Superior Court to recover damages for personal injuries alleging that the injuries resulted from a collision in California between their automobile and a car owned by the University and State of Nevada and operated by their agent acting within the scope of his agency . . .[2]

The university and the state moved to quash service on the ground that California courts do not have [subject-matter] jurisdiction over the State of Nevada and its governmental agencies. The motion was granted.

We have concluded that sister states who engage in activities within California are subject to our laws with respect to those activities and are subject to suit in California courts with respect to those activities. When the sister state enters into activities in this state, it is not exercising sovereign power over the citizens of this state and is not entitled to the benefits of the sovereign immunity doctrine as to those activities unless this state has conferred immunity by law or comity.

[The court held that California's interest in comity was outweighed by its remedial and deterrent tort policies on the facts of the case.]

---

[2] Apparently, the instant case is proceeding to trial against the special administrator or the estate of the driver. [This note has been moved in the text.—*Ed.*]

This court has repeatedly emphasized that this state and its residents and taxpayers have a substantial interest in providing a forum where a resident may seek, whatever redress is due him . . . .

To hold that the sister state may not be sued in California could result in granting greater immunity to the sister state than the immunity which our citizens have bestowed upon our state government. If a sister state has not abrogated sovereign immunity for tort, it is conceivable that a California citizen would be denied all recovery for an automobile accident in this state even though if the State of California had been the defendant, recovery would have been permitted . . . .

We conclude that the State and University of Nevada are not immune from suit in California for the driving of their agent within the scope of his employment or for the permissive use of their car within this state. This conclusion makes it unnecessary to consider plaintiffs' further contention that the State of Nevada has consented by statute to suit in California.

*The order appealed from is reversed.*

WRIGHT, C.J., and MCCOMB, TOBRINER, MOSK, BURKE, and SULLIVAN, J.J., concur.

## NOTES AND QUESTIONS

(1) For the further history, see *Hall* on remand from the denial of certiorari (*Hall v. Nevada II*), § 4.23, *infra.*

(2) Was *Hall v. Nevada* a true conflict? Did the California court consider the policies underlying Nevada's limited waiver of immunity?

(3) *The myth of comity.* If ever there were a strong case for comity in choice of law, surely it is a case in which a sister state itself stands before the forum as party defendant. Or does that feature of *Hall v. Nevada* simply make it a true conflict?

(4) **TRAMONTANA v. S.A. EMPRESA DE VIACAO AEREA RIO GRANDENSE,** 350 F.2d 468 (D.C. Cir. 1965). A U.S. Navy plane collided in midair over Rio de Janeiro with a civilian Brazilian aircraft. Survivors of a Maryland decedent who had been on board the Navy plane sued the Brazilian airline. Under the laws of all concerned American states, there was no limit on damages, but under Brazilian law, recovery was limited to 100,000 cruzeiros, or $173.00.

*Held*: Brazilian law applies. The Brazilian legislation was enacted to help Brazil develop its infant air carriage industry.

\* \* \*

The same result was reached in *Ciprari v. Servicios Aereos Cruzeiro,* 359 F.2d 855 (2d Cir. 1966). How do you suppose the Second Circuit in *Ciprari* distinguished *Kilberg,* § 4.14, *supra,* the famous 1961 New York Court of

Appeals case? Some of these conflicting interests are reflected in the negotiation of the "Montreal Agreement," raising to $75,000 the Warsaw Convention's $8,300 cap on damages for deaths occurring in international air disasters for passengers flying to or from the United States. § 49 U.S.C. 1502.

On the problems raised in this Note, see Terry Kogan, *Toward a Jurisprudence of Choice of Law: The Priority of Fairness Over Comity,* 62 N.Y.U. L. REV. 651 (1987).

(5) *Defense of compulsion of sister-state law.* A similarly strong clash of policies occurs whenever the law of one state requires conduct different from that forbidden by the law of another state. The next case exemplifies that problem.

**LAKER AIRWAYS LTD. v. SABENA, BELGIAN WORLD AIRLINES,** 731 F.2d 909 (D.C. Cir. 1984). Private action for treble damages under the Sherman Antitrust Act, alleging a conspiracy to drive the plaintiff air carrier out of business. The defense was that to effectuate British trading interests the Secretary of State of the United Kingdom had prohibited all those carrying on business in that country, except for certain American air carriers, from complying with American antitrust laws in certain cases.

*Held* (Wilkey, Circuit Judge): The Sherman Act applies.

> There is simply no room for accommodation here if the courts of each country faithfully carry out the laws which they are entrusted to enforce . . . . The suggestion has been made that this court should engage in some form of interest balancing . . . . The district court could capitulate to the British attacking law, at the cost of [failing to] implement the substantive policies established by Congress . . . . [N]ational laws do not evaporate when counteracted by the legislation of another sovereign . . . . Absent an explicit directive from Congress, this court has neither the authority nor the institutional resources to [resolve] competing claims . . . .

*See* PROBLEMS 4E-17. A TRIP HOME; 4E-18. A BUSY PHYSICIAN; 4E-19. "BRUSH YOUR TEETH TWICE A DAY"; 4E-20. THE SWEDISH NIGHTINGALE; 4E-21. CRASH IN SURINAM.

---

### TRUE CONFLICTS, HARDER CASES, AND MORE STUBBORN QUESTIONS

In one sense, the following cases are even harder cases for application of forum law. In them the forum lacks any territorial contact with the case and thus has no interest in the matter beyond its interest, as domicile, in the plaintiff's well-being.

(1) **ROSENTHAL v. WARREN,** 475 F.2d 438 (2d Cir. 1973). [The facts and opinion are found at § 3.16, *supra.*] *Held* (relying on *Kilberg,* § 4.14, *supra*): Affirmed, for the plaintiff. New York would apply its rule of unlimited recovery for wrongful death.

Dissenting, Chief Judge Lumbard conceded that Dr. Warren's liability insurance policy did not limit coverage in case of death of a patient; had Rosenthal survived with injuries of $1,250,000 (the amount claimed by the widow), the insurer would have been obligated to cover the loss. But he pointed out that the limit on death damages was fully reflected in Massachusetts' lower malpractice premiums.

\* \* \*

*Rosenthal,* like *Lilienthal,* has been widely disapproved. Critics of *Rosenthal* generally argue that, like *Lilienthal,* it offended the expectations of the parties. *See* GARY SIMSON, ISSUES AND PERSPECTIVES IN CONFLICT OF LAWS 191-3 (1985). Are you persuaded?

*Rosenthal* was rejected in *Maguire v. Exeter & Hampton Electric Co.,* 114 N.H. 589, 325 A.2d 778 (1974), and not mentioned in a recent case on somewhat similar facts, *Edwardsville National Bank and Trust Co. v. Marion Laboratories, Inc.,* 808 F.2d 648 (7th Cir. 1987). Similarly, in *Casey v. Manson Construction Co.,* 247 Or. 274, 428 P.2d 898 (1967), the court denied an Oregon woman the benefit of Oregon law on loss of consortium, since her husband was injured by the Washington defendant in Washington. The Oregon court reasoned that Washington defendants should not be required to accommodate themselves to the law of the state of residence of any traveler whom they might injure in Washington.

(2) *Want of territorial nexus.* In The Choice of Law Process 49 (1965), David Cavers argued that the defendant acting in his own state's territory should be given the benefit of his own state's law. This view probably represents the weight of authority today. *See, e.g., Veasey v. Doremus,* 103 N.J. 244, 510 A.2d 1187 (1986). *See* RUSSELL WEINTRAUB, COMMENTARY ON THE CONFLICT OF LAWS 340-42 (3d ed. 1986). *But see* David Seidelson, *Interest Analysis or the Restatement Second of Conflicts: Which is the Preferable Approach to Resolving Choice-of-Law Problems?,* 27 DUQ. L. REV. 73, 85 n. 55 (1988).

A true conflict case in which disregard of the law of the place of injury seems even more counterintuitive occurs when defendant acts on premises owned by him, while complying fully with local law regulating the safety of the site, and the plaintiff is injured there. Does it make a difference that the defendant acts at a fixed site rather than, say, in a moving car? Should it? Certainly, there is strong practical value in giving a landowner a single set of obligations that do not vary depending on where visitors to the land happen to live. *Cf. Barrett v. Foster Grant Co.,* 450 F.2d 1146 (1st Cir. 1971) (Aldrich, C. J.): "Nothing is more fixed than land, and hence . . . the duties resulting from ownership . . . . We are not convinced by plaintiffs' . . . equating the fortuity of the location of an accident during an automobile trip with an injury chargeable to the condition of a piece of real property . . . ." Do such concerns necessarily override the policy concerns of another state, in a case of true conflict?

**O'CONNOR v. LEHIGH PAVING CORP.,** 579 F.2d 194 (2d Cir.), *cert. denied,* 439 U.S. 1034 (1978). Action by a New York widow against a Virginia paving company for the death of the husband at the Virginia worksite. Under

Virginia law, an employer's immunity from suit cloaked the third-party paving company. Under New York law the action was permissible.

*Held* (Friendly, J.): For the widow. New York law applies. New York would be unlikely to depart from its long course of decision applying forum law to benefit New Yorkers in true conflict cases.

\* \* \*

In *O'Connor,* should it have made a difference to the protective policies of New York law that the place of death was out of state? Does a defendant's state pick up any additional interest by virtue of its being the place of injury?

(3) *Residence of the plaintiff, without more.* In cases like *Rosenthal v. Warren,* the forum's lack of territorial connection with an occurrence is sometimes recast as presenting a problem because the forum's sole connection with the case is as the residence of the plaintiff, without more. Some authorities recommend avoiding forum law when the forum's only contact with the case is as place where the plaintiff resides. *See, eg., Warner v. Auberge Gray Rocks Inn, Ltee.,* 827 F.2d 938 (3d Cir. 1987) (Pollak, J.); Bernard Corr, *Interest analysis and Choice of Law: The Dubious Dominance of Domicile,* 4 UTAH L. REV. 651 (1983). Do you agree that it is unreasonable for a state to assert governing power in its own courts over the welfare of its residents? Professor Weintraub even suggests that in extreme cases the forum so doing may violate due process. RUSSELL WEINTRAUB, COMMENTARY ON THE CONFLICT OF LAWS 342 n. 54 (3d ed. 1987).

(4) *Plaintiff orientation in choice of law.* In *Paul v. National Life Ins. Co.,* 352 S.E.2d 550 (W.Va. 1986), the court refused to abandon the law of the place of injury, but nevertheless applied its own plaintiff-favoring law on "public policy" grounds. The dissent complained:

> In the classic pose, Justice is blindfolded so that she can weigh the equities in a case equally without prejudice. We are peeking beneath the blindfold in conflict-of-laws cases to see if an insurance company is involved. If they are, we appear to be manipulating our conflict-of-laws rule so that the insurance company loses. I believe that even insurance companies are entitled to impartiality in the courts.

One might raise the question whether the traditional rules, in themselves, are plaintiff-favoring. Is "the place of making" for contract cases such a rule? Would "the place of injury" tend to have more remedial law than "the place of wrongful conduct?" For the argument that traditional choice-of-law rules tend to reflect the plaintiff-favoring policies underlying substantive law, *see* Louise Weinberg, *Choice of Law and Minimal Scrutiny,* 49 U. CHI. L. REV. 440, 466 (1982).

(5) *Forum shopping and forum preference.* Forum preference in choice of lawis widely criticized as parochial, and as counter to policies of comity and federalism. *See, e.g.,* Robert Jackson, *Full Faith and Credit: The Lawyer's Clause of the Constitution,* 45 COLUM. L. REV. 1 (1945). Moreover, if forum law is applied in every true conflict case, isn't that an invitation to forum-shopping plaintiffs? Under modern long-arm legislation, a plaintiff can shop

for favorable law at any forum with "minimum contacts" with the defendant. Is that a cause for concern? Why?

(6) *Forum preference and plaintiff-orientation.* When Brainerd Currie wrote, few states had as yet availed themselves of the opportunity *International Shoe* gave them to create modem long-arm legislation. Today, long-arm legislation is available in some form in all states. Thus, plaintiffs ability to shop not only for a strategically desirable forum, but for favorable law, must be enhanced in a way Currie could not have taken into account. His recommendation of residual use of forum law for non-false conflict cases was a much more evenhanded recommendation than it seems today. For the view that modern conflicts methodology is plaintiff-oriented, see Lea Brilmayer, *Interstate Federalism,* BRIGHAM YOUNG U. L. REV. 949 (1987). Is there anything to be said for plaintiff bias in the institutions of interstate litigation? *See* Louise Weinberg, *Choice of Law and Minimal Scrutiny,* 49 U. CHI. L. REV. 440, 463-9 (1982) (on "national conflicts policy").

## § 4.21 The Unprovided-for Case

*Introduction.* In later writing, Currie noticed that there were cases in which *neither* state could properly be said to have an interest. Lumped in with the "false conflicts" in his discussion in *Married Women's Contracts,* such cases are analytically quite different from false conflicts. The phenomenon of the unprovided-for case has also appeared in courts using the traditional method. *Cf Marie v. Garrison,* § 4.11, *supra.* Currie recommended that in such cases the forum apply its own law, not with any discriminatory or selfish intention, but simply because this is the rational and convenient way to try a lawsuit when no good purpose is to be served by putting the parties to the expense and the court to the trouble of ascertaining the foreign law. No useful purpose will be served by ascertaining and applying [foreign] law, since the result is a matter of entire indifference [to] both states." Brainerd Currie, *Survival of Actions: Adjudication versus Automation in the Conflict of Laws,* 10 STAN. L. REV. 205 (1958).

Was the following case rightly decided?

———

### ERWIN v. THOMAS

*Oregon Supreme Court, In Banc*
*264 Or. 454, 506 P.2d 494 (1973)*

HOLMAN, JUSTICE. This is an action for . . . loss of consortium alleged to have been suffered when plaintiffs husband was injured in an accident. Plaintiff appealed from a judgment for defendant . . . .

Defendant Thomas, while operating a truck in the state of Washington in the course of his employment for defendant Shepler, is alleged to have negligently injured plaintiff's husband. Defendant Thomas is an Oregon resident and his employer, defendant Shepler, is an Oregon corporation. Plaintiff and her injured husband are residents of Washington. Washington, by court decision, has followed the common law rule that no cause of action exists by a wife for loss of consortium. Oregon allows such an action.

The issue is whether Oregon law or Washington law is applicable. It is with some trepidation that a court enters the maze of choice of law in tort cases . . . . Until recently, this court was committed to the traditional, arbitrary, and much criticized rule that in tort cases the law of the place of the wrong, lex loci delicti commissi, governs. However, in the case of *Casey v. Manson Construction Co.*, 247 Or. 274, 428 P.2d 898 (1967), this court adopted the equally maligned and almost universally criticized "most significant relationship" approach of Restatement (Second) Conflict of Laws.

However, before engaging in the mysteries of the solution of an actual conflict, we must make certain that we have a conflict of consequence which requires a choice. All authorities agree that there is such a thing as a false conflict which requires no choice . . . .

Where, in the particular factual context, the interests and policies of one state are involved and those of the other are not (or, if they are, they are involved in only a minor way), reason would seem to dictate that the law of the state whose policies and interests are vitally involved should apply; or, if those of neither state are vitally involved, that the law of the forum should apply. It may well be that determining what interests or policies are behind the law of a particular state is far from an exact science and is something about which there can be legitimate disagreement; but, on the other hand, it is the kind of an exercise, for better or for worse, which courts do every day and, therefore, feel secure in doing. If such a claimed conflict can be so disposed of, whether it is called false or not, the disposition certainly seems preferable to wandering off into the jungle with a compass which everyone but its maker says is defective.

Let us examine the interests involved in the present case. Washington has decided that the rights of a married woman whose husband is injured are not sufficiently important to cause the negligent defendant who is responsible for the injury to pay the wife for her loss. It has weighed the matter in favor of protection of defendants. No Washington defendant is going to have to respond for damages in the present case, since the defendant is an Oregonian. Washington has little concern whether other states require non-Washingtonians to respond to such claims. Washington policy cannot be offended if the court of another state affords rights to a Washington woman which Washington does not afford, so long as a Washington defendant is not required to respond. The state of Washington appears to have no material or urgent policy or interest which would be offended by applying Oregon law.

On the other hand, what is Oregon's interest? Oregon, obviously, is protective of the rights of married women and believes that they should be allowed to recover for negligently inflicted loss of consortium. However, it is stretching the imagination more than a trifle to conceive that the Oregon Legislature was concerned about the rights of all the nonresident married women in the nation whose husbands would be injured outside of the state of Oregon. Even if Oregon were so concerned, it would offend no substantial Washington interest.

It is apparent, therefore, that neither state has a vital interest in the outcome of this litigation and there can be no conceivable material conflict of policies or interests if an Oregon court does what comes naturally and applies Oregon law. [Here the court cites an essay by Currie, *Notes on Methods and Objectives in the Conflict of Laws,* 1959 DUKE L.J. 171.]

> . . . The next question is whether our decision in *Casey v. Manson Construction Co.,* 247 Or. 274, 428 P.2d 898 (1967), is incompatible with our disposition of the present case. In Casey, which adopted and applied Restatement (Second) Conflict of Laws, an actual conflict existed. An Oregon wife brought a loss of consortium action because of an injury to her husband, also an Oregon resident, which was negligently inflicted in Washington by a Washington resident. We there held that Washington defendants should not be required to accommodate themselves to the law of the State of residence of any traveler whom they might injure in Washington; that under the given circumstances, Washington's interest in the matter, which was protective of Washington defendants, was paramount to Oregon's interest in having its resident recover for her loss; and that Washington's relationship was the more significant and Washington law applied.

Our confidence in any set body of rules as an all-encompassing and readily applicable means of solution to conflict cases is not so great that we desire to undertake the application of such rules except in those situations where the policies and interests of the respective states are in substantial opposition. We see no such conflict here, and, therefore, find it unnecessary to resort to any such set of rules. We are little concerned whether we are presented with a false conflict or with an actual conflict capable of solution by resorting to our analysis of the interests and policies of the respective states. Where such policies and interests can be identified with a fair degree of assurance and there appears to be no substantial conflict, we do not believe it is necessary to have recourse in the "contacts" of § 145(2) of Restatement (Second) Conflict of Laws.

The judgment of the trial court is reversed and the case is remanded for further proceedings.

TONGUE, J., concurs in the result.

BRYSON, JUSTICE (dissenting). . . . Regardless of whether we follow the *[Second] Restatement* or the law of the place of the wrong, I do not believe we can or should bestow Oregon statutory rights for women on women of the state of Washington . . . .

Obviously the plaintiff could not bring this action in her state, Washington, but the majority opinion holds that by merely stepping over the state boundary into Oregon she is then bestowed with the right given wives who are residents of the state of Oregon, which includes the right of action for loss of consortium of her husband.

I would affirm.

## NOTES AND QUESTIONS ON *ERWIN*

(1) *Erwin and the methodological questions.* Observe that in this case, as in *Babcock,* the forum is deciding not only a choice-of-law question, but also a methodological question. Its decision to disregard the Restatement (Second); in favor of the law of the interested state in "false conflicts" seems sound. As we shall see in Part F, *infra,* not all courts adopting the Restatement Second have perceived the utility of the *Restatement,* or indeed any set of rules, for "solving" false conflicts.

(2) *The unprovided-for case.* But was the *Erwin* court correct that "unprovided-for" cases were as easy as false conflicts? Is it possible that the unprovided-for case is even more intractable than the true conflict? Of course, whatever law is chosen in a true conflict, the interests of one of the states is going to be subordinated. But at least the law applied will be that of an *interested state.* In the unprovided-for case, on the other hand, governance under *either* state's law will be "arbitrary" in some sense. Is there a case to be made for arbitrary forum law in preference to arbitrary nonforum law? *See* Aaron Twerski, *Neumeier v. Kuehner: Where are the Emperor's Clothes?,* 1 HOFSTRA L. REV. 104 (1973).

(3) *Nonfalse conflicts and the disinterested third state.* The recommendation that forum law apply in nonfalse conflict cases seems beside the point in cases tried in states without any significant connection with the parties or occurrence. *Cf.* Brainerd Currie, *The Disinterested Third State,* 28 LAW & CONTEMP. PROB. 754 (1963). Suppose, for example, that *Lilienthal* was tried in Nevada, the defendant having been served with process there during one of his efforts to obtain financing on a new binoculars deal. Or suppose that *Erwin* was tried in California, the defendant having a place of business there. If an alternative to forum law could be found for resolution of these nonfalse conflicts, that alternative would be of use at least at the disinterested third state. Obviously, that alternative would also be of tremendous interest in any nonfalse conflict case. We turn to the search for such an alternative in the sections that follow these notes.

(4) *Current status of lex fori.* Today only a few writers continue to recommend that the interested forum generally apply its own law in a nonfalse conflict case. These include Louise Weinberg, *On Departing from Forum Law,* 35 MERCER L. REV. 595 (1984); Robert Sedler, *Interest Analysis and Forum Preference in the Conflict of Laws: A Response to the "New Critics,"* 34 MERCER L. REV. 593 (1983). *But see* Michael S. Green, Note, *Legal Realism, Lex Fori, and the Choice-of-Law Revolution,* 104 YALE L.J. 967 (1995); Larry Kramer, *Interest Analysis and the Presumption of Forum Law,* 56 U. CHI. L. REV. 1301 (1989). Resort to forum law remains substantially presumptive in some modernist jurisdictions, the presumption being most clearly expressed in Michigan, *Olmstead v. Anderson,* 400 N.W.2d 292 (Mich. 1987), and in Kentucky, *Foster v. Leggett,* 484 S.W.2d 827 (Ky. 1972). On the other hand, as the foregoing materials suggest, there is a perceived need for alternative

approaches to resolution of these cases. There is a discernible trend toward nonforum law in modernist courts.

We are now ready to survey current alternative approaches to resolution of "nonfalse" conflicts.

# PART F ALTERNATIVE MODERN METHODS FOR RESOLVING NONFALSE CONFLICTS

*Introduction.* The following materials exhibit true conflicts and unprovided-for cases in the hands of courts that are reluctant to apply forum law in such cases.

Since the widespread abandonment of territorial formalisms, the problem of resolving nonfalse conflicts has teased the minds of countless writers and judges. A feeling of unease with Currie's recommendation that the forum apply its own law to resolve nonfalse conflict cases has led to development of alternative modern choice-of-law "approaches." The approaches described in the following sections are those that are adopted in one or more states or are heavily cited in judicial opinions.

There are two things to remember about these various modernist methods. In theory, almost all of them are to be used only *after* a nonfalse conflict is identified. Most American courts today, if the question were to be put to them, probably would not admit to trying to "solve" a false conflict. Second, most modernist courts, whatever approach they *say* they follow, will often employ argumentation eclectically from other approaches. *See, e.g.,* Patrick J. Borchers, *The Choice-of-Law Revolution: An Empirical Study,* 49 WASH. & LEE L. REV. 357 (1992); William Reppy, *Eclecticism in Choice of Law: Hybrid Method or Mishmash?,* 34 MERCER L. REV. 645 (1983); Robert Leflar, *Choice of Law: A Well-Watered Plateau,* 41 LAW & CONTEMP. PROBS. 10 (1977).

## § 4.22 The Restrained Forum

*Introduction.* Interest analysis made early and distinctive headway in California, under the creative and sophisticated leadership of Chief Justice Traynor of the California Supreme Court.

(1) **PEOPLE v. ONE 1953 FORD VICTORIA,** 48 Cal. 2d 595, 311 P.2d 480 (1957) (Traynor, J.). Action by the state to declare forfeit a motor vehicle owned and driven by Willie Smith for unlawful transportation of narcotics in California. In 1953 Smith bought the car in Bexar County, Texas, financing the purchase with a loan from a finance company. The note had a clause prohibiting Smith from taking the car out of Bexar County, Texas. The car in question, containing narcotics and Smith, were seized in California. With $722.84 still unpaid on its note, the Texas finance company intervened in the California forfeiture proceeding to protect its interest. Under California law, a mortgagee's interest in a car is forfeit in these circumstances unless the mortgagee can show that it conducted a reasonable investigation of the character of the mortgagor. The Texas finance company had conducted no investigation at all of Smith's character. Under Texas law, no such investigation was required.

*Held:* For the innocent mortgagee (affirming the judgment of the court below). The California statute could not reasonably be construed so as to impose a duty of "a reasonable investigation" upon an out-of-state finance company with no way of knowing that the financed car would be driven in California. This holding would not significantly impair California's policy.

California had Smith and the narcotics and the car. Its narcotics enforcement effort would not be significantly affected by paying off the $722.84 claim of theinnocent mortgagee from the proceeds of the judicial sale of the car.

*   *   *

What result if Smith's car purchase had been financed in Nevada, a few miles from the California state line? Would it matter if the contract contained a stipulation that the car be driven only in Nevada?

(2) *Apparent true conflicts.* Note the similarities in reasoning (based on party expectations) and result (validation of an out-of-state contract) between *Milliken v. Pratt* and *One Ford Victoria.* It is an interesting feature of both these celebrated cases that the forum could depart from its own law without significantly impairing local interest. In *Milliken,* remember, the local rule had been repealed before trial. The court construed the rule narrowly, as not applying when unreasonable. In *One Ford Victoria,* California was able to achieve a substantial degree of enforcement without hardship to the innocent mortgagee. The court construed the statute narrowly, as not applying when unreasonable. Thus, both cases were only apparent true conflicts. Because forum law was, in effect, construed away in these cases, some authorities analyze such cases as "apparent true conflicts" which in fact turn out to be false conflicts. *See* Harold Horowitz, *The Law of Choice of Law in California: A Restatement,* 21 U.C.L.A. L. REV. 719 (1974).

(3) *The "moderate and restrained" forum.* Justice Traynor's conflicts decisions seem to have influenced Professor Currie. Currie came to revise his original position that forum law should always resolve true conflicts. Instead, he wrote, the very fact that a court identifies a true conflict should prompt the court to reexamine its own law "with a view to a more moderate and restrained interpretation both of the policy and of the circumstances in which it must be applied . . . ." Brainerd Currie, *The Disinterested Third State,* 28 LAW & CONTEMP. PROBS. 754, 757 (1963). Clearly, Currie was unhappy at the prospect of a court's overriding the interests of a sister state. But equally clearly, Currie saw that there would remain intractable conflicts that could not be construed away. At some point along the spectrum of possible cases, local policy could become so clear that moderate and restrained construction would no longer seem possible. What is a "restrained and moderate" application of the interested state's law? If it is only a judicial willingness to make modest compromises that *more accurately* reflect the extent of forum interest, it would seem to be immune to criticism. But what of a more consistent rule of "comity?" Does the interested forum run a risk when it extends a courteous "comity" to the laws of a sister state? In trying to answer that question, ask yourself what the possible effects of a rule of comity might be upon the tort plaintiff who has chosen the forum? Upon the tort defendant? Which of these parties will argue in support of a rule of comity? What will be the effect upon forum domestic policy? Consider Judge Wilkey's response to the defendant's argument seeking comity in the *Laker Airways* case, § 4.20, *supra.* For analysis of the unintended consequences of the rule of comity in the conflict of laws, see Louise Weinberg, *Against Comity,* 80 GEO. L.J. 53 (1991).

---

## BERNKRANT v. FOWLER

*California Supreme Court, In Bank*
*55 Cal. 2d 588, 12 Cal. Reptr. 266, 360 P.2d 906 (1961)*

TRAYNOR, JUSTICE. [This was an action by Nevada plaintiffs to enforce an oral agreement against a California estate. At a meeting in Las Vegas, the decedent, Granrud, had offered to forgive in his will any balance then due on the plaintiffs' debt to him, if, in return, the plaintiffs would prepay some of the debt now. He needed cash for a deal he was contemplating. The debt in question was a second mortgage held by Granrud on the plaintiffs' Nevada real estate. Accepting his proposition, the plaintiffs spent some $800 to roll over all their obligations, paying approximately $13,000 to Granrud, and entering a new mortgage arrangement with him on the balance of the debt. When Granrud died domiciled in California, his will made no mention of forgiving the balance of the plaintiffs' debt, by that time about $9,000. Under California law, such an agreement would have had to be in writing to be enforceable. Under Nevada law, no statute of frauds specifically covered oral agreements to provide by will. The plaintiffs appealed from a judgment for defendant.]

Preliminarily, the court held that the executrix was a proper party; that the other heirs and beneficiaries were not indispensable parties; and that the California Dead Man's Act did not bar the plaintiffs' testimony because it applied to actions "upon a claim," rather than actions seeking discharge of a debt (overruling a prior case). Later in the opinion the court also held that the Nevada statute of frauds governing transfers of real estate did not apply to alleged testamentary transfers.

We are . . . confronted with a contract that is valid under the law of Nevada but invalid under the California statute of frauds if that statute is applicable. We have no doubt that California's interest in protecting estates being probated here from false claims based on alleged oral contracts to make wills is constitutionally sufficient to justify the Legislature's making our statute of frauds applicable to all such contracts sought to be enforced against such estates. *See Rubin v. Irving Trust Co.,* 305 N.Y. 288, 298, 113 N.E.2d 424; *Emery v. Burbank,* 163 Mass. 326-329, 39 N.E. 1026. The Legislature, however, is ordinarily concerned with enacting laws to govern purely local transactions, and it has not spelled out the extent to which the statute of frauds is to apply to contracts having substantial contacts with another state. Accordingly, we must determine its scope in the light of applicable principles of the law of conflict of laws. *See People v. One 1953 Ford Victoria [supra];* Currie, *Married Women's Contracts,* 25 U.Chi. L. Rev. 227; Cheatham and Reese, *Choice of the Applicable Law,* 52 Col. L. Rev. 959.

In the present case plaintiffs were residents of Nevada, the contract was made in Nevada, and plaintiffs performed it there. If Granrud was a resident of Nevada at the time the contract was made, the California statute of frauds, in the absence of a plain legislative direction to the contrary, could not reasonably be interpreted as applying to the contract even though Granrud subsequently moved to California and died here. The basic policy of upholding the expectations of the parties by enforcing contracts valid under the only law apparently applicable would preclude an interpretation of our statute of frauds that would make it apply to and thus invalidate the contract because Granrud moved to California and died here. Such a case would be analogous to *People v. One 1953 Ford Victoria,* 48 Cal.2d 595, 311 P.2d 480, where we held that a Texas mortgagee of an automobile mortgaged in Texas did not forfeit his interest when the automobile was subsequently used to transport narcotics in California although he had failed to make the character investigation of the mortgagor required by California law. A mortgagee entering into a purely local transaction in another state could not reasonably be expected to take cognizance of the law of all the other jurisdictions where the property might possibly be taken, and accordingly, the California statute requiring an investigation to protect his interest could not reasonably be interpreted to apply to such out of state mortgagees . . . . Another analogy is found in the holding that the statute of frauds did not apply to contracts to make wills entered into before the statute was enacted [citation omitted]. Just as parties to local transactions cannot be expected to take cognizance of the law of other jurisdictions, they cannot be expected to anticipate a change in the local statute of frauds. Protection of rights growing out of valid contracts precludes interpreting the general language of the statute of frauds to destroy such rights whether the possible applicability of the statute arises from the movement of one or more of the parties across state lines or subsequent enactment of the statute.

In the present case, however, there is no finding as to where Granrud was domiciled at the time the contract was made. Since he had a bank account in California at that time and died a resident here less than two years later it may be that he was domiciled here when the contract was made. Even if he was, the result should be the same. The contract was made in Nevada and performed by plaintiffs there, and it involved the refinancing of obligations arising from the sale of Nevada land and secured by interests therein. Nevada has a substantial interest in the contract and in protecting the rights of its residents who are parties thereto, and its policy is that the contract is valid and enforceable. California's policy is also to enforce lawful contracts. That policy, however, must be subordinated in the case of any contract that does not meet the requirements of an applicable statute California of frauds. In determining whether the contract herein is subject to the statute of frauds, we must consider both the policy to protect the reasonable expectations of the parties and the policy of the statute of frauds. It is true that if Granrud was domiciled here at the time the contract was made, plaintiffs may have been alerted to the possibility that the California statute of frauds might apply. Since California, however, would have no interest in applying its own statute of frauds unless Granrud remained here until his death, plaintiffs were not bound to know that California's statute might ultimately be invoked against them. Unless they could rely on their own law, they would have to look to the laws of all of the jurisdictions to which Granrud might move regardless of where he was domiciled when the contract was made. We conclude, therefore, that the contract herein does not fall within our statute of frauds. Since there is thus no conflict between the law of California and the law of Nevada, we can give effect to the common policy of both states to enforce lawful contracts and sustain Nevada's interest in protecting its residents and their reasonable expectations growing out of a transaction substantially related to that state without subordinating any legitimate interest of this state.

*The judgment is reversed.*

---

## NOTES AND QUESTIONS ON THE RESTRAINED FORUM

(1) **EMERY v. BURBANK,** 163 Mass. 326, 39 N.E. 1026 (1895) (Holmes, J.). Action by a Maine woman to enforce an oral contract against a Massachusetts estate. In return for plaintiff's promise, made in Maine, to leave Maine and come to Massachusetts to take care of her in Massachusetts, the Massachusetts decedent promised to leave her all her property in her will. The will, however, made no provision for the plaintiff.

*Held:* For the estate. Recovery against the estate is barred under the Massachusetts statute of frauds, although the contract was made in Maine. Although the Massachusetts statute is worded "substantively" ["No agreement . . . shall be binding, unless . . . in writing"; *cf. Marie v. Garrison,* [§ 4.11[A], *supra* ], the Massachusetts statute must apply anyway. It embodies a fundamental policy for the protection of Massachusetts testators. Its purpose is to guard the assets of Massachusetts decedents from trumped up claims in Massachusetts courts. The law is also in part "procedural," because it imposes a duty upon the Massachusetts courts to husband the assets of the estate for the legatees. As to those purposes it is immaterial that the alleged agreement was made in Maine.

\* \* \*

Can *Emery* be reconciled with *Bernkrant?* Surely the plaintiff in *Emery* expected that her promisor would die domiciled in Massachusetts. Holmes recognized that the case would be even harder had the decedent been domiciled out of state at the time of the promise, but wound up surmising that forum law would be applied in that case as well, given the strength of forum policy.

Holmes's policy analysis seems strong notwithstanding his traditionalist method. Was Holmes right? Is it possible that in *Bernkrant* "moderate and restrained" interpretation of forum law was inappropriate? Although Justice Traynor explored the interests of the respective states on the issue of the validity of the contract, he gave only cursory preliminary mention to the additional local interest in applying the statute of frauds, identified by Holmes—an interest in husbanding the assets of the estate against possibly spurious claims.

(2) *The Bernkrant enigma.* A curious feature of *Bernkrant* is the evident predisposition of the court to validate the alleged oral agreement. Recall the

set of perhaps questionable preliminary rulings in favor of the plaintiffs. Moreover, it appears that the court disregarded Nevada's Dead Man's Act. Had the case been tried in Nevada, the plaintiffs could not have testified to the alleged oral agreement. *See* David Cavers, *Oral Contracts To Provide By Will and the Choice-of-Law Process,* in Perspectives Of Law—Essays for Austin Wakeman Scott 38 (Roscoe Pound ed. 1964).

(3) **RUBIN v. IRVING TRUST CO.,** 305 N.Y. 288,113 N.E.2d 424 (1953). Action by a New Yorker for breach of an alleged promise by his brother *not* to change his will. The promise was made in Florida, during a vacation. New York law required a writing, but Florida law did not.

*Held.* For the estate. Forum law applies, and enforcement of the alleged oral contract is denied. New York was the true "center of gravity" of the agreement, notwithstanding that it was made in Florida.

*   *   *

*Rubin* seems correctly decided, but does the "center of gravity" reasoning have the persuasive power of the policy analysis Holmes delivered in *Emery?*

(4) *Interest-balancing.* In both *One Ford Victoria* and *Bernkrant,* a solution is achieved by construing local law and interests narrowly. But should the interests of other concerned states be balanced against those of the forum? Although Brainerd Currie thought that interest-weighing was a political function unsuitable for courts in conflicts cases, courts do habitually weigh or balance competing interests in ordinary nonconflicts cases.

*See generally* Courtland Peterson, *Weighing Contacts in Conflicts Cases: The Handmaiden Axiom,* 9 Duq. L. Rev. 436 (1971); Peter Hay, *Full Faith and Credit and Federalism in Choice of Law,* 34 Mercer L. Rev. 709 (1983).

For recent commentary on the general problem of "the restrained forum," see Louise Weinberg, *Against Comity,* 80 Geo. L.J. 53 (1991).

## § 4.23  Comparative Impairment

*Introduction.* In *Choice of Law and the Federal System,* 16 Stan. L. Rev. 1 (1963), Professor William Baxter proposed a way of resolving true conflicts based on an analysis of *People v. One 1953 Ford Victoria,* § 4.22, *supra.* Baxter called his method, "comparative impairment." Under this approach, an interest-analytic court can resolve a true conflict by assessing the impact on its own policy of a departure from forum law, and assessing the impact on the other state's policy of applying forum law. Comparison of the two negative impacts, Baxter thought could yield a sound resolution, without the interest-balancing disfavored by Currie. The method was formally adopted for California in the following case.

# BERNHARD v. HARRAH'S CLUB

*California Supreme Court, In Bank*
*16 Cal. 3d 313, 128 Cal. Rptr. 215, 546 P.2d 719 (1976)*

SULLIVAN, JUSTICE . . . . The issue involved in the case at bench is the civil liability of defendant tavern keeper to plaintiff, a third person, for injuries allegedly caused by the former by selling and furnishing alcoholic beverages in Nevada to intoxicated patrons who subsequently injured plaintiff in California. Two states are involved: (1) California—the place of plaintiff's residence and domicile, the place where he was injured, and the forum; and (2) Nevada—the place of defendant's residence and the place of the wrong.

We observe at the start that the laws of the two states—California and Nevada—applicable to the issue involved are not identical. California imposes liability on tavern keepers in this state for conduct such as here alleged. In *Vesely v. Sager,* 486 P.2d 151 (Cal. 1971), this court rejected the contention that

> "civil liability for tavern keepers should be left to future legislative action . . . . [The rule that] the furnishing of alcoholic beverages is not the proximate cause of injuries resulting from intoxication . . . is patently unsound and totally inconsistent with the principles of proximate cause established in other areas of negligence law . . . . [The] Legislature has expressed its intention in this area with the adoption of Evidence Code section 669, and Business and Professions Code section 25602 . . . . It is clear that Business and Professions Code section 25602 (making it a misdemeanor to sell to an obviously intoxicated person) is a statute to which this presumption (of negligence, Evidence Code section 669) applies and that the policy expressed in the statute is to promote the safety of the people of California . . . ."

Nevada on the other hand refuses to impose such liability. In *Hamm v. Carson City Nuggett, Inc.,* 450 P.2d 358, 359 (Nev. 1969), the court held it would create neither common law liability nor liability based on the criminal statute banning sale of alcoholic beverages to a person who is drunk, because "if civil liability is to be imposed, it should be accomplished by legislative act after appropriate surveys, hearings, and investigations to ascertain the need for it and the expected consequences to follow." It is noteworthy that in *Hamm* the Nevada court in relying on the common law rule denying liability cited our decision in *Cole v. Rush,* 289 P.2d 450 (Cal. 1955), later overruled by us in *Vesely* to the extent that it was inconsistent with that decision.

Although California and Nevada . . . have different laws governing the issue presented in the case at bench, we encounter a problem in selecting the applicable rule of law only if both states have an interest in having their respective laws applied . . . .

Defendant contends that Nevada has a definite interest in having its rule of decision applied in this case in order to protect its resident tavern keepers like defendant from being subjected to a civil liability which Nevada has not imposed either by legislative enactment or decisional law. It is urged that in *Hamm v. Carson City Nuggett, supra,* the Supreme Court of Nevada clearly delineated the policy underlying denial of civil liability of tavern keepers who sell to obviously intoxicated patrons: "Those opposed to extending liability point out that to hold otherwise would subject the tavern owner to ruinous exposure every time he poured a drink and would multiply litigation endlessly in a claim-conscious society. Every liquor vendor visited by the patron who became intoxicated would be a likely defendant in subsequent litigation flowing from the patron's wrongful conduct . . . . [If] civil liability is to be imposed, it should be accomplished by legislative act after appropriate surveys, hearings, and investigations . . . ." Accordingly defendant argues that the Nevada rule of decision is the appropriate one for the forum to apply.

Plaintiff on the other hand points out that California also has an interest in applying its own rule of decision to the case at bench. California imposes on tavern keepers civil liability to third parties injured by persons to whom the tavern keeper has sold alcoholic beverages when they are obviously intoxicated "for the purpose of protecting members of the general public from injuries to person and damage to property resulting from the excessive use of intoxicating liquor." (*Vesely v. Sager, supra.*) California, it is urged, has a special interest in affording this protection to all California residents injured in California.

Thus, since the case at bench involves a California resident (plaintiff) injured in this state by intoxicated drivers, and a Nevada resident tavern keeper (defendant) which served alcoholic beverages to them in Nevada, it is clear that each state has an interest in the application of its respective law of non-liability. It goes without saying that these interests conflict. Therefore, . . . we are confronted with a "true" conflicts case . . . .

The search for the proper resolution of a true conflicts case, while proceeding within orthodox parameters of governmental interest analysis, has generated much scholarly examination and discussion. The father of the governmental interest approach, Professor Brainerd Currie, originally took the position that in a true conflicts situation the law of the forum should always be applied. However, upon further reflection, Currie suggested that when under the governmental interest approach a preliminary analysis reveals an apparent conflict of interest upon the forum's assertion of its own rule of decision, the forum should reexamine its policy to determine if a more restrained interpretation of it is more appropriate . . . .

Once this preliminary analysis has identified a true conflict of the governmental interests involved as applied to the parties under the particular circumstances of the case, the "comparative impairment" approach to the resolution of such conflict (Baxter, *Choice of Law and the Federal System,* 16 STAN.L.REV. 1 (1963)) seeks to determine which state's interest would be more impaired if its policy were subordinated to the policy of the other state . . . . [This] process of analysis . . . is very different from a weighing process. The court does not " 'weigh' the conflicting governmental interests in the sense of determining which conflicting law manifested the 'better' or the 'worthier' social policy on the specific issue . . . . [Emphasis] is placed on the appropriate scope of conflicting state policies rather than on the quality of those policies

. . . ." Horowitz, *The Law of Choice of Law in California-A Restatement,* 21 U.C.L.A. L. REV. 719, 753.

[This reasoning was originally] applied by Justice Traynor in his opinion for this court in *People v. One 1953 Ford Victoria* . . . .

Mindful of the above principles governing our choice of law, we proceed to reexamine the California policy underlying the imposition of civil liability upon tavern keepers. At its broadest limits this policy would afford protection to all persons injured in California by intoxicated persons who have been sold or furnished alcoholic beverages while intoxicated regardless of where such beverages were sold or furnished. Such a broad policy would naturally embrace situations where the intoxicated actor had been provided with liquor by out-of-state tavern keepers. Although the State of Nevada does not impose such *civil* liability on its tavern keepers, nevertheless they are subject to *criminal* penalties under a statute making it unlawful to sell or give intoxicating liquor to any person who is drunk or known to be a habitual drunkard. (*See* NEV. REV. STAT. 202.100; *see Hamm v. Carson City Nuggett, Inc., supra.*)

We need not, and accordingly do not here determine the outer limits to which California's policy should be extended, for it appears clear to us that it must encompass defendant, who, as alleged in the complaint, advertise[s] for and otherwise solicit[s] in California the business of California residents at defendant Harrah's Club Nevada drinking . . . . establishments, knowing and expecting said California residents in response to said advertising and solicitation, to use the Public highways of . . . California in going and coming from defendant Harrah's Club . . . ." Defendant by the course of its chosen commercial practice has put itself at the heart of California's regulatory interest, namely to prevent tavern keepers from selling alcoholic beverages to obviously intoxicated persons who are likely to act in California in the intoxicated state. It seems clear that California cannot reasonably effectuate its policy if it does not extend its regulation to include out-of-state tavern keepers such as defendant who regularly and purposely sell intoxicating beverages to California residents in places and under conditions in which it is reasonably certain these residents will return to California and act therein while still in an intoxicated state. California's interest would be very significantly impaired if its policy were not applied to defendant.

Since the act of selling alcoholic beverages to obviously intoxicated persons is already proscribed in Nevada, the application of California's rule of civil liability would not impose an entirely new duty requiring the ability to distinguish between California residents and other patrons. Rather the imposition of such liability involves an increased economic exposure, which, at least for businesses which actively solicit extensive California patronage, is a foreseeable and coverable business expense. Moreover, Nevada's interest in protecting its tavern keepers from civil liability of a boundless and unrestricted nature will not be significantly impaired when as in the instant case liability is imposed only on those tavern keepers who actively solicit California business.

Therefore, upon reexamining the policy underlying California's rule of decision and giving such policy a more restrained interpretation for the purpose of this case pursuant to the principles of the choice of law discussed above, we conclude that California has an important and abiding interest in applying its rule of decision to the case at bench, that the policy of this state would be more significantly impaired if such rule were not applied and that the trial court erred in not applying California law.

Defendant argues, however, that even if California law is applied, the demurrer was nonetheless properly sustained because the tavern keeper's duty stated in *Vesely v. Sager, supra,* is based on Business and Professions Code section 25602, which is a criminal statute and thus without extraterritorial effect. It is quite true, as defendant argues, that in *Vesely* we determined "that civil liability results when a vendor furnishes alcoholic beverages to a customer in violation of Business and Professions Code section 25602 and each of the conditions set forth in Evidence Code section 669, subdivision (a) is established."

It is also clear, as defendant's argument points out, that since, unlike the California vendor in *Vesely,* defendant was a Nevada resident which furnished the alcoholic beverage in that state, the above California statute had no extraterritorial effect and that civil liability could not be posited on defendant's violation of a California criminal law. We recognize, therefore, that we cannot make the same determination as quoted above with respect to defendant that we made with respect to the defendant vendor in *Vesely.*

However, our decision in *Vesely* was much broader than defendant would have it. There, at the very outset of our opinion, we declared that the traditional common law rule denying recovery on the ground that the furnishing of alcoholic beverage is not the proximate cause of the injuries inflicted on a third person by an intoxicated individual "is patently unsound . . . ." We reasoned: "If such furnishing is a proximate cause, it is so because the consumption, resulting intoxication, and injury-producing conduct are foreseeable intervening causes, or at least the injury-producing conduct is one of the hazards which makes such furnishing negligent . . . ."

Although we chose to impose liability on the *Vesely* defendant on the basis of his violating the applicable statute, the clear import of our decision was that there was no bar to civil liability under modern negligence law . . . . The fact then, that in the case at bench, section 25602 of the Business and Professions Code is not applicable to this defendant in Nevada so as to warrant the imposition of civil liability on the basis of its violation, does not preclude recovery on the basis of injury caused by negligence apart from the statute . . . . Everyone is responsible for an injury caused to another by his want of ordinary care or skill in the management of his property . . . .

*See* PROBLEMS 4F-1. MARCHING TO GEORGIA; 4F-2. A LIFE INSURANCE SCAM.

## NOTES ON *BERNHARD*

(1) *Comparative impairment as panacaea.* Are you satisfied that comparative impairment can resolve all true conflicts? *See* Leo Kanowitz, *Comparative*

*Impairment and Better Law: Grand Illusions in the Conflict of Laws,* 30 HASTINGS L. J. 255 (1978); Herma Hill Kay, *The Use of Comparative Impairment to Resolve True Conflicts: An Evaluation of the California Experience,* 68 CALIF L. REV. 577 (1980). In *Bernhard,* the fact that Nevada already imposed criminal liability on the allegedly tortious conduct made accommodation of Nevada's interest to the forum's interest somewhat easier. But the court overlooked the fact that the Nevada criminal liability law it cited had been repealed in 1973. Had the court taken note of the repeal, would comparative impairment have been of use in resolving the conflict? Compare the effect of the repeal in *Milliken v. Pratt,* § 4.07[A], *supra.*

(2) *Moderate and restrained construction of sister-state law?* Is comparative impairment, as used in *Bernhard,* a "moderate and restrained" construction of forum law, like that in *One 1953 Ford Victoria,* § 4.22, *supra?* Is what the court did do distinguishable from interest-balancing? How?

(3) **CABLE v. SAHARA TAHOE CORP,** 93 Cal. App. 384,155, Cal. Rptr. 770 (1979). Action by Californian employed by defendant tavern owner in Nevada. The Californian was injured in Nevada while riding as a passenger in an intoxicated Nevadan's car. The Californian became a public charge in California. The California court denied relief under Nevada law, using a comparative-impairment analysis. Was the operative distinction between *Cable and Bernhard* that the accident in *Cable* occurred in Nevada? Why should that have made a difference? Was the operative distinction between the two cases the fact that the agent of the harm in *Cable* was a Nevadan instead of a Californian? Why should that have made a difference? Ought these combined features of the case make a difference whether or not rationally related to the forum's policy concerns? The operative distinction in *Cable* in all probability lay in a post-accident change in forum law. *See* Note (6), *infra.*

Suppose that the tavern owner as well as the victim in Bernhard were Californians, but that the place of injury was Nevada, and the driver a Nevadan. How do you suppose California would decide which law to apply? *See Rong Yao Zhou v. Jennifer Mall Rest.,* 534 A.2d 1268 (D.C. App. 1987), in which the forum correctly identified the false conflict; the residence of the drunk driver was not mentioned. *See also Schmidt v. Driscoll Hotel,* 249 Minn. 376, 82 N.W.2d 365 (1957).

(4) *Advertising, solicitation, and foreseeability.* It is a prominent feature of *Bernhard* that Harrah's Club solicited its California clientele in California. But would the result have differed if Harrah's Club had not solicited California customers? *Cf. Blamey v. Brown,* 270 N.W.2d 844 (Minn. 1978) (liability imposed on non-soliciting sole proprietor).

(5) *Note on judicial process.* Note the interesting common-law reasoning in *Bernhard.* The court is unwilling to extend to extraterritorial conduct the *Veseley* "implied" private right of action under California's criminal dramshop act. But recognizing its governmental interests in making the plaintiff whole and in deterring unsafe conditions on California roads, the court creates, as a matter of California common law, a new right to sue, without regard to the criminal statute.

(6) *Ironic footnote.* The California legislature did not agree with the California Supreme Court about the wisdom of its judicially-created civil dramshop act and legislatively overruled not only *Bernhard* but also *Vesely.* In 1978, § 25.602 of the California Business & Professional Code was amended to eliminate the vicarious civil liability of bartenders and private hosts for acts of intoxicated customers or private guests. It remains a misdemeanor under California law to serve a person who is obviously intoxicated.

---

## HALL v. NEVADA [II]

*California Court of Appeal, First District*
*141 Cal. Rptr. 439, 74 Cal. App. 3d 280 (1977)*

[Hall I] is reported in § 4.20, *supra.*
The following opinion is on remand from the
United States Supreme Court's denial of certiorari.
The Supreme Court's ultimate opinion in *Nevada v. Hall*
is reported in § 5.03, *infra.*]

EMERSON, ASSOCIATE JUSTICE. [The] University of Nevada and the State of Nevada appeal from a judgment in the amount of $1,150,000 entered against them in an action . . . for damages for personal injuries. The injuries resulted from a collision between a vehicle occupied by [plaintiffs] and one driven by Helmut Bohm. It is conceded that, at the time of the accident, Bohm was an employee of the university, a governmental arm of Nevada, and was engaged in official university business . . . . The accident occurred in California . . . .

[I]mmediately [following the United State Supreme Court's denial of certiorari and] prior to the trial of this case, appellants moved for an order limiting damages to $25,000 per person pursuant to Nevada Revised Statutes section 41.035 . . . .

Nevada has chosen to waive its sovereign immunity, but to limit such waiver to $25,000 per claimant.

Appellants' motion to limit damages was denied by the trial court. The correctness of this ruling is the sole issue on appeal.

Nevada [contends] that if California accepts the waiver, it must accept the limitation.

This premise misconceives the point of *Hall [I].* The [California] Supreme Court did not hold that Nevada had waived sovereign immunity or had given its implied consent to be sued in California. It held simply that Nevada's sovereign protection does not extend beyond its own borders . . . .

That the limitation imposed by NRS § 41.035 is totally inapplicable to this case is made clear by footnote 4 of *Hall [I]* . . . .

The case of *Bernhard v. Harrah's Club* [§ 4.23, *supra*] presents both the latest definitive statement of California's choice of law rules regarding tort actions and a fact situation extremely close to the one at bench. In *Bernhard,* plaintiff, a California resident, was struck on a highway in this state by an automobile driven by another California resident who had allegedly been furnished alcoholic beverages in defendant's Nevada establishment after becoming obviously intoxicated. Plaintiff sought application of California law imposing civil liability upon tavern keepers who furnish liquor to obviously intoxicated persons . . . .

The Supreme Court, noting that it faced a "true conflicts" case, . . . pointed out that California's policy interest would be very significantly impaired if it could not extend its regulation to defendant . . . .

In the instant case Nevada advances as its policy, the fact that if its liability were not limited, its residents would suffer financially, due to the increased cost of insurance for Nevada vehicles being operated outside the state. California's policy interest lies in providing full protection to those who are injured on its highways through the negligence of both residents and nonresidents.

We consider the policy reasons for applying California law herein to be even stronger than those found in *Bernhard.* In *Bernhard,* defendant's culpable conduct occurred entirely within Nevada's own borders, yet the Supreme Court found that merely by soliciting customers from California, knowing and expecting such customers to use California's highways, defendant had "put itself at the heart of California's regulatory interest . . . ." Here, the State of Nevada's activities and respondents' resulting injuries took place within California. By thus utilizing the public highways within our state to conduct its business, Nevada should fully expect to be held accountable under California's laws.

The imposition of unlimited liability upon Nevada involves at most an increased economic exposure . . . . Given the fact that Nevada has chosen to engage in governmental and business activity in this state, the necessary acquisition of additional insurance coverage to protect itself during such activity is an entirely foreseeable and reasonable expense . . . .

[Nevada also argued unsuccessfully that application of its own law to the present case was required by the full faith and credit clause of the United States Constitution. For the fate of this contention in the Supreme Court of the United States, see *Nevada v. Hall,* § 5.03, *infra.—Ed.*]

*See* PROBLEMS 4F-3. SUICIDE OR MURDER? 4F-4. ANYTHING GOES.

---

## SAHARCESKI v. MARCURE

*Massachusetts Supreme Judicial Court*
*373 Mass. 304, 366 N.E.2d 1245 (1977)*

WILKINS, JUSTICE. The plaintiff and the defendant, Massachusetts residents and employees of a Massachusetts corporation, were acting in the course of their employment when, on June 1, 1970, in the State of Connecticut, the plaintiff, a passenger, was injured as the result of the defendant's negligent operation of a motor vehicle. If the relevant circumstances involved in this case all related to Massachusetts, the plaintiff would not be entitled to recover from his negligent fellow employee. On the other hand, if the relevant circumstances all related to Connecticut, the plaintiff would be entitled to recover . . . .

The [parties' employer] had its principal offices at its Turners Falls [Mass.] retail store outlet, of which the plaintiff was the manager. The plaintiff and the defendant were residents of this Commonwealth and had been hired here. The company had no store in Connecticut and had no employees resident or principally working there. It had purchased workmen's compensation insurance covering its employees as provided in G.L. c. 152. On June 1, 1970, the plaintiff, the defendant, and others traveled by motor vehicle on their employer's business from Massachusetts into Connecticut intending to pass through that State without stopping. Trips to Connecticut to pick up merchandise were an occasional part of the plaintiffs' duties. The vehicle, which was registered in Massachusetts, was owned by the company.

The defendant, employed as a chauffeur, was operating the vehicle when it struck the rear of a motor vehicle which was stopped in the passing lane of the Connecticut Turnpike. The plaintiff, who sustained injuries in the accident, collected workmen's compensation benefits from the company's insurance carrier.

The judge denied the defendant's motion for a directed verdict which was grounded on the claim that G.L. c. 152 prohibited a suit against a fellow employee. The jury returned a verdict for the plaintiff. However, on motion of the defendant, the judge ordered judgment for the defendant notwithstanding the verdict . . . .

In this Commonwealth, . . . an employee injured in the course of his employment by the negligence of a fellow employee may not recover from that fellow employee if he also was acting in the course of his employment. This long settled principle of Massachusetts law has not been subject to serious dispute, and is not challenged in this proceeding.

We think it clear that Massachusetts law, as expressed in its Workmen's Compensation Act, contemplates that an employee covered under the act must look solely to his employer's compensation insurer (and any independent third party tortfeasor) when he is injured in the course of his employment by the negligence of a fellow employee who is also acting in the course of his employment and that it makes no difference that the injury was received in another State.

[The] plaintiff contends that the substantive law of this Commonwealth is inapplicable to injuries arising from a tort which occurred in Connecticut. He argues that . . . appropriate conflict of laws principles require this court to look to the law of the State of Connecticut, and that the law of Connecticut would permit the plaintiff to recover against a fellow employee in these circumstances.

It is clear that an employee injured in Connecticut in the course of his employment by the negligent operation of a motor vehicle by a fellow employee may recover from that fellow employee under Connecticut law. [CONN. GEN. STAT. 31 293(a)l (1977).] Many States permit a suit against a fellow employee in such circumstances . . . .

The issue presented here has not been resolved uniformly in those cases where it has arisen and is left open by the *Restatement (Second) of Conflict of Laws. See Restatement (Second) of Conflict of Laws* § 184, Comment b (1971).[3] Some courts have undertaken to resolve the choice of law question by a largely mechanical, conclusory assertion of the result. Thus, the law of the forum has been applied, where the accident occurred out of State, by simply concluding that the forum's public policy is to deny recovery against a fellow employee. We do not regard the Connecticut rule of law as so repugnant to the declared policy of this State that we would not enforce it in appropriate circumstances.[4] On the other hand, the law of the forum allowing recovery against a fellow employee has been applied to a local accident in disregard of the [immunity] contained in the law of the State of employment, perhaps on the ground that the [immunity] of the foreign law is obnoxious to the forum's public policy, or on the simple assertion that the law of the place of the alleged tort governs all questions of law.

In situations involving a conflict of laws concerning the fellow employee's claimed [immunity] from liability, the better reasoned cases focus on the established relationship of the parties, their expectations, and the degree of interest of each jurisdiction whose law might be applied . . . .

In resolving the choice of law problem presented in this case, we believe it is appropriate to look directly to the substantive law of this Commonwealth . . . . [In] *Pevoski v. Pevoski,* 358 N.E.2d 416 (Mass. 1976), we held, as to a New York motor vehicle accident, that the law of this Commonwealth should determine the question whether one spouse may sue and recover from the other. We noted that the interest of this Commonwealth in the question was more substantial than that of New York, the place of the tort . . . .

Although the considerations involved in permitting or denying a right of action differ in this case from those present in the *Pevoski* case, there are substantial reasons for looking to the law of Massachusetts to determine whether the plaintiff should be allowed to maintain an action against his fellow employee. Most significant are the reasonable expectations of the parties, each of whom was hired and lived in Massachusetts. The workmen's compensation law of this Commonwealth bars an employee from recovering from a negligent fellow employee . . . . The plaintiff had no reasonable basis for expecting to recover in this situation, and the defendant had no reason

---

[3] The *Restatement* notes that "(s)ome workmen's compensation statutes extend immunity from liability in tort or wrongful death to certain designated persons, such as fellow employees, who are not required to provide insurance against the particular risk. It is uncertain whether such immunity will be given effect in other states."

Section 184 indicates that the plaintiffs employer would be free from liability in tort in this circumstance.

[4] If P and D while in the course of their employment in Connecticut, and while covered by the Connecticut compensation act, were involved in a motor vehicle accident in which D allegedly negligently injured P, and if P were to sue D in Massachusetts, we would not decline to permit recovery to P on the ground that the Connecticut exception to the fellow servant statute was contrary to public policy of this Commonwealth.

to expect that he would be liable. Additionally, reference to the law of the place of common employment provides both a certain source for the resolution of the issue and assurance that the ability to maintain a tort action will not turn solely on the fortuitous circumstance of where the accident takes place. The elimination of happenstance, a sort of unknowing geographical Russian roulette, as the controlling factor is particularly significant in a case where no business was to be transacted in the jurisdiction where the injury took place. As a matter of choice of law, we conclude that the substantive law of the Commonwealth should apply to bar recovery by the plaintiff in this case.

[The court noted that the same decision would be reached had it applied the whole law of the place of injury, including its conflicts rules. Citing *Levy v. Daniels U-Drive Renting Co.* [§ 4.11, *supra* ], the court pointed out that under existing Connecticut choice rules, the case was likely to be re-characterized as one of contract, and the law of the place of contracting, Massachusetts, applied.]

The conclusion that Connecticut might not apply Connecticut law in these circumstances is strengthened by the absence of strong local public policy considerations there in support of authorizing suits against fellow employees. Connecticut has abolished the right to sue a negligent fellow employee as a general principle of its law. The right to sue is limited now to motor vehicle torts or wilful or malicious conduct. Conn. Gen. Stat. § 31-293a (1977). The element of punishment for intentional or malicious wrongdoing is recognized, but Connecticut appears not to be concerned generally either with "punishment" of a negligent wrongdoer or with providing recovery for an injured employee beyond the level of his available workmen's compensation. Indeed, the legislative policy behind the [immunity] for motor vehicle torts of fellow employees may be grounded on nothing more exhilarating than the allocation of losses between insurers.[9]

It is true that the [immunity] of employers from suit by the compensation law of the place of employment involves both a detriment and a gain to the employee, who loses his tort action in exchange for the certainty of compensation benefits, while an [immunity] granted to a fellow employee involves no similar, direct exchange. However, such employees reciprocally surrender potential claims against one another in circumstances in which each is assured compensation benefits.

We suspect that the Connecticut court would regard Connecticut's transient interest in the circumstances of this case as insignificant in relation to the established, continuing employment relationship of the plaintiff, the defendant, and their employer under Massachusetts law. In any event, we elect

---

[9] If one assumes the availability of both workmen's compensation coverage and motor vehicle coverage, the difference in legislative policy between Massachusetts and Connecticut results in the insurer of the negligent fellow employee sustaining the loss in Connecticut and in the employer's . . . compensation carrier sustaining the loss in Massachusetts. This difference in policy seems not to involve a major disagreement on a subject of substantial social importance. In this Commonwealth, where coverage from two different kinds of insurance might be available, the general tendency has been to exonerate the nonworkmen's compensation carrier and to place the responsibility on the workmen's compensation insurer. [The court here cites provisions of Massachusetts law governing no-fault insurance and medical insurance.] In these circumstances, concepts of public policy which, it is said, should guide courts in their choice of law do not include punishing the wrongdoer or reimbursing the employer or its insurer . . . .

in this case to look directly to our own substantive law which, no matter where such a suit may be brought, is in the words of the Supreme Court of Connecticut "simple and easy to determine and apply" and leads "to predictable and desirable results." [Citation omitted.][10]

*Judgment affirmed.*

---

## NOTES AND QUESTIONS ON *SAHARCESKI*

(1) *A case of comparative impairment?* The *Saharceski* court seems to be following a rule that, at least in cases where Massachusetts is the joint domicile of the parties, Massachusetts law, *i.e.* forum law, will apply. But although the court is unaware of the structure of its further reasoning, and does not cite the California cases, isn't the court, in effect, doing a comparative impairment analysis? The court notes that Connecticut and Massachusetts law and policy are substantially identical. Connecticut's rule appears as a narrow exception to its more general policy, and under its own choice rules at that time Connecticut was unlikely to apply the exception.

(2) *An exercise in policy analysis.* The *Saharceski* court is not very explicit about the reasons for either the Massachusetts or the Connecticut rule. Now is your chance to try your hand at arguing the reasons for the rules in a case in which a state supreme court failed for the most part to do that. How would you argue the defendant's case, based on the reason for the Massachusetts rule? How would you argue the plaintiff's case, based on the reason for the Connecticut rule?

Why do you suppose both states' laws take the same basic position, that an injured worker ought not to be allowed to sue a fellow worker whose negligence caused the injury? It may be of some help in identifying the policy concern at work here to think about the underlying purpose of workers' compensation law in general.

Assuming the good sense of the Massachusetts rule, why would Connecticut allow such a suit? Connecticut requires only that the fellow worker's alleged negligence be in driving a motor vehicle. It might be supposed that Connecticut's concern is to deter unsafe conditions on its roads. But that is hardly a more fundamental policy than deterrence of unsafe conditions at the workplace, and under Connecticut law the fellow-worker cannot be sued for a workplace tort. Moreover, Connecticut would have allowed suit against a negligent driver/worker, as the court's citation to *Levy* reminds us, even if the negligence occurred on *Massachusetts* roads. Does the court's footnote 9 furnish a clue?

(3) *Saharceski and the Judicial Process.* Was the court right to apply forum law on the facts of *Saharceski*? Or should the court have allowed the plaintiff to collect damages? The court says, in footnote 9, that there is a legislative

---

[10] In our view, predictability is important not only after but before any claim arises, that is, the parties should have a reasonable basis for ascertaining their rights and potential obligations in advance of any conduct.

policy of protecting liability insurers from tort verdicts where workers' compensation is available to the plaintiff. But the examples given could be viewed instead as special exceptions to general state policy. As the court acknowledges, Massachusetts would freely allow the worker to sue any other third party responsible, in whole or in part, for the worker's injuries. *

How could the court have reached a result more in accord with its own general policy?

The customary solution would have been to apply Connecticut law. Connecticut had an interest in remedying an injury occurring on Connecticut roads. But the Massachusetts court was understandably reluctant to depart from its own law to deal with the rights of two Massachusetts workers *inter se,* and the Connecticut policy was narrow and apparently weak.

A better solution might have been for the court to give a more "moderate and restrained" interpretation to the Massachusetts defense. Does *Saharseski* fall within the policy purposes of the Massachusetts statutory bar?

(4) *Choice-of-law policies.* In comparative impairment cases, courts try to resolve true conflicts by narrow construction of state law. In some of these cases, narrow construction of sister-state law may offer a solution. In most of these cases, courts also take into account the expectations of the parties. What other concerns might inform a sensitive choice between competing laws? The rest of this Chapter explores this question.

---

## IS INTEREST ANALYSIS DISCRIMINATORY?

(1) *Distinction between residents and nonresidents.* Some writers have raised the question whether interest analysis is inherently defective because it suggests that a court should apply different rules to resident and nonresident parties. It seems questionable to discriminate against a party solely on the basis of residency. *See, e.g.,* John Hart Ely, *Choice of Law and the State's Interest in Protecting Its Own,* 23 WM. & MARY L. REV. 173 (1981). *But see* Louise Weinberg, *On Departing from Forum Law,* Symposium, 35 MERCER L. REV. 595, 596 n. 4, 597 n. 6 (replying to Professor Ely); Joseph Singer, *Real Conflicts,* 69 B.U. L. REV. 1, 67-74 (1989) (commenting on Ely and Weinberg). *See also* Douglas Laycock, *Equal Citizens of Equal and Territorial States: The Constitutional Foundations of Choice of Law,* 92 COLUM. L. REV. 249 (1992).

(2) *Rational basis.* Can an ordinary classification be discriminatory if it has a rational basis? Assume a variant of *Bernhard v. Harrah's Club,* in which both a Californian and a Nevadan are injured by the intoxicated driver in Nevada. Would California have a legitimate interest in remedying the tort to the nonresident as well as the resident plaintiff on such facts?

---

* Beyond these considerations, there is the possibility that if the worker were allowed to recover against an insured fellow worker, the employer's compensation insurer would then have access to equitable reimbursement of compensation paid on account of the same injury, as is customary in employee suits against third parties. Presumably, this reimbursement strengthens the insurance funding of the compensation scheme.

(3) *Lack of evenhandedness.* When a court with an interest in applying its law *withholds* the benefits of that law it may create an irrational classification. Thus, in *Bernhard,* for example, suppose the California court decided to deny the benefit of its remedial rule to the California plaintiff, on the ground that the dramshop owner was a Nevadan. Would the court have created two classes of Californians injured by intoxicated drivers? One of these classes could recover in its own state's courts, but the other could not. Is there a rational basis for the classification?

Suppose that, in *Bernhard,* a Nevada plaintiff were walking arm-in-arm with a California plaintiff when the pair were run down on a California road. If California denies recovery to the Nevada plaintiff, does California create two groups of victims of California road injuries, one which can recover against "dramshops" causing their injuries, and the other which cannot? Is there a rational basis for the classification? *Cf. Kell v. Henderson,* § 4.19, Note (2), *supra.*

(4) *Discriminatory statutory directives.* Legislation commonly contains language limiting application to events occurring within the territory, or to residents. Courts ordinarily defer, without analysis, to such express limitations. In a 1982 amendment to the Jones Act, 46 U.S.C. § 688, Congress barred American maritime tort remedies against American employers to nonresident oil workers injured on foreign waters, unless the plaintiffs have no other remedies. Is the amendment discriminatory? Unconstitutionally so?

---

## § 4.24   The Better Law and Professor Leflar

Another influential effort at finding a solution to the problem of true conflicts was made by the eminent Conflicts scholar, Professor Robert Leflar. In two very influential articles, *Choice-Influencing Considerations in Conflicts Law,* 41 N.Y.U. L. REV. 267 (1966), and *Conflicts of Law: More on Choice-Influencing Considerations,* 54 Cal. L. Rev. 1584 (1966), Leflar presented a list of "considerations" that judges might use in making choice-of-law decisions. A recent evaluation of Leflar's work is *Robert A. Leflar Symposium on Conflict of Laws,* 52 ARK. L. REV. 1 (1999) (contributions by Professors Cox, Felix, McDougal, Reynolds and Richman, Simson, Weintraub, and Whitten).

### NOTES ON "CHOICE-INFLUENCING CONSIDERATIONS"

(1) *Their Influence.* Leflar's "Considerations" have been quite influential. His methodology has influenced countless writers on choice of law, and it has been expressly adopted by the courts of five states (in order of adoption: New Hampshire (1966), Wisconsin (1967), Rhode Island (1968), Minnesota (1973), and Arkansas (1977). The whole-heartedness of these various adoptions is discussed in Robert L. Felix, *Leflar in the Courts: Judicial Adoptions of Choice-Influencing Considerations,* 52 ARK. L. REV. 35 (1999).

The reader will note that an early flurry of judicial adoptions of Leflar's Considerations ended more than two decades ago, and Professor Felix notes some back-sliding among those courts in recent years. Do you think that the popularity of the Second Conflicts Restatement might have something to do with the lack of current judicial enthusiasm for the Choice-Influencing Considerations?

(2) *Working Through the Considerations.* Leflar suggested five Considerations; he wrote that the five are not listed in any particular order, however, and none necessarily carries more weight than another in any case. Instead, the five are designed to help guide judicial analysis of difficult problems. Although the Considerations are mostly self-evident, it is useful to work through what Professor Leflar had to say about them. Leflar developed the Considerations partly by intensive study of the "escape devices" that courts used to avoid the harsh results that sometimes resulted from rigid application of the First Restatement rules. Leflar's five Considerations are described below. As you examine each one, review the cases in Part B of this Chapter and try to determine which ones may have helped Leflar to develop his list.

(a) *Predictability of Result.* Predictability of governing law reduces risks and, therefore, costs. When that happens, both the parties and society benefit. Contracting parties, in particular, want the security of knowing what risks they have undertaken so that they can assess better the deal that they are entering. Predictability is often less important in tort law; parties do not usually plan where they are going to have a serious accident. Thus, the Predictability Consideration generally will be more important in contract and property problems than in torts. Consider whether *Polson v. Stewart* from Part B might have been an influence here.

(b) *Maintenance of Interstate and International Order.* Leflar's concern here was with the free flow of interstate and international commerce. He wanted to ensure that the forum would not be parochial, that its choice-of-law decisions would not be unduly influenced by local favoritism. Not only would that be a bad thing in itself, but it easily could lead to what has been called "retaliatory comity," a sort of beggar-thy-neighbor approach to choice of law. Courts must be careful, therefore, to avoid localism. This Consideration was designed to remind judges of that goal.

(c) *Simplification of the Judicial Task.* Complicated and unfamiliar rules of law delay cases and increase the chances of a bad result, problems that are only compounded when juries are involved. Leflar thought this "Simplification" Consideration extended beyond the obvious preference for familiar forum law; it also could lead to the application of "mechanical," easily-selected choice-of-law rules. The best example here is the near-universal choice of any forum to apply its own procedural and evidentiary rules. Application of familiar forum law to such common questions—which often must be resolved quickly—greatly simplifies the judicial task and is more likely to lead to justice.

(d) *Advancement of the Forum's Governmental Interests.* Leflar cautioned against using this Consideration to apply forum law blindly. He believed that most laws do not implicate true forum interests, and that the court must be restrained in asserting them. A "justice-dispensing" court (Leflar's term) should recognize that true differences of governmental interests among the states are by no means the norm. Judges should be careful to recognize those differences that do not represent basic policy disagreements, and only consider the forum's interests, as such, when there is a fundamental policy disagreement (the legality of gambling transactions provides an example of a basic policy dispute). Consider the Arkansas *Telegraph Cases* from Part B and their possible role here.

(e) *The Better Rule of Law.* This has proven by far the most controversial of the Considerations. Leflar believed that judges often consider the relative merits of competing rules when making choice-of-law decisions; he also believed, however, that they rarely discuss that factor in their opinions. He included this Consideration to encourage honesty in judicial opinion-writing. Professor Simson recently identified the factors that courts most often use in determining the "Better Rule":

> [T]rends in state adoptions of laws like those competing for application in the case at hand; the number of states that have adopted laws of one or the other sort; patterns in judicial interpretation . . . ; the weight of scholarly comment . . . ; the competing laws' relative consistency with modern social and economic conditions; and the comparative logic or wisdom of the laws in conflict.

Gary J. Simson, *Resisting the Allure of Better Rule of Law,* 52 ARK. L. REV. 141, 146 (1999). Do you think *Milliken v. Pratt* may have influenced this Consideration?

Although Professor Simson's list sounds sensible enough, some commentators have had trouble with the Better Law concept. Objections include a concern about whether a court can ever say that forum law is not as good as that of another state, or more realistically, that a court *ever* would hold that to be the case. In practice, some cases at least have held that non-forum law is "better." *E.g., Jepson v. General Casualty Co.,* 513 S.W.2d 467 (Minn. 1994). *See generally* Robert L. Felix, *Leflar in the Courts: Judicial Adoptions of Choice-Influencing Considerations,* 52 ARK. L. REV. 35 (1999). And in some cases, at least, it would seem that a civilized court should *only* consider better law. In this respect, consider the *Holzer* decision, *supra* at § 4.14, which applied the law of Nazi Germany to defeat a breach of contract action brought by a Jewish refugee from that regime. *See also* Louise Weinberg, *Methodological Interventions and the Slavery Cases: Or, Night Thoughts of a Legal Realist,* 56 MD. L. REV. 1316 (1997) (discussing choice of law in slavery cases).

(3) *A Sample Case. Schlemmer v. Firemen's Fund Ins. Co.* 730 S.W. 2d 217 (1987), provides a typical illustration of Choice-Influencing Considerations in practice. The case involved an accident in Arkansas between a car and driver from that state and a car and driver from Tennessee. The latter car also had a passenger from Tennessee. That guest sued his host in an Arkansas court; the issue was the applicability of the Arkansas guest statute (which had been repealed after the accident). The court applied Leflar's Considerations in this way:

1. *Predictability* was not a factor in unplanned events like accidents. As for insurance, the host's rates probably were set based upon the company's experiences in Tennessee.

2. *Interstate and international Order.* Not applicable on these facts.

3. *The Judicial Task.* Also not applicable because the courts can understand both laws well enough.

4. *Advancement of the Forum's Governmental Interests.* Because Arkansas had repealed its guest statute, Arkansas had no interest to advance. That left Tennessee with the "most relevant" interest.

5. *Better Law.* Because the guest statute had been repealed, the court had no trouble in concluding that Tennessee had the better law.

\* \* \*

(4) *Other proponents of "the better law."* One author independently reaches a "better law" position, although in other ways he is a critic of modern methods. He writes: "The conscious efforts of judges to adjudicate multi-state disputes by applying rules that, in their opinion, are of superior quality ought to assure a greater number of sound decisions than any other doctrine could conceivably produce." FRIEDRICH JUENGER, GENERAL COURSE ON PRIVATE INTERNATIONAL LAW 288 (1983). A similar conclusion is reached in Joseph Singer, *Real Conflicts,* 69 B.U.L. REV. 1 (1989).

As always, there is more than one way to skin a legal cat or, more appropriately here, to get to "better law," as the next case illustrates.

## OFFSHORE RENTAL CO., INC. v. CONTINENTAL OIL CO.

*California Supreme Court, In Bank.*
*22 CaL 3d 157, 148 CaL Rptr. 867, 583 P.2d 721 (1978)*

TOBRINER, JUSTICE . . . . Plaintiff Offshore Rental Company, a California corporation, maintains its principal place of business in California, but derives its revenues in large part from leasing oil drilling equipment in Louisiana's Gulf Coast area. Headquartered in New York, defendant Continental Oil Company, a Delaware corporation, does business in California, Louisiana, and other states.

In November 1967, plaintiff opened an office in Houston, Texas, for the purpose of establishing a base closer to the Gulf Coast. In June 1968 plaintiff's vice-president, Howard C. Kaylor, went from that office to Louisiana to confer with defendant's representatives. During the course of that trip defendant negligently caused injury to Kaylor on defendant's premises in Louisiana.

At the time of his injury, Kaylor was responsible for obtaining contracts for plaintiff . . . in Louisiana. Although defendant compensated Kaylor for his injuries, plaintiff [Offshore Rental] subsequently filed [this] action in California to recover $5 million in damages occasioned by the loss of Kaylor's services.

[The court pointed out that although it would affirm the judgment of dismissal, applying Louisiana law, the trial court had made an "analytic error," applying a "most significant contacts theory," and stated that the correct approach would have been "the governmental interest analysis approach."]

The matter presently before us involves two states: California, the forum, a place of business for defendant, as well as plaintiff's state of incorporation and principal place of business; and Louisiana, the locus of the business of both plaintiff and defendant out of which the injury arose and the place of the injury.[1] As we pointed out in our decision in *Hurtado v. Superior Court* (Cal. 1974) 522 P.2d 666, however, the fact that two states are involved does not in itself indicate that there is a "conflict of laws" or "choice of laws" problem . . . . "There is obviously no problem where the laws of the two states are identical."

Here, however, the laws of Louisiana and California are not identical . . . . Although article 174 of the Louisiana code provides that "The master may bring an action against any man for beating or maiming his servant," the Louisiana [Supreme Court has] held that [a] *corporate plaintiff could* state no cause of action in modern law for the loss of services of its officer. *[Bonfanti Indus., Inc. v. Teke, Inc.* [La.Ct.App.1969) 224 So.2d 15 (aff'd. (La.1969) 226 So.2d 770).]

[The plaintiff asserts] that California Civil Code section 49 grants a cause of action against a third party for loss caused by an injury to a key employee due to the negligence of the third party. Section 49 provides that "The rights of personal relations forbid: . . . Any injury to a servant which affects his ability to serve his master . . . ."[2]

If we assume, for purposes of analysis, that section 49 does provide an employer with a cause of action for negligent injury to a key employee, the laws of California and Louisiana are directly in conflict. Nonetheless, "[a]lthough the two potentially concerned states have different laws, there is still no problem in choosing the applicable rule of law where only one of the states has an interest in having its law applied . . . ." *(Hurtado v. Superior Court, supra.)*

. . . Turning first to Louisiana, we note that Louisiana's refusal to permit recovery for loss of a key employee's services is predicated on the view that allowing recovery would lead to "undesirable social and legal consequences." *(Bonfanti Indus., Inc. v. Teke, Inc., supra.)* We interpret this conclusion as indicating Louisiana's policy to protect negligent resident tort-feasors acting within Louisiana's borders from the financial hardships caused by the assessment of excessive legal liability or exaggerated claims resulting from the loss of services of a key employee. Clearly the present defendant is a member of the class which Louisiana law seeks to protect, since defendant is a Louisiana "resident" whose negligence on its own premises has caused the injury in question. Thus Louisiana's interest in the application of its law to the present case is evident: negation of plaintiff's cause of action serves Louisiana's policy of avoidance of extended financial hardship to the negligent defendant.

Nevertheless, we recognize as equally clear the fact that application of California law to the present case will further California's interest. California, through section 49, expresses an interest in protecting California employers

---

[1] Neither party has urged that the law of Delaware or Texas is applicable.

[2] *See, e.g., Darmour Productions Corp. v. Herbert M. Baruch Corp.,* 27 P.2d 664 (Cal. 1933), in which a movie producer [was permitted to sue] under section 49 for the loss of services of one of its actresses occasioned by a third party's negligence . . . .

from economic harm because of negligent injury to a key employee inflicted by a third party. Moreover, California's policy of protection extends beyond such an injury inflicted within California, since California's economy and tax revenues are affected regardless of the situs of physical injury. Thus, California is interested in applying its law in the present case to plaintiff Offshore, a California corporate employer that suffered injury in Louisiana by the loss of the services of its key employee.[3]

Hence this case involves a true conflict between the law of Louisiana and the law of California. In *Bernhard v. Harrah's Club*, we . . . rejected the notion that in a situation of true conflict the law of the forum should always be applied. Instead, [this court adopted] the "comparative impairment" approach [which] "proceeds on the principle that true conflicts should be resolved by applying the law of the state whose interest would be the more impaired if its law were not applied."

Rather, the resolution of true conflict cases may be described as "essentially a process of allocating respective spheres of lawmaking influence." (Baxter, *Choice of Law and the Federal System* (1963) 16 STAN. L. REV. 1, 11-1 2.) The process of allocation demands several inquiries.

First, while "[i]t is not always possible to say fairly whether [the] Policy [underlying a state's law] is one that was much more *strongly* held in the past than it is now, . . . this ground of analysis should not be ignored." (Emphasis added.) (VON MEHREN & TRAUTMAN, THE LAW OF MULTISTATE PROBLEMS (1965) p. 377.)

Professor Freund has pointed out that "Statutes [in a domestic case], by reason of their pattern or their prevalence, may evidence a legal climate of opinion which makes less oppressive the responsibility of the judge in choosing between two inferences from a statute or between two possible rules of law. A similar resort may be made in multistate cases. *If one of the competing laws is archaic and isolated in the context of the laws of the federal union, it may not unreasonably have to yield to the more prevalent and progressive law, other factors of choice being roughly equal.* A married woman's disability to make a contract, imbedded in the law of one state, may be carried away by the current if contact is made with the main stream in another state. Perhaps one of the functions of conflict-of-laws decisions is to serve as growing pains for the law of a state, at all events in a federation such as our own." (Emphasis added.) (Freund, *Chief justice Stone and the Conflict of Laws* (1946) 59 HARV. L. REV. 1210, 1216.)

Thus the current status of a statute is an important factor to be considered in a determination of comparative impairment: the policy underlying a

---

[3] While this protection of the employer is the most rational policy that can be attributed to California, it is not the only one possible. The sparse legislative history of section 49 suggests that the Legislature may have retained the statutory action for injury to a servant in the belief that this statutory cause of action was necessary in order to preserve an employer's right of subrogation under the workers compensation law. As more recent cases make clear, however, the specific subrogation statutes of the worker's compensation law are sufficient, in themselves, to establish the employer's right to subrogation, and thus section 49 plays no substantial role in encouraging employers to meet their responsibility under the workers' compensation law. Moreover, the present defendant has compensated plaintiff's employee for his injuries; the record indicates no claim by defendant for indemnity.

jurisdiction's law may be deemed "attenuated and anachronistic and properly . . . be limited to domestic occurrences in the event of [a multistate] clash of interests." (Freund, *Chief Justice Stone, supra,* 59 HARV. L. REV. 1210, 1224.) Moreover, a particular statute may be an antique not only in comparison to the laws of the federal union, but also as compared with other laws of the state of its enactment. Such a Statute may be infrequently enforced or interpreted even within its own jurisdiction, and, as an anachronism in that sense, should have a limited application in a conflicts case.

Another chief criterion in the comparative impairment analysis is the "maximum attainment of underlying purpose by all governmental entities. This necessitates identifying the focal point of concern of the contending lawmaking groups and ascertaining the *comparative pertinence* of that concern to the immediate case." (Emphasis added.) (Baxter, *Choice Of Law, supra,* 16 STAN. L. REV. 1, 12.) The policy underlying a statute may be less "comparatively pertinent" if the original object of the statute is no longer of pressing importance: a statute which was once intended to remedy a matter of grave public concern may since have fallen in significance to the periphery of the state's laws. As Professor Currie observed in another context, "If the truth were known, it would probably be that [those few states which have retained the archaic law of abatement have done so] simply because of the proverbial inertia of legal institutions; and that no real policy is involved." (SELECTED ESSAYS ON THE CONFLICT OF LAWS 143 (1963)).

Moreover, the policy underlying a statute may also be less "comparatively pertinent" if the same policy may easily be satisfied by some means other than enforcement of the statute itself. Insurance, for example, may satisfy the underlying purpose of a statute originally intended to provide compensation to tort victims. The fact that parties may reasonably be expected to plan their transactions with insurance in mind may therefore constitute a relevant element in the resolution of a true conflict.

In sum, the comparative impairment approach . . . incorporates . . . : the history and current status of the states' laws; the function and purpose of those laws.

Applying the comparative impairment analysis to the present case, we first probe the history and current status of the laws before us. The majority of . . . states do not sanction actions for harm to business employees, recognizing that even if injury to the master-servant relationship were at one time the basis for an action at common law, the radical change in the nature of that relationship since medieval times nullifies any right by a modern corporate employer to recover for negligent injury to his employees. With the decision in *Bonfanti Industries, Inc. v. Teke, Inc., supra,* discarding the obsolete concept of recovery for loss of a servant's services,"[4] the Louisiana courts have thus joined the "main stream" of American jurisdictions . . . .

Indeed California has itself exhibited little concern in applying section 49 to the employer-employee relationship: despite the provisions of the antique

---

[4] In its decision precluding the corporate plaintiffs cause of action, the Louisiana court emphasized the hoary origins of article 174 . . . , [c]oncluding that article 174 was meant to apply only to "indentured servants . . ." and not [a] corporate . . . officer.

statute, no California court has heretofore squarely held that California law provides an action for harm to business employees, and no California court has recently considered the issue at all. If, as we have assumed, section 49 does provide an action for harm to key corporate employees, in Professor Freund's words the section constitutes a law "archaic and isolated in the context of the laws of the federal union." We therefore conclude that the trial judge in the present case correctly applied Louisiana, rather than California, law, since California's interest in the application of its unusual and outmoded statute is comparatively less strong than Louisiana's corollary interest, so lately expressed, in its prevalent and "progressive" law.

> An examination of the function and purpose of the respective laws before us provides additional Support for our limitation of the reach of California law in the present case. The accident in question occurred within Louisiana's borders . . . . At the heart of Louisiana's denial of liability lies the vital interest in promoting freedom of investment and enterprise *within Louisiana's borders,* among investors incorporated both in Louisiana and elsewhere. The imposition of liability on defendant, therefore, would strike at the essence of a compelling Louisiana law. Furthermore, . . . we note the realistic fact that insurance is available to guard against the exigencies of the present case . . . . The present plaintiff, a business corporation, is a potential "victim" peculiarly able to calculate such risks and to plan accordingly. Plaintiff could have obtained protection against the occurrence of injury to its corporate vice-president by purchasing key employee insurance, certainly a reasonable and foreseeable business expense. By entering Louisiana, plaintiff "exposed [it]self to the risks of the territory," and should not expect to subject defendant to a financial hazard that Louisiana law had not created. (CAVERS, THE CHOICE-OF-LAW PROCESS (1965) p. 147.) [*See* § 4.26[A], *infra.* ] [5]

Although it is equally true that defendant is a business corporation able to calculate the risks of potential tort liability and to plan accordingly, because defendant's operations in Louisiana presumably involved dealing with key employees of companies incorporated in diverse states defendant would most reasonably have anticipated a need for the protection of premises' liability insurance based on Louisiana law. Accordingly, under these circumstances, we conclude that the burden of obtaining insurance for the loss at issue here is most properly borne by the plaintiff corporation.

We have explained that Louisiana law precludes a corporate employer from stating a cause of action for losses caused by negligent injuries to a key employee. We have assumed for the purposes of the present case that California law grants a cause of action for such injuries, and thus directly conflicts with the law of Louisiana. Upon examination of the nature and purpose of the states' respective laws, however, we have determined that the California statute has historically been of minimal importance in the fabric

---

[5] We emphasize that plaintiff did not expose itself to any risk that Louisiana encourages negligent conduct by resident corporations. On the contrary, as a consequence of Louisiana's general policy against negligent behavior, defendant has already been obliged to compensate plaintiffs employee for his personal injuries.

of California law, and that the Louisiana courts have recently interpreted their analogous Louisiana statute narrowly in light of that statute's obsolescence. We do not believe that California's interests in the application of its law to the present case are so compelling as to prevent an accommodation to the stronger, more current interest of Louisiana. We conclude therefore that Louisiana's interests would be the more impaired if its law were not applied . . . .

---

## NOTES AND QUESTIONS ON *OFFSHORE RENTAL*

(1) *A "better law" case?* Although the California court cited the functionalist writers, and failed to cite Professor Leflar, is it fair to say that the court's "comparative impairment" analysis in *Offshore Rental* was substantially a "better law" analysis? Certainly, after *Offshore Rental,* comparative impairment can be said to include a "better law" component.

Indeed, as early as 1972, in *Hall v. University of Nevada [I],* reported at § 4.20, *supra,* the California Supreme Court, considering a conflict between the tort policies of the forum and the defendant state's sovereign immunity, made the distinctly "better law" remark that "in a society such as ours, which places such great value on the dignity of the individual and views the government as an instrument to secure individual rights, the doctrine of sovereign immunity must be deemed suspect."

(2) *Departing from forum law.* Is there a difference between departing from forum law in a case like *Offshore Rental* and a case like *Milliken v. Pratt?* It is true that in both cases there was little substance in the policy expressed in local law at the time of trial. But in *Milliken,* the law had been repealed. There would be no "next case" raising the capacity of married women as a defense. In *Offshore,* the law simply had not been much enforced. Thus, the California court put itself in the awkward position of explicitly disfavoring law that was on the books. What options did that leave the court in the next, wholly domestic case? Should it apply the code in that case, having explicitly disapproved it in the conflicts case?

Was this conflict necessary? Ought not the court simply to have held the forum's statute obsolete? No choice-of-law problem would then have been presented. In *Weinrot and Son, Inc. v. Jackson,* 40 Cal. 3d 327, 220 Cal. Rptr. 103, 708 P.2d 682 (1985), the California Supreme Court held that an action for loss of services of a "key employee" would not lie under the Code provision, in part for reasons spelled out *in Offshore Rental*— the Code provision was archaic and obsolescent, and corporate plaintiffs are well able to insure. *See also Thompson v. Estate of Petroff, 319* N.W.2d 400 (Minn. 1982) (striking down under the state constitution a law the forum had subordinated to "the better law" of a sister state in *Bigelow v. Halloran,* 313 N.W.2d 10 (Minn. 1981)).

Suppose the California law had been a common-law rule. Can a court ever legitimately apply foreign law as "better" law while leaving its own common-law rule intact? Once the court has identified the better rule, hasn't it actually identified its own current policy? In this situation, where the rule is non-statutory, it has been suggested, a court should change its own explicitly disfavored common-law rule. *See* Louise Weinberg, *On Departing from Forum Law,* 35 MERCER L. REV. 595 615-16 (1984). Where the forum's disfavored law is statutory, Professor Weinberg argues that a narrowing construction is often available. *See* Note (3) following *Saharceski v. Marcure,* § 4.23, *supra. See also Miree v. DeKalb County, Ga.,* 433 U.S. 25 (1977) (§ 6.09, *infra*).

*See* PROBLEMS 4F-5. AS LONG AS THEY ARE OUTSIDERS; 4F-6. VEHICLE OWNERSHIP; 4F-7. COLLATERAL SOURCE DOCTRINE; 4F-8. LEAVING THE KEYS IN THE IGNITION; 4F-9. APPLYING THE BETTER RULE?; 4F-10. COCAINE AND CONVERSION; 4F-11. THE INTRA-FAMILY EXCLUSION.

## § 4.25  The New Rules and The New Territorialism

Many scholars (and some law-makers) have reacted unfavorably to the case law that has developed under the Second Restatement and other forms of modern choice-of-law analysis. They believe that those decisions are marked by confusion, a lack of predictability, and/or marked favoritism towards forum residents. In place of that perceived anarchy, a number of scholars have suggested that choice of law should focus on territorial solutions-that is, on the law of a state chosen by certain geographic contacts. Those contacts might include domicile, the place of the accident, and so forth. This scholarship—which has earned the sobriquet "The New Territorialism"—can be traced back to the beginning of modern forms of choice-of-law analysis, and especially to the work of David Cavers, discussed in Note (2), *infra. See also* Aaron Twerski, *Enlightened Territorialism and Professor Cavers: The Pennsylvania Method,* 9 DUQ. L. REV. 373 (1971); Douglas Laycock, *Equal Citizens of Equal and Territorial States: The Constitutional Foundations of Choice of Law,* 92 COLUM. L. REV. 249 (1992); Willis L. M. Reese, *Choice of Law: Rules or Approach,* 57 CORN. L. REV. 315 (1972).

## [A]  One State's Experience with Territorialism

**CIPOLLA V. SHAPOSKA,** 439 Pa. 563, 267 A.2d 854 (1970). [Plaintiff, from Pennsylvania, a common-law state, and defendant, from Delaware, a guest-statute state, were classmates at a school in Delaware. While driving from school to plaintiff's home in Pennsylvania, they were involved in an automobile accident in Delaware. Plaintiff sued defendant in Pennsylvania.]

HELD: For defendant; Delaware law would apply.

In determining which state has the greater interest in the application of its law, one method is to see what contacts each state has with the accident, the contacts being relevant only if they relate to the "policies and interests underlying the particular issue before the court. . . ."

As it is Pennsylvania's policy that its guests should be permitted to recover for injuries caused by their hosts' negligence and as appellants are Pennsylvania residents, Pennsylvania is a concerned jurisdiction and has a contact relevant to the issue before us. This is the only relevant contact with

Pennsylvania, however. As it is Delaware's policy that its hosts should not be required to compensate their guests for their (the hosts') negligence and as appellee is a Delaware resident, Delaware is a concerned jurisdiction and has a contact relevant to the issue before us. The fact that the automobile involved in the accident is registered and housed in Delaware gives that state another contact for it appears that insurance rates will depend on the state in which the automobile is housed rather than the domicile of the owner or driver. Morris, *Enterprise Liability and the Actuarial Process—The Insignificance of Foresight,* 70 YALE L.J. 554, 574 (1961). Thus, it appears that Delaware's contacts are qualitatively greater than Pennsylvania's and that it has the greater interest in having its law applied to the issue before us.

Also, it seems only fair to permit a defendant to rely on his home state's law when he is acting within that state.

"Consider the response that would be accorded a proposal that was the opposite of this principle if it were advanced against a person living in the state of injury on behalf of a person coming there from a state having a higher standard of care or of financial protection. The proposal thus advanced would require the community the visitor entered to step up its standard of behavior for his greater safety or lift its financial protection to the level to which he was accustomed. Such a proposal would be rejected as unfair. By entering the state or nation, the visitor has exposed himself to the risk of the territory and should not subject persons living there to a financial hazard that their law had not created." DAVID CAVERS, THE CHOICE OF LAW PROCESS 146-7 (1965).

Inhabitants of a state should not be put in jeopardy of liability exceeding that created by their state's law just because a visitor from a state offering higher protection decides to visit there. This is, of course, a highly territorial approach, but "departures from the territorial view of torts ought not to be lightly undertaken." [Citation omitted]. . . . The very use of the term true conflict implies that there is no one correct answer, but as a general approach a territorial view seems preferable to a personal view.

These approaches to the solution of this true conflict lead to the conclusion that Delaware has a greater interest in the application of its law than does Pennsylvania.

## SHUDER v. McDONALD'S CORPORATION

*United States Court of Appeals for the Third Circuit*
*859 F.2d 266 (3d Cir. 1988)*

GREENBERG, Circuit Judge.

This matter is before the court on appeal from an order of the district court. . .denying a motion by defendant McDonald's Corporation for a judgment notwithstanding the verdict in this personal injury action arising from the injury of plaintiff Elizabeth F. Shuder at a McDonald's restaurant on October 17, 1982 in Virginia Beach, Virginia. We will reverse and remand the matter for entry of an order granting the motion. . . .

Mrs. [and Mr] Shuder, Pennsylvania citizens, were patrons at the McDonald's. . . . After the Shuders left the restaurant she fell on the restaurant parking lot and was injured. [The Shuders filed an action in federal court in Virginia against McDonald's Virginia (the local franchisee). The district court applied Virginia law, and the defendant won a general verdict resulting in a judgment later affirmed by the Fourth Circuit.] Subsequently, they filed this diversity of citizenship action in the United States District Court for the Western District of Pennsylvania against McDonald's [the national franchisor], Mr. Shuder joining as a plaintiff to assert a loss of consortium. They alleged that McDonald's had a duty to maintain the area in a safe condition for travel, but that [the abruptly raised portion of the parking lot]. . .where Mrs. Shuder fell was inadequately lighted and was not marked or painted to distinguish it from other portions of the parking lot. . . .

[The district judge ruled that Pennsylvania law of comparative negligence, rather than Virginia's common law contributory negligence rule, would be applied at the trial.]

The district judge instructed the jury that if it found both Mrs. Shuder and McDonald's were negligent, it should determine Mrs. Shuder's percentage of the negligence. The jury returned a verdict finding that the parking lot was negligently designed or constructed, thereby proximately causing the accident, but that Mrs. Shuder was 26% negligent. Of course, under Pennsylvania law this verdict meant that the Shuders would make a partial recovery for their damages. Accordingly, immediately after the liability trial the case was tried on damages and verdicts for the Shuders were returned. . . .

We first consider whether Pennsylvania or Virginia law should have been applied on the liability issues, our standard of review being plenary. It is well established that a district court in a diversity action will apply the choice of law rules of the forum state in determining which state's law will be applied to the substantive issues before it. Accordingly, we examine Pennsylvania law to determine whether the substantive law of Virginia or Pennsylvania should have been applied. . . .

[The court reviewed Pennsylvania's commitment to interest analysis and the *Cipolla* method of resolving true conflicts.]

We have concluded from our analysis of the foregoing authorities that this case does not involve a false conflict. Virginia has retained the common law rule that a plaintiff's contributory negligence will bar her from recovery so that her negligence will not be compared with that of the defendant. This common law policy protects defendants from claims and encourages persons to exercise care for their own safety. By limiting recovery the common law policy should tend to hold down insurance costs. To the extent it protects defendants it is not unlike the Delaware guest statute, which has been recognized by the Pennsylvania courts as furthering Delaware policy.

On the other hand, Pennsylvania has adopted comparative negligence [by statute] and thus follows a plaintiff-protecting policy. Accordingly, applying the law of either Virginia or Pennsylvania will further the policies of that state. Thus, we must determine which state has the greater interest in the application of its law by studying the contacts of each state to the accident relating to the issue before the court and comparing them on a qualitative scale. *Cipolla,* 267 A.2d at 856.

We think it is clear that Virginia has by far the more significant contacts. To start with, the accident occurred in Virginia. Further, the Shuders voluntarily went to that state. Surely Virginia has an interest in how persons conduct themselves within the state. . . . [T]he accident arose from the use of and condition of property, traditionally matters of local control. Indeed, a building permit was obtained for the driveway on which Mrs. Shuder fell. The Shuders, at trial, urged that the property was negligently constructed or designed, again matters of local concern. . . .

In considering the contacts of the states we recognize that McDonald's is a Delaware Corporation and that the plans for the property were apparently approved in Illinois. But these circumstances do not create contacts with Pennsylvania. Thus, they are neutral factors. In sum, the only contacts with Pennsylvania in this case are that the Shuders reside in that state and Mrs. Shuder received medical treatment there.

The Shuders contend, as they explain in their brief, that Pennsylvania law was properly applied as it is fairer and "more just" than Virginia law as Pennsylvania recognizes comparative negligence and Virginia retains the common law bar of contributory negligence. . . . We, however, cannot regard the alleged justness of Pennsylvania law as a valid reason for applying it. The relative liberality to plaintiffs of Pennsylvania law simply demonstrates that application of Pennsylvania law would further the policies of that state. This is a consideration quite separate from the contacts of Pennsylvania to the accident. Indeed, the Pennsylvania courts have not hesitated to apply foreign over domestic law even though they thereby bar claims by their residents. *See, e.g., Cipolla v. Shaposka*, 439 Pa. 563, 267 A.2d 854. . . .

There is a second independent reason why the judgment notwithstanding the verdict should have been granted. McDonald's urges that this action is barred by collateral estoppel, a doctrine now referred to as issue preclusion by reason of the Virginia proceedings. The parties have treated the issue as governed by Pennsylvania rather than Virginia law. . . Thus, we will consider the issue under Pennsylvania law thereby assuming, without deciding, that it is applicable. . .

The Shuders do assert that. . .[t]he Virginia action concerned McDonald's Virginia's duty to keep its premises safe. On the other hand, the issue here involves an allegation of faulty design and construction not raised in Virginia. Thus, the issues are different. Further, inasmuch as the Virginia verdict was general we cannot know what was decided by the jury. Accordingly, Mrs. Shuder may have been barred in Virginia by contributory negligence but that would not necessarily be a bar in Pennsylvania . . . .

In fact, an issue must have been decided in Virginia against Mrs. Shuder identical to an issue which had to have been found in her favor applying Virginia law in the Pennsylvania action if she was to recover against McDonald's. We know that the issues in Virginia were whether the premises were in a reasonably safe condition, whether Mrs. Shuder was guilty of contributory negligence, and whether the breach of duty by McDonald's Virginia and the contributory negligence of Mrs. Shuder if established were proximate causes of the accident. While we cannot know which of these questions was answered adversely to Mrs. Shuder, necessarily one was, and under Virginia law a finding adverse to Mrs. Shuder on any of the bases on which the first verdict could have been predicated was fatal to the action against McDonald's.

While we are aware that the Shuders have attempted to demonstrate that the issues involved in the two cases were not identical since Mrs. Shuder charged that McDonald's Virginia failed to keep and maintain the premises in a safe condition and the Shuders asserted that McDonald's [the national franchisor] was negligent by reason of defects in the design and construction of the parking lot, the fact is that if the verdict in Virginia was based on a finding that McDonald's Virginia breached no duty to Mrs. Shuder then the jury necessarily found under the judge's charge that the lot was in a reasonably safe condition. This finding would bar the Shuders from making a claim that McDonald's was liable for design or construction defects which made the property unsafe.

## MORE NOTES AND QUESTIONS ON THE NEW TERRITORIALISM

(1) *What's New About The New Territorialism?* How does the method employed in *Cipolla* and *Shuder* differ from the territorialism of the First Restatement? In other words why does it deserve to be called "new?" Suppose that in *Shuder* both the plaintiff and the defendant had been Pennsylvanians: What result under the First Restatement? What result under New Territorialism?

*Cipolla* has produced a wealth of commentary. *See, e.g., Symposium on* Cipolla v. Shaposka: *An Application of "Interest Analysis,"* 9 DUQ. L. REV. 347 (1971) (commentary by Professors Cavers, Ehrenzweig, Felix, Pelaez, Peterson Sedler, Seidelson, and Twerski)

(2) *The Work of Cavers.* Clearly the work of David Cavers, especially THE CHOICE OF LAW PROCESS (1965), provided the intellectual inspiration for the new or "enlightened" territorialism of *Cipolla* and its progeny. In that work, Cavers proposes seven "principles of preference" relying in part on John Rawls' view of justice as fairness and the "veil of ignorance:" "A practice is just if it is in accordance with the principles which all who participate in it might reasonably be expected . . . to acknowledge . . . when they are similarly circumstanced and required to make a firm commitment in advance and without knowledge of what will be their particular condition." *Id.* at 130.

Cavers acknowledges that his principles have a territorial bias as a counterbalance to the "personal" bias of interest analysis:

> An inquiry into the purposes of conflicting laws. . . leads naturally to an emphasis on the persons on whom laws have their impact when, at least it is mainly the interests of the parties to the relationship or controversy that appear to be at stake. It becomes easy in such situations for one to ascribe to the state or states with which those persons are connected a paternalistic concern for them, wherever they may be, thereby rendering the place of their actions "fortuitous" and even irrelevant to the process of choice . . . .

> I believe that there are circumstances where the citizen may properly, if metaphorically, be considered to carry a law of his state about with

him. However, I also agree with Judge Wyzanski that "departures from the territorial view of torts ought not to be lightly undertaken," and I would not confine his admonition to the law of torts. Our states and nations are territorially organized; the legal order that each has created impinges on actions and affairs which in a very high proportion of all instances, are wholly domestic to the state where they take place. To withdraw like actions and affairs from the reach of domestic law because the persons participating in them are not domestic to the state causes a wrench away from customary attitudes toward law that may lead the disadvantaged party to "regard the distinction as involving personal discrimination against him rather than as a step towards comity between states," to quote Judge Wyzanski once more.

*Id.* at 134-5. For a critique of the Cavers approach, *see* Jeffrey Shaman, *The Choice-of-Law Process: Territorialism and Functionalism,* 22 WM. & MARY L. REV. 227 (1980).

(3) *Territoriality and Expectations.* Are Cavers and *Cipolla* right about the importance of expectations in tort cases? Clearly expectations are important in consensual transactions: contracts trusts, wills and the like. Beside the normative question, what about the purely empirical question? Do ordinary people, in fact, have choice-of-law expectations at all? There is no empirical work in the area. When asked about tort choice-of-law cases, most non-lawyers hear the question as implicating *criminal law,* and routinely give a territorial response. By the time they understand that the problem is civil liability, they are already sufficiently polluted with choice-of-law theory that their responses are no longer naïve. Is this yet another example of the Heisenberg Uncertainty Principle (a phenomenon is unmeasurable if the measuring technique routinely changes the phenomenon)?

(4) *Territorialism or Significant Contacts.* Both *Cipolla* and *Shuder* are territorial in result, but the language of *Cipolla* (and of Cavers, as well) is more frankly territorial. Is *Shuder* really a new territorialist opinion, or would it fit just as easily under the "most significant contacts" rubric? Many of the modern progeny of *Cipolla* resemble *Shuder* in this respect. The two approaches are basically consistent, of course, because in non-false conflict cases the place of conduct and injury often is "the most significant contact."

(5) *Influence.* Although only one state (Pennsylvania) has "adopted" new territorialism as its principal choice-of-law methodology, the influence of the approach on modern choice-of-law practice has been considerable. New York adopted principles very similar to those suggested by Professor Cavers in *Neumeier v. Kuehner* (see § 4.25[C], *infra*), and many of the Second Restatement's sections show the influence of "enlightened" territorialism (see §§ 4.26-4.29, *infra*), as do the provisions of the Louisiana conflicts codification discussed below.

(6) *Act and Injury in Different States. Cipolla* and *Shuder* both involved conduct and injury in a single state. How should a new territorialist court treat a case where an act in one state causes injury in another? In *Troxel, v. A.I. Dupont Institute,* 431 Pa. Super. 464; 636 A.2d 1179 (1994), a Pennsylvania mother and child were referred to the defendants, a hospital and several

physicians in Delaware for treatment of cytomeglovirus ("CMV"). The defendants allegedly failed to inform the mother that the disease could be transmitted to pregnant women and their fetuses by contact and could be fatal to the fetus. Plaintiff, a pregnant Pennsylvanian, had contact with the mother and child in Pennsylvania and contracted CMV, which she transmitted to her fetus and which ultimately caused the death of the plaintiff's child three months after his birth. Relying on *Cipolla* and *Shuder,* the court held for the defendants on the choice-of-law issue and applied the law of Delaware:

> Although it must be conceded that Pennsylvania. . . has an interest in providing redress for wrongs committed against its citizens, here that interest is superseded by Delaware's interest in regulating the delivery of health care services in Delaware. DuPont is a Delaware hospital, and [defendant physicians] are licensed to practice medicine in Delaware, not Pennsylvania. . . . No services were rendered by DuPont in Pennsylvania. The services rendered and the persons delivering those services in Delaware were regulated by the laws of Delaware, not the laws of Pennsylvania. . . . [T]he hospital was required to follow and abide by the laws of Delaware. . . . [and] were entitled to rely on the duties and protections provided by Delaware law. Pennsylvania law did not follow Ashley and her mother when they traveled to Delaware to obtain medical care. Any other rule would be wholly unreasonable, for it would require hospitals and physicians to be aware of and be bound by the laws of all states from which patients came to them for treatment. This is not the law.

> Health care providers in Delaware are licensed and regulated by the State of Delaware and must comply with the laws of that state. This is not altered merely by the fact that a substantial number of its patients come from other states. Therefore, we reject appellants' argument that Pennsylvania law is applicable either because DuPont solicited patients from Pennsylvania or because it accepted referrals from Pennsylvania doctors.

According to a leading choice-of-law treatise, the result in *Troxel* is atypical. The authors distill from the cases the rule that an act in one state causing injury in another is governed by the law of the state of conduct *except* when the injury foreseeably occurs in another state that imposes a higher standard of conduct. EUGENE SCOLES, PETER HAY, PATRICK BORCHERS, AND SYMEON SYMEONIDES, CONFLICT OF LAWS 792 (3d ed. 2000). Wasn't the injury in Pennsylvania foreseeable in *Troxel?* Which solution to the true conflict is preferable: *Troxel's* reliance on the local-standards-of-conduct rule or the foreseeable-injury-in-a-state-with-higher-standards principle? Does territorialism help answer this question?

(7) *Cross References.*

(a) The court in *Shuder* makes short work of the "better law" argument. For full treatment of the issue see the discussion below.

(b) The court in *Shuder* introduces an entirely separate choice-of-law problem. Whose law of judgments (claim preclusion, issue preclusion, mutuality of estoppel) should the court apply, its own or the law of the rendering court? Section 4.24, *supra*, contains a full discussion of the issue.

## [B]  Codification

One state legislature also has embraced the New Territorialist philosophy. Louisiana, under the leadership of the distinguished Conflicts scholar, Symeon Symeonides, has adopted a code solution to choice-of-law problems. *See generally* Symeon Symeonides, *Louisiana's New Law of Choice of Law for Torts Conflicts: An Exegesis,* 66 TUL. L. REV. 677 (1992). He explains that the goal was to develop rules that are "flexible with built-in escape devices which will allow courts enough freedom to deviate in exceptional cases." *Id.* at 447. The rules are codified in Articles 3515 *et seq* of the Louisiana Civil Code. The rules adopt a form of comparative impairment with policies primarily identified by looking at domicile. Article 3544(1),for example, provides that the law of the common domicile applies when the two parties are from a state that would deny recovery in an accident, but the accident occurred in a state that would permit recovery.

Does the Code work? Professor Weintraub recently examined thirty-seven cases applying the Code sections (article 3537 and 3540) dealing with "conventional obligations." He found that fifteen of those cases "misapply the articles in the most fundamental manner. Russell J. Weintraub, *Courts Flailing in the Waters of the Louisiana Conflicts Code: Not Waving But Drowning,* 60 LA. L. REV. 1366,1367 (2000). That finding does not bode well for those who like territorial or statutory solutions to choice-of-law problems.

(8) *Other Statutory Solutions.* The Louisiana Code represents the most ambitious effort in this country to codify solutions to choice-of-law cases.[5] Codification, however, has been recommended by many. At the national level that enthusiasm takes two forms. The first is to recommend that Congress codify the *substantive* law in a particular area such as products liability. That would eliminate the choice-of-law problem because all substantive law would be the same.

The second effort would be to have Congress codify the law of choice of law much as Louisiana did. There is little doubt that Congress has the power to do so under either the Commerce or Full Faith and Credit Clauses. The real problem is that legislatures prefer tidy solutions to problems, a predilection which eventually leads to some form of territorial solution. Is it likely that Congress will solve the problem any better (or even as well) as the Louisiana legislature did under the able guidance of Professor Symeonides?

The Louisiana codification experiment provides a clear illustration of the linkage between "territorialism" and a rule-based approach to choice of law. That is not surprising. The seeming formlessness of the modern approaches to choice of law has generated a certain nostalgia for the ease of application and apparent, if elusive, certainty of rules. Some scholars have argued that in the course of decision under the modern methods, courts would eventually arrive at rules. These new rules would be superior to the traditional choice rules because derived from rational analysis of the underlying policies and interests in numerous cases. An early version of this nostalgia is found in Willis L. M. Reese, *Choice of Law: Rules or Approach,* 57 CORN. L. REV. 315

---

[5] Oregon is also considering the adoption of statutory choice-of-law solutions. *See* James A. R. Nafziger, *Oregon's Project to Codify Choice-of-Law Rules,* 60 ORE. L. REV. 1189 (2000).

(1972). The influence among law-makers of this hearkening for certainty can be seen in the Louisiana codification just discussed and in the following landmark decision.

*See* PROBLEM 4F-12. SNOWMOBILING.

## [C]   More on Rules

### NEUMEIER v. KUEHNER

*New York Court of Appeals*
*31 N. Y 2d 121, 335 N. Y.S.2d 64, 286 N.E.2d 454 (1972)*

FULD, CHIEF JUDGE. A domiciliary of Ontario, Canada, was killed when the automobile in which he was riding, owned and driven by a New York resident, collided with a train in Ontario. That jurisdiction has a guest statute, and the primary question posed by this appeal is whether in this action brought by the Ontario passenger's estate, . . . the New York defendant [should be] permitted to rely on [the Ontario] guest statute as a defense . . . .

In substance, the statute provides that the owner or driver of a motor vehicle is not liable for damages resulting from injury to, or the death of, a guest-passenger unless he was guilty of gross negligence. It is worth noting, at this point, that, although our court originally considered that the sole purpose of the Ontario statute was to protect Ontario defendants and their insurers against collusive claims (*see Babcock v. Jackson* [§ 4.19, *supra*]), "Further research; has revealed the distinct possibility that one purpose, and perhaps the only purpose, of the statute was to protect owners and drivers against ungrateful guests." (Reese, *Chief Judge Fuld and Choice of Law,* 71 Col. L.Rev. 548, 558; *see* Trautman, *Two Views on Kell v. Henderson: A Comment,* 67 Col. L. Rev. 465, 469.)

A closely-divided Appellate Division [reversing, struck the Ontario defense]. It was the court's belief that this result was dictated by *Tooker v. Lopez* [§ 4.19, *supra*].

In reaching that conclusion, the Appellate Division misread our decision in the *Tooker* case . . . . Indeed, two of the three judges who wrote for reversal—Judge Keating and Judge Burke—expressly noted that the determination then being made left open the question whether New York law would be applicable if the plaintiff passenger happened to be a domiciliary of the very jurisdiction which had a guest statute . . . .

What significantly and effectively differentiates the present case is the fact that, although the host was a domiciliary of New York, the guest, for whose death recovery is sought, was domiciled in Ontario, the place of accident and the very jurisdiction which had enacted the statute designed to protect the host from liability for ordinary negligence. It is clear that although New York has a deep interest in protecting its own residents, injured in a foreign state, against unfair or anachronistic statutes of that state, it has no legitimate interest in ignoring the public policy of a foreign jurisdiction—such as Ontario—and in protecting the plaintiff guest domiciled and injured there from legislation obviously addressed, at the very least, to a resident riding in a vehicle traveling within its borders.

To distinguish *Tooker* on such a basis is not improperly discriminatory. It is . . . , rather, the result of the existence of disparate rules of law in jurisdictions that have diverse and important connections with the litigants and the litigated issue.

The fact that insurance policies issued in this State on New York-based vehicles cover liability, regardless of the place of the accident, certainly does not call for the application of internal New York law in this case. The compulsory insurance requirement is designed to *cover* a car-owner's liability, not *create* it . . . .

When, in *Babcock v. Jackson,* we rejected the mechanical place of injury rule in personal injury cases because it failed to take account of underlying policy considerations, we were willing to sacrifice the certainty provided by the old rule for the more just, fair and practical result that may best be achieved by giving controlling effect to the law of the jurisdiction which has the greatest concern with, or interest in, the specific issue raised in the litigation. In consequence of the change effected—and this was to be anticipated—our decisions in multi-state highway accident cases, particularly in those involving guest-host controversies, have, it must be acknowledged, lacked consistency. This stemmed, in part, from the circumstance that it is frequently difficult to discover the purposes or policies underlying the relevant local law rules of the respective jurisdictions involved. It is even more difficult, assuming that these purposes or policies are found to conflict, to determine on some principled basis which should be given effect at the expense of the others.

The single all-encompassing rule which called, inexorably, for selection of the law of the place of injury was discarded, and wisely because it was too broad to prove satisfactory in application. There is, however, . . . no reason why choice-of-law rules, more narrow than those previously devised, should not be successfully developed, in order to assure a greater degree of predictability and uniformity, on the basis of our present knowledge and experience. *(See, e.g.,* Cavers, *The Choice of Law Process,* 121-122; Rosenberg, *Comments on Reich v. Purcell,* 15; UCLA L.Rev. 641, 642, 646-647.) "The time has come," I wrote in *Tooker,* "to endeavor to minimize what some have characterized as and *ad hoc* case-by-case approach by laying down guidelines, as well as we can, for the solution of guest-host conflicts problems." *Babcock* and its progeny enable us to formulate a set of basic principles that may be profitably utilized, for they have helped us uncover the underlying values and policies which are operative in this area of the law . . . :

> 1. When the guest-passenger and the host-driver are domiciled in the same state, and the car is there registered, the law of that state should control and determine the standard of care which the host owes to his guest.

> 2. When the driver's conduct occurred in the state of his domicile and that state does not cast him in liability for that conduct, he should not be held liable by reason of the fact that liability would be imposed upon him under the tort law of the state of the victim's domicile.

Conversely, when the guest was injured in the state of his own domicile and its law permits recovery, the driver who has come into that state should not—in the absence of special circumstances—be permitted to interpose the law of his state as a defense.

3. In other situations, when the passenger and the driver are domiciled in different states, the rule is necessarily less categorical. Normally, the applicable rule of decision will be that of the state where the accident occurred but not if it can be shown that displacing that normally applicable rule will advance the relevant substantive law purposes without impairing the smooth working of the multi-state system or producing great uncertainty for litigants.

The variant views expressed not only in *Tooker* but by Special Term and the divided Appellate Division in this litigation underscore and confirm the need for these rules. Since the passenger was domiciled in Ontario and the driver in New York, the present case is covered by the third stated principle. The law to be applied is that of the jurisdiction where the accident happened unless it appears that "displacing [the] normally applicable rule will advance the relevant substantive law purposes" of the jurisdictions involved. Certainly, ignoring Ontario's policy requiring proof of gross negligence in a case which involves an Ontario domiciled guest at the expense of a New Yorker does not further the substantive law purposes of New York. In point of fact, application of New York law would result in the exposure of this State's domiciliaries to a greater liability than that imposed upon resident users of Ontario's highways. Conversely, the failure to apply Ontario's law would "impair"—to cull from the rule set out above—"the smooth working of the multi-state system [and] produce great uncertainty for litigants" by sanctioning forum shopping and thereby allowing a party to select a forum which could give him a larger recovery than the court of his own domicile. In short, the plaintiff has failed to show that this State's connection with the controversy was sufficient to justify displacing the rule of *lex loci delictus.*

Professor Willis Reese, the Reporter for the current Conflict of Laws Restatement, expressed approval of rules such as those suggested above; they are, he wrote, "the sort of rules at which the courts should aim" (Reese, *Chief Judge Fuld and Choice of Law,* 71 COL. L. REV. 548, 562; *see also, Reese, Choice of Law: Rules or Approach,* 57 COM. L. REV. 315, 321, 323, 328). Indeed, in discussing the present case following the determination at Special Term that Ontario law should govern, he expressed the opinion that any other result would have been highly unreasonable . . . .

BREITEL, JUDGE (concurring). I agree that there should be a reversal, but would place the reversal on quite narrow grounds. It is undesirable to lay down prematurely major premises based on shifting ideologies in the choice of law . . . .

Problems engendered by the new departures have not gone unnoticed and they are not confined to the courts of this State (Juenger, *Choice of Law in Interstate Tort,* 118 U.PA. L. REV. 202, 214-220). They arise . . . because the departures have been accompanied by an unprecedented competition of ideologies, largely of academic origin, to explain and reconstruct a whole field of law, each purporting or aspiring to achieve a single universal principle . . . .

[The doctrine] of governmental interests developed most extensively by the late Brainerd Currie, [engaged our] court . . . in probing the psychological motivation of legislatures of other States in enacting statutes restricting recoveries in tort cases . . . .

Certain it is that States are not concerned only with their own citizens or residents. They are concerned with events that occur within their territory, and are also concerned with the "stranger within the gates" (Juenger, *op. cit., supra,* at pp. 209-210).

In this case, none would have ever assumed that New York law should be applied just because one of the two defendants was a New York resident and his automobile was New York insured, except for the overboard statements of Currie doctrine in the *Tooker case* . . . .

Consequently, I agree that there should be a reversal and the [Ontario defense] allowed to stand. The conclusion, however, rests simply on the proposition that plaintiff has failed by her allegations to establish that the relationship to this State was sufficient to displace the normal rule that the: *lex loci delictus* should be applied, the accident being associated with Ontario, from inception to tragic termination, except for adventitious facts and where the lawsuit was brought.

BERGAN, JUDGE (dissenting) . . . . There is a difference of fundamental character between justifying a departure from *lex loci delictus* because the court will not, as a matter of policy, permit a New York owner of a car licensed and insured in New York to escape a liability that would be imposed on him here; and a departure based on the fact a New York resident makes the claim for injury. The first ground of departure is justifiable as sound policy; the second is justifiable only if one is willing to treat the rights of a stranger permitted to sue in New York differently from the way a resident is treated . . . .

---

## NOTES AND QUESTIONS ON *NEUMEIER*

(1) *Rules versus analysis.* Do you agree with the *Neumeier* court that a superior solution in a case configured like *Neumeier* is to choose a non-forum defense? Was the result in *Neumeier* discriminatory, as the dissent charges? For thoughtful and creative work on the problem presented in *Neumeier,* see Robert Sedler, *Interstate Accidents and the Unprovided for Case: Reflections on Neumeier v. Kuehner,* 1 HOFSTRA L. REV. 125, 138 (1973).

(2) *The Neumeier rules.* Observe that the *Neumeier* rules appear to reflect crude understandings of interest analysis. Thus, read broadly, Rule 1 would apply in false conflicts, Rule 2 in true conflicts, and Rule 3 in unprovided-for cases. But doesn't the inevitable roughness of written restatement make the *Neumeier rules* less helpful than direct interest analysis?

Consider Rule 1. It applies the law of the state that is most likely the only interested state. But is that always so? In other words, are joint domicile cases always false conflicts? What about the interests of a place of injury when it has applicable deterrent or remedial law? In that event, Rule 1 would apply the law of the joint domicile even if New York, having no guest statute, were the place of injury, and thus might be thought to have an interest in furnishing a remedy for those injured on its territory.

Now consider Rule 2. It covers not all true conflicts, but only those in which the parties are not joint domiciliaries. For the true conflicts it does cover, it discards both forum law and notions of functional analysis, and pitches residually on the law of the place where the defendant acted. In guest cases, this is probably the place of injury, although if transposed to products liability or aviation cases it might not be. What does resort to the place of wrong accomplish? What are the costs, when an interested forum departs from its own law? Does Rule 2, at least for guest cases, inadvertently overrule New York's famous *Kilberg* case?

Now consider Rule 3. For "other" cases, Rule 3 proposes a residual choice— the law of the place "where the accident occurred," presumably the place of injury, at least for automobile torts. This choice should remind you of the dysfunctional analysis of the First Restatement's territorial rules; it will only be by happenstance that the policy of an interested state will be applied. And what of the wild card provision at the end of Rule 3? What does that mean and how would a judge ever figure it out? Is it any wonder that Rule 3 was expressly rejected in *Labree v. Major,* 111 R.I. 657, 306 A.2d 808 (1973).

Moreover, the three Rules do not even cover all guest statute cases. What happens, for example, when neither state has a guest statute, but the place of injury is in some *third* state that does? Does it make any sense to apply the law of the place of injury in such a case, as Rule 3 would require? For a case in which the court did some creative judging to avoid applying a third state's law on such facts, see *Chila v. Owens,* 348 F. Supp. 1207 (S.D.N.Y. 1972).

(4) *The impact of the Neumeier rules.* The *Neumeier* rules have been extended to tort cases not involving guest statutes, not only in New York, but in other states. In *Rosenthal v. Warren,* Chapter 1, *supra,* the Second Circuit Court of Appeals gave *Neumeier* scant mention and held itself bound by *Kilberg. But see Bader v. Purdom,* 841 F.2d 38 (2d Cir. 1988). Colorado, which formally adopted *Neumeier* rules 1 and 2 in *First National Bank v. Rostek,* 182 Colo. 437, 514 P.2d 314 (1973), today simply follows the Second Restatement. *E.g., Dworak v. Olson Constr. Co.,* 191 Colo. 161, 551 P.2d 198 (1976).

(5) *Loss-Allocation and Conduct-Regulation.* The *Neumeier* rules are based on the domicile of the parties. Thus, they are territorial in nature. The rules also draw a distinction between allocation of loss and regulation of conduct and choose a rule based solution. Thus, they are also based on presumptions (irrebuttable?) concerning the application of policy analysis. Note that Louisiana made the same choices in its codification of choice of law.

In torts, in what category do the following issues go: contributory negligence, strict (products) liability, punitive damages? Doesn't all of tort law seek to deter as well as to compensate? Is the answer the same for all punitive damages cases—compare, for example, an intentional assault action with a products liability suit based on a design defect. In contracts where do the following get placed: the absence of punitive damages, the doctrine of waiver, mutual mistake? How do you know? Is the choice between loss and conduct fundamentally any different from deciding whether something is "substance" or "procedure" or "contract" or "tort"?

And is the domicile of the parties an adequate proxy for all the policies behind all of these interests?

Despite these obvious difficulties, the Court of Appeals of New York has steadfastly maintained its adherence to the loss/conduct distinction. *See, e.g., Schultz v. Boy Scouts of Am.*, stated in § 4.19, *supra*, and *Cooney v. Osgood Mach Co., Inc.*, 81 N. Y. 2d 66, 595 N. Y. S. 2d 919, 612 N. E. 2d 277 (1993) (deciding in which category to place contribution in a products liability case). For a discussion of the problems the New York courts have had with the distinction between loss-allocation and conduct-regulation in practice, *see* Eugene Scoles, *et al.*, Conflict of Laws 750-54, 764-66 (3d ed. 2000) (discussing, respectively, *Cooney* and the issue of absolute liability of a contractor for a defective scaffold). Nonetheless, Louisiana (by the codification discussed above), Maine, and Vermont have joined New York in accepting the alleged distinction. Symeon Symeonides, *Choice of Law in the American Courts in 1998: Twelfth Annual Survey*, 47 AM. J. COMP. L. 327, 347 (1999).

(6) *The Anti-Modernists.* Few of the current writers who favor a return to territorial choice-of-law rules would advocate a return to the thoroughly discredited rules of the First Restatement. But because no one has been able to offer a workable, alternative set of rules (as the loss/distribution dichotomy just discussed illustrates), a better term for this group is probably "anti-modernist." *See* Louise Weinberg, *The Place of Trial and The Law Applied-Overhauling Constitutional Theory*, 59 U. COLO. L. REV. 87 (1988) (suggesting the term).

*See* PROBLEMS 4F-13. A TRAGEDY; 4F-14. A SAFE WORK-PLACE; 4F-15. THE OLYMPIC SPIRIT; 4F-16. AMTRAK BEWARE; 4F-17. THE FRENCH CONNECTION; 4F-18. VISITING FRIENDS; 4F-19. SASKATCHEWAN TO IDAHO BUT NOT BACK.

## [D] A Second Look at True Rules

(1) *Should There Be Rules?* Do the *Neumeier* rules seem strange to you? Do you normally expect to see such detailed "rules" as the by-product of common-law decision-making? In short, are judicially adopted rules profoundly antithetical to the judicial function? Of course, the debate between rules and approaches, between predictability and justice, is not limited to choice-of-law problems. *See generally* Louis Kaplow, *Rules vs. Standards: An Economic Analysis*, 42 DUKE L.J. 557 (1992). But it is a debate which has special poignancy in the Conflicts world, for that is a world where a rule-based system once was supreme—and not in the too—distant past.

As you consider *Neumeier* and the questions posed in the preceding paragraph, recall the experience under the First Restatement and the "escape devices" judges used to avoid the harsh results called for by the Vested Rights Doctrine. Also ask yourself whether judges ever will follow rules if they believe that doing so will lead to a result manifestly unjust. *See* William. L. Reynolds,

*Legal Process and Choice of Law,* 56 MD. L. REV. 1371 (1997) (arguing that judges will manipulate doctrine to enable themselves to "do justice" in the case before them). For the suggestion that it has been a mistake for a state's courts to hold themselves bound by a particular choice-of-law method, see Louise Weinberg, *Choosing Law, Giving Justice*, 60 LA. L. REV. 1361 (2001), a position more fully argued in Louise Weinberg, *Methodological Interventions and the Slavery Cases, or, Night-Thoughts of a Legal Realist,* 56 MD. L. REV. 1316 (1997).

(2) *A Reprise on True Rules.* Recall from § 4.25, *supra,* Professor Albert Ehrenzweig's "True Rules." A True Rule identifies outcomes that judges will try very, very hard to achieve. Thus, they will seek to legitimate children, validate marriages, uphold contracts, and they will do so regardless of the stated methodology they use (or pretend to use). Similarly, the Second Restatement contains some provisions whose wide-spread adoptions suggests that they are also True Rules (these include §§ dealing with defamation and § 193 dealing with life insurance). *See* discussion at §§ 4.26-4.32, *supra,* and William M. Richman and William L. Reynolds, *Prologomenon to an Empirical Restatement of Conflicts,* 75 IND. L. J. 417, 432-33 (2000).

Do these examples give hope that at least few strong judicial tendencies might be identified as "rules"—at least, if adequate escape devices are also available? Does New York's loss—allocation/conduct-regulating "rule"discussed above satisfy those criteria?

# PART G  THE SECOND RESTATEMENT

## § 4.26  Overview

The Restatement (Second) of Conflict of Laws adopts a complex, layered approach to choice of law that borrows from the wide array of traditional and modern choice-of-law methodologies discussed in the preceding Parts of Chapter IV. Like its predecessor, it is comprehensive and detailed, containing hundreds of territorial choice-of-law rules divided by subject matter (torts, contracts, property, etc.). It also incorporates, however, much modern learning from the choice-of-law revolution including grouping-of-contacts, interest analysis, validation, and party autonomy. To complicate matters further, the reception of the Second Restatement has varied widely. Excoriated by commentators, it has proved to be extremely popular among the courts. Adopted by more than half of the states and influential, as well, in the federal system, the Second Restatement is by far the most popular choice-of-law regime in the country today. The courts have added a final level of complexity with divergent interpretations of the Restatement's basic approach, some of which seem at odds with the intentions of the drafters.

The detailed coverage of Part G responds to this complexity as well as to the challenge Professor Weintraub voiced in a Symposium celebrating the twenty-fifth anniversary of the promulgation of the Second Restatement.

> The Restatement (Second) is an odd mixture of territorial gibberish and functional analysis. Courts, with their overloaded dockets, cannot be expected on their own to distinguish between the two. Counsel have the duty to help the courts use the Restatement (Second) in a manner that facilitates rather than impedes a content and policy-based choice between conflicting laws. In turn, law schools have the obligation to prepare their students to assume this duty.

Russell J. Weintraub, *"At Least, To Do No Harm": Does the Second Restatement of Conflicts Meet the Hippocratic Standard?*, 56 MD. L. REV. 1285, 1317-1318 (1997).

Section 4.27 treats the basic approach of the Restatement (Second), leaving to § 4.28 the exploration of the judicial interpretations of that approach. Sections 4.29-4.31 then discuss the Restatement's provisions on torts, contracts, and property.

## § 4.27  The Basic Approach

### § 6. Choice-of-Law Principles *

(1) A court, subject to constitutional restrictions, will follow a statutory directive of its own state on choice of law.

(2) When there is no such directive, the factors relevant to the choice of the applicable rule of law include:

---

* Copyright American Law Institute. Reprinted with permission. The same applies to all of the sections of the Restatement (Second) of Conflict of Laws quoted in Part H.

(a) the needs of the interstate and international systems,

(b) the relevant policies of the forum,

(c) the relevant policies of other interested states and the relative interest of those states in the determination of the particular issue,

(d) the protection of justified expectations,

(e) the basic policies underlying the particular field of law,

(f) certainty, predictability and uniformity of result, and

(g) ease in the determination and application of the law to be applied.

## § 145. The General Principle

(1) The rights and liabilities of the parties with respect to an issue in tort are determined by the local law of the state which, with respect to that issue, has the most significant relationship to the occurrence and the parties under the principles stated in § 6.

(2) Contacts to be taken into account in applying the principles of § 6 to determine the law applicable to an issue include:

(a) the place where the injury occurred,

(b) the place where the conduct causing the injury occurred,

(c) the domicil, residence, nationality, place of incorporation and place of business of the parties, and

(d) the place where the relationship, if any, between the parties is centered.

## § 188. Law Governing in Absence of Effective Choice by the Parties

(1) The rights and duties of the parties with respect to an issue in contract are determined by the local law of the state which, with respect to that issue, has the most significant relationship to the transaction and the parties under the principles stated in § 6.

(2) In the absence of an effective choice of law by the parties (see § 187), the contacts to be taken into account in applying the principles of § 6 to determine the law applicable to an issue include:

(a) the place of contracting,

(b) the place of negotiation of the contract,

(c) the place of performance,

(d) the location of the subject matter of the contract, and

(e) the domicil, residence, nationality, place of incorporation and place of business of the parties.

These contacts are to be evaluated according to their relative importance with respect to the particular issue.

(3) If the place of negotiating the contract and the place of performance are in the same state, the local law of this state will usually be applied, except as otherwise provided in §§ 189-199 and 203.

## NOTES AND QUESTIONS ON THE BASIC APPROACH

(1) *The Drafting History.* Holmes' famous aphorism that a page of history is worth a volume of logic applies with special force to the Second Restatement. It is difficult to understand the document and its hybrid method without some understanding of its eighteen-year drafting history. The project began in 1953 as an attempt to respond to the withering academic criticism of the First Restatement and to accommodate the beginnings of a conflicts revolution that was occurring in the courts. It ended in 1971 as a complex, negotiated settlement among several warring factions of choice-of-law revolutionaries. As a descriptive "restatement," it was doomed to failure from the outset because it is impossible to "restate" a revolution that is in progress and whose outcome is in doubt. As a normative "pre-statement," it has proved to be a huge success among the courts but an object of academic derision.

Repudiating the dogma of vested rights, the early drafts nevertheless retained the First Restatement's strong territorial bias but broadened its scope. Thus they contained a multitude of specific jurisdiction-selecting rules, but they also incorporated the "center of gravity" or "grouping of contacts" approach that had begun to appear in progressive judicial opinions. Conspicuously absent, however, was any serious attempt at policy analysis or consideration of the content of competing internal rules. The predictable result of those omissions was scathing criticism from the academic proponents of the more modern theories, particularly Brainerd Currie and Albert Ehrenzweig. The response of the drafters and their leader, Willis Reese, was to attempt to co-opt the critics by incorporating many of their ideas in the Choice-of-Law Principles of § 6. The result was the final 1971 draft; depending upon your point of view, either a balanced and sophisticated amalgam or an incoherent mishmash.

For more on the history of the drafting process, see William L. Reynolds, *Legal Process and Choice of Law,* 56 MD. L. REV. 1376, 1391 (1997), Patrick J. Borchers, *Courts and the Second Conflicts Restatement: Some Observations and an Empirical Note,* 56 MD. L. REV. 1233, 1236 (1997), Jeffrey M. Shaman, *The Vicissitudes of Choice of Law: The Restatement (First, Second) and Interest Analysis,* 45 BUFF. L. REV. 329, 357 (1997), Michael S. Finch, *Choice-of-Law Problems in Florida Courts: A Retrospective on the Restatement (Second),* 24 STETSON L. REV. 653, 656 (1995).

(2) *The Basic Elements.* Three basic elements define the choice-of-law approach of the Second Restatement: (a) § 6 and the most significant relationship (see notes 3 and 4, *infra*), (b) a few grouping-of-contacts sections (see note 5, *infra*), (c) numerous sections that provide choice-of-law rules for specific legal claims and issues (see note 6, *infra*).

(3) *Section 6 and the Most Significant Relationship.* The concept of the most significant relationship lies at the intellectual heart of the Restatement (Second). It appears in section after section, sometimes as a general residual choice-of-law directive to be used when no specific section applies (*e.g.,* § 145), sometimes as a check, such as a limit on party autonomy in contract (*e.g.,* § 187), and sometimes as an escape device used to avoid the irrational result of a presumptive reference section (*e.g.,* § 149, comment c).

The Restatement contains no explicit definition of the concept of "most significant relationship." Nevertheless, the implication is clear that the state of the most significant relationship is the state whose law would be applied by a court committed to the Choice-of-Law Principles of § 6. Section 6 (1) uncontroversially directs a court to follow a statutory directive of its own state on choice of law. Although the subsection is uncontroversial, its range of application is fairly narrow, as statutory directives on choice of law are quite rare. As comment c suggests, "legislatures usually legislate . . . only with the local situation in mind." There are, however, a few exceptions; the Uniform Commercial Code, for example, contains choice-of-law provisions, as do many no-fault automobile accident compensation statutes.

In the absence of a choice-of-law statute, § 6 (2) counsels a choice based on a series of factors that capture many of the themes of the choice-of-law revolution. Although the list of factors first appeared in an article co-authored by the Reporter for the Second Restatement, *see* Elliott E. Cheatham and Willis L. M. Reese, *Choice of the Applicable Law,* 52 COLUM. L. REV. 959, 962-981 (1952), it also reveals a debt to Professors Currie and Leflar, the several true-conflict-resolution devices, and even the First Restatement. The drafters deliberately chose to list the factors in no particular order of importance and acknowledged that "varying weight will be given to a particular factor, or to a group of factors, in different areas of choice of law." *See* RESTATEMENT (SECOND) § 6, comment c.

(4) *The Factors.* of § 6(2)

(a) *the needs of the interstate and international systems:* Although listed first, this factor may be the least important on the list for the resolution of individual conflicts cases. Comment d gives some indication what the drafters had in mind.

> Choice-of-law rules . . . should seek to further harmonious relations between states and to facilitate commercial intercourse between them . . . . Rules . . . formulated with regard for such needs and policies are likely to commend themselves to other states and to be adopted by these states. Adoption of the same choice-of-law rules by many states will further the needs of interstate and international systems and likewise the values of certainty, predictability and uniformity of result.

Judicial opinions rarely give strong consideration to this factor, and commentators, including the reporter for the Second Restatement acknowledge that, "it is difficult to see in the ordinary case how these needs would be affected by a decision one way or the other." Willis L. M. Reese, *The Second Restatement of Conflict of Laws Revisited,* 34 MERCER L. REV. 501, 509 (1983). *See also* Michael S. Finch, *Choice-of-Law Problems in Florida Courts: A Retrospective on the Restatement (Second),* 24 STETSON L. REV. 660, 653 (1995).

(b) *the relevant policies of the forum,*

(c) *the relevant policies of other interested states and the relative interests of those states in the determination of the particular issue*

These factors reveal the Restatement's debt to Currie and the central place of interest analysis in the Restatement's choice-of-law methodology, as does the language of comment e:

Every rule of law, whether embodied in a statute or in a common law rule was designed to achieve one or more purposes . . . . If the purposes sought to be achieved by any local statute or common law rule would be furthered by its application to out-of-state facts, this is a weighty reason why such application should be made . . . . The court must decide . . . whether the purposes sought to be achieved by a local statute or rule should be furthered at the expense of the other choice-of-law factors . . . .

Section 145, comment c, makes the point even more clearly:

The purpose sought to be achieved by the relevant tort rules of the interested states and the relation of these states to the occurrence and the parties, are important factors to be considered in determining the state of most significant relationship. This is because the interest of a state in having its . . . rule applied in the determination of a particular issue will depend upon the purpose sought to be achieved by that rule and by the relation of the state to the occurrence and the parties.

The drafters intended factors (b) and (c) to incorporate not only the basics of interest analysis, but also some of its refinements, as well. Thus § 6, comment f, shows that the drafters also had in mind the true-conflict-resolution devices of comparative impairment and relative commitment.

[T]he forum should give consideration . . . also to the relevant policies of all other interested states. The forum should seek to reach a result that will achieve the best possible accommodation of these policies. The forum should also appraise the relative interests of the states involved in the determination of the particular issue. In general, it is fitting that the state whose interests are most deeply affected should have its local law applied. Which is the state of the dominant interests may depend on the issue involved. So if a husband injures his wife in a state other than that of their domicile, it may be that the state of conduct and injury has the dominant interest in determining whether the husband's conduct was tortious or whether the wife was guilty of contributory negligence . . . On the other hand, the state of the spouse's domicile is the state of dominant interest when it comes to the question whether the husband should be held immune from tort liability to his wife . . . .

The content of the relevant local law rule of a state may be significant in determining whether this state is the state with the dominant interest. So, for example, application of a state's statute or common law rule which would absolve the defendant from liability could hardly be justified on the basis of this state's interest in the welfare of the injured plaintiff.

*(d) the protection of justified expectations.* Comment g indicates that this factor is responsible for the party autonomy and validation provisions in the Restatement, but that it should have little impact on negligence issues, "when the parties act without giving thought to the legal consequences of their conduct or to the law that may be applied." Note also that the protection of justified expectations has been used by some courts as a device for resolving

true conflicts (*see* § 4.22, *supra*); the inclusion of this factor in the § 6 list suggests that the drafters approve this use of the concept.

*(e) the basic policies underlying the particular field of law.* Comment h provides:

> This factor is of particular importance in situations where the policies of the interested states are largely the same but where there are nevertheless minor differences between their relevant local law rules. In such instances, there is good reason for the court to apply the local law of that state which will best achieve the basic policy, or policies, underlying the particular field of law involved.

This factor explains the rule of validation used in usury, rule against perpetuities, and statute of frauds cases. Professor Reese also remarks upon the role of this factor in tort cases, where the basic policy, compensation for the plaintiff, helps to explain the pro-plaintiff tendency of many modern tort choice-of-law decisions. *See* Reese, *supra,* at 513. Again, note the role of this factor as a true-conflict-resolution device in interest-analytic opinions. *See* § 4.22, *supra.*

*(f) certainty, predictability and uniformity of result.* Comment i, explaining this factor, reveals more than any other the conservative/revolutionary tension in the drafters:

> These are important values in all areas of the law. To the extent that they are attained in choice of law, forum shopping will be discouraged. These values can, however, be purchased at too great a price. In a rapidly developing area, such as choice of law, it is often more important that good rules be developed than that predictability and uniformity of results should be assured through continued adherence to existing rules.

The comment indicates that this factor helps to explain the validity and party autonomy rules as well as the decedent's-domicile rule for the distribution of movables, which is incorporated in §§ 260 and 263.

*(g) ease in the determination and application of the law to be applied.* Again tension is evident in comment j, which explains this factor, but here the tension is between rule and approach, themes that recurrently occupied the Reporter. *See* Willis L. M. Reese, *Choice of Law: Rules or Approach,* 57 CORNELL L. REV. 315 (1972).

> Ideally, choice-of-law rules should be simple and easy to apply. This policy should not be overemphasized, since it is obviously of greater importance that choice-of-law rules lead to desirable results. The policy does, however, provide a goal for which to strive.

Oddly, the comments do not cite this factor as an explanation for the forum's use of its own procedural rules, but the connection is fairly obvious. It would be massively inconvenient, for example, for the forum to determine and apply foreign pleading and evidence rules whenever it adjudicated a claim based upon foreign law.

*(h) The Missing Ingredient.* Conspicuously absent from § 6 is any mention of the better rule of law or of justice in the individual case. The omission is

somewhat surprising in that several of the drafters are on record as favoring explicit consideration of this factor. *See* Elliott E. Cheatham and Willis L. M. Reese, *Choice of the Applicable Law*, 52 COLUM. L. REV. 959, 980 (1952), ROBERT LEFLAR, AMERICAN CONFLICTS LAW 212 (3d ed. 1977). Contemporary authors also maintain that this factor is appropriate. After a review of the pre-Civil War slavery conflicts cases, Professor Weinberg suggests that it could well be the only important factor:

> The slavery cases strongly suggest, however, that it has been a mistake for courts in our time to have laid it down authoritatively that such-and-such a particular methodological analysis is the automatic requirement in every two-state case. Those cases show with too painful clarity that courts must not let the outcome of cases depend upon abstractions. Why should it matter that the slave state is "interested"? Is "the seat of the relationship"? Is, as domicile, the status-determining state? Is the forum? . . . The dangers of imposing even the best methods on the living case can be imagined, if you perform the thought experiment of resolving a conflict of slavery laws under the Restatement (Second).

Louise Weinberg, *Methodological Interventions and the Slavery Cases; Or, Night-Thoughts of a Legal Realist*, 56 MD. L. REV. 1319, 1368 (1997). She suggests at least a common law modification for Second Restatement courts: " 'The needs of the interstate and international systems' should be deleted or at the very least demoted from the top of the list, and the 'requirements of justice in the individual case' should finally be brought explicitly to bear—and be given pride of place." *Id.* at 1366.

Do you agree? Is there a danger in explicit mention and increased importance for this factor? On the other hand, is there really any need for explicit mention of this factor in § 6? Clearly the Restatement's system is flexible enough to allow manipulation of the other factors by judges who wish to apply the better law. What dangers inhere in using the explicit factors to import this missing ingredient? Is there any lesson here from the history of the escape devices used by traditionalist courts?

For a history of the struggles of Willis Reese, reporter of the Second Restatement, in developing Section 6, and for current commentary on the general principles enumerated in Section 6, see Louise Weinberg, *A Structural Revision of the Conflicts Restatement*, 75 IND. L.J. 475 (2000).

(5) *The Specific Sections: A Wide Variety of Approaches.*

(a) *Territorial Presumptions of Varying Strength.* The specific sections of the Second Restatement use a wide variety of choice-of-law strategies. Most, by far, are territorial references. Although reminiscent of the single-contact, jurisdiction-selecting rules of the First Restatement, they differ from them in this significant respect. Nearly all the jurisdiction-selecting sections of the Second Restatement are presumptive references that may be overcome by use of §§ 6, 145, and 188.

The strength of the presumption varies widely among the sections. In some cases, the presumption is very strong indeed. Thus nearly all issues of procedure and evidence except for limitations, burden of proof, and privilege are referred to the law of the forum with no "most significant relationship" exception clause. Similarly, and much more controversially, the sections dealing with real property point absolutely to the law that would be applied by the courts of the situs, and most of those dealing with the succession on death of personal property refer, without an exception clause, to the law that would be applied by the courts of decedent's domicile. (Note that these two sets of sections specifically call for application of the doctrine of renvoi and thus leave the forum court with at least the possibility of escape from the law of the situs or the decedent's domicile. The possibility of escape is not great, however, because these sections also contain provisions suggesting that the courts of the situs or decedent's domicile will "usually apply their own local law.")

The language of other sections reveals less confidence in the presumptive reference. Thus for many types of tort claims (*see, e.g.,* §§ 146, 147, 152, 154, 155, 175) and for many types of contracts (*see, e.g.,* §§ 189-197), the Second Restatement refers to a particular territorial contact, "unless, with respect to the particular issue, some other state has a more significant relationship under the principles stated in § 6 to the claim and the parties." Sections treating particular contract and tort issues are even more tentative, suggesting only that the supplied territorial reference will "usually" control. (*See, e.g.,* §§ 156-160, 164-166, 169, 172, 198, 199). The drafters do not indicate why they feel more confident in the presumptive reference with respect to particular types of contract or tort actions than they do with respect to particular contract or tort issues. Can you think of a reason?

Finally some sections include no presumptive territorial reference at all, referring instead to the appropriate general grouping-of-contacts section, which, of course, incorporates by reference the choice-of-law principles of § 6. If you adopted the Second Restatement strategy of including presumptive references of varying strengths, how would you decide the appropriate strength of presumption for any particular issue or claim? Would it depend upon your confidence in the accuracy of your choice-of-law analysis, the amount of factual variation within the particular category, or upon the degree to which reported decisions adopted the presumptive reference? For more thorough discussion of the Restatement's territorial presumptions, see Symeon C. Symeonides, *Exception Clauses in American Conflicts Law,* Jeffrey M. Shaman, *The Vicissitudes of Choice of Law: The Restatement (First, Second) and Interest Analysis,* 45 BUFF. L. REV. 329, 357-358 (1997).

b. *The Non-Territorial Sections.* In addition to its territorial presumptive references, the Second Restatement also uses other choice-of-law methodologies in several of its specific sections. Party autonomy figures importantly in the Restatement provisions governing consensual, planned transactions. Thus, the drafters give the parties total control over the construction of wills (§ 268), trusts (§§ 269, 271, 272, 277), and contracts (§ 187(1)) and substantial control over the validity of contracts (§ 187(2)) and inter vivos trusts of movables (§ 270).On the party autonomy provisions, see Larry Kramer, *Choice of Law in the American Courts in 1990: Trends and Developments,* 39 AM. J. COMP. L. 465 (1991); Andreas Lowenfeld, *"Tempora Mutantur . . ."*— *Wills and Trusts in the Conflicts Restatement,* 72 COLUM. L. REV. 382 (1972).

Substantivism—choosing law by the result that it produces—informs at least a few specific sections of the Restatement. The clearest examples are the validating provisions affecting usurious contracts, powers of appointment wills, foreign incorporations, and contract formalities. Another example is § 139, which provides for the admission into evidence of a communication if it is admissible according to the privilege law of either the forum or the state that has the most significant relationship with the communication. On substantivism as a choice-of-law strategy, see GENE SHREVE, A CONFLICT-OF-LAWS ANTHOLOGY 139-152 (1997).

Finally, a few of the specific sections of the Second Restatement are purely interest-analytic. The best examples are the sections on presumptions, as well as those on burdens of production and persuasion, which refer to the law of the forum "unless the primary purpose of the relevant rule of the state of the otherwise applicable law is to affect decision of the issue rather than to regulate the conduct of the trial."

(6) *The Grouping-of-Contacts Sections.* The grouping-of-contacts sections, §§ 145 (2) and 188 (2), serve a residual function; thus when an issue or a claim in tort is not treated by a specific choice-of-law directive, the forum should resort to the general rule of § 145.

These sections, are the lineal descendants of the "center of gravity" opinions that appeared early in the choice-of-law revolution, especially in New York. See § 4.16, *supra.* That approach, which dominated the early drafts of the Second Restatement, is vulnerable to two fundamental criticisms. *See* Michael S. Finch, *Choice-of-Law Problems in Florida Courts: A Retrospective on the Restatement (Second),* 24 STETSON L. REV. 653, 656 (1995). First, like the hard-and-fast rules of the First Restatement, it is jurisdiction-selecting; it does not take into account the contents of the competing internal rules. Second, it offers no way of measuring the significance of contacts, and, without a measure of significance, the center of gravity system amounts to little more than contract counting. *See* Jeffrey M. Shaman, *The Vicissitudes of Choice of Law: The Restatement (First, Second) and Interest Analysis,* 45 BUFF. L. REV. 329, 359 (1997).

Even the early drafts of the grouping-of-contacts sections, however, went beyond the simple contact counting of the "center-of-gravity" approach; thus an early version of § 145 provided that "in determining the relative importance of the [enumerated] contacts, the forum will consider the issues, the character of the tort and the relevant purposes of the tort rules involved." Restatement (Second) of Conflict of Laws § 379 (Tent Draft No. 8, 1963). While not extremely specific, this provision at least injected content and policy analysis into the calculation.

Later drafts of the grouping-of-contacts sections provide a greater role for policy analysis. Thus, the final version of § 145 calls for application of the law of "the state which . . . has the most significant relationship to the occurrence and the parties under the principles stated in § 6." Correspondingly, the role of the enumerated contacts is diminished; they are simply "to be taken into account in applying the principles of § 6." Comment e to § 145 demotes the contacts to mere presumptions, thus making the relative importance of policy analysis compared to contact enumeration even more clear:

In applying the principles of § 6 to determine the state of most significant relationship, the forum should give consideration to the relevant policies of all potentially interested states and the relevant interests of those states in the decision of the particular issue. Those states which are most likely to be interested are those which have one or more of the following contacts with the occurrence and the parties.

(7) *Applying the Second Restatement.* Consisting, as it does, of several disparate elements, it is not immediately apparent how the Restatement should be applied. More careful scrutiny, however, reveals what the drafters probably had in mind. In the absence of a statutory choice-of-law directive, a court should determine first whether a specific section covers the issue or claim before it. Most of the specific sections will be presumptive territorial references, but some will use other choice-of-law techniques. *See* Note 5, *supra.* Nearly all, however, will include some reference to § 6 and perhaps to one of the grouping-of-contacts sections, as well. If no specific section covers the issue or claim, the court should refer to the general grouping-of-contacts sections, which also include a reference to § 6. Thus, with either the specific sections or the general grouping-of-contacts sections, eventually the court will need to apply the factors of § 6(2).

Section 6 (2)(b) and (c) clearly contemplate performing some sort of interest analysis. Presumably if that analysis indicates a false conflict, the court should apply the law of the only interested state. If the case is a non-false conflict, the court should use the factors of § 6(2)(d)-(g) to resolve the true conflict or unprovided-for case. In no event, however, should the court use the grouping-of-contacts sections to justify a center-of-gravity or contact-counting approach. The contacts enumerated in the grouping-of-contacts sections have no independent significance and are relevant only insofar as they implicate the factors of § 6(2).

## § 4.28   Use and Abuse in the Courts

### NATIONWIDE MUTUAL INSURANCE COMPANY v. BLACK

*Court of Appeals of Ohio, Ninth Appellate District, Summit County*
*102 Ohio App. 3d 235; 656 N.E.2d 1352 (1995)*

OPINION: BAIRD, Presiding Judge.

[On September 18, 1991, an automobile owned and driven by Ruby Black, a resident of Ohio, collided in Ontario, Canada, with an automobile owned and driven by a resident of Ontario. Kay and William Black, both residents of Ohio, were passengers in Ruby Black's automobile as was Grace Bell, a resident of Pennsylvania. Kay and William Black were insured by Nationwide, an Ohio corporation; Ruby Black was insured by State Farm Insurance. State Farm is not an Ohio corporation, but Ruby Black's policy was written in Ohio.]

Kay and William Black [injured in the accident] presented claims for their injuries to State Farm, which denied them. Thereafter, [they] submitted their claims to Nationwide, seeking payment under the uninsured motorists coverage set forth in their policy of insurance with Nationwide. Nationwide paid their claim. [As their subrogee, Nationwide brought suit against Ruby Black and State Farm seeking] a determination . . . that Ohio law governed the controversy, thereby requiring State Farm to indemnify its insured, Ruby Black, for all damages . . . . [Under the no-fault regime of Ontario, Ruby Black would not be liable and State Farm would not be required to indemnify her.]

The court and the parties agreed to separately determine the issue of whether Ohio or Ontario law should be applied to the controversy. Following submission by the parties of stipulated statements of fact, the trial court ordered that the law of Ontario applied. It is from this order that Nationwide appeals . . . .

Principles of tort law govern a declaratory judgment action instituted by an insurer under the facts and circumstances . . . present here . . . . Pursuant to Ohio law and to applicable principles of tort law, a determination of which state's law applies to a controversy is to be made on a case-by-case basis. *Morgan v. Biro Mfg. Co.* (1984), 15 Ohio St. 3d 339, 340, 474 N.E.2d 286, 287. In making this decision, consideration is to be given to Restatement of the Law 2d, Conflict of Laws (1971) Sections 6, 145, and 146.

Until 1971, Ohio courts applied the rule of lex loci delicti to choice-of-law disputes in personal injury actions. Under that rule, the substantive law of the place where the injury occurred automatically governed the case. After gradually modifying the automatic application of lex loci delicti, the Supreme Court of Ohio, in *Morgan,* determined that lex loci delicti was still viable in Ohio "but it is no longer used to automatically determine the prevailing state law. Other interests of the states involved within the controversy must be thoroughly analyzed." The court concluded that choice-of-law issues in tort actions were to begin with Section 146 of the Restatement:

Pursuant to this section, a presumption is created that the law of the place of the injury controls unless another jurisdiction has a more significant relationship to the lawsuit. To determine the state with the most significant relationship, a court must then proceed to consider the general principles set forth in Section 145. The factors within this section are: (1) the place of the injury; (2) the place where the conduct causing the injury occurred; (3) the domicil, residence, nationality, place of incorporation, and place of business of the parties; (4) the place where the relationship between the parties, if any, is located; and (5) any factors under Section 6[3] which the court may deem

---

[3] Section 6 of 1 Restatement of the Law 2d, Conflict of Laws 10, provides as follows:

(1) A court, subject to constitutional restrictions, will follow a statutory directive of its own state on choice of law.

(2) When there is no such directive, the factors relevant to the choice of the applicable rule of law include

(a) the needs of the interstate and international systems,

(b) the relevant policies of the forum,

(c) the relevant policies of other interested states and the relative interests of those states in the determination of the particular issue,

(d) the protection of justified expectations,

(e) the basic policies underlying the particular field of law,

(f) certainty, predictability and uniformity of result, and

(g) ease in the determination and application of law to be applied.

relevant to the litigation. All of these factors are to be evaluated according to their relative importance to the case.

In accordance with *Morgan* and pursuant to Section 146 of the Restatement, Ontario, as the place where the injury occurred, determines the rights and liabilities of the parties, unless Ohio has a more significant relationship to the occurrence and the parties. In order to determine whether Ohio has a more significant relationship to this occurrence and the parties, we must look to the five factors set forth in *Morgan.*

With respect to two of the factors, domicil and place of relationship of parties, the trial court found that, because of the diversity of the parties' domiciles, consideration of these factors favored neither Ontario nor Ohio. In reaching its conclusion, however, the trial court stated that it was "unreasonable to suggest that only parties to a lawsuit are to be considered in a conflict-of-laws analysis since courts could reach completely different results depending on where cases are filed." Since one of the passengers in Ruby Black's automobile was domiciled in Pennsylvania and since the driver of the other automobile was domiciled in Ontario, the court determined that the "parties" had no common domicil in, or relationship to, either Ohio or Ontario.

The Restatement, however, requires the court to consider only the parties to the lawsuit. Although the term "parties" is not defined in the Restatement, several sections of the Restatement make it clear that the term "parties" is intended to mean "parties to a proceeding," and not all of the individuals involved in the occurrence that precipitated legal action, unless all such individuals are parties to such legal action. *See, e.g.,* Restatement at Sections 125 and 134. Moreover, the term "parties" is generally understood to mean parties to a lawsuit:

'Party' is a technical word having a precise meaning in legal parlance; it refers to those by or against whom a legal suit is brought, whether in law or in equity, the party plaintiff or defendant, whether composed of one or more individuals and whether natural or legal persons; all others who may be affected by the suit, indirectly or consequently, are persons interested but not parties.

BLACK'S LAW DICTIONARY (6 Ed. 1990) 1122.

In view of the foregoing, it was error for the trial court to include the Pennsylvania passenger and the Ontario driver in its analysis of the third and fourth factors of Section 145 of the Restatement. However, the error was harmless under the facts of this case.

The Restatement provides that, where the domicils and places of business of all parties are in a single state, that nexus is an important factor to be considered in determining the applicable law. Restatement Section 145. If a tortfeasor's conduct and the resultant injury occur in such a state, that state likely will be the state of the applicable law. *Id.* However, where, as here, fewer than all of the parties are domiciled in a single state,[4] the weight to be applied to this factor is not as great. Moreover, where personal injury is involved, the

---

[4] Of the two corporations that are parties to this lawsuit, only Nationwide is an Ohio corporation.

place of injury remains of particular significance. Restatement Section 145, Comment f.

With respect to two of the other factors set forth in Section 145 of the Restatement, place of injury and place of conduct causing the injury, the trial court found that those factors favored Ontario. Nationwide argues that the occurrence of the conduct and injury in Ontario was merely fortuitous, however, and should not be afforded great weight:

> The circumstances under which a guest passenger has a right of action against the driver of an automobile for injuries suffered as a result of the latter's negligence may be determined by the local law of their common domicil, if at least this is the state from which they departed on their trip and that to which they intended to return, rather than by the local law of the state where the injury occurred. Restatement Section 145, Comment d.

> Situations do arise, however, where the place of injury will not play an important role in the selection of the state of the applicable law. This will be so, for example, when the place of injury can be said to be fortuitous or when for other reasons it bears little relation to the occurrence and the parties. Restatement Section 145, Comment e.

> A possible example is where the plaintiff, who is domiciled in state X, purchases a ticket in X from the defendant airline, which is incorporated and has its principal place of business in X, for transportation from one point in state X to another point in state X. A straight line between these two points runs for a short distance over the territory of state Y. While over state Y, the pilot commits an act of negligence which causes the plane to lose an engine and the plaintiff suffers severe fright and shock as a result. The plane does not crash and continues safely to its destination. Here the relationship between the parties is centered in X and both are far more closely related to X than to Y. Even though Y is the state of both conduct and injury, its relationship to the occurrence and the parties is insubstantial. X may therefore be the state of most significant relationship. Restatement Section 146, Comment d.

Unlike the example set forth in Comment d, there is no evidence in the record that the Blacks momentarily strayed into Ontario, en route between two distinct points in Ohio, when the injuries occurred. Moreover, not all the parties to this action have the same relationship to Ohio as that set forth in Comment d to Section 146. State Farm is not a corporation organized under the laws of Ohio. The stipulated facts merely state that both Nationwide and State Farm are licensed to do business in Ohio, as they are likely licensed in other states as well.

In *Kurent v. Farmers Ins. of Columbus, Inc.* (1991), 62 Ohio St. 3d 242, 247, 581 N.E.2d 533, 537, the Supreme Court of Ohio found that the interests of an Ohio couple, injured by a Michigan driver in a collision in Michigan, were not "sufficient to override the presumption that the place where the injury occurred determines the rights and liabilities of the parties." The Michigan tortfeasor was insured by a Michigan company, and, pursuant to Michigan's no-fault insurance laws, the amount of the couple's recovery was limited because they failed to show noneconomic damage beyond a threshold level set by the state of Michigan. As a result, the couple sought recovery from their Ohio insurer under the uninsured motorists provision of their policy and pursuant to Ohio law. In finding that Michigan law applied, the court's decision emphasized the difficulty inherent in overcoming the presumption that the law of the place of the injury controls:

> Michigan law determines Karczewski's legal liability to the Kurents. He is a Michigan resident and the accident occurred in Michigan. A motorist traveling in Michigan accepts Michigan law as it pertains to accidents occurring in Michigan. That motorist does not have the option, for example, of claiming that Ohio's speed limit or traffic laws govern simply because the motorist resides in Ohio. The notion that Ohio law somehow controls the amount of damages flowing from torts committed on Michigan highways is akin to a contention that a Michigan resident who commits murder in Ohio is exempt from the death penalty because Michigan does not recognize capital punishment.

Although *Morgan* permits a court to consider, as a fifth factor, those considerations set forth in Section 6 of the Restatement that it deems relevant, those considerations largely require a weighing of the various policy interests involved. In the case sub judice, Ontario could likely advance as many policy reasons for its no-fault insurance law as Ohio could for its fault-based system. Essentially, these considerations offset one another. Even when applying the law of another state would be contrary to the public policy of Ohio, Ohio law is not to be applied unless Ohio has a significantly greater interest in having its law applied. *Sekeres v. Arbaugh* (1987), 31 Ohio St. 3d 24, 26, 31, 76-77, 508 N.E.2d 941, 943.

Although the trial court found that one of the Section 6 factors, "certainty, predictability and uniformity of result," weighed in favor of Ontario, based in part on its consideration of the Pennsylvania passenger and the Ontario driver as "parties," exclusion of them as "parties" does not change the result here. Two of the factors set forth in Section 145 of the Restatement, place of injury and place of causation of injury, squarely support the application of Ontario law. The two factors relative to domicil and relationship of the parties weigh in support of Ohio law but are not unequivocal. The final factor set forth in *Morgan,* the Section 6 considerations, can be argued in favor of either Ontario or Ohio.

Accordingly, because the presumption that Ontario law controls has not been overcome by a showing that Ohio has a more significant relationship to the case sub judice than Ontario, the decision of the trial court is affirmed.

*Judgment affirmed.*

## ESSER v. McINTYRE

*Supreme Court of Illinois*
*169 Ill. 2d 292, 661 N.E.2d 1138 (1996)*

JUSTICE HEIPLE delivered the opinion of the court:

This appeal arises from plaintiff's personal injury suit, in the circuit court of Cook County, seeking damages for injuries allegedly sustained when plaintiff slipped on unpopped popcorn kernels spilled by defendant. At the close of the evidence, the jury returned a verdict in favor of defendant. The appellate court reversed and remanded for a new trial, holding that the jury instructions improperly stated defendant's duty of care. This court granted defendant's petition for leave to appeal. We affirm.

## FACTS

In 1983, three men, Joseph McIntyre, Donald Fett, and Joseph O'Brien, along with their respective guests, Sue Pence, Joanne Walden Votava, and Eva Myers, planned a five-day vacation to Acapulco, Mexico. When Eva Myers, Joseph O'Brien's guest, became unable to go on the trip, she suggested that O'Brien invite Diane Esser, the plaintiff. After meeting O'Brien once, plaintiff agreed to accompany him and the other couples to Acapulco at O'Brien's expense.

Other than O'Brien, plaintiff did not meet her fellow travelers until she arrived at Chicago's O'Hare International Airport for the flight to Acapulco. When the six travelers arrived in Mexico, they checked into a villa at the Villa Vera Hotel. Their villa was a separate structure with three levels. The lower and upper levels contained bedrooms and the middle level contained a private pool, bar, and kitchen.

Plaintiff testified that, after checking in, the vacationers went out for dinner and then returned to the villa. Around 11 p.m., plaintiff retired to the bedroom and O'Brien followed soon after. Just after midnight, she and O'Brien heard the other vacationers pounding on their locked bedroom door and asking them to come out and "party." Plaintiff and O'Brien declined and remained in the bedroom.

Plaintiff stated that she woke up the next morning at 7 a.m. and sat on the sun deck for a short time. Wearing leather loafers, she then walked to the kitchen to order coffee from room service. As she stepped onto the kitchen's glazed tile surface she fell, hit her back on the floor, and screamed. After falling, she looked around and realized that she had slipped on unpopped popcorn kernels that were strewn across the kitchen floor.

Plaintiff testified that O'Brien and defendant McIntyre responded when she fell. Plaintiff asked defendant why no one had cleaned up the popcorn. Defendant replied that he was sorry and that he had opened the popcorn the night before and spilled it, but could not find anything to clean it up.

Plaintiff further testified that she delayed seeking medical attention until she was back in Chicago, where she could see her own doctor . . . .

Plaintiff then testified that, after returning to Chicago, she consulted her physician who prescribed a neck collar and pain medication, and advised her to keep her legs elevated. In 1984, she underwent back surgery for a ruptured disc, during which her lower spine was fused. In 1991, she underwent a second surgery for refusion of her lower spine. Plaintiff testified that, as a result of the fall, she continues to experience back pain which limits her physical activity. Further, these physical problems have caused her to suffer depression, for which she takes medication.

Defendant disputed plaintiff's testimony regarding her fall. He and the other four travelers testified that they were never aware that plaintiff fell and stated that they observed plaintiff participating in various activities after the alleged fall, including swimming, dancing, shopping and lounging on a raft in the pool. O'Brien, Pence, and Votava further testified that they noticed no bruises on plaintiff's body even though they observed her wearing a bikini in the days following the alleged fall. Photos taken of plaintiff during the vacation corroborate that there were no bruises.

Defendant and the other four vacationers also testified that there was never any popcorn in the villa during the vacation.

## PROCEDURAL HISTORY

Prior to trial, the court ruled that Illinois law, rather than Mexican law, applied to plaintiff's claim. The trial court also determined that defendant was an occupier of land and thus owed plaintiff, a licensee, a duty only to refrain from willful and wanton misconduct. At the close of the evidence, the court instructed the jury that defendant had only a duty to refrain from willful and wanton misconduct. The jury then returned a verdict for defendant. The appellate court reversed and remanded for a new trial because defendant was not an occupier of land and therefore owed plaintiff a duty of ordinary care.

Before this court, defendant argues that: (1) Mexican law rather than Illinois law applies to plaintiff's claim; (2) the trial court properly instructed the jury as to defendant's duty . . . .

## ANALYSIS

### I. Choice of Law

Initially, we must determine whether Mexican law or Illinois law applies to plaintiff's claim. The parties agree that plaintiff has no cause of action under Mexican law.

To determine which law applies, we look to the conflicts law of Illinois, the forum State. In *Ingersoll v. Klein* (1970), 46 Ill. 2d 42, 262 N.E.2d 593, this court rejected the lex loci delicti doctrine and adopted the most significant relationship test for deciding among conflicting laws (citing the preliminary draft of what is now section 145 of the Restatement (Second) of Conflict of Laws). Under this test, the law of the place of injury controls unless Illinois has a more significant relationship with the occurrence and with the parties. When applying the most significant relationship test, a court should consider

(1) where the injury occurred; (2) where the injury-causing conduct occurred; (3) the domicile of the parties; and (4) where the relationship of the parties is centered. The court must look at the contacts of the jurisdictions under these four factors and then evaluate those contacts in light of the policies underlying the laws of those jurisdictions.

The first two factors of the most significant relationship test are easily determined. First, plaintiff's injury occurred in Acapulco, Mexico, at the Villa Vera Hotel. Second, the alleged injury-causing conduct—defendant's spilling of the popcorn—also occurred in Mexico.

Third, we must determine the domicile of the parties. The parties do not dispute that defendant's domicile is Illinois. Plaintiff claims that her domicile is Illinois as well, but defendant argues that plaintiff's domicile is unclear since plaintiff has spent significant time living in Utah. However, the relevant time to examine the domicile of the parties is at the time of the accident . . . .

Fourth, and finally, we must determine where the relationship of the parties was centered. Defendant argues that his relationship with plaintiff was centered in Mexico since plaintiff and defendant had no contact until they met at the airport on the way to Mexico and have had no contact since their return, except regarding plaintiff's lawsuit. Plaintiff responds that everything about her relationship with defendant was centered in Illinois and only the destination involved Mexico. All of the vacationers were Illinois residents, the trip was planned in Illinois, plaintiff's invitation from O'Brien was issued in Illinois, and, finally, the vacationers left from and returned to O'Hare International Airport in Chicago, Illinois.

We conclude that the relationship of the parties was centered in Illinois because (1) plaintiff was invited by defendant's friend O'Brien, an Illinois resident; (2) O'Brien's invitation was issued in Illinois; and (3) defendant planned the vacation with O'Brien and Fett in Illinois.

Under the four factors of the most significant relationship test, the contacts of Mexico and Illinois are as follows: (1) the injury occurred in Mexico; (2) the injury-causing conduct occurred in Mexico; (3) both plaintiff and defendant are domiciled in Illinois; and (4) the relationship between plaintiff and defendant was centered in Illinois. In determining which jurisdiction has the most significant relationship, these contacts must be considered in light of the relevant general principles governing all choice-of-law decisions. ( . . . the seven general principles contained in section 6 of the Restatement (Second) of Conflicts of Law). Of the principles enumerated in [section 6] several are applicable here: (1) the need to foster commercial interaction between Mexico and the United States; (2) the policies and interests of Illinois and Mexico; and (3) the protection of the justified expectations of plaintiff and defendant.

In light of these general principles, Illinois law should be applied to plaintiff's claim. First, an application of Illinois law does not hinder commercial interaction between Mexico and the United States. Applying Illinois tort law will not discourage people from going to Mexico for either vacation or business because few, if any, travelers to Mexico choose that locale simply because they are less subject to tort liability.

Second, the interest of the State of Illinois in providing a remedy for an Illinois resident who has been allegedly injured by another Illinois resident outweighs Mexico's interest in limiting tort recoveries. Having provided a legal means for a plaintiff to recover for injuries caused by a defendant's culpable conduct, Illinois has a strong interest in providing that remedy in disputes between Illinois residents. That policy will be circumvented if Mexican law applies since, under Mexican law, plaintiff has no remedy for her claim against defendant. Furthermore, allowing plaintiff to state a claim under Illinois law will not impinge upon Mexican interests since the case requires no involvement by Mexican courts, Mexican defendants, or Mexican witnesses. Although Mexico has an interest in activity occurring at hotels within its borders, this is a wholly private dispute involving only Illinois residents.

Finally, defendant had no justifiable expectation that Mexican law would limit his liability for any tortious conduct he might engage in while in Acapulco. While "it would be unfair and improper to hold [defendant] liable under [Illinois] law . . . when he had justifiably molded his conduct to conform to the requirements of [Mexican law]" (Restatement (Second) of Conflict of Laws § 6, Comment g, at 15 (1971)), defendant does not contend that he acted in reliance on Mexican law. Negligent conduct is rarely, if ever, done with regard to what law will apply to a claim arising from the negligent conduct.

In light of the contacts of Mexico and Illinois under the four factors of the most significant relationship test and the evaluation of those contacts under the relevant general principles, the circuit court properly applied Illinois law. Although both Mexico and Illinois had contacts with the action, Illinois had the most significant relationship, especially considering Illinois' interest in providing tort remedies to its injured citizens.

[The court then ruled that the trial court had misapplied Illinois law and issued an erroneous jury instruction.]

## CONCLUSION

For the foregoing reasons, we affirm the judgment of the appellate court, which reversed the decision of the circuit court and remanded for a new trial.

*Affirmed.*

## NOTES AND QUESTIONS ON JUDICIAL APPLICATIONS OF THE BASIC APPROACH

(1) *Dominance in the Courts.* The Second Restatement is the dominant conflicts methodology in American courts today. *See* Patrick J. Borchers, *Courts and the Second Conflicts Restatement: Some Observations and an Empirical Note,* 56 MD. L. REV. 1233, 1234 (1997), William L. Reynolds, *Legal Process and Choice of Law,* 56 MD. L. REV. 1376, 1395 (1997). Twenty-one jurisdictions follow the Restatement's approach in tort conflicts, and twenty-five do so in contract cases. *See* Symeon Symeonides, *The Judicial Acceptance of the Second Conflicts Restatement: A Mixed Blessing,* 56 MD. L. REV.1251, 1269-1270 (1997). Additionally several other jurisdictions follow the similar "significant contacts" approach thus yielding a majority of American jurisdictions. *Id.* The next most popular American choice-of-law methodology, the traditional First Restatement approach, can claim less than half as many

adherents. William M. Richman and David Riley, *The First Restatement of Conflict of Laws on the Twenty-fifth Anniversary of its Successor: Contemporary Practice on Traditional Courts,* 56 MD. L. REV. 1196, 1201(1997).

Even these numbers, however, understate the influence of the Second Restatement. Many federal courts use the Second Restatement in federal question cases, and several jurisdictions that follow other choice-of-law methodologies nevertheless use particular sections of the Restatement (Second). Thus, New York typically uses the "center-of-gravity" approach, but nevertheless follows § 188 in some contract cases. *Allstate Ins. Co. v. Stolarz,* 613 N.E.2d 936, 939 (N.Y. 1993). Likewise, many states that still use the traditional First Restatement system have adopted Restatement (Second) §§ 187, 193, and 203 to resolve party autonomy, insurance, and usury cases respectively. *Richman and Riley, supra,* at 1213-1217, 1226. The leading observer of American conflicts decisions predicts continued dominance for the Second Restatement: "It seems that, at this point, the *Restatement (Second)* has enough momentum to justify a prediction that, if any of the jurisdictions that continue to adhere to the traditional theory chooses to abandon that theory, it will likely adopt the *Restatement (Second)."* *Symeonides, supra,* at 1278.

(2) *Reasons.* Although the dominance of the Second Restatement is now clear, the reasons for its success are the subject of conjecture. Professor Symeonides suggests that the approach has triumphed because "it provides the judge with virtually unlimited discretion, does not require hard thinking, . . . . is not ideologically 'loaded,'. . . .is a complete 'system,' . . . . carries the prestige of the American Law Institute, . . . . and has 'momentum'." *Symeonides, supra* note 1, at 1269-1277. Professor Borchers attributes the Second Restatement's popularity to its open-ended general provisions (§§ 6, 145, 188) as opposed to its many specific territorial jurisdiction-selecting sections, which, he claims, many courts ignore. *Borchers, supra* note 1, at 1233.

More charitably, Professor Reynolds argues that the Second Restatement is user-friendly and well-written and that its flexibility guides decisions rather than controlling them, thus permitting the courts to avoid unjust results. *Reynolds, supra* note 1, at 1395. *See also* Harold G. Maier, *Finding the Trees In Spite of the Metaphorist: The Problem of State Interests in Choice of Law,* 56 ALB. L. REV. 753, 771 (1993). Further, Reynolds argues, it avoids arbitrariness by requiring explanation in terms of the policies of § 6; thus its intellectual style is quite compatible with the legal process tradition, in which most contemporary judges were trained. *Reynolds, supra,* at 1393.

(3) *Use and Abuse of the Approach.* The numerical count of jurisdictions that have adopted the Second Restatement also may overstate the prevalence of that approach. As indicated in § 4.25, the Restatement adopts a layered approach that amalgamates much modern choice-of-law thinking as well as many traditional territorial references. Further, the interaction of the presumptive references, the grouping-of-contacts sections, and the principles of § 6 is subtle and easily misinterpreted. A court that misunderstands the relationship among the three central elements might well believe that it has "adopted" the Second Restatement yet apply a very different, less sophisticated choice-of-law methodology.

In this regard, consider the opinions in *Black* and *Esser*: Both the courts in these two false-conflict cases have "adopted" the Second Restatement, but are they applying the same choice-of-law approach? What motivating policies do the two opinions attribute to the laws of the competing states on no-fault liability and premises liability? What part does § 6 play in each court's decision? How about § 145? Does the *Black* court understand that the contacts of § 145 matter only in so far as they implicate the factors of § 6 (2)? Does the *Esser* court? If the *Black* court fails to grasp this central principle of the Restatement approach, how does it determine the place of the most significant relationship? Pure contact counting? And does it count the contacts correctly? Why does it matter that State Farm is not an Ohio corporation as long as the insured was an Ohioan and the policy was written in Ohio? Its method is surely a far cry from the approach outlined in § 4.25, Note 7.

In particular, note how it interprets the word "parties" by referring to the trusty law dictionary; would it have done better to use the principles of § 6 as an interpretive guide? Note also the court's misuse of the opinion in *Kurent,* in which the Supreme Court of Ohio adopts a territorial solution to a true conflict case. Whether or not such a solution is desirable in a true conflict, why would the *Black* court consider it useful precedent in a false conflict case? It certainly appears that the court's failure to take seriously the factors of § 6 (2), particularly factors (b) and (c), prevented it from performing the required interest analysis and thus allowed it to misread as controlling the higher court's opinion in *Kurent.*

*Black* and *Esser* are typical of two prevalent styles of interpretation among Second Restatement courts. While some courts understand the primacy of § 6 and use it to incorporate interest analysis, others misread §§ 145 and 188 to permit an impressionistic, contact-counting, center-of-gravity approach.

(4) *The Fault of the Second Restatement?* Professor Kramer remarked recently that, "one needs to read a lot of opinions in a single sitting fully to appreciate just how badly the Second Restatement works in practice." Larry Kramer, *Choice of Law in the American Courts in 1990: Trends and Developments,* 39 AM. J. COMP. L. 465, 486-487 (1990). Very likely, he had read too many *Black*–style and too few *Esser*–style opinions. But is it the fault of the Second Restatement that it can be misinterpreted? After all, trying to create an idiot-proof choice-of-law system may be as futile as trying to create a perpetual-motion machine.

Nevertheless, some of the fault for *Black*-style opinions belongs to the drafters of the Second Restatement. While § 6 requires an interest analysis, it does not do so in very explicit language, nor do the comments. Further, the comments *do* contain some language that easily can mislead an unsophisticated court. The hypothetical in § 146, comment d, quoted in *Black,* is a good example. It gives the impression that the court should override the place-of-injury rule only in cases where the parties stray unintentionally into the place of injury, whereas the principles of § 6 clearly justify the override in an ordinary, garden-variety false conflict like *Black.* On the unfortunate choice of this example, see Russell J. Weintraub, *"At Least, To Do No Harm": Does the Second Restatement of Conflicts Meet the Hippocratic Standard?* 56 MD. L. REV 1285, 1290 (1997).

(5) *Specific Versus General: In Practice.* Another issue that has emerged in the interpretation of the Second Restatement is the role of the specific territorial presumptions. As indicated in § 4.25, Note 7, the drafters intended that the court's choice-of-law calculation begin with the specific territorial presumptions, where applicable, and then proceed to the "most significant relationship" analysis under § 6 and the grouping-of-contacts sections. One might expect judges familiar with the traditional territorial system to be over-deferential to the presumptive references and reluctant to engage in the more free-form process required by § 6.

In fact, however, the opposite approach seems to prevail. There is now some evidence that many Second Restatement courts skip the initial presumptive reference and proceed directly to the "most significant relationship" analysis. The evidence for this counter-intuitive development is a citation study conducted by Professor Borchers. He found in tort and contract cases that the citations to §§ 145 and 188 significantly out-numbered the total of citations to all the presumptive-reference sections combined. *Borchers, supra* note 1, at 1247-1249. Thus, he concludes:

> Over time, the Second Restatement has become something different from the document it appears to be. Even the courts that claim to adhere to the Second Restatement most likely do not look at it very often . . . . Instead, courts and the attorneys practicing before them look to cases quoting sections 6, 145, 188, or some of the other popular provisions. They content themselves with block quotations of those general sections and then proceed to solve the choice-of-law problem, considering only that general section. For judges and lawyers, the Second Restatement exists not as a handsome, two-volume book authored by the American Law Institute, but rather as a kind of chain letter consisting of selective block quotations.

*Id.* at 1249. If Borchers is correct, is the courts' tendency to ignore the specific sections a good thing or not? Does your answer depend upon whether the court's treatment of the general sections is more like *Esser's* or more like *Black's*?

## § 4.29   Torts

## § 146. Personal Injuries

In an action for a personal injury, the local law of the state where the injury occurred determines the rights and liabilities of the parties unless, with respect to the particular issue, some other state has a more significant relationship, under the principles stated in § 6 to the occurrence and the parties, in which event the local law of the other state will be applied.

## § 148. Fraud and Misrepresentation

(1) When the plaintiff has suffered pecuniary harm on account of his reliance on the defendant's false representations and when the plaintiff's action in reliance took place in the state where the false representations were made

and received, the local law of this state determines the rights and liabilities of the parties unless, with respect to the particular issue, some other state has a more significant relationship under the principles stated in § 6 to the occurrence and the parties, in which event the local law of the other state will be applied.

(2) When the plaintiff's action in reliance took place in whole or in part in a state other than that where the false representations were made, the forum will consider such of the following contacts, among others, as may be present in the particular case in determining the state which, with respect to the particular issue, has the most significant relationship to the occurrence and the parties:

- (a) the place, or places, where the plaintiff acted in reliance upon the defendant's representations,

- (b) the place where the plaintiff received the representations,

- (c) the place where the defendant made the representations,

- (d) the domicile, residence, nationality, place of incorporation and place of business of the parties,

- (e) the place where a tangible thing which is the subject of the transaction between the parties was situated at the time, and

- (f) the place where the plaintiff is to render performance under a contract which he has been induced to enter by the false representation of the defendant.

## § 149. Defamation

In an action for defamation, the local law of the state where the publication occurs determines the rights and liabilities of the parties, except as stated in § 150, unless with respect to the particular issue, some other state has a more significant relationship under the principles stated in § 6 to the occurrence and the parties, in which event the local law of the other state will be applied.

## § 150. Multistate Defamation

(1) The rights and liabilities that arise from defamatory matter in any one edition of a book or newspaper, or any one broadcast over radio or television, exhibition of a motion picture, or similar aggregate communication are determined by the local law of the state which, with respect to the particular issue, has the most significant relationship to the occurrence and the parties under the principles stated in § 6.

(2) When a natural person claims that he has been defamed by an aggregate communication, the state of most significant relationship will usually be the state where the person was domiciled at the time, if the matter complained of was published in that state.

(3) When a corporation, or other legal person, claims that it has been defamed by an aggregate communication, the state of most significant relationship will usually be the state where the corporation, or other legal person, had its

principal place of business at the time, if the matter complained of was published in that state.

## § 156. Tortious Character of Conduct

(1) The law selected by the application of the rule of § 145 determines whether the actor's conduct was tortious.

(2) The applicable law will usually be the local law of the state where the injury occurred.

## § 167. Survival of actions

The law selected by application of the rule of § 145 determines whether a claim for damages for a tort survives the death of the tortfeasor or of the injured person.

## § 169. Intra-Family Immunity

(1) The law selected by application of the rule of § 145 determines whether one member of a family is immune from tort liability to another member of the family.

(2) The applicable law will usually be the local law of the state of the parties' domicil.

## § 175. Right of Action for Death

In an action for wrongful death, the local law of the state where the injury occurred determines the rights and liabilities of the parties unless, with respect to the particular issue, some other state has a more significant relationship under the principles stated in § 6 to the occurrence and the parties, in which event the local law of the other state will be applied.

## NOTES AND QUESTIONS ON THE TORTS PROVISIONS OF THE SECOND RESTATEMENT

(1) *Structure of the Chapter* Chapter 7 of the Second Restatement, denominated "Wrongs", contains one general grouping-of-contacts section for torts (§ 145, see § 4.29, *supra*), ten sections treating particular torts, and twenty sections treating particular issues in tort cases. Following the now familiar pattern, § 145 (1) calls for application of the law of the state of the most significant relationship, and § 145(2) lists a group of contacts that will typically be relevant in tort cases. The remainder of the chapter treats the particular claims and issues.

(a) *Types of Torts.* For most torts, the Restatement calls for the law of the place of injury "unless . . . some other state has a more significant relationship under the principles stated in § 6 to the occurrence and the parties . . . ." That rebuttable presumption, for example, applies to personal injuries (§ 146), injuries to personal property (§ 147), and all sections dealing with wrongful death (§§ 175-180). Application of the place-of-injury presumption results in a reference to the law of the place of publication in single-state defamation (§ 149), invasion of privacy (§ 152), and injurious falsehood (§ 151) cases; and in abuse of process cases (§ 155) to the law of the place where the proceeding occurred.

In fraud cases (§ 148), the presumption applies only when the place of the defendant's representation and the plaintiff's reliance is the same; otherwise, a grouping-of-contacts/most-significant-relationship provision controls. The place-of injury presumption does not apply to three torts. In multi-state defamation (§ 150), invasion of privacy (§ 153), and injurious falsehood (§ 151) cases, the reference is to the plaintiff's domicile; and in interference with the marriage relationship (§ 154), the place of the defendant's conduct presumptively controls.

(b) *Tort Issues.* The place-of-injury presumption is weaker in the sections dealing with particular tort issues. For many issues, it does not operate at all; and the reference is simply to the rule of § 145, which thus controls defenses (§ 161), duty or privilege to act (§ 163), survival of actions (§ 167), charitable immunity (§ 168), damages (§ 171), contribution and indemnity (§ 173), and vicarious liability (§ 174).

In other sections, the place-of-injury presumption applies, but only weakly; these sections refer to the general rule of § 145 and merely *advise* that the choice will "usually" be the law of the place of injury. *See* § 156 (tortious character of conduct), § 157 (standard of care), § 158 (interest entitled to legal protection), § 159 (duty owed plaintiff), § 160 (legal cause), § 162 (conditions of liability), § 163 (duty or privilege to act), § 164 (contributory fault), § 165 (assumption of risk), § 166 (imputed negligence), § 170 (release or covenant not to sue), and § 172 (joint torts). For one issue, intra-family immunity, § 169 refers to the general rule of § 145, but advises that the "usually" applicable law will be that of the parties' domicile, rather than the place of injury.

(2) *Deference to the Place of Injury.* Are the Second Restatement's tort provisions really different from those of its predecessor? Initially, this might seem a strange question to ask. The Introductory Note to the Chapter, after all, explicitly abandons the vested rights approach and the last event rule, and one of the drafters believed that the most notable feature of the chapter is its abandonment of the law of the place of injury rule. *See* Robert A. Leflar, *The Torts Provisions of the Restatement (Second),* 72 COLUM. L. REV. 266, 267 (1972).

Nevertheless, the place of injury is still, by far, the most common territorial reference, appearing in 21 out of 35 sections, thus leading Professor Leflar to remark that it "hovers like a ghost over the entire chapter." *Id.* at 269. The Reporter for the Second Restatement offers this rationale for the place-of-injury presumption:

> To ignore the significance of territoriality is to ignore the basic reason for the existence of choice of law. Whether we like it or not, the world is composed of many states, each having its own system of law, and it is customary for persons to travel freely from state to state . . . . The purpose of choice of law . . . is to provide a solution for the problems that inevitably arise. People naturally think in terms of

territoriality, and so have the courts. To ignore its significance is to turn one's back on the past and to ignore a vital factor that underlies the field.

Willis L. M. Reese, *The Second Restatement of Conflict of Laws Revisited,* 34 MERCER L. REV. 501, 514 (1983). Comment c to § 146 (which applies the place-of-injury presumption to personal injuries) offers the additional rationale that it furthers the § 6 choice-of-law values of certainty, predictability, uniformity of result and, ease of application.

Whether the presumption produces pernicious results in the courts depends upon how hard it is to rebut. *See* Michael S. Finch, *Choice-of-Law Problems in Florida Courts: A Retrospective on the Restatement (Second),* 24 STETSON L. REV. 653, 669 (1995). A sensible approach would be to apply the presumption only in non-false conflict cases, using interest analysis to resolve false conflicts. *See id.* at 669; Harold P. Southerland, *A Screaming Comes Across the Sky—Tort Choice-of-Law Doctrine in Florida Under the Second Restatement of Conflicts,* 40 MERCER L. REV. 781, 800 (1989) There is ample justification for such a strategy in comment c, which clearly incorporates interest analysis:

> In large part, the answer to this question [whether the presumption is rebutted] will depend upon whether some other state has a greater interest in the determination of the particular issue than the state where the injury occurred. The extent of the interest of each of the potentially interested states should be determined on the basis, among other things, of the purpose sought to be achieved by their relevant local law rules . . . .

A less sensible approach is to try to identify particular factual patterns that usually will support the place of injury presumption. Comment d to § 146 unwisely adopts this approach by maintaining that the place of injury rule usually will apply when defendant's conduct and plaintiff's injury occur in the same state. Worse, the comment suggests that the only exceptions will occur in truly unusual circumstances. (The example supplied is an airplane traveling from one point in state X to another point in state X, which passes briefly through the airspace of State Y. Over state Y, the pilot's negligence causes plaintiff, a passenger, severe fright and shock.)

Unfortunately, however the common-place-of-conduct-and-injury rule will produce irrational results in a host of cases that are much more ordinary than the cited hypothetical. *Babcock v. Jackson,* see § 4.19, *supra* is a classic example, as is any other common-domicile-false-conflict, where the conduct and injury occur in the non-domiciliary state. *See* Russell J. Weintraub, *"At Least To Do No Harm": Does the Second Restatement Meet the Hippocratic Standard?,* 56 MD. L. REV 1285, 1290 (1997). If you represented the plaintiff in a *Babcock*-type case before a committed Second Restatement court, what arguments might you use to persuade it to override the common-place-of-conduct-and-injury presumption?

The limited available empirical evidence suggests that Second Restatement courts do not rely very heavily on the place-of-injury presumption. Professor Borchers examined over 800 trial and appellate tort choice-of-law cases decided after 1960. He then compared decisions by courts using the two Restatements, interest analysis, and Leflar's system according to three parameters: the extent to which the decisions (1) chose forum law, (2) favored recovery, and (3) favored forum residents. The results for courts using the three modern systems were statistically indistinguishable, but differed substantially from the results for courts using the First Restatement. *See* Patrick J. Borchers, *The Choice-of-Law Revolution: An Empirical Study,* 49 WASH. & LEE L. REV. 357, 377-8 (1992). This suggests that courts using the Second Restatement were no more likely to defer to the territorial presumption than were courts using the other modern methods. It also suggests that the "hovering ghost" of the place-of-injury rule has not exerted the control over Second Restatement courts that the Restatement's critics feared it would.

## § 4.30   Contracts

### § 187. Law of the State Chosen by the Parties

(1) The law of the state chosen by the parties to govern their contractual rights and duties will be applied if the particular issue is one which the parties could have resolved by an explicit provision in their agreement directed to that issue.

(2) The law of the state chosen by the parties to govern their contractual rights and duties will be applied, even if the particular issue is one which the parties could not have resolved by an explicit provision in their agreement directed to that issue, unless either

(a) the chosen state has no substantial relationship to the parties or the transaction and there is no other reasonable basis for the parties' choice, or

(b) application of the law of the chosen state would be contrary to a fundamental policy of a state which has a materially greater interest than the chosen state in the determination of the particular issue and which, under the rule of § 188, would be the state of the applicable law in the absence of an effective choice of law by the parties.

(3) In the absence of a contrary indication of intention, the reference is to the local law of the state of the chosen law.

### § 193. Contracts of Fire, Surety or Casualty Insurance

The validity of a contract of fire, surety or casualty insurance and the rights created thereby are determined by the local law of the state which the parties understood was to be the principal location of the insured risk during the term of the policy, unless with respect to the particular issue, some other state has a more significant relationship under the principles stated in § 6 to the transaction and the parties, in which event the local law of the other state will be applied.

### § 196. Contract for the Rendition of Services

The validity of a contract for the rendition of services and the rights created thereby are determined in the absence of an effective choice of law by the parties by the local law of the state where the contract required that the services, or a major portion of the services, be rendered, unless, with respect to the particular issue, some other state has a more significant relationship under the principles stated in § 6 to the transaction and the parties, in which event the local law of the other state will be applied.

## § 199. Requirements of a Writing—Formalities

(1) The formalities required to make a valid contract are determined by the law selected by application of the rules of §§ 187-188.

(2) Formalities which meet the requirements of the place where the parties execute the contract will usually be acceptable.

## § 203. Usury

The validity of a contract will be sustained against the charge of usury if it provides for a rate of interest that is permissible in a state to which the contract has a substantial relationship and is not greatly in excess of the rate permitted by the general usury law of the state of the otherwise applicable law under the rule of § 188.

## § 206. Details of Performance

Issues relating to details of performance of a contract are determined by the local law of the place of performance.

## § 207. Measure of Recovery

The measure of recovery for a breach of contract is determined by the local law of the state selected by application of the rules of §§ 187-188.

## § 221. Restitution

(1) In actions for restitution, the rights and liabilities of the parties with respect to the particular issue are determined by the local law of the state which, with respect to that issue, has the most significant relationship to the occurrence and the parties under the principles stated in § 6.

(2) Contacts to be taken into account in applying the principles of § 6 to determine the law applicable to an issue include:

(a) the place where a relationship between the parties was centered, provided that the receipt of enrichment was substantially related to the relationship,

(b) the place where the benefit or enrichment was received,

(c) the place where the act conferring the benefit or enrichment was done,

(d) the domicil, residence, nationality, place of incorporation and place of business of the parties, and

(e) the place where a physical thing, such as land or a chattel which was substantially related to the enrichment, was situated at the time of enrichment.

These contacts are to be evaluated according to their relative importance with respect to the particular issue.

## NOTES AND QUESTIONS ON THE CONTRACTS PROVISIONS OF THE SECOND RESTATEMENT

(1) *Structure of the Chapter.* The Contracts chapter (Chapter Eight) of the Second Restatement provides, as might be expected, that the controlling law is either chosen in accordance with a provision resembling § 145, or in a new wrinkle, the law chosen by the parties. The latter provision permits enforcement of what is sometimes known as "party autonomy"; that concept is found in § 187 of the Second Restatement and is discussed in detail in § 4.34[B], *infra*.

In the absence of an effective choice-of-law provision, § 188 directs the use of the "local law of the state which, with respect to that issue, has the most significant relationship . . . under the principles stated in § 6." Section 188(2) then lists several factors peculiar to contract law that will help inform the § 6 choice. The rest of Chapter 8 is devoted to specific contract problems.

(2) *Types of Contracts.* For most contracts, the Second Restatement presumes that a specific law will be applied unless the presumption is rebutted by "the principles of § 6." Nine sections deal with particular contracts: Land contracts apply the *lex sitae* (§§ 189-90); a sale of a chattel involves the law of the place of delivery (§ 191); insurance contracts generally apply the law of the location of the risk (§§ 192-94), and other provisions presume application of the law of the place of repayment of money lent (§ 195), the place where services will be rendered (§ 196), or the place of shipment in transportation contracts (§ 197).

(3) *Contract Issues.* There are two dozen provisions dealing with specific contract issues. These present a hodge-podge set of presumptions; some even lack any presumption, but merely refer the reader back to the generalities of §§ 6 and 188. *E.g.*, §§ 212 and 213 involving discharge. One section refers to the domicile of one of the parties (§ 298, capacity). Place of performance is the presumptive choice in § 206, and *lex fori* appears in § 219 (enforcement of arbitration agreement). One of the more interesting choices is found in § 203, dealing with usury: An allegedly usurious contract will be enforced if the rate of interest is permissible in a "state to which the contract has a substantial relationship and is not greatly in excess of the rate permitted by the general usury law of the state [chosen under] § 188." Section 203 represents an effort to validate contracts which might be marginally usurious, but which the court believes do not deserve the Draconian penalties usually visited upon contracts which violate the usury laws—even in a technical sense. It is thus one of then few "substantivist" provisions of the Second Restatement. *See* § 4.25, Note 5(b), *supra*.

(4) *An Evaluation.* One obvious observation is that the drafters of the Second Restatement's contracts provisions expected § 187—party autonomy—to be

of great importance. In drafting the clauses dealing with the residue of agreements (that is, those without choice-of-law-clauses), the drafters chose to apply the law which most likely would be applied pursuant to the use of modern policy analysis. The faith in § 187 has been amply justified; it has long been a respected tool in the armory of the commercial lawyer.

The result in non-party autonomy cases, however, has been more mixed. Professor Borchers found that the fate of the contract provisions mirrored that of the tort sections. In other words, most provisions received scant judicial attention, while a few attracted a larger number of citations. Patrick J. Borchers, *Courts and the Second Conflicts Restatement: Some Observations and an Empirical Note,* 56 MD. L. REV. 1232, 1245 (1997) (noting relatively large numbers of citations for § 192 (life insurance contracts), § 196 (rendition of services), and § 203 (usury); also noting a much larger number for § 193 (fire, casualty, or surety insurance)). Even courts otherwise committed to the First Restatement often apply these sections of its successor. See William Richman and David Riley, *The Restatement (First) of Conflict of Laws on the Twenty-fifth Anniversary of Its Successor: Contemporary Practice on Traditionalist Courts,,* 56 MD. L. REV 1196 (1997).

What do these clauses have in common that makes them so popular? Remember: They are meant to apply only in the *absence* of a choice-of-law clause.

The sections listed above, especially § 193, are so popular that they might be called "True Rules," suggesting that courts will strain to uphold the preference because it makes so much sense. *See* William M. Richman and William L. Reynolds, *Prologemon to an Empirical Restatement of Conflicts,* 75 IND. L. J. 417, 433 (2000).

## § 4.31 Procedure

## § 122. Issues Relating to Judicial Administration

A court usually applies its own local law rules prescribing how litigation shall be conducted even when it applies the local law rules of another state to resolve other issues in the case.

## § 127. Pleading and Conduct of Proceedings

The local law of the forum governs rules of pleading and the conduct of proceedings in court.

## § 133. Burden of Proof

The forum will apply its own local law in determining which party has the burden of persuading the trier of fact on a particular issue unless the primary purpose of the relevant rule of the state of the otherwise applicable law is to affect decision of the issue rather than to regulate the conduct of the trial. In that event, the rule of the state of the otherwise applicable law will be applied.

## § 134. Burden of Going Forward with the Evidence; Presumptions

The forum will apply its own local law in determining which party has the burden of going forward with the evidence on a particular issue unless the primary purpose of the relevant rule of the state of the otherwise applicable law is to affect decision of the issue rather than to regulate the conduct of the trial. In that event the rule of the state of the otherwise applicable law will be applied.

## § 137. Witnesses

The local law of the forum determines what witnesses are competent to testify and the considerations that may affect their credibility.

## § 138. Evidence

The local law of the forum determines the admissibility of evidence, except as stated in §§ 139-141.

## § 139. Privileged Communications

(1) Evidence that is not privileged under the local law of the state which has the most significant relationship with the communication will be admitted even though it would be privileged under the local law of the forum, unless the admission of such evidence would be contrary to the strong public policy of the forum.

(2) Evidence that is privileged under the local law of the state which has the most significant relationship with the communication but which is not privileged under the local law of the forum will be admitted unless there is some special reason why the forum policy favoring admission should not be given effect.

## NOTES AND QUESTIONS ON PROCEDURE AND EVIDENCE

(1) *The Law of the Forum: Reasons.* Why should the forum apply its own law on matters of judicial administration when, following its own choice-of-law rules, it applies the tort, contract, or property law of some other state? In comment a to § 122, the drafters offer these rationales:

> The forum has compelling reasons for applying its own rules to decide such issues even if the case has foreign contacts and even if many issues in the case will be decided by reference to the local law of another state. The forum is more concerned with how its judicial machinery functions and how its court processes are administered than is any other state . . . .
>
> Parties do not usually give thought to matters of judicial administration before they enter into legal transactions. They do not usually place reliance on the applicability of the rules of a particular state to issues

that would arise only if litigation should become necessary. Accordingly, the parties have no expectations as to such eventualities, and there is no danger of unfairly disappointing their hopes by applying the forum's rules in such matters.

Enormous burdens are avoided when a court applies its own rules, rather than the rules of another state, to issues relating to judicial administration, such as the proper form of action, service of process, pleading, rules of discovery, mode of trial and execution and costs. Furthermore, the burdens the court spares itself would have been wasted effort in most instances, because usually the decision in the case would not be altered by applying the other state's rules of judicial administration . . . .

The "enormous burden" rationale is most apparent when the forum uses its own rules on pleading, discovery, and motion practice; consider how inconvenient it would be for a Michigan court to learn Louisiana pleading and practice rules simply because a Louisiana tort found its way into a Michigan forum. Thus, the Restatement refers to forum law for issues relating to subject matter jurisdiction (§ 123), forms of action (§ 124), parties (§ 125) service of process (§ 126), pleadings (§ 127), mode of trial (§ 129), attachment garnishment and contempt (§ 130), and enforcement of judgments (§ 131). The lack of party expectations on these issues is also relevant. Note also that in these cases the reference to forum law is conclusive; there is no "most significant relationship" override.

The other principal rationale for the rule, the forum's paramount interest in the functioning of its judicial machinery, explains why the forum applies its own shorter statute of limitations. *See* Restatement (Second) § 142(1) (1986). Why should the forum subordinate its own interest in protecting its courts from stale litigation to the claim state's substantive-law goal?

(2) *Burdens and Presumptions.* The Restatement characterizes these issues as falling "into a gray area between issues relating primarily to judicial administration and those concerned primarily with the rights and liabilities of the parties." The Restatement's solution in §§ 133 and 134 is interest analytic in the sense that the purpose behind the relevant foreign rule is the deciding factor. Note, however, that in the case of a true conflict, the Restatement, unlike Currie, defers to the foreign state. Is that wise? Is it supported by a "relative commitment" (see § 4.18, *supra*) argument?

(3) *Evidence.* The "enormous burden" rationale explains § 138's reference to forum law to control admissibility of evidence. The trial judge must rule promptly on evidentiary objections, so it makes sense for her to rely on the forum's familiar rules rather than having to learn a new set of rules whenever foreign substantive law applies. *See* § 138, comment a. The argument applies *a fortiori* in areas where evidentiary doctrine is complicated, such as hearsay and the best evidence rule.

The reference to forum law, however, does not control all evidence issues. For instance, although forum law supplies the standard for logical relevance, the otherwise applicable foreign substantive law necessarily controls which issues are material ("of consequence" in the language of Fed. R. Evid. 401) by specifying the elements of the parties' claims and defenses. *See* § 138, comment b. Further the Restatement sensibly treats two pseudo-evidence issues, the parol evidence rule and the statute of frauds, as matters of contract law to be controlled by §§ 187 and 188. *See* §§ 140 and 141.

(4) *Privilege*. Section 139 provides special treatment for privilege questions because privilege rules differ fundamentally from other rules of evidence. The function of most evidence rules is to enhance the truth-seeking process. By contrast, privilege rules deliberately subordinate truth seeking to some other policy goal, usually the protection or fostering of a valued relationship. The hearsay rule, for example, excludes a category of evidence because it is typically unreliable, and thus harmful to the truth seeking process. The privilege for spousal communications, on the other hand, sacrifices whatever probative help the confidential communication could offer in order to protect marriage and foster confidential communications between spouses. CHRISTO-PHER B. MUELLER AND LAIRD C. KIRKPATRICK, EVIDENCE §§ 5.1 and 5.34 (1995).

Section 139's treatment of conflict of privilege rules is one of the Second Restatement's few "substantivist" provisions. Such rules, of which the principle of validation is an example, use the preference for a particular substantive result as a choice-of-law device. Thus, § 139 chooses between the privilege rules of the forum and those of the state with the most significant relationship with the communication based upon which law will admit the evidence.

This value preference, is consistent with the general principle of evidence law that privilege rules should be construed narrowly because they deprive the court and the parties of probative evidence. In the words of the Supreme Court, "privileges contravene the fundamental principle that the public . . . has a right to every man's evidence." Thus they should be recognized "only to the very limited extent that permitting a refusal to testify or excluding relevant evidence has a public good transcending the normally predominant principle of utilizing all rational means for ascertaining truth." *Trammel v. United States*, 445 U.S. 40, 50 (1980), *United States v. Nixon*, 418 U.S. 683, 710 (1974). *See also* MICHAEL H. GRAHAM, HANDBOOK OF FEDERAL EVIDENCE § 501.1 (4th ed. 1996).

Interest analytic arguments also justify the value preference of § 139. The rule does not consider false conflicts because, in order to generate a false conflict, the forum must also be the state with the most significant relationship to the communication, and the result in such a case is so obvious as not to be treated as a choice-of-law problem at all. Section 139 (2) contemplates a true conflict between the forum's law admitting the evidence and the foreign law permitting the privilege. Interest analysis usually will not require the forum to sacrifice its own truth-seeking policy to the relationship-protecting policy of the foreign state.

Section 139 (1) contemplates an unprovided-for case where the evidence is privileged under forum law but not under the law of the place with the most significant relationship with the communication. Excluding the evidence will not advance the relationship-protecting policy of the forum, nor will admitting the evidence further the truth-seeking policy of the foreign state. However, the forum will have a residual truth-seeking policy in every case in its courts, and admission of the evidence will advance this policy.

(5) *The* Erie *Provisions of the Federal Rules of Evidence.* In civil cases where state law provides the rule of decision, Fed. R. Evid. 302, 501, and 601, call for the federal court to apply state law on issues of presumption rebuttal, privilege, and competence of witnesses, thus treating these three issues as substantive for *Erie* purposes. For choice-of-law purposes, however, Restatement (Second) § 137 always, and §§ 134 and 139 often, apply the law of the forum to those issues. Does the inconsistency trouble you, or are the policy justifications for the *Erie* rule, on the one hand, and the use of forum law in choice-of-law cases, on the other, sufficiently different to justify the discrepancy?

(6) *Lose the Labels?* With regard to the question in the preceding note, consider § 122 comment b, which advises:

> The courts have traditionally approached issues falling within the scope of the rule of this Section by determining whether the particular issue was "procedural" and therefore to be decided in accordance with the forum's local law rule, or "substantive" and therefore to be decided by reference to the otherwise applicable law. These characterizations, while harmless in themselves, have led some courts into unthinking adherence to precedents that have classified a given issue as "procedural" or "substantive", regardless of what purposes were involved in the earlier classifications. Thus, for example, a decision classifying burden of proof as "procedural" for local law purposes, such as in determining the constitutionality of a statute that retroactively shifted the burden, might mistakenly be held controlling on the question whether burden of proof is "procedural" for choice-of-law purposes. To avoid encouraging errors of that sort, the rules stated in this Chapter do not attempt to classify issues as "procedural" or "substantive". Instead they face directly the question whether the forum's rule should be applied.

Do you approve of the drafters' decision to lose the labels, or are they sufficiently convenient, and the dangers of misuse sufficiently obvious to justify their retention?

## § 4.32 Property

### [A] Land

### § 223. Validity and Effect of Conveyance of Interest in Land

(1) Whether a conveyance transfers an interest in land and the nature of the interest transferred are determined by the law that would be applied by the courts of the situs. [renvoi]

(2) These courts would usually apply their own local law in determining such questions.

## § 236. Intestate Succession to Land

(1) The devolution of interests in land upon the death of the owner intestate is determined by the law that would be applied by the courts of the situs.

(2) These courts would usually apply their own local law in determining such questions.

## § 239. Validity and Effect of Will of Land

(1) Whether a will transfers an interest in land and the nature of the interest transferred are determined by the law that would be applied by the courts of the situs.

(2) These courts would usually apply their own local law in determining such questions.

## NOTES AND QUESTIONS ON THE SECOND RESTATEMENT'S PROVISIONS FOR ISSUES INVOLVING LAND

(1) *The Situs Rule.* The situs rule is probably the broadest and most rigid of all the choice-of-law provisions of the Second Restatement. It extends to all questions involving *inter vivos* conveyances (including validity as well as construction), transfers by operation of law encumbrances, powers, marital property, equitable interests, and succession on death. Further, the drafters allow it to trump many of the values included in the principles of § 6. Thus, the law of the situs controls even when it thwarts powerful state interests, see §§ 237, 238 (legitimacy and adoption as affecting succession to land) and §§ 233, 234, 241, 242 (marital property and surviving spouse's interest in decedent's estate), or frustrates the parties' expectations, see §§ 224, 236, 240 (construction of wills and conveyances of land), and § 239 (intestate succession).

(2) *Rationales for the Situs Rule.* The drafters offer two priniocpal justifications for the situs rule.

(a) *The Situs State's Interest in Issues Involving Situs Land.* Restatement (Second) §223, Comment b states:

> [The courts of the situs] would apply their own law to determine issues in which the situs has the dominant interest. Examples of such issues are who may own the land, the conditions under which land may be held and the uses to which land may be put. So these courts would apply their own local law to determine what restrictions, if any, are imposed upon the ownership of land by a corporation or by an alien and the period during which the power to alienate interests in land may be suspended. These courts would also apply their local law to determine such issues as whether the land must be used for residential purposes only or whether it can be put to a commercial use.

The drafters recognized, however, that a non-situs state might have the dominant interest with respect to some issues:

There may . . . be occasions when the courts of the situs would apply the local law of another state on the ground that the concern of that other state in the decision of the particular issue is so great as to outweigh the values of certainty and convenience which would be served by application of the local law of the situs. So the situs courts might apply the local law of the state of the spouses' domicil to determine certain issues involving the conveyance of interests in local land from one spouse to the other, and this is particularly likely to be so when the land is one item in an aggregate of things . . . which are situated in a number of states and which it is desirable to deal with as a unit.

*Id.*

Statements like the second quoted passage appear throughout the comments to the property sections, especially those governing issues where the interest of the non-situs state is obvious and compelling. *See, e.g.,* §§ 233, 241 (rights of one spouse in other's land; state of marital domicile may have greater interest), § 236 (intestate succession; state of common domicile of decedent and heirs may have greater interest), § 240 (will construction; construction of will according to law of state of testator's domicile more likely to carry out testator's intentions). The result is that the Second Restatement's treatment of land issues has a schizophrenic quality. The comments to many sections feature subtle and nuanced interest-analytic discussions that are sensitive to the particular issue involved; by contrast, the black letter of section after section calls for the simple-minded application of the law of the situs. Is such ambivalence likely to guide the courts or confuse them? Perhaps the ambivalence results from the conflict between the descriptive and prescriptive functions of a restatement; in other words, the drafters recognized both the courts' universal application of the situs rule and the failure of the rule's interest-analytic justification.

For commentary on this justification for the situs rule, see Russell Weintraub, Commentary on the Conflict of Laws 551 (4th ed. 2001); Moffatt Hancock, *Full Faith and Credit to Foreign Laws and Judgments in Real Property Litigation: the Supreme Court and the Land Taboo,* 18 STAN. L. REV. 1299 (1966).

(b) *Recording Statutes.* The drafters also justify the situs rule even in cases where the situs does not have the dominant interest:

In the normal course of events, transactions involving land are not entered into until considerable thought has been given by the parties and their lawyers to the possible consequences. This is an area where it is peculiarly important that there be certainty, predictability and uniformity of result and ease in the determination and application of the law to be applied. For these reasons, the courts of the situs would apply their own law in situations where it is likely that a person relied on the record title before entering into a transaction involving interests in local land. Likewise, considerations of convenience make it desirable that a prospective purchaser and his agents, such as draftsman and title searchers, need consult only a single law and that is the one with which they are most familiar.

*See* Restatement (Second) § 223 comment b.

Is this explanation adequate for the universal scope of the black letter? How does it justify application of the situs rule in cases where the contest is between two sets of gratuitous transferees, none of whom have relied on the recording statutes? *See In re Barrie's Estate,* § 4.08, *supra.* Clearly, application of non-situs law could not frustrate expectations of the parties in such a case. But could it lay a trap for unwary future purchasers of the land, who relied upon situs law in determining whether the grant to one set of gratuitous transferees was valid?

It is difficult to see how that could happen. The situation usually arises when a probate court orders the distribution of an estate (testate or intestate). Regardless of the law that it uses to determine the proper distribution, it typically orders the executor to make a deed, valid according to situs law, transferring the land to the prevailing contestant, who then records that instrument in the land records of the situs. A subsequent search would show the valid deed, and the searcher would not be misled. There would seldom, if ever, be an occasion for the searcher to consider the validity of the distribution itself, because the preclusive effect of the probate court's decision usually would settle that issue conclusively.[11]

For scholarly evaluation of this rationale for the situs rule see RUSSELL WEINTRAUB, CMMENTARY ON THE CONFLICT OF LAWS 414 (3d ed. 1986); Moffatt Hancock, *Conceptual Devices for Avoiding the Land Taboo in Conflict of Laws: The Disadvantages of Disingenuousness,* 20 STAN. L. REV. 1, 22-23 (1967), reprinted in MOFFATT HANCOCK, STUDIES IN MODERN CHOICE OF LAW: TORTS, INSURANCE, LAND TITLES 372 (1984).

(c) In addition to the functional reasons for the situs rule, the drafters cite "sentimental and historical reasons." *See* Restatement (Second) Chapter 9, Topic 2 Immovables, Introductory Note. If the functional justifications for the rule are inadequate, should sentiment and history be sufficient to sustain it?

(3) *Renvoi.* Note that the reference in each of the quoted sections is to "the law that would be applied by the courts of the situs," i.e., the whole law of the situs, and thus each section calls for application of the doctrine of renvoi. The drafters give the dominant interest of the situs state in land issues as the rationale for the use of renvoi. Will the situs as situs usually have the dominant interest? *See* Note 2(a), *supra.* Do any of the other usual rationales

---

[11] *But see* Restatement (Second) §§ 236 comment a, 239 comment f (in some states, probate court order does not conclusively determine heirship or validity of a particular devise in a will). In such a state, the hard-and-fast application of the situs rule would simplify title searching; otherwise, the searcher, unable to rely on the preclusive effect of the probate court order, would need to predict the ruling of a subsequent situs court on (1) the choice-of-law issue, i.e., should the validity of the distribution be judged by situs or non-situs law, and (2) the interpretation and application by the situs court of the unfamiliar non-situs law. That is too much to expect from a title searcher.

Yet from the point of view of law reform, does it make sense to allow this oddity of preclusion law (limited preclusive effect for probate decrees in some states) to dictate the universal application of a choice-of-law rule that often subverts the interests of non-situs state and frustrates the parties' intentions. It would make more sense to advocate the retirement of this odd exception to the normal rule of preclusion.

for the doctrine of renvoi justify the situs rule? Review the materials in § 4.13, *supra*.

(4) It has been almost thirty years since the American Law Institute adopted the Second Restatement, and the First Restatement was less than 20 years old when drafting began on its successor. Is it time to begin drafting a Third Restatement? See Symposium, 57 IND. L. J. 1 (1999). One commentary in that symposium suggested the following replacement for the current Restatement's choice-of-law provisions for land issues:

## § 223. The General Principle

(1) Except as provided in § 223A, the rights and liabilities of the parties with respect to an issue involving title to immovable property are determined by the law of the state which, with respect to that issue, has the most significant relationship to the property and the parties under the principles stated in § 6.

(2) Contacts to be taken into account in applying the principles of § 6 to determine the applicable law include:

   (a)   the situs of the immovable property,

   (b)   the domicile, residence, nationality, place of incorporation, and place of business of the parties,

   (c)   the place where any relevant transaction involving the immovable occurred.

These contacts are to be evaluated with regard to their relative importance to the particular issue and the policies behind the competing internal laws.

## § 223A. The Law of the Situs of the Immovable Property

Notwithstanding the principle of § 223, the rights and liabilities of the parties with respect to an issue involving title to immovable property are determined by the whole law of the situs of the immovable if,

   (1) Application of the law of a state other than the situs would disadvantage a party that relied reasonably on the law of the situs in conducting a title search or evaluating its results.

   (2) Enforcement of the order of the court is likely to be impossible unless the court applies the law of the situs.

*See* William Richman and William Reynolds, *Prolegomenon to an Empirical Restatement of Conflicts*, 57 IND. L.J. 117, 126 (1999). Does the proposal remedy the defects of the current provision?

## [B]  Movable Property

## § 244 Validity and Effect of Conveyance of Interest in Chattel

(1) The validity and effect of a conveyance of an interest in a chattel as between the parties to the conveyance are determined by the local law of the state

which, with respect to the particular issue, has the most significant relationship to the parties, the chattel and the conveyance under the principles stated in § 6.

(2) In the absence of an effective choice of law by the parties, greater weight will usually be given to the location of the chattel, or group of chattels, at the time of the conveyance than to any other contact in determining the state of the applicable law.

## § 258. Interests in Movables Acquired during Marriage

(1) The interest of a spouse in a movable acquired by the other spouse during the marriage is determined by the local law of the state which with respect to the particular issue, has the most significant relationship to the spouses and the movable under the principles stated in § 6.

(2) In the absence of an effective choice of law by the spouses, greater weight will usually be given to the state where the spouses were domiciled at the time the movable was acquired than to any other contact in determining the state of the applicable law.

## § 260 Intestate Succession to Movables

The devolution of interests in movables upon intestacy is determined by the law that would be applied by the courts of the state where the decedent was domiciled at the time of his death.

## § 263 Validity and Effect of Will of Movables

(1) Whether a will transfers an interest in movables and the nature of the interest transferred are determined by the law that would be applied by the courts of the state where the testator was domiciled at the time of his death.

(2) These courts would usually apply their own local law in determining such questions.

## NOTES AND QUESTIONS ON THE SECOND RESTATEMENT'S TREATMENT OF MOVABLE PROPERTY

(1) *Relation to the Uniform Commercial Code.* One purpose of the Uniform Commercial Code was to produce uniformity in commercial law among the states, and the Code's success has minimized choice-of-law problems involved in non-gratuitous transactions of movables. Nevertheless, there are a few remaining issues because the official version of the Code contains alternative choices for several sections; the official version has changed over time, and not all the states have adopted each set of changes; state legislatures have enacted variations in their own Codes; and judicial interpretation of uniform sections can vary from state to state. The variations, however, are relatively minor, and have not yet caused significant controversy.

The Code deals with choice of law on the issues where there is interstate variation in two principal sections: § 1-105 and § 9-103. These sections are treated in § 4.30, *infra. See also* WILLIAM M. RICHMAN AND WILLIAM L. REYNOLDS, UNDERSTANDING CONFLICT OF LAWS § 92 (2002).

(2) *Marital Property.* Sections 257-259 of the Second Restatement deal with choice-of-law problems between common law and community property states. In common law states, a spouse does not have an interest in property acquired during the marriage by the other spouse; rather, each spouse owns property individually subject only to a forced share for the other spouse at death and a divorce court's right to distribute the assets of both spouses equitably. In community property states, each spouse owns an undivided one-half interest in all assets acquired during the marriage. For choice between the two regimes, § 258 calls for the application of the law of the state with the most significant relationship to the spouses and the property, and then specifies that the most important contact will usually be the state where the spouses were domiciled at the time the movable was acquired. The rationale for the choice is state interest and uniformity. The state of domicile will have the greatest interest in the spouses and their rights in each other's property, and it is desirable that marital property interests in movables should be governed by a single law rather than the law of the situs of each movable.

For reasons of fairness and convenience, § 259 provides that a spouse's interest in the other spouse's movable property is not affected by the mere removal of the property to a second state or a change in the spouses' common domicile. Section 257 deals with the effect of a marriage on existing interests in movables owned by one of the spouses. This question arises only between American states and foreign nations because no state of the United States vests an interest in one spouse in the pre-existing movable property of the other on the occasion of the marriage.

For more on these issues, see EUGENE SCOLES ET AL., CONFLICT OF LAWS 588-604 (3d ed. 2000).

(3) *Succession on Death.* Sections 260 and 263 apply the law of the state where the decedent was domiciled to questions of descent and distribution of movable property. The comments cite state interest, protection of justified expectations, certainty, predictability, uniformity of result, and ease in application as the rationale for the rule. *See* RESTATEMENT (SECOND) OF CONFLICT OF LAWS § 260, comment b.

Uniformity is the reason for the use of the doctrine of renvoi in these two sections; it is desirable that an estate pass as a unit, rather than being distributed according to several different schemes. Suppose, for instance, a citizen of the United States, domiciled in France, owns movable property in the United States and France. Suppose further that the French choice-of-law rule for intestacy selects the decedent's nationality and that the appropriate American state's rule selects the law of decedents domicile. If the French courts will distribute the French property according to the American scheme, and the American court does not use renvoi, it will distribute the American property according to the French scheme, thus thwarting the goal of uniformity. If, instead, the American court follows § 260, it will distribute the American property according to the law that would be applied by the French court, i.e., the intestacy law of the appropriate American state; and the entire estate will pass as a unity.

Uniformity presumably is part of the rationale for the choice of the decedent's domicile as well as for the use of renvoi. An obvious alternative reference would be the place of the movable at the time of death, but that would result in a nonuniform distribution of the estate not to mention a constant temptation to potential heirs to engage in self help by moving property as their loved ones lay dying. The protection of party expectations also enters into the calculation. The case is clearest for the validity of a will. The testator probably expected the law of domicile to control and relied on the advice of counsel in that state. But expectations matter for intestacy, as well. A state's intestacy law fashions a will for a decedent who has neglected to do so. The legislature, with concern for local family customs and relations, selects a pattern of distribution that would coincide with the wishes of the "average testator." Presumably the legislature at the decedent's domicile is best situated to perform that task. *See* Moffat Hancock, Equitable Conversion and the Land Taboo in Conflict of Laws, 70 STAN. L. REV. 1095 (1965), reprinted in MOFFAT HANCOCK, STUDIES IN MODERN CHOICE OF LAW: TORTS, INSURANCE, LAND TITLES 313 (1984).

Comment b to § 260 also cites state interest as a reason for the decedent's-domicile rule. Often the decedent's domicile will have the dominant interest, but not always. Typically the decedent's domicile will also be the situs of the movable and the domicile of many of those with competing claims to the estate. Will the state of the decedent's domicile have the dominant interest, however, when that is its only contact, and all other contacts are concentrated in some other state?

Further, there will be some cases where the decedent's-domicile rule will produce dysfunctional results. When the finding of domicile is based upon the special rules for students, prisoners, or military personnel or upon the technical rules for acquisition of a new domicile of choice (decedent's momentary presence in the new domicile sufficient), the state of domicile may have no strong interest. *See White v. Tenant, supra* at § 4.09 [B]. In such a case, will any of the other reasons for the rule—party expectations, uniformity, certainty and ease of application—supply an adequate justification?

# PART H   SOME ILLUSTRATIONS OF MODERN CHOICE-OF-LAW METHODS

*Introductory Note.* Choice-of-law theory today is obviously a "well-watered plateau," to use Professor Leflar's famous phrase. But the courts are in even more disagreement than the scholars, for, unlike most academics, some judges cling tenaciously to the discredited precepts of the Bealean Rules. They do so for a number of reasons, among them innate conservatism and an appreciation of the surface logic of First Restatement geometry. Part of the reluctance to change also stems from fear of the chaos that some believe the new methods of analysis have brought with them. Other judges, however, have felt free to experiment with modern methods, using Currie, Leflar, and the Second Restatement at various times, selecting the method which appears to be most suitable for the case at bar. Often all three are used at the same time.

Choice of law today, especially in tort, reflects the many hands on the tiller. A reader who has journeyed through the preceding sections of this Chapter knows the prevailing eclecticism all too well. Professor Juenger once wrote that most tort choice-of-law problems would disappear as obsolete law dealing with charitable immunity, guest statutes, and contributory negligence—the subject of many modern choice-of-law cases—was eliminated. *See* Friedrich Juenger, *Choice of Law in Interstate Torts,* 118 U. PA. L. REV. 202 (1969). But tort law is always evolving, and the laws of the states differ significantly today on such important tort issues as limits on recovery for pain and suffering, medical malpractice litigation, and products liability. Choice-of-law problems in torts, in other words, will not disappear, a fact readily apparent to anyone who reads the superb Annual Surveys of American choice of law which appear in the American Journal of Comparative Law. (Most of the Surveys have been written by Dean Symeon Symeonides; others have been written by Professors Borchers, Kozyris, Kramer, and Solimine.)

In this Part of the Chapter we examine choice-of-law problems today in three additional areas—property, contracts, and statutes of limitation.

## § 4.33   Property

### WILLIAMS v. WILLIAMS

*District of Columbia Court of Appeals*
*390 A.2d 4 (1978)*

PER CURIAM: This is an appeal from the court-ordered conveyance of appellant's interest in certain real property located in Maryland to appellee pursuant to an award of absolute divorce on the ground of desertion. [The parties had lived in the District of Columbia, and the couple had been divorced there. At the time of the divorce, the appellant lived in the District, and the appellee lived in Maryland] . . . .

The real property at issue, 2007 Hannon Street, Lewisdale, Maryland, was purchased by and through the sole contribution of husband one month before the wife's desertion although title was placed in joint ownership of the two parties as tenants by the entirety . . . .

The law of Maryland differs from that of the District of Columbia upon the question of the resolution of property interests between tenants by the entirety upon divorce. In this jurisdiction, the creation of a tenancy by the entirety in property acquired through the sole contribution of one spouse is a gift conditioned upon fulfillment of the marital vows and continuance of the married state. Thus desertion by a spouse and subsequent divorce upon those grounds may result in a divestiture of the conditional gift of a half interest in the property in the favor of the innocent spouse purchaser.

Under Maryland law, in the absence of proof that the acquisition as tenants by the entirety was not a voluntary act, the transaction is presumed to create an absolute gift of a one-half interest in the nonpaying spouse, and the courts will not inquire into the respective contributions of the parties or attempt an apportionment. Given the conflict in the law of the District of Columbia and Maryland, we must determine what law controls the resolution of the property interest in this case.

The District of Columbia has followed the recent trend adopting the "governmental interest analysis" approach to resolve choice-of-law questions . . . .

In our case, both parties had moved into Maryland upon purchase of the disputed property as a marital abode. The District of Columbia only obtained jurisdiction over this case because the wife deserted her husband and moved into the District, where the husband then sued for divorce. The District can have scant interest in insisting upon the application of its policy toward an innocent purchaser spouse to protect a Maryland resident when Maryland real property will be affected and that state has expressed such a strong interest in land title stability and would not protect the innocent spouse. Since "the only relationship of the District of Columbia to this claim is that it provides a forum with jurisdiction over [appellant], [t]hat is hardly a reason for the forum to prefer its own notions of policy to those embodied in the [Maryland] law . . . ." [citation omitted] We hold that Maryland law should have been applied by the trial court to the resolution of the interest in Maryland real estate between the parties . . . .

---

## NOTES AND QUESTIONS

(1) The court treats the problem before it as a false conflict (although it does not use the term). Do you agree with that analysis? The case concerned property held by a tenancy in the entirety, but bought wholly by one of the spouses. Do you agree that the relevant interests involve the family relationship (District of Columbia law) and not "land title stability" (Maryland law)?

(2) *Williams* is an unusual case. It is rare to find an opinion involving choice of law in real property which does not routinely recite and apply the law of the situs. Indeed, one commentator has said of the *Williams* decision that "[i]t

is, perhaps, as far as any court has gone toward questioning the traditional conflicts rule of property." Smith, *Choice of Law in the United States,* 38 HASTINGS L.J. 1041, 1064 (1987). Professor Reese applauds the conservatism of American courts in retaining the situs rule, *A Suggested Approach to Choice-of-Law,* 14 VT. L. REV. 1, 4 (1989), while Professor Weintraub deplores the lack of change in Russell Weintraub, Commentary on the Conflict of Laws 460 (3d ed. 1986). *See generally* Michael S. Finch, *Choice of Law and Property,* 26 STETSON L. REV. 257 (1996).

(3) Why do you think there has been such a profound absence of development in the property area? Is it because the First Restatement had something important to say about property questions? Or is the lack of change simply due to the common law's traditional conservatism when dealing with land? Have conflicts rules in these cases become "rules of property"?

*See* PROBLEMS 4H-1. IF AT FIRST YOU DON'T SUCCEED; 4H-2. IS EXERCISE GOOD FOR YOU?; 4H-3. PERPETUITIES; 4H-4. ESCHEAT; 4H-5. THE BANK SHARES; 4H-6. WHO IS DURPHY? WHERE IS DURPHY?; 4H-7. GREEN STAMPS.

## § 4.34 Contracts

### [A] Introduction

Much disagreement remains concerning the proper method of resolving true conflicts in contract cases. *See* Symeon C, Symeonides, *Choice of Law in the American Courts in 1999: Twelfth Annual Survey,* 48 AM. J. OF COMP. L.143, 145-46 (2000) (chart listing methodologies used in all fifty states). Nevertheless, there is "general agreement," as Professor Reese writes, "that protection of justified expectations is the basic policy underlying contract law. Willis L. M. Reese, A *Suggested Approach to Choice-of-Law,* 14 VT. L. REV. 1, 17 (1990). This Part considers how that "basic policy" works in one area of practice.

### [B] Party Autonomy

#### TELE-SAVE MERCHANDISING CO. v. CONSUMERS DISTRIBUTING CO.

*United States Court of Appeals for the Sixth Circuit*
*814 F.2d 1120 (1987)*

BOYCE F. MARTIN, JR., CIRCUIT JUDGE.

Tele-Save was an Ohio corporation with its principal place of business in Columbus, Ohio. Consumers is a Canadian corporation with an office in New Jersey. In early 1981, the parties began negotiation of an agreement whereby Consumers, a large chain of catalog showroom operators, would supply products and services to Tele-Save. Tele-Save would in turn operate as a catalog retail showroom under the direction of Consumers. An agreement was reached in late July 1981. Paragraph 17 of the agreement reads:

This Agreement shall be governed by, and construed in accordance with, the laws of the State of New Jersey.

Tele-Save opened its store in late September 1981 offering for sale general merchandise received from Consumers and from other suppliers who advertised in the Consumers catalog. In January 1982, Consumers notified Tele-Save that it was canceling its catalog program. Tele-Save asked Consumers to reimburse the cost of merchandise purchased through the agreement and to accept its return. Consumer's refusal prompted this lawsuit.

Count one of Tele-Save's complaint, and the only issue presented on this appeal, charged Consumers with violating Ohio's Business Opportunity Plans Act. The Act, which took effect in October 1979, regulates the sale of business opportunity plans and provides certain rights and remedies for Ohio purchasers who are defrauded by dishonest or negligent sellers. Specifically, Tele-Save alleged Consumers violated section 1334.02 by failing to provide a written disclosure statement in connection with the transaction, section 1334.03 by failing to make certain disclosures regarding potential sales, income, and profits, by making false and misleading statements, and by accepting a down payment in excess of twenty percent of the initial payment, and section 1334.06 for failing to give the required notice of cancellation and failing to follow specific procedures with regard to cancellation.

Consumers filed a motion for summary judgment arguing that the Ohio Act was inapplicable to its agreement with Tele-Save because paragraph 17 of the agreement stipulated that the contract would be governed by New Jersey law. Tele-Save opposed the motion, arguing that the contractual choice-of-law provision was ineffective because application of New Jersey law violated a fundamental public policy of Ohio and because Ohio had a materially greater interest in the resolution of the dispute than New Jersey. The district court granted the defendant's motion and never reached the merits of the claim of violations of the Act.

Federal courts sitting in diversity must apply the choice-of-law principles of the forum. *Klaxon Co. v. Stentor Elec. Mfg. Co.,* 313 U.S. 487 (1941). Accordingly, Ohio choice-of-law principles are applicable in this case.

The Ohio Supreme Court in considering the deference to give contractual choice-of-law provisions has adopted the guidelines of the Restatement (Second) of Conflict of Laws, § 187(2) (1971):

> The law of the state chosen by the parties to govern their contractual rights and duties will be applied, even if the particular issue is one which the parties could not have resolved by an explicit provision in their agreement directed to that issue, unless either
>
> > (a) the chosen state has no substantial relationship to the parties or the transaction and there is no other reasonable basis for the parties' choice, or
> >
> > (b) application of the law of the chosen state would be contrary to a fundamental policy of a state which has a materially greater interest than the chosen state in the determination of the particular issue and which, under the rule of § 188, would be the state of the

applicable law in the absence of an effective choice of law by the parties.

Ohio's receptivity to contractual choice-of-law was further discussed in the recent decision of *Jarvis v. Ashland Oil, Inc.,* 17 OHIO ST.3d 189 (1985). In *Jarvis,* the Ohio Supreme Court held that "where the parties to a contract have made an effective choice of the forum law to be applied, Restatement Section 187(2), will not be applied to contravene the choice of the parties as to the applicable law." *Id.* at 192. The court then added a narrow limitation to this rule: "[W]here the law of the chosen state sought to be applied is concededly repugnant to and in violation of the public policy of [Ohio], that law of Ohio will only be applied when it can be shown that [Ohio] has a materially greater interest than the chosen state in the determination of the particular issue." *Id.*

These recent comments by the Ohio Supreme Court indicate that Ohio choice-of-law principles strongly favor upholding the chosen law of the contracting parties. We see no reason to disturb the parties' choice absent the application of another state's law that would be concededly repugnant to Ohio public policy.

Tele-Save contends that the contractual choice-of-law provision should be ignored in this case and that Ohio law should be applied because of a non-waiver provision found in the Ohio Business Opportunity Plans Act. Section 1334.15 of the Act states:

> The remedies of sections 1334.01 to 1334.15 of the Revised Code are in addition to remedies otherwise available for the same conduct under federal, state, or local law. Any waiver by a purchaser of sections 1334.01 to 1334.15 of the Revised Code is contrary to public policy and is void and unenforceable.

Tele-Save argues that because the Ohio legislature chose to adopt the Act, including section 1334.15, we must infer that the application of another state's law would be contrary to a fundamental public policy of Ohio and that Ohio has a materially greater interest in the resolution of the conflict. We are unwilling to make these assumptions.

In order to find the first prong satisfied, we would have to find both that the Ohio statute represents *fundamental* state policy and that the parties' chosen law would be contrary to this fundamental policy. There is no hard and fast rule to determine when a state policy will be considered "fundamental." The Restatement suggests a few guidelines. For example, courts may consider a policy "fundamental" when a large number of significant contacts are grouped in the forum state as opposed to the chosen state. Restatement (Second) of Conflict of Laws, § 187 comment g (1971). In the present case, we might observe that there is no heavy concentration of significant contacts in Ohio, rather the contacts are fairly evenly divided between New Jersey and Ohio.

The Restatement also suggests that a statute may embody a "fundamental" state policy if it is "designed to protect a person against the oppressive use of superior bargaining power [as, for example, in a statute] involving the rights of an individual insured as against an insurance company . . . ." *Id.* We think it important to our decision that the parties to this contract were not of unequal bargaining strength. Their contract was freely negotiated by aggressive and successful business executives, untainted by the suspicion and misgivings characteristic of adhesion contracts. Thus, we are unable to conclude that the Ohio Business Opportunity Plans Act represents a fundamental policy of Ohio.

Further, even if we were to concede that the Ohio statute represents fundamental public policy, we are unpersuaded that the application of New Jersey law would be contrary to this policy. Both parties agree that New Jersey does not have a statute which is identical to the Ohio Act. One may not determine conclusively from this omission, however, that the application of New Jersey law would be contrary to Ohio policy. Tele-Save acknowledges that there are also common law remedies available under New Jersey law. In its original complaint, Tele-Save alleged claims for breach of contract and fraud. It is not sufficient for Tele-Save to argue nor would we hold that Ohio law should be applied merely because a different result would be reached under New Jersey law. Restatement (Second) of Conflict of Laws, § 187 comment g (1971). In order for the chosen state's law to violate the fundamental policy of Ohio, it must be shown that there are significant differences in the application of the law of the two states. *Barnes Group, Inc. v. C & C Products, Inc.*, 716 F.2d 1023, 1031 n.19 (4th Cir. 1983) (Ohio law regarding restrictive covenants not applied to a state that prohibits such covenants). We find nothing under the facts before us to indicate that application of New Jersey law would be repugnant to or clearly contrary to the public policy of Ohio. Because we find the first prong of the Restatement, section 187(2)(b) analysis to be unsatisfied, we need not address the question of whether Ohio has a materially greater interest than New Jersey in the outcome of this dispute.

As an alternative argument, Tele-Save asks that we find section 1334.15 of the Act to be a statutory directive regarding Ohio choice-of-law. Tele-Save bases its argument on section 6(1) of the Restatement (Second) of Conflict of Laws which reads: "A court, subject to constitutional restrictions, will follow a statutory directive of its own state on choice of law." Tele-Save contends that if we accept the section 6(1) Restatement argument, we need not engage in the section 187(2)(b) analysis.

In support of its theory, Tele-Save cites *Turner v. Aldens, Inc.*, 179 N.J. Super. 596, 433 A.2d 438 (1981), in which a New Jersey court chose to apply the provisions of the New Jersey Retail Installment Sales Act rather than the parties' contractual choice of Illinois law. We think it significant that Turner involved adhesion contracts. The New Jersey court, in holding that failure to apply the statute would violate a fundamental policy of New Jersey, voiced concern that individual consumers had not freely chosen Illinois law to govern their contracts. To the contrary in the present case we have a freely negotiated contract between parties of relatively equal bargaining strength. We are unpersuaded that section 1334.15 of the Ohio Act should constitute a statutory directive on Ohio choice-of-law as to these parties.

For these reasons we find the Ohio Business Opportunity Plans Act inapplicable to this case. The decision of the district court is affirmed.

MILBURN, CIRCUIT JUDGE, dissenting.

Because I believe that the Ohio Business opportunity Purchasers Protection Act is applicable in the present case, I must respectfully dissent.

The issue presented is whether an out-of-state seller of business opportunity plans may avoid application of the Act by means of a contractual choice-of-law provision. The purpose of the Act is "to regulate the sale of business opportunity plans and [to provide] significant remedies 'to those who have been mislead by dishonest or negligent franchisers,'" *Peltier v. Spaghetti Tree, Inc.,* 6 Ohio St. 3d 194, 451 N.E.2d 1219, 1221 (1983) . . . .

Although Ohio courts accord considerable deference to contractual choice-of Law provisions, the extent to which Ohio courts will allow "deft draftsmanship" to override Ohio public policy and bypass legislative judgments is limited. Fulfillment of the parties' expectations is an important consideration in contract law, but "regard must also be had for state interests and state regulation." Restatement (Second) of Conflicts of Laws § 187 comment g (1971).

Ohio has a clearly expressed fundamental policy of protecting small, inexperienced purchasers of business opportunity plans from the unfair and misleading practices often utilized by economically superior sellers of business opportunity plans. *See Business Incentives Co. v. Sony Corp.,* 397 F.Supp. 63 (S.D.N.Y. (contractual choice of New York law unenforceable because it contravened New Jersey's statutory policy of protecting small investors from unfair franchise practices); Restatement (Second) of Conflict of Laws § 187 comments(1971)("a fundamental policy may be embodied in a statute . . . which is designed to protect a person against the oppressive use of superior bargaining power."). The Act implicitly recognizes that oftentimes individuals with little economic wealth or business experience are lured into purchasing business opportunity plans "by exaggerated profit claims made by sellers who fail to provide full and complete information regarding crucial aspects of the plan." Meaney, *Ohio's Business Opportunity Law. A Practical Guide,* 11 Ohio N.U. L. Rev. 651, 652 (1984). The fact that the Ohio legislature considered these protections fundamental is evidenced by the fact that Ohio provided criminal sanctions for violations of the Act.[1]

Moreover, Ohio has a clearly expressed fundamental policy of prohibiting enforcement of contractual choice-of-law provisions abrogating the protections afforded by the Act. *See Industrial Indemnity Insurance Co. v. United States, 757* F.2d 982 (9th Cir. 1985) (Idaho expressed a fundamental policy of strict adherence to the statute of limitations period by statutorily prohibiting any condition in a contract that would reduce the period); *Foiney Industries, Inc. v. Andre,* 246 F.Supp. 333 (D.N.D. 1965) (North Dakota expressed a fundamental policy against covenants not to complete by virtue of a statute which rendered contracts in restraint of trade void). Ohio Rev. Code § 1334.15 provides that "[a]ny waiver by a purchaser of sections 1334.01 to 1334.15 of

---

[1] The majority suggests that whether a state's policy is fundamental depends on the number of contacts the state has with the transaction. To the contrary, Restatement (Second) of Conflicts of Laws § 187 comment g (1971), provides only "that the more contacts the transaction has with the chosen state, the stronger the public policy must be to overcome the stipulation." Eugene Scoles & Peter Hay, Conflict of Laws § 18.9, at 648 (1984).

the Revised Code is contrary to public policy and is void and unenforceable." Moreover, Ohio Rev. Code § 1334.06(E)(2) provides that "no seller shall . . . [i]nclude in any agreement . . . any waiver of any rights to which the purchaser is entitled under sections 1334.01 to 1334.15 of the Revised Code . . . ."[2]

Ohio also has a "materially greater interest" in than New Jersey in resolution of this controversy . . . . Ohio's interests in applying its own law are to maintain its ability to regulate the sale of business opportunity plans within the state and to protect its citizens from dishonest or negligent franchisers. In my view, Ohio courts would hold that these interests materially outweigh any generalized interest New Jersey might have in applying its own law to protect the interstate contracts of its domiciliary.

Ohio would be the state of applicable law in the absence of an effective choice of law by the parties . . . .

Even if the choice-of-law provision is not "contrary to a fundamental policy of a state which has a materially greater interest than the chosen state," section 6(1) requires application of Ohio law. "Provided that it is constitutional to do so, the court will apply a local statute in the manner intended by the legislature even when the local law of another state would be applicable under usual choice-of-law principles." RESTATEMENT (SECOND) OF CONFLICTS OF LAWS § 6 comment b (1971). The Ohio legislature expressly intended the Act to apply to these facts, and this court, while functioning as an Ohio court for purposes of diversity, may not disregard the directions of the Ohio legislature. RESTATEMENT (SECOND) OF CONFLICTS OF LAWS § 6 comment a (1971).

---

## NOTES AND QUESTIONS

(1) Which opinion do you prefer? The majority primarily links the "fundamental policy" exception in § 187(b) with contracts of adhesion; is that convincing?. In other words, does contract law have "fundamental policies" other than the one of avoiding adhesion contracts? Why did Ohio adopt the Business Opportunity Plans Act? Was the sole purpose to prevent adhesion contracts, as the majority seems to suggest, or were there other goals?

The majority also observes that there are no "significant differences" between Ohio and New Jersey law; how well is that conclusion explained? Does the opinion deal any better with the statutory choice-of-law argument?

---

[2] The majority suggests that Ohio's policy of protecting small investors and prohibiting contractual waivers of rights provided in the Act is not implicated in the present case because Tele-Save and Consumers "were not of unequal bargaining strength.' To the contrary, Consumers was one of the largest chains of catalog showroom operations in the United States and Canada, while Tele-Save, having been capitalized with only a $150,000 investment, was seriously undercapitalized. This gross disproportionality in economic strength is not indicative of equal bargaining power.

The majority also suggests that Ohio's public policy would not be undermined by requiring Tele-Save to pursue New Jersey's common law fraud remedy. To the contrary, in the absence of a fiduciary relationship, nondisclosure does not constitute fraud under New Jersey law.

(2) Does the dissent get to the heart of the problem? Judge Milburn at least thought relevant the purpose behind the Ohio Act—to protect "individuals with little economic wealth or business experience . . . ." Do you find it helpful to identify the statute's purpose before determining how "fundamental" a policy is? If you like Judge Milburn's approach, do you agree with his conclusion?

## THE HISTORY OF PARTY AUTONOMY

Section 187 and its recognition of the concept of "party autonomy" has deep roots. It can be traced back to Lord Mansfield's opinion in *Robinson v. Bland,* 2 Burr. 1077 (1760), and in this country to a statement by Chief Justice Marshall in *Wayman v. Southard,* 23 U.S. (10 Wheat.) 1, 48 (1825), who endorsed" the principle . . . that in every forum a contract is governed by the law with a view to which it was made." The leading case is *Pritchard v. Norton,* 106 U.S. 124 (1882), an action in Louisiana on a bond executed in New York. The bond was invalid in New York, the place of making, because it was not supported by consideration; the contract was enforceable in Louisiana, where it was to be performed. The Court, in a labored opinion, applied Louisiana law, expressing, along the way, a preference for party autonomy:

> The law we are in search of . . . is that which the parties have, either expressly or presumptively, incorporated into their contract as constituting its obligation.

A few years later, in *Pinney v. Nelson,* 183 U.S. 144 (1901), the Court upheld a contract provision stipulating California law, a provision illegal under the law of Colorado, the state where the defendant was incorporated. The Court noted that ordinarily "the law of the place of incorporation would control, but that "it is also true that parties in making a contract may have in view some other law . . . and when that is so that other law will control."

Although the Supreme Court a hundred years ago apparently had no difficulty with the concept of party autonomy, Professor Beale did, and it should come as no surprise, therefore, that the Restatement (First) of Conflicts rejected the notion that parties can choose their own law. Beale explained: "The fundamental objection to this in point of theory is that it involves permission to the parties to do a legislative act. It practically makes a legislative body of any two persons who choose to get together and contract." 2 JOSEPH BEALE, CONFLICT OF LAWS 1079-80 (1935). The territorialist view concerning stipulated law had some respectable intellectual support, including Learned Hand's opinion in *E. Gerli & Co. Inc., v. Cunard S.S. Co. Ltd.,* 48 F.2d 115, 117 (2d Cir. 1931) ("People cannot by agreement substitute the law of another place . . . ."). Party autonomy was not laid to rest, however, and it soon returned to the courtroom.

*Lauritzen v. Larsen,* 345 U.S. 571 (1953), was probably the key decision. That case involved a Danish seaman, injured on a Danish vessel, who sought to recover under the Jones Act, even though the accident had not occurred in American waters. Although the sailor's contract had been entered into in New York, the contract expressly stated that Danish law would govern. After labeling the place of contracting a "fortuitous" contact with the United States,

Justice Jackson's opinion observed: "Except as forbidden by some public policy, the tendency of the law is to apply in contract matters the law which the parties intended to apply."

## PARTY AUTONOMY IN PRACTICE

Choice-of-law clauses are used widely today. Courts apply them routinely. Nevertheless, some problems survive the widespread acceptance of party autonomy.

(1) *Legislation or Interpretation?* Was there anything to the vested rights objection to the idea of party autonomy? When the parties choose a law to govern their transaction, are they "making law"? Is that kind of law-making any different from the "law" routinely made by contracting parties in a purely domestic situation? Or should the law distinguish between a choice-of-law clause which *defines* a term by referring to the law of a particular state,[1] and a clause stipulating a law which, as in *Tele-Save,* leads to a result different from that which at least one interested jurisdiction would reach? In the former case, which is merely one of construction, the parties to a purely domestic contract could reach the same result as the parties to a multi-state transaction; that would not be true in the latter instance, which is one of law-selection. Does this adequately explain why Beale did not like choice-of-law clauses?

(2) *Why do Parties Choose a Governing Law* ? Consistency and predictability, as we know, reduce risk, and, therefore, also reduce costs. A choice-of-law clause certainly can achieve those ends. Why else might parties use a choice-of-law clause? Does *Tele-Save* suggest an answer?

(3) *Fundamental Policies.* Section 187(2) of the Second Restatement states that a choice-of-law clause will not be enforced if it violates a "fundamental policy" of a state "with a materially greater interest." The *Tele-Save* majority identified the avoidance of contracts of adhesion as one fundamental policy which would obviate party autonomy. Are there other such policies, or is contract law today so consistent from state-to-state that there are no fundamental policy differences?

Consider *Haisten v. Grass Valley Medical Reimbursement Fund, Ltd,* 784 F.2d 1392 (9th Cir. 1986). There, a medical malpractice action resulted in an arbitration award of $185,000. After the physician's judgment debt was discharged in bankruptcy, plaintiff sued the doctor's insurance company for indemnification. A California statute expressly permitted such suits; the contract between the doctor and the insurer, however, provided that it would be controlled by the law of the Cayman Islands, which did not.

Judge Choy threw out the reference to Cayman Islands law: "Protection of California residents from the potential risk of injury thought to be created by insurance and from the unscrupulous practices of insurance companies which profit from premiums from California constitute sufficient interest to apply California law."

---

[1] *See* RESTATEMENT (SECOND) OF CONFLICT OF LAWS Section 187(l):

(1) The law of the state chosen by the parties to govern their contractual rights and duties will be applied if the particular issue is one which the parties could have resolved by an explicit provision in their agreement directed to that issue.

Was the judge right? Can you think of any other fundamental policies in the contract area which might cause a court to ignore stipulated law? An interesting example is *Application Group, Inc. v. Hunter Group, Inc.,* 61 Cal. App.4th 881, 72 Cal. Rptr. 2d 73 (Cal. App. 1998). The issue there was the enforceability of a non-compete clause in a contract which called for the application of Maryland law. The contract had been entered into in Maryland, but an injunction was sought in California to prevent an employee from working for a competitor there. A Maryland court would issue the injunction; a California court would not. The California court held that although Maryland had all of the contacts concerning the underlying contract, the key question was enforceability in California. With respect to *that* question, California had materially greater contacts, enforcement of the non-compete clause would violate a fundamental policy of California, and, therefore, the injunction would not issue.

(4) *The "Substantial Relationship" Test.* Section 187 requires that the stipulated law bear a "substantial relationship" with the chosen jurisdiction? What does that mean? The place of making (if it is not fortuitous) or the place of performance are two places which certainly satisfy that test. What other places might?

Why would the contracting parties ever choose a law which did not bear a substantial relationship to their transaction? Perhaps a neutral law becomes a necessary compromise when each party tries to stipulate its own law. Or perhaps the contract centers on a jurisdiction lacking a sophisticated jurisprudence (either generally or in a particular area) and it is desirable to provide for a body of well-known, well-developed law.

*See* PROBLEMS 4H-8. ARBITRATION CLAUSE; 4H-9. COVENANT NOT TO COMPETE; PROBLEM 4H-10. PESOS OR DOLLARS; PROBLEM 4H-11. AN INSURABLE INTEREST?; 4H-12. A FAMILY AFFAIR.

(5) *Jurisdiction Clauses and Choice-of-Law Clauses.* What is the relation between these two? Recall the discussion in Chapter 3, *supra,* of jurisdiction clauses. Recall also that in *The Bremen v. Zapata Off-Shore Co.,* 407 U.S. 1 (1972), the Court assumed that a court in England, the chosen forum, would apply its own law to the case. Does this mean that whatever limitations may exist on the use of choice-of-law clauses can be circumvented by using a jurisdiction clause? Finally, recall that in *Burger King Corp. v. Rudzewicz,* 471 U.S. 462 (1985), the Court bolstered its finding that the Florida courts could exercise jurisdiction by referring to the contractual stipulation of Florida law. Does all of this mean that contracting parties have been given considerable freedom to evade inconvenient laws which might otherwise govern their transactions?

(6) *Renvoi and Depeçage.* Does a contractual reference to "the law of Idaho" include a reference to Idaho's "whole law" (that is, Idaho law including its choice-of-law rules)? Does it include procedural law?

**FEDERAL DEPOSIT INS. CORP. v. PETERSEN,** 770 F.2d 141 (10th Cir. 1985): Suit by a federal entity to enforce guaranty contracts executed by defendants. The guarantees stated that they "shall be governed by the law of the State of Illinois." The district court had held the claims barred by the federal statute of limitations, and plaintiff argued on appeal for application of the longer Illinois statute of limitations.

BREITENSTEIN, J: "Choice of law provisions in contracts are generally understood to incorporate only substantive law, not procedural law such as statutes of limitation . . . Absent an express statement of intent, a standard choice of law provision such as this one will not be interpreted as covering a statute of limitations."

\* \* \*

See also RESTATEMENT (SECOND) OF CONFLICT OF LAW § 187, comment (h) (accord).

(7) *The Stupid Stipulation*. What happens when the parties stipulate to a law *which invalidates* the contract? This apparently happens more often than you would think; in fact, the Reporter's Note to § 187 only cites two cases where the stipulated law superseded forum law—and in both the law chosen invalidated the contract. *See A.S. Rampell, Inc. v. Hyster Co.,* 3 N.Y.2d 369, 165 N.Y.S.2d 475, 144 N.E.2d 371 (1957); and *Gen. Elec. Credit Corp. v. Beyerlein,* 55 Misc. 2d 724, 286 N.Y.S.2d 351(1967). A more recent example is *Kipin Inds. v. Van Deilen Int'l, Inc.,* 182 F.3d 490 (4th Cir. 1999). What should a court faced with this problem do? Why would this ever happen? Is this an example of mistake in integration which should lead a court to reform the contract? *See* RESTATEMENT (SECOND) OF CONTRACTS § 155. Or did the lawyers consider the application of the stipulated law in one area without recognizing its impact in others? Is there any other explanation? *See* comment e to § 187 for the solution.

(8) *The Tort Stipulation*. Can the parties stipulate the law to govern a tort? Most cases hold that the clause does not cover torts, *e.g., Krock v. Lipsay,* 97 F.3d 640 (2d Cir. 1996); *but see Lloyd v. Loeffler,* 694 F.3d 489 (7th Cir. 1982) (tort alleged was wrongful interference with custody of a child: "stipulation of Wisconsin law was reasonable here"; the court apparently viewed the problem as similar to that raised when the parties acquiesce in forum law); *Frizzell v. Constr. Co. v. Gatlinburg, L.L.C.,* 9 S.W.3d 79 (Tenn. 1999) (clause broad enough to include claims of fraudulent inducement). *Cf. Ezell v. Hayes Oiffield Constr. Co. Inc.,* 693 F.2d 489 (5th Cir. 1982), *cert. denied,* 464 U.S. 818 (1983) (court avoided question by finding agreement on the dispositive question—in other words, a false conflict—between the two possible states).

Does a stipulation regarding tort liability raise the same concerns as a contract stipulation?

(9) *New York's Long Grasp*. New York has done its best to make itself a haven for commercial interests by enacting a law which requires New York courts to enforce, with some exceptions, a provision stipulating New York law in contracts of more than $250,000 "whether or not the contract . . . bears a reasonable relation to this state." N.Y. GEN. OBLIG. LAW § 5-1401. Is the "whether or not" provision constitutional in light of *Allstate Ins. Co. v. Hague,* 449 U.S. 302 (1981), and *Phillips Petroleum Co. v. Shutts,* 472 U.S. 797 (1985), discussed in Chapter 5, *infra?* Can New York bootstrap itself into being an

"interested" jurisdiction in this fashion?[11] *See* Note, *Title 14, New York Choice of Law Rule for Contractual Disputes: Avoiding the Unreasonable Results,* 71 CORNELL L. REV. 227 (1985) (discussing possible constitutional problems).

(10) For further materials on party autonomy, see Kilboum & Winn, *The Rules of Construction in Choice-of-Law Cases in New York,* 62 ST. JOHN'S L. REV. 243 (1988); David Trautman, *Some Notes on the Theory of Choice of Law Clauses,* 35 MERCER L. REV. 535 (1984); Gruson, *Governing-Law Clauses in International and Inter-state Loan Agreements-New York's Approach,* 1982 U. ILL. L. REV. 207; Note, *Effectiveness of Choice-of-Law Clauses in Contract Conflict of Law: Party Autonomy or Objective Determination?,* 82 COLUM. L. REV. 1659 (1982).

## [C]   The Special Problem of Usury

Usury laws are one area of contracts in which state policies do differ widely. Maximum interest rates, the transactions to which they apply, and the severity of the penalties attached for violation, all reflect basic policy disagreement, some quite fundamental. Restatement (Second) of Conflict of Laws § 203 provides:

> The validity of a contract will be sustained against the charge of usury if it provides for a rate of interest that is permissible in a state to which the contract has a substantial relationship and is not greatly in excess of the rate permitted by the general usury law of the state of the otherwise applicable law under the rule of § 188.[*]

Section 203 builds on the leading case of *Seeman v. Philadelphia Warehouse. Co.,* 274 U.S. 403 (1927). *Seeman* involved a contract with both New York and Pennsylvania contacts; the contract was usurious under Pennsylvania law. Justice Stone wrote that it is "immaterial whether the contract was entered into in New York or Pennsylvania . . . ." Rather, quoting from an earlier case, Stone wrote, "If the rate of interest be higher at the place of the contract than at the place of performance the parties may lawfully contract in that case also for the higher rate."

What policies might explain usury laws? Are usury laws really just annoying technicalities? Do legislators really care about them? *See* WILLIAM RICHMAN & WILLIAM REYNOLDS, UNDERSTANDING CONFLICT OF LAWS § 72 (3d ed. 2002).

## [D]   Commercial Law

The Uniform Commercial Code represents an heroic effort to impose order on the commercial world. Unfortunately, the Code is not as "uniform" as it might be for there is more than one official version of a number of provisions, and many states have amended the Code in one way or another. Case law

---

[11] Section 5-1402 of the same law, applying to contracts to more than $1,000,000, permits parties who stipulate for the application of New York law to consent to the jurisdiction of New York courts. Constitutional? See *Burger King Corp. v. Rudzewicz,* 471 U.S. 462 (1985), and *The Bremen v. Zapata Off-Shore Co.,* 407 U.S. 1 (1972), both discussed in Chapter 3, *supra.*

[*] Copyright American Law Institute. Reprinted with permission.

has also created cracks in the Code's uniform facade. As a result, choice-of-law remains a problem in commercial transactions.

(1) *Generally.* The drafters of the Code were quite conscious of the need to deal with choice-of-law problems. The solutions they adopted resemble closely the contract provisions of the Second Restatement. Section 1-105(1) provides the basic rule:

> Except as provided hereafter in this section, when a transaction bears a reasonable relation to this state and also to another state or nation the parties may agree that the law either of this state or of such other state or nation shall govern their rights and duties. Failing such agreement this Act applies to transactions bearing an appropriate relation to this state.**

Although the Code does not define the term "appropriate relation," the Official Comment states that "the mere fact" that suit is brought in a particular state does not create an "appropriate" relation with the forum. More helpfully, the Comment suggests that party expectations may also bear on determining whether an appropriate relation exists, at least within the general goal of promoting uniformity in Code cases.

Second, the Code permits the parties to stipulate the law which will govern their transaction if the stipulated law "bears a reasonable relation" to the transaction. That test, comment 1 to § 1-105 states, "is similar to the one laid down by the Supreme Court in *Seeman v. Philadelphia Warehouse Company.*" The comment also states that the parties may sometimes choose the law of a jurisdiction "even though the transaction has no significant contact with the jurisdiction chosen."

Because Article 1 applies to the entire Code, these two provisions of § 1-105 control choice of law in the sale of goods, commercial paper, letters of credit, secured transactions, and virtually everything else covered by the Code. The final part of the § 1-105 framework, however, creates five exceptions to the two general rules. The most significant of these exceptions involves the provisions of Article 9, dealing with the perfection of security interests. *See generally* Ryan, *Reasonable Relation and Party Autonomy Under the Uniform Commercial Code,* 63 Marq. L. Rev. 219 (1979).

(2) *The Reasonable Relation Test.* Does § 1-105 adopt the same test for stipulating law as § 187 of the Second Restatement? Consider *Travenol Labs. Inc., v. Zotal, Ltd.,* 394 Mass. 95, 474 N.E.2d 1070 (1985). Suit by a seller of goods against its Israeli distributor. The buyer asserted a set-off, an assertion valid under Israeli law, but not under Massachusetts (Code) law.

Hennessey, C.J.: "Massachusetts law applies to 'transactions bearing an appropriate relation to this State.' . . . [E]stablished conflicts principles' are a useful starting point in determining whether the Commonwealth of Massachusetts bears an 'appropriate relation' to a given transaction or occurrence."

*See also Boudreau v. Baughman,* 368 S.E.2d 849 (N.C. 1988) (accord).

(3) *Possible Revisions.* The American Law Institute has circulated a "Discussion Draft" (2000) of possible changes to Article 1 of the UCC. That Draft

---

** Copyright American Law Institute. Reprinted with permission.

would replace the current choice-of-law provision, § 1-105, and create a new set of choice-of-law rules in § 1-301. The proposed rules provide:

a) In the absence of a valid contractual choice-of-law clause, the court should apply the forum's choice-of-law principles. An "appropriate relation" to the forum would no longer be necessary or sufficient. § 1-301 (a).

b) Substantial changes would be made concerning the effectiveness of choice-of-law clauses. In contacts not involving consumers, the parties would be given greater autonomy, but, at the same time, there would be safeguard against abuse. *See* the Reporter's Note to § 1-301.

c) If the contract does involve consumers, a designation of governing law is effective only if the designation is to the consumer's residence or to the place where the consumer will receive or use the goods or services. § 1-301(b).

Is § 1-301(b) constitutional? *See* Richard K. Greenstein, *Is the Proposed U.C.C. Choice of Law Provision Unconstitutional?*, 73 TEMPLE L. REV. 1159 (2000).

*See* PROBLEMS 4H-13. REPOSSESSION; 4H-14. SELECTING THE FORUM.

(4) *Other Provisions.* The Uniform Commercial Code contains a large number of specific choice-of-law provisions, dealing with such problems as where a financing statement must be filed in order to perfect a lender's security interest in movable property. These provisions are usefully and thoroughly discussed in Russell Weintraub, Commentary on the Conflict of Laws 470-511 (3d ed. 1986). Article 9, dealing with security interests, has recently been thoroughly revised and contains a number of choice-of-law provisions. *See* generally §§ 9-301-07.

(5) *Territorialism Revisited.* One aspect of the U.C.C. is of particular interest for our purpose: those who drafted the Code chose territorial solutions to choice-of-law problems. That is not surprising given that the Code was largely drafted in the 1950s, a time when the law of conflicts was still mesmerized by the territorialism of the First Restatement. The survival of those rules for more than thirty years, however, suggests that territorial-based rules can achieve the necessary combination of certainty of application, fairness, and policy necessary for widespread acceptance in practice. Of course, that raises two further questions:

a) Is there something special about the problems the UCC deals with that makes them peculiarly susceptible to territorial solutions?

b) What price has been paid for that certainty? That is, what interests of other states have been sacrificed at the altar of territorialism and certainty?

## [E] The United Nations Convention on Contracts for the International Sale of Goods

The dramatic growth in international trade in recent years has generated pressure to provide solutions to the resulting conflicts problems. The United

Nations Convention on Contracts for the International Sale of Goods provides legal rules to govern the sale of goods between a buyer and seller who have places of business in two different countries that have ratified the Convention. The Convention, which became a part of United States law on January 1, 1988, governs only the formation of contracts and the rights and obligations of the buyer and seller arising from the contract. It is not concerned with the validity of the contract itself or the nature of property interests arising from the contract; those issues are to be resolved by domestic law. The Convention also specifically excludes certain types of sales based on the nature of the goods or the nature of the transaction; one important exclusion is consumer contracts. Contracting parties are permitted to elect out of some or all of the Convention's provisions or to vary those provisions through explicit language in the contract. The Convention, in other words, serves a "gap filling" function in that it only applies when the contract itself is silent on issues governed by the Convention.

The Convention applies to contracts for the sale of goods between parties whose "places of business" are in different states if those states have ratified the Convention; the Convention also applies when the forum's choice-of-law rules refer to the law of a nation which has ratified the Convention. The Convention also applies if the choice-of-law rules of the forum would lead to application of the law of a country which had signed the Convention. The Convention, however, permits a signatory nation to declare that it is not bound by this provision; the United States has not made that declaration. Was that a wise choice? *See* RUSSELL WEINTRAUB, COMMENTARY ON THE CONFLICT OF LAWS 75-76. (3d ed. Supp. 1989).

The Convention's choice-of-law provisions are the subject of unusually critical commentary; *see, e.g.,* Thieffry, *Sale of Goods Between French and U.S. Merchants: Choice of Law Considerations Under the U.N. Convention on Contracts for the International Sale of Goods,* 22 INT'L LAW. 1017 (1998).

The United Nations could have tried to reformulate the content or substance of the sale-of-goods rules of all signatory nations, much as the UCC changed the commercial law of almost all American jurisdictions. Instead, the Convention chose to adopt a set of rules which comes into play *only* when there are contracts between businesses operating in signatory states. *See* Russell Weintraub, *supra,* at 73. Was that wise? Consider an American manufacturer who sells to Austrian and Canadian buyers; the United States and Austria have signed the Convention, but Canada has not. In the absence of a contract provision on point, the Convention will apply to the contract with the Austrian, but not to the contract with the Canadian. Does this make sense? Can the manufacturer avoid this dilemma? Would it have been possible in any event, for the Convention to have done anything about this problem?

## § 4.35   Limitation of Actions

### [A]   Introduction

Much conflicts litigation today concerns the question of whether the suit was timely filed. It may help to explain this phenomenon that the recent tide of state legislative "tort reform" has met a strong countercurrent in litigation of toxic torts (personal injuries caused by environmental pollution or defective products) and medical malpractice. Tort reform often includes the shortening of limitation periods. Often it takes the form of abolition of the "discovery rule" under which the statute of limitations begins to run only upon discovery of the harm. There are also new statutes of repose, which terminate liabilities a fixed number of years from the date of contracting for or performance of work done, or the sale of a product. These reforms would tend to block some meritorious suits in toxic tort cases because a recurrent feature of those cases is the long latency period before manifestation of the harm. *See generally* Green, *The Paradox of Statutes of Limitations in Toxic Substances Litigation,* 76 CAL. L. REV. 965 (1988).

Challenges under state constitutional law to this sort of legislation have met with considerable success. But also potent are choice-of-law challenges, and this seems to be a large part of the activity that we are seeing.

Perhaps responding in part to this activity, the American Law Institute in 1986 began a reconsideration of § 142 of Restatement (Second) of the Conflict of Laws, under the stewardship of Professor Reese. Revised § 142 was finally promulgated, with revised Comments thereto, in 1988. Earlier, the Commission on Uniform State laws undertook a new Uniform Conflict of Laws Limitations Act, promulgated in 1983, under the stewardship of Professor Leflar.

The efforts of these groups reflect a debate over the appropriate methodology for choosing limitations law, a debate continuing in American courts. The debate has developed along lines of fairly clear demarcation. One group of courts adheres to the "traditional" view that the limitations issue is "procedural," and therefore "for the forum." Another group of courts take the position at the polar extreme, arguing that the limitations issue is always "substantive," and therefore always governed by the law of the state that governs the claim. Refreshingly, a third group argues that limitations law should be chosen precisely the way law on any other issue is chosen.

## [B]  Characterizing the Limitations Issue as "Procedural"

### SUN OIL CO. v. WORTMAN

*United States Supreme Court*
*486 U.S. 717, 108 S. Ct. 2117, 100 L. Ed. 2d 743 (1988)*

[This case is reported in § 5.04, *infra.* ]

## NOTES AND QUESTIONS ON THE PROCEDURAL MODEL AND FEDERAL TRANSFER

(1) **SCHREIBER v. ALLIS-CHALMERS CORP.,** 611 F.2d 790 (10th Cir. 1979). Action in federal trial court in Mississippi by Kansas plaintiff for personal injuries occurring in Kansas, taking advantage of Mississippi's unusual six-year statute of limitation for torts. The case was time-barred in Kansas. Mississippi's only connection with the case was that the defendant

was amenable to suit there. The case was then transferred to the more convenient federal forum in Kansas.

*Held:* For the plaintiff (reversing on the authority of *Van Dusen v. Barrack* [reported in § 6.15, *infra* ]). The federal transferee court must apply the Mississippi choice rule. Mississippi considers its limitations period procedural, and it would apply its own limitations law even in a case such as this. *Cf. Shewbrooks v. A. C & S., Inc.,* 529 So. 2d 557 (Miss. 1988). The Mississippi Supreme Court has held that its borrowing statute "only applies where a non-resident in whose favor the statute has accrued afterward moves into this state." *Louisiana & Mississippi R. Transfer Co. v. Long,* 159 Miss. 654, 667, 131 So. 84, 88 (1930). Thus, the Mississippi 6-year statute must open the door to this case in the federal court in Kansas.

(2) *The longer statute.* When the forum has no connection with the parties or the occurrence, and has a shorter statute of limitations than the more interested sister state, should the forum be allowed to apply its own period of limitations as "procedural?" Why?

What appears troubling about *Schreiber,* in the view of the *Ferens* court, is that there the uninterested forum had a *longer* period of limitations. Why should that make a difference?

## [C]  Characterizing the Limitations of Actions Issue as "Substantive"

## THE UNIFORM CONFLICT OF LAWS LIMITATIONS ACT

*12 U.L.A. 46-49 (Supp. 1983)*

§ 2. Conflict of Laws: Limitations Periods

(a) Except as provided by Section 4, if a claim is substantively based:

    (1)   upon the law of one other state, the limitation period of that state applies;

    (2)   upon the law of more than one state, the limitation period of one of those states, chosen by the law of conflict of laws of this State, applies.

(b) The limitation period of this State applies to all other claims.

§ 4. Unfairness

If the court determines that the [applicable limitations period of another state] is substantially different from the limitation period of this State and has not afforded a fair opportunity to sue upon, or imposes an unfair burden in defending against, the claim, the limitation period of this State applies.

### NOTES ON THE UNIFORM ACT

(1) *The Uniform Act and borrowing statutes.* The Uniform Act has been adopted thus far in Arkansas, Colorado, North Dakota, Oregon, and Washington. Similar legislation has been enacted recently in the United Kingdom. See

Foreign Limitations Period Act of 1984, Ch. 16; Carter, *The Foreign Limitations Period Act of 1984,* 1983 L. Q. REV. 68. How does the Act differ from the typical "borrowing" statute? Under a typical borrowing statute, the initial reference would be to the law of the place where the cause of action accrued. This might very well be the place many judges would choose to govern a case substantively. See *Dymond v. Nat'l Broadcasting Co.,* 559 F. Supp. 734 (D. Del. 1983) (state where cause of action "arises," within meaning of borrowing statute, would be state whose substantive law would be applied to merits under Delaware choice rules). However, borrowing statutes typically borrow only *shorter* limitations law, except perhaps when the plaintiff is a resident of the forum, *e.g.,* CAL. CIV. PROC. CODE § 361; N.Y. CIV. PRAC. L. & R. § 202. *See generally* David Vernon, *Statutes of Limitation in the Conflict of Laws: Borrowing Statutes,* 32 ROCKY MT. L. REV. 287 (1960).

*See* PROBLEM 4H-15. LIMITATION PERIODS.

(2) *Depeçage and the Uniform Act.* How is it possible to choose a single place of governance for all issues under any modern approach? A court working under the Act will choose one state of substantive governance from among the range of governing states, for the purpose of adopting that state's relevant limitations law. The Act makes no reference to the choice rules of the substantively-governing state; the Commissioners avoid renvoi, opting for the limitations law of the chosen state whether that state "would" apply it or not. Thus, that state's borrowing statute will be ignored. However, it was the intention of the Commissioners that the claim state's tolling and accrual rules be picked up along with its statute of limitations. *See* Robert Leflar, *The New Conflicts-Limitations Act,* 13 MERCER L. REV. 461, 465 (1984).

(3) *A new loophole.* Notice the degree of flexibility the Commissioners would afford to courts choosing limitations law, under § 4 of the Act. Is this a license to judges to disregard the relevant statute when inconvenient? Why does a similar provision not protect a *plaintiff* from unfairness in forum limitations law? The general thrust of the Act is to mandate the sister-state's statute, shorter or longer, in all cases not governed by the substantive law of the forum. Thus, as the comments accompanying the Act suggest, the "escape clause" for "unfairness" was focused primarily on the problem faced by the forum under pressure of "strong public policy" to apply its *own* longer statute. The Act restricts the escape clause to "rare" and "extreme cases," and permits no escape through renvoi. Thus, the forum is encouraged to give access under another state's law, but to avoid a local legislative mandate for access. Is there any justification for this? *Compare* RESTATEMENT (SECOND) OF CONFLICT OF LAWS § 142, *infra.* *See* ALI Proceedings 329-333 (1988) (debate and affirmative vote on motion from the floor for an amendment extending escape clause to entire section).

(4) *The song of the sirens?* The Uniform Act works by adopting for the limitations issue the law of a place that will have substantive governance of the case. In its way, it would appear to be as mechanical as its antithesis, the "procedural" approach. Yet this "substantive" model must have had considerable appeal for the Commissioners, who preferred it both to the old "procedural" model and to the analytic model preferred by modernist writers. The reasoning seems to have been that if limitations law is governed by the

place that would govern the substantive issues in a case, the choice could not be wholly irrational. At the same time, many, if not most, American courts working under the Act would choose the state "of most significant relationship" with the case, and this was likely to be the same state in all such courts. Thus, not only would there be a chance for rationality, but also for uniformity.

## PERKINS v. CLARK EQUIPMENT CO.

*United States Court of Appeals for the Eighth Circuit*
*823 F.2d 207 (8th Cir. 1987)*

FLOYD R. GIBSON, SENIOR CIRCUIT JUDGE.

## I. BACKGROUND

At all relevant times Ray and Marilyn Perkins were residents of Iowa. On January 5, 1982, while working for the City of Des Moines, Iowa, Ray Perkins fractured his right leg while attempting to mount a model 631 Bob Cat Skid-Steer Loader. Perkins' hospital bills and workers compensation disability benefits were paid by the City of Des Moines.

The loader involved in the accident was designed, manufactured, and assembled by Clark Equipment Company at its Fargo, North Dakota facility. The loader was sold and delivered to a third party in Des Moines who in turn resold it to the City of Des Moines. While in the hands of the third party, modifications were made on the loader which, Clark argues, ultimately resulted in the accident.

On December 13, 1984 the Perkinses filed this suit in the United States District Court for the District of North Dakota. Clark moved for summary judgment, arguing that the suit was barred by Iowa's two-year statute of limitations. The Perkinses resisted the motion, arguing that North Dakota's six-year statute of limitations applies. The district court granted summary judgment in favor of Clark . . . .

## II. DISCUSSION

In diversity of citizenship cases the district court must apply the choice of laws rules of the state in which it sits. *Klaxon Co. v. Stentor Elec. Mfg. Co.,* 313 U.S. 487, 496 (1941). On appeal great deference is given to the district court's interpretation of state law . . . .

In the present case the district court noted that the North Dakota Supreme Court has not specifically addressed how statutes of limitations should be characterized for choice of law purposes. In 1972 the North Dakota Supreme Court abandoned the *lex loci delicti* (law of place of injury controls) approach to choice of laws questions and adopted the most significant contacts approach. *Issendorf v. Olson,* 194 N.W.2d 750 (N.D. 1972). The Perkinses argue that *Issendorf* only applies to substantive law and that the forum should always apply its own procedural laws, including the statute of limitations. The Perkinses argue that other states which have abandoned the *lex loci delicti* approach have retained the substance/procedure distinction where statutes of limitations are involved.

The district court held that although *Issendorf* did not specifically address the issue, it did offer sufficient guidance. The court in *Issendorf* called the substance/procedure distinction "an unsatisfactory approach to the determination of the choice of law in tort cases." The court in *Issendorf* adopted the most significant contracts approach because the substance/procedure distinction was easily manipulated in hard cases and because it was more just, fair, and practical to apply the law of the state most interested in the outcome. From this reasoning the district court determined that the North Dakota Supreme Court would apply the most significant contacts approach to statutes of limitations. We agree.

The Perkinses argue that the reasons for abandoning the substance/procedure distinction do not apply to statutes of limitations and that the lack of clear guidance from the North Dakota Supreme Court suggests that the old rule, including the distinction, should be retained. Although these arguments deserve consideration, they fall short of showing that the district court's interpretation of North Dakota law is "fundamentally deficient in analysis or otherwise lacking in reasoned authority." [Citation omitted.]

Affirming the district court's application of the most significant contacts approach to the statute of limitations does not end our inquiry, however. The Perkinses argue that the district court erred in holding that Iowa had the most significant contacts under the facts in this case. The undisputed facts show the following contacts with North Dakota: 1) Clark is licensed to do and does business in North Dakota; 2) Clark designed and assembled the loader in North Dakota; and 3) the Perkinses filed this lawsuit in North Dakota.

The Iowa contacts are: 1) the accident occurred in Iowa, in the course of Ray Perkins' employment with the City of Des Moines, Iowa; 2) the Perkinses were, at all pertinent times, Iowa residents; 3) Clark is licensed to and does business in Iowa; 4) Ray Perkins' medical care was provided in Iowa; 5) the City of Des Moines paid his medical bills pursuant to Iowa worker compensation law and paid his worker compensation benefits; 6) the loader was sold and delivered by Clark to a third party in Iowa; and 7) modifications to the loader were made in Iowa.

We agree that Iowa has the more significant contacts. The Perkinses argue that the most significant contact is that since the loader was designed and manufactured in North Dakota, North Dakota's six-year statute of limitations is evidence of a strong policy to hold North Dakota manufacturers liable for an extended period of time. However, it is not our role to second guess the district court's interpretation of state law . . . . Absent clear error or an abuse of discretion we will not reverse the district court's interpretation of state law. After careful consideration we believe that the district court's interpretation was . . . correct . . . .

[W]e believe that the district court correctly predicted how the North Dakota Supreme Court would have decided the issue. The court in *Issendorf* specifically rejected the substance/procedure distinction as unsatisfactory. There is no reason to believe that the court would now welcome this "unsatisfactory approach" when statutes of limitations are involved.

[I]n 1985 the North Dakota Legislature enacted the Uniform Conflict of Laws-Limitations Act. N.D.Cent.Code §§ 28-01.2-01 through 05 (Supp. 1985). Although the effective date of the Act makes it inapplicable to this case, it nevertheless is helpful . . . . Under the Act courts will apply the statute of limitations of the state which governs the substantive issues. This result is consistent with the result we reach today . . . .

## NOTES AND QUESTIONS ON *PERKINS*

Was *Perkins* rightly decided? It seems plausible that Iowa, the place of the plaintiff's residence and the place where the injury occurred, was the "place of most significant contact." But does that resolve the choice-of-law problem presented?

What were the interests of the forum in hearing the case? In borrowing foreign law to foreclose suit? What were the interests of the claim state in shutting off foreign litigation? Didn't the *Perkins* court wind up applying the law of an uninterested state, and disregarding the law of the interested one? *Cf.* Justice Brennan's dissent in *Wortman,* § 5.04, *infra,* on the interests of "the claim state." Although North Dakota probably "would' rule this way, isn't such a result simply an embarrassment?

How much difference does it make to this analysis that the Iowa seller allegedly modified the defendant's product in Iowa before selling it to the plaintiff?

*See* PROBLEM 4H-16. RIGHT OR REMEDY.

### [D]  Modern Methods

### RESTATEMENT OF THE LAW (SECOND) OF CONFLICT OF LAWS<sup>*</sup> (As Amended, 1988)

§ 142. Statute of Limitations.

[replacing former §§ 142 and 143]

Whether a claim will be maintained against the defense of the statute of limitations is determined under the principles stated in § 6. In general, unless the exceptional circumstances of the case make such a result unreasonable:

(1)  The forum will apply its own statute of limitations barring the claim.

(2)  The forum will apply its own statute of limitations permitting the claim unless:

(a)  maintenance of the claim would serve no significant interest of the forum; and

(b) the claim would be barred under the statute of limitations of a state having a more significant relationship to the parties and the occurrence.

---

## NOTES ON REVISED § 142

(1) *The finesse of § 142.* The new revision of Restatement § 142 was intended to reject the "procedural" model and to encourage choice of limitations law using the same methods used in choice of substantive law. At the same time, the "substantive" model is rejected as well. Rather, the intention seems to be that limitations law be chosen analytically. *See* Willis L. M. Reese, *The Second Restatement of Conflict of Laws Revisited,* 34 MERCER L. REV. 502, 506-07 (1984); *see also* Cooper, *Statutes of Limitations in Minnesota Choice of Law: The Problematic Return of the Substance-Procedure Distinction,* 71 MINN. L. REV. 363 (1986); Grossman, *Statutes of limitations and the Conflict of Laws: Modern Analysis,* 1980 ARIZ. ST. L.J. 1; Martin, *Statutes of limitations and Rationality-in the Conflict of Laws,* 19 WASHBURN L.J. 405 (1980); Molhollin, *Interest Analysis and Conflicts Between Statutes of Limitations,* 27 HAST. L.J. 1 (1975).

Isn't it of enormous help here that the language of the revision moves directly to § 6, rather than to "the place of most significant contact with the parties and the occurrence with respect to the issue," as elsewhere in the Restatement? Experience under the Uniform Act demonstrates how courts might be misled by a reference to "the place of most significant contact" into doing what was done *in Perkins,* failing to choose limitations law directly and independently. Instead, § 6 opens up for immediate consideration the functional desiderata enumerated there. The same selection of methods was made in the Ninth Circuit Court of Appeals in *Tomlin v. Boeing,* 650 F.2d 1065 (9th Cir. 1981). There, the initial question was whether Washington would employ interest analysis, its adopted conflicts methodology, to choose a substantively governing state, and then would apply the limitations law of that state (the reader will recognize the "substantive" model); or whether Washington would make a direct and separate analytic choice of limitations law. The Ninth Circuit held that Washington would select the latter, analytic model.

(2) *A wrong turn?* The Comments to § 142 still contain traces of thinking more appropriate to the "substantive" model, and thus may cause some trouble.

Suppose the plaintiff resides at the forum, and the forum has a longer statute. The defendant resides at the place of injury, which has a shorter statute. In that true conflict of limitations law, how should the tie be broken?

In Comment g to revised § 142, the Restatement approves tie-breaking power for *the place of injury* in such a case except "in extreme and unusual circumstances." Does that make sense? Is there some magic tie-breaking power in the place of injury? *(See* notes accompanying *Neumeier v. Kuehner,* § 4.25[C], *supra.)*

The Committee may have reasoned that it is irrational to apply a door-closing law in a door-opening way. But wouldn't the state where the plaintiff resides have a legitimate interest in giving its resident the full benefit of whatever period the legislature has provided? As the universality of long-arm legislation suggests, there is consensus recognizing the propriety of law providing a home forum for the plaintiff. *See* ALI, Proceedings 344 (1988) (remarks of Professor Weinberg).

(3) **WARNER v. AUBERGE GRAY ROCKS INN**, 827 F.2d 938 (3d Cir. 1987) (Pollak, J.). Action by a New Jersey skier for personal injuries sustained at a Quebec ski resort. The action was timely under New Jersey law, but would have been barred under the law of Quebec.

*Held* (reversing): New Jersey would apply its longer statute to entertain the claim. New Jersey would reject Restatement's proposed Comment g. This Court reaches the result with reluctance, but this is what New Jersey would do.

*See* Klein, *A Critical Analysis of New Jersey's Domicile-Driven Choice of Law Methodology,* 17 SETON HALL L. REV. 204 (1987).

That Comment g should not discourage a result like that in *Warner* is indicated by a (surprisingly) favorable citation to *Warner* at Comment *e*.

(4) *Another wrong turn?* Comment g also suggests that the claim should not be entertained when the forum has only a slight contact with the case and the parties are both domiciled in the alternative forum under whose statute of limitations the claim would be barred." Given that modernist courts tend to disparage the place of injury as "fortuitous," is there a danger here that the interests of the place of injury may be short-changed?

(5) *A Codification.* Louisiana has codified choice of law concerning limitations. Article 3549 of the Louisiana Civil Code provides that, when an action would be barred in the forum but not in the state whose law would apply to the merits, the action should be dismissed unless the use of forum law "is warranted by compelling considerations of remedial justice." Do you find that provision better than those of the Uniform Act and of the Restatement? On the Louisiana provision, *see* Simeon Symeonides, *Louisiana Conflicts Law: Two Surprises,* 54 LA. L. REV. 497 (1994).

(6) *The Impact of Modern Methods.* Professor Symeonides reports that about a third of the states "have abandoned the traditional procedural characterization of statutes of limitation and have applied to conflicts involving these statutes the same choice-of-law analysis applied to substantive issues." Symeon C. Symeonides, *Choice of Law in the American Courts in 1999: One More Year,* 48 AM. J. COMP. L. 143, 166 (2000).

(7) *Modern methods and a hard question.* Assuming, with the Supreme Court in *Wortman,* that the forum may always apply its own longer, as well as its shorter statute of limitations, a harder question remains. Would the *Wortman* court have approved the forum's *borrowing* a longer statute?

**LEDESMA v. JACK STEWART PRODUCE, INC.,** 816 F.2d 482 (9th Cir. 1987). Action by California plaintiffs for personal injuries against Oklahoma and Arkansas defendants. The plaintiffs were injured in Arizona when their van was allegedly struck by a car driven by an Arkansas resident and owned by an Oklahoma corporation. The trial court dismissed under California's one-year statute of limitations, relying on *Nelson v. International Paint Co.,* 716 F.2d 640 (9th Cir. 1983) (forum will apply its own shorter statute).

*Held* (reversing): *Nelson* did not establish a per se rule. Unlike *Nelson,* this case involves California plaintiffs. This is a true conflict of laws which is best resolved by accommodating the interests of the place of injury, and permitting trial under its two-year statute. California's interest in protecting its courts from stale claims is "at least equally balanced by its interest in allowing its residents to recover for injuries sustained in a state that would recognize their claim as timely." California's tolling statute is further evidence that California does not insist on applying its statute inflexibly. But Arizona's interest in promoting highway safety would be gravely impaired by a dismissal.

*Dissent:* California's interest in blocking trial of stale claims remains the same whether the Californian in the case is the plaintiff or the defendant.

\*    \*    \*

When a state's general policies cannot be vindicated by application of local law, it has been the modern method to say that the state lacks an interest—not that it has an interest in applying another state's laws. Can a state with an interest in applying its statute withhold the benefit of its law from the defendant without the appearance of discrimination? Is *Ledesma* a thoughtful piece of policy analysis, or a failure of modernist reasoning? Comment e to revised § 142 of Restatement (Second) cites *Ledesma* as "espousing the modern view."

For further discussion of Section 142, see Louise Weinberg, *Choosing Law: The Limitations Debates,* 1991 U. ILL. L. REV. 683 (1991).

*See* PROBLEM 4H-17. IN THE ABSENCE OF A FEDERAL LIMITATION.

# Chapter 5

# THE CONSTITUTION AND CHOICE OF LAW

## § 5.01 Introduction

In Chapter 4, we explored the methods used by American courts in choosing law. In this chapter, we move into the more rarefied atmosphere of the Supreme Court of the United States. That tribunal sits to decide only *federal* questions. In the Supreme Court, conflicts questions become constitutional ones. What law *may* a court choose? What law *must* it choose?

The Supreme Court entertains challenges to choices of law most often under the Due Process Clause or the Full Faith and Credit Clause. As we shall see, in cases reviewing choices of law there is no modern difference, as a practical matter, between the two clauses. There is also some review under the Commerce Clause of "extra-territorial" impacts of forum law on sister states. Finally, the Supreme Court sometimes reviews state discrimination against nonresidents under the Commerce Clause, and to some extent, under the Equal Protection or Privileges and Immunities Clauses.

The Supreme Court is currently very active in reviewing interstate conflicts. But the foundation case of the modern era remains *Home Insurance Co. v. Dick*.

## PART A   THE MODERN POSITION

## § 5.02   Emergence of the Modern Position

---

### HOME INSURANCE CO. v. DICK

*United States Supreme Court*
*281 U.S. 397, 50 S. Ct. 338, 74 L. Ed. 926 (1930)*

Mr. Justice Brandeis delivered the opinion of the Court.

Dick, a citizen of Texas, brought this action in a court of that State against [an insurer incorporated in Mexico], to recover on a policy of fire insurance for the total loss of a tug. Jurisdiction was asserted *[quasi] in rem* through garnishment, by ancillary writs issued against the Home Insurance Company and Franklin Fire Insurance Company, which reinsured, by contracts with the Mexican [insurer], parts of the risk which it had assumed. The garnishees are New York corporations. Upon them, service was affected by serving their local agents in Texas. . . .

The controversy here is wholly between Dick and the garnishees. . . . [T]here is no contention that . . . jurisdiction *in personam* over [the Mexican insurer] was acquired. . . . The garnishees concede that inability to sue the Mexican [insurer] in Texas, *in personam*, is not material, if a cause of action against [the Mexican insurer] existed at the time of garnishment. . . .

Their defense rests upon the following facts. This suit was not commenced till more than one year after the date of the loss. The policy provided: "It is understood and agreed that no judicial suit or demand shall be entered before any tribunal for the collection of any claim under this policy, unless such suits or demands are filed within one year counted as from the date on which such damage occurs." This provision was in accord with the Mexican law to which the policy was expressly made subject. It was issued by the Mexican company in Mexico to one Bonner, of Tampico, Mexico, and was there duly assigned to Dick prior to the loss. It covered the vessel only in certain Mexican waters. The premium was paid in Mexico; and the loss was "payable in the City of Mexico. . . . "[2] At the time the policy was issued, when it was assigned to him, and until after the loss, Dick actually resided in Mexico, although his permanent residence was in Texas. The contracts of reinsurance were affected by correspondence between the Mexican company in Mexico and the New York companies in New York. Nothing thereunder was to be done, or was in fact done, in Texas.

. . . [A]rticle 5545 of the Texas Revised Civil Statutes (1925) provides: "No person . . . shall enter into any . . . contract . . . the time in which to sue thereon is limited to a shorter period than two years. And no . . . agreement for any such shorter limitation in which to sue shall ever be valid in this State."

. . . The garnishees appealed to this Court on the ground that the statute, as construed and applied, violated their rights under the Federal Constitution. . . .

*First.* Dick contends that this Court lacks jurisdiction of the action, because the errors assigned involve only questions of local law and of conflict of laws. . . .

The contention is unsound. There is no dispute as to the meaning of the provision in the policy. It is that the insurer shall not be liable unless suit is brought within one year of the loss. . . .

The statute is not simply one of limitation. . . . As construed, it . . . directs the disregard in Texas of contractual rights and obligations wherever created and assumed; and it commands the enforcement of obligations in excess of those contracted for. Therefore, the objection that, as applied to contracts made and to be performed outside of Texas, the statute violates the Federal Constitution, raises federal questions. . . .

*Second.* . . . A state may, of course, prohibit and declare invalid the making of certain contracts within its borders. Ordinarily, it may prohibit performance within its borders, even of contracts validly made elsewhere, if they are required to be performed within the State and their performance would violate its laws. But, in the case at bar, nothing in any way relating to the policy sued on, or to the contracts of reinsurance, was ever done or required to be

---

[2] The loss was made payable to Dick and the Texas & Gulf Steamship Company as their interests might appear. . . .

done in Texas. All acts relating to the making of the policy were done in Mexico. All [things] in relation to the making of the contracts of reinsurance were done there or in New York. And, likewise, all things in regard to performance were to be done outside of Texas. Neither the Texas laws nor the Texas courts were invoked for any purpose, except by Dick in the bringing of this suit. The fact that Dick's permanent residence was in Texas is without significance. At all times here material he was physically present and acting in Mexico. Texas was, therefore, without power to affect the terms of contracts so made. Its attempt to impose a greater obligation than that agreed upon and to seize property in payment of the imposed obligation violates the guaranty against deprivation of property without due process of law. *New York Life Ins. Co. v. Dodge,* 246 U.S. 357 (1918).[5]

. . . It is true also that a State is not bound to provide remedies and procedure to suit the wishes of individual litigants. It may prescribe the kind of remedies to be available in its courts and dictate the practice and procedure to be followed in pursuing those remedies. Contractual provisions relating to these matters, even if valid where made, are often disregarded by the court of the forum, pursuant to statute or otherwise. But the Texas statute deals neither with the kind of remedy available nor with the mode in which it is to be pursued. It purports to create rights and obligations. It may not validly affect contracts which are neither made nor are to be performed in Texas.

*Third.* Dick urges that article 5545 of the Texas law is a declaration of its public policy; and that a state may properly refuse to recognize foreign rights which violate its declared policy. Doubtless, a State may prohibit the enjoyment by persons within its borders of rights acquired elsewhere which violate its laws or public policy; and, under some circumstances, it may refuse to aid in the enforcement of such rights. But the Mexican [insurer] . . . was not before the court. The garnishees were brought in by compulsory process. Neither has asked favors. They ask only to be let alone. We need not consider how far the State may go in imposing restrictions on the conduct of its own residents, and of foreign corporations which have received permission to do business within its borders. . . . It may not abrogate the rights of parties beyond its borders having no relation to anything done or to be done within them.

*Fourth.* Finally, it is urged that the Federal Constitution does not require the states to recognize and protect rights derived from the laws of foreign countries—that as to them the full faith and credit clause has no application. The claims here asserted are not based upon the full faith and credit clause. They rest upon the Fourteenth Amendment. Its protection extends to aliens. Moreover, the [garnishee] parties in interest here are American companies. . . .

---

[5] The division of this court in . . . [the] *Dodge* [case] was not on the principle here stated, but on the question of fact whether there were . . . things done within the state of which the state could properly lay hold as the basis of the regulations there imposed. In the absence of any such things, as in this case, the Court was agreed that a state is without power to impose either public or private obligations on contracts made outside of the state and not to be performed there.

## NOTES AND QUESTIONS

(1) **NEW YORK LIFE INS. CO. v. DODGE**, 246 U. S. 357 (1918). Action by a Missouri corporation on an insurance policy. The plaintiff relied on Missouri law, which would not permit forfeiture of coverage for an immaterial breach. Forfeiture would occur under the law of the place of contracting.

*Held:* For the defendant. Only the place of contracting may regulate the contract.

*Dissent* (Brandeis, J.): The policy might fairly be found to be a Missouri policy. But even if not, Missouri should still have power to protect an insured resident from forfeiture. "The test of constitutionality to be applied here is that commonly applied when the validity of a statute . . . is questioned, namely: Is the subject-matter within the reasonable scope of regulation? Is the end legitimate? Are the means appropriate to the end sought to be obtained? If so, the act must be sustained. . . . "

(2) *Comparing Dick and Dodge. Dodge* was only one of several old cases in which the Supreme Court seemed to be making a constitutional requirement of territorialism in choice of law. The *Dick* Court purported to reconcile *Dodge* with *Dick* in its footnote 5. But with the passage of time it has become apparent that *Dodge* is obsolete while *Dick* is still good law. It is Justice Brandeis' dissent in *Dodge* that reflects modern thinking. With the exception of *Dick*, the older Supreme Court conflicts cases are no longer reliable authority, although the Court occasionally cites one. What is the difference between *Dodge* and *Dick*? In *Dick*, the Supreme Court struck down the Texas court's choice of its own law. But did the Court mandate any other law? New York law? Mexican law?

(3) *Reading Dick.* Would there be jurisdiction in the *Dick* case today?

Since plaintiff Dick claimed a permanent residency in Texas, some authorities have read *Dick* for the quite untenable proposition that a state lacks power to govern its own residents, unless it has some further contact with a case. *See, e.g.*, Martin, *The Constitution and Legislative Jurisdiction*, 10 HOFSTRA L. REV. 133, 142–46 (1981). *But see* Louise Weinberg, *Conflicts Cases and the Problem of Relevant Time: A Response to the Hague Symposium*, 10 HOFSTRA L. REV. 1023, 1026–27, nn. 16, 18 (1982) (replying to Professor Martin and arguing that "the needs of prudent governance" suggest ample state powers over a resident). Today, the Court repeatedly cites *Dick* for the broader proposition, as we shall see, that the forum with little or no interest in a case lacks power to govern it. Dick's "residence" in Texas was uncontroverted, but it was a naked allegation of the complaint. The Court treated this nominal residence as of scant relevance.

(4) *The declaration of conflicts independence. Dick*, then, stands for the proposition that the uninterested forum is not free to apply its own law. The interesting corollary of that proposition is that the interested forum *is* free to apply its own law, as Justice Brandeis saw in his *Dodge* dissent. That position became law when the Supreme Court took itself out of the business of forcing territorialist choices upon the states in 1935.

---

**ALASKA PACKERS ASS'N v. INDUSTRIAL ACC. COMM'N**, 294 U.S. 532 (1935). Action in California by California employer to reduce compensation benefits awarded under California law to an alien worker hired in California but injured during seasonal employment in Alaska. Alaska law would have provided a lesser award.

*Held* (per Justice Stone): For the plaintiff.

> California . . . had a legitimate public interest in . . . regulating this employer-employee relationship. . . . California was not required by the Fourteenth Amendment to prescribe the Alaska remedy rather than its own. . . .

> Prima facie every state is entitled to enforce in its own courts its own statutes, lawfully enacted.

> . . . A rigid and literal enforcement of the full faith and credit clause, without regard to the statute of the forum, would lead to the absurd result that, wherever . . . conflict arises, the statute of each state must be enforced in the courts of the other, but cannot be in its own.

(5) *The rejection of interest-balancing.* A suggestion in *Alaska Packers* that the Full Faith and Credit Clause might require application of the law of a state *more* interested than the forum was jettisoned in *Pacific Employers Ins. Co. v. Industrial Acc. Comm'n,* 306 U.S. 493 (1939). In *Pacific Employers,* Massachusetts was the place of the employment contract, while California was both the place of injury and the forum. As do most workers' compensation statutes, the Massachusetts statute provided that Massachusetts compensation was the sole and exclusive remedy of the injured employee. Both employer and employee were Massachusetts residents. The Court, again per Justice Stone, concluded that the California court was free to apply the law of *either* of the two interested states, without weighing or balancing their respective interests.

(6) *More on the abandonment of the forced territorialist choice.* Can it ever have made sense for the Court to try to force state courts to choose, let us say, the law of the place of contracting, when, as in *Dodge,* the Court itself could not agree where the place of contracting was? *Cf. Mutual Life Ins. Co. v. Liebing,* 259 U.S. 209 (1922) (deciding the other way in a case on *Dodge* facts, relying on a technical reading of the contract).

One writer has suggested a number of reasons for the 1935 abandonment by the Court, in *Alaska Packers, supra,* of forced territorialist choices of law. "The mandatory determinate choice" had the effect of constitutionalizing virtually every diversity or other two-state case. This entailed a questionable use of Supreme Court resources. The burden might have been borne, if the Court could have brought uniformity of result to interstate cases. "But the then-prevailing conflicts rules, no less than the approaches current today, produced results as to which reasonable people could, and did, disagree. . . . Moreover . . ., it was not clear that the rules the Court had adopted were the right rules. Yet to force the desired uniform result upon the states entailed forcing the increasingly dubious method. This left the states powerless to develop alternate rules or approaches." Louise Weinberg, *Choice of Law and Minimal Scrutiny*, 49 U. Chi. L. Rev. 440, 470–71 (1982)

(8) **WATSON v. EMPLOYERS LIABILITY ASSURANCE CORP.**, 348 U.S. 66 (1954). Action in Louisiana by a Louisiana woman for personal injuries sustained at her home when she tried to give herself a home permanent with an allegedly defective product purchased in Louisiana. Since jurisdiction over neither the manufacturer nor its parent company was obtainable, the suit was brought against the manufacturer's liability insurer under Louisiana's direct action statute. The insurance policy had a "no acceleration of liability" clause, which had the effect of prohibiting direct actions. This clause was valid under the laws of every other contact state, but was invalid under Louisiana's direct action statute.

*Held:* The forum may apply its direct action statute notwithstanding the prohibition against such actions in the policy. As place of injury, Louisiana is an interested state. The interests of the place of contracting need not displace "the interest of Louisiana in taking care of those injured in Louisiana."

\* \* \*

Query whether it could have made a difference to the interests of the forum if Ms. Watson had given herself the injurious home permanent while vacationing with friends in another state, and then had come home to suffer her injuries in Louisiana?

(9) **CLAY v. SUN INS. OFFICE, LTD.** 377 U.S. 179 (1964). Action in Florida on an insurance policy, for loss of personal property. The insured formerly resided elsewhere, where the insurance was obtained, but then moved to Florida, where the loss occurred.

*Held:* Florida may apply its law to nullify the policy clause requiring that suit be brought within twelve months. The policy coverage was "World Wide," and the insurer must have known that it could be sued [under another state's law]. "Florida has ample contacts with the present transaction and the parties to satisfy any conceivable requirement of full faith and credit or of due process."

\* \* \* \* \* \*

How would you distinguish *Clay* from *Home Ins. Co. v. Dick*, § 5.02, *supra*? *See* PROBLEM 5-1. HOW FAR DICK.

# PART B   THE MODERN POSITION: MINIMAL SCRUTINY

## § 5.03   The Modern Position: Minimal Scrutiny

### NEVADA v. HALL

*United States Supreme Court*
*440 U.S. 410, 99 S. Ct. 1182, 59 L. Ed. 2d 416*
*Rehearing Denied, 441 U.S. 917, 99 S. Ct. 2018 (1979)*

[For previous stages of this litigation, see § 4.20 and § 4.23, *supra*.]

MR. JUSTICE STEVENS delivered the opinion of the Court.

In this tort action arising out of an automobile collision in California, a California court has entered a judgment against the State of Nevada that Nevada's own courts could not have entered. We granted certiorari to decide whether federal law prohibits the California courts from entering such a judgment or, indeed, from asserting any jurisdiction over another sovereign State.

The [plaintiff/respondents] are California residents. They suffered severe injuries in an automobile collision on a California highway on May 13, 1968. The driver of the other vehicle, an employee of the University of Nevada, was killed in the collision. It is conceded that he was driving a car owned by the State, that he was engaged in official business, and that the University is an instrumentality of the State itself.

. . . The California Supreme Court held, as a matter of California law, that the State of Nevada was amenable to suit in California courts and remanded the case for trial. *Hall v. University of Nevada* [§ 4.20, *supra*]. We denied certiorari.

On remand, . . . Nevada argued that the Full Faith and Credit Clause of the United States Constitution required the California courts to enforce [Nevada's $25,000 liability limit contained in its statutory waiver of immunity]. Nevada's motion was denied, and the case went to trial.

The jury concluded that the Nevada driver was negligent and awarded damages of $1,150,000. . . .

Despite its importance, the question whether a State may claim immunity from suit in the courts of another State has never been addressed by this Court. The question is not expressly answered by any provision of the Constitution; Nevada argues that it is implicitly answered by reference to the common understanding that no sovereign is amenable to suit without its consent—an understanding prevalent when the Constitution was framed and repeatedly reflected in this Court's opinions. In order to determine whether that understanding is embodied in the Constitution, as Nevada claims,[5] it is

---

[5] No one claims that any federal statute places any relevant restriction on California's jurisdiction or lends any support to Nevada's claim of immunity. If there is a federal rule that restricts California's exercise of jurisdiction in this case, that restriction must be a part of the United States Constitution.

necessary to consider the source and scope of the traditional doctrine of sovereign immunity; the impact of the doctrine on the framing of the Constitution; the Full Faith and Credit Clause; and other aspects of the Constitution that qualify the sovereignty of the several States.

I

. . . Mr. Justice Holmes explained sovereign immunity as based "on the logical and practical ground that there can be no legal right as against the authority that makes the law on which the right depends." [Citation omitted.]

This explanation adequately supports the conclusion that no sovereign may be sued in its own courts without its consent, but it affords no support for a claim of immunity in another sovereign's courts. Such a claim necessarily implicates the power and authority of a second sovereign; its source must be found . . . in the voluntary decision of the second to respect the dignity of the first as a matter of comity. . . .

[I]f California and Nevada were independent and completely sovereign nations, Nevada's claim of immunity from suit in California's courts would be answered by reference to the law of California. . . .[13]

Nevada quite rightly does not ask us to review the California courts' interpretation of California law. Rather, it argues that California is not free, as a sovereign, to apply its own law, but is bound instead by a federal rule of law implicit in the Constitution that requires all of the States to adhere to the sovereign-immunity doctrine as it prevailed when the Constitution was adopted. Unless such a federal rule exists, we of course have no power to disturb the judgment of the California courts.

II

. . . [T]he question whether one State might be subject to suit in the courts of another State was apparently not a matter of concern when the . . . Constitution was being drafted and ratified. Regardless of whether the Framers were correct in assuming, as presumably they did, that prevailing notions of comity would provide adequate protection against the unlikely prospect of an attempt by the courts of one State to assert jurisdiction over another, the need for constitutional protection against that contingency was not discussed. . . .

The . . . Eleventh Amendment . . . places explicit limits on the powers of federal courts to entertain suits against a State.

. . . [It does] not answer the question whether the Constitution places any limit on the exercise of one's State's power to authorize its courts to assert jurisdiction over another State. . . .

---

[13] . . . [A]s concern for redress of individual injuries has enhanced, so too have moves toward the reappraisal of the practices of sovereign nations according absolute immunity to foreign sovereigns. The governing rule today, in many nations, is one of restrictive rather than absolute immunity.

## III

Nevada claims that the Full Faith and Credit Clause of the Constitution requires California to respect the limitations on Nevada's statutory waiver of its immunity from suit. That waiver only gives Nevada's consent to suits in its own courts. Moreover, even if the waiver is treated as a consent to be sued in California, California must honor the condition attached to that consent and limit respondents' recovery to $25,000, the maximum allowable in an action in Nevada's courts.

The Full Faith and Credit Clause does require [that a] judgment entered in one State must be respected in another. . . . But this Court's decision in *Pacific Insurance Co. v. Industrial Accident Comm'n*, [§ 5.02 Note (5), *supra*], clearly establishes that the Full Faith and Credit Clause does not require a State to apply another State's law in violation of its own legitimate public policy. . . .

. . . In this case, California's interest is the . . . substantial one of providing "full protection to those who are injured on its highways through the negligence of both residents and nonresidents." To effectuate this interest, California has provided by statute for jurisdiction in its courts over residents and nonresidents alike to allow those injured on its highways through the negligence of others to secure full compensation for their injuries in the California courts.

In further implementation of that policy, California has unequivocally waived its own immunity from liability for the torts committed by its own agents and authorized full recovery even against the sovereign. As the California courts have found, to require California either to surrender jurisdiction or to limit respondents' recovery to the $25,000 maximum of the Nevada statute would be obnoxious to its statutorily based policies of jurisdiction over nonresident motorists and full recovery. The Full Faith and Credit Clause does not require this result.[24]

## IV

Even apart from the Full Faith and Credit Clause, Nevada argues that the Constitution implicitly establishes a Union in which the States are not free to treat each other as unfriendly sovereigns, but must respect the sovereignty of one another. While sovereign nations are free to levy discriminatory taxes on the goods of other nations or to bar their entry altogether, the States of the Union are not. Nor are the States free to deny extradition of a fugitive when a proper demand is made by the executive of another State. And the citizens in each State are entitled to all privileges and immunities of citizens in the several States.

Each of these provisions places a specific limitation on the sovereignty of the several States. Collectively they demonstrate that ours is not a union of

---

[24] California's exercise of jurisdiction in this case poses no substantial threat to our constitutional system of cooperative federalism. Suits involving traffic accidents occurring outside of Nevada could hardly interfere with Nevada's capacity to fulfill its own sovereign responsibilities. . . .

50 wholly independent sovereigns. But these provisions do not imply that any one State's immunity from suit in the courts of another State is anything other than a matter of comity. Indeed, in view of the Tenth Amendment's reminder that powers not delegated to the Federal Government nor prohibited to the States are reserved to the States or to the people, the existence of express limitations on state sovereignty may equally imply that caution should be exercised before concluding that unstated limitations on state power were intended by the Framers. . . .

It may be wise policy, as a matter of harmonious interstate relations, for States to accord each other immunity or to respect any established limits on liability. They are free to do so. But if a federal court were to hold, by inference from the structure of our Constitution and nothing else, that California is not free in this case to enforce its policy of full compensation, that holding would constitute the real intrusion on the sovereignty of the States. . . .

Mr. Justice Blackmun, with whom The Chief Justice and Mr. Justice Rehnquist join, dissenting.

The Court, in a plausible opinion, holds that the State of Nevada is subject to an unconsented suit in a California state court for damages in tort. This result at first glance does not seem too unreasonable. One might well ask why Nevada, even though it is a State, and even though it has not given its consent, should not be responsible for the wrong its servant perpetrated on a California highway. And one might also inquire how it is that, if no provision of our national Constitution specifically prevents the nonimmunity result, these tort action plaintiffs could be denied their judgment.

But the Court paints with a very broad brush. . . .

. . . [T]he Court assumes that Nevada is "sovereign," but then concludes that . . . California can abolish the doctrine at will. By this reasoning, Nevada's amenability to suit in California is not conditioned on its agent's having committed a tortious act in California. . . . California, so far as the Federal Constitution is concerned, is able and free to treat Nevada, and any other State, just as it would treat any other litigant. . . .

The Court, by its footnote 24, purports to confine its holding to traffic-accident torts committed outside the defendant State, and perhaps even to traffic "policies." Such facts, however, play absolutely no part in the reasoning by which the Court reaches its conclusion. . . . [I]t is hard to see just how the Court could use a different analysis or reach a different result in a different case.

. . . States in all likelihood will retaliate against one another for respectively abolishing the "sovereign immunity" doctrine. States' legal officers will be required to defend suits in all other States. States probably will decide to modify their tax-collection and revenue systems in order to avoid the collection of judgments. [F]or example, Nevada evidently maintains cash balances in California banks to facilitate the collection of sales taxes from California corporations doing business in Nevada. Under the Court's decision, Nevada will have strong incentive to withdraw those balances and place them in Nevada banks so as to insulate itself from California judgments. . . .

Mr. Justice Rehnquist, with whom The Chief Justice joins, dissenting.

. . . The most recent statement by this Court on the topic appears to be that authored by Mr. Justice Black in *Western Union Telegraph Co. v. Pennsylvania,* 368 U.S. 71 (1961), which held that Western Union's due process rights would be violated if Pennsylvania escheated Western Union's unclaimed money orders. The Court found that conclusion compelled by Pennsylvania's inability to provide Western Union with a forum where all claims, including those of other States, could be resolved. The Court noted that "[i]t is plain that Pennsylvania courts, with no power to bring other States before them, cannot give such hearings."

. . . This decision cannot help but induce some "Balkanization" in state relationships as States try to isolate assets from foreign judgments and generally reduce their contacts with other jurisdictions. That will work to the detriment of smaller States—like Nevada—who are more dependent on the facilities of a dominant neighbor—in this case, California.

The problem of enforcement of a judgment against a State creates a host of additional difficulties. Assuming *Nevada* has no seizable assets in California, can the plaintiff obtain enforcement of California's judgment in Nevada courts? Can Nevada refuse to give the California judgment "full faith and credit" because it is against state policy? Can Nevada challenge the seizure of its assets by California in this Court? If not, are the States relegated to the choice between the gamesmanship and tests of strength that characterize international disputes, on the one hand, and the midnight seizure of assets associated with private debt collection on the other?. . .

*See* PROBLEM 5-2. THE HORNS OF JUSTICE BLACKMUN'S DILEMMA.

## NOTES AND QUESTIONS ON *NEVADA v. HALL*

(1) *The illusory role of federalism and comity.* Some distinguished authorities have taken the view that, whatever the Court's reasons for getting out of the full faith and credit business (*see Alaska Packers*, § 5.02 Note (4), *supra*), full faith and credit nevertheless should be given to the law of a state that clearly has predominant contacts with a case. *See* Robert Jackson, *Full Faith and Credit—The Lawyer's Clause of the Constitution*, 45 COLUM. L. REV. 1 (1945). If ever there was a case in which the argument for deference to the laws of a sister state was a strong one, *Nevada v. Hall* must be that case. The sister state itself was the defendant in the case, standing, figurative hat in hand, in another state's courts, asking for its own law to govern its own liability. Was the case rightly decided?

(2) *Foreign Sovereign Immunities Act.* It might have been helpful to the Court in *Nevada v. Hall* to cite the federal Foreign Sovereign Immunities Act of 1976, 28 U.S.C. §§ 1330, 1332 (a)(2)–(4), 1391(f), 1441(d), 1602–11 (1982). Under that Act, Congress sets out the extent to which a foreign sovereign may claim immunity from suit in any state or federal court. The foreign sovereign's own law declaring the extent of its sovereign immunity would be irrelevant to the determination.

(3) *An easy case?* Wasn't *Nevada v. Hall* to be expected, in fact, under prior law? As we have already seen, the interested forum is free to disregard the law of another interested state even when that state declares itself the

exclusive forum with exclusive lawmaking power. *E.g. Pacific Employers*, Note (5), § 5.02, *supra*.

(4) *A question of judgment.* Note that three of the Justices suggested that Nevada could refuse to enforce a California judgment which was against Nevada public policy. On the current state of the case law, however, their fears appear unfounded. The Full Faith and Credit Clause indeed may be a paper tiger when it comes to enforcement of sister-state law; but it has real teeth when it comes to enforcing sister-state judgments. For the rare exceptions, see Chapter 7, *infra*.

*See* PROBLEMS 5-3. IN HOT PURSUIT; 5-4. RECRUITING AN ATHLETE; 5-5. YSU.

---

## NOTES ON MODERN CONSTITUTIONAL THEORY

(1) *Minimal, or rational-basis, scrutiny.* Until recently, scholarly commentary on Supreme Court review of conflicts cases addressed the question, "What are the constitutional 'limits' on choice of law?" *See, e.g.*, Willis L.M. Reese, *Legislative Jurisdiction*, 78 COLUM. L. REV. 1587 (1978); Martin, *Constitutional Limitations on Choice of Law*, 60 CORNELL L. REV. 185 (1976). This sort of thinking often led writers to conclude that the Supreme Court reviews choices of law for fairness (foreseeability) or concerns of federalism (comity). But these criteria seemed only loosely related to the Court's actual decisions.

More recently, it has been suggested that the Court's conflicts cases are theoretically unifiable with other constitutional cases. In *Choice of Law and Minimal Scrutiny*, 49 U. CHI. L. REV. 440 (1982), Professor Weinberg argues that the Court's "interest" test is simply rational-basis scrutiny, familiar from other constitutional cases. In other words, the forum must have a rational basis for applying its law.

This theoretical reformulation has increasingly become the established model among writers. *See, e.g.*, Russell Weintraub, Commentary on the Conflict of Laws 525 (3d ed. 1986). (For a similar insight, see Robert Sedler, *Constitutional Limitations on Choice of Law: The Perspective of Constitutional Generalism*, 10 HOFSTRA L. REV. 59, 77–80 (1981).) Weinberg's model, however, does not reflect all of the cases. As Weinberg acknowledges, the Court has never struck down the law of an uninterested "contact" state. Is there a difference between a "contact" and an "interest"? It seems possible to hypothesize a situation in which, for example, the place of injury is "uninterested." *See, e.g., Alabama Great So. R. R. v. Carroll*, § 4.06, *supra*; *Babcock v. Jackson*, § 4.19, *supra*.

For other writing on Supreme Court review of state choices of law, *see* Kogan, *Toward a Jurisprudence of Choice of Law: The Priority of Fairness over Comity*, 62 N.Y.U. L. REV. 651 (1987); Eugene Shreve, *Interest Analysis as Constitutional Law*, 48 OHIO ST. L.J. 342 (1987); Hay, *Full Faith and Credit and Federalism in Choice of Law*, 34 HOFSTRA L. REV. 709 (1983); Ralph Whitten, *The Constitutional Limitations on State Choice of Law: Due Process*, 9 HASTINGS CONST. L.Q. 851 (1982); Ralph Whitten, *The Constitutional*

*Limitations on State Choice of Law: Full Faith and Credit*, 12 MEMPHIS ST. U.L. REV. 1 (1981); KIRGIS, *The Roles of Due Process and Full Faith and Credit in Choice of Law*, 62 CORNELL L. REV. 151 (1976).

## PART C   THE MODERN POSITION: PROBLEMS

### § 5.04   The Modern Position: Problems

Supreme Court review today, as we shall see, can be both underinclusive and overinclusive. The Court has been so permissive as to tolerate even the arbitrary and irrational law of a state without real interest in an underlying dispute, although the law of an interested contact state is available. On the other hand, the Court has been so restrictive as to interfere with the apparently reasonable law of an interested state. These problems seem to arise not so much because the law chosen by the state was unforeseeable or an offense to sister-state sovereignty, but primarily because the Court seems to have trouble giving due weight to the state's legitimate governmental interests. The following cases and materials explore these issues.

### ALLSTATE INSURANCE CO. v. HAGUE

*United States Supreme Court*
*449 U.S. 302, 101 S. Ct. 633, 66 L. Ed. 2d 521 (1981)*
*Rehearing Denied, 450 U.S. 971, 101 S. Ct. 1494 (1981)*
*(For this case in the state supreme court, see § 3.12, Note (9), supra)*

JUSTICE BRENNAN announced the judgment of the Court and delivered an opinion, in which JUSTICE WHITE, JUSTICE MARSHALL, and JUSTICE BLACKMUN joined.

. . . .

I

. . . Respondent's late husband, Ralph Hague, died of injuries suffered when a motorcycle on which he was a passenger was struck from behind by an automobile. The accident occurred in Pierce County, Wis., which is immediately across the Minnesota border from Red Wing, Minn. The operators of both vehicles were Wisconsin residents, as was the decedent, who, at the time of the accident, resided with respondent in Hager City, Wis., which is one and one-half miles from Red Wing. Mr. Hague had been employed in Red Wing for the 15 years immediately preceding his death and had commuted daily from Wisconsin to his place of employment.

Neither the operator of the motorcycle nor the operator of the automobile carried valid insurance. However, the decedent held a policy issued by petitioner Allstate Insurance Co., covering three automobiles owned by him and containing an uninsured motorist clause insuring him against loss incurred from accidents with uninsured motorists. The uninsured motorist coverage was limited to $15,000 for each automobile.[3]

After the accident, but prior to the initiation of this lawsuit, respondent moved to Red Wing [Minn.]. Subsequently, she married a Minnesota resident

---

[3] Ralph Hague paid a separate premium for each automobile including an additional separate premium for each uninsured motorist coverage.

and established residence with her new husband in Savage, Minn. At approximately the same time, a Minnesota Registrar of Probate appointed respondent personal representative of her deceased husband's estate. Following her appointment, she brought this action in Minnesota District Court seeking a declaration under Minnesota law that the $15,000 uninsured motorist coverage on each of her late husband's three automobiles could be "stacked" to provide total coverage of $45,000. Petitioner defended on the ground that whether the three uninsured motorist coverages could be stacked should be determined by Wisconsin law, since the insurance policy was delivered in Wisconsin, the accident occurred in Wisconsin, and all persons involved were Wisconsin residents at the time of the accident. . . .

## II

. . . .

In deciding constitutional choice-of-law questions, whether under the Due Process Clause or the Full Faith and Credit Clause,[10] this Court has traditionally examined the contacts of the State whose law was applied, with the parties and with the occurrence or transaction giving rise to the litigation. In order to ensure that the choice of law is neither arbitrary nor fundamentally unfair, the Court has invalidated the choice of law of a State which has had no significant contact or significant aggregation of contacts, creating state interests, with the parties and the occurrence or transaction.[11]

Two instructive examples of such invalidation are *Home Ins. Co. v. Dick*, 281 U.S. 397 (1930) [§ 5.02, *supra*], and *John Hancock Mutual Life Ins. Co. v. Yates*, 299 U.S. 178 (1936). In both cases, the selection of forum law rested exclusively on the presence of one nonsignificant forum contact. . . .

*Dick* and *Yates* stand for the proposition that if a State has only an insignificant contact with the parties and the occurrence or transaction, application of its law is unconstitutional. *Dick* concluded that nominal residence—standing alone—was inadequate; *Yates* held that a post-occurrence change of residence to the forum State—standing alone—was insufficient to justify application of forum law. Although instructive as extreme examples of selection of forum law, neither *Dick* nor *Yates* governs this case. For in

---

[10] This Court has taken a similar approach in deciding choice-of-law cases under both the Due Process Clause and the Full Faith and Credit Clause. In each instance, the Court has examined the relevant contacts and resulting interests of the State whose law was applied. *See, e.g., Nevada v. Hall,* 440 U.S. 410 (1979) [§ 5.03, *supra*]. . . .

[11] Prior to the advent of interest analysis in the state courts . . . the prevailing choice-of-law methodology focused on the jurisdiction where a particular event occurred. . . . *Hartford Accident & Indemnity Co. v. Delta & Pine Land Co., 292* U.S. 143 (1934), can, perhaps, best be explained as an example of that period. In that case, the Court struck down application by the Mississippi courts of Mississippi law which voided the limitations provision in a [Tennessee insurance policy, although both the insurer and insured] were doing business in . . . Mississippi. . . .

That case, however, has scant relevance for today. It implied a choice-of-law analysis which, for all intents and purposes, gave an isolated event—the writing of the [policy] in Tennessee—controlling constitutional significance. . . .

contrast to those decisions, here the Minnesota contacts with the parties and the occurrence are obviously significant. . . .[15]

[F]or a State's substantive law to be selected in a constitutionally permissible manner, that State must have a significant contact or significant aggregation of contacts, creating state interests, such that choice of its law is neither arbitrary nor fundamentally unfair. Application of this principle to the facts of this case persuades us that the Minnesota Supreme Court's choice of its own law did not offend the Federal Constitution.

### III

Minnesota has three contacts with the parties and the occurrence giving rise to the litigation. In the aggregate, these contacts permit selection by the Minnesota Supreme Court of Minnesota law allowing the stacking of Mr. Hague's uninsured motorist coverages.

First, and for our purposes a very important contact, Mr. Hague was a member of Minnesota's work force, having been employed by a Red Wing, Minn., enterprise for the 15 years preceding his death. While employment status may implicate a state interest less substantial than does resident status, that interest is nevertheless important. The State of employment has police power responsibilities towards the nonresident employee that are analogous, if somewhat less profound, than towards residents. Thus, such employees use state services and amenities and may call upon state facilities in appropriate circumstances.

In addition, Mr. Hague commuted to work in Minnesota . . . and was presumably covered by his uninsured motorist coverage during the commute.[18] The State's interest in its commuting nonresident employees reflects a state concern for the safety and well-being of its work force and the concomitant effect on Minnesota employers.

That Mr. Hague was not killed while commuting to work or while in Minnesota does not dictate a different result. . . . [T]he occurrence of a crash fatal to a Minnesota employee in another State is a Minnesota contact. If Mr. Hague had only been injured and missed work for a few weeks the effect on the Minnesota employer would have been palpable. . . . Mr. Hague's death affects Minnesota's interest still more acutely. . . . Minnesota's work force is surely affected by the level of protection the State extends to it, either directly or indirectly. Vindication of the rights of the estate of a Minnesota employee, therefore, is an important state concern.

Mr. Hague's residence in Wisconsin does not—as Allstate seems to argue—constitutionally mandate application of Wisconsin law to the exclusion of

---

[15] . . . While [this Court] in *Alaska Packers* [§ 5.02 Note (4), *supra*] balanced the interests of California and Alaska [under the Full Faith and Credit Clause], such balancing is no longer required.

[18] The policy issued to Mr. Hague provided that Allstate would pay to the insured, or his legal representative, damages "sustained by the insured, caused by accident and arising out of the ownership, maintenance or use of [an] uninsured automobile. . . ." No suggestion has been made that Mr. Hague's uninsured motorist protection is unavailable because he was not killed while driving one of his insured automobiles.

forum law.[21] If, in the instant case, the accident had occurred in Minnesota between Mr. Hague and an uninsured Minnesota motorist, if the insurance contract had been executed in Minnesota covering a Minnesota registered company automobile which Mr. Hague was permitted to drive, and if a Wisconsin court sought to apply Wisconsin law, certainly Mr. Hague's residence in Wisconsin, his commute between Wisconsin and Minnesota, and the insurer's presence in Wisconsin should be adequate to apply Wisconsin's law.[22]

Second, Allstate was at all times present and doing business in Minnesota.[23] By virtue of its presence, Allstate can hardly claim unfamiliarity with the laws of the host jurisdiction and surprise that the state courts might apply forum law to litigation in which the company is involved. "Particularly since the company was licensed to do business in [the forum], it must have known it might be sued there, and that [the forum] courts would feel bound by (forum) law."[24] *Clay v. Sun Insurance Office Ltd.,* 363 U.S. 207, 221 (1960)(Black, J., dissenting).[25] Moreover, Allstate's presence in Minnesota gave Minnesota an interest in regulating the company's insurance obligations insofar as they affected both a Minnesota resident and court-appointed representative—respondent—and a longstanding member of Minnesota's work force—Mr. Hague.

Third, respondent became a Minnesota resident prior to institution of this litigation. . . . There is no suggestion that Mrs. Hague moved to Minnesota

---

[21] [Allstate's] statement that the instant dispute involves the interpretation of insurance contracts which were "underwritten, applied for, and paid for by Wisconsin residents. . . . " is simply another way of stating that Mr. Hague was a Wisconsin resident. [Mrs. Hague] could have replied that the insurance contract was underwritten, applied for and paid for by a Minnesota worker. . . . [Moreover], the policy, which is part of the record, recites that Allstate signed the policy in Northbrook, Ill. . . . No party sought application of Illinois law on that basis in the court below. [Latter two sentences moved from end of footnote. —*Ed.*]

In addition, petitioner's statement that the contracts were "underwritten . . . by Wisconsin residents" is not supported by the stipulated facts, if Petitioner wishes to include itself within that phrase. . . .

[22] Of course Allstate could not be certain that Wisconsin law would necessarily govern any accident which occurred in Wisconsin, whether brought in the Wisconsin courts or elsewhere. Such an expectation would give controlling significance to the wooden *lex loci delicti* doctrine. . . .

If the law of a jurisdiction other than Wisconsin did govern, there was a substantial likelihood, with respect to uninsured motorist coverage, that stacking would be allowed. Stacking was the rule in most States at the time the policy was issued. . . . Allstate . . . cannot claim unfair surprise. . . .

[23] The Court has recognized that examination of a State's contacts may result in divergent conclusions for jurisdiction and choice-of-law purposes. Nevertheless, both inquiries are often closely related and to a substantial degree depend upon similar considerations. Here, of course, jurisdiction in the Minnesota courts is unquestioned, a factor not without significance. . . .

[24] There is no element of unfair surprise or frustration of legitimate expectations. . . . Because Allstate was doing business in Minnesota and was . . . aware that Mr. Hague was a Minnesota employee, it had to have anticipated that Minnesota law might apply to an accident in which Mr. Hague was involved. Indeed, Allstate specifically anticipated . . . an accident either in Minnesota or elsewhere . . . outside of Wisconsin, since the policy it issued offered continental coverage. [T]he policy contained no choice-of-law clause dictating application of Wisconsin law.

[25] Justice Black's dissent in the first *Clay* decision . . . subsequently commanded majority support in the second *Clay* decision. Clay v. Sun Insurance Office, Ltd., 377 U.S. 179, 181–182 (1964) (*Clay II*).

in anticipation of this litigation or for the purpose of finding a legal climate especially hospitable to her claim. . . .[28]

While *John Hancock Mutual Life Ins. Co. v. Yates, supra*, held that a postoccurrence change of residence to the forum State was insufficient in and of itself to confer power on the forum State to choose its law, that case did not hold that such a change of residence was irrelevant. Here, of course, respondent's bona fide residence in Minnesota was not the sole contact Minnesota had with this litigation. And in connection with her residence in Minnesota, respondent was appointed personal representative of Mr. Hague's estate by the Registrar of Probate for the County of Goodhue, Minn. Respondent's residence and subsequent appointment in Minnesota as personal representative of her late husband's estate constitute a Minnesota contact which gives Minnesota an interest in respondent's recovery, an interest which the court below identified as full compensation for "resident accident victims" to keep them "off welfare rolls" and able "to meet financial obligations."

In sum, Minnesota had a significant aggregation[29] of contacts with the parties and the occurrence, creating state interests, such that application of its law was neither arbitrary nor fundamentally unfair. Accordingly, the choice of Minnesota law by the Minnesota Supreme Court did not violate the Due Process Clause or the Full Faith and Credit Clause.

JUSTICE STEVENS, concurring in the judgment.

As I view this unusual case—in which neither precedent nor constitutional language provides sure guidance—two separate questions must be answered. First, does the Full Faith and Credit Clause *require* Minnesota, the forum State, to apply Wisconsin law? Second, does the Due Process Clause of the Fourteenth Amendment *prevent* Minnesota from applying its own law? The first inquiry implicates the federal interest in ensuring that Minnesota respect the sovereignty of the State of Wisconsin; the second implicates the litigants' interests in a fair adjudication of their rights.

I realize that both this Court's analysis of choice-of-law questions and scholarly criticism of those decisions have treated these two inquiries as though they were indistinguishable. Nevertheless, I am persuaded that the two constitutional provisions protect different interests and that proper analysis requires separate consideration of each.

I

The Full Faith and Credit Clause . . . does not . . . rigidly require the forum State to apply foreign law whenever another State has a valid interest in the litigation. . . . [I]n my opinion, the Clause should not invalidate a state court's choice of forum law unless that choice threatens the federal interest in national unity by unjustifiably infringing upon the legitimate interests of another State.

---

[28] The dissent suggests that considering respondent's postoccurrence change of residence as one of the Minnesota contacts will encourage forum shopping. This overlooks the fact that her change of residence was bona fide and not motivated by litigation considerations.

[29] We express no view whether the first two contacts, either together or separately, would have sufficed to sustain the choice of Minnesota law made by the Minnesota Supreme Court.

In this case, I think the Minnesota courts' decision to apply Minnesota law was plainly unsound as a matter of normal conflicts law. . . . Nevertheless, I do not believe that any threat to national unity or Wisconsin's sovereignty ensues from allowing the substantive question presented by this case to be determined by the law of another State.

. . . Since the policy provided coverage for accidents that might occur in other States, it was obvious to the parties at the time of contracting that it might give rise to the application of the law of States other than Wisconsin. . . . Therefore, while Wisconsin may have an interest in ensuring that contracts formed in Wisconsin in reliance upon Wisconsin law are interpreted in accordance with that law, that interest is not implicated in this case.

. . . Petitioner has failed to establish that Minnesota's refusal to apply Wisconsin law poses any direct or indirect threat to Wisconsin's sovereignty. . . .

## II

[A] choice-of-law decision would violate the Due Process Clause if it were totally arbitrary or if it were fundamentally unfair to either litigant. I question whether a judge's decision to apply the law of his own State could ever be described as wholly irrational. . . . The forum State's interest in the fair and efficient administration of justice is therefore sufficient, in my judgment, to attach a presumption of validity to a forum State's decision to apply its own law to a dispute over which it has jurisdiction.

. . . Concern about the [fundamental] fairness of the forum's choice of its own rule might arise if that rule favored residents over nonresidents, if it represented a dramatic departure from the rule that obtains in most American jurisdictions, or if the rule itself was unfair on its face or as applied.

The application of an otherwise acceptable rule of law may result in unfairness to the litigants if, in engaging in the activity which is the subject of the litigation, they could not reasonably have anticipated that their actions would later be judged by this rule of law. A choice-of-law decision that frustrates the justifiable expectations of the parties can be fundamentally unfair. This desire to prevent unfair surprise to a litigant has been the central concern in this Court's review of choiceof-law decisions under the Due Process Clause.[16]

Neither the "stacking" rule itself, nor Minnesota's application of that rule to these litigants, raises any serious question of fairness. . . . [T]he rule is consistent with the economics of a contractual relationship in which the policyholder paid three separate premiums for insurance coverage for three automobiles, including a separate premium for each uninsured motorist coverage. Nor am I persuaded that the decision of the Minnesota courts to apply the "stacking" rule in this case can be said to violate due process because that decision frustrates the reasonable expectations of the contracting parties. . . .

---

[16] Upon careful analysis most of the decisions of this Court that struck down on due process grounds a state court's choice of forum law can be explained as attempts to prevent a State with a minimal contact with the litigation from materially enlarging the contractual obligations of one of the parties where that party had no reason to anticipate the possibility of such enlargement.

In this case, no express indication of the parties' expectations is available. The insurance policy provided coverage for accidents throughout the United States. . . . By virtue of doing business in Minnesota, Allstate was aware that it could be sued in the Minnesota courts; Allstate also presumably was aware that Minnesota law, as well as the law of most States, permitted "stacking.". . . Therefore, the decision of the Minnesota courts to apply the law of the forum in this case does not frustrate the reasonable expectations of the contracting parties. . . .

In terms of fundamental fairness, it seems to me that two factors relied upon by the plurality—the plaintiff's post-accident move to Minnesota and the decedent's Minnesota employment—are either irrelevant to or possibly even tend to undermine the plurality's conclusion. When the expectations of the parties at the time of contracting are the central due process concern, as they are in this case, an unanticipated post-accident occurrence is clearly irrelevant for due process purposes. . . . Similarly, while the fact that the decedent regularly drove into Minnesota might be relevant to the expectations of the contracting parties, the fact that he did so because he was employed in Minnesota adds nothing to the due process analysis. The choice-of-law decision of the Minnesota courts is consistent with due process because it does not result in unfairness to either litigant, not because Minnesota now has an interest in the plaintiff as resident or formerly had an interest in the decedent as employee. . . .

JUSTICE POWELL, with whom THE CHIEF JUSTICE and JUSTICE REHNQUIST join, dissenting.

My disagreement with the plurality is narrow. I accept with few reservations Part II of the plurality opinion, which sets forth the basic principles that guide us in reviewing state choice-of-law decisions under the Constitution. The Court should invalidate a forum State's decision to apply its own law only when there are no significant contacts between the State and the litigation. This modest check on state power is mandated by the Due Process Clause of the Fourteenth Amendment and the Full Faith and Credit Clause of Art. IV, § 1. I do not believe, however, that the plurality adequately analyzes the policies such review must serve. In consequence, it has found significant what appear to me to be trivial contacts between the forum State and the litigation.

## I

. . . Two enduring policies emerge from our cases.

First, the contacts between the forum State and the litigation should not be so "slight and casual" that it would be fundamentally unfair to a litigant for the forum to apply its own State's law. The touchstone here is the reasonable expectation of the parties. *See* Weintraub, *Due Process and Full Faith and Credit Limitations on a State's Choice of Law*, 44 IOWA L. REV. 449, 445–457 (1959).

Second, the forum State must have a legitimate interest in the outcome of the litigation before it. . . .

The State has a legitimate interest in applying a rule of decision to the litigation only if the facts to which the rule will be applied have created effects within the State, toward which the State's public policy is directed. To assess the sufficiency of asserted contacts between the forum and the litigation, the court must determine if the contacts form a reasonable link between the litigation and a state policy. . . . If [so], the Constitution is satisfied.

*John Hancock Mut. Life Ins. Co. v. Yates* [relied on by the plurality], illustrates this principle. A life insurance policy was executed in New York, on a New York insured with a New York beneficiary. The insured died in New York; his beneficiary moved to Georgia and sued to recover on the policy. The insurance company defended on the ground that the insured, in the application for the policy, had made materially false statements that rendered it void under New York law. This Court reversed the Georgia court's application of its contrary rule that all questions of the policy's validity must be determined by the jury. The Court found a violation of the Full Faith and Credit Clause, because . . . Georgia had no legitimate interest in applying its own law to the legal issue of liability. Georgia's contacts with the contract of insurance were nonexistent. . . .

## II

. . . Applying these principles to the facts of this case, I do not believe, however, that Minnesota had sufficient contacts with the "persons and events" in this litigation to apply its rule permitting stacking. I would agree that no reasonable expectations of the parties were frustrated. . . .

The more doubtful question in this case is whether application of Minnesota's substantive law reasonably furthers a legitimate state interest. The plurality attempts to give substance to the tenuous contacts between Minnesota and this litigation. Upon examination, however, these contacts are either trivial or irrelevant to the furthering of any public policy in Minnesota.

First, the post-accident residence of the plaintiff-beneficiary is constitutionally irrelevant to the choice-of-law question. *John Hancock Mut. Life Ins. Co. v. Yates, supra.* The plurality today insists that *Yates* only held that a postoccurrence move to the forum State could not "in and of itself" confer power on the forum to apply its own law, but did not establish that such a change of residence was irrelevant. What the *Yates* Court held, however, was that "there was no occurrence, *nothing* done, to which the law of Georgia could apply." Any possible ambiguity in the Court's view of the significance of a postoccurrence change of residence is dispelled by *Home Ins. Co. v. Dick*, [p. 485, *supra*], where it was held squarely that *Dick's* post-accident move to the forum State was "without significance."

This rule is sound. If a plaintiff could choose the substantive rules to be applied to an action by moving to a hospitable forum, the invitation to forum shopping would be irresistible. Moreover, it would permit the defendant's reasonable expectations at the time the cause of action accrues to be frustrated, because it would permit the choice-of-law question to turn on a postaccrual circumstance. Finally, postaccrual residence has nothing to do with facts to which the forum State proposes to apply its rule; it is unrelated to the substantive legal issues presented by the litigation.

Second, the plurality finds it significant that the insurer does business in the forum State. The State does have a legitimate interest in regulating the practices of such an insurer. But this argument proves too much. The insurer here does business in all fifty States. . . .

Third, the plurality emphasizes particularly that the insured worked in the forum State.[5]

The insured's place of employment is not . . . significant in this case. . . . Minnesota does not wish its workers to die in automobile accidents, but permitting stacking will not further this interest. [W]hether the compensation provided by this policy is increased or not will have no relation to the State's employment policies or police power.

Neither taken separately nor in the aggregate do the contacts asserted by the plurality today indicate that Minnesota's application of its substantive rule in this case will further any legitimate state interest.[6] The plurality focuses only on physical contacts *vel non*, and in doing so pays scant attention to the more fundamental reasons why our precedents require reasonable policy-related contacts in choice-of-law cases. Therefore, I dissent.

-------

## NOTES AND QUESTIONS ON *HAGUE*

(1) *The sufficiency of interests in Hague.* An outpouring of criticism greeted the *Hague* decision, largely on the point made by Justice Powell: If the interests of the Minnesota forum in *Hague* were so weak as to require aggregation before forum law could be sustained, how does aggregation *help*? Three zeroes equal zero. *See* Phaedon Kozyris, *Reflections on Allstate — The Lessening of Due Process in Choice of Law*, 14 U.C.D. L. Rev. 889 (1981); Silberman, *Can the State of Minnesota Bind the Nation? Federal Choice-of-Law Constraints After Allstate Insurance Co. v. Hague,* 10 HOFSTRA L. REV. 102 (1983) ("state parochialism"); Aaron Twerski, *On Territoriality and Sovereignty: System Shock and Constitutional Choice of Law*, 10 HOFSTRA L. REV. 149, 151 (1981) ("unrestrained state chauvinism"); Arthur von Mehren & Trautman, *Constitutional Control of Choice of Law: Some Reflections on Hague*, 10 HOFSTRA L. REV. 149, 151 (1981) ("unprincipled"; "parochial").

-------

[5] The plurality exacts double service from this fact, by finding a separate contact in that the insured commuted daily to his job. This is merely a repetition of the facts that the insured lived in Wisconsin and worked in Minnesota. The State does have an interest in the safety of motorists who use its roads. . . . This safety interest, however, cannot encompass . . . the determination whether a nonresident's estate can stack benefit coverage in a policy written in another State regarding an accident that occurred on another State's roads.

[6] [Justice Stevens' opinion] supports my view that the forum State's application of its own law to this case cannot be justified by the existence of relevant . . . contacts. . . . The interesting analysis he proposes to uphold the State's judgment is, however, difficult to reconcile with our prior decisions and may create more problems than it solves. For example, it seems questionable to measure the interest of a State in a controversy by the degree of conscious reliance on that State's law by private parties to a contract. Moreover, scrutinizing the strength of the interests of a nonforum State may draw this Court back into the discredited practice of weighing the relative interests of various States in a particular controversy.

The facts of *Hague* may seem to warrant this collective outrage. Is it possible, nevertheless, that the collective judgment about the case is wrong?

(2) *A contrarian view.* At the time of trial, a Minnesota widow was suing a Minnesota insurance company under her own state's law in her own state's courts for a favorable interpretation of a Wisconsin policy of which she, as administratrix, was the designated beneficiary; arguably, the policy was thus a "Minnesota" asset of the estate of which the widow was the Minnesota administratrix. What were the reasons for Minnesota's rule prohibiting the interpretation of "other insurance" clauses so as to block stacking of paid-for coverages with a single insurer? At the time of trial, were Lavinia and Allstate within the scope of the legislation?

Are you certain that the lateness of Lavinia's arrival in Minnesota strips Minnesota of power? It has been held unconstitutional for the forum to withhold the benefits of its laws from a recently arrived resident. In *Zobel v. Williams,* 457 U.S. 55 (1982), the Supreme Court held that a state may not distribute lesser amounts of state oil revenues to more recent residents than to long-settled residents. In *Hooper v. Bernalillo,* 472 U.S. 612 (1985), the Supreme Court held on equal protection grounds that a state may not withhold Vietnam veterans' benefits from veterans who settled in the state after the Vietnam war was over. *See generally* Katheryn D. Katz, *More Equal Than Others: The Burger Court and the Newly Arrived State Resident*, 19 NEW MEX. L. REV. 330 (1989).

The Supreme Court has recently shifted its constitutional theory of such cases from the Fourteenth Amendment's Equal Protection Clause to the Fourteenth Amendment's Privileges and Immunities Clause. *See Saenz v. Roe,* 526 U.S. 489 (2002). How does this change the analysis of such cases? The Equal Protection Clause forbids the forum from withholding the benefit of its laws from the new bona fide residents. The Privileges and Immunities Clause forbids the forum from impeding the exercise of a federal right of interstate travel by so doing. But under each of these analyses, the question is the constitutionality, under federal law, of a state law depriving the newcomer of a state benefit, or putting the newcomer at a disadvantage vis-a-vis the benefit.

In *Hague*, were Wisconsin's interests so weighty that, as critics of the case strenuously urge, the Supreme Court should have fashioned a newly restrictive constitutional rule, depriving the interested forum of power? Could you argue that Wisconsin's interest in the case all but collapsed by the time of decision? Even if Wisconsin law clearly backed the insurer, can we be sure Wisconsin would have applied it? Wisconsin follows the "better law" approach to choice-of-law.

On the problems raised in this Note, *see generally* Louise Weinberg, *Conflicts Cases and the Problem of Relevant Time: A Response to the Hague Symposium*, 10 HOFSTRA L. REV. 1023 (1982). Professor Leflar observes that most American courts would decide a case on *Hague* facts the way Minnesota did, at least now that *Hague* is on the books. *See* Robert Leflar, *Choice of Law: States' Rights*, 10 HOFSTRA L. REV. 203, 204, 211 (1981).

*See* PROBLEM 5-6. THE SERVICE LETTER.

(3) **LETTIERI v. EQUITABLE LIFE ASSURANCE SOCIETY**, 627 F.2d 930 (9th Cir. 1980). This case was similar to *John Hancock Mutual Life Ins. Co. v. Yates*, discussed by both the plurality and dissent in *Hague*. The question was whether, in an action on a life insurance policy, where the decedent had misrepresented the state of his health in his written application for insurance, evidence was admissible to show that the insured had, in fact, told the agent the truth at the time of applying. In both *Yates* and *Lettieri* the widow was suing in a state to which she had moved after the underlying events had occurred. *Yates* had struck down the forum's permissive evidence rule on the theory that the law of the place of contracting must govern.

*Held* (without discussing *Yates*): The evidence is admissible under forum law.

\* \* \*

In *Hague*, need the Supreme Court have been so deferential to *Yates*?

(4) *Post-occurrence changes in law or facts.* Some of the furor *Hague* generated among observers springs from traditional concerns about vested rights or retroactivity. When are retroactive legal standards legitimate? At common law, all decisions were retroactive in effect, *cf. Hamm v. City of Rock Hill,* 379 U.S. 306 (1964). The theory was that the rule of a case was found, not fashioned. Only statutes were prospective in effect. When should post-occurrence changes in law be allowed to make a difference today? No one would argue that a taxpayer with a 1985 tax liability, finally forced to pay it in 1987, should pay at 1987 rates. Equally, no one would argue that a racially restrictive covenant, entered into prior to *Shelley v. Kraemer,* 334 U.S. 1 (1948) (courts may not enforce racially restrictive covenants), is enforceable after *Shelley v. Kraemer*. What is the difference between the two situations?

A state, of course, must have sufficient power to meet the legitimate needs of ongoing governance. *See Hanson v. Denckla,* 357 U.S. 235, 253 (1958) (the state of the after-acquired residence of the decedent settlor of a trust could determine the validity, under its own laws, of a trust created in the settler's former domicile state, the trust assets being administered in a third state); *Williams v. North Carolina [Williams I],* 317 U.S. 287 (1942) (state that is new domicile of a party to a marriage has a legitimate interest in its new domiciliary's marital status, notwithstanding that the marriage and long-term residence of the married couple was in another state).

(5) *The post-transaction departure of a party.* Suppose that state civil service workers will accept certain jobs if the state undertakes to supply a pension to the surviving spouse in the event of the worker's death. Does the state retain its interest in payment of the pension even if the surviving spouse moves to another state? If so, would a termination of benefits be discriminatory? *Cf. Gore v. Northeast Airlines,* 373 F.2d 717 (2d Cir. 1967) (holding for the widow).

On the problems raised in Notes (4) and (5), *see generally* Note, *Post Transaction or Occurrence Events in Conflict of Laws,* 69 COLUM. L. REV. 843 (1969); John K. McNulty, *Corporations and the Intertemporal Conflict of Laws,* 55 CALIF. L. REV. 12 (1967).

(6) *A destabilization of minimal scrutiny?* Note the intriguing theoretical debate going on in *Hague*. The Justices seem to be arguing not only the permissibility of Minnesota's law, but also a more fundamental question: What kind of review ought the Court to be giving?

With Justice Powell, critics of *Hague* see it as overly-permissive, and largely based on fictional interests. But the level of scrutiny in *Hague* may have been *more* strict than required by the modern, "minimal scrutiny," position. The *Hague* plurality itself put at serious constitutional discount each of the forum "contacts" it identified—Lavinia's after-acquired residence, Allstate's general presence in the forum, and Ralph's employment there. *See* Notes (1)–(3), *supra*. For the view that *Hague* destabilized rational-basis scrutiny of conflicts cases, see Louise Weinberg, *Choice of Law and Minimal Scrutiny*, 79 U. CHI. L. REV. 440, 462–63 (1982).

(7) *Foreseeability review.* Note that there seems to be a difference between "fundamental fairness" (the basic requirement of due process, which is satisfied by the finding that what the state has done is justified by a legitimate governmental interest) and "fairness" (foreseeability). Justice Brennan deals with foreseeability, but chiefly in footnotes. In *Phillips Petroleum Co. v. Shutts,* the case following these Notes, the Court does introduce a foreseeability test, but can cite as authority for this only Justice Powell's *Hague* dissent. For a debate on the extent of foreseeability review in *Hague*, see Courtland Peterson, *Jurisdiction and Choice of Law Revisited*, 59 COLO. L. REV. 37, 42 (1988); Louise Weinberg, *The Place of Trial and the Law Applied: Overhauling Constitutional Theory*, 59 COLO. L. REV. 67. 96 (1988).

How useful a test is foreseeability of the law that will be applied? In contract cases, such a requirement might seem especially sensible. Would such a requirement clash with the equally sensible and time-honored view that the parties expect law that will validate their undertakings? *See Pritchard v. Norton,* 106 U.S. 124 (1882). What is the likelihood that the parties have expectations of law in negligence cases? In cases of intentional tort, should a party be permitted to commit a wrong with interstate consequences by planning to commit it where the law shields her from liability? Can an insurer be "unfairly surprised?" *See* Russell Weintraub, *Who's Afraid of Constitutional Limitations on Choice of Law?*, 10 HOFSTRA L. REV. 17, 27 (1981).

How realistic is it to speak of expectations of governing law? Is a party likely to be concerned that the *wrong state* will hold her liable? What if there is no conflict between the two states' laws? *See* Earl Maltz, *Visions of Fairness—The Relationship Between Jurisdiction and Choice of Law*, 30 ARIZ. L. REV. 751, 767 (1988). More fundamentally, since an American court almost always has "minimum contacts" with the defendant, won't forum law affecting the defendant almost always pass a foreseeability test, as it did in *Nevada v. Hall* and *Hague*?

If the Court today were to undertake a program of scrutinizing the choice of an interested state's law for foreseeability (or comity), is there a danger that the Court would have to construct a body of federal common law, analogous to its awkward "minimum contacts" jurisdictional jurisprudence? *See* Friedrich K. Juenger, *Supreme Court Intervention in Jurisdiction and Choice of Law: A Dismal Prospect*, 14 U.C. DAVIS L. REV. 907 (1981); Louise

Weinberg, *Choice of Law and Minimal Scrutiny* 79 U. CHI. L. REV. 440, 474-78 (1982).

For other useful writing on *Hague,* see *A Response to the Hague Symposium,* 10 HOFSTRA L. REV. 973-1072 (1982), with contributions by Professors Peterson, Weinberg, Lowenfeld and Kirgis; Shreve, *In Search of a Choice-of-Law Reviewing Standard—Reflections on Allstate Insurance Co. v. Hague,* 66 MINN. L. REV. 327 (1982); *Symposium: Choice-of-Law Theory after Allstate Insurance Co. v. Hague,* 10 HOFSTRA L. REV. 1-211 (1981), with contributions by Professors Cavers, Weintraub, von Mehren & Trautman, Sedler, Silberman, Martin, Twerski, Davies, Reese and Leflar; *Symposium: Choice of Law,* 14 U.C. DAVIS L. REV. 837–918 (1981), with contributions by Professors Juenger, Lowenfeld & Silberman, Peterson, and Kozyris.

(8) *Ironic footnote.* In an apparent attempt to overturn *Hague,* the Minnesota legislature has overshot its target, and made Minnesota the only state in the country absolutely to *prohibit* the payout of "stacked" multiple uninsured motorist coverages, regardless of the number of premiums paid. *Cf. AMCO Ins. Co. v. Lang,* 420 N.W.2d 895 (Minn. 1988); *Matter of State Farm Mut. Auto Ins. Co.,* 392 N.W.2d 558 (Minn. App. 1986). The new statute apparently could block the stacking of coverages even in the absence of an anti-stacking clause in the policy. Minn. Stat. Ann. § 65B.49(3a)(6), effective October 1, 1985.

Minnesota appellate courts are refusing to apply this legislation retrospectively, even where to do so would eliminate any conflict of laws. *See Wille v. Farm Bureau Mutual Ins. Co.,* 432 N.W.2d 784 (Minn. App. 1988). Is this disregard of a post-accident change in law consistent with Minnesota's treatment of the widow's post-accident change of residence in *Hague?*

---

# PHILLIPS PETROLEUM CO. v. SHUTTS

*United States Supreme Court*
*472 U.S. 797, 105 S. Ct. 2965, 86 L. Ed. 2d 628 (1985)*

JUSTICE REHNQUIST delivered the opinion of the Court.

[The jurisdictional decision in this case is reported in § 3.12[C][2], *supra.*]

[This was a nationwide class action by some 28,000 owners of royalty rights to leased gaslands, residing throughout the United States and several foreign countries. The defendant, Phillips Petroleum Company, had suspended increases in royalty payments pending approval of new rates by the Federal Power Commission.* When the agency approved the rates, Phillips paid the suspended royalty increases to the royalty owners. However, Phillips did not pay interest for use of the monies during the years of suspension. The royalty owners sued Phillips for the interest payments withheld. The action was brought

---

* [If the Commission eventually denied Phillips' proposed price increase or reduced the proposed increase, Phillips would have had to refund to its gas customers the difference between the approved price and the higher price charged, plus interest at a rate set by statute. *See* 18 CFR § 154, 102 (1984). —*Ed.*]

in a state court in Kansas, a state where Phillips was heavily involved in gasland leasing, and where similar litigation against Phillips had already been successful.

The leased gaslands were located in 11 different States. Less than a quarter of one percent of the gas leases involved in the lawsuit concerned Kansas land. The named plaintiff was a resident of Kansas. But less than 1,000 of the 33,000 class members resided in Kansas. Defendant Phillips was a Delaware corporation with a principal place of business in Oklahoma.]

## I

As a threshold matter we must determine whether petitioner has standing to assert the claim that Kansas did not possess proper jurisdiction over the many plaintiffs in the class who were not Kansas residents and had no connection with Kansas. . . .

Respondents may be correct that petitioner does not possess standing *jus tertii*, but this is not the issue. . . .

[P]etitioner has alleged that it would be obviously and immediately injured if this class-action judgment against it became final without binding the plaintiff class. We think that such an injury is sufficient to give petitioner standing on its own right to raise the jurisdiction claim in this Court. . . .

## II

[The Court next sustained the adjudicatory jurisdiction of the Kansas forum over the absentee class-members (see the report of this part of *Shutts* in Chapter 3, § 3.12[C][2], *supra*), in part on the theory that the class-members' failure to "opt out" was tantamount to consent.]

## III

The Kansas courts applied Kansas contract and Kansas equity law to every claim in this case, notwithstanding that over 99% of the gas leases and some 97% of the plaintiffs in the case had no apparent connection to the State of Kansas except for this lawsuit. [Phillips] protested that the Kansas courts should apply the laws of the States where the leases were located, or at least apply Texas and Oklahoma law because so many of the leases came from those States. . . .

[Phillips] contends that total application of Kansas substantive law violated the constitutional limitations on choice of law mandated by the Due Process Clause of the Fourteenth Amendment and the Full Faith and Credit Clause of Article IV, § 1. We must first determine whether Kansas law conflicts in any material way with any other law which could apply. There can be no injury in applying Kansas law if it is not in conflict with that of any other jurisdiction connected to this suit.

[Phillips] claims that Kansas law conflicts with that of a number of States connected to this litigation, especially Texas and Oklahoma. . . .

The conflicts on the applicable interest rates, alone—which we do not think can be labeled "false conflicts" without a more thoroughgoing treatment than was accorded them by the Supreme Court of Kansas—certainly amounted to millions of dollars in liability.* We think that the Supreme Court of Kansas erred in deciding on the basis that it did that the application of its laws to all claims would be constitutional.

Four Terms ago we addressed a similar situation in *Allstate Ins. Co. v. Hague*[, *supra*]. In that case we . . . [stated] "that for a State's substantive law to be selected in a constitutionally permissible manner, that State must have a significant contact or significant aggregation of contacts, creating state interests, such that choice of its law is neither arbitrary nor fundamentally unfair." The dissenting Justices were in substantial agreement with this principle. . . .

[The Kansas court reasoned that Phillips] owns property and conducts substantial business in the State, so Kansas . . . has an interest in regulating petitioner's conduct in Kansas. Moreover, oil and gas extraction is an important business to Kansas, and although only a few leases in issue are located in Kansas, hundreds of Kansas plaintiffs were affected by petitioner's suspension of royalties; thus . . . the State has a real interest in protecting . . . these royalty owners. . . . [T]he Kansas court buttressed its use of Kansas law by stating that this lawsuit was analogous to a suit against a "common fund" located in Kansas.

We do not lightly discount this description of Kansas' contacts with this litigation and its interest in applying its law. There is, however, no "common fund" located in Kansas that would require or support the application of only Kansas law to all these claims. . . .

We also give little credence to the idea that Kansas law should apply to all claims because the plaintiffs, by failing to opt out, evinced their desire to be bound by Kansas law. Even if one could say that the plaintiffs "consented" to the application of Kansas law by not opting out, plaintiff's desire for forum law is rarely, if ever controlling. In most cases the plaintiff shows his obvious wish for forum law by filing there. "If a plaintiff could choose the substantive rules to be applied to an action . . . the invitation to forum shopping would be irresistible." *Allstate*, 449 U.S., at 337 (opinion of POWELL, J.). Even if a plaintiff evidences his desire for forum law by moving to the forum, we have generally accorded such a move little or no significance. In *Allstate* the plaintiff's move to the forum was only relevant because it was unrelated and prior to the litigation. Thus the plaintiffs' desire for Kansas law, manifested by their participation in this Kansas lawsuit, bears little relevance.

The Supreme Court of Kansas in its opinion in this case expressed the view that by reason of the fact that it was adjudicating a nationwide class action, it had much greater latitude in applying its own law to the transactions in question than might otherwise be the case. . . .

We think that this is something of a "bootstrap" argument. . . . [A State] may not take a transaction with little or no relationship to the forum and apply

---

* [The federal statutory rate Kansas applied as a matter of its own law went from 7 to 9% per annum, and thereafter to the average prime rate, compounded quarterly. The statutory interest rates of Texas and Oklahoma were each 6%; of Louisiana, 7%. —Ed.]

the law of the forum in order to satisfy the procedural requirement that there be a "common question of law." The issue of personal jurisdiction over plaintiffs in a class action is entirely distinct from the question of the constitutional limitations on choice of law; the latter calculus is not altered by the fact that it may be more difficult or more burdensome to comply with the constitutional limitations because of the large number of transactions which the State proposes to adjudicate and which have little connection with the forum.

. . . Given Kansas' lack of "interest" in claims unrelated to that State, and the substantive conflict with jurisdictions such as Texas, we conclude that application of Kansas law to every claim in this case is sufficiently arbitrary and unfair as to exceed constitutional limits.

When considering fairness in this context, an important element is the expectation of the parties. *See Allstate, supra*, 449 U.S., at 333 (opinion of Powell, J.). There is no indication that when the leases involving land and royalty owners outside of Kansas were executed, the parties had any idea that Kansas law would control. . . .

Here the Supreme Court of Kansas took the view that in a nationwide class action where procedural due process guarantees of notice and adequate representation were met, "the laws of the forum should be applied unless compelling reasons exist for applying a different law." Whatever practical reasons may have commended this rule to the Supreme Court of Kansas, for the reasons already stated we do not believe that it is consistent with the decisions of this Court. We make no effort to determine for ourselves which law must apply to the various transactions involved in this lawsuit, and we reaffirm our observation in *Allstate* that in many situations a state court may be free to apply one of several choices of law. But the constitutional limitations laid down in cases such as *Allstate* and *Home Insurance Co. v. Dick, supra*, must be respected even in a nationwide class action. . . .

JUSTICE POWELL took no part in the decision of this case.

JUSTICE STEVENS, concurring in part and dissenting in part.

. . . A fair reading of the Kansas Supreme Court's opinion . . . reveals that the Kansas court has examined the laws of connected jurisdictions and has correctly concluded that there is no "direct" or "substantive" conflict between the law applied by Kansas and the laws of those other States. . . .

. . . I therefore can find no due process violation in the Kansas court's decision.[24]

---

[24] Neither Phillips nor the Court contends that Kansas cannot constitutionally apply its own laws to the claims of Kansas residents, even though the leased land may lie in other states and no other apparent connection to Kansas may exist. Phillips has done business in Kansas throughout the years relevant to this litigation and it seems unarguable that application of Kansas law, or indeed the law of any of the fifty states where royalty owners reside, to the claims of at least some of the plaintiff class members was thus perceived as possible by Phillips at the time of contracting. It was also possible, of course, that any number of royalty owners might have moved to Kansas in the years Phillips held their suspense royalties, and that Kansas has a substantial interest in seeing its residents treated fairly when they invoke the jurisdiction of its courts. *See* Louise Weinberg, *Conflicts Cases and the Problem of Relevant Time*, 10 HOFSTRA L. REV. 1023, 1040–1043 (1982). . . .

## NOTES AND QUESTIONS ON *SHUTTS*

(1) *Shutts* was the first case since 1947 in which the Supreme Court struck down a choice of law. *See United Order of Com. Travelers of Am. v. Wolfe,* 331 U.S. 586 (1947) (limited to its "unique facts" in *Clay v. Sun Ins. Office,* 377 U.S. 179, 183 (1964)). Did *Shutts* warrant such treatment? The Court seems to assume that the situs of the leased gaslands could, and perhaps should, govern this equitable action for interest on suspended payments to leaseholders. Does anything justify such an assumption?

(2) *The problem of the absentee classmembers.* In the jurisdictional wing of its *Shutts* opinion, *see* § 3.12[C][2], *supra*, the Court holds that an absentee classmember's failure to "opt out," given notice and adequate representation, would be tantamount to consent to jurisdiction. But in the conflicts wing of the opinion, the Court says that even if the failure to "opt out" was also "consent" to forum law, consent would not count. Why not? Why wasn't the actual consent of the adequate class representative sufficient?

Of course the rights of the absentees were not threatened by forum law. Was there a lacuna in Justice Rehnquist's reasoning? The defendant, unlike the absent classmembers, was doing business in Kansas, and was heavily involved in gas leasing there. There was no question that Kansas had personal jurisdiction over Phillips. Phillips must have been within Kansas' regulatory power to some extent.

Once Kansas' regulatory power over the Kansas Phillips is weighed in, even supposing that Kansas' power could not extend to all the claims of absent classmembers, doesn't consent cure the deficiency? It is the general rule that courts will recognize reasonable stipulations for law. Is the forum's interest in even-handedness sufficient to justify its extending the benefit of its laws to the whole consenting class? *See* Justice Brennan's concurrence in *Sun Oil Co. v. Wortman,* § 5.04, *infra*.

(2) *General jurisdiction and choice of law.* In *Hague*, at footnote 29 (*supra*), the Court refused to decide whether defendant Allstate's forum presence was sufficient, without more, to ground the choice of forum law. Instead, the Court "aggregated" this contact with other, equally controversial contacts between the forum and the case. In *Shutts*, why weren't Kansas' contacts with defendant Phillips "aggregated" with Kansas' other contacts with the case?

The problem is not merely, as Justice Powell suggests in his *Hague* dissent, that the defendant is a resident of the forum in no greater sense than it is a resident of other states. The greater difficulty may be that the plaintiff seems to be suing the wrong defendant. If you slip and fall in a dime store in Wisconsin, and then move to Minnesota and sue the local embodiment of the dime store company, isn't there a sense in which you are suing the wrong dime store?

(3) *Shutts and complex litigation.* Is *Shutts* consistent with *Keeton v. Hustler Magazine,* § 3.10, *supra*? Justice Rehnquist was the author of *Keeton* as well as *Shutts*, and was notably optimistic in *Keeton* that the forum would have

power to govern the nationwide libels alleged in that litigation. Moreover, in *Keeton* Rehnquist argued that the forum had an interest in unitary litigation of the nationwide claims; in *Shutts*, he dismisses administrative convenience as a factor, distinguishing choice of law from jurisdiction. Does that distinction make a difference? Is it any more meaningful a distinction that there was only one claimant in *Keeton*?

If the law of a class case is to be individualized, how can adequacy of representation ever be achieved? Without the "bootstrap" so discounted by Justice Rehnquist, how can a nationwide class action ever contain a preponderance of common issues of law?

*Shutts* also seems to have constitutionalized the similar effect of *Van Dusen v. Barrack, see* § 6.15, *infra*, upon transferred consolidated cases in federal courts. Does *Shutts* mandate reference to the internal law of the individual claim state? Or to that state's conflicts rules, as does *Van Dusen?* Both cases have enormous impact on mass disaster and toxic tort litigation. *Cf. In re Agent Orange Product Liability Litigation*, § 6.15, *infra*.

(4) *Residual forum law.* Forum law is often the residual choice of courts. Residual forum law is considered inevitable by Justice Stevens in his separate opinion in *Hague*. It is woven into the fabric of interest analytic thought. After *Shutts*, when is the residual choice of forum law constitutional?

(5) *Shutts and minimal scrutiny.* Justice Rehnquist's *Shutts* opinion explicitly endorses the test for "state interest" articulated in *Hague* by Justice Brennan. But *Shutts* nevertheless seems to move the Court toward more restrictive scrutiny. *See* Louise Weinberg, *The Place of Trial and the Law Applied: Overhauling Constitutional Theory*, 59 U. COLO. L. REV. 67 (1988); Pielemeier, *Why We Should Worry About Full Faith and Credit to Laws*, 60 SO. CAL. L. REV. 1299, 1300 (1987). Justice Rehnquist states that foreseeability is a requirement, citing Justice Powell's dissent in *Hague*. Justice Rehnquist also sums up Kansas' general jurisdiction over the defendant as amounting to "little or no" significant contact between the forum and the case; yet this contact was held not constitutionally irrelevant in *Hague*. Given that the forum had *some* interests, *Shutts* seems to require a reference to the law of a *more* interested state. Does the majority's position move the law toward a Full Faith and Credit standard? *Shutts* was read precisely in this fashion by counsel for the defendant in the following case.

---

## SUN OIL CO. v. WORTMAN

*United States Supreme Court*
*486 U.S. 717, 108 S. Ct. 2117, 100 L. Ed. 2d 743 (1988)*

JUSTICE SCALIA delivered the opinion of the Court.

### I

[This case, factually similar to *Shutts*, § 5.04, *supra*, had been before the Supreme Court previously. The defendant, Sun Oil Company, was a Delaware corporation with a principal place of business in Texas. The contacts between Kansas and the claims of the class were much less substantial than in *Shutts*. When *Shutts* was reversed and remanded, this case was remanded also. On remand in both cases, the Kansas Supreme Court stuck to its earlier rulings, holding that all other concerned states "would" apply the same liability rules and interest rate that Kansas had applied.

A further issue in *Wortman* had to do with the statute of limitations. The Kansas supreme court held that it was free to apply its own 5-year statute of limitations to all the claims of the class, because the limitations issue was "procedural." Most of the claims would have been time-barred in the situs states. The Kansas supreme court distinguished the Supreme Court's ruling in *Shutts* as not involving a "procedural" issue.

Defendants sought review again in the Supreme Court in both *Shutts* and *Wortman*, and the Supreme Court granted review in *Wortman*. Wortman involved properties approximately 40% of which were located in Texas, 25% in Oklahoma, and 20% in Louisiana.]

## II-A

. . . Unable to sustain the contention that under the original understanding of the Full Faith and Credit Clause statutes of limitations would have been considered substantive, petitioner argues that we should apply the modern understanding that they are so. It is now agreed, petitioner argues, that the primary function of a statute of limitations is to balance the competing substantive values of repose and vindication of the underlying right; and we should apply that understanding here, as we have applied it in the area of choice of law for purposes of federal diversity jurisdiction, where we have held that statutes of limitation are substantive, *see Guaranty Trust Co. v. York*, 326 U.S. 99 (1945).

. . . *Guaranty Trust* itself rejects the notion that there is an equivalence between what is substantive under the *Erie* doctrine and what is substantive for purposes of conflict of laws. . . . In the context of our *Erie* jurisprudence . . . that purpose is to establish . . . substantial uniformity of predictable outcome between cases tried in a federal court and cases tried in the courts of the State in which the federal court sits. The purpose of the substance-procedure dichotomy in the context of the Full Faith and Credit Clause, by contrast, is not to establish uniformity but to delimit spheres of state legislative competence. . . .

But to address petitioner's broader point . . . that we should update our notion of what is sufficiently "substantive" to require full faith and credit: We cannot imagine what would be the basis for such an updating. . . . If we abandon the currently applied, traditional notions of such entitlement we would embark upon the enterprise of constitutionalizing choice-of-law rules, with no compass to guide us beyond our own perceptions of what seems desirable.[2] There is no more reason to consider recharacterizing statutes of

---

[2] Contrary to Justice Brennan's concurrence, there is nothing unusual about our approach. This Court has regularly relied on traditional and subsisting practice in determining the constitutionally permissible authority of courts. . . . *Hague* [ *supra*], is not to the contrary. [*Hague*] merely

limitation as substantive under the Full Faith and Credit Clause than there is to consider recharacterizing a host of other matters generally treated as procedural under conflicts law, and hence generally regarded as within the forum State's legislative jurisdiction. *See, e.g.*, Restatement (Second) of Conflict of Laws § 131 (remedies available), § 133 (placement of burden of proof), § 134 (burden of production), § 135 (sufficiency of the evidence), § 139 (privileges) (1971).

In sum, long established and still subsisting choice-of-law practices that come to be thought, by modern scholars, unwise, do not thereby become unconstitutional. If current conditions render it desirable that forum States no longer treat a particular issue as procedural for conflict-of-laws purposes, those States can themselves adopt a rule to that effect, or . . . Congress can legislate to that effect under the second sentence of the Full Faith and Credit Clause. It is not the function of this Court, however, to make departures from established choice-of-law . . . practice . . . constitutionally mandatory. We hold, therefore, that Kansas did not violate the Full Faith and Credit Clause when it applied its own statute of limitations.

## II-B

Petitioner also makes a due process attack upon the Kansas court's application of its own statute of limitations.[3] Here again neither the tradition in place when the constitutional provision was adopted nor subsequent practice supports the contention. . . . "If a thing has been practised for two hundred years by common consent, it will need a strong case for the Fourteenth Amendment to affect it." [Citation omitted].

A State's interest in regulating the work load of its courts and determining when a claim is too stale to be adjudicated certainly suffices to give it legislative jurisdiction to control the remedies available in its courts by imposing statutes of limitations. Moreover, petitioner could in no way have been unfairly surprised by the application to it of a rule that is as old as the Republic. There is, in short, nothing in Kansas' action here that is "arbitrary or unfair," *Shutts* [*supra*], and the due process challenge [to the forum's statute of limitations] is entirely without substance.

## III

In *Shutts*, we held that Kansas could not apply its own law to claims for interest by nonresidents concerning royalties from property located in other States. The Kansas Supreme Court has complied with that ruling, but petitioner claims that it has unconstitutionally distorted Texas, Oklahoma, and Louisiana law in its determination of that law.

---

rejected the view that the Constitution enshrines the rule that the law of the place of contracting governs validity of all provisions of the contract. By the time of [*Hague*], of course, such a rule could not have been characterized as a subsisting tradition, if it ever could have been, in light of escape devices such as the doctrine of public policy, characterization of an issue as procedural, and the rule that the law of the place of performance governs matters of performance.

[3] [P]etitioner takes up this issue after discussion of the full faith and credit claim, and devotes much less argument to it. . . .

To constitute a violation of the Full Faith and Credit Clause or the Due Process Clause, it is not enough that a state court misconstrue the law of another State. Rather, our cases make plain that the misconstruction must contradict law of the other State that is clearly established and that has been brought to the court's attention. . . . We cannot conclude that any of the interpretations at issue here runs afoul of this standard. . . .

JUSTICE KENNEDY took no part in the consideration or decision of this case.

JUSTICE BRENNAN, with whom JUSTICE MARSHALL and JUSTICE BLACKMUN join, concurring in part and concurring in the judgment.

I join Parts I and III of the Court's opinion. Although I also agree with the result the Court reaches in Part II, I reach that result through a somewhat different path of analysis.

For 150 years, this Court has consistently held that a forum State may apply its own statute of limitations period to out-of-state claims even though it is longer or shorter than the limitations period that would be applied by the State out of which the claim arose. *See Wells v. Simonds Abrasive Co.,* 345 U.S. 514 (1953) (shorter); *Townsend v. Jemison,* 9 How. 407, 13 L.Ed. 194 (1850) (longer); *McElmoyle v. Cohen,* 13 Pet. 312, 10 L.Ed. 177 (1839) (shorter). The main question presented in this case is whether this line of authority has been undermined by more recent case law concerning the constitutionality of state choice-of-law rules. *See Phillips Petroleum Co. v. Shutts,* 472 U.S. 797 (1985); *Allstate Ins. Co. v. Hague,* 449 U.S. 302 (1981). . . .

Were statutes of limitations purely substantive, the issue would be an easy one, for where, as here, a forum State has no contacts with the underlying dispute, it has no substantive interests and cannot apply its own law on a purely substantive matter. Nor would the issue be difficult if statutes of limitations were purely procedural, for the contacts a State has with a dispute by virtue of being the forum always create state procedural interests that make application of the forum's law on purely procedural questions "neither arbitrary nor fundamentally unfair." *Phillips Petroleum,* 472 U.S., at 818. Statutes of limitations, however, defy characterization as either purely procedural or purely substantive. The statute of limitations a State enacts represents a balance between, on the one hand, its substantive interest in vindicating substantive claims and, on the other hand, a combination of its procedural interest in freeing its courts from adjudicating stale claims and its substantive interest in giving individuals repose from ancient breaches of law. A State that has enacted a particular limitations period has simply determined that after that period the interest in vindicating claims becomes outweighed by the combination of the interests in repose and avoiding stale claims. . . .

Given the complex of interests underlying statutes of limitations, I conclude that the contact a State has with a claim simply by virtue of being the forum creates a sufficient procedural interest to make the application of its limitations period to wholly out-of-state claims consistent with the [Constitution]. This is clearest when the forum State's limitations period is shorter than that of the claim State. A forum State's procedural interest in avoiding the adjudication of stale claims is equally applicable to in-state and out-of-state claims. . .; it would be "'neither arbitrary nor fundamentally unfair'" for the forum State to conclude that its procedural interest is more weighty than that of the claim State and requires an earlier time bar, as long as the time bar applied in a nondiscriminatory manner to in-state and out-of-state claims alike.

The constitutional question is somewhat less clear where, as here, the forum State's limitations period is longer than that of the claim State. . . . Assuming, for the moment, that each State has an equal substantive interest in the repose of defendants, then a forum State that has concluded that its procedural interest is less weighty than that of the claim State does not act unfairly or arbitrarily in applying its longer limitations period. The claim State does not, after all, have any substantive interest in *not* vindicating rights it has created. Nor will it do to argue that the forum State has no interest in vindicating the substantive rights of nonresidents: the forum State cannot discriminate against nonresidents, and if it has concluded that the substantive rights of its citizens outweigh its procedural interests at that period then it cannot be faulted for applying that determination evenhandedly.

If the different limitations periods also reflect differing assessments of the substantive interests in the repose of defendants, however, the issue is more complicated. It is, to begin with, not entirely clear whether the interest in the repose of defendants is an interest the State has as a forum or wholly as the creator of the claim at issue. . . . Such efforts to break down and weigh the procedural and substantive components and interests served by the various States' limitations periods would, however, involve a difficult, unwieldy and somewhat artificial inquiry that itself implicates the strong procedural interest any forum State has in having administrable choice-of-law rules.

In light of the forum State's procedural interests and the inherent ambiguity of any more refined inquiry in this context, there is some force to the conclusion that the forum State's contacts give it sufficient procedural interests to make it "'neither arbitrary nor fundamentally unfair'" for the State to have a *per se* rule of applying its own limitations period to out-of-state claims—particularly where, as here, the states out of which the claims arise view their statutes of limitations as procedural. The issue, after all, is not whether the decision to apply forum limitations law is wise as a matter of choice-of-law doctrine but whether the decision is within the range of constitutionally permissible choices. . . . [A]ny merely arguable inconsistency with our current . . . jurisprudence surely does not merit deviating from 150 years of precedent holding that choosing the forum State's limitations period over that of the claim State is constitutionally permissible.

The Court's technique of avoiding close examination of the relevant interests by wrapping itself in the mantle of tradition is as troublesome as it is conclusory. It leads the Court to assert broadly (albeit in dicta) that States do not violate the Full Faith and Credit Clause by adjudicating out-of-state claims under the forum's own law on, *inter alia*, remedies, burdens of proof, and burdens of production. The constitutionality of refusing to apply the law of the claim State on such issues was not briefed or argued before this Court, and whether, as the Court asserts without support, there are insufficient reasons for "recharacterizing" these issues (at least in part) as substantive is a question that itself presents multiple issues of enormous difficulty and importance which deserve more than the offhand treatment the Court gives them.

Even more troublesome is the Court's sweeping dicta that *any* choice-of-law practice that is "long established and still subsisting" is constitutional. This statement on its face seems to encompass choice-of-law doctrines on purely substantive issues, and the blind reliance on tradition confuses and conflicts with the . . . test we articulated just three years ago in *Phillips Petroleum*, 472 U.S., at 818. *See also Allstate*, 449 U.S. at 308–309 n. 11 (stating that a 1934 case giving "controlling constitutional significance" to a traditional choice-of-law test "has scant relevance for today"). That certain choice-of-law practices have so far avoided constitutional scrutiny by this Court is in any event a poor reason for concluding their constitutional validity. Nor is it persuasive that the practice reflected the rule applied by States or in international law around the time of the adoption of the Constitution, since "[t]he very purpose of the full faith and credit clause was to alter the status of the several states as independent foreign sovereignties," *Milwaukee County v. M.E. White Co.*, 296 U.S. 268, 276–277 (1935), not to leave matters unchanged. The Court never offers a satisfactory explanation as to why tradition should enable States to engage in practices that, under our current test, are "arbitrary" or "fundamentally unfair." The broad range of choice-of-law practices that may, in one jurisdiction or another, be traditional are not before this Court and have not been surveyed by it, and we can only guess what practices today's opinion approves sight unseen. Nor am I much comforted by the fact that the Court opines on the constitutionality of traditional choice-of-law practices only to the extent they are "still subsisting," for few cases involve challenges to practices that no longer subsist. One wonders as well how future courts will determine which practices are traditional enough (or subsist strongly enough) to be constitutional, and about the utility of requiring courts to focus on such an uncertain and formalistic inquiry rather than on the fairness and arbitrariness of the choice-of-law rule at issue. Indeed, the disarray of the Court's test is amply demonstrated by the fact that two of the Justices necessary to form the Court leave open the issue of whether a forum State could constitutionally refuse to apply a shorter limitations period regarded as substantive by the foreign State, *see* [the opinion of] O'Connor, J., joined by Rehnquist, C.J., concurring in part and dissenting in part, even though in many States the subsisting tradition of applying the forum's limitations period recognizes no exception for limitations periods considered substantive by the foreign State.[4]

In short, I fear the Court's rationale will cause considerable mischief with no corresponding benefit. This mischief is all the more unfortunate because

---

[4] . . . The Court only heaps more confusion on its "traditional and subsisting practice" test by asserting that by the time of *Allstate* the rule that the law of the place of contracting applies" could not have been characterized as a subsisting tradition, if it ever could have been. The doubt expressed about whether this rule was ever a subsisting tradition is remarkable, given that it was once *the* dominant rule for determining what law applied in contract cases. . . . It is difficult to see why . . . "escape devices" should render this traditional rule any less of a "subsisting tradition" than the rule that the limitations period of the forum governs . . ., which [was also] subject to "escape devices," allowing application of the foreign limitations period when it [was] "built into" the statute creating the right . . . [or] when the forum State [had] a borrowing statute.

it appears to stem from the misperception that this case cannot be resolved without conclusively labeling statutes of limitations as either "procedural" or "substantive." Having asked the wrong question (and an unanswerable one), it is no wonder the Court resorts to tradition rather than analysis to answer it. Because I believe a careful examination of the . . . governmental interests created by the relevant contacts provides narrower and sounder grounds for affirming, I concur in the judgment.

JUSTICE O'CONNOR, with whom THE CHIEF JUSTICE joins, concurring in part and dissenting in part.

The Court properly concludes that Kansas did not violate the Full Faith and Credit Clause or the Due Process Clause when it chose to apply its own statute of limitations in this case. Different issues might have arisen if Texas, Oklahoma, or Louisiana regarded its own shorter statute of limitations as substantive. Such issues, however, are not presented in this case, and they are appropriately left unresolved. Accordingly, I join Parts I and II of the Court's opinion.

In my view, however, the Supreme Court of Kansas violated the Full Faith and Credit Clause when it concluded that the three States in question would apply the interest rates set forth in the regulations of the Federal Power Commission. . . . Each of the three States has a statute setting an interest rate that is different from the FPC rate, and the Supreme Court of Kansas offered no valid reason whatsoever for ignoring those statutory rates. . . .

Today's decision discards important parts of our decision in *Shutts*. . . . Faced with the constitutional obligation to apply the substantive law of another State, a court that does not like that law apparently need take only two steps in order to avoid applying it. First, invent a legal theory so novel or strange that the other State has never had an opportunity to reject it; then, on the basis of nothing but unsupported speculation, "predict" that the other State would adopt that theory if it had the chance. To call this giving full faith and credit to the law of another State ignores the language of the Constitution and leaves it without the capacity to fulfill its purpose. Rather than take such a step, I would remand this case to the Supreme Court of Kansas with instructions to give effect to the interest rates established by law in Texas, Oklahoma, and Louisiana. . . .

---

## NOTES ON *WORTMAN*

(1) *Wortman and irrationally-chosen law.* In *Wortman*, has the Court put its unqualified imprimatur on the irrational Bealeian choice?

**DAY & ZIMMERMAN, INC. v. CHALLONER**, 423 U.S. 3 (1975). This was a wrongful death/survival suit, on a theory of products liability, filed by the administrator of a Tennesee estate in federal diversity court in Texas (the place of manufacture). The defendant was a Maryland corporation with its principal place of business in Pennsylvania. The allegedly defective product was a 105 mm. howitzer round, which exploded prematurely; the plaintiff's decedent had been a United States serviceman; and the place of injury was

Cambodia. At that time Texas followed the rule of *lex loci delicti*. The defendant argued that Cambodia law would require a showing (which the plaintiff could not make) of negligence in manufacture. The plaintiff argued that Cambodia lacked legitimate governmental interest. The district court tried the case under the strict products liability rule of Texas, and the jury returned a verdict of $240,000. Judgment upon this verdict was affirmed by the Fifth Circuit Court of Appeals, on the theory that federal common law would bar a federal court from applying the law of an uninterested sovereign in a false conflict case. The plaintiff's petition to the Supreme Court for review raised the question whether the law of the uninterested place of injury, Cambodia, could be applied constitutionally.

*Held* (per curiam and without oral argument, reversing judgment on the verdict): Under *Klaxon Co. v. Stentor Elec. Mfg. Co.,* 313 U.S. 487 (1941), § 6.15, *infra*, the diversity court sitting in Texas must apply whatever law Texas would.

*Blackmun, J.* (concurring separately): ". . . [T]he Court of Appeals is not foreclosed from concluding . . . that the Texas state courts themselves would apply . . . Texas [law]. . . . I make this observation to assure the Court of Appeals that, at least in my view, today's *per curiam* opinion does not necessarily *compel* the determination that it is only the law of Cambodia that is applicable."

### (2) SCHREIBER v. ALLIS-CHALMERS CORP., 611 F.2d 1970 (10th Cir. 1979). (This case is noted § 4.35[A], *supra*.)

In *Schreiber* was forum-shopping so manipulative as to have shifted the result? How? Under the federal common law that governs choice-of-law in federal courts? *See Day & Zimmerman v. Challoner, supra.* Under the Due Process Clause or the Full Faith and Credit Clause? *See Ferens v. John Deere & Co.,* noted § 3.19, *supra*. Is there any hope for such control after *Wortman*? In *Ferens v. John Deere & Co.,* 487 U.S. 1212 (1988), the Supreme Court vacated the Third Circuit's judgment, which had held the *Schreiber* device unconstitutional, and remanded for reconsideration in light of *Wortman*.

(3) *Sun Oil's argument in Wortman*. It is somewhat accidental that the *Wortman* Court emphasized the Full Faith and Credit Clause. The Kansas court had taken the position that limitations was "procedural," and therefore for the forum. Sun Oil thus thought it had to argue that the issue was "substantive." This view was superficially appealing, bringing into play the full force of the holding in *Shutts*—that for nationwide class actions the uninterested forum must refer to the substantive law of a nonforum contact state. This, in turn, invited the more extreme (and losing) Full Faith and Credit argument, that the forum must always apply the limitations law of an interested contact state. But there is another way of dealing with the limitations issue: precisely the way one deals with any other issue. Sun Oil could have argued simply that the use of an uninterested forum's *longer* statute of limitations was a violation of either the Due Process or the Full Faith and Credit Clauses. Had it done so, the issue would simply have been whether or not Kansas had a legitimate governmental interest in opening its doors to this class action. *See* § 4.31, *supra*, on choice of limitations law.

(4) *Analyzing Wortman: The concerns of the situs.* Notice that Justice Scalia treats the situs of leased gasland as an interested state, if not the only interested state, in an action for withheld interest on suspended royalties payable under the lease. Note, too, that Justice Brennan's references to "the claim state" might be read as acceding to this assumption. But why would the situs be concerned with the rate of interest equitably imposed on suspended royalty payments? The royalty owners were for the most part people living away from the gaslands; the leases might have been executed in nonsitus states as well. The defendant Sun Oil Co. was a "resident" of most of the other situs states only in the same sense that it was a resident of Kansas.

(5) *The concerns of the forum: Administrative?* What were the interests of Kansas in *opening* its doors to those claims of the class which arose within five years of suit, but which the court assumed were time-barred under the laws of "interested" states? What do you think of Justice Brennan's suggestion that the state's interest in administrable conflicts rules might sustain its longer limitations statute?

*Regulatory?* In *Hague, supra,* the general jurisdiction of the forum was aggregated with other contacts in the case. In *Shutts,* this factor was made much of only by Justice Stevens. In *Wortman,* none of the Justices seemed to think it counted for anything at all. The question of the forum's power to govern on the basis of mere general jurisdiction over the defendant—the question the Court refused to decide in *Hague*—now seems to have been decided by default, somewhere between *Shutts* and *Wortman.*

*Reciprocal?* Was Wortman rightly decided after all? Why do all states furnish a forum for nonresidents' claims against locals? The argument that this is a service to defendants seems fanciful; defendants do not want to be sued at all, even at home. Whatever interest supports general jurisdiction, however, arguably supports application of the forum's longer statute. Conceivably, might not general jurisdiction be explained by the reciprocal interest all states share in making a forum available wherever the defendant can be found?

(6) *The problem of the fractional interest.* In footnote 24 of Justice Stevens' *Shutts* dissent, he is struggling with a pervasive and intractable problem: the problem of the fractional interest. *Shutts* and *Wortman* present the relatively simple case in which scattered nonresidents, engaged in scattered out-of-state activities, seek the benefit of forum law. Conceivably some part of Kansas' regulatory concerns could inform numerous, perhaps all, transactions between the Kansas embodiment of Phillips or Sun Oil and an absent classmember. That seems clear, at least *to the extent* that the defendants' Kansas activities might reasonably affect or be affected by nonresident leaseholders or out-of-state leases. The difficulty is that if we can identify any such interests, they will be proportional. Yet Kansas cannot apply law fractionally. It either governs or it does not.

The problem of the fractional interest, seen here in a modern class action, will be seen again in § 5.05 immediately following, in cases under the "dormant" Commerce Clause. The question in all these cases is, on how flimsy a basis of contact with a case may the forum assert the authority of an "interested" state? When does the forum's contacts with a case become so insignificant as to make the state a truly "uninterested" one?

(7) *Class and "the disinterested third state."* A federal class action sometimes is transferred arbitrarily to a federal district court having no connection with the case, perhaps because that court's docket is relatively uncrowded, or because that court has experience in handling similar complex litigation. When that happens, particularly in a multistate or diversity case likely to involve a conflict of laws, the transferee court would seem to be the very realization of Brainer Currie's "disinterested third state." For recent commentary on the opportunities and dangers confronting the disinterested third state in cases of mass tort, see Louise Weinberg, *Mass Torts at the Neutral Forum: A Critical Analysis of the American Law Institute's Proposed Choice Rule*, 56 ALB. L. REV. 807 (1993).

(8) *Jurisdiction to tax.* An even more acute problem is presented when the forum is dealing with scattered nonresidents with whom it has only fractional connections, and it seeks not to benefit, but to burden them. The jurisdiction-to-tax cases may be the easiest of these.

Generally, a state has power to tax remote activities of a taxpayer, piercing the corporate veil of the taxpayer's nonresident subsidiaries, as long as the forum has some nexus with the taxpayer (*cf. National Bellas Hess, Inc. v. Department of Revenue of the State of Illinois,* 386 U.S. 753 (1967) (state cannot collect sales taxes from out-of-state mail order firm); and as long as the state uses some reasonable apportionment formula (*Container Corp. of America v. Franchise Tax Board,* 463 U.S. 159 (1983); *Complete Auto Transit, Inc. v. Brady,* 430 U.S. 274 (1977)). It is not necessary to satisfy due process that double taxation does not occur; all that is necessary is that the sovereign use an apportionment formula reasonably calculated to avoid double taxation. *See generally* Walter Hellerstein, *Is "Internal Consistency" Foolish?: Reflections on an Emerging Commerce Clause Restraint on State Taxation*, 87 MICH. L. REV. 138 (1988).

In an ordinary case not having to do with the power to tax, where apportionment formulas won't work, what is the regulatory power of the forum with 50% of a significant contact with a case? Twenty-five percent? Two percent? When does the tail of the state begin to wag the dog of the nation? This problem is the subject of the next Part of this Chapter. As we shall see, the Court is likely to deal with this problem, as it often deals with jurisdiction to tax, under the Commerce Clause.

# PART D  THE OVERREACHING FORUM

## § 5.05  The Overreaching Forum

### NOTE ON THE OVERREACHING FORUM AND THE DORMANT COMMERCE CLAUSE

An interesting range of recent Supreme Court cases invites us now to press on a bit further in our exploration of constitutional controls on forum law. In the remainder of this chapter we will be looking at cases in which the forum, though in some sense an "interested" one, seems nevertheless unreasonable or discriminatory.

Sometimes even an interested state seems to be projecting its laws unreasonably beyond its borders. Sometimes the state seems to be exporting its burdens unfairly to its neighbors, or denying the benefit of its laws to them. So we find the Supreme Court occasionally striking down even an interested state's law. Obviously in such cases mere scrutiny for rational basis alone would not do. Only some heightened scrutiny could control an interested state's governance. As the jurisprudence of personal jurisdiction reveals, it is not always easy to find principled reasons for blocking a state from governing when it has governmental interests in doing so. So the Supreme Court seems engaged in a perennial struggle to articulate meaningful limits on an interested state's powers.

We begin with the problem of the overreaching forum. The chief vehicle of judicial control of the overreaching but interested forum has been the Commerce Clause. Complaining of extraterritoriality, the Court may strike down a choice of law as "a direct regulation of interstate commerce," or as "an undue burden on interstate commerce." The Court will strike down protectionist forum law as "discriminating against interstate commerce." An interesting subset of these cases measures the reach of a state seeking to tax interstate or international activities. In the following pair of cases the Court grapples with a state's efforts to control out-of-state takeovers of "its" corporations— companies that are in some sense local ones.

---

**EDGAR v. MITE CORP.,** 457 U.S. 624 (1982). MITE Corp., a Delaware corporation with its chief executive offices in Connecticut, made a hostile takeover bid to acquire Chicago Rivet & Machine Co., an Illinois corporation with its chief executive offices in Illinois, doing most of its business in Pennsylvania. Officials in Illinois warned MITE that it must comply with Illinois' anti-takeover statute. Arguing that the burdens and delays required by the Illinois law would, as a practical matter, wholly frustrate its takeover of Chicago Rivet, MITE brought an action in federal court for an injunction restraining enforcement of the statute.

The federal District Court held for MITE, and the United States Court of Appeals for the Seventh Circuit affirmed.

*Held* (by JUSTICE WHITE, for a plurality): *Affirmed.* First, the Illinois Act is preempted by the federal Williams Act (an amendment to the Securities and Exchange Act of 1934): "There is no question that in imposing these requirements, Congress intended to protect investors. But it is also crystal clear that a major aspect of the effort to protect the investor was to avoid favoring either management or the takeover bidder. . . . We agree with the Court of Appeals that by providing the target company with additional time within which to take steps to combat the offer, the precommencement notification provisions furnish incumbent management with a powerful tool to combat tender offers, perhaps to the detriment of the stockholders who will not have an offer before them during this period. These consequences are precisely what Congress determined should be avoided, and for this reason, the precommencement notification provision frustrates the objectives of the Williams Act. . . ." Second, the Illinois law violates the Commerce Clause: "The Illinois Act . . . directly regulates transactions which take place across state lines, even if wholly outside the State of Illinois. . . . Indeed, the Illinois law on its face would apply even if not a single one of Chicago Rivet's shareholders were a resident of Illinois, since the Act applies to every tender offer for a corporation meeting two of the following conditions: the corporation has its principal executive office in Illinois, is organized under Illinois laws, or has at least 10% of its stated capital and paid-in surplus represented in Illinois. Thus the Act could be applied to regulate a tender offer which would not affect a single Illinois shareholder.

". . . The Commerce Clause . . . precludes the application of a state statute to commerce that takes place wholly outside of the State's borders, whether or not the commerce has effects within the State. . . .

"The Illinois Act is also unconstitutional under the test of *Pike v. Bruce Church, Inc.,* 397 U.S. 137 (1970), for even when a state statute regulates interstate commerce [only] indirectly, the burden imposed on that commerce must not be excessive in relation to the local interests served by the statute. The most obvious burden the Illinois Act imposes on interstate commerce arises from the statute's previously described nationwide reach which purports to give Illinois the power to determine whether a tender offer may proceed anywhere.

"The effects of allowing the Illinois Secretary of State to block a nationwide tender offer are substantial. Shareholders are deprived of the opportunity to sell their shares at a premium. The reallocation of economic resources to their highest valued use, a process which can improve efficiency and competition, is hindered. The incentive the tender offer mechanism provides incumbent management to perform well so that stock prices remain high is reduced.

"While protecting local investors is plainly a legitimate state objective, the State has no legitimate interest in protecting nonresident shareholders. Insofar as the Illinois law burdens out-of-state transactions, there is nothing to be weighed in the balance to sustain the law. We note, furthermore, that the Act completely exempts from coverage a corporation's acquisition of its own shares. Thus Chicago Rivet was able to make a competing tender offer for its own stock without complying with the Illinois Act, leaving Chicago Rivet's shareholders to depend only on the protections afforded them by federal securities law, protections which Illinois views as inadequate to protect investors in other contexts. This distinction is at variance with Illinois' asserted legislative purpose, and tends to undermine appellant's justification for the burdens the statute imposes on interstate commerce.

"Appellant also contends that Illinois has an interest in regulating the internal affairs of a corporation incorporated under its laws. . . . [But the Act also] applies to corporations that are not incorporated in Illinois. . . . Illinois has no interest in regulating the internal affairs of foreign corporations. . . ."

JUSTICE POWELL (concurring in part): "[The] Commerce Clause . . . leaves some room for state regulation of tender offers. This period in our history is marked by conglomerate corporate formations essentially unrestricted by the antitrust laws. Often the offeror possesses resources, in terms of professional personnel experienced in takeovers as well as of capital, that vastly exceed those of the takeover target. This disparity in resources may seriously disadvantage a relatively small or regional target corporation. Inevitably there are certain adverse consequences in terms of general public interest when corporate headquarters are moved away from a city and State.* . . ."

[JUSTICE MARSHALL, joined by JUSTICE BRENNAN, and JUSTICE REHNQUIST separately, dissented on the ground of mootness, MITE having withdrawn its offer.]

---

## NOTES ON *MITE*

(1) *Commerce Clause scrutiny versus rational-basis scrutiny.* Is there any way to reconcile MITE's "direct burden" analysis with *Allstate Ins. Co. v. Hague, supra* this Chapter?

(2) MITE *and interest analysis.* Do we have to believe Justice White's statement that the Commerce Clause "precludes the application of a state statute to commerce that takes place wholly outside of the State's borders, whether or not the commerce has effects within the State"? Do we have to believe him when he says, "The State has no legitimate interest in protecting nonresident shareholders"?

What were Illinois' interests in *MITE*? White assumes that the purpose of the statute was to protect Illinois shareholders. Yet, as he himself points out, the statute could be triggered even if none of the target company's shareholders was a resident of Illinois. "The state has no legitimate interest in protecting nonresident shareholders." And Justice White also seems right when he insists that Illinois is not really interested in protecting Illinois shareholders either. After all, as White notes, shareholders are not obviously

---

* ". . . The corporate headquarters of the great national and multinational corporations tend to be located in the large cities of a few States. When corporate headquarters are transferred out of a city and State into one of these metropolitan centers, the State and locality from which the transfer is made inevitably suffer significantly. Management personnel—many of whom have provided community leadership—may move to the new corporate headquarters. Contributions to cultural, charitable, and educational life—both in terms of leadership and financial support— also tend to diminish when there is a move of corporate headquarters. . . ."

protected when a deal that would enrich them is stymied. Moreover, if Illinois were really concerned about its shareholders, it would have erected the same roadblocks to a corporation's repurchases of its own shares from Illinois shareholders.

Justice Powell is persuasive, too, that much of Illinois' concern may have been to protect incumbent local management. It is a problem for Powell's argument that the Illinois statute might have applied even in cases in which there was no local management to protect. But since the target company in *MITE* did have executive offices in Illinois, Illinois was an interested state in this case.

(3) *The interested state and "indirect regulation" of interstate commerce: a "balancing" test.* The Commerce Clause permits a state with a legitimate governmental interest in its law to have some impact on interstate commerce. The Commerce Clause question is whether that impact is so heavy as to be an "undue burden." To answer this question, the Court resorts to a "balancing" test. The national interest in the state's nonintervention is balanced against the state's legitimate need to intervene. Given the Supremacy Clause, how is it possible to weigh any merely state interest against a federal interest? Perhaps the Court should recognize that it balances two national interests in such cases: one favoring, one limiting, state governance.

(4) *"Extraterritoriality" versus "protectionism."* If Illinois' purpose in *MITE* were indeed to keep Illinois' resources in Illinois—in this case, to keep incumbent Illinois management employed, and in Illinois—would that purpose be legitimate? Or would it be protectionist or discriminatory? Does a state discriminate if it seeks to protect a valuable local resource (here, members of its managerial class) from destruction by outsiders? From export to other states? Those were the interesting—and hard—questions posed in *MITE*. Some writers argue that discriminations of that kind present the only real Commerce Clause issues. If so, Justice White's proffered analysis, with its concepts of "extraterritoriality," "direct regulation of interstate commerce," and "undue burdens on interstate commerce," is simply beside the point.

(5) *The Commerce Clause and the American common market.* There is another possibility. Surely the chief purpose of the Commerce Clause is to ensure a common market among the states. Thus, the Clause might be thought to protect free markets, free trade, and uninhibited movement across state lines, within limits established only by Congress. From this one might conclude that a state that places an undue burden on interstate commerce acts unconstitutionally whether or not it discriminates or is protectionist. Nevertheless it is not easy to find cases of pure "undue burden" to support this hypothesis. In most cases in which the Court strikes down state legislation under the dormant Commerce Clause, we find accompanying state protectionism or discrimination as well. Consider, for example, *Kassel v. Consolidated Freightways Corp.,* 450 U.S. 662 (1981). There, the Court struck down Iowa's restriction on the length of trucks within its borders because the restriction burdened interstate movement. But Justice Brennan pointed out in a separate concurrence that the vice of the Iowa restriction was that it was essentially protectionist, in effect allowing Iowa to export some of the hazards of heavy trucking to other states.

---

# CTS CORP. v. DYNAMICS CORP. OF AMERICA

*United States Supreme Court*
*481 U.S. 69, 107 S. Ct. 1637, 95 L. Ed. 2d 67 (1987)*

[CTS, an Indiana corporation, was the target of a takeover effort by an out-of-state company, Dynamics Corp. Dynamics Corp. brought an action to restrain CTS from seeking the protections of the Indiana anti-takeover statute. Following *Edgar v. MITE Corp., supra,* the federal District Court ruled that the Williams Act pre-empted the Indiana Act, and also that the Indiana Act violated the Commerce Clause. The Court of Appeals affirmed.]

JUSTICE POWELL delivered the opinion of the Court. . . .

## I

The [Indiana] Act applies only to . . . businesses incorporated in Indiana [and then only when the corporation] has its principal place of business, its principal office, or substantial assets within Indiana; and either more than ten percent of its shareholders resident in Indiana; more than ten percent of its shares owned by Indiana residents; or ten thousand shareholders resident in Indiana. . . .

## II

The first question . . . is whether the Williams Act pre-empts the Indiana Act. . . .

As the plurality opinion in *Edgar v. MITE* did not represent the views of a majority of the Court, we are not bound by its reasoning. We need not question that reasoning, however, because we believe the Indiana Act passes muster even under the broad interpretation of the Williams Act articulated by Justice WHITE in *MITE.* . . . [The] overriding concern of the *MITE* plurality was that the Illinois statute considered in that case operated to favor management against offerors, to the detriment of shareholders. By contrast, the statute now before the Court protects the independent shareholder against both of the contending parties. Thus, the Act furthers a basic purpose of the Williams Act. . . .

## III-A

As an alternative basis for its decision, the Court of Appeals held that the Act violates the Commerce Clause. . . .

The principal objects of Commerce Clause scrutiny are statutes that discriminate against interstate commerce. The Indiana Act is not such a statute. It has the same effects on tender offers whether or not the offeror is a . . . resident of Indiana. . . .

Dynamics nevertheless contends that the statute is discriminatory because it will apply most often to out-of-state entities. This argument rests on the contention that, as a practical matter, most hostile tender offers are launched by offerors outside Indiana. But . . . nothing in the Indiana Act imposes a greater burden on out-of-state offerors than it does on similarly situated Indiana offerors. . . .

## III-B

This Court's recent Commerce Clause cases also have invalidated statutes that adversely may affect interstate commerce by subjecting activities to inconsistent regulations. *E.g., Brown-Forman Distillers Corp. v. New York State Liquor Authority,* 476 U.S. 573 (1986). The Indiana Act poses no such problem. So long as each State regulates voting rights only in the corporations it has created, each corporation will be subject to the law of only one State. No principle of corporation law and practice is more firmly established than a State's authority to regulate domestic corporations, including the authority to define the voting rights of shareholders. . . .

## III-C

[The Court of Appeals found the Indiana Act unconstitutional as an undue burden on interstate commerce because of] the Act's potential to hinder tender offers. We think the Court of Appeals failed to appreciate the significance for Commerce Clause analysis of the fact that state regulation of corporate governance is regulation of entities whose very existence and attributes are a product of state law. . . . Every State in this country has enacted laws regulating corporate governance. . . . Such laws necessarily affect certain aspects of interstate commerce. . . . Large corporations that are listed on national exchanges, or even regional exchanges, will have shareholders in many States and shares that are traded frequently. . . . This beneficial free market system depends at its core upon the fact that a corporation . . . is . . . governed by the law of a single jurisdiction, traditionally the corporate law of the State of its incorporation.

These regulatory laws may affect directly a variety of corporate transactions. Mergers are a typical example. In view of the substantial effect that a merger may have on the shareholders' interests in a corporation, many States require supermajority votes to approve mergers. . . . State laws also may provide for "dissenters' rights" under which minority shareholders who disagree with corporate decisions . . . are entitled to sell their shares to the corporation at fair market value. . . . [These] laws may inhibit a corporation from engaging in the specified transactions.

It is thus an accepted part of the business landscape in this country for States to create corporations, to prescribe their powers, and to define the rights that are acquired by purchasing their shares. A State has an interest in promoting stable relationships among parties involved in the corporations it charters, as well as in ensuring that investors in such corporations have an effective voice in corporate affairs.

There can be no doubt that the [Indiana] Act reflects these concerns. . . . The primary purpose of the Act is to protect the shareholders of Indiana corporations. . . . A change of management may have important effects on the shareholders' interests. . . . The autonomy provided . . . may be especially beneficial where a hostile tender offer may coerce shareholders into tendering their shares.

. . . Dynamics [argues] that the prospect of coercive tender offers is illusory, and that tender offers generally should be favored because they reallocate corporate assets into the hands of management who can use them most effectively. . . . [But the] Constitution does not require the States to subscribe to any particular economic theory. . . .

Dynamics argues in any event that the State has "no legitimate interest in protecting the nonresident shareholders." But that comment [in MITE] was made with reference to an Illinois law that applied as well to out-of-state corporations as to in-state corporations. We agree that Indiana has no interest in protecting nonresident shareholders of nonresident corporations. . . .

## III-D

Dynamics' argument . . . ultimately rests on its contention that the Act will limit the number of successful tender offers. . . . [This] result would not substantially affect our Commerce Clause analysis. . . . The very commodity that is traded in the . . . market for corporate control—the corporation—is one that owes its existence and attributes to state law. Indiana need not define these commodities as other States do; it need only provide that residents and nonresidents have equal access to them. This Indiana has done. Accordingly, even if the Act should decrease the number of successful tender offers for Indiana corporations, this would not offend the Commerce Clause. . . .

JUSTICE SCALIA, concurring in part and concurring in the judgment.

I join parts I, III-A, and III-B of the Court's opinion hellip;.

While it has become standard practice at least since *Pike v. Bruce Church, Inc.,* 397 U.S. 137 (1970), to consider . . . whether the burden on commerce imposed by a state statute " clearly excessive in relation to the putative local benefits," such an inquiry is ill suited to the judicial function. . . . This case is a good illustration of the point. Whether the control shares statute protects shareholders of Indiana corporations, or protects incumbent management seems to me a highly debatable question, but it is extraordinary to think that the constitutionality of the Act should depend on the answer. Nothing in the Constitution says that the protection of entrenched management is any less important a "putative local benefit" than the protection of entrenched shareholders. . . .

One commentator has suggested that, at least much of the time, we do not in fact mean what we say when we declare that statutes which neither discriminate against commerce nor present a threat of . . . multiple and inconsistent burdens might nonetheless be unconstitutional under a "balancing" test. *See* Regan, *The Supreme Court and State Protectionism: Making Sense of the Dormant Commerce Clause,* 84 MICH. L. REV. 1091 (1986). As long as a State's corporation law governs only its own corporations and does not discriminate against out-of-state interests, it should survive this Court's scrutiny under the Commerce Clause, whether it promotes shareholder welfare or industrial stagnation. . . .

I do not share the Court's apparent high estimation of the beneficence of the state statute at issue here. But a law can be both economic folly and constitutional. . . .

JUSTICE WHITE, with whom JUSTICE BLACKMUN and JUSTICE STEVENS join as to Part II, dissenting. . . .

## II

. . . Given the impact of the [Indiana Act], it is clear that Indiana is directly regulating the purchase and sale of stock in interstate commerce. Appellant CTS's stock is traded on the New York Stock Exchange, and people from all over the country buy and sell CTS's shares daily. Yet, under Indiana's scheme, any prospective purchaser will be effectively precluded from purchasing CTS's shares if the purchaser crosses one of the . . . threshold ownership levels and a majority of CTS's shareholders refuse to give the purchaser voting rights. . . .

Since the restraint on the transfer of voting rights is a restraint on the transfer of shares, the Indiana [Act], like the Illinois Act in MITE, restrains [interstate commerce].

The Commerce Clause was included in our Constitution by the Framers to prevent the very type of economic protectionism Indiana's [law] represents. . . .

---

## NOTES ON *CTS*

(1) *The status of MITE.* After *CTS,* what is left of *MITE*? Can the cases be reconciled? That Indiana structured its takeover law as a restraint on the transfer of voting rights need not blind one to the consequent restraint on the transfer of control. That Indiana limited its law to Indiana corporations seems equally unhelpful in marking any fundamental distinction; an incumbent management in Indiana need only reincorporate there to gain the protections of the statute.

Certainly there is no mention in *CTS* of "extraterritoriality." Furthermore, the *CTS* Court sees no constitutional infirmity in "direct regulation of interstate commerce." Rather, Justice Powell explains patiently that much state law governing corporations can, and does, directly regulate interstate commerce. After *CTS,* can we forget about "extraterritoriality" as a constitutional limit on forum law?

Finally, *CTS* makes clear that anti-takeover legislation does not necessarily "discriminate" against interstate commerce. Justice Powell says that the state is free to protect its own interests, as long as it does so evenhandedly. In this view, wasn't *MITE* wrongly decided? Although the Illinois anti-takeover law in *MITE* made a distinction between repurchases and takeovers, it did apply evenhandedly to in-state and out-of-state offerors alike.

(2) *Protectionism and the difficulties of heightened scrutiny.* In *CTS,* Justice Powell, who had written separately in *MITE* to explain the point, must have been aware, as Justice Scalia and Justice White clearly were, of the state's likely concerns about incumbent management, and of the protectionism problem lurking in those concerns. Should the Court have dealt with the protectionism issue up front? But to strike down protectionist legislation is to strike down law for which by hypothesis a rational basis exists—the state's interest in protecting its local advantages. Thus, the Court would have to engage in some form of heightened scrutiny. Yet when a state concededly has a legitimate interest in regulating, and does so in a nondiscriminatory way, judicially-fashioned constraints on the state's regulation tend to seem arbitrary or incoherent. (*Cf.* Justice Scalia's opinion in Bendix Autolite, infra this Chapter.) This is especially so when relevant national policy is unclear. Was the Court wise in taking Commerce Clause control over state anti-takeover legislation, when national policy on business takeovers is as unclear as the badly fragmented opinions in *MITE* and *CTS* suggest?

(3) *The problem of the fractional interest.* In *CTS,* the majority says the state's interest is in protecting its shareholders. But that analysis is posited on statutory thresholds of 10% of shareholders or 10% of shares. Should this very little tail be allowed to wag the corporate dog? Should the place where only 1% of shareholders resides, holding 10% of shares, be permitted to govern all shareholders? In *CTS,* Justice Powell simply sweeps this tail-wagging problem under the rug, doesn't he?

(4) *The law of the state of incorporation.* Is the Court right in suggesting that the state of incorporation necessarily should have exclusive powers over issues affecting the corporation? It is true that a single uniform law is very desirable when multiple dispersed parties—here, the shareholders in a publicly traded company—are involved? But must that single law invariably be the law of the place of incorporation? Might it offend the Due Process Clause to apply the law of an uninterested place of incorporation, a corporate "flag-of-convenience," to an issue having nothing to do with internal corporate governance?

If the purpose of the Indiana legislation in *CTS* was to protect incumbent Indiana management, as Justice Scalia assumes, isn't the only relevant place the state where incumbent management is?

(5) *The happy Delawarization of takeover law.* There may be a short answer to the problems raised in the foregoing notes. Perhaps the Court has subtly accommodated the national interest in unitary law, as well as the several states' interests in protection of incumbent management. By insisting on the constitutional acceptability, even desirability, of the law of the place of incorporation, hasn't the Court bestowed upon much of the nation a body of law that is (notoriously) protective of the concerns of management: the law of Delaware? Any corporate management can avail itself of this protection. On this view, the interest analysis in Note (4), *supra,* though accurate enough, is naïve.

(6) *Discrimination and the Commerce Clause.* Consider the theoretically appealing proposition that as long as the state acts evenhandedly, it can burden interstate commerce as much as its legitimate interests require. The Commerce Clause, in this view, polices only attempts by a state to shift its residents' costs to outsiders. Does this view survive *MITE*? Or was *MITE* simply wrong?

(7) *Current commentary.* For recent discussion of *MITE* and *CTS* from a choice-of-law perspective, see Robert E. Suggs, *Business Combination Antitakeover Statutes: The Unintended Repudiation of the Internal Affairs Doctrine and Constitutional Constraints on Choice of Law,* 56 OHIO ST. L.J. 1097 (1995).

---

## § 5.06   The Power to Tax

### QUILL CORP. v. NORTH DAKOTA

*United States Supreme Court*
*504 U.S. 298, 112 S. Ct. 1904, 119 L. Ed. 2d 91 (1992)*

JUSTICE STEVENS delivered the opinion of the Court.

This case, like *National Bellas Hess, Inc. v. Dep't of Revenue of Illinois,* 386 U.S. 753 (1967), involves a State's attempt to require an out-of-state mail-order house that has neither outlets nor sales representatives in the State to collect and pay a use [sales] tax on goods purchased for use within the State. In *Bellas Hess* we held that a similar Illinois statute violated the Due Process Clause of the Fourteenth Amendment and created an unconstitutional burden on interstate commerce. In particular, we ruled that a "seller whose only connection with customers in the State is by common carrier or the United States mail" lacked the requisite minimum contacts with the State.

In this case, the Supreme Court of North Dakota declined to follow *Bellas Hess* because "the tremendous social, economic, commercial, and legal innovations" of the past quarter-century have rendered its holding "obsolete." Having granted certiorari, we must either reverse the State Supreme Court or overrule *Bellas Hess.* . . .

I

Quill is a Delaware corporation with offices and warehouses in Illinois, California, and Georgia. None of its employees work or reside in North Dakota, and its ownership of tangible property in that State is either insignificant or nonexistent. Quill sells office equipment and supplies; it solicits business through catalogs and flyers, advertisements in national periodicals, and telephone calls. Its annual national sales exceed $200 million, of which almost $1 million are made to about 3,000 customers in North Dakota. It is the sixth largest vendor of office supplies in the State. It delivers all of its merchandise to its North Dakota customers by mail or common carrier from out-of-state locations.

As a corollary to its [local] sales tax, North Dakota imposes a use tax upon property purchased for storage, use, or consumption within the State. [Since 1987] North Dakota requires every retailer maintaining a place of business in the State to collect the tax from the consumer and remit it to the State . . . even if they maintain no property or personnel in North Dakota.

. . . [The] State, through its Tax Commissioner, filed this action to require Quill to pay taxes (as well as interest and penalties) on all . . . sales [to North Dakota customers] made after July 1, 1987. The trial court ruled in Quill's favor, finding the case indistinguishable from *Bellas Hess*. . . .

The North Dakota Supreme Court reversed, concluding that "wholesale changes" in both the economy and the law made it inappropriate to follow Bellas Hess today. The principal economic change noted by the court was the remarkable growth of the mail-order business "from a relatively inconsequential market niche" in 1967 to a "Goliath" with annual sales that reached "the staggering figure of $183.3 billion in 1989." Moreover, the court observed, advances in computer technology greatly eased the burden of compliance with a " 'welter of complicated obligations' " imposed by state and local taxing authorities.

Equally important, in the court's view, were the changes in the "legal landscape." With respect to the Commerce Clause, the court emphasized that *Complete Auto Transit, Inc. v. Brady,* 430 U.S. 274 (1977), rejected the line of cases holding that the direct taxation of interstate commerce was impermissible. . . . This and subsequent rulings, the court maintained, indicated that the Commerce Clause no longer mandated the sort of physical-presence nexus suggested in *Bellas Hess.*

Similarly, with respect to the Due Process Clause, the North Dakota court observed that cases following *Bellas Hess* had not construed "minimum contacts" to require physical presence within a State as a prerequisite to the legitimate exercise of state power. The state court then concluded that "the Due Process requirement of a 'minimal connection' to establish nexus is encompassed within the Complete Auto test" and that the relevant inquiry under the latter test was whether "the state has provided some protection, opportunities, or benefit for which it can expect a return."

Turning to the case at hand, the state court emphasized that North Dakota had created "an economic climate that fosters demand for" Quill's products, maintained a legal infrastructure that protected that market, and disposed of 24 tons of catalogs and flyers mailed by Quill into the State every year. Based on these facts, the court concluded that Quill's "economic presence" in North Dakota depended on services and benefits provided by the State and therefore generated "a constitutionally sufficient nexus to justify imposition of the purely administrative duty of collecting and remitting the use tax."[2]

---

[2] The court also suggested that, in view of the fact that the "touchstone of Due Process is fundamental fairness" and that the "very object" of the Commerce Clause is protection of interstate business against discriminatory local practices, it would be ironic to exempt Quill from this burden and thereby allow it to enjoy a significant competitive advantage over local retailers.

## II

As in a number of other cases involving the application of state taxing statutes to out-of-state sellers, our holding in *Bellas Hess* relied on both the Due Process Clause and the Commerce Clause. Although the two claims are closely related, the Clauses pose distinct limits on the taxing powers of the States. Accordingly, while a State may, consistent with the Due Process Clause, have the authority to tax a particular taxpayer, imposition of the tax may nonetheless violate the Commerce Clause.

The two constitutional requirements differ fundamentally, in several ways. . . . [The] Due Process Clause and the Commerce Clause reflect different constitutional concerns. Moreover, while Congress has plenary power to regulate commerce among the States and thus may authorize state actions that burden interstate commerce, it does not similarly have the power to authorize violations of the Due Process Clause.

Thus, although we have not always been precise in distinguishing between the two, the Due Process Clause and the Commerce Clause are analytically distinct. . . .

## III

. . . [In] *Bellas Hess* [we] suggested that [physical] presence was not only sufficient for jurisdiction under the Due Process Clause, but also necessary. . . .

Our due process jurisprudence has evolved substantially in the 25 years since *Bellas Hess,* particularly in the area of judicial jurisdiction. . . . [To] the extent that our decisions have indicated that the Due Process Clause requires physical presence in a State for the imposition of duty to collect a use tax, we overrule those holdings as superseded by developments in the law of due process.

In this case, there is no question that Quill has purposefully directed its activities at North Dakota residents, that the magnitude of those contacts is more than sufficient for due process purposes, and that the use tax is related to the benefits Quill receives from access to the State. We therefore agree with the North Dakota Supreme Court's conclusion that the Due Process Clause does not bar enforcement of that State's use tax against Quill.

## IV

. . . Our interpretation of the "negative" or "dormant" Commerce Clause has evolved substantially over the years, particularly as that Clause concerns limitations on state taxation powers. . . . Most recently, in *Complete Auto Transit, Inc. v. Brady,* 430 U.S. 274, 285 (1977), we . . . set forth a four-part test that continues to govern the validity of state taxes under the Commerce Clause. . . .

While contemporary Commerce Clause jurisprudence might not dictate the same result were the issue to arise for the first time today, *Bellas Hess* is not inconsistent with Complete Auto and our recent cases. Under Complete Auto's four-part test, we will sustain a tax against a Commerce Clause challenge so long as the "tax (1) is applied to an activity with a substantial nexus with the taxing State, (2) is fairly apportioned, (3) does not discriminate against interstate commerce, and (4) is fairly related to the services provided by the State." 430 U.S., at 279. *Bellas Hess* concerns the first of these tests and stands for the proposition that a vendor whose only contacts with the taxing State are by mail or common carrier lacks the "substantial nexus" required by the Commerce Clause.

Thus, three weeks after Complete Auto was handed down, we cited Bellas Hess for this proposition and discussed the case at some length. *National Geographic Society v. California Bd. of Equalization,* 430 U.S. 551, 559 (1977), [affirming] the continuing vitality of *Bellas Hess. . . .* We have continued to cite *Bellas Hess* with approval ever since. . . . For these reasons, we disagree with the State Supreme Court's conclusion that our decision in Complete Auto undercut the *Bellas Hess* rule.

The State of North Dakota relies less on *Complete Auto* and more on the evolution of our due process jurisprudence. The State contends that the nexus requirements imposed by the Due Process and Commerce Clauses are equivalent and that if, as we concluded above, a mail-order house that lacks a physical presence in the taxing State nonetheless satisfies the due process "minimum contacts" test, then that corporation also meets the Commerce Clause "substantial nexus" test. We disagree. Despite the similarity in phrasing, the nexus requirements of the Due Process and Commerce Clauses are not identical. The two standards are animated by different constitutional concerns and policies.

Due process centrally concerns the fundamental fairness of governmental activity. Thus, at the most general level, the due process nexus analysis requires that we ask whether an individual's connections with a State are substantial enough to legitimate the State's exercise of power over him. We have, therefore, often identified "notice" or "fair warning" as the analytic touchstone of due process nexus analysis. In contrast, the Commerce Clause and its nexus requirement are informed not so much by concerns about fairness for the individual defendant as by structural concerns about the effects of state regulation on the national economy. Under the Articles of Confederation, state taxes and duties hindered and suppressed interstate commerce; the Framers intended the Commerce Clause as a cure for these structural ills. *See generally* The Federalist Nos. 7, 11 (Alexander Hamilton). It is in this light that we have interpreted the negative implication of the Commerce Clause. Accordingly, we have ruled that that Clause prohibits discrimination against interstate commerce, see, e.g., *Philadelphia v. New Jersey,* 437 U.S. 617 (1978), and bars state regulations that unduly burden interstate commerce, see, e.g., *Kassel v. Consolidated Freightways Corp. of Delaware,* 450 U.S. 662 (1981).

The *Complete Auto* analysis reflects these concerns about the national economy. The second and third parts of that analysis, which require fair apportionment and non-discrimination, prohibit taxes that pass an unfair share of the tax burden onto interstate commerce. The first and fourth prongs, which require a substantial nexus and a relationship between the tax and state-provided services, limit the reach of state taxing authority so as to ensure that state taxation does not unduly burden interstate commerce.[1] Thus, the "substantial nexus" requirement is not, like due process' "minimum contacts" requirement, a proxy for notice, but rather a means for limiting state burdens on interstate commerce. Accordingly, contrary to the State's suggestion, a corporation may have the "minimum contacts" with a taxing State as required by the Due Process Clause, and yet lack the "substantial nexus" with that State as required by the Commerce Clause.[7]

. . . Although we agree with the state court's assessment of the evolution of our cases, we do not share its conclusion that this evolution indicates that the Commerce Clause ruling of *Bellas Hess* is no longer good law. . . .

*Complete Auto,* it is true, renounced [prior cases] as "formalistic." But not all formalism is alike. [The old] formal distinction between taxes on the "privilege of doing business" and all other taxes served no purpose within our Commerce Clause jurisprudence, but stood "only as a trap for the unwary draftsman." Complete Auto, 430 U.S., at 279. In contrast, the bright-line rule of Bellas Hess furthers the ends of the dormant Commerce Clause. Undue burdens on interstate commerce may be avoided not only by a case-by-case evaluation of the actual burdens imposed by particular regulations or taxes, but also, in some situations, by the demarcation of a discrete realm of commercial activity that is free from interstate taxation. *Bellas Hess* followed the latter approach and created a safe harbor for vendors "whose only connection with customers in the [taxing] State is by common carrier or the United States mail." Under *Bellas Hess,* such vendors are free from state-imposed duties to collect sales and use taxes.

Like other bright-line tests, the *Bellas Hess* rule appears artificial at its edges: whether or not a State may compel a vendor to collect a sales or use tax may turn on the presence in the taxing State of a small sales force, plant, or office. This artificiality, however, is more than offset by the benefits of a clear rule. . . .

Moreover, a bright-line rule in the area of sales and use taxes also encourages settled expectations and, in doing so, fosters investment by businesses and individuals. Indeed, it is not unlikely that the mail-order industry's dramatic growth over the last quarter century is due in part to the bright-line exemption from state taxation created in *Bellas Hess.* . . .

. . . [The] *Bellas Hess* rule has engendered substantial reliance and has become part of the basic framework of a sizable industry.[1] The interest in

---

[1] North Dakota's use tax illustrates well how a state tax might unduly burden interstate commerce. On its face, North Dakota law imposes a collection duty on every vendor who advertises in the State three times in a single year. Thus, absent the *Bellas Hess* rule, a publisher who included a subscription card in three issues of its magazine, a vendor whose radio advertisements were heard in North Dakota on three occasions, and a corporation whose telephone sales force made three calls into the State, all would be subject to the collection duty. What is more significant, similar obligations might be imposed by the Nation's 6,000-plus taxing jurisdictions. . . .

[7] . . . Although . . . every tax that passes contemporary Commerce Clause analysis is also valid under the Due Process Clause, it does not follow that the converse is as well true: a tax may be consistent with due process and yet unduly burden interstate commerce. *See, e.g.,* Tyler Pipe Indus., Inc. v. Washington State Dep't of Revenue, 483 U.S. 232 (1987).

[1] Many States have enacted use taxes. See Brief for Direct Marketing Association as Amicus Curiae. An overruling of *Bellas Hess* might raise thorny questions concerning the retroactive application of those taxes and might trigger substantial unanticipated liability for mail-order houses. . . .

stability and orderly development of the law that undergirds the doctrine of stare decisis therefore counsels adherence to settled precedent.

[Although] in our cases subsequent to *Bellas Hess* and concerning other types of taxes we have not adopted a similar bright-line, physical-presence requirement, our reasoning in those cases does not compel that we now reject the rule that Bellas Hess established in the area of sales and use taxes. To the contrary, the continuing value of a bright-line rule in this area and the doctrine and principles of stare decisis indicate that the Bellas Hess rule remains good law. For these reasons, we disagree with the North Dakota Supreme Court's conclusion that the time has come to renounce the bright-line test of *Bellas Hess.*

. . . Congress remains free to disagree with our conclusions. Indeed, in recent years Congress has considered legislation that would "overrule" the *Bellas Hess* rule. Its decision not to take action in this direction may, of course, have been dictated by respect for our holding in *Bellas Hess* that the Due Process Clause prohibits States from imposing such taxes, but today we have put that problem to rest. . . .

The judgment of the Supreme Court of North Dakota is reversed, and the case is remanded for further proceedings not inconsistent with this opinion.

JUSTICE WHITE, concurring in part and dissenting in part.

. . . The Court stops short . . . of giving *Bellas Hess* the complete burial it justly deserves. In my view, the Court should also overrule that part of *Bellas Hess* which justifies its holding under the Commerce Clause. I, therefore, respectfully dissent from Part IV. . . .

. . . [There] is no relationship between the physical-presence/nexus rule the Court retains and Commerce Clause considerations that allegedly justify it. . . . [In] today's economy, physical presence frequently has very little to do with a transaction a State might seek to tax. Wire transfers of money involving billions of dollars occur every day; purchasers place orders with sellers by fax, phone, and computer linkup; sellers ship goods by air, road, and sea through sundry delivery services without leaving their place of business. It is certainly true that the days of the door-to-door salesperson are not gone. Nevertheless, an out-of-state direct marketer derives numerous commercial benefits from the State in which it does business. These advantages include laws establishing sound local banking institutions to support credit transactions; courts to ensure collection of the purchase price from the seller's customers; means of waste disposal from garbage generated by mail-order solicitations; and creation and enforcement of consumer protection laws, which protect buyers and sellers alike, the former by ensuring that they will have a ready means of protecting against fraud, and the latter by creating a climate of consumer confidence that inures to the benefit of reputable dealers in mail-order transactions. To create, for the first time, a nexus requirement under the Commerce Clause independent of that established for due process purposes is one thing; to attempt to justify an anachronistic notion of physical presence in economic terms is quite another.

The illogic of retaining the physical-presence requirement in these circumstances is palpable. Under the majority's analysis, . . . an out-of-state seller with one salesperson in a State would be subject to use tax collection burdens on its entire mail-order sales even if those sales were unrelated to the salesperson's solicitation efforts. By contrast, an out-of-state seller in a neighboring State could be the dominant business in the putative taxing State, creating the greatest infrastructure burdens and undercutting the State's home companies by its comparative price advantage in selling products free of use taxes, and yet not have to collect such taxes if it lacks a physical presence in the taxing State. The majority clings to the physical-presence rule not because of any logical relation to fairness or any economic rationale related to principles underlying the Commerce Clause, but simply out of the supposed convenience of having a bright-line rule. I am less impressed by the convenience of such adherence than the unfairness it produces. Here, convenience should give way. . . .

Also very questionable is the rationality of perpetuating a rule that creates an interstate tax shelter for one form of business—mail-order sellers—but no countervailing advantage for its competitors. If the Commerce Clause was intended to put businesses on an even playing field, the majority's rule is hardly a way to achieve that goal. . . . I would think that protectionist rules favoring a $180-billion-a-year industry might come within the scope of [the Commerce Clause's] "structural concerns." . . .

. . . Reasonable minds surely can, and will, differ over what showing is required to make out a "physical presence" adequate to justify imposing responsibilities for use tax collection. And given the estimated loss in revenue to States of more than $3.2 billion this year alone, it is a sure bet that the vagaries of "physical presence" will be tested to their fullest in our courts.

. . . [The] Court's . . . justification of encouraging settled expectations in fact connotes a substantive economic decision to favor out-of-state direct marketers to the detriment of other retailers. By justifying the *Bellas Hess* rule in terms of "the mail-order industry's dramatic growth over the last quarter century," the Court is effectively imposing its own economic preferences in deciding this case. . . .

Finally, the Court accords far greater weight to stare decisis than was given to that principle in Complete Auto itself. As that case demonstrates, we have not been averse to overruling our precedents under the Commerce Clause when they have become anachronistic in light of later decisions. . . . It is unreasonable for companies such as Quill to invoke a "settled expectation" in conducting affairs without being taxed. . . .

JUSTICE SCALIA, with whom JUSTICE KENNEDY and JUSTICE THOMAS join, concurring in part and concurring in the judgment.

. . . It is difficult to discern any principled basis for distinguishing between jurisdiction to regulate and jurisdiction to tax. . . . I agree with the Court . . . that abandonment of *Bellas Hess'* due process holding is compelled by . . . our post-1967 cases dealing with state jurisdiction to adjudicate. I do not understand this to mean that the due process standards for adjudicative jurisdiction and those for legislative (or prescriptive) jurisdiction are necessarily identical. . . .

I also agree that the Commerce Clause holding of *Bellas Hess* should not be overruled. . . . As the Court notes, "the *Bellas Hess* rule has engendered substantial reliance and has become part of the basic framework of a sizable industry." . . .

. . . Having [in cases following *Complete Auto*] affirmatively suggested that the "physical presence" rule could be reconciled with [*Complete Auto*], we ought not visit economic hardship upon those who took us at our word. . . .

---

## NOTES ON *QUILL*

(1) *The power to tax and the power to prescribe law.* Justice Scalia's partial concurrence in Quill raises the question, in passing, of the relationship between the power to tax and the power to govern generally. Under the Commerce Clause rulings in Bellas Hess, *Complete Auto,* and Quill, a state must have a certain "nexus" with a business before it may tax it, and that "nexus" requirement can be satisfied by some physical presence, but not by communication contacts alone. Is the "state interest" requirement for legislative jurisdiction under the Due Process Clause equivalent to this "nexus" requirement of the Commerce Clause? Should it be, as Justice Scalia suggests? Does he mean that a legitimate state interest should be enough to justify imposing a tax? Or does he mean that a state without some territorial contact with an issue should lack power to govern that issue by its laws?

(2) *The power to tax and the power to adjudicate.* Interestingly, the issue of power to tax was fortuitously linked to the issue of power to adjudicate by the wide readings given the Supreme Court's famous decision in International Shoe. Since the Due Process Clause, after Quill requires physical presence to ground either a state's power to adjudicate or its power to tax, are you clear why the Commerce Clause should require physical presence to ground a power to tax?

(3) *The fractional interest and the duty to apportion.* The power to tax, unlike the power to govern generally, can be conditioned, as the Complete Auto rules underscore, on reasonable apportionment. The problem of the fractional interest—is to that extent—solved, or at least solvable, in power-to-tax cases. How, then, should a state apportion its taxes when dealing with multistate or multinational enterprises? In *Container Corp. v. Franchise Tax Board,* 463 U.S. 159, 169 (1983), the Court clarified that a state's apportionment formula in such cases must be "internally and externally consistent:" An apportionment is "internally consistent" if a taxpayer would not be subjected to multiple tax liability if every other state used that formula. But nothing in this rule prevents each state remains from applying its own "internally consistent" formula, no matter what formulae other states are applying, and no matter what multiple tax liabilities ensue. As for "external consistency," An apportionment formula is "externally consistent" if it is fairly attributable to the taxpayer's economic activity within the taxing State. Do you understand the difference between "external consistency" and the separate requirement of "nexus?"

(4) *"Unitary" worldwide taxes.* May a state attribute to a company doing business there all its income worldwide, and tax a fraction of that? In

*Container Corp., supra,* the Supreme Court had before it challenges under the Due Process and Commerce Clauses to California's then "unitary" or "worldwide" corporate franchise (income) tax, as applied to a multinational enterprise. To the shock of some observers, the Supreme Court sustained California's unitary worldwide tax under both Clauses. The taxpayer in that case was an American corporation with overseas subsidiaries that were incorporated and doing business in other countries. Would *Container Corp.* permit California to tax the income of foreign corporations? Corporations with foreign parents, or foreign subsidiaries? The Supreme Court sustained California's unitary worldwide tax scheme in such cases in *Barclays Bank PLC v. Franchise Tax Board,* 512 U.S. 298 (1994).

(5) *The exception: Taxes at the point of sale.* Are there circumstances in which a state imposing a tax upon multistate activity should not be required to apportion the tax? A sales tax, for example, seems to affect a transaction that is complete at the point of sale, wherever the goods go or however they are taxed subsequently. On this thinking the Court held sales taxes free of an apportionment requirement in *McGoldrick v. Berwind-White Coal Mining Co.,* 309 U.S. 33 (1940). By analogy to a state tax on sales, may the state of origin of an interstate telephone call tax the call without apportionment? May the state of sale of an airline ticket to another state or country tax the ticket without apportionment? The court sustained an unapportioned tax on multistate calls in *Goldberg v. Sweet,* 488 U.S. 252 (1989), and on multistate bus tickets in *Oklahoma Tax Comm'n v. Jefferson Lines, Inc.,* 514 U.S. 175 (1995).

(6) *Footnote to Quill:* By late November 1997, several but not all states affected by Quill, Texas leading, were hammering out an agreement under which state legislation would be introduced to require mail order companies to compute and collect sales taxes on goods sold to customers in the customer's home state, whether or not the seller maintained a physical presence in that state. In exchange, the seller would be permitted to engage in some promotional activities in that state without subjecting itself to that state's general jurisdiction.

(7) *Recent writing.* For current discussion of Quill see Dan T. Coenen & Walter Hellerstein, *Suspect Linkage: The Interplay of State Taxing and Spending Measures in the Application of Constitutional Antidiscrimination Rules,* 95 MICH. L. REV. 2167 (1997); Barry Friedman, *Valuing Federalism,* 82 MINN. L. REV. 317 (1997); Anna M. Hoti, *Comment, Finishing What Quill Started: The Transactional Nexus Test for State Use Tax Collection,* 59 ALB. L. REV. 1449 (1996).

# PART E    THE DISCRIMINATORY FORUM

## § 5.07    Note on the Discriminatory Forum

The Supreme Court has considered discriminations in choice of law only infrequently, and has made only occasional use for the purpose of the Equal Protection Clause of the Fourteenth Amendment or of the Privileges and Immunities Clause of Article IV. Allegations of discrimination in choice of law have occasionally been successful under the Full Faith and Credit Clause, and, as is more likely today, the Commerce Clause.

## § 5.08    Discrimination Against Claimants Relying on Nonforum Law

### HUGHES v. FETTER

*United States Supreme Court*
*341 U.S. 609, 71 S. Ct. 980, 95 L. Ed. 1212 (1951)*

JUSTICE BLACK delivered the opinion of the Court.

Basing his complaint on the Illinois wrongful death statute, appellant administrator brought this action in the Wisconsin state court to recover damages for the death of Harold Hughes, who was fatally injured in an automobile accident in Illinois. The allegedly negligent driver and an insurance company were named as defendants. On their motion the trial court entered summary judgment "dismissing the complaint on the merits." It held that a Wisconsin statute, which creates a right of action only for deaths caused in that state, establishes a local public policy against Wisconsin's entertaining suits brought under the wrongful death acts of other states. The Wisconsin Supreme Court affirmed, notwithstanding the contention that the local statute so construed violated the Full Faith and Credit Clause of Art. IV § 1 of the Constitution. . . .

We are called upon to decide the narrow question whether Wisconsin, over the objection raised, can close the doors of its courts to the cause of action created by the Illinois wrongful death act. . . . We have recognized . . . that full faith and credit does not automatically compel a forum state to subordinate its own statutory policy to a conflicting public act of another state. . . . [Here,] the policy of Wisconsin, as interpreted by its highest court, [is] against permitting Wisconsin courts to entertain this wrongful death action.[1]

We hold that Wisconsin's policy must give way. That state has no real feeling of antagonism against wrongful death suits in general. To the contrary,

---

[1] The present case is not one where Wisconsin, having entertained appellant's lawsuit, chose to apply its own instead of Illinois' statute to measure the substantive rights involved. This distinguishes the present case from those where we have said that 'Prima facie every state is entitled to enforce in its own courts its own statutes, lawfully enacted.' Alaska Packers Ass'n v. Indus. Acc. Commission, 294 U.S. 532, 547 (1935).

a forum is regularly provided for cases of this nature, the exclusionary rule extending only so far as to bar actions for death not caused locally. The Wisconsin policy, moreover, cannot be considered as an application of the forum non conveniens doctrine. . . . Even if we assume that Wisconsin could refuse, by reason of particular circumstances, to hear foreign controversies to which nonresidents were parties, the present case is not one lacking a close relationship with the state. For not only were appellant, the decedent and the individual defendant all residents of Wisconsin, but also appellant was appointed administrator and the corporate defendant was created under Wisconsin laws. . . .

Under these circumstances, we conclude that Wisconsin's statutory policy which excludes this Illinois cause of action is forbidden by the national policy of the Full Faith and Credit Clause. The judgment is reversed and the cause is remanded to the Supreme Court of Wisconsin for proceedings not inconsistent with this opinion.

Mr. JUSTICE FRANKFURTER, whom Mr. JUSTICE REED, Mr. JUSTICE JACKSON, and Mr. JUSTICE MINTON, join, dissenting.

. . . This Court should certainly not require that the forum deny its own law and follow the tort law of another State where there is a reasonable basis for the forum to close its courts to the foreign cause of action. The decision of Wisconsin to open its courts to actions for wrongful deaths within the State but close them to actions for deaths outside the State may not satisfy everyone's notion of wise policy. But it is neither novel nor without reason. . . . Wisconsin may be willing to grant a right of action where witnesses will be available in Wisconsin and the courts are acquainted with a detailed local statute and cases construing it. . . . The legislature may well feel that it is better to allow the courts of the State where the accident occurred to construe and apply its own statute, and that the exceptional case where the defendant cannot be served in the State where the accident occurred does not warrant a general statute allowing suit in the Wisconsin courts. . . .

No claim is made that Wisconsin has discriminated against the citizens of other States and thus violated Art. IV, § 2 [the Privileges and Immunities Clause] of the Constitution. . . . In the present case, the decedent, the plaintiff, and the individual defendant were residents of Wisconsin. The corporate defendant was created under Wisconsin law. The suit was brought in the Wisconsin courts. No reason is apparent—and none is vouchsafed in the opinion of the Court—why the interest of Illinois is so great that it can force the courts of Wisconsin to grant relief in defiance of their own law.

Finally, it may be noted that there is no conflict here in the policies underlying the statute of Wisconsin and that of Illinois. The Illinois wrongful death statute has a proviso that "no action shall be brought or prosecuted in this State to recover damages for a death occurring outside of this State where a right of action for such death exists under the laws of the place where such death occurred and service of process in such suit may be had upon the defendant in such place." . . . Thus, in the converse of the case at bar—if Hughes had been killed in Wisconsin and suit had been brought in Illinois—the Illinois courts would apparently have dismissed the suit. There is no need to be "more Roman than the Romans."

## WELLS v. SIMONDS ABRASIVE CO.

*United States Supreme Court*
*345 U.S. 514, 73 S.Ct. 856, 97 L.Ed. 1211 (1953)*

CHIEF JUSTICE VINSON delivered the opinion of the Court.

Cheek Wells was killed in Alabama when a grinding wheel with which he was working burst. The wheel had been manufactured by the respondent, a corporation with its principal place of business in Pennsylvania. The administratrix of the estate of Cheek Wells brought an action for damages in the federal court for the Eastern District of Pennsylvania after one year, but within two years, after the death. Jurisdiction was based upon diversity of citizenship.

The section of the Alabama Code upon which petitioner predicated her action for wrongful death provided that action "must be brought within two years from and after the death. . . ." The respondent moved for summary judgment on the ground the Pennsylvania wrongful death statute required suit to be commenced within one year. . . . [T]he district judge found . . . that the Pennsylvania conflict of laws rule called for the application of its own limitation [period] rather than that of the place of the accident. . . . [H]e ordered summary judgment for the respondent. The Court of Appeals for the Third Circuit affirmed. . . .

The states are free to adopt such rules of conflict of laws as they choose, *Kryger v. Wilson*, 242 U.S. 171 (1916). . . . The Full Faith and Credit Clause does not compel a state to adopt any particular set of rules of conflict of laws; it merely sets certain minimum requirements which each state must observe when asked to apply the law of a sister state.

Long ago, we held that applying the statute of limitations of the forum to a foreign substantive right did not deny full faith and credit, *McElmoyle v. Cohen*, 13 Pet. 312 (U.S. 1839); *Townsend v. Jemison*, 9 How. 407 (U.S. 1850). . . .

The rule that the limitations of the forum apply . . . is the usual conflicts rule of the states. However, there have been divergent views when a foreign statutory right unknown to the common law has a period of limitation included in the section creating the right. The Alabama statute here involved creates such a right and contains a built-in limitation. The view is held in some jurisdictions that such a limitation is so intimately connected with the right that it must be enforced in the forum state along with the substantive right.

We are not concerned with the reasons which have led some states for their own purposes to adopt the foreign limitation, instead of their own, in such a situation. The question here is whether the Full Faith and Credit Clause compels them to do so. Our prevailing rule is that the Full Faith and Credit Clause does not compel the forum state to use the period of limitation of a foreign state. We see no reason in the present situation to graft an exception onto it. Differences based upon whether the foreign right was known to the common law or upon the arrangement of the code of the foreign state are too unsubstantial to form the basis for constitutional distinctions under the Full Faith and Credit Clause. . . .

Our [decision] in *Hughes v. Fetter,* 341 U.S. 609 (1951), [does] not call for a change in the well-established rule that the forum state is permitted to apply its own period of limitation. The crucial factor in [that case] was that the forum laid an uneven hand on causes of action arising within and without the forum state. Causes of action arising in sister states were discriminated against. Here Pennsylvania applies her one-year limitation to all wrongful death actions wherever they may arise. The judgment is affirmed.

MR. JUSTICE JACKSON, with whom MR. JUSTICE BLACK and MR. JUSTICE MINTON join, dissenting.

We are unable to accept the results or follow the reasoning of the Court. . . . Finding it impossible to serve process on the defendant in Alabama, petitioner brought an action in the United States Court for the Eastern District of Pennsylvania. Her action was based on a statute of Alabama which conferred a right of action for wrongfully causing death and required that the action be brought within two years from the death. This she did. . . .

[The] Court's opinion here refers to it as a "crucial factor" [in *Hughes*] that "the forum laid an uneven hand on causes of action arising within and without the forum state." I had supposed, before *Hughes*, that the Commonwealth of Pennsylvania could close its courts to trial of this case. But no one would have questioned, I should think, that if the cause were entertained it must be tried in accordance with the law of the place of the wrong. . . .

The Supreme Court of Alabama has held the same doctrine applicable to the very statute in question, saying, "This is not a statute of limitations, but of the essence of the cause of action. . . . " [Citation omitted.]

. . . We think that the better view of the case before us would be that it is Alabama law which giveth and only Alabama law that taketh away.

---

## NOTES ON *HUGHES* AND *WELLS*

(1) *The muddle in Hughes.* If the reasoning in *Hughes* seems opaque to you, you are not to blame. All courts and counsel in *Hughes* shared the limitations of their era; all assumed that the place of injury was the only interested state in this wrongful death case. (Justice Black's unedited opinion, as it appears in the reports, manages to get wrong even what was well understood by most others at the time.) Further obscuring the contours of the case is Justice Black's curious Footnote 10. As the dissenters point out, Wisconsin's door-closing policy, as determined by its highest court in this very case, was Wisconsin "law."

But we can think about the case straight, even if courts and counsel at the time could not.

(2) *Analyzing* Hughes. What were the interests of the respective states in *Hughes*? This was an action between two residents of Wisconsin. Wisconsin, of course, had a general interest in remedying the tort to its plaintiff; but the Wisconsin wrongful death act, with its territorial limits, legislatively stymied vindication of that interest. And so the plaintiff could not plead under the

Wisconsin statute. As the place where both parties resided, Wisconsin certainly had interests in furnishing a forum for their litigation, no matter under what law. It had zero interest in closing its doors to them. As for Illinois, that state would have had no interest, as the place of the injury, in blocking the Wisconsin trial. Illinois' only interests, as place of injury, would have been to ensure that the tort on her roads was remedied, and that future such torts were deterred.

(3) *Full faith and credit? Or equal protection?* Did Wisconsin create a discriminatory classification when it opened its courts to suits on the deaths of all of its residents except those injured elsewhere? Did Wisconsin have a rational basis for this classification? If not, then the problem in *Hughes* had more to do with equal protection than full faith and credit. Indeed, in *Wells v. Simonds Abrasive,* we see the Supreme Court explaining the recently-decided *Hughes* (which needed explanation badly) as a case in which the forum "laid an uneven hand" on the foreign cause of action. It would have been more accurate to say that in *Hughes* the forum laid an uneven hand on the resident with the foreign cause of action.

This was Brainerd Currie's analysis of *Hughes* as well. Brainerd Currie, *The Constitution and the "Transitory" Cause of Action*, (pts. 1-2), 73 HARV. L. REV. 36, 268 (1959).

(4) *Trying to distinguish between residents based on the place in which they were injured: an exercise in futility?* Indeed, discrimination between resident plaintiffs cannot be justified by the fact that one was injured outside, the other inside, the territory. The location of the spot where a resident of the forum was injured, while a matter of importance to the state where the injury occurred, is wholly irrelevant to the interest of the plaintiff's home state. Its interest is in seeing its resident made whole, no matter where she got hurt.

(5) *Territorial limits on statutory rights.* The foregoing analysis casts an ironic light on the ubiquitous territorial limits, like those seen in *Hughes,* that state legislators characteristically tack onto statutory rights. By doing so, legislators inadvertently deny some local residents the equal protections of state law. Workers' compensation statutes, for example, typically cover resident workers only for workplace accidents occurring in the state. Fortunately for employers, who otherwise would be stripped of their statutory immunity from suit, the worker usually accepts compensation under the laws of the place of injury.

(6) *Hughes and the mythical "obligation to provide a forum."* Earlier in this Chapter we saw that an interested state may furnish a forum, even though a sister state would regard the particular action as a local one within its exclusive jurisdiction; *Nevada v. Hall* and the *Pacific Employers* case, both *supra* this Chapter, stand for that proposition. *Hughes* is generally cited for the further proposition that a state must furnish a forum for a sister-state's transitory cause of action.

How can such an obligation be squared with *Wells*? Under *Wells,* a state interested in closing its doors may do so, and it does not matter if it closes its doors to a sister-state's transitory cause of action.

It would seem a more coherent formulation of the position to say that the forum without an interest in closing its doors is prohibited from doing so. The forum with no interest in hearing a case always has an economizing interest in closing its doors to that case. Thus, the forum that applies a rational local door-closing rule evenhandedly to local as well as to foreign claims acts constitutionally. The sad feature of *Wells* was that, although Pennsylvania had constitutional power to apply its short period of limitations, leaving the widow without remedy, we feel it should not have exercised its power.

(7) *Two interesting court-access analogies.* For the analogous obligation of state courts not to discriminate against plaintiffs suing under federal law, see *Testa v. Katt, infra* Chapter 6.

Interestingly, a result analogous to the result in *Hughes* also is reached at common law, without the aid of the Constitution. Recall Judge Cardozo's insistence, on a theory of vested rights, that courts "do not close their doors" to foreign claims, without some "deep-rooted" reason of public policy. *Loucks v. Standard Oil Co. of New York, supra* Chapter 4.

(8) *Recent work.* For recent writing taking *Hughes v. Fetter* into account, see H. Jefferson Powell & Benjamion Priester, *Convenient Shorthand: the Supreme Court and the Language of State Sovereignty,* 71 U. COLO. L. REV. 645 (2000); Kermit Roosevelt, *The Myth of Choice of Law: Rethinking Conflicts,* 97 MICH. L. REV. 2448 (1999); Stanley E. Cox, *The Interested Forum,* 48 MERCER L. REV. 727 (1997).

---

## § 5.09  Discrimination Against Residents With Out-of-State Interests

## NOTE ON THE EFFECT OF OUT-OF-STATE INTERESTS ON RIGHTS AT THE FORUM

We have already considered the forum's power under the Commerce Clause to overreach itself and impose burdens upon the in-state interests of nonresidents. *Cf.* the *Quill* case, *supra* this Chapter. In *Hughes v. Fetter,* also *supra* this Chapter, we examined the forum's power to deny access to its courts to a resident relying on foreign law. Now consider the further question of the forum's power to deny access to forum resources or benefits to its own residents on account of their out-of-state interests.

**CITY OF PHILADELPHIA v. NEW JERSEY,** 437 U.S. 617 (1978). Operators of New Jersey landfill sites joined with out-of-state cities to challenge a New Jersey statute [ch. 363] which, in effect, closed New Jersey's doors to most garbage originating or collected out of state. The New Jersey courts sustained the constitutionality of the statute.

*Held* (by JUSTICE STEWART): *Reversed.* "[We] reject the state court's suggestion that the banning of 'valueless' out-of-state wastes implicates no constitutional protection. Just as Congress has power to regulate the interstate movement of these wastes, States are not free from constitutional scrutiny when they restrict that movement. *Cf. Hughes v. Alexandria Scrap Corp.,* 426 U.S. 794, 802–814 (1976). . . .

"[Where] simple economic protectionism is effected by state legislation, a virtually per se rule of invalidity has been erected. *See, e. g., H. P. Hood & Sons, Inc. v. Du Mond,* 336 U.S. 525 (1949). . . . But where other legislative objectives are credibly advanced and there is no patent discrimination against interstate trade, the Court has adopted a much more flexible approach, the general contours of which were outlined in *Pike v. Bruce Church, Inc.,* 397 U.S. 137, 142 (1970): 'Where the statute regulates evenhandedly to effectuate a legitimate local public interest, and its effects on interstate commerce are only incidental, it will be upheld unless the burden imposed on such commerce is clearly excessive in relation to the putative local benefits.'. . . The crucial inquiry, therefore, must be directed to determining whether [the New Jersey law] is basically a protectionist measure, or whether it can fairly be viewed as a law directed to legitimate local concerns, with effects upon interstate commerce that are only incidental.

"The purpose of ch. 363 is set out in the statute itself as follows: 'The Legislature finds and determines that . . . the available and appropriate land fill sites within the State are being diminished, that the environment continues to be threatened by the treatment and disposal of waste which originated or was collected outside the State, and that the public health, safety and welfare require that the treatment and disposal within this State of all wastes generated outside of the State be prohibited.' The New Jersey Supreme Court accepted this statement of the state legislature's purpose. The state court additionally found that New Jersey's existing landfill sites will be exhausted within a few years; that to go on using these sites or to develop new ones will take a heavy environmental toll, both from pollution and from loss of scarce open lands; . . . and finally, that 'the extension of the lifespan of existing landfills, resulting from the exclusion of out-of-state waste, may be of crucial importance in preventing further virgin wetlands or other undeveloped lands from being devoted to landfill purposes.' Based on these findings, the court concluded that ch. 363 was designed to protect, not the State's economy, but its environment, and that its substantial benefits outweigh its 'slight' burden on interstate commerce. . . .

"Contrary to the evident assumption of the state court and the parties, the evil of protectionism can reside in legislative means as well as legislative ends. Thus, it does not matter whether the ultimate aim of ch. 363 is to reduce the waste disposal costs of New Jersey residents or to save remaining open lands from pollution, for we assume New Jersey has every right to protect its residents' pocketbooks as well as their environment. And it may be assumed as well that New Jersey may pursue those ends by slowing the flow of all waste into the State's remaining landfills, even though interstate commerce may incidentally be affected. But whatever New Jersey's ultimate purpose, it may not be accomplished by discriminating against articles of commerce coming from outside the State unless there is some reason, apart from their origin, to treat them differently. Both on its face and in its plain effect, ch. 363 violates this principle of nondiscrimination. . . . On its face, it imposes on out-of-state commercial interests the full burden of conserving the State's remaining landfill space. It is true that in our previous cases the scarce natural resource was itself the article of commerce, whereas here the scarce resource and the article of commerce are distinct. But that difference is without consequence. . . . What is crucial is the attempt by one State to isolate itself from a problem common to many by erecting a barrier against the movement of interstate trade.

"The appellees argue that not all laws which facially discriminate against out-of-state commerce are forbidden protectionist regulations. In particular, they point to quarantine laws, which this Court has repeatedly upheld even though they appear to single out interstate commerce for special treatment. But . . . [the] New Jersey statute is not . . . a quarantine law. There has been no claim here that the very movement of waste into or through New Jersey endangers health, or that waste must be disposed of as soon and as close to its point of generation as possible. The harms caused by waste are said to arise after its disposal in landfill sites, and at that point, as New Jersey concedes, there is no basis to distinguish out-of-state waste from domestic waste. . . ."

". . . Tomorrow, cities in New Jersey may find it expedient or necessary to send their waste into Pennsylvania or New York for disposal, and those States might then claim the right to close their borders. The Commerce Clause will protect New Jersey in the future, just as it protects her neighbors now, from efforts by one State to isolate itself in the stream of interstate commerce from a problem shared by all. . . ."

MR. JUSTICE REHNQUIST (with whom Chief Justice Rehnquist joins) dissenting: "A growing problem in our Nation is the sanitary treatment and disposal of solid waste. . . . The health and safety hazards associated with landfills present appellees with a currently unsolvable dilemma. Other, hopefully safer, methods of disposing of solid wastes are still in the development stage and cannot presently be used. But appellees obviously cannot completely stop the tide of solid waste that its citizens will produce in the interim. For the moment, therefore, appellees must continue to use sanitary landfills to dispose of New Jersey's own solid waste despite the critical environmental problems thereby created.

"The question presented in this case is whether New Jersey must also continue to receive and dispose of solid waste from neighboring States, even though these will inexorably increase the health problems discussed above. . . . Because past precedents establish that the Commerce Clause does not present appellees with such a Hobson's choice, I dissent.

"In my opinion, [the quarantine] cases are dispositive of the present one. . . . I simply see no way to distinguish solid waste, on the record of this case, from germ-infected rags, diseased meat, and other noxious items. . . ."

----

On the *Philadelphia* case, from the perspective of a prolific conflicts commentator, see Stanley E. Cox, *Garbage In, Garbage Out: Court Confusion about the Dormant Commerce Clause,* 50 OKLA. L. REV. 155 (1997).

**CAMPS NEWFOUND/OWATONNA, INC. v. TOWN OF HARRISON, MAINE,** 520 U.S. 564, 117 S. Ct. 1590 (1997). Camps Newfound/Owatonna, Inc. ["Camps'"] was a nonprofit organization incorporated in Maine. Camps operated a summer camp in Maine for the benefit of children of Christian Scientists. Some 95% of the campers were not residents of Maine. A Maine statute provided a general exemption from local property taxes for charitable institutions incorporated in the State, unless "conducted or operated principally for the benefit of persons who are not residents of Maine." Camps sued the taxing town to obtain the benefit of the charitable exemption, arguing that its failure to extend the exempting to Camps was not justified, because the Maine statute was unconstitutional under the Commerce Clause. The trial court ruled for Camps, but the Supreme Judicial Court of Maine reversed.

*Held* (per JUSTICE STEVENS)(reversing): The Maine statute discriminates against interstate commerce and therefore violates the Commerce Clause. "Even though petitioner's camp does not make a profit, it is unquestionably engaged in commerce, not only as a purchaser, but also as a provider of goods and services. It markets those services, together with an opportunity to enjoy the natural beauty of an inland lake in Maine, to campers who are attracted to its facility from all parts of the Nation. . . .

". . . State laws discriminating against interstate commerce on their face are virtually per se invalid. . . . The Maine law expressly distinguishes between entities that serve a principally interstate clientele and those that primarily serve an intrastate market, singling out camps that serve mostly in-staters for beneficial tax treatment, and penalizing those camps that do a principally interstate business. . . .

"If such a policy were implemented by a statutory prohibition against providing camp services to nonresidents, the statute would almost certainly be invalid. We have consistently held that the Commerce Clause precludes a state from mandating that its residents be given a preferred right of access, over out-of-state consumers, to natural resources located within its borders or to the products derived therefrom. . . . Petitioner's 'product' is in part the natural beauty of Maine itself, . . . in addition [to] the special services that the camp provides. In this way, the Maine statute is like a law that burdens out-of-state access to domestically generated hydroelectric power or to local landfills. . . . Avoiding this sort of economic Balkanization, and the retaliatory acts of other States that may follow, is one of the central purposes of our negative Commerce Clause jurisprudence. . . . By encouraging economic isolationism, prohibitions on out-of-state access to in-state resources serve the very evil that the dormant Commerce Clause was designed to prevent.

". . . With respect to those businesses—like petitioner's—that continue to engage in a primarily interstate trade, the Maine statute . . . functionally serves as an export tariff that targets out-of-state consumers by taxing the businesses that principally serve them. . . . A State may not tax a transaction or incident more heavily when it crosses state lines than when it occurs entirely within the State. . . .

". . . Though we have never had cause to address the issue directly, the applicability of the dormant Commerce Clause to the nonprofit sector of the economy follows from our prior decisions. . . . In *Edwards v. California,* 314 U.S. 160 (1941), we addressed the constitutionality of a California statute prohibiting the transport into that State of indigent persons. We struck the statute down as a violation of the dormant Commerce Clause, reasoning that the transportation of persons is 'commerce,' and that the California statute was an 'unconstitutional barrier to [that] interstate commerce.' It is immaterial whether or not the transportation is commercial in character. . . . There are a number of lines of commerce in which both for-profit and nonprofit entities participate. Some educational institutions, some hospitals, some childcare facilities, some research organizations, and some museums generate significant earnings; and some are operated by not-for-profit corporations. . . .

". . . Noting our statement in *West Lynn Creamery, Inc. v. Healy,* 512 U.S. 186, 199 (1994), that 'A pure subsidy funded out of general revenue ordinarily imposes no burden on interstate commerce, but merely assists local business,' the Town submits that since a discriminatory subsidy may be permissible, a discriminatory exemption must be too. . . . Assuming, arguendo, that the Town is correct that a direct subsidy benefitting only those nonprofits serving principally Maine residents would be permissible, our cases do not sanction a tax exemption serving similar ends. . . .

". . . The history of our Commerce Clause jurisprudence has shown that even the smallest scale discrimination can interfere with the project of our federal Union. . . . The judgment of the Maine Supreme Judicial Court is reversed."

JUSTICE SCALIA (with whom CHIEF JUSTICE REHNQUIST, JUSTICE THOMAS and JUSTICE GINSBURG join), dissenting: ". . . Facially discriminatory or not, the exemption is no more . . . economic protectionism than any state law which dispenses public assistance only to the State's residents. . . ."

JUSTICE THOMAS (with whom JUSTICE SCALIA joins, and with whom CHIEF JUSTICE REHNQUIST joins in part) dissenting: ". . . The Constitution would seem to provide an express check on the States' power to levy certain discriminatory taxes on the commerce of other States—not in the judicially created negative Commerce Clause, but in the Article I, § 10 Import-Export Clause. . . . [The] tax exemption at issue in this case [would] easily . . . survive Import-Export Clause scrutiny. . . ."

---

## NOTES ON THE *PHILADELPHIA* AND *CAMPS* CASES

(1) *A problem case. Camps* is very much a problem case. Part of the difficulty the case presents no doubt is owing to its oddly unrepresentative parties. The logic of its situation compels the "Camps" organization to make arguments on behalf of its campers. The town, too, is defending not a town ordinance, but a state statute. The case raises many other questions. Just what in *Camps,*

precisely, was in interstate commerce? Perhaps it is the nonresident campers who cross state lines; Justice Stevens likens them to the indigents in the *Edwards* case. But at other times in his opinion Justice Stevens identifies the summer camp itself as being in interstate commerce, and then again as soliciting interstate commerce.

Suppose we make the nonresident campers the fulcrum of the case, and we look for relief to the Privileges and Immunities Clause rather than the Commerce Clause. There was evidence in the record that the tax in question was passed through to the campers in the form of modest tuition and fees. But the campers were not parties. And Camps would be in no better position to avail itself of the Privileges and Immunities Clause, because the Clause protects only individuals, not corporations, and then only for denials of fundamental rights. *Paul v. Virginia,* 75 U.S. (8 Wall.) 168 (1869); *Corfield v. Coryell,* 6 F. Cas. 546 (C.C. E.D. Pa. 1823).

(2) *Exemptions and subsidies.* Possibly the greatest difficulty Camps presents is its purported distinction between exemptions and subsidies. Justice Stevens relies on *Walz v. Tax Comm'n of City of New York,* 397 U.S. 664 (1970), in which the Court held that New York's tax exemption for church property did not violate the Establishment Clause of the First Amendment. Justice Stevens claims that *Walz* rested, in part, on the premise that there is a constitutionally significant difference between subsidies and tax exemptions. But the exemption in *Walz* was applicable to all charitable organizations. An exemption singling out church property might well have run afoul of the Establishment Clause. It is true that in *New Energy Co. of Ind. v. Limbach,* 486 U.S. 269 (1988), the Court did draw a distinction between exemptions and subsidies: "Direct subsidization of domestic industry does not ordinarily run afoul of [the Commerce Clause]; discriminatory taxation . . . does." But the Court gave no reasons for this understanding. What arguments might support a distinction between subsidies and exemptions? What arguments might support treating subsidies and exemptions as functional equivalents?

(3) *The Commerce Clause and the environment.* Suppose, hypothetically, that Maine's law applied only to summer camps, and was grounded in an interest in discouraging recreational visitors. Such an interest would not be irrational where environmental resources were growing scarce. And nothing in burdening nonresidents' access to local recreational resources offends the Privileges and Immunities Clause of Article 4 where no fundamental right is involved. *Cf. Baldwin v. Fish & Game Comm'n of Montana,* 436 U.S. 371 (1978) (holding that Montana may charge license fees to nonresident elk hunters). But apparently the Commerce Clause is tougher on state policy than the Privileges and Immunities Clause. The *Camps* Court takes the view that a desire to limit consumption of scarce local resources to residents could not, under the Commerce Clause, justify doing so. And that is the position of the Court in the famous case of *Philadelphia v. New Jersey, supra.* What might the respective states have done in either the hypothetical case or in *Philadelphia v. New Jersey* to protect the environment in a way that would pass constitutional muster?

(4) *For further reading.* For commentary on some of the problems presented by these cases, see Thomas W. Merrill, *Golden Rules for Transboundary Pollution,* 46 Duke L.J. 931 (1997).

# PART F   DISCRIMINATION AGAINST NONRESIDENTS

## § 5.10   DISCRIMINATION AGAINST NONRESIDENT CLAIMANTS

### NOTE ON THE NONRESIDENT CLAIMANT

The courts have used the Commerce Clause, the Equal Protection Clause, and an implied constitutional right to travel, in measuring state discrimination against nonresidents. The Supreme Court eventually identified the right to travel as a privilege of United States citizenship, and located it in the Privileges and Immunities Clause of the Fourteenth Amendment. *Saenz v. Roe*, 526 U.S. 489 (2002). The Privileges and Immunities Clause of Article IV might seem to be the natural locus of the nonresident's claim of state discrimination, but it is important to recall that the Article IV Privileges and Immunities Clause is only of very limited utility in extending forum rights to nonresidents, for at least two reasons. First, the Court has never overruled *Paul v. Virginia,* 75 U.S. (8 Wall.) 168 (1869), holding that a corporation is not a "citizen" for purposes of the Privileges and Immunities Clause. The Clause extends only to individuals. Second, the Clause was early held, in an influential opinion by Bushrod Washington, to protect only fundamental rights. *Corfield v. Coryell,* 6 F. Cas. 546 (C.C. E.D. Pa. 1823).

The only substantial use of the Article IV Privileges and Immunities Clause in recent memory has been to strike down residency requirements for the practice of law. *See, e.g., Barnard v. Thorstenn,* 409 U.S. 546 (1989) (striking down under the Privileges and Immunities Clause the Virgin Island's 1-year residency requirement for admission to the bar); *Supreme Court of Virginia v. Friedman,* 487 U.S. 59 (1988) (same, Virginia; requirement for admission without examination); *Supreme Court of N.H. v. Piper,* 470 U.S. 274 (1984) (same, New Hampshire).

The situation of the nonresident claimant at the forum is reflected chiefly in two contexts. The first involves the nonresident's access to the courts of the forum state; the second more generally involves the nonresident's access to forum state resources or benefits. These sorts of cases typically arise as challenges to residency or licensure requirements.

*Access to courts.* It is widely believed that a state may limit to residents the use of its long-arm statute. *E.g., Amer. Int'l Pictures, Inc. v. Morgan,* 371 F. Supp. 528 (N.D. Miss. 1974). Indeed, in view of the Supreme Court's broad tolerance of *forum non conveniens* dismissals, it is hard to argue that anything in the Constitution guarantees access to courts for nonresidents. But, subject to dismissals under legitimate door-closing rules of the forum, including *forum non conveniens* and the forum's statutes of limitation, we do find occasional recognition of a nonresident's constitutional right of access to courts. *E.g., Allenberg Cotton Co., Inc. v. Pittman,* 419 U.S. 20 (1974). In *Allenberg Cotton,* a nonresident corporation filed suit for breach of a contract to grow and deliver cotton. The state permitted access to its courts only for corporations qualified to do business in the state. The Court struck down the denial of access as a violation of the Commerce Clause. In *Dahnke-Walker Milling Co. v. Bondurant,* 257 U.S. 282 (1921), the Court held that under the Supremacy Clause federal courts need not defer to state rules denying a nonresident corporation access to courts in the state.

Note that the nonresident and the recently-arrived resident are often one and the same. By imposing residency requirements, the state in effect declares the recently-arrived resident to be outside the category of "resident." But once valid residency is established, may the state distinguish between long-term residents and newer arrivals?

---

## NORDLINGER v. HAHN

*Supreme Court of the United States*
*505 U.S. 1, 112 S.Ct. 2326, 120 L.Ed.2d 1 (1992)*

JUSTICE BLACKMUN delivered the opinion of the Court.

In 1978, California voters staged what has been described as a property tax revolt by approving a statewide ballot initiative known as Proposition 13. The adoption of Proposition 13 served to amend the California Constitution to impose strict limits on the rate at which real property is taxed and on the rate at which real property assessments are increased from year to year. In this litigation, we consider a challenge under the Equal Protection Clause of the Fourteenth Amendment to the manner in which real property now is assessed under the California Constitution.

Proposition 13 followed many years of rapidly rising real property taxes in California. From fiscal years 1967-1968 to 1971-1972, revenues from these taxes increased on an average of 11.5% per year. In response, the California Legislature enacted several property tax relief measures, including a cap on tax rates in 1972. The boom in the State's real estate market persevered, however, and the median price of an existing home doubled from $31,530 in 1973 to $62,430 in 1977. As a result, tax levies continued to rise because of sharply increasing assessment values. Some homeowners saw their tax bills double or triple during this period, well outpacing any growth in their income and ability to pay.

By 1978, property tax relief had emerged as a major political issue in California. In only one month's time, tax relief advocates collected over 1.2 million signatures to qualify Proposition 13 for the June 1978 ballot. On election day, Proposition 13 received a favorable vote of 64.8% and carried 55 of the State's 58 counties. California thus had a novel constitutional amendment that led to a property tax cut of approximately $7 billion in the first year. A California homeowner with a $50,000 home enjoyed an immediate reduction of about $750 per year in property taxes.

As enacted by Proposition 13, Article XIIIA of the California Constitution . . . combines a 1% ceiling on the property tax rate with a 2% cap on annual increases in assessed valuations. The assessment limitation, however, is subject to the exception that new construction or a change of ownership triggers a reassessment up to current appraised value . . . . Real property is assessed at values related to the value of the property at the time it is acquired by the taxpayer rather than to the value it has in the current real estate market.

Over time, this acquisition-value system has created dramatic disparities in the taxes paid by persons owning similar pieces of property. Property values in California have inflated far in excess of the allowed 2% cap on increases in assessments for property that is not newly constructed or that has not changed hands. As a result, longer-term property owners pay lower property taxes reflecting historic property values, while newer owners pay higher property taxes reflecting more recent values . . . . Indeed, in dollar terms, the differences in tax burdens are staggering. By 1989, the 44% of California homeowners who have owned their homes since enactment of Proposition 13 in 1978 shouldered only 25% of the more than $4 billion in residential property taxes paid by homeowners statewide . . . .

According to her amended complaint, petitioner Stephanie Nordlinger in November 1988 purchased a house in the Baldwin Hills neighborhood of Los Angeles County for $170,000. The prior owners bought the home just two years before for $121,500 . . . .

In early 1989, petitioner received a notice from the Los Angeles County Tax Assessor, who is a respondent here, informing her that her home had been reassessed upward to $170,100 on account of its change in ownership. She learned that the reassessment resulted in a property tax increase of $453.60, up 36% to $1,701, for the 1988-1989 fiscal year.

Petitioner later discovered she was paying about five times more in taxes than some of her neighbors who owned comparable homes since 1975 within the same residential development. For example, one block away, a house of identical size on a lot slightly larger than petitioner's was subject to a general tax levy of only $358.20 (based on an assessed valuation of $35,820, which reflected the home's value in 1975 plus [an] up-to-2% per year inflation factor). According to petitioner, . . . [the] general tax levied against her modest home is only a few dollars short of that paid by a pre-1976 owner of a $2.1 million Malibu beachfront home.

After exhausting administrative remedies, petitioner brought suit against respondents in Los Angeles County Superior Court. She sought a tax refund and a declaration that her tax was unconstitutional. . . . [The] Superior Court . . . dismissed the complaint without leave to amend.

The California Court of Appeal affirmed . . . . The Supreme Court of California denied review . . . .

. . . At the outset, petitioner suggests that Article XIIIA qualifies for heightened scrutiny because it infringes upon the constitutional right to travel . . . . But the complaint does not allege that petitioner herself has been impeded from traveling or from settling in California because, as has been noted, prior to purchasing her home, petitioner lived in an apartment in Los Angeles . . . . Accordingly, petitioner may not assert the constitutional right to travel as a basis for heightened review.

. . . We have no difficulty in ascertaining at least two rational or reasonable considerations of difference or policy that justify denying petitioner the benefits of her neighbors' lower assessments. First, the State has a legitimate interest in local neighborhood preservation, continuity, and stability. The State therefore legitimately can decide to structure its tax system to discourage rapid turnover in ownership of homes and businesses, for example, in order to inhibit displacement of lower income families by the forces of gentrification or of established, "mom-and-pop" businesses by newer chain operations. By permitting older owners to pay progressively less in taxes than new owners of comparable property, the Article XIIIA assessment scheme rationally furthers this interest.

Second, the State legitimately can conclude that a new owner at the time of acquiring his property does not have the same reliance interest warranting protection against higher taxes as does an existing owner . . . . A new owner has full information about the scope of future tax liability before acquiring the property, and if he thinks the future tax burden is too demanding, he can decide not to complete the purchase at all. By contrast, the existing owner, already saddled with his purchase, does not have the option of deciding not to buy his home if taxes become prohibitively high. To meet his tax obligations, he might be forced to sell his home or to divert his income away from the purchase of food, clothing, and other necessities . . . .

Petitioner argues that Article XIIIA cannot be distinguished from the tax assessment practice found to violate the Equal Protection Clause in *Allegheny Pittsburgh Coal Co. v. County Comm'n of Webster Cty.*, 488 U.S. 336 (1989) . . . . But [there was] an obvious and critical factual difference between this case and *Allegheny Pittsburgh* . . . . Webster County's "true current value" tax law could not conceivably justify its tax assessor's acquisition value assessments] . . . .

Finally, petitioner contends that the unfairness of Article XIIIA is made worse by its exemptions from reassessment for two special classes of new owners: persons aged 55 and older, who exchange principal residences, and children who acquire property from their parents . . . . The two exemptions at issue here rationally further legitimate purposes. The people of California reasonably could have concluded that older persons in general should not be discouraged from moving to a residence more suitable to their changing family size or income. Similarly, the people of California reasonably could have concluded that the interests of family and neighborhood continuity and stability are furthered by and warrant an exemption for transfers between parents and children . . . .

Petitioner and *amici* argue with some appeal that Article XIIIA frustrates the "American dream" of home ownership for many younger and poorer California families. They argue that Article XIIIA places startup businesses that depend on ownership of property at a severe disadvantage in competing with established businesses. They argue that Article XIIIA dampens demand for and construction of new housing and buildings. And they argue that Article XIIIA constricts local tax revenues at the expense of public education and vital services.

Time and again, however, this Court has made clear . . . that . . . even improvident decisions will eventually be rectified by the democratic process and that judicial intervention is generally unwarranted no matter how unwisely we may think a political branch has acted. Certainly, California's grand experiment appears to vest benefits in a broad, powerful, and entrenched segment of society, and, as the Court of Appeal surmised, ordinary democratic processes may be unlikely to prompt its reconsideration or repeal. Yet many wise and well-intentioned laws suffer from the same malady. Article XIIIA is not palpably arbitrary, and we must decline petitioner's request to upset the will of the people of California.

The judgment of the Court of Appeal is *affirmed*.

JUSTICE THOMAS, concurring in part and concurring in the judgment.

. . . I agree with the Court that Proposition 13 is constitutional. But I also agree with JUSTICE STEVENS that *Allegheny Pittsburgh* cannot be distinguished. To me *Allegheny Pittsburgh* represents a needlessly intrusive judicial infringement on the State's legislative powers, and I write separately because I see no benefit, and much risk, in refusing to confront it directly . . .

I concur in the judgment of the Court and join Part II-A of its opinion.

JUSTICE STEVENS, dissenting.

. . . [Those] who invested in California real estate in the 1970's are among the most fortunate capitalists in the world.

Proposition 13 has provided these successful investors with a tremendous windfall and, in doing so, has created severe inequities in California's property tax scheme. These property owners (hereinafter Squires) are guaranteed that, so long as they retain their property and do not improve it, their taxes will not increase more than 2% in any given year. As a direct result of this windfall for the Squires, later purchasers must pay far more than their fair share of property taxes . . . .

. . . In my opinion, such disparate treatment of similarly situated taxpayers is arbitrary and unreasonable. Although the Court today recognizes these gross inequities, its analysis of the justification for those inequities consists largely of a restatement of the benefits that accrue to long-time property owners . . . .

. . . Just three Terms ago, this Court unanimously invalidated Webster County, West Virginia's assessment scheme under rational-basis scrutiny . . . . The "intentional systematic undervaluation" found constitutionally infirm in *Allegheny Pittsburgh* has been codified in California by Proposition 13 . . . . If anything, the inequality created by Proposition 13 is constitutionally more problematic because it is the product of a statewide policy rather than the result of an individual assessor's maladministration . . . . Our decisions have established that the Equal Protection Clause is offended as much by the arbitrary delineation of classes of property (as in this case) as by the arbitrary treatment of properties within the same class (as in *Allegheny Pittsburgh*) . . . .

. . . Under Proposition 13, a majestic estate purchased for $150,000 in 1975 (and now worth more than $2 million) is placed in the same tax class as a humble cottage purchased today for $150,000. The only feature those two properties have in common is that somewhere, sometime, a sale contract for each was executed that contained the price "$150,000." Particularly in an environment of phenomenal real property appreciation, to classify property based on its purchase price is palpably arbitrary.

. . . It is beyond question that "inhibiting the displacement of lower income families by the forces of gentrification" is a legitimate state interest; the central issue is whether the disparate treatment of earlier and later purchasers rationally furthers this goal . . . .

In my opinion, Proposition 13 sweeps too broadly and operates too indiscriminately to rationally further the State's interest in neighborhood preservation. No doubt there are some early purchasers living on fixed or limited incomes who could not afford to pay higher taxes and still maintain their homes. California has enacted special legislation to respond to their plight. Those concerns cannot provide an adequate justification for Proposition 13. A statewide, across-the-board tax windfall for *all* property owners and their descendants is no more a "rational" means for protecting this small subgroup than a blanket tax exemption for all taxpayers named Smith would be a rational means to protect a particular taxpayer named Smith who demonstrated difficulty paying her tax bill.

Even within densely populated Los Angeles County, residential property comprises less than half of the market value of the property tax roll. It cannot be said that the legitimate state interest in preserving neighborhood character is "rationally furthered" by tax benefits for owners of commercial, industrial, vacant, and other nonresidential properties. It is just short of absurd to conclude that the legitimate state interest in protecting a relatively small number of economically vulnerable families is "rationally furthered" by a tax windfall for all 9,787,887 property owners in California.

The Court's conclusion is unsound not only because of the lack of numerical fit between the posited state interest and Proposition 13's inequities but also because of the lack of logical fit between ends and means. Although the State may have a valid interest in preserving some neighborhoods,[8] Proposition 13 not only "inhibits the displacement" of settled families, it also inhibits the transfer of unimproved land, abandoned buildings, and substandard uses . . . . Proposition 13 . . . treats all property alike, giving all owners tax breaks, and discouraging the transfer or improvement of all property — the developed and the dilapidated, the neighborly and the nuisance.

In short, although I agree with the Court that "neighborhood preservation" is a legitimate state interest, . . . [the] severe inequalities created by Proposition 13 cannot be justified by such an interest.

---

[8] The ambiguous character of this interest is illustrated by the options faced by a married couple that owns a three-or four-bedroom home that suited their family needs while their children lived at home. After the children have moved out, increased taxes and maintenance expenses would absent Proposition 13 tend to motivate the sale of the home to a younger family needing a home of that size, or perhaps the rental of a room or two to generate the income necessary to pay taxes. Proposition 13, however, subsidizes the wasteful retention of unused housing capacity, making the sale of the home unwise and the rental of the extra space unnecessary.

The second state interest identified by the Court is the "reliance interests" of the earlier purchasers. Here I find the Court's reasoning difficult to follow . . . . [Those] who purchased property before Proposition 13 was enacted received no assurances that assessments would only increase at a limited rate; indeed, to the contrary, many purchased property in the hope that property values (and assessments) would appreciate substantially and quickly. It cannot be said, therefore, that the earlier purchasers of property somehow have a reliance interest in limited tax increases.

Perhaps what the Court means is that post-Proposition 13 purchasers have less reliance interests than pre-Proposition 13 purchasers . . . . To say that the later purchasers know what they are getting into does not answer the critical question: Is it reasonable and constitutional to tax early purchasers less than late purchasers when at the time of taxation their properties are comparable? This question the Court does not answer . . . . [A] statute's disparate treatment must be justified by a purpose *distinct* from the very effects created by that statute.

In my opinion, it is irrational to treat similarly situated persons differently on the basis of the date they joined the class of property owners. Until today, I would have thought this proposition far from controversial. In *Zobel v. Williams,* 457 U.S. 55 (1982), we ruled that Alaska's program of distributing cash dividends on the basis of the recipient's years of residency in the State violated the Equal Protection Clause . . . .

Similarly, the Court invalidated on equal protection grounds New Mexico's policy of providing a permanent tax exemption for Vietnam veterans who had been state residents before May 8, 1976, but not to more recent arrivals. *Hooper v. Bernalillo County Assessor,* 472 U.S. 612 (1985). The Court expressly rejected the State's claim that it had a legitimate interest in providing special rewards to veterans who lived in the State before 1976 and concluded that

"Neither the Equal Protection Clause, nor this Court's precedents, permit the State to prefer established resident veterans over newcomers in the retroactive apportionment of an economic benefit."

As these decisions demonstrate, the selective provision of benefits based on the timing of one's membership in a class (whether that class be the class of residents or the class of property owners) is rarely a "legitimate state interest." Similarly situated neighbors have an equal right to share in the benefits of local government. It would obviously be unconstitutional to provide one with more or better fire or police protection than the other; it is just as plainly unconstitutional to require one to pay five times as much in property taxes as the other for the same government services. In my opinion, the severe inequalities created by Proposition 13 are arbitrary and unreasonable and do not rationally further a legitimate state interest.

Accordingly, I respectfully dissent.

## TWO QUESTIONS ABOUT *NORDLINGER*

Note Justice Stevens' references to the interesting cases of *Zobel v. Williams* and *Hooper v. Bernalillo.* Can *Nordlinger* be reconciled with those cases? Or does it overrule them? Was *Nordlinger* right, or were *Zobel* and *Bernalillo*?

It is possible to read *Hughes v. Fetter, supra* this Chapter, as suggesting that the forum may not discriminate against one of its own residents based on the fact that at a relevant time the resident was outside the state. Can you reconcile *Hughes* with *Nordlinger*?

In cases like *Zobel* and *Bernalillo,* would it solve the problem for the new state if it furnished the benefits that the newly-arrived resident would have received in the former state? The Supreme Court granted certiorari to decide that question, see *Anderson v. Roe,* 524 U.S. 982 (1998). The case was briefed and argued with important contributions by the Justice Department and other amici, but then apparently was settled before decision.

## NOTE ON STATE BENEFITS AND EX-RESIDENTS

What happens when a recipient of an entitlement under state law takes up residence in another state? May the state strike her name from its benefit rolls? What if the state's interest in affording the benefit arises from the state's relation with a third party, as, for example, when a state pensioner dies, and her spouse then gets monthly checks as survivors' benefits? What happens when the spouse moves to another state?

**FISHER v. REISER,** 610 F.2d 629 (9th Cir. 1979). Action by a class of ex-residents challenging the constitutionality of a statute requiring increased workers' compensation benefits to be paid to residents but not to nonresidents currently receiving compensation benefits under Nevada compensation law.

*Held*: The discrimination neither violates the Equal Protection Clause nor the plaintiffs' right to travel. Nevada had a legitimate interest in confining compensation carriers' increased payments to those beneficiaries likely to spend the money within the state.

*Dissent*: The statute's denial of increased coverage for ex-residents as well as other nonresidents is "a significant penalty" on the right to travel. *Edwards v. California,* 314 U.S. 160, 181 (1941) (statute making it a criminal offense to bring nonresident indigents into the state held an undue burden on interstate travel under Commerce Clause); *Crandall v. Nevada,* 73 U.S. (6 Wall.) 35 (1867) (tax on persons leaving state violates implied constitutional right to travel, essential to right to petition the federal government).

## § 5.11    DISCRIMINATION AGAINST NONRESIDENT DEFENDANTS

### BURLINGTON NORTHERN RAILROAD CO. v. FORD

*Supreme Court of the United States*
*504 U.S. 648, 112 S.Ct. 2184, 119 L.Ed.2d 432 (1992)*

JUSTICE SOUTER delivered the opinion of the Court . . . .

Respondents William D. Ford and Thomas L. Johnson were employed by petitioner Burlington Northern Railroad Company, a corporation owing its existence to the laws of Delaware and having a principal place of business in Fort Worth, Texas. Ford and Johnson raised a claim under the Federal Employers' Liability Act (FELA), and brought suit in the state trial court for Yellowstone County, Montana, alleging injuries sustained while working at Burlington's premises in Sheridan, Wyoming. In each case, Burlington moved to change venue to Hill County, Montana, where it claimed to have its principal place of business in that State. The trial court denied each motion, and Burlington brought interlocutory appeals.

The Supreme Court of Montana consolidated the two cases and affirmed the decisions of the trial court . . . .

. . . In combination, [Montana's] venue rules, with exceptions not here relevant, permit a plaintiff to sue a domestic company in just the one county where it has its principal place of business, while a plaintiff may sue a foreign corporation in any of the State's 56 counties. Burlington claims the distinction offends the Equal Protection Clause.

The Fourteenth Amendment forbids a State to "deny to any person within its jurisdiction the equal protection of the laws." Because the Montana venue rules neither deprive Burlington of a fundamental right nor classify along suspect lines like race or religion, they do not deny equal protection to Burlington unless they fail in rationally furthering legitimate state ends.

Venue rules generally reflect . . . expediency in resolving disparate interests of parties to a lawsuit . . . . The forum preferable to one party may be undesirable to another, and the adjustment of such warring interests is a valid state concern. In striking the balance between them, a State may have a number of choices, any of which would survive scrutiny, each of them passable under the standard tolerating some play in the joints of governmental machinery. Thus, we have no doubt that a State would act within its constitutional prerogatives if it were to give so much weight to the interests of plaintiffs as to allow them to sue in the counties of their choice under all circumstances. It is equally clear that a State might temper such an "any county" rule to the extent a reasonable assessment of defendants' interests so justified.

Here, Montana has decided that the any-county rule should give way to a single-county rule where a defendant resides in Montana, arguably on the reasonable ground that a defendant should not be subjected to a plaintiff's tactical advantage of forcing a trial far from the defendant's residence. At the same time, Montana has weighed the interest of a defendant who does not reside in Montana differently, arguably on the equally reasonable ground that for most nonresident defendants the inconvenience will be great whether they have to defend in, say, Billings or Havre. Montana could thus have decided that a nonresident defendant's interest in convenience is too slight to outweigh the plaintiff's interest in suing in the forum of his choice.

Burlington does not, indeed, seriously contend that such a decision is constitutionally flawed as applied to individual nonresident defendants. Nor does it argue that such a rule is unconstitutional even when applied to corporate defendants without a fixed place of business in Montana. Burlington does claim, however, that the rule is unconstitutional as applied to a corporate defendant like Burlington that not only has its home office in some other State or country, but also has a place of business in Montana that would qualify as its "principal place of business" if it were a Montana corporation.

Burlington's claim fails. Montana could reasonably have determined that a corporate defendant's home office is generally of greater significance to the corporation's convenience in litigation than its other offices, that foreign corporations are unlikely to have their principal offices in Montana, and that Montana's domestic corporations will probably keep headquarters within the State. We cannot say, at least not on this record, that any of these assumptions is irrational. And upon them Montana may have premised the policy judgment, which we find constitutionally unimpeachable, that only the convenience to a corporate defendant of litigating in the county containing its home office is sufficiently significant to outweigh a plaintiff's interest in suing in the county of his choice.

Of course Montana's venue rules would have implemented that policy judgment with greater precision if they had turned on the location of a corporate defendant's principal place of business, not on its State of incorporation. But this is hardly enough to make the rules fail rational-basis review, for "rational distinctions may be made with substantially less than mathematical exactitude." *New Orleans v. Dukes,* 427 U.S. 297, 303 (1976). Montana may reasonably have thought that the location of a corporate defendant's principal place of business would not be as readily verifiable as its State of incorporation, that a rule hinging on the former would invite wasteful sideshows of venue litigation, and that obviating the sideshows would be worth the loss in precision. These possibilities, of course, put Burlington a far cry away from the point of discharging its burden of showing that the underinclusiveness and overinclusiveness of Montana's venue rules is so great that the rules can no longer be said rationally to implement Montana's policy judgment. Besides, Burlington, having headquarters elsewhere, would not benefit even from a scheme based on domicile, and is therefore in no position to complain of Montana's using State of incorporation as a surrogate for domicile.

Burlington is left with the argument that *Power Manufacturing Co. v. Saunders,* 274 U.S. 490, 498 (1927), controls this case. But it does not. In *Saunders,* we considered Arkansas' venue rules, which restricted suit against a domestic corporation to those counties where it maintained a place of business, but exposed foreign corporations to suit in any county. We held that the distinction lacked a rational basis and therefore deprived foreign corporate defendants of the equal protection of the laws. The statutory provision challenged in *Saunders,* however, applied only to foreign corporations authorized to do business in Arkansas, so that most of the corporations subject to its any-county rule probably had a place of business in Arkansas. In contrast, most of the corporations subject to Montana's any-county rule probably do not have their principal place of business in Montana. Thus, Arkansas' special rule for foreign corporations was tailored with significantly less precision than Montana's, and, on the assumption that *Saunders* is still good law, its holding does not invalidate Montana's venue rules.

In sum, Montana's venue rules can be understood as rationally furthering a legitimate state interest. The judgment of the Supreme Court of Montana is accordingly. . *Affirmed.*

———

**G.D. SEARLE & CO. v. COHN,** 455 U.S. 404 (1982). This was a challenge under the Equal Protection Clause to the discriminatory tolling provisions of the state's statute of limitations, whereby the statute could be tolled by resident corporations not doing business in the state, but not by nonresident corporations not doing business in the state.

*Held:* Discriminatory tolling against nonresident corporations does not violate the Equal Protection Clause. In the absence of a classification that is inherently invidious or that impinges upon fundamental rights, a state statute is to be upheld against equal protection attack if it is rationally related to the achievement of legitimate governmental ends. Under the state's law, a defendant's absence from the jurisdiction creates a problem for the plaintiff that is not alleviated by the defendant's amenability to suit under the state's long-arm statute. A local plaintiff must find the unrepresented foreign corporation before it can be served. Thus, the state has a rational basis for the discrimination, since it is harder to sue nonresident corporations than resident corporations. The case is remanded for consideration of the question whether the differential tolling for nonresidents places an undue burden on interstate commerce.

———

## NOTES ON *BURLINGTON* AND *SEARLE*

(1) *The vulnerability of the nonresident defendant.* In these cases the nonresident defendant is put in a more vulnerable position than the resident. Since rational bases can be found for the distinction, nothing in the Equal Protection Clause saves the nonresidents from the discrimination.

(2) *How about the Commerce Clause?* The Equal Protection Clause was unhelpful to the plaintiffs in *Burlington* and *Searle.* Would these cases come

out the same way under the Commerce Clause? On remand in *Searle*, the federal trial court held that the New Jersey differential tolling statute did violate the Commerce Clause, and the Court of Appeals affirmed, limiting the effect of its decision to future cases only. 784 F.2d 460 (3d Cir. 1986). The Supreme Court denied certiorari.

## BENDIX AUTOLITE CORP. v. MIDWESCO ENTERPRISES, INC.

*United States Supreme Court*
*486 U.S. 888, 108 S.Ct. 2218, 100 L.Ed.2d 896 (1988)*

JUSTICE KENNEDY delivered the opinion of the Court.

In 1974, Midwesco Enterprises, Inc., agreed with Bendix Autolite Corporation to deliver and install a boiler system at a Bendix facility in Fostoria, Ohio. Dissatisfied with the work, Bendix claimed that the boiler system had been installed improperly and that it was insufficient to produce the quantity of steam specified in the contract. This diversity action was filed against Midwesco in the United States District Court for the Northern District of Ohio in 1980. Bendix is a Delaware corporation with its principal place of business in Ohio; Midwesco is an Illinois corporation with its principal place of business in Illinois.

When Midwesco asserted the Ohio [four-year] statute of limitations as a defense, Bendix responded that the statutory period had not elapsed because under Ohio law running of the time is suspended, or tolled, for claims against entities that are not within the State and have not designated an agent for service of process. Midwesco replied that this tolling provision violated both the Commerce Clause and the Due Process Clause of the Fourteenth Amendment.

The District Court dismissed the action . . . . The Court of Appeals for the Sixth Circuit affirmed . . . .

Where the burden of a state regulation falls on interstate commerce, restricting its flow in a manner not applicable to local business and trade, there may be either a discrimination that renders the regulation invalid without more, or cause to weigh and assess the State's putative interests against the interstate restraints to determine if the burden imposed is an unreasonable one. *See Brown-Forman Distillers Corp. v. New York State Liquor Authority,* 476 U.S. 573, 578-579 (1986). The Ohio statute before us might have been held to be a discrimination that invalidates without extended inquiry. We choose, however, to assess the interests of the State to demonstrate [the reasons for our conclusion].

The burden the tolling statute places on interstate commerce is significant. Midwesco has no corporate office in Ohio, is not registered to do business there, and has not appointed an agent for service of process in the State. To gain the protection of the limitations period, Midwesco would have had to appoint a resident agent for service of process in Ohio and subject itself to the general jurisdiction of the Ohio courts. This jurisdiction would extend to any suit against Midwesco, whether or not the transaction in question had any connection with Ohio . . . .

The Ohio statutory scheme thus forces a foreign corporation to choose between exposure to the general jurisdiction of Ohio courts or forfeiture of the limitations defense, remaining subject to suit in Ohio in perpetuity . . . .

Although statute of limitations defenses are not a fundamental right, *Chase Securities Corp. v. Donaldson,* 325 U.S. 304, 314 (1945), it is obvious that they are an integral part of the legal system and are relied upon . . . . Where a State denies ordinary legal defenses or like privileges to out-of-state persons or corporations engaged in commerce, the State law will be reviewed under the Commerce Clause to determine whether the denial is discriminatory on its face or an impermissible burden on commerce. The State may not condition the exercise of the defense on the waiver or relinquishment of rights that the foreign corporation would otherwise retain. *Cf. Dahnke-Walker Milling Co. v. Bondurant,* 257 U.S. 282 (1921); *Allenberg Cotton Co. v. Pittman,* 419 U.S. 20 (1974).

. . . It is true that serving foreign corporate defendants may be more arduous than serving domestic corporations or foreign corporations with a designated agent for service, and we have held for Equal Protection purposes that a State rationally may make adjustments for this difference by curtailing limitations protection for absent foreign corporations. *G.D. Searle & Co. v. Cohn,* 455 U.S. 404 (1982). Nevertheless, State interests that are legitimate for equal protection or due process purposes may be insufficient to withstand Commerce Clause scrutiny.[3]

In the particular case before us, the Ohio tolling statute must fall under the Commerce Clause. Ohio cannot justify its statute as a means of protecting its residents from corporations who become liable for acts done within the State but later withdraw from the jurisdiction, for it is conceded by all parties that the Ohio long arm statute would have permitted service on Midwesco throughout the period of limitations. The Ohio statute of limitations is tolled only for those foreign corporations that do not subject themselves to the general jurisdiction of Ohio courts. In this manner the Ohio statute imposes a greater burden on out-of-state companies than it does on Ohio companies . . . . *Affirmed.*

JUSTICE SCALIA, concurring in the judgment.

I cannot confidently assess whether the Court's evaluation and balancing of interests in this case is right or wrong. Although the Court labels the effect of exposure to the general jurisdiction of Ohio's courts "a significant burden" on commerce, I am not sure why that is. In precise terms, it is the burden of defending in Ohio (rather than some other forum) any lawsuit having all

---

[3] In *Searle,* we . . . remanded the case "for further consideration of the Commerce Clause issue." Before the District Court ruled, However, the New Jersey Supreme Court declared its tolling statute unconstitutional under a Commerce Clause analysis as a forced licensure provision, a decision we declined to review. *Coons v. American Honda Motor Co.,* 94 N.J. 307, 463 A.2d 921 (1983), *cert. denied,* 469 U.S. 1123 (1985).

of the following features: (1) the plaintiff desires to bring it in Ohio, (2) it has so little connection to Ohio that service could not otherwise be made under Ohio's long-arm statute, and (3) it has a great enough connection to Ohio [that] it is not subject to dismissal on *forum non conveniens* grounds. The record before us supplies no indication as to how many suits fit this description (even the present suit is not an example since appellee was subject to long-arm service, and frankly I have no idea how one would go about estimating the number. It may well be "significant," but for all we know it is "negligible."

A person or firm that [declines] to appoint a general agent for service, will remain theoretically subject to suit in Ohio (as the Court says) "in perpetuity" — at least as far as the statute of limitations is concerned. But again, I do not know how we assess how significant a burden this is, unless anything that is theoretically perpetual must be significant. It seems very unlikely that anyone would intentionally wait to sue later rather than sooner — not only because the prospective defendant may die or dissolve, but also because prejudgment interest is normally not awarded, and the staleness of evidence generally harms the party with the burden of proof. The likelihood of an unintentionally delayed suit brought under this provision that could not be brought without it seems not enormously large. Moreover, whatever the likelihood is, it does not seem terribly plausible that any real-world deterrent effect on interstate transactions will be produced by the incremental cost of having to defend a *delayed* suit rather than a *timely* suit. But the point is, it seems to me we can do no more than speculate.

On the other side of the scale, the Court considers the benefit of the Ohio scheme to local interests. These are, presumably, to enable the preservation of claims against defendants who have placed themselves beyond the personal jurisdiction of Ohio Courts, and (by encouraging appointment of an agent) to facilitate service upon out-of-state defendants who might otherwise be difficult to locate. We have no way of knowing how often these ends are in fact achieved, and the Court thus says little about them . . . .

Having evaluated the interests on both sides as roughly as this, the Court then proceeds to judge which is more important. This process is ordinarily called "balancing," *Pike v. Bruce Church, Inc.,* 397 U.S. 137 (1970), but the scale analogy is not really appropriate, since the interests on both sides are incommensurate. It is more like judging whether a particular line is longer than a particular rock is heavy. All I am really persuaded of by the Court's opinion is that the burdens the Court labels "significant" are more determinative of its decision than the benefits it labels "important . . . ." I suggest an opinion could as persuasively have been written coming out the opposite way . . . .

I would therefore abandon the "balancing" approach to these negative commerce clause cases . . . .

In my view, a state statute is invalid under the Commerce Clause if, and only if, it accords discriminatory treatment to interstate commerce in a respect not required to achieve a lawful state purpose . . . . The Ohio tolling statute is on its face discriminatory because it applies only to out-of-state corporations. That facial discrimination cannot be justified . . . . A tolling statute that operated only against persons beyond the reach of Ohio's long-arm statute, or against all persons that could not be found for mail service, would be narrowly tailored to advance the legitimate purpose of preserving claims; but the present statute extends the time for suit even against corporations which (like appellee) are fully suable within Ohio, and readily reachable through the mails.

Because the present statute discriminates against interstate commerce by applying a disadvantageous rule against nonresidents for no valid state purpose that requires such a rule, I concur in the judgment that the Ohio statute violates the Commerce Clause.

Chief Justice Rehnquist, dissenting.

This case arises because of two peculiar, if not unique, rules of Ohio law. The first is that even though a foreign corporation may be subject to process under the state "long arm" statute, it is nonetheless not "present" in the State for purposes of tolling the statute of limitations. The second is that a foreign corporation installing machinery or equipment sold by it in interstate commerce is not required to appoint a statutory agent in order to transact business in Ohio. The Court dwells heavily upon the first peculiarity of Ohio law, but makes no mention of the second.

Midwesco agreed to deliver and install a boiler system at a Bendix plant in Fostoria, Ohio. On the basis of the sparse record before us, it is fair to say that while the sale may have been a transaction in interstate commerce, there is no reason at all to think that the installation was such. Cases such as *Allenberg Cotton Co. v. Pittman* and *Dahnke-Walker Milling Co. v. Bondurant*, on which the Court relies, deal with transactions respecting goods which are "in the stream of interstate commerce." A State may not require licensure of a foreign corporation which seeks only to engage in this sort of transaction. But a State may require licensure when a foreign corporation engages in intrastate commerce. *Eli Lilly & Co. v. Sav-On-Drugs, Inc.*, 366 U.S. 276 (1971). And where a foreign corporation is engaged in both interstate and intrastate commerce in a particular commodity, a State may require licensure in order to sue in connection with an intrastate aspect of the business. *Union Brokerage Co. v. Jensen*, 322 U.S. 202 (1944).

Thus, Midwesco's immunity from Ohio's requirement that foreign corporations appoint a statutory agent before doing business in the State is not by reason of any federal constitutional right, but by reason of a provision of the Ohio statutes. And if Ohio could have insisted that Midwesco appoint a statutory agent before it engaged in that portion of its transaction with Bendix which was intrastate commerce, I see no reason why it may not also treat Midwesco as it would treat any other entity which has done intrastate business in Ohio, incurred liability, and thereafter withdrawn from the State. Ohio seeks to do no more, I think, when it applies its tolling statute to Bendix's action against Midwesco under these circumstances. I see no discrimination against interstate commerce here, and I would reverse the judgment of the Court of Appeals.

## NOTES ON *BENDIX AUTOLITE*

(1) *The level-of-scrutiny debate.* Justice Scalia argues persuasively that restrictive scrutiny of the law of an interested state, on an ordinary legal question, is too hard to do and isn't worth the effort. He joins the majority only because the Ohio law at issue flunked the rational basis test, in his opinion. Chief Justice Rehnquist also sees no reason for restrictive scrutiny. If the state can regulate within its territory, and its legitimate interests produce out-of-state impacts, those are indirect, incidental, and not worth Supreme Court intervention. These let-the-extraterritorial-chips-fall-where-they-may arguments fail, however, to sway the majority. What, if anything, do you think the majority feels is at stake? If Justices Scalia and Rehnquist prevailed in their views, how would the Commerce Clause differ from the Equal Protection Clause?

(2) *The undue burden.* What was the undue burden on interstate commerce in *Bendix Autolite*? Justice Kennedy seems to be saying that the statute subjected the nonresident defendant to an unconstitutional condition, in that it required the corporation to agree to defend actions in a state lacking minimum contacts. But if the defendant had transacted business in the state and the action arose out of that very transaction, as in *Bendix Autolite,* wouldn't there *be* minimum contacts? Or perhaps the undue burden is the chilling effect on interstate commerce of coerced submission to suits in cases unrelated to the forum. But, having entered the state for business purposes, even unrelated business purposes, and having become foreseeably subject to suit there in cases related to that business, why would it be hard for a corporation to defend an unrelated case? Of course it is often a question of fact whether a corporation is doing sufficient business in the forum to come within the forum's general jurisdiction. On the other hand, isn't a decision to waive due process rights in order to earn profits a voluntary waiver?

# Chapter 6

# THE FEDERAL/STATE CONFLICT OF LAWS

## PART A  FEDERAL COMMON LAW

### § 6.01  The Federal/State Conflict of Laws

*The "vertical" conflict of laws.* Up to now we have been examining interstate or international conflicts. But in this country in addition to the laws of the several states there is also federal law. When federal and state law are in conflict, you might think of those conflicts as "vertical" conflicts, in relation to interstate conflicts, which, as compared with "vertical" conflicts, you might think of as "horizontal."

Of course, when federal and state laws collide the Supremacy Clause of Article VI resolves the conflict: federal law is the supreme law of the land, anything in state law to the contrary notwithstanding. And Article VI requires the state judges to apply federal law as the supreme law of the land.

But things are rarely as simple as that. First of all, what are the federal laws that are supreme? Is it only the Constitution, acts of Congress, and treaties made? Or does supreme federal law include ordinary case law? What is the status of federal common law after *Erie v. Tompkins,* a case that is commonly said to have struck down federal common law as unconstitutional?

That common misconception to one side, there is a further difficulty. The very existence of a conflict will be questioned. Consider that, if a party relying on state law can persuade the court that there is no conflict, the Supremacy Clause will have no operation.

*Preemption.* Sometimes, however, even when state and federal laws are saying the same thing, courts may still strike down state law, notwithstanding the absence of any conflict. In such cases, they hold that state law is wholly "preempted" by federal law: the states are not even permitted to address the issue. Federal preemption was recognized by courts as implicit in the fields of foreign relations and admiralty, and is often "implied" under acts of Congress in such fields as that of labor relations. In addition, Congress often expressly preempts a whole field, as it does for example in the statutes governing copyright, and employee benefit plans.

But here, too, nothing is simple. Parties relying on state law will try to argue that their cases are not within the preempted field.

Finally, even when federal law is held to "govern," there is quite often no federal law in point. Federal case law is less well developed than state case law, and federal common-law rules often must be fashioned on the spot. Courts fashioning federal common law often will refer to state law to furnish the content of a federal rule of decision. This is commonly thought of as "borrowed" or "incorporated" state law.

Because a choice of federal law to govern so often entails a choice of federal common law, we begin by examining that phenomenon.

---

## § 6.02   Introduction: Federal Common Law

### ERIE RAILROAD CO. v. TOMPKINS

*Supreme Court of the United States*
*304 U.S. 64, 58 S. Ct. 817, 87 L. Ed. 1188 (1938)*

Mr. Justice Brandeis delivered the opinion of the Court.

The question for decision is whether the oft-challenged doctrine of *Swift v. Tyson,*[1] shall now be disapproved.

Tompkins, a citizen of Pennsylvania, was injured on a dark night by a passing freight train of the Erie Railroad Company while walking along its right of way at Hughestown in that state. He claimed that the accident occurred through negligence in the operation, or maintenance, of the train; that he was rightfully on the premises as licensee because on a commonly used beaten footpath which ran for a short distance alongside the tracks; and that he was struck by something which looked like a door projecting from one of the moving cars.

To enforce that claim he brought an action in the federal court for Southern New York, which had jurisdiction because the company is a corporation of that state. It denied liability; and the case was tried by a jury. The Erie insisted that its duty to Tompkins was no greater than that owed to a trespasser. It contended, among other things, that its duty to Tompkins, and hence its liability, should be determined in accordance with the Pennsylvania law; that under the law of Pennsylvania, as declared by its highest court, persons who use pathways along the railroad right of way—that is, a longitudinal pathway as distinguished from a crossing—are to be deemed trespassers; and that the railroad is not liable for injuries to undiscovered trespassers resulting from its negligence, unless it be wanton or willful. Tompkins denied that any such rule had been established by the decisions of the Pennsylvania courts; and contended that, since there was no statute of the state on the subject, the railroad's duty and liability is to be determined in federal courts as a matter of general law.

The trial judge refused to rule that the applicable law precluded recovery. The jury brought in a verdict of $30,000; and the judgment entered thereon was affirmed by the [Second] Circuit Court of Appeals, which held that it was unnecessary to consider whether the law of Pennsylvania was as contended, because the question was one not of local, but of general, law. . . . "It is . . . generally recognized law that a jury may find that negligence exists toward a pedestrian using a permissive path on the railroad right of way if he is hit by some object projecting from the side of the train."

---

[1] 41 U.S. (16 Pet.) 1 (1842).

The Erie had contended that application of the Pennsylvania rule was required, among other things, by Section 34 of the Federal Judiciary Act of 1789 [the Rules of Decision Act, today at 28 U.S.C. § 1652], which provides: "The laws of the several States, except where the Constitution, treaties, or statutes of the United States otherwise require or provide, shall be regarded as rules of decision in trials at common law, in the courts of the United States, in cases where they apply."

Because of the importance of the question whether the federal court was free to disregard the alleged rule of the Pennsylvania common law, we granted certiorari.

First. *Swift v. Tyson* held that federal courts exercising jurisdiction on the ground of diversity of citizenship need not, in matters of general jurisprudence, apply the unwritten law of the state as declared by its highest court; that they are free to exercise an independent judgment as to what the common law of the state is—or should be; and that, as there stated by Mr. Justice Story:

"The true interpretation of the 34th section limited its application to state laws, strictly local, that is to say, to the positive statutes of the state, and the construction thereof adopted by the local tribunals, and to rights and titles to things having a permanent locality, such as the rights and titles to real estate, and other matters immovable and intra-territorial in their nature and character. It never has been supposed by us, that the section did apply, or was designed to apply, to questions of a more general nature, not at all dependent upon local statutes or local usages of a fixed and permanent operation, as, for example, to the construction of ordinary contracts or other written instruments, and especially to questions of general commercial law, where the state tribunals are called upon to perform the like functions as ourselves, that is, to ascertain, upon general reasoning and legal analogies, what is the true exposition of the contract or instrument, or what is the just rule furnished by the principles of commercial law to govern the case."

The Court in applying the [Rules of Decision Act] to equity cases . . ., said: "The statute, however, is merely declarative of the rule which would exist in the absence of the statute." [Citation omitted.] The federal courts assumed, in the broad field of "general law," the power to declare rules of decision which Congress was confessedly without power to enact as statutes. Doubt was repeatedly expressed as to the correctness of the construction given [the Rules of Decision Act], and as to the soundness of the rule which it introduced. But it was the more recent research of a competent scholar, who examined the original document, which established that the construction given to it by the Court was erroneous; and that the purpose of the section was merely to make certain that, in all matters except those in which some federal law is controlling, the federal courts exercising jurisdiction in diversity of citizenship cases would apply as their rules of decision the law of the state, unwritten as well as written.[5]

Criticism of the doctrine became widespread after the decision of *Black & White Taxicab Co. v. Brown & Yellow Taxicab Co.,* 276 U.S. 518 (1928). There,

---

[5] Charles Warren, *New Light on the History of the Federal Judiciary Act of 1789,* 37 HARV. L. REV. 49 (1923).

Brown & Yellow . . . and the Louisville & Nashville Railroad [both Kentucky corporations] wished that [Brown & Yellow] should have the exclusive privileges of soliciting passenger and baggage transportation at the Bowling Green, Kentucky, railroad station; and that the Black & White, a competing Kentucky corporation, should be prevented from interfering with that privilege. Knowing that such a contract would be void under the common law of Kentucky, it was arranged that the Brown & Yellow reincorporate under the law of Tennessee, and that the contract with the railroad should be executed there. The suit was then brought by the Tennessee corporation in the federal court for Western Kentucky to enjoin competition by the Black & White; an injunction issued by the District Court was sustained by the Court of Appeals; and this Court, citing many decisions in which the doctrine of *Swift & Tyson* had been applied, affirmed the decree.

*Second.* Experience in applying the doctrine of *Swift v. Tyson* had revealed its defects, political and social; and the benefits expected to flow from the rule did not accrue. Persistence of state courts in their own opinions on questions of common law prevented uniformity; and the impossibility of discovering a satisfactory line of demarcation between the province of general law and that of local law developed a new well of uncertainties.

On the other hand, the mischievous results of the doctrine had become apparent. Diversity of citizenship jurisdiction was conferred in order to prevent apprehended discrimination in state courts against those not citizens of the state. *Swift v. Tyson* introduced grave discrimination by noncitizens against citizens. It made rights enjoyed under the unwritten "general law" vary according to whether enforcement was sought in the state or in the federal court; and the privilege of selecting the court in which the right should be determined was conferred upon the noncitizen. Thus, the doctrine rendered impossible equal protection of the law. In attempting to promote uniformity of law throughout the United States, the doctrine had prevented uniformity in the administration of the law of the state.

The discrimination . . . became . . . far-reaching. This resulted in part from the broad province accorded to the so-called "general law" as to which federal courts exercised an independent judgment. In addition to questions of purely commercial law, "general law" was held to include the obligations under contracts entered into and to be performed within the state, the extent to which a carrier operating within a state may stipulate for exemption from liability for his own negligence or that of his employee; the liability for torts committed within the state upon persons resident or property located there, even where the question of liability depended upon the scope of a property right conferred by the state; and the right to exemplary or punitive damages. Furthermore, state decisions construing local deeds, mineral conveyances, and even devises of real estate were disregarded.

In part the discrimination resulted from the wide range of persons held entitled to avail themselves of the federal rule by resort to the diversity of citizenship jurisdiction. Through this jurisdiction individual citizens willing to remove from their own state and become citizens of another might avail themselves of the federal rule. And, without even change of residence, a corporate citizen of the state could avail itself of the federal rule by reincorporating under the laws of another state, as was done in the *Taxicab* case.

The injustice and confusion incident to the doctrine of *Swift v. Tyson* have been repeatedly urged as reasons for abolishing or limiting diversity of citizenship jurisdiction. Other legislative relief has been proposed. If only a question of statutory construction were involved, we should not be prepared to abandon a doctrine so widely applied throughout nearly a century. But the unconstitutionality of the course pursued has now been made clear, and compels us to do so.

*Third.* Except in matters governed by the Federal Constitution or by acts of Congress, the law to be applied in any case is the law of the state. And whether the law of the state shall be declared by its Legislature in a statute or by its highest court in a decision is not a matter of federal concern. There is no federal general common law. Congress has no power to declare substantive rules of common law applicable in a state whether they be local in their nature or "general," be they commercial law or a part of the law of torts. And no clause in the Constitution purports to confer such a power upon the federal courts. . . .

The fallacy underlying the rule declared in *Swift v. Tyson* is made clear by Mr. Justice Holmes.[3] The doctrine rests upon the assumption that there is "a transcendental body of law outside of any particular State but obligatory within it unless and until changed by statute;" that federal courts have the power to use their judgment as to what the rules of common law are; and that in the federal courts "the parties are entitled to an independent judgment on matters of general law:"

> "But law in the sense in which courts speak of it today does not exist without some definite authority behind it. The common law . . . enforced in a State . . . is not the common law generally but the law of that State existing by the authority of that State without regard to what it may have been in England or anywhere else.

> "The authority and only authority is the State, and if that be so, the voice adopted by the State as its own (whether it be of its Legislature or of its Supreme Court) should utter the last word."

Thus the doctrine of *Swift v. Tyson* is, as Mr. Justice Holmes said, "an unconstitutional assumption of powers by the Courts of the United States which no lapse of time or respectable array of opinion should make us hesitate to correct."

In disapproving that doctrine we do not hold unconstitutional section 34 of the Federal Judiciary Act of 1789 or any other act of Congress. We merely declare that in applying the doctrine this Court and the lower courts have invaded rights which in our opinion are reserved by the Constitution to the several states.

*Fourth.* The defendant contended that by the common law of Pennsylvania as declared by its highest court, the only duty owed to the plaintiff was to refrain from willful or wanton injury. The plaintiff denied that such is the Pennsylvania law. . . . The Circuit Court of Appeals ruled that the question

---

[3] *Kuhn v. Fairmont Coal Co.,* 215 U.S. 349, 370-372 (1910); *Black & White Taxicab Co. v. Brown & Yellow Taxicab Co.,* 276 U.S. 518, 532-536 (1928).

of liability is one of general law; and on that ground declined to decide the issue of state law. As we hold this was error, the judgment is reversed and the case remanded to it for further proceedings in conformity with our opinion.

## NOTES ON *ERIE*

(1) *The merits of Swift.* The Court seems to treat *Swift* as a noble experiment that failed; Justice Brandeis talks about the "benefits" expected to "flow" from that decision. What benefits? Consider, for one thing, that Justice Story had been quite right to believe that this nation needed uniform commercial law. The existence of the universally enacted Uniform Commercial Code bears him out. Consider, too, as a reading of *Swift* will demonstrate, that Story had been "right" also about the commercial-law issue in *Swift* : it *is* unfair and inconvenient to holders of negotiable paper to come up against surprising, unusual local defenses to their paper. Negotiable instruments should be able to roll across state lines without such surprises. Story's is the substantive position adopted in the Uniform Commercial Code today.

(2) *The trouble with Swift.* Under *Swift,* as Justice Brandeis complains, the states "persisted" in applying their own debtor-oriented defenses to negotiable instruments. Worse, this produced two sets of case-law rules governing the same conduct. How could such dysfunction flow from Supreme Court rulings? Consider that the Court's "general" common-law rulings under *Swift* were not *binding* on state judges under the Supremacy Clause, as true federal common-law rulings would have been. Could the Court have authorized a *genuine* federal common law of negotiable instruments in interstate cases? Is there national lawmaking power over interstate commerce?

In *Clearfield Trust Co. v. United States,* 318 U.S. 363 (1943), the Court, by Justice Douglas, held that at least the financial instruments issued by the United States itself gave rise to a genuine federal common law, binding upon the states under the Supremacy Clause. Today government contracts of all kinds are governed by federal common law. *Priebe & Sons v. United States, 332 U.S. 407 (1947).*

In his power-grab in *Swift,* Justice Story seems to have "grabbed" not too much power, but *too little.*

(3) **SOUTHERN PACIFIC CO. v. JENSEN,** 244 U.S. 205 (1917). Action challenging an award under a new New York workers' compensation statute of some $9.00 per week to Jensen's widow and children. Jensen, a longshoreman, had in effect decapitated himself by backing his forklift truck into a low hatchway on a vessel, where he was handling cargo. His employer argued that New York law could not govern a maritime case. The New York Court of Appeals approved the award to the widow, and the Supreme Court granted a writ of error.

*Held* (by JUSTICE McREYNOLDS): Reversed. "Article 3, § 2, of the Constitution, extends the judicial power of the United States 'to all cases of admiralty and maritime jurisdiction;' and article 1, § 8, confers upon the Congress power 'to make all laws which shall be necessary and proper for carrying into execution the foregoing powers and all other powers vested by this Constitution in the government of the United States or in any department or officer thereof.' Considering our former opinions, it must now be accepted as settled doctrine that, in consequence of these provisions, Congress has paramount power to fix and determine the maritime law which shall prevail throughout the country. And further, that, in the absence of some controlling statute, the general maritime law, as accepted by the Federal courts, constitutes part of our national law, applicable to matters within the admiralty and maritime jurisdiction.

". . . It certainly could not have been the intention to place the rules and limits of maritime law under the disposal and regulation of the several states, as that would have defeated the uniformity and consistency at which the Constitution aimed on all subjects of a commercial character affecting the intercourse of the states with each other or with foreign states.

"By § 9, Judiciary Act of 1789, the district courts of the United States were given 'exclusive original cognizance of all civil causes of admiralty and maritime jurisdiction, . . . saving to suitors, in all cases, the right of a common-law remedy, where the common law is competent to give it.' And this grant has been continued.*

"In view of these constitutional provisions and the Federal act it would be difficult, if not impossible, to define with exactness just how far the general maritime law may be changed, modified, or affected by state legislation. That this may be done to some extent cannot be denied. . . . [Pilotage] fees [may be] fixed under state law (*Cooley v. Port Wardens,* 53 U.S. (12 How.) 299 (1851)); and the right given to recover in death cases. *The Hamilton,* 207 U.S. 398 (1907). . . . [Plainly], we think, no such legislation is valid if it contravenes the essential purpose expressed by an act of Congress, or works material prejudice to the characteristic features of the general maritime law, or interferes with the proper harmony and uniformity of that law in its international and interstate relations. This limitation, at the least, is essential to the effective operation of the fundamental purposes for which such law was incorporated into our national laws by the Constitution itself. . . .

"If New York can subject foreign ships coming into her ports to such obligations as those imposed by her Compensation Statute, other states may do likewise. The necessary consequence would be destruction of the very uniformity in respect to maritime matters which the Constitution was designed to establish; and freedom of navigation between the states and with foreign countries would be seriously hampered and impeded. . . . The legislature exceeded its authority in attempting to extend the statute under consideration to conditions like those here disclosed. So applied, it conflicts with the Constitution and to that extent is invalid. . . . "

JUSTICE HOLMES (dissenting): . . . "No doubt there sometimes has been an air of benevolent gratuity in the admiralty's attitude about enforcing state laws. But of course there is no gratuity about it. . . . Taking it as established that a state has constitutional power to pass laws giving rights and imposing liabilities for acts done . . . when there were no such rights or liabilities before, what is there to hinder its doing so in the case of a maritime tort? Not the existence of an inconsistent law emanating from a superior source,

---

* Today, with somewhat altered language, at 28 U.S.C. § 1333. —*Ed.*

that is, from the United States. There is no such law. The maritime law is not a corpus juris—it is a very limited body of customs and ordinances of the sea. . . .

"Now, however, common-law principles have been applied to sustain a libel by a stevedore in personam against the master for personal injuries suffered while loading a ship. *Atlantic Transport Co. v. Imbrovek*, 234 U. S. 52 (1914), and . . . seamen may have similar relief. From what source do these new rights come? . . . I recognize without hesitation that judges do and must legislate, but they can do so only interstitially; they are confined from molar to molecular motions. . . .

"The common law is not a brooding omnipresence in the sky, but the articulate voice of some sovereign or quasi sovereign that can be identified; although some decisions with which I have disagreed seem to me to have forgotten the fact. . . . "

[JUSTICE HOLMES went on to state, "It always is the law of some state. . . ."]

[JUSTICE PITNEY also dissented, "in view of the momentous consequences of the decision," concurring in the dissenting opinion of Justice Holmes.]

JUSTICE REED (concurring in part): "I concur in the conclusion reached in this case, in the disapproval of the doctrine of *Swift v. Tyson*, and in the reasoning of the majority opinion, except in so far as it relies upon the unconstitutionality of the "course pursued" by the federal courts. . . .

"As the majority opinion shows, by its reference to Mr. Warren's researches and the first quotation from Mr. Justice Holmes, that this Court is now of the view that 'laws' includes 'decisions,' it is unnecessary to go further and declare that the "course pursued" was 'unconstitutional,' instead of merely erroneous. . . .

"The 'unconstitutional' course referred to in the majority opinion is apparently in the ruling in *Swift v. Tyson* that the supposed omission of Congress to legislate as to the effect of decisions leaves federal courts free to interpret general law for themselves. I am not all sure whether, in the absence of federal statutory direction, federal courts would be compelled to follow state decisions. There was sufficient doubt about the matter in 1789 to induce the first Congres to [enact the Rules of Decision Act]. No former opinions of this Court have passed upon it. Mr. Justice Holmes evidently saw nothing "unconstitutional" which required the overruling of *Swift v. Tyson*, for he said in the very opinion quoted by the majority, 'I should leave *Swift v. Tyson* undisturbed, as I indicated in *Kuhn v. Fairmont Coal Co.*, but I would not allow it to spread the assumed dominion into new fields.' If the opinion commits this Court to the position that the Congress is without power to declare what rules of substantive law shall govern the federal courts, that conclusion also seems questionable. The line between procedural and substantive law is hazy, but no one doubts federal courts, that conclusion also seems questionable. The line between procedural and substantive law is hazy, but no one doubts federal power over procedure. . . ."

---

A lot happens in *Jensen*. Building on the Constitution's grant of admiralty jurisdiction to federal courts, the Supreme Court

(a) implies maritime power in Congress, though no such power is given. And, from Congress's explicit grant of jurisdiction to federal courts, and the newly implied lawmaking power of Congress, the Court

(b) concludes that courts have lawmaking power in admiralty cases. Then the *Jensen* Court moves beyond even the foregoing rather amazing propositions, and

(c) identifies the general maritime law as federal. Admiralty case law, thus, is clearly seen as genuine federal common law. Further, the *Jensen* court clearly

(d) holds that federal common law is genuine federal law, entitled to the force of the Supremacy Clause of Article VI (unlike the general federal common law struck down in *Erie*). Federal case law in maritime cases is *binding* upon the state courts, and is supreme even over a state statute. Not only that, but the court

(e) holds that federal power in maritime cases *preempts* state power. The states may not even speak to maritime issues, because this would interfere with the "uniformity" and "harmony" of federal maritime law—even when, as in *Jensen*, there *is* no federal maritime law on point. *Jensen* is good law today, on all five points. Are you clear how it survives *Erie*?

(4) **HINDERLIDER v. LA PLATA & CHERRY CREEK DITCH CO.**, 304 U.S. 92 (1938). Action in state court, between owners of contiguous land in two states, for determination of their respective water rights. In the Supreme Court, a final question was what law governs interstate water and boundary disputes.

*Held* (by JUSTICE BRANDEIS): Federal common law governs interstate water and boundary disputes. "For whether the water of an interstate stream must be apportioned between the two States is a question of 'federal common law' upon which neither the statutes nor the decisions of either State can be conclusive."

---

*Hinderlider* was handed down by Justice Brandeis immediately following his decision in *Erie*.

(5) *Was Erie constitutionally required?* Justice Reed, concurring in part in *Erie,* thought that nothing in the Constitution required the result. Some authorities still regard *Erie* as a case of statutory reinterpretation of the Rules of Decision Act, and nothing more. Do you agree?

Note how quickly in his opinion Justice Brandeis moves to remove the Rules of Decision Act as a ground of decision. Note, too, how he insists that were the case only a matter of statutory interpretation, the Court would not overrule *Swift.* In any event, how much modern meaning can the Rules of Decision Act have, addressed as it is only to federal trial courts?

(6) *The constitutional basis of Erie.* Assuming *Erie* to have been constitutionally required, as Justice Brandeis said, what, precisely, was unconstitutional about "the course of conduct pursued" under *Swift* ? A later Supreme Court has referred to "the twin aims of the *Erie* rule" as "discouragement of forum-shopping and avoidance of inequitable administration of the laws." *Hanna v. Plumer,* 380 U.S. 460, 467-469 (1965) (Warren, C. J.). Those problems were certainly part of Justice Brandeis' critique of *Swift.* However, forum shopping is not unconstitutional; and the Fifth Amendment had no equal protection component until one was "incorporated" into the Fifth Amendment Due Process Clause in the 1954 school desegregation case arising in Washington, D.C. (*Bolling v. Sharpe,* 354 U.S. 497 (1954). Justice Brandeis' language in *Erie* about "powers reserved to the states" might suggest a Tenth Amendment basis for the decision, but Justice Brandeis does not mention the Tenth Amendment.

Wasn't Brandeis' point simply that the nation has no lawmaking power over state law? The nation has lawmaking power only over federal law:

> "Congress has no power to declare substantive rules of common law applicable in a state."

*See* John Hart Ely, *The Irrepressible Myth of Erie,* 87 Harv. L. Rev. 693, 703 (1974).

(7) *The pre-positivist "fallacy" and the Due Process Clause.* A large part of the operative portion of the opinion in *Erie* is about a "fallacy." Recall Justice Holmes' famous remark in *Jensen, supra,* that the common law is not a "brooding omnipresence in the sky," but is the "articulate voice" of some sovereign that can be identified. It was the pre-*Erie* failure of federal courts to identify the state as the source of law to be applied to that state's common-law questions that amounted to an "unconstitutional course" that federal courts pursued.

In *Erie,* the Court clarified that the nation has power only to make federal, not state, law. This raises a question whether, although *Erie* is clearly not a due process opinion, it could have been decided under the Due Process Clause of the Fifth Amendment. Under *Swift,* federal courts were making the mistake of displacing the laws of the interested state, on issues as to which the courts had not troubled to identify any national interest. When the law of a relevant sovereign is displaced by the law of an uninterested one, today the Due Process Clause in theory will strike it down. See generally the opening sections of Chapter 5. For current discussion see Stephen M. Feldman, *From Premodern to Modern American Jurisprudence: The Onset of Positivism,* 50 Vand. L. Rev. 1387 (1997).

(8) *State courts and general common law.* Do state courts retain "general" common-law powers that the nation does not? Or does the Due Process Clause stand in the way? Until very recently, Georgia asserted general common-law power (as opposed to its own specific common-law power), but only in conflict cases. Indeed, Georgia was following the precise rule of *Swift v. Tyson.* Georgia held itself free to disregard the otherwise applicable law of a sister state—if,

but only if, the sister state's law was nonstatutory—at least on general commercial questions. Georgia's practice was never challeged under either *Erie* or the Due Process Clause. *Cf. Frank Briscoe Co. v. Georgia Sprinkler Co.,* 713 F.2d 1500 (11th Cir. 1983); John B. Rees, Jr., *Choice of Law in Georgia,* 34 MERCER L. REV. 784, 787-790 (1983).

(9) *The significance of Erie.* You might want to try for yourself the experiment of consulting the *pre-Erie* cases in the federal law reports. Except for those opinions deciding clearly federal issues, or applying clearly authoritative state law, the unconstitutionality of most federal-court decisions of the period will become apparent to you. The federal judges were purporting to decide questions of state law without deferring to the actual case law of the particular state. The cases seem muddled, too pre-positivist to have any use. Indeed, they seem unconstitutional.

(10) *A movement to return to the general common law?* For a fascinating study of the antipathy of certain anti-government "militia" groups in this country to *Erie v. Tompkins,* on the ground that it destroyed the truly general common law of the people, see Susan P. Koniak, *When Law Risks Madness,* 8 CARDOZO STUD. L. & LITERATURE 65 (1996).

---

## NOTE ON THE OFFICIAL ILLEGITIMACY OF FEDERAL COMMON LAW

*Erie* furnishes the intellectual basis for the modern position that state law governs state common-law questions in both sets of courts. Properly understood, it also furnishes the intellectual basis for the modern position that federal law governs federal common-law questions in both sets of courts. (There is no federal "general" common law—no hybrid third option.) As Judge Henry Friendly famously wrote in 1964, this bipolar allocation of lawmaking power is "beautifully simple and simply beautiful." Henry Friendly, *In Praise of Erie—And of the New Federal Common Law,* 39 N.Y.U. L. REV. 383, 422 (1964). Cases decided every day illustrate this simple allocation of national power to the nation and state power to the states. But although the clarified modern position is the *actual* position, it is not the *official* position of the Supreme Court. Rather, the Court acts as though what was struck down in *Erie* was not federal "general" common law, but genuine federal common law. It turns out that federal common law has been a political football, and tends to be treated as somehow worse than state common law. Alternating waves of hostility to "judicial activism" from both the left and the right have produced an impressive body of constraints on judicial federal lawmaking power. Ironically, these constraints, for the most part, are themselves federal common law—they emerge from judicial decisions on the scope of federal judicial lawmaking power. Michael Wells, *Positivism and Antipositivism in Federal Courts Law,* 29 GA. L. REV. 655 (1995).

## THE *ERIE* MYTH

*Erie* is commonly treated by Supreme Court Justices and commentators as having struck down federal common law as unconstitutional. But there was no federal/state conflict of laws in *Erie,* was there? Whatever was declared unconstitutional, it was not federal, was it?

In fact, the Justices as well as the commentators recognize that courts simply must have power to interpret the Constitution and federal statutes. So those who believe *Erie* outlawed federal common law have had to backpedal a bit. The federal case law many believe was outlawed in Erie turns out to be not all federal case law, not cases filling the gaps in federal statutes or explicating the open-ended provisions of the Constitution, but only cases in which it is argued that courts should fashion *freestanding* federal common-law rules—cases like the following case.

## BOYLE v. UNITED TECHNOLOGIES CORP.

*Supreme Court of the United States*
*487 U.S. 500, 108 S. Ct. 2510, 101 L. Ed. 2d 442 (1988)*

JUSTICE SCALIA delivered the opinion of the Court.

This case requires us to decide when a contractor providing military equipment to the Federal Government can be held liable under state tort law for injury caused by a design defect.

On April 27, 1983, David A. Boyle, a United States Marine helicopter copilot, was killed when the . . . helicopter in which he was flying crashed off the coast of Virginia Beach, Virginia, during a training exercise. Although Boyle survived the impact of the crash, he was unable to escape from the helicopter and drowned. Boyle's father, petitioner here, brought this diversity action in Federal District Court against . . . United Technologies Corporation, which built the helicopter for the United States.

. . . [Petitioner] alleged that [the manufacturer] had defectively designed the copilot's emergency escape system: the escape hatch opened out instead of in (and was therefore ineffective in a submerged craft because of water pressure), and access to the escape hatch handle was obstructed by other equipment. The jury returned a general verdict in favor of petitioner and awarded him $725,000. . . .

The Court of Appeals reversed. . . . It found, as a matter of federal law, that [defendant] could not be held liable for the allegedly defective design of the escape hatch because, on the evidence presented, it satisfied the requirements of the "military contractor defense," which the court had recognized the same day in *Tozer v. LTV Corp.*, 792 F.2d 403 (4th Cir. 1986).

. . . Petitioner's broadest contention is that, in the absence of legislation specifically immunizing Government contractors from liability for design defects, there is no basis for judicial recognition of such a defense. We disagree. . . .

. . . [The] Federal Government's interest in the procurement of equipment is implicated by suits such as the present one—even though the dispute is one between private parties. . . . The imposition of liability on Government contractors will directly affect the terms of Government contracts: either the contractor will decline to manufacture the design specified by the Government, or it will raise its price. . . .

That the procurement of equipment by the United States is an area of uniquely federal interest does not, however, end the inquiry. . . . Displacement will occur only where . . . a "significant conflict" exists between an identifiable "federal policy or interest and the (operation) of state law," *Wallis v. Pan American Petroleum Corp.*, 384 U.S. 63, 68 (1966), or the application of state law would frustrate specific objectives of federal legislation. . . .

Here the state-imposed duty of care that is the asserted basis of the contractor's liability (specifically, the duty to equip helicopters with the sort of escape-hatch mechanism petitioner claims was necessary) is precisely contrary to the duty imposed by the Government contract (the duty to manufacture and deliver helicopters with the sort of escape-hatch mechanism shown by the specifications). . . .

There is . . . a statutory provision that [is relevant]. In the Federal Tort Claims Act (FTCA), Congress authorized damages to be recovered against the United States for harm caused by the negligent or wrongful conduct of Government employees, to the extent that a private person would be liable under the law of the place where the conduct occurred. 28 U.S.C. § 1346(b). It excepted from this consent to suit, however,

> "[any] claim . . . based upon the exercise or performance or the failure to exercise or perform a discretionary function or duty on the part of a federal agency or an employee of the Government, whether or not the discretion involved be abused." 28 U.S.C. § 2680(a).

We think that the selection of the appropriate design for military equipment to be used by our Armed Forces is assuredly a discretionary function within the meaning of this provision. It often involves not merely engineering analysis but judgment as to the balancing of many technical, military, and even social considerations, including specifically the trade-off between greater safety and greater combat effectiveness. And we are further of the view that permitting "second-guessing" of these judgments, through state tort suits against contractors, would produce the same effect sought to be avoided by the FTCA exemption. The financial burden of judgments against the contractors would ultimately be passed through, substantially if not totally, to the United States itself, since defense contractors will predictably raise their prices to cover, or to insure against, contingent liability for the Government-ordered designs. To put the point differently: It makes little sense to insulate the Government against financial liability for the judgment that a particular feature of military equipment is . . . necessary when the Government produces the equipment itself, but not when it contracts for the production. In sum, we are of the view that state law which holds Government contractors liable for design defects in military equipment does in some circumstances present a "significant conflict" with federal policy and must be displaced. . . .

We agree with the scope of displacement adopted by the Fourth Circuit here, which is also that adopted by the Ninth Circuit. . . . Liability for design defects in military equipment cannot be imposed, pursuant to state law, when (1) the United States approved reasonably precise specifications; (2) the equipment conformed to those specifications; and (3) the supplier warned the United States about the dangers in the use of the equipment that were known to the supplier but not to the United States. . . .

[The Court vacated judgment and remanded for a determination whether the defense had been made out on these facts.]

JUSTICE BRENNAN, with whom JUSTICE MARSHALL and JUSTICE BLACKMUN join, dissenting.

. . . Had respondent designed such a death trap for a commercial firm, Lt. Boyle's family could sue under Virginia tort law and be compensated for his tragic and unnecessary death. But respondent designed the helicopter for the Federal Government, and that, the Court tells us today, makes all the difference: Respondent is immune from liability so long as it obtained approval of "reasonably precise specifications"—perhaps no more than a rubber stamp from a federal procurement officer who . . . might not have noticed . . . the defects, or . . . had the expertise to discover them.

If respondent's immunity bore the legitimacy of having been prescribed by the people's elected representatives, we would be duty bound to implement their will, whether or not we approved. Congress, however, has remained silent—and conspicuously so, having resisted a sustained campaign by Government contractors to legislate for them some defense.[1] The Court—unelected and unaccountable to the people—has unabashedly stepped into the breach to legislate a rule denying Lt. Boyle's family the compensation . . . that state law assures them. This time the injustice is of this Court's own making. . . .

Before our decision in *Erie R. Co. v. Tompkins,* 304 U.S. 64 (1938), federal courts sitting in diversity were generally free, in the absence of a controlling state statute, to fashion rules of "general" federal common law. *Erie* . . . was deeply rooted in notions of federalism, and is most seriously implicated when, as here, federal judges displace the state law that would ordinarily govern with their own rules of federal common law. . . .

Accordingly, we have emphasized that federal common law can displace state law in "few and restricted" instances. "Absent some congressional authorization to formulate substantive rules of decision, federal common law exists only in such narrow areas as those concerned with the rights and obligations of the United States, interstate and international disputes implicating conflicting rights of States or our relations with foreign nations, and admiralty cases." *Texas Industries, Inc. v. Radcliff Materials, Inc.,* 451 U.S.

---

[1] *See, e.g.,* H.R. 4765, S. 2441, 99th Cong., 2d Sess. (1986) (limitations on civil liability of Government contractors). . . .

630, 641, (1981). "The enactment of a federal rule in an area of national concern, and the decision whether to displace state law in doing so, is generally made not by the federal judiciary, purposefully insulated from democratic pressures, but by the people through their elected representatives in Congress." *Milwaukee v. Illinois,* 451 U.S. 304, 312-313 (1981). . . .

. . . [Indicative] of Congress' views on the subject is the wrongful-death cause of action that Congress itself has provided under the Death on the High Seas Act (DOHSA), 46 U.S.C. § 761 *et seq.* —a cause of action that could have been asserted against United Technologies had Lt. Boyle's helicopter crashed a mere three miles further off the coast of Virginia Beach. It is beyond me how a state-law tort suit against the designer of a military helicopter could be said to present any conflict, much less a "significant conflict," with "federal interests . . . " when . . . federal law itself would provide a tort suit, but no government-contractor defense, against the same designer for an accident involving the same equipment.

At bottom, the Court's analysis is premised on the proposition that any tort liability indirectly absorbed by the Government so burdens governmental functions as to compel us to act when Congress has not. That proposition is by no means uncontroversial. The tort system is premised on the assumption that the imposition of liability encourages actors to prevent any injury whose expected cost exceeds the cost of prevention. If the system is working as it should, Government contractors will design equipment to avoid certain injuries (like the deaths of soldiers or Government employees), which would be certain to burden the Government. The Court therefore has no basis for its assumption that tort liability will result in a net burden on the Government (let alone a clearly excessive net burden) rather than a net gain. . . .

[JUSTICE STEVENS also dissented, remarking, "When judges are asked to embark on a lawmaking venture, I believe they should carefully consider whether they, or a legislative body, are better equipped to perform the task at hand. . . . "]

## NOTES ON *BOYLE*

(1) *The right rule* ? Notice that the Court fashions the new federal common-law rule on the liability of military contractors, selecting its position from among the positions advanced in the various federal circuit courts. Did the Court select the right rule? Interestingly, courts below have been grudging in their readings of *Boyle*. Before a court will insulate a government contractor from state tort liability, courts are considering such features of a case as the adequacy of warnings to users, as opposed to the government. *See, e.g., Tate v. Boeing Helicopters,* 55 F.3d 1150 (6th Cir. 1995).

(2) *The legitimacy of federal common law.* How can we believe the Court's frequent pronouncements that there is something illegitimate about federal judicial lawmaking, if the Court goes on fashioning federal common-law rules of decision, as it does in *Boyle* ? See, currently, Robert M. Ackerman, *Tort*

*Law and Federalism: Whatever Happened to Devolution ?*, 14 YALE J. ON REG. 429 (1996).

(3) *Is consistency the hobgoblin of little minds ?* In *Thompson v. Thompson,* reported below, Justice Scalia, writing separately, disapproved of new federal common-law causes of action, expressing a concern that judges will create law to mirror their own predilections. How does that view square with Justice Scalia's opinion in *Boyle ? Thompson v. Thompson* involved the propriety of judicial fashioning of a new federal cause of action. Is there a justification for federal common-law *defenses* that does not apply to federal common-law *claims*?

Does the late Justice Brennan do any better than Justice Scalia? Justice Brennan, a long-time champion of federal judicial lawmaking, hardly seems in character when he argues that something in *Erie* or the separation of powers stands in the way of federal decisional law. In *Boyle* one can see the politics on this issue changing sides in real time.

In fact there are numerous instances of federal common-law defenses to state torts. See generally, for recent discussion, Lars Noah, *Reconceptualizing Federal Preemption of Tort Claims as the Government Standards Defense,* 37 WM. & MARY L. REV. 903 (1996). Consider the body of case law on the liability of federal officials. *E.g., Westfall v. Erwin,* 484 U.S. 292 (1988) (holding that absolute immunity does not shield federal officials from state liability unless the challenged conduct is discretionary in nature; the purpose of the federal common law of official immunity is not to protect erring officials, but to insulate the official's governmental decisions from the threat of litigation). There is a similar body of federal common law limiting the liability of *state* officials in civil rights cases.

———

For theoretical background see Louise Weinberg, *Federal Common Law,* 83 NW. U. L. REV. 805 (1989). For an interesting attempt to reformulate the theoretical position of the post-*Erie* federal common law, see Bradford R. Clark, *Federal Common Law: A Structural Reinterpretation,* 144 U. PA. L. REV. 1245 (1996).

———

## NOTE ON CONSTITUTIONAL COMMON LAW

*Constitutional common law.* It is sometimes suggested that federal cases interpreting the Constitution fall into two groupings. The first grouping, which in theory Congress cannot override, is properly considered "constitutional law." The second grouping, which Congress could override, might be termed "constitutional common law." For example, no one doubts that Congress could specify the precise content of the *Miranda* warnings. Arguably for purposes of thinking about federal common law nothing is gained by drawing the distinction between "constitutional common law" and the rest of constitutional case law. As a practical matter there seems to be little difference between constitutional cases (whether or not Congress theoretically could override) and other federal cases.

See Michael Wells, Symposium, *Constitutional Torts, Common Law Torts, and Due Process of Law,* 72 CHI.-KENT L. REV. 617 (1997).

---

## § 6.03   New Federal Causes of Action

What, today, is the extent of judicial power to fashion *wholly new federal causes of action*? In answering that question, courts often face an implicit conflict of laws. Whenever a private right to sue is held unavailable under federal law, the likely outcome for the particular case is not necessarily dismissal. More often the case will be tried under the law of some state on an alternative state-law count pleaded in the complaint.

*To enforce the Constitution.* The Supreme Court has fashioned new post-*Erie* federal causes of action for violation of the Constitution. The *locus classicus* is *Bivens v. Six Unknown Named Agents of the Federal Bureau Of Narcotics,* 403 U.S. 388 (1970) (Brennan, J., recognizing a private right to sue for violation of the Fourth Amendment). In a famous separate opinion in *Bivens,* Justice Harlan, concurring, pointed out that the power of the nation to give damages for such a violation could not depend upon whether Congress had passed a statute creating a federal cause of action: "[It] would be at least anomalous to conclude that the . . . judiciary—while competent to choose among the range of traditional judicial remedies to implement statutory and common-law policies . . . is powerless to accord a damages remedy to vindicate [constitutional] policies. . . . " Justice Harlan adverted to "enclaves of federal common law that bind the states," citing cases. Moreover, the particular remedy was necessary in Bivens' case. Bivens would not have the advance notice of a wrongful search that would enable him to obtain an injunction against it; and, being innocent, would have no opportunity to avail himself of the exclusionary rule. As Justice Harlan puts this, "For people in *Bivens* ' shoes, it is damages or nothing."

Recently *Bivens* has been limited to cases in which Congress has not provided its own comprehensive remedial scheme. *See Bush v. Lucas,* 465 U.S. 367 (1983); *Schweiker v. Chilicky,* 487 U.S. 412 (1988). On the other hand, the Court has repeatedly held the Constitution actionable against state and local officials under the Civil Rights Act of 1871, *Monroe v. Pape,* 365 U.S. 167 (1961), and recently has extended this remedy to violations of the Supremacy Clause, *Golden State Transit Corp. v. City of Los Angeles,* 493 U.S. 103 (1990), and of the Commerce Clause, *Dennis v. Higgins,* 498 U.S. 439 (1991).[*] Finally, the Court has extended this remedy to state and local violations of acts of Congress. *Maine v. Thiboutot,* 448 U.S. 1 (1980).

---

[*] For analogous British litigation, *see, e.g., O'Rourke v. Camden London Borough Council,* [1997] A.E.R. 23 (H.L.) (holding that the Housing Authority's breach of a statutory duty to furnish accommodation to the homeless did not give rise to a cause of action for damages). —*Ed.*

———

*To enforce federal legislation.* The general rule at common law is that a statutory violation that causes injury, whether or not a crime, is a tort, and is actionable. Indeed, a statutory violation makes a tort obviously a more serious one. Thus, under the familiar tort rules of the several states, a statutory violation may be held negligence *per se*, or may shift the burden of proof to the defendant, or may create a presumption of liability. This heightened concern is also a feature of federal common law. *Cf. The Pennsylvania,* 86 U.S. 125 (1874) (announcing the federal common-law rule in admiralty: a statutory violation at the time of a ship collision shifts the burden to the violating vessel to show that the violation *could not* have caused the collision). Is there some reason why federal common law, unlike the common law generally, should *not* recognize the propriety of a civil remedy for harm caused by a violation of an act of Congress? Of course, Congress might want to protect defendants from tort liability for violation of the act of Congress; but presumably Congress could make that clear in the language of the statute. The following materials touch upon the current Court's positions on "implying" private rights to sue for violations of federal statutes. The question arises when an act of Congress provides for criminal or administrative enforcement only, and the plaintiff claims to be injured or to be facing injury on account of a violation, and seeks to litigate her rights against the government.

———

**TEXAS INDUSTRIES, INC. v. RADCLIFF MATERIALS, INC.,** 451 U.S. 630 (1981). In an antitrust litigation, the defendant filed a third-party complaint, seeking contribution. The District Court dismissed the third-party complaint for failure to state a claim upon which relief could be granted, holding that federal law does not allow an antitrust defendant to recover in contribution from co-conspirators. The Court of Appeals for the Fifth Circuit affirmed.

*Held* (by CHIEF JUSTICE BURGER): Affirmed. "With potentially large sums at stake, it is not surprising that the numerous and articulate *amici* disagree strongly over the basic issue raised: whether sharing of damages liability will advance or impair the objectives of the antitrust laws. . . . The contentions advanced indicate how views diverge as to the 'unfairness' of not providing contribution, the risks and trade-offs perceived by decisionmakers in business, and the various patterns for contribution that could be devised. In this vigorous debate over the advantages and disadvantages of contribution and various contribution schemes, the parties, *amici,* and commentators have paid less attention to a very significant and perhaps dispositive threshold question: whether courts have the power to create such a cause of action absent legislation and, if so, whether that authority should be exercised in this context. . . .

"Our focus, as it is in any case involving the implication of a right of action, is on the intent of Congress. Congressional intent may be discerned by looking to the legislative history and other factors: *e.g.,* the identity of the class for whose benefit the statute was enacted, the overall legislative scheme, and the traditional role of the states in providing relief. *Cort v. Ash,* 422 U.S. 66 (1975). Petitioner readily concedes that . . . there is nothing in the legislative history of the Sherman Act or the Clayton Act to indicate that Congress considered whether contribution was available to defendants in antitrust actions. . . . Moreover, it is equally clear that the Sherman Act and the provision for treble-damages actions under the Clayton Act were not adopted for the benefit of the participants in a conspiracy to restrain trade. . . . If any right to contribution exists, its source must be federal common law.

"There is, of course, 'no federal general common law.' *Erie R. Co. v. Tompkins,* 304 U.S. 64 (1938). . . . The vesting of jurisdiction in the federal courts does not in and of itself give rise to authority to formulate federal common law. . . . [Absent] some congressional authorization to formulate substantive rules of decision, federal common law exists only in such narrow areas as those concerned with the rights and obligations of the United States, interstate and international disputes implicating the conflicting rights of States or our relations with foreign nations, and admiralty cases. In these instances, our federal system does not permit the controversy to be resolved under state law, either because the authority and duties of the United States as sovereign are intimately involved or because the interstate or international nature of the controversy makes it inappropriate for state law to control.

"In areas where federal common law applies, the creation of a right to contribution may fall within the power of the federal courts. For example, in *Cooper Stevedoring Co. v. Fritz Kopke, Inc.,* 417 U.S. 106 (1974), we held that contribution is available among joint tortfeasors for injury to a longshoreman. But that claim arose within admiralty jurisdiction, one of the areas long recognized as subject to federal common law . . . ; our decision there was based, at least in part, on the traditional division of damages in admiralty not recognized at common law. . . . *Cooper Stevedoring* thus does not stand for a general federal common-law right to contribution. . . .

"Admittedly, there is a federal interest in the sense that vindication of rights arising out of these congressional enactments supplements federal enforcement and fulfills the objects of the statutory scheme. Notwithstanding that nexus, contribution among antitrust wrongdoers does not involve the duties of the Federal Government, the distribution of powers in our federal system, or matters necessarily subject to federal control even in the absence of statutory authority. In short, contribution does not implicate uniquely federal interests of the kind that oblige courts to formulate federal common law.

"Congress . . . did not intend the text of the Sherman Act to delineate the full meaning of the statute or its application in concrete situations. The legislative history makes it perfectly clear that it expected the courts to give shape to the statute's broad mandate by drawing on common-law tradition. It does not necessarily follow, however, that Congress intended to give courts as wide discretion in formulating remedies to enforce the provisions of the Sherman Act or the kind of relief sought through contribution. . . .

"In contrast to the sweeping language of §§ 1 and 2 of the Sherman Act, the remedial provisions defined in the antitrust laws are detailed and specific:

(1) violations of §§ 1 and 2 are crimes; (2) Congress has expressly authorized a private right of action for treble damages, costs, and reasonable attorney's fees. . . . The presumption that a remedy was deliberately omitted from a statute is strongest when Congress has enacted a comprehensive legislative scheme including an integrated system of procedures for enforcement. That presumption is strong indeed in the context of antitrust violations; the continuing existence of this statutory scheme for 90 years without amendments authorizing contribution is not without significance. . . . In declining to provide a right to contribution, we . . . recognize that, regardless of the merits of the conflicting arguments, this is a matter for Congress, not the courts, to resolve. . . . "

*The dubious luxury of deciding not to decide.* Is it fair to say that in *Texas Industries* the Supreme Court held that there was no contribution between joint antitrust tortfeasors? If so, isn't this now a rule of federal common law? Is it fair to say that this rule forbidding contribution claims was handed down without adequate discussion of the antitrust policies identified by Chief Justice Burger?

What might be the effect of *Texas Industries* on antitrust remedies generally? See, referring to *Texas Industries* in this connection, C. Douglas Floyd, *Antitrust Victims Without Antitrust Remedies: The Narrowing of Standing in Private Antitrust Actions,* 82 MINN. L. REV. 1 (1997).

The Supreme Court has recently recognized a right of contribution between joint tortfeasors in securities fraud litigation. *Musick, Peeler & Garrett v. Employers Insurance of Wausau,* 508 U.S. 286 (1993). On the other hand, the Court has refused to make cognizable a claim against aiders and abetters of securities fraud. *Central Bank of Denver, N.A. v. First Interstate Bank of Denver, N.A.,* 511 U.S. 164 (1994).

## THOMPSON v. THOMPSON

*Supreme Court of the United States*
*484 U.S. 174, 108 S. Ct. 513, 98 L. Ed. 2d 512 (1988)*

JUSTICE MARSHALL delivered the Opinion of the Court.

We granted certiorari in this case to determine whether the Parental Kidnaping Prevention Act of 1980, 28 U.S.C. § 1738A, furnishes an implied cause of action in federal court to determine which of two conflicting state custody decisions is valid.

I

The Parental Kidnaping Prevention Act (PKPA or Act) imposes a duty on the States to enforce a child custody determination entered by a court of a sister State if the determination is consistent with the provisions of the Act.[1] In order for a state court's custody decree to be consistent with the provisions of the Act, the State must have jurisdiction under its own local law and one of five conditions set out in § 1738A(c)(2) must be met. Briefly put, these conditions authorize the state court to enter a custody decree if the child's home is or recently has been in the State, if the child has no home State and it would be in the child's best interest for the State to assume jurisdiction, or if the child is present in the State and has been abandoned or abused. Once a State exercises jurisdiction consistently with the provisions of the Act, no other State may exercise concurrent jurisdiction over the custody dispute, § 1738A(g), even if it would have been empowered to take jurisdiction in the first instance, and all States must accord full faith and credit to the first State's ensuing custody decree.

. . . This case arises out of a jurisdictional stalemate that came to pass notwithstanding the strictures of the Act. In July 1978, respondent Susan Clay (then Susan Thompson) filed a petition in Los Angeles Superior Court asking the court to dissolve her marriage to petitioner David Thompson and seeking custody of the couple's infant son, Matthew. The court initially awarded the parents joint custody of Matthew, but that arrangement became infeasible when respondent decided to move from California to Louisiana to take a job. The court then entered an order providing that respondent would have sole custody of Matthew once she left for Louisiana. . . . This state of affairs was to remain in effect until the court investigator submitted a report on custody, after which the court intended to make a more studied custody determination.

Respondent and Matthew moved to Louisiana in December 1980. Three months later, respondent filed a petition in Louisiana state court for enforcement of the California custody decree, judgment of custody, and modification of petitioner's visitation privileges. By order dated April 7, 1981, the Louisiana court granted the petition and awarded sole custody of Matthew to respondent. Two months later, however, the California court, having received and reviewed its investigator's report, entered an order awarding sole custody of Matthew to petitioner. Thus arose the current impasse.

In August 1983, petitioner brought this action in the District Court for the Central District of California. Petitioner requested an order declaring the Louisiana decree invalid and the California decree valid, and enjoining the enforcement of the Louisiana decree. Petitioner did not attempt to enforce the California decree in a Louisiana state court before he filed suit in federal court. The District Court granted respondent's motion to dismiss the complaint for lack of subject-matter and personal jurisdiction. The Court of Appeals for the Ninth Circuit affirmed. . . .

## II

In determining whether to infer a private cause of action from a federal statute, our focal point is Congress' intent in enacting the statute. As guides

---

[1] Section 1738A reads in relevant part: "(a) The appropriate authorities of every State shall enforce according to its terms, and shall not modify except as provided in subsection (f) of this section, any child custody determination made consistently with the provisions of this section by a court of another State.". . .

to discerning that intent, we have relied on the four factors set out in *Cort v. Ash,* 422 U.S. 66, 78 (1975), along with other tools of statutory construction. *See Touche Ross & Co. v. Redington,* 442 U.S. 560, 575-576 (1979). Our focus on congressional intent does not mean that we require evidence that Members of Congress, in enacting the statute, actually had in mind the creation of a private cause of action. The implied cause of action doctrine would be a virtual dead letter were it limited to correcting drafting errors when Congress simply forgot to codify its evident intention to provide a cause of action. Rather, as [the] implied cause of action doctrine suggests, "the legislative history of a statute that does not expressly create or deny a private remedy will typically be equally silent or ambiguous on the question." *Cannon v. University of Chicago,* 441 U.S. 677, 694 (1979). We therefore have recognized that Congress' "intent may appear implicitly in the language or structure of the statute, or in the circumstances of its enactment." *Transamerica Mortgage Advisors, Inc. v. Lewis,* 444 U.S. 11, 18 (1979). The intent of Congress remains the ultimate issue, however, and "unless this congressional intent can be inferred from the language of the statute, the statutory structure, or some other source, the essential predicate for implication of a private remedy simply does not exist." *Northwest Airlines, Inc. v. Transport Workers,* 451 U.S. 77, 94 (1981). In this case, the essential predicate for implication of a private remedy plainly does not exist. None of the factors that have guided our inquiry in this difficult area points in favor of inferring a private cause of action. Indeed, the context, language, and legislative history of the PKPA all point sharply away from the remedy petitioner urges us to infer.

We examine initially the context of the PKPA with an eye toward determining Congress' perception of the law that it was shaping or reshaping. At the time Congress passed the PKPA, custody orders held a peculiar status under the full faith and credit doctrine, which requires each State to give effect to the judicial proceedings of other States. . . . Because courts entering custody orders generally retain the power to modify them, courts in other States were no less entitled to change the terms of custody according to their own views of the child's best interest. *See New York ex rel. Halvey v. Halvey,* 330 U.S. 610, 614-615 (1947). For these reasons, a parent who lost a custody battle in one State had an incentive to kidnap the child and move to another State to relitigate the issue. This circumstance contributed to widespread jurisdictional deadlocks like this one, and more importantly, to a national epidemic of parental kidnaping. At the time the PKPA was enacted, sponsors of the Act estimated that between 25,000 and 100,000 children were kidnaped by parents who had been unable to obtain custody in a legal forum.

A number of States joined in an effort to avoid these jurisdictional conflicts by adopting the Uniform Child Custody Jurisdiction Act (UCCJA), 9 U.L.A. §§ 1-28 (1979). . . . The project foundered, however, because a number of States refused to enact the UCCJA while others enacted it with modifications. In the absence of uniform national standards for allocating and enforcing custody determinations, noncustodial parents still had reason to snatch their children and petition the courts of any of a number of haven States for sole custody.

The context of the PKPA therefore suggests that the principal problem Congress was seeking to remedy was the inapplicability of full faith and credit requirements to custody determinations. . . . As Acting Deputy Attorney General Michel testified: ". . . In essence [the PKPA] would impose on States a Federal duty, under enumerated standards derived from the UCCJA, to give full faith and credit to the custody decrees of other States. Such legislation would, in effect, amount to Federal adoption of key provisions of the UCCJA for all States and would eliminate the incentive for one parent to remove a minor child to another jurisdiction."

The . . . Full Faith and Credit Clause, in either its constitutional or statutory incarnations, does not give rise to an implied federal cause of action. Rather, the Clause "only prescribes a rule by which courts, Federal and state, are to be guided when a question arises in the progress of a pending suit as to the faith and credit to be given by the court to the public acts, records, and judicial proceedings of a State other than that in which the court is sitting." *Minnesota v. Northern Securities Co.,* 194 U.S. 48, 72 (1904). Because Congress' chief aim in enacting the PKPA was to extend the requirements of the Full Faith and Credit Clause to custody determinations, the Act is most naturally construed to furnish a rule of decision for courts to use in adjudicating custody disputes and not to create an entirely new cause of action. . . .

. . . Unlike statutes that explicitly confer a right on a specified class of persons, the PKPA is a mandate directed to We agree with the Court of Appeals that "[i]t seems highly unlikely Congress would follow the pattern of the Full Faith and Credit Clause and section 1738 by structuring section 1738A as a command to state courts to give full faith and credit to the child custody decrees of other states, and yet, without comment, depart from the enforcement practice followed under the Clause and section 1738."

Finally, the legislative history of the PKPA provides unusually clear indication that Congress did not intend the federal courts to play the enforcement role that petitioner urges. . . . Congressman Fish [was] the sponsor of a competing legislative proposal—ultimately rejected by Congress—that would have extended the district courts' diversity jurisdiction to encompass actions for enforcement of state custody orders. . . . Congress considered and rejected an approach to the problem that would have resulted in a Federal court litigating between two State court decrees.

. . . [A] letter from then Assistant Attorney General Patricia Wald to the Chairman of the House Judiciary Committee . . . specifically compared proposals that would "grant jurisdiction to the federal courts to enforce state custody decrees" with an approach, such as was proposed in the PKPA, that would "impose on states a federal duty, under enumerated standards derived generally from the UCCJA, to give full faith and credit to the custody decrees of other states." The letter . . . "strongly oppose[d] . . . the creation of a federal forum for resolving custody disputes." . . . [The] Justice Department reasoned that federal enforcement of state custody decrees would increase the workload of the federal courts and entangle the federal judiciary in domestic relations disputes with which they have little experience and which traditionally have been the province of the States. . . .

. . . Instructing the federal courts to play Solomon where two state courts have issued conflicting custody orders would entangle them in traditional state-law questions that they have little expertise to resolve.[4] This is a cost that Congress made clear it did not want the PKPA to carry.[5]

In sum, the context, language, and history of the PKPA together make out a conclusive case against inferring a cause of action in federal court to determine which of two conflicting state custody decrees is valid. Against this impressive evidence, petitioner relies primarily on the argument that failure to infer a cause of action would render the PKPA nugatory. We note, as a preliminary response, that ultimate review remains available in this Court for truly intractable jurisdictional deadlocks. In addition, the unspoken presumption in petitioner's argument is that the States are either unable or unwilling to enforce the provisions of the Act. This is a presumption we are not prepared, and more importantly, Congress was not prepared, to indulge. State courts faithfully administer the Full Faith and Credit Clause every day; now that Congress has extended full faith and credit requirements to child custody orders, we can think of no reason why the courts' administration of federal law in custody disputes will be any less vigilant. Should state courts prove as obstinate as petitioner predicts, Congress may choose to revisit the issue. . . . The judgment of the Court of Appeals is affirmed. . . .

JUSTICE O'CONNOR, concurring in part and concurring in the judgment.

For the reasons expressed by JUSTICE SCALIA in Part I of his opinion in this case, I join all but the first full paragraph of Part II of the Court's opinion and judgment.

JUSTICE SCALIA, concurring in the judgment.

. . . I agree that the Parental Kidnaping Prevention Act does not create a private right of action in federal court to determine which of two conflicting child custody decrees is valid. . . .

"[But] I . . . find misleading the Court's statement that, in determining the existence of a private right of action, we [rely] on the four factors set out in *Cort v. Ash* . . . . That is not an accurate description of what we have done. It could not be plainer that we effectively overruled the *Cort v. Ash* analysis in *Touche Ross & Co. v. Redington,* 442 U.S. 560, 575-76 (1979) and *Transamerica Mortgage Advisors, Inc. v. Lewis,* 444 U.S. 11, 18 (1979), converting one of its four factors (congressional intent) into *the determinative factor,* with the other three merely indicative of its presence or absence. . . .

---

**4** . . . Petitioner argues that determining which of two conflicting custody decrees should be given effect under the PKPA would not require the federal courts to resolve the merits of custody disputes and thus would not offend the longstanding tradition of reserving domestic relations matters to the States. Petitioner contends that the cause of action he champions would require federal courts only to analyze which of two States is given exclusive jurisdiction under a federal statute, a task for which the federal courts are well qualified. We cannot agree with petitioner that making a jurisdictional determination under the PKPA would not involve the federal courts in substantive domestic relations determinations. Under the Act, jurisdiction can turn on the child's "best interest" or on proof that the child has been abandoned or abused. . . .

**5** . . . Petitioner essentially asks that federal district courts exercise appellate review of state-court judgments. This is an unusual cause of action for Congress to grant, either expressly or by implication. Petitioner's proposal is all the more remarkable in the present case, in which he seeks to have a Federal District Court in California enjoin enforcement of a Louisiana state-court judgment before the intermediate and highest appellate courts of Louisiana even have had an opportunity to review that judgment.

Contrary to what the language of today's opinion suggests, this Court has long since abandoned its hospitable attitude towards implied rights of action. In the 23 years since Justice Clark's opinion for the court in *J.I. Case Co. v. Borak,* 377 U.S. 426 (1964), we have twice narrowed the test for implying a private right, first in *Cort v. Ash,* itself, and then again in *Touche Ross* and *Transamerica.* The recent history of our holdings is one of repeated rejection of claims of an implied right. This has been true in nine of eleven recent private right of action cases heard by this Court, including the instant case. . . .

I have found the Court's dicta in the present case particularly provocative of response because it is my view that, if the current state of the law were to be changed, it should be moved in precisely the opposite direction—away from our current congressional intent test to the categorical position that federal private rights of action will not be implied. . . .

It is, to be sure, not beyond imagination that in a particular case Congress may intend to create a private right of action, but choose to do so by implication. One must wonder, however, whether the good produced by a judicial rule that accommodates this remote possibility is outweighed by its adverse effects. . . . [It is] dangerous to assume that, even with the utmost self-discipline, judges can prevent the implications they see from mirroring the policies they favor. . . .

If a change is to be made, we should get out of the business of implied private rights of action altogether.

---

For further reading, see Susan J. Stabile, *The Role of Congressional Intent in Determining the Existence of Implied Private Rights of Action,* 71 NOTRE DAME L. REV. 861 (1996).

---

## § 6.04   Freestanding Federal Common-Law Causes of Action

### MORAGNE v. STATES MARINE LINES, INC.

*Supreme Court of the United States*
*398 U.S. 375, 90 S. Ct. 1772, 26 L. Ed. 2d 339 (1970)*

[This began as an action in admiralty by a widow against a shipowner for the wrongful death of her husband, a longshoreman, in the territorial waters of Florida. The complaint alleged no negligence on the part of the owner, but rather that the ship was unseaworthy (an admiralty remedy amounting to strict liability for even a transient defect on board). Unfortunately for Moragne's widow, the case fell between the cracks of the patchwork of federal statutory wrongful death remedies, and although Florida's wrongful death statute would have worked had the widow pleaded negligence, under Florida law the tort of unseaworthiness was not cognizable.* Consequently, the District Court dismissed, and the Court of Appeals affirmed the dismissal, over the widow's argument that she should be entitled to recover under the general maritime law without regard to the federal statutes.]

MR. JUSTICE HARLAN delivered the opinion of the Court.

. . . [The] rule of maritime law that "in the absence of a statute there is no action for wrongful death," [was] first announced in *The Harrisburg,* 119 U.S. 199 (1886). . . .

## I

. . . Our analysis of the history of the common-law rule indicates that it was based on a particular set of factors that had, when *The Harrisburg* was decided, long since been thrown into discard even in England, and that had never existed in this country at all. . . .

. . . Because the primary duty already exists, the decision whether to allow recovery for violations causing death is entirely a remedial matter. . . .

Legal historians have concluded that the sole substantial basis for the rule at common law is a feature of the early English law that did not survive into this century—the felony-merger doctrine. . . . The . . . punishment for the felony was the death of the felon and the forfeiture of his property to the Crown; thus, after the crime had been punished, nothing remained of the felon or his property on which to base a civil action . . . for wrongful death. . . .

[In] this country the felony punishment did not include forfeiture of property; therefore, there was nothing, even in those limited instances, to bar a subsequent civil suit. . . . Nevertheless, . . . American courts generally adopted the English rule as the common law of this country as well. . . .

## II

We need not . . . pronounce a verdict on whether *The Harrisburg,* when decided, was a correct extrapolation of the principles of decisional law then in existence. A development of major significance has intervened, making clear that the rule against recovery for wrongful death is sharply out of keeping with the policies of modern American maritime law. This development is the wholesale abandonment of the rule in most of the area where it once held sway, quite evidently prompted by the same sense of the rule's injustice that generated so much criticism of its original promulgation. . . .

[The] legislatures both here and in England began to evidence unanimous disapproval of the rule against recovery for wrongful death. The first statute partially abrogating the rule was Lord Campbell's Act, 9 & 10 Vict., c. 93 (1846), which granted recovery to the families of persons killed by tortious conduct. . . .

---

* It was held that admiralty could employ the law of the state to remedy a death in the state's territorial waters, if the state intended its law to have such scope. [The] law of [the] State could be applied to a death on the high seas, if the State intended its law to have such scope. *The Hamilton,* 207 U.S. 398 (1907). —*Ed.*

In the United States, every State today has enacted a wrongful-death statute. The Congress has created actions for wrongful deaths of railroad employees, Federal Employers' Liability Act, 45 U.S.C. §§ 51-59; of merchant seamen, Jones Act, 46 U.S.C. § 688; and of persons on the high seas, Death on the High Seas Act, 46 U.S.C. §§ 761, 762. Congress has also, in the Federal Tort Claims Act, 28 U.S.C. § 1346(b), made the United States subject to liability in certain circumstances for negligently caused wrongful death to the same extent as a private person. . . .

These numerous and broadly applicable statutes, taken as a whole, make it clear that there is no present public policy against allowing recovery for wrongful death. The statutes evidence a wide rejection by the legislatures of whatever justifications may once have existed for a general refusal to allow such recovery. This legislative establishment of policy carries significance beyond the particular scope of each of the statutes involved. The policy thus established has become itself a part of our law, to be given its appropriate weight not only in matters of statutory construction but also in those of decisional law. . . .

### III

. . . Congress acted in 1920 to furnish the remedy denied by the courts for deaths beyond the jurisdiction of any State, by passing two landmark statutes. The first of these was the Death on the High Seas Act. . . . The second statute was the Jones Act, . . . which . . . provided a right of recovery [to seamen] against their employers for negligence resulting in injury or death. This right follows from the seaman's employment status and is not limited to injury or death occurring on the high seas.[11]

The United States, participating as *amicus curiae,* contended at oral argument that these statutes, if construed to forbid recognition of a general maritime remedy for wrongful death within territorial waters, would perpetuate three anomalies of present law. The first of these is simply the discrepancy produced whenever the rule of *The Harrisburg* holds sway: within territorial waters, identical conduct violating federal law (here the furnishing of an unseaworthy vessel) produces liability if the victim is merely injured, but frequently not if he is killed. . . .

The second incongruity is that identical breaches of the duty to provide a seaworthy ship, resulting in death, produce liability outside the three-mile limit—since a claim under the Death on the High Seas Act may be founded on unseaworthiness . . . but not within the territorial waters of a State whose local statute excludes unseaworthiness claims. . . .

The third, and assertedly the "strangest" anomaly is that a true seaman— that is, a member of a ship's company, covered by the Jones Act—is provided

---

[11] In 1927 Congress passed the Longshoremen's and Harbor Workers' Compensation Act, . . . granting to longshoremen the right to receive workmen's compensation benefits from their employers for accidental injury or death arising out of their employment. . . . The Act does not . . . affect the longshoreman's remedies against . . . a shipowner, and therefore does not bear on the problem before us except perhaps to serve as yet another example of congressional action to allow recovery for death in circumstances where recovery is allowed for nonfatal injuries.

no remedy for death caused by unseaworthiness within territorial waters, while a longshoreman, to whom the duty of seaworthiness was extended only because he performs work traditionally done by seamen, does have such a remedy when allowed by a state statute.

There is much force to the United States' argument that these distinctions are so lacking in any apparent justification that we should not, in the absence of compelling evidence, presume that Congress affirmatively intended to freeze them into maritime law. There should be no presumption that Congress has removed this Court's traditional responsibility to vindicate the policies of maritime law by ceding that function exclusively to the States. However, respondents argue that an intent to do just that is manifested by . . . portions of the Death on the High Seas Act. . . .

The legislative history of the Act suggests that respondents misconceive the thrust of the congressional concern. . . . The discussion of the bill on the floor of the House evidenced . . . concern that a cause of action be provided "in cases where there is now no remedy," 59 Cong. Rec. 4486, and at the same time that "the power of the States to create actions for wrongful death in no way be affected by enactment of the federal law." . . .

Congress intended to ensure the continued availability of a remedy, historically provided by the States, for deaths in territorial waters. . . . The void that existed in maritime law up until 1920 was the absence of any remedy for wrongful death on the high seas. Congress, in acting to fill that void, legislated only to the three-mile limit because that was the extent of the problem. The express provision that state remedies in territorial waters were not disturbed by the Act ensured that Congress' solution of one problem would not create another by inviting the courts to find that the Act pre-empted the entire field, destroying the state remedies that had previously existed.

. . . Congress in 1920 . . . legislated against a backdrop of state laws that imposed a standard of behavior generally the same as—and in some respects perhaps more favorable than—that imposed by federal maritime law.

Since that time the equation has changed drastically, through this Court's transformation of the shipowner's duty to provide a seaworthy ship into an absolute duty not satisfied by due diligence. . . . The unseaworthiness doctrine has become the principal vehicle for recovery by seamen for injury or death, overshadowing the negligence action made available by the Jones Act . . . ; and it has achieved equal importance for longshoremen and other harbor workers to whom the duty of seaworthiness was extended because they perform work on the vessel traditionally done by seamen. . . . The resulting discrepancy between the remedies for deaths covered by the Death on the High Seas Act and for deaths that happen to fall within a state wrongful-death statute not encompassing unseaworthiness could not have been foreseen by Congress. Congress merely declined to disturb state remedies at a time when they appeared adequate to effectuate the substantive duties imposed by general maritime law. That action cannot be read as an instruction to the federal courts that deaths in territorial waters, caused by breaches of the evolving duty of seaworthiness, must be *damnum absque injuria* unless the States expand their remedies to match the scope of the federal duty. . . .

Our recognition of a right to recover for wrongful death under general maritime law will assure uniform vindication of federal policies, removing the tensions and discrepancies that have resulted from the necessity to accommodate state remedial statutes to exclusively maritime substantive concepts. . . . Such uniformity not only will further the concerns of both of the 1920 Acts but also will give effect to the constitutionally based principle that federal admiralty law should be "a system of law coextensive with, and operating uniformly in, the whole country." *The Lottawanna,* 88 U.S. (21 Wall.) 558, 575 (1875). . . .

## IV

. . . The . . . established expectations of both those who own ships and those who work on them are that there is a duty to make the ship seaworthy and that a breach of that federally imposed duty will generally provide a basis for recovery. . . .

. . . Respect for the process of adjudication should be enhanced, not diminished, by our ruling today.

## V

Respondents argue that [our ruling today] will necessitate a long course of decisions to spell out the elements of the new "cause of action." We believe these fears are exaggerated, because our decision does not require the fashioning of a whole new body of federal law, but merely removes a bar to access to the existing general maritime law. . . .

Respondents argue, for example, that a statute of limitations must be devised . . . for the new wrongful-death claim. However, petitioner and the United States respond that . . . there is no reason . . . that such actions should not share the doctrine of laches immemorially applied to admiralty claims. In applying that doctrine, the argument runs, the courts should give consideration to the two-year statute of limitations in the Death on the High Seas Act, just as they have always looked for analogy to appropriate state or foreign statutes of limitations. . . . We need not decide this question now, because the present case was brought within a few months of the accident and no question of timeliness has been raised. The argument demonstrates, however, that the difficulties should be slight in applying accepted maritime law to actions for wrongful death.

The one aspect of a claim for wrongful death that has no precise counterpart in the established law governing nonfatal injuries is the determination of the beneficiaries who are entitled to recover. General maritime law, which denied any recovery for wrongful death, found no need to specify which dependents should receive such recovery. On this question, petitioner and the United States argue that we may look for guidance to the expressions of Congress, which has spoken on this subject in the Death on the High Seas Act, the Jones Act, and the Longshoremen's and Harbor Workers' Compensation Act. Though very similar, each of these provisions differs slightly in the naming of dependent relatives who may recover and in the priority given to their claims. . . .

The United States contends that, of the three, the provision that should be borrowed for wrongful-death actions under general maritime law is that of the Death on the High Seas Act. It is the congressional enactment that deals specifically and exclusively with actions for wrongful death, and that simply provides a remedy—for deaths on the high seas—for breaches of the duties imposed by general maritime law. . . .

We do not determine this issue now, for we think its final resolution should await further sifting through the lower courts in future litigation. . . . If still other subsidiary issues should require resolution, such as particular questions of the measure of damages, the courts will not be without persuasive analogy for guidance. Both the Death on the High Seas Act and the numerous state wrongful-death acts have been implemented with success for decades. The experience thus built up counsels that a suit for wrongful death raises no problems unlike those that have long been grist for the judicial mill. . . .

Reversed and remanded.

## NOTES ON *MORAGNE*

(1) *Federal common law in admiralty.* As *Moragne* exhibits, the post-*Erie* view is that federal common law is freely fashioned for admiralty cases. The Court hammered the point home early. See, e.g., *Garrett v. Moore-McCormack Co.,* 317 U.S. 239 (1942) (federal common law governs the validity of seamen's releases in state as in federal courts; one who sets up a seaman's release has the burden of proving there was no overreaching in obtaining it).

In *Pope & Talbot, Inc. v. Hawn,* 346 U.S. 406 (1953), the plaintiff, an injured maritime worker, sued shipowners in a federal diversity court. The shipowners relied on state law, which would have barred Hawn for contributory negligence. They argued that this suit was not brought on "the admiralty side" of the District Court, but on the "law side," in diversity; and that *Erie R. Co. v. Tompkins* required the application of state law in diversity cases. Justice Black, for the Court, gave short shrift to this argument: "Thus we are asked to use the *Erie-Tompkins* case to bring about the same kind of unfairness it was designed to end. Once again, the substantial rights of parties would depend on which courthouse, or even on which 'side' of the same courthouse, a lawyer might guess to be in the best interests of his client." The Court held that federal common law governed Hawn's claim.

(2) *Moragne as acute example of federal common law-making. Moragne* was the first judicially created remedy for wrongful death in Anglo-American history. As such it was an impressive exercise of judicial federal lawmaking power. See also the later case of *Carlson v. Green,* 556 U.S. 14 (1980), (implying a cause of action under the Eighth Amendment on behalf of survivors of a decedent federal prisoner).

(3) *The parallel legislation.* The *Moragne* cause of action was not implied "under" any of the several federal statutes dealing with maritime wrongful death. To today's reader, *Moragne* may seem to have been decided almost

*in the teeth* of the federal wrongful death statutes. But Justice Harlan identifies the policy underlying those statutes, and argues that this national policy itself had become part of the common law. Which of these views of the relationship between new common-law rights and existing statutory rights is the correct view?

(4) *Justice Harlan's use of the existing legislation: National policy and judge-made law.* It is a bedrock principle of the legal process that lawyers and courts consider how statutes and doctrine may apply to the facts of particular cases by identifying the "reason for the rule." Once the likely policies underlying law are ascertained, the application of the law to particular facts is clarified. Thus, the common law-making process inevitably seems to begin with the identification of the relevant sovereign's policy. And thus, in *Moragne,* when Justice Harlan saw existing acts of Congress as (in effect) establishing a national policy in favor of recovery for maritime wrongful deaths, he was able to fashion a common-law remedy to vindicate that policy more evenly. "The policy thus established has become itself a part of our law, to be given its appropriate weight not only in matters of statutory construction but also in those of decisional law. . . . "

But see *Kirkpatrick & Co., Inc. v. Environmental Tectonics Corporation, International,* 493 U.S. 400 (1990). There, in holding that the defendant could not avail itself of the defense that its conduct involved the nonjusticiable action of a foreign state, the Court, per Justice Scalia, went on to say: "Petitioners insist, however, that the policies underlying the act of state doctrine are implicated in the present case. . . . These urgings are deceptively similar to what we said in [*Banco Nacional de Cuba v. Sabbatino,* 493 U.S. 398, 428 (1964)], where we observed that sometimes . . . the policies underlying the [doctrine] may not justify its application. . . . [I]t is something quite different to suggest that those underlying policies are a doctrine unto themselves. . . . " What does Justice Scalia mean by this language in *Kirkpatrick*? Once having identified what national policy is, is a court free, under the Supremacy Clause, to disregard it?

Justice Harlan also argues in *Moragne* that universal state enactment of wrongful death statutes tells us what *national* policy is, or at least what it is not. Is this persuasive? Suppose all states enacted laws segregating the races in public schools. Doesn't *Brown v. Board of Education* suggest that supreme national policy would be quite different, and would have to be accepted by the states as state policy?

(5) *Expanding the Moragne cause of action: A federal tort for loss of consortium.* In *Sea-Land Services, Inc. v. Gaudet,* 414 U.S. 573 (1974), the Court, Justice Brennan, held that the nonstatutory maritime wrongful death action fashioned in *Moragne* would permit the widow of a maritime worker to recover damages for loss of "society." Six years later, in an action by the spouse of an injured but living worker for "loss of consortium," a plurality of Justices, Justice Brennan writing, was unable to distinguish *Gaudet,* and approved the remedy. *Am. Export Lines, Inc. v. Alvez,* 446 U.S. 274 (1980).

(6) *More on the problem of parallel legislation.* Some rules of law are in their nature so arbitrary or detailed that only a legislature would feel comfortable in creating them. Courts traditionally do not like to establish arbitrary periods

of limitation, for example. The defendant in *Moragne* argued that wrongful death is too statutory in nature for judicial lawmaking. Wrongful death statutes typically contain such inherently legislative matter as periods of limitation and schedules of beneficiaries. Should the Court have deferred to Congress? Should it at least have spelled out the content of the *Moragne* action, in the legislative manner, for example, of *Miranda v. Arizona*?

*Moragne* was limited to state territorial waters in *Mobile Oil Corp. v. Higginbotham,* 436 U.S. 618 (1978), on the theory that to do otherwise would be to allow end runs around the federal Death on the High Seas Act. Did *Higginbotham* reintroduce the remedial patchwork in admiralty wrongful death suits (Justice Harlan's term was "disparities") that *Moragne* had fairly cured? The dissenters in *Higginbotham* chastised the Court with the celebrated language of *The Sea Gull,* 21 F. Cas. 909, 910 (C.C.D. Md. 1865), by Chief Justice Chase, sitting on circuit:

> "[Certainly] it better becomes the humane and liberal character of proceedings in admiralty to give than to withhold the remedy, when not required to withhold it by established and inflexible rules."

State law was allowed to govern the wrongful death of a non-seaman engaged in recreational activity in territorial waters in *Yamaha Motor Corp. v. Calhoun,* 516 U.S. 199 (1996). Could an airline passenger's survivors sue under the general maritime law for a death on the high seas?

(7) *Lawmaking power implied from a special constitutional grant of jurisdiction.* Where did the *Moragne* Court get its power to fashion a new and utterly unprecedented common-law remedy as a matter *of federal law*? Interestingly, nothing in Article I explicitly gives Congress lawmaking power over maritime affairs. Under the early understandings of the scope of the commerce power, had the omission from Article I of an express delegation of maritime power been taken seriously, intrastate disputes arising on navigable waters would have been beyond the governance of Congress. *Cf. S. Pac. Co. v. Jensen, supra* this Chapter.

(8) *Unique legitimacy of federal common law in admiralty?* Is it appropriate to conclude that judge-made law, legitimate in admiralty, is uniquely legitimate in admiralty? Under that view, federal case law created by judges sitting in admiralty might not be legitimate if Congress' power to make maritime law derived not by implication from the Article III grant of jurisdiction, but from the Article I commerce power. Yet surely there are wellsprings of maritime legislative power in the Commerce Clause; the two streams of power flow in tandem and converge. Cf. *The Genesee Chief v. Fitzhugh,* 53 U.S. 443 (1851) (the true test of admiralty jurisdiction in tort is whether the claim arose on navigable waters); *The Daniel Ball,* 77 U.S. 557 (1871) (a stream is navigable if it is part of a "continued highway over which commerce may be carried on with other states or foreign countries").

And how relevant to judicial maritime lawmaking can admiralty *jurisdiction* be, anyway, when the power is exercised, as in *Moragne,* in diversity cases, and in state courts?

# PART B  SUPREMACY AND PREEMPTION

## PRELIMINARY NOTES ON FEDERAL LAW IN STATE AS WELL AS FEDERAL COURTS

Under Article VI of the Constitution of the United States, all judges, state and federal, like all other officials, must take an oath to support "this Constitution."[1] Under the Supremacy Clause,[2] all judges, state judges explicitly, are bound by federal law.[3] State courts not only can apply federal law, and do apply it every day, but also, under the Supremacy Clause, *must* apply it, when it is applicable.

Some students are surprised to learn that most issues of federal law were in the exclusive jurisdiction of the state courts until 1875. Until then, Congress had failed to enact a statute granting federal courts general jurisdiction over cases arising under federal law, like the one we have today.[4] Even after 1875, state courts had exclusive jurisdiction of cases arising under federal law in which the claims fell short of the statutory jurisdictional amount, until the jurisdictional amount was finally repealed. And the fact that state courts have a larger criminal jurisdiction than the federal courts means that they administer the bulk of federal constitutional defenses to criminal procedures under cases like *Mapp v. Ohio,* 367 U.S. 643 (1961) (holding that the Fourth Amendment exclusionary rule applies to the states) and *Miranda v. Arizona,* 384 U.S. 436 (1966) (holding that the Fifth Amendment privilege against unwarned confessions applies to the states).

---

## WHEN FEDERAL LAW GOVERNS: INTRODUCTORY NOTES ON SUPREMACY AND PREEMPTION

(1) *The presumption of dual governance and the vitality of state law.*  In thinking about the federal/state conflict of laws—the "vertical" conflict of laws, so to say—it may seem odd that any such conflict can occur. Under the Supremacy Clause, federal law should always trump, notwithstanding state law to the contrary.

But it turns out that state law has considerable scope notwithstanding the supremacy of federal law. The coexistence of state and federal laws does not always create a conflict. So state law and federal law often exist side by side.

---

[1] "The Senators and Representatives before mentioned, and the Members of the several State Legislatures, and all executive and judicial Officers, both of the United States and of the several States, shall be bound by Oath or Affirmation, to support this Constitution." U.S. Const., Art. VI, cl. 3.

[2] "This Constitution, and the Laws of the United States which shall be made in Pursuance thereof; and all Treaties made, or which shall be made, under the Authority of the United States, shall be the supreme Law of the Land." U.S. Const., Art. VI, cl. 2.

[3] "[And] the Judges in every State shall be bound thereby, any Thing in the Constitution or Laws of any State to the Contrary notwithstanding." U.S. Const., Art. VI, cl. 2.

[4] 28 U.S.C. § 1331.

If a national interest requires new federal law, by far the most usual recourse is to presume that both sovereigns can continue to govern together, each within its respective sphere.

American lawyers are comfortable with this dual governance. We understand that a client might have to pay both state and federal taxes. We are comfortable joining state and federal counts in a complaint, as alternative theories of recovery. Nothing in the federal count will necessarily diminish anything in the state count.

(2) **MONROE v. PAPE,** 365 U.S. 167 (1961). This was an action under the Civil Rights Act of 1871, 42 U.S.C. § 1983. The defendant police officers broke into the plaintiff's home in the early morning, made him stand naked in his living room, and ransacked his belongings—without warrant or probable cause. Section 1983, the statutory civil rights cause of action, had previously been little used because of narrow Supreme Court interpretations. The Court, by Justice Douglas, swept these away, in effect creating a modern action against state and local officials for damages for constitutional tort.[*]

JUSTICE FRANKFURTER (dissenting): "The cost . . . of providing a federal judicial remedy for every constitutional violation involves preemption by the National Government . . . of matters of intimate concern to state and local governments. . . . "

_____

Are Justice Frankfurter's fears of "preemption" warranted? State trespass theories are pleadable alongside the federal civil rights claim recognized in *Monroe.* The two counts may be freely joined in a complaint. In federal courts, the state count is within federal "pendent" jurisdiction, without regard to diversity of citizenship. And of course the civil rights tort that is brought to life in *Monroe* supplements state law only in cases in which the defendant is a government official.

(3) *Traditional spheres of governance.* It is true that, traditionally, there are matters that are understood to be more appropriately governed locally, and others that are felt to be properly governed by the nation. For example, in counseling a corporate client, American lawyers look to state law to govern the basic powers of corporate management and the corporation's ordinary contracts. But we look to federal law when the corporation's transactions implicate, for example, federal antitrust, securities, labor, or patent policies.

(4) *"Conflict preemption."* Federal *supremacy,* on the other hand, does come into play when there is some specific conflict between state and federal law. The existence of an actual conflict overcomes the presumption in favor of dual governance. Some members of the Supreme Court describe the operation of federal supremacy in such cases as "conflict preemption." *See generally* Louise Weinberg, *The Federal-State Conflict of Laws: "Actual" Conflicts,* in Symposium, "Federal Conflicts Law," 70 TEX. L. REV. 1743-1798 (1992).

---

[*] *See* Louise Weinberg, *The Monroe Mystery Solved: Beyond the "Unhappy History" Theory of Civil Rights Litigation,* 1991 B.Y.U. L. REV. 737 (1991).

(5) *"Field preemption."* On the other hand, when federal law is held to *preempt an entire field,* it does not matter whether or not there is some specific actual conflict. It does not even matter whether or not there exists any federal law in point. It does not matter even if state and federal law are *identical.* If the *field* is held "preempted," state law purporting to govern within the preempted field is simply a nullity. The states may not even speak to those issues.

(6) *Jurisdiction and choice of law.* In thinking about these issues, hang on to this: Jurisdiction is essentially *disjunct* from choice of law, even more so in "vertical" than in "horizontal" conflicts cases. The reasons should be pretty obvious. Under *Erie,* ultimate governance on state-law issues—in any court—belongs to some state. Similarly, under the Supremacy Clause, ultimate governance on federal-law issues—in any court—belongs to the nation. In both instances, the identity of the particular court simply does not matter. *See generally* Louise Weinberg, *The Power of Congress over Courts in Nonfederal Cases,* 1995 B.Y.U. L. Rev. 731-817 (1995).

---

## § 6.05 Supremacy

### TESTA v. KATT

*Supreme Court of the United States*
*330 U.S. 386, 67 S. Ct. 810, 91 L. Ed. 967 (1947)*

Mr. Justice Black delivered the opinion of the Court.

Section 205(e) of the Emergency Price Control Act provides that a buyer of goods at above the prescribed ceiling price may sue the seller "in any court of competent jurisdiction" for not more than three times the amount of the overcharge plus costs and a reasonable attorney's fee. Section 205(c) provides that the federal district courts shall have jurisdiction of such suits "concurrently with state and territorial courts.". . .

[Katt] was in the automobile business in Providence, . . . Rhode Island. In 1944 he sold an automobile to petitioner Testa, who also resides in Providence, for $1100, $210 above the ceiling price. [Testa] . . . filed this suit against [Katt] in the state District Court in Providence. Recovery was sought under § 205(e). The court awarded a judgment of treble damages and costs. . . . On appeal, the state Supreme Court reversed. . . . It held that an action for violation of § 205(e) could not be maintained in the courts of that state. The state Supreme Court . . . reasoned that: A state need not enforce the penal laws of a government which is foreign in the international sense; § 205(e) is treated by Rhode Island as penal in that sense; the Unite States is "foreign" to the state in the "private international" as distinguished from the "public international" sense; hence Rhode Island courts, though their jurisdiction is adequate to enforce similar Rhode Island "penal" statutes, need not enforce § 205(e). . . .

For the purposes of this case, we assume, without deciding, that § 205(e) is a penal statute in the "public international," "private international," or any other sense.[*] So far as the question of whether the Rhode Island courts properly declined to try this action, it makes no difference into which of these categories the Rhode Island court chose to place the statute which Congress has passed. For we cannot accept the basic premise on which the Rhode Island Supreme Court held that it has no more obligation to enforce a valid penal law of the United States than it has to enforce a penal law of another state or a foreign country. Such a broad assumption flies in the face of the fact that the states of the Union constitute a nation. It disregards the purpose and effect of article VI of the Constitution which provides:

> "This Constitution, and the Laws of the United States which shall be made in Pursuance thereof; and all Treaties made, or which shall be made, under the Authority of the United States, shall be the supreme Law of the Land; and the Judges in every State shall be bound thereby, any Thing in the Constitution or Laws of any State to the Contrary notwithstanding."

It cannot be assumed, the supremacy clause considered, that the responsibilities of a state to enforce the laws of a sister state are identical with its responsibilities to enforce federal laws. . . .

Violent public controversies existed throughout the first part of the 19th century . . . concerning the extent of the constitutional supremacy of the federal government. . . . But after the fundamental issues over the extent of federal supremacy had been resolved by war, this Court repudiated the assumption that federal laws can be considered by the states as though they were laws emanating from a foreign sovereign. . . .

. . . [In] *Mondou v. New York, N.H. & H.R. Co.,* 223 U.S. 1 (1912), this Court was presented with a case testing the power and duty of states to enforce federal laws. . . . This Court held that the Connecticut court could not decline to entertain [a Federal Employers' Liability Act claim]. The contention that enforcement of the congressionally created right was contrary to Connecticut policy was answered as follows:

> ". . . When Congress . . . adopted that act, it spoke for all the . . . states, and thereby established a policy for all. That policy is as much the policy of Connecticut as if the act had emanated from its own legislature. . . ."

So here, the fact that Rhode Island has an established policy against enforcement by its courts of statutes of other states and the United States which it deems penal, cannot be accepted as a "valid excuse." *Cf. Douglas v. New York, N.H. & H.R. Co.,* 279 U.S. 377, 388 (1929). For the policy of the federal act is the prevailing policy in every state. . . . [A] state court cannot refuse to enforce the right arising from the law of the United States because

---

[*] "Private international law" is an old-fashioned term for the conflict of laws in private litigation. "Public international law," on the other hand, deals with the work product of international organizations, conferences, and world courts, and tends to involve the rights of nations vis-á-vis each other. —Ed.

of conceptions of impolicy or want of wisdom on the part of Congress in having called into play its lawful powers.

The Rhode Island court . . . cites cases of this Court which [appear to have held to the contrary concerning the obligation of states to apply the laws of sister states under the full faith and credit clause]. But those holdings have no relevance here, for this case raises no full faith and credit question. . . . [Those] decisions did not bring before us our instant problem of the effect of the supremacy clause on the relation of federal laws to state courts. . . .

It is conceded that this same type of claim arising under Rhode Island law would be enforced by that state's courts. . . . Thus the Rhode Island courts have jurisdiction adequate and appropriate under established local law to adjudicate this action. Under these circumstances the state courts are not free to refuse enforcement of [Testa's] claim. The case is reversed and remanded for proceedings not inconsistent with this opinion.

## NOTES ON *TESTA*

(1) *The limited scope of federal supremacy.* In *Testa,* note that although Rhode Island's rule not recognizing "the penal law of another sovereign" was struck down under the Supremacy Clause, nothing in the opinion preempts Rhode Island's powers over its conflicts rules generally or even over its specific conflicts rule refusing to apply the penal law of another sovereign. The Supremacy Clause blocks only the feature of Rhode Island law that is in actual conflict with federal law: the state's rule declining jurisdiction in a case in which Congress has mandated that it take jurisdiction.

(2) *The "otherwise valid excuse."* Consider the analogy between *Testa* and *Hughes v. Fetter,* Chapter 5, *supra.* Under *Testa,* the state may not discriminate against the claimant with a federal claim. Under *Hughes,* a state may not discriminate against the claimant with a sister-state claim. But in both cases alike, any reasonable *procedural* bar applied *evenhandedly* should enable the state to decline jurisdiction. The state would have an "otherwise valid excuse." *Douglas v. New York, N.H. & H.R. Co.,* 279 U.S. 377, 388 (1929) (Holmes, J.). In *Douglas,* a state statute permitted discretionary dismissal of a claim for *forum non conveniens* when neither the plaintiff nor the defendant was a resident of the forum state. The state courts did not avail themselves of this "excuse," reasoning that *Douglas* was a claim under a federal statute, the Federal Employer's Liability Act (FELA), and that under the Supremacy Clause, state courts were under a duty to adjudicate the federal claim. But, perhaps surprisingly, the Supreme Court reversed and remanded, instructing the state that "there is nothing in the Act of Congress that purports to force a duty upon [state] courts as against an otherwise valid excuse."

Suppose state law differs from federal as a matter of the state's *substantive* policy. Should that furnish the state with an "otherwise valid excuse" from having to adjudicate a federal claim? In *Mondou v. New York, N.H. & H.R. Co.,* 223 U.S. 1, 57 (1912), the state court rejected an FELA claim as against state public policy. The Supreme Court held that the state must take the federal case, remarking, in effect, that under the Supremacy Clause, national policy *was* state policy.

**HOWLETT v. ROSE,** 496 U.S. 356 (1990). This case began as an action under the federal Civil Rights Act of 1871, 42 U.S.C. § 1983, in Florida state court. Plaintiff, a student, sought damages and injunctive relief for violation of his federal constitutional rights. He alleged that school officials had engaged in an unconstitutional search of his car on school premises, and had suspended him from classes without due process of law. He named as a defendant, among others, the school board. Under Florida law, a school board enjoys absolute sovereign immunity from suit in Florida courts. A Florida statute waived sovereign immunity, but the Florida Supreme Court had held that the waiver was only for claims under state tort law, and, specifically, that it did not apply to federal civil rights claims in Florida courts.

The trial court dismissed the student's civil rights claim against the school board. An appellate court affirmed the dismissal, and the Florida Supreme Court denied review.

*Held* (per JUSTICE STEVENS): Florida must take the federal civil rights case. "We conclude that whether the question is framed in preemption terms, as petitioner would have it, or in the obligation to assume jurisdiction over a 'federal' cause of action, as respondent would have it, the Florida court's refusal to entertain one discrete category of § 1983 claims, when the court entertains similar state law actions against state defendants, violates the Supremacy Clause.

"If Florida's law on the school board's immunity is treated as a 'substantive' difference between federal and state laws governing defenses of governments to § 1983 claims, it is preempted by federal law to the contrary. If it is treated as a 'procedural' characteristic of state courts, it is not an 'otherwise valid excuse' because it is not neutral. The state here, clearly, is 'discriminating against federal causes of action.'. . . Federal law is enforceable in state courts . . . because the Constitution and laws passed pursuant to it are as much laws in the States as laws passed by the state legislature. The Supremacy Clause makes those laws 'the supreme Law of the Land,' and charges state courts with a coordinate responsibility to enforce that law according to their regular modes of procedure. . . . "

For recent comment on trial of federal civil rights cases in state courts, see R. Perry Sentell, Jr., *Local Government and Constitutional Torts: In the Georgia Courts,* 49 MERCER L. REV. 1 (1997).

(3) *The disingenuous "excuse."* To what extent can a state further a substantive policy preference by imposing a disingenuous procedural or jurisdictional hurdle in the way of trial of a federal claim? On this question Justice Stevens remarked in *Howlett* : "The force of the Supremacy Clause is not so weak that it can be evaded by mere mention of the word 'jurisdiction.'. . . The Supremacy Clause requires more than that." Something of this sort might, in fact, have been in the background in *Howlett.* Florida's refusal to waive its immunity in federal civil rights cases, and its adherence to this position in *Howlett* —a case against a school board—might reflect a substantive state policy hostile

to judicially supervised racial desegregation of schools. As this hypothesis suggests, the more substantive the state policy that is in conflict with federal, the quicker, under the Supremacy Clause, it should fall.

(4) *The discriminatory procedural bar.* Both *Testa* and *Howlett* embrace the notion that the state courts may not *discriminate* against plaintiffs relying on federal law. Under both *Howlett* and *Testa* the discriminatory state procedural bar will be ineffective.

*McKnett v. St. Louis & S. F. Ry.,* 292 U.S. 230 (1934), was factually similar to *Howlett* in this respect. In *McKnett,* the Alabama Supreme Court dismissed an action under the FELA for an accident which had occurred out of the state. The reason given was that an Alabama statute required dismissal of cases arising out of state. The statute had been repealed, *but only with respect to state-law claims.* In reversing dismissal of the federal claim, the Supreme Court, per Justice Brandeis, pointed out that the Alabama dismissal was based solely on "the source of law to be enforced. . . . The plaintiff is cast out because he is suing to enforce a federal act. A state may not discriminate against rights arising under federal laws."

In *Testa,* Rhode Island courts did purport evenhandedly to refuse to enforce the penal laws of other sovereigns, whether state or federal. Justice Black found discrimination nevertheless in the fact that Rhode Island enforced similar Rhode Island statutes. Suppose, in *Testa,* Rhode Island refused to enforce *all* civil penal laws, including those of Rhode Island. Shouldn't its obligation under the Supremacy Clause still be to take the federal statutory claim for treble damages? Given the imperatives of federal supremacy, why should a state's procedures ever excuse it from its obligation to take federal cases? Even if a state procedure bars state and federal claims evenhandedly, what difference can that make to the national interest in enforcement of the particular right? For example, if in *Howlett* the state had evenhandedly refused to enforce all actions against school boards, including actions under state law, wouldn't its obligation under the Supremacy Clause still be to take a federal civil rights suit against a school board? *Cf. State Dep't of Public Safety v. Brown,* 794 P.2d 108 (Alaska 1991), in which the Alaska supreme court held that Alaska must take a federal Jones Act case against the statutory "employer" even when the employer was Alaska itself. Under the Supremacy Clause, the Alaska court reasoned, neither Alaska's sovereign immunity nor the Alaska Workers' Compensation Act could bar the federal suit.

(5) *The relation between the "supremacy" cases and cases of "conflict preemption."* We tend to think of *Testa* as speaking to the obligation of state courts to give access to federal claims. But in *Testa,* isn't there simply a conflict between state law and federal law? Is there any good reason for treating the case as one of access or subject-matter jurisdiction? Since federal law conflicts with state law in *Testa,* why doesn't it simply preempt state law?

We seem to have two doctrinally separate but overlapping lines of federal cases. The first, the *supremacy* cases, deal with cases of conflict between federal and state law in state courts. The second, the cases of *preemption of conflicting state law,* deal with cases of conflict between federal and state law in *both* sets of courts. What justifies this doctrinal duplicativeness? In *Howlett,* indeed, Justice Stevens remarks that it does not matter whether he analyzes the case under supremacy doctrines or as a case of preemption: it would come out the same under either theory.

To be sure, the problem of conflicting state *procedure* can arise only in state court. Is that a good enough reason for preserving the doctrinal separateness of the supremacy cases, with all its baggage: the discrimination against the federal claims, and the "otherwise valid excuse?"

(6) *The tyranny of state procedure: Taking state courts as we find them.* It is commonly said that federal law takes the state courts as it finds them. Henry Hart, *The Relations Between State and Federal Law,* 54 COLUM. L. REV. 489, 508 (1954). This view has its source in the notion that the states are under no duty to build courts in the first place. See *Douglas, supra,* 279 U.S. at 387 (noting that Congress does not purport to compel states to create courts to hear a federal claim). From this bizarre hypothesis of a courtless state, the Supreme Court reasons that when litigants adjudicate in state courts they must generally be bound by state procedural and administrative rules. Thus, the state usually is free to vindicate any nondiscriminatory procedural policy in the trial of a federal as well as a state case. If that means a federal claim in fact does not get heard, no matter. The state has an "otherwise valid excuse."

---

## § 6.06 "Reverse-*Erie*:" The Administration of Federal Law in State Courts

### INTRODUCTION: FEDERAL SUBSTANCE AND STATE PROCEDURE

Under the Supremacy Clause, state judges often will have to fashion an answer to a federal question. They must in good faith discern the resolution in light of national, rather than local, policies. But it is one of the ironies of federal supremacy that procedural policies of the state might be effective to bar enforcement of a federal claim, while state substantive policies could not. The more strongly the state's policy is held, the more quickly it falls, under the Supremacy Clause. A state dismissing a school desegregation suit under the federal Civil Rights Act, could, within limits, do so on the ground that a relevant statute of limitations had run for all personal injuries claims of that vintage in that state. *See, e.g., Wilson v. Garcia,* 471 U.S. 261 (1985). But the state could not dismiss on the ground that its own *substantive* law and policy favored segregated schools.

Should state courts be free in all cases to apply their own procedures to federal claims? What happens if the state procedure seriously impedes vindication of federal policy? In such a case, the Supremacy Clause might well require a state court to follow federal procedure. The following remains the classic case on the problem.

# DICE v. AKRON

*Supreme Court of the United States*
*342 U.S. 359, 72 S. Ct. 312, 96 L. Ed. 398 (1952)*

Opinion of the Court by MR. JUSTICE BLACK, announced by MR. JUSTICE DOUGLAS.

Petitioner, a railroad fireman, was seriously injured when an engine in which he was riding jumped the track. Alleging that his injuries were due to respondent's negligence, he brought this action for damages under the Federal Employers' Liability Act, in an Ohio court of common pleas. Respondent's defenses were (1) a denial of negligence and (2) a written document signed by petitioner purporting to release respondent in full for $924.63. Petitioner admitted that he had signed several receipts for payments made him in connection with his injuries but denied that he had made a full and complete settlement of all his claims. He alleged that the purported release was void because he had signed it relying on respondent's deliberately false statement that the document was nothing more than a mere receipt for back wages.

After both parties had introduced considerable evidence the jury found in favor of petitioner and awarded him a $25,000 verdict. The trial judge later entered judgment notwithstanding the verdict. In doing so he reappraised the evidence as to fraud, found that petitioner had been "guilty of supine negligence" in failing to read the release, and accordingly held that the facts did not "sustain either in law or equity the allegations of fraud by clear, unequivocal and convincing evidence."[1] This judgment notwithstanding the verdict was reversed by the Court of Appeals of Summit County, Ohio, on the ground that under federal law, which controlled, the jury's verdict must stand because there was ample evidence to support its finding of fraud. The Ohio Supreme Court, one judge dissenting, reversed the Court of Appeals' judgment and sustained the trial court's action, holding that: (1) Ohio, not federal, law governed; (2) under that law petitioner, a man of ordinary intelligence who could read, was bound by the release even though he had been induced to sign it by the deliberately false statement that it was only a receipt for back wages; and (3) under controlling Ohio law factual issues as to fraud in the execution of this release were properly decided by the judge rather than by the jury. We granted certiorari because the decision of the Supreme Court of Ohio appeared to deviate from previous decisions of this Court that federal law governs cases arising under the Federal Employers' Liability Act.

*First.* We agree with the Court of Appeals of Summit County, Ohio, and the dissenting judge in the Ohio Supreme Court and hold that validity of releases under the Federal Employers' Liability Act raises a federal question

---

[1] The trial judge had charged the jury that petitioner's claim of fraud must be sustained "by clear and convincing evidence," but since the verdict was for petitioner, he does not here challenge this charge as imposing too heavy a burden under controlling federal law.

to be determined by federal rather than state law. Congress in § 1 of the Act granted petitioner a right to recover against his employer for damages negligently inflicted. State laws are not controlling in determining what the incidents of this federal right shall be. Manifestly the federal rights affording relief to injured railroad employees under a federally declared standard could be defeated if states were permitted to have the final say as to what defenses could and could not be properly interposed to suits under the Act. Moreover, only if federal law controls can the federal Act be given that uniform application throughout the country essential to effectuate its purposes. Releases and other devices designed to liquidate or defeat injured employees' claims play an important part in the federal Act's administration. Their validity is but one of the many interrelated questions that must constantly be determined in these cases according to a uniform federal law.

*Second.* In effect the Supreme Court of Ohio held that an employee trusts his employer at his peril, and that the negligence of an innocent worker is sufficient to enable his employer to benefit by its deliberate fraud. Application of so harsh a rule to defeat a railroad employee's claim is wholly incongruous with the general policy of the Act to give railroad employees a right to recover just compensation for injuries negligently inflicted by their employers. And this Ohio rule is out of harmony with modern judicial and legislative practice to relieve injured persons from the effect of releases fraudulently obtained. We hold that the correct federal rule is that announced by the Court of Appeals of Summit County, Ohio, and the dissenting judge in the Ohio Supreme Court—a release of rights under the Act is void when the employee is induced to sign it by the deliberately false and material statements of the railroad's authorized representatives made to deceive the employee as to the contents of the release. The trial court's charge to the jury correctly stated this rule of law.

*Third.* Ohio provides and has here accorded petitioner the usual jury trial of factual issues relating to negligence. But Ohio treats factual questions of fraudulent releases differently. It permits the judge trying a negligence case to resolve all factual questions of fraud "other than fraud in the factum." The factual issue of fraud is thus split into fragments, some to be determined by the judge, others by the jury.

It is contended that since a state may consistently with the Federal Constitution provide for trial of cases under the Act by a nonunanimous verdict, *Minneapolis & St. Louis R. Co. v. Bombolis,* 241 U.S. 211 (1916), Ohio may lawfully eliminate trial by jury as to one phase of fraud while allowing jury trial as to all other issues raised. The *Bombolis* case might be more in point had Ohio abolished trial by jury in all negligence cases including those arising under the federal Act. But Ohio has not done this. It has provided jury trials for cases arising under the federal Act but seeks to single out one phase of the question of fraudulent releases for determination by a judge rather than by a jury.

. . . The right to trial by jury is a basic and fundamental feature of our system of federal jurisprudence and . . . it is part and parcel of the remedy afforded railroad workers under the Employers' Liability Act. . . . [To] deprive railroad workers of the benefit of a jury trial where there is evidence to support negligence is to take away a goodly portion of the relief which Congress has afforded them. It follows that the right to trial by jury is too substantial a part of the rights accorded by the Act to permit it to be classified as a mere local rule of procedure for denial in the manner that Ohio has here used.

The trial judge and the Ohio Supreme Court erred in holding that petitioner's rights were to be determined by Ohio law and in taking away petitioner's verdict when the issues of fraud had been submitted to the jury on conflicting evidence and determined in petitioner's favor. The judgment of the Court of Appeals of Summit County, Ohio, was correct and should not have been reversed by the Supreme Court of Ohio. The cause is reversed and remanded to the Supreme Court of Ohio for further action not inconsistent with this opinion. . . .

MR. JUSTICE FRANKFURTER, whom MR. JUSTICE REED, MR. JUSTICE JACKSON and MR. JUSTICE BURTON join, concurring for reversal but dissenting from the Court's opinion.

. . . To require Ohio to try a particular issue before a different fact-finder in negligence actions brought under the Employers' Liability Act from the fact-finder on the identical issue in every other negligence case disregards the settled distribution of judicial power between Federal and State courts where Congress authorizes concurrent enforcement of federally-created rights.

It has been settled ever since the *Second Employers' Liability Cases* (*Mondou v. New York, N.H. & H.R. Co.*), 223 U.S. 1 ( — —), that no State which gives its courts jurisdiction over common law actions for negligence may deny access to its courts for a negligence action founded on the Federal Employers' Liability Act. Nor may a State discriminate disadvantageously against actions for negligence under the Federal Act as compared with local causes of action in negligence. *McKnett v. St. Louis & S.F.R. Co.*, 292 U.S. 230, 234 (1934); *Missouri ex rel. Southern R. Co. v. Mayfield*, 340 U.S. 1, 4 (1950). Conversely, however, simply because there is concurrent jurisdiction in Federal and State courts over actions under the Employers' Liability Act, a State is under no duty to treat actions arising under that Act differently from the way it adjudicates local actions for negligence, so far as the mechanics of litigation, the forms in which law is administered, are concerned. . . .

Ohio and her sister States with a similar division of functions between law and equity are not trying to evade their duty under the Federal Employers' Liability Act; nor are they trying to make it more difficult for railroad workers to recover, than for those suing under local law. The States merely exercise a preference in adhering to historic ways of dealing with a claim of fraud; they prefer the traditional way of making unavailable through equity an otherwise valid defense. . . . The fact that Congress authorized actions under the Federal Employers' Liability Act to be brought in State as well as in Federal courts seems a strange basis for the inference that Congress overrode State procedural arrangements controlling all other negligence suits in a State, by imposing upon State courts to which plaintiffs choose to go the rules prevailing in the Federal courts regarding juries. Such an inference is admissible, so it seems to me, only on the theory that Congress included as part of the right created by the Employers' Liability Act an assumed likelihood that trying all issues to juries is more favorable to plaintiffs. . . .

. . . [Two] questions remain for decision: Should the validity of the release be tested by a Federal or a State standard? And if by a Federal one, did the Ohio courts in the present case correctly administer the standard? If the States afford courts for enforcing the Federal Act, they must enforce the substance of the right given by Congress. They cannot depreciate the legislative currency issued by Congress—either expressly or by local methods of enforcement that accomplish the same result. . . . In order to prevent diminution of railroad workers' nationally-uniform right to recover, the standard for the validity of a release of contested liability must be Federal. . . . One who attacks a settlement must bear the burden of showing that the contract he has made is tainted with invalidity, either by fraud practiced upon him or by a mutual mistake under with both parties acted. [Federal citation omitted.] . . .

The judgment of the Ohio Supreme Court must be reversed for it applied the State rule as to validity of releases. . . . [We] would return the case for further proceedings on the sole question of fraud in the release.

---

## NOTES ON *DICE*

(1) *The federal right to trial by jury in Dice.* Are you clear why the Seventh Amendment right to trial by jury in civil cases was not an issue in *Dice*? The right to trial by jury is a statutory right under the FELA. But suppose the statute had been silent, and that the Supreme Court had declared the same right to trial by jury as a matter of federal common law. Would the result be the same?

(2) *The release.* Note the insistence of the Court that a contract of release of a federal statutory claim, or at least this statutory claim, cannot be governed by state law. Instead, apparently there is a federal common law of contracts for this issue.

The Court fashions the federal common-law rule for the case, deriving it from previous authority. The Court places an extraordinary burden on the railway defendant in an FELA case. From the discussion in the case, can you identify the national policy that justifies this? See also *Garrett v. Moore-McCormack Co.*, 317 U.S. 239 (1942) (holding that a state court must apply federal common law to determine the validity of a seaman's release, and imposing substantial burdens on a shipowner pleading a defense of release, a seaman being the ward of the admiralty). Note that the Jones Act, which furnishes a negligence remedy to seamen as against their employers, simply incorporates the FELA.

# AMERICAN DREDGING CO. v. MILLER

*Supreme Court of the United States*
*510 U.S. 443, 114 S. Ct. 981, 127 L. Ed. 2d 285 (1994)*

JUSTICE SCALIA delivered the opinion of the Court.

This case presents the question whether, in admiralty cases filed in a state court . . ., federal law preempts state law regarding the doctrine of *forum non conveniens.*

## I

William Robert Miller, a resident of Mississippi, . . . [worked] as a seaman aboard the M/V JOHN R., a tug operating on the Delaware River. In the course of that employment [Miller] was injured. . . . [He] returned to Mississippi where he continued to be treated by local physicians.

. . . [Miller] filed this action in the [state court] in . . . Louisiana. He sought relief under the Jones Act, which authorizes a seaman who suffers personal injury "in the course of his employment" to bring "an action for damages at law," 46 U.S.C. § 688, and over which state and federal courts have concurrent jurisdiction. [Miller] also requested relief under general maritime law. . . .

The [Louisiana] trial court granted [American Dredging's] motion to dismiss the action under the doctrine of *forum non conveniens,* holding that it was bound to apply that doctrine by federal maritime law. The Louisiana Court of Appeal . . . affirmed. The Supreme Court of Louisiana reversed, holding that Article 123 of the Louisiana Code of Civil Procedure, which renders the doctrine of *forum non conveniens* unavailable [in maritime cases] in Louisiana state courts, is not preempted by federal maritime law. . . .

## II

. . . In exercising [its concurrent admiralty] jurisdiction, . . . a state court may "adopt such remedies, and . . . attach to them such incidents, as it sees fit so long as it does not attempt to make changes in the substantive maritime law." *Red Cross Line v. Atlantic Fruit Co.,* 264 U.S. 109, 124 (1924). That proviso is violated when the state remedy "works material prejudice to the characteristic features of the general maritime law or interferes with the proper harmony and uniformity of that law in its international and interstate relations." *Southern Pacific Co. v. Jensen,* 244 U.S. 205, 216 (1917). The issue before us here is whether the doctrine of *forum non conveniens* is either a "characteristic feature" of admiralty or a doctrine whose uniform application is necessary to maintain the "proper harmony" of maritime law. . . .[1]

---

[1] JUSTICE STEVENS asserts that we should not test the Louisiana law against the standards of *Jensen,* a case which, though never explicitly overruled, is in his view as discredited as *Lochner v. New York,* 198 U.S. 45 (1905). [American Dredging's] preemption argument was primarily based

## A

Under the federal doctrine of *forum non conveniens,* "when an alternative forum has jurisdiction to hear [a] case, and when trial in the chosen forum would 'establish . . . oppressiveness and vexation to a defendant . . . out of all proportion to plaintiff's convenience,' or when the 'chosen forum [is] inappropriate because of considerations affecting the court's own administrative and legal problems,' the court may, in the exercise of its sound discretion, dismiss the case, even if jurisdiction and proper venue are established." *Piper Aircraft Co. v. Reyno,* 454 U.S. 235 (1981). . . .

. . . Our most recent opinion dealing with *forum non conveniens, Piper,* at 248, recognized that the doctrine "originated in Scotland, and became part of the common law of many States," and treated the *forum non conveniens* analysis of . . . an admiralty case as binding precedent in the nonadmiralty context.

[The] doctrine of *forum non conveniens* neither originated in admiralty nor has exclusive application there. To the contrary, it is and has long been a doctrine of general application. Louisiana's refusal to apply *forum non conveniens* does not, therefore, work "material prejudice to [a] characteristic [feature] of the general maritime law." *Southern Pacific Co. v. Jensen,* 244 U.S., at 216.

## B

[American Dredging] correctly points out that the decision here under review produces disuniformity. . . . We must therefore consider whether Louisiana's rule "interferes with the proper harmony and uniformity" of maritime law, *Southern Pacific Co. v. Jensen,* at 216. . . .

. . . [We] disallowed in *Jensen* the application of state workers' compensation statutes to injuries covered by the admiralty jurisdiction. Later, in *Knickerbocker Ice Co. v. Stewart,* 253 U.S. 149, 163-164 (1920), we held that not even Congress itself could permit such application and thereby sanction destruction of the constitutionally prescribed uniformity. . . .

The requirement of uniformity is not, however, absolute. . . :

". . . State-created liens are enforced in admiralty. State remedies for wrongful death and state statutes providing for the survival of actions . . . have been upheld when applied to maritime causes of action. . . . State rules for the partition and sale of ships, state laws governing the specific performance of arbitration agreements, state laws regulating the effect of a breach of warranty under contracts of maritime insurance—all these laws and others have been accepted as rules of decision in admiralty cases, even, at times, when they conflicted with

---

upon the principles established in *Jensen,* as repeated in . . . later cases (which JUSTICE STEVENS also disparages). . . . [Miller] did not assert that those principles had been repudiated; nor did the Solicitor General, who, in support of [Miller], discussed *Jensen* at length. Since we ultimately find that the Louisiana law meets the standards of *Jensen* anyway, we think it inappropriate to overrule *Jensen* in dictum, and without argument or even invitation.

a rule of maritime law which did not require uniformity." *Romero v. International Terminal Operating Co.,* 358 U.S. 354, 373-374 (1959)).

. . . *[Forum] non conveniens* . . . is in two respects quite dissimilar from any other matter that our opinions have held to be governed by federal admiralty law: it is procedural rather than substantive, and it is most unlikely to produce uniform results.

Because the doctrine is one of procedure rather than substance, [American Dredging] is wrong to claim support from our decision in *Pope & Talbot, Inc. v. Hawn,* 346 U.S. 406 (1953), which held that Pennsylvania courts must apply the admiralty rule that contributory negligence is no bar to recovery. The other case [American Dredging] relies on, *Garrett v. Moore-McCormack Co.,* 317 U.S. 239, 248-249 (1942), held that the traditional maritime rule placing the burden of proving the validity of a release upon the defendant preempts state law placing the burden of proving invalidity upon the plaintiff. . . . Unlike burden of proof . . ., *forum non conveniens* does not bear upon the substantive right to recover, and is not a rule upon which maritime actors rely in making decisions about primary conduct—how to manage their business and what precautions to take.[4] . . .

C

. . . [We] have held that the Jones Act [which replicates for seamen the negligence remedy against employers provided for railway workers in the Federal Employers Liability Act, like the FELA requires] state courts to apply a uniform federal law. *Garrett v. Moore-McCormack Co.,* 317 U.S. 239, 244 (1942). [Despite] that uniformity requirement we held in *Missouri ex rel. Southern R. Co. v. Mayfield,* 340 U.S. 1, 4-5 (1950), that a state court presiding over an action pursuant to the FELA "should be freed to decide the availability of the principle of *forum non conveniens* in these suits according to its own local law." We declared *forum non conveniens* to be a matter of "local policy," a proposition well substantiated by the local nature of the "public factors" relevant to the *forum non conveniens* determination.

We think it evident that the rule which *Mayfield* announced for the FELA applies as well to the Jones Act. . . . [For] practical reasons, a seaman will almost always combine in a single action claims for relief under the Jones Act and general maritime law. It would produce dissonance rather than harmony to hold that his claims for unseaworthiness and maintenance and cure, but not his Jones Act claim, could be dismissed for *forum non conveniens* . . . .

JUSTICE SOUTER, concurring.

I join in the opinion of the Court because I agree that in most cases the characterization of a state rule as substantive or procedural will be a sound

---

[4] . . . The dissent is wrong to say . . . that the federal court in a State with the Louisiana rule may as well accept jurisdiction, since otherwise the state court will. That is no more true of *forum non conveniens* than it is of venue. . . . Federal courts will continue to invoke *forum non conveniens* to decline jurisdiction in appropriate cases, whether or not the State in which they sit chooses to burden its judiciary with litigation better handled elsewhere.

surrogate for the conclusion that would follow from a more discursive preemption analysis. The distinction between substance and procedure will, however, sometimes be obscure. As to those close cases, how a given rule is characterized for purposes of determining whether federal maritime law preempts state law will turn on whether the state rule unduly interferes with the federal interest in maintaining the free flow of maritime commerce.

JUSTICE STEVENS, concurring in part and concurring in the judgment.

. . . In my view, *Jensen* is just as untrustworthy a guide in an admiralty case today as *Lochner v. New York,* 198 U.S. 45 (1905), would be in a case under the Due Process Clause.* . . . We should jettison *Jensen* 's special maritime preemption doctrine and its abstract standards of "proper harmony" and "characteristic features."

The *Jensen* decision and its progeny all rested upon the view that a strong preemption doctrine was necessary [for the] protection of maritime commerce. . . . [We] should recognize that, today, . . . to the extent that the mere assertion of state judicial power may threaten maritime commerce, the Due Process Clause provides an important measure of protection for out-of-state defendants, especially foreigners. See *Asahi Metal Industry Co. v. Superior Court of California,* 480 U.S. 102 (1987); *Helicopteros Nacionales de Colombia v. Hall,* 466 U.S. 408 (1984). Extension of the ill-advised doctrine of *Jensen* is not the appropriate remedy for unreasonable state venue rules. Accordingly, I concur in the judgment and in Part II-C of the opinion of the Court.

JUSTICE KENNEDY, with whom JUSTICE THOMAS joins, dissenting.

. . . From the historical evidence, there seems little doubt to me that *forum non conveniens* is an essential and salutary feature of admiralty law. It gives ship owners and operators a way to avoid vexatious litigation on a distant and unfamiliar shore. By denying this defense in all maritime cases, Louisiana upsets international and interstate comity and obstructs maritime trade, and by sanctioning Louisiana's law, a rule explicable only by some desire to disfavor maritime defendants, the Court condones the forum shopping and disuniformity that the admiralty jurisdiction is supposed to prevent.

In committing their ships to the general maritime trade, owners and operators run an unusual risk of being sued in venues with little or no connection to the subject matter of the suit. A wage dispute between crewman and captain or an accident on board the vessel may erupt into litigation when the ship docks in a faraway port. Taking jurisdiction in these cases, instead of allowing them to be resolved when the ship returns home, disrupts the schedule of the ship and may aggravate relations with the state from which it hales. . . .

. . . These realities cannot be obscured by characterizing the defense as procedural. . . . Procedural or substantive, the *forum non conveniens* defense promotes comity and trade. The States are not free to undermine these goals.

---

*In *Lochner v. New York,* 198 U.S. 45 (1905), the Supreme Court struck down a New York statute providing a 12-hour maximum workday for bakers. The Court reasoned that the legislature had violated the parties' liberty of contract, within the meaning of "liberty" in the Due Process Clause of the Fourteenth Amendment. Today *Lochner* is discredited. —*Ed.*

It is true that in *Missouri ex rel. Southern R. Co. v. Mayfield,* 340 U.S. 1 (1950), we held the state courts free to ignore *forum non conveniens* in FELA cases. But we did not consider the maritime context. Unlike [the] FELA, . . . admiralty law is international in its concern. A state court adjudicating [an] FELA dispute interposes no obstacle to our foreign relations. . . .

Amicus the Solicitor General has urged that we limit our holding, that forum non conveniens is not part of the uniform law of admiralty, to cases involving domestic entities. We think it unnecessary to do that. Since the parties to this suit are domestic entities it is quite impossible for our holding to be any broader. . . .

---

# NOTES ON *MILLER*

(1) *Background: The problem in the Fifth Circuit.* At the time of *Miller,* the United States Court of Appeals for the Fifth Circuit was struggling with the difficulty that two major maritime states in that Circuit, Texas and Louisiana, were unwilling to follow federal *forum non conveniens* doctrine in transnational maritime cases brought to their courts. Compare *Exxon Corp. v. Chick Kam Choo,* 817 F.2d 307 (5th Cir.), reversed on other grounds, 486 U.S. 140 (1988) (holding that state courts in the geographical area covered by the Fifth Circuit must apply federal forum non conveniens rules in admiralty saving-clause cases), with *In re Aircrash Disaster in New Orleans,* 821 F.2d 1147 (5th Cir. 1987), vacated on other grounds sub nom. *Pan Am. World Airways, Inc., v. Lopez,* 490 U.S. 1032 (1989) (holding that in diversity cases in the Fifth Circuit federal courts are free to apply federal forum-non-conveniens rules). To what extent, precisely, does *Miller* speak to these Fifth Circuit cases? After Miller, are Louisiana and Texas free in maritime cases to hold themselves bound by *Miller*?

(2) *Is forum non conveniens outcome-determinative*? Justice Scalia, for the *Miller* Court, argues that forum non conveniens is "procedural," and technically, of course, forum non conveniens is a matter apart from the merits of a case. But he does not address the question whether in federal cases the doctrine is likely to be outcome-determinative where applied. In federal courts common-law forum non conveniens is limited to transnational litigation, because the transfer statute supersedes the doctrine in domestic cases. But can a transnational personal-injuries case survive dismissal from an American court and separation from American contingency-fee lawyers? *See* Louise Weinberg, *The Helicopter Case and the Jurisprudence of Jurisdiction,* 58 So. CAL. L. REV. 913, & nn. 110-111 (1985).

(3) *Miller and the coordinate national powers.* The Jones Act, as amended, denies a federal maritime cause of action to foreign oil rig workers injured in foreign waters, unless no other remedy is available. 46 U.S.C. § 688(b). Could a Louisiana court refuse to dismiss a Jones Act claim barred by § 688(b)? If the Louisiana court is bound to apply the Act of Congress, why should it not be bound to apply federal case law on forum non conveniens? Why not,

for example, in an action by a foreign maritime worker not engaged in oil-drilling and therefore not covered by the statute?

(4) *Miller and American litigants.* Both the Court and the parties in *Miller* assume without discussion that federal courts can close their doors to an American citizen suing an American company, while reserving the question whether federal courts can close their doors to a foreigner. Yet in *Piper Aircraft Co. v. Reyno*, 454 U.S. 235, 255 (1981), the Supreme Court took the view that American plaintiffs in a transnational case generally should have a home forum. And how is it possible for an American defendant to argue that it is inconvenient for it to stand trial at home?

(5) *Justice Scalia's slight overstatement.* Justice Scalia quotes language from the 1959 *Romero* case intended to show that state law is alive and well in admiralty. But the *Romero* examples are obsolete. To be sure, state law *is* alive and well in admiralty. State law is habitually adopted in maritime cases to flesh out federal rules of decision. But as to nonstatutory maritime death claims, federal law has governed those ever since *Moragne v. States Marine Lines, Inc., supra.* [a] Federal common law also determines the validity and meaning of maritime contracts.[b] As for maritime arbitration agreements, today, under the influence of the Federal Arbitration Act, federal and not state law governs the specific performance of maritime agreements to arbitrate.

(6) *Other state remedies and federal admiralty.* Could a state court adjudicating a maritime case give *relief* of a kind unknown to federal admiralty courts? The Supreme Court has never held that federal courts sitting in admiralty have general power to issue injunctions, and it is often said that there is no such power. (*But see Pino v. Protection Maritime Ins. Co., Ltd.,* 599 F.2d 10 (1st Cir.), cert. denied, 444 U.S. 900 (1979)). Should state courts adjudicating maritime cases be permitted to issue injunctions? *Cf. Red Cross Line v. Atlantic Fruit Co.,* 264 U.S. 109 (1924).

———

See for a recent attempt to re-think federal common lawmaking authority in admiralty, Jonathan M. Gutoff, *Federal Common Law and Congressional Delegation: A Reconceptualization of Admiralty,* 42 VA. J. INT'L L. 513 (2002). For current commentary on the general problem of the administration of federal maritime law in state courts, see David W. Robertson, *Admiralty and Maritime Litigation in State Court,* 55 LA. L. REV. 685 (1995); David W. Robertson, *Displacement of State Law by Federal Maritime Law,* 26 J. MARIT. L. & COMM. 326 (1995).

---

[a] For a current limiting case see *Yamaha Motor Corp. v. Calhoun,* 516 U.S. 199 (1996), holding that federal admiralty law does not preempt the damages available under state wrongful death and survival statutes for deaths of recreational boaters within state territorial waters.

[b] But see *Wilburn Boat Co. v. Fireman's Fund Ins. Co.,* 348 U.S. 310 (1955), applying state law to prevent a forfeiture of marine insurance for breach of a nonmaterial term in a case involving a small houseboat and landlocked waters.

# THE CURIOUS EXAMPLE OF THE FEDERAL ARBITRATION ACT

The Federal Arbitration Act (FAA) has been held to preempt state arbitration law in contracts in interstate commerce. *Southland Corp. v. Keating,* 476 U.S. 1 (1984). Thus, even in state courts, arbitration clauses in such contracts must be enforced. This result would have come as something of a surprise to the drafters of the FAA. The FAA in terms applies to federal courts only. Indeed, in *Bernhard v. Polygraphic Co.,* 350 U.S. 198 (1956), the Supreme Court had upheld application of *state* arbitration law to an arbitration provision in an intrastate contract in a diversity case, despite the Federal Arbitration Act. But in *Prima Paint Corp. v. Flood & Conklin Mfg. Co.,* 388 U.S. 395 (1967), the FAA was held to oust state law to the contrary, in federal courts, in disputes arising on contracts in interstate commerce; a concurrence suggested that the FAA also might be binding on state courts in interstate commerce cases, because the Commerce Clause probably was the only source of power for Congress to enact the FAA. Finally, in *Southland, supra,* the Federal Arbitration Act was recognized as preempting state arbitration laws in cases affecting interstate commerce, notwithstanding the apparent limitation of the FAA itself to federal courts.

**ALLIED-BRUCE TERMINIX COMPANIES, INC. v. DOBSON,** 513 U.S. 265 (1995). The plaintiff purchased a house in Alabama and employed the services of the defendant termite control company. The plaintiff later found the house to be infested with termites, and filed suit against the company in an Alabama state court.

Applying Alabama law invalidating arbitration clauses, the state court denied the company's motion for a stay pursuant to the Federal Arbitration Act and to the arbitration clause in the service contract. The Alabama Supreme Court affirmed, reasoning that the Federal Arbitration Act applies to contracts contemplating substantial interstate activity in interstate commerce, not primarily local activity.

*Held* (per JUSTICE BREYER): Reversed and remanded. The parties do not contest that interstate activity in fact was involved in this transaction, and the commerce power of Congress reaches such activity. Congress intended the preemptive reach of the Federal Arbitration act to be as broad as the commerce power.

JUSTICE SCALIA (dissenting): "I shall not in the future dissent from judgments that rest on *Southland.* I will, however, stand ready to join four other Justices in overruling it, since *Southland* will not become more correct over time, the course of future lawmaking seems unlikely to be affected by its existence, and the accumulated private reliance will not likely increase beyond the level it has already achieved (few contracts not terminable at will have more than a 5-year term). . . . "

JUSTICE THOMAS (joined by JUSTICE SCALIA, dissenting): "I disagree with the majority at the threshold of this case, and so I do not reach the question that it decides. In my view, the Federal Arbitration Act does not apply in state courts. . . . "

---

## § 6.07  Conflict Preemption

### INTRODUCTORY NOTE

Because the Supremacy Clause would defeat any state law in conflict with federal, the litigated question in "vertical" conflicts cases tends to become whether in fact there is a conflict, as the following case demonstrates.

---

### CALIFORNIA v. ARC AMERICA CORP.

*Supreme Court of the United States*
*490 U.S. 93, 109 S. Ct. 1661, 104 L. Ed. 2d 86 (1989)*

JUSTICE WHITE delivered the opinion of the Court.

In *Illinois Brick Co. v. Illinois,* 431 U.S. 720 (1977), the State of Illinois brought suit on its own behalf and on behalf of a number of local governmental entities seeking treble damages under § 4 of the Clayton Act[1] . . . for an alleged conspiracy to fix the price of concrete block in violation of § 1 of the Sherman Act.[*] The state and the local governments were all indirect purchasers of concrete block—that is, they did not purchase concrete block directly from the price-fixing defendants but rather purchased products or contracted for construction into which the concrete block was incorporated by a prior purchaser. The Court held that, with limited exceptions, only overcharged direct purchasers, and not subsequent indirect purchasers, were persons "injured in [their] business or property" within the meaning of § 4, and that therefore the State of Illinois was not entitled to recover under federal law for the portion of the overcharge passed on to it.

Appellants in the present case, the States of Alabama, Arizona, California, and Minnesota, brought suit in the appropriate federal courts on their own

---

[1] Section 4 provides as follows:

"[Any] person who shall be injured in his business or property by reason of anything forbidden in the antitrust laws may sue therefor in any district court of the United States in the district in which the defendant resides or is found or has an agent, without respect to the amount in controversy, and shall recover threefold the damages by him sustained, and the cost of suit, including a reasonable attorney's fee." 15 U.S.C. § 15(a)."

[*] 15 U.S.C. § 1. —*Ed.*

behalf and on behalf of classes of all governmental entities within each State, excluding the Federal Government, seeking treble damages under § 4 of the Clayton Act for an alleged nationwide conspiracy to fix prices of cement in violation of § 1 of the Sherman Act. Appellants are, at least in part, indirect purchasers of cement, and so under *Illinois Brick,* like the State of Illinois in that case, would not be entitled to recover on their indirect purchaser claims under § 4 unless those claims fell within one of the exceptions. In their complaints, however, appellants also alleged violations of their respective state antitrust laws under which, as a matter of state law, indirect purchasers arguably are allowed to recover for all overcharges passed on to them by direct purchasers. The claims under these state indirect purchaser statutes are the focus of this case.

Numerous similar actions were filed by other plaintiffs in various district courts, and the actions were transferred to the United States District Court for the District of Arizona for coordinated pretrial proceedings. The District Court certified the actions as class actions and established a number of plaintiff classes. Between July 1979 and October 1981, several major defendants settled with the various classes, resulting in a settlement fund in excess of $32 million. The settlements left distribution of the fund for later resolution, subject to approval of the District Court.

Appellants sought payment out of the settlement fund for their state indirect purchaser claims. Appellees, class members who are direct purchasers, objected. When the District Court approved a plan for distributing the settlement fund, it refused to allow the claims against the fund pursuant to state indirect purchaser statutes. According to the District Court, "Such statutes are clear attempts to frustrate the purposes and objectives of Congress, as interpreted by the Supreme Court in *Illinois Brick,* and, accordingly, are pre-empted by federal law."

The Ninth Circuit affirmed. The Court of Appeals identified "three purposes or objectives of federal antitrust law in this context," as defined by *Illinois Brick* and *Hanover Shoe, Inc. v. United Shoe Machinery Corp.,* 392 U.S. 481 (1968): avoiding unnecessarily complicated litigation; providing direct purchasers with incentives to bring private antitrust actions; and avoiding multiple liability of defendants. If state laws permitting indirect purchasers to recover were construed to restrict direct purchasers to suing only for the amount of any overcharge they have absorbed, the Court of Appeals was of the view that state law conflicted directly with federal law as construed in *Illinois Brick.* Alternatively, if state law permitted indirect purchasers to bring claims for damages in addition to the claims brought by direct purchasers, it would "impermissibly interfere with the three policy goals outlined in *Hanover Shoe* and *Illinois Brick.*" The Court of Appeals therefore held that state indirect purchaser claims that did not satisfy any exception to *Illinois Brick* were pre-empted. . . .

We should first make it clear exactly what the issue is before us. These cases alleged violations of both the Sherman Act and state antitrust acts. The settlements, as we understand it, covered both the federal and the state-law claims; the settlement fund was intended to be distributed in complete satisfaction of those claims. Under federal law, no indirect purchaser is entitled to sue for damages for a Sherman Act violation, and there is no claim here that state law could provide a remedy for the federal violation that federal law forbids. Had these cases gone to trial and a Sherman Act violation been proved, only direct purchasers would have been entitled to damages for that violation, and there is no suggestion by the parties that the same rule should not apply to distributing that part of the fund that was meant to settle the Sherman Act claims. The issue before us is whether this rule limiting recoveries under the Sherman Act also prevents indirect purchasers from recovering damages flowing from violations of state law, despite express state statutory provisions giving such purchasers a damages cause of action.

The path to be followed in pre-emption cases is laid out by our cases. It is accepted that Congress has the authority, in exercising its Article I powers, to pre-empt state law. In the absence of an express statement by Congress that state law is pre-empted, there are two other bases for finding pre-emption. First, when Congress intends that federal law occupy a given field, state law in that field is pre-empted. *Pacific Gas & Electric Co. v. State Energy Resources Conservation and Development Comm'n*, 461 U.S. 190 (1983). Second, even if Congress has not occupied the field, state law is nevertheless pre-empted to the extent it actually conflicts with federal law, that is, when compliance with both state and federal law is impossible, *Florida Lime & Avocado Growers, Inc. v. Paul*, 373 U.S. 132 (1963), or when the state law "stands as an obstacle to the accomplishment and execution of the full purposes and objectives of Congress," *Hines v. Davidowitz*, 312 U.S. 52 (1941). *See, e.g., Silkwood v. Kerr-McGee Corp.*, 464 U.S. 238 (1984).

In this case, in addition, appellees must overcome the presumption against finding pre-emption of state law in areas traditionally regulated by the States. When Congress legislates in a field traditionally occupied by the States, "we start with the assumption that the historic police powers of the States were not to be superseded by the Federal Act unless that was the clear and manifest purpose of Congress." *Rice v. Santa Fe Elevator Corp.*, 331 U.S. 218, 230 (1947). Given the long history of state common-law and statutory remedies against monopolies and unfair business practices,[4] it is plain that this is an area traditionally regulated by the States. . . .

In light of these principles, the Court of Appeals erred in holding that the state indirect purchaser statutes are pre-empted. There is no claim that the federal antitrust laws expressly pre-empt state laws permitting indirect purchaser recovery. Moreover, appellees concede that Congress has not pre-empted the field of antitrust law. Congress intended the federal antitrust laws to supplement, not displace, state antitrust remedies. . . .

Appellees' only contention is that state laws permitting indirect purchaser recoveries pose an obstacle to the accomplishment of the purposes and objectives of Congress. State laws to this effect are consistent with the broad purposes of the federal antitrust laws: deterring anticompetitive conduct and

---

[4] At the time of the enactment of the Sherman Act, 21 States had already adopted their own antitrust laws . . . . Moreover, the Sherman Act itself, in the words of Senator Sherman, "does not announce a new principle of law, but applies old and well recognized principles of the common law . . . ." 21 Cong. Rec. 2456 (1890).

ensuring the compensation of victims of that conduct. . . .[6] In this respect, the Court of Appeals has misunderstood both *Hanover Shoe* and *Illinois Brick*.

Neither of those cases addressed the preemptive force of the federal antitrust laws. Neither case contains any discussion of state law or of the relevant standards for pre-emption of state law. As we made clear in *Illinois Brick*, the issue before the Court in both that case and in *Hanover Shoe* was strictly a question of statutory interpretation—what was the proper construction of § 4 of the Clayton Act. . . .

It is one thing to consider the congressional policies identified in *Illinois Brick*  and *Hanover Shoe* in defining what sort of recovery federal antitrust law authorizes; it is something altogether different, and in our view inappropriate, to consider them as defining what federal law allows States to do under their own antitrust law. . . .

The Court of Appeals . . . concluded that state indirect purchaser statutes interfere with the congressional purpose of avoiding unnecessarily complicated proceedings on federal antitrust claims. But these state statutes cannot and do not purport to affect remedies available under federal law. Furthermore, state indirect purchaser actions will not necessarily be brought in federal court. Unlike the federal indirect purchaser claims asserted in *Illinois Brick*, which would have been exclusively within the jurisdiction of the federal courts, 15 U.S.C. §§ 15(a), 26, claims under state indirect purchaser statutes could be brought in state court, separately from federal actions brought by direct purchasers. Moreover, federal courts have the discretion to decline to exercise pendent jurisdiction over state indirect purchaser claims, even if those claims are brought in the first instance in federal court. Since many state indirect purchaser actions would be heard in state courts, at least when the federal courts determined that hearing those claims would be overly burdensome, any complication of federal direct purchaser actions in federal court would be minimal.

Second, the Court of Appeals reasoned that allowing state indirect purchaser claims could reduce the incentives of direct purchasers to bring antitrust actions by reducing their potential recoveries. The presence of indirect purchaser claims would reduce settlement offers to direct purchasers, the Court of Appeals believed, and if the total liability were to exhaust a defendant's assets, the direct purchasers would have to share the defendant's estate in bankruptcy with indirect purchasers. But the Court in *Illinois Brick* was not concerned with the risk that a plaintiff might not be able to recover its entire damages award or might be offered less to settle. Indeed, taken to its extreme, the Court of Appeals' logic would lead to the pre-emption of any state-law claims against antitrust defendants, even if wholly unrelated, because the presence of other litigation could threaten the defendants with

---

[6] In one respect, the Court of Appeals was overly narrow in its description of the congressional purposes identified in *Illinois Brick*. In *Illinois Brick,*  the Court was concerned not merely that direct purchasers have sufficient incentive to bring suit under the antitrust laws, as the Court of Appeals asserted, but rather that at least some party have sufficient incentive to bring suit. Indeed, we implicitly recognized as much in noting that indirect purchasers might be allowed to bring suit in cases in which it would be easy to prove the extent to which the overcharge was passed on to them. *See* 431 U.S., at 732, n. 12.

bankruptcy and reduce their willingness to settle. *Illinois Brick* was concerned that requiring direct and indirect purchasers to apportion the recovery under a single statute—§ 4 of the Clayton Act—would result in no one plaintiff having a sufficient incentive to sue under that statute. State indirect purchaser statutes pose no similar risk to the enforcement of the federal law.

Appellees argue that because the defendants in these antitrust actions have settled and there is a limited settlement fund, the indirect purchasers' claims are pre-empted because those claims will likely reduce the amount that can be paid from the fund to direct purchasers. But as we said earlier, the settlement covered both federal and state-law claims, and whatever amount is allocable to federal claims will be distributed only to direct purchasers. Indirect purchasers will participate only in distributing the funds available to claimants under state law. Even if the settlement fund is not to be divided between state and federal law claimants, the settlement necessarily was intended to dispose of all claimants, whether claiming under federal or state law and whether direct or indirect purchasers. That direct purchasers may have to share with indirect purchasers is a function of the fact and form of settlement rather than the impermissible operation of state indirect purchaser statutes.

Third, the Court of Appeals concluded that state indirect purchaser claims might subject antitrust defendants to multiple liability, in contravention of the "express federal policy" condemning multiple liability. But [the cases on which the Court of Appeals relied] all were cases construing § 4 of the Clayton Act; in none of those cases did the Court identify a federal policy against States imposing liability in addition to that imposed by federal law. Ordinarily, state causes of action are not pre-empted solely because they impose liability over and above that authorized by federal law; . . . and no clear purpose of Congress indicates that we should decide otherwise in this case.

. . . The congressional purposes on which *Illinois Brick* was based provide no support for a finding that state indirect purchaser statutes are pre-empted by federal law. The judgment of the Court of Appeals is therefore reversed. . . .

JUSTICE STEVENS and JUSTICE O'CONNOR took no part in the consideration or decision of this case.

---

## NOTES ON *ARC AMERICA*

(1) *The litigated question: Was there a conflict?* There was just one liquidated settlement fund in *ARC America.* Either the direct-purchaser claimants were entitled to the whole fund, under *Illinois Brick,* or they would have to share it with the indirect-purchaser claimants. Does the fact that the fund was allocable to both state and federal claims clear up this difficulty?

Even if there were only unliquidated claims for damages, doesn't *ARC America* conflict with *Illinois Brick*? Consider the possible scenarios. There is no option, of course, for bringing suit on both federal and state claims in state court; federal antitrust claims are held to be within the exclusive jurisdiction of federal courts. But suppose parallel litigation, with state claims in state court, and federal claims in federal court. In such a case, the tortfeasor would have to defend expensively in both sets of courts, under serious risk of multiple liability: trebled entire damages to direct purchasers under federal law in federal court, and apportioned damages to indirect purchasers under state law in state court—the very multiple liability that *Illinois Brick* sought to avoid.

Or suppose an action in federal court, combining antitrust claims with pendent state claims. If, under *Illinois Brick,* the direct purchaser must be given an entire remedy, the defendant in such a case would have to face exposure to entire trebled damages to the direct purchasers, plus apportioned damages to the indirect purchasers. Multiple liability occurs again. Moreover, on the state claim, the federal court would have to do the sort of complex calculation of passed-through injury which *Illinois Brick* was supposed to obviate.

Alternatively, the defendants' liabilities might be liquidated to some fixed sum; and then, under *ARC America,* the inevitable apportionment of the damages would occur. But this would mean that some of the direct-purchaser plaintiffs' damages could not be recovered, at least not trebly, contrary to the intention of Congress; and the defendant in this scenario would get the set-off that *Illinois Brick* and its predecessor *Hanover Shoe* held unavailable.

In *ARC America,* should the Court have found that the presumption against preemption was in fact overcome, in the sense that a conflict was made out between national policy and state law?

Does it say anything about the national policies underlying *Illinois Brick* that the *ARC America* Court was comfortable with state law to the contrary?

(2) *After ARC America: What about contribution?* In *Texas Industries v. Radcliff Materials,* 451 U.S. 630 (1981), *supra* this Chapter, the Court held that it would not infer a private federal right to contribution between joint tortfeasors in antitrust. This opinion has been widely understood as holding that there is no right to contribution between joint tortfeasors in antitrust actions. Thus, a state-court adjudicating an antitrust claim raised by way of defense or counterclaim, where the antitrust tortfeasor seeks contribution, under the Supremacy Clause would be bound to deny a right to contribution between antitrust tortfeasors. But suppose the tortfeasor seeks to assert a right to contribution under some analogous *state-law* theory? Does *ARC America* permit contribution, under state law? If so, what sort of impact would that have on the difficult questions of antitrust policy the Court refused to tackle in *Texas Industries*?

(3) *If ARC-America is national policy.* Reliance on state-law theories for vindication of national policies may not always work. For widespread antitrust injury, the only state likely to have legislative jurisdiction over the whole case would be the defendant's state, or a state in which the defendant chose to contract or conspire. But in the broad run of cases, that state's laws on unfair competition would tend to be protective of the defendant, who chose that state in which to contract or conspire.

(4) *Footnotes.* In *Kansas v. Utilicorp United, Inc.,* 497 U.S. 199 (1990), the Court held that *Illinois Brick* was still good law, notwithstanding the

intervening decision in *ARC America.* Justice White, dissenting, complained that, under both cases it had been thought that indirect purchasers might be allowed to bring suit in cases in which the calculation of damages passed on to them would not be difficult.

*ARC America* has emerged as importantly affecting the allocation of adjudicatory power over antitrust claims in the United States. For further discussion of the problems raised by *ARC America* see Louise Weinberg, *The Federal-State Conflict of Laws: "Actual" Conflicts,* 70 Tex. L. Rev. 1743, 1760-1772; 1783-1784 (1992).

(5) *A civil rights cause of action for violation of the Supremacy Clause?*

**GOLDEN STATE TRANSIT CORP. v. CITY OF LOS ANGELES,** 493 U.S. 103 (1989). Under the National Labor Relations Act (NLRA), an employer's failure to make a concession during collective bargaining is not an unfair labor practice. In an earlier stage of this litigation, the Supreme Court held, in *Golden State I,* that Los Angeles had acted in a manner inconsistent with the Act when it conditioned renewal of Golden State's taxicab franchise on its settling its pending labor dispute. The Act, the Court reasoned, gives management a right to refuse to make concessions, and thus preempts the imposition of a condition like that imposed by Los Angeles.

On remand, Golden State pursued a claim for damages under the Civil Rights Act of 1871, 42 U.S.C. § 1983, which provides:

"Every person who, under color of any statute, ordinance, regulation, custom, or usage, of any State or Territory or the District of Columbia, subjects, or causes to be subjected, any citizen of the United States or other person within the jurisdiction thereof to the deprivation of any rights, privileges, or immunities secured by the Constitution and laws, shall be liable to the party injured in an action at law, suit in equity, or other proper proceeding for redress . . . ."

The District Court dismissed. It reasoned that a civil rights action would not lie because Los Angeles had not violated federal labor law; the court noted that Los Angeles *could* not violate federal labor law, since Los Angeles was not a party to the collective bargaining agreement, and the National Labor Relations Act imposed duties only on parties to collective bargaining agreements. Rather, Los Angeles' conduct was *preempted* by the Act. But the Supremacy Clause in itself could not give rise to a civil rights claim. The Court of Appeals affirmed.

*Held* (per Justice Stevens): For the plaintiff. "[The city] argues that the Supremacy Clause, of its own force, does not create rights enforceable under [the Civil Rights Act]. We agree . . . . Given the variety of situations in which preemption claims may be asserted, in state court and in federal court, it would obviously be incorrect to assume that a federal right of action . . . exists every time a federal rule of law preempts state regulatory authority . . . . In all cases, the availability of the . . . remedy turns on whether the statute, by its terms or as interpreted, creates obligations sufficiently specific and definite to be within the competence of the judiciary to enforce, is intended to benefit the putative plaintiff, and is not foreclosed by express provision or other specific evidence from the statute itself . . . .

"The nub of the controversy between the parties is whether the NLRA creates 'rights' in labor and management that are protected against governmental interference. The city does not argue, nor could it, that a § 1983 action is precluded by the existence of a comprehensive enforcement scheme. Although the National Labor Relations Board has exclusive jurisdiction to prevent and remedy unfair labor practices by employers and unions, it has no authority to address conduct protected by the NLRA against governmental interference . . . . Nor can there be any substantial question that our holding in *Golden State I* that the city's conduct was preempted was within the competence of the judiciary to enforce. Rather, the city argues that it cannot be held liable under § 1983 because its conduct did not violate any rights secured by the NLRA . . . .

"The city's . . . refusal to renew [Golden State's] franchise violated [Golden State's] right to use permissible economic tactics to withstand the strike . . . . [The] case does not come within any recognized exception from the broad remedial scope of § 1983. . . . "

JUSTICE KENNEDY (joined by CHIEF JUSTICE REHNQUIST and JUSTICE O'CONNOR, dissenting): "[The] Court should not interpret [the Civil Rights Act] to give a cause of action for damages when the only wrong committed by the State or its local entities is misapprehending the precise location of the boundaries between state and federal power. The dispute over the taxicab franchise involves no greater transgression than this. . . .

"The NLRA creates two relations which encompass different legal interests. The statute creates the first relation between Golden State and the striking union . . . . The NLRA also creates a jural relation between the city and Golden State. Although the NLRA does not provide in any detailed way how a city should act when renewing an operating franchise, the statute does have a preemptive effect under the Supremacy Clause . . . .

"The city's lack of power gives rise to a correlative legal interest . . . . The majority has chosen to call the interest a right. I would prefer to follow the familiar Hohfeldian terminology and say that Golden State has an immunity from the city's interference with the NLRA. See Hohfeld, *Some Fundamental Legal Conceptions as Applied in Judicial Reasoning,* 23 YALE L.J. 16, 55-58 (1913) (defining the correlative of no power as an immunity) . . . .

"Golden State's immunity . . . permits the company to object only that the wrong sovereign has attempted to regulate its labor relations. Golden State's immunity does not benefit the company as an individual, but instead results from the Supremacy Clause's separate protection of the federal structure and from the division of power in the constitutional system. . . . "

## § 6.08   Field Preemption

### BANCO NACIONAL DE CUBA v. BANCO NACIONAL DE CUBA v. SABBATINO

*Supreme Court of the United States*
*376 U.S. 398, 84 S. Ct. 923, 11 L. Ed. 2d 804 (1964)*

[This was a complicated litigation to try title to a shipload of sugar. The ship was arrested in United States waters, and its cargo, still on board, was, in effect, interpleaded in federal court between two claimants: Sabbatino, a New York court-appointed receiver, and Banco, an instrumentality of the Cuban government. The sugar had been expropriated by Cuba. Sabbatino argued that Cuba's title was no good because the expropriation was discriminatory, retaliatory, and confiscatory, and hence invalid under international law. Banco countered that the common-law "act of state" doctrine forbade courts from scrutinizing the validity of the acts of foreign states, including their expropriations.]

MR. JUSTICE HARLAN delivered the opinion of the Court.

The question . . . is whether the so-called act of state doctrine serves to sustain petitioner's claims in this litigation. . . .

### IV.

The classic American statement of the act of state doctrine . . . is found in *Underhill v. Hernandez,* 168 U.S. 250, 252 (1897), where Chief Justice Fuller said for a unanimous Court:

> ". . . [The] courts of one country will not sit in judgment on the acts of the government of another, done within its own territory. Redress of grievances by reason of such acts must be obtained through the means open to be availed of by sovereign powers as between themselves."

. . . [The] Court in that case refused to inquire into acts of Hernandez, a revolutionary Venezuelan military commander . . ., [in] a damage action in this country by Underhill, an American citizen, who claimed that he had unlawfully assaulted, coerced, and detained in Venezuela by Hernandez.

. . . [In] *Oetjen v. Central Leather Co.,* 246 U.S. 297, (1918), . . . *Underhill* was reaffirmed in unequivocal terms. . . :

> "The principle that the conduct of one independent government cannot be successfully questioned in the courts of another is as applicable to a case involving the title to property brought within the custody of a court, such as we have here, as it was held to be to the cases . . . in which claims for damages were based upon acts done in a foreign country. . . . [To] permit the validity of the acts of one sovereign state to be reexamined and perhaps condemned by the courts of another would very certainly imperil the amicable relations between governments. . . ."

## V.

Preliminarily, we discuss the foundations on which we deem the act of state doctrine to rest, and more particularly the question of whether state or federal law governs its application in a federal diversity case.[20]

We do not believe that this doctrine is compelled either by the inherent nature of sovereign authority, as some of the earlier decisions seem to imply, or by some principle of international law. If a transaction takes place in one jurisdiction and the forum is in another, the forum does not by dismissing an action or by applying its own law purport to divest the first jurisdiction of its territorial sovereignty; it merely declines to adjudicate or makes applicable its own law to parties or property before it. The refusal of one country to enforce the penal laws of another is a typical example of an instance when a court will not entertain a cause of action arising in another jurisdiction. While historic notions of sovereign authority do bear upon the wisdom of employing the act of state doctrine, they do not dictate its existence.

. . . Although it is, of course, true that United States courts apply international law as a part of our own in appropriate circumstances, *Ware v. Hylton,* 3 U.S. (3 Dall.) 199 (1796); *The Paquete Habana,* 175 U.S. 677, 700 (1900), the public law of nations can hardly dictate to a country which is in theory wronged how to treat that wrong within its domestic borders.

Despite the broad statement in *Oetjen* that "The conduct of the foreign relations of our government is committed by the Constitution to the executive and legislative departments," it cannot of course be thought that every case or controversy which touches foreign relations lies beyond judicial cognizance. The text of the Constitution does not require the act of state doctrine; it does not irrevocably remove from the judiciary the capacity to review the validity of foreign acts of state.

The act of state doctrine does, however, have "constitutional" underpinnings. It arises out of the basic relationships between branches of government in a system of separation of powers. It concerns the competency of dissimilar institutions to make and implement particular kinds of decisions in the area of international relations. The doctrine as formulated in past decisions expresses the strong sense of the Judicial Branch that its engagement in the task of passing on the validity of foreign acts of state may hinder rather than further this country's pursuit of goals both for itself and for the community of nations as a whole in the international sphere. . . . Whatever considerations are thought to predominate, it is plain that the problems involved are uniquely federal in nature. If federal authority, in this instance this Court, orders the field of judicial competence in this area for the federal courts, and the state courts are left free to formulate their own rules, the purposes behind the doctrine could be as effectively undermined as if there had been no federal pronouncement on the subject.

We could perhaps in this diversity action avoid the question of deciding whether federal or state law is applicable to this aspect of the litigation. New

---

[20] Although the complaint in this case alleged both diversity and federal question jurisdiction, the Court of Appeals reached jurisdiction only on the former ground. We need not decide, for reasons appearing hereafter, whether federal question jurisdiction also existed.

York has enunciated the act of state doctrine in terms that echo those of federal decisions decided during the reign of *Swift v. Tyson* . . . . Thus our conclusions might well be the same whether we dealt with this problem as one of state law, see *Erie R. Co. v. Tompkins,* 304 U.S. 64 (1938), or federal law.

However, we are constrained to make it clear that an issue concerned with a basic choice regarding the competence and function of the Judiciary and the National Executive in ordering our relationships with other members of the international community must be treated exclusively as an aspect of federal law.[23] It seems fair to assume that the Court did not have rules like the act of state doctrine in mind when it decided *Erie R. Co. v. Tompkins.* Soon thereafter, Professor Philip C. Jessup, now a judge of the International Court of Justice, recognized the potential dangers were *Erie* extended to legal problems affecting international relations.[24] He cautioned that rules of international law should not be left to divergent and perhaps parochial state interpretations. His basic rationale is equally applicable to the act of state doctrine.

The Court in the pre-*Erie* act of state cases, although not burdened by the problem of the source of applicable law, used language sufficiently strong and broadsweeping to suggest that state courts were not left free to develop their own doctrines (as they would have been had this Court merely been interpreting common law under *Swift v. Tyson, supra*). . . . We are not without . . . precedent for a determination that federal law governs; there are enclaves of federal judge-made law which bind the States. A national body of federal-court-built law has been held to have been contemplated by § 301 of the Labor Management Relations Act, *Textile Workers Union of America v. Lincoln Mills,* 353 U.S. 448 (1957). Principles formulated by federal judicial law have been thought by this Court to be necessary to protect uniquely federal interests, *D'Oench, Duhme & Co. v. Federal Deposit Ins. Corp.,* 315 U.S. 447 (1942); *Clearfield Trust Co. v. United States,* 318 U.S. 363 (1943). Of course the federal interest guarded in all these cases is one the ultimate statement of which is derived from a federal statute. Perhaps more directly in point are the bodies of law applied between States over boundaries and in regard to the apportionment of interstate waters.

In *Hinderlider v. La Plata River Co.,* 304 U.S. 92 (1938), in an opinion handed down the same day as *Erie* and by the same author, Mr. Justice Brandeis, the Court declared, "For whether the water of an interstate stream must be apportioned between the two States is a question of 'federal common law' upon which neither the statutes nor the decisions of either State can be conclusive." Although the [state-court] suit was between two private litigants and the relevant States could not be made parties, the Court considered itself free to determine the effect of an interstate compact regulating water apportionment. The decision implies that no State can undermine the federal

---

[23] At least this is true when the Court limits the scope of judicial inquiry. We need not now consider whether a state court might, in certain circumstances, adhere to a more restrictive view concerning the scope of examination of foreign acts than that required by this Court.

[24] *The Doctrine of Erie Railroad v. Tompkins Applied to International Law,* 33 AM. J. INT'L L. 740 (1939).

interest in equitably apportioned interstate waters even if it deals with private parties. . . . The problems surrounding the act of state doctrine are, albeit for different reasons, as intrinsically federal as are those involved in water apportionment or boundary disputes. The considerations supporting exclusion of state authority here are much like those which led the Court in *United States v. California,* 332 U.S. 19 (1947), to hold that the Federal Government possessed paramount rights in submerged lands though within the three-mile limit of coastal States. We conclude that the scope of the act of state doctrine must be determined according to federal law.[25]

## VI.

If the act of state doctrine is a principle of decision binding on federal and state courts alike but compelled by neither international law nor the Constitution, its continuing vitality depends on its capacity to reflect the proper distribution of functions between the judicial and political branches of the Government on matters bearing upon foreign affairs. It should be apparent that the greater the degree of codification or consensus concerning a particular area of international law, the more appropriate it is for the judiciary to render decisions regarding it, since the courts can then focus on the application of an agreed principle to circumstances of fact rather than on the sensitive task of establishing a principle not inconsistent with the national interest or with international justice. It is also evident that some aspects of international law touch much more sharply on national nerves than do others; the less important the implications of an issue are for our foreign relations, the weaker the justification for exclusivity in the political branches. The balance of relevant considerations may also be shifted if the government which perpetrated the challenged act of state is no longer in existence, for the political interest of this country may, as a result, be measurably altered. Therefore, rather than laying down or reaffirming an inflexible and all-encompassing rule in this case, we decide only that the Judicial Branch will not examine the validity of a taking of property within its own territory by a foreign sovereign government, extant and recognized by this country at the time of suit, in the absence of a treaty or other unambiguous agreement regarding controlling legal principles, even if the complaint alleges that the taking violates customary international law. . . .

When we consider the prospect of the courts characterizing foreign expropriations, however justifiably, as invalid under international law and ineffective to pass title, the wisdom of the precedents is confirmed. While each of the leading cases in this Court may be argued to be distinguishable in its facts from this one—*Underhill* because sovereign immunity provided an independent ground and *Oetjen* . . . because there was actually no violation of international law— . . . the plain implication of . . . these opinions . . . is that the act of state doctrine is applicable even if international law has been violated. . . .

---

[25] Various constitutional and statutory provisions indirectly support this determination, see U.S. Const., Art. I, § 8, cls. 3, 10; Art. II, §§ 2, 3; Art. III, § 2; 28 U.S.C. §§ 1251(a)(2), (b)(1), (b)(3), 1332(a)(2), 1333, 1350, 1351, by reflecting a concern for uniformity in this country's dealings with foreign nations and indicating a desire to give matters of international significance to the jurisdiction of federal institutions . . . .

The possible adverse consequences of a conclusion to the contrary of that implicit in these cases in highlighted by contrasting the practices of the political branch with the limitations of the judicial process in matters of this kind. Following an expropriation of any significance, the Executive engages in diplomacy aimed to assure that United States citizens who are harmed are compensated fairly. Representing all claimants of this country, it will often be able, either by bilateral or multilateral talks, by submission to the United Nations, or by the employment of economic and political sanctions, to achieve some degree of general redress. Judicial determinations of invalidity of title can, on the other hand, have only an occasional impact, since they depend on the fortuitous circumstance of the property in question being brought into this country. Such decisions would, if the acts involved were declared invalid, often be likely to give offense to the expropriating country; since the concept of territorial sovereignty is so deep seated, any state may resent the refusal of the courts of another sovereign to accord validity to acts within its territorial borders. Piecemeal dispositions of this sort involving the probability of affront to another state could seriously interfere with negotiations being carried on by the Executive Branch and might prevent or render less favorable the terms of an agreement that could otherwise be reached. Relations with third countries which have engaged in similar expropriations would not be immune from effect.

The dangers of such adjudication are present regardless of whether the State Department has, as it did in this case, asserted that the relevant act violated international law. If the Executive Branch has undertaken negotiations with an expropriating country, but has refrained from claims of violation of the law of nations, a determination to that effect by a court might be regarded as a serious insult, while a finding of compliance with international law would greatly strengthen the bargaining hand of the other state with consequent detriment to American interests.

Even if the State Department has proclaimed the impropriety of the expropriation, the stamp of approval of its view by a judicial tribunal, however, impartial, might increase any affront and the judicial decision might occur at a time, almost always well after the taking, when such an impact would be contrary to our national interest. Considerably more serious and far-reaching consequences would flow from a judicial finding that international law standards had been met if that determination flew in the face of a State Department proclamation to the contrary. When articulating principles of international law in its relations with other states, the Executive Branch speaks not only as an interpreter of generally accepted and traditional rules, as would the courts, but also as an advocate of standards it believes desirable for the community of nations and protective of national concerns. In short, whatever way the matter is cut, the possibility of conflict between the Judicial and Executive Branches could hardly be avoided. . . .

Another serious consequence of the exception pressed by respondents would be to render uncertain titles in foreign commerce, with the possible consequence of altering the flow of international trade. If the attitude of the United States courts were unclear, one buying expropriated goods would not know if he could safely import them into this country. Even were takings known to be invalid, one would have difficulty determining after goods had changed hands several times whether the particular articles in question were the product of an ineffective state act.[38] . . .

It is contended that regardless of the fortuitous circumstances necessary for United States jurisdiction over a case involving a foreign act of state and the resultant isolated application to any expropriation program taken as a whole, it is the function of the courts to justly decide individual disputes before them. Perhaps the most typical act of state case involves the original owner or his assignee suing one not in association with the expropriating state who has had "title" transferred to him. But it is difficult to regard the claim of the original owner, who otherwise may be recompensed through diplomatic channels, as more demanding of judicial cognizance than the claim of title by the innocent third party purchaser, who, if the property is taken from him, is without any remedy. . . .

It is suggested that if the act of state doctrine is applicable to violations of international law, it should only be so when the Executive Branch expressly stipulates that it does not wish the courts to pass on the question of validity. . . . It is highly questionable whether the examination of validity by the judiciary should depend on an educated guess by the Executive as to probable result and, at any rate, should a prediction be wrong, the Executive might be embarrassed in its dealings with other countries. . . .

However offensive to the public policy of this country and its constituent States an expropriation of this kind may be, we conclude that both the national interest and progress toward the goal of establishing the rule of law among nations are best served by maintaining intact the act of state doctrine in this realm of its application. . . .

The judgment of the Court of Appeals is reversed and the case is remanded to the District Court for proceedings consistent with this opinion. . . .

Mr. Justice White, dissenting.

I am dismayed that the Court has, with one broad stroke, declared the ascertainment and application of international law beyond the competence of the courts of the United States in a large and important category of cases. I am also disappointed in the Court's declaration that the acts of a sovereign state with regard to the property of aliens within its borders are beyond the reach of international law in the courts of this country. However clearly established that law may be, a sovereign may violate it with impunity, except insofar as the political branches of the government may provide a remedy. This backward-looking doctrine, never before declared in this Court, is carried a disconcerting step further: not only are the courts powerless to question acts of state proscribed by international law but they are likewise powerless to refuse to adjudicate the claim founded upon a foreign law; they must render judgment and thereby validate the lawless act. Since the Court expressly extends its ruling to all acts of state expropriating property, however clearly

---

[38] This possibility is consistent with the view that the deterrent effect of court invalidations would not ordinarily be great. If the expropriating country could find other buyers for its products at roughly the same price, the deterrent effect might be minimal although patterns of trade would be significantly changed.

inconsistent with the international community, all discriminatory expropriations of the property of aliens, as for example the taking of properties of persons belonging to certain races, religions or nationalities, are entitled to automatic validation in the courts of the United States. No other civilized country has found such a rigid rule necessary for the survival of the executive branch of its government; the executive of no other government seems to require such insulation from international law adjudications in its courts; and no other judiciary is apparently so incompetent to ascertain and apply international law. . . .

## NOTES ON *SABBATINO*

(1) *Federalization.* Note the moment of federalization in *Sabbatino,* when the Court feels "constrained" to make clear that the question whether the act of state doctrine applies is a federal one, although New York law would come out the same way.

*Sabbatino* was a diversity case. Are you clear why *Erie* did not require state law?

(2) *The act-of-state doctrine.* The Court holds that a foreign government's act may not be scrutinized in the courts of this country. Is there a good argument that *Sabbatino,* even if right on choice of law, was wrong on in approving the act-of-state doctrine? Should the federal common-law rule have been that the legality of an expropriation of property later brought to this country *is* justiciable?

Note here that federal common law is freestanding, although Justice Harlan insists it has strong constitutional "underpinnings." The rule of the case is compelled not by any authoritative text, but by perceived national policy.

*The "Hickenlooper Amendment. "* As it happens, Congress did not agree with Justice Harlan on the act-of-state doctrine. In the so-called "Hickenlooper Amendment," Congress legislatively revised *Sabbatino* on its facts, authorizing courts to scrutinize the validity of foreign expropriations of property when found in this country. But nothing in the Hickenlooper Amendment disturbs the broader holding of *Sabbatino,* on the preemptive effect of national lawmaking power over the foreign relations of the United States. (For retroactive application of the Hickenlooper Amendment to *Sabbatino* itself on remand, see *Banco Nacional v. Farr,* 383 F.2d 166 (2d Cir. 1967)).

(3) *Preemption of foreign relations law.* Isn't it clear, after *Sabbatino,* that the states cannot speak at all—with their "divergent and perhaps parochial voices"—in the field of foreign relations of the United States?

The Court's arguments in *Sabbatino* support exclusive national authority over all of the foreign relations law of the United States. But see American Law Institute, Restatement (Third) of the Foreign Relations Law of the United States § 2 (1987) (taking the view that the sources of United States foreign relations law include international law and state law).

Complete preemption of any field, even this one, may be tougher to achieve than *Sabbatino* suggests. For example, in the wake of the lifting of restrictions on trade with South Africa, the Bush administration discovered that American state and local governments were putting their own trade restrictions into effect.

For comment on *Sabbatino,* see Jack L. Goldsmith, *Federal Courts, Foreign Affairs, and Federalism,* 83 VA. L. REV. 1617 (1997).

(4) *Separation of powers.* Consider also *Sabbatino'*s identification of federal intragovernmental relations as a federal question. The allocation of power among the branches of the federal government, like the foreign relations of the United States, presents questions that, in Justice Harlan's words, are "uniquely" and "exclusively" federal. State governance on such questions would be inappropriate.

(5) *The scope of foreign relations preemption.*

**ZSCHERNIG v. MILLER,** 389 U.S. 429 (1968). This began as an action by East German heirs of an American citizen who died intestate in Oregon. The heirs challenged a state law providing for escheat of personalty claimed by an alien unless (1) a United States citizen would enjoy a reciprocal right to claim property in that alien's country; (2) American citizens would have the right to receive payment here of funds from estates in the foreign country; and (3) foreign heirs would have the right to receive the proceeds of Oregon estates without confiscation. Under these provisions the Oregon supreme court denied the East German heirs' right to take.

*Held* (per JUSTICE DOUGLAS): For the East German heirs: "[The] history and operation of this Oregon statute make clear that [it] is an intrusion by the state into the field of foreign affairs which the Constitution entrusts to the President and the Congress. . . .

"As one reads the Oregon decisions, it seems that foreign policy attitudes, the freezing or thawing of the 'cold war,' and the like are the real desiderata. Yet they of course are matters for the Federal Government, not for the local probate courts. . . .

". . . Oregon judges . . . seek to ascertain whether 'rights' protected by foreign law are the same 'rights' that citizens of Oregon enjoy. . . . The statute as construed seems to make unavoidable judicial criticism of nations established on a more authoritarian basis than our own.

"It seems inescapable that the type of probate law that Oregon enforces affects international relations in a persistent and subtle way. The practice of state courts in withholding remittances to legatees residing in Communist countries or in preventing them from assigning them is notorious. The several States, of course, have traditionally regulated the descent and distribution of estates. But those regulations must give way if they impair the effective exercise of the Nation's foreign policy. . . .

JUSTICE HARLAN (concurring in the result): "The appellants concede that Oregon might deny inheritance rights to all nonresident aliens. Assuming that this is so, . . . a foreign government can hardly object to the denial of rights which it does not itself accord to the citizens of other countries. . . . "

JUSTICE WHITE (dissenting): ". . . Generally for reasons stated by Justice Harlan in . . . his separate opinion, I do not consider the Oregon statute to be an impermissible interference with foreign affairs. . . . "

(6) *Silencing the state voice.* Is complete preemption of the field of foreign affairs necessarily a good thing? *Crosby v. Nat'l Foreign Trade Council*, 530 U.S. 363 (2000), was an action by a trade association challenging a Massachusetts statute which imposed sanctions upon Myanmar (Burma) for its human rights violations. The law prohibited only the state and its agencies from contracting with Burma, except to provide news, telecommunications, or medical supplies. In 1996, three months after the Massachusetts law was enacted, Congress passed a statute imposing both mandatory and conditional sanctions on Burma. The federal District Court permanently enjoined enforcement of the state Act, holding that it "unconstitutionally impinged on the federal government's exclusive authority to regulate foreign affairs," and the Court of Appeals for the First Circuit affirmed. The Supreme Court, by Justice Souter, did not reach this question. Rather, the Court read the statute as implying an actual conflict between state and federal law, such that the state law could not stand. The combination of "carrots" and "sticks" Congress had enacted, together with broad discretion in the President to use them, was intended to encourage Burma to improve its human rights record. By prohibiting most state contracts with Burma, Massachusetts had taken away some of the President's carrots and sticks.

Was this conflict substantial? Should the state have been permitted to regulate its own contracts? Is the state now forced to associate itself with a government which, in its judgment, is evil? When national policy must be compromised by balancing forces, would it necessarily be harmful either to national policy or to that delicate balance to permit divergent and perhaps parochial state voices to be heard? In *Crosby*, should the voice of Massachusetts, with its clearer moral message, have been allowed to be heard?

---

# SUMMING UP

We have seen that when a court decides that state law cannot govern an issue, *Erie* is out of the picture: federal law is held to govern that issue under the Supremacy Clause, and state law does not matter. Nevertheless, the general pattern is one of dual governance, in which state and federal laws exist side by side with little conflict. When state law is thought to have no role at all in administration of the subject, the field is said to be "completely preempted" by federal law; state regulation is prohibited even though it does not conflict with federal. "Supremacy" and "preemption" cases are one-step, either-or sorts of cases. Crude policy analyses are employed to sustain what appear largely intuitive decisions about what is "uniquely" or "inherently" federal on the one hand or "traditionally for the states" on the other. The federal-state choice-of-law process in these sorts of cases seems without substantial analytic content.

# PART C   WHEN STATE LAW GOVERNS

## § 6.09   Notes on Federal Incorporation of State Law

(1) *"Borrowed" or "incorporated" state law.* Even when it seems obvious that a given matter is appropriately governed by the nation, a variety of motives may encourage a court to pick up as the federal rule of decision whatever the state rule happens to be. Federal incorporation of state law is sometimes statutory: Congress may explicitly adopt state law to deal with federal questions, as it does, for example, in the Federal Tort Claims Act, 28 U.S.C. § 1346(b). More frequently federal incorporation of state law is nonstatutory. A court may "borrow" state law to supply the meaning of an undefined term in a statute, or to fill some statutory gap. Sometimes state law is incorporated because the court wishes to avoid disturbing settled local understandings when no overriding national interest seems to warrant that. Sometimes the national interest may be better served by local solutions.

*Incorporated state law or federal common law.* The question whether federal law should incorporate state law is often entangled with questions of the legitimacy of federal common law. That is because a holding that federal law applies commonly requires a court to fashion a federal common-law rule of decision. On the desirability of federal common law as opposed to federal incorporation of state statutes of limitation, see Abner J. Mikva and James E. Pfander, *On the Meaning of Congressional Silence: Using Federal Common Law to fill the Gap in Congress's Residual Statute of Limitations,* 107 YALE L. J. 529 (1997). But it is the official position of the Supreme Court that the fashioning of federal common law is not to be undertaken casually. State law is commonly "incorporated" in admiralty cases, or permitted to govern in some "residual" sense. See Joel K. Goldstein, *The Life and Times of Wilburn Boat: A Critical Guide, Part One,* 28 J. MARIT. L. & COMM. 395 (1997). For current writing on the complexity of the vertical choice-of-law problem in admiralty, see Steven F. Friedell, *Searching for a Compass: Federal and State law Making Authority in Admiralty,* 57 LA. L. REV. 825 (1997).

(2) *The source of incorporated state law.* From time to time a court will treat incorporated state law as if it governed of its own force. More often it seems clear that the incorporated state law is not operating of its own force, but as a matter of federal law. Can you think of a situation in which a theoretical distinction between incorporated state law "operating of its own force" and incorporated state law "operating as a matter of federal law" would make a practical difference? For one practical consequence of this distinction see the final segment of this Chapter, on "Federal Choice Rules for Interstate Conflicts."

(3) *How state law is incorporated: A two-step process.* Federal incorporation of state law tends to occur in a distinctive two-step process. At the first stage, the court perceives that the issue before it presents a federal question, and that therefore *Erie* is irrelevant, and the issue will be reviewable as a federal question in the United States Supreme Court. But then, at the second stage, the court poses the separate question whether or not it would be desirable to adopt state law anyway.

**DeSYLVA v. BALLENTINE,** 351 U.S. 570 (1956). This was a dispute between the widow of a deceased songwriter and his illegitimate child, over their statutory shares of copyright renewal rights. Under the then Copyright Act, a copyright was good for only 28 years; but a right to renew the copyright for another 28 years returned to the author, free of obligation under any conveyance by the author of the original copyright. In the event of the death of the author, the Act provided a statutory schedule of takers of the right to renew. This schedule included the "children" of the author. The big issue in *DeSylva* was whether an illegitimate child was a "child" within the meaning of the Copyright Act.

*Held* (per JUSTICE HARLAN): For the child, applying California's Probate Code. "The scope of a federal right is, of course, a federal question, but that does not mean that its content is not to be determined by state, rather than federal law. This is especially true where a statute deals with a familial relationship; there is no federal law of domestic relations, which is primarily a matter of state concern. . . . The evident purpose [of the renewal provision] is to provide for the family of the author after his death. . . . [It] takes the form of a compulsory bequest of the copyright to the designated persons. This is really a question of the descent of property, and we think the controlling question under state law should be whether the child would be an heir of the author. . . . "

JUSTICE DOUGLAS (joined by JUSTICE BLACK, concurring): "The meaning of the word 'children' as used in . . . the Copyright Act is a federal question. Congress could of course give the word the meaning it has under the laws of the several States. . . . I would think the statutory policy of protecting dependents would be better served by uniformity, rather than by the diversity which would flow from incorporating into the Act the laws of forty-eight States. I would . . . hold that illegitimate children were 'children' within the meaning of . . . the Copyright Act, whether or not state law would allow them dependency benefits."

---

State law in *DeSylva* clearly protects settled local expectations. But *DeSylva* on its facts is today considerably modified by federal constitutional rulings protecting illegitimates from discrimination.

Is there an argument that *DeSylva* gave insufficient consideration to federal *copyright* policy?*

---

* Congress agreed with Justice Douglas, overriding *DeSylva* in the current copyright statute. 17 U.S.C. § 101. (The statute abolished renewals, but existing renewal rights were "grandfathered" in.) For a policy analysis critical of *DeSylva*, see LOUISE WEINBERG, FEDERAL COURTS: CASES AND COMMENTS ON JUDICIAL FEDERALISM AND JUDICIAL POWER 232-233 (1994). —*Ed.*

# MIREE v. DeKALB COUNTY, GEORGIA

*Supreme Court of the United States*
*433 U.S. 25, 97 S. Ct. 2490, 53 L. Ed. 2d 557 (1977)*

MR. JUSTICE REHNQUIST delivered the opinion of the Court.

These consolidated cases arise out of the 1973 crash of a Lear Jet shortly after takeoff from the DeKalb-Peachtree Airport.[1] The United States Court of Appeals for the Fifth Circuit, *en banc,* affirmed the dismissal of petitioners' complaint against respondent DeKalb County . . ., holding that principles of federal common law were applicable to the resolution of petitioners' breach-of-contract claim. We granted certiorari to consider whether federal or state law should have been applied to that claim. . . .

## I

Petitioners are, respectively, the survivors of deceased passengers, the assignee of the jet aircraft owner, and a burn victim. They brought separate lawsuits, later consolidated, against [DeKalb County, as operator of the airport,] in the United States District Court for the Northern District of Georgia. The basis for federal jurisdiction was diversity of citizenship, and the complaints asserted that [the County] was liable on three independent theories: negligence, nuisance, and breach of contract. . . . The courts below have unanimously agreed that the negligence and nuisance theories are without merit; only the propriety of the dismissal of the contract claims remains in the cases.

Petitioners seek to impose liability on [the County] as third-party beneficiaries of contracts between [the County] and the Federal Aviation Administration (FAA). Their complaints allege that respondent entered into . . . agreements with the FAA. Under the terms of the contracts respondent agreed to "take action to restrict the use of land adjacent to or in the immediate vicinity of the Airport to activities and purposes compatible with normal airport operations including landing and takeoff of aircraft."

Petitioners assert that respondent breached the FAA contracts by owning and maintaining a garbage dump adjacent to the airport, and that the cause of the crash was the ingestion of birds swarming from the dump into the jet engines of the aircraft. . . .

## II

Since the only basis of federal jurisdiction . . . is diversity of citizenship, the case would unquestionably be governed by Georgia law, *Erie Railroad Co.*

---

[1] Petitioners also sued the United States under the Federal Tort Claims Act. The litigation before us arises out of the District Court's granting of respondent DeKalb County's motion to dismiss. . . . The United States has made no similar motion, and is not a party to the cases in this Court.

*v. Tompkins,* 304 U.S. 64 (1938), but for the fact that the United States is a party to the contracts in question, entered into pursuant to federal statute. The *en banc* majority of the Court of Appeals adopted . . . the view that, given these factors, application of federal common law was required. . . .

We do not agree with the conclusion of the Court of Appeals. The litigation before us raises no question regarding the liability of the United States or the responsibilities of the United States under the contracts. The relevant inquiry is a narrow one: whether petitioners as third-party beneficiaries of the contracts have standing to sue respondent. While federal common law may govern even in diversity cases where a uniform national rule is necessary to further the interests of the Federal Government, *Clearfield Trust Co. v. United States,* 318 U.S. 363 (1943), the application of federal common law to resolve the issue presented here would promote no federal interests even approaching the magnitude of those found in *Clearfield Trust* hellip;. [In] this case, the resolution of petitioners' breach-of-contract claim against respondent will have no direct effect upon the United States or its Treasury.[4] The Solicitor General, waiving his right to respond in these cases advised us: "In the course of the proceedings below, the United States determined that its interests would not be directly affected by the resolution of these issues. . . . The operations of the United States in connection with FAA grants such as these are undoubtedly of considerable magnitude. However, we see no reason for concluding that these operations would be burdened or subjected to uncertainty by variant state-law interpretations regarding whether those with whom the United States contracts might be sued by third-party beneficiaries to the contracts. . . .

We think our conclusion that these cases do not fit within the *Clearfield Trust* rule follows from the Court's later decision in *Bank of America National Trust & Savings Assn. v. Parnell,* 352 U.S. 29 (1956), in which the Court declined to apply that rule in a fact situation analogous to this one. *Parnell* was a diversity action between private parties involving United States bonds. The Bank of America had sued *Parnell* to recover funds that he had obtained by cashing the bonds, which had been stolen from the bank. There were two issues: whether the bonds were "overdue" and whether Parnell had taken the bonds in good faith. The Court of Appeals, over a dissent, applied federal law to resolve both issues; this Court reversed with respect to the good-faith issue . . . "Securities issued by the Government generate immediate interests of the Government. These were dealt with in *Clearfield Trust* . . . . But they also radiate interests in transactions between private parties. The present litigation is purely between private parties. . . . " 352 U.S. at 33.

The Court recognized, as we do here, that the application of state law to the issue of good faith did not preclude the application of federal law to questions directly involving the rights and duties of the Federal Government, and found: "Federal law of course governs the interpretation of the nature of the rights and obligations created by the Government bonds themselves. A decision with respect to the 'overdueness' of the bonds is therefore a matter of federal law. . . . " *Id.,* at 34.

---

[4] There is no indication that petitioners' tort claim against the United States will be affected by the resolution of this issue. Indeed, the Federal Tort Claims Act itself looks to state law in determining liability. 28 U.S.C. § 1346(b).

The parallel between *Parnell* and these cases is obvious. The question . . . whether petitioners may sue respondent does not require decision under federal common law since the litigation is among private parties and no substantial rights or duties of the United States hinge on its outcome. On the other hand, nothing we say here forecloses the applicability of federal common law in interpreting the rights and duties of the United States under federal contracts.

Nor is the fact that the United States has a substantial interest in regulating aircraft travel and promoting air travel safety sufficient, given the narrow question before us, to call into play the rule of *Clearfield Trust.* In *Wallis v. Pan American Petroleum Corporation,* 384 U.S. 63, 68 (1966) [Harlan, J.], the Court discussed the nature of a federal interest sufficient to bring forth the application of federal common law:

> "In deciding whether rules of federal common law should be fashioned, normally the guiding principle is that a *significant conflict between some federal policy or interest and the use of state law in the premises must first be specifically shown.* It is by no means enough that, as we may assume, Congress could under the Constitution readily enact a complete code of law governing transactions in federal mineral leases among private parties. Whether latent federal power should be exercised to displace state law is primarily a decision for Congress." (Emphasis added.)

The question . . . whether private parties may, as third-party beneficiaries, sue a municipality for breach of FAA contracts involves this federal interest only insofar as such lawsuits might be thought to advance federal aviation policy by inducing compliance with FAA safety provisions. However, even assuming the correctness of this notion, we adhere to the language in *Wallis,* cited above, stating that the issue of whether to displace state law on an issue such as this is primarily a decision for Congress. Congress has chosen not to do so in this case.[5] Actually the application of federal common law, as interpreted by the Court of Appeals here would frustrate this federal interest *pro tanto,* since that court held that this breach-of-contract lawsuit would not lie under federal law. On the other hand, at least in the opinion of the majority of the panel below, Georgia law would countenance the action. Even assuming that a different result were to be reached under federal common law, we think this language from *Wallis* all but forecloses its application to these cases: "Apart from the highly abstract nature of [the federal] interest, there has been no showing that state law is not adequate to achieve it." 384 U.S., at 71.

We conclude that any federal interest in the outcome of the question before us "is far too speculative, far too remote a possibility to justify the application of federal law to transactions essentially of local concern." *Parnell,* 352 U.S., at 33-34.

Although we have determined that Georgia law should be applied to the question raised by respondent's motion to dismiss, we shall not undertake to

---

[5] The Congress has considered, but not passed, a bill to provide for a federal cause of action arising out of aircraft disasters. See Hearings on S. 961 before the Subcommittee on Improvements in Judicial Machinery of the Senate Committee on the Judiciary, pt. 2, 91st Cong., 1st Sess. (1969).

decide the correct outcome under Georgia law. The dissent to the panel opinion, in a footnote, stated that Georgia law would preclude petitioners from suing as third-party beneficiaries. The panel opinion, of course, held otherwise. . . . We therefore vacate the judgment and remand to the Court of Appeals for consideration of the claim under applicable Georgia law.

### III

Petitioners have argued in this Court that the Airport and Airway Development Act of 1970 provides an implied civil right of action to recover for death or injury due to violation of the Act. 49 U.S.C. § 1701 *et seq.*[6] Petitioners, however, allege only diversity of citizenship as the basis for federal jurisdiction of their lawsuits; they do not rely upon federal-question jurisdiction, which would be more consistent with a theory of an implied federal cause of action under that Act. The complaints sought recovery solely on the grounds of negligence, nuisance, and breach of contract. There is no indication that petitioners alleged a violation of a federal statute and a right to recovery for such a violation. The fact that this asserted basis of liability is so obviously an afterthought may be some indication of its merit, but since it was neither pleaded, argued, nor briefed either in the District Court or in the Court of Appeals, we will not consider it.

The judgment is vacated, and the cases are remanded to the Court of Appeals for further proceedings consistent with this opinion.

Mr. Chief Justice Burger, concurring in the judgment.

There is language in the Court's opinion which might be misinterpreted as rigidly limiting the application of "federal common law" to only those situations where the rights and obligations of the Federal Government are at issue. I do not agree with such a restrictive approach.

I cannot read *Clearfield Trust* and *Parnell* as, in all circumstances, precluding the application of "federal common law" to all matters involving only the rights of private citizens. . . .

I would not read *Wallis v. Pan American Petroleum Corporation,* 384 U.S. 63 (1966), to preclude a choice of "federal common law" simply because there is no specific federal legislation governing the particular transaction at issue. Once it has been determined that it would be inappropriate to apply state law and that federal law must govern, "the inevitable incompleteness presented by all legislation means that interstitial federal lawmaking is a basic responsibility of the federal courts." *United States v. Little Lake Misere Land Co.,* 412 U.S. 580, 593 (1973). In short, although federal courts will be called upon to invoke it infrequently, there must be " 'ederal judicial competence to declare the governing law in an area comprising issues substantially related to an established program of government operation.' " *Ibid.,* quoting Paul Mishkin, *The Variousness of "Federal Law": Competence and Discretion in the*

---

[6] In language similar to that used in the FAA . . . agreements, §§ 1718(3) and (4) require, as a condition precedent to approval of an airport development project, written assurances that the airport approaches will be safely maintained and that the use of land adjacent to the airport will be restricted to uses compatible with aircraft takeoff and landing.

*Choice of National and State Rules for Decision,* 105 U. PA. L. REV. 797, 800 (1957).

Although in my view the issue is close, I conclude, on balance, that the cause of action asserted by the plaintiffs is not so intimately related to the purpose of the Airport and Airway Development Act of 1970 as to require the application of federal law in this case. Accordingly, the rule of *Erie R. Co. v. Tompkins,* 304 U.S. 64 (1938), applies, and I join the judgment of the Court remanding the cases for a determination of the correct outcome under Georgia law.

---

## NOTES ON *MIREE*

(1) *Miree and aviation disaster litigation.* Though not sounding in tort, *Miree* is widely presumed to make unavailable a federal common law of aviation tort.

(2) *Federal common law and judicial process.* Didn't the *Miree* Court hold that third-party beneficiaries have no federal common-law action for breach of federal contracts for the maintenance of safe airports? Isn't that a federal common-law rule?

One of Justice Rehnquist's rationales for *Miree* was that state law better vindicated the national interest in airport safety. Putting to one side the problem that would be presented if, in some subsequent case, state law might be unhelpful to the identified national interest, the trouble with such a reading of *Miree* is that the *Miree* Court did not know what Georgia law *was.* The Court remanded for a determination. Indeed, on remand the question was certified to the Georgia Supreme Court, and on the basis of the Georgia court's answers, the Fifth Circuit held that the plaintiffs in fact could *not* sue under Georgia law as third-party beneficiaries. 588 F.2d 453 (5th Cir. 1979).

Did the *Miree* court also need a clearer determination of what *federal* law was? Are you certain that there is a federal common-law rule against third-party beneficiaries in aviation cases? The Court cites no authority, reaching the issue by "assuming" such a federal common-law rule would block the suit, as the court below held.

Sometimes an alleged federal rule has its origins in pre-*Erie* cases, and may lack authority.

(3) *No law for the case.*

**In re "AGENT ORANGE" PRODUCT LIABILITY LITIGATION,** 635 F.2d 987 (2d Cir. 1980). Consolidated actions by war veterans against the United States government and various companies which supplied the government with the herbicide "Agent Orange" for deforestation purposes during the Viet Nam war. The complaint alleged personal injuries and deaths caused by "Agent Orange," and damage to the veterans' offspring. The trial court held that there was federal-question jurisdiction, treating the claim as one of federal common law, but certified the jurisdictional question for expedited review to the Court of Appeals.

*Held* (per Judge Kearse): These cases evoke national policy concerns, but the content of national policy is unclear. It might be national policy to protect the military supplier, or it might be national policy to compensate the veterans and their families. "The extent to which either group *should* be favored . . . is preeminently a policy determination of the sort reserved in the first instance for Congress." Under the circumstances, residual state law governs, and the case is remanded for trial under state law in the diversity, rather than federal-question, jurisdiction of the district court.

Interestingly, at the time of this opinion in *Agent Orange*, every federal circuit that had considered the question had held that there was some version of a federal common-law defense of immunity for military contractors.

## § 6.10 Statutory Incorporation of State Law

*Introduction.* Sometimes Congress itself explicitly directs that state law should supply a federal rule of decision. Familiar examples include the Federal Tort Claims Act, which makes the United States liable under state law for certain torts by its employees, as a private party would be under the law of the place of the defendant's act or omission; and the Foreign Sovereign Immunities Act of 1976, which makes foreign sovereigns liable in our courts in certain cases, as a private party would be under the law of the place of the defendant's act or omission. The interpretation of such a statutory directive can give some trouble, as the following case demonstrates.

————

## ROBERTSON v. WEGMANN

*Supreme Court of the United States*
*436 U.S. 584, 98 S. Ct. 1991, 56 L. Ed. 2d 554 (1978)*

MR. JUSTICE MARSHALL delivered the opinion of the Court.

I

. . . In 1969, Clay Shaw was tried in a Louisiana state court on charges of having participated in a conspiracy to assassinate President John F. Kennedy. He was acquitted by a jury but within days was arrested on charges of having committed perjury in his testimony at the conspiracy trial. Alleging that these prosecutions were undertaken in bad faith, Shaw [filed a civil rights case under 42 U.S.C. § 1983 in federal district court, naming] as defendants the then District Attorney of Orleans Parish, Jim Garrison, and five other persons, including petitioner . . . Robertson, who was alleged to have lent financial support to Garrison's investigation of Shaw through an organization known as "Truth or Consequences." On Shaw's application, the District Court enjoined prosecution of the perjury action, and the Court of Appeals affirmed.

Since Shaw had filed an action seeking damages, the parties continued with discovery after the injunction issued. Trial was set for November 1974, but in August 1974 Shaw died. The executor of his estate, respondent . . . Wegmann, moved to be substituted as plaintiff, and the District Court granted the motion. Petitioner and other defendants then moved to dismiss the action on the ground that it had abated on Shaw's death.

The District Court denied the motion to dismiss. It began its analysis by referring to 42 U.S.C. § 1988; this statute provides that, when federal law is "deficient" with regard to "suitable remedies" in federal civil rights actions, federal courts are to be governed by "the common law, as modified and changed by the constitution and statutes of the State wherein the court having jurisdiction of [the] civil . . . cause is held, so far as the same is not inconsistent with the Constitution and laws of the United States."

The court found the federal civil rights laws to be "deficient in not providing for survival." It then held that, under Louisiana law, an action like Shaw's would survive only in favor of a spouse, children, parents, or siblings.[3] Since no person with the requisite relationship to Shaw was alive at the time of his death, his action would have abated had state law been adopted as the federal rule. But the court refused to apply state law, finding it inconsistent with federal law, and in its place created "a federal common law of survival in civil rights actions in favor of the personal representative of the deceased."

On . . . interlocutory appeal . . ., the United States Court of Appeals for the Fifth Circuit affirmed. . . . It offered a number of justifications for creating a federal common-law rule allowing respondent to continue Shaw's action: Such a rule would better further the policies underlying § 1983; would "[foster] the uniform application of the civil rights laws;" and would be consistent with "[t]he marked tendency of the federal courts to allow actions to survive in other areas of particular federal concern." The court concluded that, "as a matter of federal common law, a § 1983 action instituted by a plaintiff prior to his death survives in favor of his estate. . . . "[5]

## II

As both courts below held, and as both parties here have assumed, the decision as to the applicable survivorship rule is governed by 42 U.S.C. § 1988. This statute recognizes that . . . federal law simply does not cover every issue that may arise in the context of a federal civil rights action. When federal law is thus "deficient," § 1988 instructs us to turn to "the common law, as modified and changed by the constitution and statutes of the [forum] State," as long as these are "not inconsistent with the Constitution and laws of the

---

[3] See FED. RULE CIV. PROC. 25(a)(1). . . . . [This] Rule does not resolve the question of what law of survival of actions should be applied in this case. It simply describes the manner in which parties are to be substituted in federal court once it is determined that the applicable substantive law allows the action to survive a party's death.

[5] Section 1988's reference to "the common law" might be interpreted as a reference to the decisional law of the forum State, or as a reference to the kind of general common law that was an established part of our federal jurisprudence by the time of § 1988's passage in 1866, see *Swift v. Tyson,* 41 U.S. (16 Pet.) 1 (1842). The latter interpretation has received some judicial and scholarly support. It makes no difference for our purposes which interpretation is the correct one, because Louisiana has a survivorship statute that, under the terms of § 1988, plainly governs this case.

United States." Regardless of the source of the law applied in a particular case, however, it is clear that the ultimate rule adopted under § 1988 "is a federal rule responsive to the need whenever a federal right is impaired." *Sullivan v. Little Hunting Park, Inc.,* 396 U.S. 229, 240 (1969).

. . . [One] specific area not covered by federal law is that relating to the survival of civil rights actions under § 1983 upon the death of either the plaintiff or defendant. State statutes governing the survival of state actions do exist, however. These statutes, which vary widely with regard to both the types of claims that survive and the parties as to whom survivorship is allowed, were intended to modify the simple, if harsh, 19th-century common-law rule [by which] an injured party's personal claim was . . . extinguished upon the death of either the injured party himself or the alleged wrongdoer. Under § 1988, this state statutory law, modifying the common law, provides the principal reference point in determining survival of civil rights actions, subject to the important proviso that state law may not be applied when it is "inconsistent with the Constitution and laws of the United States." Because of this proviso, the courts below refused to adopt as federal law the Louisiana survivorship statute and in its place created a federal common-law rule.

### III

In resolving questions of inconsistency between state and federal law raised under § 1988, courts must look not only at particular federal statutes and constitutional provisions, but also at the policies expressed in them. Of particular importance is whether application of state law would be inconsistent with the federal policy underlying the cause of action under consideration. The instant cause of action arises under 42 U.S.C. § 1983, one of the Reconstruction civil rights statutes. . . .

Despite the broad sweep of § 1983, we can find nothing in the statute or its underlying policies to indicate that a state law causing abatement of a particular action should invariably be ignored in favor of a rule of absolute survivorship. The policies underlying § 1983 include compensation of persons injured by deprivation of federal rights and prevention of abuses of power by those acting under color of state law. No claim is made here that Louisiana's survivorship laws are in general inconsistent with these policies, and indeed most Louisiana actions survive the plaintiff's death. Moreover, certain types of actions that would abate automatically on the plaintiff's death in many States—for example, actions for defamation and malicious prosecution— would apparently survive in Louisiana. In actions other than those for damage to property however, Louisiana does not allow the deceased's personal representative to be substituted as plaintiff; rather, the action survives only in favor of a spouse, children, parents, or siblings. But surely few persons are not survived by one of these close relatives, and in any event no contention is made here that Louisiana's decision to restrict certain survivorship rights in this manner is an unreasonable one.

It is therefore difficult to see how any of § 1983's policies would be undermined if Shaw's action were to abate. The goal of compensating those injured by a deprivation of rights provides no basis for requiring compensation of one who is merely suing as the executor of the deceased's estate. And, given that most Louisiana actions survive the plaintiff's death, the fact that a particular action might abate surely would not adversely affect § 1983's role in preventing official illegality, at least in situations in which there is no claim that the illegality caused the plaintiff's death. A state official contemplating illegal activity must always be prepared to face the prospect of a § 1983 action being filed against him. In light of this prospect, even an official aware of the intricacies of Louisiana survivorship law would hardly be influenced in his behavior by its provisions.

. . . That a federal remedy should be available . . . does not mean that a § 1983 plaintiff (or his representative) must be allowed to continue an action in disregard of the state law to which § 1988 refers us. A state statute cannot be considered "inconsistent" with federal law merely because the statute causes the plaintiff to lose the litigation. If success of the § 1983 action were the only benchmark, there would be no reason at all to look to state law, for the appropriate rule would then always be the one favoring the plaintiff, and its source would be essentially irrelevant. But § 1988 quite clearly instructs us to refer to state statutes; it does not say that state law is to be accepted or rejected based solely on which side is advantaged thereby. Under the circumstances presented here, the fact that Shaw was not survived by one of several close relatives should not itself be sufficient to cause the Louisiana survivorship provisions to be deemed "inconsistent with the Constitution and laws of the United States."

## IV

Our holding today is a narrow one, limited to situations in which no claim is made that state law generally is inhospitable to survival of § 1983 actions and in which the particular application of state survivorship law, while it may cause abatement of the action, has no independent adverse effect on the policies underlying § 1983. A different situation might well be presented, as the District Court noted, if state law "did not provide for survival of any tort actions," or if it significantly restricted the types of actions that survive. . . . We intimate no view, moreover, about whether abatement based on state law could be allowed in a situation in which deprivation of federal rights caused death. . . .

MR. JUSTICE BLACKMUN, with whom MR. JUSTICE BRENNAN and MR. JUSTICE WHITE join, dissenting.

. . . I do not read the emphasis of § 1988, as the Court does, to the effect that the Federal District Court "was required to adopt" the Louisiana statute, and was free to look to federal common law only as a secondary matter. It seems to me that this places the cart before the horse. Section 1988 requires the utilization of federal law ("shall be exercised and enforced in conformity with the laws of the United States"). It authorizes resort to the state statute only if the federal laws "are not adapted to the object" of "protection of all persons in the United States in their civil rights, and for their vindication" or are "deficient in the provisions necessary to furnish suitable remedies and punish offenses against law." Even then, state statutes are an alternative source of law only if "not inconsistent with the Constitution and laws of the United States." Surely, federal law is the rule and not the exception.

Accepting this as the proper starting point, it necessarily follows, it seems to me, that the judgment of the Court of Appeals must be affirmed, not reversed. To be sure, survivorship of a civil rights action under § 1983 upon the death of either party is not specifically covered by the federal statute. But that does not mean that "the laws of the United States" are not "suitable" or are "not adapted to the object" or are "deficient in the provisions necessary." The federal law and the underlying federal policy stand bright and clear. And in the light of that brightness and of that clarity, I see no need to resort to the myriad of state rules governing the survival of state actions.

*First.* In *Sullivan v. Little Hunting Park, Inc.,* 396 U.S. 229 (1969), a case that concerned the availability of compensatory damages for a violation of § 1982, a remedial question, as here, not governed explicitly by any federal statute other than § 1988, Mr. Justice Douglas, writing for the Court, painted with a broad brush the scope of the federal court's choice-of-law authority:

> "As we read § 1988, . . . both federal and state rules on damages may be utilized, whichever better serves the policies expressed in the federal statutes. . . . "

*Second.* The Court's reading of § 1988 cannot easily be squared with its treatment of the problems of immunity and damages under the Civil Rights Acts. Only this Term, in *Carey v. Piphus,* 435 U.S. 247 (1978), the Court set a rule for the award of damages under § 1983 for deprivation of procedural due process by resort to "federal common law." Though the case arose from Illinois, the Court did not feel compelled to inquire into Illinois' statutory or decisional law of damages, nor to test that law for possible "inconsistency" with the federal scheme, before embracing a federal common-law rule. Instead, the Court fashioned a federal damages rule, from common-law sources and its view of the type of injury, to govern such cases uniformly State to State.

Similarly, in constructing immunities under § 1983, the Court has consistently relied on federal common-law rules . . . in attributing immunity to prosecutors and to other officials, matters on which the language of § 1983 is silent. [W]e have not felt bound by the tort immunities recognized in the particular forum State and, only after finding an "inconsistency" with federal standards, then considered a uniform federal rule. Instead, the immunities have been fashioned in light of historic common-law concerns and the policies of the Civil Rights Acts.

*Third.* A flexible reading of § 1988, permitting resort to a federal rule of survival because it "better serves" the policies of the Civil Rights Acts, would be consistent with the methodology employed in the other major choice-of-law provision in the federal structure, namely, the Rules of Decision Act. § 28 U.S.C. § 1652. That Act provides that state law is to govern a civil trial in a federal court "except where the Constitution or treaties of the United States or Acts of Congress otherwise require or provide." The exception has not been interpreted in a crabbed or wooden fashion, but, instead, has been used to give expression to important federal interests. Thus, for example, the exception has been used to apply a federal common law of labor contracts in suits under § 301 of the Labor Management Relations Act of 1947, *Textile Workers Union v. Lincoln Mills,* 353 U.S. 448 (1957); to apply federal common law to transactions in commercial paper issued by the United States where the United States is a party, *Clearfield Trust Co. v. United States,* 318 U.S. 363 (1943); and to avoid application of governing state law to the reservation of mineral rights in a land acquisition agreement to which the United States was a party and that bore heavily upon a federal wildlife regulatory program, *United States v. Little Lake Misere Land Co.,* 412 U.S. 580 (1973).

Just as the Rules of Decision Act cases disregard state law where there is conflict with federal policy, even though no explicit conflict with the terms of a federal statute, so, too, state remedial and procedural law must be disregarded under § 1988 where that law fails to give adequate expression to important federal concerns. . . .

*Fourth* . . .The unsuitability of Louisiana's law is shown by the very case at hand. . . . The Louisiana survivorship rule applies no matter how malicious or ill-intentioned a defendant's action was. In this case, as the Court acknowledges, the District Court found that defendant Garrison brought state perjury charges against plaintiff Shaw "in bad faith and for purposes of harassment," a finding that the Court of Appeals affirmed as not clearly erroneous. The federal interest in specific deterrence, when there was malicious intention to deprive a person of his constitutional rights, is particularly strong. . . . Insuring a specific deterrent under federal law gains importance from the very premise of the Civil Rights Act that state tort policy often is inadequate to deter violations of the constitutional rights of disfavored groups. . . .

The Louisiana rule requiring abatement appears to apply even where the death was intentional and caused, say, by a beating delivered by a defendant. The Court does not deny this result, merely declaring that in such a case it might reconsider the applicability of the Louisiana survivorship statute. . . .

. . . The Court opines that no official aware of the intricacies of Louisiana survivorship law would "be influenced in his behavior by its provisions." But the defendants in Shaw's litigation obviously have been "sweating it out" through the several years of proceedings and litigation in this case. One can imagine the relief occasioned when the realization dawned that Shaw's death might—just might—abate the action. To that extent, the deterrent against behavior such as that attributed to the defendants in this case surely has been lessened.

As to compensation, . . . the Court does not purport to explain why it is consistent with the purposes of § 1983 to recognize a derivative or independent interest in a brother or parent, while denying similar interest to a nephew, grandparent, or legatee.

*Fifth* . . .Does it make sense to apply a federal rule of survivorship in [some] States while preserving a different state rule, stingier than the federal rule, in Louisiana?

A federal rule of survivorship allows uniformity, and counsel immediately know the answer. . . . Nor will federal rights depend on the arcane intricacies of state survival law—which differs in Louisiana according to whether the right is "strictly personal;" [or] whether the action concerns property damage. . . .

. . . A defendant who has violated someone's constitutional rights has no legitimate interest in a windfall release upon the death of the victim. . . .

---

## NOTES ON *WEGMANN*

(1) *A misreading?* Has the Court stood § 1988 on its head? The *Wegmann* dissent points out that there is indeed a vast body of federal common law on civil rights. If the *Wegmann* court is correct, before federal common law was fashioned for the punitive damages and immunities issues in civil rights cases, federal law should have been perceived as "deficient," and reference should have been made to state law. Would such a procedure have served the policies underlying the civil rights laws? Is federal law "deficient" when, even in the absence of specific case law, the result national policy would require is reasonably clear?

(2) **HARDIN v. STRAUB,** 490 U.S. 536 (1989). Action by Michigan state prisoner under the Civil Rights Act of 1871, 42 U.S.C. § 1983, for deprivation of civil rights. The trial court dismissed because the complaint was filed after the expiration of Michigan's 3-year statute of limitations for personal injury torts. On appeal, the prisoner argued that the Michigan statute of limitations contained a standard tolling provision for prisoners; but the Court of Appeals affirmed the dismissal, holding that under § 1988, the tolling provision was "inconsistent" with a national policy in favor of expeditious handling of civil rights cases, identified by the Supreme Court in *New York University v. Tomanio,* 446 U.S. 478 (1980).

*Held* (per JUSTICE STEVENS): The Michigan statute and its tolling provision should have been applied. In *Wilson v. Garcia,* 471 U.S. 261 (1985), this Court held that the personal-injuries statute of limitations of the state should be applied in federal civil rights actions. It is true that in *Tomanio* we held that there is no federal common-law rule that tolls the statute of limitation for prisoners; we refused to toll the state personal-injuries statute, since state law did not contain a tolling provision, either. But the underlying goals of civil rights legislation are compensatory and deterrent, and those goals would best be served by permitting tolling, if the state permits it.

(3) *Alternative reference and former Federal Rule 43(a).* Before promulgation of the Federal Rules of Evidence, former FED. R. CIV. P. 43(a) governed choice of evidence law in federal litigation. The rule provided that federal or state law could be chosen, *whichever would favor admissibility.* This was a rule of alternative reference, with a policy tie-breaker. Under this rule, evidence could be excluded only if both sovereigns' decided cases would exclude it. Thus, federal policy favoring admissibility of evidence was effectuated, without regard to the problem of consistency in "choice." In his *Wegmann* dissent, is Justice Blackmun suggesting that § 1983 should be read similarly, as a rule of alternative reference, with a policy tie-breaker?

(4) *The Rules of Decision Act as a statutory reference to state law.* The dissent in *Wegmann* refers to another familiar federal statutory incorporation of state law, the Rules of Decision Act. Is the dissent correct, that the Act cannot be implemented where state law conflicts with federal policy? This is the view of the Court in *United States v. Little Lake Misere Land Co.,* 412 U.S. 580, 592-593 (1973). In part this view rests on the language of the Rules of Decision Act itself, that state law applies unless the Constitution or an act of Congress otherwise "requires." *See* Louise Weinberg, *The Curious Notion that the Rules of Decision Act Blocks Supreme Federal Common Law,* 83 Nw. U. L. Rev. 860 (1989).

## § 6.11   Administering Federal Courts in State-Law Cases

*Of federal procedure and state substance: A review.* The body of federal law which governs the conduct of federal judicial proceedings is composed of acts of Congress, rules of court, and ordinary case law. All of it is indubitably legitimate. The national lawmaking power over federal courts is established both in the Tribunals Clause of Article I, Section 8, and in Article III, Section 1. As Justice Reed remarked, dissenting in *Erie,* no one doubts federal power over federal procedure.

Nevertheless conflicts between federal procedural and state substantive law have given considerable trouble. The difficulty is that federal procedural law is, indeed, a ghost of *Swift v. Tyson.* Like the "general federal common law" declared unconstitutional in *Erie,* federal procedural law is typically available in federal courts only; it is generally not binding on state courts. So federal procedures can seem to replicate today the chief defect of the pre-*Erie* regime: disparate outcomes in similar cases.

The Court has handled this difficulty by developing the following guidelines:

1. Where an act of Congress, or a rule with the force of an act of Congress, is clearly on point, and is "arguably procedural," it is presumptively constitutional. *Hanna v. Plumer,* 380 U.S. 460 (1965).

2. Where the procedural rule is a federal common-law rule, the test of its constitutionality is whether or not it is "outcome determinative." *Guaranty Trust Co. v. York,* 326 U.S. 99 (1945).

3. However, even where "outcome determinative," if the federal procedural rule manifests strong federal policies, those policies may properly be allowed to outweigh state policies to the contrary. *Byrd v. Blue Ridge Rural Elec. Cooperative, Inc.,* 356 U.S. 525 (1958).

On the other hand, where a federal procedural rule affects trial of an issue as to which *federal* law supplies the rule of decision, federal power is complete, even where important state policies may be offended. That is because, in such cases, federal power over federal tribunals is supplemented by federal substantive power over the particular substantive issue.

---

## GASPERINI v. CENTER FOR HUMANITIES, INC.

*Supreme Court of the United States*
*518 U.S. 415, 116 S. Ct. 2211, 135 L. Ed. 2d 659 (1996)*

Justice Ginsburg delivered the opinion of the Court.

I

. . . Petitioner William Gasperini, a journalist for CBS News and the Christian Science Monitor, began reporting on events in Central America in 1984. . . . During the course of his seven-year stint in Central America, Gasperini took over 5,000 slide transparencies, depicting active war zones, political leaders, and scenes from daily life. In 1990, Gasperini agreed to supply his original color transparencies to The Center for Humanities, Inc. (Center) for use in an educational videotape, "Conflict in Central America." Gasperini selected 300 of his slides for the Center; its videotape included 110 of them. The Center agreed to return the original transparencies, but upon the completion of the project, it could not find them.

Gasperini commenced suit in the United States District Court for the Southern District of New York, invoking the court's diversity jurisdiction. . . . He alleged several state-law claims for relief, including breach of contract, conversion, and negligence. The Center conceded liability for the lost transparencies and the issue of damages was tried before a jury.

At trial, Gasperini's expert witness testified that the "industry standard" within the photographic publishing community valued a lost transparency at $1,500. This industry standard, the expert explained, represented the average license fee a commercial photograph could earn over the full course of the photographer's copyright, *i.e.*, in Gasperini's case, his lifetime plus 50 years. Gasperini estimated that his earnings from photography totaled just over $10,000 for the period from 1984 through 1993. He also testified that he intended to produce a book containing his best photographs from Central America.

After a three-day trial, the jury awarded Gasperini $450,000 in compensatory damages. This sum, the jury foreperson announced, "is $1500 each, for 300 slides." Moving for a new trial under Federal Rule of Civil Procedure 59, the Center attacked the verdict on various grounds, including excessiveness. Without comment, the District Court denied the motion.

The Court of Appeals for the Second Circuit vacated the judgment entered on the jury's verdict. Mindful that New York law governed the controversy, the Court of Appeals endeavored to apply CPLR § 5501(c), which instructs that, when a jury returns an itemized verdict, as the jury did in this case, the New York Appellate Division "shall determine that an award is excessive or inadequate if it deviates materially from what would be reasonable compensation." The Second Circuit's application of § 5501(c) as a check on the size of the jury's verdict followed Circuit precedent elaborated two weeks earlier in *Consorti v. Armstrong World Industries, Inc.*, 64 F.3d 781, superseded, 72 F.3d 1003 (1995). . . .

## II

Before 1986, state and federal courts in New York generally invoked the same judge-made formulation in responding to excessiveness attacks on jury verdicts: courts would not disturb an award unless the amount was so exorbitant that it "shocked the conscience of the court." *See Consorti*, 72 F.3d, at 1012-1013 (collecting cases). . . .

In both state and federal courts, trial judges made the excessiveness assessment in the first instance, and appellate judges ordinarily deferred to the trial court's judgment. . . .

In 1986, as part of a series of tort reform measures, New York codified a standard for judicial review of the size of jury awards. Placed in CPLR § 5501(c), the prescription reads:

> "In reviewing a money judgment . . . in which it is contended that the award is excessive or inadequate and that a new trial should have been granted unless a stipulation is entered to a different award, the appellate division shall determine that an award is excessive or inadequate if it deviates materially from what would be reasonable compensation."

As stated in Legislative Findings and Declarations accompanying New York's adoption of the "deviates materially" formulation, the lawmakers found the "shock the conscience" test an insufficient check on damage awards; the legislature therefore installed a standard "inviting more careful appellate scrutiny." Ch. 266, 1986 N.Y. Laws 470. At the same time, the legislature instructed the Appellate Division, in amended § 5522, to state the reasons for the court's rulings on the size of verdicts, and the factors the court considered in complying with § 5501(c). In his signing statement, then-Governor Mario Cuomo emphasized that the CPLR amendments were meant to ratchet up the review standard. . . .

Although phrased as a direction to New York's intermediate appellate courts, § 5501(c)'s "deviates materially" standard, as construed by New York's courts, instructs state trial judges as well. . . . [Citations omitted.] To determine whether an award "deviates materially from what would be reasonable compensation," New York state courts look to awards approved in similar cases. . . . [Citations omitted.]

## III

In cases like Gasperini's, in which New York law governs the claims for relief, does New York law also supply the test for federal court review of the size of the verdict? The Center answers yes. The "deviates materially" standard, it argues, is a substantive standard that must be applied by federal appellate courts in diversity cases. The Second Circuit agreed. . . . Gasperini . . . characterizes the provision as procedural, an allocation of decisionmaking authority regarding damages, not a hard cap on the amount recoverable. Correctly comprehended, Gasperini urges, § 5501(c)'s direction to the Appellate Division cannot be given effect by federal appellate courts without violating the Seventh Amendment's re-examination clause.

As the parties' arguments suggest, CPLR § 5501(c), appraised under *Erie R. Co. v. Tompkins*, 304 U.S. 64 (1938), and decisions in *Erie* 's path, is both "substantive" and "procedural:" "substantive" in that § 5501(c)'s "deviates materially" standard controls how much a plaintiff can be awarded; "procedural" in that § 5501(c) assigns decisionmaking authority to New York's Appellate Division. Parallel application of § 5501(c) at the federal appellate level would be out of sync with the federal system's division of trial and appellate court functions, an allocation weighted by the Seventh Amendment. The dispositive question, therefore, is whether federal courts can give effect to the substantive thrust of § 5501(c) without untoward alteration of the federal scheme for the trial and decision of civil cases. . . .

## B

. . . Acting essentially as a surrogate for a New York appellate forum, the Court of Appeals reviewed Gasperini's award to determine if it "deviated materially" from damage awards the Appellate Division permitted in similar circumstances. The Court of Appeals performed this task without benefit of an opinion from the District Court, which had denied "without comment" the Center's Rule 59 motion. Concentrating on the authority § 5501(c) gives to the Appellate Division, Gasperini urges that the provision shifts fact-finding responsibility from the jury and the trial judge to the appellate court. Assigning such responsibility to an appellate court, he maintains, is incompatible with the Seventh Amendment's re-examination clause, and therefore, Gasperini concludes, § 5501(c) cannot be given effect in federal court. Although we reach a different conclusion than Gasperini, we agree that the Second Circuit did not attend to "an essential characteristic of [the federal-court] system," *Byrd v. Blue Ridge Rural Elec. Cooperative, Inc.*, 356 U.S. 525, 537 (1958), when it used § 5501(c) as the standard for federal appellate review." . . .

. . . *Byrd* [was] a diversity suit for negligence in which a pivotal issue of fact would have been tried by a judge were the case in state court. The *Byrd* Court held that, despite the state practice, the plaintiff was entitled to a jury trial in federal court. In so ruling, the Court said that the *Guaranty Trust* "outcome-determination" test was an insufficient guide in cases presenting countervailing federal interests. The Court described the countervailing federal interests present in *Byrd* this way:

> ". . . An essential characteristic of [federal courts] is the manner in which, in civil common-law actions, [they distribute] trial functions between judge and jury and, under the influence—if not the command—of the Seventh Amendment, [assign] the decisions of disputed questions of fact to the jury."

The Seventh Amendment . . . also controls the allocation of authority to review verdicts, the issue of concern here. The Amendment reads:

"In Suits at common law, where the value in controversy shall exceed twenty dollars, the right of trial by jury shall be preserved, and no fact tried by a jury, shall be otherwise re-examined in any Court of the United States, than according to the rules of the common law." U.S. Const., Amdt. 7.

*Byrd* involved the first clause of the Amendment, the "trial by jury" clause. This case involves the second, the "re-examination" clause. In keeping with the historic understanding, the re-examination clause does not inhibit the authority of trial judges to grant new trials "for any of the reasons for which new trials have heretofore been granted in actions at law in the courts of the United States." Fed. Rule Civ. Proc. 59(a). That authority is large. . . .

. . . Before today, we have not "expressly [held] that the Seventh Amendment allows appellate review of a district court's denial of a motion to set aside an award as excessive." . . .

As the Second Circuit explained, appellate review for abuse of discretion is reconcilable with the Seventh Amendment as a control necessary and proper to the fair administration of justice. . . . All other Circuits agree. . . .

## C

In *Byrd*, the Court faced a one-or-the-other choice: trial by judge as in state court, or trial by jury according to the federal practice. In the case before us, a choice of that order is not required, for the principal state and federal interests can be accommodated. . . . New York's dominant interest can be respected, without disrupting the federal system, once it is recognized that the federal district court . . . can apply the State's "deviates materially" standard. . . . We recall, in this regard, that the "deviates materially" standard serves as the guide to be applied in trial as well as appellate courts in New York.

Within the federal system, practical reasons combine with Seventh Amendment constraints to lodge in the district court, not the court of appeals, primary responsibility for application of § 5501(c)'s "deviates materially" check. Trial judges have the "unique opportunity to consider the evidence in the living courtroom context," while appellate judges see only the "cold paper record." [Citation omitted.]

District court applications of the "deviates materially" standard would be subject to appellate review under the standard the Circuits now employ when inadequacy or excessiveness is asserted on appeal: abuse of discretion. . . .

## IV

. . . Accordingly, we vacate the judgment of the Court of Appeals and instruct that court to remand the case to the District Court so that the trial judge, revisiting his ruling on the new trial motion, may test the jury's verdict against CLPR § 5501(c)'s "deviates materially" standard. . . .

[JUSTICE STEVENS' dissent is omitted.]

JUSTICE SCALIA, with whom the CHIEF JUSTICE and JUSTICE THOMAS join, dissenting.

Today the Court overrules a longstanding and well-reasoned line of precedent that has for years prohibited federal appellate courts from reviewing refusals by district courts to set aside civil jury awards as contrary to the weight of the evidence. One reason is given for overruling these cases: that the courts of appeals have, for some time now, decided to ignore them. Such unreasoned capitulation to the nullification of what was long regarded as a core component of the Bill of Rights—the Seventh Amendment's prohibition on appellate reexamination of civil jury awards—is wrong. It is not for us, much less for the courts of appeals, to decide that the Seventh Amendment's restriction on federal-court review of jury findings has outlived its usefulness.

The Court also holds today that a state practice that relates to the division of duties between state judges and juries must be followed by federal courts in diversity cases. On this issue, too, our prior cases are directly to the contrary.

As I would reverse the judgment of the Court of Appeals, I respectfully dissent. . . .

## II

The Court acknowledges that state procedural rules cannot, as a general matter, be permitted to interfere with the allocation of functions in the federal court system. . . . But the . . . Court approves the "accommodation" achieved by having district courts review jury verdicts under the "deviates materially" standard, because it regards that as a means of giving effect to the State's purposes "without disrupting the federal system." But changing the standard by which trial judges review jury verdicts does disrupt the federal system, and is plainly inconsistent with "the strong federal policy against allowing state rules to disrupt the judge-jury relationship in federal court." *Byrd v. Blue Ridge Rural Elec. Cooperative, Inc.*, 356 U.S. 525, 538 (1958). . . .

We discussed precisely the point at issue here in *Browning-Ferris Industries of Vt., Inc. v. Kelco Disposal, Inc.*, 492 U.S. 257 (1989), and gave an answer altogether contrary to the one provided today. *Browning-Ferris* rejected a request to fashion a federal common-law rule limiting the size of punitive-damages awards in federal courts, reaffirming the principle of *Erie R. Co. v. Tompkins*, 304 U.S. 64 (1938), that "In . . . any . . . lawsuit where state law provides the basis of decision, the propriety of an award of punitive damages . . . and the factors the jury may consider in determining their amount, are questions of state law." 492 U.S., at 278. But the opinion expressly stated that "Federal law . . . will control on those issues involving the proper review of the jury award by a federal district court and court of appeals." *Id.*, at 278-279. . . . The same distinction necessarily applies where the judgment under review is for compensatory damages: State substantive law controls what injuries are compensable and in what amount; but federal standards determine whether the award exceeds what is lawful to such degree that it may be set aside by order for new trial or remittitur.

The Court does not disavow those statements in *Browning-Ferris* (indeed, it does not even discuss them), but it presumably overrules them, at least where the state rule that governs "whether a new trial or remittitur should be ordered" is characterized as "substantive" in nature. . . .

I do not see how this can be so. It seems to me quite wrong to regard [New York's] provision as a "substantive" rule for *Erie* purposes. The analogy to a statutory cap on damages fails utterly. There is an absolutely fundamental distinction between a rule of law such as that, which would ordinarily be imposed upon the jury in the trial court's instructions, and a rule of review, which simply determines how closely the jury verdict will be scrutinized for compliance with the instructions. . . .

To say that application of § 5501(c) in place of the federal standard will not consistently produce disparate results is not to suggest that the decision the Court has made today is not a momentous one. The principle that the state standard governs is of great importance, since it bears the potential to destroy the uniformity of federal practice and the integrity of the federal court system. Under the Court's view, a state rule that directed courts "to determine that an award is excessive or inadequate if it deviates in any degree from the proper measure of compensation" would have to be applied in federal courts, effectively requiring federal judges to determine the amount of damages *de novo*, and effectively taking the matter away from the jury entirely. *Cf. Byrd*, 356 U.S., at 537-538. . . .

. . . [In] my view, one does not even reach the *Erie* question in this case. The standard to be applied by a district court in ruling on a motion for a new trial is set forth in Rule 59 of the Federal Rules of Civil Procedure, which provides that "A new trial may be granted . . . for any of the reasons for which new trials have heretofore been granted in actions at law in the courts of the United States." That is undeniably a federal standard. . . .

\* \* \*

There is no small irony in the Court's declaration today that appellate review of refusals to grant new trials for error of fact is a control necessary and proper to the fair administration of justice. It is objection to precisely that sort of control by federal appellate judges that gave birth to the Reexamination Clause of the Seventh Amendment. Alas, those who drew the Amendment, and the citizens who approved it, did not envision an age in which the Constitution means whatever this Court thinks it ought to mean—or indeed, whatever the courts of appeals have recently thought it ought to mean.

When there is added to the revision of the Seventh Amendment the Court's precedent-setting disregard of Congress's instructions in Rule 59, one must conclude that this is a bad day for the Constitution's distinctive Article III courts in general, and for the role of the jury in those courts in particular. I respectfully dissent.

---

For recent writing see Douglas Floyd, *Erie Awry: A Comment on Gasperini v. Center for Humanities, Inc.,* 1997 B.Y.U. L. REV. 267 (1997). On the general problem of federal procedure for procedure for state-law cases, see Joseph P. Bauer, *The Erie Doctrine Revisited: How a Conflicts Perspective Can Aid the Analysis,* 74 NOTRE DAME L. REV. 1235 (1999).

## PART D   FEDERAL CONFLICTS LAW

### INTRODUCTORY NOTES ON FEDERAL CHOICE RULES

Thus far, this Chapter has been concerned with the federal-state choice-of-law process. We might conceptualize federal-state conflicts as "vertical" ones. We turn now to the subject of federal conflicts law to govern "horizontal" conflicts. The example that may occur to you first is the body of federal conflicts law that deals with conflicts between the law of this country and a foreign country.

There also exist rules of federal law that are used to guide resolution of interstate conflicts. For example, when state law is incorporated into federal law, the question may arise, "*Which* state's law?" There are federal "horizontal" conflicts cases that address this question. The federal conflicts rules for both the international cases and the incorporated state-law cases apply in both federal and state courts. For ordinary state-law cases in federal courts, the Supreme Court has developed a third body of federal choice rules for determining which state's law a federal court must apply. These latter rules typically require a renvoi-like reference to the conflicts rules of a particular state. But as an initial proposition they are conflicts rules for federal courts only.

As you review these bodies of federal conflicts law for interstate cases, consider the propriety and feasibility of a new, fourth body of federal conflicts law, to govern ordinary interstate conflicts *in all courts*. This new conflicts law might take the form, perhaps, of national legislation, or, perhaps, of a federal common law of the conflict of laws.

---

### § 6.12   Interstate Choices in Federal Cases

### PRELIMINARY NOTES ON FEDERAL LAW AND INTERSTATE CONFLICTS

(1) *The interstate conflict in federal cases.* In *DeSylva v. Ballentine, supra,* recall that the Supreme Court held that courts nevertheless should refer to state law to determine who was a "child" for purposes of federal copyright renewal. But the Court had no occasion to reach the question *which* state's law. What if in *DeSylva* the author had died domiciled in New York, but had lived there only very briefly, and indeed had lived most of his adult life with the illegitimate child in California? Which state's law would apply? In such a case, federal courts are not bound to apply the choice rules of the states in which they sit, but are free to choose law by any method available to them. *Cf. Scott v. Eastern Air Lines,* 399 F.2d 14 (3d Cir. 1968). Although the Supreme Court has never endorsed any single method in such cases, lower courts typically resort to the formula, "place of most significant contact," lifted from the Second Restatement.

(2) *The question of national policy.* Whatever the merits of the Restatement formula, perhaps the choice of law in such cases should depend, rather, on

what would best serve the national policy underlying the federal law at issue. Consider the following example. When dealing with actions under older acts of Congress, federal courts typically refer to state law to supply periods of limitation for federal claims[1] But suppose there are two relevant states? Depending on the strength of national enforcement policy, arguably the longer of the two statutes should be chosen, in preference to the statute of the state "of most significant contact" with the case.

(3) *Statutory choices.* Occasionally Congress explicitly specifies a mandatory choice among incorporated state laws. For example, the Social Security Act refers to the law of the state where a deceased insured died domiciled, to govern the question whether the surviving spouse was married to the insured. To take another example, the Federal Tort Claims Act mandates the law of the state of the wrongful act or omission to govern the liability of the United States for the torts of its employees.

(4) *A federal rule of renvoi.* In the case of the Federal Tort Claims Act, the Supreme Court has construed the statutory reference to the state of wrongful act or omission, to be to that state's "whole law," including its choice rules. *Richards v. United States,* 369 U.S. 1 (1962). In other words, the Court read the doctrine of "renvoi" into the statute.

## § 6.13  Federal Statutory Choices Among State Laws

**INTERNATIONAL PAPER CO. v. OUELLETTE,** 479 U.S. 481 (1987). Action for damages for pollution by a paper mill operating in New York on the bank of Lake Champlain. The action was filed in Vermont Court under the Vermont common law of nuisance. The plaintiffs were property owners residing on the Vermont shore of Lake Champlain. They alleged that the paper mill made their water "foul, unhealthy, smelly, and . . . unfit for recreational use," thereby diminishing the value of their property in the amount of $20 million. They also sought $100 million in punitive damages. The defendant paper mill argued that the suit was preempted by the federal Clean Water Act.

*Held* (per JUSTICE POWELL): The Vermont property owners' suit as framed is preempted by the Clean Water Act. It is true that the Clean Water Act has a saving clause, saving state common law. "[But after] examining the [Act] as a whole, its purposes and its history, we are convinced that if affected States were allowed to impose separate discharge standards on a single point source, the inevitable result would be a serious interference with the achievement of the full purposes and objectives of Congress." Thus, the only state common

---

[1] In 1990 Congress provided a prospective uniform 4-year federal statute of limitations for actions under all later federal statutes. 28 U.S.C. § 1658 provides: "Except as otherwise provided by law, a civil action arising under an Act of Congress enacted after the date of this section may not be commenced later than 4 years after the cause of actions accrues."

For personal-injuries actions under general as well as statutory maritime law, in 1980 Congress provided a uniform 3-year statute. 46 U.S.C. § 763a provides, "Unless otherwise specified by law, a suit for recovery of damages for personal injury or death, or both, arising out of a maritime tort, shall not be maintained unless commenced within three years from the date the cause of action accrued."

law that can be "saved" is the law of the state where the pollution source is located.

JUSTICE BRENNAN (joined by JUSTICES MARSHALL and BLACKMUN, dissenting in part): "I disagree . . . with the Court's view that a Vermont court must apply New York nuisance law. . . . " The language of the statute saves, rather than preempts, state law for these cases.

[JUSTICE STEVENS, joined by JUSTICE BLACKMUN, also filed a separate opinion dissenting in part.]

---

## NOTES ON *OUELLETTE*

(1) *Law and the degradation of the environment.* By allowing the polluter to locate in a state that permits the pollution, has the Supreme Court done a disservice to national environmental policy?

In *Arkansas v. Oklahoma,* 501 U.S. 91 (1992), the Court, per Justice Stevens, unanimously sustained an EPA permit *requiring* compliance with the water-quality standards of downstream states. The Court explained:

> "Unlike [*Milwaukee* and *Ouellette*], this litigation involves not a state-issued permit, but a federally issued permit. . . . Although [the provisions of the Clean Water Act] do not authorize the downstream State to veto the issuance of a permit for a new point source in another State, the Administrator retains authority to block the issuance of any state-issued permit that is outside the . . . requirements of the Act. . . . *Ouellette* . . . [does] not in any way constrain the EPA's authority to require a point source to comply with downstream water quality standards."

But the Court refrained from endorsing the views of the Tenth Circuit Court of Appeals in the case, views critical of *Ouellette.* The Tenth Circuit had characterized the law of the state of the pollution source as "the lowest common denominator." The Tenth Circuit had also noted evidence of significant degradation to the Illinois River, and little or no enforcement action.

*See,* recently, Joshua D. Sarnoff, *The Continuing Imperative (But Only from a National Perspective) for Federal Environmental Protection,* 7 DUKE ENVTL. L. & POL'Y F. 225 (1997).

---

## § 6.14  Federal Common-Law Choices Among State Laws

**TEXAS v. NEW JERSEY,** 379 U.S. 674 (1965). Action in the original jurisdiction of the Supreme Court, to determine under the federal common law of interstate relations which of two states was entitled to escheat intangible unclaimed property. In this case the Sun Oil Company, over a period of four decades, had accumulated some 1700 small creditors who had never claimed the moneys due them or cashed checks sent them. The right to escheat was claimed both by Texas and Pennsylvania as "the" principal place of business of Sun Oil, and also by New Jersey, as Sun Oil's state of incorporation.

*Held* (per Justice Black): "Since the States separately are without constitutional power to provide a rule to settle this interstate controversy and since there is no applicable federal statute, it becomes our responsibility in the exercise of our original jurisdiction to adopt a rule which will settle the question. . . . Since this Court has held in *Western Union Tel. Co. v. Pennsylvania,* 368 U.S. 71 (1961), that the same property cannot constitutionally be escheated by more than one State," we must choose exclusively the only law that can apply. The test of significant contacts would be too vague for this purpose. States would lose more in litigation expenses than they might gain in escheats. We hold that unclaimed intangible property may be escheated only by the State of the last known address of the creditor, as shown by the debtor's books. In the absence of any address for the creditor, or if the creditor's state has failed to make a timely escheat, the right to escheat is lodged, within certain constraints, in the state of incorporation of the debtor.

---

## NOTE ON *TEXAS v. NEW JERSEY*

*What does it mean?* Does the rule of *Texas v. New Jersey* speak to choice of law or jurisdiction? Or both?**

In *California v. Texas,* 437 U.S. 601 (1978), the Court refused to decide within its original jurisdiction a similar interstate controversy over the right to tax the estate of the multimillionaire, Howard Hughes. Then, in *Cory v. White,* 457 U.S. 85 (1982), the Court held that the Federal Interpleader Act provides no jurisdictional basis for federal trial courts to resolve inconsistent death tax claims against the Hughes estate. Recall, however, that in *Nevada v. Hall,* Chapter 5, *supra,* the Court recognized the power of a state to take jurisdiction over claims against a sister state.

---

## § 6.15  Interstate Choices for Federal Courts Only

In the preceding materials we observed federal choice rules which, under the Supremacy Clause, undoubtedly would be binding on state courts if similar questions were to arise in state courts.

In this section, we deal with a different body of federal choice-of-law rules, one evolved for handling issues which, under *Erie,* are governed exclusively by state law. These latter choice rules mandatory, like other federal "procedural" rules, only in federal courts.

---

* The Supreme Court's efforts to deal with the problem of conflicting state escheatment claims are now superseded by an act of Congress. *See* 12 U.S.C. §§ 2501-03.

**KLAXON CO. v. STENTOR ELECTRIC MFG. CO., INC.,** 313 U.S. 487 (1941). This began as an action on the contract tried under New York law in a federal diversity court in Delaware. After judgment in the plaintiff's favor, the plaintiff moved the district court for an award of pre-judgment interest. The trial judge granted the award of interest as mandatory under New York law. The Court of Appeals affirmed on the ground that an award of interest was "substantive," and that the "better view" was that interest, like damages, was governed by the law of the place of performance, New York.

*Held* (per JUSTICE REED): When a federal court is applying state law under the compulsion of *Erie,* the question *which* state's law must also be decided by state law. There is no general federal common law of the conflict of laws. *Erie* requires that the law to be applied in such cases be the whole law of the state in which the federal court is sitting, including its choice-of-law rules. "Any other ruling would do violence to the principle of uniformity within a state. . . . "

---

Was the *Klaxon* Court right, that *Erie* requires a reference to the choice rules of the forum state in a state-law case in federal court? In *Erie* itself, the Court remanded for trial under the law of the place of injury, without consulting the choice rules of the forum state. Nor did the Rules of Decision Act, 28 U.S.C. § 1652, make such a choice, specifying only that "The laws of the several states" shall govern in cases where they apply, "except where the Constitution . . . or Acts of Congress otherwise require or provide." But isn't the Court right, that any other initial reference would evoke disturbing echoes of the pre-*Erie* regime?

For current writing on the duty of federal judges under *Klaxon,* see Bradford R. Clark, *Ascertaining the Laws of the Several States: Positivism and Judicial Federalism after Erie,* 145 U. PA. L. REV. 1459 (1997).

---

## VAN DUSEN v. BARRACK

*Supreme Court of the United States*
*376 U.S. 612, 84 S. Ct. 805, 11 L. Ed. 2d 945 (1964)*

MR. JUSTICE GOLDBERG delivered the opinion of the Court.

. . . On October 4, 1960, shortly after departing from a Boston airport, a commercial airliner, scheduled to fly from Boston to Philadelphia, plunged into Boston Harbor. As a result of the crash, over 150 actions for personal injury and wrongful death have been instituted against the airline, various manufacturers, the United States, and, in some cases, the Massachusetts Port Authority. In most of these actions the plaintiffs have alleged that the crash resulted from the defendants' negligence in permitting the aircraft's engines to ingest some birds. More than 100 actions were brought in the United States

District Court for the District of Massachusetts, and more than 45 actions in the United States District Court for the Eastern District of Pennsylvania. The present case concerns 40 of the wrongful death actions brought in the Eastern District of Pennsylvania by personal representatives of victims of the crash. The defendants, petitioners in this Court, moved under § 1404(a) to transfer these actions to the District of Massachusetts, where it was alleged that most of the witnesses resided and where over 100 other actions are pending. The District Court granted the motion, holding that the transfer was justified regardless of whether the transferred actions would be governed by the laws and choice-of-law rules of Pennsylvania or of Massachusetts. The District Court also specifically held that transfer was not precluded by the fact that the plaintiffs had not qualified under Massachusetts law to sue as representatives of the decedents. The plaintiffs, respondents in this Court, sought a writ of mandamus from the Court of Appeals and successfully contended that the District Court erred and should vacate its order of transfer. The Court of Appeals held that a § 1404(a) transfer could be granted only if at the time the suits were brought, the plaintiffs had qualified to sue in Massachusetts, the State of the transferee District Court. . . .

## I. WHERE THE ACTION "MIGHT HAVE BEEN BROUGHT."

Section 1404(a) reflects an increased desire to have federal civil suits tried in the federal system at the place called for in the particular case by considerations of convenience and justice. . . . To this end it empowers a district court to transfer "any civil action" to another district court . . . in which the action "might have been brought." Although in the present case the plaintiffs were qualified to bring suit as personal representatives under Pennsylvania law (the law of the State of the transferor federal court), the Court of Appeals ruled that the defendants' transfer motion must be denied because at the time the suits were brought in Pennsylvania (the transferor forum) the complainants had not obtained the appointments requisite to initiate such actions in Massachusetts (the transferee forum). [Justice Goldberg first decided that this action "might have been brought" in Massachusetts, as a matter of statutory interpretation of the federal transfer statute: "We cannot agree that the final clause of § 1404(a) was intended to restrict the availability of convenient federal forums by referring to state-law rules, such as those concerning capacity to sue, which would have applied if the action had originally been instituted in the transferee federal court."]

. . . [In] our opinion the underlying and fundamental question is whether, in a case such as the present, a change of venue within the federal system is to be accompanied by a change in the applicable state law. . . .

## II. "THE INTEREST OF JUSTICE": EFFECT OF A CHANGE OF VENUE UPON APPLICABLE STATE LAW.

. . . [The] plaintiffs emphasize the likelihood that the defendants' "ultimate reason for seeking transfer is to move to a forum where recoveries for wrongful death are restricted to sharply limited punitive damages rather than compensation for the loss suffered." It is argued that Pennsylvania choice-of-law rules would result in the application of laws substantially different from those that would be applied by courts sitting in Massachusetts. . . .

If conflict of laws rules are laid aside, it is clear that Massachusetts (the State of the transferee court) and Pennsylvania (the State of the transferor court) have significantly different laws concerning recovery for wrongful death. The Massachusetts Death Act provides that one who negligently causes the death of another "shall be liable in damages in the sum of not less than two thousand nor more than twenty thousand dollars, to be assessed with reference to the degree of his culpability." By contrast, under Pennsylvania law the recovery of damages is based upon the more common principle of compensation for losses rather than upon the degree of the tortfeasor's culpability and is not limited to $20,000. Some of the defendants urge, however, that these differences are irrelevant to the present case because Pennsylvania state courts, applying their own choice of law rules, would require that the Massachusetts Death Act be applied in its entirety, including its culpability principle and damage limitation. It follows that a federal district court sitting in Pennsylvania, and referring, as is required by *Klaxon Co. v. Stentor Elec. Mfg. Co., Inc.,* 313 U.S. 487 (1941), to Pennsylvania choice-of-law rules, would therefore be applying the same substantive rules as would a state or federal court in Massachusetts if the actions had been commenced there. . . . The plaintiffs, however, [argue] that Pennsylvania, in light of its laws and policies, might not apply the culpability and damage limitation aspects of the Massachusetts statute. . . .

The possibilities suggested by the plaintiffs' argument illustrate the difficulties that would arise if a change of venue, granted at the motion of a defendant, were to result in a change of law. Although in the present case the contentions concern rules relating to capacity to sue and damages, in other cases the transferee forum might have a shorter statute of limitations or might refuse to adjudicate a claim which would have been actionable in the transferor State. In such cases a defendant's motion to transfer could be tantamount to a motion to dismiss. . . . [The] potential prejudice to the plaintiffs is so substantial as to require review of the assumption that a change of state law would be a permissible result of transfer. . . .

The decisions of the lower federal courts, taken as a whole, reveal that courts . . . have been strongly inclined to protect plaintiffs against the risk that transfer might be accompanied by a prejudicial change in applicable state laws. . . .

Of course these cases allow plaintiffs to retain whatever advantages may flow from the state laws of the forum they have initially selected. There is nothing, however, in the language or policy of § 1404(a) to justify its use by defendants to defeat the advantages accruing to plaintiffs who have chosen a forum which, although it was inconvenient, was a proper venue. In this regard the transfer provisions of § 1404(a) may be compared with those of § 1406(a). Although both sections were broadly designed to allow transfer instead of dismissal, § 1406(a) provides for transfer from forums in which venue is wrongly or improperly laid, whereas, in contrast, § 1404(a) operates on the premises that the plaintiff has properly exercised his venue privilege. . . .

The legislative history . . . certainly does not justify the rather startling conclusion that one might "get a change of law as a bonus for a change of venue.". . . . If a change of law were in the offing, the parties might well regard the section primarily as a forum-shopping instrument. And, more importantly, courts would at least be reluctant to grant transfers, despite considerations of convenience, if to do so might conceivably prejudice the claim of a plaintiff who had initially selected a permissible forum. We believe, therefore, that both the history and purposes of § 1404(a) indicate that it should be regarded as a federal judicial housekeeping measure, dealing with the placement of litigation in the federal courts and generally intended, on the basis of convenience and fairness, simply to authorize a change of courtrooms.

Although we deal here with a congressional statute apportioning the business of the federal courts, our interpretation of that statute fully accords with and is supported by the policy underlying *Erie R. Co. v. Tompkins.* This Court has often formulated the *Erie* doctrine by stating that it establishes "the principle of uniformity within a state," *Klaxon,* 313 U.S. at 496. . . . A superficial reading of these formulations might suggest that a transferee federal court should apply the law of the State in which it sits rather than the law of the transferor State. Such a reading, however, directly contradicts the fundamental *Erie* doctrine which the quoted formulations were designed to express. As this Court said in *Guaranty Trust Co. of New York v. York,* 326 U.S. 99, 109 (1945):

> ". . . The nub of the policy that underlies *Erie R. Co. v. Tompkins* is that for the same transaction the accident of a suit by a nonresident litigant in a federal court instead of in a State court a block away, should not lead to a substantially different result."

Applying this analysis to § 1404(a), we should ensure that the "accident" of federal diversity jurisdiction does not enable a party to utilize a transfer to achieve a result in federal court which could not have been achieved in the courts of the State where the action was filed. . . .

We conclude, therefore, that in cases such as the present, where the defendants seek transfer, the transferee district court must be obligated to apply the state law that would have been applied if there had been no change of venue. . . .

In so ruling, however, we do not and need not consider whether in all cases § 1404(a) would require the application of the law of the transferor, as opposed to the transferee, State. We do not attempt to determine whether, for example, the same considerations would govern if a plaintiff sought transfer . . . or if it was contended that the transferor State would simply have dismissed the action on the ground of forum non conveniens. . . .

[The Court went on to hold, in this part of its opinion, that the reference in the Federal capacity rule, 17(b), to the state "in which the district court is held," was also to be interpreted in transfer cases as a reference to the transferor court.]

## III. APPLICABLE LAW: EFFECT ON THE CONVENIENCE OF PARTIES AND WITNESSES.

The holding that a § 1404(a) transfer would not alter the state law to be applied does not dispose of the question of whether the proposed transfer can be justified when measured against the relevant criteria of convenience and fairness. . . .

[We] are fully aware that the District Court concluded that the relevant Pennsylvania law was unsettled, that its determination involved difficult questions, and that in the near future Pennsylvania courts might provide guidance. We think that this uncertainty, however, should itself have been considered as a factor bearing on the desirability of transfer. . . . We do not suggest that elements of uncertainty in transferor state law would alone justify a denial of transfer; but we do think that the uncertainty is one factor, among others, to be considered in assessing the desirability of transfer. . . .

. . . [The] District Court ignored [such] considerations which might well have been more clearly appraised and might have been considered controlling had not that court assumed that even after transfer to Massachusetts the transferee District Court would be free to decide that the law of its State might apply. It is appropriate, therefore, to reverse the judgment of the Court of Appeals and to remand to the District Court to reconsider the motion to transfer. . . .

MR. JUSTICE BLACK concurs in the reversal substantially for the reasons set forth in the opinion of the Court, but he believes that, under the circumstances shown in the opinion, this Court should now hold it was error to order these actions transferred to the District of Massachusetts.

---

## NOTES ON *VAN DUSEN*

(1) *Multidistrict litigation.* After *Van Dusen* was decided, Congress enacted legislation providing for transfer and consolidation of mass cases with scattered numerous filings. See Multidistrict Litigation Act of 1968, 28 U.S.C. § 1407. The legislation has no statutory choice-of-law directive. Nevertheless courts generally administer the statute under the rule of *Van Dusen* (see, e.g., *In re Air Crash Disaster at Boston, Mass.,* 399 F.Supp. 1106 (D. Mass. 1975); but see, e.g., *In re Paris Air Crash,* 399 F.Supp. 732 (C.D. Cal. 1975) (damages law of transferee forum applied).

(2) *The interests of justice and law-shopping.* Should the defendant be able to work a change in governing law by obtaining a change of venue? If not, why should the plaintiff be able to shop for favorable law at the outset? Is there any way to reconcile the viewpoints of the *Van Dusen* Court and the Court in *Piper Aircraft Co. v. Reyno*? Since, in the international case, there is no way of controlling the law that would be applied in a foreign forum, should the concerns undergirding the opinion in *Van Dusen* have counted for more in *Reyno*? Recall that such concerns also traditionally justify the elaborate conditions imposed on dismissals for forum non conveniens.

(3) **SCHREIBER v. ALLIS-CHALMERS CORP.,** 611 F.2d 790 (10th Cir. 1979). Action by Kansas plaintiff for personal injuries sustained in Kansas, brought in federal district court in Mississippi. Mississippi's only contact with the case was that the defendant manufacturer was doing business there. But the lure of Mississippi as a forum was its long (6-year) statute of limitations, and the absence of a "borrowing statute" Mississippi would apply to cut off stale out-of-state claims. The defendant moved under 28 U.S.C. § 1404(a) for transfer to federal district court in Kansas. This motion was granted. Once in Kansas, the defendant moved to dismiss because the Kansas statute of limitations had expired. The federal court in Kansas denied the motion, applying Mississippi's 6-year statute.

*Held*: For the plaintiff. Mississippi's statute governs. Kansas' choice rules are immaterial. Mississippi characterizes its limitations statute as "procedural" and would apply the statute in this case, and under *Klaxon* and *Van Dusen,* the transferee court was bound by the choices that the transferor state would make.

---

In *Ferens v. John Deere & Co.,* 494 U.S. 516 (1990), the Supreme Court sustained the *Schreiber* device in a case in which transfer was on the plaintiff's motion.

(4) *Mass tort.* What are the implications of *Van Dusen* for mass disaster litigation? In aviation cases, where the victims will tend to be similarly situated at least with respect to the defendant's liability, the choice-of-law process under *Van Dusen* may be manageable. But what of mass toxic tort cases? Not infrequently, the litigational complexity of a mass disaster case is compounded by international contacts.

Recall, in this regard, that the Due Process Clause has now been held to impose a constitutional burden on courts similar to the statutory burden imposed on federal courts by *Van Dusen. See Phillips Petroleum Co. v. Shutts, supra.*

(5) *Substantive federal tort rules?* Of course, substantive federal tort law for mass disasters would clear up the conflicts difficulties. But Congress has repeatedly rejected bills that would authorize uniform federal tort law for mass disasters.

Courts are generally even less hospitable than Congress to the notion of fashioning substantive federal common law for mass disaster cases. See, e.g., the rejection of the defendant's effort to obtain federal common law in the closely divided decision in *Jackson v. Johns-Manville Corp.,* 750 F.2d 1314 (5th Cir. 1985) (en banc).

---

# In re "AGENT ORANGE" PRODUCT LIABILITY LITIGATION

[On remand from 635 F.2d 987 (2d Cir. 1980)]
*United States District Court*
*580 F.Supp. 690 (E.D. N.Y. 1984)*

WEINSTEIN, Chief Judge. A considerable number of Vietnam war veterans . . . claim to have suffered injury as a result of . . . exposure to herbicides in Vietnam. Defendants produced those herbicides. Individual claims, originally filed in all parts of the country, were transferred for pretrial purposes to this court. Subject to some powers to opt out, common issues presented by plaintiffs' claims will now be tried together since a class has been certified pursuant to Rule 23. . . .

## *INTRODUCTION*

Plaintiffs originally sought to [rely] on federal question jurisdiction. 28 U.S.C. § 1331. This court sustained their contention. The Second Circuit reversed, concluding . . . that if the action was to continue in the federal courts, jurisdiction must be based on diversity of citizenship.

In applying state law, following what is assumed to be the mandate of *Klaxon,* the choice of law methodology used by the states in which transferor courts sit has been examined to predict what law each state would apply.

We recognize that *Klaxon* has been widely criticized and that learned scholars have suggested on the basis of policy and possible constitutional grounds that a federal conflicts of law rule should be applied in diversity cases such as the one before us. The Supreme Court has, however, made it clear that the *Klaxon* rule is not to yield to the more modern thinking of conflicts-of-laws scholars. *See, e.g., Day and Zimmerman, Inc. v. Challoner,* 423 U.S. 3 (1975).

## [I. *THE POSSIBLE SOURCES OF LAW.* [*] ]

### A. *Federal Law*

. . .[The] Court of Appeals has decided that there is no federal substantive law directly controlling in this case. . . .

Even though federal substantive law does not control by its own force, states will often look to non-controlling federal decisions, statutes, executive orders and administrative decisions in deciding what state policy and substantive law ought to be. . . . Often, then, federal substantive law becomes state substantive law, not because the federal government has willed it so, but because the state has deemed it should be so through its governing institutions including the state's courts.

---

[*] Heading supplied. —*Ed.*

## B. *State Law*

. . .[As] to those claims originally filed in this court, [this court] sits much as a state trial court would in New York, applying New York substantive law except when, under the New York law of conflicts, a New York court would look to substantive law other than New York's in deciding what substantive law would apply. Cases commenced in other districts are treated as if they are pending in those other districts whether transferred to this court for pretrial purposes under the multi-district litigation statute, 28 U.S.C. § 1407, or transferred for trial for the convenience of witnesses, 28 U.S.C. § 1404. *See Van Dusen v. Barrack,* 376 U.S. 612 (1964).

Certifying this as a class action with residents of different states as plaintiffs does not, we assume for present purposes, by analogy to *Van Dusen v. Barrack,* reduce all disputes within the litigation to one subject to the substantive and conflicts of laws rules of New York. This is arguably clear where the suits were begun in other states and transferred to this court under section 1404 or 1407 of Title 28. . . .

C. *National-Consensus Law.* While those close to the American law scene tend to emphasize the diversity of substantive law among the states and between the states and the federal government, to outside observers much of the differences must appear as significant as that among the Lilliputians to Swift's hero. Faced with a unique problem, American lawmakers and judges tend to react in much the same way, arriving at much the same result. . . .

Institutions such as the American Law Institute with its Restatements, the National Commissioners on Uniform State Laws with many widely-adopted uniform statutes and the National Municipal League with its uniform charters aid these unifying national tendencies. . . .

We need not leave to speculation the assumption that states recognize this Agent Orange litigation as one with strong national overtones. . . . Some states have enacted statutes of limitation expressly extending the time available for "Agent Orange" plaintiffs to sue. Other state legislatures have set up commissions and outreach programs to study the problem and assist veterans or their dependents in pursuing Agent Orange claims against the United States.

## II. *CLAIMS OF DEFENDANTS AND MISUNDERSTANDING OF POSTURE CASE*

. . . [The defendants] . . . argue . . . that (1) federal common law may only be applied where there is a substantial federal interest at stake, (2) the Second Circuit's decision constitutes a determination binding on this court that there is no such federal interest in this litigation, and (3) therefore, although they do not suggest any rational way by which a state may choose one state's law to apply, they conclude that this court may not apply federal or national consensus common law to any issue. Further, they suggest that there is no single national consensus substantive law (although at least one defendant on oral argument urged that the government contract defense rested on a national consensus).

Defendants misstate the holding of the Court of Appeals. That decision was jurisdictional only—that the federal courts did not have jurisdiction under 28 U.S.C. § 1331. It did not constitute a determination that the state courts could not or would not look to other law, whether state, federal, or national consensus, if their choice of law rules so dictated. There is no necessary congruity between the basis for competence of a court and the basis for choice of law. Nor did the Court of Appeals decide that there was no substantial federal interest in the case. On the contrary, it is clear from the opinion that it did not disagree with this court's conclusion that there are "substantial federal interests that would be adversely affected by application of state law to the instant claims and . . . that there [are] no substantial state interests in having state law applied." Rather, the Court of Appeals found that although the federal government had an interest in . . . the plaintiffs as former servicemen and the defendants as defense contractors, those "two interests have been placed in sharp contrast with one another." Because of this clash and the fact that "the federal government's . . . interest in the *outcome* of the litigation, *i.e.,* in how the parties' welfares should be balanced, is as yet undetermined," the Court of Appeals determined that there was no "significant conflict between (identifiable) federal policy or interest and the use of state law." As a result, the strict requirements for the application of federal common law . . . were, according to the Court of Appeals, not met. . . .

. . . [The] Second Circuit's holding was premised at least in part on the fact that the claims "do not directly implicate the rights and duties of the United States" and that "no substantial rights or duties of the government hinge on the outcome." While not decisive in connection with the instant conflicts of laws opinion, that is no longer true. The government is a third-party defendant at least as to those claims alleging independent injury to wives, as by miscarriages, and to children, as by genetic damage. *In re "Agent Orange" Product Liability Litigation,* 580 F.Supp. 1242 (E.D.N.Y.), mandamus denied, 733 F.2d 10 (2d Cir. 1984).

The difference between federal law applying of its own force under the Supremacy Clause, which the Second Circuit's decision forbids in part, and applying a form of national consensus law or of federal law itself because a state court chooses to look to it as the rule of decision is well accepted. For example, state courts, in interpreting their state's constitution and statutes, will often follow the federal constitution and statutory authority although they may not be required to do so. . . . States will often look to federal tax laws and federal rules of procedure in formulating and interpreting their own. . . . *See* Note, *Supreme Court Review of State Interpretations of Federal Law Incorporated by Reference,* 66 HARV. L. REV. 1498 (1953).

. . . Federal courts recognize this state practice when they apply federal law to a situation because they find the state court would apply it as a matter of policy. . . . Similarly, a state in applying a sister state's law, will generally do so as a matter of policy, not because the federal Constitution compels such application. . . .

## III. *CONFLICT OF LAWS RULES**

Much of the law of conflicts is in a state of flux, development and refinement. Any dogmatism as to the result were the issue to be certified to the highest court of each jurisdiction involved is unwarranted. . . .

Essentially, there are five different conflicts of laws methodologies widely used in this country. These may be summarized as (1) traditional or Restatement (First) based upon Professor Beale's work, (2) Restatement (Second) being in large part a pragmatic and conservative revision by Professor Reese of Professor Currie's interest analysis school, (3) governmental interest, (4) Leflar, and (5) forum. . . .

Some states use a combination or variation of these techniques. For purposes of this opinion, we have eschewed specific discussion of the effects of . . . renvoi, or the increased likelihood of depeçage, applying the law of different jurisdictions to different aspects of the case, though, as will be seen, both doctrines are implicated in the present case. Finally, it is unnecessary to consider whether any state's conflict of law rule would deprive a litigant of due process, equal protection, or other constitutional right since each of the states whose conflict rule might apply has sufficient nexus with the matter through residence or the like.

Modern approaches, although differing in their formulations, mandate an analytical inquiry which is essentially the same. As Professor Leflar put it:

> "It appears that the various scholarly views concerning choice of law, developed during the last couple of decades, are being accepted by the courts as though they constituted one somewhat multi-faceted approach to the subject. Essentially, they are consistent with each other. Any one of them is likely to produce about the same result on a given set of facts as will another."

R. Leflar, American Conflicts Law 218 (3d ed. 1977). The *Restatement Second* is the most comprehensive of the modern approaches. To the extent that they differ from the current *Restatement,* other approaches are analyzed below. . . .

### A. *Restatement (Second)*

. . . Injuries arguably occurred in the fifty states and other nations where the plaintiffs now live or at one time lived. The original exposure to Agent Orange was at a variety of places in and near Vietnam—*i.e.,* South Vietnam, Cambodia and Laos. The conduct causing the injury was the manufacture of Agent Orange by the defendants and the alleged failure by the defendants to warn the government of the dangers of Agent Orange. Agent Orange was manufactured in factories in New Jersey, Michigan, Arkansas, West Virginia, Missouri and Canada, and perhaps Germany and elsewhere. The basic decision to use it was made in and around Washington, D.C. and in South Vietnam by our government officials and those of South Vietnam. The

---

* Portions of the material in this section are rearranged or moved from other parts of the opinion. —*Ed.*

companies responsible for its manufacture are incorporated and have as their main place of business the states of Delaware, New Jersey, Ohio, Michigan, Missouri, Kansas and Connecticut; treated as a unit, their combined sales run into the billions of dollars and have a substantial impact in every state of the union and in many foreign countries. It is difficult to pinpoint any particular states as the location of the failure to warn since what is alleged is inaction, not action. However, the meetings and conferences which plaintiffs allege furthered what they refer to as the "conspiracy of silence" took place in the various states where defendants have their principal place of business. Other states with relevant contacts include Pennsylvania and Texas, where the Herbicide Management Team of the United States armed forces was located, Alabama and Mississippi, the states from where the Agent Orange was shipped, and South Vietnam, where it was stored and used.

Adding to the factual complexity is that of mixture. The products manufactured were so mixed and so labeled that it is not possible to determine which manufacturer's product was used at any time or place.

. . . The three most important issues whose policies must be analyzed for this preliminary conflicts-of-laws opinion are products liability, the government contract defense and punitive damages. The articulation of the substantive rules relating to these issues will be restated in a more definite form in subsequent decisions; a rough approximation of these rules for the purposes of this conflicts opinion suffices.

### 1. Product Liability Law

Virtually all, if not every one, of the states in question has adopted some form of products liability law either by case-law or by statute. The general policy behind such a rule of law to shift costs from the injured plaintiff to the manufacturer is reflected in the oft quoted statement in *Greenman v. Yuba Power Products, Inc.,* 377 P.2d 897, 900 (Calif. 1962):

> "The purpose of such liability is to ensure that the costs of injuries resulting from defective products are borne by the manufacturers that put such products on the market rather than by the injured persons who are powerless to protect themselves."

. . . [Much] the same considerations controlling choice of law in the government contract defense, discussed at length below, apply to product liability law generally. They tend to lead to application of federal law or of a law of national consensus.

### 2. Government Contract Defense

. . . Two related policies have been expressed by . . . state courts in allowing the government contract defense. . . . The first views the government contract defense as following from the notion of sovereign immunity.

Another policy has been referred to as the "efficiency" rationale, *i.e.,* that the defense is necessary to ensure the smooth operation of government procurement programs. . . .

Other courts have rejected the government contract defense, at least where the claim was grounded in strict product liability. *See Challoner v. Day and Zimmerman, Inc.,* 512 F.2d 77, 84 (5th Cir.) (applying Texas law), *rev'd on other grounds,* 423 U.S. 3 (1975). They reason that the . . . defense, having its source in ordinary negligence, does not apply to actions grounded in strict liability. [These] . . . tip the balance in favor of the injured plaintiff rather than the contractor, asking:

> "On what principled ground . . . could it be justified that the cost of manufacturing defects will be passed along, through higher contract prices to the government to all of us who are taxpayers, while the design defect 'tax' will fall only on a few unfortunate, innocent, randomly selected victims?"

Having [summarized] the relevant policies of the various forum states, it is suggested that we select the law . . . to be applied to one or more of the substantive issues in this litigation. Yet it has already been pointed out that considering only the defendants' principal places of business and manufacture and principal contacts relevant to the conduct causing the injury, we count more than twenty jurisdictions. If to these jurisdictions are added the states and counties which bear much of the expense of caring for the service people, spouses and children who need public assistance, the number of jurisdictions far exceeds fifty. This complexity is compounded by the fact that at least three of the foreign countries involved—Canada, Australia and New Zealand—are themselves federal republics with federal-state issues not unlike our own.

The class action nature of the litigation, as already indicated, will not be assumed to control the choice-of-law aspect of the case. Nevertheless, a state court passing on the claims of an individual or a group of veterans might well recognize the unfairness in treating differently legally identical claims involving servicemen who fought a difficult foreign war shoulder-to-shoulder and were exposed to virtually identical risks. Similarly, it would make little sense to have a serviceman's recovery (or that of a spouse or child) in this suit depend on the fortuity of where he manifested his injuries or where he filed suit.

It quickly becomes apparent that it is impossible through sensible applica-tion of *Restatement (Second)* . . . analysis to identify the interest of any one state as being sufficiently greater than that of any others to a degree sufficient to justify the application of that state's law in resolving the issues in this litigation. Any narrow and mechanical state choice of law system simply col-lapses under the weight of the multiplicity of contacts, policies and unar-ticulated or conflicting state interests in this unique case. A state court, therefore, because of its inability to identify and select any other state's law to be applied as the rule of decision and because of the need for uniformity across the country, would seek to divine what the national rule of decision with regard to product liability law would be so that such law would appropri-ately reflect the national and international characteristics of this case. By contrast, the application of an individual state's law rather than a federal law or a national consensus law would be irrational and unfair.

The use of federal or national common law is also justified by *Restatement of Conflict of Laws (Second)* § 6(2)(c), which requires an analysis of "the relevant policies of other interested states and the relative interest of those states in the determination of the particular issue." The other interested state whose interest and policies must be considered is, of course, the United States which, under § 3 comment (c) of the *Restatement,* "is a state in the sense here used as to matters that are governed by federal law."

The policies of the United States, broadly speaking, parallel the states': on the one hand, it has a policy of compensating servicemen who are injured in the course of military service. On the other hand, there is the policy expressed by the government contract defense of insulating defense contractors who merely produced military equipment according to the specifications set forth by the government. How the balance should be struck in this case between those two conflicting policies need not be decided at this point. What is important is that these federal policies are far more specific than those of the states and the national interest in this litigation is far greater than that of any individual state.

While somewhat inchoate, the sense of the nation's interest is paramount to any state's. In matters affecting the nation as a whole, the concept of a single nation with interests overriding those of any state on some matters has never been doubted since the Civil War. . . . Seldom will the law . . . depart from the sense of the situation that the facts of the real world present.

This suit involves tens of thousands of servicemen and their wives and children alleging injury abroad in time of war as a result of a military decision. As opposed to the general policy behind products liability which encompasses all those injured by defective products, there is a far more specific federal policy of ensuring compensation for injured members and veterans of the armed forces. See 10 U.S.C. §§ 1071-87 (program of medical care for members of uniformed services and dependents); 38 U.S.C. §§ 310-15 (schedule of compensation to veterans and dependents for wartime disabilities); §§ 321-22 (schedule of compensation to survivors of veterans for wartime death), §§ 331-35 (same, peacetime disabilities), §§ 34-42 (same, peacetime death). Furthermore, Congress has recently expressed a specific policy in favor of the plaintiffs, not just as servicemen, but as "Agent Orange" victims. In Pub. L. No. 97-72, 95 Stat. 1047 (1981), Congress authorized the Veterans Administration to provide veterans who allege injury by exposure to Agent Orange with out-patient and in-patient hospital and nursing care at VA facilities without proving a causal relationship between the exposure and the illness and without regard to ability to pay. The same law also significantly expanded the scope of the study of the effects of Agent Orange on Vietnam veterans originally ordered by Pub. L. No. 96-151, 93 Stat. 1097 (1979). While such federal regulation does not mean that the federal government has preempted state tort law, it is an expression of federal policy that state courts would not be likely to ignore.

For much the same reasons, the national interest is far greater than that of the individual states. While the individual states may have a general interest in having their citizens recover or their chemical companies protected from liability, the nation as a whole has a far more specific interest in both the plaintiffs, as servicemen, and the defendants, as government contractors. . . .

Moreover, ordinarily federal law controls the construction and applicability of government contracts. *Priebe & Sons, Inc. v. United States,* 332 U.S. 407 (1947).

The existence and scope of a contractor's liability, if any, will undoubtedly affect future dealings between the contractor and the government. For example, war contractors may increase the price of war materials to reflect their potential liability. They may balk at supplying the military with particular products. As a result, the government's military capabilities may be affected. In addition, the importance of large government war contractors to the national economy implicates a national interest transcending state boundaries. Defendants, who include many of the nation's largest chemical manufacturers, face claims which may result in billions of dollars in liability. The sudden onset of substantial liabilities, even if they fell short of defendants' total assets, may affect national interests both in the sense that it may affect the federal treasury and in the sense that it would seriously affect the national economy. Furthermore, this litigation involves defoliants and other toxic chemicals whose use and misuse are increasingly governed by federal law. Comprehensive federal legislation has, in large part, taken these products out of the domain of state regulation.

### 3. *Punitive Damages*

The third issue of substantive law whose policies must be analyzed for choice-of-law purposes is punitive damages. The states of the veterans' domicile do not have an interest in whether or not punitive damages are imposed on the defendants. The legitimate interests of those states are limited to assuring that the plaintiffs are adequately compensated for their injuries and that the proceeds of any award are distributed to the appropriate beneficiaries. The only jurisdictions concerned with punitive damages are those, including the federal government, with whom the defendants have contacts significant for choice of law purposes. Those contacts include defendants' place of incorporation, principal place of business, location of the plants that manufactured Agent Orange, and the site of any action taken in furtherance of what plaintiffs refer to as "the conspiracy of silence."

The purposes underlying the allowance of punitive damages are punishment of the defendant and deterrence of future wrongdoing. The purpose underlying the disallowance is protection of defendants from excessive financial liability.

Courts disagree as to whether, as between the place of misconduct and the primary place of business, the former or the latter has the greater interest in awarding punitive damages. It is not necessary to decide that question for purposes of this litigation. The same reasons that justified the application of a single federal law or national consensus law to the government contract defense and to the standard of liability in this product liability case apply to the question of punitive damages. There is no rational method by which a state court could choose the law of any one state to govern the issue. The allegedly wrongful activity has contacts significant for choice of law purposes with at least twelve different jurisdictions. The Agent Orange was manufactured in many states by companies having their principal places of business in many other states, and the meetings and conferences which furthered the alleged "conspiracy of silence" took place in a variety of states.

On the other hand, there is an overriding federal interest in the award of punitive damages. The federal government is interested in the defense contractors' continued willingness and ability to supply material vitally needed for the national defense. The government also has an interest in assuring that defective war material does not injure American soldiers. How the balance should be struck in this case need not be decided now. It is enough to recognize that the federal government's interest parallels its interest in the defendants as war contractors, outlined above, and is demonstrably greater and more specific than the interest of any individual state.

## B. *Governmental Interest*

Under the governmental interest approach, the court must consider whether the public policy of a particular legislature would be furthered, frustrated or is irrelevant if applied in the case at bar. The law of the forum will be displaced only if the policy of the legislature of another [state] has a stronger interest. What was said above in connection with the discussion of the *Restatement* approach applies to an analysis of the application of the governmental interest analysis. It makes no difference whether this litigation poses a false conflict or a true conflict. There is no rational method by which a state could choose one state's law to govern some or all of the issues in the case and a state would look to a single national common law. Furthermore, the legislature of another [state], in this case the United States, has a far stronger interest than the legislature of any other [state]. . . .

## C. *Leflar—Better Law*

The Leflar approach requires that a court take into account "five choice-influencing considerations" and weigh each consideration in the light of the specific facts, with no more intrinsic importance attached to any consideration than to another. *See generally* R. Leflar, American Conflicts Law, 96 (3d ed. 1977); Leflar, *Choice-Influencing Considerations in Conflicts Law,* 41 N.Y.U. L. REV., 267, 269 (1966). . . . The only relevant consideration which has not thus far been discussed is the fifth, a preference for application of the better rule of law. This last factor calls into play the notion of the national law as the "more progressive" law and possibly provides further support for the application of federal common law. . . .

## D. *Traditional Approaches*

As with the states using the *Restatement,* governmental interests, and Leflar approaches, states using traditional approaches such as *lex loci* have never been faced with a case involving the number and quality of different state contacts presented by this litigation. Any conclusion, therefore, as to what such a state would do must, of necessity, be somewhat hypothetical. Nevertheless, we can reasonably conclude that the *lex loci* states would apply a federal or national consensus common law. . . .

Under the *Restatement (First) of Conflicts* § 377, which embodies the *lex loci* approach, the general rule is that the law to be applied is the law of "the place of the wrong." The "place of the wrong," in turn, is defined in personal injury cases to be "the place where the harmful force takes effect upon the body." In this case that would be South Vietnam, Laos or Cambodia as to the members of the Armed Forces and a variety of states and countries as to spouses and children. Although many of the more serious symptoms did not manifest themselves until years later, apparently the "harmful force (took) effect upon the body" of each affected servicemen immediately. . . . So far as wives or children are concerned, the place of coitus, if that could be determined, would probably be decisive.

Although the *lex loci* approach would normally look to South Vietnam, Laos, or Cambodia as the place of the wrong to the servicepeople, none of the parties have argued that the laws of those countries should be applied, even if their contents could be known. The theory behind *lex loci* is that "each state has legislative jurisdiction to determine the legal effect of facts done or events caused within its territory." § 377 Comment a. That rationale does not apply here: the jurisdiction where most of the use of herbicides took place, South Vietnam, no longer exists and Cambodia appears to be an independent state in name only now taken over by Vietnam. North Vietnam, the jurisdiction that has replaced South Vietnam and Cambodia, was at war with the United States and it was in the prosecution of the war that the exposure to Agent Orange took place. It would be ludicrous to allow North Vietnam (or France or the Soviet Union, whose laws undoubtedly have a strong influence on Vietnamese jurisprudence) to determine the law of this case.

Even if it is argued that the alleged adverse effects of exposure to Agent Orange did not manifest themselves until after the veterans returned from Vietnam and thus the normally applicable *Restatement (First)* rule is that the law of the state where those first manifestations occurred would apply, it is still probable that a state court would apply federal or national consensus law to all substantive issues in the litigation. The fact that a state uses the *lex loci* approach in most cases does not mean that it is immune to arguments based on the relative interests of jurisdictions. Thus, for example, a number of states that generally apply the *lex loci* approach in tort cases will apply the law of the parties' domicile to the issue of spousal immunity. . . .

Pragmatic [avoidance] of *lex loci* is particularly likely here where the jurisdiction with the greater interest is the federal government. As already pointed out, states have long looked to federal law for the rule of decision in particular cases even though it was not mandated by the Supremacy Clause.

The rationale given by state courts for adhering to the *lex loci* approach does not apply here. As the Supreme Court of Virginia stated in refusing to abandon the *lex loci* approach, "the components of the [modern approaches] can be viewed differently from case to case, thereby creating uncertainty and confusion in the application of the theory. . . . Thus, we do not think that the uniformity, predictability, and ease of application of the [*lex loci* ] rule should be abandoned in exchange for a concept which is so susceptible to inconstancy . . ." *McMillan v. McMillan,* 219 S.E.2d 662, 664 (Va. 1979). When the choice is between forum law and a federal or national consensus law as distinguished from a choice between forum law and a sister state's law, that danger of "inconstancy" does not exist. For close to two hundred years, state courts have had to choose between federal and state law in a particular case based not on *lex loci,* but on the . . . Supremacy Clause. Nonetheless, the same factors that decide whether federal law controls under the Supremacy Clause suggest whether it or national consensus law should control as a matter of choice of law. Finally, the *sui generis* nature of this litigation means that application of federal or national consensus common law to this litigation would not require a wholesale abandonment of *lex loci* . . . .

E. *Forum*

The decision to apply a national law is further reinforced by an analysis of what a court does when its choice of law rules point to foreign law and that law is not pleaded or proved by the parties. In such cases, a court will generally apply forum law or dismiss the case. . . .

[It] has been clearly shown in this litigation why the law of the forum should be displaced in the face of the overwhelmingly national and federal aspects of the case. . . . A state court in such a position, having no preexisting applicable conflicts rule, would turn to federal or national consensus law.

In the litigation most closely analogous to *Agent Orange* for present purposes, the federal court for the District of Columbia, sitting in a diversity case as a local District of Columbia court, had to decide the law applicable to claims arising out of the crash near Saigon of an Air Force C-5A carrying United States military and civilian personnel and 226 Vietnamese orphans. *In re Air Crash Disaster Near Saigon, South Vietnam on April 4, 1975,* 476 F.Supp. 521 (D.D.C. 1979). . . . It applied District of Columbia law of survival to all parties despite the fact that plaintiffs resided all over the United States, and that Lockheed Aircraft Corp., a defendant with the United States, had its chief place of business and place of incorporation outside the District. District of Columbia law was really only a euphemism for a national substantive law of liability. Rejecting traditional conflicts of law, the court relied upon the *sui generis* nature of the case.[*]

The federal and national interests in this litigation are far greater than those implicated in . . . the *Saigon* [case]. . . .

The overwhelming need for a uniform approach and a single substantive standard is obvious. Normally we would expect Congress to recognize this and provide a federal statute which would be all encompassing or which would leave lacunae to be filled by the federal courts directly or through absorption of state law. Although it could do so under its commerce or war powers, Congress has not enacted such a statute.

Given a failure of the legislature and the executive, the federal courts could be expected to step in by creating federal common law to cover a national problem. But the Second Circuit has blocked that route by denying that federal substantive law controls of its own force. Thus, under *Klaxon,* we look to the states to accomplish the sound result. . . .

Given the strong state-federal interest in uniformity, the lack of a federal statute or of a uniform state statute, and the Second Circuit opinion denying

---

[*] This paragraph is moved from a later position in the opinion. —*Ed.*

that federal common law controls of its own force all substantive issues in *Agent Orange,* what would state courts do? Would they not look to the first court that dealt with the issue or to a neutral body to formulate the uniform rules they could all accept for this unique litigation? And is not a federal court charged with adjudicating all or nearly all the *Agent Orange* cases such a body? . . .

. . . Thus, the law is driven in this most unusual case to either federal or national consensus substantive law as the only workable approach.

. . . But for the fact that arguably the federal government has not allowed itself to be sued, federal law might apply under *Clearfield Trust Co. v. United States,* 318 U.S. 363 (1943) [holding that federal common law governs the commercial obligations of the United States].

. . . [A] number of state and federal courts have had occasion to deal with choice of law issues in mass tort situations where the interests of dozens of jurisdictions, including the United States, have been implicated.

In the litigation most closely analogous to Agent Orange for present purposes, the federal court for the District of Columbia, sitting . . . as a local District of Columbia court, had to decide the law applicable to claims arising out of the crash near Saigon of an Air Force C-5A carrying United States military and civilian personnel and 226 Vietnamese orphans. *In re Air Crash Disaster Near Saigon, South Vietnam on April 4, 1975,* 476 F.Supp. 521, 526-27 (D.D.C. 1979). The specific issue before the court related to the survival of decedents' causes of action. It noted that the District of Columbia follows the "interest analysis" method in choice of law. It analyzed the relevant interests [and concluded]: "It is a 'paramount' interest and concern of the United States federal government that its courts provide a just and reasonable resolution of claims such as those on behalf of the estates of the deceased orphans." [The court] applied District of Columbia law of survival to all parties despite the fact that plaintiffs resided all over the United States, and that Lockheed Aircraft Corp., a defendant with the United States, had its chief place of business and place of incorporation outside the District. District of Columbia law was really only a euphemism for a national substantive law of liability. Rejecting traditional conflicts of law, the court relied upon the *sui generis* nature of the case.

With only slight paraphrasing, [what] was said by the District of Columbia court applies with even greater force to this litigation. . . .

*In re Paris Air Crash of March 3, 1974,* 399 F.Supp. 732 (C.D. Cal. 1975), also dealt with claims arising out of an air disaster occurring in a foreign country—the crash of a Turkish Air Lines DC-10 in France. The specific issue before the court was what law to apply in determining damages, liability having been conceded. Claimants were from 26 foreign countries and at least twelve states of the United States, a total of 38 jurisdictions. The court considered at length the interests of the United States. It gave special weight to the fact that the DC-10 which crashed was "designed, constructed, manufactured, and tested in California," and that "the state of residence of designers and manufacturers has a most significant interest in applying its measure of damages to a product distributed throughout the world for the sake of uniformity of decisions involving such designers and manufacturers." There-fore, the court concluded, "clearly the United States and the State of California both have governmental interests in applying the law of California, a state of the United States, in the measure of damages for each claimant, which interests are significantly greater than the interests of countries or states of which either the decedents or claimants are citizens."

An analysis of the rationale of both of the above decisions leads to the conclusion that a state using either "modern" or traditional choice of law methodology would apply federal or national consensus law to this litigation. The federal and national interests in this litigation are far greater than those implicated in either the *Saigon* or *Paris* cases. On the other side of the balance there is no single contact in this case equivalent to the contact of the place of manufacture and design as in *Paris*. A state court would therefore have no rational choice but to apply federal or national consensus common law. . . .

Because of the *sui generis* nature of this litigation, it is not surprising that there are no cases directly on point. It is, however, common to find state courts and federal courts sitting as state courts under *Erie* applying federal law, because of the predominant federal interest in the litigation. *See, e.g., Filardo v. Foley Bros.,* 297 N.Y. 217, 78 N.E.2d 480, 79 N.Y.S.2d 217 (1948), rev'd on other grounds, 336 U.S. 281 (1949); *Weinberger v. New York Stock Exchange,* 335 F.Supp. 139, 143 (S.D.N.Y. 1971); *McLaughlin v. Sikorsky Aircraft,* 148 Cal.App.3d 203, 195 Cal.Rptr. 764 (1983). Thus, state courts will often look to federal law if they feel it is appropriate.

That neither New York nor, as far as we have ascertained, any state has had a case such as this one before us does not permit our throwing up our hands and refusing to decide the question. Perhaps it would have been better if certification rules permitted posing the conflicts question to the more than half-a-hundred jurisdictions involved. But no such procedure is presently in place. . . . In the meantime, this court must ascertain the living state law as best it can. . . .

---

## NOTES ON *AGENT ORANGE*

(1) *Is mass tort administrable?* The compound task of federal courts in complex litigations like *Agent Orange* appears to be to examine the choice-of-law decisions in all transferor states, as well as the substantive law decisions of the states variously chosen by this method. This laborious process must be repeated for each issue in a case. It seems fair to say that under *Erie, Klaxon,* and *Van Dusen,* the Supreme Court has rendered mass tort and other multistate litigation administrable only with difficulty in federal courts.

Nor would state courts be much better forums for mass tort cases. They lack any mechanism for interstate transfer and consolidation. Even apart from that difficulty, state and federal courts alike are under heightened Due Process Clause constraints when choosing law in multistate cases. The forum may not apply unitary law to all claims on all issues in disregard of the possibly stronger claims of other states. *Phillips Petroleum Co. v. Shutts,* 472

U.S. 797 (1985). Thus, the Supreme Court seems to contemplate an exhaustive exploration even in state courts of what law other states "would" choose in a mass tort case.

(2) *National consensus law.*  Can you describe the law chosen in *Agent Orange* ? Was it federal law, like a Supreme Court case or act of Congress? Or was it a common-law version of uniform state law?

What is the difference between Judge Weinstein's "national consensus law" and federal common law? Are you persuaded that all states "would" apply federal common law in *Agent Orange*? Does Judge Weinstein's purported "interest analysis" support that view? In *Bowen v. United States,* 370 F.2d 1311 (7th Cir. 1978), an aviation case under the Federal Tort Claims Act, it was argued that "the place where the act or omission occurred" would, in fact, apply not its own law, but federal common law; and that, therefore, federal common law would become the law of "the place where the act or omission occurred." The court rejected this argument, noting the Supreme Court inhospitable attitude toward a federal common law of aviation disaster, and citing *Miree v. DeKalb County, supra.*

In a 1991 study on enterprise liability for personal injury, the American Law Institute recommended the application of "national consensus" state law in mass tort cases.

(3) *Federalization.*  Would it help the administration of mass tort cases to federalize the *substantive*  tort issues? If there were a federal common law of mass tort, no choice among state laws would be necessary, of course, unless courts perversely persisted in borrowing state law on each issue. Moreover, diversity jurisdiction would not be necessary to federal litigation. In consolidated federal litigation, the state-court cases of nondiverse parties would be subject to removal and consolidation. As matters now stand, if a defendant understandably seeks unitary litigation, the only practical alternative to federalization appears to be the forum provided under the bankruptcy laws. And even then, under the 1984 Bankruptcy Amendments, some personal injuries cases must be tried separately in any event.

Congress could federalize aviation tort. Could the Supreme Court? Does *Miree v. DeKalb County*  affect your view?

Could Congress or the Court federalize the law of multistate asbestos tort? Of mass product liability? Does *Boyle v. United Technologies Corp.*  affect your view?

(4) *Alternatives.* Would it be preferable for Congress to leave substantive state law intact for mass torts, but to legislate special federal choice-of-law rules for mass tort cases?

This was the recommendation of the American Law Institute's Complex Litigation Project (approved May, 1993). The Project proposes for enactment by Congress a discouragingly complicated hierarchy of hard-and-fast rules for choosing among the laws of interested states, with a residual place-of-conduct rule that would make a race to the regulatory bottom a foregone conclusion. See Louise Weinberg, *Mass Torts at the Neutral Forum: A Critical Analysis of the American Law Institute's Proposed Choice Rule,* 56 ALBANY L. REV.

807-854 (1993). The Institute's unappealing proposal has been widely ignored by courts dealing with mass disasters.

Given that *Klaxon* and *Van Dusen* account for most of the administrative difficulty experienced by federal courts in mass tort cases, would the cleaner, more direct statutory solution be a simple legislative override of those cases? This would free federal courts to fashion federal choice-of-law rules for mass tort cases. To resolve any doubt, Congress could authorize the fashioning of federal-common law choice rules explicitly. But would federal common-law choice rules in cases otherwise governed by state law create the sort of dysfunction that in *Erie* Justice Brandeis attributed to the doctrine of *Swift v. Tyson?*

---

**In re RHONE-POULENC RORER, INC.,** 51 F.3d 1293 (7th Cir. 1995). This case began as a class action on behalf hemophiliacs infected by AIDS, against manufacturers of allegedly contaminated blood transfusion products. The District Court certified the class, and certified its decision of this issue for interlocutory review.

*Held* (per Circuit Judge Posner): The District Judge must decertify the class. He proposes to instruct the jury on a single legal standard of negligence combining the negligence standards of all 50 states. The jury would receive "a kind of Esperanto instruction." This is like the pre-*Erie* "general common law," a "brooding omnipresence in the sky." But the reality is that the "articulate voices" of the sovereigns in this case "sing negligence" in 50 different pitches. If there is no single body of law that governs the duty of the defendants, then there can be no "common issues of law" within the meaning of Rule (23).

[One Circuit Judge dissented, on other grounds.]

---

## § 6.16  A Genuine Federal Common Law of Choice of Law

We have yet to consider a final option. In the silence of Congress, would it be advisable or feasible for courts to develop a federal common law of conflicts for all interstate conflicts, in all courts? Interstate conflicts do seem to present an "intrinsically" federal question. That is an implication of the Supreme Court's original jurisdiction over disputes between states, and is further suggested by the Full Faith and Credit and Interstate Commerce Clauses. The really difficult question would seem to be: just what should such federal common-law conflicts rules provide?

## Donald T. Trautman, THE RELATION BETWEEN FEDERAL COMMON LAW AND CONFLICT OF LAWS

*41 Law and Contemporary Problems* 105 (Spring 1977)

The late Professor Trautman proposed a federal common law of the conflict of laws.[*] By this Trautman means *genuine* federal law, binding on all courts under the Supremacy Clause. All courts could fashion federal conflicts law (with final review in the United States Supreme Court), much as today all courts fashion rules of decision on other federal issues, subject only to final review in the Supreme Court.

Trautman did not see his proposed federal common law of conflicts as preemptive. Rather, he saw it as an expedient supplementary resource in the resolution of intractable conflicts. Courts would resort to it when helpful in resolving true conflicts:

> "It seems to me that the development of a conception that a judge, whether in a state or in a federal court, was free to consult, and to find authority in, a body of law distinct from the law of the particular states involved in a conflict dispute would go far toward removing some of the most troublesome aspects of functional analysis as it is now practiced and promote an atmosphere conducive to a sounder development of the field. . . . [In] *Bernkrant* Justice Traynor would not need to be confined to the multi-jurisdictional policies of California, nor to 'shared' policies of California and Nevada, to explain how the California court can restrict the scope of California domestic law. . . . "

But what would be the *content* of this federal common law of conflicts? Professor Trautman contemplated the sort of "functional analysis" elsewhere proposed by himself with Professor von Mehren, and by Professor Weintraub. With functional analysis, courts could weigh the local policies of the concerned states against widely shared, multistate policies.

Lest it be thought that this suggestion was too radical, Professor Trautman argued that in fact such a "functional" federal common law of the conflict of laws already exists, in a sense, and is already applied in all courts. As a celebrated example, he cited *Milliken v. Pratt.*

--------

## NOTES ON A FEDERAL COMMON LAW OF CHOICE OF LAW

(1) *The principled departure from forum law.* Did Professor Trautman find a solution to the problems engendered when courts depart from forum law? He saw his suggestion's chief merit in this feature:

---

[*] Professor Trautman was building on work by Harold W. Horowitz, *Toward a Federal Common Law of Choice of Law,* 14 UCLA. L. REV. 1191 (1967); William F. Baxter, *Choice of Law and the Federal System,* 16 STAN. L. REV. 1 (1963). Recently Trautman expanded on his own views in Donald T. Trautman, *Toward Federalizing Choice of Law,* 70 TEX. L. REV. 1715 (1992).

"To a large extent, the only significant contribution of federal common law . . . would be to free . . . judges from any compulsions they might otherwise find in local law to prefer local law or local residents and to provide them with the intellectual equipment needed . . . to view multistate problems from the perspective of the overarching federal order."

(2) *The problem of judicial performance.* For all its appeal, there is at least one practical obstacle to his suggestion with which Professor Trautman did not deal. Such functional analyses as most courts engage in today seem to take place on a crude, jurisdiction-selecting level. What assurance do we have that courts would not choose law precisely as they have been doing, whether or not they say they are employing a "functional analysis" that is part of the federal common law? And, given the Supreme Court's recent performance in constitutional conflicts cases and in jurisdiction cases, what assurance do we have that the Court can supervise the federal common law of conflicts with greater wisdom?

(3) *A hypothetical: Hilton v. Guyot.* In *Hilton v. Guyot,* 159 U.S. 113 (1895), the Supreme Court set forth general rules regarding the recognition and enforcement of foreign judgments. In the Court's view, comity, reciprocity, and the policy of finality, required that ordinarily such judgments be enforced. However, where the foreign country whose judgment was sought to be enforced would not enforce an American judgment, the Court held, by Justice Gray (over Chief Justice Fuller's strong dissent, joined by Justices Harlan, Brewer, and Jackson) that a court in this country need not enforce the foreign judgment.

Suppose that a case similar to *Hilton* arose today. Suppose that a French national appeared in an Ohio state court and commenced an action on a French judgment against an Ohio corporation, seeking recognition of the foreign judgment. Suppose that France still follows its rule of non-recognition of a foreign judgment, reviewing all such judgments *au fond.* A French court would not enforce an American judgment without re-trying the whole case. The defendant argues that *Hilton v. Guyot,* a Supreme Court case, is the binding federal common law on this point, and that under *Guyot* 's rule of reciprocity, an American court cannot enforce the foreign judgment. The defendant also makes an argument in reliance on *Sabbatino, supra,* to the effect that a foreign judgment is an act of state and that an American court may not inquire into its validity. The defendant argues, further, that even if an American court could so inquire, it does so as part of the foreign relations law of the United States, and thus is controlled by the rule of retaliatory nonrecognition announced in *Guyot.* You represent the plaintiff judgment creditor. What do you argue? Need *Sabbatino* hurt? Can it help?

# Chapter 7

# JUDGMENTS

## PART A  BASIC PRINCIPLES

### § 7.01  Finality in the Rendering State—Res Judicata[1]

Conflict of laws has been concerned traditionally with the interstate recognition and enforcement of judgments. The focus of concern has been this question: What effect does a judgment rendered in one state have in the courts of a *sister state?* Before investigating this question in detail, however, it makes sense to consider what effect a judgment has *in the state where it was rendered.* The law of res judicata or former adjudication controls that question. A full exposition of the topic is beyond the scope of this book; it is well treated in civil procedure courses and treatises.[2] Nevertheless, a brief treatment is warranted here because so much of the law of full faith and credit depends upon the policies and doctrines embodied in the law of res judicata.

### [A]  The Policies Behind Finality

The policies behind the law of res judicata are easy to articulate.[3] For the litigant, finality is an important goal; the purpose of litigation is dispute resolution, and the parties want a resolution that they can rely on. A certain and final resolution permits the parties to order their affairs and plan in a sensible way; otherwise, they cannot. Society is no less interested in finality than are the litigants. Resolving a single dispute more than once wastes limited societal resources. But there are also, of course, countervailing policies of justice. Enforcing broad and strict rules of finality may occasionally deprive a litigant of important rights, merely because they were not asserted at the proper time. These two goals—judicial economy and justice—have been the principal forces that have forged the modern doctrine of res judicata.

### [B]  Claim Preclusion and Issue Preclusion

The law of res judicata is composed of two major branches: claim preclusion (in older terminology, bar and merger) and issue preclusion (in older terminology, direct and collateral estoppel).[4] Claim preclusion prohibits a second suit

---

[1] This section is adapted from WILLIAM RICHMAN & WILLIAM REYNOLDS, UNDERSTANDING CONFLICT OF LAWS § 109 (3d ed. 2002).

[2] Excellent treatments are: 18A, 18B CHARLES WRIGHT, ARTHUR MILLER, & EDWARD COOPER, FEDERAL PRACTICE AND PROCEDURE (2002); GENE SHREVE & PETER RAVEN-HANSEN, UNDERSTANDING CIVIL PROCEDURE, Ch. 15 (3d ed. 2002); FLEMING JAMES, GEOFFREY HAZARD & JOHN LEUBSDORF, CIVIL PROCEDURE, Ch. 11 (5th ed. 2001). *See also* RESTATEMENT (SECOND) OF JUDGMENTS, Ch. 3 and 4 (1982); *Developments in the Law-Res Judicata,* 65 HARV. L. REV. 818 (1952).

[3] *Developments in the Law-Res Judicata, supra* n. 2, at 820.

[4] For a famous rendition of the distinction, *see* Cromwell v. County of Sac, 94 U.S. 351 (1876). *See also* RESTATEMENT (SECOND) OF JUDGMENTS § 17, comments a, b, and c.

on a *claim* or *cause of action* that was asserted in a prior suit that proceeded to a final judgment on the merits. The judgment in the first action precludes not only all questions that were actually litigated, but also all issues that might have been litigated. More limited in scope, issue preclusion prohibits relitigation *of factual issues* actually decided in a prior proceeding, regardless of whether the second proceeding is based upon the same claim or cause of action.

A series of three examples illustrates the distinction. Suppose that plaintiff has been injured twice in two entirely unrelated accidents by ambulance drivers who are both employees of defendant hospital. Further, suppose that the jurisdiction where the lawsuits occur has a rule of charitable immunity. The following chart shows three possible sequences of litigation. In each case, assume that litigation #1 occurs before litigation #2.

|  | Litigation | Cause of Action | Issue Litigated |
|---|---|---|---|
| **I.** | 1. P. v. Hospital | Accident # 1 | Issue A: Did ambulance #1 run the stop sign? |
|  | 2. P. v. Hospital | Accident # 1 | Issue B: Did ambulance # 1 exceed the speed limit? |
| **II.** | 1. P. v. Hospital | Accident # 1 | Issue C: Is the hospital a charitable institution? |
|  | 2. P. v Hospital | Accident # 2 | Issue C: Is the hospital a charitable institution? |
| **III.** | 1. P. v. Hospital | Accident #1 | Issue A: Did ambulance # 1 run the stop sign? |
|  | 2. P. v. Hospital | Accident # 2 | Issue C: Is the hospital a charitable institution? |

In example I, claim preclusion will prohibit the second suit entirely. Because both suits are based on the same cause of action (Accident #1), the second suit is precluded, even though it raises an issue that was not litigated in the first suit (the ambulance's speed). That issue *might have* been litigated in the first suit.

In example II, issue preclusion will prohibit relitigation of the charitable immunity issue in the second suit, even though the two suits are based on different causes of action. That issue was already litigated between the parties in the first suit.

Lastly, in example III, neither doctrine applies; claim preclusion does not apply because the two suits are based on different causes of action (different accidents), and issue preclusion does not apply because the charitable immunity issue was not litigated in the first suit.

*See* PROBLEMS 7A-1. ISSUE PRECLUSION AFTER APPEAL; 7A-2. IS THE FEDERAL GOVERNMENT BARRED?

## [C]   The Dimensions of a Claim or Cause of Action

A comparison of claim preclusion and issue preclusion illustrates the importance of determining the dimensions of a single claim or cause of action. If two suits are based upon the same cause of action, the second is precluded entirely, even though new issues are raised; by contrast, if the two suits are on different causes of action, only issues actually litigated in the first suit are precluded in the later action. So the important question becomes: What constitutes a single claim or cause of action?

There are several answers to the question, but two predominate.[5] The primary right theory holds that a single cause of action consists of the violation of a single primary right. Suppose, for instance, defendant shop owner accuses plaintiff customer of shoplifting and then has him physically detained. According to the primary right theory, plaintiff has two causes of action—one to vindicate his right not to be defamed, and another to vindicate his right not to be falsely imprisoned. The transactional theory defines a cause of action as a single transaction or occurrence, or an interlocked series of transactions or occurrences. In the example posed above, the transactional theory would indicate only one cause of action because the defamation and the false imprisonment arise out of one transaction or occurrence.

## [D]   Persons Affected by Res Judicata—Parties and Privies

Who is bound by a judgment, and who may benefit from a judgment? The answer typically given is: the parties to the action and those in privity with them.[6] Determining the parties to a suit seldom presents a problem; they are usually the people named in the action and subject to the jurisdiction of the court. The concept of privity is more difficult. The term is conclusory, just shorthand for the conclusion that a person is so closely related to a party that it is fair to bind her to the results of the litigation. The question, then, is: What relationships establish privity?

A person may be considered a privy of a party if the party is her legal representative. Thus, if a trustee sues defendant and loses, the beneficiary of the trust will be precluded from suing defendant on the same cause of action.[7] Another classic privity situation involves successive owners of property. Suppose Owner owns a piece of land over which Defendant claims an easement. Owner sues Defendant to quiet her title in the land free of the easement, but loses. Owner then conveys to Owner #2. Owner #2 is precluded from claiming the land free of the easement because she is considered a privy

---

[5] The two views of cause of action are discussed in Restatement (Second) of Judgments § 24, comment a. The Restatement adopted the transactional theory.

[6] *See* James, Hazard & Leubsdorf, *supra* n. 2, at § 11.23.

[7] Restatement (Second) of Judgments § 41.

of Owner.[8] A final example of privity concerns persons who control the litigation, even though they are not parties. Suppose Plaintiff sues Defendant for negligence. Defendant's insurer assumes the defense of the action. A judgment against Defendant will also bind Defendant's insurer because, although not a party, it controlled the defense of the first action.

*See* PROBLEM 7A-3. PRECLUDING THE VICTIM'S SPOUSE?; 7A-4. DOUBLE JEOPARDY?; 7A-5. A TAIWANESE CONVICTION.

## [E] Strangers to the Litigation—Mutuality of Estoppel

The Due Process Clause prohibits depriving a person of property without affording her notice of a claim against her and an opportunity to be heard in her defense. The implication of this principle is that a court may not apply the doctrines of claim or issue preclusion to the detriment of strangers to the litigation. The principles of res judicata are constitutional as long as they bind only those who have had a day in court. Suppose, for example, Defendant drives his car into a car containing Plaintiff #1 and Plaintiff #2. Plaintiff #1 sues Defendant, contending Defendant was negligent, and loses. In a later negligence action by Plaintiff #2 against Defendant, Defendant may not use the results of the first suit against Plaintiff #2, because she has not had a day in court on the issue of Defendant's negligence.

An entirely different question is whether a stranger to the litigation may *benefit* from the doctrines of claim and issue preclusion. The stranger cannot be bound by findings in the litigation, but can she use those findings (in a subsequent action) against one who was a party? Once again, suppose Defendant drives his car into a car containing Plaintiff #1 and Plaintiff #2. Plaintiff #1 sues Defendant contending that Defendant was negligent, and this time wins. Can Plaintiff #2 now use that determination in a later action against Defendant? The older cases, relying on a doctrine known as mutuality of estoppel, said Plaintiff #2 could not.[9] Because Plaintiff #2 would not have been bound by the result in *Plaintiff #1 v. Defendant* (because Plaintiff #2 was not a party), she could not benefit from the result either.

Commentators have had harsh words for the doctrine of mutuality,[10] and many courts have abandoned it.[11] Some have rejected it completely, permitting a stranger to use the results of a prior litigation in nearly all circumstances. Others have been more cautious and have permitted a stranger to the litigation to benefit only to the extent that she wishes to use the result defensively—to protect herself from recovery by one who was a losing party in the first action.

---

[8] *Id.* at § 43.

[9] *See, e.g. Ralph Woff & Sons v. New Zealand Ins. Co.,* 248 Ky. 304, 53 S.W.2d 623 (1933).

[10] Fleming James, citing Brainerd Currie and Jeremy Bentham, said:

    Here as elsewhere in the law a requirement of mutuality as an independent principle of justice has been aptly described as a "tinkling cymbal, an empty and fatuous formula productive of more harm than good." It is indeed a notion more appropriate to the gaming table than to the bench.

Fleming James, Civil Procedure § 11.31 (1965).

[11] *See Parklane Hosiery Co. v. Shore,* 439 U.S. 322 (1979), *Bernhard v. Bank of Am. Nat'l Trust & Sav. Ass'n,* 19 Cal. 2d 807, 122 P.2d 892 (1942).

## § 7.02  Interstate Finality—Full Faith and Credit

The Full Faith and Credit Clause provides that "Full Faith and Credit shall be given in each State to the public Acts, Records and judicial Proceedings of every other State. And the Congress may by general Laws prescribe the Manner in which the Acts, Records and Proceedings shall be proved, and the Effect thereof." The Clause is the first section of Article IV, the Article dealing with relations among the several states. (Article IV also provides, *inter alia,* for extradition of fugitives from justice and from slavery, and the admission of states; it also contains the Privileges and Immunities Clause.)

Congress first exercised its authority to legislate under the Clause in 1790,[12] legislation which has remained in force to the present. The statute, codified as 28 U.S.C. § 1738, now provides that:

> The Acts of the legislature of any State . . . shall be authenticated by affixing the seal of such State thereto.

> The records and judicial proceedings of any court of any such state . . . shall be proved . . . by the attestation of the clerk . . . together with a certificate of a judge of the court that the said attestation is in proper form.

> Such Acts, records and judicial proceedings or copies thereof so authenticated, shall have the same full faith and credit in every court within the United States . . . as they have by law or usage in the courts from which they are taken.

The Clause is modeled on provisions found in several state constitutions and in the Articles of Confederation. On the history of the Clause, see Ralph Whitten, *The Constitutional Limitation on State-Court Jurisdiction: A Historical-Interpretive Reexamination of the Full Faith and Credit and Due Process Clauses,* 14 CREIGHTON L. REV. 499 (1981); Kurt Nadelmann, *Full Faith and Credit to Judgments and Public Acts: A Historical-Analytical Reappraisal,* 56 MICH. L. REV. 33 (1957). Although the Full Faith and Credit Clause does not distinguish between the respect that must be accorded statutes and the respect that must be given judgments, both the implementing statute and the case law have long drawn that distinction. As Chief Justice Stone explained, the Full Faith and Credit Clause and implementing Act have "placed a judgment on a different footing from a statute of one state, judicial recognition of which is sought in another." *Magnolia Petroleum Co. v. Hunt,* 320 U.S. 430 (1943). In Chapter 5, *supra,* we examined the statutory end of the dichotomy and how compelling state interests are accommodated. This Chapter treats the judgment end of the equation.

The cornerstone of the policy underlying the Full Faith and Credit Clause is national unity:

> Full faith and credit is a national policy, not a state policy. Its purpose is not merely to demand respect from one state for another, but rather to give us the benefits of a unified nation by altering the status of otherwise independent, sovereign states.

---

[12] Act of May 26, 1790, Stat. 122, ch. 11 § 1. Although the language has changed a bit from that day to this, the changes were not meant to be substantive.

Willis Reese & Vincent Johnson, *The Scope of Full Faith and Credit to Judgments*, 49 COLUM. L. REV. 153, 1610-62 (1949). That policy of national unity can help the analyst through many a tight spot.

The national mandate of full faith and credit applies to all cases involving state court recognition of judgments of other states; that much is clear from the language of the implementing statute. Case law has made clear that state courts also must recognize federal judgments, *Stoll v. Gottlieb,* 305 U.S. 165 (1938), and that federal courts must recognize state court judgments, *St. John v. Wisconsin Employment Relations Bd.,* 340 U.S. 411 (1951).

Finally, note that the implementing statute clearly ties the scope of the required recognition to the level of recognition the judgment would receive *at home.* Why should that be so?

## § 7.03  Whose Law of Finality

When a litigant presents the judgment of one state in the courts of another, the Full Faith and Credit Clause and its implementing statute require the second state to give the judgment full faith and credit, but exactly how much faith and credit is required? Or, in other words, what does "full" mean? The answer to the question is to be found in the law of judgments—claim preclusion and issue preclusion.

That answer, however, raises in turn another question: Whose law of judgments—the law of the rendering state or the law of the enforcing or recognizing state? The states differ on several significant issues: the dimensions of a cause of action (what counts as splitting a cause of action), the kinds of dismissals that are "on the merits," the persons considered parties and privies, and the rule of mutuality. Different positions on these questions will produce different preclusive effects for the judgment. Can the second forum apply its own law to resolve these issues, or must it apply the law of the rendering state? The materials that follow explore this question. *See generally* WILLIAM RICHMAN & WILLIAM REYNOLDS, UNDERSTANDING CONFLICT OF LAWS § 110[c] (3d ed. 2002).

## FINLEY v. KESLING

*Illinois Appellate Court*
*105 Ill. App. 3d 1, 433 N.E.2d 1112 (1982)*

ROMITI, JUSTICE

The plaintiff in this case was previously a party to a divorce action in Indiana. In that case he testified, under oath, that he owned 31% of certain stock, his wife 29% and his children 40%. The Indiana court accepted this testimony and so divided the particular property. Now the plaintiff has filed a lawsuit in Illinois claiming beneficial ownership of the stock which in Indiana he had testified was owned by the children. The trial court, while aware that Indiana will not apply collateral estoppel unless mutuality is present, held that even though the children were not parties to the Indiana action, it would be contrary to Illinois public policy to allow plaintiff to deny either his own previous testimony or the Indiana decree and to carry this issue further, and dismissed the action. We agree and affirm.

In 1954 the plaintiff, Charles Finley, organized a previously founded insurance brokerage business into Charles O. Finley & Co., Inc., an Illinois corporation. At that time, in view of his poor medical history and for tax reasons in the event of his early death, he put 10% of the stock in each of his four children's names. The remaining 60% was divided between Finley and his wife. Although other children were born after 1954, no stock was given to them.

At the time of its formation in 1954, the total capitalization of the corporation was $5,000, all of which was contributed by Finley. In 1961, the corporation became the owner and operator of a major league professional baseball franchise; this was sold in 1980. At the same time the corporation, which now has a shareholder equity in excess of $20,000,000, adopted a plan of liquidation and distribution. Finley in the present action claims that although 40% of the stock is registered in the children's names they are not entitled to any part of the liquidating distributions of the corporation.

As already stated, Finley filed this declaratory judgment action seeking a declaration that the children are not beneficial owners of the stock and that he is the beneficial owner of the stock. Defendants filed a motion to dismiss . . . on the grounds of *res judicata*. The pleadings and briefs of the parties in the trial court disclose that in about 1974, Shirley M. Finley, then the wife of the plaintiff, filed a suit for divorce in Indiana. At the hearing on her motion for temporary support, Finley testified:

. . . So I said, "Well, that does sound like a good idea to give the stock to the kids and the wife." So I decided that I'd give her 29 percent and the four children 10 percent each. That was a total of 69 percent of the stock that I gave at the time I formed the corporation for tax purposes. That was my thinking in the event of an early death. . . .

. . . The trial court in its decree of dissolution found that:

> The capital stock of Charles O. Finley of Illinois and Charles O. Finley of Indiana is now and has been for many years owned in these proportions: 31 percent by the husband, 29 percent by the wife and 40 percent in equal proportions by four of their children. Thus as to these two corporations we are concerned only with 60 percent of their authorized, issued and outstanding capital stock.

The court decreed that the parties should retain as their separate property the shares of the capital stock issued to them in the corporation, namely 31% to Finley and 29% to his wife. In addition, the Indiana appellate court in 1977 on an appeal from an interlocutory order stated, "The husband holds thirty-one percent of the corporate stock and the wife holds twenty-nine percent of the corporate stock. The remaining forty percent of the corporate stock which is not part of the marital estate is divided equally among four of their children." *Finley v. Finley* (Ind. App. 1977), 367 N.E.2d 1126, 1127.

The Illinois trial judge granted the motion to dismiss and dismissed the proceedings with prejudice. The written order expressly adopted his oral opinion in which he stated in part:

Every relevant stage along the way to the final divorce decree, the Plaintiff either affirmatively stated or acquiesced in the trial [and] in the Appellate Court case that he owned 31 percent and the four children owned the total of 40 percent. . . .

If the text writers need a classic example of the folly of requiring mutuality of estoppel for estoppel by verdict, these facts and the plaintiffs inconsistent positions taken in sister states supply it. . . .

Finley does not deny the statements he made and caused to be made in the Indiana Court proceedings. Nor does he claim they were made by mistake, accidentally or without full knowledge of the facts. Likewise, he does not deny that the Indiana trial court found that the children owned the stock and that the Indiana appellate court stated the children owned the stock and it was not marital property. . . . What he does contend is that, despite all this, he is not bound by the Indiana holdings because the children were not parties to the lawsuit and thus there could be no mutuality of estoppel and that Illinois is constitutionally required under the Full Faith and Credit Clause to follow Indiana's doctrine of collateral estoppel rather than its own. It is not disputed that under the Illinois doctrine of collateral estoppel, Finley would be barred from bringing this action.

I

Indiana, unlike Illinois, still requires mutuality before it applies the doctrine of collateral estoppel. . . . We have difficulty believing that even Indiana, reluctant as it may be to follow the modern trend of cases abandoning the requirement of mutuality, would permit Finley to avoid the effect of a ruling set forth not only in the judgment but in an appellate court decision, a ruling which he himself apparently had sought and which was based on his own pleadings and testimony and that of one of his witnesses. But it is not necessary to guess whether Indiana would cling to the doctrine of mutuality under these peculiar circumstances at the price of "[subjecting] the law to ridicule." While we are required by the full faith and credit clause to give effect to the Indiana judgment, we are not required to give effect to the Indiana rules limiting application of the doctrine of collateral estoppel at the price of "[generating] absurd results."

Article 4, § I of the Federal constitution requires that "Full Faith and Credit shall be given in each State to the public, Acts, Records, and Judicial Proceedings of every other State." The intended purpose of this clause is "to alter the status of the several states as independent foreign sovereignties, each free to ignore obligations created under the laws or by the judicial proceedings of the others, and to make them integral parts of a single nation throughout which a remedy upon a just obligation might be demanded as of right, irrespective of the state of its origin." Its intended function is to avoid the relitigation in other states of adjudicated issues. On the other hand this clause does not compel the courts of one state to subordinate the local policies of that state to the policies and laws of another state. *Williams v. State of North Carolina* [*Williams I*]; (1942), 317 U.S. 287.

It is undisputed that, as Finley contends, the judgment of a state court is entitled to the same validity and effect in another state as it has in its own and that the only pleas which can be raised against it in a second state are those which would be good to a suit thereon in the first state. The Full Faith and Credit Clause is intended to establish as constitutional law the principles embodied in the common law doctrine of *res judicata*. So that just as the doctrine of *res judicata* bars parties from relitigating a cause of action in the same state, it, through the constitutional provision, bars them from relitigating the cause of action in a different state.

It is also true, as Finley contends, that a judgment has no constitutional claim to a greater effect in the second state than it had in the first. *New York ex rel. Halvey v. Halvey* (1947), 330 U.S. 610. . . .

However this does not mean that even though a state is not required by the Constitution to give greater effect to a judgment than would the courts of the first state, it cannot give greater effect to the adjudication of the issue therein than would the first state. Finley has cited no case, and we have found none, which holds that a state is barred either by the Full Faith and Credit Clause or by section 1738 of the United States Code of Judiciary and Judicial Procedure from applying its own doctrine of collateral estoppel but instead must give effect not only to the judgment of the first state but to the rules of that state as to when collateral estoppel is to be applied. . . .

We recognize, although Finley does not raise the point, that as a simple choice of laws question, the effect of a judgment on the issues involved may be determined by the local law of the state where the judgment was rendered. Restatement of Conflict of Laws (Second) § 95, *but see* criticism in Carrington, *Collateral Estoppel and Foreign Judgments,* 24 Ohio St. L. J. 381 (1963). But the applicability of such conflict of laws principles is always subject to the public policy of the forum state. This policy was accurately set forth by the trial court in this case.

*Affirmed.*

## NOTES AND QUESTIONS ON *FINLEY* AND THE CONTOURS OF THE FULL FAITH AND CREDIT OBLIGATION

(1) *At Least as Much Preclusive Effect.* Suppose the opposite of *Finley,* that is, a situation where the state that rendered the judgment has abandoned the mutuality rule but the forum has not. Must the forum apply the law of the rendering state or can it apply its own less preclusive rule? The problem also can arise in a claim preclusion context. Suppose Ohio has adopted the transactional theory of cause of action and thus requires an automobile accident plaintiff to bring all claims arising out of a particular incident in a single action. In contrast, Indiana, adhering to the older primary right theory, permits splitting the claim into one action for property damage and another for personal injury. If plaintiff sues first in Ohio for property damage and later in Indiana for personal injuries, what is Indiana's obligation under the Full Faith and Credit Clause? Must it apply Ohio's law precluding the personal injury claim or can it apply its own less preclusive rule?

The orthodox answer to this question is that the forum must give the judgment "at least the res judicata effect which the judgment would be accorded in the State which rendered it." *Durfee v. Duke,* 375 U.S. 106, 109

(1963). In other words, the forum must use the law of judgments of the rendering state when that law is *more* preclusive than the forum's. *See also* Restatement (Second) of Conflict of Laws (§§ 94 and 95 (1971) (what issues and what persons affected by the judgment determined by the law of the rendering state). Is the "at least as much effect" rule required to satisfy the goals of the full faith and credit clause? Instead of the "at least as much effect" rule, the Court might have adopted the less ambitious "anti-discrimination" rule which would require only that the enforcing state treat a judgment from the rendering state exactly as it would treat a judgment of its own courts. How would it offend the dignity of the rendering state for the enforcing state to apply its own law and thus give the judgment the exact same effect it would give to a judgment of its own courts? *See* Paul Carrington, *Collateral Estoppel and Foreign Judgments,* 24 OHIO ST. L.J. 381, 383 (1963).

Despite the apparent rigidity of this rule, it has at least one settled exception. The forum can apply its own statute of limitations barring an action to enforce the judgment even though the suit would not be time-barred in the rendering state. *McElmoyle v. Cohen,* 38 U.S. (13 Pet.) 312 (1839). *See also Watkins v. Conway,* 385 U.S. 188 (1966).

Professors Wright, Miller, and Cooper challenge the premise that the forum should invariably use the law of judgments of the rendering court. In their view:

> [T]he central core of rules must of course be followed to support the finality, repose, and reliance values that are common to res judicata policy in all states. Many other rules should be followed to support the first court's power to control its own procedures. Nonetheless, it is not desirable to suppose that every last variation of preclusion policy is so far part of the judgment that full faith and credit commands obedience. To the contrary, there are many situations in which the *res judicata* effects of a state court judgment are properly controlled by the domestic rules of a second state.

18B CHARLES WRIGHT, ARTHUR MILLER, & EDWARD COOPER, FEDERAL PRACTICE AND PROCEDURE § 4467 (2002).[*] But how is the core to be distinguished from the periphery? The authors counsel a painstaking analysis of the purposes that underlie the individual preclusion rules. Within the core, they conclude, are enforcement of a money judgment, preclusion of defenses, claim preclusion (bar and merger); toward the periphery are many questions of issue preclusion such as privity and mutuality. Given the underlying difficulty of the individual *res judicata* questions, how easy will it be to convince a court to undertake the recommended issue-by-issue purposive analysis? Further, is the game worth the candle? How often will the enforcing state actually be offended by having to apply the rendering state's preclusion rules?

(2) *More Preclusive Effect.* What should happen in a case like *Finley* when the forum's law of judgments is more preclusive than the law of the rendering state? Can the forum give the judgment more preclusive effect (more faith and credit) than it would receive in the rendering state? Is the case for rigid application of the law of the rendering state less clear here than in Note (1)?

---

[*] Reprinted with permission. Copyright 1981, West Publishing Co.

Does the language of the Full Faith and Credit Clause permit an argument that, although less preclusive effect is not permitted, more is? *See* Jeffrey Lewis, *Mutuality in Conflict: Flexibility and Full Faith and Credit,* 23 DRAKE L. REV. 364, 374 (1974). Leaving the semantics aside, does it make sense to allow a mutuality state to force a nonmutuality forum to expend judicial resources adjudicating an issue that it considers settled? *See* Robert Casad, *Intersystem Issue Preclusion and the Restatement (Second) of Judgments,* 66 CORNELL L. REV. 510, 523 (1981).

On the other hand, can the forum's use of its own more preclusive rules generate unfairness?

---

**HART v. AMERICAN AIRLINES**, 61 Misc. 2d 41, 304 N.Y.S.2d 810 (Sup. Ct. 1969). Action by two New York plaintiffs, whose decedents died in a crash of defendant's airliner in Kentucky. Plaintiffs urged the preclusive effect of a finding of defendant's negligence made in a prior Texas proceeding involving the same disaster but different plaintiffs. Texas retained the mutuality of estoppel rule, which New York had abandoned.

*Held:* For plaintiffs; New York can apply its own rules of issue preclusion and give the Texas proceedings more faith and credit than would Texas. "The State of Texas has no legitimate interest in imposing its rules of collateral estoppel upon these New York residents."

\* \* \*

Suppose in *Hart* that the Texas suit had involved only property damage or minor personal injuries. Should that change the result? Would defendant have a strong reliance argument if it could show that its litigation of the issue in Texas was less than complete because it reasonably believed that the stakes were limited by the low damage claim and the Texas mutuality rule? *See* WILLIAM RICHMAN & WILLIAM REYNOLDS, UNDERSTANDING CONFLICT OF LAWS § 110[c] (3d ed. 2002). On the effect that preclusion law has on the behavior of litigants, see Howard M. Erichson, *Interjurisdictional Preclusion,* 96 MICH. L. REV. 945, 992-993 (1998).

These nicely balanced arguments notwithstanding, the Supreme Court may have settled the issue in *Marrese v. American Academy of Orthopedic Surgeons,* 470 U.S. 373 (1985); the Court held that a federal court could not give a state court judgment more preclusive effect than it would receive in the state's own courts. Might the holding apply only when the second forum is a federal court and thus leave state courts free to grant more preclusive effect to a sister-state judgment? There is no reason to think so, but the Court's most forceful statements on the more faith and credit issue have all involved federal courts. *See* GENE SHREVE & PETER RAVEN-HANSEN, UNDERSTANDING CIVIL PROCEDURE 527 (3d ed. 2002). *Marrese* is treated in greater detail in § 7.12, *infra. See also* Gene Shreve, *Preclusion and Federal Choice of Law,* 64 TEX. L. REV. 1209 (1986); Stephen Burbank, *Afterwords: A Response to Professor Hazard and a Comment on Marrese,* 70 CORNELL L. REV. 659 (1985).

*Marrese* may have settled the issue, but apparently many state courts judges remain confused. A recent empirical study considered 286 cases where a state court was called upon to give full faith and credit to a federal court judgment. It found that the state courts most often applied their own preclusion law rather than the preclusion law of the rendering court, and that many state court decisions showed a blissful lack of awareness that there was any choice-of-preclusion-law problem at all. *See Erichson, supra,* 1008-1009. Do you suspect that this is the result of bad lawyering?

*See* PROBLEM 7A-6. ARE YOU ENTITLED TO ONE FREE BITE?

## § 7.04 Full Faith and Credit for In Rem Proceedings

When a court exercises some form of in rem jurisdiction over property within the state, are the proceedings entitled to full faith and credit in the courts of sister states? As posed, the question is too broad and thus confusing. In fact it encompasses at least three constituent questions: First, what effect must the forum give to a sister-state judgment that purports to create or destroy interests in the property? Second, what if the rendering state exceeds its limited authority and issues a judgment that purports to create or destroy personal obligations? Is that judgment entitled to full faith and credit? Finally, what respect does the forum owe to the findings made by the rendering court on contested issues of fact? The cases and notes that follow explore these questions.

## HARNISCHFEGER SALES CORP. v. STERNBERG DREDGING CO.

*Mississippi Supreme Court*
*189 Miss. 73, 191 So. 94 (1939)*

[Harnischfeger sold a dredge to Sternberg and received in return a series of notes for the purchase price and a chattel mortgage on the dredge. Sternberg defaulted, and Harnischfeger sued in Louisiana to foreclose the mortgage and to obtain a personal judgment, as well. Sternberg moved to dismiss on the ground that there was no personal jurisdiction over it in Louisiana. After the trial court denied the motion, the parties litigated the merits of the case. Sternberg's defense was based on breach of Harnischfeger's warranty that the dredge could operate a "two-yard bucket." The trial court found no breach of warranty, foreclosed the chattel mortgage, and ordered the dredge sold. It also rendered a personal judgment against Sternberg for the amount of the notes. On appeal, the Supreme Court of Louisiana affirmed the trial court's order foreclosing the mortgage on the dredge but reversed the deficiency judgment, holding that Louisiana lacked personal jurisdiction over Sternberg.

Harnischfeger then sued Sternberg in Mississippi, and Sternberg, again relying on the "two-yard bucket" issue, pleaded breach of warranty and fraud as a defense. Harnischfeger interposed a plea of res judicata based on the

Louisiana proceedings. The Mississippi trial court struck the plea of res judicata, heard the "two-yard bucket" issue, and found for Sternberg. Harnischfeger appealed to the Supreme Court of Mississippi.]

McGOWAN, J., delivered the opinion of the court. . . .

. . . Two questions are presented by the appellant corporation for decision, which are, in substance, as follows: (1) That the Louisiana proceedings constituted res adjudicata or estoppel as against Sternberg Dredging Company to again set up the defense and representations as to the two-yard bucket; and (2) that all the allegations and proof as to fraud and deceit for material representations were incompetent in the light of the peculiar language of the written sales contract.

We shall only consider the first question—that the Louisiana litigation constitutes res adjudicata or estoppel as to the defense sought to be interposed in the Mississippi court.

It is to be stated with reference to the facts that practically the same evidence was offered in both proceedings by the Sternberg Dredging Company as to the breach-of-warranty theory. The case on the evidence offered by the appellee is perhaps stronger, but it tends to the same ultimate conclusion. In the Mississippi Court, in the case at bar, the appellee changed its pleading subsequent to the filing of the plea of res adjudicata. The proof in both cases tended to establish the same ultimate fact, and it is unnecessary for us to detail the evidence. . . .

At the outset we will state that the effect of the estoppel by the final decree of the Supreme Court of Louisiana is to be determined by the laws of that state where the decree was rendered, and this seems to be an accepted and universal rule.

. . . [In the Louisiana court] appellee . . . offered its defense, and resisted to the utmost the enforcement of the lien . . . for the reasons we have stated. The ultimate facts as to whether or not a debt existed that would authorize the enforcement of a lien are the same in both the Louisiana and the Mississippi courts. The litigation was between the same parties, the same subject, the only difference in the pleas and proof in the two courts being a change in the name of the pleading. The same cause of action was alleged in the Louisiana Court as was interposed and allowed by the lower court in this state, and that cause of action was, when the case is stripped to the bone, that the machine delivered would not and did not carry a two-yard bucket, and by this we understand it to mean that the machine was not capacitated to be filled with two yards of earth and successfully dumped therefrom.

It is said that the Louisiana decree cannot operate as res adjudicata or estoppel because the Supreme Court held that the proceeding was in rem. The appellant, Harnischfeger Sales Corporation, is not seeking here to bring a suit on the contention that the Louisiana judgment and action of that court, on the defense thereto, operated as a judgment which concluded the parties as to the amount of the judgment. The contention of the appellant is, as we understand it, that the Sternberg Dredging Company interposed the same defense in the Louisiana court as it interposed in the case at bar, and as to that defense the doctrine of res adjudicata is interposed and effective to conclude it, even though the proceedings in Louisiana to enforce a chattel mortgage on the thing mortgaged in that state were in rem. The appellee had its option to stand on the want of jurisdiction of the Court, but it did not do so. It appeared there. Sternberg, the main witness in both trials, testified to the same salient facts as to this defense in the Louisiana court as was testified by him in the Mississippi Court in the case at bar. We are of the opinion that the defense was adjudged and concluded as to that defense and that every court everywhere would be bound to so hold. . . .

Many authorities are collated by both sides, but our attention has not been called to a case where a defendant in a proceeding in rem against him appeared in court and by plea sought to defeat the proceeding in rem to enforce a chattel mortgage because of a particular defense thereto which, if successful, would defeat the debt, and, of course, thereby prevent the enforcement of any lien. The cases cited are those in which there was no appearance by the defendant and no issue raised and actually litigated. . . .

When the Sternberg Dredging Company decided and elected to resist the entry of any decree in rem against the machine and to interpose the breach-of-warranty defense, it thereby concluded itself irrevocably. Suppose the Louisiana Court had taken the opposite view and had determined in the court of last resort that the defense was valid in that it extinguished the debt? By that decree it would have retained the machine free from the lien; and, certainly where both parties appeared and contested the issue, debt or no debt, because of a breach of warranty, that decree would be final and conclusive on that issue actually litigated, and we think under . . . Louisiana [law] would be res adjudicata. . . .

It appears to us that whatever may be said about the decisions of the Louisiana court . . . the claim interposed in the case at bar . . . wherein Sternberg Dredging Company sought to extinguish the debt by plea and proof of a breach of warranty on the cause of action, that the bucket would carry two yards of earth when in actual operation such warrant failed because the bucket would not so function, the same claim is here res adjudicata. We think there is no merit in the contention that by changing the name of the facts the cause of action was changed; and we have examined all the authorities cited from that Court on that question and can find no reason for saying that the cause of action was not identical. . . .

We are, therefore, of the opinion that the court below erred in striking the plea of res adjudicata and declining to allow it as an estoppel to the defense here involved. . . .

*Reversed, and judgment appellant.*

## NOTES AND QUESTIONS ON *HARNISCHFEGER* AND RECOGNITION OF IN REM PROCEEDINGS

(1) *Recognition of the Interests in the Property.*

(a) Assume in a case like *Harnischfeger,* Sternberg, not subject to personal jurisdiction in Louisiana, defaults after being notified of the Louisiana foreclosure action. The court finds Sternberg indebted to Harnischfeger, orders the dredge sold and the proceeds paid to Harnischfeger. Purchaser buys the dredge at the judicial sale. Later Purchaser takes the dredge to Mississippi where Sternberg sues him for it. Purchaser sets up the Louisiana judgment as a defense. What result?

(b) Probate of Testator's will in Iowa. Son and Nephew, neither subject to personal jurisdiction in Iowa, are notified of the action. Nephew appears; Son does not. The probate court validates the will and, pursuant to its terms, gives Nephew title to Testator's car. Nephew drives the car to Illinois where Son, as an intestate heir, sues Nephew for the car claiming the will to be invalid. What result?

(c) How could preclusion be justified in hypotheticals (a) and (b)? Sternberg and Son were not subject to personal jurisdiction, and neither had a day in court; would it be unfair to preclude their claims? Is there a justification in necessity?

(2) *Binding the Parties Personally.* Suppose in a case like *Harnischfeger,* that Sternberg, not subject to personal jurisdiction in Louisiana, defaults after being notified of the Louisiana foreclosure action. The court finds Sternberg indebted to Harnischfeger in the amount of $16,000 and orders the dredge sold and the proceeds paid to Harnischfeger. The dredge brings $8,000 at the judicial sale, and the court then enters a deficiency judgment against Sternberg for $8,000. Harnischfeger then sues Sternberg in Mississippi on the deficiency judgment. What result? For help with this question consider the following case.

**COMBS v. COMBS**, 249 Ky. 155, 60 S.W.2d 368 (1933). Debtor owed creditors a considerable sum of money and, to secure that debt, gave creditors a lien on debtor's land in Arkansas. Creditors sued debtor in Kentucky on the debt. Before process could be served on debtor, however, he sued creditors in Arkansas to remove the lien on the Arkansas land. The creditors were not subject to the in personam jurisdiction of the Arkansas court. Debtor alleged that he was indebted to creditors, that creditors had a lien on his land, and that he had paid a part of the debt. Debtor asked the court to permit him to pay the remainder into court and to cancel the lien as a cloud on his title. The Arkansas court granted debtor's request; it fixed the sum he owed (the original debt less the amount he claimed to have paid), ordered debtor to pay the balance into the court, and extinguished the lien. Debtor then appeared in the Kentucky action and argued that the Arkansas proceeding was entitled to full faith and credit in Kentucky and that it precluded the creditors' claim.

*Held:* For the creditors. The judgment of the Arkansas court is:

> obligatory on [creditors] . . . in so far as it released their lien upon the land in that state. But, when the court undertook to grant additional relief strictly in personam, it transgressed its jurisdiction so as to render such unauthorized additional relief of no force and effect whatever. That relief in this case was the adjudication that [Debtor] had paid to [creditors] . . . any part of his debt and thereby discharged a part of his obligation to them, and that the court could and did fix the amount due. . . . It may be that the Arkansas court was vested with authority to lift the lien from the land involved, and

for that purpose to incidentally determine the amount of the lien, and whether or not it had been paid, but the only binding effect of such adjudications would be that of releasing the lien as an encumbrance upon the title to the res. Such adjudications in so far as they affected the personal obligations and rights of the parties were and are not binding upon [creditors] herein, nor do they operate as a res adjudicata estoppel in any future action.

(3) *Preclusion of Litigated Issues.* How is *Harnischfeger* different from *Combs* and the hypothetical in Note (2)? In all three cases, the rendering court lacked personal jurisdiction over the party against whom preclusion was later argued. Is the distinction that Sternberg appeared in *Harnischfeger* and litigated the issue? What effect did the hypothetical Harnischfeger in Note (2) want for the Louisiana proceedings? What effect did the real Harnischfeger want for those proceedings in the actual case? Exactly what did the Mississippi court give full faith and credit to in *Harnischfeger*—the Louisiana court's judgment, or its findings on the "two-yard bucket" issue? Finally, what would have happened in *Harnischfeger* if Sternberg had interposed another defense in the Mississippi action, say, lack of contractual capacity?

(4) The Restatement (Second) of Judgments deals with the issues in Notes (1)-(3), *supra,* as follows: *

§ 30. Judgments Based on Jurisdiction to Determine Interests in Things

A valid and final judgment in an action based only on jurisdiction to determine interests in a thing:

(1) Is conclusive as to those interests with regard to all persons, if the judgment purports to have that effect (traditionally described as "in rem"), or with regard to the named parties, if the judgment purports to have that effect (traditionally described as "quasi in rem"); and

(2) Does not bind anyone with respect to a personal liability; and

(3) Is conclusive between parties, in accordance with the rules of issue preclusion, as to any issues actually litigated by them and determined in the action.

(5) Harnischfeger *Evaluated.* Does the holding in *Harnischfeger* make sense? Its principal application occurs in cases in which the defendant has made a limited appearance, a device that permits a defense on the merits of the defendant's interest in the attached property without requiring the defendant to submit to the court's personal jurisdiction. The limited appearance was created to ameliorate some of the unfairness to the defendant caused by traditional attachment jurisdiction; without it, the defendant could be forced to choose between forfeiting the attached property and consenting to the court's personal jurisdiction. *See* § 3.16, Note (6), *supra.* What arguments support the issue preclusion rule of *Harnischfeger?* Does the rule destroy the value of the limited appearance? *See* WILLIAM RICHMAN & WILLIAM REYNOLDS, UNDERSTANDING CONFLICT OF LAWS §111[c] (3d ed. 2002).

---

*In Harnischfeger,* the property was worth a large fraction of plaintiffs claim; would it be fair to apply issue preclusion against the defendant in a case in which the value of the attached property was only a small fraction of the total amount of plaintiffs claim? *See* Eugene Scoles, *Interstate Preclusion by Prior Litigation,* 74 Nw. U.L. REV. 742, 755 (1979). For a detailed, if dated, discussion of *Harnischifeger, see* Charles W. Taintor II, *Foreign Judgment In Rem: Full Faith and Credit v. Res Judicata In Personam,* 8 PITT. L. REV. 223 (1942). How much does the *Harnischfeger problem* matter after *Shaffer v. Heitner? See* § 3.16, *supra.*

(6) *More Faith and Credit.* Not all states adhere to the *Harnischfeger* principle; some permit relitigation of issues determined in a prior in rem action in which defendant has made a limited appearance. Suppose plaintiff brings an in rem action against defendant in such a state; defendant makes a limited appearance, litigates the merits, and loses. Plaintiff now brings an in personam action against defendant in a state that adheres to the *Harnisch-feger* rule. Can the second state preclude defendant from relitigating the issues even though the first state would not? *See* § 7.03, *supra;* Michael H. Hoff-heimer, *Mississippi Conflict of Laws,* 67 MISS. L.J. 175, 198 (1997), Robert Casad, *Intersystem Issue Preclusion and the Restatement (Second) of Judg-ments,* 66 CORNELL L. REV. 510, 530 (1981).

## § 7.05  Recognition of Judgments of Foreign Nations

### HILTON v. GUYOT

*United States Supreme Court*
*159 U.S. 113, 16 S. Ct. 139, 140 L. Ed 95 (1895)*

[Plaintiff, a citizen of France, obtained a judgment against defendants, citizens of New York, in a French court. He then sought to enforce the judgment in a federal court in New York. Defendants defended upon the ground, *inter alia,* that the French judgment should not be enforced without re-examination of the merits because an American judgment against a French citizen would be subject to reexamination in the courts of France. The trial court enforced the judgment without a retrial of the merits.]

MR. JUSTICE GRAY  . . .  delivered the opinion of the court. . . .

No law has any effect, of its own force, beyond the limits of the sovereignty from which its authority is derived. The extent to which the law of one nation, as put in force within its territory, whether by executive order, by legislative act, or by judicial decree, shall be allowed to operate within the dominion of another nation, depends upon what our greatest jurists have been content to call "the comity of nations." Although the phrase has been often criticized, no satisfactory substitute has been suggested.

"Comity," in the legal sense, is neither a matter of absolute obligation, on the one hand, nor of mere courtesy and good will, upon the other. But it is the recognition which one nation allows within its territory to the legislative, executive or judicial acts of another nation, having due regard both to international duty and convenience, and to the rights of its own citizens or of other persons who are under the protection of its laws. . . .

In order to appreciate the weight of the various authorities cited at the bar, it is important to distinguish different kinds of judgments. Every foreign judgment, of whatever nature, in order to be entitled to any effect, must have been rendered by a court having jurisdiction of the cause, and upon regular proceedings and due notice. In alluding to different kinds of judgments, therefore, such jurisdiction, proceedings and notice will be assumed. It will also be assumed that they are untainted by fraud, the effect of which will be considered later.

A judgment *in rem,* adjudicating the title to a ship or other movable property within the custody of the court, is treated as valid everywhere. As said by Chief Justice Marshall:

The sentence of a competent court, proceeding *in rem,* is conclusive with respect to the thing itself, and operates as an absolute change of the property. By such sentence, the right of the former owner is lost, and a complete title given to the person who claims under the decree. No court of co-ordinate jurisdiction can examine the sentence. The question, therefore, respecting its conformity to general or municipal law can never arise, for no co-ordinate tribunal is capable of making the inquiry.

*Williams v. Armroyd,* 7 Cranch, 423, 432. The most common illustrations of this are decrees of courts of admiralty and prize, which proceed upon principles of international law. But the same rule applies to judgments *in rem* under municipal law.

A judgment affecting the status of persons, such as a decree confirming or dissolving a marriage, is recognized as valid in every country, unless contrary to the policy of its own law. . . .

Other judgments, not strictly *in rem,* under which a person has been compelled to pay money, are so far conclusive that the justice of the payment cannot be impeached in another country, so as to compel him to pay it again. For instance, a judgment in foreign attachment is conclusive, as between the parties, of the right to the property or money attached. . . .

Other foreign judgments which have been held conclusive of the matter adjudged were judgments discharging obligations contracted in the foreign country between citizens or residents thereof . . .

The extraterritorial effect of judgments *in personam,* at law or in equity, may differ, according to the parties to the cause. A judgment of that kind between two citizens or residents of the country, and thereby subject to the jurisdiction in which it is rendered, may be held conclusive as between them everywhere. So, if a foreigner invokes the jurisdiction by bringing an action against a citizen, both may be held bound by a judgment in favor of either, and if a citizen sues a foreigner, and judgment is rendered in favor of the latter, both may be held equally bound.

The effect to which a judgment, purely executory, rendered in favor of a citizen or resident of the country, in a suit there brought by him against a foreigner, may be entitled in an action thereon against the latter in his own country—as is the case now before us—presents a more difficult question, upon which there has been some diversity of opinion. . . .

In view of all the authorities upon the subject, and of the trend of judicial opinion in this country and in England, following the lead of Kent and Story, we are satisfied that, where there has been opportunity for a full and fair trial abroad before a court of competent jurisdiction, conducting the trial upon regular proceedings, after due citation or voluntary appearance of the defendant, and under a system of jurisprudence likely to secure an impartial administration of justice between the citizens of its own country and those of other countries, and there is nothing to show either prejudice in the court, or in the system of laws under which it was sitting, or fraud in procuring the judgment, or any other special reason why the comity of this nation should not allow it full effect, the merits of the case should not, in an action brought in this country upon the judgment, be tried afresh, as on a new trial or an appeal, upon the mere assertion of the party that the judgment was erroneous in law or in fact. The defendants, therefore, cannot be permitted, upon that general ground, to contest the validity or the effect of the judgment sued on.

But they have sought to impeach that judgment upon several other grounds, which require separate consideration.

It is objected that the appearance and litigation of the defendants in the French tribunals were not voluntary, but by legal compulsion, and therefore that the French courts never acquired such jurisdiction over the defendants, that they should be held bound by the judgment.

Upon the question what should be considered such a voluntary appearance, as to amount to a submission to the jurisdiction of a foreign court, there has been some difference of opinion in England. . . .

The present case is not one of a person travelling through or casually found in a foreign country. The defendants, although they were not citizens or residents of France, but were citizens and residents of the State of New York, and their principal place of business was in the city of New York, yet had a storehouse and an agent in Paris, and were accustomed to purchase large quantities of goods there, although they did not make sales in France. Under such circumstances, evidence that their sole object in appearing and carrying on the litigation in the French courts was to prevent property, in their storehouse at Paris, belonging to them, and within the jurisdiction, but not in the custody, of those courts, from being taken in satisfaction of any judgment that might be recovered against them, would not, according to our law, show that those courts did not acquire jurisdiction of the persons of the defendants.

It is next objected that in those courts one of the plaintiffs was permitted to testify not under oath, and was not subjected to cross-examination by the opposite party, and that the defendants were, therefore, deprived of safeguards which are by our law considered essential to secure honesty and to detect fraud in a witness; and also that documents and papers were admitted in evidence, with which the defendants had no connection, and which would not be admissible under our own system of jurisprudence. But it having been shown by the plaintiffs, and hardly denied by the defendants, that the practice followed and the method of examining witnesses were according to the laws of France, we are not prepared to hold that the fact that the procedure in these respects differed from that of our own courts is, of itself, a sufficient ground for impeaching the foreign judgment. . . .

When an action is brought in a court of this country, by a citizen of a foreign country against one of our own citizens, to recover a sum of money adjudged by a court of that country to be due from the defendant to the plaintiff, and the foreign judgment appears to have been rendered by a competent court, having jurisdiction of the cause and of the parties, and upon due allegations and proofs, and opportunity to defend against them, and its proceedings are according to the course of a civilized jurisprudence, and are stated in a clear and formal record, the judgment is *prima facie* evidence, at least, of the truth of the matter adjudged; and it should be held conclusive upon the merits tried in the foreign court, unless some special ground is shown for impeaching the judgment, as by showing that it was affected by fraud or prejudice, or that, by the principles of international law, and by the comity of our own country, it should not be given full credit and effect.

There is no doubt that both in this country, as appears by the authorities already cited, and in England, a foreign judgment may be impeached for fraud. . . .

But whether those decisions can be followed in regard to foreign judgments, consistently with our own decisions as to impeaching domestic judgments for fraud, it is unnecessary in this case to determine, because there is a distinct and independent ground upon which we are satisfied that the comity of our nation does not require us to give conclusive effect to the judgments of the courts of France; and that ground is, the want of reciprocity, on the part of France, as to the effect to be given to the judgments of this and other foreign countries.

[The Court reviewed the French statutes dealing with the recognition of foreign judgments.] . . .

The defendants, in their answer, cited the above provisions of the statutes of France, and alleged, and at the trial offered to prove, that, by the construction given to these statues by the judicial tribunals of France, when the judgments of tribunals of foreign countries against the citizens of France are sued upon in the courts of France, the merits of the controversies upon which those judgments are based are examined anew, unless a treaty to the contrary effect exists between the Republic of France and the country in which such judgment is obtained, (which is not the case between the Republic of France and the United States) and that the tribunals of the Republic of France give no force and effect, within the jurisdiction of that country, to the judgments duly rendered by courts of competent jurisdiction of the United States against citizens of France after proper personal service of the process of those courts has been made thereon in this country. We are of opinion that this evidence should have been admitted. . . .

It appears, therefore, that there is hardly a civilized nation on either continent, which, by its general law, allows conclusive effect to an executory foreign judgment for the recovery of money. In France, and in a few smaller

States—Norway, Portugal, Greece, Monaco, and Haiti—the merits of the controversy are reviewed, as of course, allowing to the foreign judgment, at the most, no more effect than of being *prima facie* evidence of the justice of the claim. In the great majority of the countries on the continent of Europe—in Belgium, Holland, Denmark, Sweden, Germany, in many cantons of Switzerland, in Russia and Poland, in Romania, in Austria and Hungary, (perhaps in Italy) and in Spain—as well as in Egypt, in Mexico, and in a great part of South America, the judgment rendered in a foreign country is allowed the same effect only as the courts of that country allow to the judgments of the country in which the judgment in question is sought to be executed.

The prediction of Mr. Justice Story has thus been fulfilled, and the rule of reciprocity has worked itself firmly into the structure of international jurisprudence.

The reasonable, if not the necessary, conclusion appears to us to be that judgments rendered in France, or in any other foreign country, by the laws of which our own judgments are reviewable upon the merits, are not entitled to full credit and conclusive effect when sued upon in this country, but are *prima facie* evidence only of the justice of the plaintiffs' claim.

In holding such a judgment, for want of reciprocity, not to be conclusive evidence of the merits of the claim, we do not proceed upon any theory of retaliation upon one person by reason of injustice done to another; but upon the broad ground that international law is founded upon mutuality and reciprocity, and that by the principles of international law recognized in most civilized nations, and by the comity of our own country, which it is our judicial duty to know and to declare, the judgment is not entitled to be considered conclusive. . . .

. . . If the judgment had been rendered in this country, or in any other outside of the jurisdiction of France, the French courts would not have executed or enforced it, except after examining into its merits. The very judgment now sued on would be held inconclusive in almost any other country than France. . . . In the courts of nearly every other nation, it would be subject to re-examination, either merely because it was a foreign judgment, or because judgments of that nation would be re-examinable in the courts of France.

For these reasons  . . .  *the Judgment is reversed*  . . .   . . .

MR. CHIEF JUSTICE FULLER, with whom concurred MR. JUSTICE HARLAN, MR. JUSTICE BREWER, and MR. JUSTICE JACKSON, dissenting.

I cannot yield my assent to the proposition that because by legislation and judicial decision in France that effect is not there given to judgments recovered in this country which, according to our jurisprudence, we think should be given to judgments wherever recovered, (subject, of course, to the recognized exceptions) therefore we should pursue the same line of conduct as respects the judgments of French tribunals. The application of the doctrine of *res judicata does* not rest in discretion; and it is for the government, and not for its courts, to adopt the principle of retorsion, if deemed under any circumstances desirable or necessary.

As the court expressly abstains from deciding whether the judgment is impeachable on the ground of fraud, I refrain from any observations on that branch of the case.

*See* PROBLEM 7A-7. SEPARATION OF POWERS.

---

## NOTES AND QUESTIONS ON *HILTON* AND THE RECOGNITION OF FOREIGN NATION JUDGMENTS

(1) *Early Case Law.* Before *Hilton,* early English and American case law held that a foreign nation judgment was only *prima facie* evidence of the justice of the underlying claim. Thus all defenses that could have been raised to the original claim could also be interposed in the suit on the foreign judgment. Isolated examples of this view survived until very late; *see Svenska Handelsbanken v. Carlson,* 258 F. Supp. 448 (D. Mass 1966) (a federal court read 150-year-old Massachusetts case law to give *only prima facie effect* to a Swedish judgment). For a discussion of the early cases, see Courtland Peterson, *Foreign Country Judgments and the Second Restatement of Conflict of Laws,* 72 COLUM. L. REV. 220, 225 (1972).

(2) *Hilton and the Reciprocity Rule. Hilton* is an advance over the *prima facie* evidence position since it provides for conclusive effect for the foreign judgment in most cases; in others, however, the Court injected a reciprocity requirement. What criterion does the Court use to determine the cases in which the reciprocity requirement applies? Does the reciprocity rule make sense? Is it wise policy, in other words, to penalize a private person (the foreign plaintiff) for the acts of his country's courts? Is it likely that reciprocity would work to influence foreign courts to recognize American judgments, or might it have the opposite effect and produce retaliation against those judgments? Based on considerations such as these, the commentators have been quite critical of *Hilton; see, e.g.,* ROBERT LEFLAR, LUTHER MCDOUGAL & ROBERT FELIX, AMERICAN CONFLICTS LAW 250 (4th ed. 1986); Arthur Lenhoff, *Reciprocity and the Law of Foreign Judgments: A Historical-Critical Analysis,* 16 LA. L. REV. 465 (1956).

The issue of reciprocity, of course, implicates the more basic question of what policy bases support the recognition of foreign nation judgments by American courts. One commentator suggests the following:

1. the policy of economy of judicial resources;

2. the policy of fairness to private litigants;

3. the policy of fostering a desirable international order;

4. the policy of promoting acceptance abroad of domestic judgments; and

5. the policy of encouraging the initial selection of the most appropriate forum for litigation of the case.

Robert Casad, *Issue Preclusion and Foreign Country Judgments: Whose Law?* 70 IOWA L. REV. 53, 61 (1984). What do these goals suggest about the reciprocity requirement?

(3) *The Impact of* Hilton. Despite its influential source, *Hilton's* impact has been minor. Because *Hilton* was a diversity case, and the Court based its

decision not on the constitution or federal statute, but on federal common law, the decision did not bind the states under the Supremacy Clause. Many states have rejected the reciprocity principle. *See, e.g., Johnston v. Compagnie Generale Transatlantique*, 242 N.Y. 381, 152 N.E. 121 (1926). *See also* Uniform Foreign Money-Judgments Recognition Act, §§ 3, 4, 13 U.L.A. 263 (1962) (rejecting reciprocity) (adopted in 18 states). Further limiting the influence of *Hilton* is the holding of federal courts that the *Erie* decision compels them to apply state rather than federal law on the issue of recognition of foreign nation judgments. *See Somportex Ltd. v. Philadelphia Chewing Gum Corp.*, 453 F.2d 435 (1971), *cert. denied*, 405 U.S. 1017 (1972).

(4) Restatement (Second) of Conflict of Laws § 98 (1971) provides:

> A valid judgment rendered in a foreign nation after a fair trial in a contested proceeding will be recognized in the United States so far as the immediate parties and the underlying cause of action are concerned.

Section 98 requires a "fair trial." How much variation from American procedure should be tolerated before the foreign proceeding is held to fail this text? What guidance does the *Hilton* opinion provide?

The Restatement also requires "a contested proceeding," thus casting doubt upon default judgments. Comment d provides that usually default judgments should be recognized if the foreign court had jurisdiction. But according to what standards should jurisdiction be measured, the minimum contacts standard of *International Shoe? See* Courtland Peterson, *Foreign Country Judgments and the Second Restatement of Conflict of Laws*, 72 COLUM. L. REV. 220, 245-247 (1972). What if the defendant litigates the jurisdictional issue in the foreign court or waives his opportunity to do so? *See Somportex, Ltd. v. Philadelphia Chewing Gum Corp.*, 453 F.2d 435 (1971), *cert. denied*, 405 U.S. 1017 (1972).

*See* PROBLEM 7A-8. RECIPROCITY IN STATE COURT.

(5) *Defenses.* The defenses to a foreign nation judgment generally parallel those available against a sister state judgment. Thus a foreign judgment may be attacked for lack of jurisdiction (see Note (4), *supra*), fraud in the procurement, or because it was based upon a penal cause of action.

One defense operates very differently, however. Although a state court cannot refuse to recognize a sister-state judgment because the underlying claim violates the public policy of the recognizing state (*see Fauntleroy v. Lum*, § 7.07, *supra*), it may refuse to recognize a foreign judgment on that ground. *See* Restatement (Second) of Conflict of Laws § 117, comment c (1971) (recognition except when "the original claim is repugnant to fundamental notions of what is decent and just in the State where enforcement is sought"); *see also* RESTATEMENT (REVISED) OF FOREIGN RELATIONS LAW OF THE UNITED STATES § 482(2)(d)(1986).

*See* PROBLEM 7A-9. THE GUARANTEE.

(6) *Whose Law?* Given that the foreign judgment will be recognized and that there is no applicable defense, what is its effect? Should its effect be determined by the law of judgments of the rendering or the recognizing forum? The

answer is fairly clear when the rendering forum is an American state (see § 7.03, *supra*), but not when it is a foreign nation. *See* Casad, *supra* Note (2).

(7) *Federal Law or State Law.* Since *Aetna Life Ins. Co. v. Tremblay,* 223 U.S. 185 (1912), in which the Supreme Court held that a Maine court's failure to recognize a Canadian judgment did not raise a federal question, it has been assumed that the recognition and effect to be accorded to foreign nation judgments is largely a matter of state law. Does that allocation of law-making responsibility make sense? Or is this an issue where it is important for the United States to speak with one voice instead of fifty, and where disparate state court pronouncements could embarrass or frustrate the federal government's foreign policy?

Commentators have preferred a uniform federal solution under federal statutory or common law. *See* EUGENE SCOLES ET AL., CONFLICT OF LAWS 1149 (3d ed. 2000); Casad, *supra* Note (2), 77-80. *But see* Peterson, *supra* Note (1), 238. (Most issues concerning recognition and effect of judgments—priority, mutuality, jurisdiction, and even public policy—can be left safely to the states without fear of disrupting foreign policy.) The commentators favoring a federal common law approach were encouraged by *Zschernig v. Miller,* § 6.08, *supra,* in which the Supreme Court struck down an Oregon law that prohibited distribution from Oregon estates to claimants who resided in foreign countries unless (1) American citizens enjoyed the reciprocal right to take from decedent's estates in those countries, and (2) the foreign claimant had the right to receive the proceeds "without confiscation." The Court held the statute "an intrusion in the federal domain" of foreign policy. *Zschernig,* however, seems to have been an isolated occurrence; a federal common law of recognition of foreign nation judgments does not seem to be forthcoming from the Supreme Court.

(8) *Treaties.* A sensible way to produce a uniform national law of recognition of foreign-nation judgments would be to enter mutual recognition treaties with our principal trading partners. This has been the approach of the member states of the European Union. The 1968 Brussels Convention on Jurisdiction and the Recognition and Enforcement of Judgments establishes permissible bases for judicial jurisdiction and then provides for recognition of a judgment from a court of a member state provided that the judgment rests upon a jurisdictional basis sanctioned by the Convention. The Lugano Convention (1988) establishes a similar regime between members of the European Union and the member states of the European Free Trade Association. Together the conventions constitute for Europe an analogue of the American full faith and credit clause. For commentary on the two conventions, see Scoles et al., 1198, Robert Reuland, *The Recognition of Judgments in the European Community: The Twenty-Fifth Anniversary of the Brussels Convention,* 14 MICH. J. INT'L L. 559 (1993).

Like current American law, the conventions permit *general* jurisdiction based on domicile of natural persons and the "seat of the company" for business entities, appearance, and the agreement of the parties. Notably absent is "tag" jurisdiction and jurisdiction based on "doing business" (when the plaintiff's claim does not arise out of the defendant's forum based activities). The provisions on *specific* jurisdiction are roughly similar to an

American-style enumerated act long-arm statute with two main differences: (1) the rules pay more attention to the relationship of the controversy to the *forum* in contrast to American law, which insists on forum contacts with the *individual defendant*; and (2) there is jurisdiction over all defendants where any defendant is domiciled. For a useful comparison of the conventions and the American law of jurisdiction, see Linda J. Silberman, *Judicial Jurisdiction in the Conflict of Laws Course: Adding a Comparative Dimension,* 28 VAND. J. TRANSNAT'L L. 389 (1995). (Especially useful is the author's resolution under the conventions of hypotheticals paralleling the facts of recent Supreme Court jurisdiction cases.)

The prospects that the United States will adopt a similar strategy are uncertain. Until recently, there seemed little likelihood that the United States would participate in an international judgments recognition regime. After extensive negotiations between the United States and the United Kingdom between 1974 and 1976, the parties initialed a draft convention, but there was resistance in Britain based on unwillingness to recognize "excessive" American tort damage awards and treble-damage antitrust judgments. In 1980, the negotiations were suspended indefinitely. *See* ANDREAS LOWENFELD, CONFLICT OF LAWS 732-734 (2d ed. 1998).

In 1993, however, the Hague Conference on Private International Law undertook to prepare a Convention on International Jurisdiction And Foreign Judgments In Civil And Commercial Matters. *See* Peter H. Pfund, *The Project of the Hague Conference on Private International law to Prepare a Convention on Jurisdiction and the Recognition/Enforcement of Judgments in Civil and Commercial Matters,* 24 BROOK. J INT'L L. 7, 8 (1998). A series of articles on the prospects for the project appears in Symposium, *Enforcing Judgments Abroad: The Global Challenge,* 24 BROOK. J. INT'L L. 1-221 (1998) (articles by Mary Ellen Fullerton, Peter Pfund, Arthur von Mehren, Louise Lussier, Paul Beaumont, Friedrich Juenger, Ronald Brand, Patrick Borchers, and Russell Weintraub). *See also* Kevin Clermont, *Jurisdictional Salvation and the Hague Treaty,* 85 CORNELL L. REV. 89 (1999).

The most current draft of the Convention is entitled "Summary of the Outcome of the Discussion in Commission II of the First Part of the Diplomatic Conference 6-20 June 2001." That current draft is a "mixed convention," a designation that can be understood only by consideration of some additional terminology. A "single" convention regulates judgment recognition only; it does not purport to regulate the jurisdictional law of the signatory states. A "double" convention, by contrast, regulates both judgment recognition and the internal law of jurisdiction of the signatory states. The current draft is a "mixed" convention because it regulates judgment recognition but only partially regulates jurisdiction. It produces that result by creating three lists of jurisdictional bases: (1) a white list of jurisdictional bases which are permitted and which guaranty recognition of a resulting judgment (Articles 3-13); (2) a black list of jurisdictional bases which are prohibited (Article 18); and (3) a gray list of jurisdictional bases which are not prohibited but which do not guaranty recognition of a resulting judgment (Article 17).

Unfortunately, several of the bases on the black list, including tag jurisdiction, and general jurisdiction based on "doing business" are well-recognized bases under American law; and some of the bases on the white list are prohibited by recent decisions of the Supreme Court. Other controversial provisions from the American point of view are those dealing with awards of punitive damages, lis pendens, inconsistent judgments, forum non conveniens, and public policy. Whether the provisions of the Convention would trump the United States Supreme Court's rulings on the jurisdictional limitations imposed by the due process clause is treated in Symposium, *"Could a Treaty Trump Supreme Court Jurisdictional Doctrine?"* 61 ALB. L. REV. 1159-1309 (1998) (articles by Professors Patrick Borchers, Stanley Cox, Harold Maier, Andrew Strauss, Russell Weintraub, and Joachim Zekoll).

Currently prospects for a draft that would be acceptable to all of the Hague Conference states do not appear good. If a draft is not adopted or is adopted by the Conference but not ratified by the United States, an alternative for the United States is a federal statute that would regulate recognition of the judgments of foreign states and thus achieve some of the goals of ratification of the Convention. Currently the American Law Institute is in the process of drafting such a statute.

Ironically, in the United States recognition of foreign arbitral awards is on sounder footing than recognition of judgments. The United States is a party to the United Nations Convention on the Recognition and Enforcement of Foreign Arbitral Awards, 21 U.S.T. 2517, T.I.A.S. No. 6997, 330 U.N. T.S. 38. It requires American courts to enforce agreements to arbitrate and to recognize arbitral awards. For extensive commentary on the Convention, the American implementing legislation, and practice under both, see Comment, *International Commercial Arbitration Under the United Nations Convention and the Amended Federal Arbitration Statute,* 47 WASH. L. REV. 441 (1972).

---

## TELNIKOFF v. MATUSEVITCH[1]

*Court of Appeals of Maryland*
*347 Md. 561, 702 A.2d 230 (1997)*

ELDRIDGE, Judge.

The issue presented in this certified question case is whether a particular English libel judgment, under the circumstances presented, is contrary to the public policy of Maryland so that it should be denied recognition under principles of comity.

### I.

Matusevitch, a resident of Maryland, who works in Washington, D.C., was sued in a British court for libel by Telnikoff, a British citizen living in Germany. The action arose out of an article written by Telnikoff in the London Daily Telegraph concerning the hiring practices of the British Broadcasting

---

[1] This opinion has been heavily edited; deletions are not marked by ellipses [–*Eds*].

Corporation. Matusevitch then wrote a letter to the Daily Telegraph which Telnikoff believed accused him of racism. The jury agreed with Telnikoff and awarded him 240,000 pounds in damages.

[Telnikoff then sought to enforce the judgment. Eventually, the Court of Appeals of Maryland was asked to decide whether recognition of the judgment would be "repugnant to the public policy of Maryland."]

The justification for the public policy exception to the recognition of foreign judgments was articulated by the United States Court of Appeals for the District of Columbia Circuit in *Laker Airways v. Sabena, Belgian World Airlines,* 731 F.2d 909, 937 (D.C.Cir.1984), as follows:

> There are limitations to the application of comity. When the foreign act is inherently inconsistent with the policies underlying comity, domestic recognition could tend either to legitimize the aberration or to encourage retaliation, undercutting the realization of the goals served by comity. No nation is under an unremitting obligation to enforce foreign interests which are fundamentally prejudicial to those of the domestic forum. Thus, from the earliest times, authorities have recognized that the obligation of comity expires when the strong public policies of the forum are vitiated by the foreign act.

The principles underlying comity, including the public policy exception, have been codified in the Maryland Uniform Foreign-Money Judgments Recognition Act. Section 10-704(b)(2) of the Act specifically states that a "foreign judgment need not be recognized if the cause of action on which the judgment is based is repugnant to the public policy of the State."

The question before us is whether Telnikoff's English libel judgment is based upon principles which are so contrary to Maryland's public policy concerning freedom of the press and defamation actions that recognition of the judgment should be denied.

> While we shall rest our decision in this case upon the non-constitutional ground of Maryland public policy, nonetheless, in ascertaining that public policy, it is appropriate to examine and rely upon the history, policies, and requirements of the First Amendment and Article 40 of the Declaration of Rights . . . as well as the present relationship between those provisions and defamation actions in Maryland.

American and Maryland history reflects a public policy in favor of a much broader and more protective freedom of the press than ever provided for under English law.

The stark contrast between English and Maryland law is clearly illustrated by the underlying litigation between Telnikoff and Matusevitch. Telnikoff, an employee of the publicly funded Radio Free Europe/Radio Liberty, was undisputably a public official or public figure. In this country, he would have had to prove, by clear and convincing evidence, that Matusevitch's letter contained false statements of fact and that Matusevitch acted maliciously in the sense that he knew of the falsity or acted with reckless disregard of whether the statements were false or not. The English courts, however, held that there was no evidence supporting Telnikoff's allegations that Matusevitch acted with actual malice, either under the *New York Times Co. v. Sullivan* definition or in the sense of ill-will, spite or intent to injure. Despite the absence of actual malice under any definition, Telnikoff was allowed to recover. He was not even required to prove negligence, which is the minimum a purely private defamation plaintiff must establish to recover under Maryland law.

In addition, Telnikoff was not required to prove that Matusevitch's letter contained a false statement of fact, which would have been required under present Maryland law. Instead, falsity was presumed, and the defendant had the risky choice of whether to attempt to prove truth. Furthermore, Telnikoff did not have to establish that the alleged defamation even contained defamatory statements of fact; the burden was upon the defendant to establish that the alleged defamatory language amounted to comment and not statements of fact.

Finally, contrary to the decisions of the Supreme Court and this Court, Matusevitch's letter was not examined in context but in isolation. It must be remembered that Telnikoff began the public debate with his published article, and Matusevitch's letter constituted his rebuttal. Undoubtedly, in this country, Matusevitch's alleged defamatory language would, as a matter of law, be treated as "rhetorical hyperbole" in the course of rebuttal during a vigorous public debate.

The principles governing defamation actions under English law, which were applied to Telnikoff's libel suit, are so contrary to Maryland defamation law, and to the policy of freedom of the press underlying Maryland law, that Telnikoff's judgment should be denied recognition under principles of comity. In the language of the Uniform Foreign-Money Judgments Recognition Act, Telnikoff's English "cause of action on which the judgment is based is repugnant to the public policy of the State . . . ."

"At the heart of the First Amendment," as well as Article 40 of the Maryland Declaration of Rights and Maryland public policy, "is the recognition of the fundamental importance of the free flow of ideas and opinions on matters of public interest and concern." *Hustler Magazine v. Falwell*. The importance of that free flow of ideas and opinions on matters of public concern precludes Maryland's recognition of Telnikoff's English libel judgment.

CHASANOW, Judge, dissenting.

I believe Maryland's public policy should not preclude enforcement of this judgment. The majority opinion devotes page after page to a stirring tribute to freedom of the press, but this case does not involve freedom of the press. This is a libel judgment obtained by one resident of England against another resident of England. The libel was contained in a letter written by the defendant. The letter was libelous regardless of whether the newspaper chose to reprint it. Freedom of the press is not implicated, nor was any United States interest implicated. I trust the majority is not somehow suggesting that it is freedom of speech that protects speaking, but it is freedom of the press that protects printing or writing; that simply is wrong. Article 40 of the Maryland Declaration of Rights also clearly differentiates between the "liberty of the press" and a citizen's right to speak, write, or publish.

There is another public policy that should also be considered by this Court. Our interest in international good will, comity, and res judicata fostered by recognition of foreign judgments must be weighed against our minimal interest in giving the benefits of our local libel public policy to residents of another country who defame foreign public figures in foreign publications and who have no reasonable expectation that they will be protected by the Maryland Constitution. Unless there is some United States interest that should be protected, there is no good reason to offend a friendly nation like England by refusing to recognize a purely local libel judgment for a purely local defamation. In the instant case, there is no United States interest that might necessitate non-recognition or non-enforcement of the English defamation judgment.

It is unwarranted to simply refuse, on the basis of freedom of the press and Maryland public policy, to enforce all English libel judgments. England has an interest in protecting its residents, including its own public officials and public figures, from even unintentionally false and defamatory statements damaging to their reputation. It should not violate our public policy to recognize that interest as long as it does not endanger our interest in the free dissemination of information by our media and those people shielded by our Constitution. Our national interest might necessitate non-recognition of an English libel judgment if it was a judgment against a United States publication that was circulated abroad, or even perhaps a defamation judgment obtained in a foreign country by a United States public figure who cannot sue for merely negligent or unintended defamation under our Constitutions and public policy. Each case should be examined on its own facts to see if the United States freedom of the press is implicated or if the free speech rights of people entitled to the protection of our First Amendment are implicated.

## NOTES AND COMMENTS ON *TELNIKOFF*

(1) *Choice of Law.* The majority opposition does not discuss expressly choice of law. Why do you think that is? (Hint: What *was* the issue before the Court?) If choice of law had been discussed, what result should have been reached?

(2) *Choice of Law Again.* If the majority *had* engaged in some form of choice-of-law interest analysis, what result would it have reached? Maryland is one of the few states to retain (at least in theory) the First Restatement approach to torts; what result would have been reached under the Vested Rights Doctrine?

(3) *The Dissent.* Dissenting Judge Chasanow makes a powerful case for enforcing the British judgment. But he has an easy case: British courts, after all, are the essence of fairness (or so they say). What if the judgment had issued from an Iraqi court? What if it had been a libel judgment entered by a court in favor of the Prime Minister of a country suing the New York Times for criticizing her regime?

(4) *Another Dissent.* The American Law Institute has undertaken a study of common themes in the civil procedure of civilized nations. The hope is that by identifying those themes, it will be possible to alleviate the stress caused by multi-national litigation. The ALI study expressly disapproves of the result

in *Telnikoff:* "[P]ublic policy should be used to defeat recognition of foreign judgments in the United States only when a U.S. interest is implicated. *Ad hoc* judicial assertions of public policy must be avoided." ALI, *International Jurisdiction and Judgments Project: Report,* 27 & n.23 (April 14, 2000). Why do you think that the blue-ribbon ALI drafters took that position? *See also* Linda Andreas, *A Different Challenge for the ALI: Herein of Foreign Country Judgments, An International treaty, and An American Statute,* 75 IND. L. J. 535 (2000).

# PART B   THE REACH AND LIMITS OF FULL FAITH AND CREDIT

## § 7.06   Overview

The mandate of full faith and credit is strict, but it is not absolute; limitations on a state's obligations under the Full Faith and Credit Clause do exist. These can be divided into two groups: The first involves situations where the judgment is not valid in the rendering state; the second group consists of a limited group of cases where a judgment, although valid in the rendering state, will not be recognized elsewhere. This Part of Chapter 7 first lays out the "Iron Law" of full faith and credit established in *Fauntleroy v. Lum;* it then examines limitations on that Iron Law.

## § 7.07   The Iron Law of Full Faith and Credit

### FAUNTLEROY v. LUM

*United States Supreme Court*
*210 U.S. 230, 28 S. Ct. 641 (1908)*

MR. JUSTICE HOLMES delivered the opinion of the court.

This is an action upon a Missouri judgment brought in a court of Mississippi. The declaration set forth the record of the judgment. The defendant pleaded that the original cause of action arose in Mississippi out of a gambling transaction in cotton futures; that he declined to pay the loss; that the controversy was submitted to arbitration, the question as to the illegality of the transaction, however, not being included in the submission, that an award was rendered against the defendant; that thereafter, finding the defendant temporarily in Missouri, the plaintiff brought suit there upon the award; that the trial court refused to allow the defendant to show the nature of the transaction and that by the laws of Mississippi the same was illegal and void, but directed a verdict if the jury should find that the submission and award were made, and remained unpaid; and that a verdict was rendered and the judgment in suit entered upon the same.

The laws of Mississippi make dealing in futures a misdemeanor, and provide that contracts of that sort, made without intent to deliver the commodity or to pay the price, "shall not be enforced by any court." The defendant contends that this language deprives the Mississippi courts of jurisdiction.

The doctrine laid down by Chief Justice Marshall was "that the judgment of a state court should have the same credit, validity, and effect in every other court in the United States, which it had in the State where it was pronounced, and that whatever pleas would be good to a suit thereon in such State, and none others, could be pleaded in any other court of the United States." *Hampton v. McConnel,* 3 Wheat. 234 [1818]. There is no doubt that this quotation was supposed to be an accurate statement of the law as late as *Christmas v. Russell,* 5 Wall. 290 [1866], where an attempt of Mississippi, by statute, to go behind judgments recovered in other States was declared void, and it was held that such judgments could not be impeached even for fraud.

We assume that the statement of Chief Justice Marshall is correct. It is confirmed by the Act of May 26, 1790, c.11, 1 Stat. 122 (Rev. Stat. § 905), providing that the said records and judicial proceedings "shall have such faith and credit given to them in every court within the United States, as they have by law or usage in the courts of the State from whence the said records are or shall be taken." Whether the award would or would not have been conclusive, and whether the ruling of the Missouri court upon that matter was right or wrong, there can be no question that the judgment was conclusive in Missouri on the validity of the cause of action. A judgment is conclusive as to all the *media concludendi,* and it needs no authority to show that it cannot be impeached either in or out of the State by showing that it was based upon a mistake of law. Of course, a want of jurisdiction over either the person or the subject-matter might be shown. But as the jurisdiction of the Missouri court is not open to dispute, the judgment cannot be impeached in Mississippi even if it went upon a misapprehension of the Mississippi law.

We feel no apprehensions that painful or humiliating consequences will follow upon our decision. No court would give judgment for a plaintiff unless it believed that the facts were a cause of action by the law determining their effect. Mistakes will be rare. In this case the Missouri court no doubt supposed that the award was binding by the law of Mississippi. If it was mistaken, it made a natural mistake. The validity of its judgment, even in Mississippi, is, as we believe, the result of the Constitution as it always has been understood, and is not a matter to arouse the susceptibilities of the States, all of which are equally concerned in the question and equally on both sides.

*Judgment reversed.*

MR. JUSTICE WHITE, with whom concurred MR. JUSTICE HARLAN, MR. JUSTICE McKENNA and MR. JUSTICE DAY, dissenting.

Admonished that the considerations which control me are presumptively faulty, as the court holds them to be without merit, yet so strong is my belief that the decision now made unduly expands the Due Faith and Credit Clause of the Constitution, I state the reasons for my dissent.

The foundation upon which our system of government rests is the possession by the States of the right, except as restricted by the Constitution, to exert their police powers as they may deem best for the happiness and welfare of those subject to their authority. The whole theory upon which the Constitution was framed, and by which alone, it seems to me, it can continue, is the recognition of the fact that different conditions may exist in the different States, rendering necessary the enactment of regulations of a particular subject in one State when such subject may not in another be deemed to require regulation; in other words, that in Massachusetts, owing to conditions which may there prevail, the legislature may deem it necessary to make police regulations on a particular subject, although like regulations may not obtain in other States. And, of course, such also may be the case in Louisiana or any other State. If it be that the ruling now made deprives the States of powers admittedly theirs, it follows that the ruling must be wrong. Indeed the principle, as understood by me, goes further than this, since it not only gives to each of the States in the cases suggested the power to render possible an evasion of the police laws of all the other States, but it gives to each State the authority to compel the other States, through their courts, to give effect to illegal transactions done within their borders. It may not be denied that a State which has lawfully prohibited the enforcement of a particular character of transaction and made the same criminal has an interest in seeing that its laws are enforced and will be subjected to the gravest humiliation if it be compelled to give effect to acts done within its borders which are in violation of its valid police or criminal laws. And the consciousness of the enforced debasement to which it would be subjected if compelled to enter a decree giving effect to acts of residents of Mississippi, done within that State, which were violative of the public policy of the State and which were criminal, was clearly shown in the opinion of the Supreme Court of the State in this case.

When the Constitution was adopted the principles of comity by which the decrees of the courts of one State were entitled to be enforced in another were generally known, but the enforcement of those principles by the several States had no absolute sanction, since they rested but in comity. Now it cannot be denied that under the rules of comity recognized at the time of the adoption of the Constitution, and which at this time universally prevail, no sovereignty was or is under the slightest moral obligation to give effect to a judgment of a court of another sovereignty, when to do so would compel the State in which the judgment was sought to be executed to enforce an illegal and prohibited contract, when both the contract and all the acts done in connection with its performance had taken place in the latter state. This seems to me conclusive of this case, since both in treatises of authoritative writers (Story, Conflict of Law 609), and by repeated adjudications of this court it has been settled that the purpose of the Due Faith and Credit Clause was not to confer any new power, but simply to make obligatory that duty which, when the Constitution was adopted rested, as has been said, in comity alone.

Certainly if such was the purpose of the framers in regard to the clause referred to, a like purpose must have been intended with reference to the due faith and credit clause. If a judgment for a penalty in money rendered in one State may not be enforced in another, by the same principle a judgment rendered in one State, giving to the party the results of prohibited and criminal acts done in another State, is not entitled to be enforced in the State whose laws have been violated.

---

## NOTES AND QUESTIONS ON *FAUNTLEROY*

(1) *The Clash Between Federalism and State Interests.* Mississippi made it a crime to deal in cotton futures. A contract to do so was entered into in Mississippi, and it later was the subject of litigation there. And yet, a Missouri court held the contract in question enforceable. How could it do that? Do you think the parties failed to point out the illegality of the transaction?

The Mississippi Supreme Court wrote:

[W]e are unwilling to believe that it will ever be held that a court is precluded by the Constitution of the United States from ascertaining whether the claim on which a judgment is rendered in another state is such a one as the courts of the state in which suit on the judgment is brought are, on grounds of public policy, expressly prohibited from enforcing.

If this be law, all that is necessary to free the most corrupt transaction from all objection is to obtain service on a party and get judgment in another state.

*Lum v. Fauntleroy,* 80 Miss. 757, 763, 32 So. 290, 291 (1902). Is that dire forecast correct? Or is the Mississippi court leaving something out of the equation? Put differently, is there anything that defendant's lawyer did not do which ought to have been done?

Obviously there is some very high level disagreement in *Fauntleroy* concerning the nature of the federal system. Justice Holmes, characteristically, took a rigid position on the importance of preclusion, contenting himself with the observation that "mistakes will be rare." Justice McKenna's dissent, on the other hand, emphasizes comity and respect for policies of other states. Some questions:

— Which position do you think is more in tune with the original understanding of the Full Faith and Credit Clause?

— Which position better suits the needs of our modem federal system?

— Which position is more like the formal, territorialist view, and which is more akin to modern interest analysis.[13]

*See* PROBLEMS 7B-1. HOW STALE CAN THE CLAIM BE?; 7B-2. THE NEW FAMILY.

(2) *Correcting Errors.* If "mistakes" of fact or law cannot be corrected by collateral attack, how does Justice Holmes expect them to be corrected? Is this expectation realistic? Consider; the discussion of inconsistent judgments which follows.

## INCONSISTENT JUDGMENTS

(1) *The Treinies Litigation.* Plaintiff sues defendant and wins in F-1. She then sues on that judgment in F-2 but loses when the court there holds that F-1 lacked personal jurisdiction. Plaintiff then sues on the F-1 judgment in F-3; defendant, of course, sets up the F-2 judgment as a bar. You are a judge in F-3; how do you analyze the problem? Does it matter if you are convinced that the F-2 decision was flatly wrong? Does the national policy favoring finality of judgment, in other words, obviate the search for justice?

The Supreme Court answered those questions in *Treinies v. Sunshine Mining Co.,* 308 U.S. 66 (1939), a messy contest between stepfather and stepdaughter over mining stock. The stepfather won the first round in the Washington probate court (F-1). That court decided that it had both personal

---

[13] If this answer surprises you, *see* Holmes' very territorialist, formalistic opinion on conflicts in *Slater v. Mexican Nat'l Ry. Co.,* 194 U.S. 120 (1904).

and subject matter jurisdiction. The stepfather then sought to use that judgment in litigation pending in Idaho involving the same stock. The Idaho court (F-2), however, refused to recognize the Washington (F-1)judgment on the ground that the Washington court had lacked subject matter jurisdiction. The Idaho Supreme Court affirmed as to jurisdiction but remanded on another issue, and the Supreme Court of the United States denied certiorari. The stepfather did not appeal the order entered on remand in Idaho; rather, he sued again in Washington, and the mining company filed an interpleader action in federal court. This time the Supreme Court exercised jurisdiction over the case.

Justice Reed, speaking for a unanimous Court, made clear the proper procedure to follow in such a case; even if the F-2 judgment was wrong, the right to review that error was in those (the Idaho) [*i.e.,* F-2] proceedings. While petitioner sought review from the decree of the Supreme Court of Idaho by petition for certiorari to this court, which was denied, no review was sought from the final decree of the Idaho District Court [on remand].

The power of the Idaho Court to examine into the jurisdiction of the Washington court is beyond question. Even where the decision against the validity of the original judgment is erroneous, it is a valid exercise of judicial power by the second court.

One trial of an issue is enough. 308 U.S. at 77-78.

(2) *The Last-in-Time Rule.* The rule in *Treinies* has become known as "the last-in-time" rule. *See generally* Ruth Bader Ginsburg, *Judgments in Search of Full Faith and Credit: The Last-in-Time Rule for Conflicting Judgments,* 82 HARV. L. REV. 798 (1969). The lesson is clear: If you think an F-2 court messed up, your proper course is to appeal the judgment in F-2, and, if you still think you've been wronged, to ask the Supreme Court to review the case. Otherwise you're stuck with the F-2 judgment which, itself, must be given full faith and credit.[14] The policy is also clear: The law wants to encourage both finality and comity by dealing with the problem when it occurs. *See* Restatement (Second) of Conflict of Laws 114, comment b; Restatement (Second) of Judgments § 15.

What is perhaps not clear is whether it is realistic to expect the Supreme Court to play much of a role as final adjudicator of state court errors. In the 1997 Term, for example, the Court reviewed on the merits only 80 of 6718 cases (a bit more than 1%) disposed of during the Term. *See* Table, 112 HARV. L. Rv. at 372 (1998).[15] Or do we not worry about hostility to sister-state judgments anymore; if we do not, then *Treinies* clearly is correct, for there is no reason to believe that either F-2 or F-1 is more likely to reach the correct result. Hence, finality, as represented by the lasting time rule, should be the trump card.

---

[14] In case you're confused by the fact that the stepfather in *Treinies* did ask the Supreme Court to hear his case, consider Justice Ginsburg's observation that the F-2 decree was not a final judgment when certiorari was sought. *See* 82 HARV. L. REV. at 803.

[15] In contrast, during the 1939 Term, when *Treinies* was decided, the Court decided on the merits 238 of the 1007 cases (24%) it was asked to hear. Henry Hart, *The Business of the Supreme Court at the October Terms 1937 and 1938,* 53 HARV. L. REV. 579, 582 (1940).

*Treinies* thus serves the goal of finality. It also makes the job of the F-3 court easier, for that tribunal need not be forced to choose between the F-I and F-2 decisions.

Finally, *Treinies* seems compelled by *Fauntleroy v. Lum:* Any correction of erroneous judgment must be by way of appeal, and not by collateral attack. As the court observed in *First Tennessee Bank N.A. Memphis v. Smith,* 764 F.2d 255, 259 (6th Cir. 1985): "This last-in-time rule is based not only upon principles of comity and the need for finality, but upon the obligation of the litigants to exercise all due diligence in the full and forthright presentation of their controversy."

(3) *A Variation.* What if F-3 is also F-1? Consider *Colby v. Colby,* 78 Nev. 150, 369 P.2d 1019 (1962). There, a Nevada court had granted a divorce which was later set aside in Maryland. Must Nevada recognize the Maryland decree? The *Colby* court said no, and the Supreme Court, amazingly, denied certiorari. 371 U.S. 888 (1962).

*Colby* has been criticized harshly as being inconsistent with the general rule on inconsistent judgments. *See* Ruth Bader Ginsburg's article, *supra Note* (1) at 819-20. *See also Layton v. Layton,* 538 S.W.2d 642 (Tex. Civ. App. 1976) (same facts as *Colby,* but F-1 (Texas) respected the F-2 decision).

The Iron Law of preclusion established in *Fauntleroy* is very tough, indeed. Nevertheless, its scope has some limits. *See generally* William L. Reynolds, *The Iron Law of Full Faith and Credit,* 53 MD. L. REV. 412 (1994). The following section discusses some of those limits based on the nature of the original judgment.

*See* PROBLEM 7B-3. THE INTEREST OF THE SECOND OR THIRD STATE.

## § 7.08   Exceptions to the Iron Law I—Problems with the F-1 Decree

*Fauntleroy v. Lum* lays down a very strong rule in favor of preclusion and in favor of finality. But the strength of the finality principle depends on how much credit the judgment would get in the jurisdiction which rendered it. A judgment in other words, must be recognized, but only to the extent that it would be recognized in the rendering state. *See* RESTATEMENT (SECOND) OF CONFLICT OF LAWS § 93. "[A] judgment has no constitutional claim to a more conclusive or final effect in the State of the forum than it has in the State where rendered. [I]t is clear that the State of the forum has at least as much leeway to disregard the judgment, to qualify it, or to depart from it as does the State where it was rendered." *New York ex. rel Halvey v. Halvey,* 330 U.S. 610, 614-15 (1947). An easy example illustrates the principle: Assume a judgment is entered by a Vermont court which has the power to revise it within thirty days. During that period, no court in Vermont will, under Vermont law, enforce the judgment. If the plaintiff should seek to enforce the judgment in New York during the thirty-day period, a New York court could also properly refuse to enforce the judgment without violating the Full Faith and Credit Clause.

Once that basic principle is understood, many problems in the law of judgments become much easier to solve. This Section examines some problems with the decree which may prevent the rule of recognition from coming into play.

## [A]   Judgments Not on the Merits

Imagine a suit for breach of contract that was dismissed on motion for having been filed after the statute of limitations had run. Can plaintiff then re-file the action in another state which has a more favorable limitations period? This was the situation in the leading case of *Warner v. Buffalo Drydock Co.,* 67 F.2d 540, 542 (2d Cir. 1933), where Judge Augustus Hand wrote:

> The Ohio [F-1] decree does not fail to bar the remedy in the present action because it is not res judicata as to everything which it decided, but because it did not decide that the claim was extinguished, but only that plaintiff could not sue in Ohio on account of the local statute of limitations.

Why is that? Is the plaintiff getting a second bite at the litigation apple? Should a dismissal for failure to state a claim be treated differently than a dismissal based on limitation? What of a voluntary dismissal? Dismissal for lack of jurisdiction? Misjoinder? *See generally* Restatement (Second) of Judgments § 20 (dismissals for venue, joinder, or jurisdictional reasons, as well as voluntary dismissals, are not on the merits, and, therefore, they lack claim-preclusive effect). Should all of these problems be treated the same? Or could it be argued that some of them, such as limitations, are so "substantive" that they should be treated as decisions on the merits? FED. R. CIV. PROC. 41 prescribes the preclusive to be attached to "voluntary dismissals" in the federal system.

What happens if the dismissal was on alternative grounds, one procedural and the other substantive? Is plaintiff barred from refiling in another state? *See* Restatement (Second) of Judgments § 20, comment.

## [B]   Lack of Finality

A judgment need not be respected until it is final in the state which rendered it. RESTATEMENT (SECOND) OF JUDGMENTS § 13. This follows naturally from the basic rule of preclusion, of course, as does the fact that finality is determined by the law of the state which rendered the order. *See* RESTATEMENT (SECOND) OF CONFLICT OF LAWS § 107. The rule of finality has proven troublesome only when dealing with judgments that can be modified, a particular problem in domestic relations litigation. *See* William M. Richman and William L. Reynolds, Understanding Conflict of Laws § 98 (3d ed. 2002). This problem is discussed in Parts C and D of Chapter 8, *infra.*

Even if a judgment is not final, nothing prevents a court from recognizing it out of comity, that is, out of respect for a decision made elsewhere. *See, e.g., Worthley v. Worthley,* 44 Cal. 2d 465, 283 P.2d 19 (1955). Or is that unconstitutional because it involves giving the judgment more faith and credit than it would receive in the rendering state? *See* discussion in § 7.03 Note (2), *supra.*

*See* PROBLEMS 7B-4. DEFERRING TO NEW JERSEY?; 7C-5. MODIFIABLE: BY WHOSE LAW?

Sometimes, of course, "final" doesn't really mean final. In *Gondeck v. Pan American World Airways, Inc.,* 382 U.S. 25 (1965), the Court granted a second petition for rehearing from a denial of certiorari made *three* years earlier: "We therefore grant the motion for leave to file the petition for rehearing, grant the petition for rehearing, vacate this order denying certiorari, grant the petition for certiorari, and reverse the judgment of the Court of Appeals." The lesson? Never give up hope.

## [C]   The Judgment and Fraud

Assume the defendant in the enforcing state alleges that the judgment was procured by fraud. Is that a valid ground for denying recognition? Does it matter whether fraud is a ground for collateral attack in the rendering state?

The law has long recognized a distinction in this area between "intrinsic" and "extrinsic" fraud. The former involves "a fraudulent instrument, or perjured evidence, or any matter which was actually presented and considered in the judgment assailed." *United States v. Throckmorton,* 98 U.S. 61, 66 (1878). Extrinsic fraud, in contrast, occurs when "the unsuccessful party has been prevented from exhibiting fully his case as by keeping him away from court or where the defendant never had knowledge of the suit." *Id.* at 65-66. In most states, only the latter type of fraud can lead to the setting aside of a judgment because "the mischief of retrying every case in which the judgment or decree rendered on false testimony would be greater than any compensation arising from doing justice in individual cases." *Id.* at 68-69.

The most widely cited example is *Levin v. Gladstein,* 142 N.C. 482, 55 S.E. 371 (1906). There, a dispute over a sale of goods led to litigation in Maryland, the parties then resolved their differences, and the plaintiff told the defendant that the suit would be withdrawn. Relying on that promise, the defendant left Maryland. The plaintiff, however, did not dismiss and took a default judgment against defendant in Maryland. When plaintiff brought suit in North Carolina to enforce the judgment, however, the defendant successfully pleaded the fraud in the Maryland litigation.

Recent years have seen a weakening of the intrinsic/extrinsic dichotomy, however, and courts are now more willing to grant relief, regardless of the type of fraud involved. As Justice Brennan observed when he was a state court judge: "Plainly, the encouragement of vexatious litigation is the lesser evil. We prefer to follow the equity of the matter and to take away an unjust judgment obtained by vital perjury when the injustice and inequity of allowing it to stand are made evident." *Shammas v. Shammas,* 9 N.J. 321, 88 A.2d 204, 209 (1952). Accordingly, FED. R. CIV. P. 60 (b)(3) now permits relief for verdicts obtained by "fraud (whether heretofore denominated intrinsic or extrinsic), misrepresentation, or other misconduct of an adverse party." *See generally* 11 C. WRIGHT & A. MILLER, FEDERAL PRACTICE AND PROCEDURE §§ 2860-61. The Restatement (Second) of Judgments § 68 (default judgments) and § 70 (judgments in contested actions) also would abolish the distinction between the two types of fraud and permit recovery in a number of circumstances.[16] The problem of fraudulent judgments is thoughtfully discussed in Michael Pryles, *The Impeachment of Sister State Judgments for Fraud,* 25 Sw. L.J. 697 (1971).

*See* PROBLEM 7B-6. EXTRINSIC FRAUD.

## [D]  Lack of Personal Jurisdiction

As you learned in Chapter 3, the Due Process Clause of the federal constitution requires that a defendant have minimum contacts with the forum before its courts can exercise jurisdiction over her. That protection would not be worth much if she had to travel from her home in Oregon to a court in Georgia to assert her jurisdictional objection. For that reason, the defendant has always had the choice of defaulting in the forum and then, when sued on the judgment elsewhere, defending on the ground that the original judgment was entered by a court without jurisdiction.

But what happens if the defendant does not default? What if the defendant appears specially in the forum to assert the lack of jurisdiction and she loses? Can she still raise the lack of jurisdiction in a collateral attack? What happens, in other words, when due process and full faith and credit run into one another?

---

[16] Those sections provide:

§ 68. Fraud, Mistake, and Other Grounds of Relief from Default Judgment Subject to the limitations stated in § 74, a judgment by default may be avoided if the judgment

(1) Resulted from the defaulting party's being induced by fraud or duress to submit to the jurisdiction of the court or to refrain from contesting the action;

(2) Was based on a claim that the party obtaining the judgment knew it to be fraudulent;

(3) Resulted from the defaulting party's failure to contest the action by reason of justifiable mistake or from a substantial mistake by the court;

(4) Was against a minor, a person adjudicated as incompetent, or a person known by the party obtaining the judgment to be incapable of adequately defending the action, and no representative was appointed to act for the defaulting party; or

(5) Ought to be set aside on account of changed circumstances, as stated in § 73.

§ 70. Judgment Procured by Corruption, Duress, or Fraud

(1) Subject to the limitations stated in § 74, a judgment in a contested action may be avoided if the judgment:

(a) Resulted from corruption of or duress upon the court or the attorney for the party against whom the judgment was rendered, or duress upon that party; or

(b) Was based on a claim that the party obtaining the judgment knew to be fraudulent.

(2) A party seeking relief under Subsection 11 must:

(a) Have acted with due diligence in discovering the facts constituting the basis for relief;

(b) Assert his claim with particularity; and

(c) Where his claim is based on falsity of the evidence on which the judgment was based, show that he has made a reasonable effort in the original action to ascertain the truth of the matter to appear at all. If, in the absence of appearance, the court had proceeded to judgment, and the present suit had been brought thereon, respondent could have raised and tried out the issue in the present action, because it would never have had its day in court with respect to jurisdiction.

**BALDWIN v. IOWA STATE MEN'S TRAVELING ASS'N**, 283 U.S. 522 (1931): Suit brought in F-1; defendant appeared specially to contest personal jurisdiction. The trial court held jurisdiction proper. Defendant did not appeal from that ruling, and suffered a default judgment on the merits. Suit to enforce was then brought in F-2; the defense was lack of personal jurisdiction in F-1.

Held. For Plaintiff, the collateral attack was precluded. For the Court, Justice Roberts wrote:

> [R]espondent entered the Missouri [F-1] court for the very purpose of litigating the question of jurisdiction over its person.

> Public policy dictates that there be an end of litigation. We see no reason why this doctrine should not apply in every case, where one voluntarily appears, presents his case and is fully heard, and why he should not, in the absence of fraud, be thereafter concluded by the judgment of the tribunal to which he has submitted his cause.

The rule in *Baldwin* is the flip side of that *bete noire* of beginning law students, *Pennoyer v. Neff,* 95 U.S. 714 (1878), which held that the Constitution requires that the issue of jurisdiction be subject, in the proper circumstances, to collateral attack. In *Thompson v. Whitman,* 85 U.S. (18 Wall.) 457 (1874), the Court had held that mere recitals of jurisdiction in a decree could not be conclusive as to the facts recited therein. That result is plainly correct after *Pennoyer;* otherwise, a court simply could bootstrap itself out of the constraints of the Due Process Clause by making the appropriate recitals concerning jurisdiction. But why did the holding in *Thompson* not control the result in *Baldwin?*

Is *Baldwin* consistent with the holding in *Treinies v. Sunshine Mining Co., supra,* (the "last-in-time" rule)? What does *Baldwin* tell an attorney she must do when she loses her special appearance? What do both cases tell us about the right and wrong way to correct an error in the proceeding?

*See* PROBLEMS 7B-7. DEFAULT JUDGMENT; 7B-8. HOW BINDING IS BINDING?

## [E]   Lack of Subject Matter Jurisdiction

### DURFEE v. DUKE

*United States Supreme Court*
*375 U.S. 106, 84 S. Ct. 242, 11 L. Ed. 2d 186 (1963)*

MR. JUSTICE STEWART delivered the opinion of the Court.

In 1956 the petitioners brought an action against the respondent in a Nebraska court to quiet title to certain bottom land situated on the Missouri River. The main channel of that river forms the boundary between the States of Nebraska and Missouri. The Nebraska court had jurisdiction over the subject matter of the controversy only if the land in question was in Nebraska. Whether the land was Nebraska land depended entirely upon a factual question —whether a shift in the river's course had been caused by avulsion or accretion. The respondent appeared in the Nebraska court and through counsel fully litigated the issues, explicitly contesting the court's jurisdiction over the subject matter of the controversy.[17] After a hearing the court found the issues in favor of the petitioners and ordered that title to the land be quieted in them . . . The respondent appealed, and the Supreme Court of Nebraska affirmed the judgment after a trial de novo on the record made in the lower court. The State Supreme Court specifically found that the rule of avulsion was applicable, that the land in question was in Nebraska, that the Nebraska courts therefore had jurisdiction of the subject matter of the litigation, and that title to the land was in the petitioners. The respondent did not petition this Court for a writ of certiorari to review that judgment.

Two months later the respondent filed a suit against the petitioners in a Missouri court to quiet title to the same land. Her complaint alleged that the land was in Missouri. The suit was removed to a Federal District Court by reason of diversity of citizenship. The District Court after hearing evidence expressed the view that the land was in Missouri, but held that all the issues had been adjudicated and determined in the Nebraska litigation, and that the judgment of the Nebraska Supreme Court was res judicata and "is now binding upon this court." The Court of Appeals reversed, holding that the District Court was not required to give full faith and credit to the Nebraska judgment, and that normal res judicata principles were not applicable because the controversy involved land and a court in Missouri was therefore free to retry the question of the Nebraska court's jurisdiction over the subject matter. We granted certiorari to consider a question important to the administration of justice in our federal system. For the reasons that follow, we reverse the judgment before us.

The constitutional command of full faith and credit, as implemented by Congress, requires that "judicial proceedings shall have the same full faith and credit in every court within the United States as they have by law or usage in the courts of such State from which they are taken." Full faith and credit thus generally requires every State to give to a judgment at least the res judicata effect which the judgment would be accorded in the State which rendered it. "By the Constitutional provision for full faith and credit, the local doctrines of res judicata, speaking generally, become a part of national jurisprudence, and therefore federal questions cognizable here." *Riley v. New York Trust Co.,* 315 U.S. 343, 349.

\* \* \*

[R]espondent relies upon the many decisions of this Court which have held that a judgment of a court in one State is conclusive upon the merits in a court in another State only if the court in the first State had power to pass on the merits—had jurisdiction, that is, to render the judgment. As Mr. Justice

---

[17] This is, therefore, not a case in which a party, although afforded an opportunity to contest subject-matter jurisdiction, did not litigate the issue. *Cf. Chicot County Drainage Dist. v. Baxter State Bank,* 308 U.S. 371.

Bradley stated the doctrine in the leading case of *Thompson v. Whitman,* 18 Wall. 457, "we think it clear that the jurisdiction of the court by which a judgment is rendered in any State may be questioned in a collateral proceeding in another State, notwithstanding the provision of the fourth article of the Constitution and the law of 1790, and notwithstanding the averments contained in the record of the judgment itself." The principle has been restated and applied in a variety of contexts.

However, while it is established that a court in one State, when asked to give effect to the judgment of a court in another State, may constitutionally inquire into the foreign court's jurisdiction to render that judgment, the modern decisions of this Court have carefully delineated the permissible scope of such an inquiry. From these decisions there emerges the general rule that a judgment is entitled to full faith and credit—even as to questions of jurisdiction—when the second court's inquiry discloses that those questions have been fully and fairly litigated and finally decided in the court which rendered the original judgment.

With respect to questions of jurisdiction over the person, this principle was unambiguously established in *Baldwin v. Iowa State Traveling Men's Assn.,* 283 U.S. 522. There it was held that a federal court in Iowa must give binding effect to the judgment of a federal court in Missouri despite the claim that the original court did not have jurisdiction over the defendant's person, once it was shown to the court in Iowa that that question had been fully litigated in the Missouri forum. "Public policy," said the Court, "dictates that there be an end of litigation; that those who have contested an issue shall be bound by the result of the contest, and that matters once tried shall be considered forever settled as between the parties. We see no reason why this doctrine should not apply in every case where one voluntarily appears, presents his case and is fully heard, and why he should not, in the absence of fraud, be thereafter concluded by the judgment of the tribunal to which he has submitted his cause."[18]

Following the *Baldwin* case, this Court soon made clear in a series of decisions that the general rule is no different when the claim is made that the original forum did not have jurisdiction over the subject matter. In each of these cases the claim was made that a court, when asked to enforce the judgment of another forum, was free to retry the question of that forum's jurisdiction over the subject matter. In each case this Court held that since the question of subject-matter jurisdiction had been fully litigated in the original forum, the issue could not be retried in a subsequent action between the parties.

The reasons for such a rule are apparent. In the words of the Court's opinion in *Stoll v. Gottlieb* 305 U.S. 1651.

> We see no reason why a court, in the absence of an allegation of fraud in obtaining the judgment, should examine, again the question whether the court making the earlier determination on an actual

---

[18] This decision was adhered to the following year in *American Surety Co. v. Baldwin,* 287 U.S. 156 (1932). In his opinion for a unanimous Court in that case, Mr. Justice Brandeis said: "The principles of res judicata apply to questions of jurisdiction as well as to other issues."

contest over jurisdiction between the parties, did have jurisdiction of the subject matter of the litigation. Courts to determine the rights of parties are an integral part of our system of government. It is just as important that there should be a place to end as that there should be a place to begin litigation. After a party has his day in court, with opportunity to present his evidence and his view of the law, a collateral attack upon the decision as to jurisdiction there rendered merely retries the issue previously determined. There is no reason to expect that the second decision will be more satisfactory than the first.

305 U.S., at 172.

To be sure, the general rule of finality of jurisdictional determinations is not without exceptions. Doctrines of federal preemption or sovereign immunity may in some contexts be controlling. *Kalb v. Feuerstein,* 308 U.S. 433; *United States v. United States Fid. Co.,* 309 U.S. 506.[19] But no such overriding considerations are present here. While this Court has not before had occasion to consider the applicability of the rule to a case involving real property, we can discern no reason why the rule should not be fully applicable.

It is argued that an exception to this rule of jurisdictional finality should be made with respect to cases involving real property because of this Court's emphatic expressions of the doctrine that courts of one State are completely without jurisdiction directly to affect title to land in other States. This argument is wide of the mark. Courts of one State are equally without jurisdiction to dissolve the marriages of those domiciled in other States. But the location of land, like the domicile of a party to a divorce action, is a matter "to be resolved by judicial determination." *Sherrer v. Sherrer,* 334 U.S. 343, at 349. The question remains whether, once the matter has been fully litigated and judicially determined, it can be retried in another State in litigation between the same parties. Upon the reason and authority of the cases we have discussed, it is clear that the answer must be in the negative.

It is to be emphasized that all that was ultimately determined in the Nebraska litigation was title to the land in question as between the parties to the litigation there. Nothing there decided, and nothing that could be decided in litigation between the same parties or their privies in Missouri, could bind either Missouri or Nebraska with respect to any controversy they might have, now or in the future, as to the location of the boundary between them, or as to their respective sovereignty over the land in question. Either State may at any time protect its interest by initiating independent judicial proceedings here.

For the reasons stated, we hold in this case that the federal court in Missouri had the power and, upon proper averments, the duty to inquire into the jurisdiction of the Nebraska courts to render the decree quieting title to the land in the petitioners. We further hold that when that inquiry disclosed, as it did, that the jurisdictional issues had been fully and fairly litigated by the parties and finally determined in the Nebraska courts, the federal court in Missouri was correct in ruling that further inquiry was precluded. Accordingly

---

[19] In neither of these cases had the jurisdictional issues actually been litigated in the first forum.

the judgment of the Court of Appeals is reversed, and that of the District Court is affirmed.

MR. JUSTICE BLACK, concurring.

Petitioners and respondent dispute the ownership of a tract of land adjacent to the Missouri River, which is the boundary between Nebraska and Missouri. Resolution of this question turns on whether the land is in Nebraska or Missouri. Neither State, of course, has power to make a determination binding on the other as to which State the land is in. However, in a private action brought by these Nebraska petitioners, the Nebraska Supreme Court has held that the disputed tract is in Nebraska. In the present suit, brought by this Missouri respondent in Missouri, the United States Court of Appeals has refused to be bound by the Nebraska court's judgment. I concur in today's reversal of the Court of Appeals' judgment, but with the understanding that we are not deciding the question whether the respondent would continue to be bound by the Nebraska judgment should it later be authoritatively decided, either in an original proceeding between the States in this Court or by a compact between the two States under Art. 1, § 10, that the disputed tract is in Missouri.

*See* PROBLEMS 7B-9. CLAMMING IN COUNTY WATERS; 7B-10. A CHARGE ON HIS ESTATE.

## THE "BOOTSTRAP" PRINCIPLE

(1) *The Bootstrap.* If the land in dispute in *Durfee v. Duke* is "really" located in Missouri, then should not the courts of *that* state have jurisdiction to determine title to "Missouri" land? (Remember that a federal district court in Missouri had made that finding.) How does Nebraska get the power to rob Missouri of authority over its "own" land?

*Durfee* illustrates what Professor Dobbs has called the "Bootstrap Principle." *See* Dan Dobbs, *The Validation of Void Judgments—The Bootstrap Principle,* 53 VA. L. REV. 1003, 1241 (Parts 1 and 2) (1967), and *Beyond Bootstrap: Foreclosing the Issue of Subject-Matter Jurisdiction Before Final Judgment,* 51; MINN. L. REV. 491 (1967). That principle, simply put, combines the axiom that a court always has jurisdiction to determine its own jurisdiction with the doctrine of res judicata. In other words, once a court holds that it has jurisdiction, it has, for practical purposes, "bootstrapped" itself into having jurisdiction. The bootstrap is successful because the jurisdictional finding binds all who participated in the litigation of the issue.

What is the meaning of Justice Black's opinion? If petitioner today "owns" the land because it has been held to be located in Nebraska, can the Nebraska Attorney General (or a congressionally-approved Interstate Compact such as that mentioned by Black) change her rights in the property? Perhaps Black is trying to say that the decision does not bind persons, such as the State of Missouri, who were not parties before the Court. If so, why did he think that needed to be said?

(2) *How Much is Needed for a Bootstrap?* The issue of subject matter jurisdiction was litigated in F-1 in *Durfee.* Is actual litigation required in order

to trigger the Bootstrap Principle or is it sufficient that there was an opportunity to litigate the issue of subject matter jurisdiction? The normal rule, of course, is that subject matter jurisdiction can be raised at any time; and it can be raised, not only by the parties, but by the court, *sua sponte. See* F.R. CIV. P. 12(h)(3). Can that rule expand the scope of the bootstrap rule?

**CHICOT COUNTY DRAINAGE DIST. v. BAXTER STATE BANK,** 308 U.S. 371 (1940). Suit in Arkansas federal court by holders of public bonds. The bonds had been the subject of an earlier bankruptcy proceeding in federal court leading to a court-approved plan which effectively rendered the bond holders' position in the present litigation untenable; no objection had been made to that plan. The bondholders, however, relied upon the fact that the Supreme Court, between the two actions, had declared unconstitutional in an unrelated proceeding—the statute which had led to the decree in the first case. The lower courts had held that the declaration of unconstitutionality had rendered the law "inoperative," and that it provided "no basis for the challenged decree."

HUGHES, C.J.: The question is simply whether respondents having failed to raise the [constitutional] question in the proceeding to which they were parties and in which they could have raised it and had it finally determined, were privileged to remain quiet and raise it in a subsequent suit. Such a view is contrary to the well-settled principle that *res judicata* may be pleaded as a bar, not only as respects matters actually presented to sustain or defeat the right asserted in the earlier proceeding, "but also as respects any other available matter which might have been presented to that end."

\*    \*    \*

Can *Chicot County* be squared with *Durfee? See also Sherrer v. Sherrer,* 334 U.S 343 (1948) (litigation of jurisdiction to divorce—the wife's domicile—consisted only of husband's general appearance and denial of jurisdiction without proffer of proof, the Court held the finding of subject matter jurisdiction could not be attacked collaterally).

This expanded version of the bootstrap principle has an interesting application in diversity of citizenship cases. In *McCormick v. Sullivant,* 23 U.S. (10 Wheat.) 192 (1825), the Supreme Court held that a collateral attack could not be made on a federal diversity judgment even where the pleading failed to disclose the citizenship of the parties. The *McCormick* holding was expanded in *Des Moines Navigation and Railroad Co. v. Iowa Homestead Co.,* 123 U.S. 552 (1887), to preclude collateral attack by a state court of a federal diversity judgment even when the record in the federal case (F-1) demonstrated; that the parties were not diverse, and where the issue of subject matter jurisdiction had never been litigated.

Whatever happened to the principle that jurisdiction cannot be conferred on the court by the parties? Or is there something "different" about diversity litigation? Are there, in other words, some federal interests in preserving federal judgments against collateral attack in (hostile) state courts which might justify the *McCormack* and *Des Moines* cases?

(3) *Federal Policy and the Bootstrap.* Can a state court bootstrap itself into subject matter jurisdiction of a case that Congress has entrusted to the

*exclusive* jurisdiction of the federal courts, or does the importance of the federal policy underlying the grant of exclusive jurisdiction trump the bootstrap principle?

**KALB v. FEURERSTEIN,** 308 U.S. 433 (1940). Two farmers had their farms foreclosed and sold under state judicial authority by state officials. At the time of sale, the farmers had pending in bankruptcy court a petition to stay the proceedings under the federal farm bankruptcy (Frazier-Lemke) Act, whose jurisdiction over these matters would be exclusive. Rather than taking a direct appeal from the foreclosure actions, the farmers attacked the sales collaterally in another state court action.

BLACK, J.: It is generally true that a judgment by a court of competent jurisdiction bears a presumption of regularity and is not thereafter subject to collateral attack [citing *Chicot County, supra*]. But Congress may by specific bankruptcy legislation create an exception to that principle. The Constitution grants Congress exclusive power to regulate bankruptcy and under this power Congress can limit the jurisdiction which courts, State or Federal, can exercise over the person and property of a debtor who duly invokes the bankruptcy law.

Congress manifested its intention that the issue of jurisdiction in the foreclosing court need not be contested or even raised by the distressed farmer-debtor. [W]hether the issue of jurisdiction was actually contested or whether it could have been contested, are not applicable where the plenary power of Congress over bankruptcy has been exercised as in this Act.

\*   \*   \*

Can *Kalb* and *Chicot County* be reconciled? The two cases, decided on the same day more than half a century ago, suggest a line of analysis. Both, after all, involve an important federal interest (bankruptcy) addressed by Congress in recent legislation. Yet, collateral attack was permitted only in *Kalb*. Is Justice Black's reliance there on statutory language and purpose persuasive? Suppose Congress wants to be sure that federal interests will be adequately protected in litigation by requiring that litigation involving those interests only be heard in a Federal court. Does *Kalb* insure that the Iron Law of preclusion will not be able to overcome that Congressional desire? Is that concern sufficient to overcome the Iron Law of finality?

*Kalb* and *Chicot County* are just two of a clutch of cases decided at the end of the Depression in which the Court discussed the problem of collateral attack on a final judgment for lack of subject matter jurisdiction when federal interests were at stake. *See* Bennett Boskey & Robert Braucher, *Jurisdiction and Collateral Attack, October Term, 1939,* 40; COLUM. L. REV. 1006, 1018-19 (1940), who wrote that, after *Kalb,* "the Court has established that the newly dominant doctrine of res judicata may be overridden by a countervailing policy, at least when that policy is embodied in an act of Congress." How do you know when a "countervailing policy" is present? The authors suggest "analytical dissection of jurisdiction doctrines in each specific situation presented." *Id.* at 1029. *See also United States v. United States Fidelity & Guaranty Co.,* 309 U.S. 506 (1939) (res judicata does not preclude a collateral attack based on sovereign immunity). (For a rare state court opinion holding that a strong federal interest inproper subject matter jurisdiction can overcome the res judicata effect of an earlier state court decision, see *Salisbury v. Salisbury,* 657 S.W.2d 761 (Tenn. App. 1983); the required strong federal interest was the Parental Kidnapping Prevention Act, *see* § 8.14, *infra.)* More generally Restatement (Second) of Judgments, § 86, comment b, states:

> The judgment by the state court is *prima facie* entitled to recognition even though the court's interpretation of federal law is not ultimately authoritative. However, the fact that federal substantive interests are at stake is a factor militating, in some degree, against treating the state court judgment as conclusive. The weight accorded this factor depends on the nature of the federal substantive policy involved and the possibility that it might have been inaccurately comprehended by the state court.

(4) *Federal Policy in Federal Courts.* Can the same concern for federal interests arise when the initial judgments were rendered by a *federal* court?

**CONSOLIDATED RAIL CORP. v. ILLINOIS**, 423 F. Supp. 941 (Regional Rail Reorg. Ct. 1976), *cert. denied,* 420 U.S. 1095 (1977): A federal district court had enjoined plaintiff railroad from certain activity. The Regional Rail Reorganization Act of 1973, however, had given exclusive jurisdiction of various forms of litigation involving railroads to a specially designated court made up of Article III judges. The problem, therefore, was whether the first decree—by a federal court, remember—must be respected by the special court.

WISDOM, J.: Although the policies of terminating litigation, avoiding inconsistent results, and repose, which support application of res judicata to questions of subject matter jurisdiction, may vindicate the general rule that litigated questions of subject matter jurisdiction cannot be collaterally attacked, the policy basis for the rule should make us wary of its procrustean application. Here, countervailing policy considerations support the conclusion that Congress, in passing the Act and § 209(e) in particular, intended to void determinations made by other courts, when these determinations were reserved for our exclusive consideration. The legislative mandate overpowers the general rule.

In sum, the purposes of the Act and [its] language compel us to hold that Congress concluded that the policies supporting our exclusive jurisdiction outweigh the policies of res judicata.

\* \* \*

Restatement (Second) of Judgments § 12 provides:[20]

§ 12. Contesting Subject Matter Jurisdiction

When a court has rendered a judgment in a contested action, the judgment precludes the parties from litigating the question of the court's subject matter jurisdiction in subsequent litigation except if:

---

[20] Copyright American Law Institute. Reprinted with permission.

(1) The subject matter of the action was so plainly beyond the court's jurisdiction that its entertaining the action was a manifest abuse of authority; or

(2) Allowing the judgment to stand would substantially infringe the authority of anothertribunal or agency of government; or

(3) The judgment was rendered by a court lacking capability to make an adequately informed determination of a question concerning its own jurisdiction and as a matter of procedural fairness the party seeking to avoid the judgment should have opportunity belatedly to attack the court's subject matter jurisdiction.

Does § 12 restate the law properly? Consider the support in other case law and in policy for each of the provisions of § 12.

## [F] The Land Taboo

### FALL v. EASTIN

*United States Supreme Court*
*215 U.S. 1, 30 S. Ct. 3, 54 L. Ed. 65 (1909)*

MR. JUSTICE McKENNA delivered the opinion of the Court.

The question in this case is whether a deed to land situated in Nebraska, made by a commissioner under the decree of a court of the State of Washington in an action for divorce, must be recognized in Nebraska under the due faith and credit clause of the Constitution of the United States.

Plaintiff alleged the following facts: She and E. W. Fall, who was a defendant in the trial court, were married in Indiana in 1876. Subsequently they went to Nebraska, and while living there, "by their joint efforts, accumulations and earnings, acquired jointly and by the same conveyance" the land in controversy. In 1889 they removed to the State of Washington, and continued to reside there as husband and wife until January, 1895, when they separated. On the twenty seventh of February, 1895, her husband brought suit against her for divorce in the Superior Court of that county.

[Plaintiff] further alleges that a decree was entered granting her a divorce, and setting apart to her the land in controversy as her own separate property forever, free and unencumbered from any claim of the plaintiff thereto, and that he was ordered and directed by the court to convey all his right, title and interest in and to the land within five days from the date of the decree.

She also alleges the execution of the deed to her by the commissioner appointed by the court, the execution and recording of the mortgage to W. H. Fall and the deed to defendant;[21] that the deed and mortgage were each made without consideration and for the purpose of defrauding her, and that they cast a cloud upon her title derived by her under the decree of divorce

---

[21] E. W. Fall and W. H. Fall were brothers; the defendant, to whom the land had been conveyed, was their sister. The allegation, in short, was that the conveyance and mortgage were attempts to defraud plaintiff. *See* RUSSELL WEINTRAUB, COMMENTARY ON THE CONFLICT OF LAWS 508 (4th ed. 2001) –*Eds.*

and the commissioner's deed. She prays that her title be quieted and that the deed and mortgage be declared null and void.

W. H. Fall disclaimed any interest in the premises, and executed a release of the mortgage made to him by E. W. Fall. No personal service was had upon E. W. Fall, and he did not appear. A decree was passed in favor of plaintiff, which was affirmed by the supreme court [of Nebraska]. A rehearing was granted and the decree was reversed.

*     *     *

The contentions of the parties, it will be observed, put in prominence and as controlling, different propositions. Plaintiff urges the equities which arose between her and her husband, on account of their relation as husband and wife, in the state of Washington, and under the laws of that state. The defendant urges the policy of the state of Nebraska, and the inability of the court of Washington, by its decree alone or the deed executed through the commissioners, to convey the land situated in Nebraska. To the defendant's view the supreme court of the state finally gave its assent, as we have seen.

In considering these propositions, we must start with a concession of jurisdiction in the Washington court over both the parties and the subject-matter. Jurisdiction in that court is the first essential, but the ultimate question is: What is the effect of the decree upon the land, and of the deed executed under it? The supreme court of the state concedes, as we understand its opinion, the jurisdiction in the Washington court to render the decree. The court said:

> We think there can be no doubt that where a court of chancery has by its decree ordered and directed persons properly within its jurisdiction to do or refrain from doing a certain act, it may compel obedience to this decree by appropriate proceedings, and that any action taken by reason of such compulsion is valid and effectual wherever it may be assailed. In the instant case, if Fall had obeyed the order of the Washington court and made a deed of conveyance to his wife of the Nebraska land, even under the threat of contempt proceedings, or after duress by imprisonment, the title thereby conveyed to Mrs. Fall would have been of equal weight and dignity with that which he himself possessed at the time of the execution of the deed.

But Fall, not having executed a deed, the court's conclusion was, to quote its language, that "neither the decree nor the commissioner's deed conferred any right or title upon her." This conclusion was deduced, not only from the absence of power generally of the courts of one state over lands situated in another, but also from the laws of Nebraska providing for the disposition of real estate in divorce proceedings.

The territorial limitation of the jurisdiction of courts of a state over property in another state has a limited exception in the jurisdiction of a court of equity, but it is an exception well defined. A court of equity, having authority to act upon the person, may indirectly act upon real estate in another state, through the instrumentality of this authority over the person. Whatever it may do through the party, it may do to give effect to its decree respecting property, whether it goes to the entire disposition of it or only to effect it with liens or burdens.

Whether the doctrine that a decree of a court rendered in consummation of equities, or the deed of a master under it, will not convey title, and that the deed of a party coerced by the decree will have such effect, is illogical or inconsequent, we need not inquire, nor consider whether the other view would not more completely fulfill the Constitution of the United States, and that whatever may be done between the parties in one state may be adjudged to be done by the courts of another, and that the decree might be regarded to have the same legal effect as the act of the party which was ordered to be done.

[H]owever plausibly the contrary view may be sustained, we think that the doctrine that the court, not having jurisdiction of the *res* cannot affect it by its decree, nor by a deed made by a master in accordance with the decree, is firmly established. The embarrassment which sometimes results from it has been obviated by legislation in many states. In some states the decree is made to operate *per se* as a source of title. This operation is given a decree in Nebraska. In other states power is given to certain officers to carry the decree into effect. Such power is given in Washington to commissioners appointed by the court. It was in pursuance of this power that the deed in the suit at bar was executed. But this legislation does not affect the doctrine which we have expressed, which rests, as we have said, on the well-recognized principle that, when the subject-matter of a suit in a court of equity is within another state or country, but the parties within the jurisdiction of the court, the suit may be maintained and remedies granted which may directly affect and operate upon the person of the defendant and not upon the subject-matter, although the subject-matter is referred to in the decree, and the defendant is ordered to do or refrain from certain acts toward it, and it is thus ultimately but *indirectly* affected by the relief granted. In such case, the decree is not of itself legal title, nor does it transfer the legal title. It must be executed by the party, and obedience is compelled by proceedings in the nature of contempt, attachment, or sequestration. On the other hand, where the suit is strictly local, the subject-matter is specific property, and the relief when granted is such that it *must* act directly upon the subject-matter, and not upon the person of the defendant, the jurisdiction must be exercised in the state where the subject-matter is situated.

This doctrine is entirely consistent with the provision of the Constitution of the United States, which requires a judgment in any state to be given full faith and credit in the courts of every other state. This provision does not extend the jurisdiction of the courts of one state to property situated in another, but only makes the judgment rendered conclusive on the merits of the claim or subject matter of the suit. "It does not carry with it into another state the efficacy of a judgment upon property or persons, to be enforced by execution. To give it the force of a judgment in another State it must become a judgment there; and can only be executed in the latter as its laws permit." *M'Elmoyle v. Cohen,* 13 Pet. 312.

There is, however, much temptation in the facts of this case to [hold for Plaintiff]. As we have seen, the husband of the plaintiff brought suit against her in Washington for divorce, and, attempting to avail himself of the laws of Washington, prayed also that the land now in controversy be awarded to him. She appeared in the action, and, submitting to the jurisdiction which he had invoked, made counter charges and prayers for relief. She established her charges, she was granted a divorce, and the land decreed to her. He, then, to defeat the decree, and in fraud of her rights, conveyed the land to the defendant in this suit. This is the finding of the trial court. It is not questioned by the supreme court; but, as the ruling of the latter court, that the decree in Washington gave no such equities as could be recognized in Nebraska as justifying an action to quiet title does not offend the Constitution of the United States, we are constrained to affirm its judgment.

MR. JUSTICE HARLAN and MR. JUSTICE BREWER dissent.

MR. JUSTICE HOLMES, concurring specially.

I am not prepared to dissent from the judgment of the court, but my reasons are different from those that have been stated.

The real question concerns the effect of the Washington decree. As between the parties to it, that decree established in Washington a personal obligation of the husband to convey to his former wife. A personal obligation goes with the person. If the husband had made a contract, valid by the law of Washington, to do the same thing, I think there is no doubt that the contract would have been binding in Nebraska. So I conceive that a Washington decree for the specific performance of such a contract would be entitled to full faith and credit as between the parties in Nebraska. But it does not matter to its constitutional effect what the ground of the decree may be, whether a contract or something else. *Fauntleroy v. Lum,* 210 U.S. 230. (In this case it may have been that the wife contributed equally to the accumulation of the property, and so had an equitable claim.) A personal decree is equally within the jurisdiction of a court having the person within its power, whatever its ground and whatever it orders the defendant to do. Therefore, I think that this decree was entitled to full faith and credit in Nebraska.

But the Nebraska court carefully avoids saying that the decree would not be binding between the original parties, had the husband been before the court. The ground on which it goes is that to allow the judgment to affect the conscience of purchasers would be giving it an effect *in rem.* It treats the case as standing on the same footing as that of an innocent purchaser. Now, if the court saw fit to deny the effect of a judgment upon privies in title, or if it considered the defendant an innocent purchaser, I do not see what we have to do with its decision, however wrong. I do not see why it is not within the power of the State to do away with equity or with the equitable doctrine as to purchasers with notice if it sees fit. Still less do I see how a mistake as to notice could give us jurisdiction. If the judgment binds the defendant, it is not by its own operation, even with the Constitution behind it, but by the obligation imposed by equity upon a purchaser with notice. The ground of decision below was that there was no such obligation. The decision, even if wrong, did not deny to the Washington decree its full effect.

## NOTES AND QUESTIONS ON *FALL* AND THE LAND TABOO

(1) *The Fall Decision.* Mr. Fall had transferred the land to his sister. It's hard to argue that she was a bona fide purchaser who took without notice of Mrs. Fall's earlier and inconsistent claim. If that is correct, then what value is served by the Court's holding?

What of Nebraska's interest in the sanctity of its land records? Is that a convincing justification? Think about the process by which land records would get changed if the Fall litigation had been entirely domestic. Is there any reason why Nebraska's land records could not be adequately protected by requiring, say, that Mrs. Fall register (or sue on) the Washington decree in a Nebraska court before making that decree effective? The order of the Nebraska court could then be placed in the land records, thereby informing any title searcher of Mrs. Fall's interest in the property. If so, it is very hard, is it not, to justify Nebraska's refusal to recognize the foreign decree? A more sympathetic writer on the plight of a Nebraska lawyer examining a title" is Brainerd Currie, *Full Faith and Credit to Foreign Land Decrees,* 21 U. Chi. L. Rev. 620, 641 (1954).

Or does Nebraska have a unique interest, as situs, in having its own law applied (and, as a corollary, an interest in its courts having exclusive jurisdiction over Nebraska land)? First, recall *Fauntleroy v. Lum, see* § 7.07, *supra;* does that case and its Iron Law of preclusion supply a pretty good answer here? Second, is Nebraska an *interested* jurisdiction; and, therefore, entitled to have its law applied? Does the dispute between the Falls (and Ms. Eastin) have *anything* at all to do with Nebraska law? Does that question also supply a pretty good answer to the first question in this paragraph?

*See* PROBLEMS 7B-11. THE HOTEL; 7B-12. THE SUMMER COTTAGE; 7B-13. ANOTHER HAPPY FAMILY.

(2) *The Alternatives.* One of the great joys of our legal system is that there is usually more than one way to skin a legal cat. It has become commonplace to suggest that all that was wrong in *Fall* was that Mrs. Fall sought legal the wrong remedy.

At least two alternatives were available. First, she could have sued in Nebraska on the Washington equity decree itself. One difficulty, as discussed in § 7.09 [C], *supra,* is that at the time of the decision, equity decrees were not thought entitled to recognition.

The California Supreme Court endorsed this alternative in *Rozan v. Rozan,* 49 Cal. 2d 322, 331, 317 P.2d 11, 16 (1957). There, the court expressed its belief that a California divorce decree which ordered a conveyance of land in North Dakota would be honored in North Dakota. The Court distinguished Fall on the ground that in that case a court-appointed commissioner had executed the conveyance of Nebraska land which had "directly affected title to land in Nebraska." Is this a difference amounting to a distinction?

A second alternative would have been to force Mr. Fall to execute a deed under threat of contempt. Such compelled deeds are apparently enforced routinely. *See* Russell Weintraub, Commentary on the Conflicts of Laws 515 (4th ed. 2001); Gene Picotte, Note, *Validity of Deed Given Under Compulsion of "Foreign" Court,* 12 MONT. L. REV. 59 (1951). Although the deed would have been executed under duress, the Nebraska court in *Fall* certainly indicated that it would have had no problem with this end-run around the land taboo. *See* 75 Neb. at 125, 113 N.W. at 178. Does the Nebraska court's position exalt form over substance? For a recent example of a court ordering someone to act concerning property in another state, *see Eckard v. Eckard,* 333 Md.531, 636 A.2d 455 (1994).

*See* PROBLEMS 7B-14. 1000 ACRES OF PRIME FARM LAND; 7B-15. FIRST IN TIME, FIRST IN RIGHT?

(3) *The Holmes Opinion.* Were you surprised that Justice Holmes, who wrote the majority opinion in *Fauntleroy v. Lum,* did not dissent? And if he was not going to dissent, why did he not join the majority opinion? Holmes believed that if the defendant were a bona fide purchaser and not privy with Mr. Fall, it would be a question of *state* (Nebraska) law whether the Washington conveyance could affect the bona fide purchaser's title. Is that statement consistent with the well-established doctrine that the rendering state controls the preclusive effects of its judgments?

---

## CLARKE v. CLARKE

*United States Supreme Court*
*178 U.S. 186, 20 S. Ct. 873, 44 L. Ed. 1028 (1900)*

[The Clarke family lived in South Carolina. When Mrs. Clarke died, she left land she owned in Connecticut to be divided equally among her husband and two daughters. Unfortunately, one daughter (Julia) died shortly thereafter, and Mr. Clarke sued to obtain guidance from a South Carolina Court as to whether he the executor of his wife's estate, could sell the land. The court, after appointing a guardian ad litem for the other daughter (Nancy), held that the land could be sold because the will had equitably converted it.

Suit was then brought in Connecticut to obtain the guidance of a court of that state. Applying Connecticut law, the Court gave all of Julia's share to Nancy; the proceeds of the land sale would have been split equally between Nancy and her father under South Carolina law.

The perplexed father then asked for guidance from the Supreme Court.]

MR. JUSTICE WHITE, delivered the opinion of the court.

It is a doctrine firmly established that the law of a state in which land is situated controls and governs its transmission by will or its passage in case of intestacy. This familiar rule has been frequently declared by this court.

It is conceded that, had the will been presented to the courts of Connecticut in the first instance and rights been asserted under it, the operative force of its provisions upon real estate in Connecticut would have been within the control of such courts. But it is said a different rule must be applied where the will has been presented to a South Carolina court and a construction has been there given to it; for, in such a case, not the will but the decree of the South Carolina court, construing the will, is the measure of the rights of the parties, as to real estate in Connecticut. The proposition, when truly comprehended, amounts but to the contention that the laws of the respective states controlling the transmission of real property by will, or in case of intestacy, are operative only so long as there does not exist in a foreign jurisdiction a judgment or decree which in legal effect has changed the law of the situs of the real estate.

[T]he question as to the operative effect of the will of Mrs. Clarke, upon the status of land situated in Connecticut, was one directly involving the mode of passing title to lands in that state. This resulted from the fact that if the will worked a conversion into personalty immediately upon the death of Mrs. Clarke, as contended, it necessarily vested her executor with authority at once to sell and convey the real estate in Connecticut by a deed sufficient, under the laws of that State, to transfer title to real estate—a power which was held by the courts of Connecticut not to have been conferred. Had the executor assumed to exercise such a power, however, the validity or invalidity of a conveyance thus executed would have been one exclusively for the courts of Connecticut to determine, just as would have been the question of the sufficiency of the will to vest title. Such being the case, there is no basis for the contention that it was not the exclusive province of the courts of Connecticut to determine, prior to the execution of such a conveyance, whether or not the power to do so existed.

[W]hether Mr. Clarke, as executor and trustee under the will of his wife, had any power, duty or estate with respect to lands situated in Connecticut, depended upon the laws of that State. The courts of the domicile of Mrs. Clarke could properly be called upon to construe her will so far as it affected property which was within or might properly come under the jurisdiction of those tribunals. If, however, by the law as enforced in Connecticut, land in Connecticut owned by Mrs. Clarke at her decease was real estate for all purposes, despite the provisions contained in her will, that land was a subject matter not directly amenable to the jurisdiction of the courts of another state, however much those courts might indirectly affect and operate upon it in controversies, where the court, by reason of its jurisdiction over persons and the nature of the controversy, might coerce the execution of a conveyance of or other instrument encumbering such land.

And the cogency of the reasons just given is further demonstrated by considering the case from another though somewhat similar aspect. The decree of the South Carolina court, which, it is contended, had the effect of converting real estate situated in Connecticut into personal property, was not one rendered between persons who were *sui juris*. Nancy B. Clarke, one of the parties to the suit in South Carolina, and whom the Connecticut court has held inherited, to the exclusion of the father, under the laws of Connecticut, the whole of the real estate belonging to her sister, was a minor.

It cannot be doubted that the courts of a state where real estate is situated have the exclusive right to appoint a guardian of a non-resident minor, and vest in such guardian the exclusive control and management of land belonging to said minor, situated within the state.

Of what efficacy, however, would be the power of one state to control the administration, through its own courts, of real estate within the state, belonging to minors, without regard to the domicile of the minor, if all such real estate could be disposed of and the administration thereof be controlled by the decree of the court of another state.

When, therefore, Henry P. Clarke, as administrator, appointed in Connecticut, of the estate of his deceased daughter, Julia Clarke, applied to the Connecticut probate court to determine who was entitled to the—real estate— owned by the intestate, it was the province of the Connecticut court to decide such question solely with reference to the law of Connecticut. Its power in this regard was not limited by the fact that in order to determine who owned the real estate, it was necessary for the court to construe the will of the mother of the intestate, and to determine what effect it had upon the status of the real estate under the law of Connecticut. Having a right to decide these questions, it was not constrained to adopt the construction of the will which had been announced by the court of South Carolina. From these conclusions, it follows that because the court of Connecticut applied the law of that state in determining the devolution of title to real estate there situated, thereby no violation of the constitutional requirement that full faith and credit must be given in one state to the judgments and decrees of the courts of another state, was brought about, as the decree of the South Carolina court, in the particular under consideration, was not entitled to be followed by the courts of Connecticut, by reason of a want of jurisdiction in the court of South Carolina over the particular subject matter which was sought to be concluded in Connecticut by such decree.

*Judgment affirmed.*

*See* PROBLEM 7B-16. PERSONALTY AND REALTY.

## NOTES AND QUESTIONS

(1) *Equitable Conversion and the Land Taboo.* Is the real holding in *Clarke* that you cannot fool the Supreme Court (at least if you're dealing with land)? After all, if equitable conversion could be used successfully as an end-run around the "land taboo," it could destroy the rule in *Fall* pretty quickly.

Recall the earlier discussion of equitable conversion in Section 4.1 [E], *supra.* Why is it that land is so important in the problem presented by *Clarke?* Why can't the South Carolina court authoritatively decide, as the first court to hear the case, that this is really a problem in "personal" rather than "real" property and, as a result, that jurisdiction quite properly was exercised by the South Carolina courts?

Can the *Clarke* holding be squared with *Durfee v. Duke?* If Nebraska in *that* case had jurisdiction to decide whether it had subject matter jurisdiction (over land?) why does the South Carolina court in *Clarke* lack equivalent jurisdiction?

Professor Moffatt Hancock points out that Mrs. Clarke also owned land in Kansas, New York, and South Carolina. Each state would have reached a different result on the merits: respectively, all to father, life estate to father with remainder to Nancy, to father and Nancy in equal shares, and, in Connecticut, all to Nancy. *See* Moffatt Hancock, *Full Faith and Credit to Foreign Laws and Judgments in Real Property Litigation: The Supreme Court and the Land Taboo,* 18 STAN. L. REV. 327 (1966). South Carolina's attempt to harmonize the disparate results can be seen as an attempt to impose order on this chaos. In this sense equitable conversion is a very useful "legal fiction," *see* L. L. Fuller, *Legal Fictions,* 25 ILL. L. REV. 363, 513 (1930), for it permits the same result to be achieved in each state. *See generally* Moffatt Hancock, *"In the Parish of St. Mary le Bow, in the Ward of Cheap": Choice of Law Problems Resolved by Statutory Construction: The Charitable Testamentary Gift Cases,* 16 STAN. L. REV. 561 (1964). Robby Alden, *Modernizing the Situs Rule for Real Property Conflicts,* 65 TEX. L.REV. 585 (1987).

Is it relevant, as Professor Hancock observes, that South Carolina was the *only* interested jurisdiction because the real question was one of succession? Although the laws of the four states where Mrs. Clarke owned property differed on the succession issue, do you believe those differences reflect fundamental policy differences or are they merely quirky? If the latter, the result is certainly harder to justify. And why should it matter that Nancy Clarke was a minor? In thinking about this question, recall where Nancy was domiciled and reflect on the comparative strengths of the interests of Connecticut and South Carolina in protecting her and her property rights.

Think of the enormous legal fees the Clarke litigation must have run up in order to resolve what should have been a very simple problem. Is this any way to run a legal system?

(2) *The "Land Taboo" Today.* The body of law exemplified by *Fall* and *Clarke* has been under heavy attack for a long time. Perhaps the most prominent critic has been Professor Hancock, whose very influential articles, most written in the 1960's, have been collected in Moffatt Hancock, Studies in Modern Choice-of-Law: Torts, Insurance, Land Titles (1984). The result really hinges on the common law's historic preoccupation with land as something special—a view we saw earlier in § 3.20, *supra,* in connection with the "local action" exception in jurisdiction, and in § 4.08, supra, in connection with the situs rule in choice of law. Professor Hancock's styling of this fetish as the "land taboo" is quite telling.

Modern courts have become much more willing to violate the land taboo. In yet another case involving Nebraska land, the court held that it would recognize the foreign decree at least "if the related public policy of the situs state is in substantial accord with that of the other state." *Weesner v. Weesner,* 168 Neb. 346, 95 N.W.2d 682, 690 (1952) (the *Weesner* opinion weakly attempted to distinguish *Fall* by noting that Nebraska courts now had the power to award land as alimony). The court in *McElreath v. McElreath,* 162 Tex. 195, 345 S.W.2d 722 (1961), when faced with a situation similar to that in *Fall,* explained why the land taboo should be exorcised:

> [W]hat difference does it make to the State of Texas whether the property here involved is awarded to the ex-husband or the ex-wife of a broken Oklahoma marriage? Is there in Texas a public policy which prefers land tenure by males rather than by females? Is there

a reasonable probability of the return of feudal tenures to Anglo-American jurisprudence so that one owning land would be burdened with Knight Service? Texas should have no concern with the methods adopted by Oklahoma in settling the matrimonial differences of its citizens and their property rights.

Sounds good doesn't it?

## § 7.09 Exceptions to the Iron Law II—F-2's Ability to Ignore a Valid F-1 Judgment

### [A] Lack of a Competent Court in F-2

**KENNEY v. SUPREME LODGE OF THE WORLD, LOYAL ORDER OF MOOSE**, 252 U.S. 411 (1920). Wrongful death action in Alabama; judgment for plaintiff. Suit was brought to enforce the judgment in Illinois, but an Illinois statute prohibited its courts from hearing causes of action for wrongful death which arose in other states. The Illinois courts refused to hear the case.

HOLMES, J. [R]eliance was placed upon *Anglo-American Provision Co. v. Davis Provision Co.,* 191 U.S. 373 [1903].

*Anglo-American* was a suit by a foreign corporation on a foreign judgment against a foreign corporation. The decision is sufficiently explained without more by the views about foreign corporations that had prevailed unquestioned since *Bank of Augusta v. Earle,* 13 Pet. 519 [1839]. Moreover, no doubt there is truth in the proposition that the Constitution does not require the State to furnish a court. But it also is true that there are limits to the power of exclusion and to the power to consider the nature of the cause of action before the foreign judgment upon it is given effect.

In *Fauntleroy v. Lum* the policy of Mississippi was more actively contravened in that case than the policy of Illinois in this. Therefore the fact that here the original cause of action could not have been maintained in Illinois is not an answer to a suit upon the judgment. But this being true, it is plain that a state cannot escape its constitutional obligations by the simple device of denying jurisdiction in such cases to courts otherwise competent.

---

## NOTES AND QUESTIONS

(1) *Lack of Capacity to Sue.* Chief Justice Marshall had opined in *Bank of Augusta v. Earle* that a corporation "must dwell in the place of its creation, and cannot migrate to another sovereignty." Does this mean that *Kenney* carves out a special rule for foreign corporations or is *Anglo-American* (referred to by Holmes in his opinion in *Kenney*) over-ruled? Consider also *Weidman v. Weidman,* 274 Mass. 118, 174 N.E. 206 (1931), where a wife obtained alimony from a New York Court and then sought to enforce the New York judgment in Massachusetts. That court declined to do so on the ground

that Massachusetts law does not permit suits between spouses. Constitutional?

These cases led Professor Stumberg to conclude that the forum could deny relief to those who lacked *capacity* to sue under forum law. *See* GEORGE STUM-BERG, PRINCIPLES OF CONFLICT OF LAWS 119 (3d ed. 1963); RESTATEMENT (SECOND) OF CONFLICT OF LAWS § 117, comment d. But why should the Constitution distinguish between policies and persons in this fashion?

*Kenney* is undoubtedly correct and seems to be compelled by *Fauntleroy*. Justice Holmes, who wrote both opinions, certainly thought so. If *Kenney* had come out the other way, what would stop Mississippi, in a case like *Fauntleroy*, from accomplishing its purpose by forbidding its courts to exercise jurisdiction over a suit upon a judgment based on a futures contract?

(2) *Closing the Court to a Foreign Cause of Action.* Consider also the discussion of *Hughes v. Fetter* in Section 5.06[A], *supra*. If a state must open its courts to a foreign cause of action, it certainly is difficult to argue that those courts can be closed to a foreign judgment.

(3) *Type of Relief.* There is one additional limitation to the *Kenney* doctrine. Plaintiff who seeks to enforce a judgment of a sister state must seek a type of relief that courts of the enforcing state are empowered to grant. Thus, if courts of the enforcing state cannot grant specific performance in domestic cases, they need not do so in a suit to enforce a sister state judgment. Usually, however, this limitation presents no real barrier to full faith and credit because the typical remedy sought in an action on a sister state judgment is money damages and all states provide for that type of remedy. *See* W. RICHMAN & W. REYNOLDS, UNDERSTANDING CONFLICT OF LAWS § 103 (2002).

## [B]  Penal and Tax Judgments

**HUNTINGTON v. ATTRILL**, 146 U. S. 657 (1892): New York made corporate directors personally liable for certain corporate debts if the directors had sworn falsely that the corporation was fully capitalized. After a New York court found against the defendant, suit was brought in Maryland to enforce the judgment. The Maryland court refused, saying, "it is well settled that no State will enforce penalties imposed by the laws of another State."

GRAY, J.: The question whether a statute may be called penal in the international sense, so that it cannot be enforced in the courts of another state, depends upon the question whether its purpose is to punish an offense against the public justice of the state or to afford a private remedy to a person injured by the wrongful act.

Penal laws, strictly and properly, are those imposing punishment for an offense committed against the state, and which, by the English and American constitutions, the executive of the State has the power to pardon.

\* \* \*

The holding in *Huntington* can be traced back to a famous utterance of Chief Justice Marshall: "The Courts of no country execute the penal laws of another." *The Antelope*, 23 U.S. (10 Wheat.) 66, 123 (1825). *See* Brainerd

Currie, *The Constitution and the Transitory Cause of Action,* 73 HARV. L. REV. 268, 279-80 (1959), for a discussion of the complete irrelevance of the quoted language to the facts in *The Antelope.*

In any event, when is a judgment based on a "penal law in the international sense"? As Professor Leflar points out, courts have used this loophole to deny litigants in a wide variety of cases, including those involving usury forfeiture provisions, and punitive damages in tort cases. *See* Robert; Leflar, *Extrastate Enforcement of Penal and Governmental Claims,* 46 HARV. L. REV 193 (1932) (citing, *e.g.,* cases refusing to enforce wrongful death actions and claims for punitive damages in ordinary tort cases).

**MILWAUKEE COUNTY v. M.E. WHITE CO.**, 296 U.S. 268 (1935). Suit to enforce a judgment for taxes rendered in another state.

STONE, J.: "Whether one state must enforce the revenue laws of another" remains an open question in this court.

A cause of action on a judgment is different from that upon which the judgment was entered.

We can perceive no greater possibility of embarrassment in litigating the validity of a judgment for taxes and enforcing it than any other for the payment of money.

[N]o state can be said to have a legitimate policy against payment of its neighbor's taxes, the obligation of which has been judicially established.

We conclude that a judgment is not to be denied full faith and credit in state and federal courts merely because it is for taxes.

---

## NOTES

The *Milwaukee County* Court expressly reserved the question of whether a judgment "created by the penal law, in the international sense"—remember *Huntington v. Attrill*—was entitled to full faith and credit. After *Milwaukee County,* how could any case decided by an American court be denied recognition because it is "penal"? Or do state judgments which liquidate tax claims somehow differ from those based on wrongful death actions? Or from civil fines? After all, every American judgment is rendered, at least in this post-Warren Court era, under the full protection of the federal constitution, isn't it?

The modern trend is certainly toward recognizing such claims, even when they have not been liquidated. The leading case is *Oklahoma ex rel. Oklahoma Tax Comm'n v. Neeley,* 225 Ark. 230, 282 S.W.2d 150 (1955).

For a discussion of the problem of recognizing international tax judgments, see *British Columbia v. Gilbertson* 433 F. Supp. 410 (D. Or. 1979), *aff'd,* 597 F.2d 1161 (9th Cir. 1979) (refusing to enforce a judgment for taxes obtained in a provincial court in British Columbia). English courts will not enforce a judgment based on foreign penal or revenue laws, although they do construe those terms strictly." *See* CHESHIRE AND NORTH, PRIVATE INTERNATIONAL LAW 374 (11th ed. 1987).

*See* PROBLEMS 7B-17. FINES FOR FAILURE TO PAY TAXES; 7B-18. LISTENING IN.

## [C] The Special Problem of Equity Decrees

Anglo-American jurisprudence long distinguished between courts of law and equity, although in very recent times the two systems have been merged almost everywhere. Should that distinction be carried over into the area of recognition of judgments? There is a fair amount of support for the notion that foreign equity decrees need not be recognized. The maxim that "equity acts upon the person" has long influenced the law in this area and has led courts to conclude that different rules apply when equitable decrees are involved; a court, after all, cannot "act upon the person" of someone not actually, before it.

Most of the cases involve recognition of foreign decrees affecting land in the forum; that special problem is discussed earlier in this section in connection with *Fall v. Eastin* and *Durfee v. Duke*. And there is clear authority that an order by an equity court to pay a definite amount of money must be recognized. *Lynde v. Lynde,* 181 U.S. 183 (1901). *See generally* Willis L. M. Reese, *Full Faith and Credit to Foreign Equity Decrees,* 42 IOWA L. REV. 183 (1957).

The problem becomes a bit more difficult when one court enjoins a litigant from pursuing an action brought in another state. What if the litigant who has been enjoined turns around and gets an injunction himself. The next case discusses that problem.

———

## JAMES v. GRAND TRUNK WESTERN RAILROAD CO.

*Illinois Supreme Court*
*14 Ill. 2d 356, 152 N.E.2d 858,*
*cert. denied, 358 U.S. 915 (1958)*

MR. JUSTICE BRISTOW delivered the opinion of the court:

[Action brought in Illinois under the Michigan wrongful death act. Defendant employer then obtained an *ex parte* injunction from a Michigan court, which ordered the plaintiff not to proceed with the Illinois suit. After being threatened with imprisonment for contempt in Michigan, for failing to withdraw the Illinois suit, plaintiff asked an Illinois court to stop the defendant from harassing her. In response, an Illinois judge ordered defendant to refrain from proceeding against plaintiff in Michigan. The Illinois Supreme Court then considered the problem.]

With reference to the Michigan injunction, while we quite agree with defendant's repeated assertion that a court of equity has power to restrain persons within its jurisdiction from instituting or proceeding with foreign actions, we note that the exercise of such power by equity courts has been deemed a matter of great delicacy, invoked with great restraint to avoid distressing conflicts and reciprocal interference with jurisdiction.

Illinois has consistently followed the course of refusing to restrain the prosecution of a prior instituted action pending in a sister State unless a clear equity is presented requiring the interposition of the court to prevent a manifest wrong and injustice; and neither a difference of remedy afforded by the domicile and the forum nor mere inconvenience and expense of defending will constitute grounds for such an injunction. That course is based on the policy that after suits are commenced in one State, it is inconsistent with inter-State harmony if their prosecution be controlled by the courts of another State.

Conversely, where other States have enjoined litigants from proceeding with a previously instituted Illinois action, this jurisdiction has followed the overwhelming judicial opinion that neither the full-faith-and-credit clause nor rules of comity require compulsory recognition of such injunctions so as to abate or preclude the disposition of the pending case.

Therefore, it is evident that legal consistency, as well as the weight of authority, do not require us to recognize the Michigan injunction, and we may retain jurisdiction and proceed with plaintiffs wrongful death action. Such a course, however, is not practicable in the instant case, unless plaintiff, who is subject to imprisonment and other coercive tactics if she fails to dismiss her Illinois action, is protected by enjoining defendant from enforcing the Michigan injunction by contempt proceedings. A plaintiff cannot be expected or required to risk imprisonment so that the court may retain jurisdiction of a cause.

This brings us to the ultimate issue in this case: whether the court which first acquires jurisdiction of the parties and of the merits of the cause can issue a counter-injunction restraining a party before it from enforcing an out-of-State injunction which requires the dismissal of the local cause and ousts the forum of jurisdiction.

[W]e cannot close our eyes to the fact that the intended effect of the Michigan injunction, though directed at the parties and not at this court, is to prevent the Illinois court from adjudicating a cause of action of which it had proper jurisdiction. For it is patent that if the litigants are coerced to dismiss the Illinois action, it is our rightfully acquired jurisdiction that is thereby destroyed. Therefore, the Michigan injunction was in everything but form an order restraining the Illinois court and determining the cases it may properly try.

[T]he Illinois court should be entitled to the same respect for its jurisdiction that it accords the courts of other States, and in the absence of such respect, should be able to protect its jurisdiction from unjustifiable interference by the courts of other States. It is one thing for Illinois to have a policy against enjoining pending litigation on the merits in other States, in the absence of cogent equitable grounds, but it is quite another to stand by impotently and see a litigant, in a case of which the Illinois court has prior jurisdiction of the merits, forced by an out-of-State injunction to dismiss that legitimate cause of action for no reason other than that defendant would prefer to defend the lawsuit elsewhere. Reluctance to be an interloper is not synonymous with abdication.

The Illinois court is not so barren of authority, nor so calcified in its reasoning, as to cower behind the equitable maxim that "equity acts *in personam*," and to parrot, as defendant urges, that it is only the litigants and not the jurisdiction of this court that is being interfered with by the Michigan injunction. We are entitled to recognize that their coercion destroys our jurisdiction, and unless we can protect the litigant from such coercion, it is idle to say that we can protect our jurisdiction.

*Reversed and remanded.*

MR. JUSTICE SCHAEFER, dissenting:

I agree with the majority that in situations like the present one, the useful maxim "equity acts *in personam*" does not tell the full story. By concentrating upon the immediate effect of the injunction it overlooks the purpose for which it was sought and the result that it must achieve if it is to accomplish its purpose. When the Chancellor, in Bacon's day, enjoined the successful party from enforcing the judgment he had obtained at law, the end result was an interference with the processes of the law courts. In the same way, if the Michigan injunction accomplishes its purpose, the operation of the Illinois courts will have been interfered with. It is this inevitable interference with the operation of the courts of sister States that has largely prompted this court's reluctance to authorize the issuance of such injunctions. And I think that this inevitable interference has a bearing upon the claim of such an injunction to recognition under the full-faith-and-credit clause.

So far as I have been able to ascertain, no court has as yet held that such an injunction is entitled to full faith and credit in the sense that the action toward which the injunction is directed must be abated. When such injunctions have been recognized, it has been because the state in which the action is pending has chosen to do so as a matter of comity, and not because it was required to do so by constitutional command.

But the question in this case goes a step beyond the issue as to full faith and credit. What is here sought is a counter-injunction to restrain the railroad from enforcing the injunction entered by the Michigan court.

The place to stop this unseemly kind of judicial disorder is where it begins. The peculiar preference of one State for a particular venue in a single class of cases does not, it seems to me, afford a basis for indirect interference with litigation pending in another jurisdiction. The salutary power of a court of equity to restrain the prosecution of inequitable actions in a foreign court originated and developed upon more substantial considerations. But we are not called upon to review the propriety of the Michigan injunction. Plaintiff did not seek to review it in the Michigan courts.

HERSHEY and DAVIS, JJ., join in this dissent.

## NOTES AND QUESTIONS ON *JAMES*

(1) *Anti-Suit Injunctions.* The majority thought that an injunction directed at litigation elsewhere should be granted but rarely. Yet the court thought the decree under review proper. Why? Is the Michigan litigation "vexatious"? Why?

Justice Schaefer is surely correct in dissent that this whole mess is unseemly. But does he pay enough attention to the plight of the poor plaintiff who is trying to recover for the alleged wrongful death of her husband? Or is there something that plaintiff could have done—but did not do—in Michigan which might have alleviated this whole problem?

In our federal system, is there any longer any reason to tolerate situations like that in *James?* Can't the Chancellor's wise use of his discretionary powers, along with the doctrine of *forum non conveniens,* eliminate situations such as that found in *James?* For a view that injunctions like the one issued by the Michigan Court are entitled to full faith and credit, *see* Comment, *Full Faith and Credit to Foreign Injunctions,* 29 U. CHI. L. REV. 740 (1962).

The injunction against intrastate divorce litigation has been a particular thorn in the judicial side. *See* Robert Leflar, et al., American Conflicts Law § 229 (4th ed. 1986).

(2) *The International Problem.* The problem of injunctions against litigation conducted in other countries has grown rapidly in recent years. Two leading cases are *In re Unterweser Reederei,* GMBH, 428 F.2d 888 (5th Cir. 1970), *aff'd on reh'g en banc,* 446 F.2d 907 (5th Cir. 1971), *vacated on other grounds, sub nom, The Bremen v. Zapata Off-Shore Co.,* 407 U.S. 1 (1972), and *Laker Airways, Ltd v. Sabena, Belgian World Airlines,* 731 F.2d 909 (D.C. Cir. 1984).

*Unterweser* held that it was proper to enjoin a party from proceeding in a foreign forum if the American court has jurisdiction; if the actions are essentially duplicative; and if the foreign action is vexatious, threatens the American court's jurisdiction, or involves an important policy of the American forum. *Laker* involved a much more narrow use of the injunction against foreign litigation. The American court was petitioned to enjoin attempts in England to restrain proceedings in this country; no attempt was made to enjoin the parties from going to judgment abroad on the underlying claim. The injunction was granted in order to preserve the jurisdiction of the American court, and because its issuance would not violate generally accepted notions of international comity.[22]

The European Union, in contrast to the American practice, follows a first-in-time rule. *See* Peter Herzog, *The Common Market Convention on Jurisdiction and the Enforcement of Judgment,* 17 VA. J. INT'L. L.J. 417 (1977). *See*

---

[22] American attempts to enforce American law in other countries have been deeply resented. *See, e.g.,* Comment, *Foreign Nondisclosure Laws and Domestic Discovery Orders in Antitrust Litigation,* 88 YALE L.J. 612 (1979). *See generally* RESTATEMENT (THIRD) OF THE FOREIGN RELATIONS LAW OF THE UNITED STATES (REVISED) § 437.

*generally* Teresa Baer, Note, *Injunctions Against Prosecution of Litigation Abroad: Towards a Transnational Approach,* 37 STAN. L. REV. 155 (1984).

(3)  *The Preclusive Effect of Injunction Proceedings.*

(a) *The Injunction Denied in F-1.* Should any preclusive effect attach to the denial of injunctive relief? Does it matter whether relief was denied because the Chancellor exercised her discretion as a dispenser of equity not to grant it or because the Chancellor found that the facts did not entitle the petitioner to relief. (Hint: Is either of those decisions "on the merits"?) For an argument that recognition would be proper in both situations, *see Developments in the Law—Injunctions, Problems of the Injunction in a Multi-Jurisdictional Context,* 78 HARV. L. REV. 1031, 1041-42 (1965).

(b) *The Injunction Granted in F-1.* Consider a baseball player under contract to the Philadelphia Phillies who "jumps" teams to play for the Cleveland Indians. The Phillies then obtain an injunction in Pennsylvania, ordering the player not to play for any other team during his contract term with the Phillies if the Phillies ask an Ohio court to enjoin the player from playing in Ohio, must the courts of that state recognize the earlier Pennsylvania injunction? In *Philadelphia Baseball Club Co. v. Lajoie,* 13 Ohio Dec. 504 (C.P. 1902), the court said no. [23] It reasoned that the injunction ordered by the Pennsylvania court was based on the legal theory of negative enforcement of employment contracts, a theory not recognized in Ohio because it infringes personal liberty. What does *Fauntleroy v. Lum* (*see* § 7.07, *supra*) have to say on that point?

Or could the Chancellor simply refuse to issue the order because supervising its enforcement would impose too great a strain on the legal system—an especially appealing argument where the case is one in which the forum has little interest. Does it matter that an enforcing Chancellor would not have the opportunity to decide whether to exercise his discretion? It is generally said that full faith and credit need not be given a decree such as that rendered by the Pennsylvania court in *Lajoie. See, e.g., Developments in the Law—Injunctions,* 78 HARV. L. REV. 1031 (1965). For more on the *Lajoie* case, see J. Weistart & C. Lowell, The Law of Sports 472-73 (1979). Although the Restatement (First) of Conflict of Laws § 449 agreed that an equity decree based on an exercise of discretion need not be recognized, the Second Restatement refused to take a position on the issue. *See* § 102, comment *c.*

Consider, in response, Professor Barbour's argument made long ago:

> The doctrine that a cause of action is distinguished by or merged in a legal judgment results from the policy that there be an end of litigation. The same considerations of policy demand that equal effect be given to the equitable decree.

Willard Barbour, *The Extra-Territorial Effect of The Equitable Decree,* 17 MICH. L. REV. 527, 545 (1919).

(4) The *Baker* case. The question of whether the same full faith credit should be applied to both legal and equitable decrees was addressed again by the Supreme Court in *Baker v. General Motors,* discussed in § 7.09[D], *infra.*

---

[23] The player in the case was Napoleon Lajoie, one of the greatest second basemen ever to play the game.

## [D]   Public Policy and Full Faith and Credit

## YARBOROUGH v. YARBOROUGH

*United States Supreme Court*
*290 U.S. 202, 54 S. Ct. 181, 78 L. Ed 269 (1933)*

[The Yarboroughs lived in Georgia until their separation in 1927. The Georgia divorce court awarded custody of Sadie, the daughter, to her mother, and ordered the father to make one lump sum payment of $1,750 as support for Sadie. Sadie, who was not a party to the divorce action, moved to South Carolina to live with her grandfather. She later sued her father for more support, alleging that unless she received more she "will be denied the necessities of life and an education, and will be dependent upon the charity of others." The South Carolina court obtained personal jurisdiction over Mr. Yarborough and ordered him to pay Sadie $50/month.]

MR. JUSTICE BRANDEIS delivered the opinion of the Court.

[The Court first found that the Georgia support order was "intended" to absolve Sadie's father from further obligation to support her."]

Second. The Georgia decisions have settled that a consent decree or order fixing permanent alimony for a minor child, at whatever stage of the divorce proceedings it may have been entered, has the same effect as if based upon, and specifically mentioned in, the second verdict of a jury; and that such an order, like any other judgment, becomes unalterable after the expiration of the term.

Third. It is contended that the Georgia decree is not binding upon Sadie, because she was not a formal party to the suit, was not served with process and no guardian ad item was appointed for her therein. In Georgia, as elsewhere, a property right of a minor can ordinarily be affected by legal proceedings only if these requirements are complied with. But the obligation imposed by the Georgia law upon the father to support his minor child does not vest in the child a property right. The provision which the Georgia law makes of permanent alimony for the child during minority is a legal incident of the divorce proceeding. As that suit embraces within its scope the disposition and care of minor children, jurisdiction over the parents confers *eo ipso* jurisdiction over the minor's custody and support. Hence, by the Georgia law, a consent (or other) decree in a divorce suit, fixing permanent alimony for a minor child is binding upon it, although the child was not served with process, was not made a formal party to the suit, and no guardian ad litem was appointed therein.

Fourth. It is contended that the order for permanent alimony is not binding upon Sadie because she was not a resident of Georgia at the time it was entered. Being a minor, Sadie's domicile was Georgia, that of her father; and her domicile continued to be in Georgia until entry of the judgment in question. She was not capable by her own act of changing her domicile. The character and extent of the father's obligation, and the status of the minor, are determined ordinarily not by the place of the minor's residence but by the law of the father's domicile. Moreover, this is not a case where the scope of the jurisdiction acquired by the Georgia court rests upon the effectiveness of service by publication upon a nonresident. Mrs. Yarborough filed a cross-bill, as well as an answer; and in the cross-bill prayed "that provision for permanent alimony be made for the" support and education of Sadie. Thus the court acquired complete jurisdiction of the marriage status and, as an incident, power to finally determine the extent of her father's obligation to support his minor child.

Fifth. The fact that Sadie had become a resident of South Carolina does not impair the finality of the judgment. South Carolina thereby acquired the jurisdiction to determine her status and the incidents of that status. Upon residents of that state it could impose duties for her benefit. Doubtless, it might have imposed upon her grandfather who was resident there a duty to support Sadie. But the mere fact of Sadie's residence in South Carolina does not give that state the power to impose such a duty upon the father who is not a resident and who long has been domiciled in Georgia. He has fulfilled the duty which he owes her by the law of his domicile and the judgment of its court. Upon that judgment he is entitled to rely. It was settled by *Sistare v. Sistare,* 218 U.S. 1, that the Full Faith and Credit Clause applies to an unalterable decree of alimony for a divorced wife. The clause applies, likewise, to an unalterable decree of alimony for a minor child. We need not consider whether South Carolina would have power to require the father, if he were domiciled there, to make further provision for the support, maintenance, or education of his daughter.

*Reversed.*

MR. JUSTICE STONE, dissenting.

I think the judgment should be affirmed.

The divorce decree of the Georgia court purported to adjudicate finally, both for the present and for the future, the right of a minor child of the marriage to support and maintenance, by directing her father to make a lump sum payment for that purpose. More than two years later, after the minor had become a domiciled resident of South Carolina, and after the sum paid had been exhausted, a court of that State, on the basis of her need as then shown, has rendered a judgment directing further payments for her support out of property of the father in South Carolina, in addition to that already commanded by the Georgia judgment.

[T]here is nothing in the decree itself, or in the history of the proceedings which led to it, to suggest that it was rendered with any purpose or intent to regulate or control the relationship of parent and child, or the duties which flow from it, in places outside the State of Georgia where they might later come to reside. It would hardly be thought that Georgia, by judgment of its courts more than by its statutes, would attempt to regulate the relationship of parent and child domiciled outside of the State at the very time the decree was rendered; and, in the face of constitutional doubts that arise here, it is far from clear that its decree is to be interpreted as attempting to do more than to regulate that relationship while the infant continued to be domiciled within the State. But if we are to read the decree as though it contained a clause, in terms, restricting the power of any other state, in which the minor might come to reside, to make provision for her support, then, in the absence of some law of Congress requiring it, I am not persuaded that the Full Faith and Credit Clause gives sanction to such control by one state of the internal affairs of another. —

. . . In the assertion of rights, defined by a judgment of one state, within the territory of another, there is often an inescapable conflict of interest of the two States, and there comes a point beyond which the imposition of the will of one state beyond its own border involves a forbidden infringement of some legitimate domestic interest of the other. That point may vary with the circumstances of the case; and in the absence of provisions more specific than the general terms of the congressional enactment this Court must determine for itself the extent to which one state may qualify or deny rights claimed under proceedings or records of other states.

More than once this Court has approved the doctrine that a state need give no effect to judgments for conviction of crime or for penalties procured in a sister state. And the intervention of a sister state's judgment will not overcome a local policy against allowing to foreign corporations the use of local courts in settling foreign disputes. The Full Faith and Credit Clause does not require one state, at the behest of the courts of another, to surrender its powers to decide what criminal penalties it shall impose, to circumscribe, within limits, the classes of disputes to which its courts must give ear, or to protect its residents from undue interference with the marriage relationship.

The question presented here is whether the support and maintenance of a minor child, domiciled in South Carolina, is so peculiarly a subject of domestic concern that Georgia law cannot impair South Carolina's authority. The subject matter of the judgment in each state is the duty which government may impose on a parent to support a minor child. The maintenance and support of children domiciled within a state, like their education and custody, is a subject in which government itself is deemed to have a peculiar interest and concern . . . The states very generally make some provision from their own resources for the maintenance and support of orphans or destitute children, but in order that children may not become public charges the duty of maintenance is one imposed primarily upon the parents, according to the needs of the child and their ability to meet those needs . . . The measure of the duty is the needs of the child and the ability of the parent to meet those needs at the very time when performance of the duty is invoked. Hence, it is no answer in such a suit that at some earlier time provision was made for the child, which is no longer available or suitable because of his greater needs, or because of the increased financial ability of the parent to provide for them, or that the child may be maintained from other sources.

In view of the universality of these principles, it comes as a surprise that any state, merely because it has made some provision for the support of a child, should, either by statute or judicial decree, so tie its own hands as to foreclose all future inquiry into the duty of maintenance however affected by changed conditions.

Even though the Constitution does not deny to Georgia the power to indulge in such a policy for itself, it by no means follows that it gives to Georgia the privilege of prescribing that policy for other states in which the child comes to live. South Carolina has adopted a different policy. It imposes in the father or his property located within the state the duty to support his minor child domiciled there. It enforces the duty by criminal prosecution and also permits suit by the minor child maintained by guardian *ad litem*. The measure of the duty is the present need of the child and the ability of the parent to provide for it.

The Fourteenth Amendment does not enable a father, by the expedient of choosing a domicile other than the state where the child is rightfully domiciled, to avoid the duty which that state may impose for support of his child. The reason seems plain. The locality of the child's residence must see to his welfare. While it might be more convenient for creditors of the father to look to the law of his residence as fixing all his obligations, it would seem that the compelling interest in the welfare of children, to which performance of the duties of parentage is a necessary incident, outweighs commercial convenience; the more so where, as in this case, the obligation is to be satisfied from the father's property within the state of the child's domicile.

[I]t would not seem open to serious question that every state has an interest in securing the maintenance and support of minor children residing within its own territory so complete and so vital to the performance of its functions as a government that no other state could set limits upon it. Of that interest, South Carolina is the sole mistress within her own territory. Even though we might appraise it more lightly than does South Carolina, it is not for us to say that a state is not free, within constitutional limitations, to regard that interest as fully as important and as completely within the realm of state power as the legal incidents of land located within its boundaries, or of a marriage relationship, wherever entered into but of which it is the domicile, or its power to pass upon the sanity of its own residents, notwithstanding the earlier pronouncements of the courts of other states.

Here the Georgia decree did not end the relationship of parent and child, as a decree of divorce may end the marriage relationship. Had the infant continued to reside in Georgia, and had she sought in the courts of South Carolina to compel the application of property of her father, found there, to her further maintenance and support, full faith and credit to the Georgia decree applied to its own domiciled resident might have required the denial of any relief. But when she became a domiciled resident of South Carolina, a new interest came into being—the interest of the State of South Carolina as a measure of self-preservation to secure the adequate protection and maintenance of helpless members of its own community and its prospective citizens. That interest was distinct from any which Georgia could constitutionally regulate or control by its judgment, even though rendered while the child was domiciled in Georgia. The present decision extends the operation of the Full Faith and Credit Clause beyond its proper function of affording protection to the domestic interests of Georgia and makes it an instrument for encroachment by Georgia upon the domestic concerns of South Carolina.

MR. JUSTICE CARDOZO concurs in this opinion.

---

## NOTES AND QUESTIONS

(1) *The Georgia Decree.* The Georgian support order at issue in *Yarborough* is very strange in its finality. Support orders are almost always modifiable, at least prospectively. *See* § 8.17, *infra.* That makes Sadie's claim all the more appealing, doesn't it? Are you surprised by the mechanical nature of Justice Brandeis' majority opinion? Does he think this case differs at all from any other piece of civil litigation?

(2) *The Dissent.* Justice Stone's dissent is justly famous. It is certainly eloquent about the plight of poor Sadie; but what is Stone's legal theory? Does he believe that Sadie's welfare is essentially a local concern, to be tested by whatever state may happen to be her current domicile?

Is a better rationale available? Hint: Was Sadie a party to the Georgia action? Should that matter? Or are her interests adequately protected by her parents so that she can properly be said to be in privity with them, and, therefore, bound by ordinary principles of preclusion?

*See* PROBLEM 7B-19. TRAYNOR, J. AND *YARBOROUGH.*

---

## THOMAS v. WASHINGTON GAS LIGHT CO.

*United States Supreme Court*
*448 U.S. 261, 100 S. Ct. 2647, 65 L. Ed. 2d 757 (1980)*

MR. JUSTICE STEVENS announced the judgment of the Court and delivered an opinion, in which MR. JUSTICE BRENNAN, MR. JUSTICE STEWART, and MR. JUSTICE BLACKMUN joined.

Petitioner received an award of disability benefits under the Virginia Workmen's Compensation Act. The question presented is whether the obligation of the District of Columbia to give full faith and credit to that award bars a supplemental award under the District's Workmen's Compensation Act.

Petitioner is a resident of the District of Columbia and was hired in the District of Columbia. He sustained a back injury while at work in Arlington, Va., on January 22, 1971. Several weeks later the Virginia Industrial Commission issued its award directing that payments continue "during incapacity," subject to various contingencies and changes set forth in the Virginia statute.

In 1974, petitioner notified the Department of Labor of his intention to seek compensation under the District of Columbia Act. Respondent opposed the claim primarily on the ground that since, as a matter of Virginia law, the Virginia award excluded any other recovery "at common law or otherwise" on account of the injury in Virginia,[4] the District of Columbia's obligation to give that award full faith and credit precluded a second, supplemental award in the District.

The Administrative Law Judge held that the Virginia award, by its terms, did not preclude a further award of compensation in Virginia. Moreover, he construed the statutory prohibition against additional recovery "at common law or otherwise" as merely covering "common law and other remedies under Virginia law." [P]etitioner was awarded permanent total disability benefits with a credit for the amounts previously paid under the Virginia award.

## I

Respondent contends that the District of Columbia was without power to award petitioner additional compensation because of the Full Faith and Credit Clause of the Constitution or, more precisely, because of the federal statute implementing that Clause.[10] An analysis of this contention must begin with two decisions from the 1940's that are almost directly on point: *Magnolia Petroleum Co. v. Hunt,* 320 U.S. 430, and *Industrial Commission of Wisconsin v. McCartin,* 330 U.S. 622.

In *Magnolia* the employer hired a Louisiana worker in Louisiana. The employee was later injured during the course of his employment in Texas. A tenuous majority[11] held that Louisiana was not permitted to award the injured worker supplementary compensation under the Louisiana Act after he had already obtained a recovery from the Texas Industrial Accident Board:

> Respondent was free to pursue his remedy in either state but, having chosen to seek it in Texas, where the award was res judicata, the full faith and credit clause precludes him from again seeking a remedy in Louisiana upon the same grounds.

Little more than three years later, the Court severely curtailed the impact of *Magnolia.* In *McCartin,* the employer and the employee executed a contract for payment of a specific sum in full settlement of the employee's right under Illinois law. The contract expressly provided, however, that it would "'not affect any rights that applicant may have under the Workmen's Compensation Act of the State of Wisconsin.'" The employee then obtained a supplemental award from the Wisconsin Industrial Commission; but the Wisconsin state courts vacated it under felt compulsion of the intervening decision in *Magnolia.*

---

[4] Virginia Code § 65.1-40 (1980) provides:

> "Employee's rights under Act exclude all other.— The rights and remedies herein granted to an employee when he and his employer have excepted the provisions of this Act respectively to pay and accept compensation on account of personal injury or death by accident shall exclude all other rights and remedies of such employee, his personal representative, parents, dependents or next of kin, at common law or otherwise, on account of such injury, loss of service or death."

[10] The statute places on courts in the District of Columbia the same obligation to respect state judgments as is imposed on the courts of the several States.

[11] Four Members of the Court—Justices Black, Douglas, Murphy, and Rutledge dissented, expressing the opinion that the holding was not supported by precedent and did not accord proper respect to the States' interests in implementing their policies of compensating injured workmen.

This Court reversed, holding without dissent that *Magnolia* was not controlling. Although the Court could have relied exclusively on the contract provision reserving the employee's rights under Wisconsin law to distinguish the case from *Magnolia,* Mr. Justice Murphy's opinion provided a significantly different ground for the Court's holding when it said:

> "[T]he reservation spells out what we believe to be implicit in [the Illinois Workmen's Compensation] Act— namely, that an award of the type here involved does not foreclose an additional award under the laws of another state. And in the setting of this case, that fact is of decisive significance."

Earlier in the opinion, the Court had stated that "[o]nly some unmistakable language by a state legislature or judiciary would warrant our accepting a construction" that a workmen's compensation statute "is designed to preclude any recovery by proceedings brought in another state."

The Virginia Workmen's Compensation Act's exclusive-remedy provision, *see* fn. 4, *supra,* is not exactly the same as Illinois' but it contains no "unmistakable language" directed at precluding a supplemental compensation award in another State that was not also in the Illinois Act. Consequently, *McCartin* by its terms, rather than the earlier *Magnolia* decision, is controlling as between the two precedents. Nevertheless, the fact that we find ourselves comparing the language of two state statutes, neither of which has been construed by the highest court of either State, in an attempt to resolve an issue arising under the Full Faith and Credit Clause makes us pause to inquire whether there is a fundamental flaw in our analysis of this federal question.

## II

We cannot fail to observe that, in the Court's haste to retreat from *Magnolia,* it fashioned a rule that clashes with normally accepted full faith and credit principles. It has long been the law that "the judgment of a state court should have the same credit, validity, and effect, in every other court in the United States, which it had in the state where it was pronounced." *Hampton v. McConnel, 3* Wheat. 234, 235 (Marshall, C. J.). This rule, if not compelled by the Full Faith and Credit Clause itself, is surely required by 28 U.S.C. § 1738. Thus, in effect, by virtue of the full faith and credit obligations of the several States, a State is permitted to determine the extraterritorial effect of its judgments; but it may only do so indirectly, by prescribing the effect of its judgments within the State.

The *McCartin* rule, however, focusing as it does on the extraterritorial intent of the rendering State, is fundamentally different. It authorizes a State, by drafting or construing its legislation in "unmistakable language," directly to determine the extraterritorial effect of its workmen's compensation awards. [T]he *McCartin* unmistakable language rule represents an unwarranted delegation to the States of this Court's responsibility for the final arbitration of full faith and credit questions. To vest the power of determining the extraterritorial effect of a State's own laws and judgments in the State itself risks the very kind of parochial entrenchment on the interests of other States that it was the purpose of the Full Faith and Credit Clause and other provisions of Art. IV of the Constitution to prevent.

Thus, a re-examination of *McCartin's* "unmistakable language" test reinforces our tentative conclusion that it does not provide an acceptable basis on which to distinguish *Magnolia*. But if we reject that test, we must decide whether to overrule either *Magnolia* or *McCartin*.

### III

[A]s a practical matter the "unmistakable language" rule of construction announced in *McCartin* left only the narrowest area in which *Magnolia* could have any further precedential value. For the exclusivity language in the Illinois Act construed in *McCartin* was typical of most state workmen's compensation laws. Consequently, it was immediately recognized that *Magnolia* no longer had any significant practical impact. Moreover, since a state legislature seldom focuses on the extraterritorial effect of its enactments, and since a state court has even less occasion to consider whether an award under its State's law is intended to preclude a supplemental award under another State's Workmen's Compensation Act, the probability that any State would thereafter announce a new rule against supplemental awards in other States was extremely remote. As a matter of fact, subsequent cases in the state courts have overwhelmingly followed *McCartin* and permitted successive state workmen's compensation awards. Thus, all that really remained of *Magnolia* after *McCartin* was a largely theoretical difference between what the Court described as "unmistakable language" and the broad language of the exclusive-remedy provision in the Illinois Workmen's Compensation Act involved in *McCartin*.

This history indicates that the principal values underlying the doctrine of stare decisis would not be served either by attempting to revive *Magnolia* or by attempting to preserve the uneasy coexistence of *Magnolia* and *McCartin*. The latter attempt could only breed uncertainty and unpredictability, since the application of the "unmistakable language" rule of *McCartin* necessarily depends on a determination by one state tribunal of the effect to be given to statutory language enacted by the legislature of a different State. And the former would represent a rather dramatic change that surely would not promote stability in the law. Moreover, since *Magnolia* has been so rarely followed, there appears to be little danger that there has been any significant reliance on its rule. We conclude that a fresh examination of the full faith and credit issue is therefore entirely appropriate.

### IV

Three different state interests are affected by the potential conflict between Virginia and the District of Columbia. Virginia has a valid interest in placing a limit on the potential liability of companies that transact business within its borders. Both jurisdictions have a valid interest in the welfare of the injured employee—Virginia because the injury occurred within that State, and the District because the injured party was employed and resided there. And finally, Virginia has an interest in having the integrity of its formal determinations of contested issues respected by other sovereigns.

The conflict between the first two interests was resolved in *Alaska Packers Assn. v. Industrial Accident Commission,* 294 U.S. 532, and a series of later cases. In *Alaska Packers,* California, the State where the employment contract was made, was allowed to apply its own workmen's compensation statute despite the statute of Alaska, the place where the injury occurred, which was said to afford the exclusive remedy for injuries occurring there. The Court held that the conflict between the statutes of two States ought not to be resolved "by giving automatic effect to the full faith and credit clause, compelling the courts of each state to subordinate its own statutes to those of the other, but by appraising the governmental interests of each jurisdiction, and turning the scale of decision according to their weight."

It is thus perfectly clear that petitioner could have sought a compensation award in the first instance either in Virginia, the State in which the injury occurred, or in the District of Columbia, where petitioner resided, his employer was principally located, and the employment relation was formed. Compensation could have been sought under either compensation scheme even if one statute or the other purported to confer an exclusive remedy on petitioner. Thus, for all practical purposes, respondent and its insurer would have had to measure their potential liability exposure by the more generous of the two workmen's compensation schemes in any event. It follows that a State's interest in limiting the potential liability of businesses within the State is not of controlling importance.

It is also manifest that the interest in providing adequate compensation to the injured worker would be fully served by the allowance of successive awards. In this respect, the two jurisdictions share a common interest and there is no danger of significant conflict.

The ultimate issue, therefore, is whether Virginia's interest in the integrity of its tribunal's determinations forecloses a second proceeding to obtain a supplemental award in the District of Columbia. We return to the Court's prior resolution of this question in *Magnolia.*

[N]either *Magnolia* nor this case concerns a second State's contrary resolution of a factual matter determined in the first State's proceeding. [C]ompensation could be obtained under either Virginia's or the District's workmen's compensation statutes on the basis of the same set of facts. A supplemental award gives full effect to the facts determined by the first award and also allows full credit for payments pursuant to the earlier award. There is neither inconsistency nor double recovery.

But the critical differences between a court of general jurisdiction and an administrative agency with limited statutory authority forecloses the conclusion that constitutional rules applicable to court judgments are necessarily applicable to workmen's compensation awards.

A final judgment entered by a court of general jurisdiction normally establishes not only the measure of the plaintiffs rights but also the limits of the defendant's liability. A traditional application of res judicata principles enables either party to claim the benefit of the judgment insofar as it resolved issues the court had jurisdiction to decide. Although a Virginia court is free to recognize the perhaps paramount interests of another State by choosing to apply that State's law in a particular case, the Industrial Commission of Virginia does not have that power. Its jurisdiction is limited to questions arising under the Virginia Workmen's Compensation Act. Full faith and credit must be given to the determination that the Virginia Commission had the authority to make; but by a parity of reasoning, full faith and credit need not be given to determinations that it had no power to make. Since it was not requested, and had no authority, to pass on petitioner's rights under District of Columbia law, there can be no constitutional objection to a fresh adjudication of those rights.

It is true, of course, that after Virginia entered its award, that State has an interest in preserving the integrity of what it had done. And it is squarely within the purpose of the Full Faith and Credit Clause, as explained in *Pacific Employers* [306 U.S. 493, 501], "to preserve rights acquired or confirmed under the public acts" of Virginia by requiring other States to recognize their validity. Thus, Virginia had an interest in having respondent pay petitioner the amounts specified in its award. Allowing a supplementary recovery in the District does not conflict with that interest.

As we have already noted, Virginia also has a separate interest in placing a ceiling on the potential liability of companies that transact business within the State. But past cases have established that interest is not strong enough to prevent other States with overlapping jurisdiction over particular injuries from giving effect to their more generous compensation policies when the employee selects the most favorable forum in the first instance. Thus, the only situations in which the *Magnolia* rule would tend to serve that interest are those in which an injured workman has either been constrained by circumstances to seek relief in the less generous forum or has simply made an ill-advised choice of his first forum.

But in neither of those cases is there any reason to give extra weight to the first State's interest in placing a ceiling on the employer's liability than it otherwise would have had. For neither the first nor the second State has any overriding interest in requiring an injured employee to proceed with special caution when first asserting his claim. Compensation proceedings are often initiated informally, without the advice of counsel, and without special attention to the choice of the most appropriate forum. Often the worker is still hospitalized when benefits are sought as was true in this case. And indeed, it is not always the injured worker who institutes the claim. This informality is consistent with the interests of both States. A rule forbidding supplemental recoveries under more favorable workmen's compensation schemes would require a far more formal and careful choice on the part of the injured worker than may be possible or desirable when immediate commencement of benefits may be essential.

Thus, whether or not the worker has sought an award from the less generous jurisdiction in the first instance, the vindication of that State's interest in placing a ceiling on employers' liability would inevitably impinge upon the substantial interests of the second jurisdiction in the welfare and subsistence of disabled workers—interests that a court of general jurisdiction might consider, but which must be ignored by the Virginia Industrial Commission.

Of course, it is for each State to formulate its own policy whether to grant supplemental awards according to its perception of its own interests. We simply conclude that the substantial interests of the second State in these circumstances should not be overridden by another State through an unnecessarily aggressive application of the Full Faith and Credit Clause, as was implicitly recognized at the time of *McCartin.*

We therefore would hold that a State has no legitimate interest within the context of our federal system in preventing another State from granting a supplemental compensation award when that second State would have had the power to apply its workmen's compensation law in the first instance. The Full Faith and Credit Clause should not be construed to Preclude successive workmen's compensation awards. Accordingly, *Magnolia Petroleum Co. v. Hunt* should be overruled.

The judgment of the Court of Appeals is reversed, and the case is remanded.

MR. JUSTICE WHITE, with whom THE CHIEF JUSTICE and MR. JUSTICE POWELL join, concurring in the judgment.

I agree that the judgment of the Court of Appeals should be reversed, but I am unable to join in the reasoning by which the plurality reaches that result. Although the plurality argues strenuously that the rule of today's decision is limited to awards by state workmen's compensation boards, it seems to me that the underlying rationale goes much further. If the employer had exercised its statutory right of appeal to the Supreme Court of Virginia and that Court upheld the award, I presume that the plurality's rationale would nevertheless permit a subsequent award in the District of Columbia. Otherwise, employers interested in cutting off the possibility of a subsequent award in another jurisdiction need only seek judicial review of the award in the first forum. But if such a judicial decision is not preclusive in the second forum, then it appears that the plurality's rationale is not limited in its effect to judgments of administrative tribunals.

The plurality contends that unlike courts of general jurisdiction, workmen's compensation tribunals generally have no power to apply the law of another State and thus cannot determine the rights of the parties thereunder. Yet I see no reason why a judgment should not be entitled to full res judicata effect under the Full Faith and Credit Clause merely because the rendering tribunal was obligated to apply the law of the forum—provided, of course, as was certainly the case here, that the forum could constitutionally apply its law. The plurality's analysis seems to grant state legislatures the power to delimit the scope of a cause of action for federal full faith and credit purposes merely by enacting choice-of-law rules binding on the State's workmen's compensation tribunals. The plurality criticizes the *McCartin* case for vesting in the State the power to determine the extraterritorial effect of its own laws and judgments, yet it seems that its opinion is subject to the same objection.

As a matter of logic, the plurality's analysis would seemingly apply to many everyday tort actions. I see no difference for full faith and credit purposes between a statute which lays down a forum-favoring choice-of-law rule and a common-law doctrine stating the same principle. Hence when a court, having power in the abstract to apply the law of another State, determines by application of the forum's choice-of-law rules to apply the substantive law of the forum, I would think that under the plurality's analysis the judgment would not determine rights arising under the law of some other State. Suppose, for example, that in a wrongful-death action the court enters judgment on liability against the defendant, and determines to apply the law of the forum which sets a limit on the recovery allowed. The plurality's analysis would seem to permit the plaintiff to obtain a subsequent judgment in a second forum for damages exceeding the first forum's liability limit.

The plurality does say that factual determinations by a workmen's compensation board will be entitled to collateral-estoppel effect in a second forum. While this rule does, to an extent, circumscribe the broadest possible implications of the plurality's reasoning, there would remain many cases, such as the wrongful-death example discussed above, in which the second forum could provide additional recovery as a matter of substantive law while remaining true to the first forum's factual determinations. Moreover, the dispositive issues in tort actions are frequently mixed questions of law and fact as to which the second forum might apply its own rule of decision without obvious violation of the principles articulated by four Members of the Court. Actions by the defendant which satisfy the relevant standard of care in the first forum might nevertheless be considered "negligent" under the law of the second forum.

Hence the plurality's rationale would portend a wide-ranging reassessment of the principles of full faith and credit in many areas.

One purpose of the Full Faith and Credit Clause is to bring an end to litigation. The plurality's opinion is at odds with this principle of finality. Plaintiffs dissatisfied with a judgment would have every incentive to seek additional recovery elsewhere, so long as the first forum applied its own law and there was a colorable argument that as a matter of law the second forum would permit a greater recovery. It seems to me grossly unfair that the plaintiff, having the initial choice of the forum, should be given the additional advantage of a second adjudication should his choice prove disappointing. Defendants, on the other hand, would no longer be assured that the judgment of the first forum is conclusive as to their obligations, and would face the prospect of burdensome and multiple litigation based on the same operative facts. Such litigation would also impose added strain on an already overworked judicial system.

Perhaps the major purpose of the Full Faith and Credit Clause is to act as a nationally unifying force. The plurality's rationale would substantially undercut that function. When a former judgment is set up as a defense under the Full Faith and Credit Clause, the court would be obliged to balance the various state interests involved. But the State of the second forum is not a neutral party to this balance. There seems to be a substantial danger—not presented by the firmer rule of res judicata—that the court in evaluating a full faith and credit defense would give controlling weight to its own parochial interests in concluding that the judgment of the first forum is not res judicata in the subsequent suit.

I would not overrule either *Magnolia* or *McCartin*. To my mind, Mr. Chief Justice Stone's opinion in *Magnolia* states the sounder doctrine; as noted, I do not see any overriding differences between Workmen's compensation awards and court judgments that justify different treatment for the two. However, *McCartin* has been on the books for over 30 years and has been widely interpreted by state and federal courts as substantially limiting *Magnolia*. Unlike the plurality's opinion, *McCartin* is not subject to the objection that its principles are applicable outside the workmen's compensation area. Although I find *McCartin* to rest on questionable foundations, I am not now prepared to overrule it. And I agree with the plurality that *McCartin,* rather than *Magnolia,* is controlling as between the two precedents since the Virginia Workmen's Compensation Act lacks the "unmistakable language" which *McCartin* requires if a workmen's compensation award is to preclude a subsequent award in another State. I therefore concur in the judgment.

MR. JUSTICE REHNQUIST, with whom MR. JUSTICE MARSHALL joins, dissenting.

This is clearly a case where the whole is less than the sum of its parts. In choosing between two admittedly inconsistent precedents, *Magnolia Petroleum Co. v. Hunt,* and *Industrial Comm'n of Wisconsin v. McCartin,* six of us agree that the latter decision, *McCartin,* is analytically indefensible. The remaining three Members of the Court concede that it rest[s] on questionable foundations." Nevertheless, when the smoke clears, it is *Magnolia* rather than *McCartin* that the plurality suggests should be overruled. Because I believe that Magnolia was correctly decided, and because I fear that the rule proposed by the plurality is both ill-considered and ill-defined, I dissent.

One might suppose that, having destroyed *McCartin's* ratio decidendi, the plurality would return to the eminently defensible position adopted in *Magnolia.* But such is not the case. The plurality instead raises the banner of "stare decisis" and sets out in search of a new rationale to support the result reached in *McCartin,* significantly failing to even attempt to do the same thing for *Magnolia.*

If such *post hoc* rationalization seems a bit odd, the theory ultimately chosen by the plurality is even odder. It would seem that, contrary to the assumption of this Court for at least the past 40 years, a judgment awarding workmen's compensation benefits is no longer entitled to full faith and credit unless, and only to the extent that, such, a judgment resolves a disputed issue of fact. I believe that the plurality's justification for such a theory, which apparently first surfaced in a cluster of articles written in the wake of *Magnolia,* does not withstand close scrutiny.

The plurality identifies three different "state interests" at stake in the present case: Virginia's interest in placing a limit on the potential liability of companies doing business in that State; Virginia's interest in the "integrity of its formal determinations of contested issue"; and a shared interest of Virginia and the District of Columbia in the welfare of the injured employee. The plurality then undertakes to balance these interests and concludes that none of Virginia's concerns outweighs the concern of the District of Columbia for the welfare of petitioner.

Whenever this Court, or any court, attempts to balance competing interests it risks undervaluing or even overlooking important concerns. I believe that the plurality's analysis incorporates both errors. First, it asserts that Virginia's interest in limiting the liability of businesses operating within its borders can never outweigh the District of Columbia's interest in protecting its residents. In support of this proposition it cites *Alaska Packers* and *Pacific Employers*. Both of those cases, however, involved the degree of faith and credit to be afforded statutes of one State by the courts of another State. The present case involves an enforceable judgment entered by Virginia after adjudicatory proceedings. In *Magnolia*, Mr. Chief Justice Stone, who authored both *Alaska Packers* and *Pacific Employers*, distinguished those two decisions for precisely this reason, chastising the lower court in that case for overlooking "the distinction, long recognized and applied by this Court, between the faith and credit required to be given to judgments and that to which local common and statutory law is entitled under the Constitution and laws of the United States." This distinction, which has also been overlooked by the plurality here, makes perfect sense, since Virginia surely has a stronger interest in limiting an employer's liability to a fixed amount when that employer has already been haled before a Virginia tribunal and adjudged liable than when the employer simply claims the benefit of a Virginia statute in a proceeding brought in another State.

In a similar vein, the plurality completely ignores any interest that Virginia might assert in the finality of its adjudications. While workmen's compensation awards may be "non-final" in the sense that they are subject to continuing supervision and modification, Virginia nevertheless has a cognizable interest in requiring persons who avail themselves of its statutory remedy to eschew other alternative remedies that might be available to them. Otherwise, as apparently is the result here, Virginia's efforts and expense on an applicant's behalf are wasted when that applicant obtains a duplicative remedy in another State.

At base, the plurality's balancing analysis is incorrect because it recognizes no significant difference between the events that transpired in this case and those that would have transpired had petitioner initially sought his remedy in the District of Columbia. But there are differences. The Commonwealth of Virginia has expended its resources, at petitioner's behest, to provide petitioner with a remedy for his injury and a resolution of his "dispute" with his employer. That employer similarly has expended its resources, again at petitioner's behest, in complying with the judgment entered by Virginia. These efforts, and the corresponding interests in seeing that those efforts are not wasted, lie at the very heart of the divergent constitutional treatment of judgments and statutes.

In further support of its novel rule, the plurality attempts to distinguish the judgment entered in this case from one entered by a "court of general jurisdiction." Specifically, the plurality points out that the Industrial Commission of Virginia, unlike a state court of general jurisdiction, was limited by statute to consideration of Virginia law. According to the plurality, because the Commission "was not requested, and had no authority, to pass on petitioner's rights under District of Columbia law, there can be no constitutional objection to a fresh adjudication of those rights."

This argument might have some force if petitioner had somehow had Virginia law thrust upon him against his will. In this case, however, petitioner was free to choose the applicable law simply by choosing the forum in which he filed his initial claim. Unless the District of Columbia has an interest in forcing its residents to accept its law regardless of their wishes, I fail to see how the Virginia Commission's inability to look to District of Columbia law impinged upon that latter jurisdiction's interests. I thus fail to see why petitioner's election, as consummated in his Virginia award, should not be given the same full faith and credit as would be afforded a judgment entered by a court of general jurisdiction.

I suspect that my Brethren's insistence on ratifying *McCartin's* result despite condemnation of its rationale is grounded in no small part upon their concern that injured workers are often coerced or maneuvered into filing their claims in jurisdictions amenable to their employers. There is, however, absolutely no evidence of such overreaching in the present case. Indeed, had there been "fraud, imposition, [or] mistake" in the filing of petitioner's claim, he would have been permitted, upon timely motion, to vacate the award.

I fear that the plurality, in its zeal to remedy a perceived imbalance in bargaining power, would badly distort an important constitutional tenet. Its "interest analysis," once removed from the statutory choice-of-law context considered by the Court in *Alaska Packers* and *Pacific Employers,* knows no metes or bounds. Given the modem proliferation of quasi-judicial methods for resolving disputes and of various tribunals of limited jurisdiction, such a rule could only lead to confusion. I find such uncertainty unacceptable, and prefer the rule originally announced in *Magnolia Petroleum Co. v. Hunt,* a rule whose analytical validity is, even yet, unchallenged.

The Full Faith and Credit Clause did not allot to this Court the task of "balancing" interests where the "public Acts, Records, and judicial Proceedings" of a State were involved. It simply directed that they be given the "Full Faith and Credit" that the Court today denies to those of Virginia. I would affirm the judgment of the court below.

*See* PROBLEM 7B-20. THE PIPE STABBER.

---

## CONFUSION AT THE TOP:
## NOTES AND QUESTIONS ON *THOMAS v. WASHINGTON GAS LIGHT*

(1) *The Plurality.* The plurality rejects the *McCartin* "unmistakable language" approach because the extraterritorial effect of the state court judgment is a question for the Supreme Court rather than for state legislatures. That makes sense. Yet, it certainly is hornbook law that the preclusive effect of an opinion is determined by the law of the rendering jurisdiction. *See* Restatement (Second) of Conflict of Laws § 97. Can you resolve this apparent contradiction?

The plurality opinion rejected both *McCartin* and *Magnolia.* The problem with *McCartin* was the "not intended" language. Justice Stevens argued that a state can prescribe the extraterritorial effects of its judgment only indirectly, by determining what the effect of a judgment will be *within* the state; a state cannot, he argued, directly determine the extra-territorial effects of its judgments by statutory expressions of its "intent." Does Steven's argument make sense? Is it consistent with the law of full faith and credit generally. The Stevens opinion then rejected *Magnolia* because it was contrary to long-standing practice in the states, and because *Magnolia* had been severely undercut by *McCartin*. Stevens accordingly, did not feel constrained to follow either precedent.

Justice Stevens then considered what the rule should be. He identified three interests that might be relevant. The first two—Virginia's interest in limiting the liability of its employees and each jurisdiction's interest in protecting injured workers—got short shrift from the plurality. What arguments did the opinion use to discount these interests? How sound were they? The third interest—Virginia's concern over the integrity of its quasi-judicial proceeding—receives more extended treatment. Do you think the plurality dealt adequately with this issue? Is there any difference between workers' compensation cases and other tort actions? If not, then isn't the effect of the plurality opinion in *Thomas*—if it were the law—to render the Full Faith and Credit Clause nugatory? In other words, if Virginia workers' compensation awards are not entitled to full faith and credit, why should other Virginia awards (such as one made in an automobile accident case) be recognized?

Or is there something special about the nature of the tribunal that made the award in *Thomas?*

Professor Sterk writes that because the object of the Full Faith and Credit Clause is "national unification within the context of a federal system" the forum a state chooses to resolve disputes should be irrelevant: "[T]he state's resolutions should be no less binding because the rendering tribunal is not a traditional court. It is the determination, not the determiner, that requires full faith and credit." Stewart Sterk, *Full Faith and Credit, More or Less, To Judgments: Doubts About Thomas v. Washington Gas Light Co.,* 69 GEO. L.J. 1329, 1355-56 (1981). Do you agree? Note also the dissent's argument that arbitration awards are generally entitled to recognition. Is there any real difference between the workers' compensation panel in *Thomas* and an arbitration panel?

What of Justice Stevens's point that the Virginia compensation tribunal could *not* consider the laws of other states? Does that mean, as Justice White argues, that a decision resting on a statute which imposes a rigid, statutory choice of law rule does not have to be recognized? *Cf.* Md. Ann. Code Cts. & Jud. Proc., § 3903(a) (les locus delictus to be applied in wrongful death cases).

(2) *The Concurrence.* Is Justice White's concurring opinion any more satisfactory? His attack on the plurality opinion is quite strong, especially his exposure of the fallacy of the argument that anything turns on the fact that the Workmen's Compensation Commission could not consider applying the laws of any other state. Justice White settled on the *McCartin,* approach; even though it rests on "questionable foundations." Nevertheless, he voted to keep it alive, albeit limited to workers' compensation cases.

What do you think of White's resolution of the problem? It certainly limits the scope (damage?) of the plurality opinion, doesn't it? And who really is upset if an injuredworker gets a little money from a big public utility? Some commentators like Justice White's approach, expressing the opinion, for example, that this is an issue "which is more important to settle than to settle correctly." WILLIAM M. RICHMAN & WILLIAM L. Reynolds, UNDERSTANDING CONFLICT OF LAWS § 106 (3d ed. 2002).

Nevertheless, there is (or should be) a nagging concern: Does our system of precedent really permit the carving out by courts of special exceptions which are not based on precedent as Justice White would do? Isn't precedent supposed to extend to all situations covered by the ratio decidendi of the case? *See generally* WILLIAM L. REYNOLDS, JUDICIAL PROCESS IN A NUTSHELL (3d ed. 2002). Obviously, Justice White's ad hoc approach violates that tenet.

(3) *The Dissent.* That leaves us with the dissent. That opinion is clearly correct, is it not? Or would it be wrong to overrule precedent that has stood for forty years? Has anyone relied on the *McCartin* rule? If not, should it be consigned to the dustbin of history? If you don't like the three proposed solutions to the problem, can you think of a better one?

Finally, can you think of any other case in which Justices Marshall and Rehnquist were united in the way they are in *Thomas?* Does that give you a clue as to the strangeness of the problem (and of its result)?

(4) *An Evaluation of Thomas By a Test Case.* Should it matter that Thomas had an option, following his injury, to sue either in Virginia or the District of Columbia? An instructive case is *Semler v. Psychiatric Institute of Washington, D.C.,* 575 F.2d 922 (D.C. Cir. 1978), involving an attempt, following a successful wrongful death action in Virginia, to recover survivor's benefits under District of Columbia law. The court rejected that attempt, in part because plaintiff could have sued originally in either jurisdiction. Plaintiff attempted to analogize her case to *McCartin* because District of Columbia law, unlike Virginia law, distinguished between wrongful death and survivor's recovery. As a result, a District of Columbia court, sitting in a domestic case, would hold that the plaintiff had not split her cause of action and would permit the later recovery. Judge Wilkey, writing before *Thomas* was decided, had no difficulty in distinguishing the workers' compensation cases: "[W]hile the principles enunciated in *Magnolia Petroleum* may have been modified by *McCartin* in the context of workmen's compensation cases, they retain their vitality in the ordinary choice-of-law case." 575 F.2d at 930 fn. 41. In other words, plaintiff's suit in the District was barred because it would have been barred in Virginia, the rendering state.

What would the result have been if *Semler* had arisen after the decision in *Thomas?* Does the extra-territorial intent argument of *McCartin* help plaintiff? What about the *Thomas* plaintiff's argument based on the limited authority of the tribunal?

(5) A few years after the decision in *Thomas,* the Court held that the basic Full Faith and Credit statute, 28 U.S.C. § 1738, does not apply either to administrative or arbitral decisions. *See,* respectively, *Univ. of Tenn. v. Elliott,* 478 U.S. 788 (1986), and *McDonald v. City of W. Branch,* 466 U.S. 284 (1984).

## NOTE ON PUBLIC POLICY, FULL FAITH AND CREDIT AND § 103 OF THE RESTATEMENT (SECOND)

Restatement (Second) of Conflict of Laws § 103 provides: *

A judgment rendered in one State of the United States need not be recognized or enforced in a sister State if such recognition or enforcement is not required by the national policy of full faith and credit because it would involve an improper interference with important interests of the sister State.

Comment; b to § 103 explains that "[t]here will be extremely rare occasions when the policy embodied in full faith and credit will give way before the national policy that requires protection of the dignity and of the fundamental interests of each individual State." As authority, the Reporter's Reporter's Note to § 103 refers the reader to Justice Stone's dissenting opinion in *Yarborough* and to his majority opinions in *Magnolia Petroleum* and *Milwaukee County v. M. E. White Co.*, 296 U.S. 268 (1935). The Note also refers to *McCartin*, two concurring opinions in domestic relation cases, and an article co-authored by the Reporter of the Second Restatement, Willis L. M. Reese and Vincent Johnson, *The Scope of Full Faith and Credit to Judgments*, 49 COLUM. L. REV. 153 (1949).[1]

Does § 103 "restate" the law accurately? Or does it run up against the brick wall built by *Fauntleroy v. Lum* ? Expressed differently, does interest analysis have a role to play when it comes time to enforce a judgment? Or should the balance-of-interests test found in the *Thomas* plurality be discarded?

Is there a fundamental difference between balancing interests while litigation is pending and doing so after a judgment has been rendered? As Professor Sterk observes: "The authority to resolve disputes between the parties over whom the sovereign has power is one of the basic attributes of sovereignty." Stewart Sterk, *Full Faith and Credit, More or Less, to Judgment: Doubts About Thomas v. Washington Gas Light Co.*, 69 GEO. L.J. 1329, 1346-47 (1981). Is there really an answer to that argument? Do you agree that § 103 is "totally unsupported by authority, policy, or reason." ALBERT EHRENZWEIG & DAVID Louisell, JURISDICTION IN A NUTSHELL (3d ed. 1973).

One last thought on § 103. Suppose Notre Dame and Miami play for the national championship in football. The governors of Indiana and Florida, each certain of victory, make a wager. Each promises that if his team loses, he will not run for re-election. Miami wins, and Florida's governor sues his Indiana counterpart for specific performance in a Florida court, obtaining jurisdiction by personal service in Florida. The Florida court enjoins the defendant's

---

* Copyright American Law Institute. Reprinted with permission.

[1] This article supplied much of the thinking for the plurality opinion in the *Thomas* case, although strangely enough, it was cited only in Justice White's concurring opinion.

running for re-election in Indiana. What happens when plaintiff attempts to get full faith and credit for that order in Indiana?

## BAKER and THOMAS v. GENERAL MOTORS CORP.

*Supreme Court of the United States*
*522 U.S. 222 (1998)*

Justice GINSBURG delivered the opinion of the Court.

This case concerns the authority of one State's court to order that a witness' testimony shall not be heard in any court of the United States . . . .

Two lawsuits, initiated by different parties in different states, gave rise to the full faith and credit issue before us. One suit involved a severed employment relationship, the other, a wrongful-death complaint. We describe each controversy in turn.

### The Suit Between Elwell and General Motors

Ronald Elwell was a GM employee from 1959 until 1989. For fifteen of those years, beginning in 1971, Elwell was assigned to the Engineering Analysis Group, which studied the performance of GM vehicles, most particularly vehicles involved in product liability litigation. Elwell's studies and research concentrated on vehicular fires . . . Beginning in 1987, the Elwell-GM employment relationship soured. GM and Elwell first negotiated an agreement under which Elwell would retire after serving as a GM consultant for two years. When the time came for Elwell to retire, however, disagreement again surfaced and continued into 1991.

In May 1991, plaintiffs in a product liability action pending in Georgia deposed Elwell. The Georgia case involved a GM pickup truck fuel tank that burst into flames just after a collision. During the deposition, and over the objection of counsel for GM, Elwell gave testimony that differed markedly from testimony he had given when serving as an in-house expert witness for GM . . . .

A month later, Elwell sued GM in a Michigan County Court, alleging wrongful discharge and other tort and contract claims. GM counterclaimed, contending that Elwell had breached his fiduciary duty to GM by disclosing privileged and confidential information and misappropriating documents. In response to GM's motion for a preliminary injunction, and after a hearing, the Michigan trial court enjoined Elwell from "consulting or discussing with or disclosing to any person any of General Motors Corporation's trade secrets[,] confidential information or matters of attorney-client work product relating in any manner to the subject matter of any products liability litigation whether already filed or [to be] filed in the future which Ronald Elwell received, had knowledge of, or was entrusted with during his employments with General Motors Corporation." . . .

In August 1992, GM and Elwell entered into a settlement under which Elwell received an undisclosed sum of money. The parties also stipulated to the entry of a permanent injunction and jointly filed with the Michigan court both the stipulation and the agreed-upon injunction. The proposed permanent injunction contained two proscriptions. The first substantially repeated the terms of the preliminary injunction; the second comprehensively enjoined Elwell from "testifying, without the prior written consent of General Motors Corporation, either upon deposition or at trial, as an expert witness, or as a witness of any kind, and from consulting with attorneys or their agents in any litigation already filed, or to be filed in the future, involving General Motors Corporation as an owner, seller, manufacturer and/or designer of the product(s) in issue." . . .

To this encompassing bar, the consent injunction made an exception: "[This provision] shall not operate to interfere with the jurisdiction of the Court in . . . Georgia [where the litigation involving the fuel tank was still pending]." *Ibid.* (emphasis added). No other noninterference provision appears in the stipulated decree. On August 26, 1992, with no further hearing, the Michigan court entered the injunction precisely as tendered by the parties.

Although the stipulated injunction contained an exception only for the Georgia action then pending, Elwell and GM included in their separate settlement agreement a more general limitation. If a court or other tribunal ordered Elwell to testify, his testimony would "in no way" support a GM action for violation of the injunction or the settlement agreement: "'It is agreed that [Elwell's] appearance and testimony, if any, at hearings on Motions to quash subpoena or at deposition or trial or other official proceeding, if the Court or other tribunal so orders, will in no way form a basis for an action in violation of the Permanent Injunction or this Agreement.'" . . .

In the six years since the Elwell-GM settlement, Elwell has testified against GM both in Georgia (pursuant to the exception contained in the injunction) and in several other jurisdictions in which Elwell has been subpoenaed to testify.

### The Suit Between the Bakers and General Motors

The decedent, Beverly Garner, was a front-seat passenger in a 1985 Chevrolet S-10 Blazer involved in a February 1990 Missouri highway accident. The Blazer's engine caught fire, and both driver and passenger died. In September 1991, Garner's sons, Kenneth and Steven Baker, commenced a wrongful death product liability action against GM in a Missouri state court . . .

The Bakers sought both to depose Elwell and to call him as a witness at trial. GM objected to Elwell's appearance as a deponent or trial witness on the ground that the Michigan injunction barred his testimony. In response, the Bakers urged that the Michigan injunction did not override a Missouri subpoena for Elwell's testimony. The Bakers further noted that, under the Elwell-GM settlement agreement, Elwell could testify if a court so ordered, and such testimony would not be actionable as a violation of the Michigan injunction.

[T]he Federal District Court in Missouri allowed the Bakers to depose Elwell and to call him as a witness at trial . . .

At trial, Elwell testified in support of the Bakers' claim . . . .Following trial, the jury awarded the Bakers $11.3 million in damages, and the District Court entered judgment on the jury's verdict.]

## II

Our precedent differentiates the credit owed to laws (legislative measures and common law) and to judgments . . . Regarding judgments, however, the full faith and credit obligation is exacting. A final judgment in one State, if rendered by a court with adjudicatory authority over the subject matter and persons governed by the judgment, qualifies for recognition throughout the land. For claim and issue preclusion (res judicata) purposes, in other words, the judgment of the rendering State gains nationwide force.

A court may be guided by the forum State's "public policy" in determining the law applicable to a controversy. *See Nevada v. Hall,* 440 U.S. 410, 421-424 (1979). But our decisions support no "roving public policy exception" to the full faith and credit due judgments. *See Estin,* 334 U.S., at 546 (Full Faith and Credit Clause "ordered submission . . . even to hostile policies reflected in the judgment of another State, because the practical operation of the federal system, which the Constitution designed, demanded it."); *Fauntleroy v. Lum,* 210 U.S. 230, 237 (1908) (judgment of Missouri court entitled to full faith and credit in Mississippi even if Missouri judgment rested on a misapprehension of Mississippi law). In assuming the existence of a ubiquitous "public policy exception" permitting one State to resist recognition of another State's judgment, the District Court in the Bakers' wrongful-death action, see *supra,* at 662, misread our precedent. "The full faith and credit clause is one of the provisions incorporated into the Constitution by its framers for the purpose of transforming an aggregation of independent, sovereign States into a nation." *Sherrer v. Sherrer,* 334 U.S. 343, 355 (1948). We are "aware of [no] considerations of local policy or law which could rightly be deemed to impair the force and effect which the full faith and credit clause and the Act of Congress require to be given to [a money] judgment outside the state of its rendition." *Magnolia Petroleum Co. v. Hunt,* 320 U.S. 430 (1943).

The Court has never placed equity decrees outside the full faith and credit domain. Equity decrees for the payment of money have long been considered equivalent to judgments at law entitled to nationwide recognition.; See, e.g., *Barber v. Barber,* 323 U.S. 77 (1944) (unconditional adjudication of petitioner's right to recover a sum of money is entitled to full faith and credit); see also A. Ehrenzweig, Conflict of Laws § 51, p. 182 (rev. ed.1962) (describing as "indefensible" the old doctrine that an equity decree, because it does not "merge" the claim into the judgment, does not qualify for recognition). We see no reason why the preclusive effects of an adjudication on parties and those "in privity" with them, i.e., claim preclusion and issue preclusion (res judicata and collateral estoppel), should differ depending solely upon the type of relief sought in a civil action. Cf. Barber, 323 U.S., at 87 (Jackson, J., concurring) (FullFaith and Credit Clause and its implementing statute speak not of "judgments" but of " 'judicial proceedings' without limitation"); Fed. Rule Civ. Proc. 2 (providing for "one form of action to be known as 'civil action,' " in lieu of discretely labeled actions at law and suits in equity).

Full faith and credit, however, does not mean that States must adopt the practices of other States regarding the time, manner, and mechanisms for enforcing judgments. Enforcement measures do not travel with the sister state judgment as preclusive effects do; such measures remain subject to the even-handed control of forum law. See *McElmoyle ex rel. Bailey v. Cohen,* 13 Pet. 312, 325 (1839) (judgment may be enforced only as "laws [of enforcing forum] may permit"); see also Restatement (Second) of Conflict of Laws § 99 (1969) ("The local law of the forum determines the methods by which a judgment of another state is enforced.").

Orders commanding action or inaction have been denied enforcement in a sister State when they purported to accomplish an official act within the exclusive province of that other State or interfered with litigation over which the ordering State had no authority. Thus, a sister State's decree concerning land ownership in another State has been held ineffective to transfer title, see *Fall v. Eastin,* 215 U.S. 1, (1909), although such a decree may indeed preclusively adjudicate the rights and obligations running between the parties to the foreign litigation, see, e.g., *Robertson v. Howard,* 229 U.S. 254, 261 (1913) ("[I]t may not be doubted that a court of equity in one State in a proper case could compel a defendant before it to convey property situated in another State."). And antisuit injunctions regarding litigation elsewhere, even if compatible with due process as a direction constraining parties to the decree, see *Cole v. Cunningham,* 133 U.S. 107 (1890), in fact have not controlled the second court's actions regarding litigation in that court . . . .Sanctions for violations of an injunction, in any event, are generally administered by the court that issued the injunction.

As earlier recounted, the parties before the Michigan County Court, Elwell and GM, submitted an agreed-upon injunction, which the presiding judge signed. While no issue was joined, expressly litigated, and determined in the Michigan proceeding,[11] that order is claim preclusive between Elwell and GM. Elwell's claim for wrongful discharge and his related contract and tort claims have "merged in the judgment," and he cannot sue again to recover more. Similarly, GM cannot sue Elwell elsewhere on the counterclaim GM asserted in Michigan.

Most essentially, Michigan lacks authority to control courts elsewhere by precluding them, in actions brought by strangers to the Michigan litigation,

---

[11] In no event, we have observed, can issue preclusion be invoked against one who did not participate in the prior adjudication. See *Blonder-Tongue Laboratories Inc., v. University of Ill. Foundation,* 402 U.S. 313, 329, 28 L. Ed. 2d 788, 91 S. Ct. 1434 (1971); *Hansberry v. Lee,* 311 U.S. 32, 40, 85 L. Ed. 22, 61 S. Ct. 115 (1940). Thus, Justice KENNEDY emphasizes the obvious in noting that the Michigan judgment has no preclusive effect on the Bakers, for they were not parties to the Michigan litigation. See *post,* at 5-7. Such an observation misses the thrust of GM's argument. GM readily acknowledges "the commonplace rule that a person may not be bound by a judgment *in personam* in a case to which he was not made a party." Brief for Respondent 35. But, GM adds, the Michigan decree does not bind the Bakers; it binds *Elwell* only. Most forcibly, GM insists that the Bakers cannot object to the binding effect GM seeks for the Michigan judgment because the Bakers have no constitutionally protected interest in obtaining the testitmony of a particular witness. See *id.,* at 39 ("The only party being 'bound' to the injunction is Elwell, and holding him to his legal obligations does not violate anyone's due process rights."). Given this argument, it is clear that issue preclusion principles, standing alone, cannot resolve the controversy GM presents.

from determining for themselves what witnesses are competent to testify and what evidence is relevant and admissible in their search for the truth.

. . . Michigan's decree could operate against Elwell to preclude him from volunteering his testimony. But a Michigan court cannot, by entering the injunction to which Elwell and GM stipulated, dictate to a court in another jurisdiction that evidence relevant in the Bakers' case—a controversy to which Michigan is foreign—shall be inadmissible. This conclusion creates no general exception to the full faith and credit command, and surely does not permit a State to refuse to honor a sister state judgment based on the forum's choice of law or policy preferences. Rather, we simply recognize that, just as the mechanisms for enforcing a judgment do not travel with the judgment itself for purposes of Full Faith and Credit . . . and just as one State's judgment cannot automatically transfer title to land in another State, see *Fall v. Eastin*, 215 U.S. 1, (1909), similarly the Michigan decree cannot determine evidentiary issues in a lawsuit brought by parties who were not subject to the jurisdiction of the Michigan court. *Cf. United States v. Nixon*, 418 U.S. 683, 710, (1974). ("[E]xceptions to the demand for every man's evidence are not lightly created nor expansively construed, for they are in derogation of the search for truth.").[12]

The language of the consent decree is informative in this regard. Excluding the then-pending Georgia action from the ban on testimony by Elwell without GM's permission, the decree provides that it "shall not operate to interfere with the jurisdiction of the Court in . . . Georgia." But if the Michigan order, extended to the Georgia case, would have "interfer[ed] with the jurisdiction" of the Georgia court, Michigan's ban would, in the same way, "interfere with the jurisdiction" of courts in other States in cases similar to the one pending in Georgia.

. . . Michigan's power does not reach into a Missouri courtroom to displace the forum's own determination whether to admit or exclude evidence relevant in the Bakers' wrongful-death case before it. In that light, we see no altruism in GM's agreement not to institute contempt or breach-of-contract proceedings against Elwell in Michigan for giving subpoenaed testimony elsewhere. Rather, we find it telling that GM ruled out resort to the court that entered the injunction, for injunctions are ordinarily enforced by the enjoining court, not by a surrogate tribunal.

In sum, Michigan has no authority to shield a witness from another jurisdiction's subpoena power in a case involving persons and causes outside Michigan's governance. Recognition, under full faith and credit, is owed to

---

[12] Justice KENNEDY inexplicably reads into our decision a sweeping exception to full faith and credit based solely on "the integrity of Missouri's judicial processes." The Michigan judgment is not entitled to full faith and credit, we have endeavored to make plain, because it impermissibly interferes with Missouri's control of litigation brought by parties who were not before the Michigan court. Thus, Justice KENNEDY's hypothetical, misses the mark. If the Bakers had been parties to the Michigan proceedings and had actually litigated the privileged character of Elwell's testimony, the Bakers would of course be precluded from relitigating that issue in Missouri. See *Comwell v. County of Sac*, 94 U.S. 351, 354 (1876) ("[D]etermination of a question directly involved in one action in conclusive as to that question in a second suit between the same parties . . . ."); see also *supra*, n.5.

dispositions Michigan has authority to order. But a Michigan decree cannot command obedience elsewhere on a matter the Michigan court lacks authority to resolve . . .

\* \* \*

For the reasons stated, the judgment of the Court of Appeals for the Eighth Circuit is reversed, and the case is remanded for further proceedings consistent with this opinion.

Justice SCALIA, concurring in the judgment.

I agree with the Court that enforcement measures do not travel with sister-state judgments as preclusive effects do. Ante, at 665. It has long been established that "the judgment of a state Court cannot be enforced out of the state by an execution issued within it." *McElmoyle ex rel. Bailey v. Cohen,* 13 Pet. 312, 325, 10 L.Ed. 177 (1839). To recite that principle is to decide this case.

General Motors asked a District Court in Missouri to enforce a Michigan injunction. The Missouri court was no more obliged to enforce the Michigan injunction by preventing Elwell from presenting his testimony than it was obliged to enforce it by holding Elwell in contempt. The Full Faith and Credit Clause " 'did not make the judgments of other States domestic judgments to all intents and purposes, but only gave a general validity, faith, and credit to them, as evidence. No execution can issue upon such judgments without a new suit in the tribunals of other States.' " *Thompson v. Whitman,* 18 Wall. 457, 462-463, 21 L.Ed. 897 (1873) (emphasis added) (quoting J. Story, Conflict of Laws § 609). A judgment or decree of one State, to be sure, may be grounds for an action (or a defense to one) in another. But the Clause and its implementing statute "establish a rule of evidence, rather than of jurisdiction. While they make the record of a judgment, rendered after due notice in one State, conclusive evidence in the courts of another State, or of the United States, of the matter adjudged, they do not affect the jurisdiction, either of the court in which the judgment is rendered, or of the court in which it is offered in evidence. Judgments recovered in one State of the Union, when proved in the courts of another government, whether state or national, within the United States, differ from judgments recovered in a foreign country in no other respect than in not being reexaminable on their merits, nor impeachable for fraud in obtaining them, if rendered by a court having jurisdiction of the cause and of the parties." *Wisconsin v. Pelican Ins. Co.,* 127 U.S. 265, 291-292.

The judgment that General Motors obtained in Michigan " 'does not carry with it, into another State, the efficacy of a judgment upon property or persons, to be enforced by execution. To give it the force of a judgment in another State, it must be made a judgment there; and can only be executed in the latter as its laws may permit.' " *Lynde v. Lynde,* 181 U.S. 183. Because neither the Full Faith and Credit Clause nor its implementing statute requires Missouri to execute the injunction issued by the courts of Michigan, I concur in the judgment.

Justice KENNEDY, with whom Justices O'CONNOR and THOMAS join, concurring in the judgment.

I concur in the judgment. In my view the case is controlled by well-settled full faith and credit principles which render the majority's extended analysis unnecessary and, with all due respect, problematic in some degree. This separate opinion explains my approach.

The majority, of course, is correct to hold that when a judgment is presented to the courts of a second State it may not be denied enforcement based upon some disagreement with the laws of the State of rendition. Full faith and credit forbids the second State from questioning a judgment on these grounds. There can be little doubt of this proposition. We have often recognized the second State's obligation to give effect to another State's judgments even when the law underlying those judgments contravenes the public policy of the second State.

My concern is that the majority, having stated the principle, proceeds to disregard it by announcing two broad exceptions. First, the majority would allow courts outside the issuing State to decline to enforce those judgments "purport[ing] to accomplish an official act within the exclusive province of [a sister] State." Second, the basic rule of full faith and credit is said not to cover injunctions "interfer[ing] with litigation over which the ordering State had no authority." The exceptions the majority recognizes are neither consistent with its rejection of a public policy exception to full faith and credit nor in accord with established rules implementing the Full Faith and Credit Clause. As employed to resolve this case, furthermore, the exceptions to full faith and credit have a potential for disrupting judgments, and this ought to give us considerable pause . . .

In any event, the rule would be an exception. Full faith and credit requires courts to do more than provide for direct enforcement of the judgments issued by other States. It also "requires federal courts to give the same preclusive effect to state court judgments that those judgments would be given in the courts of the State from which the judgments emerged." *Kremer v. Chemical Constr. Corp.*, 456 U.S. 461, 466, (1982) . . .

In the case before us, of course, the Bakers were neither parties to the earlier litigation nor subject to the jurisdiction of the Michigan courts. The majority pays scantattention to this circumstance, which becomes critical. The beginning point of full faith and credit analysis requires a determination of the effect the judgment has in the courts of the issuing State. In our most recent full faith and credit cases, we have said that determining the force and effect of a judgment should be the first step in our analysis. A conclusion that the issuing State would not give the prior judgment preclusive effect ends the inquiry, making it unnecessary to determine the existence of any exceptions to full faith and credit. *Id.*, at 383, 386. We cannot decline to inquire into these state-law questions when the inquiry will obviate new extensions or exceptions to full faith and credit.

If we honor the undoubted principle that courts need give a prior judgment no more force or effect that the issuing State gives it, the case before us is resolved. Here the Court of Appeals and both parties in their arguments before our Court seemed to embrace the assumption that Michigan would apply the full force of its judgment to the Bakers. Michigan law does not appear to support the assumption . . .

In all events, determining as a threshold matter the extent to which Michigan law gives preclusive effect to the injunction eliminates the need to decide whether full faith and credit applies to equitable decrees as a general matter or the extent to which the general rules of full faith and credit are subject to exceptions. Michigan law would not seek to bind the Bakers to the injunction and that suffices to resolve the case. For these reasons, I concur in the judgment.

## NOTES AND QUESTIONS ON THE *BAKER* CASE

(1) *The Majority Opinion.* The majority shows the classic signs of a compromise opinion: Lots of helpful dicta, but a holding that is a bit difficult to explain.

(a) *Clearing Away the Underbrush.* Justice Ginsburg's majority opinion clears away a lot of conflicts underbrush before it gets to the holding. (No doubt that reflects her own background as a teacher and scholar in the area.)

(i) *Equity Decrees.* We learn, for example, that equity decrees are entitled to the constitutional requirement of full faith and credit; that is something that should have known generally for a hundred years, but it was not made clear by the Court until *Baker.* See the discussion of *James v. Grand Trunk Rd., supra* § 7.09[C]. *See generally* Polly J. Price, *Full Faith and Credit and the Equity Conflict,* 84 VA. L. REV. 747 (1998).

(ii) *Public Policy.* More important, perhaps, is the slaying of the § 103 dragon (at least for the time being), of the notion that there is, as Justice Ginsburg put it, a "roving 'public policy exception' to the full faith and credit due judgments." Do you find it interesting that the opinion somehow fails to mention § 103 in this part of the discussion?

But does the majority then bring a public policy exception in through the back door when it states (in dictum) that judgments have been "denied enforcement when they purported to accomplish an official act within the exclusive province of . . . [another] State or interfered with litigation over which the ordering State had no authority"? The opinion cites at that point to *Fall v. Eastin* and cases involving anti-suit injunctions, suggesting, perhaps, that any exception would be quite limited..

(b) *Complex Litigation.* The opinion also highlights—in footnote 11—an increasingly serious problem in today's world of complex, multi-party litigation. That problem, of course, stems from a decree like the one in *Baker* itself that purports to bind only the parties thereto, but also necessarily affects the rights of non-parties. On the surface that is not a new problem. A finding in a simple two-party contract action that a defendant owes money to a plaintiff may force the former into bankruptcy and change the legal and economic status of many others. But the situation in *Baker* and many other similar cases presents a fundamentally different situation in that the Michigan decree has the potential to effect the rights of persons who have no connection with that litigation. The problem becomes especially acute when, as in *Baker,* the "judgment" is the result of a consent decree. *Baker* does not resolve that problem, but it certainly highlights the issue. Is there a proper resolution? (Hint: Think Due Process rather than Full Faith and Credit.) *See generally* Katherine C.

Pearson, *Common Law Preclusion, Full Faith and Credit, and Consent Judgments: The Analytical Challenge,* 48 CATH. L. REV. 419 (1999); Howard M. Erichson, *Interstate Preclusion,* 96 MICH. L. REV. 945 (1998).

What happened to the contract between GM and Elwell? Why did GM not rely on that also? (Hint: Remember the list of defenses to contract enforcement.)

(b) *The Holding.* What exactly is the holding in *Baker* ? In other words, what do you make of the statement by the majority that "a Michigan decree cannot command obedience elsewhere on a matter the Michigan court lacks authority to resolve"? Is that mere question-begging? Why can't the Michigan court "resolve the question" of Elwell's later testimony? Is that because Missouri has some "right" to determine who may testify in its courts? If so, where does that "right' come from—what constitutional provision makes that rule clear? (Hint: Good luck in finding the answer in the majority opinion.)

Another way of looking at the holding is to ask why Missouri might not wish to enforce the Michigan decree. If the F-1 order were simply to pay a sum of money, and the plaintiff sought to enforce the decree through garnishment, would Missouri have any grounds for objection? On the other hand, would Michigan have any grounds for objections, if Missouri enforced the decree through its own garnishment procedures? In which of these categories does *Baker* fall?

On the other hand, did Missouri have any legitimate objection to enforcing the injunction? Do Missouri courts not routinely issue injunctions? Did GM ask Missouri to establish some sort of special enforcement mechanism?

(2) *The Scalia Concurrence.* Justice Scalia attempts to provide an answer to the last question. The Michigan decree, he writes, has preclusive effect, but it is not self-executing; in other words, suit has to be brought in Missouri to enforce the Michigan decree. That result has a certain plausibility in the *Baker* context: Injunctions are not normally thought of as self-executing—someone wearing a black robe has to enter the picture as a result of a lawsuit and lecture the respondent about right and wrong. Is Scalia really saying only that the case was not ripe to consider the preclusion issue?

But does Scalia really mean to say as a sweeping statement that preclusive effect never comes into play unless there has been a separate enforcement action? Consider the situation where F-1 holds in the *A v. B* action that A breached the contract; if A were later to sue to enforce the contract in F-2, must B bring a separate enforcement action in F-2 before it can assert a preclusion defense? It seems very unlikely that Scalia meant to go that far. If he did not, the question then becomes—what is the functional difference, if any, between the two situations? (Hint: Good luck in finding an explanation.)

(3) *The Kennedy Concurrence.* This opinion is much more traditional. Justice Kennedy starts out with the proposition that serious, quasi-constitutional issues should be avoided if there is any legitimate way to do so. That much is certainly hornbook law. He then adds the basic point that if F-1 (Michigan) would not enforce the injunction against the Bakers, then F-2 (Missouri) is certainly under no obligation to do so. Justice Kennedy's review of Michigan case law leads him to the conclusion that F-1 would not so limit Elwell's

testimony. As a result, Missouri was under no obligation to do either. Justice Kennedy, therefore, felt no need to inquire into the more sensitive Full Faith and Credit questions discussed by the majority.

(4) *The Iron Law and Baker. Baker* certainly reinforces the Iron Law of Full Faith and Credit, for it makes clear that there is no general, policy-based exception to the Full Faith and Credit Clause; the enforcing state, in other words, has no business rejecting the judgment of another state based on its own policy objectives. On the other hand, we learn, the enforcing state may follow its own rules of enforcement. Drawing the line, as law students learn early in the first semester, often can be difficult; for example, is it clear why the Elwell decree is on the enforcement side of the line?

How the Court will police the intersection between the two will be interesting to see. After all, if there is no enforcement mechanism, then preclusion means little, if anything. The basic constitutional rule of non-discrimination seems to have little impact here; although Missouri obviously was treating a foreign injunction differently than it would its own injunctions, the Court seems little troubled by that discrimination. Perhaps that suggests that the *real* concern of the majority was with the problem mentioned in footnote 11 (see Note 1(a), *supra*), but that the members of the majority could not find a way to resolve it. That would explain the unsatisfactory nature of the holding—it was a way to buy time while the Court decided how to resolve the *real* problem.

(5) *A Last Word.* Is it possible to consider *Baker* as another retrogade opinion emphasizing territorialism? Consider the following quote:

> *Baker* epitomizes the persistent appeal of the traditional approach to choice of law issues in the face of the unrelenting disdain of the academic community. The appeal in turn reflects the fact that the traditional approach embodies very basic notions of sovereignty and power that are deeply embedded in the Americal political and legal culture.

Earl M. Maltz, *The Full Faith and Credit Clause and the First Restatement: The Place of* Baker v. General Motors Corp. *in Choice of Law Theory,* 73 TULANE L. REV. 305 (1998).

## PART C   FEDERAL-STATE PRECLUSION

### § 7.10   Federal-State Preclusion

## INTRODUCTION

We have been focusing on the preclusive effect that the judgment of one state has in the courts of another. But in order to know the full effect of a state judgment we must also know how that judgment would be treated in federal courts.

That question logically breaks down into two more precise ones:

(1) How must a federal court treat a state-court judgment in an ordinary state-law case? And,

(2) How must a federal court treat a state-court judgment in a case that was pleaded, or could have been pleaded, under federal substantive law?

With those questions raised, it becomes clear that we have left open another. What is the scope of a federal court judgment? In turn, this would appear to break down into two further questions:

(3) What is the effect in all courts of a federal judgment in a federal-law case?

(4) What is the effect in all courts of a federal judgment in a state-law case?

American judges and lawyers tend to expect that the law of the judgment-rendering sovereign determines the scope of that sovereign's judgments. The late Professor Degnan proposed just such a general rule in a well-known article, Ron Degnan, *Federalized Res Judicata*, 85 YALE L.J. 741 (1976). But persuasive counter-arguments are continually surfacing. *See generally* Gene Shreve, *Preclusion and Federal Choice of Law*, 64 TEX. L. REV. 1209 (1986).

---

### § 7.11   Recognition of State Judgments on State Questions

Suppose a federal court must determine the scope of a state-court judgment in a state-law case. What law governs that issue? The answer is that federal law governs it, just as federal law governs the same question when it arises in a state court. The full faith and credit statute, 28 U.S.C. § 1738, requires that faith and credit be given to state judgments by "every court within the United States." But remember that federal law governs only at this first level of analysis. State law will govern in the end; in the full faith and credit statute Congress makes a mandatory reference to the law of the judgment-rendering state.

## § 7.12　Recognition of State Judgments on Federal Questions

When a court, federal or state, must determine the scope of a state judgment in a federal-law case, the plot thickens. It is true that § 1738 mandates a reference to the law of the judgment-rendering state. But what if federal jurisdiction is exclusive, as it is under the federal antitrust laws. Does a state-court judgment sounding in antitrust preclude a statutory federal suit against a violator of the antitrust laws? Or should an exception be made in such cases? Consider, also, that the full faith and credit statute is only a statute. An after-enacted substantive statute, like the Sherman [Antitrust] Act, arguably might require that judgments thereunder be given preclusive effect whether or not state law would do so. How would you come out on these questions?

## MARRESE v. AMERICAN ACADEMY OF ORTHOPAEDIC SURGEONS

*Supreme Court of the United States*
*470 U.S. 373, 105 S.Ct. 1327, 84 L.Ed.2d 274 (1985)*

Justice O'CONNOR delivered the opinion of the Court.

### I

Petitioners are board-certified orthopaedic surgeons who applied for membership in respondent American Academy of Orthopaedic Surgeons (Academy). Respondent denied the membership applications without providing a hearing or a statement of reasons. In November 1976, petitioner Dr. Treister filed suit in the Circuit Court of Cook County, State of Illinois, alleging that the denial of membership in the Academy violated associational rights protected by Illinois common law. Petitioner Dr. Marrese separately filed a similar action in state court. Neither petitioner alleged a violation of state antitrust law in his state court action; nor did either petitioner contemporaneously file a federal antitrust suit. The Illinois Appellate Court ultimately held that Dr. Treister's complaint failed to state a cause of action . . . . After the Appellate Court ruled against Dr. Treister, the Circuit Court dismissed Dr. Marrese's complaint.

In March 1980, petitioners filed a federal antitrust suit in the United States District Court for the Northern District of Illinois based on the same events underlying their unsuccessful state court actions. As amended, the complaint alleged that respondent Academy possesses monopoly power, that petitioners were denied membership in order to discourage competition, and that their exclusion constituted a boycott in violation of § 1 of the Sherman Act, 15 U.S.C. § 1. Respondent filed a motion to dismiss arguing that claim preclusion barred the federal antitrust claim because the earlier state court actions concerned the same facts and were dismissed with prejudice. In denying this motion, the District Court reasoned that state courts lack jurisdiction over federal antitrust claims, and therefore a state court judgment cannot have claim preclusive effect in a subsequent federal antitrust suit . . . .

The Court of Appeals . . . en banc . . . held that claim preclusion barred the federal antitrust suit . . . . .

### III

The issue presented by this case is whether a state court judgment may have preclusive effect on a federal antitrust claim that could not have been raised in the state proceeding. Although federal antitrust claims are within the exclusive jurisdiction of the federal courts, the Court of Appeals ruled that the dismissal of petitioners' complaints in state court barred them from bringing a claim based on the same facts under the Sherman Act. The Court of Appeals erred by suggesting that in these circumstances a federal court should determine the preclusive effect of a state court judgment without regard to the law of the State in which judgment was rendered.

The preclusive effect of a state court judgment in a subsequent federal lawsuit generally is determined by the full faith and credit statute, which provides that state judicial proceedings "shall have the same full faith and credit in every court within the United States . . . as they have by law or usage in the courts of such State . . . from which they are taken." 28 U.S.C. § 1738. This statute directs a federal court to refer to the preclusion law of the State in which judgment was rendered . . . .

The fact that petitioners' antitrust claim is within the exclusive jurisdiction of the federal courts does not necessarily make § 1738 inapplicable to this case. Our decisions indicate that a state court judgment may in some circumstances have preclusive effect in a subsequent action within the exclusive jurisdiction of the federal courts. Without discussing § 1738, this Court has held that the issue-preclusive effect of a state court judgment barred a subsequent patent suit that could not have been brought in state court [citation omitted]. Moreover, Kremer held that § 1738 applies to a claim of employment discrimination under Title VII of the Civil Rights Act of 1964, although the Court expressly declined to decide whether Title VII claims can be brought only in federal courts. Kremer implies that absent an exception to § 1738, state law determines at least the issue preclusive effect of a prior state judgment in a subsequent action involving a claim within the exclusive jurisdiction of the federal courts.

More generally, Kremer indicates that § 1738 requires a federal court to look first to state preclusion law in determining the preclusive effects of a state court judgment. Cf. Smith, *Full Faith and Credit and § 1983: A Reappraisal,* 63 N.C. L.Rev. 59, 110-111 (1984). The Court's analysis in Kremer began with the finding that state law would in fact bar relitigation of the discrimination issue decided in the earlier state proceedings. That finding implied that the plaintiff could not relitigate the same issue in federal court unless some exception to § 1738 applied. Kremer observed that "an exception to § 1738 will not be recognized unless a later statute contains an express or implied repeal." Title VII does not expressly repeal § 1738, and the Court concluded that the statutory provisions and legislative history do not support a finding of implied repeal. We conclude that the basic approach adopted in Kremer applies in a lawsuit involving a claim within the exclusive jurisdiction of the federal courts.

To be sure, a state court will not have occasion to address the specific question whether a state judgment has issue or claim preclusive effect in a later action that can be brought only in federal court. Nevertheless, a federal court may rely in the first instance on state preclusion principles to determine the extent to which an earlier state judgment bars subsequent litigation . . . .

If state preclusion law includes [a] requirement of prior jurisdictional competency, which is generally true, a state judgment will not have claim preclusive effect on a cause of action within the exclusive jurisdiction of the federal courts. Even in the event that a party asserting the affirmative defense of claim preclusion can show that state preclusion rules in some circumstances bar a claim outside the jurisdiction of the court that rendered the initial judgment, the federal court should first consider whether application of the state rules would bar the particular federal claim.

Reference to state preclusion law may make it unnecessary to determine if the federal court, as an exception to § 1738, should refuse to give preclusive effect to a state court judgment. The issue whether there is an exception to § 1738 arises only if state law indicates that litigation of a particular claim or issue should be barred in the subsequent federal proceeding. To the extent that state preclusion law indicates that a judgment normally does not have claim preclusive effect as to matters that the court lacked jurisdiction to entertain . . . a state court judgment does not bar a subsequent federal antitrust claim. Unless application of Illinois preclusion law suggests, contrary to the usual view, that petitioners' federal antitrust claim is somehow barred, there will be no need to decide in this case if there is an exception to § 1738.[3]

We are unwilling to create a special exception to § 1738 for federal antitrust claims that would give state court judgments greater preclusive effect than would the courts of the State rendering the judgment . . . .

If we had a single system of courts and our only concerns were efficiency and finality, it might be desirable to fashion claim preclusion rules that would require a plaintiff to bring suit initially in the forum of most general jurisdiction, thereby resolving as many issues as possible in one proceeding. The decision of the Court of Appeals approximates such a rule inasmuch as it encourages plaintiffs to file suit initially in federal district court and to attempt to bring any state law claims pendent to their federal antitrust claims. Whether this result would reduce the overall burden of litigation is debatable, and we decline to base our interpretation of § 1738 on our opinion on this question.

---

[3] . . . Although a particular State's preclusion principles conceivably could support a rule similar to that proposed by THE CHIEF JUSTICE where state preclusion rules do not indicate that a claim is barred, we do not believe that federal courts should fashion a federal rule to preclude a claim that could not have been raised in the state proceedings . . . .

More importantly, we have parallel systems of state and federal courts, and the concerns of comity reflected in § 1738 . . . are not made less compelling because state courts lack jurisdiction over federal antitrust claims. We therefore reject a judicially created exception to § 1738 that effectively holds as a matter of federal law that a plaintiff can bring state law claims initially in state court only at the cost of forgoing subsequent federal antitrust claims . . . .

Although for purposes of this case, we need not decide if . . . an exception exists for federal antitrust claims, we observe that the more general question is whether the concerns underlying a particular grant of exclusive jurisdiction justify a finding of an implied partial repeal of § 1738. Resolution of this question will depend on the particular federal statute as well as the nature of the claim or issue involved in the subsequent federal action. Our previous decisions indicate that the primary consideration must be the intent of Congress.

## IV

Before this Court, the parties have continued to disagree about the content of Illinois preclusion law. We believe that this dispute is best resolved in the first instance by the District Court . . . .

Justice BLACKMUN and Justice STEVENS took no part in the consideration or decision of this case.

Chief Justice BURGER, concurring in the judgment.

I agree with the Court's . . . conclusion that . . . a fair reading of § 1738 requires federal courts to look first to general principles of state preclusion law . . . .

I cannot agree with the Court's interpretation of the jurisdictional competency requirement. If state law provides a cause of action that is virtually identical with a federal statutory cause of action, a plaintiff suing in state court is able to rely on the same theory of the case and obtain the same remedy as would be available in federal court, even when the plaintiff cannot expressly invoke the federal statute because it is within the exclusive jurisdiction of the federal courts. In this situation, the jurisdictional competency requirement is effectively satisfied . . . .

No Illinois court has considered how the jurisdictional competency requirement should apply in the type of situation presented by this case, where the same theory of recovery may be asserted under different statutes. Nor has any Illinois court considered whether res judicata precludes splitting a cause of action between a court of limited jurisdiction and one of general jurisdiction.

In this situation, it may be consistent with § 1738 for a federal court to formulate a federal rule to resolve the matter. If state law is simply indeterminate, the concerns of comity and federalism underlying § 1738 do not come into play. At the same time, the federal courts have direct interests in ensuring that their resources are used efficiently and not as a means of harassing defendants with repetitive lawsuits, as well as in ensuring that parties asserting federal rights have an adequate opportunity to litigate those rights. Given the insubstantiality of the state interests and the weight of federal interests a strong argument could be made that a federal rule would be more appropriate than a creative interpretation of ambiguous state law . . . .[4]

A federal rule might be fashioned from the test, which this Court has applied in other contexts, that a party is precluded from asserting a claim that he had a "full and fair opportunity" to litigate in a prior action. Thus, if a state statute is identical in all material respects with a federal statute within exclusive federal jurisdiction, a party's ability to assert a claim under the state statute in a prior state court action might be said to have provided, in effect, a "full and fair opportunity" to litigate his rights under the federal statute.

The Court will eventually have to face these questions; I would resolve them now.

---

## NOTES ON *MARRESE*

(1) *A tale of two statutes.* The policies underlying the full faith and credit statute are doubtless very strong, but so also are the substantive policies underlying other national legislation—on civil rights, antitrust, securities, trade, the environment. Should res judicata policy sometimes have to give way to overriding substantive policy? Does the Marrese Court's "implied partial repeal" analysis provide a sufficient safety net for concerns of national substantive policy?

(2) **ALLEN v. McCURRY,** 449 U.S. 90 (1980). Federal civil rights action alleging McCurry had been convicted on the strength of unconstitutionally obtained evidence. The state prosecutor pleaded res judicata because McCurry had had a full and fair opportunity to litigate the issue in a suppression hearing during the state criminal proceeding.

*Held* (per Justice Stewart): McCurry is precluded from suit. The rules of collateral estoppel apply to actions brought under the Civil Rights Act of 1871, and apply to state-court judgments, civil and criminal. There is no evident intention behind the Civil Rights Act to work a partial repeal of the full faith and credit statute. Nor does it matter to this result that, since McCurry had enjoyed "a full and fair opportunity" to litigate his Fourth Amendment claim in the state court, he is unable, under federal common-law rules, to obtain federal habeas corpus relief.

[Justice Blackmun, joined by Justices Brennan and Marshall, dissented.]

---

Should it have made a difference in *McCurry* that, like all defendants in criminal prosecutions, McCurry was an involuntary litigant without a choice

---

[4] By contrast, when a federal court construes substantive rights and obligations under state law in the context of a diversity action, the federal interest is insignificant and the state's interest is much more direct than it is in the present situation, even if the relevant state law is ambiguous.

of forum? Are there other distinctions between prosecutions and civil suits which arguably might justify an exception to the usual preclusion rules in a situation like McCurry's?

(3) *The full and fair opportunity.* What does Justice O'Connor mean in *Marrese,* when she says the Court is unwilling to fashion a rule that would give a judgment in an antitrust case greater preclusive effect than the rendering court would give it? The Chief Justice points to what in fact has become a large body of federal common law on the "full and fair opportunity" to litigate a federal question, as foreclosing further federal hearings. Is the Chief Justice right, that, notwithstanding § 1738's reference to state law, it might be appropriate to apply this federal standard in *Marrese?*

(4) *The stakes.* Isn't the more compelling question whether an antitrust judgment should be given less preclusive effect than the rendering court would give it? After all, national substantive enforcement policies are at stake, and in a proper case would seem to outweigh the procedural policies underlying the full faith and credit statute. But after *Allen v. McCurry,* note (2) *supra,* in which the Court refused to make an exception to § 1738 for civil rights cases, even though the prior judgment was in a criminal case, how could the Court do so for antitrust cases?

---

## § 7.13 Recognition of Federal Judgments on Federal Questions

That there is a general obligation of due faith and credit to a federal judgment should come as no surprise, and seems necessary and proper to federal supremacy. It is well settled that all courts owe full faith and credit to federal judgments, and that the preclusive effect of a federal judgment is a question of federal common law.

---

**FEDERATED DEPARTMENT STORES v. MOITIE,** 452 U.S. 394 (1981). In the wake of a suit by the Justice Department against a department store empire alleging price-fixing violations of the antitrust laws, a number of civil suits were filed by retail purchasers in state and federal court, alleging both federal antitrust and state-law business torts. The federal courts dismissed all such claims on the ground that retail purchasers could not suffer antitrust "injury." Moitie, one of these retail purchasers, without appealing the dismissal, brought a fresh suit in state court, on a state-law theory of unfair competition. Meanwhile, the Supreme Court held, in an unrelated case, that retail purchasers indeed could suffer antitrust "injury."

Defendant Federated, meanwhile, removed Moitie's new suit as "really federal," and then moved the federal court to dismiss it as res judicata. Plaintiff Moitie argued that the recent Supreme Court case on antitrust "injury" showed that the District Court's original dismissal was wrong, and should be considered res judicata. But the District Court held that that first dismissal was indeed res judicata, even if in error, and granted the defendant's motion to dismiss. This time Moitie appealed. The United States Court of Appeals reversed, holding that there was an equitable exception to res judicata in such cases, to prevent substantial injustice.

*Held* (per Justice Rehnquist): *Reversed.* The original dismissal was res judicata as to Moitie's antitrust suit, notwithstanding that Moitie tried to plead it exclusively under state law, and notwithstanding the intervening change in federal antitrust law. There is no federal common-law equitable exception to the rules of claim preclusion for "substantial injustice."

---

As *Moitie* suggests, federal control of federal judgments in federal-law cases is plenary. Not only does the Supreme Court sit to correct an errant state (or federal) court on the point, but, as a codified exception to the Anti-Injunction Act, 28 U.S.C. § 2283, a federal injunction is available to restrain relitigation by a state court of a decided federal question. Can you think of a way, in the teeth of all this, a state court could nevertheless effectively negate a federal judgment? Consider the following case.

---

# PARSONS STEEL, INC. v. FIRST ALABAMA BANK

*Supreme Court of the United States*
*474 U.S. 518, 106 S.Ct. 768, 88 L.Ed.2d 877 (1986)*

Justice REHNQUIST delivered the opinion of the Court.

Parsons Steel . . . sued respondents First Alabama Bank . . . in Alabama state court in February 1979, essentially alleging that the bank had fraudulently induced . . . Parsons to permit a third person to take control of a subsidiary of Parsons Steel and eventually to obtain complete ownership of the subsidiary. The subsidiary was adjudicated an involuntary bankrupt in April 1979 . . . . In May 1979 Parsons Steel . . . sued the bank in the United States District Court for the District of Alabama, alleging that the same conduct on the part of the bank that was the subject of the state-court suit also violated the [federal] Bank Holding Company Act (BHCA) . . . .

The parties conducted joint discovery in the federal and state actions. The federal action proceeded to trial on the issue of liability before the state action went to trial. A jury returned a verdict in favor of petitioners, but the District Court granted judgment n.o.v. to the bank. That judgment was affirmed on appeal. After the federal judgment was entered, respondents pleaded in the state action the defenses of res judicata and collateral estoppel based on that judgment. The Alabama court, however, ruled that res judicata did not bar the state action . . . . A jury returned a general verdict in favor of [Parsons], awarding a total of four million and one dollars in damages.

Having lost in state court, [the bank] returned to the District Court that had previously entered judgment in the bank's favor and filed the present injunctive action against petitioners, the plaintiffs in the state action. The District Court found that the federal BHCA suit and the state action were based on the same factual allegations and claimed substantially the same damages. The court held that the state claims should have been raised in the federal action as pendent to the BHCA claim and accordingly that the BHCA judgment barred the state claims under res judicata. Determining that the Alabama judgment in effect nullified the earlier federal-court judgment in favor of the bank, the District Court enjoined petitioners from further prosecuting the state action.

A divided panel of the Court of Appeals affirmed in relevant part, holding that the issuance of the injunction was not "an abuse of discretion" by the District Court. The majority . . . agreed with the District Court that the fraud . . . [claim] . . . could have been . . . raised in the same action as the BHCA claim. Thus the parties to the BHCA action and their privies . . . were barred by res judicata from raising these claims in state court after the entry of the federal judgment.

The majority then held that the injunction was proper under the so-called "relitigation exception" to the Anti-Injunction Act, 28 U.S.C. § 2283, which provides:

> "A court of the United States may not grant an injunction to stay proceedings in a State court except as expressly authorized by Act of Congress, or where necessary in aid of its jurisdiction, *or to protect or effectuate its judgments*" (emphasis added).

In reaching this holding, the majority explicitly declined to consider the possible preclusive effect, pursuant to the Full Faith and Credit Act, 28 U.S.C. § 1738, of the state court's determination after full litigation by the parties that the earlier federal-court judgment did not bar the state action. According to the majority, "while a federal court is generally bound by other state court determinations, the relitigation exception empowers a federal court to be the final adjudicator as to the res judicata effects of its prior judgments on a subsequent state action."

The dissenting judge rejected "the majority's conclusion that the Anti-Injunction Act . . . implicitly amended the Full Faith and Credit Act, 28 U.S.C. § 1738." He . . . would have held in cases where the state court has decided the res judicata issue that "section 1738 requires the federal court to afford full faith and credit to the state court's resolution of the issue."

In our view, the majority of the Court of Appeals gave unwarrantedly short shrift to the important values of federalism and comity embodied in the Full Faith and Credit Act . . . .

[The] Court of Appeals did not consider the possible preclusive effect under Alabama law of the state-court judgment, and particularly of the state court's resolution of the res judicata issue, concluding instead that the relitigation exception to the Anti-Injunction Act limits the Full Faith and Credit Act. We do not agree . . . . We believe that the Anti-Injunction Act and the Full Faith and Credit Act can be construed consistently, simply by limiting the relitigation exception of the Anti-Injunction Act to those situations in which the state court has not yet ruled on the merits of the res judicata issue. Once the state court has finally rejected a claim of res judicata, then the Full Faith and Credit Act becomes applicable and federal courts must turn to state law to determine the preclusive effect of the state court's decision.

The Court of Appeals also felt that the District Court's injunction would discourage inefficient simultaneous litigation in state and federal courts on the same issue—that is, the res judicata effect of the prior federal judgment. But this is one of the costs of our dual court system:

> "In short, the state and federal courts had concurrent jurisdiction in this case, and neither court was free to prevent either party from simultaneously pursuing claims in both courts." *Atlantic Coast Line R. Co. v. Locomotive Engineers,* 398 U.S. 281 (1970).

Should the District Court conclude that the state-court judgment is not entitled to preclusive effect under Alabama law and the Full Faith and Credit Act, it would then be in the best position to decide the propriety of a federal-court injunction under the general principles of equity, comity, and federalism . . . .

---

### NOTES ON *PARSONS STEEL*

(1) Full faith and credit and federal injunctions against suit. In *Parsons Steel,* the full faith and credit statute trumps not only the policies underlying the federal Bank Holding Company Act, but also those underlying the statute enabling federal courts to issue injunctions to protect and effectuate their judgments. Was this the right result?

(2) The last-in-time rule and litigation strategy. What could the bank have done to protect itself from the outcome in Parsons Steel? Suppose it had sought the federal injunction before the state suit went to judgment?

---

### § 7.14 Recognition of Federal Judgments on State Questions

Although it seems reasonable to suppose that the effect of a federal judgment always presents a federal question, it seems equally reasonable to suppose that, under the rule of *Erie v. Tompkins,* the effect of a federal judgment in a state-law case must be governed by state law. Finding it difficult to recconcile these two principles, federal appeals courts, forced to choose, began to hold, under the influence of Restatement (Second) of Judgments, that federal judgments in cases under state law were governed not by federal but by state law. Eventually, in 2001, the Supreme Court found a way not only to reconcile these two copeting principles with each other, but with the recent appellate cases as well. For this resolution, see the *Semtek* case, Note (1) *infra*.

## NOTES ON THE PRECLUSIVE EFFECT OF FEDERAL JUDGMENTS IN STATE-LAW CASES

**(1) SEMTEK INTERNAT'L INC. v. LOCKHEED MARTIN CORP.,** 531 U.S. 497 (2001). Defendant Lockheed removed this California case to a federal district court in the same state, and then moved successfully to dismiss the case "on the merits" as barred by California's statute of limitations. It is the general federal rule that a federal court's dismissal of a claim as time-barred is "on the merits," although such a judgment would not be "on the merits" in a number of states. Semtek then filed the identical lawsuit anew, this time in a Maryland state court. Under the relevant Maryland statute of limitations, Semtek's claim was still good. The state court nevertheless granted Lockheed's motion to dismiss on the ground of res judicata, and this judgment was affirmed by the Maryland Court of Special Appeals. The Maryland court reasoned that the federal dismissal in California now barred suit in Maryland because the scope of a federal judgment, even a diversity judgment, was governed by federal law. Because the Maryland court's decision was in conflict with recent decisions of federal appeals courts, which increasingly were holding that state law governed the scope of a federal diversity judgment, the Supreme Court granted certiorari.

*Held* (by Justice Scalia, for a unanimous Court): *Reversed.* "Petitioner contends that the outcome of this case is controlled by Dupasseur v. Rochereau, [an 1875 Supreme Court case,] which held that the res judicata effect of a federal diversity judgment [is governed by state law. However,] Dupasseur is not dispositive because it was decided [before Erie]. Respondent, for its part, contends that the outcome of this case is controlled by Federal Rule of Civil Procedure 41(b), [which provides that a federal dismissal except on grounds not relevant to this case] 'operates as an adjudication on the merits.' . . . Implicit in this reasoning is the unstated minor premise that all judgments denominated 'on the merits' are entitled to claim-preclusive effect. . . . [O]ver the years the meaning of the term 'judgment on the merits' has gradually undergone change, and it has come to be applied to some judgments (such as the one involved here) that do not pass upon the substantive merits of a claim and hence do not (in many jurisdictions) entail claim-preclusive effect. That is why the Restatement of Judgments has abandoned the use of the term. . . . [Moreover, if read literally], Rule 41(b) would in many cases violate the federalism principle of Erie R. Co. v. Tompkins, by engendering substantial variations in outcomes between state and federal litigation which would likely influence the choice of a forum. . . . [I]n the present case, for example, the traditional rule is that expiration of the applicable statute of limitations merely bars the remedy and does not extinguish the substantive right, so that dismissal on that ground does not have claim-preclusive effect in other jurisdictions with longer, unexpired limitations periods. Out-of-state defendants sued on stale claims in California and in other States adhering to this traditional rule would systematically remove state-law suits brought against them to federal court—where, unless otherwise specified, a statute-of-limitations dismissal would bar suit everywhere. . . . We think, then, that the effect of the 'adjudication upon the merits' default provision of Rule 41(b) [in this case] is simply that, unlike a dismissal 'without prejudice,' the dismissal in the present case barred refiling of the same claim in the United States District Court for the Central District of California. . . . Federal common law governs the claim-preclusive effect of a dismissal by a federal court [in a federal case, and similarly must govern the claim-preclusive effect of a dismissal by a federal court] sitting in diversity. . . . [D]espite the sea change that [Erie has effected] in the background law since Dupasseur was decided, . . . we think the result decreed by Dupasseur continues to be correct for diversity cases. Since state, rather than federal, substantive law is at issue there is no need for a uniform federal rule. And indeed, nationwide uniformity in the substance of the matter is better served by having the same claim-preclusive rule (the state rule) apply whether the dismissal has been ordered by a state or a federal court. This is, it seems to us, a classic case for adopting, as the federally prescribed rule of decision, the law that would be applied by state courts in the State in which the federal diversity court sits. . . . {A]ny other rule would produce the sort of 'forum-shopping. . .and. . .inequitable administration of the laws' that Erie seeks to avoid. . . . This federal reference to state law will not obtain, of course, in situations in which the state law is incompatible with federal interests. If, for example, state law did not accord claim-preclusive effect to dismissals for willful violation of discovery orders, federal courts' interest in the integrity of their own processes might justify a contrary federal rule. No such conflict with potential federal interests exists in the present case. Dismissal of this state cause of action was decreed by the California federal court only because the California statute of limitations so required; and there is no conceivable federal interest in giving that time bar more effect in other courts than the California courts themselves would impose. . . .

\*    \*    \*

Why do you suppose the full faith and credit statute did not govern in Semtek? For background on federal incorporation of state law, refer to § 6.09.

(2) *A hypothetical.* Suppose that a passenger injured in a bus accident sues the bus company in federal diversity court, and recovers. Then suppose that a second passenger files suit in a state court in the same state, and moves for summary judgment on the issue of liability, arguing that the liability of the bus company is res judicata. Suppose that the rule of mutuality of estoppel is followed in this state. The federal common-law rule is one of non-mutuality. See *Parklane Hosiery Co., Inc. v. Shore,* 439 U.S. 322 (1979) (binding a party to an adverse determination in a federal-question case in federal court, in a second federal case brought by a third person, in the absence of special circumstances). Should the state court in the hypothetical case grant or deny summary judgment as to liability? Why?

Now suppose that a third passenger files suit in a federal diversity court in the same state. Should the federal judge grant or deny summary judgment as to liability? Why?

(3) *State preclusion rules and the possibility of renvoi.* In *St. Paul Guardian Ins. Co. v. Old Republic Ins. Co.,* 47 F.3d 1176 (9th Cir. 1995) [unpublished], the court managed to apply state and federal preclusion rules at the same time: "The Rule in this circuit is that, in a diversity action, the forum state's law applies to determine the preclusive effect of a previous judgment, even where the previous judgment was issued by a federal court under diversity jurisdiction. *Bates v. Union Oil Co.,* 944 F.2d 647, 649 (9th Cir. 1991), *cert. denied,* 112 S.Ct. 1761 (1992). However, the court in Bates determined: 'Oregon has yet to resolve whether it would apply its own law or federal to determine the preclusive effect of a prior federal diversity judgment. We assume that Oregon, like Washington and California, would apply federal law to determine the preclusive effect of a prior federal judgment. Therefore, we apply federal law to determine the preclusive effect of the . . . judgment.' We must therefore look to federal law in determining whether [the appellant] should be estopped . . . ."

# Chapter 8

# FAMILY LAW

## § 8.01  Scope Note

Family law occupies a unique area in conflicts jurisprudence, sometimes creating difficult problems. There are two main reasons for this. *First,* family law problems often involve dual interests: sometimes they are treated like other personal problems in torts or contracts or property law; at other times, however, the state takes an active interest in the relationship or status of the parties—in divorce and custody, for example—and uses that interest to treat these issues in a special way. *Second,* legal relationships such as custody or support often need continuing adjustment; but, because our society is so mobile, the family members are often located in two or more states, each of which may arguably have an interest in the family's legal arrangement. Interstate family law issues, therefore, pose interesting and instructive contrasts to, as well as a review of, much of the material studied earlier in this course. For that reason, it makes a good concluding chapter. The first two Parts of this Chapter discuss marriage and divorce; the second two Parts deal with problems involving children: custody and support.

## PART A  MARRIAGE

### § 8.02  The Place of Celebration

#### IN RE MAY'S ESTATE

*New York Court of Appeals*
*305 N. Y 486, 122 N.Y.S.2d 486, 114 N.E.2d 4 (1953)*

LEWIS, Ch. J. In this proceeding, involving the administration of the estate of Fannie May, deceased, we are to determine whether the marriage in 1913 between the respondent Sam May and the decedent, who was his niece by the half blood—which marriage was celebrated in Rhode Island, where concededly such marriage is invalid—is to be given legal effect in New York where statute law declares incestuous and void a marriage between uncle and niece. (Domestic Relations Law, § 5, subd. 3.). . . .

Sam May . . . came to New York in December, 1912, and within a month thereafter he and the decedent—both of whom were adherents of the Jewish faith— went to Providence, Rhode Island, where, on January 21, 1913, they entered into a ceremonial marriage performed by and at the home of a Jewish rabbi. The certificate issued upon that marriage gave the age of each party as twenty-six years and the residence of each as "New York, N.Y." Two weeks after their marriage in Rhode Island the respondent May and the decedent

793

returned to Ulster County, New York, where they lived as man and wife for thirty-two years until the decedent's death in 1945. Meantime the six children were born who are parties to this proceeding.

[I]n Rhode Island on January 21, 1913, the date of the marriage here involved, there were effective statutes which prohibited the marriage of an uncle and a niece, excluding, however, those instances—of which the present case is one—where the marriage solemnized is between persons of the Jewish faith within the degrees of affinity and consanguinity allowed by their religion. . . .

We regard the law as settled that, subject to two exceptions presently to be considered, and in the absence of a statute expressly regulating within the domiciliary State marriages solemnized abroad, the legality of a marriage between persons *sui juris* is to be determined by the law of the place where it is celebrated.

The statute of New York upon which the appellants rely is subdivision 3 of section 5 of the Domestic Relations Law which, insofar as relevant to our problem, provides:

"§ 5. Incestuous and void marriages.

"A marriage is incestuous and void whether the relatives are legitimate or illegitimate between either:

"1. * * *

"2. * * *

"3. An uncle and niece or an aunt and nephew.

"If a marriage prohibited by the foregoing provisions of this section be solemnized it shall be void, and the parties thereto shall each be fined not less than fifty nor more than one hundred dollars and may, in the discretion of the court in addition to said fine, be imprisoned for a term not exceeding six months. Any person who shall knowingly and wilfully solemnize such marriage, or procure or aid in the solemnization of the same, shall be deemed guilty of a misdemeanor and shall be fined or imprisoned in like manner."

Although the New York statute quoted above declares to be incestuous and void a marriage between an uncle and a niece and imposes penal measures upon the parties thereto, it is important to note that the statute does not by express terms regulate a marriage solemnized in another State where, as in our present case, the marriage was concededly legal.

As section 5 of the New York Domestic Relations Law does not expressly declare void a marriage of its domiciliaries solemnized in a foreign State where such marriage is valid, the statute's scope should not be extended by judicial construction. Accordingly, as to the first exception to the general rule that a marriage valid where performed is valid everywhere, we conclude that, absent any New York statute expressing clearly the Legislature's intent to regulate within this State marriages of its domiciliaries solemnized abroad, there is no "positive law" in this jurisdiction which serves to interdict the 1913 marriage in Rhode Island of the respondent Sam May and the decedent.

As to the application of the second exception to the marriage here involved between persons of the Jewish faith whose kinship was not in the direct ascending or descending line of consanguinity and who were not brother and sister—we conclude that such marriage, solemnized, as it was, in accord with the ritual of the Jewish faith in a State whose legislative body has declared such a marriage to be "good and valid in law", was not offensive to the public sense of morality to a degree regarded generally with abhorrence and thus was not within the inhibitions of natural law.

*Decree Affirmed.*

DESMOND, J. (dissenting). It is fundamental that every State has the right to determine the marital status of its own citizens. Exercising that right, New York has declared in section 5 of the Domestic Relations Law that a marriage between uncle and niece is incestuous, void and criminal. Such marriages, while not within the Levitical forbidden degrees of the Old Testament, have been condemned by public opinion for centuries and are void, by statute in (it would seem) forty-seven of the States of the Union and except, also, that Rhode Island, one of the forty-seven, exempts from its local statute "any marriage which shall be solemnized among the Jews, within the degrees of affinity or consanguinity allowed by their religion", Gen. L. of R.I., ch. 415, § 4). It is undisputed here that this uncle and niece were both domiciled in New York in 1913, when they left New York for the sole purpose of going to Rhode Island to be married there, and that they were married in that State conformably to its laws *(see* above) and immediately returned to New York and ever afterwards resided in this State. That Rhode Island marriage, between two New York residents, was, in New York, absolutely void for any and all purposes, by positive New York law which declares a strong public policy of this State *(see* Penal Law, § 1110).

The general rule that "a marriage valid where solemnized is valid everywhere" (see Restatement, Conflict of Laws, § 121) does not apply. To that rule there is a proviso or exception, recognized, it would seem, by all the States, as follows: "unless contrary to the prohibitions of natural law or the express prohibitions of a statute". Section 132 of the Restatement of Conflict of Laws states the rule apparently followed throughout America: "A marriage which is against the law of the state of domicil of either party, though the requirements of the law of the state of celebration have been complied with, will be invalid everywhere in the following cases."

The old and famous New York case of *Wightman v. Wightman* (4 Johns. Ch. 343, 349, 350), decided in 1820 when there were no marriage statutes in our State, says that marriages may be declared by "appropriate legislation", to be incestuous. New York, as a sovereign State with absolute powers over the marital status of its citizens, has enacted such legislation, but we, by this decision, are denying it efficacy.

Section 5 of the Domestic Relations Law, the one we are concerned with here, lists the marriages which are "incestuous and void" in New York, as being those between parent and child, brother and sister, uncle and niece, and aunt and nephew. All such misalliances are incestuous, and all, equally, are void. The policy, language, meaning and validity of the statute are beyond dispute. It should be enforced by the courts.

*See* PROBLEMS 8A-1. HER MOTHER'S HUSBAND; 8A-2. A CHILD BRIDE.

## NOTES AND QUESTIONS ON CELEBRATING THE LAW OF THE PLACE OF CELEBRATION

(1) *A True Rule.* What does the New York court mean when it says that, generally speaking, "the legality of a marriage between persons *sui juris* is to be determined by the law of the place where it is celebrated?" Both the Restatement (Second) of Conflict of Laws § 283 and commentators, *e.g.*, ROBERT LEFLAR, ET AL, AMERICAN CONFLICTS LAW § 22 (4th ed. 1986), agree.

The law of celebration (or "lex celebrationis") is closely related to one of Professor Ehrenzweig's "True Rules," the rule of validation. *See* Albert Ehrenzweig, Conflict of Laws 352-53 (2d ed. 1962). Ehrenzweig generally would have courts validate consensual arrangements such as contracts and marriages. Isn't there a stronger case for enforcing expectations about marital status, especially when children are involved, than there is for ordinary contracts? Or, is that argument backwards: Doesn't the state have a *stronger* concern with marriages than it does with ordinary commercial arrangements?

(2) *Interest Analysis.* Was Rhode Island an interested jurisdiction? How strong were *its* interests? How strong was New York's interest in preventing incestuous marriage? Is this a true conflict? How important are party expectations when they fly in the face of a strongly held policy of the joint domicile?

(3) *Public Policy and Morals.* The majority opinion in *May's Estate* suggests that either a statutory prohibition of validity or a marriage "offensive to the public sense of morality" might trump the natural desire to carry out the couple's expectations that they have a legal marriage. Statutory prohibitions of the sort required are rare, with the exception of polygamy and incest. Why didn't the marriage in *May's Estate* fit the statutory prohibition exception? Is it because the New York law did not expressly invalidate all uncle-niece marriages by New York domiciliaries, *wherever celebrated* How common is that sort of legislation? Why didn't the marriage in *May's Estate* fall into the category of "offensive to the public sense or morality"? Does the majority even attempt to analyze this issue? How would you go about doing so? Why does a state prohibit polygamy and incest anyway? Does the court or legislature tell you?

Whose social policy are we talking about? Does the policy deterring to the place of celebration apply with equal force when the marriage took place abroad? What if a polygamous marriage iscontracted ina country where it is legal and the menage then moves to America? Can they live together here legally? The most famous case is *In re Dalip Singh Bits Estate,* 83 Cal. App. 2d 256, 188 P. 2d 499 (1948), where the court split an estate between the two widows of a foreign polygamous marriage. *See generally* Schuz, When is a Polygamous Marriage Not a Polygamous Marriage, 46 MOD. L. REV. 653 (1983).

Many American jurisdictions at one time had laws prohibiting miscegenation (and much of the case law in this area involved those archaic prohibitions), but such laws, of course, are unconstitutional today. A few states still recognize informal, "common-law" marriages. These are usually, but not always, validated when the issue arises in a conflicts context. *See generally* EUGENE SCOLES & PETER HAY, CONFLICT OF LAWS § 13.16 (2d ed. 1991).

*See* PROBLEMS 8A-3. BACK HOME AGAIN; 8A-4. A CHURCH WEDDING; 8A-5. MEMBERS OF THE PEACE CORPS; 8A-6. FIRST COUSINS; 8A-7. COMPETING WIDOWERS; 8A-8. THE COMMON-LAW MARRIAGE.

## § 8.03 Annulment

Annulment is the converse of divorce: it is a legal proceeding which dissolves the marriage, and it is granted only for problems which existed at the time the marriage was celebrated. Again, both choice of law and jurisdictional issues can be raised.

**WILKINS v. ZELICHOWSKI,** 26 N.J. 370, 140 A.2d 65 (1958): The bride and groom were domiciled in New Jersey. They ran away to Indiana to be married, returning "immediately" to New Jersey. The bride later sought to annul the marriage because she was not 18 when she married, that being the minimum age for marriages in New Jersey. Indiana, however, permitted girls to marry at 16.

*Held:* The marriage was invalid: "New Jersey was the only state having any interest [and the] purpose in having the ceremony take place in Indiana was to evade New Jersey's marriage policy.

\* \* \*

What does it mean to have an "interest" in the annulment? Restatement (Second) of Conflict of Laws § 283 states that the law to be applied is that of the place with "the most significant relationship to the spouses and the marriage."

What of jurisdiction? Is annulment a local action, in which subject-matter jurisdiction is vested only in a particular contact state? Which state ought that to be? Some courts have held that any interested state can hear an annulment action, *see, e.g., Bramble v. Kemper,* 227 Ark. 186, 297 S.W. 2d 104 (1957). Why? How about any other state which, in the language of *Wilkins,* has an "interest"? Again, some think so. *E.g., Whealton v. Whealton,* 67 Cal. 2d 656, 432 P.2d 979, 63 Cal. Rptr. 291 (1967). *See generally* David Vernon, *Labyrinthine Ways: Jurisdiction to Annul,* 10 J. PUB. L. 47 (1961).

*See* PROBLEM 8A-9. IS ANNULMENT A TRANSITORY ACTION?

## § 8.04 The Incidental Question

**IN RE ESTATE OF LENHERR,** 455 Cal. 225, 314 A.2d 255 (1974): Leo and Sarah Lenherr were divorced in 1930 from their former spouses. The ground for divorce in each case was adultery; that is, adultery committed between Leo and Sarah. After their divorces, the couple married in West Virginia and returned to Pennsylvania, their former and future domicile, to live. Leo died in 1971, and Sarah sought the benefit of a tax exemption available to widows under Pennsylvania's inheritance tax.

The problem arose because the Lenherrs' marriage, although valid in West Virginia, was invalid under Pennsylvania law. That state forbade marriages between two persons who had committed adultery with each other.

*Held:* Sarah was entitled to the exemption. The purpose behind the prohibition against remarriage, the court observed, was "to protect the sensibilities of the injured spouse," and to deter adulterous conduct. Because neither purpose would be served by denying the tax exemption, and because doing so would defeat the purpose underlying the exemption, the court decided to give "extraterritorial effect" to the Pennsylvania statute.

## NOTES AND QUESTIONS

*Lenherr's Estate* is an example of what has become known as the "incidental question," so-called because the validity of the marriage is questioned only incidentally in connection with resolving another legal question (such as whether a party is a surviving spouse entitled to a tax exemption). Most discussions of the incidental question usually involve marriage, but it can arise in other areas as well.

The resolution of *Lenherr's Estate* may remind you of the technique of comparative impairment, discussed in § 4.23, *supra.* Of course, there is this (crucial) difference: the two statutes being compared in *Lenherr* are both from the same jurisdiction—Pennsylvania. *See generally* Gotlieb, *The Incidental Question Revisited—Theory and Practice in the Conflict of Laws,* 26 INT'L. & Comp. L. Q. 734 (1977); Rosa, *Marriage in American Conflicts of Laws,* 26 I'NT'L . & COMP. L. Q. 952 (1977).

## THE DEFENSE OF MARRIAGE ACT

Congress adopted the Defense of Marriage Act ("DOMA") in 1996. DOMA, codified at 1 U.S.C. § 7 and 28 U.S.C. § 1738C, provides that "No state . . . is required to give effect to any public act, record, or judicial proceeding of any other state . . . respecting a relationship between persons of the same sex that is treated as a marriage under the laws of such state. . . . "

DOMA was enacted in response to a decision by the Hawaiian Supreme Court that the Hawaiian constitution required that same-sex couples who wanted to marry had to be permitted to do so. *Baehr v. Lewin* , 852 P. 2d 44 (Haw. 1993). DOMA was very controversial at the time it was adopted, and it remains so today.

The commentary on DOMA is voluminous. *See, e.g.* , Symposium, *Interjuris-dictional Marriage Recognition,* 32 CREIGHTON L. REV. 3 (1998) (contributions by many professors); Andrew Koppelman, *Same-Sex Marriage, Choice of Law, and Public Policy*, 76 TEXAS L. REV. 921 (1998); Larry Kramer, *Same Sex Marriage, Conflict of Laws, and the Unconstitutional Public Policy Exception*, 106 YALE L.J. 1965 (1997); Julie L.B. Johnson, Note, *The Meaning of "General Laws": The Extent of Congress' Powers Under the Full Faith and Credit Clause and the Constitutionality of the defense of Marriage Act,* 145 U.PA. L. REV. 151 (1996); Jennifer Gerarda Brown, *Extraterritorial Recognition of Same-Sex Marriage: When Theory Confronts Praxis*, 16 QUINIPPIAC L. REV. 1 (1996); Daniel Crane, *The Original Understanding of the "Effects Clause" of Article IV, Section 1 and Implication of the Defense of Marriage Act*, GEORGE MASON L. REV. 307 (1998). *See also* Joseph W. Hovermill, *A Conflict of Laws and*

*Morals: The Choice of Law Implications of Hawaii's Recognition of Same-Sex Marriages,* 53 MD. L. REV. 450 (1994).

1. *Why the Fuss?* One of the editors of this book was asked to testify before Congress about DOMA. The editor's response was that there was little to say, because DOMA merely codified existing full faith and credit law. Can there be any doubt that the editor was correct, at least if *In Re May's Estate* is constitutionally sound, and of its soundness there was little doubt until the furor over DOMA erupted?

2. *Is the Traditional Wisdom Wrong?* Remember the discussion in § 7.02, *supra,* of the practical problems involved in giving full faith and credit to statutes. Would it be desirable or even possible to establish a constitutional regime where full faith and credit to legislative enactments was a serious constitutional requirement?

3. *Maybe Some Full Faith and Credit?* Should the full faith and credit question raised by DOMA turn on the specific issue at stake—that is on whether the same-sex marriage should be recognized for purposes of granting alimony in a divorce action, survivor's rights in a wrongful death action, or visitation rights in a custody dispute? Does such bifurcation of marital rights make sense? See the discussion of the "Incidental Question" in § 8.04, *supra.*

4. *Other Problems with DOMA.* DOMA, of course, also raises other serious constitutional questions. Does the discrimination against same-sex marriages violate other protections afforded by the Constitution, such as Equal Protection or Due Process? *See generally* Mark Strasser, *Loving the Romer Out for Baehr On Acts in Defense of Marriage and the Constitution,* 58 U. PITT. L. REV. 279 (1997).

# PART B  DIVORCE AND MARITAL SUPPORT

This Part treats the authority of a court to sunder the marital relation. Because marriage creates both status and personal relations, a divorce can raise very interesting jurisdictional questions, which, in turn, can lead to difficult enforcement issues.

## § 8.05  Jurisdiction to Divorce

### WILLIAMS v. NORTH CAROLINA [WILLIAMS I]

*United States Supreme Court*
*317 U.S. 287, 63 S. Ct. 207, 87 L. Ed. 279 (1942)*

Mr. Justice Douglas delivered the opinion of the Court.

Petitioners were tried and convicted of bigamous cohabitation under § 4342 of the North Carolina Code, and each was sentenced for a term of years in a state prison. The judgment of conviction was affirmed by the Supreme Court of North Carolina. The case is here on certiorari.

Petitioner Williams was married to Carrie Wyke in 1916 in North Carolina and lived with her there until May, 1940. Petitioner Hendrix was married to Thomas Hendrix in 1920 in North Carolina and lived with him there until May, 1940. At that time petitioners went to Las Vegas, Nevada, and on June 26, 1940, each filed a divorce action in the Nevada court. The defendants in those divorce actions entered no appearance nor were they served with process in Nevada. In the case of defendant Thomas Hendrix, service by publication was had by publication of the summons in a Las Vegas newspaper and by mailing a copy of the summons and complaint to his last post-office address. In the case of defendant Carrie Williams, a North Carolina sheriff delivered to her in North Carolina a copy of the summons and complaint. A decree of divorce was granted petitioner Williams by the Nevada court on August 26, 1940, on the ground of extreme cruelty, the court finding that "the plaintiff has been and now is a bona fide and continuous resident of the County of Clark, State of Nevada, and had been such resident for more than six weeks immediately preceding the commencement of this action in the manner prescribed by law." The Nevada court granted petitioner Hendrix a divorce on October 4, 1940, on the grounds of wilful neglect and extreme cruelty, and made the same finding as to this petitioner's bona fide residence in Nevada as it made in the case of Williams. Petitioners were married to each other in Nevada on October 4, 1940. Thereafter they returned to North Carolina where they lived together until the indictment was returned. Petitioners pleaded not guilty and offered in evidence exemplified copies of the Nevada proceedings, contending that the divorce decrees and the Nevada marriage were valid in North Carolina as well as in Nevada. The State contended that since neither of the defendants in the Nevada actions was served in Nevada nor entered an appearance there, the Nevada decrees would not be recognized as valid in North Carolina. On this issue the court charged the jury in substance that a Nevada divorce decree based on substituted service where the defendant made no appearance would not be recognized in North Carolina. The State further contended that petitioners went to Nevada not to establish a bona fide residence but solely for the purpose of taking advantage of the laws of that State to obtain a divorce through fraud upon that court. On that issue the court charged the jury that the defendants had the burden of satisfying the jury, but not beyond a reasonable doubt, of the bona fides of their residence in Nevada for the required time . . .

The historical view that a proceeding for a divorce was a proceeding in rem was rejected by [*Haddock v. Haddock*, 201 U.S. 562 (1906)]. We likewise agree that it does not aid in the solution of the problem presented by this case to label these proceedings as proceedings in rem. Such a suit, however, is not a mere in personam action. Domicile of the plaintiff, immaterial to jurisdiction ina personal action, is recognized in the Haddock case and elsewhere as essential in order to give the court jurisdiction which will entitle the divorce decree to extraterritorial effect, at least when the defendant has neither been personally served nor entered an appearance. The findings made in the divorce decrees in the instant case must be treated on the issue before us as meeting those requirements. For it seems clear that the provision of the Nevada statute that a plaintiff in this type of case must reside" in the State for the required period requires him to have a domicile as distinguished from a mere residence, in the state. Hence, the decrees in this case, like other divorce decrees, are more than in personam judgments. They involve the marital status of the parties. Domicil creates a relationship to the state which is adequate for numerous exercises of state power. Each state as a sovereign has a rightful and legitimate concern in the marital status of persons domiciled within its borders. The marriage relation creates problems of large social importance. Protection of offspring, property interests, and the enforcement of marital responsibilities are but a few of commanding problems in the field of domestic relations with which the state must deal. Thus it is plain that each state, by virtue of its command over its domiciliaries and its large interest in the institution of marriage, can alter within its own borders the marriage status of the spouse domiciled there, even though the other spouse is absent.

This Court stated in *Atherton v. Atherton* [181 U.S. 155] that "A husband without a wife, or a wife without a husband, is unknown to the law." But if one is lawfully divorced and remarried in Nevada and still married to the first spouse in North Carolina, an even more complicated and serious condition would be realized. Under the circumstances of this case, a man would have two wives, a wife two husbands. The reality of a sentence to prison proves that is no mere play on words. Each would be a bigamist for living in one state with the only one with whom the other state would permit him lawfully to live. Children of the second marriage would be bastards in one state but legitimate in the other. And all that would flow from the legalistic notion that where one spouse is wrongfully deserted he retains power over the matrimonial domicil so that the domicil of the other spouse follows him wherever he may go, while, if he is to blame, he retains no such power. But such considerations are inapposite. As stated by Mr. Justice Holmes in his dissent in the *Haddock* case, they constitute a "pure fiction, and fiction always is a poor ground for changing substantial rights." Furthermore, the fault or wrong of one spouse in leaving the other becomes under that view a jurisdictional fact on which this Court would ultimately have to pass. Whatever may be said as to the practical effect which such a rule would have in clouding divorce decrees, the question as to where the fault lies has no relevancy to the existence of state power in such circumstances. The existence of the power of a state to alter the marital status of its domiciliaries, as distinguished from the wisdom of its exercise, is not dependent on the underlying causes of the domestic rift. As we have said, it is dependent on the relationship which domicil creates and the pervasive control which a state has over marriage and divorce within its own borders. Moreover, so far as state power is concerned, no distinction between a matrimonial domicil and a domicil later acquired has been suggested or isapparent. It is one thing to say as a matter of state law that jurisdiction to grant a divorce from an absent spouse should depend on whether by consent or by conduct the latter has subjected his interest in the marriage status to the law of the separate domicil acquired by the other spouse. But where a state adopts, as it has the power to do, a less strict rule, it is quite another thing to say that its decrees affecting the marital status of its domiciliaries are not entitled to full faith and credit in sister states. Certainly if decrees of a state altering the marital status of its domiciliaries are not valid throughout the Union even though the requirements of proce- dural due process are wholly met, a rule would be fostered which could not help but bring "considerable disaster to innocent persons" and "bastardize children hitherto supposed to be the offspring of lawful marriage" (Mr. Justice Holmes dissenting in *Haddock v. Haddock*), or else encourage collusive divorces. These intensely practical considerations emphasize for us the essential function of the full faith and credit clause in substituting a command for the former principles of comity and in altering the "status of the several states as independent foreign sovereignties" by making them "integral parts of a single nation."

It is objected, however, that if such divorce decrees must be given full faith and credit, a substantial dilution of the sovereignty of other states will be effected. For it is pointed out that under such a rule one state's policy of strict control over the institution of marriage could be thwarted by the decree of a more lax state. But such an objection goes to the application of the full faith and credit clause to many situations. It is an objection in varying degrees of intensity to the enforcement of a judgment of a sister state based on a cause of action which could not be enforced in the state of the forum. Mississippi's policy against gambling transactions was overridden in *Fauntleroy v. Lum* [210 U.S. 230] when a Missouri judgment based on such a Mississippi contract was enforced by this Court. Such is part of the price of our federal system.

[I]n this case we must assume that petitioners had a bona fide domicil in Nevada, not that the Nevada domicil was a sham. We thus have no question on the present record whether a divorce decree granted by the courts of one state to a resident, as distinguished from a domiciliary, is entitled to full faith and credit in another state. Nor do we reach here the question as to the power of North Carolina to refuse full faith and credit to Nevada divorce decrees because, contrary to the findings of the Nevada court, North Carolina finds that no bona fide domicil was acquired in Nevada. In the second place, the question as to what is a permissible limitation on the full faith and credit clause does not involve a decision on our part as to which state policy on divorce is the most desirable one. It does not involve selection of a rule which will encourage on the one hand or discourage on the other the practice of divorce. That choice in the realm of morals and religion rests with the legislatures of the states. Our own views as to the marriage institution and the avenues of escape which some states have created are immaterial. It is a Constitution which we are expounding—a Constitution which in no small measure brings separate sovereign states into an integrated whole through the medium of the full faith and credit clause. Within the limits of her political power North Carolina may, of course, enforce her own policy regarding the marriage relation—an institution more basic in our civilization than any other. But society also has an interest in the avoidance of polygamous marriages and in the protection of innocent offspring of marriages deemed legitimate in other jurisdictions. And other states have an equally legitimate concern in the status of persons domiciled there as respects the institution of marriage. So, when a court of one state acting in accord with the requirements of procedural due process alters the marital status of one domiciled in that state by granting him a divorce from his absent spouse, we cannot say its decree should be excepted from the full faith and credit clause merely because itsenforcement or recognition in another state would conflict with the policy of the latter. Whether Congress has the power to create exceptions *(see Yarborough v. Yarborough, 290* U.S. 202, 215, nt. 2, dissenting opinion) is a question on which we express no view.

Mr. Justice Frankfurter, concurring:

We are not authorized nor are we qualified to formulate a national code of domestic relations. We cannot, by making "jurisdiction" depend upon a determination of who is the deserter and who the deserted, or upon the shifting notions of policy concealed by the cloudy abstraction of "matrimonial domicile," turn this into a divorce and probate court for the United States. The need for securing national uniformity in dealing with divorce, either through constitutional amendment or by some other means, has long been the concern of the Conference of Governors and of special bodies convened to consider this problem. This Court should abstain from trying to reach the same end by indirection.

There is but one respect in which this Court can, within its traditional authority and professional competence, contribute uniformity to the law of marriage and divorce, and that is to enforce respect for the judgment of a state by its sister states when the judgment was rendered in accordance with settled procedural standards . . .

The duty of a state to respect the judgments of a sister state arises only where such judgments meet the tests of justice and fair dealing that are embodied in the historic phrase, "due process of law." But in this case all talk about due process is beside the mark. If the actions of the Nevada court had been taken "without due process of law," the divorces which it purported to decree would have been without legal sanction in every state, including Nevada. There would be no occasion to consider the applicability of the Full Faith and Credit Clause. It is precisely because the Nevada decrees do satisfy the requirements of the Due Process Clause and are binding in Nevada upon the absent spouses that we are called upon to decide whether these judgments, unassailable in the state which rendered them, are, despite the commands of the Full Faith and Credit Clause, null and void elsewhere.

North Carolina did not base its disregard of the Nevada decrees on the claim that they were a fraud and a sham, and no claim was made here on behalf of North Carolina that the decrees were not valid in Nevada . . .

MR. JUSTICE MURPHY: I dissent.

This case cannot be considered as one involving the Constitution alone; rather the case involves the interaction of public policy upon the Constitution. This is not to say that our function is to become censors of public morals and decide this case in accordance with what we may think is the wisest rule for society with respect to divorce. But the question of public policy enters to this degree—marriage and the family have generally been regarded as basic components of our national life, and the solution of the problems engendered by the marital relation, the formulation of standards of public morality in connection therewith, and the supervision of domestic (in the sense of family) affairs, have been left to the individual states.

In recognition of the paramount interest of the state of domicile over the marital status of its citizens, this Court has held that actual good faith domicile of at least one party is essential to confer authority and jurisdiction on the courts of a state to render a decree of divorce that will be entitled to extraterritorial effect under the Full Faith and Credit Clause. Did petitioners acquire a bona fide domicile in Nevada? I agree with my brother Jackson that the only proper answer on the record is, no. North Carolina is the state in which petitioners have their roots, the state to which they immediately returned after a brief absence just sufficient to achieve their purpose under Nevada's requirements. It follows that the Nevada decrees are entitled to no extraterritorial effect when challenged in another state.

This is not to say that the Nevada decrees are without any legal effect in the State of Nevada. That question is not before us.

We have recognized an area of flexibility in the application of the Clause to preserve and protect state policies in matters of vital public concern. We have said that conflicts between such state policies should be resolved, "not by giving automatic effect to the full faith and credit clause, but by appraising the governmental interests of each jurisdiction, and turning the scale of decision according to their weight." *Alaska Packers Ass'n v. Comm'n* [294 U.S. 532]. (*See also Milwaukee County v. White Co., and compare* the dissenting opinion in *Yarborough v. Yarborough.*) That Clause should no more be read "with literal exactness like a mathematical formula" than are other great and general clauses of the Constitution placing limitations upon the States to weld us into a Nation. Rather it should be construed to harmonize its direction "with the necessary residuum of state power . . ."

There is an element of tragic incongruity in the fact that an individual may be validly divorced in one state but not in another. But our dual system of government and the fact that we have no uniform laws on many subjects give rise to other incongruities as well—for example, the common law took the logical position that an individual could have but one domicile at a time, but this Court has nevertheless said that the Full Faith and Credit Clause does not prevent conflicting state decisions on the question of an individual's domicile.

Mr. Justice Jackson, dissenting:

I cannot join in exerting the judicial power of the Federal Government to compel the State of North Carolina to subordinate its own law to the Nevada divorce decrees. The Court's decision to do so reaches far beyond the immediate case. It subjects matrimonial laws of each state to important limitations and exceptions that it must recognize within its own borders and as to its own permanent population. It nullifies the power of each state to protect its own citizens against dissolution of their marriages by the courts of other states which have an easier system of divorce. It subjects every marriage to a new infirmity, in that one dissatisfied spouse may choose a state of easy divorce, in which neither party has ever lived, and there commence proceedings without personal service of process. The spouse remaining within the state of domicile need never know of the proceedings. Or, if they come to one's knowledge, the choice is between equally useless alternatives: one is to ignore the foreign proceedings, in which case the marriage **is** quite certain to be dissolved; the other is to follow the complaining spouse to the state of his choice and there defend under the laws which grant the dissolution on relatively trivial grounds. To declare that a state is powerless to protect either its own policy or the family rights of its people against such consequences has serious constitutional implications. It is not an exaggeration to say that this decision repeals the divorce laws of all the states and substitutes the law of Nevada as to all marriages one of the parties to which can afford a short trip there.

I doubt that it promotes clarity of thinking to deal with marriage in terms of a res, like a piece of land or a chattel. It might be more helpful to think of marriage as just marriage—a relationship out of which spring duties to both spouse and society and from which are derived rights—such as the right to society and services and to conjugal love and affection—rights which generally prove to be either priceless or worthless, but which none the less the law sometimes attempts to evaluate in terms of money when one is deprived of them by the negligence or design of a third party.

It does not seem consistent with our legal system that one who has these continuing rights should be deprived of them without a hearing. Neither does it seem that he or she should be summoned by mail, publication, or otherwise to a remote jurisdiction chosen by the other party and there be obliged to submit marital rights to adjudication under a state policy at odds with that of the state under which the marriage was contracted and the matrimonial domicile was established.

\*    \*    \*

While a state can no doubt set up its own standards of domicile as to its internal concerns, I do not think it can require us to accept and in the name of the Constitution impose them on other states. If Nevada may prescribe six weeks of indefinite-permanent abode in a motor court as constituting domicile, she may as readily prescribe six days. Indeed, if the Court's opinion is carried to its logical conclusion, a state could grant a constructive domicile for divorce purposes upon the filing of some sort of declaration of intention. Then it would follow that we would be required to accept it as sufficient and to force all states to recognize mail-order divorces as well as tourist divorces. Indeed, the difference is in the bother and expense—not in the principle of the thing.

The Court advances two "intensely practical considerations" in support of its present decision. One is the "complicated and serious condition" if "one is lawfully divorced and remarried in Nevada and still married to the first spouse in North Carolina." This of course begs the question, for the divorces were completely ineffectual for any purpose relevant to this case. I agree that it is serious if a Nevada court without jurisdiction for divorce purports to say that the sojourn of two spouses gives four spouses rights to acquire four more, but I think it far more serious to force North Carolina to acquiesce in any such proposition. The other consideration advanced is that if the Court doesn't enforce divorces such as these it will, as it puts it, "bastardize" children of the divorcees. When thirty-seven years ago Mr. Justice Holmes perpetrated this quip, it had point, for the Court was then holding divorces invalid which many, due to the confused state of the law, had thought to be good. It is difficult to find that it has point now that the shoe is on the other foot. In any event, I had supposed that our judicial responsibility is for the regularity of the law, not for the regularity of pedigrees.

## NOTES AND QUESTIONS ON *WILLIAMS I* AND THE DOMICILE RULE

(1) *The Majority Opinion.* Why did North Carolina wish to challenge the validity of the divorces? Does it seem strange to you that the state prosecuted Mr. and Mrs. Williams? Obviously, small town mores in North Carolina in 1940 were a far cry from the permissive society that was to follow. A beguiling recitation of the Williams' plight can be found in Thomas Reed Powell, *And Repent at Leisure,* 58 HARV. L. REV. 930 (1945).[1] *Williams* was a very important decision, for it was rendered in an era when a divorce was generally very difficult to obtain. Hence, it provided a way for an unhappy spouse effectively to dissolve a marriage.

What gives Nevada subject matter jurisdiction to grant the divorces? Was it an "interested" jurisdiction? What legitimate state interests does the Nevada legislation serve? Would it have been more interested if the divorcing petitioners had been long-term Nevada residents?

Why did Justice Douglas accept the common law view that domicile was the key jurisdictional element? Recall the discussion of domicile in Chapter Two, *supra.* Do you think it has the talismanic qualities attributed to it by Justice Douglas? How long did Nevada require to establish domicile? Is it possible to establish domicile in a shorter period?

Undoubtedly, the (new) Williams couple had planned all along to return to North Carolina. Don't you think that the Supreme Court must have realized

---

[1] Among the facts Professor Powell found: The two couples were from Granite Falls, North Carolina, population 2,417. When the Williams' returned to North Carolina they "set up housekeeping" in Pineole, population 306. Mr. Hendrix had worked in Mrs. Williams's store.

that? Apparently, then, *Williams I* would permit a state to exercise jurisdiction to divorce on fraudulent recitations of jurisdictional facts. Assuming that the parties have enough money, is there anything to prevent them from lying to the Nevada court about their status as domiciliaries, securing the divorce, and returning home? If they can do that, what becomes of the domestic relations policies of North Carolina embodied in its restrictive grounds for divorce statutes? And does Nevada have any incentive to ensure that the parties do not perjure themselves concerning their status as domiciliaries?

(2)  *The Frankfurter Concurrence.* What did he write? Why did he write?

(3)  *The Murphy Dissent.*  In contrast, it is perfectly clear why Justice Murphy dissented: He saw the handwriting on the wall. How would he have solved the problem he identified? Do any of the opinions in *Thomas v. Washington Gas Light Co.,*  448 U.S. 261 (1980), discussed in § 7.09, *supra,* support Murphy's position?

(4)  *The Jackson Dissent.* Justice Jackson also saw the handwriting on the wall, but, unlike Murphy, Jackson was worried about personal rights, as well as state interests. But whose personal rights are more important: The spouse who wants a divorce, or the one who stays at home?

## § 8.06  Recognition and Collateral Attack

### WILLIAMS v. NORTH CAROLINA [WILLIAMS II]

*United States Supreme Court*
*325 U.S. 226, 65 S. Ct. 1092, 89 L. Ed.1577 (1945).*

Mr. Justice Frankfurter delivered the opinion of the Court.

This case is here to review judgments of the Supreme Court of North Carolina, affirming convictions for bigamous cohabitation, assailed on the ground that full faith and credit, as required by the Constitution of the United States, was not accorded divorces decreed by one of the courts of Nevada. *Williams v. North Carolina* [ *Williams I*], decided an earlier aspect of the controversy. It was there held that a divorce granted by Nevada, on a finding that one spouse was domiciled in Nevada, must be respected in North Carolina, where Nevada's finding of domicil was not questioned, though the other spouse had neither appeared nor been served with process in Nevada and though recognition of such a divorce offended the policy of North Carolina. The record then before us did not present the question whether North Carolina had the power "to refuse full faith and credit to Nevada divorce decrees because, contrary to the findings of the Nevada court, North Carolina finds that no bona fide domicil was acquired in Nevada." [*Williams I*]. This is the precise issue which has emerged after retrial of the cause following our reversal. Its obvious importance brought the case here.

Under our system of law, judicial power to grant a divorce—jurisdiction, strictly speaking—is founded on domicile. In view of *Williams* [I],  the jurisdictional requirement of domicil is freed from confusing refinements about "matrimonial domicile" and the like. Divorce, like marriage, is of concern not merely to the immediate parties. It affects personal rights of the deepest significance. It also touches basic interests of society. Since divorce, like marriage, creates a new status, every consideration of policy makes it desirable that the effect should be the same wherever the question arises.

It is one thing to reopen an issue that has been settled after appropriate opportunity to present their contentions has been afforded to all who had an interest in its adjudication. This applies also to jurisdictional questions. After a contest these cannot be relitigated as between the parties. But those not parties to a litigation ought not to be foreclosed by the interested actions of others; especially not a State which is concerned with the vindication of its own social policy and has no means, certainly no effective means, to protect that interest against the selfish action of those outside its borders. The State of domiciliary origin should not be bound by an unfounded, even if not collusive, recital in the record of a court of another State. As to the truth or existence of a fact, like that of domicile upon which depends the power to exert judicial authority, a State not a party to the exertion of such judicial authority in another State but seriously affected by it has a right, when asserting its own unquestioned authority, to ascertain the truth or existence of that crucial fact.[2]

These considerations of policy are equally applicable whether power was assumed by the court of the first State or claimed after inquiry. This may lead, no doubt, to conflicting determinations of what judicial power is founded upon. Such conflict is inherent in the practical application of the concept of domicil in the context of our federal system.[3] If a finding by the court of one State that domicil in another State has been abandoned were conclusive upon the old domiciliary State, the policy of each State in matters of most intimate concern could be subverted by the policy of every other State. This Court has long ago denied the existence of such destructive power. The issue has a far reach. For domicil is the foundation of probate jurisdiction precisely as it is that of divorce.

[T]he decree of divorce is a conclusive adjudication of everything except the jurisdictional facts upon which it is founded, and domicil is a jurisdictional fact. To permit the necessary finding of domicil by one State to foreclose all States in the protection of their social institutions would be intolerable.

But to endow each State with controlling authority to nullify the power of a sister State to grant a divorce based upon a finding that one spouse had acquired a new domicil within the divorcing State would, in the proper functioning of our federal system, be equally indefensible. The necessary accommodation between the right of one State to safeguard its interest in the family relation of its own people and the power of another State to grant divorces can be left to neither State . . .

If it is a matter turning on local law, great deference is owed by the courts of one State to what a court of another State has done. But when we are

---

[2] We have not here a situation where a State disregards the adjudication of another State on the issue of domicile squarely litigated in a truly adversary proceeding.

[3] Since an appeal to the Full Faith and Credit Clause raises questions arising under the Constitution of the United States, the proper criteria for ascertaining domicile should these be in dispute, become matters for federal determination.

dealing as here with an historic notion common to all English-speaking courts, that of domicil, we should not find a want of deference to a sister State on the part of a court of another State which finds an absence of domicil where such a conclusion iswarranted by the record.

Against the charge of bigamous cohabitation under the North Carolina General Statutes, petitioners stood on their Nevada divorces and offered exemplified copies of the Nevada proceedings. The trial judge charged that the State had the burden of proving beyond a reasonable doubt that (1) each petitioner was lawfully married to one person; (2) thereafter each petitioner contracted a second marriage with another person outside North Carolina; (3) the spouses of petitioners were living at the time of this second marriage; (4) petitioners cohabited with one another in North Carolina after the second marriage. The burden, it was charged, then devolved upon petitioners "to satisfy the trial jury, not beyond a reasonable doubt nor by the greater weight of the evidence, but simply to satisfy" the jury from all the evidence, that petitioners were domiciled in Nevada at the time they obtained their divorces. The court further charged that "the recitation" of bona fide domicil in the Nevada decree was "prima facie evidence" sufficient to warrant a finding of domicil in Nevada but not compelling "such an inference." If the jury found, as they were told, that petitioners had domicils in North Carolina and went to Nevada "simply and solely for the purpose of obtaining" divorces, intending to return to North Carolina on obtaining them, they never lost their North Carolina domicils nor acquired new domicils in Nevada. Domicil, the jury was instructed, was that place where a person "has voluntarily fixed his abode not for a mere special or temporary purpose, but with a present intention of making it his home, either permanently or for an indefinite or unlimited length of time . . ."

If a State cannot foreclose, on review here, all the other States by its finding that one spouse is domiciled within its bounds, persons may, no doubt, place themselves in situations that create unhappy consequences for them. This is merely one of those untoward results inevitable in a federal system in which regulation of domestic relations has been left with the States and not given to the national authority. But the occasional disregard by any one State of the reciprocal obligations of the forty-eight States to respect the constitutional power of each to deal with domestic relations of those domiciled within its borders is hardly an argument for allowing one State to deprive the other forty-seven States of their constitutional rights.

In seeking a decree of divorce outside the State in which he has theretofore maintained his marriage, a person is necessarily involved in the legal situation created by our federal system whereby one State can grant a divorce of validity in other States only if the applicant has a bona fide domicil in the State of the court purporting to dissolve a prior legal marriage. The petitioners therefore assumed the risk that this Court would find that North Carolina justifiably concluded that they had not been domiciled in Nevada. Since the divorces which they sought and received in Nevada had no legal validity in North Carolina and their North Carolina spouses were still alive, they subjected themselves to prosecution for bigamous cohabitation under North Carolina law. A man's fate often depends, as for instance in the enforcement of the Sherman Law, on far greater risks that he will estimate "rightly, that is, as the jury subsequently estimates it, some matter of degree."

We conclude that North Carolina was not required to yield her State policy because a Nevada court found that petitioners were domiciled in Nevada when it granted them decrees of divorce. North Carolina was entitled to find, as she did, that they did not acquire domicils in Nevada and that the Nevada court was therefore without power to liberate the petitioners from amenability to the laws of North Carolina governing domestic relations. And, as was said in connection with another aspect of the Full Faith and Credit Clause, our conclusion "is not a matter to arouse the susceptibilities of the States, all of which are equally concerned in the question and equally on both sides." *Fauntleroy v. Lum,* 210 U.S. 230, 238.

*Affirmed.*

MR. JUSTICE MURPHY, concurring.

By being domiciled and living in North Carolina, petitioners secure all the benefits and advantages of its government and participated in its social and economic life. As long as petitioners and their respective spouses lived there and retained that domicile North Carolina had the exclusive right to regulate the dissolution of their marriage relationships. However harsh and unjust North Carolina's divorce laws may be thought to be, petitioners were bound to obey them while retaining residential and domiciliary ties in that state.

No justifiable purpose is served by imparting constitutional sanctity to the efforts of petitioners to establish a false and fictitious domicil in Nevada. Such a result would only tend to promote wholesale disregard of North Carolina's divorce laws by its citizens, thus putting an end to "the existence of all efficacious power on the subject of divorce." Certainly no policy of Nevada dictates lending the full faith and credit clause to protect actions grounded in deceit. Nevada has a recognizable interest in granting only two types of ex parte divorces: (a) those effective solely within the borders of Nevada, and (b) those effective everywhere on the ground that at least one of the parties had a bona fide domicil in the state at the time the decree was granted. Neither type of divorce is involved here. And Nevada has no interest that we can respect in issuing divorce decrees with extraterritorial effect to those who are domiciled elsewhere and who secure sham domicils in Nevada solely for divorce purposes.

Whatever embarrassment or inconvenience resulting to those who have made property settlements, contracted new marriages or otherwise acted in reliance upon divorce decrees obtained under conditions found to exist in this case is not insurmountable. The states have adequate power, if they desire to exercise it, to enact legislation providing for means of validating any such property settlements or marriages or of relieving persons from other unfortunate consequences.

Nor are any issues of civil liberties at stake here.

The CHIEF JUSTICE AND MR. JUSTICE JACKSON join in these views.

MR. JUSTICE RUTLEDGE, dissenting.

Once again the ghost of "unitary domicil" returns on its perpetual round, in the guise of "jurisdictional fact," to upset judgments, marriages, divorces, undermine the relations founded upon them, and make this Court the unwilling and uncertain arbiter between the concededly valid laws and decrees of sister states. From *Bell* and *Andrews* to *Davis* to *Haddock* to *Williams* and now back to *Haddock* and *Davis* through *Williams* again—is the maze the Court has traveled in a domiciliary wilderness, only to come out with no settled constitutional policy where one is needed most.

No more unstable foundation, for state policies or marital relations, could be formulated or applied. In no region of adjudication or legislation is stability more essential for jurisdictional foundations. Beyond abnegating our function, we make instability itself the constitutional policy when the crux is so conceived and pivoted.

The question is not simply pertinent, it is imperative, whether "matrimonial domicil" has not merely been recast and returned to the play under the common law's more ancient name of "domicil of origin." For North Carolina is the only state which, upon the facts, conceivably could qualify either as "matrimonial domicil" or as "domicil of origin," whether or not they differ.

Unless "matrimonial domicile" banished in *Williams I,* has returned renamed in *Williams II* , every decree becomes vulnerable in every state. Every divorce, wherever granted, whether upon a residence of sixweeks, six months or six years, may now be reexamined by every other state, upon the same or different evidence, to redetermine the "jurisdictional fact," always the ultimate conclusion of "domicil . . ."

Stripped of its common-law gloss, the basic constitutional issue inherent in the problem is whether the states shall have power to adopt so-called "liberal" divorce policies and grant divorces to persons coming from other states while there transiently or for only short periods not sufficient in themselves, absent other objective criteria, to establish more than casual relations with the community.

I, therefore, dissent from the judgment which, in my opinion, has permitted North Carolina at her substantially unfettered will to deny all faith and credit to the Nevada decree, without in any way impeaching or attempting to impeach that judgment's constitutional validity. But if she is not to be required thus to give the faith and credit due, in my opinion she should not be allowed to deny it by any standard of proof which is less than generally is required to overturn or disregard a judgment upon direct attack. The solemnity of the judicial act and the very minimum of "respect" due the action of a sister state should compel adherence to this standard, though doing so would not give the full faith and credit which the Constitution commands. To approximate the constitutional policy would be better than to nullify it.

MR. JUSTICE BLACK, dissenting.

Anglo-American law has, until today, steadfastly maintained the principle that before an accused can be convicted of crime, he must be proven guilty beyond a reasonable doubt. These petitioners have been sentenced to prison because they were unable to prove their innocence to the satisfaction of the State of North Carolina. They have been convicted under a statute so uncertain in its application that not even the most learned member of the bar could have advised them in advance as to whether their conduct would violate the law. In reality the petitioners are being deprived of their freedom because the State of Nevada, through its legislature and courts, follows a liberal policy in granting divorces.

Who after today's decision can know or guess what "right" he can safely exercise under a divorce decree in the intervening period between the day of its entry and the day of its invalidation by a jury?

MR. JUSTICE DOUGLAS joins in this dissent.

## NOTES AND QUESTIONS ON *WILLIAMS II*

(1) *Of Mills, Havens, and Magnet Forums.* Laws widely perceived as oppressive, unreasonable, or inconvenient nevertheless sometimes remain widely in force. It is not unusual when that happens to find one state or country stepping in to supply the demand for more convenient law. Tax "havens" like the Cayman Islands provide a familiar example; the divorce "mill" provides another. Is this merely a kind of "fraud on the law" or do the Nevadas, Monacos, and Switzerlands of this world meet important demands? A more important question is whether it is fair to limit those who cannot afford to take advantage of more flexible foreign law away from home with the inflexible law of their home state. During the heyday of the adultery requirement for granting a divorce, the rich in this country generally had effective freedom to make second marriages through the suitcase divorce route, an avenue denied to the poor.

(2) *Gresham's Law and Federalism.* Justice Frankfurter's opinion holds that F-2 may question the "jurisdictional facts" upon which the F-1 decree was based. Is that simply because North Carolina was not a party to the earlier proceedings, and, therefore, was not barred under ordinary preclusion principles from attacking the earlier decree?

Or was Frankfurter stalking bigger game? Consider what would happen if the case had gone the other way. A spouse would be able to go to a state with friendly divorce laws, fake the domicile requirement, and return to the only state with a real interest in the marriage, having successfully evaded that state's public policy limiting the grant of divorce. Would not, then, a kind of "Gresham's Law" of divorce operate, with lenient state laws driving out strict?

> If the holding in *Williams II* is, in fact, based on the interest of the state of the marital domicile, does it provide support for the notion found in Restatement (Second) of Conflict of Laws § 103, that the Iron Law of Full Faith and Credit is subject to policy exceptions? *See* § 7.09[D], *supra.*

(3) *Define domicile.* Whose concept of domicile are we using: Nevada's, North Carolina's, or the "common law's"? (Hint: see footnote 3 of the Court's opinion.) If domicile is a federal question, does that mean that every "challenge to a divorcing court's jurisdiction raises a federal question appropriate for Supreme Court review? *Cf. Cook v. Cook,* 336 U.S. 674 (1949) (affirming finding by a Connecticut court that domicile was lacking in Nevada). *Cf. Indiana ex rel. Anderson v. Brand,* 303 U.S. 95 (1938) (federal common law determines whether a contract exists for purposes of Contract Clause litigation.)

*See* PROBLEMS 8B-1. A BROODING OMNIPRESENCE?; 8B-2. PHYSICIAN HEAL THYSELF.

(4) *Review.* What standard of review should a court in the position of the North Carolina court use? Does it (or did it) matter that the Nevada decree was found invalid in a criminal prosecution? Was Justice Black right in being concerned about civil liberties? And what of Justice Rutledge's concern that "every decree becomes vulnerable in every state"? Or, as Justice Frankfurter put it, are these just the inevitable costs of our wonderful federal system?

Nevada has attempted toobstruct collateral attacks by holding that perjury with respect to domicile is intrinsic fraud, and, therefore, does not render the divorce vulnerable on that ground when Nevada is the divorcing state. *See Colby v. Colby*, 78 Nev. 150, 369 P.2d 1019 (1962) (Nevada refused to recognize a Maryland decision not to recognize a Nevada divorce). What do you think the Supreme Court which decided the *Williams* cases would have said about *Colby* ? Does the combination of *Colby* and *Williams II* create a curious phenomenon—the judgment that is final in the state of rendition and open to collateral attack elsewhere? It is true that Maryland denied full faith and credit to a judgment Nevada would hold binding. But of two prior inconsistent judgments, wasn't Nevada obligated to give full faith and credit to the one that was last in time? *See* Chapter 7, Part B, *supra.*

## § 8.07   Precluding Collateral Attack—Bilateral Divorces

### SHERRER v. SHERRER

*United States Supreme Court*
*334 U.S. 343, 68 S. Ct. 1087, 92 L. Ed. 1429 (1948)*

Mr. Chief Justice Vinson delivered the opinion of the Court.

Petitioner Margaret E. Sherrer and the respondent, Edward C. Sherrer, were married in New Jersey in 1930, and from 1932 until April 3, 1944, lived together in Monterey, Massachusetts. Following a long period of marital discord, petitioner, accompanied by the two children of the marriage, left Massachusetts on the latter date, ostensibly for the purpose of spending a vacation in the State of Florida. Shortly after her arrival in Florida, however, petitioner informed her husband that she did not intend to return to him. Petitioner obtained housing accommodations in Florida, placed her older child in school, and secured employment for herself.

On July 6, 1944, a bill of complaint for divorce was filed at petitioner's direction in Florida. The bill alleged extreme cruelty as grounds for divorce and also alleged that petitioner was a "bona fide legal resident of the State of Florida." The respondent received notice by mail of the pendency of the divorce proceedings. He retained Florida counsel who entered a general appearance and filed an answer denying the allegations of petitioner's complaint, including the allegation as to petitioner's Florida residence.

On November 14, 1944, hearings were held in the divorce proceedings. Respondent appeared personally to testify with respect to a stipulation entered into by the parties relating to the custody of the children. Throughout the entire proceedings respondent was represented by counsel.[4] Petitioner introduced evidence to establish her Florida residence and testified generally to the allegations of her complaint. Counsel for respondent failed to cross-examine or to introduce evidence in rebuttal.

The Florida court on November 29, 1944, entered a decree of divorce after specifically finding that petitioner "is a bona fide resident of the State of Florida, and that this court has jurisdiction of the parties and the subject matter in said cause." Respondent failed to challenge the decree by appeal to the Florida Supreme Court.

On December 1, 1944, petitioner was married in Florida to one Henry A. Phelps, whom petitioner had known while both were residing in Massachusetts and who had come to Florida shortly after petitioner's arrival in that State. Phelps and petitioner lived together as husband and wife in Florida, where they were both employed, until February 5, 1945, when they returned to Massachusetts.

In June, 1945, respondent instituted an action in the Probate Court of Berkshire County, Massachusetts, which has given rise to the issues of this case. Respondent alleged that he is the lawful husband of petitioner, that the Florida decree of divorce is invalid, and that petitioner's subsequent marriage is void. Respondent prayed that he might be permitted to convey his real estate as if he were sole and that the court declare that he was living apart from his wife for justifiable cause.

The Probate Court found that petitioner was never domiciled in Florida, and granted respondent the relief he had requested. The Supreme Judicial Court of Massachusetts affirmed.

At the outset, it should be observed that the proceedings in the Florida court prior to the entry of the decree of divorce were in no way inconsistent with the requirements of procedural due process. We do not understand respondent to urge the contrary. The respondent personally appeared in the Florida proceedings. Through his attorney he filed pleadings denying the substantial allegations of petitioner's complaint.

It should also be observed that there has been no suggestion that under the law of Florida, the decree of divorce in question is in any respect invalid or could successfully be subjected to the type of attack permitted by the Massachusetts court.

[T]he requirements of full faith and credit bar a defendant from collaterally attacking a divorce decree on jurisdictional grounds in the courts of a sister State where there has been participation by the defendant in the divorce proceedings, where the defendant has been accorded full opportunity to contest the jurisdictional issues, and where the decree is not susceptible to such collateral attack in the courts of the State which rendered the decree.

Applying these principles to this case, we hold that the Massachusetts courts erred in permitting the Florida divorce decree to be subjected to attack on

---

[4] It is said that throughout most of the proceedings respondent did not appear in the courtroom but remained "in a side room."

the ground that petitioner was not domiciled in Florida at the time the decree was entered. Respondent participated in the Florida proceedings by entering a general appearance, filing pleadings placing in issue the very matters he sought subsequently to contest in the Massachusetts courts, personally appearing before the Florida court and giving testimony in the case, and by retaining attorneys who represented him throughout the entire proceedings. It has not been contended that respondent was given less than a full opportunity to contest the issue of petitioner's domicile or any other issue relevant to the litigation. There is nothing to indicate that the Florida court would not have evaluated fairly and in good faith all relevant evidence submitted to it. Respondent does not even contend that on the basis of the evidence introduced in the Florida proceedings, that court reached an erroneous result on the issue of petitioner's domicile. If respondent failed to take advantage of the opportunities afforded him, the responsibility is his own. We do not believe that the dereliction of a defendant under such circumstances should be permitted to provide a basis for subsequent attack in the courts of a sister State on a decree valid in the State in which it was rendered.

But the recognition of the importance of a State's power to determine the incidents of basic social relationships into which its domiciliaries enter does not resolve the issues of this case. This is not a situation in which a State has merely sought to exert such power over a domiciliary. This is, rather, a case involving inconsistent assertions of power by courts of two States of the Federal Union and thus presents considerations which go beyond the interests of local policy, however vital. In resolving the issues here presented, we do not conceive it to be a part of our function to weigh the relative merits of the policies of Florida and Massachusetts with respect to divorce and related matters. Nor do we understand the decisions of this Court to support the proposition that the obligation imposed by Article IV, § I of the Constitution and the Act of Congress passed thereunder amounts to something less than the duty to accord full faith and credit to decrees of divorce entered by courts of sister States. The full faith and credit clause is one of the provisions incorporated into the Constitution by its framers for the purpose of transforming an aggregation of independent, sovereign States into a nation . . .[5]

It is one thing to recognize as permissible the judicial reexamination of findings of jurisdictional fact where such findings have been made by a court of a sister State which has entered a divorce decree in ex parte proceedings. It is quite another thing to hold that the vital rights and interests involved in divorce litigation may be held in suspense pending the scrutiny by courts of sister States of findings of jurisdictional fact made by a competent court in proceedings conducted in a manner consistent with the highest requirements of due process and in which the defendant has participated. We do not conceive it to be in accord with the purposes of the full faith and credit requirement to hold that a judgment rendered under the circumstances of this case may be required to run the gauntlet of such collateral attack in the courts of sister States before its validity outside of the State which rendered it is established or rejected. That vital interests are involved in divorce litigation

---

[5] If in its application local policy must at times be required to give way, such, is part of the price of our federal system. "*Williams I,* 317 U.S. 287, 302, (1942).

indicates to us that it is a matter of greater rather than lesser importance that there should be a place to end such litigation. And where a decree of divorce is rendered by a competent court under the circumstances of this case, the obligation of full faith and credit requires that such litigation should end in the courts of the State in which the judgment was rendered.

*Reversed.*

MR. JUSTICE FRANKFURTER, with whom MR. JUSTICE MURPHY concurs, dissenting.

If all that were necessary in order to decide the validity in one State of a divorce granted in another was to read the Full Faith and Credit Clause of the Constitution, generations of judges would not have found the problem so troublesome as they have, nor would a divided Court have successively pronounced a series of discordant decisions. "Full faith and credit" must be given to a judgment of a sister State. But a "judgment" implies the power of the State to deal with the subject matter in controversy. A State court which has entered what professes to be a judgment must have had something on which to act. That something is what is conveyed by the word "jurisdiction," and, when it comes to dissolving a marriage status, throughout the English-speaking world the basis of power to act is domicile. Whether or not in a particular situation a person is domiciled in a given State depends on circumstances, and circumstances have myriad diversities. But there is a consensus of opinion among English-speaking courts the world over that domicile requires some sense of permanence of connection between the individual who claims it and the State which he asks to recognize it.

If the marriage contract were no different from a contract to sell an automobile, the parties thereto might well be permitted to bargain away all interests involved, in or out of court. But the State has an interest in the family relations of its citizens vastly different from the interest it has in an ordinary commercial transaction. That interest cannot be bartered or bargained away by the immediate parties to the controversy by a default or an arranged contest in a proceeding for divorce in a State to which the parties are strangers. Therefore, the constitutional power of a State to determine the marriage status of two of its citizens should not be deemed foreclosed by a proceeding between the parties in another State, even though in other types of controversy considerations making it desirable to put an end to litigation might foreclose the parties themselves from reopening the dispute. I cannot agree that the Constitution forbids a State from insisting that it is not bound by any such proceedings in a distant State wanting in the power that domicile alone gives, and that its courts need not honor such an intrinsically sham proceeding, no matter who brings the issue to their attention . . .

Today's decision may stir hope of contributing toward greater certainty of status of those divorced. But when people choose to avail themselves of laws laxer than those of the State in which they permanently abide, and where, barring only the interlude necessary to get a divorce, they choose to continue to abide, doubts and conflicts are inevitable, so long as the divorce laws of the forty-eight States remain diverse, and so long as we respect the law that a judgment without jurisdictional foundation is not constitutionally entitled to recognition everywhere. These are difficulties, as this Court has often reminded, inherent in our federal system, in which governmental power over domestic relations is not given to the central government.

I cannot bring myself to believe that the Full Faith and Credit Clause gave to the few States which offer bargain-counter divorces constitutional power to control the social policy governing domestic relations of the many States which do not.

## NOTES AND QUESTIONS ON *SHERRER*

(1) *Attack by the F-I Petitioner.*  Mrs. Sherrer could not have attacked the divorce she procured. Local law notions of fairness estop the F-I petitioner from seeking the divorce. *See*  Charles Clark, *Estoppel Against Jurisdictional Attack on Decrees of Divorce,* 70 YALE L.J. 45 (1960).

*See*  PROBLEMS 8B-3. Mental Cruelty; 8B-4. A HORSE TRAINER AND A JOCKEY; 8B-5. FIRST IN TIME, FIRST IN RIGHT?; 8B-6. MODIFYING THE NONMODIFIABLE?; PROBLEM 8B-7. VACATING THE DECREE; 8B-8. THE TRIBAL COURT.

(2) *Attack by the F-1 Respondent. Sherrer*  involved, of course, the more interesting question of when the F-1 respondent  can challenge the divorce. Does this question present a real problem under traditional notions of res judicata? Recall the discussion of the "bootstrap" principle in § 7.08[E], *supra.* Would Mr. Sherrer have been able to attack the decree if it had been issued in a contracts case? Should it matter that the issue of jurisdiction (domicile) was not litigated?

So why the hoopla? What *is*  this case doing in the Supreme Court? Is the problem that we all *know*  that the Florida domicile was a fake? Should we care about that trickery when the only parties affected by the decree were present and willing to abide by the results of that fakery? After all, as Chief Justice Vinson observed, the "vital interests" involved in divorce litigation suggest "that it is a matter of greater rather than lesser importance that there should be a place to end such litigation."

Does *Sherrer* require a *real* adversarial proceeding? Some cases say yes, *see* Restatement (Second) Conflict of Laws § 73, Reporter's Note, and *Durfee v. Duke,* 375 U.S. 106 (1963), discussed in § 7.08, *supra,* but see the facts in *Sherrer* itself.

(3) *Collateral Attack and Fraud.*  What is the effect of fraud? In *Day v. Day,* 273 Md. 229, 205 A.2d 798 (1965), the husband had obtained his wife's consent to jurisdiction in another state by fraudulent means. Her subsequent attack on the decree was successful, the court holding that her consent to jurisdiction was ineffective because it had been procured by fraud.

## COLLATERAL ATTACK BY THIRD PARTIES

Can third parties be estopped from raising the jurisdictional issue?

**JOHNSON v. MEULBERGER**, 340 U.S. 581 (1953): Bruce Johnson's first wife died in 1939. He then married Madaline Ham. The couple lived in New York. In 1942, Ham obtained a Florida divorce "although the undisputed facts show that she did not comply with the jurisdictional ninety-day residence requirement." Johnson appeared by attorney in the Florida action, but did not contest that court's jurisdiction. Bruce then married petitioner Genevieve Johnson in 1944. He died the next year, leaving, by will, his entire estate to his daughter, Eleanor. Petitioner sought to take her statutory third of Bruce's estate; Eleanor objected, on the ground that her father's divorce from Madaline was invalid.

*Held:* for Johnson; collateral attack was not permitted:

Such an attack is barred when the party attacking would not be permitted to make a collateral attack in the courts of the granting state.

If the laws of Florida should be that a surviving child is in privity with its parent, as to that parent's estate, surely the Florida doctrine of res judicata would apply to the child's collateral attack as it would to the father's.

We conclude that Florida would not permit [Eleanor] to attack the Florida decree of divorce as beyond the jurisdiction of the rendering court. In that case New York cannot permit such an attack.

[JUSTICE FRANKFURTER dissented.]

\* \* \*

Does the holding in *Johnson* preclude collateral attack situations where it otherwise would be available? Recall the discussion of issue preclusion in Chapter 7, Part A, *supra*.

## § 8.08   Divisible Divorce

### ESTIN v. ESTIN

*United States Supreme Court*
*334 U.S. 541, 68 S. Ct. 1213, 92 L. Ed. 1561 (1948)*

Opinion of the Court by MR. JUSTICE DOUGLAS, announced by MR. JUSTICE REED.

The parties were married in 1937 and lived together in New York until 1942 when the husband left the wife. There was no issue of the marriage. In 1943 she brought an action against him for a separation. He entered a general appearance. The court, finding that he had abandoned her, granted her a decree of separation and awarded her $180 per month as permanent alimony. In January 1944, he went to Nevada where in 1945 he instituted an action for divorce. She was notified of the action by constructive service but entered no appearance in it. In May, 1945, the Nevada court, finding that petitioner had been a bona fide resident of Nevada since January 30, 1944, granted him an absolute divorce "on the ground of three years continual separation, without cohabitation." The Nevada decree made no provision for alimony, though the Nevada court had been advised of the New York decree.

Prior to that time petitioner had made payments of alimony under the New York decree. After entry of the Nevada decree he ceased paying. Thereupon respondent sued in New York for a supplementary judgment for the amount of the arrears. Petitioner appeared in the action and moved to eliminate the alimony provisions of the separation decree by reason of the Nevada decree.

We held in *Williams v. North Carolina* [*Williams* I] that a divorce decree granted by a State to one of its domiciliaries is entitled to full faith and credit in a bigamy prosecution brought in another State, even though the other spouse was given notice of the divorce proceeding only through constructive service; and (2) that while the finding of domicile by the court that granted the decree is entitled to prima facie weight, it is not conclusive in a sister State but might be relitigated there. The latter course was followed in this case, as a consequence of which the Supreme Court of New York found, in accord with the Nevada court, that petitioner "is now and since January, 1944, has been a bona fide resident of the State of Nevada."

Petitioner's argument therefore is that the tail must go with the hide—that since by the Nevada decree, recognized in New York, he and respondent are no longer husband and wife, no legal incidence of the marriage remains.

The difficulty with that argument is that the highest court in New York has held in this case that a support order can survive divorce and that this one has survived petitioner's divorce. That conclusion is binding on us, except as it conflicts with the Full Faith and Credit Clause.

We can put to one side the case where the wife was personally served or where she appeared in the divorce proceedings. The only service on her in this case was by publication and she made no appearance in the Nevada proceeding. The requirements of procedural due process were satisfied and the domicile of the husband in Nevada was foundation for a decree effecting a change in the marital capacity of both parties in all the other States of the Union, as well as in Nevada. But the fact that marital capacity was changed does not mean that every other legal incidence of the marriage was necessarily affected.

An absolutist might demand a rule that once a divorce is granted, the whole of the marriage relation is dissolved, leaving no roots or tendrils of any kind. But there are few areas of the law in black and white. The greys are dominant and even among them the shades are innumerable. For the eternal problem of the law is one of making accommodations between conflicting interests. This is why most legal problems end as questions of degree. That is true of the present problem under the Full Faith and Credit Clause. The question involves important considerations both of law and of policy which it is essential to state.

The situations where a judgment of one State has been denied full faith and credit in another State, because its enforcement would contravene the latter's policy, have been few and far between. The Full Faith and Credit Clause is not to be applied, accordion-like, to accommodate our personal predilections. It substituted a command for the earlier principles of comity and thus basically altered the status of the States as independent sovereigns. It ordered submission by one State even to hostile policies reflected in the judgment of another State, because the practical operation of the federal system, which the Constitution designed, demanded it. The fact that the requirements of full faith and credit, so far as judgments are concerned, are exacting, if not inexorable, does not mean, however, that the State of the domicile of one spouse may, through the use of constructive service, enter a decree that changes every legal incidence of the marriage relationship.

New York was rightly concerned lest the abandoned spouse be left impoverished and perhaps become a public charge. The problem of her livelihood and support is plainly a matter in which her community had a legitimate interest. The New York court, having jurisdiction over both parties, undertook to protect her by granting her a judgment of permanent alimony. Nevada, however, apparently follows the rule that dissolution of the marriage puts an end to a support order.

The New York judgment is a property interest of respondent, created by New York in a proceeding in which both parties were present. It imposed obligations on petitioner and granted rights to respondent. The property interest which it created was an intangible, jurisdiction over which cannot be exerted through control over a physical thing. Jurisdiction over an intangible can indeed only arise from control or power over the persons whose relationships are the source of the rights and obligations.

We know of no source of power which would take the present case out of that category. The Nevada decree that is said to wipe out respondent's claim for alimony under the New York judgment is nothing less than an attempt by Nevada to restrain respondent from asserting her claim under that judgment. That is an attempt to exercise an in personam jurisdiction over a person not before the court. That may not be done. Since Nevada had no power to adjudicate respondent's rights in the New York judgment, New York need not give full faith and credit to that phase of Nevada's judgment.

The result in this situation is to make the divorce divisible—to give effect to the Nevada decree insofar as it affects marital status and to make it ineffective on the issue of alimony. It accommodates the interests of both Nevada and New York in this broken marriage by restricting each State to the matters of her dominant concern.

Since Nevada had no jurisdiction to alter respondent's rights in the New York judgment, we do not reach the further question whether in any event that judgment would be entitled to full faith and credit in Nevada.

MR. JUSTICE FRANKFURTER, dissenting.

[T]he crucial issue, as I see it, is whether New York has held that no "ex parte" divorce decree could terminate a prior New York separate maintenance decree, or whether it has decided merely that no "ex parte" divorce decree of another State could. New York may legitimately decline to allow any "ex parte" divorce to dissolve its prior separate maintenance decree, but it may not, consistently with *Williams v. North Carolina,* discriminate against a Nevada decree granted to one there domiciled, and afford it less effect than it gives to a decree of its own with similar jurisdictional foundation. I cannot be sure which it has done.

I would therefore remand the case to the New York Court of Appeals for clarification of its rationale.

MR. JUSTICE JACKSON, dissenting.

If there is one thing that the people are entitled to expect from their lawmakers, it is rules of law that will enable individuals to tell whether they are married and, if so, to whom. Today many people who have simply lived in more than one state do not know, and the most learned lawyer cannot advise them with any confidence. The uncertainties that result are not merely technical, nor are they trivial; they affect fundamental rights and relations such as the lawfulness of their cohabitation, their children's legitimacy, their title to property, and even whether they are law-abiding persons or criminals. In a society as mobile and nomadic as ours, such uncertainties affect large numbers of people and create a social problem of some magnitude. It is therefore important that, whatever we do, we shall not add to the confusion. 1 think that this decision does just that . . .

The Court reaches the Solomon-like conclusion that the Nevada decree is half good and half bad under the Full Faith and Credit Clause. It is good to free the husband from the marriage; it is not good to free him from its incidental obligations. Assuming the judgment to be one which the Constitution requires to be recognized at all, I do not see how we can square this decision with the command that it be given full faith and credit. For reasons which I stated in dissenting in *Williams v. North Carolina,* I would not give standing under the clause to constructive service divorces obtained on short residence. But if we are to hold this divorce good, I do not see how it can be less good than a divorce would be if rendered by the courts of New York.

## NOTES AND QUESTIONS ON DIVISIBLE DIVORCE

(1) *Divisible Divorce.* How did the Court conceptualize Mrs. Estin's interest? Once it is labeled a "property interest," of course, the full panoply of due process rights attaches. Does that characterization make sense? Was it compelled?

Or is Justice Jackson's sneer that the Nevada decree is "half good and half bad" well-founded? Was any other result possible after *Williams I*?

The combination of *Williams I* and *Estin* protects a non-consenting spouse's economic rights, but not any interest she might have in preserving her marital ties. Has the Court made the right choice here? Some think not. *See* Robert Drinan, *What are the Rights of the Involuntary Divorcee: Reflections on Divisible Divorce,* 53 Ky. L.J. 209 (1965).

(2) *Individual Rights and State's Rights.* Is the holding in *Estin* based on the due process rights of the stay-at-home spouse not to be deprived of property by a Nevada court which lacked jurisdiction over her? If so, would it have been unconstitutional for a New York court to give full faith and credit to the part of the Nevada decree that cut off her right to alimony? The alternative explanation of the holdings is that the Nevada decrees did not violate due process, but that New York was not required to recognize them—an explanation which focuses on the rights of the absent spouse rather than on the rights of the state of New York. Does this reading of the holding support Restatement (Second) of Conflict of Laws § 103, discussed in § 7.09[D], *supra*?

*See* PROBLEMS 8B-9. THE PENSION FUNDS; 8B-IO. PERMANENT TERMINATION OF ALIMONY; 8B-I 1. CONTRACT CONSIDERATION AND ONE-DAY DISSOLUTIONS.

(3) *The Vanderbilt Case. Estin* involved a support order entered before the divorce decree. Does the same rule apply when the decree was entered *after* the divorce?

The Court answered this question in *Vanderbilt v. Vanderbilt,* 359 U.S. 416 (1957). Mrs. Vanderbilt obtained a New York support order *after* her husband had obtained a Nevada *ex parte* divorce. New York had not been the marital domicile, but Mrs. Vanderbilt had moved there before the divorce. The Court found New York had a sufficient interest in Mrs. Vanderbilt to create a property right for her: "Since the wife was not subject to its jurisdiction, the Nevada divorce court had no power to extinguish any right which [the wife] had under the laws of New York to financial support from her husband."

What happens if the wife establishes her New York domicile after the divorce? In *Loeb v. Loeb,* 4 N.Y.2d 542, 176 N.Y.S.2d 590, 152 N.E.2d 36 (1958), *cert. denied,* 359 U.S. 913 (1959), the couple was domiciled in Vermont, the husband obtained an *ex parte* divorce in Nevada, and the wife later moved to New York and sought an alimony award from a court in that state. The court denied her claim, interpreting the relevant New York statute to preclude relief. Did that deny her due process? *Cf. Zobel v. Williams,* 457 U.S. 55 (1982) (Alaska cannot pay less oil bounty money to more recent residents without violating Equal Protection Clauses.) On the other hand, if the court had read the New York statute otherwise, would providing relief to Mrs. Loeb have violated the Full Faith and Credit Clause?

## SIMONS v. MIAMI BEACH FIRST NATIONAL BANK

*United States Supreme Court*
*381 U.S. 81, 85 S. Ct. 1315, 14 L. Ed. 2d 232 (1965)*

MR. JUSTICE BRENNAN delivered the opinion of the Court.

The question to be decided in this case is whether a husband's valid Florida divorce, obtained in a proceeding wherein his nonresident wife was served by publication only and did not make a personal appearance, unconstitutionally extinguished her dower right in his Florida estate.

The petitioner and Sol Simons were domiciled in New York when, in 1946, she obtained a New York separation decree that included an award of monthly alimony. Sol Simons moved to Florida in 1951 and, a year later, obtained there a divorce in an action of which petitioner had valid constructive notice but in which she did not enter a personal appearance.[6] After Sol Simons' death in Florida in 1960, respondent, the executor of his estate, offered his will for probate in the Probate Court of Dade County, Florida. Petitioner appeared in the proceeding and filed an election to take dower under Florida law, rather than have her rights in the estate governed by the terms of the will, which made no provision for her. The respondent opposed the dower claim, asserting that since Sol Simons had divorced petitioner she had not been his wife at his death, and consequently was not entitled to dower under Florida law.

---

[6] Petitioner was served by publication while still living in New York and received copies of the order for publication and the divorce complaint. She did not enter an appearance in the Florida proceeding on advice of counsel.

Petitioner thereupon brought the instant action in the Circuit Court for Dade County in order to set aside the divorce decree and to obtain a declaration that the divorce, even if valid to alter her marital status, did not destroy or impair her claim to dower. The action was dismissed after trial, and the Florida District Court of Appeal for the Third District affirmed. The Supreme Court of Florida declined to review the case.

We proceed to the decision of the question whether the Florida courts unconstitutionally denied petitioner's dower claim. [7]

Petitioner argues that since she had not appeared in the Florida divorce action the Florida divorce court had no power to extinguish any right which she had acquired under the New York decree. She invokes the principle of *Estin v. Estin,* where this Court decided that a Nevada divorce court, which had no personal jurisdiction over the wife, had no power to terminate a husband's obligation to provide the wife support as required by a pre-existing New York separation decree . . .

[T]he only obligation imposed on Sol Simons by the New York decree, and the only rights granted petitioner under it, concerned monthly alimony for petitioner's support. Unlike the ex-husband in *Estin,* Sol Simons made the support payments called for by the separate maintenance decree notwithstanding his *ex parte* divorce. In making these payments until his death he complied with the full measure of the New York decree; when he died there was consequently nothing left of the New York decree for Florida to dishonor.

This conclusion embodies our judgment that there is nothing in the New York decree itself that can be construed as creating or preserving any interest in the nature of or in lieu of dower in any property of the decedent, wherever located. Petitioner refers us to no New York law that treats such a decree as having that effect, or, for that matter, to any New York law that has such an effect irrespective of the existence of the decree.

Insofar as petitioner argues that since she was not subject to the jurisdiction of the Florida divorce court, its decree could not extinguish any dower right existing under Florida law, *Vanderbilt v. Vanderbilt,* 354 U.S. 416, 418, the answer is that under Florida law no dower right survived the decree. The Supreme Court of Florida has said that dower rights in Florida property, being inchoate, are extinguished by a divorce decree predicated upon substituted or constructive service. *Pawley v. Pawley.* [8]

---

[7] Neither the Florida trial court nor the District Court of Appeal expressly discussed the merits of petitioner's claim that the divorce, even if valid, did not destroy or impair her dower rights. But since Florida law allows dower only to a decedent's wife, *see* note 6, *infra* , we interpret the Florida courts' decisions sustaining the validity of the divorce as also holding that the divorce extinguished petitioner's dower rights.

[8] In Pawley, the Supreme Court of Florida distinguished the dower right from the right to support saying:

"In this, if not in every jurisdiction, right of dower can never be made the subject of a wholly independent issue in any divorce suit. It stands or falls as a result of the decree which denies or grants divorce. It arises upon marriage, as an institution of the law. The inchoate right of dower has some of the incidents of property. It partakes of the nature of a lien or encumbrance. It is not a right which is originated by or is derived from the husband; nor is it a personal obligation to be met or fulfilled by him, but it is a creature of the law, is born at the marriage altar, cradled in the bosom of the marital status as an integral and component part thereof, survives during

It follows that the Florida courts transgressed no constitutional bounds in denying petitioner dower in her ex-husband's Florida estate.

*Affirmed.*

MR. JUSTICE HARLAN, concurring.

I am happy to join the opinion of the Court because it makes a partial retreat from *Vanderbilt v. Vanderbilt,* 354 U.S. 416, a decision which I believe must eventually be rerationalized, if not entirely overruled.

Two rules emerged from the case, neither of which, I suggest with deference, commends itself. (1) an ex parte divorce can have no effect on property rights; (2) a State in which a wife subsequently establishes domicile can award support to her regardless of her connection with that State at the time of the ex parte divorce and regardless of the law in her former State of domicile.[9]

The first rule slips unobtrusively into oblivion in today's decision, for Florida is allowed to turn property rights on its ex parte decree. A concurrence disputes this, but I do not understand how the Court's language in this case can be read as anything less. If I may paraphrase only slightly, the Court says, "Insofar as petitioner argues that since she was not subject to the jurisdiction of the Florida divorce court, its decree could not extinguish any dower right existing under Florida law, *Vanderbilt v. Vanderbilt,* 354 U.S. 416, 418, the answer is that the Florida decree extinguished petitioner's dower rights." The Court goes on to state and accept the Florida law that an *ex parte* divorce extinguishes dower rights. I do not see how a withdrawal from the due process phase of *Vanderbilt* could be clearer.

Because New York was petitioner's State of domicile at all times relevant to this case and did not purport to invest her with any rights to property beyond those she received from her husband, the second rule is not involved here. My hope is that its time will come too. I continue to believe that the views expressed in my *Vanderbilt* dissent embody a more satisfactory and workable approach to the law of "divisible divorce" *(Estin v. Estin,* 334 U.S. 541) than can be distilled from existing Court opinions.

MR. JUSTICE BLACK with whom MR. JUSTICE DOUGLAS joins, concurring.

I agree completely with the Court's judgment and opinion, and add these few words only in reply to the suggestion of my Brother HARLAN that the Court

the life of the wife as such and finds its sepulcher in divorce. Alimony too is an institution of the law but it is a personal obligation of the husband which is based upon the duty imposed upon him by the common law to support his wife and gives rise to a personal right of the wife to insist upon, if she be entitled to, it. It has none of the incidents of, and is in no sense a lien upon or interest in, property. Consequently, the right of the wife to be heard on the question of alimony should not, indeed lawfully it cannot, be destroyed by a divorce decree sought and secured by the husband in an action wherein only constructive service of process was effected."

[9] The Vanderbilt result might have been proper on any of three grounds. (1) If New York was Mrs. Vanderbilt's State of domicile at the time of the ex parte Nevada divorce, New York law investing a wife with support rights should not be overbore by an ex parte decree in another State. (2) If California was Mrs. Vanderbilt's domicile at the time of the Nevada divorce and under California law support could have been awarded, New York should also be free (though not bound) to award support. (3) If Mr. Vanderbilt owned property in New York at the time of the ex parte divorce, New York might arguably be free to hold that ownership of New York property carries with it the obligation to support one's wife, at least to the extent of the value of that property.

here is making "a partial retreat from *Vanderbilt v. Vanderbilt,* 354 U.S. 416." I do not think that today's decision marks any "retreat" at all from the opinion or holding in *Vanderbilt,* and I do not understand the Court so to regard it. *Vanderbilt* held that a wife's right to support could not be cut off by an *ex parte* divorce. In the case before us, Mrs. Simons' Florida dower was not terminated by the *ex parte* divorce. It simply never came into existence. Unless this Court were to make the novel declaration that Florida cannot limit dower rights to widows, I see no possible way in which the *Vanderbilt* case, which dealt with rights which a State did give to divorced wives, could be thought to apply.

MR. JUSTICE STEWART and MR. JUSTICE GOLDBERG, dissenting.

We would dismiss the writ of certiorari in this case as improvidently granted, believing that, as the Court's opinion clearly demonstrates, no federal question is presented.

## NOTES AND QUESTIONS ON *SIMONS*

(1) *Inchoateness.* Justice Reed's opinion in *Simons* is not a model of clarity. His failure to explain the state of Florida law is particularly quirky. Why does it matter that dower rights are "inchoate"? What does that term mean, anyway? Is it relevant how Florida law (as opposed to constitutional law) characterizes the right? Isn't alimony an "inchoate" right? After all, the judge might dissolve the marriage, but refuse to award alimony.

(2) If Mrs. Simons had contested the divorce on the merits, she could have preserved her dower right, couldn't she? But to contest *on the merits* she would have had to a) travel to Florida, b) consent to the jurisdiction of that court, and c) contest the divorce. What risks would she have run if she had decided to contest? Is it consistent with due process to force Mrs. Simons to choose between the loss of her dower rights and the inconvenience and risk of making a general appearance in Florida?

(3) What happens if the Court had not dissolved Mrs. Simon s dower rights? If Mr. Simons had remarried before dying, there could be *two* widows claiming an interest in his property. That would be a fine kettle of fish, wouldn't it, one guaranteed to feed Florida lawyers for many years.

(4) If you are having trouble reconciling *Simons* and *Estin, see* David Currie's excellent article, *Suitcase Divorce in the Conflict of Laws,* 34 U. CHI. L. REV. 26 (1967).

*See* PROBLEMS 8B-12. IS THE STATE BOUND? PROBLEM 8B-13. WAS SHE MARRIED?

## RE-THINKING THE *WILLIAMS* DOCTRINE

Does the holding in *Simons* make you want to rethink *Williams I?* Don't the two cases demonstrate that, despite the *Estin* divisible divorce compromise, there is an irreconcilable conflict between the interests of Nevada and Florida in the marital status of their domiciliaries on the one hand and the due process rights of the stay-at-home spouses on the other? Who should prevail in such a contest? If the *Williams I* / *Simons* answer made sense in the era of fault-only divorce law, does it still make sense today?

And you might want to think about the larger issues as well. Do you think the Court (or at least Justice Douglas) foresaw the ultimate result at the time of *Williams I.* Were at least some Justices primarily interested in destroying highly restrictive divorce laws? Is that a proper role for the Court? Was the result "good" in some ultimate sense—was the freedom from oppressive and hateful marriages worth the impoverishment of vast numbers of persons, overwhelmingly women and children?

## § 8.09  Dividing Marital Property

Common law jurisdictions have developed over the years a variety of methods for determining what happens to property owned by the husband or wife or both when the marriage is dissolved. In most states today, statutory law provides—with a large variation in details—for an equitable distribution of marital property at divorce. Several states, as well as many foreign countries, have community property systems which, generally speaking, divide the property equally between the spouses. These different schemes can create interesting conflicts problems. Does the situs rule apply, for example, to the distribution of a foreign couple's land? *See generally* Peter N. Swisher,*et al.*, Family Law: Cases, Materials, and Problems (2d ed. 1998); Eugene Scoles & Peter Hay, Conflict of Laws, ch. 14 (2d ed. 1992); Friedrich Juenger, *Marital Property and the Conflict of Laws: A Tale of Two Countries,* 81 COLUM. L. REV. 1081 (1981).

Of course, the conflict between community and common law property states is particularly interesting. This has led to the development of a concept called "quasi-community property." This is property which would have been community property except it was acquired during marriage in a state other than the forum. *See, e.g.,* William M. Reppy, *Community Property Comes to Texas,* 9 COMM. PROP. 171 (1982); Herma Schreter, *Quasi-Community Property in the Conflict of Laws,* 50 CALIF L. REV. 206 (1962).

## § 8.10  Alternative Bases for Divorce Jurisdiction

### ALTON v. ALTON

*United States Court of Appeals for the Third Circuit*
*207 F.2d 667 (1953)*

GOODRICH, CIRCUIT JUDGE. This case involves an important and novel question with regard to jurisdiction for divorce. The plaintiff, Sonia Alton, left her home in West Hartford, Connecticut, and went to the Virgin Islands, where she arrived February 10, 1953. After six weeks and one day continuous presence there she filed a suit for divorce on March 25, 1953. Her husband, David Alton, defendant, entered an appearance and waived service of summons. He did not contest the allegations of the complaint. When the case came to the judge of the district court he asked for further proof on the question of domicile. This was not furnished. He thereupon denied the plaintiff the relief sought, and the case comes here on her appeal. The defendant has filed no brief and made no argument.

We turn first to the opening clause of the [Virgin Islands divorce] statute. Continuous physical presence in the Islands for six weeks prior to the filing of a complaint in a divorce action is declared to be prima facie evidence of domicile.

The problem we must answer is whether six weeks' physical presence creates, without more, a rational foundation on which to base a finding of domicile.

A six-weeks' sojourn without proof of the intent with which one makes it, we think, tends to establish nothing but the fact of six weeks' physical presence. Thousands and thousands of people spend six weeks or more in a place every year on business, for pleasure, for reasons of health, to visit relatives and all the other different reasons which make Americans move about, without the faintest intention of making a change in their homes.

In considering this statute, we do not think that we can ignore the facts of life with respect to migratory divorce in America. It is well known to all of us that increasingly large numbers of persons who are dissatisfied with their marital lot are repairing to other jurisdictions, the Virgin Islands among them, where short residence requirements and liberal grounds for divorce appear to offer them the relief they desire. In very few of these instances do the parties intend to remain longer than necessary to obtain the decree sought. Consequently in these cases the court's finding of domicile usually is contrary to the fact and frequently is based upon evasive or even perjured testimony. The statutory presumption in the present case will doubtless eliminate the temptation to such perjury but the findings based upon it will still be contrary to the true fact in the great majority of cases. The presumption must, therefore, be regarded as either an unreasonable interference by the legislative branch of the insular government with the exercise of the judicial power by the judicial branch or as an attempt by the legislature to convert the suit for divorce into what is in fact a transitory action masquerading under a fiction of domiciliary jurisdiction. We think that looked at in any of these ways the portion of the statute which provides for such a prima facie conclusion is invalid.

The second part of the statute goes on to provide that the court shall have jurisdiction, after six weeks' residence by the plaintiff, where the defendant has been personally served or appeared, "without further reference to domicile." In other words, if the defendant is before the court, the case is to proceed without reference to domicile. The action, in other words, is to become a simple transitory action like a suit for tort or breach of contract where, the defendant being in court and the court competent to proceed in this type of action, all the requisites for jurisdiction are satisfied. Can divorce be turned into a simple, transitory action at the will of any legislature?[10]

---

[10] The legislative history of the statute shows without a doubt that the Legislative Assembly intended to confer jurisdiction to divorce regardless of domicile, rather than merely to establish a rule of evidence.

The background of divorce legislation and litigation shows that it has not been considered a simple transitory personal action. The principle said to govern is that marriage is a matter of public concern, as well as a matter of interest to the parties involved. Because it is a matter of public concern, the public, through the state, has an interest both in its formation and in its dissolution, and the state which has that interest is the state of domicile, because that is where the party "dwelleth and hath his home."

We now go out beyond the place where legal trails end. The Supreme Court has never had occasion to say what would happen in a case where two parties, being personally before the court, are purportedly divorced by a state which has no domiciliary jurisdiction, and the question of the validity of the decree comes up in a second state in a prosecution for bigamy, or in a suit for necessaries by a creditor, or in some other such fashion. Granted that the parties are precluded from attacking the decree, does that immunity extend only to attacks by them or by those in privity with them? Here is an unanswered question. The answer would be conclusive in this case if Mrs. Alton had got her divorce, had re-married, and had been prosecuted for adultery in Connecticut.

We think that adherence to the domiciliary requirement is necessary if our states are really to have control over the domestic relations of their citizens. The instant case would be typical. In the Virgin Islands incompatibility of temperament constitutes grounds for divorce. In Connecticut it does not. We take it that it is all very well for the Virgin Islands to provide for whatever matrimonial regime it pleases for people who live there. But the same privilege should be afforded to those who control affairs in Connecticut.

Our conclusion is that the second part of this statute-conflicts with the Due Process Clause of the Fifth Amendment and the Organic Act. Domestic relations are a matter of concern to the state where a person is domiciled. An attempt by another jurisdiction to affect the relation of a foreign domiciliary is unconstitutional even though both parties are in court and neither one raises the question. The question may well be asked as to what the lack of due process is. The defendant is not complaining. Nevertheless, if the jurisdiction for divorce continues to be based on domicile, as we think it does, we believe it to be lack of due process for one state to take to itself the readjustment of domestic relations between those domiciled elsewhere. The Supreme Court has in a number of cases used the due process clause to correct states which have passed beyond what that court has considered proper choice-of-law rules.

If we are right so far in holding that the Virgin Islands have no jurisdiction to give divorces to persons not domiciled there, the second part of the statute quoted cannot aid the plaintiffs case. That part of the statute seems to say that if the parties are in court and do not object the court may not exercise its curiosity by finding out if there really is a domicile in the forum. It is well settled, of course, that parties cannot by their consent confer jurisdiction of the subject matter upon a court which does not have authority to deal with that subject matter.

The judgment of the district court will be affirmed.

HASTIE, CIRCUIT JUDGE, dissenting:

Whom does the questioned rule of evidence deprive of anything without due process of law? The Fifth Amendment says "No person shall be" denied the essentials of fair procedure. But the present rule deprives no defendant of a fair and full opportunity to challenge the domiciliary claims of the plaintiff and the jurisdiction of the court.

[T]his court now says that the Fifth Amendment requires that the exercise of legal power to grant divorce be restricted to those cases where one party at least is a local domiciliary. The agreed starting point in this phase of the case is the fact that English and American judges in recent times have refrained, in the absence of statute, from exercising their divorce power except in cases involving local domiciliaries. But what is it that raises this judicial rule of self-restraint to the status of an invariable Constitutional principle? What makes any legislative effort to establish an alternative basis upon which state power may be exercised in divorce cases a violation of due process of law?

I can find nothing in the history of the present judge-made rule which entitles it to Constitutional sanction. Certainly it is no ancient landmark of the common law.

The common law courts in England had no divorce jurisdiction at the time of the American Revolution and I know of none which was exercised by the courts in the North American British colonies. The English ecclesiastical courts could grant a form of relief analogous to our present separation from bed and board. And Parliament could legislate an absolute divorce, presumably for any subject of the King wherever he might make his home. But it was not until 1857 that the common law courts in England were for the first time given authority to entertain divorce causes.

In the United States our Constitutional scheme placed this power among those relegated to the several states. [T]he rule that divorce jurisdiction will be exercised only by the courts of a state which has a domiciliary connection with the spouses is a creation of nineteenth century American judges. It is also clear that the rule did not become settled in England, the normal source of common law tradition, until the 1895 decision of the Privy Council in *Le Mesurier v. Le Mesurier,* [1895] A.C. 517. Thus, we seem to have the curious chronology of the American courts adopting a rule of practice in the first half of the nineteenth century under the influence of the creative scholarship of a distinguished writer [Justice Story in his treatise on Conflicts], the British courts adopting this doctrine in the latter half of the nineteenth century, and now in mid-twentieth century, American judges saying that the doctrine is one of those fundamental ideas which must be read into the original provisions of our Constitution. My conclusion is that, on such evidence as is at hand, the limitation of the divorce power to the domiciliary state has no such ancient roots or impressive history as to suggest its entitlement to perpetuation as a Constitutional requirement.

[T]he court concludes "that adherence to the domiciliary requirement is necessary if our states are really to have control over the domestic relations of their citizens", and that any departure from the domiciliary rule would be a denial of procedural due process. This statement of social justification of a legal rule presupposes a stable and intimate attachment of both spouses to a single community which in fact and alone has a genuine interest in their relationship. But this picture is no longer characteristic of our society or of the conduct of estranged spouses in it. In their activities and their careers men are increasingly mobile. Community attachments tend to be less intimate and less lasting than heretofore. And when the unsettling factor of domestic estrangement is added there is considerable likelihood that the spouses will go their separate ways in different communities. One need not approve these patterns of behavior to recognize what doubt they cast upon the essentiality of a legal rule which must be justified by premising a single community which alone and intimately is concerned with each unsuccessful marriage.

[T]he concept of domicil as a basis of jurisdiction is in practice elusive and very unsatisfactory for several reasons. It is a highly technical concept depending upon the proof of the mental attitude of a person toward a place. Whether in taxation or in divorce, the use of domicil as a jurisdictional base gives trouble when it is applied to people who really have no "home feeling" toward any place or, at the other end of the scale, to those who have more than one home. And, as already pointed out, in the divorce field difficulties are multiplied because the estranged spouses so often establish separate homes. Thus, when a court is asked to grant a divorce it very often finds that not one domicil but at least two—potentially more through refinements of the "marital domicil" concept—may be interested in the parties and their relationship. In these all too familiar situations of divided domicile the jurisdictional requirement which the majority regards as so essential to fairness that it can not be changed is a troublemaker and a potential source of injustice.

In this very case, suppose Mrs. Alton had proved to the satisfaction of the majority of this court that her six weeks stay in the Virgin Islands had been attended by the intention to remain there permanently, while Mr. Alton continued a domiciliary of Connecticut. Under the rule of the power of the domicil of one spouse as settled in *Williams v. State of North Carolina* [*Williams II,*] it is clear that the Virgin Islands would have plenary divorce power in this situation. But what of the interest of Connecticut, the home of the husband, the place of marriage, and the last matrimonial domicile which must be very important under the rationalization offered to justify the domiciliary rules?

In the Virgin Islands it has seemed to the legislature that an alternative to the domiciliary rule is worth a trial. And in selecting the alternative of personal jurisdiction over both parties, the legislature has obviated that very disregard of interests on the defendant's side which is the great weakness of the domiciliary rule. In this action I can find nothing arbitrary or unfair; hence, nothing inconsistent with the Fifth Amendment.

One other matter should be mentioned. Although the court recognizes that, as concerns authoritative precedents, this case requires us to travel beyond the place "where legal trails end", the majority opinion places some reliance upon the less than pellucid body of case law: which is concerned with various aspects of the problem of recognition of divorce granted in one state of the union by a sister state. For present purposes I do not find these cases very helpful. The due process question in divorce jurisdiction which we have to decide is whether it is fair for a state and its courts to adjudicate the merits of a petition for the dissolution of a particular marriage. The problem of the full faith and credit cases is to what extent a second state must subordinate its notions of policy about a marital matter in which it wants to have a voice to what a sister state has already decided. Perhaps full faith should be given to every American divorce decree which satisfies due process. But until the Supreme Court makes it clear that in this area due process and full faith are of the same dimensions, I mistrust any inversion of reasoning which would extract from the not invariant line of decisions on full faith and credit the essentials of due process in the original exercise of divorce power.

[I]t seems proper to point out that if a state proceeds upon this new basis of divorce jurisdiction another conflict of laws difficulty must be faced before the merits of the claim can be decided. That difficulty is the proper choice of the law to govern the controversy.

So long as one of the spouses has had a domiciliary relationship to the forum it has been conventional theory that the forum has sufficient connection with the domestic relation which is the subject matter of suit to justify not only the exercise of its judicial power to decide the controversy but also the application of its own substantive law of divorce as well. It is quite possible that some of the difficulties which have arisen in this field are the result of failure to keep in view that these are distinct problems although the existence of a domiciliary relationship is thought to solve both.

But once the power to decide the case is based merely upon personal jurisdiction a court must decide as a separate question upon what basis, if any, the local substantive law of divorce can properly be applied to determine whether the plaintiff is entitled to the relief sought. In this case, if it should appear that Mr. and Mrs. Alton were both domiciled in Connecticut at the time of suit in the Virgin Islands and that their estrangement had resulted from conduct in the matrimonial home state, it may well be that under correct application of conflict of laws doctrine, and even under the due process clause, it is incumbent upon the Virgin Islands, lacking connection with the subject matter, to apply the divorce law of some state that has such connection, here Connecticut.

Of course such a solution would be a novelty in divorce procedure. But the entire situation presented by this statute is very unusual. And the legislation is an innovation in a very important area. I am authorized to state that CHIEF JUDGE BIGGS and CIRCUIT JUDGE KALODNER concur in the views stated in this opinion.

## NOTES AND QUESTIONS ON OTHER BASES FOR DIVORCE JURISDICTION

(1) *The Goodrich Opinion.* There are few cases questioning the need for one state to have a domiciliary relation with one spouse to grant a divorce. *Alton* is the leading case; perhaps that is why Judge Goodrich, a leading conflicts scholar of the vested rights school, said he had been forced to "go out beyond where legal trails end."

*See* PROBLEM 8B-14. DOMICILE AS THE SOLE BASIS FOR EX PARTE DISSOLUTIONS.

(2) *The Constitutional Issue in Alton.* That the Virgin Islands was merely a sham domicile was not the real problem in *Alton,* was it? This defect in subject matter jurisdiction presented a question of Virgin Islands law, quickly answered by referring to the statute. Rather, the court holds the statute itself unconstitutional. Was the court saying that true domicile was a constitutional requirement in divorce cases? Or was it saying something broader? Isn't what really troubled the majority the fact that the forum was not a legitimately interested one? If so, then under the rule of *Home Ins. Co. v. Dick,* discussed in § 5.02, *supra,* the forum had no power to apply its statute for the benefit of these parties. To do so would violate the Due Process Clause.

A difficulty with this view, noted by Judge Goodrich, is that no one was complaining. Whose fifth amendment due process rights were offended? Surely not Mr. Alton's—he cheerfully waived any claim of unfairness.

Why then is the domicile requirement a *constitutional* mandate? How can a non-domiciliary divorce between consenting persons violate the Fifth Amendment? That provision, after all, protects *persons,* and the territorial court *had* personal jurisdiction over Mr. Alton. Perhaps the majority was trying to use the Due Process Clause as a necessary surrogate to protect the interests of other states (here, Connecticut). If so, can that attempt survive footnote 10 of the Supreme Court's opinion in the *Bauxites* case (discussed in § 3.10, *supra*)? Would it make more sense to protect the domiciliary state's interests via the Full Faith and Credit Clause and require the non-domiciliary forum (here, the Virgin Islands) to apply the divorce laws of the state of domicile? Why do you think the law has not developed in that direction?

(3) *Alton and the Problem of Consensual Divorce.* The obvious frustration of the judges in *Alton* seems inevitable given the nature of the Court's holdings in bilateral consensual divorce cases. The parties, if able to afford the divorce, have it in their power, apparently, to bind themselves under the Full Faith and Credit Clause to a valid divorce, waiving every objection of personal and subject matter jurisdiction, and with their presence bestowing on the otherwise sham litigation the critical feature that the parties each had a full and fair opportunity to litigate every issue.

But what of the interests of the marital domicile? The parties are clearly evading otherwise governing law. Can the two spouses bind a third party? Can the parties—the narrow issue in *Alton*—consent to *irrelevant law* for their case? When are stipulations for irrelevant law valid?

Does Goodrich's argument come into conflict with the holding in *Hughes v. Fetter,* see § 5.08, *supra,* requiring state courts to hear transitory causes of action? Or are divorces not transitory causes of action? If not, why not?

(4) *The Hastie dissent.* Judge Hastie's analysis focused on fairness concerns. But does he undervalue the interests of the (real) domiciliary state? What are those interests, anyway? Is a divorce really no different, as Justice Jackson wrote in *Williams I,* from a suit "to collect a grocery bill"?

Judge Hastie's dissent makes the important point that adjudicative and legislative jurisdiction are two very different aspects of forum power. Does anything but tradition compels that divorce be a local action? Hastie points out that the Virgin Islands legislature has simply converted the action to a transitory one, and that the forum accordingly can take jurisdiction. Hastie's suggestion assumes, probably correctly, that a court with no interest in taking a case may adjudicate it. Then, addressing the central problem in *Alton,* of the forum's lack of interest in applying its own law, Judge Hastie makes the further suggestion that the forum apply the law of the marital domicile. But, if that suggestion were adopted, how many couples do you think you would see flocking to the Virgin Islands to obtain the "benefit" of their own state's laws on divorce?

(5) *Recent Developments.* What is the impact of recent developments in divorce law? Today, virtually all states recognize no-fault divorce. Homer Clark, The Law of Domestic Relations in the United States 496 & n.1 (2d ed. 1987). Professor Garfield has written that the near-universal enactment of no-fault divorce laws undercuts the argument that the domiciliary state has a significant substantive interest in the divorce. Helen Garfield, *The Transitory Divorce Action: Jurisdiction in the No-Fault Era,* 58 TEX. L. REV. 501, 522-26 (1980). On the other hand, a number of states have adopted special administrative procedures, such as conciliation and mediation, in divorce actions; and many states provide for the adjustment of marital property under equitable apportionment statutes. Do these provisions show that states are still interested in questions presented by marital dissolution? If so, does that affect your analysis of the *Alton* problem?

There is some relaxation of the domicile requirement when armed forces personnel are involved. *See* William M. Richman & William L. Reynolds, Understanding Conflict of Laws 367 (2d ed. 1993). Should the same hold for other forced non-domiciliaries such as prisoners? See the discussion of this point in connection with the domicile requirement for voting in Chapter II. Professor Garfield argues that because one has the constitutional "right to freedom of choice in marriage," a state may be unable to deny a divorce to non-domiciliaries. Garfield, *supra,* at 517-22. Is *Williams I* then unconstitutional? *See also Developments in the Law, The Constitution and the Family,* 93 HARV. L. REV. 56, 1308-13 (1980).

The signs since *Alton* have been mixed. Restatement (Second) Conflict of Laws § 72 permits a non-domiciliary state to grant a divorce when it is "reasonable" to do so. In *Sosna v. Iowa,* 419 U.S. 393 (1975), however, the Court, in dictum, observed that it "has often been stated that judicial power to grant a divorce jurisdiction strictly speaking—is founded on domicile."

(6) *The subsequent history of Alton.* Mrs. Alton, weary of her struggle for freedom in the Virgin Islands, obtained her divorce, and the Supreme Court never did address the interesting questions the case raised because *Alton* was vacated as moot, 343 U.S. 610 (1954). The Virgin Islands legislation was later held unconstitutional because it conflicted with the Congressional enabling act concerning territorial legislation. *Granville-Smith v. Granville-Smith,* 349 U.S. 1 (1955).

## § 8.11 International Divorces

The Full Faith and Credit Clause does not apply to decrees rendered by foreign nations; in the absence of treaty obligations, recognition is a matter for each state to decide. Two problems present themselves. The first is jurisdiction. Other countries may award divorces on a basis other than domicile. American courts are more likely to recognize a foreign divorce if jurisdiction abroad was based on something that looks like domicile, or other strong ties between a party and the forum. *See* WILLLIAM M. RICHMAN AND WILLIAM L. REYNOLDS, UNDERSTANDING CONFLICT OF LAWS §120 (3d ed. 2002). Friedrich Juenger, *Recognition of Foreign Divorces,* 50 AM. J. OF COMP. L. (1972).

The more difficult problem involves "quickie" divorces rendered by a nation which has only the most minimal of contacts with a party—often by appearance of counsel only—and whose jurisdiction obviously is invoked to evade more stringent rules at home.

Consider *Rosensteil v. Rosensteil,* 16 N.Y.2d 64, 262 N.Y.S.2d 86, 209 N.E. 2d 709 (1965): A divorce was granted a New Yorker by a Mexican court. Plaintiff had been in Mexico for less than a day when he appeared before the court. His wife had entered an appearance, but did not go to Mexico. The New York court recognized the Mexican decree. The court did not seem bothered by the mere technical jurisdiction of the Mexican court, a jurisdiction it believed to be no different than that exercised by Nevada in analogous cases: After all, "Nevada gets no closer to the real public concern with the marriage than Chihuahua."

What is the difference between Nevada and Chihuahua when the question is recognition of a divorce rendered elsewhere? Not all courts have treated the Mexican one-day divorce with the blase attitude of the New York courts; the cases are collected in Homer Clark The Law of Domestic Relations in the United States 432 (2d ed. 1987). Does the *Sherrer* estoppel principle apply to foreign divorces as well as to domestic ones? *See, e.g., id.* at 433.

The Internal Revenue Service, for one, will not recognize a non-colorable divorce and will assess taxes based on what it believes are the realities of the situation. *See* REV. RUL. 76-225; *Borax's Estate v. C.I.R.,* 349 F.2d 666 (2nd Cir. 1965).

A fascinating question involves divorces awarded by non-judicial religious tribunals. Of course, they are invalid if the tribunal was in this country. E.g., *Shikoff v. Murff,* 257 F.2d 306 (2d Cir. 1958). Why? But what if recognition is sought here of a divorce of foreign domicilaries made by a *foreign* tribunal. Some courts have recognized such divorces. *E.g., Sherif v. Sherif,* 76 Misc. 2d 905, 352 N.Y.S.2d 781 (1974); *Machransky v. Machransky,* 31 Ohio App. 482, 166 N.E. 423 (1927).

*See* PROBLEMS 8B-15. THE HAITIAN TOUR; 8B-16. TO HAITI AND BACK-TWICE; 8B-17. A MEXICAN DIVORCE.

## § 8.12   Choice of Law

*A Very Brief Note on Choice of Law in Divorce.* American courts virtually always apply forum law in divorce actions. *See* RESTATEMENT (SECOND) OF CONFLICT OF LAWS § 285. As long as domicile is a jurisdictional prerequisite to divorce, the forum will be an interested jurisdiction. Hence, the revolution in choice of law theory has bypassed altogether the field of divorce. *See generally* WILLIAM M. RICHMAN & WILLIAM L. REYNOLDS, UNDERSTANDING CONFLICT OF LAWS 368-69 (3d ed. 2002) .

## PART C   CUSTODY

### § 8.13   Jurisdiction

### INTRODUCTORY NOTES

(1) *The Traditional View.*  The First Conflicts Restatement (§ 117) treated custody as a status question; custody jurisdiction, therefore, lay exclusively in the state where the child was domiciled. That position came under heavy fire as too simplistic and not concerned enough with the welfare of the child. *See, e.g.,* George Stumberg, *The Status of Children in the Conflict of Laws,* 8 U. Chi. L. Rev. 42 (1940).

**SAMPSELL v. SUPERIOR COURT**, 32 Cal. 2d 763, 197 F.2d 739 (1948), was a very influential opinion seeking a more enlightened road. This was a divorce action filed in California. The couple had been married in California, the child had been born there, and had lived there until he moved out of state when he was two and his parents separated. The mother took the child to Utah. The father sought custody, alleging that the child was taken out of state without his consent.

Traynor J: In the interest of the child, there is no reason why the state where the child is actually living may not have jurisdiction to act to protect the child's welfare, and there is likewise no reason why other states should not also have jurisdiction. It does not follow, however, that the courts of both states will exercise jurisdiction and reach conflicting results. The courts of one state may determine that the other state has a more substantial interest in the child and leave the matter to be settled there. On the other hand, there is no reason why, if the welfare of the particular child is a matter of real concern to the courts of another state, those courts may not also have jurisdiction, which might be exercised in the interest of the child.

(2) *Child Snatching.*  Of course, Justice Traynor and the "best interests" position won. It did not lead to Nirvana. The best interests test encouraged parents, unsuccessful in one state in a custody battle, to take their children—often in flagrant violation of court orders—to another state in hopes of changing the result by asking a court to favor the local parent. "Child Snatching" became a national problem, a problem compounded by judicial favoring of local parents. Of course, this was devastating for the child who was shunted from state to state and suffered not only from uncertainty, but also from the bitter fights of the parents.

(3) *The UCCJA.*  As divorce became more frequent and Americans more mobile, the situation rapidly became intolerable. The solution was the Uniform Child Custody Jurisdiction Act (UCCJA), written under the leadership of Professor Brigitte Bodenheimer. (Professor Bodenheimer's contributions are discussed in Sanford N. Katz, *Brigitte Bodenheimer:Protector of the Children,* 16 U.C. Davis L. Rev. vii (1982), and Carol Bruch, *Brigitte M. Bodenheimer,* 14 Fam. L.Q. vii (1981).) *See generally* Brigitte Bodenheimer, *The Uniform Child Custody Jurisdiction Act: A Legislative Remedy for Children Caught in the Conflict of Laws,* 22 Vand. L. Rev. 1207 (1969). By the early 1980s, all states had adopted the UCCJA.

The goal of the UCCJA was to "limit custody jurisdiction to the state where the child has his home or where there are other strong contacts with the child and his family." Commissioner's Prefatory Note, 9 U.L.A. 118. Only the court which rendered the decree can modify it (if it still has jurisdiction), and the decree must be recognized everywhere. Congress has helped implement the UCCJA by adopting the Parental Kidnaping Prevention Act, discussed in § 8.14, *infra*. The following case shows the basic jurisdictional workings of the UCCJA.

## REXFORD v. REXFORD

*Alaska Supreme Court*
*631 P.2d 475 (1980)*

DIMOND, SENIOR JUSTICE.

Thomas and Sandra Rexford were married in Alaska about ten years ago, in 1969. Their two children, ages nine and seven, were born of this marriage. The family lived in Alaska at all times before this controversy arose. In November, 1978, Sandra left the family home in Anchorage, taking the children without Thomas's consent, and went to Los Angeles where they began to reside with Sandra's mother. After being in California for about eight days, on November 29, 1978, Sandra filed a petition in the Los Angeles Superior Court for legal separation from her husband and for legal custody of the children.

Through counsel, Thomas made an appearance before the court to oppose Sandra's action to have custody of the children awarded to her. The court awarded temporary custody to Sandra, and ordered an investigation by the California probation department to assist in determining which parent should have permanent custody. Following this action, Thomas filed a suit for divorce and custody of the children in the superior court in Alaska. That court ordered a stay of the proceedings relative to custody because of the pending custody proceedings in California. From this order Thomas Rexford has appealed.

This case involves the Uniform Child Custody jurisdiction Act. ("Act") The purposes of the Act are stated in section I (AS 25.30.010).[11]

---

[11] AS 25.30.010 provides:

Purpose. The general purposes of this chapter are to:

(1) avoid jurisdictional competition and conflict with courts of other states in matters of child custody which have in the past resulted in the shifting of children from state to state with harmful effects on their well-being:

(2) promote cooperation with the courts of other states to the end that a custody decree is rendered in that state which can best decide the case in the interest of the child;

(3) assure that litigation concerning the custody of a child takes place ordinarily in the state with which the child and his family have the closest connection and where significant evidence concerning his care, protection, training, and personal relationships is most readily available, and that courts of this state decline the exercise of jurisdiction when the child and his family have a closer connection with another state.

(4) discourage continuing controversies over child custody in the interest of greater stability of home environment and of secure family relationships for the child;

(5) deter abductions and other unilateral removals of children undertaken to obtain custody awards;

To promote the purposes of the Act, section 6 (AS 25.30.050) provides in part, that a court of the adopting state may not exercise its jurisdiction if a custody proceeding is pending in a court of another state that is exercising its jurisdiction in substantial conformity with the Act.[12] In this case, the Alaska court determined that Thomas was participating in a custody action pending in California at the time he filed the Alaska suit and therefore stayed the Alaska action on the basis of AS 25.30.050.

The problem here is whether the California court exercised its jurisdiction in this custody dispute substantially in conformity with the Act. Section 3 of the Act sets forth the limited circumstances under which a court has subject matter jurisdiction to make a child custody determination. It provides as follows:

(a) A court of this State which is competent to decide child custody matters has jurisdiction to make a child custody determination by initial or modification decree if:

(1) this State (i) is the home state of the child at the time of commencement of the proceedings, or (ii) had been the child's home state within 6 months before commencement of the proceeding and the child is absent from this State because of his removal or retention by a person claiming his custody or for other reasons, and a parent or person acting as parent continues to live in this State; or

(2) it is in the best interest of the child that a court of this State assume jurisdiction because (i) the child and his parents, or the child and at least one contestant, have a significant connection with this State, and (ii) there is available in this State substantial evidence concerning the child's present or future care, protection, training, and personal relationships; or

(3) the child is physically present in this State and (I) the child has been abandoned or (ii) it is necessary in an emergency—to protect the child because he has been subjected to or threatened with mistreatment or abuse or is otherwise neglected [or dependent]; or

---

(6) avoid re-litigation of custody decisions of other states in this state insofar as feasible;

(7) facilitate the enforcement of custody decrees of other states;

(8) promote and expand the exchange of information and other forms of mutual assistance between the courts of this state and those of other states concerned with the same child; and

(9) make uniform the law of those states which enact it.

[12] AS 25.30.050 provides in part:

Simultaneous proceedings in other states.

(a) The superior court may not exercise its jurisdiction under this chapter if at the time of filing the petition a proceeding concerning the custody of the child was pending in a court of another state exercising jurisdiction substantially in conformity with this chapter, unless the proceeding is stayed by the court of the other state because this state is a more appropriate forum or for other reasons.

(c) If the court is informed during the course of the proceeding that a proceeding concerning the custody of the child was pending in another state before the court assumed jurisdiction, it shall stay the proceeding and communicate with the court in which the other proceeding is pending so that the issue my be litigated in the more appropriate forum and information may be exchanged in accordance with §§ 180-210 of this chapter. If a court of this state has made a custody decree before being informed that a proceeding was commenced in another state after it assumed jurisdiction, it shall likewise inform the other court to the end that the issues may be litigated in the more appropriate forum.

(4)(i) it appears that no other state would have jurisdiction under prerequisites substantially in accordance with paragraphs (1), (2), or (3), or another state has declined to exercise jurisdiction on the ground that this State is the more appropriate forum to determine the custody of the child, and (ii) it is in the best interest of the child that this court assume jurisdiction.

(b) Except under paragraphs (3) and (4) of subsection (a), physical presence in this State of the child, or of the child and one of the contestants, is not alone sufficient to confer jurisdiction on a court of this State to make a child custody determination.

(c) Physical presence of the child, while desirable, is not a prerequisite for jurisdiction to determine his custody.

The relevant California statute, Civil Code § 5152, is virtually identical, while the Alaska statute, AS 25.30.020, omits the "significant connection" basis described in subsection 2. Alaska clearly has jurisdiction under the "home state" basis described in subsection I (AS 25.30.020(a)(1)) because Alaska had been the children's home state within six months before commencement of the California proceeding and the children are absent from this state because of their removal by Sandra, who is claiming custody. The record does not disclose upon which basis the California court assumed jurisdiction.

It appears, however, that it must have been upon the "significant connection" basis of subsection 2.[13]

Thomas argues that the California court did not have jurisdiction under this or any of the sections and hence the Alaska court's order staying the proceedings was improper because, for purposes of the simultaneous proceedings section, California did not exercise jurisdiction substantially in conformity with the Act.

Under circumstances very similar to this case, California ruled in its decision in *In re Marriage of Ben-Yehoshua,* 91 Cal.App.3d 259, 154 Cal.Rptr. 80 (1979), that the superior court did not have jurisdiction. In that case the parties had lived in Israel for thirteen years when the mother visited in California with the children. Fourteen days after her arrival she filed an action for separation and custody of the children. The husband came to California, accepted service of process and retained counsel to represent him in the case. He appeared personally at the order to show cause hearing and entered into a stipulation with his wife that she have temporary custody over the children. The husband cooperated in the preparation of a probation report.

Upon appeal by the husband from the interlocutory decree that, in part, awarded custody to the wife, the court of appeal held that the superior court had not had jurisdiction under Civil Code § 5152(1)(b) to pass upon the custody issue. The appellate court found it "readily apparent that the children in this case did not have the requisite significant relationship to this state and that Israel was the state having the maximum contacts." The court quoted from the Commissioners' Note to § 3 of the Act, "Short-term presence in the state is not enough [to establish subject matter jurisdiction] even though there may

---

[13] California Civil Code § 5152(1)(b). It could not have been upon the "home state" basis because California was the state where the children lived for only eight days, and not the required six months, before Sandra filed her petition. The other grounds are clearly inapplicable.

be an intent to stay longer, perhaps an intent to establish a technical 'domicile' for divorce or other purposes."

The only difference between the facts of Ben-Yehoshua and this case is that in this case the children remained with Sandra in California, while the children in Ben-Yehoshua returned to Israel with the husband. This distinction cannot be considered significant for two reasons. First, a major purpose of the Act is to "deter abductions and other unilateral removals of children undertaken to obtain custody awards." To give any consideration to the fact that the children have been with Sandra in California since November 21, 1978, would be contrary to this purpose. Second, subject matter jurisdiction either exists or does not exist at the time when the petition is filed with the court. Facts developing after that, such as the length of time the children have now been in California, cannot be considered when determining whether the court initially had jurisdiction to hear the action.

It should be noted that Thomas's appearance in the California proceeding and his cooperation with the state's Child Custody Investigator in the preparation of a probation report did not waive or confer jurisdiction upon the court.

Thus, we conclude that the Los Angeles Superior Court did not have jurisdiction to determine this custody proceeding. However, we hold that the Alaska Superior Court did not abuse its discretion in deferring to California in this case and staying the Alaska proceedings. The Commissioners' Note to § 6 of the Act provides:

> while jurisdiction need not be yielded under subsection (a) if the other court would not have jurisdiction under the criteria of this Act, the policy against simultaneous custody proceedings is so strong that it might in a particular situation be appropriate to leave the case to the other court even under such circumstances.

Given the strength of the policy reasons, this seems to be one of the "particular situations" when it is more appropriate to leave the case to California. The factor weighing most heavily is not the lapse of time that has occurred since Sandra removed the children to California, but the extensive investigation that California has conducted into the abilities of both parents to care for the children. The probation report, prepared by the Child Custody Investigator, is thirty-five pages long. It is based upon interviews with Sandra, Thomas, and the children, and reports completed by witnesses for both spouses as well as statements submitted by the physicians of both parties. Thomas has the opportunity under provisions of the Act adopted both in California and Alaska to transmit to California any and all information gathered by the Child Custody Investigator in this state.[14] A major purpose of the Act is to ensure that the state making the custody determination has significant evidence concerning the child's care, protection, training, and personal relationships.[15]

---

[14] Section 18 of the Act permits the taking of testimony in another state; § 19 permits the court of one state to request that the court of another state forward its evidence and any social studies prepared for it.

[15] See AS 25.30.010(3), set forth in note 5 supra. See also AS 25.30.060(c)(3), which provides that a court may decline jurisdiction on grounds of forum non conveniens "if better evidence concerning the child's present or future care, protection, training, and personal relationships is available in another state, or if equally substantial evidence is more readily available in another state."

California either has in its possession or has available to it the fullest amount of information possible to make a fair and just determination of the custody issue. It would subject the parties to needless expense and the possibility of being held in contempt by one court for complying with an order of the other court to permit Alaska to continue its proceedings. Under these circumstances, it is less important which court exercises jurisdiction than that an informed decision is made which provides the stability of home environment and secure family relationships needed by the children.

While the superior court was authorized by AS 25.30.050(c) to stay its proceeding, in view of the pending action in California, the statute indicates that the court should have "communicated with the court in which the other proceeding is pending so that the issue may be litigated in the more appropriate forum and information may be exchanged in accordance with §§ 180-210 of this chapter."[16] In the event a final decree has not yet been entered in the California proceeding, we remand the case to the superior court for it to communicate with the California court pursuant to this statute. If a final decree has already been entered in California, then the stay on the proceeding in this state should be continued, pending the outcome of any appeal that Thomas might take in California on the issue of jurisdiction. Should a California appellate court conclude that the superior court in California did not have jurisdiction to hear the matter, Thomas's petition in this state may be renewed.

## NOTES AND QUESTIONS ON *REXFORD*

(1) Why was Alaska the "home state"? Had the Rexford children been there for six months when the Alaska case was filed? The court believed that the key date was when the *California* suit was filed. Do you agree? What about the Court's statement that the length of the children's stay in California was irrelevant? Do you agree that it was?

(2) Nevertheless, the Alaska court declined to exercise jurisdiction. Why did it decline? Do you agree with this result? Is the deference to California consistent with the statutory effort "to deter abduction"? What of the court's emphasis on the fact that a custody investigation had been conducted in California; do you think it wise to have considered that? After *Rexford,* should an attorney advise a client in Thomas' position not to cooperate with the authorities?

(3) In a later case with somewhat analogous facts, *S.J. v. L. T.,* 727 P.2d 789 (Alaska 1986), the Alaska court approved the exercise of jurisdiction when Alaska had "sufficient information available to it to make a fair determination of the custody issue."

(4) The well-known *Ben-Yehoshua* case from California, referred to in *Rexford,* also concluded that subject matter jurisdiction had to exist when the custody petition is filed with the court. What made *Ben-Yehoshua* difficult was that the father lived in Israel and the home state of the children was there.

---

[16] *See* note 6 *supra; see Vanneck v. Vanneck,* 49 N.Y.2d 602, 427 N.Y.S.2d 735, 404 N.E.2d 1278 (1980).

Should it matter, in other words, that a foreign country, rather than another state is involved?

*See* PROBLEMS 8C-1. WALTZING MATILDA; 8C-2. FRENCH CUSTODY; 8C-3. LEARNING ENGLISH.

(5) *Rexford's* careful concern with how best to proceed in order both to help the child and keep down litigation exemplifies the goals of many state courts and of the Commissioners who wrote the UCCJA.

## [A]   Analysis of The UCCJA

### [1]   *Jurisdiction*

The UCCJA has a number of jurisdictional provisions. (Most are in § 3 of the Act which is reprinted in the *Rexford* case.) Because they are not mutually exclusive, more than one may apply in any case.

(a) *Home-state jurisdiction.* This is the key concept. A state has jurisdiction under § 3(a)(1) if it is the child's home state, or if it had been the child's home state within 6 months before commencement of the proceeding. What is the home state? That place where the child lives with a parent "for at least 6 consecutive months" immediately preceding the filing of the action. Section 2(5). The six-month period was selected "in order to have a definite and certain test which is at the same time based on a reasonable assumption of fact." Commissioner's Comment, 9 U.L.A. 144. The "fact" assumed is that "[m]ost American children are integrated into an American community after living there six months. *Id.*, quoting David Ratner, *Child Custody in a Federal System,* 62 MICH. L. REV. 795, 818 (1964).

The time requirement of home state jurisdiction means that it can be lost if the child lives elsewhere for six months with a parent. When a couple splits up, therefore, and one parent moves to another state with the child, the stay-at-home parent should sue for custody within six months or risk losing the home court (state) advantage.

(b) *Significant connection jurisdiction.* A state may also assume jurisdiction if it is in the best interest of the child, *and* if, under § 3(a)(2), the child and at least one parent "have a significant connection" with the state, *and* that state has available "substantial evidence concerning. the child's present or future care, protection, training, and personal relationships." "Significant connection" jurisdiction is to be exercised only "if there is no home state or the child and his family have equal or stronger ties with another state." Commissioner's Note.

The "significant connection" test has generated a fair amount of litigation, often in connection with the question of whether a former home state where one parent continues to live retains jurisdiction over the decree it rendered. *See* the discussion of *Harris v. Melnick,* below.

(c) *Emergency jurisdiction.* Jurisdiction is also proper, under § 3(a)(3), if the child is present in the state and either has been "abandoned" or there is an "emergency" need to protect her from "mistreatment or abuse" or from neglect. According to the Commissioner's Comment, "[t]his extraordinary jurisdiction is reserved for extraordinary circumstances. When there is child neglect without emergency or abandonment, jurisdiction cannot be based on this paragraph."

Professor Brigitte Bodenheimer believed that emergency jurisdiction "exists when a child is in immediate danger from a source within the state's borders." Her examples are a child whose parents are killed in an accident or one who is threatened with violence. She also believed jurisdiction was proper where the parents are fighting over custody in a state which is not a home state and there has been no custody adjudication; thus, "it is urgent to settle the dispute by way of a temporary custody order pending adjudication in the proper state." Brigitte Bodenheimer, *Progress Under the Uniform Child Custody Jurisdiction Act and Remaining Problems: Punitive Decrees, Joint Custody, and Excessive Modifications,* 65 CALIF. L. REV. 978, 993 (1977).

(d) *Residual jurisdiction.* Finally, if no other state has jurisdiction, then, if it is in the child's best interest, § 3(a)(4) permits jurisdiction to be exercised. The Act does not expressly provide for jurisdiction by consent of the litigating parties. Would that be wise? Should a guardian be appointed to protect the child's interests in a consent case? This problem is discussed in David Ratner, *Procedural Due Process and Jurisdiction to Adjudicate,* 75 Nw. U. L. REV. 363, 406-10 (1980).

(e) *Jurisdiction and Conduct.* Section 8(a) of the UCCJA authorizes a court to decline jurisdiction if the petitioner "has wrongfully taken the child from another state or has engaged in similar reprehensible conduct". This refusal can extend, if similar cause be shown, to modification of decrees. Section 8(b). This, of course, is a codification of the "clean hands" doctrine traditionally applied by equity courts. The Commissioner's Note tells a court to refuse jurisdiction "unless the harm done to the child by a denial of jurisdiction outweighs the parental misconduct" 9 U.L.A. 252. This provision has created significant difficulty in application. *See* Homer Clark, The Domestic Relations Law of the United States 473-76 (2d ed. 1987).

Does a mother who takes her child without permission to another state in order to escape physical (or emotional) violence to her or to the child have unclean hands?

*See* PROBLEMS 8C-4. ARIZONA, TENNESSEE AND X; 8C-5.; PARENTS v. GRANDPARENTS.

(f) *Concurrent jurisdiction.* The flexibility of the UCCJA's jurisdiction standards make it quite possible that more than one state will feel it has jurisdiction. The Act addresses this problem in § 6 (reprinted in the *Rexford* case) with a first-in time rule: The second state should stay its action "and communicate with the court in which the other proceeding is pending § 6(c), to determine the more appropriate forum to hear the case. After consultation, the second forum may decline to exercise jurisdiction, as the court in *Rexford* did. The court has a duty to consult on its own, even if the parties do not raise the issue. Indeed, consultation with another court may be quite proper, even when no foreign action is pending, when "gray area decision-making" is involved in order to head off conflicts at the start. *See* Lucy S. McGough and Anne R. Hughes, *Charted Territory: The Louisiana Experience with the Uniform Child Custody Jurisdiction Act,* 44 LA. L. REV. 19, 46 (1983).

## [2]  *Modification*

Concurrent jurisdiction can exist only before a decree is entered. There is no concurrent jurisdiction afterwards: only the decree-rendering state can modify it. This is perhaps the most important part of the UCCJA, for it vitiates the major incentive to engage in child snatching. There is a catch however; "§ 14 permits modification of another court's award only if the decree rendering court has lost jurisdiction."[17] Obviously, this can create difficulties, for a modifying court can "cheat" if it is so inclined, by concluding that the decree rendering state has indeed lost jurisdiction, and under the last-in-time rule of *Treinies v. Sunshine Mining Co.,* 308 U.S. 66 (1939) (*see* § 7.07, Inconsistent Judgments, Note (1) *supra*), that second decision must be recognized.

Perhaps the biggest "loss of jurisdiction" problem involves custody decisions made by former home states where a non-custodial parent continues to live, a relationship which satisfies, at least arguably, the "significant connection" jurisdiction test.

An example is *Harris v. Melnick,* 314 Md. 539, 552 A.2d 38 (1989). The couple in that case lived in Maryland and their son was born there. While divorce proceedings were pending in Maryland, the mother and son moved to Colorado. The Maryland court awarded her custody of the son, and the two of them continued to live in Colorado; the father remained in Maryland. Ten years later, the father asked the Maryland court to resolve a dispute concerning custody and visitation. Did that court have jurisdiction to do so, even when it was conceded that Colorado was the home state?

The Maryland court thought so. Judge Rodowsky's opinion framed the question as one of modifiability. UCCJA § 14 clearly provides that only the court which rendered the original decree can modify it, unless that court has lost jurisdiction. The court relied on the Commissioner's Note to § 14 and Professor Bodenheimer's writings to conclude that § 14 means what it says: Modification can take place only in the rendering state if that court retains jurisdiction.

The question then became whether Maryland *had* retained jurisdiction even though Colorado was now the child's home state and the divorce had taken place ten years earlier. The court found that a substantial connection existed, pointing to such factors as the child's continued visits to his father in Maryland and the presence of witnesses to the relationship between father and son there. The court observed: "Courts generally give the decree-rendering state a strong presumption of continuing modification jurisdiction until all or almost all connection with the parents and the child is lost."

The court wrote that it is "not uncommon in divorce situations for the non-custodial parent to remain in the state which rendered the original custody decree and in which that parent enjoys visitation rights, while the custodial parent lives in another state. The Uniform Act does not require more for the jurisdiction of the originating state to continue."

---

[17] Section 14(a) provides that another State's custody decree "shall not" be modified unless the rendering court either lacks jurisdiction or has declined to exercise it and the forum now has jurisdiction.

Finally, the court noted that the trial court properly could have declined to exercise jurisdiction, using the discretion granted it under UCCJA § 7.[18] The mother had argued for that result, emphasizing that substantially all of her son's personal relationships, as well as his school records, were in Colorado. Should the trial court have declined jurisdiction?

But is that fair? Should the custodial parent really have to travel from Colorado to Maryland to litigate custody when the child has a new home state in Colorado and most of the relevant evidence is there? After all, the move to another state may be caused by strong economic need (perhaps caused by the stay-at-home parent's failure to make support payments); should a court consider those factors? Or is the fear of child-snatching and its attendant problems so strong that the price paid by the custodial parent is worth it? For an expression of this point of view, see *McAtee v. McAtee,* 323 S.E.2d 611 (W. Va. 1984).

Professor Bodenheimer certainly would have approved of the result in *Harris.* She wrote that § 14 puts the lid on the myth of concurrent jurisdiction: "[T]he state of the prior decree alone has jurisdiction to modify its decree. This jurisdiction is exclusive. No other state has authority to hear a petition for modification. Brigitte Bodenheimer, *Interstate Custody: Initial Jurisdiction and Continuing Jurisdiction Under the UCCJA,* 14 Fam. L.Q. 203, 216-17 (1981).

*See* PROBLEMS 8C-6. BACK AND FORTH; 8C-7. THE CONSOLIDATION; 8C-8. SUMMER VACATION; 8C-9. ABROGATING VISITATION RIGHTS.

### [3] *An Evaluation*

The effectiveness of the UCCJA's modification provisions has drawn mixed reviews. Nevertheless, a reading of reported decisions gives a strong feeling that courts (or at least appellate courts) are trying very hard to carry out the spirit as well as the letter of the UCCJA. Of course, a court's failure to pay attention to the modification rules can at times be frustrating. In *Salisbury v. Salisbury,* 657 S.W. 2d 761, 768 (Tenn. App. 1983), for example, a Texas court had ignored an earlier Tennessee custody order. When the case was heard again in Tennessee, the court remarked that "the Tennessee decree is entitled to enforcement by the state of Texas, which we would point out would still be a Mexican province had Tennesseans not fought at the Alamo."

## § 8.14   Recognition

Traditionally, interstate recognition was a problem with custody decrees; because they could always be modified in the best interests of the child, they were not considered final decrees entitled to recognition. *See, e.g., New York ex rel. Halvey v. Halvey,* 330 U.S. 610 (1947). The UCCJA changed that. A decree rendered by a court with proper jurisdiction under the UCCJA must

---

[18] Section 7 provides a kind of "inconvenient forum" checklist for a court to use in deciding whether to permit another state to assume jurisdiction. The Commissioners' Comment stresses the need for "interstate judicial communication and cooperation." 9 U.L.A. 234.

be recognized and enforced by other states. When combined with the no modification rule in § 14, the recognition rules of §§ 13 and 15 come close to eliminating the problem of parental child-snatching. The UCCJA recognition principle does raise, however, an intriguing constitutional problem. To analyze that problem, we must first examine an old chestnut.

## MAY v. ANDERSON

*United States Supreme Court*
*345 U.S. 528, 73 S. Ct. 840, 97 L. Ed. 1221 (1953)*

MR. JUSTICE BURTON delivered the opinion of the Court.

The question presented is whether, in a habeas corpus proceeding attacking the right of a mother to retain possession of her minor children, an Ohio court must give full faith and credit to a Wisconsin decree awarding custody of the children to their father when that decree is obtained by the father in an ex parte divorce action in a Wisconsin court which had no personal jurisdiction over the mother. For the reasons hereafter stated, our answer is no.

The parties were married in Wisconsin and, until 1947, both were domiciled there. After marital troubles developed, they agreed in December, 1946, that appellant should take their children to Lisbon, Columbian County, Ohio, and there think over her future course. By New Year's Day, she had decided not to return to Wisconsin and, by telephone, she informed her husband of that decision.

Within a few days he filed suit in Wisconsin, seeking both an absolute divorce and custody of the children. The only service of process upon appellant consisted of the delivery to her personally, in Ohio, of a copy of the Wisconsin summons and petition. Such service is authorized by a Wisconsin statute for use in an action for a divorce but that statute makes no mention of its availability in a proceeding for the custody of children. Appellant entered no appearance and took no part in this Wisconsin proceeding which produced not only a decree divorcing the parties from the bonds of matrimony but a decree purporting to award the custody of the children to their father, subject to a right of their mother to visit them at reasonable times. Appellant contests only the validity of the decree as to custody.

Armed with a copy of the decree and accompanied by a local police officer, appellee, in Lisbon, Ohio, demanded and obtained the children from their mother. The record does not disclose what took place between 1947 and 1951, except that the children remained with their father in Wisconsin until July 1, 1951. He then brought them back to Lisbon and permitted them to visit their mother. This time, when he demanded their return, she refused to surrender them.

Relying upon the Wisconsin decree, he promptly filed in the Probate Court of Columbian County, Ohio, the petition for a writ of habeas corpus now before us. Under Ohio procedure that writ tests only the immediate right to possession of the children. It does not open the door for the modification of any prior award of custody on a showing of changed circumstances. Nor is it available as a procedure for settling the future custody of children in the first instance.

Separated as our issue is from that of the future interests of the children, we have before us the elemental question whether a court of a state, where a mother is neither domiciled, resident nor present, may cut off her immediate right to the care, custody, management and companionship of her minor children without having jurisdiction over her in personam. Rights far more precious to appellant than property rights will be cut off if she is to be bound by the Wisconsin award of custody.

In *Estin v. Estin,* [334 U.S. 541], and *Kreiger v. Kreiger,* [334 U.S. 555], this Court upheld the validity of a Nevada divorce obtained ex parte by a husband, resident in Nevada, insofar as it dissolved the bonds of matrimony. At the same time, we held Nevada powerless to cut off, in that proceeding, a spouse's right to financial support under the prior decree of another state. In the instant case, we recognize that a mother's right to custody of her children is a personal right entitled to at least as much protection as her right to alimony.

In the instant case, the Ohio courts gave weight to appellee's contention that the Wisconsin award of custody binds appellant because, at the time it was issued, her children had a technical domicile in Wisconsin, although they were neither resident nor present there. [19] We find it unnecessary to determine the children's legal domicile because, even if it be with their father, that does not give Wisconsin, certainly as against Ohio, the personal jurisdiction that it must have in order to deprive their mother of her personal right to their immediate possessions. [20]

The judgment of the Supreme Court of Ohio, accordingly, is reversed and the cause is remanded to it for further proceedings not inconsistent with this opinion.

MR. JUSTICE FRANKFURTER, concurring.

---

[19] For the general rule that in cases of the separation of parents, apart from any award of custody of the children, the domicile of the children is that of the parent with whom they live and that only the state of that domicile may award their custody. *See* Restatement, Conflict of Laws (1934), §§ 32 and 146, Illustrations 1 and 2.

[20] "The weight of authority is in favor of confining the jurisdiction of the court in an action for divorce, where the defendant is a non-resident and does not appear, and process upon the defendant is by substituted service only, to a determination of the status of the parties. This rule of law extends to children who are not within the jurisdiction of the court when the decree is rendered, where the defendant is not a resident of the state of the seat of the court, and has neither been personally served with process nor appeared to the action" [citation omitted].

The instant case does not present the special considerations that arise where a parent, with or without minor children, leaves a jurisdiction for the purpose of escaping process or otherwise evading jurisdiction, and we do not have here the considerations that arise when children are unlawfully or surreptitiously taken by one parent from the other.

The Court's decision holds that the state in which a child and one parent are domiciled and which is primarily concerned about his welfare cannot constitutionally adjudicate controversies as to his guardianship. The state's power here is defeated by the absence of the other parent for a period of two months. The convenience of a leave-taking parent is placed above the welfare of the child, but neither party is greatly aided in obtaining a decision. The Wisconsin courts cannot bind the mother, and the Ohio courts cannot bind the father. A state of the law such as this, where possession apparently is not merely nine points of the law but all of them and self-help the ultimate authority, has little to commend it in legal logic or as a principle of order in a federal system.

The views expressed by my brother Jackson make it important that I state, in joining the Court's opinion, what I understand the Court to be deciding and what it is not deciding in this case.

What is decided—the only thing the Court decides—is that the Full Faith and Credit Clause does not require Ohio, in disposing of the custody of children in Ohio, to accept, in the circumstances before us, the disposition made by Wisconsin. The Ohio Supreme Court felt itself so bound. This Court does not decide that Ohio would be precluded from recognizing, as a matter of local law, the disposition made by the Wisconsin court. For Ohio to give respect to the Wisconsin decree would not offend the Due Process Clause. Ohio is no more precluded from doing so than a court of Ontario or Manitoba would be, were the mother to bring the children into one of these provinces.

Property, personal claims, and even the marriage status, generally give rise to interests different from those relevant to the discharge of a State's continuing responsibility to children within her borders. Children have a very special place in life which law should reflect. Legal theories and their phrasing in other cases readily lead to fallacious reasoning if uncritically transferred to determination of a State's duty towards children. There are, of course, adjudications other than those pertaining to children, as for instance decrees of alimony, which may not be definitive even in the decreeing State, let alone binding under the Full Faith and Credit Clause. Interests of a State other than its duty towards children may also prevail over the interest of national unity that underlies the Full Faith and Credit Clause. But the child's welfare in a custody case has such a claim upon the State that its responsibility is obviously not to be foreclosed by a prior adjudication reflecting another State's discharge of its responsibility at another time. Reliance on opinions regarding out-of-State adjudications of property rights, personal claims or the marital status is bound to confuse analysis when a claim to the custody of children before the courts of one State is based on an award previously made by another State. Whatever light may be had from such opinions, they cannot give conclusive answers.

MR. JUSTICE JACKSON, whom MR. JUSTICE REED joins, dissenting.

The Court apparently is holding that the Federal Constitution prohibits Ohio from recognizing the validity of this Wisconsin divorce decree insofar as it settles custody of the couple's children. In the light of settled and unchallenged precedents of this Court, such a decision can only rest upon the proposition that Wisconsin's courts had no jurisdiction to make such a decree binding upon appellant.

A conclusion that a state must not recognize a judgment of a sister commonwealth involves very different considerations than a conclusion that it must do so. . .

The Ohio courts reasoned that although personal jurisdiction over the wife was lacking, domicile of the children in Wisconsin was a sufficient jurisdictional basis to enable Wisconsin to bind all parties interested in their custody. This determination that the children were domiciled in Wisconsin has not been contested either at our bar or below. Therefore, under our precedents, it is conclusive. *Williams v. North Carolina [Williams I]*, 317 U.S. 287, 302.

In this situation Wisconsin was no meddler reaching out to draw to its courts controversies that arose in and concerned other legal communities. If ever domicile of the children plus that of one spouse is sufficient to support a custody decree binding all interested parties, it should be in this case. *Cf. Yarborough v. Yarborough,* 290 U.S. 202, 210.

I am quite aware that in recent times this Court has been chipping away at the concept of domicile as a connecting factor between the state and the individual to determine rights and obligations. We are a mobile people, historically on the move, and perhaps the rigid concept of domicile derived by common law from feudal attachment to the land is too rigid for a society so restless as ours. But if our federal system is to maintain separate legal communities, as the Full Faith and Credit Clause evidently contemplates, there must be some test for determining to which of these a person belongs. If, for this purpose, there is a better concept than domicile, we have not yet hit upon it. Abandonment of this ancient doctrine would leave partial vacuums in many branches of the law. It seems to be abandoned here.

Nor can I agree on principle with the Court's treatment of-the question of personal jurisdiction of the wife. But here the Court requires personal service upon a spouse who decamps before the State of good-faith domicile can make provision for custody and support of the children still legally domiciled within it. Wisconsin had a far more real concern with the transactions here litigated than have many of the divorce-mill forums whose judgments we have commanded their sister states to recognize.

*   *   *

The difference between a proceeding involving the status, custody and support of children and one involving adjudication of property rights is too apparent to require elaboration. In the former, courts are no longer concerned primarily with the proprietary claims of the contestants for the "res" before the court, but with the welfare of the "res" itself Custody is viewed not with the idea of adjudicating rights in the children, as if they were chattels, but rather with the idea of making the best disposition possible for the welfare of the children. To speak of a court's "cutting off" a mother's right to custody of her children, as if it raised problems similar to those involved in "cutting off" her rights in a plot of ground, is to obliterate these obvious distinctions. Personal jurisdiction of all parties to be affected by a proceeding is highly desirable, to make certain that they have had valid notice and opportunity to be heard. But the assumption that it overrides all other considerations and in its absence a state is constitutionally impotent to resolve questions of custody flies in the face of our own cases. The wife's marital ties may be dissolved without personal jurisdiction over her by a state where the husband has a genuine domicile because the concern of that state with the welfare and marital status of its domiciliary is felt to be sufficiently urgent. Certainly the claim of the domiciled parent to relief for himself from the leave-taking parent does not exhaust the power of the state. The claim of children as well as the home keeping parent to have their status determined with reasonable certainty, and to be free from an incessant tug of war between squabbling parents, is equally urgent.

*See*  PROBLEM 8C-10. A HABEAS CORPUS PROCEEDING.

## NOTES AND QUESTIONS ON CUSTODY AND THE CONSTITUTION

(1) *The Holding.* What *exactly* did *May* hold?

(a) Did the Court hold that custody is a kind of property right which cannot be terminated without personal jurisdiction over the defendant? Is this what the Court meant with its reference to "in personam" jurisdiction and its observation that "[r]ights far more precious than 'property rights might be terminated?

(b) Or did the Court merely hold that Ohio was not *required* to follow the Wisconsin order, but could do so if it felt like it. Justice Burton's opinion does seem to frame the issue in terms of giving Wisconsin "the right" as against Ohio to determine custody. Is it significant that Burton did not discuss the Due Process Clause?

(c) Justice Frankfurter obviously thought (b) was the correct answer. So why did he concur?

(d) What grade would you give Justice Burton's opinion for clarity?

(e) The Court seemed to treat a custody problem like any other problem involving property and did not seem concerned with such issues as the welfare of the child and the state's interest in protecting that welfare. *See* Homer Clark, The Domestic Relations Law of the United States 461 (2d ed. 1987). Is that because those issues are irrelevant in a property rights case?

*See* PROBLEM 8C-11. "BUT I NEVER LIVED IN Y!"

(2) *Minimum contacts. Shaffer v. Heitner,* 433  U.S. 186 (1977), extended the minimum contacts requirement to in rem cases. No longer can it be argued that minimum contacts can be avoided because custody (*i.e.* , status) disputes are proceedings in rem. *See* WILLIAM M. RICHMAN & WILLIAM L. REYNOLDS, UNDERSTANDING CONFLICT OF LAWS 384 (3d ed. 2002). *Shaffer* expressly left open its application to cases involving "adjudications of status." 433 U.S. 208 at n.30. Curiously, footnote 30 does not cite *May.* "Does this mean," Professor Clark asks, "that the Court does not consider a custody case to involve status"? Homer Clark, *supra,* at 462 n 53.

Consider also that minimum contacts is a standard with some play in the joints. Might that standard not be bent a bit when dealing with the welfare of children? Or is the right to have ones claim to be a custodial parent heard by a convenient forum equally important? Should it matter why the parent left?

In *Stanley v. Illinois,*  405 U.S. 645 (1972), the Court suggested that an unwed father's rights could be terminated in an adoption proceeding by publication, when personal service was availalable. Does that overrule *May,* sub silentio? Professor Clark thinks it might. *See*  Homer Clark, *supra* Note (1). *See also In re Marriage of Leonard,*  122 Cal. App. 3d 443, 175 Cal. Rptr. 903 (1981). On the other hand, as Professor Garfield observes, "Viewing *May* as a right-to-hearing case makes it more consistent with *Stanley* and requires rejection of Professor Clark's suggestion that *Stanley* may have overruled *May* sub silentio." Helen Garfield, *Due Process Rights of Absent Parents in Interstate Custody Conflicts,* 16 IND. L. REV. 445, 456 n.71. Is Garfield's argument helped by the fact that *Stanley* really was about the procedure needed in adoption cases when it wasn't known who was the father, and the case involved for that reason a very different issue from those presented in the custody cases?

In *Kulko v. Superior Court,* 436 U.S. 84 (1978), discussed in § 8.17, *infra,* the court refused to uphold jurisdiction in a child support case when minimum contacts were not present. The *Kulko* majority noted, however, that there was an alternative procedure available (URESA), and that California had not asserted a "particularized interest" in child support cases by adopting a "special jurisdictional statute." 436 U.S. 84 at 98. Could the UCCJA be both the alternative and " particularized" statute? *See In re Marriage of Leonard,* 122 Cal. App. 3d 443, 459, 175 Cal. Rptr 903, 912 (1983):

The [UCCJA] with an integrated, detailed plan for jurisdiction in child custody proceedings, is such a statute. Given the importance of a custody award in the life of a child, it is fair and reasonable to require a parent to submit to the jurisdiction of a forum which, under the standards of the Act, is most suited to make that determination.

Do you agree?

## NOTES AND QUESTIONS ON *MAY v. ANDERSON* AND THE UCCJA

(1) *Frankfurter's Position.* The jurisdictional sections of the UCCJA do not require that the Court have personal jurisdiction over both parents. According to § 4, an absent parent is entitled only to "reasonable notice and opportunity to be heard." This raises, of course, the issue of how *May* should be construed today. The UCCJA obviously adopts Justice Frankfurter's position that personal jurisdiction is not needed over both spouses. Professor Garfield's illuminating article, after thoughtfully analyzing the precedents, proposes that the absent parent is entitled to some kind of hearing before permanent custody can be constitutionally awarded. Who's right?

(2) *The Hudson Case.* Consider a couple married in Indiana, who live there briefly, and who then move to Iceland where two children are born. Everyone moves to Washington, but the mother later returns to Indiana with the children. The mother sues for divorce there, notifying the father of the action by mail. He then takes the children to Spain without permission. Can the Indiana court decide custody?

It did. Relying on the "status" exception footnote in *Shaffer,* the court believed that a custody case should be viewed as an in rem proceeding; the "res" (the child's status) was properly before the court because it had significant connection jurisdiction under UCCJA § 3(a)(2). Hence, the court was able to hold that "traditional notions of fair play and substantial justice" were satisfied if the UCCJA's *notice* requirements had been met. In *re Hudson,* 434 N.E.2d 107, 119 (Ind. App. 1982), *cert. denied,* 459 U.S. 1202 (1983).

The *Hudson* court's adoption of the "status" solution to the personal juris-diction problem has met with approval elsewhere. *E.g., McAtee v. McAtee,* 323 S.E.2d 611 (W. Va. 1984); Bodenheimer & Neeley-Kvarme, *Jurisdiction Over Child Custody and Adoption After Shaffer and Kulko,* 12 U. C. DAVIS L. REV. 229 (1979).

(3) *Due Process for the Absent Parent.* Not all courts believe that personal jurisdiction over the absent spouse can be dispensed with, however. In *Ex Parte Dean,* 447 So. 2d 733, 737 (Ala. 1984), for example the court, relying heavily on *Kulko* and the majority opinion in *May* held that it need not respect a Florida custody decree because it was made "by a court lacking *in personam* jurisdiction over affected parties." Professor Helen Garfield, after stressing that the *Hudson* approach does not address the problem of minimum contacts, notes that "Notice alone does not satisfy due process if it does no more than inform a defendant of a hearing taking place in a distant forum." 16 Ind. L. Rev. at 473-74. Professor Ratner has also expressed unease over the proce-dural due process problem. *See* David Ratner, *Procedural Due Process and Jurisdiction to Adjudicate,* 7 5 Nw. U. L. REV. 363, 417-19 (1980). But how do you solve the problem that if personal jurisdiction over both parents is required, there may be no state capable of entering a binding decree, a dilemma which brings you back full circle to the situation before the adoption of the UCCJA?

(4) *Termination.* Is the same result proper if the question is not custody, but termination of parental rights? That issue was reached in the following case.

**IN RE M.L.K.,** 13 Kans. App. 2d 251, 768 P.2d 316 (1989). A child, born in Colorado, was placed with a couple who then moved to Kansas. After several years, the couple moved to terminate the parental rights of the natural parents. The father was not known, and the mother could not be found; ser-vice, therefore, was by publication. An attorney, appointed to represent the absent parent, challenged the court's jurisdiction.

ANDERSON, J: [I]n recent years, the Supreme Court has ruled that the rights of a parent in termination and/or custody proceedings warrant protection.

> On first impression, the rules handed down in *International Shoe* would seem to control our case, since the natural parents of M.L.K. did not have the [required] "minimum contacts". However, [i]n *Shaffer v. Heitner,* the court carved out an exception to the "minimum con-tacts" rule [and] recognized that status adjudication based on special-ized jurisdictional rules meets due process requirements of fairness without the need for "minimum contacts" of the parties with the forum state.

Is there any reason to view termination cases any differently from divorce or custody cases? We think not. Termination of parental rights is nothing more than a determination of legal status between the natural parent and the child. In both custody and termination proceedings, the court principally determines where and with whom a child should or should not live. All these proceedings are determinations of status and, as such, are within the "status exception" to the minimum contacts rule.

[W]e are well aware of the potential inequities. [T]he danger exists that parental rights might be wrongfully terminated.[S]hould such a situation arise in any future case, the trial court has the necessary equitable powers to deal with the problem.

\* \* \*

Do you think termination of parental rights is a better or worse case for applying the status exception than custody? Are you worried that the decision in *M.L.K* might lead to abuse?

## THE PARENTAL KIDNAPPING PREVENTION ACT

The Parental Kidnapping Prevention Act (PKPA), 28 U.S.C. § 1738A, adopted in 1980, implements the promise of the Full Faith and Credit Clause for custody cases.[21] The magnitude of the interstate custody problem is underscored by the fact that the PKPA was Congress' first legislation passed under the authority of the Full Faith and Credit Clause, apart from the general implementing statute, 28 U.S.C. § 1738 (discussed in § 7.02, *supra*).

Although the PKPA has a number of other provisions.[22] its main provisions were designed to make enforceable custody decrees rendered under the UCCJA. The PKPA's provisions therefore, closely parallel, but are not identical to, those of the UCCJA.[23] The main difference between the two statutes

---

[21] *See generally* Russell Coombs, *Interstate Child Custody: Jurisdiction, Recognition, and Enforcement.* 66 Minn. L. Rev. 711 (1982). *See also* Michael Dorsaneo, *Due Process, Full Faith and Credit, and Family Law Litigation,* 36 Sw. L.J. 1085 (1983).

[22] One provision of the PKPA provides for the use of the Parent Locator Service, which appears in the Social Security Act. 42 U.S.C. § 653. The Service provides information for locating a parent or child in order to enforce certain state or federal laws. Hence, the Service may be used in order to enforce a law regarding the "unlawful taking or restraint of a child," or to make or enforce a custody determination.

The last provision of the Act makes 18 U.S.C. § 1073 applicable to "cases involving parental kidnaping and interstate or international flight to avoid prosecution under applicable state felony statutes." A state which makes parental kidnaping a crime may seek the help of the FBI in locating the abducting parent. This is the only section of the Act with international implications—the other sections only apply to states and United States territories and possessions.

[23] The PKPA provides:

§ 1738A. Full faith and credit given to child custody determinations.

(a) The appropriate authorities of every State shall enforce according to its terms, and shall not modify except as provided in subsection (f) of this section, any child custody determination made consistently with the provisions of this section by a court of another State.

(b) . . .

(4) "Home State" means the State in which, immediately preceding the time involved, the child lived with his parents, a parent, or a person acting as parent, for at least six consecutive months, and in the case of a child less than six months old, the State in which the child lived from birth, with any of such persons. Periods of temporary absence of any of such persons are counted as part of the six-month or other period;

(c) A child custody determination made by a court of a State is consistent with the provisions of this section only.

(2) If one of the following conditions is met:

(A) such State (I) is the home State of the child on the date of the commencement of the

involves the federal requirement that a court must defer to the state which first validly exercises jurisdiction.[24] The PKPA contains an important exception to this race to the courthouse rule; a second state, which is also the home state, may exercise jurisdiction if the first state's jurisdictional basis was only "significant connection" jurisdiction. In other words, because a home state decree can always trump a significant connection state's order, only home state decrees can be sure of being honored elsewhere. *See generally* McGough and Hughes, *Charted Territory: The Louisiana Experience with the Uniform Child Custody Jurisdiction Act,* 44 LA. L. REV. 19, 62-64 (1983).

The PKPA is a very important statute, for it places the authority of the national government, and the Supremacy Clause, behind efforts to end the child-snatching problem. It is also important because Congress rejected the "in personam" reading of *May v. Anderson* and adopted instead the "status" interpretation. Thus, Congress has placed its imprimatur on the interpretation of *May* which does not require jurisdiction over both parents to adjudicate

---

proceeding, or (ii) had been the child's home State within six months before the date of the commencement of the proceeding and the child is absent from such State because of his removal or retention by a contestant or for other reasons, and a contestant continues to live in such State;

(B) (i) it appears that no other State would have jurisdiction under subparagraph (A), and (ii) it is in the best interest of the child that a court of such State assume jurisdiction because (1) the child and his parents, or the child and at least one contestant, have a significant connection with such State other than mere physical presence in such State, and (II) there is available in such State substantial evidence concerning the child's present or future care, protection, training, and personal relationships;

(C) the child is physically present in such State and (I) the child has been abandoned, or (ii) it is necessary in an emergency to protect the child because he has been subjected to or threatened with mistreatment or abuse;

(D) (i) it appears that no other State would have jurisdiction under subparagraph (A), (B), (C) or (E), or another State has declined to exercise jurisdiction on the ground that the State whose jurisdiction is in issue is the more appropriate forum to determine the custody of the child; and (ii) it is in the best interest of the child that such court assume jurisdiction; or

(E) the court has continuing jurisdiction pursuant to subsection (d) of this section.

(d) The jurisdiction of a court of a State which has made a child custody determination consistently with the provisions of this section continues as long as the requirement of subsection (c)(1) of this section continues to be met and such State remains the residence of the child or of any contestant.

(f) A court of a State may modify a determination of the custody of the same child made by a court of another State, if—

(1) it has jurisdiction to make such a child custody determination; and

(2) the court of the other State no longer has jurisdiction, or it has declined to exercise such jurisdiction to modify such determination.

(g) A court of a State shall not exercise jurisdiction in any proceeding for a custody determination commenced during the pendency of a proceeding in a court of another State where such court of that other State is exercising jurisdiction consistently with the provisions of this section to make a custody determination.

[24] The relationship between the two statutes is discussed in Foster, *Child Custody Jurisdiction: UCCJA and PKPA,* 27 N.Y.L. SCH. L. REV. 297, 331-42 (1981); Professor Foster argues that the PKPA is the less flexible statute because Congress has required that all custody decrees entered by courts having jurisdiction under the PKPA must be recognized.

Another difference between the two is that under the PKPA there can be no overlap between "substantial connection" and "home state" jurisdiction; the former can exist only when the latter is not present. HOMER CLARK, THE DOMESTIC RELATIONS LAW OF THE UNITED STATES 480 (2d ed. 1988).

a custody problem. Does that approval help solve the riddle of the constitutionality of that reading?

## A NOTE ON THE UCCJEA

A new Uniform Act, the Uniform Child Custody Jurisdiction and Enforcement Act ("UCCJEA"), was promulgated in 1998. The UCCJEA makes few substantive changes in the UCCJA, although it resolves a number of problems that had arisen under the older statute. Some things worth noting about the later statute:

1. The Act reconciles the UCCJA with the PKPA. The most important reconciliation gives "home state" jurisdiction the same priority that it has under the PKPA.

2. The new Act makes clear that modification of an existing order can *only* be done by the issuing court, as long as that court retains jurisdiction over either parent or the child. (Some courts had been ignoring the UCCJA's mandate in § 14 to the same effect and confirmed in *Harris v. Melnick, supra.*)

3. The UCCJEA provides a welcome panoply of new enforcement mechanisms, including a central custody registry and enforcement by public officials.

The UCCJEA does not address adoption, which is covered by the Uniform Adoption Act. *See generally* Patricia M. Hoff, *The ABC's of the UCCJEA: Interstate Child-Custody Practice Under the New Act*, 32 Fam. L.Q. 267 (1998).

*See* PROBLEM 8C-12. WHOSE CHILDREN ARE THEY?

## § 8.15　International Problems

Congress has addressed the even more vexatious problem of international custody by adopting in 1988 the International Child Abduction Remedies Act, 42 U.S.C. §§ 11601, *et seq.* That Act provides an enforcement mechanism to implement the Hague Convention on the Civil Aspect of International Child Abduction (1980).[25] Concurrent jurisdiction to enforce that Convention is given to state and federal courts.[26] The Hague Convention is described in Cheshire and North's Private International Law 728-729 (11th ed. 1987). *See also* Linda Silberman, *Hague Int'l Child Abduction Convention: A Progress*

---

[25] The text of the Hague Convention and the International Child Abduction Remedies Act, along with a State Department analysis of the Convention and Regulations promulgated under the Act, are reproduced in the Family Law Reporter (July 18, 1989) (Supp. No. 122).

[26] The provision for federal jurisdiction in a domestic relations case is striking. There has long been a judge-made "domestic relations" exception to federal jurisdiction. *See generally* Roger M. Baron, *Federal Preemption in the Resolution of Child Custody Jurisdiction Disputes*, 45 Ark. L. Rev. 885 (1993). Some commentators thought the PKPA would be read to override that exception, but the Court held otherwise in *Thompson v. Thompson*, 484 U.S.174 (1988) (Congress did not intend to create federal question jurisdiction); the *Thompson* decision is discussed in Chapter 6.02, *supra.* A thorough discussion of federalism questions and the PKPA is Finch and Kasriel, *Federal Court Correction of State Court Error: The Singular Case of Interstate Custody Disputes,* 48 Ohio St. L.J. 927 (1987).

*Report* , 57 L. &. CONTEMP. PROBS. 210 (1994); Adair Dyer, *The International-ization of Family Law,* 30 U. C. DAVIS. L. REV. 625 (1997).

# PART D    CHILD SUPPORT

## § 8.16    The Problem

The enforcement of child support orders and the issues encountered in this course have come increasingly into conflict. The mobility of American society, the high frequency of divorce, and the large numbers of children born out of wedlock have made the workings of the interstate child support system a very serious national issue. Indeed, the twin problems of obtaining child support orders and then of getting them enforced probably present the most common of all conflicts problems. Exacerbating the situation is the fact that many unsatisfied support orders involve relatively small sums of money; although the amounts may be too small to attract the attention of lawyers sophisticated enough to know how to manipulate the system, the orders are often of critical importance to the custodial parent who may need the money desperately.

The divorce revolution which *Williams I* and its progeny helped so much to foster undoubtedly relieved much human suffering. But it has come at a great price—the impoverishment of vast numbers of women and children. To give you just one datum, in 1998 child support arrearages amounted to close to $50 *billion*. Naturally, the burden of this debt falls overwhelmingly on the poor and less well-off. This disaster generally is not a "conflicts" problem, of course, although the collection of support when the parties live in different states is far worse than a "pure" intra-state problem. Thus, many support problems fall well within the Conflicts ambit. At least some solutions, therefore, must be found there.

Child support presents the legal community with an enormous and unique challenge. Vast numbers of cases must be processed quickly and, at the same time, without doing violence to constitutional principles developed elsewhere. This Part of Chapter 8 re-examines conflicts questions in light of special child support issues and explores the unusual statutory attempts to solve the problem; this Part also examines the recent and very strong federal concern and legislation in this area.

## § 8.17    Jurisdiction

### KULKO v. CALIFORNIA SUPERIOR COURT

*United States Supreme Court*
*436 U.S. 84, 98 S. Ct. 1690, 56 L. Ed. 2d 132 (1978)*

MR. JUSTICE MARSHALL delivered the opinion of the Court.

The issue before us is whether, in this action for child support, the California state courts may exercise in personam jurisdiction over a nonresident, nondomiciliary parent of minor children domiciled within the State. For reasons set forth below, we hold that the exercise of such jurisdiction would violate the Due Process Clause of the Fourteenth Amendment.

Appellant Ezra Kulko married appellee Sharon Kulko Horn in 1959, during appellant's three-day stopover in California en route from a military base in

Texas to a tour of duty in Korea. At the time of this marriage, both parties were domiciled in and residents of New York State. Immediately following the marriage, Sharon Kulko returned to New York, as did appellant after his tour of duty. Their first child, Darwin, was born to the Kulkos in New York in 1961, and a year later their second child, Ilsa, was born, also in New York. The Kulkos and their two children resided together as a family in New York City continuously until March 1972, when the Kulkos separated.

Following the separation, Sharon Kulko moved to San Francisco, California. A written separation agreement was drawn up in New York; in September 1972, Sharon Kulko flew to New York City in order to sign this agreement. The agreement provided, inter alia, that the children would remain with their father during the school year but would spend their Christmas, Easter, and summer vacations with their mother. While Sharon Kulko waived any claim for her own support or maintenance, Ezra Kulko agreed to pay his wife $3,000 per year in child support for the periods when the children were in her care, custody, and control. Immediately after execution of the separation agreement, Sharon Kulko flew to Haiti and procured a divorce there; the divorce decree incorporated the terms of the agreement. She then returned to California, where she remarried and took the name Horn.

The children resided with appellant during the school year and with their mother on vacations, as provided by the separation agreement, until December 1973. At this time, just before Ilsa was to leave New York to spend Christmas vacation with her mother, she told her father that she wanted to remain in California after her vacation. Appellant bought his daughter a one-way plane ticket, and Ilsa left, taking her clothing with her. Ilsa then commenced living in California with her mother during the school year and spending vacations with her father. In January 1976, appellant's other child, Darwin, called his mother from New York and advised her that he wanted to live with her in California. Unbeknownst to appellant, appellee Horn sent a plane ticket to her son, which he used to fly to California where he took up residence with his mother and sister.

Less than one month after Darwin's arrival in California, appellee Horn commenced this action against appellant in the California Superior Court. She sought to establish the Haitian divorce decree as a California judgment; to modify the judgment so as to award her full custody of the children; and to increase appellant's child-support obligations. Appellant appeared specially and moved to quash service of the summons on the ground that he was not a resident of California and lacked sufficient "minimum contacts" with the State under *International Shoe Co. v. Washington,* 326 U.S. 310, 316 (1945), to warrant the State's assertion of personal jurisdiction over him.

[The California Supreme Court affirmed the denial of the motion to quash.]

II

The Due Process Clause of the Fourteenth Amendment operates as a limitation on the jurisdiction of state courts to enter judgments affecting rights or interests of nonresident defendants. It has long been the rule that a valid judgment imposing a personal obligation or duty in favor of the plaintiff may be entered only by a court having jurisdiction over the person of the defendant. The existence of personal jurisdiction, in turn, depends upon the presence of reasonable notice to the defendant that an action has been brought, and a sufficient connection between the defendant and the forum State to make it fair to require defense of the action in the forum. In this case, appellant contends that his connection with the State of California is too attenuated, under the standards, implicit in, the Due Process Clause of the Constitution, to justify imposing upon him the burden and inconvenience of defense in California.

Like any standard that requires a determination of "reasonableness," the "minimum contacts" test of *International Shoe* is not susceptible of mechanical application; rather, the facts of each case must be weighed to determine whether the requisite "affiliating circumstances" are present. We recognize that this determination is one in which few answers will be written "in black and white. The greys are dominant and even among them the shades are innumerable." *Estin v. Estin,* 334 U.S. 541, 545 (1948). But we believe that the California Supreme Court's application of the minimum-contacts test in this case represents an unwarranted extension of International Shoe and would, if sustained, sanction a result that is neither fair, just, nor reasonable.

## A

In reaching its result, the California Supreme Court did not rely on appellant's glancing presence in the State some 13 years before the events that led to this controversy, nor could it have. Appellant has been in California on only two occasions, once in 1959 for a three-day military stopover on his way to Korea, and again in 1960 for a 24-hour stopover on his return from Korean service. To hold such temporary visits to a State a basis for the assertion of in personam jurisdiction over unrelated actions arising in the future would make a mockery of the limitations on state jurisdiction imposed by the Fourteenth Amendment. Nor did the California court rely on the fact that appellant was actually married in California on one of his two brief visits. We agree that where two New York domiciliaries, for reasons of convenience, marry in the State of California and thereafter spend their entire married life in New York, the fact of their California marriage by itself cannot support a California court's exercise of jurisdiction over a spouse who remains a New York resident in an action relating to child support.

Finally, in holding that personal jurisdiction existed, the court below carefully disclaimed reliance on the fact that appellant had agreed at the time of separation to allow his children to live with their mother three months a year and that he had sent them to California each year pursuant to this agreement. [T]o to find personal jurisdiction in a State on this basis, merely because the mother was residing there, would discourage parents from entering into reasonable visitation agreements. Moreover, it could arbitrarily subject one parent to suit in any State of the Union where the other parent chose to spend time while having custody of their offspring pursuant to a separation agreement. As we have emphasized:

The unilateral activity of those who claim some relationship with a nonresident defendant cannot satisfy the requirement of contact with

the forum State. [I]t is essential in each case that there be some act
by which the defendant purposefully avails [him]self of the privilege
of conducting activities within the forum State.

*Hanson v. Denckla,*  357 U.S., at 253.

The "purposeful act" that the California Supreme Court believed did
warrant the exercise of personal jurisdiction over appellant in California was
his "actively and fully consent[ing] to Ilsa living in California for the school
year and sen[ding] her to California for that purpose." We cannot accept the
proposition that appellant's acquiescence in Ilsa's desire to live with her
mother conferred jurisdiction over appellant in the California courts in this
action. A father who agrees, in the interests of family harmony and his
children's preferences, to allow them to spend more time in California than
was required under a separation agreement can hardly be said to have
"purposefully availed himself" of the "benefits and protections" of California's
laws.[27] *See Shaffer v. Heitner,*  433 U.S., at 216.

Nor can we agree with the assertion of the court below that the exercise
of in personam jurisdiction here was warranted by the financial benefit
appellant derived from his daughter's presence in California for nine months
of the year. This argument rests on the premise that, while appellant's liability
for support payments remained unchanged, his yearly expenses for supporting
the child in New York decreased. But this circumstance, even if true, does
not support California's assertion of jurisdiction here. Any diminution in
appellant's household costs resulted, not from the child's presence in California, but rather from her absence from appellant's home. Moreover, an action
by appellee Horn to increase support payments could now be brought, and
could have been brought when Ilsa first moved to California, in the State of
New York; a New York court would clearly have personal jurisdiction over
appellant and, if a judgment were entered by a New York court increasing
appellant's child-support obligations, it could properly be enforced against him
in both New York and California. Any ultimate financial advantage to
appellant thus results not from the child's presence in California, but, from
appellee's failure earlier to seek an increase in payments under the separation
agreement. The argument below to the contrary in our view, confuses the
question of appellant's liability with that of the proper forum in which to
determine that liability.

B

The circumstances in this case clearly render "unreasonable" California's
assertion of personal jurisdiction. There is no claim that appellant has visited
physical injury on either property or persons within the State of California.
The cause of action herein asserted arises, not from the defendant's commercial transactions in interstate commerce, but rather from his personal,
domestic relations. It thus cannot be said that appellant has sought a

---

[27] The court below stated that the presence in California of appellant's daughter gave appellant
the benefit of California's "police and fire protection, its school system, its hospital services, its
recreational facilities, its libraries and museums." But, in the circumstances presented here, these
services provided by the State were essentially benefits to the child, not the father, and in any
event were not benefits that appellant purposefully sought for himself.

commercial benefit from solicitation of business from a resident of California that could reasonably render him liable to suit in state court; appellant's activities cannot fairly be analogized to an insurer's sending an insurance contract and premium notices into the State to an insured resident of the State. Furthermore, the controversy between the parties arises from a separation that occurred in the State of New York; appellee Horn seeks modification of a contract that was negotiated in New York and that she flew to New York to sign. As in *Hanson v. Denckla,* the instant action involves an agreement that was entered into with virtually no connection with the forum State.

Finally, basic considerations of fairness point decisively in favor of appellant's State of domicile as the proper forum for adjudication of this case, whatever the merits of appellee's underlying claim. It is appellant who has remained in the State of the marital domicile, whereas it is appellee who has moved across the continent. Appellant has at all times resided in New York State, and, until the separation and appellee's move to California, his entire family resided there as well. As noted above, appellant did no more than acquiesce in the stated preference of one of his children to live with her mother in California. This single act is surely not one that a reasonable parent would expect to result in the substantial financial burden and personal strain of litigating a child-support suit in a forum 3,000 miles away, and we therefore see no basis on which it can be said that appellant could reasonably have anticipated being "haled before a [California] court," *Shaffer v. Heitner,* 433 U.S., at 216. To make jurisdiction in a case such as this turn on whether appellant bought his daughter her ticket or instead unsuccessfully sought to prevent her departure would impose an unreasonable burden on family relations, and one wholly unjustified by the "quality and nature" of appellant's activities in or relating to the State of California. *International Shoe Co. v. Washington,* 326 U.S., at 319.

## III

[A]ppellee argues that California has substantial interests in protecting the welfare of its minor residents and in promoting to the fullest extent possible a healthy and supportive family environment in which the children of the State are to be raised. These interests are unquestionably important. But while the presence of the children and one parent in California arguably might favor application of California law in a lawsuit in New York, the fact that California may be the "'center of gravity'" for choice-of-law purposes does not mean that California has personal jurisdiction over the defendant. And California has not attempted to assert any particularized interest in trying such cases in its courts by, *e.g.,* enacting a special jurisdictional statute.

California's legitimate interest in ensuring the support of children resident in California without unduly disrupting the children's lives, moreover, is already being served by the State's participation in the Revised Uniform Reciprocal Enforcement of Support Act of 1968. This statute provides a mechanism for communication between court systems in different States, in order to facilitate the procurement and enforcement of child-support decrees where the dependent children reside in a State that cannot obtain personal jurisdiction over the defendant. California's version of the Act essentially permits a California resident claiming support from a nonresident to file a petition in California and have its merits adjudicated in the State of the alleged obligor's residence, without either party's having to leave his or her own State. New York State is a signatory to a similar Act. Thus, not only may plaintiff-appellee here vindicate her claimed right to additional child support from her former husband in a New York court, but also the Uniform Acts will facilitate both her prosecution of a claim for additional support and collection of any support payments found to be owed by appellant.[28]

It cannot be disputed that California has substantial interests in protecting resident children and in facilitating child-support actions on behalf of those children. But these interests simply do not make California a "fair forum," *Shaffer v. Heitner,* in which to require appellant, who derives no personal or commercial benefit from his child's presence in California and who lacks any other relevant contact with the State, either to defend a child-support suit or to suffer liability by default.

## IV

[T]he mere act of sending a child to California to live with her mother is not a commercial act and connotes no intent to obtain or expectancy of receiving a corresponding benefit in the State that would make fair the assertion of that State's judicial jurisdiction.

*Reversed.*

MR. JUSTICE BRENNAN, with whom MR. JUSTICE WHITE and MR. JUSTICE POWELL join, dissenting.

The Court properly treats this case as presenting a single narrow question. That question is whether the California Supreme Court correctly "weighed" "the facts" of this particular case in applying the settled "constitutional standard" that before state courts may exercise in personam jurisdiction over a nonresident, nondomiciliary parent of minor children domiciled in the State, it must appear that the nonresident has "certain minimum contacts [with the forum State] such that the maintenance of the suit does not offend 'traditional notions of fair play and substantial justice." *Int'l Shoe Co. v. Washington,* 326 U.S. 310, 316 (I 945). The Court recognizes that "his determination is one in which few answers will be written 'in black and white.'" I cannot say that the Court's determination against state-court in personam jurisdiction is implausible, but, though the issue is close, my independent weighing of the facts leads me to conclude, in agreement with the analysis and determination of the California Supreme Court, that appellant's connection with the State of California was not too attenuated, under the standards of reasonableness and fairness implicit in the Due Process Clause, to require him to conduct his defense in the California courts. I therefore dissent.

---

[28] Thus, it cannot here be concluded, as it was in *McGee v. International Life Insurance Co.,* with respect to actions on insurance contracts, that resident plaintiffs would be at a "severe disadvantage" if in personam jurisdiction over out-of-state defendants were sometimes unavailable.

## NOTES AND QUESTIONS ON *KULKO*

(1)  For commentary on *Kulko,* see WILLIAM M. RICHMAN AND WILLIAM L. REYNOLDS, UNDERSTANDING CONFLICT OF LAWS 377-78 (3d ed. 2002).

(2)  Are you bothered by the Court's emphasis on unfairness to the father? What of unfairness to Mrs. Kulko? After all, she is now the custodial parent, but has to travel across the country to get an increase in support. Is that the way a rational legal system should operate?

(3)  The Court cites *International Shoe, McGee,* and *Hanson* in Part II of its opinion, but which case furnishes the "purposefully availing" rule which is actually applied in Part II A? Note also that in footnote 7 the Court rejects the arguments of the California courts that the defendant "purposefully availed" himself of the benefits of California. Why? What else would defendant have to have done to meet the test?

(4)  In Part II B, the Court indicates that a defendant who has not "purposefully availed" nevertheless may be amenable to jurisdiction if he caused "effects" within the forum. The opinion limits the effects test, however, to cases where defendant engages in wrongful activity outside the state which causes injury inside the state or where defendant engages in commercial activity which affects state residents. *See* ROBERT CASAD AND WILLIAM M. RICHMAN, JURISDICTION IN CIVIL ACTIONS (3d ed. 1998). In this vein, the *Kulko* Court comments: "The cause of action herein asserted arises, not from the defendant's commercial transactions, but rather from his personal, domestic relations." The commercial/personal distinction is puzzling. Would the case have come out as it did if the defendant had actively initiated his daughter's move to California rather than merely acquiescing in her expressed desire? If so, is initiation a more significant jurisdictional concept than the personal/commercial distinction? *See* WILLIAM M. RICHMAN AND WILLIAM L. REYNOLDS, UNDERSTANDING CONFLICT OF LAWS § 36 (3d ed. 2002) (advocating a "who went to whom" test as a component of the jurisdictional calculation).

(5)  The Court generally treats the child support question as akin to other jurisdictional questions; child support does not differ, in other words, from car accidents. Does that make sense? Does the emphasis in the plurality opinion in *Asahi Metal Industry Co., Ltd v. Supreme Court of California,* see § 3.10, *supra,* on California's interest (or lack thereof, in the indemnity claim between the Taiwanese tire manufacturer and the Japanese supplier suggest a different result if *Kulko* were to be decided today?

(6)  Reasons of policy may also have motivated the result in *Kulko.* If the Court had ruled the defendant amenable in California, it would have punished him for socially desirable conduct—allowing his children to choose to live with their mother. Such a result might lead counsel to advise a parent against permitting the child to live with the other parent because doing so could result in child support litigation in a distant and inconvenient forum. *See* John McDermott, *Personal Jurisdiction: The Hidden Agendas in the Supreme Court Decisions,* 10 VT. L. REV. 1, 23 (1985).

(7)  What about California's interest in the welfare of its children? The Court discounts that interest by pointing out that California has not expressed its concern by enacting a long arm statute which addresses child support cases

specifically. This argument is unsatisfactory of course, for it implies that a state can change the constitutional reach of its judicial jurisdiction simply by passing a statute. *See also* Russell Weintraub, *Due Process Limitations on the Personal Jurisdiction of State Courts: Time for a Change,* 63 OR. L. REV. 475, 495-6 (1984).

(8) The Court suggests that a proceeding under URESA (the Uniform Reciprocal Enforcement of Support Act), at least in theory, provides a practical alternative method for Mrs. Kulko. That statute is discussed in § 8.20, *infra;* after reading that section, consider again the correctness of the *Kulko* Court's observation.

(9) *Kulko* involved an assertion of jurisdiction under California's long-arm statute which extends jurisdiction as far as the Constitution permits. Are there other bases for asserting jurisdiction over non-paying parents? Some suggestions (and a handy review of jurisdiction issues) follow:

(a) *Domestic Long-Arm Statutes.* A number of states have adopted specialized long-arm statutes for domestic relations matters. These statutes permit a court to award support or alimony based on certain contacts the obligor has had with the forum. Examples of those contacts include living as a family in the forum and becoming a parent there. Domestic relations long-arm statutes are particularly useful in a state whose general long-arm statute does not reach as far as the Constitution permits. Statutory authorization, of course, is only part of the inquiry; the assertion of jurisdiction must still satisfy the demands of due process. Perhaps a specific statute in addition to filling in gaps in a general long-arm statute, might also be useful in demonstrating the strength of the state's interest.

Would the result in *Kulko* have been different if California had had an enumerated-act long-arm statute with a provision for tortious activity outside of California which causes injury in California? Could the mother have pleaded the case, then, as one where the father had negligently failed to perform his duty to support his children in California? Doesn't the failure of a parent to support a child in another state cause harm there just as much as failure to make a product properly causes harm? Aren't they both "torts"? If they aren't, what does that say about our definition of what is a "civil wrong"—the domain of the field of torts? *See generally* Anne Bradford Stevens, *Is Failure to Support a Minor Child in the State Sufficient Contact with that to Justify in Personam Jurisdiction,* 17 SO. ILL. U. L. REV. 491 (1993).

(b) *Enumerated Act Long-Arm Statutes.* Creativity can be important here. Remember that jurisdiction generally can be asserted for committing a tort or conducting business in the forum. Non-support of a dependent in the state where the family has been domiciled, for example, has been held to be a tort. *E.g., In re Miller,* 86 Wash. 2d 712, 548 P.2d 542 (1976). Does it help that non-support can be criminal? Does entering into a separation agreement in the forum constitute "doing business" for purposes of a long-arm statute? *See Van Wagenberg v. Van Wagenberg,* 241 Md. 154, 215 A.2d 812, *cert. denied,* 385 U.S. 833 (1966).

(c) *Continuing Jurisdiction.* A court which has properly obtained jurisdiction over the defendant may maintain that jurisdiction as long as the litigation lasts. Justice Holmes wrote that once a party has been properly served or has submitted to the court's jurisdiction, "we dispense with the necessity of maintaining the physical power, and attribute the same force to the judgment or decree whether the party remain within the jurisdiction or not." *Michigan Trust Co. v. Ferry,* 228 U.S. 346, 353 (1913).

The concept of continuing jurisdiction has special importance in child support cases. Because child support decrees are generally freely modifiable, at least prospectively, a court which makes an award has the power to change it later on. Should a court exercise continuing jurisdiction if both parties have left the forum? Do you agree?

(d) *Consent and Appearance.* A defendant may always consent to a court's exercise of personal jurisdiction. Consent often is made by contract or in the form of an express waiver; even a standard form contract can contain a consent to jurisdiction clause. Recall *National Equipment Rental, Ltd. v. Szukhent,* 375 U.S. 311 (1964), § 3.12[C][2] *supra.* Jurisdiction also may be based on a defendant's general appearance to defend the action; it does not take much participation to rise to the level of a general appearance.

An important variation on consent jurisdiction involves counterclaims. The forum has jurisdiction to hear a counterclaim against a *plaintiff* who files there. *Adam v. Saenger,* 303 U.S. 59 (1938). The theory is that the plaintiff, by seeking the help of the forum, has agreed to permit the court to pass on all issues related to her claim. This is an important rule for it means that an obligee who seeks to enforce a support order in a jurisdiction which otherwise would lack jurisdiction over her has submitted herself to its jurisdiction. Thus, if the forum modifies the support order, the obligee is bound even if she has had no other contacts with the forum. Fortunately, most states' version of URESA only permits litigation of support questions, and not issues such as custody, in actions brought under URESA.

(e) *In rem Jurisdiction.* What if the defaulting parent has assets located in a state other than the one where he lives? Can the custodial parent attach the assets to satisfy the judgment? This, of course, raises the question of whether *Shaffer v. Heitner,* 433 U.S. 186 (1977), requires minimum contacts for post-judgment attachment jurisdiction. As the Court said in a famous footnote in *Shaffer.* "Once it has been determined that the defendant is a debtor of the plaintiff, there would seem to be no unfairness in allowing an action to realize on that debt in a State where the defendant has property. 433 U.S. at 210 n.36.

**HUGGINS v. DEINHARD**, 134 Ariz. 98, 654 P.2d 32 (1982), posed this issue in the child support context. *Huggins* involved a divorce granted by a California court with personal jurisdiction over the father, who was ordered to pay $200 per month child support. He moved to London and fell behind on his payments. Ten years later, he opened a bank account in Arizona by sending $21,000 from his home in London; the bank account was "appellant's only contact with the State of Arizona." When the mother learned of the Arizona account, she asked an Arizona court to garnish the bank account in order to satisfy the arrearages. The trial court held for the mother.

*Held,* in an opinion by BROOKS, J.:

It is clear from the language of the California Civil Code that the amount of child support which is past due is not subject to modification. Accordingly, we find that as to accrued child support, the judgment of divorce which ordered support is final and entitled to full faith and credit.

[The court then quoted footnote 36 in *Shaffer*.] We find that *Shaffer* did not prevent the trial court from asserting *quasi in rem* jurisdiction over the bank account. The California court having had *in personam* jurisdiction over both parties, its judgment ordering payment of child support is entitled to full faith and credit, and there is no unfairness in allowing appellee to realize on that debt in Arizona where appellant has property, whether or not the Arizona court would have jurisdiction to determine the existence of the debt as an original matter.

Post-judgment attachment of the obligor's assets can be very important in child support cases. Of course, jurisdiction over the asset holder is necessary, but a creative lawyer can work wonders. An illustrative case is *Goodyear Tire & Rubber Co. v. Ruby,* 312 Md. 413, 540 A.2d 482 (1988). The Rubys had made Maryland their marital domicile, but Mr. Ruby moved to Texas where he worked for Goodyear. Mrs. Ruby obtained a divorce in Maryland, after her husband had been personally served there. The court ordered Mr. Ruby to pay $400 each month in child support. When he had not paid after two months, Mrs. Ruby obtained a wage lien, from the Maryland court, on the wages Goodyear owed Mr. Ruby. Goodyear contested, claiming that Maryland could not exercise jurisdiction over Goodyear in an action "entirely unrelated" to Goodyear's contacts with the state. The court made short shrift of that argument. As long as Goodyear's contacts with Maryland reflect "continuing and systematic general business conduct," jurisdiction was properly exercised.

This result is correct, isn't it? *See also Champion Intl Corp. v. Ayars,* 587 F. Supp. 1274 (D. Conn. 1984). Did the Maryland court need personal jurisdiction over the father/obligor in order to attach his wages?

## § 8.18  Recognition

[Re-read *Yarborough v. Yarborough,* 290 U.S. 202 (1933), § 7.09[D], *supra.*]

(1) *Equity Decrees.* For a long time, recognition of child support orders presented substantial problems even for a court sympathetic to child support claims. The first problem is that old red herring, the equity decree. Child support orders traditionally come from "equity" courts, whose decrees, you will recall, have never been held entitled to full faith and credit. *See* § 8.14, *supra.* No good reason exists for this rule. In any event, the Supreme Court has held that an equitable decree must be accorded full faith and credit if a fixed sum is owed under it *Lynde v. Lynde,* 181 U.S. 183 (1901). Thus, at least non-modifiable support arrearages are entitled to full faith and credit.

(2) *Lack of Finality.* Child support orders are almost always modifiable, both retroactively and prospectively (in contrast to the order in *Yarborough*). Simply enforcing the judgment, therefore, might give it *more* faith and credit than it would receive in the rendering state. Courts have worked out a sensible solution to this dilemma. Although decrees which can still be modified in the

rendering state are not entitled to full faith and credit, *Sistare v. Sistare,* 218 U.S. 1 (1910) (dictum), another state may adopt the decree as its own. *Griffin v. Griffin,* 327 U.S. 220 (1946). *See also Light v. Light,* 12 Ill. 2d 502, 147 N.E.2d 34 (1957) (Schaefer, J.) (enforcing as to future installments); *Worthley v. Worthley,* 44 Cal. 2d 465, 283 P.2d 19 (1955) (Traynor, J.) (enforcing decree modifiable both prospectively and retroactively). Does the modifiability problem disappear if the arrearages are first reduced to judgment in F-I?

Congress has recently addressed the problem of finality of support orders. Its solution, the Bradley Amendment, is discussed, *infra,* § 8.20 Note (7).

### § 8.19  Choice of Law

There are a number of common choice-of-law questions concerning child support. These include determining whether the defendant has a duty to support a child, the proper interpretation of the order, determining the age of emancipation, defenses to enforcement, the limitations period on arrearages, and retroactive modification of orders. Because both the state where the obligor lives and the state where the obligee lives have a substantial interest in those questions, either state could probably choose to apply its own law.

The common law referred these types of questions to the law of the state where the dependent lives. Today, however, almost all choice-of-law questions in the child support area are controlled by statute.

### § 8.20  Statutory Solutions

Large-scale national involvement in child support issues began with the rise in divorce which followed World War II, and the government's concern that the children of those divorces receive adequate private financial support. Under that impetus, the Uniform Reciprocal Enforcement of Support Act (URESA),[1] 9 U. L.A. 553, was approved in 1950. (Significant amendments were made to URESA in 1952, 1958, and 1962.) URESA was designed to provide a simple solution to interstate enforcement of child support orders. URESA proved difficult to administer, however, and was replaced in the 1990's with the Uniform Interstate Family Support Act ("UIFSA"). Today, all states, thanks in large part to effective federal prodding, have adopted UIFSA. The next case shows how UIFSA works.

### WELSHER v. RAGER

*Court of Appeals of North Carolina*
*127 N.C.App. 521, 491 S.E.2d 661 (1997)*

TIMMONS-GOODSON, JUDGE.

This action arises out of plaintiff Rosemarie Welsher's attempt to enforce a New York child support order. Plaintiff and defendant Paul Rager were divorced in 1980. In 1985, plaintiff petitioned for a court order recognizing

---

[1] A revised version of URESA is known as "RURESA."

an agreement for support executed by plaintiff and defendant on 17 January 1985 . . . The order obligated defendant to make payments of $45.00 per week . . .

Plaintiff still resides in New York. However, defendant has moved to Winston-Salem, North Carolina; and has refused to make any of the $45.00 payments since 6 July 1995. At that time, Jeremy and Michael were twenty-one and eighteen, respectively, and Michael had just graduated from high school.

Plaintiff initiated the present action by filing a petition requesting registration and enforcement of the 1985 New York child support order in Forsyth County, North Carolina. At the time that this petition was filed, Jeremy and Michael were aged twenty-two and nineteen, respectively. The petition claimed arrearage of $1,789.64 as of 11 April 1996 . . .

Defendant responded by filing an "Answer for Civil Suit," which alleged, in pertinent part, that the couple's original 1980 divorce decree only obligated him to support the children until they were eighteen and out of high school; that he did not knowingly agree to pay support until the children reached twenty-one; and that he felt that making support payments to an "adult" over the age of eighteen was unjustifiable. Accordingly, defendant asked that the court relieve him of any obligation under the 1985 order for support. The answer was made in an unverified written statement and included no documentation pertaining to the divorce decree. We note that at no time did defendant seek to modify his obligation based on Jeremy's emancipation.

*    *    *

Plaintiff . . . argues that the trial court erred in failing to apply New York law in deciding whether to enforce the 1985 New York support order. Plaintiff contends that the Uniform Interstate Family Support Act (UIFSA), recently enacted by the North Carolina General Assembly, requires that a support order be interpreted according to the law of the state in which it is issued. We agree.

The Uniform Reciprocal Enforcement of Support Act (URESA) was repealed by the North Carolina General Assembly effective 1 January 1996. In its place, the legislature adopted UIFSA in Chapter 52C of our General Statutes. Both URESA and UIFSA were promulgated and intended to be used as procedural mechanisms for the establishment, modification, and enforcement of child and spousal support obligations. Under URESA, a state had jurisdiction to establish, vacate, or modify an obligor's support obligation even when that obligation had been created in another jurisdiction. The result was often multiple, inconsistent obligations existing for the same obligor and injustice in that obligors could avoid their responsibility by moving to another jurisdiction and having their support obligations modified or even vacated.

UIFSA was designed to correct this problem. *See* Patricia Wick Hatamyar, *Critical Applications and Proposals for Improvement of the Uniform Interstate Family Support Act and The Full Faith and Credit for Child Support Orders Act* , 71 ST. JOHN'S L.REV. 1 (1997); David H. Levy & Cecilia A. Hynes, *Highlights of the Uniform Interstate Family Support Act* , 83 ILL. B.J. 647 (1997).

UIFSA establishes a one order system whereby all states adopting UIFSA are required to recognize and enforce the same obligation consistently. A priority scheme is established for the recognition and enforcement of multiple existing support obligations. In instances where only one tribunal has issued a support order, that order becomes the one order to be recognized and enforced by states adopting UIFSA. For example, the official comment to section 52C-6-603 of the North Carolina General Statutes notes, [a]lthough RURESA specifically subjects a registered order to "proceedings for reopening, vacating, or staying as a support order of this State," these remedies are not authorized under UIFSA. While a foreign support order is to be enforced and satisfied in the same manner as if it had been issued by a tribunal of the registering state, the order to be enforced remains an order of the issuing state. Conceptually, the responding state is enforcing the order of another state, not its own order.

The one order system is applicable even where the state initiating the order has not adopted UIFSA.

Once the validity of the one order is determined, enforcement by the registering tribunal is obligatory, with two exceptions. The registering tribunal may vacate or modify the order if (1) both parties consent to the modification, or (2) the child, the obligor and the individual obligee have all permanently left the issuing state and the registering state can claim personal jurisdiction over all of them.

A non-registering party may also avoid enforcement of an order by successfully contesting its registration. Upon filing, a support order becomes registered in North Carolina and, unless successfully contested, must be recognized and enforced. The procedure for contesting a registered order is set out in Part Two of Article 6 of UIFSA, entitled "Contest of Validity of Enforcement. [A] party seeking to vacate an order's registration has the burden of proving at least one of seven narrowly-defined defenses. The possible defenses are as follows: (1) the issuing tribunal lacked jurisdiction; (2) the order was fraudulently obtained; (3) the order has been vacated, suspended or modified; (4) the issuing tribunal has been stayed pending appeal; (5) the remedy sought is not available in this state; (6) payment has been made in full or in part; and (7) enforcement is precluded by the statute of limitations. If the defending party either fails to contest the registration or does not establish a defense, the registering tribunal is required by law to confirm the order.

In terms of choice of law, URESA generally required that the law applied in interpreting and/or enforcing the support order be that of the state in which enforcement was sought. *See Pieper v. Pieper*, 90 N.C.App. 405, 368 S.E.2d 422 (holding that URESA could not be used to enforce a foreign support order requiring support until age 22 since such an order could not have been issued under North Carolina law), *aff'd*, 323 N.C. 617, 374 S.E.2d 275 (1988). However, UIFSA provides, "The law of the issuing state governs the nature, extent, amount, and duration of current payments and other obligations of support and the payment of arrears under the order." The official comment to section 52C-6-604 notes that this means "an order for the support of a child until age 21 must be recognized and enforced in that manner in a state in which the duty of support of a child ends at age 18."

* * *

Plaintiff's support order became registered in North Carolina upon filing. Applying the appropriate law, UIFSA, the record is devoid of a defense which would justify vacating a properly registered support order. Under UIFSA, unless the court finds that the defendant has met his burden of proving one of the specified defenses, enforcement is compulsory. The trial court's single finding of fact in the present case was that the children had reached eighteen. Under URESA, such a finding may have been sufficient to deny enforcement since North Carolina lawwould have governed interpretation of the order, and provided for emancipation at eighteen. *See Pieper*, 90 N.C.App. 405, 368 S.E.2d 422. However, as URESA has been repealed, New York law, which provides that the age of emancipation is twenty-one, must be applied in enforcing the 11 February 1985 foreign order.

Moreover, the record is devoid of any evidence that either (1) both parties consented to a modification, or (2) the issuing state had lost continuing, exclusive jurisdiction over the order. Hence, no court of this jurisdiction may properly vacate or modify this order. If defendant wishes to have the order modified or vacated, he must pursue the matter in New York, which maintains continuing, exclusive jurisdiction over the order. *Id.*

* * *

In her final assignment of error, plaintiff contends that the trial court erred in failing to use New York law in interpreting the order, as required by the Federal Full Faith and Credit for Child Support Orders Act (FFCCSOA), 28 U.S.C. § 1738B. Again, we agree.

FFCCSOA, which became effective [in] 1994, is extremely similar to UIFSA both in terms of structure and intent. The federal statute also obligates states to enforce, according to its terms, a child support order issued by another state which is made consistent with the Act's jurisdiction and due process standards. *See Kelly v. Otte*, 123 N.C.App. 585, 589-90, 474 S.E.2d 131, 134, *disc. review denied*, 345 N.C. 180, 479 S.E.2d 204 (1996). Modification of a valid order is only allowed if: (1) all parties have consented to the jurisdiction of the forum state to modify the order; or (2) neither the child nor any of the parties remains in the issuing state and the forum state has personal jurisdiction over the parties. *Id.* This Court has previously held that, while the law of the forum state may apply to the enforcement and remedy applied to a registered foreign support order under URESA, FFCCSOA requires that the law of the rendering state govern the order's interpretation. *Id.*

In light of this Court's decision in *Kelly*, the trial court's findings and conclusions are not consistent with the requirements of FFCCSOA. Absent a finding concerning both parties' consent to the jurisdiction of this state to modify this order, or New York's lack of continuing, exclusive jurisdiction over the order, the trial court was required to give the order full faith and credit, enforcing the order and interpreting it according to the law of New York. Failure to do so was error.

We note that the trial court, applying New York law could properly find that defendant was not liable for any arrearage as to Jeremy, because Jeremy had reached the age of 21 prior to the 6 July 1995 date on which defendant ceased to make court-ordered support payment. However, the trial court is still without authority to modify the $45.00 a week payment, as such modification is not allowed under UIFSA and FFCCSOA. The New York order does not provide a per child break-down regarding defendant's support obligation, but merely provides that $45.00 per week is to be paid for both children. Absent further knowledge as to whether an adjustment would be permitted under New York law for Jeremy's emancipation, and in what proportion, enforcement of the order in any amount less than $45.00 per week would be an impermissible modification of the New York order. Defendant's only recourse, in this case, then, is to seek modification of his child support obligation in New York, based upon Jeremy's emancipation. *See State, Dept. of Rev. v. Skladanuk* , 683 So.2d 624 (Fla.Dist.Ct.App. 1996)(holding that FFCCSOA prevented Florida court from modifying the terms of a New York order as written regardless of the defendant's inability to pay and that the defendant was required to seek modification of his child support obligation in New York).

In sum, because the trial court failed to apply New York law in accordance with UIFSA and FFCCSOA, its order is vacated, and this matter is remanded to the trial court for hearing and the entry of an order not inconsistent with this opinion.

*Reversed and remanded.*

## NOTES AND QUESTIONS ON *WELSHER*

The opinion in *Welsher v. Rager* nicely describes the differences between URESA and UIFSA. The former permitted the existence of multiple support orders because it required a separate enforcement action in each state where the obligor lived. The drafters of UIFSA, on the other hand, sought ease of enforcement by adopting the "one controlling order" concept, a close version of the "home state" jurisdiction which is the basis of the Uniform Child Custody Jurisdiction Act. *See generally* John J. Sampson, *Uniform Interstate Family Support Act (1996) (with More Unofficial Annotations)*, 32 FAM. L. Q. 385 (1998); Janet E. Atkinson & Susan F. Paikin, *Interstate Child Support*, in Eric Pierson, ED. 200 WILEY FAMILY LAW UPDATE (2000); Margaret Campbell Haynes, *Interstate Enforcement of Support*, in MARION F. DOBBS, ENFORCING CHILD AND SPOUSAL SUPPORT (1995). The chart at the very end of this Chapter captures very nicely the workings of UIFSA and the one controlling order concept. (The chart was prepared by the Center for the Support of Children and is reproduced with its permission.)

(1) *The controlling order.* This doctrine requires that there be one—and only one—controlling order. That order can be entered only be a court that has personal jurisdiction over the child and at least one of its parents. (Jurisdiction can also be attained by consent). Only a court in the state which entered the controlling order may modify it. If all concerned (parents and children) leave the state, modification may occur only if another state enters a new controlling order. That state, of course, must have personal jurisdiction over the obligor to enter a new order. Why?

(2)  *Choice of Law.* Under the old URESA regime, forum law was applied to most significant issues. It was thought that judges would be more willing to apply a law with which they were familiar. The drafters of UIFSA decided, however, to have the law of the controlling order apply to all questions concerning the order. Why do you think that the drafters of UIFSA made that choice? (There is a major exception: forum law controls the actual methods of enforcement—*e.g.*, garnishment.)

(3)  *Jurisdiction.*  UIFSA specifies a number of specific jurisdictional bases. Among these are the following: (3) the individual resided with the child in this State; (4) the individual resided in this State and provided prenatal expenses or support for the child; (5) the child resides in this State as a result of the acts or directives of the individual. Do you think that these contacts satisfy the constitutional requirements for jurisdiction discussed in Chapter 3? Do you think, in particular, that (5) can be squared with *Kulko*? UIFSA also has an "any other basis" jurisdictional section, similar to the "California-style" long-arm statutes discussed in Chapter 3.

Some members of the UIFSA Advisory Group suggested that the California-style approach to jurisdiction be the only one. The drafters, however, settled on an enumerated long-arm statute, despite its obvious constitutional difficulties in likely fact patterns. Their reasoning was that judges needed more specific guidance than "do whatever the Constitution permits." Do you agree?

(4)  *Judgments.*  The "one controlling order"of UIFSA should make enforcement much easier than under URESA. There is a problem, however; what happens if the F-2 court does not know that F-1 has previously issued an outstanding controlling order? (This problem is more common than you would think; the parties, for various reasons, often do not tell the lawyers and judges about previous orders.) When that occurs, the F-2 order will be entered without ostensible subject matter jurisdiction. In other words, the second order is arguably void. In that situation, which order controls? (*Hint: See* F.R.C.P. 60(b).)

(5)  *Federal Law. Welscher* also discusses in some detail the Full Faith and Credit for Child Support Orders Act, 28 U.S.C. § 1738B (1994) (widely, but not euphonically, known as FFCCSOA). That statute is to UIFSA what the Parental Kidnaping Prevention Act is to the Uniform Child Custody Jurisdiction Act (*see* § 8.13, *supra*). In other words, FFCCSOA codifies the Full Faith and Credit Clause with respect to UIFSA orders. Because the federal statute closely parallels the Uniform Act (as is also true concerning the two custody statutes), a valid child support order entered under UIFSA is entitled to Full Faith and Credit. Question: Was passage of FFCCSOA necessary? For more on federal statutes affecting child support orders, *see* PETER N. SWISHER, ET AL., FAMILY LAW: CASES, MATERIALS, AND PROBLEMS 1074-1077 (2d ed. 1998).

(6)  *Foreign Support Orders.* One might expect enforcement of support orders entered by the court of another country to be governed by federal law. One would be wrong. In, fact, the federal government has been remarkably unready to enforce foreign support orders. As a result, a number of states, with the tacit blessings of the State Department, at least, have entered into "arrangements" with foreign countries concerning the actual enforcement of child support orders. Is it constitutional for a state to have "foreign relations"

with other countries? *See generally* Gloria DeHart, *Comity, Conventions, and the Constitutions: State and Federal Initiatives in International Support Enforcement* , 28 FAM. L.Q. 89 (1994). *See also* Russell Weintraub, *Recognition and Enforcement of Judgments and Child Support Obligations in United States and Canadian Courts,* 34 TEX. INT'L L.J. 361 (1999).

(7) *Federal Intervention.* Traditionally, the family has been considered a matter of local concern, best left to the states. In recent years, however, Congress has adopted a good deal of legislation dealing specifically with child support.

Congress enacted Title IV-D of the Social Security Act to deal generally with the problems posed by the failure of parents to support their children adequately. *See* 42 U.S.C. §§ 651-662. The federal government has seen two national interests here—helping children live better lives and saving tax dollars which might otherwise have to be paid to destitute parents. To that end, federal intervention in the child support world has increasingly taken the form of a carrot-and-stick approach. The carrot is federal payments to support children in need of assistance, and the stick is the threat that those funds will be denied to a state unless it complies with federal requirements designed to insure better collection of child support orders.[16]

Under Title IV-D, states must establish procedures for determining paternity and for enforcing support obligations. Title IV-D was strengthened significantly by the adoption of the Child Support Enforcement Amendments of 1984, 42 U.S.C. §§ 651 *et seq.* Those amendments established a number of programs to help ensure child support is paid. Among these are mandatory wage withholding provisions in original support orders, tax refund intercept procedures, expedited processes for collection, and various monitoring systems. The 1984 amendments also required each state to adopt specified procedures for dealing with interstate wage withholding cases. *See* 42 U.S.C. 666(b)(9) and 45 C.F.R. § 303.100(g).

In 1987, Congress, exasperated with the continuing difficulties in enforcing child support orders, adopted the so called Bradley Amendment to Title IV-D, P.L. 100-485, 42 U.S.C. § 666(a)(9). This law requires states to adopt legislation providing that child support orders become final judgments as soon as any arrearages arise. Although the Bradley Amendment may solve the finality problem, its effect on the bureaucratic quagmire is problematic. Since then, as *Welscher* describes, Congress has required the states to adopt a number of provisions which make it easier for the custodial parent to collect child support. These measures include the "intercept" of tax returns and the location of obligors through the Parent Locator Service. A number of states have also imposed penalties on "dead-beat" parents that include the loss of licenses ranging from operating a boat or a car to practicing a profession (including the practice of law (!)).

Is the solution to make interstate (or maybe all) child support enforcement a problem for the federal government? Enforcement could then be placed in agencies reporting to the federal judiciary. Many problems discussed in this

---

[16] *See* note 6 *supra; see Vanneck v. Vanneck,* 49 N.Y.2d 602, 427 N.Y.S.2d 735, 404 N.E.2d 1278 (1980).

part of the Chapter would either disappear or at least ameliorate with the national service of process that could be made available to federal courts; modification problems could be addressed in conference calls or other less formal mechanisms; and standard definitions of questions such as the age of emancipation would eliminate a lot of conflict. If this sounds attractive, you might ask whether the states would have any remaining role in what was once thought to be a quintessential local concern. Does that bother you?

✳

## Determining the Controlling Order and CEJ Under UIFSA

STEP 1: Are there any valid support orders? ——— No ——→ Either obligor or obligee may petition to establish a support and/or paternity order using UIFSA's long arm provisions (§201) or two state procedures (§401). That order is controlling and sets the non-modifiable terms. **STOP**

Yes ↓

STEP 2: List all valid support orders:

| Date of Order | State Where Entered | Amount of Order | Who Still Lives There? (obligor/ individual obligee/ child/ none) |
|---|---|---|---|
| ——— | ——— | ——— | ——— |
| ——— | ——— | ——— | ——— |
| ——— | ——— | ——— | ——— |

ANY TRIBUNAL WITH A VALID SUPPORT ORDER AND WHERE EITHER THE OBLIGOR, INDIVIDUAL OBLIGEE OR CHILD CONTINUES TO RESIDE IS A STATE WITH CONTINUING, EXCLUSIVE JURISDICTION OVER THE ORDER.

STEP 3: How many valid support orders exist? ——— 1 ——→ That order must be recognized as controlling and sets the non-modifiable terms. (§207(A)) State: _____ **STOP**

2 or more ↓

STEP 4: Do any of the Tribunals have CEJ? ——— No ——→ A State with jurisdiction over the non-requesting party may issue a new child support order. That order must be recognized as controlling and sets the non-modifiable terms. (§207 (B)(3)) State: _____ **STOP**

Yes ↓

STEP 5: List all Tribunals with CEJ:
_____
_____
_____

STEP 6: How many Tribunals have CEJ? ——— 1 ——→ That order must be recognized as controlling and sets the non-modifiable terms. (§207 (B)(1)) State: _____ **STOP**

2 or more ↓

STEP 7: Are any of the orders in the child's home state (the state in which the child lived at least 6 months immediately before the UIFSA petition was filed or since birth for a child under 6 months)? ——— Yes ——→ That order must be recognized as controlling and sets the non-modifiable terms. (§207 (B)(2)) State: _____ **STOP**

No ↓

STEP 8: Which is the most recent order? ——→ That order must be recognized as controlling and sets the non-modifiable terms. (§207 (B)(2)) State: _____ **STOP**

*Reprinted with permission, Center for the Support of Children (1997)

# PROBLEM SUPPLEMENT

# PROBLEM SUPPLEMENT

## TABLE OF CONTENTS

(Page references are to pages in Problem Supplement.)

## CHAPTER 1. INTRODUCTION

## CHAPTER 2. DOMICILE

§ 2.01     The Concept

§ 2.02     Domicile of Origin

§ 2.03     Domicile of Choice

## CHAPTER 3. JURISDICTION

## PART C. JURISDICTION AFTER 1977

§ 3.10     The More Recent Cases

## PART D. BASES FOR JURISDICTION

### PART C. ESCAPE DEVICES

### PART D. THE CHOICE-OF-LAW REVOLUTION

**[The following two problems in this Part are not referred to in the main text, but may be used for additional practice.]**

## PART E. INTEREST ANALYSIS

§ 4.18.    Doing Interest Analysis

§ 4.19.    False Conflict

§ 4.20.    True Conflicts: Currie's Solution—Forum Law

## PART F. ALTERNATIVE MODERN METHODS FOR RESOLVING NONFALSE CONFLICTS

§ 4.23.    Comparative Impairment

§ 4.24    The Better Law and Professor Leflar

## PART G. THE SECOND RESTATEMENT

**[The following problems in this Part are not referred to in the main text, but may be used for additional practice.]**

## PART H. SOME ILLUSTRATIONS OF MODERN CHOICE-OF-LAW METHODS

§ 4.33    Property

§ 4.34    Contracts

[B]    Party Autonomy

[D]    Commercial Law

## CHAPTER 5. THE CONSTITUTION AND CHOICE OF LAW

## PART E. THE DISCRIMINATORY FORUM
**[The following problems in this Part are not referred to in the
main text, but may be used for additional practice.]**

## CHAPTER 6. FEDERAL/STATE CONFLICT OF LAWS

## PART B. SUPREMACY AND PREEMPTION
**[The following two problems in this Part are not referred to in the
main text, but may be used for additional practice.]**

## CHAPTER 7. JUDGMENTS

## PART A. BASIC PRINCIPLES

## PART B. THE REACH AND LIMITS AND FULL FAITH AND CREDIT

## CHAPTER 8. DOMESTIC RELATIONS

## PART A. MARRIAGE

## PART B. DIVORCE AND MARITAL SUPPORT

## PART C. CUSTODY

§ 8.13    Jurisdiction

# PROBLEM SUPPLEMENT

## TABLE OF CASES

# Chapter 1

# INTRODUCTION

**PROBLEM 1-1. THE CAR RENTAL**

*Using the background you have acquired in and the common sense you brought to law school, try to answer the questions in Problem 1-1. As you go through the choice-of-law materials in the course keep returning to the Car Rental Problem to see whether your choice of forum was in your client's interest.*

Alice Adams, who lived in State *X*, rented a car there from the local office of Mavis, a national car rental agency doing business in all states, incorporated in State *U*, and having its main office in State *V*. Alice drove to her daughter Barb's home in State Y so that Barb could join her for a trip to California to attend a wedding there. While en route and driving in State Z, Alice negligently drove the car into a bridge abutment. Barb was seriously injured in the accident.

Disregarding the choice-of-law issues:

> (i) By the law of *X* and *Y*, Alice would be liable to Barb in a negligence action, and Mavis, as owner of the car, would be vicariously liable for Alice's tort.

> (ii) By the law of Z, Alice would not be liable to Barb because under Z's guest statute, the host's liability to a guest arises only in cases of wilful negligence. Further, Z had no provision for an owner's vicarious liability for torts committed by a person driving a car with consent of the owner.

The choice-of-law rules in the three states provide:

> (i) *X* and *Y* look to the law of the place of impact in determining tort liability.

> (ii) *Z* applies the law of the place having the most significant relationship with the issue presented.

As counsel for Barb, where would you file suit against Alice? Mavis? Why?

---

**PROBLEM 1-2. UNIFORMITY WHATEVER THE FORUM**

The articulated basis for the traditional choice-of-law approach is that "[f]airness to the parties requires that the fortuitous choice of a geographic place of suit should, as far as is possible, not vary the way in which the suit will be decided." Goodrich, Handbook of the Conflict of Laws 5 (4th ed. Scoles

1964). Justice Jackson echoed the same sentiment in *Lauritzen v. Larsen*, 345 U.S. 571,591 (1953), a maritime case, saying that the "purpose of conflict-of-laws doctrine is to assure that a case will be treated in the same way under the appropriate law regardless of the fortuitous circumstances which often determine the forum."

On the other side, it has been suggested "in all solemnity" that if uniformity is truly the goal of the ideal choice-of-law system, an ideal rule would be to have all states adopt the choice-of-law rule of the "state first in alphabetical order." Currie, "The Verdict of the Quiescent Years," *Selected Essays on the Conflict of Laws* 609 (1963). Thus, Alabama's choice-of-law rule would be applied in all states, at least until a fifty-first state with a name such as Aaronia is admitted to the Union, in which event its choice-of-law rules would be applied. For variety, the same author suggested that an inverse alphabetical order might be adopted as the rule for transactions occurring in odd-numbered years. *See also*, Katzenbach, *Conflicts on an Unruly Horse*, 65 Yale L.J. 1087, 1098–99 (1956), for a critique of uniformity as the primary goal of choice of law.

Uniformity as a primary choice-of-law goal is currently out of fashion. In essence, forum shopping seems to be invited by the enactment of broad long-arm statutes by the states and the concurrence of the United States Supreme Court in the expansion of state court jurisdiction in such cases as *International Shoe Co. v. Washington*, 326 U.S. 310 (1945). Is such forum shopping undesirable? Why? If uniformity of result without regard to forum is not achieved, is it likely that plaintiff's forum selection will become the key factor in conflict-of-laws cases?

Uniformity of result for cases arising in the United States and tried in the United States might be achieved by (1) an interstate choice-of-law compact; (2) making the laws—substantive and procedural—of all states uniform; (3) the United States Supreme Court imposing uniformity by invoking the due process, equal protection, and full faith and credit provisions of the Constitution, or (4) Congress exercising its powers under the Full Faith and Credit Clause. Should efforts be made in one or more of these directions? As you consider the desirability of uniformity as a primary goal, ask yourself whether it makes sense to support or reject uniformity without knowing what uniform result will be reached. Injustice applied uniformly is not an attractive goal.

# Chapter 2

# DOMICILE

## § 2.01 The Concept

### PROBLEM 2-1. ENEMY NATIONALS

Vera Vincze and her son, Vern, filed filed a claim with the United States Attorney General seeking the return of property vested in the Attorney General by federal statute. The statute, World War II legislation designed to freeze property of enemy aliens, restricted the right to reclaim such property to "persons other than nationals of Hungary, as defined in Executive Order 8389, who are successors in interest to the owner of the property held." The Executive Order defined the word "national" to include "any person who has been domiciled in, or a subject, citizen, or resident of Hungary at any time since July 1, 1940."

Claimants are the widow and only child of Erno Vincze, a Jew who was killed in the Dachau concentration camp on January 14, 1945 after five years of imprisonment. In view of the increasing Nazi orientation of the Hungarian government, Erno, prior to his arrest in 1940, had transferred funds to a New York bank and had obtained United States visas for himself and his family. It was these funds Vera and Vern were claiming. The family had lived in Hungary all of their lives until Vera and Vern came to the United States shortly after the end of World War II. (Both became United States citizens before they filed their claim.)

Erno Vincze's only "crime" was being a Jew. During the years Erno was in prison, his wife and son spent virtually all of their time seeking his release. They stayed in Hungary only for that purpose. Both were imprisoned off and on over the five years. All of Erno's Hungarian property was confiscated by the Hungarian government. Vera and Vern were forced out of their home and placed in quarters designated as "Jewish Housing," where they lived in a single room with a dozen strangers. Ultimately, they remained out of prison only by hiding in fields and cellars. From the time of Erno's arrest until Vera and Vern finally left Hungary after his death, they were barred from voting or earning a living, and had no access to police protection or the courts.

What arguments would you make on behalf of Vera and Vern to persuade the Attorney General to release the funds to them? Are you likely to succeed? Why? *See Roboz v. Kennedy*, 219 F. Supp. 892 (D.D.C. 1963).

––––––

## PROBLEM 2-2. ONE VOTE SHORT

The statutory requirements for having the State Board of Education remove a portion of a school district from an existing district and assign it to another include a vote approving the removal by "more than two-thirds of the legal voters in each of the districts involved." The statute defined a "legal voter" as "any citizen 18 years old or older who is registered to vote and who has resided in the school district for 30 days or more at the time of the balloting." The records of the Ginger Creek District, one of the two districts involved, listed 900 "legal voters." The election resulted in 600 votes favoring removal, one vote short of the statutory requirement if the records were accurate.

Your clients, leaders of the drive for removal, have asked that you "do what you can to have the removal approved." Your investigation shows that Marnie Mullins and her parents were listed as "legal voters" although they had moved out of the district six weeks before the election because their house had been razed by fire and was not habitable. The house was in the process of being rebuilt, and the parents planned to move back in as soon as it was completed. Marnie, however, planned to get married before the rebuilding process was completed and to move into new living quarters outside of the district. In fact, she and her husband-to-be had already signed a lease on new quarters.

Would the facts revealed by your investigation give you confidence in advising your clients that the 600 votes met the statutory requirements? Why? *See Stein v. County Board of School Trustees*, 85 Ill. App. 2d 251, 229 N.E.2d 165 (1967), *aff'd*, 40 Ill. 2d 477, 240 N.E.2d 668 (1968).

––––––

## PROBLEM 2-3. ON THE MOVE AGAIN

A venue statute in State $X$ provided that suit against a "resident" of $X$ must be brought in the county of defendant's "residence," but that suit against a "nonresident" could be filed in any county where service was obtained. John Jaines had lived in Jones County in $X$ for thirty years. He sold his house there and, while traveling to his new home in Smythe County in $X$, was served with process in Hart County in $X$, mid-way between his old and new homes.

Will an objection to venue be sustained? *See Cohen v. Daniels*, 25 Iowa 88 (1868).

---

## § 2.02     Domicile of Origin

### PROBLEM 2-4. GAINING A NEW DOMICILE

Alex Andes, a potential defendant in a malpractice suit you wish to file on behalf of Clara Cole, a State $Y$ domiciliary, had lived in and practiced medicine in State Y for four years before being drafted into the Army. Upon being drafted, Alex sold his house in $Y$ and moved, along with his wife and children, to State $X$ where he was stationed. Alex rented a house in $X$, and his children attended school there.

After a year, Alex was sent to the Far East. His family remained in the rented house in $X$.

Alex had two cars, one registered in $X$ and the other in $Y$. He and his wife continued to vote (absentee) in $Y$ elections, and Alex retained his membership in the $Y$ Medical Association. The evidence showed that Alex did not plan to remain in $X$ after he was discharged from the Army, but planned to do advanced work in Dermatology at a medical school in State $Z$ and to seek a faculty appointment at a medical school "somewhere" when he completed his advanced training.

You would prefer to file Clara's claim in a Federal District Court rather than in a state court, and you must decide whether to file in the federal court in $X$ or $Y$. Would it make any difference which of the two federal courts you chose? Why? *See Ferrara v. Ibach*, 285 F. Supp. 1017 (D.S.C. 1968).

---

## § 2.03     Domicile of Choice

### PROBLEM 2-5. ESTABLISHING DIVERSITY FOR PURPOSES OF SUIT

Dan Daniels was having serious difficulties with his wife, Donna, and was convinced that her affections were being alienated by Ed Edsel, her secretary. All three parties lived in State $X$. Donna was a political power there, and Dan was convinced — rightly or wrongly — that she could influence the result of a state court proceeding in $X$.

For the sole purpose of bringing an alienation of affections suit in the Federal District Court for $X$, Dan moved to State $Y$, determined to stay there for as long as it took to establish a "domicile" sufficient to support a diversity action in *X*. Two months later, he filed suit in the federal court in *X*. Would the court take jurisdiction? Why? *See Williamson v. Ostenton*, 232 U.S. 619 (1914).

———

## PROBLEM 2-6. A FAMILY THAT STAYS TOGETHER

An action was filed in State Court of Delaware by Charles Chad against several members of his family and a Delaware corporation having its principal place of business in Puerto Rico. Defendants had the action removed to the United States District Court for Delaware and the hearing is on the removal petition, which alleged that two of the defendants were "residents" of New Jersey, and the third was a "resident" of Puerto Rico. On behalf of Charles, you challenged the removal on the ground that he was a "resident" of Puerto Rico and not New York.

The parties stipulated to the following facts:

(1). Charles lived in New Jersey with his family until he was 18 when he enrolled at Columbia University in New York. After two years at Columbia, he went into the army and for two years was stationed at a variety of bases around the world. After his discharge, he completed his education at a school in Ohio, went into the family business in New Jersey, was married there, and lived in a house he bought there.

(2) Within a few years, Charles and his wife and children moved to Puerto Rico where he took over the day-to-day management of the company's Puerto Rican plant and moved into a company owned home. About half of his time was spent working in Puerto Rico and half was spent working in New York. He paid income taxes and voted in the Commonwealth of Puerto Rico.

(3) Three years later, a strain developed in the marriage and Charles' wife took the children and returned to New Jersey to live.

(4) For several months thereafter, Charles continued to live in the house in Puerto Rico and to split his work between Puerto Rico and New York as he had in the past. The only change was that rather than staying at his parents' home in New Jersey when he worked in New York, as he had previously, he lived in different New York hotels and the New York Athletic Club.

(5) Charles was then made president of the company and one of his brothers went to Puerto Rico to assume Charles' old position. Charles turned over the company house in Puerto Rico to his brother and bought a condominium there for himself. He continued to split his time evenly between New York and Puerto Rico, and, tiring of hotel living, bought a condominium in New York.

(6) A few years later, Charles filed for divorce in New York and in that suit alleged that he was a New York domiciliary. He later dropped the suit and obtained a Mexican divorce.

(7) A family dispute arose, partially as the result of the divorce, and Charles left the company and filed the present suit.

Is it likely that the challenge to the removal petition will succeed? Why? Discuss in full. *See Unanue v. Caribbean Canneries, Inc.*, 323 F. Supp. 63 (D. Del. 1971).

In considering Problem 2-6, keep in mind the provisions of 28 U.S.C. § 1332:

(a) The district courts shall have original jurisdiction of all civil action where the matter in controversy exceeds the sum of $10,000. . . .and is between—

(1) citizens of different States;

(2) citizens of a State and citizens or subjects of a foreign state;

(3) citizens of different States and in which citizens or subjects of a foreign state are additional parties . . . .

. . . .

(c) For purposes of this section . . ., a corporation shall be deemed a citizen of any State by which it has been incorporated and of the State where it has its principal place of business . . . .

(d) The word "States", as used in this section include the Territories, the District of Columbia, and the Commonwealth of Puerto Rico.

---

## PROBLEM 2-7. BONDED ALIENS

A "bonded alien" is defined in the immigration law as:

An alien having a residence in a foreign country which he or she has no intention of abandoning who is coming temporarily to the United States (i) to perform services of an exceptional nature; or (ii) to perform temporary services or labor, if unemployed persons capable of performing such service or labor cannot be found in this country; or (iii) as a trainee.

Alan, Barb, and Carol were "bonded aliens," who lived in State *X*. Alan had lived in *X* for ten years before applying for an *ex parte* dissolution of his marriage; Barb had lived in *X* for four years before she filed for dissolution of her marriage to another bonded alien who also lived there; Carol had lived in *X* for 18 months before filing a petition to adopt a young orphan who was being cared in by a State *X* institution.

In all three cases, the judge believes that she lacks jurisdiction to grant the requested relief unless the parties are domiciliaries of *X*. What argument would you make to persuade her that the petitioners are domiciliaries of State *X* for the purposes of the suits they have filed? Are your arguments likely to prevail? *See Williams v. Williams*, 328 F. Supp. 1380 (D.V.I. 1971).

————————

## PROBLEM 2-8. VOTING RIGHTS

Frank Full, a 19-year-old sophomore at the State University of *X*, requested that he be classified as a resident for tuition purposes despite the fact that he was being supported by his parents and spent the summer months at their home in State *Y*. After a full hearing, Frank's request was denied by a student-faculty administrative panel. He did not appeal the decision.

A few months later, Frank attempted to register to vote in *X*. The County Registrar rejected his application on the ground that the University's determination that he was a nonresident for purposes of tuition precluded him from voting in *X* unless he could show a change of circumstances. Would you advise him to contest the Registrar's decision? Why? *See Jolicoeur v. Mihaly*, 5 Cal. 3d 565, 488 P.2d 1 (1971).

————————

## PROBLEM 2-9. THE PRISONER

Alice Able had lived all of her life in State *X*. Her only forays outside of the State were for the purpose of practicing her profession, assassination. She was apprehended in State *Y* after she had successfully assassinated two people. Alice was convicted and sentenced to life in the *Y* penitentiary. After having served ten years of the sentence (and with seven remaining before she became eligible to be considered for parole), Alice asked you, a lawyer in a prisoner legal assistance clinic, to obtain a dissolution for her from Bob, her husband, who lived in State *Z*. In response to your question about her plans if and when she was released, Alice said she planned to settle in *Y* because she had come to like its climate.

Your research discloses that the dissolution law of *Y* requires that a person filing for dissolution "have been a bona fide resident of *Y* for at least one full year prior to filing." You know, of course, that as a general rule only a domiciliary of a state may obtain an ex parte dissolution there. You also discover that *X* has a similar one-year provision and, in addition, requires at least six weeks of "continuous residence" in the county in which the dissolution action is filed.

Would you be able to honor Alice's request? Why? *See McKenna v. McKenna*, 282 Pa. Super. 45, 422 A.2d 668 (1980).

# Chapter 3

# JURISDICTION

## PART C.   JURISDICTION AFTER 1977

### § 3.10    The More Recent Cases

#### PROBLEM 3C-1. THE HITCH AND TRAILER

Agnes Ault, an itinerant horse trader, bought a two-horse trailer and hitch from Bourne, Inc., a local retailer in State $X$. At the time of the sale, Agnes told the Bourne manager of her plan to drive all over the country hauling horses in the trailer. The trailer and hitch were manufactured in State $Y$ by Clarice, Inc., and distributed by it in a two-state area — $X$ and $Y$. Shortly after the sale while Agnes was driving in State $Z$, the hitch snapped, causing the trailer to overturn. The two horses in the trailer were injured so badly that they had to be destroyed.

Agnes has asked you, a lawyer in $Z$, to represent her in a suit against Bourne and Clarice. $X$, $Y$, and $Z$ all have long-arm statutes extending jurisdiction of the courts as far as permitted by the Constitution. Your experience is such that it seems clear that a $Z$ jury will award substantially higher damages than juries in $X$ or $Y$. The product liability and warranty rules in the three states are identical. Where would you advise Agnes to file suit? Why? *See Edmundson v. Miley Trailer Co.*, 211 N.W.2d 269 (Iowa 1973). *But see Smalley v. Dewberry*, 379 N.W.2d 922 (Iowa 1986), overruling *Edmundson*. Would your advice be influenced by the fact that the vehicle Agnes was driving was registered in $Z$ or that when she bought the trailer and hitch she told Bourne's manager that she planned to drive to $Z$? Why? *See Kellan v. Holster*, 518 F. Supp. 175 (M.D. Fla. 1981).

---

#### PROBLEM 3C-2. THE TRADE SHOW

Mary Marks, a domiciliary of State $X$, filed a products liability diversity action in the Federal District Court for $X$ against Bong Industries, Inc., a State $Y$ corporation, for injuries suffered in $X$ when a ladder manufactured by Bong collapsed as Mary was climbing it. Bong, asserting a lack of in personam jurisdiction, moved for a dismissal under Rule 12(b) of the Federal Rules of Civil Procedure. (It conceded that it had received proper notice.) A statute in $X$ conferred jurisdiction on the $X$ courts to the full extent permitted by the Constitution.

The parties stipulated the following facts: In February 1980, Mary attended a trade show in State $X$ at which Bong and a number of other manufacturing concerns had sales booths. She was given literature describing a special offer on Bong ladders, which provided that customers who purchased ladders at the show would get "free freight." Mary bought and paid for the ladder while at the show, and indicated on the purchase order that Bong should ship the ladder to her State $X$ address. The purchase order was approved at Bong's home office in State $Y$, and Bong shipped the ladder to Ms. Able in $X$ by common carrier "FOB $Y$."

It is undisputed that Bong has no employees, agents, or offices in $X$, does not advertise there, and has made no other shipments to the state.

Should Bong's motion be granted? Why? *See Moore v. Little Giant Industries, Inc.*, 513 F. Supp. 1043 (D. Del. 1981), *aff'd without opinion*, 681 F.2d 807 (3d Cir. 1982).

---

## PROBLEM 3C-3. THE AUDIT

Allan & Bruce (A & B), a Bahamian partnership of certified public accountants, did business only in the Bahamas. In the regular course of its business, A & B did an audit of Clarice, Ltd., a local company doing business only in the Bahamas.

While Dave Duns, an American businessman, was vacationing in the Bahamas, he became acquainted with Clarice's operation and decided to make an effort to acquire a controlling interest in it. At Dave's request, A & B turned over to Dave a copy of the audit with knowledge that Dave planned to use it to raise funds in the United States to carry out his acquisition plan.

Dave sought funds from Ethel Edge in State $X$. On the strength of the A & B audit and Dave's persuasiveness, Ethel committed $2,500,000 to the acquisition. When the investment turned sour, Ethel filed suit in $X$ against A & B, alleging that its audit was false and fraudulent. $X$'s long-arm statute extended the court's jurisdiction as far as permitted by the Constitution. In challenging the $X$ court's jurisdiction by means of a special appearance, what arguments would you make on behalf of A & B? Are the arguments likely to be persuasive? Would it make any difference if Dave, when he received a copy of the audit, told the A & B partners of his plan to raise money in $X$ rather than his general statement of an intention to raise funds in the United States? Why? *See Coopers & Lybrand v. Cocklereece*, 157 Ga. App. 240, 276 S.E.2d 845 (1981).

---

## PROBLEM 3C-4. SHE CAN'T GO HOME AGAIN

In the course of preparing to visit a friend in State $X$, Paula Pack, a domiciliary of State $Y$, drove her motor home to the $Y$ Propane Gas outlet in her home town and had the propane gas tank on her motor home filled. She told the dealer of her plan to visit $X$. Shortly after she arrived in $X$, the propane tank exploded while Paula was sleeping in the motor home. She was so severely injured that she could not be moved back to $Y$ and she remained hospitalized in $X$.

About 14 months after the explosion — two months after the $Y$ limitation period had run — Paula's friend came to your office in $X$ to ask you to represent Paula in a suit against $Y$ Propane. Your investigation reveals that $Y$ Propane does business only in $Y$. If $X$'s long-arm statute extends the court's jurisdiction to the full extent permitted by the Constitution, $X$ had no borrowing statute, and $X$'s limitation period was two years, would you advise Paula to file suit in $X$. Why? Would you take the case on a contingency? *See Northern Propane Gas Co. v. Kipps*, 127 Ariz. 522, 622 P.2d 469 (1981).

---

## PROBLEM 3C-5. THE MICHELINS

Rhoda Roual, a domiciliary of State $X$, purchased four Michelin tires from Shorte, Inc., a small retailer located in $X$. Shorte balanced the tires and mounted them on Rhoda's car. A few months later while Rhoda was driving in State $Y$, one of the tires failed causing the car to overturn. Rhoda was seriously injured in the accident.

Although Le Manufacture Francaise Pneumatiques (Michelin of France) had manufacturing plants in the United States, the tires on Rhoda's car had been made in France and exported to the United States.

As counsel for Rhoda, what facts would you seek to discover and what legal research would you do before advising her whether to file suit against Michelin of France, and, if so, where to file the suit? *See Le Manufacture Francaise v. District Court*, 620 P.2d 1040 (Colo. 1980).

———

## PROBLEM 3C-6. A NIGHT TO FORGET

Tim Tempe, a State $X$ domiciliary, was visiting a cousin in State $Y$ when he was introduced to Vera Vaint, a $Y$ domiciliary. Tim and Vera did a substantial amount of drinking the night they met and before the evening ended, they engaged in sexual intercourse. Tim returned to $X$ on the following day and never returned to $Y$. About a year later, State $Y$ welfare officials filed a paternity action in $Y$ against Tim, claiming that he was the father of Vera's child. (In fact, the blood tests were consistent with Tim's paternity.)

On advice of counsel, Tim filed a special appearance in the $Y$ proceeding challenging the court's jurisdiction. As counsel for the $Y$ welfare officials, what arguments would you make in resisting Tim's efforts to have the case dismissed on jurisdictional grounds? Are your arguments likely to prevail? (Assume that $Y$'s long-arm statute conferred jurisdiction on the courts to the full extent permitted by the Constitution.) *See Larsen v. Scholl*, 296 N.W.2d 785 (Iowa 1980). *But see Department of Health & Rehab. Services v. Wright*, 522 So. 2d 838 (Fla. 1988).

———

## PROBLEM 3C-7. SENDING A LETTER

Frieda Fallan, head of General Surgery at a hospital in Ohio, brought to the President of the hospital and the hospital's Medical Executive Committee some concerns she had about the competence of Henry Heins, a surgeon on the staff. As a result, Henry's hospital privileges were restricted.

In an effort to force a reinstatement, Henry distributed as packet of materials to local media. The packet contained a letter from Larry Long, a South Carolina resident and physician, written to the President of the Hospital. Copies of Larry's letter had been sent from South Carolina to Henry in Ohio and to two persons in Texas.

Frieda filed an action in Ohio against Henry and Larry asserting, among other things, that Larry's letter contained defamatory materials about Frieda. Assuming that the Ohio long-arm statute permits such a suit, would the Ohio court meet constitutional standards if it asserted jurisdiction over Larry? *See Fallang v. Hickey*, 40 Ohio St. 3d 106, 532 N.E.2d 117 (1988).

## PROBLEM 3C-8. WHO OWES WHAT TO WHOM?

In a diversity action in the Federal District Court for Kansas, the husband of a woman who died of toxic shock syndrome after using tampons manufactured by Playtex in Delaware recovered $1,525,000 in actual damages and $10,000,000 in punitive damages. Playtex paid the punitive damage award. Its excess insurers sought a declaratory judgment in state court in Kansas that they were not obligated to indemnify Playtex for the punitive damage award against it.

Playtex is a Delaware corporation and has its principal office in that state. The trial court ruled that it had both subject matter and personal jurisdiction and that as a matter of public policy under Kansas law the excess insurers were not required to repay Playtex for the punitive damages assessed against it. Playtex challenged the jurisdiction of the Kansas court to determine the issue presented and objected to the court's application of Kansas law to decide the issue. Assuming that the Kansas long-arm statute extends the court's jurisdiction as far as permitted by the Constitution, is the trial court likely to be reversed on appeal? *See St. Paul Surplus Lines v. Intern. Playtex*, 245 Kan. 258, 777 P.2d 1259 (1989), *cert. denied*, 110 S. Ct. 758 (1990).

## PROBLEM 3C-9. TURBINES FOR SALE

In the course of a telephone conversation between Tim Thoms, an Arkansas resident, and Jane Mills, President of Turbines, Inc., an Indiana-based corporation, Tim agreed to buy part of an aircraft engine from Turbines. Jane, who was vacationing in Florida when the phone call was made, had called the Texas office of the owner of two aircraft engines and offered to buy the engines. Tim, who was in the seller's office when the call came in, took the phone and agreed that if Turbine bought the engines Tim would buy part of one of them from Turbine. Shortly after the conversation, Turbines offer was accepted by the Texas seller. Turbine then sent one of its employees from Indiana to Texas to pick up engines and drive them back to Indiana.

Since the route from Texas to Indiana took the employee within three miles of Tim's place of business in Arkansas, Jane instructed the employee to leave the front end of the engine with Tim. When the employee attempted to do so, a disagreement arose, with Tim claiming he had agreed to buy a different portion of the engine. Turbines' employee then left Tim's place and business without leaving anything and drove back to Indiana. Tim filed a breach of contract action in an Arkansas state court. Turbines removed the action to the Federal District Court for Arkansas and moved to have the action dismissed for lack of personal jurisdiction.

Assuming the Arkansas long-arm statute extended as far as permitted by the Constitution, is it likely that Turbines' motion would be granted? *See Papachristou v. Turbines, Inc.*, 884 F.2d 1116 (8th Cir. 1989).

---

## PROBLEM 3C-10. ALCOHOL ABUSE TRAINING

Health Communications Industries (HCI) is incorporated in the District of Columbia and has its only office there. It trains persons who serve and sell alcoholic beverages to recognize alcohol abusers. Marner Company, a hotel management firm, is incorporated and has its principal office in Texas. It manages hotels in several locations, but not in the District.

Marner contacted HCI by phone and mail asking the latter to provide training for some of Marner's employees. (Some insurance companies give lower rates to companies whose employees have gone through the HCI program.) A contract ultimately was signed at a meeting in Texas.

HCI held four two-day workshop sessions at various locations where Marner operated hotels. Each participant took an examination after the sessions were over and sent them to HCI's home office where they were graded. HCI sent a "one-year" certificate to each Marner employee who passed the examination. The certificate authorized the certified personnel to train other Marner employees in approved HCI methods for a period of one year (after which they could be recertified). Those trained by Marner certified employees took examinations that were sent to HCI's office for grading.

HCI filed suit in the District of Columbia against Marner alleging nonpayment. Assuming that the jurisdiction of the court extends to the full extent permitted by the Constitution, should HCI's claim be dismissed? Why? *See Health Communications, Inc. v. Mariner Corp.*, 860 F.2d 460 (D.C. Cir. 1988).

---

## PROBLEM 3C-11. THE LIQUIDATION

National Insurance Co., a State $X$ company, became insolvent, and, as provided by the $X$ statute, the $X$ Commissioner of Insurance, Ilsa Interl, was appointed liquidator. In winding up the company's affairs, Ilsa filed suit in $X$ against two State $Y$ insurance companies that acted as agents for National in $Y$ and two personal guarantors from $Y$ who guaranteed the defendant companies' accounts with National. She sought to recover unpaid premiums from the defendants.

As liquidator, Ilsa was charged by statute with collecting "all debts and money due and claims belonging to the insurer" and the X statute conferred jurisdiction on X courts in the situation presented. The defendants were served under the X long-arm statute. As a matter of constitutional law, may the X court assume jurisdiction over the Y debtors? Why? *See Hager v. Doubletree*, 440 N.W.2d 603 (Iowa 1989), *cert. denied*, 110 S. Ct. 325 (1989).

---

## PROBLEM 3C-12. A HIGH-SPEED BOAT

Carly Carnon, a New Jersey resident, met a sales representative of Everglade Maritime, a Florida company, at a boat show in New York. Over the next two years, Everglade's employees wrote to Carly at her New Jersey home and called her there at least twenty times in an effort to interest her in a boat. In one of the phone conversations Carly finally agreed to buy a boat. Everglade forwarded a contract to Carly at her home. She signed it there and mailed it to Everglade in Florida.

Although Carly took delivery of the boat in Florida and registered it there, she had made it clear to Everglade employees throughout the two year period that she planned to keep the boat in New Jersey. A few weeks after taking possession, Carly hired a third-party shipper to bring the boat to New Jersey. The carrier had an accident en route and the vessel was seriously damaged. Carly had the boat sent back to Everglade, which subsequently resold it.

In the course of negotiating with Everglade about the resale, Carly discovered that it may have defrauded her in the original sale. She then filed suit against Everglade in New Jersey seeking a return of the purchase price. Assuming that New Jersey's statutory requirements were met, are the New Jersey courts free to assert jurisdiction over Everglade? Why? *See Lebel v. Everglades Marina, Inc.*, 115 N.J. 317, 558 A.2d 1252 (1989).

---

## PROBLEM 3C-13. IMPORTED ASBESTOS

Julie Jones, a former employee of Uvalde, a Texas corporation, filed suit against Jugometal, a Yugoslavian trading company that annually supplied about 5,000 metric tons of asbestos to Uvalde over the fifteen years Julie worked for Uvalde.

Jugometal sold the asbestos to a New York broker who resold it to Uvalde. Jugometal dealt only with the broker, delivered the asbestos as directed by the broker, and was paid by the broker. Assuming that the Texas long-arm statute extends jurisdiction as far as constitutionally permitted, is it likely that the Federal District Court for Texas has jurisdiction over Jugometal? *See Irving v. OwensCorning Fiberglas Corp.*, 864 F.2d 383 (5th Cir. 1989). *cert. denied*, 110 S. Ct. 83 (1989).

---

# PART D.   BASES FOR JURISDICTION

## § 3.12     Traditional Bases for Jurisdiction

### [A]—Personal Service Within the State

### PROBLEM 3D-1. AN INVITATION TO ATTEND

Will White, the manager of Nutra-Fair, a Wyoming company with its main office there, met Geri Gibson, a Californian, at a chiropractor's meeting in Omaha, Nebraska. About a month later, he called Geri at her home in California and asked if she would be interested in an exclusive California distributorship for Nutra-Fair products. Will flew to California twice thereafter to meet with Geri and her husband, and ultimately Geri agreed to the terms he proposed.

Will mailed a distributorship contract to Geri at her home. As previously agreed, Geri, her husband, and two associates signed the contract in California and returned it to Will in Wyoming. The four persons who signed the agreement formed a partnership called Nutra-Fair of California to sell Nutra-Fair products in California. They used the phone or mail to order products from the manufacturer's home office in Wyoming.

The Nutra-Fair management was not pleased with the partners' performance and in early June filed an action in Wyoming seeking to terminate the distributorship. About two weeks after the suit was filed, Geri went to Wyoming to attend a convention sponsored by Nutra-Fair. While she was there, she was served with four copies of the complaint and four summonses naming Geri and her three partners as defendants.

The four defendants entered special appearances seeking to quash service and to contest the court's jurisdiction. Assuming that the requirements of the Wyoming statute were met, would the Wyoming court be acting constitutionally if it asserted jurisdiction? Why? *See Nutri-West v. Gibson*, 764 P.2d 693 (Wyo. 1988).

---

## § 3.16    The In Rem Revolution

### PROBLEM 3D-2. THE ACCIDENTAL SHOOTING

Anne and Bill Barnes owned and operated a farm that straddled the border between States *X* and *Y*. They lived in a farm house located on the *X* side of the line. Clara Chale owned and operated a farm that was contiguous with the Barnes farm and also straddled the border between *X* and *Y*. She lived in a farm house located on the *Y* side of the line. While Anne and Bill were inspecting a portion of their farm located in *Y*, Clara, who was hunting on the *Y* portion of her farm, accidentally shot and killed Anne.

After the *Y* statute of limitations had run, but before the *X* statute had run, Bill filed a wrongful death action against Clara in the state court in *X*. *X*'s long-arm statute extended jurisdiction of its courts as broadly as permitted by the Constitution. Clara was served in *Y* as provided by *X*'s statute. In addition, Bill attached the *X* portion of Clara's farm. Thus, Bill claimed that both in personam and quasi in rem jurisdiction were present. Would you advise Clara to make a special appearance in the *X* proceeding to challenge both strands of Bill's assertion of jurisdiction, or would you advise her to remain aloof from the *X* proceeding? Why? *See Rhoades v. Wright*, 622 P.2d 343 (Utah 1980), *cert. denied*, 454 U.S. 897 (1981).

---

# PART F.    LIMITATIONS ON THE EXERCISE OF JURISDICTION

## § 3.18    Forum Non Conveniens

### PROBLEM 3F-1. IN TRINIDAD

In January, 1980, a vessel owned by Alyse, Inc., a Liberian company, negligently collided with an ore pier located in Trinidad and owned by Bobble, Inc., a State *X* corporation. The pier was damaged when the ship's captain, in violation of Trinidad law, failed to take on a local pilot before attempting to dock. The pier suffered an estimated $8,000,000 in damages.

Bobble filed an admiralty action in the Federal District Court for State *X*, with service being made on Alyse's agent in State *X*. The trial court granted Alyse's motion to dismiss on forum non conveniens grounds, saying:

This Court is persuaded that the lack of a substantial nexus between this controversy and State $X$ combined with the inconvenience and possible prejudice to the defendant resulting from retention of jurisdiction here — which substantially outweigh any inconvenience plaintiff may suffer— renders this an inappropriate forum; an evaluation of the contentions of the parties compels the conclusion that the litigation of this case can be conducted most expeditiously and inexpensively in Trinidad.

Dismissal will not leave plaintiff without any remedy. Defendant has agreed to submit to the jurisdiction of the courts of Trinidad as a condition of dismissal of this suit; moreover, defendant has already commenced a suit in Trinidad which establishes its presence there for purposes of suit by plaintiff. Defendant has also offered a letter of guaranty that a Trinidad judgment will be satisfied and agreed that this may be made a condition of the dismissal of this action.

Defendant's motion to dismiss is granted, subject to reinstatement in the event that defendant shall fail to submit to jurisdiction in Trinidad with respect to the subject matter of this action and execute the guaranty of satisfaction of judgment described above.

Bobble has appealed the dismissal on the grounds that the trial court abused its discretion because: (1) Bobble resided in and had its principal office in $X$; and (2) damages available in the Trinidad action could not exceed $560,000 despite the $8,000,000 in damages actually suffered. What is the likely result of Bobble's appeal? Why? *See Alcoa S.S. Co., Inc. v. M/V Nordic Regent*, 654 F.2d 147 (2d Cir.), *cert. denied*, 449 U.S. 890 (1980).

---

## PROBLEM 3F-2. CAIRO OR CONNECTICUT

Two Egyptian Air Force pilots were killed when their F-16 crashed in Egypt. The F-16 was designed and assembled by Dynamics, Inc., a Delaware corporation with headquarters in Missouri. The plane was assembled in Texas. Technologies, Inc., also a Delaware corporation, had its principal place of business in Connecticut and designed and manufactured the F-16's engine in that state. Evans, Inc., designed and manufactured the F-16's fuel pump in Connecticut. The three companies were defendants in a product liability action filed in a state court in Connecticut by Stan Slithe, the temporary administrator of the estates of the deceased pilots.

The defendants moved to dismiss on the basis of forum non conveniens. As part of their motion, they agreed to submit to the jurisdiction of the Egyptian court, to make their personnel and production records available, to waive any applicable limitations periods, to satisfy any judgment against them, and to refrain from objecting to a reopening in Connecticut if the conditions were not met. The Egyptian court had statutory authority over the claim, and the court found that plaintiffs would have a remedy in the Egyptian court. Thus, Egypt would be an adequate alternative forum. What other findings would the court have to make before determining whether to grant defendant's motion to dismiss? Why? *See Miller v. United Technologies Corp.*, 40 Conn. Supp. 457, 515 A.2d 390 (1986).

## § 3.20    Forum Selection Clauses

### PROBLEM 3F-3. PARTNERS IN DISPUTE

Willa Wand, a physician, suffered serious injuries in an automobile accident while driving her Volkswagen Beetle in State *X*. She filed suit in *X* against the vehicle's manufacturer, Volkswagenwerk, A.G. (VWAG), and its importer, Volkswagen of America (VWoA). Willa's claim was based on the fact that the seat belt in the car was defective and that the defect was a proximate cause of her injuries. The jury awarded Willa $9,300,000 against VWAG and VWoA. While the case was on appeal, Willa and the two defendants settled the matter for $5,015,000.

VWAG and VWoA then filed suit in *X* against Klippan, GmbH, the German manufacturer of the seat belts found by the jury to be defective. The suit sought payment of all or part of the judgment on contractual grounds and under *X*'s statutory and equitable principles of indemnity and contribution. (Klippan had refused VWAG's tender of the defense prior to the trial of Willa's suit.)

The contracts between VWAG and Klippan, and VWoA and VWAG each contained the following clause:

> Venue for all disputes that may result from this contract or orders hereunder is the court of competent jurisdiction for Wolfsburg, Germany.

In the absence of a showing of the applicable German law, should the *X* court honor the quoted clause? Would the result be the same if the clause were one under which the parties agreed "to submit to the jurisdiction of the court in Wolfsburg, Germany"? *See Volkswagenwerk, A. G. v. Klippan, GmbH*, 611 P.2d 498 (Alaska), *cert. denied*, 449 U.S. 974 (1980). *But see Felix v. Bomoro Kommanditgesellschaft*, 196 Cal. App. 3d 106, 241 Cal. Rptr. 670 (1988).

### PROBLEM 3F-4. THE ARBITRATION CLAUSE

For more than 35 years, Able & Daughter, a State *X* firm, had acted as exclusive sales representative in the United States for Eteco, a large Belgium wire products manufacturer. About 20 years before the present dispute arose over Eteco's plan to open its own sales offices in the United States, the parties had entered an agency contract containing an arbitration clause that required that all disputes be settled by arbitration in Coutrai, Belgium. When Eteco opened the sales offices, Able filed an action against it in the Federal District Court for State *X*. In addition to alleging breach of contract, Able asserted a tort claim arising from misuse of confidential customer information and alleged antitrust violation based on Eteco's refusal to deal.

Eteco moved for a stay pending arbitration in Coutrai, Belgium. Able resisted the stay and argued that under the *Bremen* test, Coutrai would be an unreasonable forum because of Eteco's economic dominance in the area and the inconvenience and expense to Able if it were forced to arbitrate in a forum in which it would have to present its case in a foreign language.

Would Able's arguments succeed? Why? *See Sam Reisfeld & Son Import Co. v. S. A. Eteco*, 530 F.2d 679 (5th Cir. 1976).

---

# PROBLEM 3F-5. THE AFFILIATION AGREEMENT

Plaintiffs owned and operated the Red Bull motel in New York. They signed an affiliation agreement with defendant, Best Western, an Arizona corporation, under which Red Bull was allowed to use the Best Western name, logo, emblems, and registered marks, all of which are valuable assets for a motel. The contract with Best Western, renewed annually, contained a clause that stipulated that any dispute arising out of the contract could be brought only in Arizona.

Under the contract, Best Western was permitted to monitor the maintenance and housekeeping standards of the motel twice a year. If the motel failed to pass inspection, it was placed on a 90 day probation, and a second failing score was a ground for terminating the affiliation. Plaintiffs were placed on probation once, but were removed from that status during the second inspection. Several months later, Best Western's inspector gave Red Bull a failing score despite the fact that extensive refurbishing had occurred.

Red Bull alleged that the inspector's negative comments were directed almost exclusively to the fact that many of Red Bull's guests were black or hispanic. (In fact, under a contact with the New York Department of Social Services, 35 of the 145 room at Red Bull were used as temporary shelter for homeless families, many of whom (although not all) were black or hispanic. Shortly after the inspection, Best Western terminated the affiliation.

In a suit filed in the Federal District Court for the Southern District of New York, Red Bull alleged that the termination was due to racial bias and requested an injunction. Best Western, citing the exclusive forum selection clause in the contract, moved to have the case transferred to the District of

Arizona under 28 U.S.C. § 1404(a). Is it likely that the case will be transferred? Why? *See Red Bull Associates v. Best Western Intern., Inc.*, 862 F.2d 963 (2d Cir. 1988).

---

## PROBLEM 3F-6. THE SALES AGENT

Lois Lane, a domiciliary of State $X$, filed a diversity action in the Federal District Court for $X$ against Kettle, Inc., a corporation organized and having its principal place of business in State $Y$. Lois alleged breach of contract, unlawful price discrimination, and tortious interference with prospective economic advantage. Under the contract in question, Lois was to act as Kettle's exclusive sales agent in States $X$ and $Z$. The contract, a form provided by Kettle, established $Y$ as "the exclusive forum for any dispute arising under the contract or related to it." Kettle moved for a transfer of venue to $Y$.

(a) If by the law of $X$ selection clauses were not enforceable, would the court be free to apply federal standards or would it be bound by $X$'s law?

(b) If the law of $X$ was consistent with the federal standard, would the motion to transfer venue be granted if, in addition to the facts set forth above: (1) $X$ was located on the east coast and $Y$ on the west coast; (2) the witnesses in the case were located in $X$, $Y$, and $Z$; and (3) most of the documents involved in the case were located in $Y$? *See Kolendo v. Jerell, Inc.*, 489 F. Supp. 983 (S.D. W. Va. 1980).

# Chapter 4

# CHOICE-OF-LAW THEORY

## PART A.  A PRELIMINARY LOOK

### § 4.02    An Introductory Problem

### PROBLEM 4A-1. FORUM'S POLICY

In thinking about the question, "[W]hat does 'policy' have to do with the [Kalmich] case?", consider what policies might dictate the court's decision to hear or dismiss the following two cases. In essence, what policies undergird limitation periods?

| Case | Forum's Period of Limitations | Foreign Period of Limitations | Time Claim Asserted After Accrual |
|------|-------------------------------|-------------------------------|-----------------------------------|
| 1 | Three Years | One Year | Two Years |
| 2 | One Year | Three Years | Two Years |

---

### § 4.04    Proving Foreign Law

### PROBLEM 4A-2. THE ISRAELI LAWYER

Aril Avens, an Israeli attorney, filed a diversity action in the United States District Court for State $X$ alleging she had been defamed by a former client, Bernard Bland, who had employed her to represent him in a matter involving the inheritance of real property in Israel. Bernard, whose last known residence was in $X$, sent four letters and a cable to officials of the Israeli bar and members of the executive and judicial branches in Israel accusing Aril of collaborating with adverse parties and manipulating false documents to plaintiff's detriment. After reviewing the charges against Aril, Israeli officials found that she had acted properly and that the charges were completely groundless.

The court, applying $X$'s choice-of-law rules, held that Israeli law normally would govern since all of the relevant actions and injuries occurred there. Neither party pleaded or proved Israeli law, however. Should the court follow the state or federal rule in determining the content of Israeli law? Why? *See Wachs v. Winter*, 569 F. Supp. 1438 (E.D.N.Y. 1983). If the federal rule is deemed to control, what specific result would you expect?

————————

## PROBLEM 4A-3. THE LAW WHEN?

Amy Alyse, who lived in State *X* and farmed in States *X* and *Y*, filed a conversion action in *X* against the Blanch Bank, a State *Y* lending institution. Amy alleged that Blanch had sold her tractor at a foreclosure sale after she had paid the underlying debt.

Blanch had advanced the money to Amy in *Y* on the security of the tractor and Amy's promise to keep the tractor in *Y*. Applying its own choice-of-law rule, the *X* court decided that the law of *Y* governed the conversion issue. The law of *Y* was neither pleaded or proved, however; and *X* followed the rule that in the absence of proof, the law of *Y* would be presumed to be the same as the statutory and case law of *X*. The loan was made prior to the adoption of the Uniform Commercial Code in either state. Both had adopted the Code thereafter. Under U.C.C. § 1-01, the Code applied only "to transactions entered into and events occurring after the . . ." Code's effective date.

The trial court has concluded that the result in the case depended on whether its applied the law of *X* as it was (i) prior to the adoption of the Code; (ii) at the time of the foreclosure sale; (iii) at the time suit was filed; or (iv) at the time of trial. The judge has asked you, a law clerk, to brief the "time" issue and to provide her with an answer. Please do so. *See Zeman v. Canton State Bank*, 211 N.W.2d 346 (Iowa 1973).

————————

## PROBLEM 4A-4. "I SHOT HIM FIVE TIMES IN SELF-DEFENSE."

Ginny Grant filed a claim for widow's benefits under the Social Security Act. A regulation under the Act provided:

> A person who has been finally convicted by a court of competent jurisdiction of the felonious and intentional homicide of an insured individual shall not be entitled to monthly benefits or to the lump-sum death payment based on the earnings of such deceased individual and such felon shall be considered nonexistent in determining the entitlement of other persons to monthly benefits or the lump-sum death payment based on the deceased individual's earnings.

The administrative agency applied the regulation in denying Ginny's claim.

Ginny had been convicted in Iran of "willful homicide" and sentenced to death under the following provisions of the Iranian Code:

> Whoever willfully, but without intention to kill, inflicts a wound or deals a blow to another person, causing the death of the victim, shall be punished by hard labor from three to ten years, provided that the instrument used shall ordinarily not be suitable for causing death.
>
> If the instrument used proves to be ordinarily suitable for causing death, the offender shall be deemed to have committed murder.
>
> The penalty prescribed for an offender who commits murder shall be death, except if otherwise provided by law.

The Iranian officials commuted Ginny's death sentence to life imprisonment and she was released under a general amnesty after having spent five years in solitary confinement.

Ginny argued that she had killed her husband in self defense and that she had not had a fair trial because: (1) she had been questioned interminably without having been given the *Miranda* warnings; (2) she had been tortured during the course of her interrogation; and (3) she could not communicate with the lawyer appointed to represent her because the lawyer neither spoke nor understood English very well. She admitted that she shot her husband five times, but insisted that she had done so in self defense.

The court found that the procedures of the Iranian court were consistent with those normally followed in Iran and that the Iranian court had jurisdiction. As counsel for Ginny, what arguments would you make that she should be permitted to introduce evidence that she had not killed her husband feloniously and intentionally? Are your arguments likely to prevail? *See Cooley v. Weinberger*, 518 F.2d 1151 (10th Cir. 1975).

---

## PROBLEM 4A-5. DID TWO UNINSURED MOTORISTS MEET?

In a diversity case appealed to the Circuit Court of Appeals, the panel certified three questions to the Supreme Court of *X* in an effort to determine the applicable *X* law.

The *X* court had adopted the following rule:

> When it appears . . . to any circuit court of appeals of the United States, that there are involved in any proceeding before it questions or propositions of law of this state which are determinative of said cause independently of any other questions involved . . . and that there are no clear controlling precedents in the decisions of the Supreme Court of this State, such federal court before rendering a decision may certify such questions or proposition of law of this state to the . . . Court . . . for rendition of a judgment or opinion concerning such questions or propositions of *X* law. This Court may, in its discretion, decline to answer the questions certified to it.

The case involved a refusal by defendant insurance company to honor an uninsured motorist clause in a policy issued by the company in State $Y$ to an army Colonel stationed in State $Z$. (The company issued policies only to members of the armed forces and members of their families.) The car involved in the $X$ accident was driven by the insured's son, a college student in $X$ who was spending the summer there working for a relative. The son was driving a car he was in the process of purchasing from a dealer, but at the time of the accident title had not passed to him. The car, thus, was not one of the three cars listed in the policy.

The insurance policy excluded from uninsured motorist coverage any accident in which an uninsured "owned" vehicle was being driven by the injured party and the issue presented was whether the son "owned" the vehicle he was driving. By $Z$ law, the "uninsured owned vehicle" exclusion was valid and applicable, while by $X$ law, the exclusion was invalid and did not preclude recovery.

The three questions certified by the Court of Appeals were:

1. Would $X$ or $Z$ law apply in construing the insurance policy; or, stated differently, under the $X$ "center of gravity" test, which state would be deemed to have the most significant contacts with the insurance policy for choice of-law-purposes?

2. Would $X$ or $Z$ law govern the validity of the uninsured motorist exclusionary clause; or stated differently, if $Z$ law is held to govern the insurance contract, does $X$ public policy prevent the enforcement of the exclusionary clause?

3. Would $X$ or $Z$ law govern the issue of vehicle ownership, or stated differently, would $X$ under its "center of gravity" test consider $X$ or $Z$ to have the most significant contacts for the purposes of establishing the law governing vehicle ownership?

What responses would you expect from the $X$ court? Why? *See Boardman v. United Service Auto. Ass'n*, 470 So. 2d 1024 (Miss.), *cert. denied*, 474 U.S. 980 (1985).

---

## PART B. THE TRADITIONAL SYSTEM

## § 4.05    Introduction

### PROBLEM 4B-1. A MEXICAN TRAIN CRASH

Alyse Railway, Inc., a Colorado corporation, operated a rail line from Texas to Mexico City. On a trip that started in Texas, Brad Baird, a Texas resident and an Alyse employee, was killed in Mexico when, as part of his duties, he tried to couple two freight cars. Brad's widow and children, alleging negligence by Alyse, filed a diversity action against Alyse in Texas.

Alyse concedes that its negligence created civil liability under the Mexican equivalent of a wrongful death statute. Texas also had wrongful death legislation. The Mexican law called for periodic support payments to Brad's widow during what would have been his normal life expectancy and to his children until they reached the age of emancipation. Texas law made no provision for periodic payments and permitted the recovery of the economic loss to Brad's estate as the result of his death plus the loss of companionship.

What law should govern the action? Why? (Modified facts of *Slater, id.*)

---

## § 4.06    Torts

### PROBLEM 4B-2. VICARIOUS LIABILITY BY NEW YORK LAW

A New York statute provides that "[e]very owner of a motor vehicle . . . shall be liable . . . for death or injuries . . . resulting from negligence in the operation of such motor vehicle . . . by a person legally using . . . the same with the permission, express or implied, of such owner."

Frieda Fernald loaned her car to George Gage in New Jersey without restriction on its use. (Both Frieda and George were New Jersey residents.) Just as George drove the car across the George Washington Bridge into New York, he struck and injured a pedestrian, Hana Hosle, who was a New York resident.

Hana filed suit in New Jersey against Frieda and asserted that the New York statute applied. Under New Jersey law, the owner of the vehicle would be not be liable vicariously for George's tort.

Is the New Jersey court likely to apply the New York statute and hold Frieda liable? Would the application of the New York statute to a person such as Frieda, who had no personal contact with New York, raise serious constitutional problems? *See Young v. Masci,* 289 U.S. 253 (1933).

Would the result be the same (i) if Frieda, when she turned possession of the car over to George, had directed him not to go to New York? (ii) if Frieda and George lived in Illinois and she assumed reasonably that he would use the car in Illinois and Indiana, but George drove it to New York and had the accident?

## PROBLEM 4B-3. OWNER'S LIABILITY

Clara Chad, a New York domiciliary, rented an automobile for 30 days in New York from Davis, Inc., a national rental agency. The car was registered in New York and was delivered to Clara there. She drove to State *Y* on a vacation trip. Shortly after arriving in State *Y*, Clara, who was intoxicated, drove the car onto the sidewalk where it struck and severely injured Edna Erle, a *Y* domiciliary.

Edna filed a diversity action against Clara and Davis in United States District Court for *Y*. Under the New York statute, Davis, as owner-lessor of the car, would be liable to Edna if Clara were liable. By the law of *Y*, however, owner-lessors of automobiles are not vicariously liable for torts committed by their lessees. A *Y* statute required lessees to obtain liability insurance as a condition precedent to renting a car.

If *Y* followed traditional choice-of-law analysis, what arguments would you make on behalf of Edna to persuade the court to hold Davis liable? (Clara was judgment-proof.) Are your arguments likely to prevail? *See Kline v. Wheels by Kinney, Inc.*, 464 F.2d 184 (4th Cir. 1972).

As a legislator, would you support a bill establishing an "alternate reference" approach under which car rental agencies would be held responsible for the negligence of their lessees if such liability was called for by the law of the place of rental or the law of the place of the accident? What arguments would be made against such an approach? Assuming the approach was desirable in most cases, would you want the legislation to apply to rental agreements that prohibited lessees from taking the car outside of the rental state?

## PROBLEM 4B-4. WHEN EAST MEETS WEST

Donna Dunn, a domiciliary of State *X*, was killed in State *Y* while driving west on I-70 when her automobile was struck head-on by a car driven by Chet Chad, also a domiciliary of *X*. (Chet fell asleep at the wheel while driving east on I-70, lost control of his vehicle, and crossed the median.)

Both *X* and *Y* had wrongful death statutes under which Chet would be liable for causing Donna's death. If the law of *X* were applied, Donna's estate could recover an unlimited amount for the economic loss to her estate based on the present value of her likely earnings during her life expectancy, an amount concededly equal to $750,000. If the law of Y were applied, Donna's husband and children could recover a maximum of $50,000 for loss of companionship and financial support.

Would some economic, political, or social policy of Y be forwarded by the application of its rule? If so, what policy? If not, what would justify applying Y's law to limit the amount of recovery? *See Reich v. Purcell*, 67 Cal. 2d 551, 432 P.2d 727 (1967).

---

## PROBLEM 4B-5. ALIENATION OF AFFECTIONS

Gloria and Harry Holb, a married couple, lived in State X. While Gloria was in State Y visiting her mother, she had an affair with Ivan Indel, a Y domiciliary. Harry filed an alienation of affections action against Ivan in State Y.

Alienation of affection actions had been abolished by statute in X. Such suits were permitted in Y. Under the place of impact theory enunciated in *Alabama Great Southern*, what law would govern Harry's suit? *See Gordon v. Parker*, 83 F. Supp. 40 (D.Mass.), *aff'd*, 178 F.2d 888 (1st Cir. 1949).

---

## § 4.07     Contracts

### [A]—The Place of Contracting

### PROBLEM 4B-6. COME FLY WITH ME CLARICE

Clarice Chad and Dave Drake, domiciliaries of state X and Y respectively, met for the first time when they sat beside each other on a cross country flight. During the course of the flight, while the plane was flying over State Z, they shook hands on an agreement under which Dave agreed to perform services for Clarice in States X, Y, and Z in return for specified payments to be made to him by Clarice.

If the law of X or Y were applied, the oral agreement would be enforceable and Clarice, who was eighteen, would have full capacity to contract. If the law of Z were applied, the agreement would be unenforceable under the statute of frauds and Clarice would lack the capacity to contract, the age of majority being nineteen.

Would the agreement be enforceable? If so, on what theory? Would it make any difference where suit was filed?

––––––––––

## PROBLEM 4B-7. SUPPORTING OUR CHILDREN

Edna East, a New Yorker, became pregnant as a result of having sexual relations in New York with Frank Fulde, a wealthy Illinois resident. He supported Edna during the last four months of her pregnancy and, at his request, she went to Illinois to have the baby. Frank paid all of her living and hospital expenses. Edna then returned to New York with the child. Eighteen months later, she returned to Illinois, employed counsel (whose fee Frank paid), and entered into a written agreement with Frank under which she released him from all liability to the child in return for his agreement to pay $325 per month in child support until the child reached the age of 19. The contract recited that the law of Illinois was to govern all aspects of the agreement.

Edna then returned to New York where she and the child have continued to live over the past several years. By New York law, child support agreements required approval by a court to be binding. New York also required that the child be provided with something more than the "bare necessities otherwise required to be provided by the community, with the child's welfare being the paramount consideration." By Illinois law, court approval was not required and the amount provided ($325 per month) was adequate.

Edna is now demanding that Frank quadruple the child support payments. He has offered to increase them to $525 per month. Edna asks you whether she should accept Frank's offer or litigate. What advice would you give her? Why? *See Haag v. Barnes*, 9 N.Y.2d 554, 175 N.E.2d 441 (1961).

––––––––––

## § 4.08     Land — The Situs Rule

### [B]—The Performance Exeption

## PROBLEM 4B-8. LAW OF THE SITUS

Real property located in State *Y* was owned by Alan Axel at the time he died intestate. Alan had lived his entire life in *X*. He left two children and a widow, all of whom had always lived in *X*.

By the law of *Y*, Alan's widow would receive one-half of his real property, and the children would share equally in the balance. By the law of *X*, his widow would receive one-quarter of his real property, and the children would share equally in the balance.

If the rationale of *Barrie* and the traditional situs rule applied, the law of *Y* would govern the intestate distribution of Alan's estate. Is such a result justified on policy grounds? Why?

## PROBLEM 4B-9. INCORPORATION BY REFERENCE

Fran Fuld lived and died a domiciliary of State *X*. Her brother, George Gage, a domiciliary of State *Y*, invested money for her in *Y* oil and gas properties. By the time Fran died, she had acquired $5,000,000 worth of such property. In 1958, George had his lawyers prepare wills for himself and Fran. Fran's will was forwarded to her in *X* where she executed it in 1959. When George died in 1962, he left a portion of his estate, $25,500,000, to the George Gage Trust, a charitable trust located in *Y*.

After Fran died, a dispute arose in the *X* Probate Court between the trustees of the Gage Trust and Fran's sole surviving relative, Clarice Chad, over the validity of a clause in her will purporting to leave the $5,000,000 in *Y* oil and gas property to the Gage Trust by incorporating by reference the terms of the trust. By the law of *X*, the incorporation by reference was too indefinite to be sustained. By the law of *Y*, the incorporation by reference provision was enforceable.

(a) What law should the *X* Probate Court apply in determining the validity of the clause? Why?

(b) If the *X* Probate Court invalidates the incorporation-by-reference provision and the *X* Supreme Court sustains that decision on the trustee's appeal, would the trustees be barred constitutionally from raising the issue of the validity of the provision in a later proceeding in *Y*? *See Welch v. Trustees of Robert A. Welch Foundation*, 465 S.W.2d 195 (Tex. Civ. App. 1971).

(c) Would the result in the *Y* proceeding be different if *Y* had adopted the following provision of the Uniform Probate Code:

> Section 3-408. FORMAL TESTACY PROCEEDING; WILL CON-STRUCTION; EFFECT OF FINAL ORDER IN ANOTHER JURISDICTION.
>
> A final order of a court of another state determining testacy, the validity or construction of a will, made in a proceeding involving notice to and an opportunity for contest by all interested persons must be accepted as determinative by the courts of this state if it includes, or is based upon, a finding that the decedent was domiciled at his death in the state where the order was made.

---

## PROBLEM 4B-10. A GIFT TO CHARITY

At the time of his death, John Jacks, a widower domiciled in State $X$, owned 600 acres of $X$ farm land valued at $1,000 an acre ($600,000), 1200 acres of $Y$ farm land valued at $3,000 an acre ($3,600,000), shares of stock worth $180,000, half of the stock being located in $X$ and half being located in a safety deposit box in $Y$, $1,000,000 in farm equipment equally divided between the two farms, and $60,000 in cash.

In his will, John left the stock and the cash to his three children to share and share alike; he then directed that the land and farm equipment in $X$ and $Y$ be sold, with the proceeds to be used first to pay debts, cost of administration, and state and federal tax obligations, and the remainder to be turned over to a charitable corporation located in $X$.

In a State $X$ probate proceeding, Alan's children challenged the devise to the charity to the extent that it involved $Y$ land and farm equipment. The children argued that (1) $Y$'s mortmain statute voided the charitable bequest to the extent of 75% of the value of all of the property located in $Y$, and (2) the $X$ court lacked jurisdiction to make a determination as to the validity of the disposition of $Y$ property.

The $X$ probate court rejected the challenge, saying that the direction in the will ordering the sale of the property amounted to an equitable conversion of the $Y$ land to personalty and that the domicile at death had jurisdiction to dispose of the decedent's personalty. State $X$ had no restrictions on bequests to charities.

In subsequent probate proceedings in $Y$:

(a) Is the $Y$ court bound by the determination in State $X$?

(b) Would it make any difference if the children appeared in the $X$ proceeding and did not challenge the devise to the charity or the jurisdiction of the $X$ court?

(c) Would it make any difference if two of the children were domiciliaries of State $X$ and appeared in the proceeding there to challenge the court's jurisdiction while the third child, a domiciliary of $Y$ did not appear in the $X$ proceeding despite having received notice of it by registered mail? *See Durfee v. Duke*, Chapter 7[E], *infra*; *Clarke v. Clarke*, Chapter 7[F], *infra*.

---

## PART C.   ESCAPE DEVICES

## § 4.11     Characterization

### [A]—Substance/Procedure

### PROBLEM 4C-1. THE PROMISED LAND

While in Rio de Janeiro for a short vacation, Mabel Mach, a State X resident, purchased three gems from H. Stern Com. E. Ind. S.A. for $50,000. Before going to the H. Stern store, Mabel had seen a flyer in her hotel room in Rio stating in English that H. Stern provided a "one-year guarantee for refund either at our Rio store or in your own country. H. Stern Jewelers on 5th Avenue, New York City, our wholly-owned subsidiary, are at your disposal for help and service." Within one year of the sale, Mabel tendered the gems to H. Stern in New York City and asked for a full refund. Her request was denied, but she was offered $25,000 in return for the gems and a release of any claim.

After telling you the facts set forth above, Mabel showed you a copy of the flyer and told you that at the time of the sale in Rio, the person in charge of the Stern store there had assured her that she could obtain a refund. Your research has indicated that under the law of both Brazil and X, Mabel would be barred from introducing the flyer and from testifying about her conversation with the person in charge of the Rio store; New York's rule would permit the introduction of both items. Would you advise Mabel to settle for the $25,000, or, indeed, anything under $45,000? Why? *See Kristinus v. H. Stern Com. E. Ind. S.A.*, 463 F. Supp. 1263 (S.D.N.Y. 1979).

---

### PROBLEM 4C-2. COMMITTEE OF INQUIRY

The Ghana Supply Commission (GSC), an official agency of the Republic of Ghana, filed a diversity action in the United States District Court for State X against NEPCO, a privately owned X corporation, alleging that NEPCO owed it for fuel oil GSC had delivered to NEPCO. Prior to suit, a Committee of Inquiry had been established by the government of Ghana to investigate the transaction under which NEPCO obtained the oil. The Committee's proceedings were in camera as required by the law of Ghana. By means of requests for documents and answers to interrogatories, NEPCO sought to obtain the substance of the testimony introduced before the Committee of Inquiry. NEPCO filed a motion to compel the production of the materials held by the Committee. In response, the Republic of Ghana submitted an official "Claim of Executive Privilege" signed by the then head of state, now deposed, and resisted all efforts to force the production of the evidence gathered by the Committee.

Should NEPCO's motion be granted? Why? (Assume that State $X$ has adopted a mix of the most significant relationship and interest theories, but that it characterizes privilege questions as procedural.) Would the result be the same if $X$ characterized the privilege as substantive? *See Ghana Supply Com'n v. New England Power Co.*, 83 F.R.D. 586 (D. Mass. 1979). *But see, Zenith Radio Corp. v.* United States, 588 F. Supp. 1443 (Ct. Int'l Trade 1984), *aff'd*, 823 F.2d 518 (Fed.Cir. 1987). *See also Societe Nat. Ind. Aero. v. United States Dist. Court*, 482 U.S. 522 (1987).

---

## PROBLEM 4C-3. SLOT MACHINE JURISPRUDENCE

Alan Arthur and Bob Bose, both residents of State $X$, met while they were in the Army. Bob was discharged before Alan, and when Alan was to be discharged, Bob agreed to drive from State $X$ to State $Y$, pick up Alan, and drive him back to his home in $X$. (Alan agreed to pay Bob $25 for the assistance.) While Bob was driving Alan back home — and doing so negligently — the car was involved in an accident in $Y$ and both Alan and Bob were killed.

Alan's personal representative filed a wrongful death action in $X$ against Bob's estate, the suit being filed 30 months after the accident. Both $X$ and $Y$ had two-year limitation periods applicable to wrongful death actions. In prior cases, the Supreme Court of $X$ had held that the two-year $X$ statute was "built-in," and, thus, substantive; and the $Y$ Supreme Court had held that the $Y$ two-year period was procedural. $X$ had a five-year general statute of limitations. As counsel for the insurance company that issued liability insurance to Bob, would you advise it to make a substantial settlement offer. Why? *See Nelson v. Eckert*, 231 Ark. 348, 329 S.W.2d 426 (1959).

---

## PROBLEM 4C-4. STATUTES OF FRAUDS ARE SUBSTANTIVE

While in New York, Naomi Nown, a Delaware resident, purchased a $10,000 bond from Orville Orcutt, a sales representative for P.J. Pond Co., a New York brokerage house with offices throughout the country, and received a writing signed by Orville promising that Pond would repurchase the bond at face value plus accrued interest at any time within three years of the sale. When Pond refused her timely demand, Naomi filed suit against it in Delaware.

By the law of New York, the agent's authority to bind Pond was not required to be in writing. By the law of Delaware, the agent's authority was required to be in writing. If New York law applied, Naomi would prevail. If Delaware law applied, she would not.

The Delaware court held that statutes of frauds, both domestic and foreign, should be deemed substantive in *all* cases in order to provide maximum protection for Delaware citizens.

Is the court right in concluding that the substantive classification of all statutes of frauds would provide the greatest protection for Delaware citizens in all cases? Why? *See Lams v. F.H. Smith Co.*, 36 Del. 477, 178 A. 651 (1935).

----

## PROBLEM 4C-5. A FINDER'S FEE

Cynthia Cole, an investment advisor living and working in State $X$, phoned Dave Downs, President of Downs, Inc., a Delaware corporation having its principal place of business in State $Y$ and proposed that she attempt to interest Northern, Inc., a Canadian corporation, in a merger with Downs. Dave assented to the suggestion and agreed to pay a finder's fee to Cynthia if the merger occurred. Seven months after Cynthia brought the parties together, the two companies merged. The merged company refused Cynthia's demand that it pay her a $400,000 finders's fee.

The Canadian and $Y$ statutes of frauds do not bar Cynthia's recovery, but the statute in $X$, if applied, would bar her claim. Delaware's internal law would also bar the claim.

As counsel for Cynthia, where would you advise her to file suit, assuming jurisdiction is available in Canada, Delaware, and States $X$ and $Y$? Why? What additional information would you seek before giving the requested advice? Why? *See Ehrman v. Cook Electric Co.*, 468 F. Supp. 98 (N.D. Ill. 1979).

----

## [C]—Property and Contract

## PROBLEM 4C-6. THE COMMUNITY

Level Loan Company, organized and having its only office in State $X$, agreed to lend $4,000 to Fay Frank, a domiciliary of State $Y$ who worked in $X$, on condition that Fay's brother, Fred, co-sign the note. Fred, a $Y$ domiciliary, cosigned the note as requested and did so in Level's office. He did not inform his wife, Gert, of the commitment he had made. Fay failed to pay the note, and Fred refused Level's demand that he pay it.

$Y$'s community property law provides that community assets are liable for the suretyship debts incurred by a husband or wife only if the community benefited by the undertaking. If $Y$ law applies, Level could obtain a judgment against Fred individually, but the only assets Fred had or was likely to have were community assets. $X$, also a community property state, holds the community liable for suretyship debts even if the community as such received no benefit.

Both $X$ and $Y$ follow the same choice-of-law rules. Representing Level, how would you urge the court to characterize the case? Why? What characterization would be urged by Gert's counsel? Why? Is it likely that the same result would be reached whether the suit were filed in $X$ or $Y$? Why? *See Potlach Fed. Credit Union v. Kennedy*, 76 Wash. 2d 806, 459 P.2d 32 (1969).

---

## § 4.12    Depeçage

### PROBLEM 4C-7. APPLYING THE LAW OF DIFFERENT STATES?

Paula Page, a State $X$ domiciliary, was employed as a truck driver by the PIE Company, a corporation organized in $X$ and having its principal office there. While driving a load of pinon nuts from $X$ to State $Z$, Paula pulled her tractor-trailer off the road in State $Y$ to give aid to a trucker whose rig had overturned. Paula's rig was completely off the highway except that the left rear corner of the trailer extended by about 12 inches over the traveled portion of the road. Paula lit flares and put them out to warn approaching drivers that the rig extended slightly onto the roadway.

Harry Henks, an $X$ domiciliary, was employed as a truck driver by the BNI Company, a corporation organized and having its principal office in $X$. While in the process of driving a load of pinon logs from $X$ to $Z$, Harry's rig skidded as it was passing Paula's rig and the right rear corner of his trailer struck the left rear corner of Paula's trailer.

Harry filed suit against Paula and PIE in $X$ for personal injuries suffered. BNI filed suit in $X$ against the same two defendants for damages to the tractor-trailer Harry was driving.

By the law of $Y$, Harry, since he was guilty of contributory negligence, would not be permitted to recover for his personal injuries; nor would BNI be able to recover for property damages. A $Y$ statute provided: "No standing vehicle or any part thereof shall be left on the paved portion of a highway." The $Y$ Supreme Court had held that any violation of the statute was negligence per se. By the law of $X$, Harry's contributory negligence would not operate to deny him recovery, $X$ being a comparative negligence state and Harry being only 20% at fault for the accident. Although the $X$ "standing vehicle" statute was the same as $Y$'s, the $X$ Supreme Court had held that a violation of the statute was merely evidence of negligence which could be overcome by additional evidence such as placing of flares.

What would be the result of the two actions if the $X$ court attempted to sort out the state interests involved? Why? *See Sabell v. Pacific Intermountain Express Co.*, 36 Colo. App. 60, 536 P.2d 1160 (1975).

---------

## § 4.13　　　Renvoi

### PROBLEM 4C-8. FROM ENGLAND TO FRANCE TO ENGLAND AND BACK?

Sybil Annesley lived in France for the last 58 years of her life in a chateau she and her husband purchased. Sybil, who was born and raised in England, movee to France several years after she was married in England to an Englishman. After her husband died, she continued to live in the chateau and visited England only to attend the weddings of her three children.

Fifteen years before she died, she executed her final will in France. The will purported to dispose of all of her real and personal property. Other than modest bequests to five servants, she left everything to her daughter, Elizabeth. Clause eight of the will, which was in English and in English form, read as follows:

> I declare that although I live in France and own a chateau there, it has not been and is not my intention to abandon my domicil of origin, namely England, and I have not made any application under Article 13 of the French Civil Code or any other law for a decree to fix my domicil in France nor have I done anything to become a naturalised subject of France. I intend to remain a British subject.

By the law of France, Sybil's could dispose of only one-third of her personal property because two children, in addition to Elizabeth, survived her. By the law of England, the bequest to Elizabeth was valid. Further, by English law, the disposition of personalty at death was governed by the law of domicile at death. By the law of France, it was governed by the law of nationality at death.

Would the two children who were not included in the will prevail if they challenged it in England? Would the English court look only to the internal or municipal law of France (the law of the domicile) or would it look to the whole law of France, including its choice-of-law rule, and take a reference back to the law of England? And if it took a reference back to the law of England, would that reference be to the internal law of England or to its whole law?

As a matter of policy, would it be preferable for England simply to apply the internal law of France? Why? *See In re Annesley*, [1926] Ch. 692.

----

## PROBLEM 4C-9. FROM TINKER TO EVERS TO CHANCES I, II, and III

Ken Keen, an *X* national, died domiciled in *Y* leaving personalty in *X, Y* and *Z*.

(i) The choice-of-law rules of *X* and *Y* direct the courts to imitate the courts of the decedent's nationality at death. *Z's* rules direct the courts to imitate the courts of the domicile at death. What law would govern the disposition of the personalty in each of the countries? Would the result be different if Ken died domiciled in *Z*?

(ii) The choice-of-law rules of *X* and *Y* direct the courts to look to the law of nationality at death and to take a single reference from that law. *Z's* rules direct the courts to look to the law of the domicile at death and to take a single reference from that law. What law would govern the disposition of the personalty in each of the countries? Would the result be different if *Z's* law directed the court to take a double reference from the law of the domicile at death?

(iii) The choice-of-law rules of *Y* direct its courts to look to the law of nationality at death and to take a single reference from it. The *X* and *Z* rules direct the courts to look to the law of domicile at death and to take a single reference from it. What law would govern the distribution of the personalty in each country? What would be the result if the courts in *X* and *Z* were directed to take two references from the law of the domicile at death?

----

## PROBLEM 4C-10. A WIFE'S CAPACITY

George Grade, who was domiciled in State *Y* with his wife Helen, owned land in State *X*. George arranged a $200,000 loan from InterBank of State *X* with the land as collateral. InterBank sent the necessary note and trust deed to the Grades in *Y*, with the notation that, as a condition to the loan, Helen, who was independently wealthy, would have to join George in signing the documents. After signing the documents in *Y*, the Grades mailed them back to InterBank's main office in *X*, and the money was advanced by means of a deposit in an InterBank account in George's name. When George failed to pay the debt, InterBank demanded that Helen pay it.

After Helen came to you for advice, you did some research and discovered that (1) by the law of *Y*, Helen lacked the capacity to guaranty her husband's debt; and (2) by the law of *X*, Helen clearly had sufficient capacity to commit herself. Your research further revealed that *X*'s highest court, in *B v. B*, had voided an *X* wife's promise to guaranty her husband's debt when the wife had signed the note and trust deed on *X* land while in State *Z*, where she was vacationing. *Z*'s law concerning a wife's capacity was the same as *Y*'s.

Would you advise Helen to accept InterBank's offer to settle for $100,000? Why? If InterBank filed suit against Helen in *Y*, what argument(s) would you make on her behalf if you discovered that by *Y*'s choice-of-law rule, the law of the situs of real property governed transactions in which land was used as collateral? Why? *See University of Chicago v. Dater*, 277 Mich. 658, 270 N.W. 175 (1936).

---

## PROBLEM 4C-11. THE TRUCK STOP

Debra Doone, a truck driver domiciled in Indiana, was seriously injured at a truck stop in State *X* as the result of the negligence of members of the truck stop's staff. Stop, Inc., the owner of the truck stop, was incorporated and had its principal office in State *Y*. It operated truck stops in seven states, including State *Z*.

Eighteen months after the accident — six months after the limitation period in *X*, had run — Debra asked you to act as her counsel in a suit against Stop. Your research indicates that six of the seven states in which Stop operated had borrowing statutes that accepted the bar of the place of accrual. Thus, suit would be barred in all six states because it was barred in *X*. The seventh state, *Z*, had a two-year limitations period for tort actions and a borrowing statute that accepted the bar of the place where defendant "had previously resided." In addition, you discovered that *Y* which borrowed the bar of the place of accrual, had a five-year limitations period for tort actions.

Would you advise Debra to file suit in State *Z*? Why? What problem or problems do you foresee in persuading the court that it should reach the merits of Debra's claim? *See Drudge v. Overland Plazas Co.*, 531 F. Supp. 210 (S.D. Iowa 1981), *aff'd*, 670 F.2d 92 (8th Cir. 1982).

---

## PROBLEM 4C-12. FEDERAL TORT CLAIMS ACT APPLIED

If a United States Army vehicle with its brake off is parked on a hill in State *X* and rolls down the hill into State *Y* where it strikes an *X* resident who had just crossed the state line, and suit is filed in the United States District Court for State $Y$, what process would the federal judge go through in determining what law to apply? If $X$'s conflict-of-laws rule calls for the application of the law of the place having the most significant contact with the tort and $Y$'s rule calls for the application of the law of the place of physical impact, would the court apply the internal law of State $X$ or State $Y$? Is any additional information necessary to answer the latter question? If so, what information?

---

## PROBLEM 4C-13. NO SOVEREIGNTY AND NO FAULT

An Air New Zealand aircraft crashed into Mount Erebus in Antarctica and all persons on board were killed. Plaintiffs, all New Zealand citizens and survivors of those killed, filed an action against the United States in the District of Columbia. They sought recovery for wrongful death under the Federal Tort Claims Act (FTCA), alleging negligence by officials of the Department of Defense in the selection, training, and supervision of personnel at McMurdo (a United States Naval Air Station in Antarctica), and of Navy Air Traffic Controllers at McMurdo. The government has appealed the denial of its motion to dismiss.

The FTCA exempts from the waiver of sovereign immunity claims that arise in a "foreign country." Antarctica, a large continent, is unique in that by treaty in 1959, it is not subject to the sovereignty of any nation. The United States has four year-round bases in Antarctica, including McMurdo, which has a summer population of 850 persons, and a winter population of 90. The trial court rejected the government's argument that Antarctica was a "foreign country" within the FTCA. On appeal, what arguments would you make on behalf of the government to persuade the court to reverse? Why?

The issues presented are almost *sui generis* in that Antarctica has no civil tort law. Thus, the court is faced with deciding what law should govern the aspects of the case that involve the allegedly negligent actions by McMurdo personnel and those that involved negligent training of personnel in Maryland.

What law should govern the substantive (negligence) issues in the case? Why? *See Beattie v. United States*, 756 F.2d 91 (D.C. Cir. 1984). *But see Smith v. United States*, 702 F. Supp. 1480, 1482 (D. Or. 1989). In considering the case, keep in mind that New Zealand has a no-fault system that bars tort action for personal injuries caused by the negligence of another.

---

## PROBLEM 4C-14. JUDGE SCALIA'S HYPO

Karla Kraft, a resident of *X*, filed suit under the Federal Tort Claims Act in the United States District Court for *X*, alleging that she was injured in State *Y* by a federal employee, also an *X* resident, who, in the course of his employment, was driving a privately owned vehicle registered in *X*. Karla alleged that she was injured as the result of the excessive speed of the vehicle, attributable to the negligent (1) driving of the federal employee; (2) training the driver received at the federal training center in State *Z*; and (3) selection of the driver by supervisors in the District of Columbia.

Keeping in mind the FTCA choice of law rule calling for the application of the law of the place where the act or omission occurred, what law would apply to the various facets of the case? Why? *See Beattie v. United States*, 756 F.2d 91, 127–130 (Dissent by Scalia, J.), 138-143 (Concurring opinion, Wald, J.) (D.C. Cir. 1984).

---

## § 4.14    Public Policy

## PROBLEM 4C-15. THE GOLDEN RULE AND PROSTITUTION

In *Loucks*, Justice Cardozo articulated the public-policy standard as calling for a refusal to enforce a foreign statute only if it "would violate some fundamental principle of justice, some prevalent conception of good morals, some deep-rooted tradition of the common weal." In *Intercontinental Hotels Corp. (P.R.) v. Golden*, 15 N.Y.2d 9, 203 N.E.2d 210 (1964), Judge Burke, while recognizing the *Louks* standard, said that "foreign based rights should be enforced unless the judicial enforcement . . . would be the approval of a transaction which is inherently vicious, wicked or immoral, and shocking to the prevailing moral sense of a sister state." Can you imagine a state court or legislature adopting a rule or statute that was inherently vicious, wicked, or shocking to the prevailing moral sense? Would the following facts qualify?

George Golde operated a house of prostitution in State *X* where such operations were legal. Hana Holte operated an employment agency in *X* and supplied prostitutes to George under an agreement whereby he agreed to pay $400 to Hana for each prostitute who remained in George's employ for 60 days or more. George left State *X* owing $4,000 to Hana under the arrangement. Hana located George in State *Y* and filed suit against him there. By the law of *Y*, prostitution was illegal. What would be the result of Bob's suit? Why?

---

## PROBLEM 4C-16. BUYING BACK YOUR OWN GOODS

Root, Inc., purchased a large piece of movable equipment in State *X*. The equipment was stolen from Root's plant in *X* by an unknown party. Equip, Inc., acting in good faith and in ordinary course, purchased the equipment in question in State *Y* and shipped it to its plant in State *Z*.

Root traced the equipment and filed a writ of replevin in *Z* seeking to recover the equipment. By the law of *X*, the true owner can recover stolen property from a good faith purchaser (BFP) *only* if the true owner tenders to the BFP the full purchase price the BFP had paid. By the law of *Y* and *Z*, the true owner prevails against the BFP.

What law is likely to govern the rights of the parties if *Z* followed modern choice-of-law theory? Why? As counsel for Equip, what fall-back position would you develop if the *Z* court indicated that its choice-of-law rules called for the application of *X* law? Why? *See Brown & Root v. Ring Power Corp.*, 450 So. 2d 1245 (Fla. App. 1984).

---

## PROBLEM 4C-17. A COUPLE IN A HURRY

Mary and Mark Mers were married and lived in State *X* for seven years before deciding to have their marriage dissolved. They entered an agreement settling their property rights, agreeing that their minor child would live with Mary, and providing for adequate support for the child. They discovered, however, that the backlog of cases in the *X* courts was such that it would take more than a year before the dissolution action was heard.

Mary comes to your office, explains the situation, and tells you that she wants the marriage dissolved within the next few months because she is two months pregnant and wishes to marry the father before her pregnancy becomes obvious. Mary then shows you a brochure a friend of hers had given her advertising packaged three-day divorces in the Dominican Republic. For $3,500, Mary's air fare, hotel and meal costs, filing fees, and charges by attorneys for both parties would be covered. She explains that she had discussed the matter with Mark and that he was willing to sign any necessary documents consenting to the jurisdiction of the Dominican courts. Mary asks whether the Dominican divorce would be valid in State *X*? What answer would you give? Why? *See Hyde v. Hyde*, 562 S.W.2d 194 (Tenn. 1978).

## PROBLEM 4C-18. INTERSPOUSAL IMMUNITY

Sarah and Tom Toblie, a married couple living in State *X*, were killed in the crash of a private plane crash in State *Y*, the crash having been caused by Bob's negligence. Sarah's estate filed a wrongful death action in *Y* against Tom's estate.

By the law of *X*, there was no interspousal immunity. State *Y*, however, had a statute that barred tort action between spouses. Should *Y*'s public policy as expressed in its statute be applied to bar the action? Why? *See Robertson v. McKnight*, 609 S.W.2d 534 (Tex. 1980). Would the result be the same if Sarah and Tom were domiciled in *Y* and the plane crashed in *X*? Why? *See Linton v. Linton*, 46 Md. App. 660, 420 A.2d 1249 (1980); *McMillan v. McMillan*, 219 Va. 1127, 253 S.E.2d 662 (1979).

## PROBLEM 4C-19. A "TALAK" DIVORCE

In a dissolution proceeding in State *X* filed by Wife 2 against Husband, Wife 1 intervened alleging that she was Husband's lawful wife and that Wife 2 had never lawfully married him.

The following facts were stipulated:

In 1970, Husband and Wife 1 were married in India, where they lived. In 1974, Husband left Wife 1 and started cohabiting with Wife 2. In 1976, he was granted permanent resident alien status in the United States. About eight years later, Husband and Wife 2 converted to Islam in India. Shortly thereafter, Husband, while in Kuwait, divorced Wife 1 according to Islamic law by pronouncing three times: "I divorce you." (Wife 1 was not informed of the procedure, known as "talak.") On the following day, Husband and Wife 2 were married in Kuwait in a Muslim ceremony. Within a few months, Wife 2 was granted permanent resident alien status in the United States as the lawful wife of one who already had that status. Husband and Wife 2 lived together in the United States for several years before the dissolution proceeding was filed. All of the parties remain citizens of India.

Assuming that by Islamic law, the "talak" process was effective to constitute a valid divorce, what would be the likely result of the suit in *X* if that state followed a Restatement (Second) approach? Why? *See Seth v. Seth*, 694 S.W.2d 459 (Tex. App. 1985).

----

### PROBLEM 4C-20. "I SIMPLY OBEYED THE LAW"

Alice Alber, a German citizen, and Gestalt Co., a German corporation, entered into a seven-year employment contract in Germany. The contract was signed in 1933. By decree of Adolph Hitler in 1935, Jews were barred from employment by German companies. As soon as the decree was issued, Gestalt dismissed Alice, although her services had been completely satisfactory. Alice was arrested shortly thereafter and was placed in a concentration camp for three years. (Her "crime" was being Jewish.) Alice escaped from the camp in 1938 and went to New York where she filed a breach of contract action against Gestalt. Suit was commenced by personal service on Gestalt's New York agent. Would the New York court accept as a valid defense Gestalt's claim that it was merely obeying a government decree? The German decree is an example of a foreign rule that violated the *Golden* rule (Problem 4C-14, *supra*). How does it differ from *Louks* and *Golden*? *See Holzer v. Deutsche Reichsbahn-Gesellschaft*, 277 N.Y. 474, 14 N.E.2d 798 (1938). For the post-war German treatment of the same problem, *see* Bundesgerichtsat, Decision of May 25, 1955, 8 Neue Juristche Wochenschrift 1274 (1955). Nazi legislation adversely affecting Jews was abrogated by Control Council Law No. 1, Official Gazette of the Control Council of Germany, No. 1, pp. 10 and 11.

----

## PART D.  THE CHOICE-OF-LAW REVOLUTION

[The following two problems in this Part are not referred to in the main text, but may be used for additional practice.]

### PROBLEM 4D-1. DOES THE CENTER OF GRAVITY SHIFT?

According to the record, the younger Auten child was born in 1921 and the older in 1919. Thus, the children had reached their majority by 1947 when Mrs. Auten filed suit in New York and they were 33 and 35 respectively when the Court of Appeals handed down its decision. While England may have been the "center of gravity" in 1933, when the settlement agreement was executed, should the center shift as the years passed and the urgency of their father's obligation to support them was converted to making up for a past deficiency?

The Court of Appeals in *Auten* said, "It hardly needs stating that it is England which has all the truly significant contacts. . .." In view of the fact that the issue before the court was whether a contract made in New York and with performance by the husband being payment to a New York trustee, why are the English contacts so clearly more significant? Did the court treat the case as a contracts case or as case involving child support? If it was treated as a family law issue, would England have had all the truly significant contacts if Mr. Auten lived in New York, remarried there, and had two children of the second marriage to support? Had the issue been the adequacy of the writing under the statute of frauds, would England's contacts be more significant that New York's?

---

## PROBLEM 4D-2. 2¢ PLAIN

Ann Ablet applied for and was issued a life insurance policy while she was domiciled in State $X$. The policy was issued by the Bond Life Insurance Co., incorporated and having its main office in State $Y$, through Bond's resident agent in $X$. A few years after the policy was issued, Ann moved to State $Z$ where she resided until her death. She kept the policy in force and ten years after her move to $Z$ borrowed $12,000 on the policy. When the next premium became due, the loan indebtedness on the policy was $12,500.02—the $12,000 loan plus $500.02 in interest. The cash surrender value of the policy was $12,500, or $.02 less than the indebtedness. Because of the $.02 deficiency, the policy's automatic loan provision to pay premiums did not become operative. The premium notice that Bond sent did not indicate that the automatic loan provision was inoperative.

As soon as the 30-day grace period had run, Bond informed Ann that the policy had been cancelled and could be reinstated only upon the filing of a new application, the payment of a premium, and a satisfactory medical report. Ann did not respond, but did tender the premium that was due. She died a few days later.

By the law of $X$ and $Y$, Ann had received appropriate notice. The policy, thus, had lapsed before her death. By the law of $Z$, however, the notice was inadequate and the policy was in force when she died.

The beneficiary of the policy was willing to accept 80% of the face value in full settlement. As counsel to Bond, would you advise it to settle for 80%? Why? *See Lester v. Aetna Life Ins. Co.*, 433 F.2d 884 (5th Cir. 1970), *cert. denied*, 402 U.S. 909 (1971).

## PART E.   INTEREST ANALYSIS

## § 4.18     Doing Interest Analysis

### PROBLEM 4E-1. CURRIED CONFLICTS

In *Grant v. McAuliffe*, § 4.11, *supra*, the court dealt with a two-car accident in Arizona involving California parties. The defendant died and the issue was whether the claim survived his death in light of the fact that by Arizona law the claim died with the defendant and by California law it survived his death. In commenting on the case in *Survival of Action: Adjudication versus Automation in Conflict of Laws*, 10 Stan. L. Rev. 205 (1958), Professor Brainerd Currie hypothesized a series of 16 cases, set forth below. In each case, it should be assumed, as in *Grant*, that in California, tort actions survive the death of the tortfeasor and in Arizona, they do not. Assume also that the policies behind California's survival statute are: (1) to prevent injured parties from becoming a burden on California taxpayers by reason of their inability to support themselves because of their injuries; and (2) to assure that medical creditors will not be deterred from providing assistance to persons injured in California because of the injured party's prospective inability to pay for the services. Finally, assume that Arizona's interest in failing to permit claims to survive is to protect estates of Arizonan's being administered in Arizona from claims against which the estate cannot effectively defend itself.

| CASE | DOMICILE OF PLAINTIFF | DOMICILE OF DEFENDANT | PLACE OF INJURY | FORUM |
|------|------------------------|------------------------|------------------|--------|
| 1.   | Calif | Calif | Calif | Calif |
| 2.   | Ariz  | Calif | Calif | Calif |
| 3.   | Calif | Ariz  | Calif | Calif |
| 4.   | Calif | Calif | Ariz  | Calif |
| 5.   | Calif | Calif | Calif | Ariz  |
| 6.   | Ariz  | Ariz  | Calif | Calif |
| 7.   | Calif | Ariz  | Ariz  | Calif |
| 8.   | Calif | Calif | Ariz  | Ariz  |
| 9.   | Ariz  | Calif | Calif | Ariz  |
| 10.  | Ariz  | Calif | Ariz  | Calif |
| 11.  | Calif | Ariz  | Calif | Ariz  |
| 12.  | Ariz  | Ariz  | Ariz  | Calif |
| 13.  | Ariz  | Ariz  | Calif | Ariz  |
| 14.  | Ariz  | Calif | Ariz  | Ariz  |
| 15.  | Calif | Ariz  | Ariz  | Ariz  |
| 16.  | Ariz  | Ariz  | Ariz  | Ariz  |

(a) In which cases would the interest of the forum state not be forwarded by applying the law of the place of impact? In which state would the interest of the forum state not be forwarded by classifying California's survival statute as procedural?

(b) What would be the interests of California and Arizona in Case 10? How should that case be decided?

(c) What other state policies might explain the rules in the two states? Would these additional interests change the result if the court adopted an interest analysis?

---

## § 4.19     False Conflicts

### PROBLEM 4E-2. REVERSING *BABCOCK*

Helen Holden was killed when the car in which she was a passenger swerved off the road and struck a telephone pole in State $X$. The car was owned and being driven by George Groat. George and Helen both resided in State $Y$, and the car was registered, garaged, and insured there. The two were returning to $Y$ after having had lunch with a mutual friend in $X$. The accident was caused by George's negligent driving, although his conduct did not amount to willful negligence.

By the law of $X$, George, and therefore his insurance company, would have been liable to Helen. $Y$'s guest statute required that the driver's negligence rise to the level of willful negligence as a condition to a passenger's recovery. Under the Babcock analysis, what would be the result of a suit in $X$ by Helen's personal representative against George? Why? If the suit were filed in $Y$ and $Y$ followed the Babcock analysis, what would be the result? Why? Would the result be different in either state if Helen, rather than having been killed, was severely injured? Why? *See Fuerste v. Bemis*, 156 N.W.2d 831 (Iowa 1968).

---

### PROBLEM 4E-3. THE CASE FOR THE OPPOSITION

Assume an action between two residents of Louisiana in a Louisiana court for injuries incurred in Arkansas on a trip that started and was to end in Louisiana, with the host driving negligently but not willfully so. Arkansas had a guest statute that required a showing of wilful negligence; Louisiana required only ordinary negligence. The judge assigned to write the opinion has asked you to develop as strong a series of arguments as possible against departing from the traditional lex loci delicti position the court had taken in prior cases. What arguments would you make? *See Johnson v. St. Paul*

*Mercury Ins. Co.*, 256 La. 289, 236 So. 2d 216 (1970). *But see Jagers v. Royal Indemnity Co.*, 276 So. 2d 309 (La. 1973).

———

## PROBLEM 4E-4. PRESUMPTION OF DEATH

The three children of Sarah Sands brought suit in a State $X$ court against Federal Life Assurance Co., Inc., to recover on an insurance policy their father had taken out on their mother's life. The policy named the children as beneficiaries. The children, all adults, live in States $X$, $Y$, and $Z$. The family lived in State $X$ when the policy was issued and their father still lives there.

After a dispute with her husband, the insured left home carrying only a small clutch purse. She had tried to persuade her husband to move to State $Z$, and, indeed, his refusal was the cause of the dispute. After she left home, no one in the family ever saw or heard from her again except that she cashed some traveler's checks in State $Z$ a few weeks after she left.

State $X$ and $Z$ both have seven year statutes to establish the presumption of death. The laws differ, however, in the requirement in $Z$ that a diligent search precede a finding of death and the absence of that requirement in $X$. No such search was undertaken.

Assuming that $X$'s approach to choice of law follows the choice-influencing considerations enunciated by Professor Leflar, are the children likely to prevail? Why? *See Gavers v. Federal Life Ins. Co.*, 118 Wis. 2d 113, 345 N.W.2d 900 (Wis. App. 1984).

———

## PROBLEM 4E-5. UNLIMITED RECOVERY?

Bob Boors, a State $X$ domiciliary, drove his car to Mexico for a vacation. While driving negligently there, he struck and seriously injured Roberta Robble, a Mexican national and domiciliary.

By Mexican law, a person negligently injured in an automobile accident may recover a maximum of $2,000. By $X$ law, no such limitation exists.

(a) If Roberta sues Bob in State $X$ and $X$ follows the California choice-of-law analysis (interest and comparative impairment), would the $2,000 limitation be applied to Roberta's claim? Why? If the Currie interest analysis were applied by $X$, would the result be the same? Why? *See Hernandez v. Burger*, 102 Cal. App. 3d 795, 162 Cal. Rptr. 564 (1980).

(b) Would your analysis be different if Bob, rather than being a domiciliary of $X$ was a Mexican national and domiciliary, and Roberta, rather than being a Mexican national and domiciliary, was a domiciliary of X who was injured by Bob's negligence while she was vacationing in Mexico? Why? (Assume personal service on Bob in State X while he was there for a weekend visiting a friend.)

## PROBLEM 4E-6. THE U-TURN

Tina Tell, a domiciliary of Indiana, rented a car in New York from Ronde Rental Company for the purpose of driving to Pennsylvania to pick up friends and take them to a resort hotel in New Jersey. After picking up her friends and while she was in New Jersey en route to the hotel, Clara Cole, one of Tina's friends, mentioned that she had left her hat at a restaurant where the group had stopped for lunch. Tina, who forgot she was driving on a divided interstate highway, immediately made a U-turn on the highway for the purpose of going back to the restaurant to retrieve Clara's hat. As the result of the U-turn, Tina was driving the wrong way on the highway. Within a few minutes and while still in New Jersey, Tina's car ran head-on into a car being driven by Dave Dombey, a domiciliary of Pennsylvania, whose car was registered there.

Investigation has indicated that the car Tina was driving was owned by its manufacturer, Chrysler Corporation, and was on a long-term lease to Ronde. Chrysler was incorporated in Michigan, had its home office there, and did business in all 50 states. Ronde also operated in all 50 states. It was incorporated in Delaware and had its main office in Pennsylvania.

By the law of Pennsylvania and New Jersey, neither Ronde nor Chrysler would be liable to Dave for injuries sustained as the result of Tina's negligent driving. By the law of Indiana and New York, both Chrysler and Ronde would be liable to Dave for Tina's negligent driving. By the law of Delaware and Michigan, Chrysler, as owner, would be liable to Dave, but Ronde, as lessor, would not be liable to him.

If Dave filed suit in New Jersey against Ronde and Chrysler, what arguments would you, as counsel for Dave, make on his behalf? Is it likely that your arguments would be persuasive? Assume that New Jersey follows interest analysis in deciding choice-of-law questions. *See White v. Smith*, 398 F. Supp. 130 (D.N.J. 1975). *See also, Caldararo v. Au*, 570 F. Supp. 39 (S.D.N.Y. 1983).

## PROBLEM 4E-7. THE MEXICAN SAFARI

Andrea Alber, a domiciliary of Missouri, was in California on vacation when she decided to join some friends in a hunting expedition in Novajoa, Mexico. She bought a 12-gauge Remington shotgun and four boxes of Remington ammunition in California and flew down to Navajoa with her friends. After using the ammunition she brought with her, Andrea bought more ammunition in Navajoa. The ammunition was labeled "Remington" and looked the same as the ammunition she had purchased in California except that the package said it had been manufactured in Mexico by Cartuchos Deportivos De Mexico, S.A., under a license issued by Remington Corporation, a Connecticut company doing business and advertising heavily throughout the United States. Remington owned 40% of the shares of Cartuchos and under the licensing agreement, Cartuchos agreed to maintain standards of manufacturing established by Remington. Remington employees from the United States periodically inspected Cartuchos' plant to assure that the standards were being met.

One of the shells purchased in Mexico contained an excessive powder charge and when Andrea attempted to fire the shotgun, the shell exploded in the gun and severely injured Andrea's eyes.

Andrea filed suit in California against Remington. By the law of California, Remington would be liable to her on the theory that it was an integral part of the Mexican enterprise. By the law of Mexico, Remington would not be liable. (It was stipulated that Mexico did not recognize any right of recovery on a product liability theory.) Missouri's domestic law was the same as California's, but its choice-of-law rule would have directed its courts to look to the law of the place of impact, Mexico. What would be the likely result of Andrea's suit in California? Why? Would the analysis or result be different if Andrea had been a domiciliary of California rather than Missouri? *See Kasel v. Remington Arms Co.*, 24 Cal. App. 3d 711, 101 Cal. Rptr. 314 (1972).

## PROBLEM 4E-8. THE STATE LINE TAVERN

The Line Tavern, which did not advertise, was located in State $X$ about 20 miles from the State $Y$ line. About 20% of Line Line's patrons were from $Y$. On April 20, Dot Dombey arrived at Line at 9:00 p.m. and consumed nine very dry martinis before she left at midnight, when Line closed. Immediately upon leaving, she drove to $Y$ in search of an open bar. Shortly after she crossed into $Y$ and while driving 90 miles per hour, Dot ran into a legally parked car.

Ed Englert, who was in the parked car, was severely injured and filed suit in *X* against Line and its owner, Larry Line. (Dot was convicted in *Y* of driving while intoxicated.)

State *Y* had no dram shop act and its highest court had held that the supplier of liquor was not liable for damage done by persons to whom the liquor had been given or sold. State *X* had the following Dram Shop Act:

> Every person who shall be injured by any intoxicated person shall have a right of action against any person who shall by selling intoxicating liquors cause the intoxication of such person, for all damages actually sustained, as well as exemplary damages.

Assume that *X* courts followed California's comparative-impairment choice-of-law approach, would Ed prevail? Why? Would it make any difference whether Dot was an *X* or a *Y* domiciliary? Would it make any difference whether Ed was an *X* or a *Y* domiciliary? What result would you expect if *X* followed the choice-of-law rules of Restatement (Second) of Conflict of Laws? If the suit was filed in *Y*, and *Y* followed the California's choice-of-laws rules, would Bob prevail? *See Bankord v. DeRock*, 423 F. Supp. 602 (N.D. Iowa 1976).

## PROBLEM 4E-9. KLM AND PAN AM

Sally Sander, a State *X* domiciliary who boarded the plane in *X*, was killed in Spain when the Pan American 747 on which she was a passenger collided with a KLM 747 on an airport runway. Sally's executor filed suit against KLM in the United States District Court for State *X*; the suit was among more than 100 transferred to State *Y* by the Judicial Panel on Multidistrict Litigation. (28 U.S.C. § 1407(a)) KLM is a Dutch corporation with its principal place of business in the Netherlands. State *X* has adopted interest analysis. State *Y* has continued to follow traditional choice-of-law rules.

The executor argued that the court in *X*, applying interest analysis, would apply *X*'s wrongful death act in its entirety, including its punitive damage provision, and, thus, that the court in *Y* should do the same. As counsel for KLM, what arguments would you make in resisting the executor's argument? Are your arguments likely to succeed? (Assume that neither Spanish nor Dutch law permits an award of punitive damages.) *See Sibley v. KLM-Royal Dutch Airlines*, 454 F. Supp. 425 (S.D.N.Y. 1978). What law would you expect to be applied if *X* followed traditional choice-of-law rules? *See Kilberg v. Northeast Airlines*, 9 N.Y.2d 34, 172 N.E.2d 526 (1961).

---

## PROBLEM 4E-10. THE DANGERS OF RAIL TRAVEL

Dan Doule boarded an Amtrak passenger train in New York to return to his home in Pennsylvania. While the train was traveling in New Jersey, a fifteen-foot section of a steel rail being carried by an Amtrak work train going in the other direction penetrated the passenger train and killed several passengers. Dan incurred only minor physical injuries, but he suffered acute depression as the result of having witnessed the havoc. Despite receiving the best of psychiatric care, Dan's mental condition continued to deteriorate until his life became a complete shambles— break-up of marriage, loss of job, etc.

Despite the fact that Amtrak trains had been involved in a similar incident ten weeks before the accident in question, Amtrak had taken little effective action to avoid a repetition. (Amtrak is a corporation established by an Act of Congress and is deemed to be a citizen of, and to have its principal place of business in, the District of Columbia.)

Dan filed suit in the United States District Court for the Southern District of New York. The court, applying New York's choice-of-law rules, assessed compensatory and punitive damages by application of the law of Pennsylvania, plaintiff's domicile. Amtrak objects only to the imposition of punitive damages.

On that issue, both Pennsylvania and New Jersey recognize that punitive damages may be applied on a showing "that there has been a deliberate act or omission with knowledge of a high degree of probability of harm and reckless indifference to consequences." The two states differ, however, on the treatment of punitive damages in vicarious liability cases. Pennsylvania applies the more liberal standard and holds corporations liable for acts of agents done within the scope of their authority. New Jersey requires that the corporation authorize, ratify, or participate in committing the act in question.

Should the court have applied New Jersey or Pennsylvania law to the punitive damage issue? Why? Would it be more appropriate to apply the law of the District of Columbia or New York to the issue? Why? *See Dobelle v. National R.R. Passenger Corp.*, 628 F. Supp. 1518 (S.D.N.Y. 1986).

---

## PROBLEM 4E-11. LIFE CAN BE DANGEROUS

Alan Axel, a customer at a gas station in State *X*, was killed when a truck tire that was being inflated by an employee of the station exploded. His widow, who had lived with her husband for thirty years in State *X*, filed a survival action against General Tire, which designed and manufacturer the tire at its plant in State *Y*; the Tire and Rim Association, which approved the specifications for the tire rim at its laboratory in State *Y*; and the Rubber Manufacturers Association, which approved the specifications for the tire at its office in State *Z*. The suit sought recovery of compensatory and punitive damages.

State *X* law barred the recovery of punitive damages in survival actions. The law in *Y* and *Z* permitted such recoveries. Assuming that an appropriate showing can be made, is it likely that the *X* court would permit plaintiff to recover punitive damages? Why? *See Beasock v. Dioguardi Enterprises, Inc.*, 100 A.D.2d 50, 472 N.Y.S.2d 798 (1984).

---

## § 4.20 True Conflicts: Currie's Solution — Forum Law

### PROBLEM 4E-12. EVEN STEVEN

The Alert Coal Co., a Kentucky corporation doing business only in that state, bought a bulldozer from a Kentucky dealer. The bulldozer, manufactured in Illinois by Bobble Bulldozers, Inc., a Delaware corporation having its principal office in Chicago, never worked properly and finally caught fire and was damaged severely. Alleging design and production defects, Alert filed a product liability suit against Bobble in the United States District Court for Illinois seeking recovery of its economic losses. By Kentucky law, recovery would be allowed if the defects could be shown. By Illinois law, however, no recovery was available on a product liability claim in the absence of personal injuries.

Assume that Illinois follows Restatement (Second) choice-of-law theory. Bobble moved for a dismissal on the ground that the law of Illinois was applicable and, thus, that Alert had not stated a valid claim. The court made the following findings:

> Illinois has a legitimate interest in the liability to be imposed on Illinois-based manufacturers under strict liability or negligence principles. Kentucky has an equally legitimate interest in the remedies to be afforded its residents who suffer such tort injuries. And if it is assumed that the substantive law of the two jurisdictions looks in different directions, each state would seem to have an equal interest in having its tort rule applied in the determination of the issue presented by this case.

As counsel for Bobble, what arguments would you make to persuade the court to apply Illinois law? Are your arguments likely to be persuasive? *See Hardly Able Coal v. International Harvester*, 494 F. Supp. 249 (N.D. Ill. 1980).

_____

## PROBLEM 4E-13. COMPARATIVE NEGLIGENCE

The parties to a suit that involved a truck-automobile accident in State $X$ included the owner of the automobile (a State $Y$ resident), the owner of the truck (an $X$ corporation authorized to do business in $Y$), and the drivers of the car and the truck (both $Y$ residents).

The suit was tried in $Y$. The trial court charged the jury in accordance with $X$'s modified comparative negligence statute, which provided that there would be no recovery by a party whose negligence was greater that the negligence of the party against whom the claim is made. The jury found that the driver of the car was 60% at fault, as compared with the 40% fault of the truck driver. Thus, the owner of the car was denied any recovery for property damage, and the driver of the car was denied any recovery for personal injuries. Under $Y$'s version of comparative negligence, they would have recovered 40% of the damage they suffered.

The owner and the driver have appealed. As their counsel, what analysis would you present to persuade the appellate court that the trial court was in error? Why? Do you believe that your argument would prevail? (Assume that $Y$ had adopted a modern interest analysis approach to choice of law.) *See Hicks v. Graves Truck Lines, Inc.*, 707 S.W.2d 439 (Mo. App. 1986).

_____

## PROBLEM 4E-14. BEAUTIFUL HAWAII

Ramona Ross, a title contractor licensed and registered as such in State $X$, entered into a contract to install teak parquet floor tiles in a condominium project in Hawaii being built by the Kaanapali Corporation, a Hawaiian company. Orville Opel, a State $X$ resident, owned all of the stock in Kaanapali and signed the contract on its behalf in Ramona's $X$ office. After completing the installation, Ramona filed suit in $X$ against Kaanapali for extra expenses incurred as the result of Kaanapali's acceleration of the work schedule.

Kaanapali has asked for a summary judgment on the ground that Ramona was not a licensed contractor in Hawaii and by Hawaiian law, unlicensed contractors were barred from recovering for work done, either on the contract as such or on the basis of value given. The $X$ law also required a license and barred contract actions by unlicensed contractors. It permitted them to recover the value of the work done, however. $X$'s choice-of-law rules were patterned after Restatement (Second).

Kaanapali has offered to pay Ramona 25¢ on the dollar. Would you advise her to accept the settlement offer? Why? *See Nelson v. Kaanapali Properties,* 19 Wash. App. 893, 578 P.2d 1319 (1978); *Wood Bros. Homes, Inc. v. Walker Adjustment Bureau,* 198 Colo. 444, 601 P.2d 1369 (1979). *See also* Restatement (Second) of Conflict of Laws § 196 (1971).

## PROBLEM 4E-15. THE *LAURITZEN-ROMERO-RHODITIS* TRILOGY

Plaintiff, a Greek seaman who had joined the crew of M/V Proso in the Netherlands, was injured while the ship was anchored at a Maryland anchorage when he fell from the radar mast in the course of his employment. The ship, sailing under a Greek flag, was owned by a Liberian corporation, which, in turn, was owned by a Panamanian corporation. All of the officers and a majority of the crew were Greek citizens.

Plaintiff filed a claim in the United States District Court for Maryland under the court's maritime jurisdiction. What elements should the court taking into account in determining what law to apply? Why? *See Vlachos v. M/V Proso,* 637 F. Supp. 1354 (D.Md. 1986), applying what the court described as "the *Lauritzen-Romero-Rhoditis* . . . trilogy." *Id.* at 1361. *See, thus, Lauritzen v. Larson,* 345 U.S. 571 (1953); *Romero v. International Terminal Operating Co.,* 358 U.S. 354 (1959); *Hellenic Lines Ltd. v. Rhoditis,* 398 U.S. 306 (1970).

## PROBLEM 4E-16. THE CARD COUNTER

Mary Marvans, a Pennsylvania domiciliary, was participating in a blackjack game at a casino in Atlantic City, New Jersey, when the dealer called her a "card counter" and a "scum" and refused to let her play any more. Mary filed a diversity action for defamation in Pennsylvania against the Casino and the dealer.

By the law of New Jersey, plaintiff failed to state a claim for relief; by the law of Pennsylvania, she had. What law is likely to govern? Why? *See Lamelza v. Bally's Park Place, Inc.,* 580 F. Supp. 445 (E.D. Pa. 1984).

———

## PROBLEM 4E-17. A TRIP HOME

Mary Marvis, who resided with her parents in Delaware, and Ted Noun, who resided with his parents in Pennsylvania were both 17 years old and were attending a technical school in Delaware. During the term they became friends and on most days Mary would drive Ted from school to his home in Pennsylvania, a distance of about two miles. On one of those trips and while still in Delaware, Mary, who was driving negligently but not willfully so, ran her the car into a telephone pole. Ted was seriously injured. Ted and his parents filed suit in Pennsylvania against Mary and her mother, who owned the car.

Delaware had a guest statute which shielded Mary and her mother from liability for ordinary negligence. By Pennsylvania law, they would be liable. Pennsylvania followed a mix of interest and Restatement (Second) analysis in choice-of-law cases. What is the likely result of the action? Why? *See Cipolla v. Shaposka*, 439 Pa. 563, 267 A.2d 854 (1970).

———

## PROBLEM 4E-18. A BUSY PHYSICIAN

Mary Marsh, a New Jersey resident, was operated on in New York by Dr. Ned Noone, a New York resident. Ned provided post-operative care for Mary at his New York office for three years after the operation. At the end of that time, Mary learned that the operation had been completely unnecessary, and a year after that she filed a malpractice action in New Jersey against Ned. The New York limitation period on Mary's claim ran before she filed suit in New Jersey. The two-year New Jersey statute, however, did not start running until Mary discovered, or reasonably should have discovered, that she bad an actionable claim.

Ned's primary practice was in New York and he never saw Mary except in New York. He was licensed to practice in New Jersey, however, was a staff member of two New Jersey hospitals, and occasionally performed surgery in New Jersey.

Would you file suit for Mary suit in New Jersey on a wholly contingent fee arrangement? Why? *See Schum v. Bailey*, 578 F.2d 493 (3d Cir. 1978).

## PROBLEM 4E-19. "BRUSH YOUR TEETH TWICE A DAY"

Terry Tone, a State $X$ resident, had his wisdom teeth removed by a local dentist. During the procedure, his right lingual nerve was damaged causing a numbness in the right side of his tongue and giving him "electric shock-like" sensations in the same place. After the problem arose, Terry visited an oral surgery clinic in $X$ and was advised to consult with Dr. Barb Blake on her next scheduled visit to the clinic. He did this and Barb, a State $Y$ oral surgeon who specialized in repairing of damaged nerves, suggested the removal of the neuroma on his lingual nerve and the grafting of a section of the greater auricular nerve located in his neck below his left ear to replace the damaged nerve. Barb indicated that the procedure would leave a small area of numbness in Terry's temple area and possibly part of his ear, but that other patients who had undergone similar surgery had not had problems with that kind of numbness.

Barb rejected Terry's request that the surgery be done at the clinic in $X$. She indicated that it could only be done at her own clinic in $Y$. Barb operated on Terry in $Y$. She did not graft the greater auricular nerve as she had indicated, but rather, and without explanation, grafted an alternative nerve from Terry's neck onto the damaged lingual nerve in his tongue. Terry continued to have the same problems he had before the surgery, and in addition, the removal of the alternative donor nerve left him with a highly unpleasant sensation of strangulation and chocking when anything touched the area of his neck from which the donor nerve had been removed.

Terry filed a diversity action in the United States District Court for State $X$, and a jury awarded him $800,000 on a charge that applied the law of State $X$. The $X$ law of informed consent was more favorable to plaintiff than $Y$'s rule. Barb appealed on the ground that $Y$ law should have been applied. Assuming the $X$ court use of potpourri of modern choice-of-law theories, what result would you expect? Why? *See Blakesley v. Wolford*, 789 F.2d 236 (2d Cir. 1986).

## PROBLEM 4E-20. THE SWEDISH NIGHTINGALE

Myann Morgan, a Swedish opera singer, filed a product liability claim in the United States District Court for State $X$ against MS&D, Inc., a State $Y$ corporation that manufactured a hepatitis vaccine approved by the U.S. Food and Drug Administration. The vaccine, manufactured at a MS&D plant in State $Z$, was administered to Myann in Sweden, the drug having been sold to the Swedish government by MS&D. Plaintiff claims to have developed severe arthritis as the result of the two shots of the vaccine she received.

MS&D, asserting forum non conveniens, has moved for dismissal. As part of its motion, MS&D, which is not amenable to the jurisdiction of the Swedish court, pledged to submit to its jurisdiction and to pay any judgment entered against it by a court there. A remedy would be available in Sweden, although not as generous a remedy as a product liability recovery in this country.

Is it likely that the court will dismiss the action on the basis of defendant's motion? Why? Assuming that the claim is not dismissed and modern choice-of-law theory is applied, what law will govern the product liability issue? Why? *See Carlenstople v. Merck & Co.*, 638 F. Supp. 901 (S.D.N.Y. 1986).

--------

### PROBLEM 4E-21. CRASH IN SURINAM

Alyse Anchor, a Canadian domiciliary, was severely injured when the Bell helicopter she was flying crashed in Surinam where she was working temporarily for her Canadian employer, Chad, Inc. The helicopter, manufactured in Texas by Bell, Inc., a Texas corporation, had passed through several hands before Chad purchased it. Alyse filed an action in the United States District Court for Texas against Bell on a product liability theory for design and manufacturing defects and against Chad for negligent repairs and maintenance of the helicopter.

Texas recognized strict product liability. Canada and Surinam did not. Texas required equal contribution among joint tortfeasors. Canada also required contribution among joint tortfeasors, but in accordance with their percentage of fault. The law of Surinam on the contribution issue was not known. The damage rules of the three jurisdictions were the same except that substantially more damages were available for pain and suffering under Texas law than under the law of Surinam or Canada.

What law should the court apply to each of the issues? Why? *See Baird v. Bell Helicopter Textron*, 491 F. Supp. 1129 (N.D. Tex. 1980).

## PART F. ALTERNATIVE MODERN METHODS FOR RESOLVING NONFALSE CONFLICTS

### § 4.23    Comparative Impairment

### PROBLEM 4F-1. MARCHING TO GEORGIA

Sonya Sands, a New York resident, applied for and was issued a $100,000 life insurance policy by a Massachusetts insurance company. Sonya died 30 days after the policy was issued. The insurance company refused to pay the designated beneficiary, Sonya's husband, Tom, on the ground that Sonya had falsely stated in the insurance application that to her knowledge she was in good health. At that time, she knew she was suffering from terminal cancer.

Shortly after Sonya died, Tom moved permanently to a vacation home he and Sonya had owned in Georgia. Tom filed suit in Georgia against the insurance company, which did business in Georgia, alleging that the broker through whom the insurance policy had been obtained knew that Sonya suffered from terminal cancer and had advised her to fill out the application as she had. The insurance company moved to dismiss on the grounds that by the law of both New York and Massachusetts, the false statement in the application form invalidated the insurance policy, and oral evidence of statements made by the broker was not admissible. By Georgia law, oral evidence of the broker's statements would be admissible and, if believed, would be treated as a waiver of the insurance company's invalidation defense. Further, Georgia classified its admissibility-waiver rule as procedural while the other two states treated their rules as substantive.

Would you advise your client, Tom, to accept a $20,000 settlement offer from the company? Why? *See John Hancock Ins. Co. v. Yates*, 299 U.S. 178 (1936).

---

## PROBLEM 4F-2. A LIFE INSURANCE SCAM

Lean Literas, a New Jersey resident, applied for a $1,000,000 five-year term life insurance policy from Equis Life Company through a New York agent. Lean named his son, Joe, a California resident, and his wife, Mary, who lived with him in New Jersey, as beneficiaries. Lean signed the an application that contained several significant misstatements about his health, and the required medical history and examination were provided by a New York doctor whose report was inaccurate from start to finish in that it failed to report a variety of serious medical problems Lean had. In reliance on the misinformation, Equis issued the policy. Lean died four months later. Equis then investigated the claim and uncovered the falsehoods and omissions in the insurance application. When the insurer denied liability, Joe and Mary, who had moved to California, filed suit against Equis in that state.

Under the law of both New York and California, an insurer may avoid liability on a policy procured through material misrepresentation by the insured. Under New York law an insurer has an absolute right to rescind the policy on the ground that false statements or omissions about health are conclusively presumed to be material misrepresentations and Equis had an absolute right to rescind the contract. Under California law, an insurer has no absolute right to rescind; it permits the plaintiff to present plausible explanations for the falsehoods to the trier of fact, and the insurance company can then rebut them.

In light of *Bernhard*, § 4.23, *supra*, would the California court apply the New York or California rule? *See Lettieri v. Equitable Life Assur. Soc. of U.S.*, 627 F.2d 930 (9th Cir. 1980).

---

## PROBLEM 4F-3. SUICIDE OR MURDER?

Two California police officers filed a diversity action in California against two New York forensic pathologists, alleging that they had defamed plaintiffs. A prisoner in the custody of the two officers was found dead in his cell in a California jail. He was hanging by the neck from a mattress cover that had been looped over the cell's door jamb. (The prisoner was a New York domiciliary who was attending college in California.) The coroner in California found that the prisoner had committed suicide. Because of extensive publicity about the case, the Coroner, after making her initial finding, convened a nine-person coroner's jury to advise her. The panel found by 5-4 vote that the death was not a suicide but had been caused by an unknown person or persons. As was her right, the Coroner disregarded the panel vote and again indicated that in her opinion the death was a suicide.

At the request of the decedent's family, the two defendants agreed to conduct another autopsy. The body was flown to New York for examination there. At a press conference in New York the two reported their conclusion that the death was not a suicide. In their suit, the police officers alleged that they had been defamed during the press conference.

New York and California law differed on the extent of privileges available to defendants. Plaintiffs urged that New York law governed and defendants that California law did. What law would you expect the court to apply? Why? Is it likely that a court in New York would reach the same result? Why? *See Matter of Yagman*, 796 F.2d 1165, *modified*, 803 F.2d 1085 (9th Cir. 1986). *But see Carolco Pictures, Inc. v. Sirota*, 700 F. Supp. 169 (S.D.N.Y. 1988).

---

## PROBLEM 4F-4. ANYTHING GOES

Pamella Payne and James Johns, attorneys with the U.S. Department of Justice, filed a libel action in the United States District Court, District of Columbia, against the publisher and managing editor of a national daily newspaper, and the reporter who wrote the article in question. The article reported that the two plaintiffs had developed and implemented an unethical plan to force S.R. Calabres, a convicted felon with reputed organized crime connections, to cooperate with the government against other alleged organized crime figures, including Sam Snare, a Las Vegas casino owner. (The article reported a series of serious violations of S.R.'s rights in an effort to force him to cooperate.) The plaintiffs worked with the Justice Department in Washington,

D.C. during the period in question, but were working in California as members of the Department's San Francisco Strike Force when the articles appeared.

By statute in California, plaintiffs' alleged failure to demand a retraction within a specified period of time warranted dismissal of the suit. The other states involved had no such mandatory retraction provision.

Assuming that the court applied a "governmental interest" analysis, would defendants' motion to dismiss be granted? Why? Would the same result follow if the court applied California's comparative-impairment approach to choice-of-law cases? Why? *See Dowd v. Calabrese*, 589 F. Supp. 1206 (D.D.C. 1984).

## § 4.24　The Better Law and Professor Leflar

### PROBLEM 4F-5. AS LONG AS THEY ARE OUTSIDERS

Alyce Co., Incorporated and having its main office in State $X$, marketed birth control pills in the United States until the U.S. Food and Drug Administration directed that the pills be labeled to indicate possible severe side effects, including disabling thromnoembolic incidents. Alyce immediately withdrew the pill from the United States market and sold them without any warning through wholly owned subsidiaries in England and New Zealand.

Alyse was sued in state court in $X$ by three women, two from England and one from New Zealand, who used the pills over a three-year period. Each of the women suffered a disabling thromnoebolic incident that resulted in an impairment of leftside bodily functions, partial paralysis, and impairment of speech. The women sought compensatory and punitive damages for: (1) negligent manufacture and failure to warn; (2) intentional misrepresentation and fraudulent concealment; (3) breach of express and implied warranties; and (4) violation of strict liability in tort by unreasonably putting into commerce as a contraceptive a defective and dangerous product, made the more dangerous for failure to warn.

By the law of $X$, the plaintiffs could recover both compensatory and punitive damages on all counts. By the law of England, recovery required that negligence be shown and punitive damages are not available. New Zealand has an accident compensation system under which tort liability has been abolished. New Zealand law, which limited recovery to lost earnings and cost of medical care, requires that all claim be filed against the Accident Compensation Board rather than against Alyce.

What law would be applied by the $X$ court? Why? *See Bewers v. American Home Products Corp.*, 117 Misc. 2d 991, 459 N.Y.S.2d 666 (Sup. Ct. 1982), *rev'd on other grounds*, 99 A.D.2d 949, 472 N.Y.S.2d 637 (1984), *aff'd*, 64 N.Y.2d 630, 474 N.E.2d 247 (1984).

## PROBLEM 4F-6. VEHICLE OWNERSHIP

Mary Maas, a resident of State $X$ was injured in $X$ as she was crossing the street in front of her home. The car, driven by Ned Norman, an $X$ resident, had been purchased by him in State $Y$ several weeks before the accident. The $Y$ dealer had not complied with the title transfer rules in $Y$ and, thus, by $Y$ law, the dealer continued to own the vehicle, and was vicariously liable as owner. By $X$ law, the dealer would not be liable vicariously. $X$ followed the choice-of-law approach of Restatement (Second), and $Y$ followed the approach suggested by Leflar's choiceinfluencing considerations, with a very strong emphasis, however, on applying the better rule.

Assuming that Ned had neither insurance nor assets, as counsel for Mary, where would you recommend she file suit against the dealer? Why? *See Goetz v. Wells Ford Mercury, Inc.*, 405 N.W.2d 842 (Iowa 1987).

## PROBLEM 4F-7. COLLATERAL SOURCE DOCTRINE

Anna Andrews filed an action in Florida to confirm an arbitration award of $300,000 under the uninsured motorist coverage of a liability insurance policy she had purchased in Maine. Anna, a Maine resident, was injured in a two-car accident in Florida while she was vacationing there. The driver of the other vehicle, a Florida resident, was uninsured.

When Anna and her insurance company, Bolt, could not agree on the total amount of damages, the issue was submitted by the parties to arbitration in $X$. Bolt concedes that it owes Anna $236,000 but challenges $64,000 of the award on the ground that it represented $64,000 in medical expenses that had been paid by Medicare rather than by Anna. Florida's collateral source statute calls for the deduction of that amount from the $300,000, while Maine's does not.

Assuming that the Florida court takes a modern choice of law approach that combines "interest" and "most significant relationship" analysis, would Anna be permitted to retain the full $300,000? Why? *See Andrews v. Continental Ins. Co.*, 444 So. 2d 479 (Fla. App.), *review denied*, 451 So. 2d 847 (Fla. 1984).

---

## PROBLEM 4F-8. LEAVING THE KEYS IN THE IGNITION

Tom Tobbler, a 17-year old who lived with his parents in Wisconsin, was observed walking down the street by a police officer who was sitting in a police car outside of the police garage just prior to going off duty at midnight. The officer's partner had just left the police car to pick up his own vehicle so that he could drive himself and the other officer to their respective homes.

The officer who remained in the police vehicle got out and started to question Tom. He suspected that he was a juvenile who was out in violation of a local 10 p.m. curfew. While he was talking to Tom, his partner drove up, observed Tom being questioned, and left his vehicle to join in the interrogation. He left the engine running, however, and Tom immediately darted away, got into the officer's private vehicle, and drove off. Tom, driving at speeds in excess of 100 miles per hour, drove the car out of Wisconsin into Illinois where he lost control of the car and smashed into a car being driven by Vern Verlas, an Illinois resident. Vern was severely injured in the crash, and Tom was killed.

Vern filed suit in Wisconsin against the officer whose car had been stolen. By the law of Wisconsin, the act of leaving the vehicle running did not give rise to liability. By the law of Illinois, it was sufficient to give Vern a right to recover.

What would be the likely result of Vern's suit? Why? (Wisconsin generally follows Leflar's choice-influencing considerations in choice-of-law cases.) Is it likely that the result would be different had suit been filed in Illinois, which generally follows the Restatement (Second) choice-of-law approach? *See Lichter v. Fritsch*, 77 Wis. 2d 178, 252 N.W.2d 360 (1977), and *Dodge v. Stine*, 739 F.2d 1279 (7th Cir. 1984).

---

## PROBLEM 4F-9. APPLYING THE BETTER RULE?

Flora Franc, a Minnesota resident, was driving in Indiana en route to an Indiana lake where she planned to spend her vacation fishing. Joe Jossie, a New York resident, was driving a truck registered in New Jersey and owned by Clarice Trucking, a national operation with offices in all fifty states. Clarice's home office was in Massachusetts. The car driven by Flora and the truck driven by Joe collided on an Indiana highway. (Joe's trip had started in New York and he was en route to New Mexico.) Both drivers survived the crash. A few months after the accident, Flora had recovered sufficiently to take an ambulance plane to a hospital near her home in Minnesota. She remained in the Minnesota hospital for three months and was then confined to her Minnesota home for six months.

Flora filed suit against Clarice in Minnesota. Comparative negligence had been adopted by the Minnesota legislature. All of the other states possibly involved followed the common-law rule of contributory negligence. The parties stipulated that Joe was 80% and Flora 20% responsible for the accident. What is the likely outcome of Flora's suit? Why? *See Schwartz v. Consolidated Freightways Corp. of Del.*, 300 Minn. 487, 221 N.W.2d 665 (1974).

## PROBLEM 4F-10. COCAINE AND CONVERSION

Business Air, Inc., a State *X* corporation having its main office there, owned an aircraft that was covered by an insurance policy issued by Pure Insurance, Inc., a State *Y* corporation doing business in all fifty states. The policy contained a clause disavowing liability "for loss or damage due to conversion or embezzlement by any person in possession of the aircraft under a bailment or lease." The policy had been issued to Business Air by Pure's aviation manager, an independent State *Z* corporation. The policy was issued in State *Z*, delivered to Pure in *Y*, and forwarded by Pure to Business Air in *X*.

Business Air leased the aircraft to Clara Clear. The plane was destroyed when it crashed in *X* while Clara was flying it. At the time of the crash, Clara was attempting to smuggle cocaine into the United States and was intentionally flying below the minimum allowable altitude to avoid radar detection.

Pure denied liability for property damage under the "disavowal" clause on the ground that the lessee's use of the aircraft for illegal smuggling amounted to "conversion" of the aircraft. By the law of *X*, the clause did not apply because it was read as being limited to conversion in the criminal sense. *Y*'s courts viewed Clara's activities as misuse of the leased aircraft and, therefore, as a conversion as that word was used in the policy. The *Z* law on the issue is unclear.

Business Air wishes to sue Pure and has asked you where it should file suit. State *X* follows the choice-influencing considerations approach recommended by Leflar; *Y* uses the Restatement (Second) approach; *Z* follows the comparative impairment pattern enunciated by the California courts. Please advise Business Air and explain why you decided to give the advice you did. *See Business Air Center, Inc. v. Puritan Ins. Co.*, 593 F. Supp. 1048 (W.D. La. 1984).

----

## PROBLEM 4F-11. THE INTRAFAMILY EXCLUSION

Tim Tower, a Florida resident, purchased automobile liability insurance in Florida on a car registered and normally garaged there. The policy, issued by State Farm, insured Tim against all sums for which he legally could be required to pay as damages because of bodily injury suffered by others as the result of the operation of the motor vehicle. It excluded from that coverage, however, bodily injury to any member of Tim's family residing the the same household as Tim. (The exclusion was valid under Florida law, but invalid under Minnesota law.)

After the policy had been in effect fort several years, Tim and his wife were driving in Minnesota where they had gone for a summer vacation when there was a two-car accident in which Tim's wife, Sandy, was seriously injured. At trial in Minnesota, the jury awarded Sandy $400,000 in damages and determined that the other driver was 40 percent responsible for the accident and that Tim was 60 percent responsible. The damages, thus, were apportioned, and Tim owed Sandy $240,000.

State Farm, relying on the exclusion clause, refused to represent Tim or to pay the judgment. Tim filed an indemnification action against State Farm. The trial court found for Tim. It held that the Minnesota law applied and that the intrafamily exclusion clause was invalid.

What would be the result of State Farm's appeal? Why? (In choice of law cases, Minnesota follows the choice-influencing considerations developed by Leflar, with some substantial emphasis on the better rule consideration.) *See Hime v. State Farm Fire & Casualty Co.*, 284 N.W.2d 829 (1979), *cert. denied*, 444 U.S. 1032 (1980).

----

## § 4.25    The New Rules and the New Territorialism

## PROBLEM 4F-12. SNOWMOBILING

While snowmobiling in Pennsylvania, Bob Broome, a New York resident, hit a steel cable strung across an access road to the Antlers Hunting Club. He died instantly of a broken neck. Bob's personal representative filed a survival action against Antlers. By the common-law survival rules of both New York and Pennsylvania, Antlers was liable to the plaintiff. By the law of New York, however, damages in a survival action were limited to those accruing before death and did not include damages "for and by reason of death," except funeral expenses. Since death was instantaneous, plaintiff could prove neither pain and suffering by decedent nor medical expenses. Lost earnings, since they arose by reason of death, were also excluded under New York law. Pennsylvania's law permitted the personal representative to recover pecuniary losses to a decedent's estate as the result of lost future earnings.

Assuming that the Pennsylvania court applied a mix of modern theories to choice-of-law questions, what law is likely to be applied to measure damages? Why? As counsel for Antlers, how would you counter an argument based on Cavers' principled preferences that out-of-state plaintiffs should recover the more liberal benefits of the state of injury? *See Broome v. Antlers' Hunting Club*, 595 F.2d 921 (3d Cir. 1979).

---

## PROBLEM 4F-13. A TRAGEDY

Henry House wrote a book that purported to be a nonfiction report of the death in Chile of a young American citizen at the time of the overthrow of President Allende, and the efforts of the young man's wife and father to find out what had happened. The book (published in 1978) was a best seller; a paperback edition was issued in 1980; and a movie, "Missing," based on parts of the book, was released in 1982.

In 1983, the American ambassador to Chile at the time President Allende was overthrown, two of his aides, and the chief of the U.S. Naval Mission to Santiago at that time filed libel actions against the author, the publisher of the hardcover edition, the distributor of the paperback editions, and the filmmakers. They alleged that the book and film falsely accused them of ordering, or approving the order for, the murder of the young American. The plaintiffs all are domiciled in Virginia.

Suit was filed in the Federal District Court for the Eastern District of Virginia and transferred under § 1404(a) to the United States District Court for the Southern District of New York. The court found that federal venue in the libel action would not have been proper in the Eastern District of Virginia because Virginia's long-arm statute did not authorize jurisdiction over all of the defendants. (Only one of the defendants was subject to the jurisdiction of the Virginia courts under its long-arm statute.)

Virginia and New York impose one-year limitation periods on libel actions. New York, however follows the single publication doctrine, while Virginia recognizes the common-law rule that each sale give rise to a separate cause of action. By Virginia law, the author and original publisher are liable for authorized republications. By New York law, they are liable only if they exercised authority or control over the republication.

Does the single or multiple publication rule govern? Why? What substantive law should the court in New York apply? Why? *See Davis v. Costa-Gavras,*

580 F. Supp. 1082 (S.D.N.Y. 1984). *See also, McFadden v. Burton*, 645 F. Supp. 457 (E.D. Pa. 1986).

## PROBLEM 4F-14. A SAFE WORKPLACE

Fran Foraker, a State $X$ resident and an employee of Maintenance, Inc., was severely burned while cleaning an environmental control device at the Cyclops plant in State $Y$. The device was made in State $Z$ and sold there to Cyclops by Mikropul, Inc., a State $Z$ corporation doing business in all fifty states. Fran's employer, an $X$ corporation, provided maintenance services to factories in $X$ and $Y$, and had its only office in $X$. Fran filed a diversity action in the federal court in State $X$ against Cyclops and Mikropul, alleging an unsafe workplace.

Assume appropriate jurisdiction and a choice-of-law approach in $X$ that applied *lex loci delicti* unless a compelling governmental interest to the contrary existed.

Fran urges that $X$ rules governing safe workplaces should control rather than the law of the place where the accident happened or where the machine was manufactured. Is she likely to prevail? Why? *See Foraker v. Cyclops Corp.*, 605 F. Supp. 641 (N.D. Ohio 1985).

## PROBLEM 4F-15. THE OLYMPIC SPIRIT

As part of the effort to raise funds for the Olympic games, Congress authorized the United States Mint to produce commemorative coins for issue by the United State Treasury Department. As authorized under the Act, the Treasury assigned to plaintiff, a French company, the "exclusive right to market the Coins in all areas outside of the United States or its possessions except United States Military and Diplomatic establishments outside of the United States." Under that contract, the Treasury agreed that it would "prohibit domestic bulk purchasers from selling the Coins directly or indirectly to persons outside of the United States."

Defendant, a bulk purchaser for domestic sale, arranged for the resale of the coins in Germany in violation of the Treasury's agreement with plaintiff and in violation of a specific clause in defendant's contract with the Treasury. Defendant's arrangements to have the coins resold in Germany were conceived and executed in New York, and arrangements were made there to ship, receive payment, and cover up the transactions.

Plaintiff's suit in United States District Court for New York included claims for relief as a third party beneficiary of defendant's contract with the Treasury and for tortious interference with an advantageous business relation plaintiff had with the Treasury. Plaintiff's tort claim was based on a New York statute. Defendant urges that German law, as the place where the contract was allegedly breached and the tort occurred, should govern. Keeping in mind the developments in New York, including the decisions in *Neumeier v. Kuehner*, 31 N.Y.2d 121, 286 N.E.2d 454 (1972), and *Cousins v. Instrument Flyers, Inc.*, 44 N.Y.2d 698, 376 N.E.2d 914 (1978), what result would you expect on the choice-of-law issue? Why? *See Maison Lazard v. Manfra, Tordella & Brooks, Inc.*, 585 F. Supp. 1286 (S.D.N.Y. 1984).

----

## PROBLEM 4F-16. AMTRAK BEWARE

Belle Ballou was traveling on an Amtrak passenger train from her home in New York to visit her mother in South Carolina. Chad Canon, who was observably intoxicated, boarded the train in the District of Columbia. As the train was proceeding through Virginia, Chad, without any provocation, pulled out a pocket knife and slashed Belle twice in the hand and once in the face.

Belle filed a tort action against Amtrak in the United States District Court for the Southern District of New York. On the facts stated, Amtrak would not be liable under Virginia law and would be liable under New York law. Virginia follows the traditional "place of impact" rule in choice-of-law cases. New York looks to the law of the place having the strongest interest in the resolution of the particular issue presented, and when "the parties are from different states, this is usually the law of the place of injury (*i.e., lex loci delictus*), unless it can be shown that displacing this rule would advance the substantive law purposes of the states involved." *Wachs v. Winter*, 569 F. Supp. 1438, 1442 (E.D.N.Y. 1983).

Are there circumstances that would take the case out of the *lex loci delicti* rule? Why? *See German-Bey v. Nat'l R.R. Passenger Corp.*, 546 F. Supp. 253 (S.D.N.Y. 1982), *rev'd*, 703 F.2d 54 (1983). Would it make any difference if Belle were from Virginia or South Carolina rather than New York, or if she boarded the train in the District of Columbia? Why?

----

## PROBLEM 4F-17. THE FRENCH CONNECTION

After reading an advertisement in the New York Times, Grace Gown, a New York domiciliary, called a local phone number and made arrangements to rent a car in France for a three-week period for $600, the price to include "all necessary insurance." The agency through which she made arrangements was a wholly-owned subsidiary of Renault France, a French automobile manufacturer created by and owned by the government of France.

Grace took possession of the vehicle shortly after she arrived in France, and was injured when the car crashed into a telephone pole just outside of Paris. At the time, Grace was a passenger in the car, which was being driven by a friend from home with whom she was vacationing. The friend was listed in the rental agreement as an authorized driver.

Grace filed suit against Renault France in the United States District Court for the Southern District of New York. She claimed the right to recover against the "owner" of the vehicle under § 388 of the New York Vehicle and Traffic Law, that provided:

> Every owner of a vehicle . . . shall be liable . . . for injuries to persons . . . resulting from negligence in the use or operation of such vehicle. . . by any person using or operating the same with the permission, express or implied, of such owner.

Under French law, the owner of a rented vehicle was not liable for injuries caused by the negligent operation of the vehicle, and, in fact, the lessee was deemed the "owner" for liability purposes. Renault France had arranged for the insurance coverage usually obtained when cars were rented there.

Keeping in mind the developments in New York, including the decisions in *Neumeier* and *Cousins*, is it likely that Grace will be able to recover from defendant? Why? Under other modern choice-of-law theories, what result would you expect? Why? *See Boxer v. Gottlieb*, 652 F. Supp. 1056 (S.D.N.Y. 1987).

---

## PROBLEM 4F-18. VISITING FRIENDS

Jane Jarvis, a State $X$ resident, drove to State $Y$ to visit friends, Leona and Larry Libre, at their home. After she arrived, the three decided to ride in Jane's car to visit a battleship that was moored in $Y$. Jane and Larry sat in the front seat. Leona sat in the back. En route, Jane drove negligently and rammed her car into the car in front of it. Leona, who was pregnant, struck her stomach on the back of the front seat and was seriously injured.

State $Y$ had a guest statute that permitted recovery against the operator only if gross negligence was shown and it limited liability for prenatal injuries to cases in which the unborn child was viable at the time of the accident. State $X$ permitted guests to recover for ordinary negligence and did not require viability as a condition to recovery for prenatal injures. At the time of the accident, the child Leona was carrying was not viable. The child, Emily, was born with some injuries as a result of the accident.

Leona and Emily filed suit against Jane in the United States District Court for Rhode Island. Some Rhode Island cases had followed the choice-influencing considerations developed by Leflar, and some cases had patterned the choice-of-law analysis after the New York line of cases from *Babcock* (§ 4.19, *supra*) to *Neumiyer* (§ 4.25[C], *supra*). What would be the probable result of the suits? Why? *See Labree v. Major*, 111 R.I. 657, 306 A.2d 808 (1973).

-----

## PROBLEM 4F-19. SASKATCHEWAN TO IDAHO BUT NOT BACK

A Cessna, owned by Flying Services, Ltd., a Canadian company having its only office in Saskatchewan, Canada, was being flown by John James, the primary owner of the company, when it crashed in Idaho while carrying three passengers who resided in Saskatchewan. The plane was on the first leg of a round trip from Saskatchewan to Boise, Idaho, and back, and had stopped in North Dakota and Montana before crossing into Idaho and crashing. The passengers all worked for the same company and were on a business trip. The pilot and one of the passengers were killed in the crash. Two passengers survived. They were rescued after an intensive air search conducted by the Idaho National Guard.

The two passengers who survived and John's family and that of the deceased passenger received worker's compensation payments under the Saskatchewan Worker's Compensation Act. The Act insulated from third-party tort liability not only the worker's immediately employer, but all employers, such as Flying Service, which make payments into the fund. Under that Act, Flying Service was shielded. Idaho law contained no such shield.

Eighteen months after the crash, the families of the two who died filed wrongful death claims in Idaho against Flying Service and Cessna, Inc., the manufacturer of the plane, a Kansas corporation doing business in all states and in Canada. (The plane had been manufactured in Kansas.) The two survivors filed personal injury claims against the same two defendants, asserting the right to recover against Cessna on a strict liability theory. Saskatchewan required negligence as a basis for recovery. Idaho and Kansas had adopted the strict liability theory. Saskatchewan's wrongful death act contained a one-year limitation period. Idaho's had a two-year statutory period. Both had two-year limitation periods applicable to the claims by the two parties who survived the crash.

What is the likely result of the suits? Why? Would it make any difference which of the modern choice-of-law theories Idaho followed? Why? *See Johnson v. Pischke*, 108 Idaho 397, 700 P.2d 19 (1985).

[The following problems in this Part are not referred to in the main text, but may be used for additional practice.]

## PROBLEM 4F-20. AN UNDERINSURED MOTORIST

Sara Sams, a State $X$ domiciliary, was injured in State $Y$ when Tom Thiel, a $Y$ domiciliary, negligently rammed the car Sara was driving. Sara filed suit in $Y$ against Tom and against the Aries Insurance Company on a liability policy it had issued to her in $X$. She alleged that Tom was *underinsured* and that Aries was obligated under the *uninsured* motorist provision of the liability policy to pay the excess of the damages she suffered over the amount of Tom's insurance coverage. By $X$ law, the uninsured motorist provision did not provide coverage when the defendant was underinsured. $Y$'s law was to the contrary. Would Aries be liable for the excess? Why? (Assume that $Y$ applies Restatement (Second) analysis in choice-of-law cases.) *See Brawner v. Kaufman*, 496 F. Supp. 961 (E.D. La. 1980).

## PROBLEM 4F-21. A COMMUNITY DEBT?

Connie Durward owned 100% of the shares in the Cosine Fruit Company, a Colorado corporation. Several years after acquiring the stock, Connie married Dave Durward in Colorado where they both lived. Under Colorado law, the shares in the company remained Connie's sole property.

Shortly after the marriage, the Cosine company suffered financial reverses. Pacific Gamble Company agreed to continue to provide Cosine with inventory if Connie signed a note on which she would be liable personally along with the company. Connie agreed and signed a $50,000 note for the Company and for herself.

Several months later, Cosine and Connie defaulted on the note, and a few months later she and Dave moved to the State of Washington. Both found jobs, and their only assets were the salaries they earned after moving to Washington. By Washington law, that property was community property and not subject to claims for other than community debts.

Within a short time, Pacific Gamble filed suit in Washington against Cosine, Connie, and the Durward marital community to recover the balance due on the note. The trial court entered summary judgment against Cosine and Connie individually, but dismissed the action against the marital community. Pacific Gamble has appealed.

The court defined the issue presented as follows: "Is the creditor on a obligation incurred by one spouse in a foreign, noncommunity property state in which both spouses were domiciled, restricted in its recovery to the separate property of the obligor spouse, as the the term 'separate property' is defined by Washington law, after the couple moves to Washington?"

Washington follows the "most significant relationship" test of Restatement (Second). As counsel for Pacific Gamble, what argument would you make in an effort to persuade the appellate court to reverse the lower court? Is it likely that your arguments would prevail? *See Pacific Gamble Robinson Co. v. Lapp*, 95 Wash. 2d 341, 622 P.2d 850 (1980).

---

## PROBLEM 4F-22. MAP MAKER, MAP MAKER, MAKE ME A MAP

Wanda Will, who was an experienced commercial pilot for Braniff, was killed along with her son and father in a plane crash in West Virginia. Wanda was on vacation and flying her own Beechcraft at the time of the crash. She was en route from Dallas, Texas, back to her home in Danbury, Connecticut.

Jones & Co., a Colorado company, produced charts and maps that Braniff provided its pilots for their professional and personal use. The Jones charts, in use when the plane crashed, incorrectly described the equipment available at the West Virginia airport. It is conceded that errors in the charts caused the crash.

Representatives of the decedents filed wrongful death actions against Jones & Co. in the United States District Court for Connecticut. The claims were based on breach of implied and express warranties and strict product liability. The jury found for plaintiffs on both theories.

Jones & Co. has appealed on the ground that the trial court erred in applying the substantive law of Colorado. (Had West Virginia or Connecticut law been applied, defendant would not have been held liable.)

Assuming that in choice-of-law cases Connecticut followed the most-significant-relationship approach of Restatement (Second), is it likely that the appeal will succeed? Why? *See Saloomey v. Jeppesen & Co.*, 707 F.2d 671 (2d Cir. 1983). *But see Myers v. Hayes Intern. Corp.*, 701 F. Supp. 618 (M.D. Tenn. 1988).

## PROBLEM 4F-23. THE AIR FLORIDA CRASH

A Boeing 737 owned and operated by Air Florida crashed as it was taking off from National Airport, a major airport for Washington, D.C., but located in Virginia. The aircraft crashed into a bridge that connects Virginia and Washington, D.C., and struck cars driving over the bridge as well as the commuter train tracks that cross the bridge. Seventy people were killed in the crash, which was caused in part because the plane was inadequately de-iced before taking off. American Airlines, which provided the de-icing service to Air Florida at National Airport, allegedly failed to de-ice the plane properly.

Suits were filed in the District of Columbia, Georgia, Illinois, Maryland, Massachusetts, Pennsylvania, Texas, and Virginia, and transferred to the District of Columbia pursuant to 28 U.S.C. § 1407(a). Under § 1407(a), the transferee court applies the choice-of-law rules of the transferor states. Each of the three corporate defendants were incorporated and had their principal offices in a single state: Air Florida (Florida), Boeing (Washington), and American Airlines (Texas).

The District of Columbia, Illinois, Massachusetts, Pennsylvania, and Texas have discarded the old *lex loci delicti* test in favor of a more modern approach. Georgia, Maryland, and Virginia retain the older rule.

The parties urge several different approaches. Some plaintiffs urge that the law of the District of Columbia or Florida (where the pilots were trained) be applied. Both permit punitive damages. Air Florida and American urge that Virginia law apply (their actions having occurred there); Boeing urged that Washington law govern its possible obligation (it designed and manufactured the plane there). Virginia and Washington do not allow punitive damages. Several plaintiffs from states with laws that allow punitive damages urge that the law of their domiciles apply on the issue.

What analytical framework should the court establish to determine the appropriate law to apply to the punitive damage issue? Why? *See In re Aircrash Disaster at Washington, D.C.*, 559 F. Supp. 333 (D.D.C. 1983).

## PROBLEM 4F-24. AN INTERNATIONAL DISGRACE

Dr. Jose Filartiga and his daughter Dolly, citizens of Paraguay now residing in the United States, filed suit in the United States District Court for the Eastern District of New York under 28 U.S.C. § 1350, which grants district courts "original jurisdiction of any civil action by an alien for a tort only, committed in violation of the law of nations or a treaty of the United States."

Defendant, Juan Pena, a Paraguayan who was formerly Inspector General of Police that country, allegedly tortured and murdered Jose's son in retaliation for Jose's opposition to President Alfredo Stroessner's government. The court originally dismissed on the ground that violations of the law of nations do not occur when the parties are nationals of the country in question. The Court of Appeals reversed. At that point, Juan took no further part in the proceeding.

The court has asked for argument on the following questions: (1) Does the act-of-state doctrine call for dismissal?; (2) Does forum non conveniens theory warrant a dismissal?; and (3) What law governs the rights of parties, *e.g.*, Paraguay, International, New York, Federal, or some other law? *See Filartiga v. Pena-Irala*, 577 F. Supp. 860 (E.D.N.Y. 1984).

# PART H.   SOME ILLUSTRATIONS OF MODERN CHOICE-OF-LAW METHODS

## § 4.33    Property

### PROBLEM 4H-1. IF AT FIRST YOU DON'T SUCCEED

In 1955, Meg Maher, a New York resident, established a trust with March Trust Company of New York as trustee, with a life estate for her son, Edward. The trust provided that when Edward died, the corpus was to be held in trust for his son, Frank. On Frank's death, the trustee was to distribute the corpus as Frank appointed by will, or, failing the exercise of such power, to his distributees as in intestacy.

When Frank died in 1988, he was domiciled in California, and was survived by his widow, Helen, their daughter, Linda, and five children by previous marriages. Frank's will exercised the power by dividing the corpus into two trusts, one for benefit of his widow and the other for the benefit of Linda, with the latter to terminate 21 years after the death of the last survivor of his wife, Helen, his daughter, Linda, and Linda's children living at the time of Frank's death.

In the probate proceeding in California, a California statute was applied so that the trust to Linda terminated at the death of her mother, if not terminated earlier by Linda's death. The disposition in Frank's will violated California's rule against perpetuities and would have failed but for the change. Thus, the five children of Frank's earlier marriages would have taken a share by intestacy had the court not saved the disposition by changing it. (The change also saved the disposition under the New York rule against perpetuities.)

The five children who were excluded had received notice of the California probate proceeding, but did not appear. Six months later (after learning of the ruling), they applied to the California court for permission to appear on the ground that they had failed to do so inadvertently. Their application was rejected on the ground that it had not been inadvertence but a calculated strategic decision that led them to stay out of the California proceeding. The late appearance was deemed a general appearance. The New York Trustee did not appear in the California proceeding.

Assuming that New York is not constitutionally compelled to recognize and enforce the California decree, as a matter of choice of law is it likely that New York would recognize the decree? Why? Would the type of property being held in trust be an important consideration in the choice-of-law decision to be made? Why? *See Matter of Acheson*, 28 N.Y.2d 155, 269 N.E.2d 571, *cert. denied*, 404 U.S. 826 (1971).

———

## PROBLEM 4H-2. IS EXERCISE GOOD FOR YOU?

Charlotte Cole, who died domiciled in New York, established a testamentary trust consisting of stocks and bonds to be held by a New York bank as trustee. The trust provided life income to her son, Donald, and granted him an unrestricted power of appointment over any interest remaining upon his death. In the event Donald failed to exercise the trust, the property was to pass to his issue.

Donald, a long-term domiciliary of Indiana before his death, did not mention the trust in his will. After some bequests to designated charities, Donald's will contained a general residuary clause dividing the estate among his three children. The will was probated in Indiana.

The Internal Revenue Service, arguing that New York law governed, asserted that the trust property passed through Donald's estate and was subject to estate taxes. The executor of Donald's estate urged that Indiana law governed, and that the property, rather than passing through the estate, passed to the children directly from the trustee.

By statute in New York, a testate decedent is presumed to have exercised a power of appointment unless a different testamentary intent appears expressly or by necessary implication, and, thus, the property would be deemed to have passed through Donald's estate. Indiana's statutory law created the opposite presumption, *i.e.*, that absent a specific testamentary indication that the decedent intended to exercise the power, it is deemed unexercised, and the property would pass through the trust rather than the estate.

Assuming that Indiana follows adopted an interest analysis approach to choice of law, what result would you anticipate in the executor's resistance to the IRS claim? Why? Is it likely that the same result would be reached if the suit were tried in New York? Why? *See White v. United States*, 680 F.2d 1156 (7th Cir. 1982).

---

## PROBLEM 4H-3. PERPETUITIES

Sarah Scone, then a New York domiciliary, executed an irrevocable trust designating a New York corporate trustee and stipulating that she was to receive the income for life, with the remainder to her husband. If he predeceased her, the property was to be distributed as she appointed in her will. Failing a valid exercise of the power by will, the property was to pass to her next-of-kin pursuant to New York law.

Sarah's husband predeceased her. She died in England where she had lived for 48 years prior to her death. In her will, she attempted to exercise her power of appointment by designating an English trustee to take and hold the property for her two nieces for life, with the remainder to go to a designated English charity. Under the will's residuary clause, the trustee was to take the property on behalf of the English charity.

By New York law, her exercise of the power failed because the gift to the charity after the nieces' life estate violated New York's rule against perpetuities. By

English law, the exercise of the power was valid; if invalid, however, the property would pass under the residuary clause of the will.

As counsel for the English charity, would you recommend that it accept a settlement offer under which the nieces would take one-half of the property outright, with the other half passing to the charity on the nieces' death? Why? *See Matter of Bauer*, 14 N.Y.2d 272, 200 N.E.2d 207 (1964).

---

## PROBLEM 4H-4. ESCHEAT

In a dispute among the states about escheating unclaimed accounts payable held by Sun Oil Company, the United States Supreme Court exercising its "housekeeping" authority to resolve disputes among the states, held that:

(1) the State of the creditor's last known address is entitled to escheat the creditor's property, but

(2) if the last known address (i) is not reflected on the creditor's books, or (ii) is an a state that has no escheat provision for intangibles, the state of the debtor's place of incorporation may escheat and hold the property until another state comes forward and proves that it has a superior right.

*Texas v. New Jersey*, 379 U.S. 674, *final decree*, 380 U.S. 518 (1965).

Western Union, incorporated and having its principal office in New York, issues money orders throughout the country. If the payee cannot be located within 72 hours, the office of destination notifies the sending office, which, in turn, notifies the original sender. A refund in the form of a negotiable draft is given to the sender, who can either cash it or keep it for use in the future. Over the years, thousands of money orders are sent. In some cases, the payee does not appear, and Western Union is unable to locate the sender. Western Union, thus, holds a substantial amount of money that has not been claimed.

Pennsylvania filed an original action against New York in the United States Supreme Court, claiming all funds held by Western Union for unclaimed money orders sent from Western Union offices in Pennsylvania. The case would be very much *Texas v. New Jersey, id.*, except that Western Union's records did not contain the addresses of either the sender or the designated payee. Unless an exception was made for the situation presented, therefore, virtually all of the unclaimed funds would go to New York, the state of incorporation.

What arguments would you make in trying to persuade the Court to modify the *Texas v. New Jersey* holding? It is likely that your arguments would prevail? *See Pennsylvania v. New York*, 407 U.S. 206, *reh'g denied*, 409 U.S. 897 (1972).

---

## PROBLEM 4H-5. THE BANK SHARES

An action was commenced in State *X* by the *X* Commissioner of Revenue seeking to escheat unclaimed shares of stock and unclaimed cash dividends of the Allain Bank, an *X* corporation. Allain's records indicate that the last known addresses of some shareholders of record who had not claimed their property are outside of State *X*, in States *R, S, T, U,* and *V*, and in the United Kingdom. Of the states, only *R* and *S* have statutes by which all of the property in question would escheat. State *T* would escheat the cash dividends but not the shares of stock. States *U* and *V* would not escheat any of the property. The United Kingdom's escheat rules were not pleaded and proved in the proceeding. Assuming that notice of the escheat proceeding was sent by registered mail to the last known addresses of persons in States *R, T,* and *V* but not to persons in *S, U,* and the United Kingdom, what would be the result of the proceeding in *X*? *See State v. New Jersey National Bank & Trust Co.*, 117 N.J. Super. 38, 283 A.2d 543 (1971), *rev'd in part*, 62 N.J. 50 (1972).

## PROBLEM 4H-6. WHO IS DURPHY? WHERE IS DURPHY?

Alyse Arnold, the State *X* Escheator, filed suit against Bronson Corporation, a national company organized in *X*, in an effort to escheat shares of Bronson stock and unpaid cash dividends held by Bronson.

In December of 1951, Bronson issued 200 shares to Clarice Chad, whose address was listed on its books as being in State *Y*. Sometime later, Clarice transferred the shares to a person named Durphy. At present, Clarice has no recollection of Durphy's first name or where he lived at the time of the transfer. No request was made by Durphy to have the transfer noted on Bronson's books.

From April 1955 to August 1956, Bronson mailed dividend checks to Clarice. She returned them with a notation that she had sold the shares. Since that time, stock splits and stock dividends increased the 200 shares to 7,200, and unpaid cash dividends to $245,000. The shares remained listed in Clarice's name because it was the only name Bronson had.

The only evidence concerning the identity of Durphy was testimony that a Daniel D. Durphy of State *Y* was actively seeking to acquire Bronson shares from 1951 to 1954. That person, however, died in 1955 and the shares were not included in the inventory of his estate.

Bronson challenged Alyse's right to escheat the property on behalf of State *X*. As counsel for Bronson, what arguments would you make? Is it likely that your arguments would prevail? *See Nellius v. Tampax, Inc.*, 394 A.2d 233 (Del. Ch. 1978).

## PROBLEM 4H-7. GREEN STAMPS

Unredeemed trading stamps issued by retailers represent a tremendous potential source of escheatable property. Since there appears to be no method for identifying the addresses of persons holding the unredeemed stamps, is there any reasonable possibility that any state other than the state of incorporation of the company issuing the stamp can escheat their value? *See Sperry & Hutchinson Co. v. O'Connor*, 488 Pa. 340, 412 A.2d 539 (1980), in which the State sought to escheat more than $3,000,000 in unredeemed trading stamps generated in Pennsylvania sales.

---

## § 4.34    Contracts

### [B]—Party Autonomy

### PROBLEM 4H-8. ARBITRATION CLAUSE

Rose Rundle, a small Iowa steel processor, ordered some steel from Ted Thomas, a Louisiana steel broker. In turn, Ted ordered the steel from Sunwell Steel, Inc., a New York dealer. Sunwell mailed an acknowledgement of the order to Rose, who initialed the acknowledgement and returned it to Sunwell.

The acknowledgement contained the following arbitration clause:

> Any controversy or claim arising out of or relating to this order and its acceptance shall be settled by arbitration in accordance with the rules, then obtaining, of the American Arbitration Association (AAA); and judgment may be entered upon the award rendered in the highest court of the forum, State or Federal.

A dispute arose about the quality of steel Sunwell shipped, and Rose withheld a portion of the payment due. Sunwell filed a demand for arbitration with the AAA, including a request that the arbitration be held in New York. Rose responded, set forth her defense, and requested that Ottumwa, Iowa, be fixed as the site of the arbitration. Under AAA rules, if the parties are unable to agree on the location of the arbitration, AAA is granted the power to designate the place. In accordance with that rule, the AAA designated New York as the place for arbitration.

Rose then filed notice that it was withdrawing from the proceeding. In accordance with AAA rules, the arbitration went forward, and a $10,000 award was made to Sunshine. After giving appropriate noticeto Rose, Sunshine obtained a judgment from the New York Supreme Court and subsequently filed suit on it in Iowa.

By Iowa law, pre-dispute arbitration clauses were not enforceable. By New York law, such clauses were valid and enforceable. If Iowa take a Restatement (Second) approach to choice-of-law disputes, what is the likely result of Sunwell's claim? Why? *See Joseph L. Wilmotte & Co. v. Rosenman Bros.*, 258 N.W.2d 317 (Iowa 1977). *See also Southland Corporation. v. Keating*, 465 U.S. 1 (1984).

---

## PROBLEM 4H-9. COVENANT NOT TO COMPETE

Bowman Bolts, Inc., sold nuts, bolts, and other parts used in the production and repair of machinery. It was incorporated in Ohio, had its principal office there, and relied exclusively on its national sales force to market its products. Its sales force was made up of personnel who were independent contractors. They worked under contracts that were terminable by either party at will, and had nonexclusive territories.

The contract provided that for two years after they severed their relations with Bowman, sales personnel would not sell "Bowman-like" products to customers with whom they had dealt over their final two years with Bowman. The contract also provided that it was to be "construed in accordance with the laws of Ohio."

Over a two-year period, six members of Bowman's sales staff were induced to leave Bowman and join the staff of Cash, Inc., a Bowman competitor. Three of them, residents of Alabama, had worked for Bowman in that state and continued to do so for Cash. One was from Maryland and worked there as well as in the District of Columbia while with Bowman. Cash expanded her territory to include Virginia. Another member of the staff lived and worked for Bowman in Louisiana. Cash had him retain the same territory. Finally, a staff member who lived in and worked for Bowman in South Carolina became sales manager there for Cash and sold directly to customers as well.

Bowman filed a diversity action against Cash in the United States District Court for Ohio, alleging tortious interference with an advantageous contractual relationship. The case was transferred under § 1404(a) to the Federal District Court for South Carolina. The trial court there, applying the Ohio law as directed by the contract, found that a valid restrictive covenant had been violated by Cash and awarded Bowman $243,000 in compensatory damages and $250,000 in punitive damages.

Cash, conceding that it was liable under Ohio law, has appealed on the ground that the trial court erred in applying that law. As counsel for Cash, what arguments would you make to persuade the appellate court to reverse on the general liability issue? On the punitive damage issue? Why? What information would you need before developing your arguments? Why? *See Barnes Group, Inc. v. C & C Products, Inc.*, 716 F.2d 1023 (4th Cir. 1983).

## PROBLEM 4H-10. PESOS OR DOLLARS

Netty Noel, a United States citizen, moved to Cuba in 1946 to operate an export-import business there. While living in Cuba she met and married a Cuban citizen. Netty and her husband continued to live in Cuba until 1959 when they fled to the United States just after Castro took power.

In 1948 and again in 1950, Netty took out life insurance policies through the Havana office of Canadian Insurance Federation (CIF), which had its head office in Toronto and did business in the United States and 22 other countries. The policies contained a clause that "all sums payable under this policy— premiums proceeds, and loans—shall be paid at Havana, Cuba in the lawful currency of the United States of America."

Shortly after Netty obtained the second policy, Cuban law was changed. Prior to the change, although both Cuban pesos and United States dollars were legal tender in Cuba, *creditors* could determine which of the two to accept. With the change, however, *debtors* were given the option of paying debts in either currency, and creditors were required to accept persos on a one-to-one basis in extinguishment of obligations expressed in dollars. Both the dollar and the peso remained legal tender and Netty continued to pay premiums in dollars. A few years later, the Cuban government again changed the law. Only the peso remained as legal tender, and all debts contracted in dollars were required to be discharged in pesos. Netty continued to pay premiums in dollars and CIF to accept the payments despite new rule. When Castro took power in 1959, it became illegal for persons in Cuba to hold dollars. Since 1959, the peso has diminished in value until currently it is substantially worthless in terms of dollars. Netty has continued to pay premiums in dollars.

Netty filed suit in the United States District Court for the State *X* for a declaratory judgment that on her death, CIF will be required to pay the proceeds of the insurance policies to the designated beneficiaries (1) in dollars and (2) in the United States, where the beneficiaries live. As counsel for CIF, what arguments would you make to persuade the court to dismiss Netty's suit? Are your arguments likely to be persuasive? *See Johansen v. Confederation Life Association*, 447 F.2d 175 (2nd Cir. 1971).

## PROBLEM 4H-11. AN INSURABLE INTEREST?

Priscilla Point and Orville Orcutt, long-time residents of State *X*, entered into an agreement there to undertake a business venture in *Y* under the name,

Media S & M, Inc., with Priscilla to furnish the experience necessary to set up and run the company and Orville to provide the start-up capital.

As planned, Priscilla moved temporarily to State *Y* to set up the company office there. To protect his investment and with Priscilla's consent, Orville took out a $250,000 insurance policy on her life. Media S & M, Inc., was designated the beneficiary. He applied for the policy from his home in *X* and it was issued by a *Z* insurance company from its home office in *Z*.

About twenty days after the one-year incontestability clause in the insurance policy had run, an unknown person shot and killed Priscilla. Acting on behalf of Media, Orville claimed $500,000 from the insurance company, the policy having a double indemnity clause in case of accidental death. Under the law of *X*, the new company did not have an insurable interest that would support the claim and, thus, the policy was void ab initio. The insurance claim was valid under the laws of *Y* and *Z*.

What law would govern under traditional choice-of-law theory? Under modern choice-of-law theory? Why? *See New York Life Ins. Co. v. Baum*, 700 F.2d 928 (5th Cir. 1983).

---

## PROBLEM 4H-12. A FAMILY AFFAIR

Two ships, the Queeny (a chemical carrier) and the Corinthos (a tanker), collided in Pennsylvania waters causing the Corinthos to sink. Plaintiff's son, a crew member on the Corinthos and an Indian resident, was killed in the accident. Plaintiff's son-in-law (an Indian resident), purporting to act under a power of attorney plaintiff executed in India, employed Louisiana lawyers to represent her. At their recommendation, he signed a release in India in full settlement of plaintiff's claim in admiralty for the loss of her son. At the time of the settlement, plaintiff had become a permanent resident of Bangladesh.

Plaintiff filed suit in the United States District Court for the Eastern District of Pennsylvania to set aside the settlement and release. She claimed that the power of attorney was improperly executed and that, if it was properly executed, her son-in-law exceeded his authority in agreeing to the settlement and release of her claim. (Although the amount due under the settlement was paid to the son-in-law, plaintiff claimed that she had not received any of the money and, in fact, had not learned of the settlement for several years after it was executed.) She also claimed that the release had been improperly executed under Indian law.

The parties stipulated that (1) the issues presented involved two separate documents—the special power of attorney and the release—that raised independent issues of contracts, agency, admiralty, and wrongful death; and (2) the court had to determine whether the issues, viewed individually, raised problems of procedural or substantive law before it determined what law governed.

Would state or federal (maritime) choice-of-law rules govern the issues relating to the power of attorney? the release? Why? What additional information, if any, would you seek before answering the questions? *See Complaint of Bankers Trust Co.*, 752 F.2d 874 (3rd Cir. 1985).

———

## [D]—Commercial Law

### PROBLEM 4H-13. REPOSSESSION

Paula Purle, an enrolled member of the Navajo Nation residing on the tribal reservation, purchased an automobile from Model Motors, Inc., a State *X* dealer. She paid 20% of the purchase price and signed a note for the balance along with a security agreement that Model filed in accordance with *X* law.

Several months before Paula bought the car, the Navajo Tribal Council enacted a rule, approved by the Secretary of the Interior, requiring that as a condition precedent to a repossession on the reservation of chattels, (1) the buyer in possession must consent to the repossession; or (2) permission to repossess must be obtained from the Tribal Council. If a repossession in violation of the rule occurred, the buyer could recover an amount equal to the total credit service charge plus 10% of the debt unpaid at the time of repossession. Model repossessed the car on the reservation in conformity with State X's law but in violation of the Council rule.

In a suit in State *X* by Paula, is *X* constitutionally compelled to recognize the tribal council rule and award Paula the damages provided? Why? *See Jim v. CIT Financial Services Corp.*, 87 N.M. 362, 533 P.2d 751 (1975), *rev'g*, 86 N.M. 784, 527 P.2d 1222 (Ct. App. 1974).

———

### PROBLEM 4H-14. SELECTING THE FORUM

While Alan Alton, a State *X* domiciliary, was undergoing intensive combat training at an army base in State *Y*, he was severely injured when a hand grenade he was about to throw exploded prematurely. The grenade was manufactured in Texas by Bobble Bros., Inc., and contained a fuse produced in Kentucky by Char Co., Inc. The grenade, of course, had been purchased by the Department of Defense.

All of the states involved had adopted U.C.C. § 2-318, which extended a seller's warranty "to any natural person who is in the family or household of his buyer or who is a guest in his home if it is reasonable to expect that such person may use. . . .the goods. . . ." By the law of the place of injury, Y, Alan could not recover in warranty from the manufacturers in the absence of privity. By the law of Kentucky, Texas and State X, privity was not required as a condition to recovery in warranty.

Alan consulted you after the limitation periods had run in all four states on a product liability action. The only action possibly available is one in warranty. None of the states had decided a case under U.C.C. § 1-105. In other choice-of-law cases, however, State Y had followed traditional choice-of-law theories; State X had adopted Leflar's choice-influencing considerations theory, but had expressed doubts about its "better rule" aspects; Texas had adopted the most-significantrelationship test of Restatement (Second); and Kentucky had adopted a rule under which it applies Kentucky law to any issue having a substantial relationship—not necessarily the most significant relationship — to Kentucky. *See Foster v. Leggett*, 484 S.W.2d 827 (Ky. 1972).

As a lawyer admitted to practice in Y, you must determine where suit should be filed in the best interest of your client, Alan. What choice would you make? Why? *See Whitaker v. Harvell-Kilgore Corp.*, 418 F.2d 1010 (5th Cir. 1969), and 424 F.2d 549 (1970) (denying a petition for rehearing).

---

## § 4.35     Limitation of Actions

### [B]—Characterizing the Limitations Issue as "Substantive"

### PROBLEM 4H-15. LIMITATION PERIODS

The United States District Court for State X certified the following questions to the X Supreme Court:

> Which state's law provides the statute of limitations applicable to a negligence action brought in X by a Y resident against an X defendant for personal injuries resulting from an automobile accident in Z when:
>
> 1. The action would be time-barred under the X limitation period but not under the Z period; and
>
> 2. The X borrowing statute is inapplicable?

Assuming that X has adopted a generally modern posture in choice-of-law cases, what arguments would you make to persuade the court that the law of Z should control and, thus, that the case should be heard? Is it likely that your arguments would succeed? Why? *See Cameron v. Hardisty*, 407 N.W.2d 595 (Iowa 1987).

---

## PROBLEM 4H-16. RIGHT OR REMEDY

Claude Cranch, an $X$ resident, was fatally injured in $X$ while he was repairing a leak in a supply line at his employers plant. The machinery in the plant had been designed, manufactured, and installed by Denton Design, Inc., a company incorporated and having its only plant in State $Y$.

Claude's suit in $X$ against Denton was dismissed on the ground that the limitation period in $X$ had run. Claude then filed suit in $Y$. The $Y$ statutory period had not run and $Y$'s borrowing statute only accepted the bar of the place where defendant resided.

Denton argued that because by $X$ law, the $X$ time bar went to the right rather than the remedy, $Y$ either was constitutionally compelled to recognize the finality of the dismissal in $X$ or should recognize the $X$ time bar as a matter of choice of law. Is it likely that the $Y$ court will grant Denton's motion to dismiss? Why? *See Harris v. Clinton Corn Processing Co.*, 360 N.W.2d 812 (Iowa 1985).

---

## [C]—Modern Methods

## PROBLEM 4H-17. IN THE ABSENCE OF A FEDERAL LIMITATION PERIOD

In part of the litigation stemming from the Washington Public Power Supply System (WPPSS) bond issue, more than a thousand bondholders filed claims against the underwriters and vendors of the bonds. The claims were based on alleged violations of (1) § 10(b) of the Securities and Exchange Act of 1934; (2) the Racketeer Influenced and Corrupt Organizations Act of 1970 (RICO); and (3) violations of state laws relating to fraud and deceit, misrepresentation, and breach of fiduciary duties. Neither of the Federal statutes contained a limitation period. (In such situations, the federal courts apply state limitation periods.)

Some of the claims were filed in the United States District Court for New Jersey. Defendants moved to dismiss the § 10(b) and the RICO claims on the ground that they were not filed within the appropriate limitation period. The issues, thus, are (1) which state's limitation law should governed; (2) once that is decided, which of the several limitations periods within the state chosen would apply; and (3) what law will be use to determine when the applicable limitation periods started to run. The bonds were issued and payable in

Washington. Most of the plaintiffs came from New Jersey and many, although not all of the sales were made there.

New Jersey limitation periods are: (1) two years for violations of its securities statute; (2) six years for claims based on common law fraud; and (3) two years on civil actions predicated on the violation of its criminal law. Washington, the state in which the bonds were issued, had four-year limitation periods for (1) and (3) and a five-year period for (2).

What choice-of-law model will the federal court follow in determining which state's limitations to apply? Why? Once the court determines which state's limitation periods to apply, what pattern will it follow in determining which periods in that state should apply? Why? Once the court determines which limitation periods to apply, what law will be applied to determine when the selected limitation period starts to run? Why? *See Kronfeld v. First Jersey Nat. Bank*, 638 F. Supp. 1454 (D.N.J. 1986).

# Chapter 5

# THE CONSTITUTION AND CHOICE OF LAW

## § 5.02    Emergence of the Modern Position

### PROBLEM 5-1. HOW FAR *DICK*?

An automobile liability insurance policy issued in State $X$ by an $X$ insurance company to Rob Root, a resident of $X$, provided that a condition precedent to the company's liability was that the insured give notice of all accidents "as soon as practicable" after the event. The $X$ Court had construed the provision as requiring notice if a person of ordinary and reasonable prudence would believe that liability might arise as the result of an accident. By statute in State $Y$, such notice requirements were not effective against a person injured by an insured as long as notice was given to the insurance company before the injured person recovered a judgment against the insured.

Clara Colot, a resident of $Y$, was injured when her car veered off a $Y$ highway and went into a ditch. She claimed that her car was forced off the highway by a car being driven by Rob. Rob filed an accident report with the $Y$ State Police, but because there had been no collision, he did not inform his insurance company. Clara's insurance company sent a representative to interview Rob concerning the accident, and Rob signed a statement for the representative. Several months later, Clara filed suit in $Y$ against Rob. Rob then notified his insurance company for the first time. Assuming that the insurance company is not liable under the law of $X$, is the $Y$ court constitutionally required to apply the $X$ rule and hold that the insurance company is not liable to Clara? *See Security Insurance Group v. Emery*, 272 A.2d 736 (Me. 1971).

----

## § 5.03    The Modern Position: Minimal Scrutiny

### PROBLEM 5-2. THE HORNS OF BLACKMUN, J.'S DILEMMA

In a portion of his dissent in *Nevada v. Hall*, omitted above, Justice Blackmun said "[i]f respondents were forced to seek satisfaction of their judgment in Nevada, that State, of course, might endeavor to refuse to enforce that judgment, or enforce it only on Nevada's terms." Assume that at the time Hall and the others filed suit against Nevada, the only assets Nevada had outside of the State were $5,000,000 in deposits in various banks and that on advice of counsel, the State transferred all of the money to Nevada banks as soon a suit was threatened. Plaintiffs have now retained you to help them realize on the $1,150,000 judgment.

Pointing to the quoted language in Justice Blackmun's opinion, the Nevada Attorney General has offered to settle for $200,000. How would you respond to your clients' inquiry concerning the wisdom of accepting the offer? Why? *See Fauntleroy v. Lum,* § 7.07, *infra.*

---

## PROBLEM 5-3. IN HOT PURSUIT

Following a bank robbery in Virginia, an Arlington County police officer driving a police car chased a car that fit the description of the car in which the robbers had escaped. He followed the car into the District of Columbia and gave chase with lights flashing and siren going. The chase took the officer through the heart of the District at speeds exceeding 80 miles per hour, more than 50 miles over the speed limit. The robbers' vehicle went through a red light and smashed into a car being driven carefully by Sarah Shaw. Sarah was not seriously injured, but her husband, Sean, who was a passenger in the car, lost both legs as the result of the accident.

Sarah and Sean, employees of the federal government who worked in the District and lived in Maryland, filed suit in the District of Columbia against Arlington County. They alleged that the police officer had received inadequate training at the Virginia Police Academy and that he had violated the rules of both Virginia and the District of Columbia in conducting a high speed chase in a manner that endangered innocent bystanders.

By Virginia law, Arlington County had sovereign immunity and, thus, was immune from liability. The District of Columbia had no similar sovereign immunity law. At trial, the County was held liable to Sean for $4 million and to Sarah for $350,000. The County appealed on both full faith and credit and comity grounds, arguing that footnote 24 in *Nevada v. Hall,* § 4.20, *supra* was intended to apply to cases like the one before the court.

In essence, the County argued that the denial of sovereign immunity in this case would impede its law enforcement ability. Is it likely that the County will prevail in its appeal? Why? Would the case be treated differently if plaintiffs were residents of Virginia rather than Maryland? Why? *See Biscoe v. Arlington County,* 738 F.2d 1352 (D.C. Cir. 1984), *cert. denied,* 469 U.S. 1159 (1985); *Bays v. Jenks,* 573 F. Supp. 306 (W.D. Va. 1983).

---

## PROBLEM 5-4. RECRUITING AN ATHLETE

Clarice Cole, who was living with her family in State *Y*, was recruited to play basketball for State *X* University (SXU). Under the terms of the agreement, as long as Clarice remained academically eligible to compete, she would receive room, board, tuition, and books for four years, as well as proper medical care if she was injured while playing basketball.

She attended SXU and played basketball for the first two years. During the middle of the second year, Clarice broke her wrist in a game. She alleges that the SXU medical staff provided no medical treatment, but merely taped the wrist before each game. She completed the season and then entered the hospital in $X$ to have the wrist repaired. Because of the delay, the bones did not knit properly and Clarice has lost most of the strength in her hand.

She filed suit in State $Y$ against SXU, alleging breach of contract by virtue of its failure to provide proper medical treatment as promised. Among other things, SXU pleaded sovereign immunity and the bar of the statute of limitations. By the law of $X$, the University was immune from suit as a state agency. By the law of $Y$, the University would not be immune.

$Y$'s had a two-year limitation period on the claim and suit was filed more than two years after it arose. Thus, the claim would be stale unless the limitation period was tolled by the fact that SXU was located outside of $Y$ for the entire statutory period. The tolling statute provided that "[w]hen a cause of action accrues against a person, if he is out of the state . . . the period of limitation for the commencement of the action . . . does not begin to run until he comes into the state. . . ."

Assume that (1) SXU's activities in $Y$ incident to recruiting Clarice were sufficient contact to make it amenable to process there; and (2) $Y$'s approach to choice of law tended to be an eclectic mix of modern theories. As counsel for SXU, what arguments would make to persuade the court on both the sovereign immunity and tolling issues? Why? Is it likely that your arguments will prevail? *See Barile v. University of Virginia*, 30 Ohio App. 3d 190, 507 N.E.2d 448 (1986). On the "tolling" issue, *see Bendix Autolite Corp. v. Midwesco Enterprises, Inc.*, § 5.05, *supra*.

---

## PROBLEM 5-5. YSU

Maud Mabel, a private lender in State $X$, filed suit in $X$ against $Y$ State University (YSU), a public institution, seeking to recover for the breach of two "reverse purchase" agreements she had made with YSU. Under the agreements, YSU sold securities to Maud and agreed to repurchase them on a specified date for the original purchase price plus interest. In essence, the transaction was a loan from Maud with the securities as collateral.

The transactions were arranged by phone calls to Maud in $X$ from YSU's financial officer in $Y$, and were confirmed by mail. As soon as she received a written confirmation, Maud would deposit funds to YSU's account with an $X$ bank and, in turn, receive the securities from the $X$ bank. Maud alleged that YSU had refused her tender of the securities for repurchase and that she had been forced to sell them on the market for $500,000 less than YSU had promised to pay.

By statute in *Y*, YSU, a state agency, is only amenable to suit in a specified county in *Y* and "shall have sovereign immunity from suit in any other place within or without State *Y*." By the law of *X*, institutions such as YSU have no sovereign immunity.

As counsel for YSU, would you move for dismissal on grounds of sovereign immunity? Why? Is such a motion likely to succeed? Why? If the motion fails, what other argument would you make for dismissal? If the *X* court renders judgment for Maud, and YSU had no assets in any place but *Y*, could you successfully resist enforcement of the judgment in *Y*? *See Ehrlich-Bober & Co. v. University of Houston*, 49 N.Y.2d 574, 404 N.E.2d 726 (1980).

---

## § 5.04     The Modern Position: Problems

### PROBLEM 5–6. THE SERVICE LETTER

Alice Able was vice president of Bobble Brewers, Inc., when the company was taken over by Clitz Brewery, Ltd., a national company incorporated and having its main office in State X. At the time of the take-over, Clitz hired Alice as the industrial relations manager for its State Y plant. (Alice had been living in Y and working there at Bobble's plant.) Seven years later, Alice was promoted to plant manager of the Y plant, and eight years thereafter was promoted again to plant manager of a much larger Clitz plant in State Z. After working in Z for five years, Alice was offered a position at the Clitz home office in X as vice president of plant operations for the entire company. Shortly after Alice moved to X, a dispute arose between Alice and the company President, Don Daniels, and Alice was dismissed.

She returned to State Z for a few months and then settled in State Y. Shortly after arriving in Y, Alice requested a "service letter" from Don "setting forth the nature and character of services [she had] rendered and stating for what cause [her] service had ended". Such a "service letter" was required by a Y statute and the failure to send one on request was a misdemeanor. The Y court had held that a civil right of action existed for violation of the statute. Neither X nor Z had comparable legislation. Don failed to send the requested letter. Alice filed suit in X and received a jury verdict of $1 in real damages and $400,000 in punitive damages. The trial court charged the jury in accordance with the Y law.

You have been asked by Clitz to advise it concerning the wisdom of an appeal in face of Alice's offer to settle for $200,000. What advice would you give? Why? What additional information would you need before giving the requested advice? *See McCluney v. Jos. Schlitz Brewing Co.*, 649 F.2d 578 (8th Cir.), *aff'd*, 454 U.S. 1071 (1981)(Justice Stevens opinion in dissent).

# PART E.   THE DISCRIMINATORY FORUM

[The following problems in this Part are not referred to in the main text, but may be used for additional practice.]

## PROBLEM 5-7. CAN TRANSITORY ACTIONS BE LOCALIZED?

Jane Josse lived and worked in State $X$. She was injured on the job by the malfunctioning of a machine owned by her employer, Bee, Inc., a company with plants in States $X$, $Y$ and $Z$. Under an $X$ statute, employers are liable to employees injured as the result of machinery malfunctions despite the fact that the employee's carelessness contributed substantially to the injury. The $X$ statute contained a proviso that "any action brought under this statute must be brought in a court of competent jurisdiction in this state and not elsewhere." Jane, who remained an $X$ resident, filed suit against Bee in $Y$ asserting her right to recover under the $X$ statute.

Does the Full Faith and Credit Clause require that $Y$'s courts honor the localizing provision in the $X$ statute? *See Tennessee Coal, Iron & R.R. Co. v. George*, 233 U.S. 354 (1914) and *Atchison, Topeka & Santa Fe Ry. v. Sowers*, 213 U.S. 55 (1909).

Would the Constitution require the same result if Alice resided and worked in a foreign country which had a statute identical with that in $X$ and she sued in $Y$? *See Slater v. Mexican Nat'l R.R. Co.*, 194 U.S. 120 (1904).

## PROBLEM 5-8. THE BONDING COMPANY

Torsion, Inc., a general contractor incorporated in $X$, entered a contract with State $X$ to construct a large classroom building on the campus of $X$ State University (XSU). As required by $X$ statute, Torsion provided a performance and payment bond. The bond was issued by U.S.F. & G., a national bonding company. When Torsion failed to pay for supplies from ALV Supplies, Inc., a State $Y$ company, ALV filed suit in $Y$ against U.S.F. & G. A clause in the bond, required by $X$ statute, provided that suit on the bond could be brought "only in the district court of State $X$ in the district in which the construction contract was to be performed."

Is the $Y$ court constitutionally bound to dismiss ALV's suit? Why? *See State ex rel. U.S. Fid. & Guar. v. Mehan*, 581 S.W.2d 837 (Mo. App. 1979).

————

## PROBLEM 5-9. WHAT IS A TRANSITORY ACTION?

Raoul Randall filed a diversity action in the United States District Court for State *X* against his former employer, ARAMCO, alleging wrongful discharge. Raoul worked for ARAMCO for seven years in Saudi Arabia and all of the acts involved occurred there. By Saudi law, the Saudi Labor Commission had exclusive authority to hear wrongful discharge cases. Both parties concede that Saudi substantive law governed the rights and duties of the parties. They disagree, however, about the exclusivity clause in the Saudi law.

As counsel for Raoul, what reasonable arguments would you make in an effort to persuade the court to ignore the exclusivity clause? Why? Do you believe it likely that your arguments would prevail? Why? *See Randall v. Arabian American Oil Co.*, 778 F.2d 1146 (5th Cir. 1985), *reh'g denied*, 782 F.2d 1040 (1986).

————

## PROBLEM 5-10. REVERSING THE WHEEL

Assume that the grinding wheel mentioned in *Wells* had (1) been manufactured in Alabama and (2) caused injury in Pennsylvania, and (3) that suit was filed in Alabama 18 months after the injury. Thus, Alabama's two-year statute would permit recovery but Pennsylavania's one-year "substantive" statute would bar relief. Would it be constitutional for Alabama to grant relief despite the fact that the running of Pennsylvania's time period extinguished the right in Pennsylvania? Why?

————

## PROBLEM 5-11. THE XYZ AFFAIR

Boone Brokers, Inc., organized in State *X* and having its principal office there, operated real estate offices in 30 states, including State *Y*. Boone failed to comply with the statutory requirement of *Y* that real estate brokers operating there either obtain a *Y* license or forfeit access to its courts. Boone filed suit in *Y*, alleging that Chad Channing, a *Y* resident, had breached an exclusive brokerage contract entered into and to be performed in State *Z*, a state in which Boone was licensed. Would the *Y* court be acting constitutionally if it dismissed Boone's claim on the ground that it had failed to obtain a *Y* brokers license? *See Sun Sales Corp. v. Block Land, Inc.*, 456 F.2d 857 (3d Cir. 1972). Does the decision in *Bendix* call for a reexamination of the issue raised in *Sun Sales*?

# Chapter 6

# FEDERAL/STATE CONFLICT OF LAWS

## § 6.03    FEDERAL LAW OR STATE LAW

### PROBLEM 6-1. WHAT LAW GOVERNS FEDERAL PAPER I?

A check for $100, payable to the order of Charles Chad for services rendered, was drawn by the Treasurer of the United States through the Federal Reserve Bank of Philadelphia and mailed to Charles. He never received it. An unknown person endorsed the check and presented it to the Philadelphia branch of a national department store, which cashed it. The store endorsed the check over to the Clearfield Trust Company, which accepted it as agent for the purpose of collection and endorsed it as follows: "Pay to the order of Federal Reserve Bank of Philadelphia, Prior Endorsements Guaranteed." The check was paid and the store's account credited. Neither the store nor Clearfield had any knowledge or suspicion of the forgery, and each acted in good faith.

When the facts came to light, the Federal Reserve filed suit against Clearfield on its endorsement and the store intervened. Under Pennsylvania law, the Federal Reserve would be barred from recovering because it had unreasonably delayed giving notice of the forgery to Clearfield. Under the federal rule, however, the Federal Reserve would prevail. What law is likely to be applied? Why? If federal law were applied, what would be the source of that law? *See Clearfield Trust Co. v. United States*, 318 U.S. 363 (1943).

---

### PROBLEM 6-2. WHAT LAW GOVERNS FEDERAL PAPER II?

Rhoda Rosa owned one hundred H.O.L.C. bearer bonds, with payment guaranteed by the federal government. The bonds were due to mature in ten years, but were called early as permitted by the terms of the bonding agreement. A few days after the bonds were called, they disappeared and did not surface again for four years when Sam Sample presented them for payment to Trent State Bank in *X*. Trent forwarded the bonds to the Federal Reserve Bank located in State *Y*. It returned the face value to Trent in ordinary course. Trent deposited the proceeds in Sam's account and Sam spent the money.

Both Sam and Trent refused Rhoda's demand that they reimburse her for the value of the bonds. She comes to you for advice. Your investigation reveals that (1) Sam has sufficient assets to pay a judgment; (2) under the laws of *X* and *Y*, Rhoda was entitled to recover the value of the bonds because Sam and Trent were aware that the bonds were overdue when they were presented to the Federal Reserve Bank; (3) under federal law, the defendants' good faith overrode the staleness and Sam and the bank would prevail; and (4) Rhoda was a domiciliary of State *Z*.

What advice would you give Rhoda about whether and where to file suit? Why? *See Bank of America v. Parnell*, 352 U.S. 29 (1956).

———

# Chapter 7

# JUDGMENTS

## PART A. BASIC PRINCIPLES

## § 7.01 Finality in the Rendering State

### PROBLEM 7A-1. ISSUE PRECLUSION AFTER APPEAL

Nora Neth, the owner of a gasoline service station, and Pete Pall, a customer of Nora's, filed suit in State $X$ against Angela Archer for injuries they suffered when gas pumps Angela had leased to Nora exploded and destroyed Pete's car and Nora's service station. The suit was based on dual theories of negligence and strict product liability.

The trial court found for Angela, holding that evidence of plaintiff's contributory negligence destroyed the negligence count and that evidence of abnormal use destroyed the strict product liability count. Nora and Pete appealed to the $X$ Supreme Court which affirmed on the grounds that (1) the record contained no evidence that Angela was negligent; and (2) as a matter of law, a lessor of equipment was not liable in strict product liability.

Nora and Pete then filed suit in State $Y$ against the Goode Tire and Rubber Company alleging that the explosion resulted from a leak in a defective hose Goode had supplied to Angela. Again the dual grounds of negligence and strict product liability were alleged. Is State $Y$ constitutionally bound to dismiss the suit against Goode? *See Speyer, Inc. v. Goodyear Tire and Rubber Co.*, 222 Pa. Super. 261, 295 A.2d 143 (1972).

---

### PROBLEM 7A-2. IS THE FEDERAL GOVERNMENT BARRED?

The United States Attorney General filed suit in the United States District Court for State $X$, attacking the multi-member ward system for electing members of the City of Alyse school board. It was alleged that the electoral system violated the Voting Rights Act, 42 U.S.C. §§ 1971 and 1973. The defendant school board moved to dismiss on the ground that the action was barred by virtue of a prior determination that the system did not violate the Voting Rights Act in a suit in federal court filed against the school board by a group of parents. Should the motion to dismiss be granted? Why? *See United States v. East Baton Rouge Parish Sch. Bd.*, 594 F.2d 56 (5th Cir. 1979).

## PROBLEM 7A-3. PRECLUDING THE VICTIM'S SPOUSE?

Dr. Karla Kane, a State X physician, was convicted in X of the second degree murder of Larry Lane, one of her patients, by virtue of having shot him 4 times. By X law, such a conviction required a finding of "an unlawful killing with malice aforethought." After Karla appealed and lost, Mamie, Larry's widow, brought a wrongful death action against Karla in X and won a default judgment for $2,000,000.

Mamie then filed suit in State Y against the Downs Insurance Company, which had issued a $5,000,000 liability insurance policy to Karla. Mamie claimed that the policy covered Karla's action in killing Bob. Downs argued that (1) the policy specifically exempted coverage for acts committed with "intent to cause personal injury"; (2) an X statute prohibited insurers from covering losses caused by the wilful act of the insured; and (3) Karla's conviction in X precluded Mamie from relitigating the issue of the wilfulness of Karla's act. Mamie conceded that the policy did not cover wilful acts. She argued, however, that she should be permitted to prove that Karla had not acted wilfully. Would you advise Downs to settle for $500,000? Why? Would X or Y preclusion rules be applied? Why? *See Clemmer v. Hartford Ins. Co.*, 135 Cal. Rptr. 848 (Cal. App. 1977), *rev'd*, 22 Cal. 3d 865, 587 P.2d 1098 (1978).

## PROBLEM 7A-4. DOUBLE JEOPARDY?

Edna Ernest was acquitted in State X of having murdered her father, Bob Beard, a domiciliary of State Y. Shortly after the acquittal, Edna's sister, Clarice Chad, asked the Y probate court to bar Edna from taking any property under Bob's will on the ground that Edna had wilfully murdered him.

In an earlier case, the Y Supreme Court had held that a person convicted of murdering his wife was precluded from relitigating his role in his wife's death in a later probate proceeding. Edna urged that such a preclusion operated in her favor and that her acquittal barred relitigation of the question whether she had murdered her father. Is it likely that Edna's argument would prevail? Why? Would the X or Y preclusion rules be applied? *See Matter of Estate of Congdon*, 309 N.W.2d 261 (Minn. 1981). *See also* Uniform Probate Code § 2-803.

## PROBLEM 7A-5. A TAIWANESE CONVICTION

Jong, a Taiwanese national living in State $X$, killed his wife in $X$. He then fled to Taiwan, surrendered to the authorities there, and was tried and convicted of homicide by a Taiwanese court. Jong was the primary beneficiary of a $100,000 life insurance policy on his wife's life. Tang, Jong's mother-in-law, was the alternate beneficiary.

Tang filed suit in $X$ against Aetna Life Insurance Company to collect on the policy on the theory that Jong was barred from collecting by virtue of his conviction in Taiwan. Jong, still in prison in Taiwan, received notice of the $X$ proceeding and appeared by counsel. An $X$ statute provides:

> No person who has unlawfully and intentionally caused the death of a decedent shall be entitled to succeed to any portion of the estate. For the purposes of this section, a conviction or acquittal on a charge of murder or voluntary manslaughter shall be a conclusive determination of the unlawfulness or lawfulness of a causing of death.

Jong's counsel tendered evidence that Jong was temporarily insane when he killed his wife and, thus, should not be barred by the statutes from collecting the insurance proceeds. Tang moved to bar the evidence on the ground that Jong was precluded by the Taiwanese conviction from claiming that he did not unlawfully and intentionally cause his wife's death.

As counsel for Jong, what facts would you attempt to present in an effort to meet Tang's argument? What arguments would you make? *See Haung Tang v. Aetna Life Ins. Co.*, 523 F.2d 811 (9th Cir. 1975).

## § 7.03    Whose Law of Finality?

## PROBLEM 7A-6. ARE YOU ENTITLED TO ONE FREE BITE?

A State $X$ statute requires that all milk dealers be licensed periodically and empowers the State Milk Markets Commission to deny a license if the applicant (1) is not qualified by character to conduct the business; (2) has been a party to a combination to fix prices contrary to law; or (3) has been convicted of a felony.

While its application for the extension of its $X$ license was pending, Farmland Dairies was convicted in State $Y$ of fixing prices illegally there. Under $X$ law, the $Y$ conviction would (1) be admissible in the Commission proceeding, (2) be conclusive proof of the underlying facts, and (3) warrant denial of the application. The $Y$ judgment, however, contained a provision that it was not to be used for evidentiary purposes in any civil proceeding.

Is the $X$ Commission under a constitutional compulsion to refrain from applying its own rules in considering whether to extend Farmland's license? Why? *See Farmland Dairies v. Barber*, 65 N.Y.2d 51, 478 N.E. 2d 1314 (1985).

---

## § 7.05    Recognition of Judgments from Foreign Nations

### PROBLEM 7A-7. SEPARATION OF POWERS

In a constitutional system which by and large contemplates a division of functions and which vests the conduct of foreign affairs primarily in the executive branch, often with the advise and consent of the Senate, should the United States Supreme Court be empowered to establish a reciprocity rule governing the recognition of judgments rendered in other countries? Should such questions be certified to the State Department for a statement of the applicable rule much in the way questions are referred to state courts in Eric and other situations? In view of the fact that the United States Supreme Court has adopted a reciprocity rule for the recognition of judgments from other countries, should that rule be binding on state courts or, in a federal system, should the state courts be free to adopt other rules for the recognition of judgments of foreign nations?

---

### PROBLEM 7A-8. RECIPROCITY IN STATE COURT

Hana Haft, a German citizen, obtained a default judgment in Germany declaring George Grange, a U.S. citizen, to be father of her child and ordering him to pay $150 per month in child support. George, who met Hana while he was stationed at a U.S. Army facility in West Germany, was served with process while he was in Germany. During the pendency of the trial, he signed a statement admitting paternity. Although he was in Germany at the time of the hearing, he did not appear.

Hana has filed suit in state court in State $X$ of the United States seeking to have the Germany judgment enforced for back payments of $6,400 plus interest and to establish the German decree as a State $X$ decree. Hana's counsel did not submit any evidence that German courts would enforce the State $X$ judgment in comparable circumstances. George's counsel, citing *Hilton v. Guyot*, has moved to dismiss. Is it likely that the motion will be granted? Why? If the suit is not dismissed, George's counsel has indicated an intention to submit evidence that George was not the father of the child and that he was intoxicated when he signed the statement admitting paternity. Is it likely that the court will admit the evidence? Why? *See Nicol v. Tanner*, 310 Minn. 68, 256 N.W.2d 796 (1976).

---

## PROBLEM 7A-9. THE GUARANTEE

The Royal Bank of Canada (Royal) filed suit against Alice Able, a State *X* domiciliary, in Federal District Court for *X* on a default judgment Royal had obtained against Alice in Alberta, Canada. The Canadian action was based on a guarantee Alice had signed in *X* and forwarded to Royal's home office in Alberta. The guarantee called for repayment in *X* of up to $250,000 if Royal advanced that amount to Bobble Company, Ltd., an Alberta corporation, and Bobble failed to repay the loan. Bobble defaulted and Royal filed suit in Alberta when Alice rejected its demand that she honor her commitment.

Notice of the suit was given to Alice by a process that was consistent with Alberta's procedural requirements and was reasonably calculated to give her notice, but which did not satisfy *X*'s statutory notice requirements. Further, the long-arm jurisdiction asserted by the Canadian court was consistent with the due process requirements of the U.S. Constitution, but was inconsistent with the *X* statutory requirements which were narrower than those permitted by the U.S. Constitution. By Canadian law, a United States judgment would be recognized only if the defendant had been served personally in the decreeing state.

Would the Federal District Court for *X* follow the rules established in *Hilton v. Guyot* or would it follow *X*'s rules governing recognition of foreign-state judgments? What issues would properly be before the court in *X* as it seeks to determine whether to recognize the Canadian judgment? *See Royal Bank of Canada v. Trentham Corp.*, 491 F. Supp. 404 (S.D. Tex. 1980), *judgment vacated*, 665 F.2d 515 (5th Cir. 1981).

---

## PART B.  THE REACH AND LIMITS OF FULL FAITH AND CREDIT

### § 7.07    The Iron Law of Full Faith and Credit

#### PROBLEM 7B-1. HOW STALE CAN THE CLAIM BE?

State $X$ has a ten-year limitation period on money judgments and does not permit the revival of judgments beyond the initial ten-year period. State $Y$ has a twenty-year limitation period on money judgments and permits the repeated revival of such judgments for additional twenty year periods.

Nineteen years after the issuance of an $X$ money judgment, Jane Joel, the judgment creditor, filed suit on the $X$ judgment in State $Y$ and received a $Y$ judgment over the objection of Ken Krath, the judgment debtor, that the $X$ limitation period had run. Nineteen years after the issuing of the $Y$ judgment, Jane revived it a $Y$ proceeding. Ken again appeared to object that the $X$ statute had run. Nine years after the revival—and 47 years after the $X$ judgment was originally issued—Jane filed suit in State $X$ on the revived $Y$ judgment. Is $X$ constitutionally required to enforce the $Y$ judgment? *See Union Nat'l Bank v. Lamb*, 337 U.S. 38, *reh'g denied*, 337 U.S. 928 (1949).

---

#### PROBLEM 7B-2. THE NEW FAMILY

A State $X$ dissolution decree ordered Dave Donald to pay $15,000 in alimony to his former wife, Clara, at the rate of $150 per month until fully paid. The decree stated that it was final and that execution would issue for any payment or payments in default. Dave failed to make the required payments, and two years later Clara filed suit in State $Y$, where Dave had lived since the dissolution, (i) to establish the $X$ decree as a judgment of $Y$; (ii) to obtain a judgment for the arrearage of $3,600 (24 months at $150 per month) plus interest; and (iii) to recover reasonable attorney's fees. Dave defended by proving that he and his second wife had triplets and that he could not pay $150 per month and still support his new wife and family.

During a recess, Dave's counsel suggested that Dave would be willing to pay past due installments at a rate of $25 per month and future installments at $35 per month if Clara waived past due interest. As counsel for Clara, what advice would you give if she asked whether she should accept the offer? Why?

If Clara remarried two days after filing suit in $Y$ and by the law of $Y$ the remarriage of a divorced wife cuts off her right to alimony, is the $Y$ court constitutionally free to apply the $Y$ rule in face of an $X$ rule to the contrary? Why? Would your analysis be different if Clara and her new husband were domiciled in $Y$? Why?

## PROBLEM 7B-3. THE INTEREST OF THE SECOND OR THIRD STATE

Charles and Donna Ryman were married in State $X$ in 1969. They lived there together for 12 years before separating. Charles then filed a divorce action in $X$. His petition was denied and a legal separation order issued.

Throughout the marriage, Charles was in the Navy and stationed in State $X$. After the separation order was issued, Charles left the Navy and moved to State $Y$ seeking work. After he had been in $Y$ for three months, he filed a dissolution action. Donna, who was given appropriate notice, did not appear.

About one month later, the $Y$ court declared the marriage dissolved. Donna immediately filed a petition before the $X$ court that had issued the separation order and asked that the $Y$ dissolution be declared null and void on the ground that Charles was not a domiciliary of $Y$ and, thus, that the $Y$ court had no jurisdiction. Charles was given appropriate notice, but did not appear. The $X$ court declared the $Y$ decree null and void.

A few weeks after the $Y$ decree was issued and before the $X$ court had acted on Donna's petition, Charles received notice that a position as a civilian employee of the Navy was available to him in State $Z$ and he moved there to accept it. Within six months Charles remarried, and a year or so later his wife gave birth to twins. Charles and his new family continue to live in Z.

Donna filed a petition in a $Z$ court, asking it to adopt the $X$ decree as its own and to declare the $Y$ dissolution invalid. Had the issue of the validity of the $Y$ decree been raised initially in a $Z$ court, it would have held that recognition of the $Y$ decree was mandated by the Full Faith and Credit Clause. Is $Z$ free to apply its own law and hold the $Y$ dissolution decree valid in light of the holding of the $X$ court? *See Rymanowski v. Rymanowski*, 105 R.I. 89, 249 A.2d 407 (1969). If the $Z$ court declares the $Y$ dissolution valid, is the $X$ constitutionally mandated to accept that determination? Why?

## § 7.08    Exceptions to the Iron Law I: Problems With the F-1 Decree

### [B]—Lack of Finality

### PROBLEM 7B-4. DEFERRING TO NEW JERSEY?

Jan and Jack Jonis were married in New Jersey; they lived there for three years before Jan filed a separate maintenance action. Jack appeared personally, and the court issued a support order directing Jack to pay Jan $700 per month.

Jack left New Jersey a few weeks later and moved to Nevada. Two years later be obtained an ex parte dissolution of the marriage in Nevada. Jan received appropriate notice. Until the dissolution decree was issued, Jack paid Jan as directed by the New Jersey decree. When Nevada issued the dissolution decree, it made no mention of support or alimony, and Jack simply stopped making the monthly payments.

Jack moved to California 18 months after the Nevada decree; subsequently Jan filed an action in California, asking that Jack be ordered to pay back alimony of $12,600 ($700 per month for 18 months) plus interest and that the New Jersey decree be established as a California decree as regards future payments. The California court, applying New Jersey law, determined that the Nevada dissolution decree had not cut off Jan's right to support. It must determine what force and effect to give the New Jersey support decree, which, by New Jersey law, is modifiable both retroactively and prospectively.

As counsel for Jan, what arguments would you make to persuade the court to enforce the New Jersey decree? Is it likely that you arguments will prevail? Why? *See Worthley v. Worthley*, 44 Cal. 2d 465, 283 P.2d 19 (1955).

### PROBLEM 7B-5. MODIFIABLE BY WHOSE LAW?

Betsy Blom filed suit in State $X$ on a $190,000 lump sum State $Y$ judgment for arrears arising from the failure of her former husband, Charles, to pay $1,600 monthly alimony payments to Betsy as directed by a $Y$ dissolution decree. Charles resisted on the ground that by the law of both $X$ and $Y$, lump sum judgments for back alimony were modifiable.

Is the $X$ court under constitutional compulsion to apply $Y$ law in determining whether the $Y$ decree is modifiable? Assuming it is modifiable, is $X$ free to apply the doctrine of comity and treat the *Y* judgment as final and binding? *See Barber v. Barber*, 323 U.S. 77 (1944).

---

## [C]—The Judgment and Fraud

### PROBLEM 7B-6. EXTRINSIC FRAUD

Fran Fuld, a State *X* domiciliary, filed an action in *X* for dissolution of her marriage and for child custody and support. George, her husband, received appropriate notice. Two days later, the couple reconciled and, in fact, lived together for two years thereafter. Throughout the two years of reconciliation, Fran assured George that the dissolution action had been dismissed. George, thus, did not retain counsel. A few months before the couple split up again, the *X* court issued a decree dissolving the marriage. The decree awarded custody to Fran and fixed child support payments. George, who had no actual knowledge of the proceeding until after the decree was issued, did not appear. He found out that the decree had been issued only when the Social Service Officer for the district notified him that he was behind in his support payments.

George, who was incensed, immediately left *X*, moved to State *Y*, and refused to make the child support payments. About a year later, Fran filed suit in *Y* for back child support. George responded by challenging the entire *X* judgment on the ground that he had been lulled into believing that the action had been dismissed.

By the laws of both *X* and *Y*, extrinsic fraud of the kind practiced by Fran was sufficient to set aside the decree. By the law of *X*, however, the decree would not be set aside in the absence of (1) a showing that the challenging party had a meritorious defense to the claim; and (2) clear and convincing evidence of the fraud. By the law of *Y*, the showing of a meritorious defense was irrelevant to setting aside the decree and the fraud could be shown by a preponderance of the evidence. Is the *Y* court free to set aside the decree by application of the *Y* standards? *See In re Marriage of Short*, 263 N.W.2d 720 (Iowa 1978).

---

## [D]—Lack of Personal Jurisdiction

### PROBLEM 7B-7. DEFAULT JUDGMENT

George Grand obtained a default judgment in State *X* against Barb Blounde and her husband Bill. Barb and Bill, at all times residents of State *Y*, were served in *Y* with a copy of the *X* summons and complaint. The Bloundes responded by personal letter to the clerk of the *X* court saying that George's claim was contingent on his success in helping them obtain a loan and that, since no loan had been obtained, they did not owe him any money. (By the law of *X*, submission of the letter amounted to a general appearance.)

The clerk responded by means of a form letter informing the Bloundes that they were required to comply with certain requirements concerning the filing of an original will. The Bloundes returned a copy of their original letter to the clerk and indicated that the form letter did not appear to relate to their problem. The clerk then wrote a letter telling them that they must pay a $36 appearance fee and file their answer on 28-line pleading paper and that a failure to file an answer within thirty days would amount to a default. The Bloundes responded that they could not afford to comply and asked that the special paper and appearance fee be waived. They received no response from the clerk, who did not file their letter as a formal answer. The Bloundes assumed that the waiver had been granted, however.

A default judgment was entered in *X*, and George filed suit on it in State *Y*. Is *Y* constitutionally compelled to recognize and enforce the *X* judgment? Why? Would a prior *X* determination that the procedure followed satisfied due process be controlling? Why? *See R.R. Gable, Inc. v. Burrows*, 32 Wash. App. 749, 649 P.2d 177 (1982), *cert. denied*, 461 U.S. 957 (1983).

---

## PROBLEM 7B-8. HOW BINDING IS BINDING?

Arlene Andes, a State *X* resident, was injured in a two-car accident in State *X*. Two years later, she obtained a default judgment in State *X* against Chet Chundee, a State *Y* resident. Chet, who had never been in *X*, was served by mail at his home in *Y*. He did not appear. Arlene filed suit in *Y* on the *X* judgment. Chet challenged the *X* court's jurisdiction to render a judgment against him.

An *X* statute provides that in automobile negligence actions, ownership of the vehicle is "prima facie" proof that the vehicle was "being operated and used with the authority, consent, and knowledge of the owner," and further, that registration of the vehicle is "prima facie" proof that the vehicle was "owned by the person in whose name it was registered." The *X* nonresident motorist statute permitted service on nonresidents owners who authorized or consented to their cars being used in *X*. At the time of the accident, the car was registered in Chet's name.

In the *Y* proceeding, the trial court rejected Chet's offer to prove that he had sold the car to Clarice Cole nine months before the accident, that he had assigned the certificate of title to her, and that she had promised to have the car registration transferred. The trial judge held that full faith and credit required that she enforce the *X* judgment.

On appeal to the *Y* Supreme Court, would the trial court be sustained? Why? *See James v. Francesco*, 61 N.J. 480, 295 A.2d 633 (1972).

---

## [E]—Lack of Subject Matter Jurisdiction

### PROBLEM 7B-9. CLAMMING IN COUNTY WATERS

State *X* had a statute that authorized the forfeiture of any boat or vessel seized while being used for illegal clamming and made it unlawful for persons who were not residents of *X* to take or gather clams in *X* "waters." The statute provided that immediately after seizure, the sheriff of the county in which the boat or vessel was seized was to give information about the seizure to two justices of the peace "of the county where the seizure was made." The justices were to conduct a trial to determine whether the alleged illegal clamming had occurred and, upon such a finding, to direct the sheriff to sell the vessel at a public auction.

Tim Thomson, sheriff of Monmouth County in *X*, seized a vessel owned by Walt Whitman, a State *Y* resident, on the ground that Walt had been clamming in violation of the *X* statute. Tim followed the statutory process and, after a hearing as provided, sold the Walt's vessel at public auction.

Walt filed an in personam action against Tim in State *Y*, alleging that Tim had illegally seized his vessel in State *Y* waters and converted the vessel Tim, who was properly served with process, produced the record of the proceeding before the two justices, which recited that the vessel had been seized within Monmouth county and that it had been engaged in clamming in violation of the *X* statute. Tim then moved for dismissal on the ground that under the Full Faith and Credit Clause and the full faith and credit statute, the record was conclusive both as to the jurisdiction of the court and the merits of the case.

Tim's motion was denied and the case was put to a jury, which found that the vessel had been seized in State *X*, but not in Monmouth County. Judgment was then rendered for Walt.

Is it likely that the lower court's determination will be sustained on appeal? Why? *See Thompson v. Whitman*, 85 U.S. 457 (1873).

---

### PROBLEM 7B-10. A CHARGE ON HIS ESTATE

A marriage dissolution decree in State *X* ordered Bill Bober to pay $700 a month to his former wife, Doris, "as permanent alimony." The decree provided that in the event of Bill's death, the $700 monthly payment was to "became a charge on Mr. Bober's estate during Mrs. Bober's lifetime." Neither party appealed the order.

Ten years later, Bill died testate as a domiciliary of State $Y$ leaving $250,000 worth of $Y$ real property. Doris filed a claim against his estate on the basis of the $X$ decree. The $Y$ court rejected her claim an the grounds that the $X$ divorce court had no authority under $X$ law to place a "charge" on Bill's estate for the $700 monthly alimony payments or to place what amounted to a lien on $Y$ real property.

On appeal to the $Y$ Supreme Court, the question of $X$ law was certified to the $X$ Supreme Court, which verified that the decree charging Bob's estate was improper under $X$ law. The $X$ court also said, however, that in the absence of an appeal, the decree was final and enforceable. What decision is likely to be made by the $Y$ Supreme Court? Why? *See Aldrich v. Aldrich*, 378 U.S. 540 (1964).

————

## [F]—The Land Taboo

### PROBLEM 7B-11. THE HOTEL

Lynne Lyon obtained a State $X$ separate maintenance decree against her husband, Harry. When Harry failed to make the required payments, Lynne reduced her claim for past due payment to a $30,000 money judgment and levied on an $X$ hotel Harry owned. Lynne bought the hotel at the sheriff's sale in satisfaction of her $30,000 judgment.

Shortly thereafter, Harry filed for divorce in State $Y$. Lynne appeared generally in the $Y$ proceeding. Despite the State $X$ levy and sale, the $Y$ court erroneously held that the hotel belonged to Harry, and it ordered Lynne to execute a quitclaim deed conveying to Harry any interest she had in the hotel. Lynne executed the deed as directed. She then returned to State $X$ and sought to quiet her title to the hotel property. As counsel for Lynne, what advice would you give her about accepting Harry's offer to sell the hotel and divide the proceeds with her? Why? *See Porter v. Porter*, 101 Ariz. 131, 416 P.2d 564 (1966), *cert. denied*, 386 U.S. 957 (1967).

————

### PROBLEM 7B-12. THE SUMMER COTTAGE

Diana and Ed Dombey, a married couple living in State $X$, bought a summer cottage located in State $Y$. When the couple separated several years later, Ed stayed in the family home in $X$, and Diana moved to the cottage in $Y$. Nine months after the separation, Ed filed a dissolution action in $X$. Diana, although served in $Y$, did not appear. The court ordered the marriage dissolved and awarded "sole title" of the $Y$ cottage to Ed. Shortly after the $X$ decree became final, Diana filed suit in $Y$, asking that the $Y$ cottage be sold and the proceeds divided equally. In response, Ed submitted the $X$ decree and asked for a dismissal of the suit, a declaration that he was the sole owner of the cottage, and an order evicting Diana from the cottage.

As counsel for Diana, what arguments would you make in resisting Ed's various motions? Is it likely that your arguments will be persuasive? *See Manfrini v. Manfrini*, 136 N.J. Super. 390, 346 A.2d 430 (1975), *cert. denied*, 70 N.J. 526, 361 A.2d 540 (1976).

---

## PROBLEM 7B-13. ANOTHER HAPPY FAMILY

Fran Franson's father died domiciled in State $X$, leaving a will in which he expressed his intention to disinherit Fran, also an $X$ domiciliary. The primary asset in the estate was oil and gas property located in State $Y$. By the law of $Y$, Fran could not be disinherited unless her father in his will set forth with specificity reasons for the disinheritance and the court deemed the reasons valid. No statement of reason was contained in the will. By $X$ law, Fran was subject to being disinherited without any statement of reasons.

The will was probated in $X$. Over Fran's objection, the provision disinheriting her was sustained. Fran refused to obey an $X$ court order to execute a quitclaim deed conveying "all right, title and interest" in the $Y$ property to her brother, George, the beneficiary under the will. A master appointed by the court executed the deed on Fran's behalf.

George, who wished to sell the $Y$ property, filed a quiet title action there, seeking a declaration that he had merchantable title to the property. Fran filed an objection. Prior to trial, George offered Fran 16.6% of the proceeds of the sale if she would withdraw her resistance and sign a release. (If Fran prevails at the trial, she would recover a 50 percent interest in the property.)

As counsel for Fran, would you advise her to accept the settlement offer? Why? *See Alexander v. Alexander*, 357 So. 2d 1260 (La. App. 1978).

---

## PROBLEM 7B-14. 1000 ACRES OF PRIME FARM LAND

At the time of the dissolution of their marriage in a bilateral proceeding in State $X$, Winnie and Walter Wexsty owned 1,000 acres of prime State $Y$

farm land as joint tenants with right of survivorship. The dissolution decree, which was not appealed, declared that Winnie was the sole owner of the 1,000 acres. It did not, however, order Walter to convey the land to Winnie, and no deed was ever executed.

Both parties remarried and continued to live in X. After Winnie died a few years later, an ancillary probate proceeding was started in Y, with her second husband designated as her personal representative. Walter appeared and claimed title to the Y property as the surviving joint tenant. He argued that the X court had no jurisdiction in transfer the Y property to Winnie.

What would be the likely disposition of Walter's claim? Why? Is the claim constitutionally based? Why? *See Matter of Estate of Mack*, 373 N.W.2d 97 (Iowa 1985).

--------

## PROBLEM 7B-15. FIRST IN TIME, FIRST IN RIGHT?

Laura Lang filed suit in State X, alleging that Richard Roberts had misappropriated funds belonging to Laura and had used them to buy land in State Y. She asked the X court to impose a constructive trust for her benefit on the Y land. After a full hearing, the Y court did as Laura requested.

While the X suit was pending, Laura filed a complaint in Y containing the same allegations. After the X court decree was issued, she amended the complaint in Y to set forth the X judgment and asked the Y court to enforce the equitable trust established by the X decree. She contended that the decree was entitled to full faith and credit.

Before the Y court could respond, Richard filed a petition in bankruptcy. After a hearing, the Bankruptcy Court held that the X judgment was entitled to full faith and credit to the extent that it created a constructive trust on Y land. The trial court in Y then held that it was required to give res judicata effect to the Bankruptcy Court's conclusion that the X judgment was enforceable.

Did the trial court act appropriately in holding itself bound by the Bankruptcy Court's determination? Why? If the Bankruptcy Court had held that the X decree was not entitled to full faith and credit, is the Y court free to disagree and hold that it was so entitled? Why? *See Andre v. Morrow*, 106 Idaho 455, 680 P.2d 1355 (1984).

## PROBLEM 7B-16. PERSONALTY AND REALTY

Although the power may be exercised in a more restrained manner when personalty rather than real property is involved, do situs courts have the same power over personal property and rights in such property as do situs courts that deal with real property? *See Green v. Van Buskirk*, 74 U.S. 139 (1868).

## § 7.09 Exceptions to the Iron Law II: F-2's Ability to Ignore a Valid F-1 Judgment

### [B]—Penal and Tax Judgments

### PROBLEM 7B-17. FINES FOR FAILURE TO PAY TAXES

James Johns, a New Jersey resident who worked in Philadelphia, was sued in New Jersey by the City of Philadelphia for failure to pay an income tax imposed on all persons employed within the city. In addition to seeking back taxes and interest, the City asked the court to impose a $300 fine as provided for in the tax ordinance for failure to file a return.

James' counsel urged that the $300 fine was penal and, thus, not enforceable in New Jersey. What arguments would you make on behalf of the City to overcome the penal statute argument? Is it likely that you will succeed? *See Philadelphia v. Smith*, 82 N.J.429, 413 A.2d 952 (1980); *Philadelphia v. Austin*, 171 N.J. Super. 118, 407 A.2d 1294 (1979), *aff'd*, 86 N.J. 55, 429 A.2d 568 (1981). For background, *see Huntington v. Attrill*, 146 U.S. 657 (1892).

## PROBLEM 7B-18. LISTENING IN

Plaintiff, Bob Bobble, a resident of State $X$ who was office manager of defendant's $X$ office, filed an action for wrongful discharge in $X$. The defendant, Computer Science, Inc., is a State $Y$ corporation doing business in $X$ as well as twenty other states. Computer filed a counterclaim when, in the course of discovery proceedings, it learned that over the years Bob had taped many of his telephone conversations with Computer's *Y* employees, an activity that violated *Y*, but not *X*, law. The *Y* statute subjects persons convicted of violating it to criminal penalties and provides a private litigant damages of $3,000, or three times the amount of actual damages, whichever is greater.

In an effort to have the counterclaim dismissed, Bob argued that the *Y* statute was unenforceable in *X* because it was penal and, if not penal, violated *X*'s public policy. State *X* follows the Restatement (Second) approach to choice-of-law issues.

As counsel for Computer, what arguments would you make in resisting Bob's attempt to have the counterclaim dismissed? Why? Do you believe your arguments would prevail? *See Becker v. Computer Science Corp.*, 541 F. Supp. 694 (S.D. Tex. 1982).

---

## [D]—Public Policy and Full Faith and Credit

### PROBLEM 7B-19. TRAYNOR, J. AND *YARBOROUGH*

Carol and David Donald were married and lived in New York. Their daughter, Kim, was born there. When Kim was a year old, Carol and Dave were divorced in a bilateral proceeding in Georgia.

The Georgia decree incorporated a "complete and final" settlement agreement signed by Carol and David under which Carol was to have custody of Kim and David was to deposit $60,000 as the corpus of a trust held by a Georgia trustee for Kim's support until she became eighteen. The agreement recited that it was "in lieu of any claim Kim now has or may hereafter be entitled to from her father or his estate for past, present, and future support and maintenance. . .." The agreement also recited that no changes in the parties' financial circumstances should be taken into account or authorize a change in David's obligation to Kim. The trustee, which was to pay the income from the fund monthly to Kim, was authorized to invade the corpus in specified circumstances. The Georgia law was the same as it had been when *Yarborough* was decided.

Several years later, Carol, who lived in New York with Kim, filed a URESA action there, seeking to increase the child support payments to $2,000 per month. The petition was transmitted to California, where David resided. Under URESA, in force in California, Georgia, and New York, the duty of support is that imposed by the law of state where the obligor was present during the period for which support is sought.

The trial court, feeling bound by *Yarborough*, dismissed the petition. What is the likely outcome of an appeal? Why? *See Elkind v. Byck*, 68 Cal. 2d 453, 439 P.2d 316 (1968).

————

## PROBLEM 7B-20. THE PIPE STABBER

Carla Combs worked as a pipe stabber on a pipeline being built through States $X$, $Y$ and $Z$. On the morning of the day she was injured, Carla parked her car in State $X$, about 100 feet from the State $Y$ boundary, and started working in $X$. By 10 a.m., the work had progressed into State $Y$, and Carla worked in $Y$ for the balance of the day. At 5 p.m., the end of the work day, a company truck picked up the employees in $Y$ to drive them back to $X$ where they had parked their cars. A gate had been erected on the boundary between $Y$ and $X$. When the truck reached that point, Carla jumped off the back to open the gate. She fell as she jumped, however, and suffered severe injuries. Carla's claim for worker's compensation was denied by the Compensation Board in $Y$ on the ground that she had not been injured in the course of her employment. Carla appealed the Board's ruling to the $Y$ Supreme Court, which affirmed.

Carla has asked you to represent her in filing a worker's compensation claim in State $X$. What would you have to learn before agreeing to take on the case? Would you anticipate a constitutional bar to the claim in $X$? Why? *See La Rue v. El Paso Natural Gas Co.*, 57 N.M. 93, 254 P.2d 1059 (1953).

————

# Chapter 8

# DOMESTIC RELATIONS

## PART A.   MARRIAGE

### § 8.02    The Place of Celebration

#### PROBLEM 8A-1. HER MOTHER'S HUSBAND

Many states limit their incest statutes to situations involving persons related by blood. Other states extend the prohibition to include marriages between persons related by affinity. State $X$'s prohibition extended to relationships by affinity, and its statute stated: "No man shall marry his wife's daughter; no woman shall marry her mother's husband." State $Y$ had no such prohibition.

Gloria Grand, the daughter of her mother's first marriage, married her mother's second husband, Henry, shortly after Henry's marriage to her mother was dissolved. All of the parties were domiciliaries of $X$. Gloria's marriage took place in State $Y$, and the couple returned to $X$ immediately after the ceremony. Gloria and Henry lived together in $X$ for 27 years and had three children before he died, leaving real and personal property worth $6,000,000 in States $X$, $Y$ and $Z$. ($Z$'s law was similar to that of $X$.)

By will, Henry left Gloria $500,000 and provided that if she sought and was denied a forced share (1/3), rather than taking the designated amount, she was to take nothing under the will. Gloria has asked you whether she should elect a forced share rather than taking what she described as a "measly $500,000." What advice would you give her? Why? *See Rhodes v. McAfee*, 224 Tenn. 495, 457 S.W.2d 522 (1970).

———

#### PROBLEM 8A-2. A CHILD BRIDE

Sandra Spears, a 13-year-old girl, and Harold Hunt, a 17-year-old boy, both living in State x, were married in State $Y$ at a wedding attended by their parents. The couple and their parents then returned to their respective homes in $X$. Sandra and Harold lived together in $X$ for four days when Harold and Sandra's parents were charged with contributing to the delinquency of a minor. The case against them depends on a determination about the validity of the marriage.

By the law of $Y$, the marriage was valid because the parents had consented. By the law of $X$ it was null and void.

As counsel for State $X$, what arguments would you make to persuade the court that the marriage was invalid? Is it likely that your arguments would persuade the court? Why? *See State v. Graves*, 228 Ark. 378, 307 S.W.2d 545 (1957).

---

## PROBLEM 8A-3. BACK HOME AGAIN

The final decree of State $X$ dissolving Toby Tyler's marriage prohibited her from remarrying for six months. Within a month of the decree being issued, Toby went to State $Y$ with Seth Salway, married him there, and returned to the house they had been sharing in $X$.

Toby comes to your office to ask whether she is legally married to Chet. What answer would you give her? What additional facts, if any, would you want before answering? Why? *See Bogen v. Bogen*, 261 N.W.2d 606 (Minn. 1977).

---

## PROBLEM 8A-4. A CHURCH WEDDING

Vera Versale, an American citizen, was married in Poland to Walt Wentz, a Polish citizen, in a Roman Catholic ceremony. Although the couple obtained the appropriate marriage license, they did not go through the civil ceremony required by Polish law as an absolute condition precedent to a valid marriage. (Many European countries have requirements similar to Poland's.)

After having lived with Walt in Poland for five years and having two children, Vera left him and returned to her former home in State $X$. (She took the children with her.) A few months after her return, she married Raoul Rhode in $X$ and lived there with him for several years. Raoul left Vera when he discovered that her marriage to Walt had not been dissolved. He filed suit to annul his marriage to Vera on the ground that it was bigamous.

As counsel for Raoul, what arguments would you make to persuade a court that the marriage was void? Are your arguments likely to prevail? Why? *See Bronislawa K. v. Tadeusz K.*, 393 N.Y.S.2d 534 (Fam. Ct. 1977).

## PROBLEM 8A-5. MEMBERS OF THE PEACE CORPS

Two Peace Corps volunteers were married in the newly created African nation in which they worked. An American missionary performed the ceremony in traditional form. A marriage license had been issued by the appropriate official of the nation. While the marriage would have been valid by the laws of all states of the United States, it was invalid where it was performed because by statute all marriage ceremonies had to be performed in the official language of the nation, and the ceremony in question had been performed in English and Latin. (Seventeen different languages were spoken in the country and the national government adopted the statute in question as part of an attempt to unify the country by having all persons speak a single language.)

Would the marriage be recognized as valid in this country? Why? Would you need more facts before answering the question? If so, what facts?

## PROBLEM 8A-6. FIRST COUSINS

Two first cousins, who were domiciled in State $X$, took a vacation together in State $Y$. While there, they decided to get married and did so in a $Y$ ceremony. They then returned to $X$ where they made their home. By the law of $Y$, first-cousin marriages were declared by statute to be "absolutely void and incestuous." By the law of $X$, first-cousin marriages were valid.

The couple separated after having lived together in $X$ for six months. The husband comes to your office to ask whether it will be necessary for him to obtain an annulment or a divorce before he marries again. What advice would you give him? Why? If the law of $Y$ validated first cousin marriages and the law of $X$ declared them absolutely void, what advice would you give? Why? Are the courts likely to view the marital status differently if the issue arises 20 years and three children later? Why? *See In re Miller's Estate*, 239 Mich. 455, 214 N.W. 428 (1927); *Toth v. Toth*, 50 Mich. App. 150, 212 N.W.2d 812 (1973). *See also In re Mortenson's Estate*, 83 Ariz. 87, 316 P.2d 1106 (1957).

———————

## PROBLEM 8A-7. COMPETING WIDOWERS

Wendy Waltz and Vern Verity were married in Missouri during a visit there. A few weeks later they returned to their home in New York and lived there as husband and wife for two years. Vern then left Wendy. She moved to Connecticut. A few years later she met and married Charles Chad. The couple was married in Maryland and established their home in Connecticut. (Charles had been living in New York prior to the marriage.) Shortly after the marriage to Charles, Wendy obtained a job with the Veterans Administration in Connecticut and worked there until she died 22 years later.

Shortly after her death, Vern filed a claim, as widower, as beneficiary of a $50,000 group life insurance policy Wendy had obtained as a federal employee. Since Charles also claimed the proceeds, the insurance company paid the money into the United States District Court for New York in an interpleader action.

Wendy had not designated a beneficiary of the policy. Under the terms of the federal statute regulating the group policy, if the insured failed to designate a beneficiary, the proceeds were payable to her "widower." Vern claimed that his marriage to Wendy had never been dissolved and, thus, that he was her widower. By what law should the federal court determine whether Vern or Charles should prevail? Why? *See Metropolitan Life Ins. Co. v. Manning*, 568 F.2d 922 (2d Cir. 1977).

———————

## PROBLEM 8A-8. THE COMMON-LAW MARRIAGE

Flo Forest's husband filed a petition to dissolve the marriage in State $X$ where they had lived for several years. Three months before the $X$ dissolution decree was issued, Flo "married" Greg Gerand in a marriage ceremony in France. Over the next 15 years, Flo and Greg lived together as husband and wife in France, Germany, and Laos. Greg then retired, and they moved to State $T$. Greg died four years later.

During the time they lived in $T$, Flo and Greg visited friends in various parts of the United States, including a two-week visit to State $X$ and a one-month visit to State $Y$. From the time of the ceremonial marriage in France, the couple regarded themselves as being married and held themselves out as such.

Common law marriages are recognized in $X$ and $Y$, but not $T$.

(i) Would the probate court in *T* view the marriage as being valid? Why? *See Metropolitan Life Insurance Co. v. Holding*, 293 F. Supp. 854 (E.D. Va. 1968). *But see Laikola v. Engineered Concrete*, 277 N.W.2d 653 (Minn. 1979).

(ii) If Greg had not retired, but had moved to *T* to work and had been killed in an industrial accident, is it likely that Flo could receive workers' compensation as Greg's "widow" under a statute that defined "widow" as "only the decedent's wife living with him or dependent for support on him at the time of his death"? (Assume that the visits described above did not occur.) *See Gibson v. Hughes*, 192 F. Supp. 564 (S.D.N.Y. 1961).

---

## § 8.03    Annulment

### PROBLEM 8A-9. IS ANNULMENT A TRANSITORY ACTION?

Clara and Don Clarice were married in State *X* and lived there for six weeks. Clara, a petty officer in the Navy, was transferred to sea duty on the U.S.S. Repose, a ship having its "home port" in State *Y*. Three months after being transferred, Clara filed suit in *Y* to annul the marriage. Don, who remained in *X*, was notified appropriately. He did not appear; rather, he informed the court that he wished to contest the annulment action but was having difficulty locating a lawyer. The court treated Don's letter as a default, heard testimony ex parte, and granted the requested annulment about five weeks after the petition had been filed. One week later, Don moved to set aside the default and to permit him to answer. His motion was denied.

Don appealed. He argued that (1) the *Y* court, having no personal jurisdiction over him, had no jurisdiction to proceed ex parte; and (2) even if the court had personal jurisdiction over him, it lacked jurisdiction to annul the marriage because *Y* was neither the place where the marriage occurred nor the domicile of either party. Is Don's appeal likely to succeed? Why? *See Whealton v. Whealton*, 67 Cal. 2d 656, 432 P.2d 979 (1967).

---

# PART B.   DIVORCE AND MARITAL SUPPORT

## § 8.06    Recognition and Collateral Attack

### PROBLEM 8B-1. A BROODING OMNIPRESENCE?

In *Williams II*, Mr. Justice Frankfurter said in note 7 of the opinion: "Since an appeal to the Full Faith and Credit Clause raises questions arising under the Constitution of the United States, the proper criteria for ascertaining domicil, should these be in dispute, become matters for federal determination." At a later point in the opinion, he said: "Neither a rational system of law nor hard practicality calls for our independent determination, in reviewing the judgment of a State court, of that rather elusive relation between person and place which establishes domicil." In *Williams II*, it was clear that Nevada and North Carolina did not agree on what constituted domicile for the purpose of establishing divorce jurisdiction. Should the Supreme Court have interposed itself and articulated a federal standard of domicile for use in determining divorce jurisdiction? If the standard is not federal, what standard should be applied? Could North Carolina refuse to recognize an ex parte divorce obtained in a sister state in which the party had resided for two years on the ground that North Carolina's residency requirement was three years?

## PROBLEM 8B-2. PHYSICIAN HEAL THYSELF

After 23 years of married life, Sarah Sage, a physician, separated from her husband, Tom Tule, and went to State $Y$. After living in $Y$ for ninety days, Sarah filed for an ex parte dissolution there. (Tom, who remained in the family home in State $X$, was given appropriate notice of the proceeding, but did not appear.) A short time after the petition was filed, the requested dissolution was granted, and ten days later Sarah returned to $X$. Within a few weeks, she married Phil Polte in $X$. The couple lived together in $X$ until Sarah died 18 months later.

In the course of the probate of Sarah's estate, Tom and Phil both claimed as surviving spouse. They stipulated the following facts:

1. Sarah rented an apartment in $Y$, obtained a license to practice medicine there, and joined the staff of a $Y$ hospital. She also opened a bank account in $Y$ and obtained a $Y$ driver's license. She did not change the $X$ registration on her car, however.

2. Sarah tried, but was unable to obtain $Y$ certification to practice her specialty, anesthesiology.

3. While she was in $Y$, Sarah left her $X$ office open. It was staffed by a nurse whose only activity during Alice's absence was to collect unpaid bills.

4. Sarah said in a letter to her 16-year old son:

   I'm way out in the golden west and I'm sure you know why. After all those years of harassment, I'm applying for the divorce I could never get at home. I might even stay here as it is a wonderful climate. Be good to your father.

As counsel for Phil, what arguments would you make that $X$ is constitutionally barred from invalidating the dissolution? Are your arguments likely to prevail? If X is not barred under full faith and credit principles from invalidating the Y decree, may it recognize the decree as valid as a matter of comity? Why? *See Cooper v. Cooper*, 217 N.W.2d 584 (Iowa 1974).

## § 8.07    Precluding Collateral Attack — Bilateral Divorces

### PROBLEM 8B-3. MENTAL CRUELTY

Two years after her marriage was dissolved in the Virgin Islands in a proceeding in which her husband, Alex, was represented by counsel, Alice Andler filed suit in State X seeking a declaratory judgment that the dissolution decree was void. She alleged that the decree was based on her fraudulent residency and collusive agreement to the ground of mental cruelty; that her husband had trumped up a false charge of adultery against her and thereafter coerced her to dissolve the marriage and to use his attorney who arranged the trip to the Virgin Islands. The trial court found as a matter of fact that Alice's residence in the Virgin Islands was for the sole purpose of dissolving the marriage and that as soon as it was dissolved, she returned to her home in X; that she had been pressured into using her husband's lawyer; and that the mental cruelty ground was based on false and fraudulent evidence. The trial court, however, held that the decree was entitled to full faith and credit. On appeal, what arguments would you make as counsel for Alice that the trial court was in error? Are your arguments likely to prevail? *See Teich v. Teich*, 132 Ill. App. 2d 348, 270 N.E.2d 525 (1971).

### PROBLEM 8B-4. A HORSE TRAINER AND A JOCKEY

Sandra and Ted Tiller, a jockey and horse trainer respectively, spent virtually all of their time following the horse racing circuit around the country. Their normal pattern was to be "on the road" more than 11 months a year, and to spend a vacation in a resort hotel in State X, where they had been born and married.

Seven years after the marriage, while they were at the race meeting at Raton, New Mexico, the couple had their fiftieth serious argument. Sandra stormed out of their trailer, and on the next day filed a petition to dissolve their marriage. The petition falsely stated that Sandra and Ted had continuously resided in New Mexico for more than the six-month New Mexico residency requirement. Ted entered an appearance, did not dispute the residency statement, and the dissolution decree was issued a few months later.

About eight months after the New Mexico decree was issued, Ted, who was spending a few days in *X*, came to your office. He told you what had happened, explained that he wished to remarry, and asked if the New Mexico decree was valid. Your research uncovered *Heckathorn v. Heckathorn*, 77 N.M. 369, 423 P.2d 410 (1967), in which the wife's divorce petition failed to allege either domicile in New Mexico or that the statutory residency period had been satisfied. The husband's response denied the couple's residency in general terms. In its final decree, the court stated that the parties were residents of the state, but did not state that the statutory residency period had been met. Thirty months later, the husband filed a petition in New Mexico to void the divorce decree. On a finding that the couple had been domiciled in California at the time of the earlier petition and decree, the New Mexico court voided the divorce.

What advice would you give Ted? Why? *See Murphy v. Murphy*, 581 P.2d 489 (Okla. App. 1978). *See also Murphy v. Murphy*, 96 N.M. 401, 631 P.2d 307 (1981).

———

## PROBLEM 8B-5. FIRST IN TIME, FIRST IN RIGHT?

Dan and Edna Fult were married in State *X* and lived there for ten years before they separated. On the day of the separation, Dan moved to State *Y*. About thirty days after the separation, Edna filed a separate maintenance action in *X*, with service being had on Dan in *Y* by means of a registered letter sent to him there. (X had a long-arm statute extending the court's jurisdiction to the fullest extent permitted by the Constitution.)

Dan failed to appear in the *X* proceeding. Despite his absence, the *X* court found that it had personal jurisdiction over him and decreed that Edna and Dan were legally separated, awarded her $2,000 a month as separate mainte- nance, and an additional $1,500 a month for the support of the two children of the marriage. The decree recited that the *X* court retained continuing juris- diction over "the matter." By the law of *X*, maintenance and support orders were subject to being modified prospectively and retroactively.

Two years after the separation, Dan moved to State *Z*. About four months after his arrival, he filed a dissolution petition in *Z*. Notice was given to Edna in *X* by registered mail. She did not appear, however. The *Z* court's dissolution decree made no mention of support or alimony. By the law of both *X* and *Z*, an ex parte decree of dissolution that was silent on the subject cut off the absent spouse's right to support. By the law of *Z*, alimony was never awarded. By the law of *X*, a spouse could obtain alimony only if provided for in the original dissolution decree.

Within two months of the Z decree being issued, Dan moved back to Y. Although he continued to pay $1,500 per month in child support, he stopped paying the $2,000 maintenance money to Edna as soon as the Z decree became final.

Edna then filed suit in X, asking for a declaratory judgment to the effect that the Z dissolution decree was invalid and for a judgment for all back maintenance. Dan was served by means of a registered letter sent to him in Y. He did not appear. The X court held the Z decree invalid on the ground that Dan had not been a domiciliary of Z either at the time he filed suit there or at the time the decree was issued. It also gave Edna a lump-sum judgment for all back maintenance payments.

Edna filed suit in Y on the X lump-sum judgment and asked that the X maintenance-support order be established as a Y decree under the Uniform Interstate Family Support Act (UIFSA) in force in all three states.

The Y case authorities were clear that whether or not Dan had established a domicile in Z, his physical presence there for four months established a sufficient nexus with Z to authorize its courts to dissolve the marriage. The Y court held that the Z decree was valid and that Edna's right to maintenance or alimony did not survive it. The Y court refused to enforce the X judgment for back maintenance payments. At Dan's request, the Y court also reviewed the child support portion of the X decree and reduced the monthly payments to $500 per month.

(a) What arguments would you make on behalf of Edna in an appeal of the Y decree? Are your arguments likely to succeed? *See Rymanowski v. Rymanowski*, 105 R.I. 89, 249 A.2d 407 (1969).

(b) Assume that X's version of URESA provided that X support decrees shall not be deemed nullified by a support order of another state and that whatever payments were made pursuant to another state's support order would be credited to the amount due under the X decree. Assume further that Dan paid $500 per month pursuant to the Y court child support order for one year; that Edna then obtained a judgment for $6,000 in X for the amount not paid under the X decree; and that she filed suit on the judgment in State T where Bob had moved. (Assume Bob received notice of the X proceeding by registered mail.) Is your strongest argument that the X decree was entitled to full faith and credit in T? Why? What other arguments would you make on Edna's behalf?

---

## PROBLEM 8B-6. MODIFYING THE NONMODIFIABLE?

Donna and Ernie Ext lived together in State X for the twelve years of their marriage. While both still lived there, they separated and entered into a property settlement calling for an equal division of all of their property, specifying support for Donna, including all of her medical expenses, and providing that such support would continue in the form of alimony in the event of a divorce. The agreement provided that it "shall be governed by the law of X and in the event of a dissolution, the decree shall contain no provision for alimony or property rights, this agreement being intended by the parties to be final and binding on such matters." In addition, the agreement stated it "shall survive and not be merged in any final divorce between the parties."

The marriage was then dissolved in a bilateral proceeding in X. The decree stated that the agreement for spousal support was "ratified, approved and confirmed," but made no express provision for support payments. Further, the decree did not purport to merge the agreement in the decree. By X law, spousal support agreements entered into prior to divorce were not subject to modification by the court.

Ernie moved to State Y shortly after the dissolution. Four years later, Donna filed a breach of contract action against Ernie in Y seeking $2,100 in medical expenses due her under the separation agreement. Ernie conceded that the payment was due under the agreement, moved to establish the X decree as a Y decree, and requested that the decree be modified to exclude any requirement that he pay for Donna's medical expenses, past due or arising in the future.

Donna did not object to the establishment of the X decree as a Y decree, but argued that Y had a constitutional obligation to recognize the finality doctrine of X. By the law of Y, agreements such as that between Donna and Ernie were modifiable at any time "pursuant to equitable considerations." Is the Y court free to apply its own law to the modification-finality issue as to past due payments? Future payments? *See Knodel v. Knodel,* 14 Cal. 3d 752, 537 P.2d 353 (1975).

---

## PROBLEM 8B-7. VACATING THE DECREE

Trish and Tom Toland were married in Tennessee and lived there throughout their ten-year marriage. They separated and executed an agreement by which they divided their property, gave Trish custody of their two children, and provided for Tom to pay $900 per month for the support of each of the children. Trish then filed a dissolution petition in Tennessee. The petition was granted after a hearing in which Tom participated. The terms of the agreement were incorporated in the court's decree.

After the dissolution, Tom moved to New York. A few weeks after the Tennessee decree became final, Tom was killed in an employment-related automobile accident. When Trish learned of Tom's death, she petitioned the court in Tennessee to vacate the dissolution decree on grounds of personal hardship in that his death left her and her children destitute. The court declared the decree vacated and void ab initio. Trish then filed a claim as Tom's widow for benefits under the New York Workers' Compensation statute.

As counsel for Trish, what arguments would you make that the Compensation Board is constitutionally required to recognize the validity of the Tennessee decree and, thus, recognize her status as Tom's widow? Are your arguments likely to prevail? *See Wheeler v. Stewart Mapping Serv.*, 50 A.D.2d 308, 377 N.Y.S.2d 965 (1976), *aff'd*, 42 N.Y.2d 847, 366 N.E.2d 286 (1977).

---

## PROBLEM 8B-8. THE TRIBAL COURT

Sue and Sam Streff, Native American members of the Itachi Tribe, were married on the tribal reservation and lived there as husband and wife for three years. Sam then left Sue and moved off the reservation to State *X* in which the reservation was located. Two years later, while Sam was visiting his mother at her reservation home, he was served with notice that Sue had filed a petition in the Tribal Court to dissolve their marriage and that the hearing was scheduled in two months. About a month later, Sam was notified at his home off the reservation that the hearing date had been advanced and would commence two days later at 2 P.M.

Sam immediately visited your office in State *X*, told you what had happened, and asked you to represent him. You called the Clerk of the Tribal Court and asked about the procedure for entering an appearance on Sam's behalf and for arranging a delay to permit you to familiarize yourself with the case. The Clerk reported accurately that no appearance was allowed by anyone but a "Tribal Spokesperson" and that once the final time of a hearing was set, the Tribal Court would not change it. Sam did not appear at the hearing, and the Tribal Court dissolved the marriage.

At Sam's request, you filed a dissolution action for him in the state court in *X*. What arguments would you present on Sam's behalf in response to Sue's motion to dismiss on the ground that the marriage had already been dissolved? Are your arguments likely to prevail? *See Red Fox and Red Fox*, 23 Or. App. 393, 542 P.2d 918 (1975).

---

## § 8.08    Divisible Divorce

## PROBLEM 8B-9. THE PENSION FUNDS

Tammy and Tom Tapir were married and lived in California, a community property state, throughout their married life. Tammy, a California judge for 30 years, retired. Tom was a public school teacher for the same period of time. He retired about a year later. Shortly thereafter, the couple decided to separate. As a retired judge, Tammy had a vested interest in a relatively large retirement fund. As a retired school teacher, Tom had a vested interest in a relatively small retirement fund.

Tommy moved to Nevada and about nine months after her arrival filed a petition to dissolve the marriage. Tom received appropriate notice. An ex parte decree was issued under which the parties were awarded full ownership of their respective retirement funds.

(i) Several months later, Tammy returned to California, and Tom filed an action challenging that part of the Nevada decree denying to the parties any share of the community property represented by the retirement funds of the other. As counsel for Tammy, what arguments would you make to persuade the court that the entire Nevada decree was entitled to full faith and credit? Are your arguments likely to be persuasive? Why? *See Waite v. Waite*, 6 Cal. 3d 461, 492 P.2d 13 (1972).

(ii) Assume the same facts set forth above, except that Tammy, in addition to her interest in the retirement fund, owned a ranch in Nevada worth $2,500,000 and that in the ex parte proceeding there, the court found that (1) she owned the ranch as her separate property and (2) Tom had no community property interest in the ranch. Would California be bound by the Nevada court's determination as to ownership of the ranch? Why? If California is bound to recognize the decree as to the ownership of the ranch and if $700,000 worth of community property remained in California, would you advise Tom to accept $350,000 as his full share of the California community property? Why? *See Leff v. Leff*, 25 Cal. App. 3d 630, 102 Cal. Rptr. 195 (1972).

---

## PROBLEM 8B-10. PERMANENT TERMINATION OF ALIMONY

Helen and Henry Howly's marriage was dissolved in State $X$ in a bilateral proceeding. At that time, Henry was ordered to pay $400 per month in child support and $250 per month to Helen as alimony. Two years later, Henry remarried and adopted his second wife's two children by a former marriage. Within a few months of the remarriage, Henry applied to the $X$ court for a modification of the alimony portion of the decree. Helen, who had moved to State $Y$, was served there personally but did not appear except by means of a letter she wrote to the judge indicating her opposition to any modification and asking in lieu thereof that a substantial increase be granted. The $X$ court issued the following order:

> All decrees concerning alimony heretofore made are modified and alimony is hereby permanently terminated. This court does not reserve jurisdiction to make any further award of alimony.

Several years later, Helen filed suit in State $Z$, obtained personal service on Henry there, and asked for an alimony award. What result? Why?

---

## PROBLEM 8B-11. CONTRACT CONSIDERATION AND ONE-DAY DISSOLUTIONS

Joan and Jack Jasper, a married couple living in Massachusetts, separated and agreed to cooperate in obtaining a Mexican divorce. Jack appeared personally in the Mexican proceeding, with Joan appearing only by counsel. (She agreed to appear only after Jack conveyed to her his interest in the family home.) A dissolution was decreed, although Jack had been in Mexico for less than three hours at the time of the decree. The Mexican decree not only dissolved the marriage but provided that "any and all duties the husband theretofore or hereafter had, may have had, or may have to support his wife are hereby canceled."

Assuming that Massachusetts normally does not recognize Mexican one-day dissolutions in the absence of remarriages in reliance thereon, *see Poor v. Poor*, 381 Mass. 392, 409 N.E.2d 758 (1980), is it likely that Joan would be bound by the portion of the decree cutting off Jack's duty to support Alice? Why? *See McCarthy v. McCarthy*, 361 Mass. 359, 280 N.E.2d 151 (1972).

---

## PROBLEM 8B-12. IS THE STATE BOUND?

Under *Sherrer* and *Johnson*, neither party to a dissolution proceeding nor a person claiming through such party may attack the validity of a dissolution decree if the decreeing state would not permit such an attack. Do the cases stand for the proposition that a state is similarly barred from challenging the validity of a bilateral dissolution? Thus, if in *Johnson*, New York filed bigamy charges against E. Bruce Johnson when he married his third wife, would the State of New York be bound by the Florida decree as Mr. Johnson's daughter was bound?

---

## PROBLEM 8B-13. WAS SHE MARRIED?

In a bilateral proceeding in State *X*, Sara Samper's marriage to Tim Samper was dissolved and Sara was awarded $500 per month in alimony to be paid "for as long as Sara shall remain unmarried." About 18 months after the divorce, Sara married Chuck Chandra in a State $Y$ ceremony. Immediately preceding the marriage, Chuck had obtained a decree in $Y$, dissolving his marriage to his first wife, Dawn, in an ex parte proceeding. Within a week of the marriage, Sara and Chuck moved to State $Z$, where Chuck had lived prior to establishing a threemonth residence in State $Y$ to satisfy its dissolution-residence rule. When Tim learned of Sara's marriage, he stopped making payments under the $X$ decree.

Two years later, Dawn filed suit in $Z$ for separate maintenance and a declaration that the $Y$ dissolution was null and void. As soon as Dawn's suit was filed, Sara left Chuck. Dawn prevailed in her suit and Sara then filed in $Z$ for an annulment. It was granted. Sara has come to your office and asked you to represent her in her efforts to reinstate the $X$ alimony decree as to the future and to obtain back payments for the two years during which Tim had not made payments. Would you advise Sara that it was likely she could reinstate Tim's obligation as to the future, and that it was similarly likely that he could be forced to pay back alimony? *See Sutton v. Lieb*, 342 U.S. 402, *reh'g denied*, 343 U.S. 921 (1952).

---

## § 8.10    Alternative Bases for Divorce Jurisdiction

### PROBLEM 8B-14. DOMICILE AS THE SOLE BASIS FOR EX PARTE DISSOLUTIONS

John Jaines, a naval officer, came to State $X$ as the result of having been ordered to join the crew of the U.S.S. Enterprise. He lived aboard ship for 90 days and then filed for an ex parte dissolution of his marriage to Karla Kane. During the 90 days, the ship was undergoing tests at sea. Thus, John was in State $X$ territory for a total of 24 days of the 90 days in question. The ship left State $X$ permanently a few days after the petition was filed. Neither John nor Karla were domiciliaries of $X$.

In order to accommodate the needs of members of the armed forces, State $X$, along with several other states, passed special legislation permitting members of the armed forced to file for dissolution after having maintained a "military presence" in $X$ for 90 days. Karla filed a special appearance challenging the jurisdiction of the $X$ court to dissolve the marriage. Is her challenge likely to be sustained? Why? *See In re Marriage of Ways*, 85 Wash. 2d 693, 538 P.2d 1225 (1975); *Wallace v. Wallace*, 63 N.M. 414, 320 P.2d 1020 (1958).

## § 8.11    International Divorces

### PROBLEM 8B-15. THE HAITIAN TOUR

Haitian Tours, Inc., a State $X$ corporation, sold package tours which included air travel to Haiti, lodging and meals for two days, a Haitian guide, and a lawyer to represent the traveler in a dissolution action, either ex parte or bilateral. For a two-party proceeding, Haitian Tours, Inc. made arrangements for the spouse who went to Haiti (1) to file an appropriate dissolution petition; (2) to submit to the Haitian court an affidavit of marriage; (3) to present to the court the consenting spouse's waiver of personal appearance, submission to jurisdiction, and notarized power of attorney. The powers of attorney named the same lawyer to represent all of the absent spouses. For one-party proceeding, Haitian Tours, Inc., made arrangements to have service of process made on the nonappearing spouse wherever he or she resided. The package cost $3,125 for a unilateral dissolution tour and $3,275 for a bilateral dissolution tour. Air fare and lodgings accounted for one-third of the tour fee, with the balance going to pay the various legal and administrative fees involved.

State $X$'s Attorney General filed suit to enjoin Haitian Tours, Inc., from sponsoring the tours. The Attorney General urged that the tours violated a State $X$ statute prohibiting deceptive and fraudulent commercial practices. What arguments would you, as counsel for Haitian Tours, Inc., make in resisting the efforts of the Attorney General? Are your arguments likely to prevail? Why? *See Kugler v. Haitian Tours, Inc.*, 120 N.J. Super. 260, 293 A.2d 706 (1972).

### PROBLEM 8B-16. TO HAITI AND BACK — TWICE

Louise and Kevin Kola were married in State $X$ and had lived there for five years as husband and wife when Kevin went to Haiti, stayed there for two days, and obtained an ex parte dissolution of the marriage. He immediately returned to State $X$.

About a year later while vacationing in Jamaica, British West Indies, Kevin met and married Clarice Cole, a barrister who was domiciled in Jamaica and who specialized in domestic relations cases. When Kevin proposed to Clarice, he told her about the ex parte divorce he had received in Haiti. As a condition to obtaining a marriage license in Jamaica, Kevin was required to submit to

Jamaican officials a certified copy of the ex parte Haitian dissolution decree. Jamaica recognized such decrees as being valid.

A few weeks after the wedding, as they had planned, Kevin and Clarice moved to *X* where they lived as husband and wife for five years. They had three children during that period and separated after several severe arguments about the proper way to raise children. Kevin then took a two days tour to Haiti and, while there, obtained an ex parte dissolution of his marriage to Clarice. (Clarice received notice of the proceeding.) Kevin immediately returned to State *X*.

   (i)   When Clarice threatened to file a separate maintenance action against him in *X*, Kevin came to your office and asked you to file an action to annul his marriage to her on the ground that he was legally married to Louise at the time he married Clarice and was still legally married to her. Would you advise Bob to file such an action? Why? Discuss.

   (ii)   Disregard (i) and assume that a short time after he returned to *X* from Haiti, Kevin was killed in the course of his employment in *X* and that Louise and Clarice both filed compensation claims as his "widow." As counsel for Clarice, what arguments would you make to persuade the court to find that she is Kevin's widow? Are your arguments likely to prevail?

*See Mouscardy v. Mouscardy*, 52 App. Div. 2d 841, 382 N.Y.S.2d 820 (1976), *vacated and new decision*, 63 App. Div. 2d. 973 (1978).

———

## PROBLEM 8B-17. A MEXICAN DIVORCE

Alice and Bob Branch were married in New York and lived there as husband and wife until by agreement of the parties, Alice went to Jaurez, Mexico for 24 hours for the purpose of obtaining a dissolution of their marriage. Bob appeared by counsel, and the decree was issued 24 hours after Alice's petition was filed. By New York law, the dissolution was valid. Alice returned to New York to live.

A few months later, she met Charles Chad, a New Jersey domiciliary, and shortly thereafter Alice and Charles were married in New Jersey. Alice continued to work in New York, but lived in New Jersey with Charles. About six months after the marriage, Alice and Charles moved to Pennsylvania where they lived for several years before separating.

Charles filed an annulment action in Pennsylvania on the ground that Alice's divorce from Bob was invalid by the law of New Jersey and Pennsylvania and, thus, her marriage to Charles was bigamous. As counsel for Alice, would you urge that full faith and credit required the Pennsylvania court to recognize the validity of the Mexican dissolution? Why? What arguments would you make in an effort to persuade the court to recognize the validity of the decree? *See Rosen v. Sitner*, 274 Pa. Super. 445, 418 A.2d 490 (1980); *Zwerling v. Zwerling*, 270 S.C. 685, 244 S.E.2d 311 (1978).

---

# PART C.   CUSTODY

## § 8.13   Jurisdiction

### PROBLEM 8C-1. WALTZING MATILDA

Wendy Wales, a United States citizen and California domiciliary, met and married Les Wales while she was touring Australia. Les, who had never been outside of Australia, and Wendy lived together in Australia for ten years. Two children were born during that period. When the oldest child was four years old, the couple separated and obtained a bilateral divorce in Australia. When the divorce became final, Wendy, with Les's consent, returned with the children to California. After having been in California for four years, Wendy met and married Chuck, an Australian citizen who was living in California temporarily. Shortly after the marriage, Wendy, Chuck, and the two children moved to Australia.

About three years later, after several months of bickering about the appropriateness of the schooling Wendy was providing for the children, Les asked the Australian Family Court to issue a custody order granting him specific visitation rights and giving him control of the children's education. Wendy resisted the petition, but after a full hearing the Australian court issued a decree directing that Les control the children's education. The decree also specified Les's visitation rights, enjoined Wendy from leaving Australia with the children without permission of the Court, and ordered her to leave the children with Les whenever she left Australia. A few weeks after the decree, Wendy, who had separated from her second husband, left Australia with the children and went to California where she planned to live permanently. She did not inform Les or the Australian Court that she was leaving.

When Les discovered that Wendy had left Australia with the children, he petitioned the Australian Family Court to have custody awarded to him. He alleged the facts set forth and also that Wendy was emotionally upset and unstable as the result of the break-up of her second marriage. Les's petition was served on Clarice, Wendy's solicitor of record in the prior custody proceeding. Clarice, who did not know where Wendy was, declined to participate in the proceeding on the ground that she had not been retained for that purpose and, thus, was not authorized to appear for a client. Five days after Les's petition was filed and with no one present representing Wendy, the Australian Family Court granted Les temporary custody pending a full hearing after the children were located.

About three weeks after the decree, Les learned that Wendy was living in California. He immediately employed California counsel and instituted proceedings under California's Uniform Child Custody Jurisdiction Act, asking that the Australian decree be recognized and that Wendy be directed to turn the children over to him so that he could return with them to Australia. What would be the likely result of Bob's action? *See Miller v. Superior Court,* 22 Cal. 3d 923, 587 P.2d 723 (1978).

---

## PROBLEM 8C-2. FRENCH CUSTODY

Gerald Plas, a French resident and citizen, and his wife, Melinda Plas, an American citizen with a permanent French resident card, were married in France and lived there together for several years except when Melinda visited her parents in State $X$ for six weeks every year. Gwen, a child of the marriage with dual citizenship, lived in France with her parents except for the annual six-week visits to her grandparents.

Melinda did not return to France after a recent visit. Instead, she informed Gerald that she was leaving him and planned to stay in State $X$ with Gwen. Gerald came to $X$ three months after receiving Melinda's letter. Over Melinda's objection, he took Gwen with the intention of returning with her to France via Canada. At Melinda's request, Gerald was stopped by Canadian officials and Gwen was returned to Melinda, who filed a custody proceeding in $X$ a few weeks later.

Does $X$ have jurisdiction under the Uniform Child Custody Jurisdiction Act? Why? *See Plas v. Superior Court (Plas),* 155 Cal. App. 3d 1008, 202 Cal. Rptr. 490 (1984).

---

## PROBLEM 8C-3. LEARNING ENGLISH

Sarah and Tad Towicz, citizens of Poland, were often separated when the job of one or the other called for travel. Tad came to the United States as part of a two-year scientific mission, while Sarah remained in Poland with the couple's 12-year-old daughter, Vera. About two months after arriving in the United States, Tad decided that he did not wish to return to Poland. He did not inform Sarah of his decision; rather, he wrote to her suggesting that she send Vera to join him for a few months so that Vera could improve her English. Sarah did as Tad suggested and sent Vera to join him. Four months after Vera's arrival, Tad informed Sarah of his intention to remain in the United States and to keep Vera with him permanently.

As soon as she learned of Tad's intentions, Sarah filed a custody proceeding in Poland. Tad was served through the Polish consul in State $X$ where he was living. Bob did not appear in the Polish proceeding. The Polish family court, having doubts about its jurisdiction in the absence of the both parents, certified the case to the Polish Supreme Court for a decision on the jurisdictional issue. That court held that "because Vera's last place of domicile as determined by the will of both parents was Poland, the Polish courts had jurisdiction to determine the custody issue." Applying a welfare-of-the-child test, the court awarded custody to Sarah.

Assuming that the UCCJA was in force in State *X*, what arguments would you make on Sarah's behalf to persuade the *X* court to honor the Polish decree? Are your arguments likely to be persuasive? *See Rzeszotarski v. Rzeszotarski*, 296 A.2d 431 (D.C. Ct. App. 1972).

---

## PROBLEM 8C-4. ARIZONA, TENNESSEE AND *X*

Anne Abele, a Tennessee lawyer representing the father in a custody proceeding, wrote the following memorandum to you, a State *X* lawyer, asking that you (1) evaluate the likelihood that the mother will be able to have the decision of the *X* trial court overturned, and (2) prepare the brief and make the oral argument in the case. How would you assess the mother's chances of success? Would you accept the referral? Why? (State *X* has enacted the UCCJA.)

"The facts in the case occurred over three calendar years, and in an effort to avoid confusion, I have divided the events into annual segments.

**"Year One**

"(a) November: The mother was granted custody and the father visitation rights in a bilateral dissolution proceeding in Arizona.

"(b) December: The Arizona decree was modified and both parties were prohibited from removing the children from Arizona.

**"Year Two**

"(c) January: The father moved to Tennessee and has resided there ever since.

"(d) February: The mother moved to State *X* with the children in violation of the Arizona decree.

"(e) July: The mother took the children to Hawaii for two months during the period when the father was scheduled to have custody.

"(f) September: The father moved in Arizona for a modification of the Arizona decree.

"(g) October: While the Arizona proceeding was pending, the father removed the children to Tennessee (from *X*) without the knowledge or consent of the mother. He immediately filed a custody action in Tennessee. (*X* later charged the husband with the felony of child stealing.)

**"Year Three**

"(h) January: The Arizona court heard the father's motion to modify, with the mother present, but the father absent (although represented by counsel).

"(i) February: The Arizona court denied the father's motion but granted the wife's motion that she be permitted to remove the children from Arizona and to reside wherever she wished to reside.

"(j) February (a few days later): The Tennessee court denied the mother's motion to dismiss for lack of jurisdiction. She then made a general appearance. At the hearing, the mother and the two children testified. With the court being aware of all of the prior proceedings, including the criminal proceedings pending in X, the court awarded custody to the father on the ground that such an award would be in the best interest of the children.

"(k) April: The mother sought in X to enforce the latest Arizona decree. She asked that the children be returned to her and that the father be held in contempt for failure to comply with the Arizona decree.

"(l) May: The father filed the Tennessee custody decree in the X proceeding and moved to dismiss the mother's action on grounds of lack of jurisdiction.

"(m) July: The matter was heard in X. The trial court granted the father's motion to dismiss for lack of jurisdiction and accorded full faith and credit to the Tennessee decree. The mother appealed.

"This is the current posture of the case."

*See In re Marriage of Hopson*, 110 Cal. App. 3d 884, 168 Cal. Rptr. 345 (1980). *See also Plas v. Superior Court (Plas)*, 155 Cal. App. 3d 1008, 202 Cal. Rptr. 490 (1984).

---

## PROBLEM 8C-5. PARENTS V. GRANDPARENTS

Alice Andes, the paternal grandmother of Mike Andes, was appointed his guardian by a State X court. Mike's parents, Ned and Paula, consented to the appointment because Ned was serving a prison term on a drug charge and Paula was an outpatient in a heroin addiction clinic. At the time of the appointment, all parties were domiciliaries of State X.

About two years after Alice's appointment, she and Mike's grandfather, Dave, sold their home and were making plans to move to State Y. Ned, who had been released from prison, and Paula obtained a temporary ex parte restraining order from the X court prohibiting Alice from leaving X with Mike. Alice, Dave, and Mike left X before the restraining order was served on them, and they did so in violation of an X statute requiring a guardian to obtain permission of the court before taking the ward out of state.

Seven months after the move to Y, Ned and Paula filed a petition in X, seeking to have Alice's guardianship terminated and to have custody returned to them. Alice appeared by counsel and contested the merits of the petition. The X court granted the parents' petition on the ground that the conditions that made the guardianship necessary no longer existed.

Ned and Paula went to Alice's Y home to pick up their son. Alice and Dave were willing to surrender the child, but asked the parents to wait a few hours while they said goodbye to him. When Ned and Paula insisted that Mike leave immediately, Alice and Dave resisted their efforts physically. A scuffle ensued resulting in the arrest of the parents and the filing of assault and battery charges against them. Alice immediately filed a custody petition in Y. The Y court issued an order granting temporary custody to Alice and temporarily enjoining the parents from any further contact with Mike. The parents filed an original proceeding in the Y appellate court seeking to enjoin the Y court from exercising jurisdiction over Mike's custody.

As counsel for Alice, what arguments would you make in resisting the petition? Are your arguments likely to prevail? *See Fry v. Ball*, 190 Colo. 128, 544 P.2d 402 (1975).

## PROBLEM 8C-6. BACK AND FORTH

About five months after a State X bilateral dissolution decree awarded custody of five children to their mother, Alice Altar, the court in X modified its decree and granted custody to their father, Bob. Within a week, Bob moved with the five children to State Y, and one month later the X court again modified the decree and awarded custody to Alice. Bob, who was given notice of the proceeding, did not appear.

Shortly after the decree granting custody to Alice for a second time, Bob filed a petition in Y, asking that he be granted custody and that Alice be restrained temporarily from removing the children from Y. The requested restraining order was issued. Eighteen months later, the merits of Bob's custody petition came to trial. Alice appeared specially to challenge the court's jurisdiction. After concluding that it had jurisdiction, the trial court awarded custody to Bob. What would be the result of an appeal on the jurisdiction issue? Why? *See Pierce v. Pierce*, 287 N.W.2d 879 (Iowa 1980).

## PROBLEM 8C-7. THE CONSOLIDATION

While Sarah Sams was residing in State X with her child, Stan, she petitioned the X court for a modification of a seven-year-old custody decree and for increased child support from her former husband, Tim. (The couple had been divorced several years earlier in a bilateral X proceeding.) Tim counter-petitioned in X, asking that he be granted custody. At Tim's request, the X court ordered Sarah to produce the child. She ignored the court's order and moved to State Y with the child.

Three years later, Sarah initiated a URESA proceeding in Y asking for past due and future child support payments. As provided in URESA, the proceedings were transferred to X where Tim still lived. He responded by asking for a consolidation of the URESA proceeding and the earlier custody-support proceeding Sarah had initiated. Sarah did not appear in the X proceeding, although she filed an answer to Tim's counterpetition. The X court granted custody to Tim.

Acting on Tim's behalf, you filed a habeas corpus petition seeking to have the Y court recognize the X decree. What arguments would you expect to be made by counsel for Sarah? How would you respond to them? It is likely that your arguments would prevail? *See Slidell v. Valentine*, 298 N.W.2d 599 (Iowa 1980).

---

## PROBLEM 8C-8. SUMMER VACATION

The marriage of Helen and Ike Holme, domiciliaries of State X, was dissolved in a proceeding there. The custody portion of the decree awarded custody to Ike during the week and to Helen on weekends. Ike was required to support the children.

Helen moved to State Y and remarried. She and Ike entered into a written agreement under which Ike agreed to have the children stay with Helen during the summer months. Helen and Ike shared the cost of the air fare, and Helen agreed to support the children while they were with her. The agreement provided that Helen was to return the children to Ike one week before school started in X.

One week before she was supposed to return the children to Ike, Helen started an action in Y to have the X decree modified so that she had full custody. She also asked for a modification of the support portion of the X decree. Ike appeared specially to challenge the jurisdiction of the Y court. The Y long-arm statute granted the courts in Y jurisdiction to the fullest extent permitted by the Constitution.

Assuming the UCCJA is in force in both states, what arguments would counsel for the parties make? Which side would prevail? *See Titus v. Superior Court*, 23 Cal. App. 3d 792, 100 Cal. Rptr. 477 (1972).

---

## PROBLEM 8C-9. ABROGATING VISITATION RIGHTS

Joan Janes was awarded custody of her son, Ken, by a State $X$ court as part of a dissolution decree in a bilateral proceeding. Ken's father, Larry, was granted visitation rights. Three months before the $X$ dissolution decree was issued, Joan had moved from $X$ to State $Y$ and had taken Ken with her. Five months after the $X$ decree was issued and eight months after she had moved to $Y$, Joan petitioned the $Y$ court to cut off Larry's visitation rights. Larry appeared specially to challenge the jurisdiction of the $Y$ court.

Both states had enacted the UCCJA. What arguments would you make on behalf of Joan to persuade the $Y$ court to take jurisdiction? How would your arguments differ if the $X$ decree prohibited Alice from removing Ken from $X$ without the court's permission and she had not obtained such permission? Is Joan likely to prevail in both situations? *See Moore v. Moore*, 379 So. 2d 1153 (La. App. 1980).

---

## § 8.14    Recognition

## PROBLEM 8C-10. A HABEAS CORPUS PROCEEDING

In a State $X$ proceeding, Sandy Smythe, Rob Round's grandmother, was awarded custody of Rob. Rob's father, Ralph, was in the State $X$ penitentiary at the time of the custody proceeding and he consented to awarding custody to Sandy. Rob's mother, Clarice, was not in $X$ at the time of the custody proceeding and her whereabouts were unknown. Notice by publication was given and, in addition, notice was given to all of Rob's known relatives as required by $X$ law.

A few months later, Clarice returned to $X$ and demanded that Alice turn Rob's custody over to her. Sandy refused and Clarice filed a habeas corpus proceeding asserting her right to immediate custody of Rob. The $X$ court refused to issue the writ on the ground that Clarice was bound by the earlier custody proceeding and suggested that Clarice file a formal custody proceeding if she wished to obtain custody of Rob. The court indicated that in order to prevail, Clarice would have to show a change of circumstances. Rather than following the court's advice, Clarice went to Rob's school and took him with her to State $Y$ where she had been living about a year. She filed for dissolution in $Y$ and for custody of Rob.

Both $X$ and $Y$ had adopted the UCCJA. As counsel for Sandy, what arguments would you make in an effort to persuade the $Y$ court to reject the custody portion of Clarice's petition and order Clarice to return Rob? Are your arguments likely to succeed? *See In Re Marriage of Saucido*, 85 Wash. 2d 653, 538 P.2d 1219 (1975).

---

## PROBLEM 8C-11. "BUT I NEVER LIVED IN Y!"

Two years after a State $X$ bilateral dissolution that made no mention of child custody, Rose Reller, the children's mother, moved to State $Y$ with the children. She had custody under an agreement she and their father, Rex, had entered into at the time of the dissolution. Rex left $X$ at about the same time Alice did and moved to State $Z$. As provided in the agreement, Rose sent the children to $Z$ to spend the summer with Rex. When he refused to return them at the end of the third summer, Rose filed a child custody proceeding in $Y$. Rex appeared specially and moved to dismiss Alice's petition on the ground that the $Y$ court had no jurisdiction over him. His motion was denied, and he withdrew from the proceeding. Permanent custody was awarded to Rose, and Bob appealed on the jurisdiction issue. What arguments would you make as counsel for Rose to persuade the court to sustain the decision? Are your arguments likely to be persuasive? *See Goldfarb v. Goldfarb*, 246 Ga. 24, 268 S.E.2d 648 (1980).

---

## PROBLEM 8C-12. WHOSE CHILDREN ARE THEY?

The marriage of Teri and Gerald Towns was dissolved in a State $X$ proceeding. The decree awarded Teri custody of the four children of the marriage on condition that she not take the children out of $X$. Two years later, the $X$ court modified the decree at the request of the parties and permitted Teri to take the children out of $X$. (Gerald was awarded custody during the summer months.) Teri then moved with the children to State $Y$.

When the children returned to $X$ five months later to visit relatives during the Thanksgiving holiday, Gerald obtained an ex parte order awarding him custody of the children. A few days later at Teri's request, the $X$ court rescinded the order, and Teri returned with the children to $Y$. About one month thereafter, Teri and the children moved to State $Z$. A few weeks later, the $X$ court ordered Teri to show cause why Gerald should not be awarded custody of the children. An $X$ attorney made a limited appearance for Teri, and seven months later, the $X$ court ordered that custody be transferred to Gerald.

As soon as that order was issued, Gerald went to Z, seized two of the children, and returned with them to X. Teri then filed suit in Z, asking that custody of the four children be awarded to her. Six weeks later she went to X and sought to have the X decree modified to grant her custody of the children. On the same day, she attempted to abduct the two children Gerald had abducted. She succeeded in removing one of them and took her back to Z.

Eleven months later, the Z court held that it was the proper forum under the Uniform Child Custody Jurisdiction Act to resolve the custody dispute and denied Gerald's effort to have the X decree enforced. After a six month investigation, the Z court awarded custody of the four children to Teri. Teri then sought unsuccessfully to abduct the child who remained in X with Gerald.

The courts in X and Z each refuse to enforce the custody decree of the other. What remedy, if any, is available to the parties to get the dispute settled? Does either the UCCJA or the Parental Kidnapping Prevention Act provide a mechanism for settlement? Section 1738A mandates that a state court:

> shall not exercise jurisdiction in any proceeding for a custody determination commenced during the pendency of a proceeding in a court of another State where such court of that other State is exercising jurisdiction consistently with the provisions of this section to make a custody determination.

The United States Supreme Court is the final arbiter of federal legislation. Is access to that Court the only means to enforce 1738A?

# TABLE OF CASES

[Principal cases appear in capital letters with italic references; all references are to pages.]

[Principal cases appear in capital letters with italic references; all references are to pages.]

[Principal cases appear in capital letters with italic references; all references are to pages.]

[Principal cases appear in capital letters with italic references; all references are to pages.]

[Principal cases appear in capital letters with italic references; all references are to pages.]

[Principal cases appear in capital letters with italic references; all references are to pages.]

[Principal cases appear in capital letters with italic references; all references are to pages.]

[Principal cases appear in capital letters with italic references; all references are to pages.]

[Principal cases appear in capital letters with italic references; all references are to pages.]

[Principal cases appear in capital letters with italic references; all references are to pages.]

# TABLE OF AUTHORITIES

[References are to pages.]

[References are to pages.]

[References are to pages.]

# C

[References are to pages.]

[References are to pages.]

[References are to pages.]

[References are to pages.]

[References are to pages.]

[References are to pages.]

[References are to pages.]

[References are to pages.]

[References are to pages.]

# R

[References are to pages.]

[References are to pages.]

[References are to pages.]

# T

[References are to pages.]

[References are to pages.]

[References are to pages.]

# INDEX

[References are to pages.]

[References are to pages.]

[References are to pages.]

[References are to pages.]